BEST POEMS OF 1997

BEST POEMS
OF 1997

The National Library of Poetry

Howard Ely, Editor

Best Poems of 1997

Copyright © 1997 by The National Library of Poetry
as a compilation.

Rights to individual poems reside with the artists themselves.
This collection of poetry contains works submitted to the Publisher by individual authors who confirm that the work is their original creation. Based upon the authors' confirmations and to the Publisher's actual knowledge, these poems were written by the listed poets. The National Library of Poetry does not guarantee or assume responsibility for verifying the authorship of each work.

The views expressed within certain poems contained in this anthology do not necessarily reflect the views of the editors or staff of The National Library of Poetry.

All rights reserved under International and Pan-American copyright conventions. No part of this book may be reproduced, stored in a retrieval system or transmitted in any form, electronic, mechanical, or by other means, without written permission of the publisher. Address all inquiries to Jeffrey Franz, Publisher, One Poetry Plaza, Owings Mills, MD 21117.

Library of Congress
Cataloging in Publication Data
ISBN 1-57553-674-9

Proudly manufactured in The United States of America by
Watermark Press
One Poetry Plaza, Suite G
Owings Mills, MD 21117

Foreword

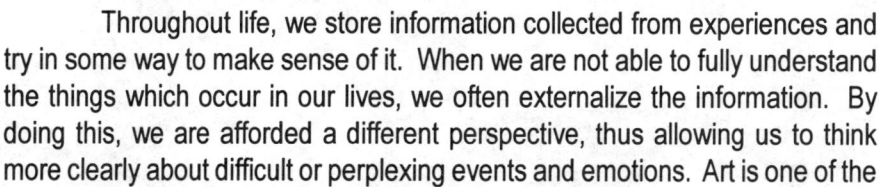

      Throughout life, we store information collected from experiences and try in some way to make sense of it. When we are not able to fully understand the things which occur in our lives, we often externalize the information. By doing this, we are afforded a different perspective, thus allowing us to think more clearly about difficult or perplexing events and emotions. Art is one of the ways in which people choose to externalize their thoughts.

      Within the arts, modes of expression differ, but poetry is a very powerful tool by which people can share sometimes confusing, sometimes perfectly clear concepts and feelings with others. Intentions can run the gamut as well: the artists may simply want to share something that has touched their lives in some way, or they may want to get help to allay anxiety or uncertainty. The poetry within *The Best Poems of 1997* is from every point on the spectrum: every topic, every intention, every event or emotion imaginable. Some poems will speak to certain readers more than others, but it is always important to keep in mind that each verse is the voice of a poet, of a mind which needs to make sense of this world, of a heart which feels the effects of every moment in this life, and perhaps of a memory which is striving to surface. Nonetheless, recalling our yesterdays gives birth to our many forms of expression.

Melisa S. Mitchell
Editor

Editor's Note

Poetry comes nearer to vital truth than history.
— *Plato*

What is truth? Is it as simple as a recitation of fact, or is there more? Countless philosophers have tried to answer these questions since time immemorial, yet none has found a satisfactory answer.

History, as Plato implies in the quote above, is merely a chronology of events. Poetry, because it is colored by the experiences and emotions of the poet, comes closer to explaining why historical events have occurred. The search for truth demands a reason *why* something has happened; perhaps this is the underlying message of Plato's assertion. That often ephemeral reason why is the intangible thing that breathes life into fact and makes it truth. In this case truth, like poetry, becomes intensely personal, while facts remain detached and impersonal.

In his poem "To the Lehigh Cement Company, of Union Bridge, Maryland," Richard Eichman attempts to reveal the truth behind the facts. One can imagine that this cement company provides employment for the townsfolk; perhaps it even brings prosperity to the entire town. Surely they should be grateful for this, yet the residents do not praise the company, or even "hold [its] practice harmless." Eichman attempts to explain the reason for the town's discontent:

> *From native rock, 'tis said, our Rinehart got*
>   *Results when sculpturing on his father's farm; less*
> *Fam'd hands might do as well. Was it the lot*
>   *Of some great work unborn, as fine as th'armless*
> *Venus discover'd on the isle of Milo,*
> *To be ground up and stor'd within your silo?*

In other words, a sculptor used the local rock to create important and beautiful works of art. Eichman laments that it is entirely possible that other works, potentially of equal or even greater beauty, were never made because the stone from which they would have been crafted was ground up to make cement. What the cement company sees as mere product, Eichman views as unformed statues, and so he refers to the company's actions as "a new class of old iconoclasm" — literally a destruction of religious images, but in this case a more general demolition of sculpture. This wanton destruction is viewed as

> *...either saintly act or scandal,*
> *According as one's own enthusiasm*
> *Leads one to side with Rome or with the Vandal.*

Those in favor of commercial progress will no doubt applaud the cement company's efficient actions, while those who are concerned more with aesthetics will damn them.

Eichman leaves no doubt as to where his sympathies lie. He acknowledges that while the destruction of statuary is nothing new:

> *Fanatics (every tribe and era has 'em)*
> *Are drawn to marble works and known to handle*
> *Them roughly...*

He must condemn the company with this stinging line:

> *But you alone demolish them ere made.*

The truth is, in this case, that progress is not to be celebrated if it comes at the expense of beauty.

"To the Lehigh Cement Company, of Union Bridge, Maryland" is a sharp, well-formulated criticism of industrial advancements which mourns the toll they have taken upon the creative side of society. Richard Eichman has expressed this criticism clearly and concisely, with a definite economy of language, using the poetic form known as *ottava rima* to convey this message. *Ottava rima* is an Italian form, used with great success by Lord Byron (note the parenthetical explanation below the title: "comic ottava rima stanzas in the manner of Lord Byron"). Each stanza is eight lines of iambic pentameter, and the rhyme scheme is *abababcc*. This form is especially difficult to use in English poetry, because of the complexity of the rhyme scheme and the rhythms of the language, but Eichman demonstrates considerable poetic skill with its application here. It is because of this masterful use of a difficult form, in addition to the clear, succinct, and persuasive expression of his opinion, that the judges at the National Library of Poetry have awarded Richard Eichman the Grand Prize for the contest associated with **Best Poems of 1997**.

Another poem that reveals truth more clearly than does history is Patricia Kelly's "Yesterday's Table." A brief glance at the family chronicled in this work might reveal nothing out of the ordinary, but the persona who narrates this piece tells a different story. She speaks of sitting at a table with her mother and her sister, trying to recall her dead father — but they do not recall him fondly or even clearly:

> *A shadow is the most that can be conjured.*
> *Blood ties, yet even your voice has thinned,*
> *an echo I can live with.*

There is a sense of relief in this poem, not that any of the father's suffering has been ended, but that their own has:

> *The hand, still poised to strike is safely buried,*
> *your lips finally sealed.*
> *The beating that did not raise welts, raised questions*
> *you will never answer, and shame, your only legacy,*
> *has faded. Even that.*

The women are also relieved that they have survived, and that they now have the chance to achieve some kind of serenity in their lives: "We have outlived the need for explanations, / outgrown your noise, your little tyranny." Perhaps they shall never make peace with the man who caused them so much pain during his lifetime, but at least, now that he is gone, the women can admit the truth to themselves and even to others.

Photographs cannot even be considered accurate recorders of history's truth, as evidenced in Austin Lin's "Waiting for Lillián at Café Premo." This piece is a reminiscence of a vacation just ended; the narrator sits in an airport café and watches the comings and goings of travelers. The persona feels separate from the travelers' world, and begins to recall the previous summer, using as touching-off points both memories ("the lucid taste of raspberry daiquiris that my tongue remembers") and physical mementos:

> *...do-it-yourself group photos from Kodak Funsavers*
> *shot at arm's length — just far enough away to capture our nervous embraces*
> *that are unperformed (as only we Fantasists would have it)*
> *so that we can rehearse them to ourselves, perfecting Atlanta's first Platonic hug.*

The "nervous embraces" in these photographs seem to have a certain distance to them, as implied in the phrase "arm's length," but the subjects of the photographs (at least in the persona's case) treasure these embraces and consider them to be tokens of a more serious affection. In this instance, "Platonic" seems to refer to a love that aspires to an ideal of passion and ecstasy — "platonic" with a lower-case "p" usually indicates non-sexual love. The persona would rather return to those days captured in the photographs (a fantasy world) than to move forward into real life: "I'll trade you these tickets to first-class / for an Alice-Through-the Plexiglass." The photographs do not capture the truth as the persona remembers it; and the persona can use them as a means to escape reality.

A poem in this anthology that effectively uses language to expose truth is Robert Rembecki's "Breakthrough." This piece tells the story of a writing career from beginning to end. However, key words in the story are juxtaposed with other, more telling words which reveal a more accurate reality. The following is a good example:

> *You become a published author (charlatan)*
> *and with proper marketing (brainwashing) techniques*
> *you earn (buy) the respect of your colleagues*
> *becoming a wealthy (insecure) individual*

The parenthetical words represent the truth of the situation, while the preceding euphemisms only show what the public is allowed to see. This particular work is an especially apt representation of Plato's assertion about poetry, history, and truth.

There are many other poems in this anthology which you should read with special attention to the truths they may reveal: "Birthing an Image," by Frances Boyle; "Out Back," by Steve Handley; "Pitchpipe," by Jeff Kelly; "Displaced," by Diane Nye; "Ode to Galileo Galilei," by Wilmo C. Orejola; "Somnolence," by William Santos; and "On Reading Milton," by Michael Schronce. Each of these poems is commendably well crafted and worthy of praise. It is important to note as well all of the fine works published within this volume; time and space do not permit a detailed critique of every poem contained herein, but every work that appears on these pages deserves the honor of being among the **Best Poems of 1997**.

The publication of **Best Poems of 1997** is the culmination of the efforts of a great many individuals. Assistant editors, customer service, administrative, and general services staff have all contributed their considerable talents to the production of this volume. The editorial staff of the National Library of Poetry is sincerely grateful to them, and to you, the poets, for making this anthology a success.

Diana Zeiger
Editor
and the Editorial Board of the National Library of Poetry

Grand Prize

Richard Eichman / Union Bridge, MD

Second Prize

Frances Boyle / Colorado Springs, CO
Steve Handley / Dublin, OH
Jeff Kelly / Seattle, WA
Patricia Kelly / College Point, NY
Austin Lin / Signal Mountain, TN

Diane Bishop Nye / Eureka, CA
Wilmo C. Orejola / Pompton Plains, NJ
Robert Rembecki / Warren, MI
William Santos / Elmwood Park, NJ
Michael Schronce / Bessemer City, NJ

Third Prize

David Edwards Allen Jr / Los Altos, CA
Ruth Sigler Avery / Tulsa, OK
Jesse Battis / Chillwack, BC, CANADA
Vera Baxter / Thornhill, ON, CANADA
Phyllis I. Behrens / Arlington, TX
Dorothy L. Blundell / Oklahoma City, OK
Beth A. Boettcher / Reading, PA
Jim Bosiljevac / Cincinnati, OH
Barbara Rose Brooker / San Francisco, CA
Tania Bruce / Dubuque, IA
Michael Sean Conway / San Ysidro, CA
Eric Day / Backus, MN
Patsy Estep / Logan, WV
Jack Fahey / Marlborough, MA
Rich Fiegelman / Shickshinny, PA
Richard Fullerton / Winston-Salem, NC
Bree Gale / Bolingbrook, IL
Dave Gerardi / Garden City, NY
Dave Gifford / Beverly, MA
Seth L. Ginsburg / Plano, TX
Matthew Goeglein / Fort Wayne, IN
Mildred Gomoll / Stouffville, ON, CANADA
Gretchen Haller / Pittsburgh, PA
Matthew Henderson / Milwaukie, OR
Mary Ellen Huddy / North Fork, CA
Thom Ingram / Germantown, NY
Linda Lee Jacobsen / Harlan, IA
Magali Gueits Kain / Port Charlotte, FL
Mary Karsten / Denver, CO
Mary Kellerman / Louisville, KY

Elizabeth Kelly / West Chester, OH
Angelika Klien / Phoenix, AZ
Lucas Klotzbach / Decorah, IA
Esaku Kondo / Bloomfield Hills, MI
Toni Leeber / Cool Ridge, WV
Harold W. Mann / Durham, NC
Raymond Marcus / Queens Village, NY
Ginny Marsh / Winter Haven, FL
William E. Mays / Adrian, MI
Barbara Moyer / Winnipeg, MB, CANADA
Jill Naponelli / Ontario, CA
Constance Plumley / Akron, OH
Edna May Quentin / Toronto, ON, CANADA
Mev Borso Rozsman / Greensboro, GA
Karol Ruding / Arlington, VA
Marilyn Sanders / N. Hollywood, CA
Patricia Saphier / Pacific Palisades, CA
Robert Schalit / Schenectady, NY
Ernest Serna / Laurel, MD
E. McIntire Slee / Fairfield, CA
Halina Stolar / Waco, TX
Nilofer Sultana / Rawalpindi Cault, PAKISTAN
Kimberly A. Terlap / Evanston, IL
Ana Lee Thorn / Louisville, KY
Theresa Trout / Grand Junction, CO
Huldah M. Turner / NSW, AUSTRALIA
Bryan VanDyke / Richland, MI
Mike B. Weltz / Washington, DC
Mr. Woollybear / Federal Way, WA

Grand Prize Winner

To the Lehigh Cement Company of Union Bridge, Maryland

(comic ottava rima stanzas in the manner of Lord Byron)

Stone-crushing Lehigh, shame! The town does not
   Intone your praise or hold your practice harmless:
From native rock, 'tis said, our Rinehart got
   Results when sculpturing on his father's farm; less
Fam'd hands might do as well. Was it the lot
   Of some great work unborn, as fine as th' armless
Venus discover'd on the isle of Milo,
To be ground up and stor'd within your silo?

'Tis a new class of old iconoclasm,
   Consider'd either saintly act or scandal,
According as one's own enthusiasm
   Leads one to side with Rome or with the Vandal.
Fanatics (every tribe and era has 'em)
   Are drawn to marble works and known to handle
Them roughly, on a lark or on crusade;
But you alone demolish them ere made.

Richard Eichman

Beginnings: 1960-1980: Jacques Brel And Saigon

The bull, the arena and . . .
       and your freedom
        has been misplaced
    while cheering multitudes
      wave
       blood
              red
              flags
  and bowing
    beg
      for a
        white
         flag
           to signal
            as signal
the matadors have lain down
in the dirt
of mushrooming ceremonies.
    Phyllis I. Behrens

On Reading Milton

Wait first, and see, that
the blinded-ness which serves thee e'er
now is spent, or too ostentatious

Perhaps a man be. Is fallacy
resented? those eyes that can trick, or
dull a capacity for the spirited

Quick? I myself have touched shadows that
danced, heard laughter un-sourced, sensed
visions on walls, smelt air's

Discourse. What's more, but more,
and meaning for that! Half my bread's
a bite, and a mountain to a gnat.

Then—Stand! Do you find your God
in dark? That we know now sight's by you
town apart, yet I fear my portion's

Got, and given: I have more bread to
make, and keep away that gnat's eye fondly
I must, and 'Thou art That' define.
    Michael Schronce

Iwo Jima

Rest, as the light burns low,
dying soldier, nor ever know
the least chagrin as memory seeks
a ghoulish wake to keep.
Do not lament on this strange shore
where life is spent with such extravagance
you scorned the power to bring great joy
in fragile syllables.
Nor in this hour impatiently recall
as pain burns bright
youth asked more than phrases trite,
less ridicule would pierce the
  fragile crust of vows
how eloquent you phrase it now,
o, swaggering, bragging youth
for, crimson on black sand, we read the truth!
    Theresa Trout

Ladies, Waiting

Sitting in rooms emptied of dying men,
their widows weave with dignity
the tattered ends of plans through gracious years.

My dears, my dears,

the emptiness that crouches in your halls
was not bequeathed the day they read the will
or featured boldly in the family crest.

The best, the Best

shines in the silver chest, the crystal case,
waiting to be handed down again
beneath the ranks of framed and silent eyes.
    Richard Fullerton

Yesterday's Table

Three of us is all I can imagine,
reaching into the distant past, groping for your face.
A shadow is the most that can be conjured.
Blood ties, yet even your voice has thinned,
an echo I can live with.
The hand, still poised to strike is safely buried,
your lips finally sealed.
The beating that did not raise welts, raised questions
you will never answer, and shame, your only legacy,
has faded. Even that.
Three of us only sit at yesterday's table,
spooning the just dessert you always missed,
watching the evening light through ninon curtains,
a delicacy, an elegance, a memory fragile as a woman's wrist.
Mother, daughter, sister, all of your women, grown.
We have outlived the need for explanations,
outgrown your noise, your little tyranny.
The chair at the head of the table now is vacant,
three of us sit here, only three.
    Patricia Kelly

Husk Mind

Zealots eyes, recreant reasons, yellow hides
your call expanded with lies
inventions that should have expired

A battered record echoing aged lessons
transported as though novel, nothing fresh here to master
yet, employed again by cowards who must exploit

Concerns contemporary, not unique
grasping their own ilk
by assessing like regard

Your kind halted before, yesterday accurately related
now in your twisted custom you would postulate
that nothing transpired

You are waste, we abhor you as all preceding did
your attitude disdained no sympathy, nor shelter
purge you we must

No one feature, nor shape nothing left to reach
cast, distant further till you no longer wait
nor can prey

And entreat we shall for your absolute demise
telling the morrow to guard your zealots eyes
never neglect remember
    Karol Ruding

birdwoman

where are you now
that i need your
inspiration?
the sea gulls, too, are on the look-out
scanning sand for your covered eyes
your long blowing blighted hair
your fit and insecure legs;
perhaps you don't know

that the sun-stained, weather-worn
conversation of your arms
is inviting
casting heaven by handful to these coastline majesties;
perhaps you do know, and that's why you come here
encircled in caws and raucous flight
extending the best of you, as they
gleefully grub your last-night's bread.
   Patricia Saphier

Valentino's Dance

You came to me suddenly, from the depths of my prescient memory.
   My soul had sought you an eternity, all the while listening for
the rhapsody of deception, in tune with the color of
   your passions, alert to the sounds of my fear.
You drew me, in swift and seductive two-quarter time. You,
   wearing your ancient aegis and I wearing my hopeful smile.

Who could deny the dancer, so measured his call and primitive.
   Your breath leaps across my senses enveloping my being
and I am beguiled by the staccato of your silent need,
   aroused by the pretense of my souls completeness so near.
Joined with you in this movement and stillness,
                    I miss a step.

   I hear your music and
      my vigilant soul resists;
   a war dance of spirits ravaged
      by too many tangos.

Yet, the wonder and magic touch me with the promise for
   another lifetime, whispering adagios across my ageless mind.
            A dream of a past not yet fulfilled.

Dance with me again, Valentino.
   Magali Gueits Kain

Out Back

I saw the naked electric light in the darkness,
And life, as it was slowed down a bit.
Tiny beams from small ships and those from larger ones
Were broken into a million selfish rays
By the warm, black waters of the harbour.
The dark faces of store fronts stared blankly out onto the road,
And the air that had been so thick was clear,
Because the street was empty.
The dull florescent lights that anchored themselves
Along that long green corridor seemed to numb even the colors
That were trying to break free from the tiles.
The sound of a radio, out of tune, sat in the corner of my room,
I didn't have the courage to get up and turn it off.
Without that, the room would be silent,
And I alone to explore the remnant of my mind.
The smell of sweat and sex lingered
In the stagnant air that lay just below the ceiling.
Death was coming to pay us a visit here tonight.
The atmosphere was that of the time before a hurricane,
Calm and Serene, trying desperately to hide the truth.
   Steve Handley

Yet Unspoken

Time is overfed
and the hush of twilight conspicuous.
Time is overfed on fratricide
and the motion of images
through the fuming air:
The immortal sin of it — breathless,
clinging to the skin like pitch,
ringing the fettered bellows loud . . .
like trousers knee-blown
there is an odd oldness about it:
Over-used and ridiculous,
sad with the aching ennui of rain drops
shrinking diminutive
on the flat glass coasts of window panes . . .
like bulb burnt black
there is a final gesture of resignation
in it: In the smile printed solemnly
on puppet faces, on our own faces,
to face the twilight — the hush
of twilight.
   Raymond Marcus

Rooftop Elegy

they've found us again,
sitting at the edge of
the world
feet dangling
glaring at the single
solemn star in the sky

helicopters float by
and their lights
coax us to come in
a man screams
beneath the blades
but we're not ready to go

the cotton sea flows
deep and steady
as the lights across the
way begin to fade and
fluctuate
the bare earth pulls on
our shoe strings
but we're not ready to go.
   Mike B. Weltz

Of Paper Cups And Dreams

Talk to me
of paper cups and dreams
of brooks, rivers, clouds or chalkboards
electrical sockets or grass
mountain lakes and books
Tell me about
baskets and blankets
trees and old trunks
clothes, jewelry,
and the stories of stars
Speak lightly
of quilts and carpets
rocks and brass buttons
smoke and spirits, or
kisses and vines
Teach me
to love living
   Ana Lee Thorn

The Nature Of Winter

I plunge headlong
into the maelstrom of desire
shake loose the wheel from the wagon
tear asunder the room
the blessed roster of names
of the century now flurry
in the ubiquitous snow
the rush of atoms in the blood
tantamount profusion of sanguine leaves
the flutter and sputter
of birds gathered in evergreens
the emergence in my heart
the shards of restlessness
break open the wound
bitter as walnuts cracked
on the wooden floor
perhaps not for longing
but for the hot lust raged.
Tania Bruce

Drought

Saharan sky
a boundless sea of misty blue
devoid of white sails open to the breeze
or billowy clouds to carry ships
across your vast expanse.
Nothing to hide that fiery ball
that beats down on the plain
fifteen hours every day
scorching everything below to golden brown
as crackling spikes of burned out crops
support the weary tramp of men.

Saharan sky
when will the fleet arrive
and sail across an ocean churned
by winds that make the heavens cry
with tears to turn a deadened earth to green
and brighten all life forms
with seasons of full growth
to gladden every hopeful heart
by the largess of a harvest scene.
William E. Mays

Eclipse

Luna was shrouded in eclipse,
old town streetlamps aglow in her stead.
Come midnight, the chandeliered sequins,
timely beckoned sly boys from their beds.
Through windows and once secured doorways,
urchins climbed, and crept, and then soared.
Unchained of the fetters familiar.
Alive with a life so adored.
106 whistles past in an hour,
pounding trackline while distancing ties.
Open boxcar, and pubescent hoboes,
railroaders, the crossing, goodbyes.
One by one breathy leap to continuum,
an entrancing, cold maw of rust steel.
As they landed each surely scathed mortal,
hear my pulse, that is still how I feel.
Surging growth every mile we travelled,
bridge of years, the horizon, and soon.
Youth with soul to spare, where eaglets dare,
as Sol repainted countenance Moon.
Rich Fiegelman

Breakthrough

So much time spent(wasted) on this
always hoping(begging) it would pay off
Suddenly, someone knows the right(rich) person
and your wishes(matins) are answered

You become a published author(charlatan)
and with proper marketing(brainwashing) techniques
you earn(buy) the respect of your colleagues
becoming a wealthy(insecure) individual

All of your friends(tools) adore you
Basking in(stealing) all of your success
you remember(lose) them with numerous parties
Dedicating yourself to work(plagiarize) harder

And when, in later years, your career wavers(plummets)
friends and associates are there for(abandon) you
Alone and peaceful(resentful) you spend your days
Planning(Plotting) your retirement(revenge)

Near death you are comfortable(bitter) with your life
a highly esteemed(scorned) writer(cheat)
Although eccentric(loony) you are yet adored(reviled)
You owe it all to hard work(luck) and dedication(chance)
Robert Rembecki

Midnight Zoo

I decide to write to those who
wish to read, pretending that
I write to one.

You gave me fear, taught me
unbalanced and lunatic, like a child
that a mother must rear . . .

The destitution of dreams holds
me as if in the palm of something
larger, yellow perhaps, and full of the maker.

Playmate descendant grant me a wish
of kindred play, gardens and flowers,
candlelit meetings and bright walls
with decorate smiles . . .

Bottles of pride wash up on shores
(Long since walked, long since comforting)
On sand erased — play, too, forgotten
in the fires of others, in the fires of
blood . . . that is me
that is you (my apparition)
in this midnight zoo.
Matthew Henderson

Sylvia Plath Pacing In The Dark (An Acrostic)

Stumbling through my padded cell,
Anesthesia thoughts blur like
Chalk on wet pavement. Useless
Repetition, hollow thud
Inside my empty head. Smell
Leaks like faulty pipes. Sound, like
Echoes in a tunnel. Taste,
Garbage on a thick tongue. My
Insides turn to dust. Bones can
Only take so much. Lock me
Up inside a padded cloud.
Send me off to Hell.
Halina Stolar

Gerst

There were words in the very beginning; quick and sure.
A rapid fire exchange at the bar, late at night,
in the middle of my first fall alone, 21 and new to this place.
Mountains, not oceans, seasons, not coasts; Knowing no one well:

Smoke and Scotch; Fire and Ice.
Friday nights after long shifts of work and school
Friends at The Fox . . . carouse and close the joint at 2 AM
before the breakfast run along highways, where pianos fell, waiting.

Like I fell, waiting, between then and now or two and four.
And you were sane and strong and real in ways I'd never known,
and the craving ran long and hard through blood and cells like raw lightning,
held in memory, to erupt in long, cold nights to follow.

Our hands ran sure and straight to the heat of all matter,
like 2 AM Highways . . . slick and hard and true. Not able to stop,
or brake, or slow down, for so long, that finally there was wonder
and joy and neither of us could get enough for a long, long time.

Autumn stirs the passioned dreams and desires of wildfires.
For these hot spots were missed by the passage of time — distance.
And they flare and heat these shortened days in bursts of words
that touch like hands, which how the way on highways of 2 AM.

Mary Karsten

Anarchy Through A Sideways Eight

Dried pages litter a camouflaged, plastic highway
Their author discards them as the finishes
Their words melt into tiny pools of ink
Rolling off the bowed landscape
And onto the edge of poisoned grass
The author walks farther down the road
Beyond caring
Beyond purpose
And tired of walking
His sweat falls as pebbles of salt
Moisture lifts up
Pages fall down
He walks away

Dave Gerardi

Ode To Galileo Galilei

Let this discourse not second-guess your judgment, learned one,
Served not by doubt or debate, recanting truth prevailed upon,
Silenced by the church for the evil of questioning mind,
Your telescope rebuked what Ptolemaic church defined.

Pardon the inquisitor who sought the truth like a child
For when the brain runs short of facts, the perverse heart goes wild;
Who cared if false were truths believed, the mind was bound and broke
This mirror of the universe dulled, trashed in cobweb nook.

If man knew it all, truth won't hurt, he need not tell a lie,
If man were perfect, what then is life for, why even try,
But man is so inadequate, must be by grand design,
He be the rich, the mighty, or even the most divine.

Man invented religion to set life's goals and meaning
That science may serve to make better life's chances for living;
Mere science may not resolve the mysteries church dogmas sealed,
For truth but waits discovery our consciousness fulfilled.

Popes, potentates bend truth to fit what's deemed a nobler cause,
Laws and expediencies ameliorate friends, alienate foes;
Take comfort, truth-seeking galileos gagged, chastised, banished,
From madness, learns sanity. From life, hard-learned truths hold best.

Wilmo C. Orejola

Divided Between The Blinds

Divided light slips,
knifing between the blinds.
Not seen before,
sedentary grains of dust float aimlessly,
about a room once full of joy.

A one-time safe haven,
the empty crib by the wall.
Once seen before,
as the center of attention.
Now gathers the sedentary,
you and I.

In religious circles,
to wander aimlessly about.
Each to blame the other,
our child we lost.
So divided this light slips,
knifing between the blinds.

Ernest Serna

Narcissist

Doggedly refuse the day
eclipse a shuddering sky
with a deliberate moon dancing
and a heart betrayed as night
for the love of God, or the love
of you, sitting a pedestal.

Sugar sweet in a delirium
slowly seeking equilibrium
with those five - fingered toes
so that you are Poseidon in a
shimmering sea, this and this
always to be.

What is your unrest?
the shells bell and call if only
lonely sounds in your head.
What things fill you blood red,
as you step coldly into bed?

Constance Plumley

Bones Along the Baja

Blank shots shot into the darkness,
like a hand reaching,
like a voice calling;
and only the broken wind whispers
back in dull reply.

And in the futility
of the moment,
in the myth of the dream,
waiting for editors
to return my notes,
needing something to scream . . .

Feel I'm a creep stepping my way
to a shallow, cramped grave.

I should've been a plumber,
I should've been a crow.

. . . Back to these old
ecclesiastical bones
here along the Baja.

Michael Sean Conway

Come, Come

Come, come, hold my hands,
Take me to the distant lands,
Away, away from the freezing chill,
Towards the life of a blissful thrill,
From the memories, agonizing, painful,
From the strife, traumatic, stressful,
Take me to the offshore sands,
Come, tightly clasp my hands,
Drag me away from the mumbo jumbo futile,
From my own thoughts, vacuous, puerile,
From the words acerbic, bitter, bombastic,
From the looks dour, censorious, sarcastic,
Take me to a quietude, away from the shrill bands,
Come gingerly and lovingly hold my hands,
Fed up am I with false pretensions,
pompous, fustian, baseless assertions,
I need an antidote, a surcease, a cure,
For the pains I no longer can endure,
Take me to far off, sequestered islands,
Come, come, hold these outstretched hands.
Nilofer Sultana

Pithy

Standing in a shadow-tied night
A slattern gazes without conscious thought
Time pulls her tortuous heresies
Like the moon shifts the vigorous tide
Cowering behind her mind's flesh parapet
She dreams a dream
And thinks she thinks of tomorrow
Temptations spawn in front of her eyes
Posed like a nocturnal bird without a spine
Drawn to the sweet carrion scent
Of a hopeless prey
Beliefs and thinking queue in her head
Ready to pierce her tender skull
None register sincere
And none will be the savior
She rests hollow, cold steel against her brain
Then impulsively thinks of her distraught life
But she didn't think for very long.
Eric Day

Heaven's Milk — Quest For The Innocence

Behold her fragile majesty [the gate to heaven's way]
Amongst the crippled sky and vile sea
And in the dark [the black you breathe]
Inside this bitter hell
Sweet Salvation cries a cry for me
I spread my wings to penetrate this All Infernal Reign
Cast my humble eyes upon her face
Virgin Pure [like heaven's milk]
The winds of rapture rage
Surging [like a symphony of grace]

There is no other feeling that can set my soul to flight
There is no creature meek enough to radiate such might
There is no shelter strong enough to veil such the bliss
No darker shade of morbid loss could make me slit my wrists

  Until my soul is numb
  And my fortitude effete
  I must endure
  I will endure
  My quest is for the innocence.
Mr. Woollybear

Growing Into This Silence

In the silence of this one heartbeat—
longing, longing to be something greater
than itself—I know you are here.
The whisper of God curves all around me, a structure
made of other people's light. Your presence
breaks the sound barrier, and Lamb roars out
from the infected places of the world. Lion is
subdued, remembering how it was, then.

The star of oldest memory is still tucked
between the fingers of each adolescent boy;
wonderful creature, burning and outreaching
himself every time. The night is steep like a pillar
of antiquated sunlight, and he takes it into him, pushes
every war in him against it, and the steam is thick
leaving only fire behind.

He is still alive after all of this, still orbiting
in rings that scrape the bed where Sun is resting.
Moon holds him, pillows him in harp-threads
of that same silence.
He weeps with the rocking motion.
He can only laugh or weep.
Jesse Battis

Faeroe

This is not your scorched Neptune
Caught in the slowly revolving blue-green
  of split treasure crashed, ceasing
this haloed veil shorn free of Those seeing
this alone next to nearness.
Thistled china-deep now twisting,
now, and lashing and turning from salt-weeded vines
is not aching for vindication, seen
crowned in dark marine wind
I will go there now,
greened from the salt of
  Light rising to meet me,
under the watch of Turning to Never,
from this thorn I am now smitten.
This broken sceptre taken,
  sailing on, listens
    across now, and falls.
Elizabeth Kelly

Kalamazoo: A Traveller's Vignette

Autumn comes slowly here this year,
First leaves falling yellow
As across the street a green tractor
Rolls up the hill, bending down
Row after row of the final crop of corn.

The sky fills with crisp brown cuttings,
Husk pieces turning end over end
Long, dying wings of the briefly airborne—
Headed east with the wind,
Instead of south with the geese.

This city packs away its possessions,
Rustling through all the oranges and yellows—

September drips from the faucet,
Noon suns warm only the blacktop—
After a summer, merely one week to go—
Rows falling under the blade
Shreds of dying corn taking to the sky.
Bryan VanDyke

Somnolence

In the nights after sunny binges
Ones that hold her tight all day long
Some of which release her at twilight
She treads upon slippery ledges
Under the watchful eyes of peering cats
Who flee the scene when her scent draws near

Once again, as the moon rises
She leaves her cenotaph empty

She, who covets the piercing gravel
Beneath her feet, between her toes
Has more to say when the moment is
Timely than she ever hoped to say
When the time is proper
And who, having fallen to earth far too many times
During the turmoil of subsequent journeys
Suddenly...remembers why she is there, and
Methodically returns to her nascent berth

Another sun tumbled about a minute ago
Which explains why her hair was soaked and her
Fingers were not at the ends of her hands
William Santos

Convent At Bruges

The cobbled track, well trodden, wanders proud
    And paveless, close walled against the raucous street
Which lippens on the note, re-echoed sweet,
    From one Parhelion pealing bell. While loud
The human forces paganly compete,
    That undulating bell, with hammered beat,
And phonologic harmonies replete
    Rolls, and then recedes above the crowd.

Behind the sheltering wall cumulate,
    From sombre buildings, heads inclined,
Converging nuns, their habits sharp defined,
    Enter the church in peace quite irrefutable.
One russet cow, with Titian glowing hide,
    Fresh milked, contented on the lush green square
Before the porch, protective moves, to where
    Her calf is roaming, free, preoccupied.

The final ringing note so clear,
    Echoes and ebbs, its tidal forces spent.
Gregorian chanting voices, God intent,
    Zephyr the air, and mollify the ear.
Vera Baxter

Silently Adrift

Meanwhile . . . on the distant horizon,
the ship of Socrates approaches,
a sanctuary set adrift in a fool's ocean
beckoning all like-minded outlaws to her with creaking charms,
a gliding fortress of Neptune thought,
pale white ash in the blue
— we the coral in the mischief sea,
a strange fusion of oar and axe,
high water jackals are we.
Below deck we philosophize and hide our eyes,
pale white and creaking
from the prying fingers of dawn,
our confusion once again drawn
to the sight of Socrates, the trident outlaw,
now upon us.
Matthew Goeglein

Waiting Host

I'll visit you when winter quiet settles
and grief fades into shadows of a cloud
night rustling garbs of thickening dusk
I'll come
reluctant
to give you me
your sting piercing the ripened years
of this wretched shape of clay.
I'll lie with you in a silent bed of earth,
kiss you with my summer
before darkness pours light
from your bedroom into my sleep
flowing down my body's paths,
leaving dusty mounds for other seasons to scatter.
I'll visit you
tomorrow
after
tomorrow.
Dorothy L. Blundell

Poughkeepsie, 1970

There are no toilet seats in this man's town.
We dangle in the water, dead fish in a pail.
The Fisher King has left us and his catch goes bad.

We guess at their suspicions.

Could some McMurphy of a man
Unhinge a seat, and with that rude and simple discus,
Drop an orderly at forty feet?

Or would some Billy Bibbitt of a boy
Along a plastic rim more wicked than obsidian
Slit his wrists in expiation of his sin?

Or would the thinker think
To link a chain of seats together
Like Rapunzel's hair, and climb
That Jacob's ladder from the grave?

There are no toilet seats in this man's town,
Nor men to sit on them if they were there.
Robert Schalit

A Musing On The Vagaries Of Epiphany

came earlier today
driving home from school
a new cigarette just past Towne
Shirley singing about what she'd do
for the one she loves
and quietly quietly quietly
crept round my brain
whispering bit louder each time
words hardly daring to form on my
tongue but finally spilling out
in a flash blinding revelation
unquestionable realization that is
my one true possession
in imitation of the clichTd phoenix resurrected
at last
renewed passion that makes my fingers ache
and bliss in silly things
like clouds and lemons and orchids
i even smile when i remember
the scent of burnt firecrackers in Tokyo night
Jill Naponelli

In the Orchard of Life

Like fallen leaves that cup the rain
That bounces off a window pane,
I've felt depressed and battered down
With others like me all around.

We were on top amidst the tree
Of what was high society
Until that fateful saw came 'round
And tossed us spinning to the ground.

It pruned the limbs as we hung on
With little warning we were gone.
No longer needed! We were told
By owners who were very cold.

I want to scream in our defense.
To say to them, "From this point hence,
You'll rue the day you cut away
My friends and I!" That's what I'll say!

But saws keep running. They can't hear.
I'm stuck in muck up to my ear.
The liquid muddles thoughts I think.
With tilted head I take a drink.

Jack Fahey

Vainglory (Or Pickett's Folly)

Somewhere the sound of a crow is heard
through the Summer morning's haze,
and the guns have fallen silent
for the first time in many days.

How different it was the day before
when the hellish business began,
as the long gray lines with flags unfurled
moved out as though one man.

Their bayonets flashed defiance
to the blue coats on the hill,
as across the open fields they came
one spirit, one purpose, one will.

Rank upon rank moved swiftly now
as one by one they fell,
and the cannon's voice was challenged
by the familiar rebel yell.

Oh the vainglory that accomplished naught
over bloodied fields where brave men fought,
at Cemetery Ridge - how apt the name -
where Southern manhood died in vain.

E. McIntire Slee

The Trunk

Octogenarian figure kneeling nostalgic
solitude,
hesitant fingers unwrapping precious bundles.
Perfumed aromas opening delicate echoes,
skeletal arms caressing Battenburg lace.
Pressed violets stirring autumn memories,
butterfly ribbons hugging blushed whispers.
Sepia photograph peering silent dignity,
buried emotions
surfacing
celadon
eyes.

Barbara Moyer

Advertising 1997

Offices filled with repaired chairs and refurbished carpets
Eroded chromed intersections
Left over from limo nights of
Wall Street smoke and cocaine dreams
Eccentric geniuses and creative freedom

Now covered by quick cautious steps of overworked juniors
Tense in earnest swagger
Racing to curry favor
From overseers who have begun to realize
They have staked their lives on illusions of security

In times of right-sized nervous clients
With faces tight as production schedules
Pony-tailed Republicans engage in turf fight
Subterfuge in the service of professional survival

Veterans just wonder
Where the fun has gone

Seth L. Ginsburg

Displaced

Un-manned, she spins into the dark
dreams with no forgiving
sleep; she walks against the chill
closed window light in evening streets;
in bars, she cools with scotch
the burning track behind her
Riding Greyhounds, she watches bright homes,
green yards with trees and swings glide by;
conjures happy owners of the lights within

   The dinner table shared
   with robust children,
   love and laughter

Each bright isle of home holds fast
its own; claims away a further portion
of her thinning expectations;
her windows streak with constant trickling
rain; soon she thinks she will make no more
plans; but given time, now she sees wet leaves
sparkle in weak sunlight and knows that she will.

Diane Bishop Nye

Animal King

Anger crackles ten miles high, Blazing red across the sky.
Eating away the bright clear blue,
Devouring whole my love for you.
Like acid rain falling from my eyes,
Too many times, I've sat and cried.
Venomous rays, poison tipped tears, forgotten sun relived my fears.
Replayed my thoughts on a drive-in screen,
In open view, for all to see.
My pain was a living breathing thing, ruling all as the animal king
Vicious lies entangled its heart,
It snared my soul as it tore me apart.
Settling deep its darkening hold, gripping tight to never let go.
It whispered to me a lullaby
That gave me nightmares with your smile
It settled low into my sleep
To finish off what was left of me.
Until there was nothing but bitter bones
Black cold eyes like hollow stones.
And that, my love, is the animal king
Whose spider web songs destroyed my dreams.

Patsy Estep

To One I Remember

Long ago, she wore white—spotless white,
As she finished her rounds
And completed her report.
It was good to sit down and rest tired feet,
Then go home for a sound sleep.

Today in the "Home," she still makes her rounds;
No white uniform, but nondescript dress,
Wrinkled hose tumble down her legs
Toward her comfortable black shoes,
One lace bouncing gaily along.

She slowly opens my door and walks to the window,
Draws back the drapes and gazes at a tree,
Then turns again to my open door.
Often a frozen smile, but no recognition of me,
She switches on (or off) my night light,
Then moves on down the corridor.

Dear Lord, please help me to be kind!
One day, she will again finish her rounds
And leave for her Home Sweet Home
For a long, long, rest. Requiescat!
   Mildred Gomoll

Flight Over Antarctica

We flew above the clouds,
cleaving translucent blue of sky
and soft Antarctic sunlight.

Then we dropped below the clouds
into a sunless world of water, ice and snow —
sculptured whiteness, marble-still,
silent as sleep.

Aeons of snow falling on snow
blanketed the Pole.
Ice-floes in spiral drifts,
slow-cruising ice-berg islands,
enormous, deep-creviced, indigo-slashed,
glistening glacier skeins cascading into ice-froth,
all owe fealty to ice-blue Antarctic seas —
only the inky smudge of Erebus,
peaking high into the clouds,
stained the pure whiteness of Antarctic snow.

We left this other world of silent whiteness,
this alabaster dreaming
in a sleep of time.
   Huldah M. Turner

A Toronto Night

The face of night is soft and strangely fair
From hidden flowers
A shadowed fragrance fills the air.

So near our roof but to the right
There hangs the moon
A round and silvered bowl of light.

How soft and hushed this magic hour
Let my heart drink
The beauty, fragile as a flower.

A song has burst its bars and taken flight
It's soaring forth
To praise a white Toronto night.
   Edna May Quentin

Failed Quest

Laboring lungs, pregnant with gasps,
An accordion sucking and ousting breath.
Volcanic giggles spew forth unchecked—
A child chases a firefly.
Halos in a Mason crystal cocoon,
Igniting the night with Tinker Bell's dust.
A reverent peek at the winged constellation,
Now flush the quarry and seek anew!

And so I recall youth's sojourn with me,
Its effervescence revisiting now and then,
Declining my invitation to stay.
I forgive the treason of this insubordinate frame,
This resolute visage seeping through Maybelline veneer.
Yet how I would shed the shackles of utility
For fabrication, foolery, and a true guffaw!
I want the child heart.

I chased a firefly tonight and reclaimed the prize...
But it was just a Lampyris
In a glass jar.
   Toni Leeber

Birthing an Image

Mountains etched against the sunset
stand there only two dimensional
while bubbling champagne becomes just a flat dry wine.

The depth of long held friendship retreats to pleasantries,
and music, the redeemer of my moods,
washes helplessly at the glass door of my soul,
while sidereal space echoes only
the silence of God.
On an endless stretch of nothingness I float becalmed

Until . . . from some hidden soul-spring
a soundless struggle surfaces.
Myriad impressions
contract and then rush up
clamoring for order and expression.
Chaotic words eddy round the edges of my mind
swirling to combine and recombine
searching out linguistic chemistry
until at last in intimate liaison
they metamorphose into metaphor.
   Frances Boyle

Mighty Aphrodite

Mighty Aphrodite
have you come here to love me
wake me from my long sleep
lean on me when you weep
letting me rest upon your beauty
showing off your maternity
endorsing me in your loneliness
showing me shear utter happiness
you will no longer have to roam
I will give you a new home
please admit this one invasion
just trying to reach your salvation
let me crawl back into your brain
I promise you I will cause no pain
O'Mighty Aphrodite from heaven above
are you hear for me to love
   Tom Jackson

Tristan

Seedlings sprung from the fields
These pines were summoned
By his defiant hand.
Held by the arid winds
Beside these stones well set
To make a wall against the west.

Darker than the dial at dawn
They sadden the dim hot noons
As though there were
Or might have been
A rare tranquility and fallen rain.

I look away to speak of vervain
It blooms as it did a year before.
A pungent silence
Gray clouded leaves
Shadowed in spice and forgetfulness.

Old stones quivering in a new season
Shudder with the tides beneath
And a moon full of storms.
If these are tears
Say I am mourning a lost province.

Mary Kellerman

Standing Tall

Towering apparitions betray
fluid purity
fuming in fog abyss,
swaying against the mistral,
tethered in harmony.
Glass and steel,
coterie to gothic icons,
grace and elegance
echoes their simplicity.
Born of Mies,
side-by-side,
orphans,
that pirouette amid the shadows,
unmasking regal rhapsody
to gargoyles.
Undaunted and sublime.
Contemporary.
Innocent symmetry
embraced by monsters.

Bree Gale

Waiting

She waits
in a sepulchral chamber
and the sense of loss
is deeper than pain.
Hopefully she scans each face,
for the memory
hidden deep
of soft arms and gentle breath
is just beyond her reach,
teasing her
like the words to the tune
she hums
as she rocks
and memories bounce
off the walls of her mind.
Yet today she stares
in confusion
as a smiling young woman
takes her hands,
and says, "Hi Mama."

Ginny Marsh

Hunger

We spoke of revolution on young summer nights
Listening to the radio for news of the fall
While we flew proud flags, misunderstood
On our arms and our backs
Torn field jackets sewn with emblems
Of our fathers' war, long gone

How we prayed for peace, begged for release
Cursed Lyndon Johnson, Robert McNamara, William Westmoreland
Lifted our eyes to heaven and shook with righteous outrage
While we lifted cold cans of beer
To wash away our guilty innocence

In the end, the war didn't push them down
Dominos toppling neatly, suddenly red
But young men died anyway, screaming
Or silent, too shattered to scream
And the revolution never scratched
Corporate government on its marble Olympus
But it did rip our cities with riots
That, suicidal, ate themselves
Out of a desperate hunger for justice

Dave Gifford

Grandpa's Place

The trees flow graciously along my side like green buffalo herding
toward their favorite drinking hole.
No one speaks, as faces are studied.
To ourselves, we recall our first visit to the place—
The day the box fell . . . .

   His first daughter sees the snow fall as sent from heaven,
   His wife feels the paralyzing chill of fate and,
   My mother, feels the sacred essence of life.
    I, however see him . . . Gone.

Our arrival into the cryptic world holds us captivate.
Anguish floods my soul.

Souvenirs of him clutched firmly in my hand.
Dampness disguises my face, my eyes are heated.

Outside, the June air radiates against my skin . . . as I kneel to
plant my flower, his caffeine, his tobacco.

Kimberly A. Terlap

Tell Me The Day And You Will Tell Me A Lie

The muscles of my thighs
checked the descent
Into the angled drain
Of the two hills,
Filled with clay and serpentine rock
And roots of California oaks.
Alongside stark yellow madness
And deadened manzanitas
Beneath where banana slugs
Slither innocently.
And imminence is yesterday
And yesterday is tomorrow;
Yet my muscles tense
To check the slide
Into the grasping space of always inimical time.

David Edwards Allen Jr.

Waiting for Lilián At Café Premo

Fluorescent, hanging City-scene, urban banks and towers, crystalline.
This poster is the Realist's bane, this Time delayed behind airport picture-frames.

On this side of the mural, in my half-dozing state, between
dried-contact-lens-views of late comers sprinting toward their gates,
and the lucid taste of raspberry daiquiris that my tongue remembers,
and do-it-yourself group photos from Kodak Funsavers
shot at arm's length — just far enough away to capture our nervous embraces
that are unperformed (as only we Fantasists would have it)
so we can rehearse them to ourselves, perfecting Atlanta's first Platonic hug.

So this autumnal shutter stills our condensing sighs
and puts them away, dusty-trunk-in-the-attic-style. Click.
Well, that's it for this roll of twenty-four

Hours. Would that these impatient second-hands,
help me catch these dissolving hour-glass sands
and wrap them into packets of Equal, of Sweet 'N' Low
mixed in cafe mocha, in espresso.

Let me keep my soulful cobblestone scene
as I throw down the rest of this caffeine.
I'll trade you these tickets to first-class
for an Alice-Through-the-Plexiglas.
    Austin Lin

Moderns

Who knows my tribe knows who I am
Yet foreigner am I to most.
No chosen Khosa I, nor Kirghiz caravanner,
No Lett or Dutch, nor Basque on Biscay's coast.

The ancients liked their ditches, village fires.
Thereby, costumed, they spiraled, seared their fears,
Raw guards stood menacing at river passes: Toltec and Celt,
Bold Ainu, Bhote — fierce tribesmen shook their spears.

We moderns, whelp of nations, boast of one
Fused canton, yet adore each tribal residue;
Bird totems, phalluses, head wear, unknowing masks.
Old and primitive? What glamour! No cachet in the new!

Meantime the Tamil-Sinhalese brouhaha appalls us;
Somalis puzzle — Chechnya; Bosnian, Croat, and Serb;
The Tigre-Eritrean fight befuddled; Afghan wars;
Armenian pocket; Tajik tangle; Irish bombs. These all disturb.

My tribe is Plato's. Western values overpower; the Psalmist sings.
Augustine teaches all are sinners. Max Weber moderns praise.
Tom Jefferson hoisted nation's sights yond tribal-ness.
And Wilson (almost) conned a globe past ditching ways.
    Harold W. Mann

Who'll Come Tonight?

I live on a hill that has too many rooms.
Within there, wanderers never walk, except at night.
I smile and nod to him who helps my child.
And thank the girl who found my doll; then it is light.

With disregard of time or place — (prerogative of dreams)
I glide from Maid to Grand Mama! Then crawl in babyhood afright.
Gray mist obliterates the years.
My fellow visitors wander here or there, with age not right.

My lover's soft brown eyes go warm and moist.
We reach, but do not touch, each other's sight.
A caring teacher points a defect in my sums.
Two girls I bore (now grown) engage their childish fight.

I look down, while skimming up my hill;
Or is it up, while plodding down my toes do light?
When suddenly I pause for contemplation:
The wild gulls swoop, and so I too must soar, my form upright.

From them, I'll learn the answers they'll not give
To jumbled mixed-up goals for which I live; forgive my fright,
For I live on a hill that has too many rooms.
The children play. Men go. I'm always here. Who'll come tonight?
    Ruth Sigler Avery

Requiem

As once a proud, straight oak indelibly etched its leafless branches
Against a luminous winter sunset, and against my memory,
So stand you, my love, etched against my broken heart.
And I, stunned and dazed, beneath the ruthless crush of separation,
See you with an insight I knew not when you held me in your arms:
For then you were a part of me - - - warm and feeling, flesh and blood
But now the part of me is torn away,
I stand aside and gaze at the framework and structure
Of what you were.

And in that long, cogent look, I find dignity and strength
To meet with courage the gnawing ache and emptiness
Which will mark the passing of days
Until Time's non-committal and aloof but healing hand
Will soothe the ache which only reunion in immortality will cure.

But oh, my beloved, could I beg back but one hour of the relentless past,
Would I pour out my heart in a tender flow of endearing words
Which would perfectly express my love for you,
Or would I only lie mute and content in your sweet embrace
Secure in the knowledge that you understood?
Mary Ellen Huddy

Subterranean Visions

A strange magic hangs in the balance of a shy mystic
strangled in the consciousness that drowns
in a black-light eye sit down

Transcriptions of her royal soul
approach my dispelled mind
in a walk down Fifth Avenue

I'm wanting to hold her close hand, but it seems
to lie in a forbidden heaven and
universal hypnotism delays the first star
from enlightening the glory of
a fractured style of thought
that cringes at its own ideas
with a contorted face

Nirvana and an angel ride above the overcast sky
and we speak silent, doing nothing but attempting
to create memories in a day yet to come;
thinking of mixing new Coca-Cola with cheap bottles of rum
in a hunt for a time when legends will live
and the stars won't appear as torn lamp shades
Lucas Klotzbach

Secret

"Pupils! Attention please! Make deep bows!"
The grand marshal's voice pierced high into the sky,
Imperial princess "Shigeko," one year junior than he, followed
As swirling highborn fragrance caressed his lowered skinhead.
This narrow pebblestone walk to the sanctuary echoed
As if hundreds of followers were stepping "Riverdance" rhythm.

A midsummer sun was burning all over the Shrine of Mishima
While "Shigeko" prayed for victory to her ancestor.
Nineteen thirty seven's Far East was wavering in chaos after
Japan plunged into the endless battles against Mainland China.

Though born in poverty a commercial trade school freshman,
His unrequited adoration toward her gushed out with a rush.
"Is it really blasphemous sin being a roadside commoner?"
Asked himself. Heard was another voice, "Go with your thought!"

July twenty third, nineteen sixty one, at only age thirty six
Princess "Shigeko" journeyed to her origin, "Goddess Amaterasu."

Like a kaleidoscope, his vague sentimental memories loom large
In Southern skyline along the forest misted beyond silky drizzle.
At age seventy two, he still warms a vivid longing for her in secret
While Michigan's February stagnates low in the leaden universe.
Esaku Kondo

Pitchpipe

Sitting on the hood of his Mercedes,
the overdressed, overtanned bass
sneaks a cigarette in the gray evening,
flicking, tapping out off beats. Already inside
the cold rehearsal room, the bike-
helmeted tenor snacks in his spandex.
Crossing the street in tie-dyed sweats without
underwear, the earphoned bari sings quietly
with the group he saw Saturday. An enormous
belch half a block away signals the approach of
the beer-gut lead, still in his whites,
his stethoscope taps against the name tag.
Chatting comes to an end inside
when the A-flat is blown.
Magic begins, their voices mold into that
perfect tonic, causing three squirrels
on the window ledge
to drop stolen nuts
and applaud.

Jeff Kelly

Stephan's Kirche

347 steps to the top.
Aeolus gusting through the casement.
Birds spinning an interlacing canopy of air.
The city spread out below,
A tapestry of life, ever-moving.
The people below,
Gliding across the square,
Mere Threads
In the ever-changing Tapestry.
Gazing across the city,
Seeing the weaving
Continuing to the horizon and beyond.
The stairs is lead downward,
One . . .
  two . . .
    three . . .
      four . . .
        five . . . 347 steps to the bottom.
Stepping into the Tapestry,
Continuing the weaving my own Thread.

Angelika Klien

Ghost Of Time

Past
Tall, red, its pride revealed,
   dawn spilled through open doors.
Cocks cried greetings to first light,
   wagon wheels left squiggly tracks behind.
Field mice raced, scampered to hide,
   a cat pursued, out of sight.
Dusk darkened earth-streaked windows,
   tall, sturdy, in its prime.

Present
Weakened by the elements of age,
   shades of gray replace peeling red coats.
Morning sun shines through unopened doors,
   tracks come this way, no more.
Cobwebs encompass within, life moved on,
   meek, humble, an empty cocoon in time.

Future
Visions and thoughts will just assemble,
   only tomorrows can bring forth the words.

Linda Lee Jacobsen

Native Veil

Wintering in a terrace keystone,
Festering, a sympathy;
Partake of inhalation in stagnant catacombs...
the listener plays the role and holds the nectar for the bee

with armored gear and a nine yard pole,
half a mile inland from the embankment of the sea.

No touch so light could blister skin
like the attempt given, and the motive within.

Digging through the terrace layers
and spackling the rubble fallen below;
like icing on this trembling finger,
out of place and offering devotion
with a taste of betrayal in its creamy center,
Try it on the threshold of emotion.

Shifting foot to foot, to shuffling,
pieces of the terrace crackling, crumbling underfoot...
this once-sturdy foundation was established
too long ago, the mammoth recalled, hacking
the beekeeper's concoction: particles of benevolence and soot.

The archaeologists wanted to leave it buried.

Beth A. Boettcher

My Whispered Friend

How strange that I should feel this way.
How strange that you will never know.
Seems like I wasted time because
Destiny decided not to wait on me.
But my love is strong enough to
make this worst criminal a saint.
To make the wind call out your name.
And someday, I might tell you.
So when you're all alone and
you think someone has called your name,
Remember me, my whispered friend.

Michelle McMillan

The Visit

I make spaghetti
twisted red
squirted with lemon juice.

You squeeze lemon juice on
your hands
Your floral robe decorates your plum body like a lamp.
Your hair rests like delicate threads.

I don't visit you
Do I want to see the bronze plaque
with your husband's names
listening like dead soldiers?
Do I want to see the empty metal pot
Devoid of orchids?
Do I want to feel your hurt steam through cold marble?
Do I want to see my reflection in the empty bronze plaque?
Do I want to see my grandmother's legacy carved like a
lovesick teenager?

Do I want to grieve?

Barbara Rose Brooker

River Hill Geneology

I study the hilltop looking for I know not what, until they find me.

Bold and unlikely, Augustine and Philomena and Emma and
  great-great grandmother Mary Agatha
    (courteously stepped to the rear)
  and then
  Joseph and Mary — established presences
hinting at who they were that I have yet to learn
  — promising, promising —
and Grammy and Leo and Leone, and somewhere, Sam
and Daddy yearning, from elsewhere, farther south with other
  brothers to be closer to Mary Ann — still searching?
and nearby, I was told, my little lost child, but I cannot find her
  Perhaps they have.

I do not wonder about the others, though they, too, were communities.
That would be like looking at halls of mirrors facing each other —
  eternally diminishing aspects, peering uselessly.

They have settled amongst themselves, and I am here with mine
  seeing the same stars and sunsets, facing the same cold rain
connected to the spine of the land beneath the trees
  from which the rivers have lapped loose soil and leaves and stone.

      Gretchen Haller

Playing Basketball With God

I see you out there in the driveway, Big Brother,
throwing the ball at the rim time and again.
Just you and your crazy dreams.
You're twenty now; when will you realize that?
Your days of stardom have passed like the ball
which sails left of the hoop and into the trees.
I remember your days of slam dunks, shots that never missed
and a ball dribbled into a blur.
Who are you yelling at out there?
I watch you throw yourself into a bush behind the basket
and shout, "Foul! That's a foul!"
You shoot your free throws, missing both,
and grumble something about someone playing unfairly.
Still you continue on, dribbling around,
a muted ghost of your old dribble,
shooting over an imaginary opponent and talking to yourself.
When you come inside, I ask, "Did you win?"
"Not today. He was really on top of his game."

      Jim Bosiljevac

Little Things

It's not the confusion; nor the repetitiveness
Not even the sporadic anger that balls your fists
Not even that so much as
The awful blankness of the last minute
The inability to synapse the ordinary, the mundane
The damn banality of everydayness
The irrevocable loss of the infinitesimal connections between
this and that; here and there; now and later; you and I.

My anger, a vortex. Singular and witless
Rallying against an errant eraser that smears white into black
Tabula rasa in reverse. Leaving behind specks of
this and that; here and there; now and later;
You and I.

Oh sweet love of my life, my solo wayfarer
Hellbent on this inverse journey to your father's smile
Your old dog's antics; your mother's honeyed scent
I bow to the inevitable. Bid farewell to my anger.
Say "Godspeed" to you.
Not a little thing.

      Mev Borso Rozsman

Lines

Twenty . . .
Nineteen . . .
Eighteen . . .
Every word, taken away
by need, power, commerce,
"We must charge a nominal fee."
You must reconsider me.
Let me be whom I choose to be.
Give into this mystery,
this needing to see.

These words
are who
I am.

These
are
my
lines.

      Thom Ingram

Survivor

She wears the night like a shroud
  daylight interrupting denial
  memories clouded by fragmented chapters
  laughter conspicuously absent

Derailed and demoralized
  she clutches the bedsheets,
  grasping for answers to questions
  she is not capable of asking

The quilt of her world
  lays tattered at her feet
  in patterns of self-annihilation
  her antecedents claiming their victory

Four walls close in like a dedicated posse
  then, somewhere beyond consciousness
  the transient inferno dies to embers
  turmoil and stagnation sheds its ugly skin

Serenity embraces like a loving mother's arms
  her existence, once crimped and wrinkled
  remains behind like the bedsheets
  she has now escaped

      Marilyn Sanders

A Melody In Rose

At night, when dreams from slumber's state
Drift in the sky where stars devise
Their fixed positions to await
The brightness of a rapture's rise:
A melody in rose-quaffed notes,
My soul's refreshment, needs suppose,
And showers bliss on other folks
Whose thirsting lives would seek repose.
\Floats softly into billowed breeze
Bouquets of lovely hope, and, then,
Enchanting blossoms through the trees,
It rings, like chimes, past hill and glen;
The scattered petals--far and wide--
Feign dance in merry waltzing time,
And glide upon a swelling tide
Whose voice sings of a rose sublime.
   Dollyna K. Perry

Beauty Is The Hem Of God's Own Garment

"Beauty is the hem of God's own garment"
Look quietly and intently for a while,
Fragile things that are so very delicate
Are often those most favored by our smile.

Lovely things in any form or color
Delight us as we go upon our way,
So it is that we're most apt to worship
It's easy then to turn to Him and pray.

But, storms are beautiful the same as flowers,
The stones that cut our feet, He made them, too;
Waters rough are part of His own beauty,
And woodlands dark are worth our struggling through.

Beauty is the hem of God's own garment,
Let us touch it, let us hold it as we go;
The moonlight only comes to us in darkness
But darkness is not dark with Him, you know.
   Marguerite H. Atkins

The Country Doctor

He clings to a time that never was
  In his lifetime a reality
He believes in the good that every man has
  Tho' buried too deep to see

He believes if he hangs on that Good will win
  And I hope that he is right
But now the town's evil has festered
  And he's in for a hell of a fight

He believes in doctoring rich or poor
  Each person according to need
He would never refuse a man who can't pay,
  But his is a vanishing breed

Some of the doctors still new to the town
  Genuflect to a God called Greed
They keep bankers' hours, then go to the golf course
  And occasionally fix a nose bleed

In spite of the strife, he's nice to his wife
  And spoils his pets and his mom
We all wish him well - Send the bad guys to hell!
  Three cheers to my Brüderlein Tom.
   Jan Carroll Cole

Teen And Parent: A Driving Experience

"Don't worry, I'm behind the wheel!"
  (Of my not-yet-paid-for automobile!)
"Do you know how fast this car will go?"
  "Up to the speed limit, and no mo'!"
"Gee, I'm only going 35, and we aren't going far."
  "Why does it seem so fast on this side of the car?"
"Now I can drive and I feel so free!"
  (Just wait 'til you start paying the fees!)
"We need to get there quick, there are people waiting!"
  "That's no excuse for your tail-gating!"
"These other drivers go too slow."
  "It's most important to arrive safely, you know."
"All these other cars are passing me!"
  "It's OK, nothing says You have to speed."
"Look, we've arrived!"
  (And we're still alive!)
"When we drive home, is it still my turn?"
  "It's the only way you're going to learn."
   Edna Pakele

Oklahoma Tears -- April 19, 1995

Even though I'm just a teen
I'm affected by this scene

People running, screaming, crying
Others staring, falling, dying

Fear and terror all around
Grasping everyone in town

Disbelief and rage abundant
Suffering, anguish, all apparent

For little children, husbands, wives
Broken hearts and shattered lives

Lost in a moment of unreality
Cowardly, cruel insanity

All for a moment of personal gain
Causing a lifetime of unending pain

Through rivers of Oklahoma tears
Hands clasped together for future years

Saddened Americans side by side
With heads bowed for all who died
   Susie Simmons
   Oklahoman

The Navigators

To greater horizons
our 'Mentor Spirits' deftly *soar* . . .
Entrusting 'the traverse'
of souls . . . left traveling
(the wrong roads),
To We, who, have not yet,
found the path.
   Lindy Atkinson-Matalone

Eclipse

As the sun breaks the veil of night
A new hope appears in the sky
A joy comes over the land
And warms our weary hearts
It summons us to the day
And dispels the night
It is our guide by day
It is our dreams at night
It stays constant in its chase
Catching the moon from time to time
In the grand clash of the eclipse
There the sky is darken
But the sun emerges triumphant
As the moon withdrawals into the night
   Carl Hartman

Changes

   Tossed wildly about
by cold March wind,
snowflakes silently drift
into April's waiting arms.

Their frozen glitter
becomes glistening raindrops.

Their frozen glitter
Becomes glistening raindrops.

Vanishing into frozen earth
they whisper
To sleeping grass

"Come forth and show your colors"
Beauty welcomed
By May's soft music
Of birds soft music
Of birds and bees
Having a feast
At Nature's bounteous table.
   Agnes M. Phillips

A Bird Song

I knew something must have waked me up!
I did not know just what I had heard,
But getting out of bed was alright!
And it might have been the Mocking Bird.

I rose to stand at Bedroom window,
to make my eyes at window lookout!
as glancing to really see the Bird,
I knew I must not have my voice shout.

I stood there for a moment or two,
When its sound did truly reach my ear,
the sound of bird was a lovely song!
And the song did seem to be so near.

It was as sweet as an angels voice!
I knew that God had sent me the Bird,
to have me know the Bird is so good!
I'll always love the song I have heard.

And it truly was the Mocking bird.
I'm glad it sing at my home so long!
The Mocking bird makes me so happy,
That I can truly hear its sweet song.
   Violet Henson Anderson

Jinnah (The Founder Of Pakistan)

If Washington is for the dignity,
So, is Jefferson for the simplicity;
Then, Lincoln is admired, democratic polity;
But Jinnah, the Quaid-e-Azam, father of Nationality.

Oh! Weep for him, who wept and wept;
Wept with pain and agony, who seldom slept.

In whose mind, emerged a land of dream;
Where stands Himalayas, and flow five streams.

After Mughal, Pakistan's bounty once more to rejoice;
Mass movement leap'd on his heavenly voice.

It was he, who dug and discovered;
cut and polished, then defined;
Koh-e-Noor of Pakistani nationhood;
Saved from Hindu neo-colonists, best understood.

He made the Pakistan history, whole world admired;
A manifesto of freedom, Third World adhered.

His throat-cancer, T.B.-chest, bled;
Restless, penniless, fragile, but seldom slept!

At his mausoleum, together with the angels;
The wreath we lay, the tears we shed'll stay.
   Shah Salim Ahmed

Remembrance Of You

Walking through the whispering willow trees
Listening to the whispers of the night
Thinking of you with each heartbeat
Turning with sudden fright of being alone
Looking up to see the stars shining bright
The moon peeping from the edge of my world
Shivers embrace me, in the gentle breeze
The willows swaying, as the leaves play a soft melody
The night is young, the day left behind
Thoughts of you linger on
As with the wind, you're here then gone
The feelings of you still left within my arms
A feeling of wanting and a strong desire
The notion of being close at your side
Here all alone, with the secret of you
locked tight within my heart
Feeling the loneliness, the heartache,
And the emptiness of being without you
Looking forward to the light of day
When we'll be together once more.
   Glenda M. Pazhedath

Thru His Eyes

When I was a child, I spoke and understood the ways of children.
I approached manhood but kept my youthful spirit.
The pitch of my voice fell, while I climbed to maturity.
My mind, keep its virginity.
Its thoughts were simple, innocent, an untouched domain.
An invisible shield protects my imperfections,
Just long enough to master its disguise.
A challenge, a hurdle, a stumbling block
Weave an intricate pattern thru my life,
I have been given this fountain of youth, capable of
Spilling over on others who desire to drink.
My visions are sometimes clouded.
God's will is clear.
It's thru his eyes I am perfected.
   Christine Taylor Carr

An American Prayer

Pictures of women stare back at me
and I am at once amazed
what gluttony it must be to watch the world's queens
want me for reasons I'll never know
she tells me oh, don't go, please stay
I think why?!? My throat is dry
and too many dreams have told me that sweetness
only leads to cavities; huh huh I laugh
as I think about how she tells me that
I'm so nice and funny and with her Argentinean accent
she tells me you are a crazy guy and I laugh
as she tries to figure out our American jokes
and commonplace words such as "dude," and "dope"

In this dim forest candles are our only light
the calm sounds of the American Night ring in my ear
bon fire breathes life; charred wood (logs)

Young girl....
Vahaken Depoyan

Best Friends

I looked up and saw his face, and in an instant all time is removed.
A flash back to our childhood, with memories held throughout the
    years.
Just fourteen, the best of friends.
We took on the world together, without thought to the future.
Knowing friendships last forever, and ours would never end.
Yet fate travels many highways, and some we must walk alone.
He went off to college, I to fight a war so far away from home.
Now as his car pulls ever closer, I want to smile and call out his
    name.
But then, reality hits me and my heart tears in pain.
The window rolls down so easily, on his fine expensive car.
His arm is extended in my direction, holding a crumpled bill.
I lower my head and take it, for my face he doesn't see
Or he would recognize,
Best friends are forever and friendships never die.

John J. Sloan

My Mask

Behind my mask I hide my pain,
    and the war that is raging inside my body.

Behind my mask I hide my emotions,
    which are churning and clouding my thoughts.

If I show my pain,
    you will grow tired of my complaints,
    you will grow tired of my illness,
    you will question my honesty,
    you will tell me I must like the attention,
    you will eventually turn away, and leave me.

If I show my feelings,
    you will see my frustration,
    you will see my loss of control,
    you will see I am telling the truth,
    you will see my wish to escape,
    you will see my endless tears, because I am alone.

So, I put on my mask.
    I try to smile. I try to laugh.
    I try to act like you want to act.
    But, this is not who I am. My mask is a lie.

Kim Kingsbaker Jones

Praying For A Lady III

I'm kneeling now to say a prayer
I beg you Lord to please be fair
I'm praying for a lady dear
Please help this lady not to fear

The lady friend at times you see
Has helped to calm and comfort me
Her smile, her wit, her charming way
Is why I'm on my knees to pray

She needs you Lord, so I will pray
She needs you now in every way
She needs a hand from up above
To calm her fear, to soothe, to love

Dear God listen to my plea
I pray with deep humility
I beg you Lord, to set her free
My friend you see, is Norma G.

J. Patrick Stephens

At The Portal (An Epitaph)

At the portal
The mortal
Chortled
In the face
Of eternity.
"Don't chortle,
Mortal,
At my portal,
Or you will be sorry
For eternity
Gets even
Sooner or later."

James W. Cole III

A Quiet Talk

A quiet, whispered call to God
Is just a prayer away.
I have only just to call His name
and ask for guidance through my day.

I know, without a doubt, He's there
I feel His presence every where.
There is no friend so dear
As the one who understand my prayers.

He gives me peace and happiness
And love beyond compare.
I have only just to call His name
and I find He's always there.

Irene Hicks

Nieve

I search deep into my soul,
    so lost and cold.
The answers seem so few.
The eyes and ears hold close to you.
The tears fall, the heart races.
Why you? Asked so much through my mind.
Why did I have to be the target.
I open my heart, mind and soul.
Only to have it torrent apart
    like some sick form of art.

Lindsay Gaken

At The Cabin At Tahoe

There was rain in the pine trees,
Wind in the eaves;
Fire in the fireplace,
You close to me.
Blue eyes so piercing,
Dark curly hair,
Lips full of passion
When I kissed you there.
Finally coals in the fire place,
Music volume down;
There was bliss of a lifetime
In the happiness we found.

Louise Butts Hendrix

Mirror

To be an inspiration,
Is how I would aspire;
As when a creative thought,
Becomes a consuming desire . . .

I am an apparition,
Of what's within your soul;
To give a glimpse inside yourself,
Is my only goal.

Like on a pool of water,
Your reflection, you see;
But the image that looks back at you,
Isn't you—It's me!

We Are One!

L. S. Waldo

In The Labor Of Love

When someone hears of the family I have
They say, "Oh, your poor woman"
    And I've often wondered,
Why can't they, just once in a while,
    Say, "Oh, you poor tired man!"
He's the one who puts bread on the table,
Shirts on their back and shoes on their feet.
Sure, I cook, wash and mend
Wipe runny noses and heal skinned knees
    It's true, my work is never done!
But when the kids are in bed
And the clock has been wound,
His book he puts down,
My mending is laid aside.
We clasp hands, and with a smile on our face
Offer a prayer of thanks
To the One up above
For our family, our health and our strength
And the day just spent
In the labor of love.

Martha Dobbs

Just Plain Tired!

I'm happy, I'm sad, my emotional state is a mess,
it changes from one to the other I do confess.

Mixed up, confused, are all in the world like me?
I'm not alone, I've got 3 kids and a husband you see.

Should I not be happy all of the time?
I'm very tired, worn out, is this such a crime?

Dusting, cleaning bathrooms, it never does stop,
cooking and cleaning, "Who took the mop?"

Strong and supportive, I am a good mother,
to Amanda and Ryan and their little brother.

Do they see the inside me, the one that's distraught?
Money? "Oh crap! More socks to be bought?"

Restraint, composure, I'm told, it can be done.
"Oh" psychiatric help, is this how its won?

Up and down, sideways? My thoughts tends to go,
be content, just relax, "Ouch! You stepped on my toe."

Cody is whining, water is boiling, cats in my lap,
the ball through the window I'm taking a nap!

Sarah Cummins

For Wendy And Jeff

A child is our messenger to a time we will not see
    A voyager to be sent out on uncharted waters
    "Where will they go?"
    "What will they be?"
    Many questions - few answers
Some things we know
    Our love will fill their sails with a strong, but gentle wind
    Guidance we give, a compass to guide them on their way
    Like young birds we teach them to fly, then let them go
We are fortunate to have the experience
It is part of our own voyage
A cycle, repeated, into eternity

    Mackenzie is your messenger
    The voyage has begun.

Eli Isaac Chyatte

God

My life was quite complete, secure
I do believe in God.
But people say that God is dead,
That God does not exist . . .
I look around me and get so scared
The emptiness crawls slow in my heart.
I feel so small, alone and lost
And troubled with so many questions.
If God does not exist, If God is dead
To whom we cry for help in desperate moments
Or pray when our child is sick?
Who give us beauty of majestic mountains
The valleys, lakes, and forest with the singing birds?
Who scatter millions of shining stars
Like diamonds on the purple velvet?
Oh, no, God does exist.
He is all around us
From little flower to the highest sky
And deep as hope in us.

Liudmilla Palumbo

Self Analysis

None can stay or stop the hand of time,
As it moves in its own relentless rhyme.
The clock moves the same for pauper or king,
And in the end all feel the sting!
The hair grows gray; the eyes grow dim!
Each year sees less of pep and vim!
You see your friends are growing old,
But fail to see the lines your face does hold.
None can see a true picture of me,
Perhaps that is to save our sanity!
For how much more difficult life might be,
Should I ever see the me that others see!
As we see ourselves through glasses of rose,
Others see what we unknowingly disclose,
All our faults we wish not to see,
Are apparent to those other than me!
So gloat not too much you are not as other men,
Lest you see the real you now and then!
And find to your sadness your words are true!
That sadly; most men are better than you!

Jesse D. Peay Jr.

Both Sides

The pessimist has no desire to spread his wings,
and fly over the moon.
The optimist can swallow the sea if encountered.
One of the above sees beauty, the other torment.
One embraces his senses, the other gasps.
One will soar without direction or boundaries,
the other will be frozen forever in a dark reality,
or maybe it only feels like forever.
As they both grow old, one will leave a mesmerizing
tapestry of his life, the other will recede into his dark
cave until his heart is still.

Virginia L. Ganley

These (Little) Insipid

Frail (Rosebuds)...did not...grow!! (?)
...in Texas or Rome!! (?) But come-
What (May)?-From upper west side.../-
Fire escape (?)...-burnt out by rosered-

Fingertips (?)-unlike (our heroine)-
Clytemenstra (with(tiny wrists)they..)
Wrestle...(like (baby tigers)!! (?) (?)))
She should (have known) in 100% humidity-

....-(Nothing(can grow))!!-a reminder...
of(her past)...and Russian(vodka and drunk-
Lips)!! (?)-so sweet...in(blue cup)...but
...in control (limp(as soft kisses?)....

Bent(over(unfurled)like-(little girls)?)
Serrated and-(set) (-in stone)yet-whispering...
Like whippoorwill or nightingale-to(this-day)/
-Just (4) common(limp lilies)..-in (despair!)?

-Like(Baby rabbits)...throats (torn) beyond (repair)?

Philip Sherrod

Cool Stand Earth

The image of the big hot sun
fell into the rose garden
Leaving us little design
But to cool stand earth

Waiting on the rising Saturn
We grin that in between
Old sol and tribal semi-sonic
Was the cool stand shade earth

Rising as the shadow
Calypso to event
Paradise sugar middle east
Cool stand earth

Some believe midway
Between wonder reggae
Was the power beneath wings
Cool stand earth

Active as the aura
of the promote natural
commute cross walk
Cool stand earth

Isabelle Hunter

My Daily Prayer

Help me, Dear Lord, as days go by,
To look ahead without a sigh.
And though at times I may be weak,
Help me to turn the other cheek.
May I behave as a child,
And let my angers all be mild.
Give me the strength to forgive,
Everyday that I live.
When a friend is in need,
Let me help in word and deed.
Give me the power to be humane,
And love my brethren more than gain.
To meet the stress that life poses,
And always stop to smell and roses.

Audrey T. Furr

Valley Woman

Held fast to the plains
Trapped in the mire of living
I bloody the earth with frustration,
Salt the wound with bitter tears.
For I know a man
Who walks the mountain tops,
Carries the sky within his eyes,
Tracks the path of falling snow
Traps the wind.
Leaving me
In the mountains shadow
To be taunted by the wind,
Bruised
By the falling snow...

Sandra Hudgins

Untitled

Lay down your shield
For I am here to help you.
Invite me in so I can protect you
From the pain.

I feel the sorrow
That boils inside.
I feel the cracks
In the broken heart.

Don't build that wall,
For I am part of you.
If you close me out
I will not come back.

We are one together
And two alone.
Take off your mask
Let me feel the pain.

I will ease it for you.
So we can share
And prosper together,
As one

Mary Saffrin

An Artist's Lament

I stand by coffin, in wonder
to see me, so stiffly, lying there
with cheeks that are "far to healthy"
and the curl, removed from my hair.
My chest, so broad and muscular, in life
now, sunken, and shallow, from care and strife
my hands are folded, at last, in peace
no more to draw - reduce, increase, but wait
there's a hint of a smile on my lips
at last, in death, I've found a way to rob
all who were guilty, of, that quip or quips
that "time worn" phrase "thank you Bob"

Robert Champ

Everything

Missing you is a state of being
  I can never leave behind
Wanting you is a magical thought
  I embrace and ponder in my mind
Needing you is a constant feeling
  I dance with throughout the day
Loving you is a wondrous magic
  I hope will never go away
Missing you, wanting you
  needing you, loving you
Not a day has passed without these
  Since the day I felt
  Your heart as it was touching mine
Missing you, wanting you
  needing you, loving you
Never shall a day pass without these
  gifts so rare and beautiful
  growing stronger throughout time.

Rhonda McCulley

The Old Buckley House...

I love you old house! I can't say just why...
So snug on the knoll, out lined 'gainst the sky.
The charm of your shape, the old lovely trees,
And, even the bent fence somehow doth please.
The family who built you, way back in the past,
I'm sure are just filled with memories that last.
The running of feet on the sturdy stairway,
The banging of doors, as they went out to play.
The pleasant large kitchen, with flies buzzing 'round
And, all thro' the orchard the fruit on the ground.
The lilacs in back, which scented the air,
The rich dark earth gardened with care.
And, looking thro' windows stained different hues
One saw the waters with various blues...
Sometimes they were calm and restful to see
But sometimes were angry, and dashed on the lee.
Those glorious sunsets of red, yellow, gold...
Some wispy and fragile, some solid and bold.
Could I just paint this picture, plus islands afar,
The soft evening color... and in it a star.
Oh! Beauties around us... how it helps us to live!
What comfort... what pleasure... what succor it gives!

Emelia L. Bave

You Were There

You were there, when we laughed the day through
That was when my sky was blue

You were there, when the storm clouds gathered
And my dreams shattered

You were there, when I had a broken heart
My world seem to had fallen apart

You were there, when my tears flowed
And my life was on over load

You were there, to listen and listen again
You were my good friend

You gave me hope, that soon the sun would shine
And a smile I would find

Thank you for being my friend
With the help of God and a friend, I know that I will win

Ludema M. Garza

A Poetry Day

Just before dawn when every-thing is still
I dream of rolling meadows and green hills
It seems as if I'm floating away
I know that I'm embarking on a poetry day.

Trouble seems unimportant or not at all
My mind fill with images short and small
They just won't go away
So I embark on a poetry day

All problems are solved with the stroke of a pen
I forget when they started and where they end
All of my troubles seem to go away
As I embark on a poetry day.

Suddenly there is inspiration all around
All I have to do is write it down
When I'm disturbed I say, "go away"
I'm embarking on a poetry day.

Maureen H. Cottonham

Heart Of A Poet

You hit a snag wanting to give up on tomorrow,
thinking it easier to hide the hurt inside.
Puffs of subtlety and clever idioms cloud the issues,
building walls to conceal whatever.

We spend so much time wasting time,
hiding behind facades to mask the pain.
We could be doing so much more.
Like drafting in the rain, drops;
or create a line or two expresses
the tide flowing boldly to the shore and back again.

Touch the heart of a poet and walk with angels, know life in
simpler form.
Look to the sky, and think about the sun giving itself to the sea.
And then, at the time of dawn, the sky calls to bring it home again.
It's important to know the dark times,
making tomorrow's light a road to somewhere else.

The midnight pit awaits.
But think about the lone branch inside
that stretches out to break the fall for the chance to start again.
Believe it or not, tomorrow will come. It always does you know.

Rodney Drake

No Longer

I can no longer brush my teeth or comb my hair.
I can no longer get dressed up or wear jeans.
I can no longer go on vacations or take short trips.
I can no longer watch the change of seasons or make plans for the
future.
I can no longer watch the children grow or play in the snow.
I can no longer be with you, my family, in the way I have been.
I can no longer see my dreams fulfilled or be a part of my family's
life.
I am no longer my parents' son or my brother's brother on earth.
I am no longer my friend's friend on earth, but I am your son,
brother, and friend in heaven.
I am no longer with you, I am with God.
I wish I were still there, but unfortunately, I am not.
You see, someone took my life from me.
It was not my choice to have my life end at this time.
Know that I am with you—in your heart, in your mind, and in your
soul.
Please remember me, do not grieve, I am happy with God.

Pattye Probasco

Our Life Together

You walked into my life over thirty years ago
Carrying a box of chocolates as I recall
It took only six months for us to tie the knot
We went through the years loving, sharing and
having a ball

Had many wonderful years and a few not so hot
But we hung in there and I'm so very glad we did
Now in our retirement years as I look back over our lot
I know it was fate that brought us together so
very long ago

But it is the love we share that keep us on the
straight and narrow
And it is that love that will carry us beyond
today and through all our tomorrows

Audrey R. Kachelriess

A Red Rose

A scarlet red rose
As delicate as porcelain,
As precious as gold.

Jessica Reilly

Picasso

I walk down the street
with my red painted lips
nose in the air
men look and stare

They like what they see
the enigma in me
a lovely Picasso, a rare find
surely, one of a kind

They want me but can't have me
can't afford me
I'm the works of a Spanish milegro
a lively Picasso

Yolanda Aldape

In Shakespeare, Lost

Perched high and far
above the crowds,
in Shakespeare, lost.

This spot chose I
to stimulate
all my senses.

In the corner
alone I sit,
fifth floor, alone.

Dreaming of dreams
Of days to come,
Of tests at nine.

Perched high and far
above the crowds,
in Shakespeare, lost.

Christopher S. Robertson

A Gentle Soul

I gaze upon a mountain and great
  Majesty I see,
And from the autumn forest, each
  Tree is there for me.

It is from thy wisdom that lies
  Deep down inside,
That allows by deceptive grace
  My heart to fill with pride.

Thou art my every waking breath
  And prayer from bended knee,
For it is by your strength alone
  That I remain just me.

While others are destructive
  Waves upon a sandy shoal,
I am but an aging shroud, for
  Thee, my gentle soul.

James W. Duncan

Universal Soul

Time cannot erode our universal soul
Conscious stream of every being...
Dignity its mantel...clarity its name
Change its wonder...passion its flame...
Entwined in ancient spirits of long ago...
Listen! Hear music of our soul....

It will weave a story of wisdom
That is ours...each must tend it
And play their parts...know this
Truth and let its magic start...
Elusive thought it be broken world's
Weep and heal within its heart...

Bridge from past to future days
Each strand memories braid
Mosaic pattern of our ways
Power of its source beyond ken
Of men...mortal though we be
Let all strive to seek its mystery...

Celestine H. Smith

Riding Piggy-Back

Big fluffy snowflakes
Floated lazily from the sky;
Smaller ones drifted aimlessly,
Catching bigger ones drifting by.

I watched the erratic flutters,
Playing "Catch me if you can!"
Skittering with the whims
Of the west wind's capricious plan.

They varied their winding pathways
With puffs of breezes, making no sound;
Little popcorn snowflakes riding
Piggy-back down to the ground!

Edna May Hermann

The Girls I Knew

The girls I knew
When I was young
Are wrinkled now
And go unsung.

The girls whose looks
Turned knees to jelly
Have straggled locks
And sagging belly.

The girls I loved
So way back when,
Do those girls know
I'd love again?

Have they an inkling
Of this truth:
Behind my wrinkling
Laughs a youth?

For me their truth
Must be the same:
They dance their youth
Just slightly lame.

Ralph E. Grimes

First Frost

A heavy dew covered everything that night.
The temperature dropped suddenly during
the first hour of the morning and covered the
brilliant fall-colored leaves and everything else
with an icy white frosting. The crimson sunrise
crept up over the horizon and painted the few
fluffy white clouds in the sky dusty-pink as it
flooded the deep blue sky with light. As the
warmth of the sun melted the icy frosting off
of the brilliant-colored tree leaves, large drops
of water splattered onto the ground. The white-
frosted stone fence turned back to its gray-black
hue and the late crop of hay in the field once
more became golden. Until the tree leaves started
to fall when the brisk wind began to blow, the
brilliant-colored leaves sparkled like multicolored
diamonds. Jack Frost's white-frosted beauty melted
away, then we enjoyed a warm autumn day.

Alyce M. Nielson

Ballad Of The Homeless

From cardboard coffins buried beneath freeways
they rise
Like roots of a well-watered weed
they rise
Each morning city streets explode under their maniacal gaze
These jobless ministers of begging seeking to fill a need
they rise
To patrol the unholy streets they have converted from a maze
they rise
driven by an inborn American greed
they rise
these merchants of this begging craze
determined to be successful, to have a good day, to fulfill
a creed
they rise
as determined to be on time as the office workers
rushing to the safety of the high-rises
Be slow in nailing the coffin shut
For they are us
these souls that have fallen into the dust

Lee Harris

Autumn Leaves

My mind is like unto a pile of fallen leaves;
Wherein a mouse doth move this way and that;
Stirring the crumpled confusion of leaves,
Sniffing for a strayed tibit of thought that
Vanishes 'er the scent is found.
I must write it quickly for the thought
Can ne'er be retrieved. It goes and comes no more.
Unless, in another form, unrecognized,
Amid the scurry of fallen leaves;
Wind driven. Mouse moved. Touched with fairy kisses.
For the leaves within the mind are but compost
For future thoughts, changed to fit the new.
The prickly, dusty edges softened so that
Flowers may bloom among them. Shining thoughts
Bright with new found truth and beauty
That ever grows new thoughts and feelings,
From the litter of the past
Experience, loves, talk, thoughts and prayers
Mixed together as a pile of fallen leaves.

Carol Kinch

Dance Of Life

Pull and part we pulsate the rhythm of life...
Music of our journey orchestrates our friendship.
Our rhapsodical imagination draw us together
Embraced in oneness with our Creator.
Quietly moving we express our passion to be fully human.
Compassionately we listen to our fluctuating feelings
   as we trust in our whimsical dreams.
Joyfully relaxed in God's love we risk being alive and
   creatively leap to the
     ..."Dance of Life".

Corene K. Besetzny

I Listened To You, Mom

You told me not to drink.
You told me not to give into peer pressure.
I listened to you, mom.
I did not drink a sip.
But how come I am the one lying here in a pool of my own blood?
I listened to you, mom.
How come the person who decided to drink,
Is not lying on the cold pavement surround be her own blood?
I listened to you, mom.
How come her heart is still beating?
Why, oh why, am I the one to die?
I listened to you, mom.
I am dying because somebody else decided to drink and drive.
I guess that person gave into peer pressure.
I listened to you, mom.
I guess she was just a weak girl.
I hear the sirens coming up the block now, I know I am to die.
I listened to you, mom.
If only that girl listened to her mom.
I would still be alive.

Janice Smith

The Lady In White

In the foggy mist of the night air
the lady in white drifted past the lamp post
in a dark corner of an alley way.
He caught a glimpse of her black hair
which flowed in the evening breeze like a wave.
As he blinked,
she was gone in an instant.
Among a midnight glow of the moon
shadowed by dark gray clouds,
a soft, flowing veil began to unfold.
he followed her into a white picker fence park.
A sunlight began to appear from the clouds,
he spotted a silhouette.
Among the greenery,
he was captivated by the liveliness he felt
in the morning air.
When he looked down at his feet,
the cold stone beneath him read
Abigail Foxbury
1928-1961.

Janice M. Chang

Smooth As Silk

Who? Shows his gratitude,
Endearing qualities,
Unconsciously plays
his nonjudgmental role
with Perpetual
Infantile Innocence,
Protection and support;
Unconsciously accepts
my care; my love?
My dog, silk.

Mary Lou Wire

A Bride's Song Of Love

"Come, my love, make love to me;
Show me how lovely true love can be?
Come deep within, until I can hold you
   tightly, beneath my skin:
This is how all life must begin.
And, what a lovely way to start!
Holding each other close, heart to heart,
No longer alone, no longer apart!
Now we belong to nature's history;
Now we are a part of life's great mystery!
for, life's greatest mystery is life itself.

Gloria R. Barron

New Snow

A soft white mantle God has laid
Of sparkling snow in morning light
His busy hands have changed the world
With flake by flake throughout the night
The first dim rays of the coming dawn
Begin to change the black starlit sky
To blues and grays with a pinkish hue
So birds can fly and soar on high
Stream beds sleeping 'neath the snow
Waiting patiently for a breath of Spring
Tiny rivulets then silent flows
As Mother Nature turns the snows
From soft white blankets of crystal glows
To feed the streams and ponds below
First with a whisper so soft and low
Then louder and louder to a huge crescendo
It cries to all the land and trees
To all creatures in the land to see
The new snow will be changed to Spring

Keith John Nichol

Wisdom

Wisdom, is gained by growing each day
   finding the answers, in our own way.
This helps to, give us new insight
   with the candle of understanding, to
   sheds new light.

Helping others, to see what's right
learning, as we go our own way.
To hopefully now, gain insight
by seeking the answers each day.

Karen P. Gilley

The Party

Smiling faces and rambling talk,
ribbons of laughter drift from the walk;
words belying an inner feeling,
eyes looking down or at the ceiling.

Boredom masked by glasses of gin,
covetous eyes drinking for sin
with any girl who flashes a smile
and willing to go that extra mile.

Winding ribbons of exposed flesh
aching for flattery from the press;
cynical smiles concealing disdain
for others seeking corresponding acclaim.

Jubilation and sorrow faintly entwined
where flesh presses flesh of mingling mankind;
silent rebuke of the whole affair
but planning ahead when all will be there.

Harold Corey

I Miss You

Sometimes I'm surprised
To find how much
You're still with me.
How easily my mind finds you
In searching for a place to rest.

It seems that somewhere
In the months and miles
Between us,
The thoughts of you
Should have faded....

But no,
At the slightest reason...
Indeed,
for no reason at all...
I think of you.

I miss you.

Verley Lloyd Boyd

Walking In The Early Morning

I put on my walking socks and shoes,
Starting my daily exercise.
Just around the sunrise.

I look upward to the last side,
What a splendid display on the sky!
Who painted it so well and so high!

The neighborhood streets are very quiet,
The surrounding looks peace and calm,
Only the busy birds joyously sing and fly.

They try to wake up those people,
Who are still in their dreams,
To search their own inside.

They never enjoyed the
early morning delicious fresh air
Which millions money cannot buy.

The excitement speeds my walking pace,
I feel that I just want to fly.

Patricia Kao

Mom

My mother, so dear my earliest memories.
I fondly recall.
A slim, pretty lady . . .
with red lipstick and purse . . .
She'd let me sleep with her for
my afternoon nap
Sometimes in the night
I'd cuddle between her and dad.
She'd lay my head on her lap,
and stroke my hair . . .
And the world was perfect . . .
I was happy right there.
She helped me with homework,
and cooked my favorite foods . . .
she called me her baby when I was fourteen years old.
Mom now you're eighty, and I am fifty . . .
You are so cherished . . .
you'll never know . . . .
I love you mom, now are a lady . . .
my darling mother . . .
I am still your baby.

Eva A. Ness

A Cloud

Look up at the sky.
Take a moment and look around.
Especially on a sunny day.
No matter where you are.
It could be a incredible discovery.
That touches the imagination of all ages.
Look at the different shapes forming.
It's such an irresistible
play on the eyes and mind.
Which gives the feeling of a peaceful refrain
A cloud may come, glossy white or grey,
They seem to be so soft and fluffy.
See how the wind blows, around and through each one.
Just watch them float by. Way up high, in the sky.
Try comparing one cloud to
Something you've seen.
No matter where it may be.
Take a moment to glance at the cloud.
Look up at the sky.
And see them as they go rolling bye.

Mamie Lou G. Williams

Lost

Lost in a world of wonder.
Not knowing what to expect next.
The thrill of all the wondrous details of my fantasy.
Lost in a sky of vivid blue desert.
Watching the vivid colors change from hour to hour.
Lost in a ball of emotions.
It is love or fun?
Do I mourn or celebrate.
Speed up or slow down?
Lost not knowing what to do next.
My mind is filling with great expectations,
that will probably never be real.
Lost isn't so bad,
if you have someone to be lost with.

Kristy Smith

My Garden Of Prayer

There is a place so beautiful, so fair
Where I can go with my burdens and cares
A place so vast and spacious
and filled with a heavenly aurora to grace it.
A place of quiet solitude and gracious air
I call it "Garden of Prayer."

This is a beautiful place with no doors to close
No rules, no limits, you may enter as oft as you choose.
A place, once you enter, you will return
Because anguish within will no longer churn.
My friend, it's a place to seek God and pray
But, seek Him in, "My Garden of Prayer."

Each night as I enter "My Garden of Prayer"
To ask the Lord's blessing on those for whom I care
And His voice, soft as a whisper speaks to me
My child, just be what I ask you to be
I'll carry your burdens and bless your day
But first, you must enter, "My Garden of Prayer."

Meryl M. Schiess

Man In The Mirror

Who is that Man in the Mirror.
Man in the Mirror Reminds Me of a very special Person.
Man in the Mirror wonders where He has been or
Where He is going.
Man in the Mirror is He lost?
Man in the Mirror just realized He is an Adult.
Man in the Mirror confused, Shy, unsure of His abilities.
Man in the Mirror, A stranger staring back.
Man in the Mirror, Worries, feels unloved, seeks help, but
in Public appears confident.
Who is the Man in the Mirror someone's Husband, Brother,
Father, or is the Man in the Mirror every Man in the World.

John Sanchez

Open Eye Soul

My open eye soul was serene in solitude,
like the white clouds diversed in the blue sky,
forming unsimilar shapes in full magnitude,
suspended in space, a new world in height.

The dark, penetrating shadows in seclusion
reflected on the ocean, sired a ructious drubbing,
enclosing me in distrust and disconcertation,
relinquishing, serenity, emerging, high binding.

My rebellious soul confronted its darkness
with fortitude, wisdom and a cosmic courage.
It cried for freedom, content and lightness,
in the new world of altitude and bondage.

The cotton balls became my only inspiration
The eagle strengthened my languished energy,
a white, round pond heightened my contemplation,
a legion of angels restored my placidity.

A dozen of white pines on isolated bareness,
sparking as heavenly queens in shining places,
penetrated my soul in a sublime gentleness,
in the round ball of the wide open spaces.

Arlene F. De Rodriguez

Voices Of The Past

Voices of the past are calling
  as echoes of herds abound.
    The soft sweet swish of the arrow
    as the buffalo hits the ground.

The sounds of dancing with war paint
  the settler's wagons are near.
    And the drums build up to a fury
    drumming out any doubts or fears.

The feathers that are worn so proudly
  speak of their victories past.
    Eyes that light up in terror
    as the enemy's guns start to blast.

Innocence, pride and glory;
  centuries of freedom are gone.
    Once a proud and happy people
    Whose voices have been quiet too long.

Ron Nicely

My Choice

With idleness, inertia is born,
Indulgence from dust to morn.
By hiding, dozing, playing, lying,
And constant non attending;
Inoculating, drinking, sniffing,
Crashing, torturing, sleeping,
Procrastinating, loafing, evading,
It's my mind I'm destroying.

In quietness, a fortress rises,
From bits of changing sizes.
By watching, hearing, feeling, smelling,
Expostulating, mulling,
Meditating, hypothesizing,
Judging, telling, inferring,
Manipulating, discovering,
That's my mind I'm constructing.

Evelyn N. Burrows

Like Romeo And Juliet

I want us to be like Romeo and Juliet,
So in love with each other, so set;
In our ways.

I want us to go through triumph and pain,
To test our strength,
Tell whether we're crazy or sane.

I want us to be so absorbed in our love,
We only care about each other,
And no one above.

I want us to love each other,
Till death do us part,
With all of our soul,
And all of our heart.

Kristin Sforzo

My Heart

My heart aches from the pain.
My body wants to be held.
But he doesn't love me anymore
and I doubt he ever will.
It's not the way it was before
and it never will be
but maybe one day he will understand
all the pain he caused me.
The sky is dark cause I hurt so bad
and in my heart it is always raining.
I can't waste my life on just one man
and I know my destiny is gaining.
   Rebekkah Plummer

Vows

Radiant, reverently the couple,
exchange marriage vows.
Hearing them recite in "sickness
and health", my mind strays.

Lost in thought, remembering my
grandfather, a inspiration model.
Faithfully loyal, in caring for my
bedridden grandmother.

Drawing up a mental image, of him,
methodically braiding her hair.
Rummaging through a box of ribbons,
adorning her with pastel bows.

Recalling him carrying her outside,
and inadvertently forgetting her.
Panicky over the lapse, desiring
only she remain with him.

Refocused, listening to the words,
"I pronounce you husband and wife."
Time only revealing, what challenges
the couple will face.
   Pat Bordner

I Think Of Youth!

I think of Youth!
I think of Youth!
I often think of Youth!

Just a glimpse of the serpents tooth ..
Poisoned at the root..
In the taste of bitter fruit...
We come to know the final truth..

I think of Youth!
I think of Youth!
I often think of Youth!

A super sleuth in a suit..
The cheerful expressions of a mute..
Piano lessons and the flute..
That girl next door was very cute..

I think of Youth!
I think of Youth!
I often think of Youth!

I think of Youth!
I think of Youth!
I often think of Youth!
   Brettioes Spurling

Restoration Of Peace

At a time in our life we begin to see
the meaning of our direction

In the event we experience the 'sting
of death' of one close to us

The promises our Creator made to all
of us, expressed as the 'Resurrection'

Not a restoration of life to pain, sorrow
or tears of this system.

But a life promised of peace, beauty and wisdom.

The Creators purpose for the earth
to enjoy and inherit as his children

We can choose freely the knowledge
that gives that direction promised.

To have part in the restoration of
the earth to the purposed paradise

To welcome back loved ones, who
like Lazarus given restored life

As a result of our choosing of knowledge
that will give us that future so precious

Can the appreciation of life through
the loss of a dear one remind us
of this promised 'Restoration'?
   Annette Vessey Garvin

The Raindrop

As I watched the falling rain,
It fell upon my window pain.
As I watched the raindrops trickle down
And fall upon the thirsty ground.

As I watched the grass, the trees, the buttercups,
They soon drank all the raindrops up.
This is God's way of quenching the thirst
Of he plants, the flowers, the trees of this earth.
   Anita G. Sowers

Drifters From Safe Land

She climbs azure tides spritzed soft with fragrant summer mist.
Drifting her crimson vessel across blue crystal wisps.
On a misguided voyage toward wildly chanting seas,
tossing her splintering wood skiff, windswept, carelessly.

Through surging wrath, a shielding reef, would be, if she knew,
the lofty coastal compass watch, if only once in view.
While thirsting swells in her breast, sinking her with each wave,
she spews out death to reject the typhoon's cryptic grave.

As saturating gloom drips from black Van Gogh like skies,
her boiling remorse escapes her in prayerful cries.
Then from somber petition, His glaring shaft appears.
So to the cresting rocky cliff is where she saw to steer.

Like her resurrecting hope, Supreme warrior dressed
against the ebon tempest blear, His bright beacon pressed.
Returning souls as many times as drifters from safe land,
boldly guides the lighthouse ray, much like the Savior's hand.
   Susan Stowe Phillips

Caretakers

As you give of yourself so I shall return of me
The love only we can share
for it includes no one
as it is ours.

Caretaker's are the chosen to carry the emotions of all
Takers are suppose to look to caretaker's for sorting and answers
the burden's of the selected roles are heavy
One no more than the other.

Trauma is something out of the ordinary
for someone who has not experienced it
there is no explanation,
all that can be expected is caring
for understanding is a realm only for the traumatized of which
the traumatized fear giving there trauma and suffering to others.
There isn't a person who hasn't had a traumatic experience
from the age of a newborn child found in a dumpster
To the elderly fearing the unknown as the past becomes clearer than
the present.
   Barbara J. Bartow

Disciple's Dilemma

Life is a river coursing from an unknown stream;
A jungle spring, unexplored, mysterious as a woman's dream,
Not hinting — what around the bend may bring.

It was cold emptiness of failure - not warm peace of success.
We had sorely worked while seeking to reach a futile goal,
Unknowingly, but ultimately so, none-the-less.

Our attempt to Christianize had failed - turned cold.
what could we do but petition of our Lord —
A pardon or a mercy to unfold?

And for that in solitude we wait praying,
To celebrate what eludes us now — at yet a future date!
Thus having dreamed to serve; but having failed thru fear,
Or lack of faith; or perhaps an unknown hold —
Could not, this also be - a refining of the gold?

Oh, would that we could only know for sure.
Though we had failed, yet had we not also endured?
What was lost in the striving; cannot we win another day?

But knowing that in the balance, this matter must be weighed;
With heavy heart we wait the final judgment —
And the price that needs be paid.
   Helen Hastings

On Star Gazing

O divine one, your star-gems glitter only at night!
They and the moon are your only light;
Are they solely for your delight?
Your holy dawn-sun puts them easily to flight!

What hidden mysteries do they reveal?
Or what silent thoughts do they steal!
Are your vast expanses really real?
What ponderous thunderous wonders
  their innocent light doth conceal!

O mighty eternal one, your star-gems of night,
Do silently, stealthily put to flight,
 A rude, ruddy, red setting sun;
When yet, another day is finally done!
   Albert P. Boettcher

Do You Love Me

I went about my daily tasks
Thinking about my pleasures,
The things I had collected
My lifetime of treasures.

Then across my mind a memory came
Of Grandma in the garden singing,
How her voice filled the air
As though the Bells of Heaven ringing.

When They Ring Those Golden Bells
Seemed to echo all around,
When Grandma sang that song
I knew she was "Heaven" bound!

My thoughts switched gear to days gone by
Of Grandpa at his chair a praying,
"Don't you love me child"
A voice seemed to be saying.

"A new love will come to you
You'll have courage of your convictions,
There will be freedom to love others
Not bound by the world's restrictions."
   Joyce E. Shafer

Candyland For Louis

I'm going to build a playhouse
  Upon the meadow green,
Using beams of golden sunshine,
  Bright as you've ever seen.

Giant sugar cane will thatch the roof;
  Black licorice for the floors;
Striped Peppermint sticks for windows
  And candy bars for doors.

The yard will have a merry-go-round
  Atop a strawberry cake.
The kids may ride and eat and then
  Drink from a chocolate lake.
Jelly Bean will make the walkway;
  Lined with flowers and clover.
And when I'm through, that ever day,
  I'll ask you to come over.
   Jackie St. Cyr

Third Of My Soul

Today I lost a third
of my soul
it fled through my eyes
and sorrow mirrored in its windows

I had lost my soul before
bits of pieces here and there
but never a third

Do I have enough soul left
to go on living?
yes, and whatever
the size of it
I will be stingy with it

Meanwhile, I'll stretch it
to adorn my eyes with it.
   Aida Ophelia Saldana

Dear God, For This I Pray

Strength for the task begun
Something attempted
Something done

Courage in time of trial
Not only to the end
But the extra mile.

Wisdom another to understand
And aid by a smile
Or a helping hand

Live for my fellow man
A life to live
The best I can.

Strength, courage, wisdom, love
And gentle guidance
From above.

Mary Elizabeth Chapman

Love On Wings

Sentiment opened the door
I don't smell cinnamon and spice
but looking at someone nice
love came through the door.
Sentiment not a bottle of perfume
but love entered the room.
Sentiment not the flavor of a mint
in a dish that pleases the eye
but love that does try.
Sentiment not lace covered glows
given to a friend
but love within.
Sentiment not a basket of flowers
that fills the room with fragrance
but love at an everyday pace.
Sentiment not a pair of love birds
but love taking its turn
Sentiment not flowers and lace
now I'm at the bottom line
What I see is God's grace.

Lola I. Hansell

The Shadow Painter

His shadow shapes beguile the mind,
Brushed in shades this artist finds
Upon his palette, black to gray.
More subtle tones for hazy days.

He fells tall trees, trails the swallows.
Swings the doors to deadwood hollows.
Casts silhouettes on lakes of glass,
And rides the waves of prairie grass.

He's masterful in all the modes.
From pyramids to tiny toads.
Creating art of curves or block,
Of motion quick, or still as rock.

The world's his canvas, there to test,
No mountain range or valley rests.
With sun and moonlight at his call,
The shadow painter paints them all.

Ernest Hodson

Writer's Block

I get so sick of the way that I write.
I release all my feelings on paper of my sorrow and spite.
The rhymes run together like earlier ones you've heard.
My sentences make noise instead of the words.
I can't change my style for it all sounds the same.
No matter what is written I still find it quite lame.
A very dissatisfied writer am I.
But Why?!?!?
With words running as high as the sky, you would think
that I could find some to fit I.
I only yearn to describe my world of flowers, heart
and smiles like pearls.
I want it to sound so very lush but my hopes are only
crushed by the little fact that I have so much to say
and can not seem to put it in a way that all will help
people to understand the emotions and feelings I have
for a man.
I suppose the best way to communicate across the
miles is with one simple tool...a smile.

Lisa Sorensen

"Daddy"

Wise as an owl and shy as a fox,
I called him "Daddy," some called him cop.

Some even say he's a pig, but if they could see,
The hurt and pain in his family.

When he came home with tears in his eyes,
Of the things he saw in others lives.

A look only to his families faces,
A different man took up those spaces.

He truly believed the most men were good,
Only a few didn't act as they should.

In thirty years he never drew his gun,
This proud fact was known to everyone.

A respected man by friends and foes alike,
We hated to see "Daddy" go out each night.

In uniform of blue and badge of gold,
Stories of pain and suffering he could've told.

But the stories "Daddy" told to me had a happy ending,
So with a prayer to "Daddy" I sending.

From his little girl to "Daddy" the man I love,
Some day we'll be together in heaven above.

Lois E. Cole

The Whole Tone

Now music is very pleasing to the ear,
And the sound of music at times
delivers pleasure to the mind.
You see, God invented music for his pleasure
and we are blessed that He shares it with you and me.
It lifts our spirits up high,
the sweet sounds of music in the sky,
shell echoes near and far,
will always bring peace, love, and joy to our hearts.
And from you, love is the delight,
that music brings out into the light,
and makes everything just right.
The sweet sounds of music, in the night.

Calvin Robinson

Its Ok To Cry

When a good friend dies in the midst of war
and you pray and ask God why-
After the fighting is done and you stop to rest
it's okay for a soldier to cry.

When the battle is only you try to survive
from ground fire and death from the sky-
you must do you part till the battle is won
then it's okay for a soldier to cry.

When the orders you give as a leader of men
causes many a good man to die -
you must put it aside till the fighting is through
only then is it okay to cry.

When the battles are won and at last you're at home
Feel no remorse that you didn't die-
Just remember your friends and the job that was done
It's okay for a soldier to cry.
            Jesse F. Harvey

Time

For some your cup is full and round
The nectar sweet and sound
For others your dole is but a sip
A bitter stain upon the lip

Enchanting youth like the tune of the piper
You lie in wait like a coiled viper
Forceful wind, you nudge ever onward,
Ahead, tomorrow
Your shadow veils the truth, the pain the sorrow

Time, you ambiguous friend
You hint at horizon without end
Your shadow quells the flame of passion as it burns
Darkens the path as it turns

The future counted now, day by day
The golden tresses now a pale grey
Time, you cruel thief, your face is shone
I feel your laughter in my bones.
            Janice Roach

Through My Window

Ice crystals crazing across the glass
Brown frozen stubs of summers grass

Trees dozing, some in deep slumber
Their colors range from white to burnt umber

Snowflakes falling like pillow soft down
Each finding their place upon the ground

Winds moaning thru lifeless branches
Warm cups of tea, through which life enhances

Tiny tracks crisscrossing the snow
A hole, where a squirrel found something to go

Few birds remain to eat at the feeder
The rest have gone, follow the leader

Bundled children, scuffling with the snow
Their puffy little cheeks all rosy and aglow

Shadowy patterns moving lickety splinter
Gosh I love winter
            Roland J. Fiorini

Family

A family means togetherness,
Addressing each others need.

Alleviating any bitterness,
By doing a very good deed.

By struggling through life,
As if it were a wilderness.

To eliminating any strife,
That would cause any bewilderment.

That to aid one another,
When one is down and out.

It surely is not a bother.
This is without a doubt.

It's the love of one another,
That helps a family to succeed.
            Nicholas J. Kayganich

Paradise

It does not really matter
If I live or die
All my so called friends
Already said good-bye

They say that they avoid me
Because they are afraid
To say something reminding me
Of the plans we've made

I feel that they are lying
They do not really care
Their life would still be normal
Even if I was not there

I only need some of your
Attention and advice
Then once again I'll obtain
The perfect paradise
            Melissa Harp

My Friend...

My friend, I need not your generosity
you try to give to me

My friend, I need your voice
so that I can listen

My friend, I need your eyes
so that I can see

My friend, I need your ears
so that I can speak

My friend, I need your hand
so that I can be assured

My friend, I need your trust
so that I can turn my back

My friend, I need not what you can give
I need only for you to live
            Howard P. Butterstein

Love

Love is a strange thing.
It is a flower so delicate.
That a touch will bruise it.
And yet so strong that
nothing will stop its growth...
Think how often we miss love
in a lifetime
by a wrong gesture
by an unspoken word
by not keeping silent
at the right time...
We lose it by - lack of money.
By - the interference of
other people.
By - a quarrel over a trifle,
and yet we can't love
without it...
Essie Fink

Love

Love is innocence
loving someone is like riding on air
after taking the plunge from the plane
free falling
feeling the wind
blowing
whisking you away
on a warm day
feeling invincible
glowing for all to see
for all to know
you're in love,
and it's wonderful.
Karmen Sellers

November Tempest

In the deceased lightning sky
the moon pulls forward,
through the yellow fog.
A light mist performs in the wind,
gives rise to new clouds.
It beckons to the whims of a storm.
Stillness confiscates the sky.
The leaves listen,
a confession to their owner.

The night's hand moves the dead limbs
in a symphony, to call upon those
who seek the dryness.
Rain paints the world
to bring us back to color,
a psalm to the night.

As the thunder walks upon darkness,
the tempest spins his web,
only to entangle the light
in a drop of dew.
Kerry Frieben

Cigarette Butts In A Coffee Cup

On rare occasions he could be seen
A fleeting image, as through a screen
Or a voice heard in the dead of night
Muffled words; terse; discordant; uptight.

He was present in the redolence of shaving cream
That lingered a while, as though to blaspheme
Then he was gone, as he'd gone before
Leaving an empty screen behind a forbidding door.

The children searched for him after sunup
Finding only cigarette butts in his coffee cup
Her bedroom door was closed and locked tightly
They would hear her anger raging nightly.

He'd come back before; would he come back again?
Her anger festered; erupted; the children were in pain
They cringed beneath the molten bitterness
So young; so small; they were defenseless.

He came back once more and stayed a while
Another child was born in the crumbling domicile
Then he was gone to never again show up
Leaving cigarette butts in his coffee cup.
Elaine E. Kelso

The Vineyard

Night is real.
Loneliness subsides to shuttered eye dreams
The only things real.
Vineyards etched into the land,
clawing roots milking the soil.
Stone cottages, a foreign tongue,
Cypress trees forever holding time—The Ruins of Pompeii.
Man. Woman.
Wears featherweight white dresses,
each dimpled with dancing impressions
As her body moves.

Vines resurrect to the sky,
Tumbling over one another against stone.
Flowers in high Bloom:
Forget-Me-Nots, powder roses, lilacs—
All floating on a breeze.

Man. Woman. Barefoot. Eden.
Down a Roman, cobblestoned, narrow street village.
Chariots and Maseratis Rumble somewhere lost between walls.
Azure sky forever.
Danielle Sciaretta

The Mountains

Far in the distance the mountains lay
Appearing to be close but miles away
Over the top the clouds hand heavy and low
A blue grey mist surrounds from below

The trees full of dew appear to be weeping
Ferns and wildflowers look up as if to be seeking
Falling to the ground the water joins the stream
Clean and pure the water is a dream

The cool water brings birds, bear and deer
With the rushing sound there isn't any fear
God has made the mountains their home
All his creatures are free to roam
Pat Brehm

This Is My Dream

I've got a dream that man should realize
That there's a great hand that holds out the prize
When hope fails and dream shatters.
Still love whispers when some have nothing on their platters.
I dream for everyone to climb up to the top of the mountain
Searching every path until they find the fountain
That leads down the foothills to quench man's thirst
Giving peace of mind to the last, the second, and the first.
I dream of the day when man will walk hand in hand
Hugging each other and joining the band;
Opening doors for the children who lost their dreams
Making way for the old who live with screams.
I dream of the day when violence will cease
Taking our love ones as morality decrease;
Authoritative forces quench man's spirit and make him weak
Leaving him breathless and with a streak.
Can't we get along each day we meet?
Can't we touch everyone we see on the street?
Opening doors, the quench the fires that have been set
Relieving each life from down to the very sunset.

Everton L. Hohn

The Road To Nowhere

The long, long trail so lacking in care,
has branches scattered everywhere;
it empties off into a horizon bare
that oft' traveled road...to Nowhere!

Past mountains high and cities of glass...
palm trees tall and stone grass,
Scorched mercilessly by an unrelenting sun,
It seeks soothing coolness
of which there is none!

Thru the desert's far reaches it runs.
To valley's wide...and oasis of dust,
Finding cactus, prairie dog, and towering rock forms,
but not a river...one!

Far beyond vision it trails on and on,
To what? We haven't a clue!
For those that travel it—returneth not from the blue!

Bernadette M. Bland

As You Marry

As you are married, I hope you will find,
   All you've ever hoped for in life;
May your dreams become your realities,
   As you become husband and wife.
To begin your life together,
   Knowing not what the future may hold,
Is an act of faith in each other,
   Worth more than all riches and gold.
Not all your days will be smooth ones;
   You'll have your share of bumps through the years;
So keep loving and working together
   Through the good times, and through the tears.
And as days join to build a lifetime,
   May God be with you each day;
And no matter what you may encounter,
   Keep you in His care always!

Charlotte A. Fife

Did You Know....

Did you know....that there is no one
In my world besides you with whom I
Can spend an entire day doing whatever
Comes along with never a thought for
Anyone else—Feeling completely
Satisfied because we are together?

Did you know....that there is no one
Besides you whom I can talk to openly
And honestly knowing our love will only
Grow and feeling a need for nothing but
Our conversation?

Did you know....that there is no one
More comfortable for me than you -
Whom I can enjoy silence with and never
Have a need to fill the space between us
Because there is no space?.....

Did you know...that no one has ever
Made me as happy as you have or loved me
So completely - never have I known true
Intimacy until we grew to where we are?

Did you know...that in loving you, I
Have experienced feelings far beyond
Any I could have imagined and far better
Than any I believed possible?

Kevin T. Durkin

I See A New Bright Future

I see a bright new future,
In all a new dawn,
In all humanity,
Like dewdrops on the lawn.

The sun rises in the sky,
The moon fills the heavens, too.
I know things are getting better,
For me and for you.

If we are together, friends,
Standing hand and hand,
Our world means better things,
For people throughout the land.

Ted Harris

Saying Goodbye

The first day seemed dark and gloom.
I couldn't help but feel the doom.
But as we got closer to see,
we knew that it just had to be.
How could it have happened so fast?
You had lived not long in your past.
You've been through the good and the bad.
I wish that it were more good you've had.
You mean so much to me
and now you have to go, I see.
Saying goodbye could be real rough,
but now I have to be real tough.
Forever seems to be so long.
The strength in you will keep me strong.

Traci Hanff

Major Prophette

Purity infested
with inquisitional love
whose retriever was tamed
to recapture strays
disinfecting from
repuzzled truths
inflicted by rubied eyes
hallowing the spirituality
of burnished gold
postured carnivorously.

Unenergized lore
muddled to ridicule
sought its asylum
in eccentric minds
of tomorrow's abstractionists
inhabiting parables.

Wilbur J. Childs

Nightmare

A realm beyond control
Secreted, from universal black holes

Worst fears controlling destinies
Brutal attacks by fabricated entities

The situation with no escape
Realizing, you can not wake

The state of being senseless
Memories that are relentless

Tears of sweat, consumed by fire
The torches emotion, desire

When traveling in forbidden zones
The outcome, will be unknown

William C. Leppo

How Are You?

At one time "How are you?" and "I'm
  fine" were automatic greetings.
But as my friends and I age and
  say, "Hello, how are you?"
We really want to know:
How are you doing day by day?
How are your chronic aches and pains?
How is your athritis, your migraine,
  you breathing, your shingles, it all?
How are you coping with all the
  change that aging brings—both
  physical and emotional?
But it's not as dreadful and depressing
  as this may sound.
It's wonderful to have friends who
  do not want an automatic answer,
But friends who truly care.

Druscilla L. Radloff

Paradise

Behind that domed mountain of many diamonds
Beyond the rows of upright arrow pines
Ever spinning in silk soft sun beams
Where the sly breeze whispers to idle clouds
Where the recluse mystics murmur recitals
And twilight tavern doors are about to close
They say: There is a Paradise.
A dream, a lifelong dream
A dream, wherein all desires reflect
A dream, through which brightens a monotracing path
A pathway leading to a dim-flaring hope
A dream portraying a pilgrim of seclusion
Who paces along misty dale of yore.
My eager aspiration enquires,
Oh pilgrim, beyond all whimsical illusions,
on the other face of unseen horizon,
They say: Extends the adorning paradise.
And in response, the pilgrim sights:
Paradise is in your noble heart!

M. K. Sherkat

The Place I Belong

Will you take me, Mamma, to the Garden of Eden
Will you take me, Mamma, to the Garden of Love
Will you take me, Mamma, to the place I belong

Will you play sweet soothing tunes for me, Mamma
The sweetest tunes I've never heard in my lifetime
Will you play sweet soothing tunes for me, Mamma
The sweetest tunes I've never heard before
Will you play those soothing tunes for me, Mamma
The sweetest tunes I'm dying for

Will you sing a lullaby to me, Mamma
The lullaby of my childhood
Will you sing that lullaby to me, Mamma
The lullaby from my child's years
Will you sing that lullaby to me, Mamma
The lullaby that'll bring me to rest

I'm a lone steppen wolf, Mamma, and ain't got no home at all
I'm a lone steppen wolf, Mamma, and I don't know where to go
It's no trail, nor road I follow
Yet I know I'll reach that place I belong

Guennadi N. Slasten

Vampira's Reign

I am the Vampira that arises forth into the night
to drink thy blood with thunderous delight.
Carnal blood filled treasure in thy veins of the living
be my every pleasure to drink in each night for all eternity.
Electric thunder burning in my eyes.
The sweet heady taste of thy livings blood on my tips.
Nectar of the undead blood be thy name for me to claim.
Each night I arise from my earthly bed of undead slumber
to venture forth into the dark and cruel night
in search for my living plunder.
    As I loom ever more closer to my prey
I shall capture you once more and again
as the blood feast it does begin.
Enter the realm of my blood-filled reign
and I shall feed upon you once more and again.
Daylight comes soon as I go back to lay in my earthly tomb
till the next night's bloody doom.

Melanie R. Price

Ontology

Having come this far
Complex organisms, birthed from a star
Thought patterns, which regard our existence
As something more than mere coincidence
Billions of years, after the quake
For ever evolving, lost in wake
Coming to the conclusion of self-aware
Longing to winnow the solitaire
Individual God's? Or the creation from one
Absolute knowledge, overrun
Designed entitles, locked in a cage
After images of the omnipotent sage
Peering deep into the great expanse
Hoping to find a glimpse of Jehovah's trance
Universe within a universe
The mind becomes immersed
And in the parallels we get distraught
Perplexing these dimensions of space and thought
Creation or evolution? Where it all begins
Spirituality, is the search from within.
Michael J. Hawks

The Rescue

I walked along the seashore looking for a place in the sun.
I looked for shade among the dunes and found there was none.
I rode the waves of the ocean until I thought I would drown.
A rip-tide tugged at my soul and pulled me swiftly down.

Then the angel of the morning pulled me back to shore.
She left me alone and crying against the ocean's roar.
I cried, "Oh morning angel, why did you leave me here to die?
There is no shade, no solace, no matter how I try.

The angel of the evening covered me with a blanket from the deep.
She sang a haunting lullaby as I drifted off to sleep.
When I awoke, my heart stood still, filled with awesome fright.
Clothed before me in robes black was the angel of the night.

He sighed "Come fly with me ore' the ocean to a distant shore,
where there is rest, the endless sleep and peace forever more."
In the blackness of the night, my soul longed for the sun.
The darkness hid the light beyond, there was no place for me to run.

Then reflected on the ocean's walls pristine wings I could see.
Drenched with dew from Heaven a loving angel beckoned me.
A powerful gust of wind rose suddenly and I began to run,
beneath the wings of my guardian angel to a shade tree in the sun.
Doris Hartsell Brewer

Home

My heart went out to her sitting there
rocking back and forth in her old rocking chair
Tears falling freely from her eyes so blue
the ache in her heart so fresh and new.
The doctor had said she could live alone no more
and slowly turned and walked out the door.
How could she leave her home she loved so
what could she do, where could she go?
I walked over, took her hand in mine
to express how I felt the words I couldn't find.
She smiled up at me with a glow on her face
and said, "Let's not fret, just trust in God's grace".
With that she closed her eyes and all was quiet
God called her home she would live with him tonight.
Carol Steele

Lament At Winter

My flora are fading;
the petals wither
one by one, shedding
singular spice where
pilings turn brown.

Each ghost-like erasure
of blossomed being
takes sequent treasure
from joy of living;
slowly I drown

Barrened to nothingness.
Mistermed "Useless things",
wildest weeds would bless
with sunshine's blooming's
gracing my gown,

But no more sap remains
so soaked is my growth.
Once strong, bark restrains
former call, now loathe
to lift cold's frown.
Florence Raush Ehlers

Holocausts

Woven in history
  many secrets . . . countless torments
Through famines . . . ghettos . . . camps
  multitude of faces through a fence

Stripped of all dignity
  treated humanly less
Taken in the night
  held in the darkness

They took them one by one
  they took them in a crowd
They couldn't keep them silent
  they heard their crying loud

Imposed . . . destroyed
  conquered . . . overpowered
Life drained . . . breath gone
  thousands of tears showered

Persecuted . . . crucified in hatred
  to the very point of defeat
Stopped . . . by God's love
  in every man's heartbeat
Ann Marie Mushinski

The Peak

Combing the clouds,
Touching the blue.
Upright and proud,
A symbol of what is true.

The brave attempt to ascend it,
Climbing each step at a time.
The weak give up and surrender it,
Not knowing the feelings sublime.

My peak is high,
It seems so far,
But I know if I try,
I'll reach it and brush the stars.
Amy Sherman

A Rodeo Cowboy

He says "I'm a rodeo cowboy"
the "cock of the walk"
ya can bet that I'll brag
but I ain't all just talk!

I do everything with a flair
from my clothes to my rig
live life to the fullest
why not do it up big!

I ride the rodeo circuit
it's a really fast pace
ride in least three events
an try darn hard to place!

Ya, it takes a lot mere than braggin
to stay on bronc's and bulls
that "eight seconds a lifetime"
when that chute tender pulls!

"Morewood"
Daniel L. Rice

Night Time Praise

In the still
of the night
while the stars
are shining bright.

That's the time
when I love
to give thanks
to the heavens above.

Give thanks to God
for all he's done
especially for sending
down His Son.

Alonzo D. Easley Sr.

To See With Eyes And Heart

To see with one's own eyes.
Can fool oneself in so many ways.
For the eyes can mislead you away.
So easily and without warning.
But to see with one's heart.
Can not only tell the whole story
but can open one's eyes.
How we view ourselves and others
can not only come from our eyes.
It can also come from one's heart.
To see and feel through one's
heart is so deep but yet, it can
be so tender and wise.
The heart can pump and filter
the blood.
The heart can see and feel with
such depth and honesty.
The heart can have everlasting
love.

Joyce L. Higgs

Greedy Woodpecker

This fine figure of sculptured wood
  was once upon a time a live young bird.
From tree to tree fast in flight,
  in search of food from morning till night.

Just so happened in this very limb
  lived a nest of termites.
It was a large hole at the bottom of that limb;
  a magnificent bird so young and slim.

With greedy thoughts the woodpecker entered that nest.
Standing so straight and tall anticipating his exit,
  becoming the largest, so becoming king of them all.

As he ate his way up the inside of that inhabited hollow,
He didn't allow not one pair
  of insects to escape to carry on tomorrow.

From the narrow hole in the top of the limb
  his head did erupt,
And as he took down that last greedy gulp,
  high up in that might pine tree,
  the woodpecker got stuck and could not get free.
With pen and chisel in hand, I carved him out for the world to see.

Millard G. Pendergraph

Examined

There comes a time that we must go, to check the place that doesn't show. The thought inside to do this task, could cause a person to wear a mask. As I wait in the room, I watch the clock, before the doom. The time for this has to come, but it makes you want to run. Just say a prayer, so when the doctor enters, you can prepare. Exchange some words to express, why you're here and no excess. As you are examined, do not fret, because it's for your leveled best. All is for our health you see, as we leave happily. Now we wait the time, as days go past, to see results that we must grasp. Good or bad we must face, even though our life's a race. Take the time to mend this place, so we can resume our pace. Except for those who have no time, can make the end with God in mind.

Rose Jenkins

I Blame It On The Storm

After all, it's easy to love in the calm,
when souls unite, and dance to the tune
of passions - flowing...ebbing...flowing
hearts unbarred/vulnerable
As you stroke my being with words whispered in the dark,
Your voice hesitates at the sound of distant thunder.
Our eyes adjust to the approach of destructive energy pulsating...
Illuminating - truths uncovered
Darkness Overtaking - hiding bonds
Souls cover...grasping for each other
seeking strength and security
From the winds that buffet and threaten the vow
that locked two hearts together.
Hidden in the darkness, my heart
screams silently in search of you.
I am being swept away - alone -
Left to battle the storm's fury.
In brief illumination, I see your back as you walk away
And the tear that dripped from my cheek
touched you in midnight's shower.

Bobette L. Hedges

Discovery

As the light of day disintegrates,
   the fires roar takes over.
My room is dark with shadows
   dancing on the walls.
I am mesmerized by the blaze,
   fearful of its power.
It beckons me closer, I move with caution.
My eyes blur then refocus
   as all surroundings disappear.
My ears block even the tinniest of sound,
   careful not to intrude.
My mind is for one second clear and I am at peace.
For a brief moment
   my roller coaster is stationary.
In the distance beyond the flames,
   the world I know is no longer.
At this second I find my answers.
I see inside my soul.
No question, No doubts.
I can see who I truly am.
   Kelly Hibbard

The Busy Little Bee

The busy little bee that's buzzing there
Is making its hive with the greatest of care.
It needs a good home, but still likes to roam,
As its busily buzzing away.
Buzz, buzz buzz, buzz as its busily buzzing away.

The busy little bee that's buzzing there
Is getting its food from the flower so fair.
The nectar is sweet and the bee's greatest treat,
As its busily buzzing away.
Buzz, buzz buzz, buzz as its busily buzzing away.

The busily little bee that's buzzing there
Is working hard, just to do his share.
For the queen on the throne and the great big drone.
As its busily buzzing away.
Buzz, buzz buzz, buzz as it's busily buzzing away.
The busy little bee that's buzzing there
May be a honey, but won't take a dare.
Stay out of its home, it's making honey comb,
As it's busily buzzing away.
Buzz, buzz buzz, buzz as it's busily buzzing away.

The busy little bee that's buzzing there
Is serenely happy in its world so rare.
It's a master of art, just from God's part,
As it's busily buzzing away.
Buzz, buzz buzz, buzz as it's busily buzzing away.
   Rebecca Ensor

The Catacomb

Porcupines and lightning battle the wind
   More cakes to light the lamps of friendship
Yet, in amazing struggle, priest meets pauper
   I have this necklace, leather book and little lend
We are not to fight for material wealth
   Nor create a bomber to boast pride out of stealth
Clandestine hootenannies glide with enemies
   And the light of little children in threnodies
The Bible lawyers of boastful nonsense in pride of envy
   Are on excuse for flesh-begotten mammals, too trendy
   Scott C. Harrison

Love Song

My love is an irish potato
   With laughing light blue eyes
With a bit of wit and humor
   He just cannot disguise!
He has tied a string to his finger
   That he jiggles from time to time
And the other end is twined around

This captive heart of mine!
Oh, I love that irish potato
   Who's all the world to me
And I know my love will last
   Thru all eternity!
   Roberta J. Crowe

No Escape

I wanted it to be me that died
Not one who was great and faithful
I loved her so very much
And in my mind there is no such
A person to ever take her place...
I struggle and fight
Trying to pull myself up,
But all that's accomplished
Is a torn and ripped self-
Till I'm worn and I stop.
After all my tries and attempts
To become one as a whole
I fall - an all that's left for me to do.
Is give up and die.
I lower myself to this way out
Only as a call for help and a way to escape.
The sadness surrounds me!
I'm tired of living!
I'm sure I'm right.
   LeAnna Heard

Winter Flight

The smell of juniper filled the air.
Flowers nestled sweetly in her hair.
Dogs kept watch on a darker side.
Rivers were muddied, there was no tide.
Music swelled to fill what was lost.
Business calculated with relish the cost.
Tissues tried to absorb human grief.
Hugs and words gave no relief.
Rocks were ground to give a blush,
Or carved with chisel amid the hush.
Artists tried to paint a face,
No match for nature's human race.
Hearts no longer beat with blood,
But drown and gasp in sorrow's flood.
For what had once to dance and sing,
Is empty now, a hollow thing.
Pink's become a yellow hue.
Softest supple has hardened too.
Wherever souls take flight to flee,
Today is too far to comfort me.
   Susan Rains

Changes

No one owns a mountain.
No one owns the sea.
No one can hold a snowflake.
It melts away so fast.

There have been many
changes over the years.
Trying to accept them is the
hardest part of all.

Up and down is how life goes,
but if we look around us
we see the beauty
of each day.

We have regrets for the things
too late to change.
What is done is meant to be.
Tomorrow is another day.

Margaret Roy

Lonely Soul Ache

I seem so sad
Even when I feel glad
Depression comforts me
In mu time of need
I can feel my lonely heart bleed

No more poor pitiful me
Set my lonely heart free
I walk along a razor
Me and my empty soul
Pain is like a radio
The dial keeps me in control

Loren Bill Ennis

Epigram

I passed by a park to see
children fast at play.
I stopped and watched them silently
frolic in the rain.
The girl, is her name Mary?
The boy, perhaps the a Jay?
And the one beneath the oak tree
who doesn't join the games
The tattered dress on Mary
The leather shoes on Jay
The oak tree doesn't notice
what the boy has on today.
Such rosy cheeks on Mary
and darker skin on Jay
The oak tree doesn't care
if the boy is blue or gray.
And still they play together
as if they were the same
The boy, Jay and Mary,
The oak tree and the rain.

Kathy Hutchison

Panacea

She came in a time of anguish, and grief
  Like an Angel transposed from above
With tiny rose petal cheeks
  And glistening radiant eyes, filled with love

She brought smiles to our solemn faces
  A new innocence, filled the air
Where before there was a lingering sadness
  There is now joy, and happiness there

From infancy, to a Little Princess
  So swift, she seems to grow
No longer a bundle of fragile stillness
  Inquisitively funny, she now seems so

She claims, two snowy little kittens
  "Peanuts and Snoopy", she whispers with a grin
But there's Big Bird and Elmo
  And others goo, she calls her friends

She came in a most troubled, and difficult time
  And no one knows better than me
Like an Angel sent, from heaven above
  My Granddaughter - Kasey Marie

Charles R. Smith

Steel City

Aw, great powerful mass of crude mystery!
If you had a tongue within your gate,
Many tales of the tired and weary
Bewildering sometimes tragic could you relate.
Noisy monster with dirty massive wheels
Belching blazes that blister the sky
Huge ugly boulders where the workman kneels
Bright lights that dazzle the eye.
Smoldering clouds of smog and smoke
Mingle with a workers shrill harsh cry.
The old blends with the new cloak
Planning, inventing, building as the days go by
Factory mill workers with harsh laws
Each with their special duty
Melting, molding, sorting without flaws
In this amazing city.
City? Yes, a city of steel,
With citizens of a hard working class,
With their shoulder to the wheel
Making many wonders come to pass.

Eunice Abby Reding

Get Well

Get well, my dearest heart,
for you are very bright and smart.
Get well, for we will be there to see you,
through obstacles and triumphs, don't be blue.
Get well, stand tall and hold your head up high,
keep believing in the Lord, he's just above the sky.
Get well, to this very day,
God is a miracle worker, if you just pray.
Get well, we're singing and clapping our hands,
of the greatest joy with us, in the stands.
Get well, and praise the Lord,
for He is our Saviour, so come aboard.
Get Well, Get Well, Get Well.

Cynthia Howard

Memories

Son, as I sit here thinking of you,
I feel a cool wind caressing my face.
As I caress the memory of you when you were born.
A moment in time when I felt
I could turn the world upside down,
Because I had a son.

The cool wind is turning cold with the memory,
How I watched you struggle for life . . .
But I couldn't help you.
O, how helpless I did feel,
Watching you through those panes of glass.

Unable to hold you,
To tell you, Daddy loves you.
To feel the weight of your little body,
To touch your little round face,
With that button nose
To see your bright eyes shining.

These are the things Son,
I miss in my memories of you.

I love you Jimmy,
—Dad
James R. Osborne

Knowing Our Fellow Man

I am so content!
Living in a small town,
You know most people and greetings are always sent,
I know if I lived in the city, I would be down.

I believe that people living in a small town care.
In large cities, they just don't know anyone; they don't dare.
But that isn't fair!
I swear!

Maybe that's the key,
To help violence flee!

If you know someone,
Maybe that's the day to put out violence's flame,
A small victory won!
Doing violence to someone we know should cause shame!

So we should get to know our fellow man,
Trying to be kind,
Hopefully this can spread throughout our land!
Easing violence and our minds!

Paula Patterson-Stevenson

The Road Kill

Wild steps muffled in the night,
   Are betrayed in eyes marked by a flash of light.
A fine line surpassed overhead,
   Under stars and black stillness left for dead.
Hours turn colder before the dawn is unveiled,
   And a fear of death is lost in a body that failed.
To memorialize a wild heart with only a thought,
   Ends the story of what it sought,
And despite the urgency at which life begins and ends,
   A message is revealed from what the future sends.
Colors of a giver often become the taker searching to find,
   Another spirit taking flight,
Beyond the imagination of physical mind.

Vincent Shane Hesting

Hummingbird

Little bird with wings a flicker,
Sipping from my home made nectar,
Early morning you are nipping,
As my coffee I am sipping.
Feathers black with sheen of green,
In the sunlight how they gleam.
Summer's flowers are almost gone,
Soon you'll fly to winter home.
Yes, to the south you'll fly away,
But you'll be back one day in May.
So, my little feathered friend,
I'll see you when Spring comes again.

Charlotte Higgins

Carl's Eyes

Carl's eyes are loving,
Yet can be cruel and mean.
Carl's eyes are exiting,
but haven't seen all to be seen.
Carl's eyes have loved,
but lied about how true.
Carl's eyes are devious.
You never know what they'll do.
Carl's eyes show pain,
but no own knows how great.
Carl's eyes show love,
but it quickly becomes hate.
Carl's eyes are giving,
but greedy they can be.
Carl's eyes are deep,
too deep for me to see.
Carl's eyes tell a story,
but no one knows the theme.
Carl's eyes are beautiful,
but never what they seem.

Tracy Lynn McKenzie

190. Segments Of Now

Do we know where we are
Maybe
On which point of the star
On which side of the sea
On which branch of the tree
On which shade of the rainbow
On which pane of the window

On which segment of now

Do we know where or how
Many
Points of the star there are
Sides of the sea that be
Binate branches of the tree
Shades of the rainbow glow
Panes of the window show

Segments of now?

Floyd Caplow

Special Light

To all is given a special light.
In some it's dim, in some it's bright.
To say it's love that makes it dim,
Is but a lie, it's lust to him.
Lose your light you've lost your look,
People can read you like a book.
A man that dims is not the one,
But he should help you reach the sun.
People change when light is lost.
But change is not the only cost,
Friends and family disappear
A nothingness is all you hear.
So get down on your knees and pray,
Listen to what God has to say.
He'll tell you my child come back to me
And with the light, happy you'll be.

Wolfgang Bleached Kiwi

Cast Shadows

They are subtle, go unnoticed
But affect their surroundings
Take time to notice them

Where you are, do they lend
Warmth or Austereness mayhap blandness?

Look at them and decide for yourself

Things is, these shadows can be
A comforting part of your surroundings

They can shade the harshest of reality
They can soften starkness
They can enhance and extend comfort

Have you noticed? Did you see?
Now, you must be wondering
What a kind of a shadow do I cast?
Am I a shadow?
Do I cast comfort?

Joan A. Shonk

Paradise

On fire...In Eden.
We forgot about the tree,
and God's righteous anger.
The garden's vacancy we had
not contemplated.

You sensed the desire of my touch,
so it seemed the right thing...to
run away, as thickets of misunderstanding
were irrationally threaded;

I chased you, caught you, then gently
you threw soft arms around me
face to face, warm moist lips
manipulating, our tongues entwined
until this special place sang like
a burning bough in willing submission
eager bodies captured in the rhythm of
passion's embrace.

Thus, evermore the tedium ceased.
'Twas, then ecstasy and paradise...
Was found.

Jay Warren Downs

Seasons

In every year we have four seasons
We love them all for different reasons.
We know for sure that it is spring
When tulips bloom and Robins sing
the rain falls gently to the ground
And everywhere new life abounds.
Shades of green beneath a sky of blue
Summer's here: So many things to do.
Picnics, swimming and campfires that spark
Boating, baseball and walks in the park
Cooler weather's here and summer takes her leave
Glorious tints of red and gold decorate the trees
Harvest time, Halloween and then thanksgiving day
Winter comes blowing in and autumn cannot stay
Children playing in snowmen, they'll melt in the sun
Memories of Christmas fade, a brand new year begins
Winter winds go away and we dream again of spring.

Barbara Clark

Blue Gray

Blue gray, Platinum dawn

  how densely, you blend with my colorful thoughts
  how softly, you melt with my colorless dreams

As I rise with you, Platinum dawn
the day will pass with, pleasure and joy, prosperity and hope
till the last drop of light, till the last dew of tears

I don't just dream, I see it with my own eyes
the rainbows of joy, the colors of peace, the hues of love

As your luminous sunrise, stretches upward with such grace
  hence, from horizon I face

As your morning star showers purity
  over the mountains, the plains, the trees,
over the garden of my childhood limpid memories

I hasten towards you,
  from the dark indigo of night, toward the blue threshold of day
hoping, maybe, one day, you'll tuck me, into your spangled
  saddlebag
carry me, to the sweet times, to the sweet home, to the sweet land

where for a long time now
in the innocent distance, of two halves of a glance
love is stoned...love is hanged

Parvin Bavafa

Fury

The sun skulks slowly behind the clouds;
Shadows overcast as the storm surges in.
Vivid lightening scores the heavens with a slash
And thunder explodes with ear-shattering din!
Rain dances sporadically across the field.
The obsidian sky flashes with brilliant fire.
Kettle drum-beat rumbles echo through the valley
As all nature expends excess energy in ire.
Glistening sheets of water inundates the earth;
The tempo of celestial fury increases its pace.
On and on the cacophonous discord clashes;
Element at their worst presenting a hateful face!
Violence of the wind rampages in savage force
As with blazing zeal, the monstrous tempest rages on;
Until — finally exhausting itself — the clamor ceases
And quiet tranquillity resolves with break of dawn.

D. J. Knoll

The Great Seahawk

Once captain of this sailing ship,
I won't forget that ocean might
That smashed our bow like its know how,
Was gusty winds that tells no lies into the night.
When hurricanes just go insane,
They have no name.

They called my ship the great seahawk.
The keel was laid by restless men
Who think wood strength cannot be bent,
By hurricanes.

Who lives for sight for what it's worth
When ocean birth make men just curse,
That wicked eye.
Right off Cape Hatteras where wishful tides,
Reach for the sky.

What held are sails
Was thirsty ropes that gave us hope,
I'd steer my ship.
Between two rocks that act like locks.

Strong winds wear veils
If we just fail,
To outthink fate.
If ships are names with only graves.
We will prevail.
The great seahawk makes sailors talk
That challenges met,
We won't forget.

Peter E. Barrow

A Rose In Mind

I ask myself what it is I want?
The day passes and still no answers . . .
On the next day——I ask again and my thoughts are,
need, want . . . or desires.
Closing my eyes now for answers
an image comes over me . . .
And what I saw was the most beautiful sight I ever saw!
A garden of white roses—
I couldn't speak nor could I think.
As though the wind blew the sweetest scent
I ever smelled—in thought, this was heaven.
I couldn't believe before our very eyes—
this sight I was seeing!
My heart started to pound . . .
as though it never pounded before.
I kneeled down to pray what it was that I wanted?
I was told to reach deep down into my heart and find that single
white rose, and you too shall have
Heaven!

Rhonda Russell

Leave In Fall

You're the only one that made me feel right
And you turned my soul from black to white
And you put the fires in me
And you showed me how to love you and me
Now that you are gone I don't know what to do
And my broken heart turned blue
With you I was colorful as the leaves in fall
But without you I'm dying just like the leaves in fall

Allan Picardy

Lighted Path

Angels are sent
from heaven above;
To guide and support
Each day with love.

The faith you hold
has shown me the way;
I've learned to give thanks
at the end of my day.

Gentle encouragement
you've given it's true;
with hope and love
and good advice, too.

The light you hold
is there for me;
It inspires my life
it's plain to see.

Hold on to that light
you know what to do;
When God made angels
He found one in you.

Rita Hensel

Christmas

The fire is crackling on the logs
Carolers singing Christmas songs
Santa's Elves finish the toys
For all the little girls and boys

Out shopping for last minute gifts
Children writing their Christmas lists
People putting on a Christmas play
Santa Claus is packing his sleigh

Over the city Santa will go
And he will yell Ho! Ho! Ho!
Hanging all of the Christmas stockings
Giving the cookies icing toppings

Putting up the Christmas tree
Parents going out to ski
Into bed everyone goes
When Santa will come, nobody knows

Dianna Bastien

In You!

In you I place my confidence,
In you I place my trust.
From you I gain the will to do.
All of the things I must.
In you I see a guiding light.
That guides me on my way.
Within you is the happiness,
That thrills me day by day,
From you I gain a love that's rare
You hold my deepest heart
And that is why I long to hold you
And from you never part
With you all my dreams come true
And paradise I see
From you I will never part
Only death can take me away

Frank Sass

Untitled

The warm soft glow of your face
is like that of the radiant sun
It sets my heart on fire
for you are the only one
The way you wrap my body
With all your care and love
It is like a blanket of fog
that fits over me like a glove
The shining stars in the sky
your eyes they reflect so bright
as a full moon glows amidst
on a warm July's summer night
with one touch of your hand
I feel completely at ease
the blood runs thru my veins
like the air of an afternoon breeze
while walking along the beach
staring out at the water and land
wherever I am you're always at reach
our external love is hand in hand.

Michele Barks

Untitled

I have experienced catharsis,
And purged my inner self.
Hoping that is what I love,
Is not a fading phase.
Growing comfortable can cause pain,
But it is a welcome pain.
During the day the pain lingers,
But the night brings reassurance.
Embraces, touches, and words,
Are a step towards bliss.
Ending quickly as an intruder enters,
And resuming as soon as safety returns.
Phases and choices float in my mind,
Decisions are made in real life.

Daniel Stephen Frechette

Easter!

The sky was black
The sun refused to shine
Upon the scene on yon
Gol gothas' brow.

The Son of God
In nakedness displayed
The Thorn crown caused his blood
to trickle down.

The Silence rent
The thunder pierced the sky
the lightning flashed
His suffering betrayed.

Within a borrowed tomb
They placed His frame
Disciples sorrowed and
Their souls dismayed.

But Lo! On Easter morn
Behold Him there
The Son of God
In glory, all arrayed.

Laura Spencer Silek

Sanctuary

A glimpse of sunlight peeks through the fog-covered sky
Seagulls perched on the rocks as the waves crash on by

Meditate, while listening to the waves break on the shore

Peaceful, serene——

  Heaven

Therese Nadeau

For Carole Lee
(Who Finally Had The Courage To Leave)

He caught her off-guard slapping her face, swinging
A red hand-print splayed on a creamy white cheek,
each finger-mark stinging, tomorrow's blue bruising

The second came close-fisted, harder, ears ringing
Experience motivating, she fought to escape
but her neck snapped, huge fingers tangled hair, pulling

He wrenched, turned and threw her roughly, rage screaming
Her back smashed wall, splintering bone, hands at her throat
Black eyes danced mean, and he sneered at her, panting

She moaned...her fear, pain and tears stimulating, arousing
turning him on, strengthening his power, control
Full of lust, calloused hands groped, tore, probing

Clothes shed, soft body parts exposed, weakening
He laughed, as he broke, violated and humiliated her
Then left her lay naked, broken and bleeding

She curled fetal, protective, softly crying, surviving,
feeling him near, smelling his musky sweat, waiting
She prayed he was done with her, this time...
A scratched match...inhaling, shuffling, fabric rustling,
pants zipping, heavy footsteps walking away. He was humming!

Paulette A. Burrier

Life's Song

Life keeps us singing a song
Even when things go wrong.
Sometimes the years go swiftly by
And I try not to ask why
Things happen the way they do.
There is a path for each of us to go
Sometimes to hurry, sometimes to go slow
Though we can't always see it we know
At the end we'll see a rainbow.
We need faith as we go through life
To see past the problems of worry and strife
To ever onward to day by day
Never looking back at our yesterday.
What happened in the past cannot be redone
But we look forward to victory to be won.
And at the end of each day to say "Well done."
Because someone's day we made a little brighter
Or some one's burden a little lighter.
These are the things that brighten our day
As we travel along life's way.

Elizabeth Peters

Incredibly October

An over-burdened sun releases molten silver on the sea
The shape, womanlike - wide, narrow, wide
Slides to shore
Wave treads are dark
And darker surfers idling on the brink
Seem never to fall.
Sand-dirty babies plod ecstatic
To the bright promise of lace-trimmed ripples.
A Mexican, short, sturdy, enigmatic behind dark glasses,
Gazes stolid outward.
Seabirds swooping on discarded scraps
Less raucous now in their delight
Than hard-bodied, hard-headed marines
Screaming in mock fight
A line separates swimmers from surfers
And those between, walk the pier tidily unabashed
At their detachment.
Later, the young and old leave stealthily
So as not to steal the day from those remaining
Who, perhaps, can hold the scene together.

Mary V. Carter

My Grandparents

Diligent workers
Thinkers
Peacemakers
My grandparents.
A World War II veteran
A hard-working housewife and mother
Come together to form apart of my history
My grandparents.
Their smiling eyes
And well-worn features
Show their generations strength
My grandparents.
Grandpa instilled in me my creativity
Granny her gentle and caring nature
Contributions that make me a dynamic combination of them
My grandparents.
My heroes.

Laura Harrison

Tongue-Tied

"I see you off in the distance,
so I search for something clever to say;
But the words that I speak
come out as a 'squeak',
For my tongue always gets in the way.

With my pen I can write with great eloquence.
In my mind, the words all make perfect sense;
but as my mouth starts to utter,
my tongue starts to stutter,
and thus is the beginning of consequence.

So if chance one day we should meet,
and you find my words few and discreet;
be they ever so humble, I'll try not to humble,
and keep my tongue out form under my feet."

Michael Eric Hanemann

"Ugly..."

Broken glass in the corner 'n white
dust all over the floor:
 'n Little Jack Horner ain't gettin'
his fur pie no more!
 Hope you had fun girl, cuz now
there's Be-Elzee to pay
 We gettin' ugly wit' each other;
'n you best not to stand in my way!
 Home should be somewhere we
both can escape from the shit;
 But, dig, somethin's wrong here
they's too many shakes snakes in dis pit!
 Don't wann'em to eat'ya so you
gonna feed 'em a mouse?
 Well, I ain't yer rodent:
You will not bring death to my house!
 Gettin' ugly wit each other....

Billy Christian

Sunrise

In the cold darkness at the crack of dawn
A faint glimmer of light appears
and streaks across the sky at the horizon
etching in silver the crest of the mountain.
Soon a tinge of saffron appears,
rimmed with a band of crimson.
The light increases and expands
into a meld of rosy blue.
It is the glory of the morning!
One wonders at its effulgence,
heralding the day that is yet to come.
It is a silent trumpet of the brightness
that is slowly descending upon us.
As the darkness fades into obscurity,
we are bathed in a heavenly light
which awakens all nature and us,
from a night of slumber and rest.
So that we may again go forth
to do the tasks which will enrich our lives
and give more reason to our being.

Gordon Pierce

Some Things Are Hard To Do

When you grow up
Time goes so fast
Then you're a senior
Ready to graduate

You look back on friends
Old and new
The friendships you have lost
And the ones you've kept

You remember the good times
And even the bad
One thing you always remember
How much you love them

It's hard growing up
It's hard thinking of friends
Then having to say goodbye
For the first time and last.

Kristina M. Groover

The Seduction Of The Bottle

The bottle set on the table
  gleaming in soft candle light;
Enticing the young man close to it,
  flirting with all its might!

"Come - sit here beside me,"
  said the bottle to the man.
"Drown your troubles in my nectar,"
  "Let me take your hand".

The man sat down at the table
  and reached out to the bottle of wine.
He was feeling tired and lonely,
  so he drank - time, after time, after time.

Night and day - he held the bottle,
  consumed by its warmth and taste.
He thoughts he had found the perfect union,
  and nothing could take its place.

As time went by, nothing-else was important,
  and the bottle possessed his soul.
It devoured the man it had befriended,
  leaving him withered and old.

    Mary A. Calain

Ode To A Golden Bridle

Dear heart, in days gone past,
we rode our winged horse.
How he loved to carry us
to Camelot and neuschwanstein
or gamboling above the Rhine.

We rode the diamond skies of night
To wherever was our yen.
I in drifting gossamer
You in tiger skin.

He'll give us flight until we die
And all our dreams a bate.
Then he will gently set us down
Somewhere near heaven's gate.

    Nell Huddleston

Dream of Peace

World Peace is a dream not yet realized.
Different creeds and races are feared
        and despised.

Lord, if You're listening, I implore
Please end this Nightmare of Hatred
        and War!

How I wish all children could grow up free,
Never knowing hunger or disease.

Oh, what a miracle if men could live as
        brothers,
Sharing riches of The Earth and caring for
        each other!

Every child's pure at birth and beautiful
        inside,
All 'created equal' in God's Eyes!

    Marian Hallet

Time On Target

St. Laurent De Cuves 5 August, 1944
They killed my radio operator that day.
The famed German eighty-eight!
Shell from a tank, eight hundred yards away.

Enemy infantry battalion and tanks,
Ready to attack from a woods half-a-mile square.
Report coordinates and situation by radio.
Request T-O-T as soon as they can prepare.

All first rounds will explode together.
A T-O-T is the deadliest kind of artillery fire,
There will be five battalions in "fire for effect".
Adjusting rounds burst at edge of woods as I desire.

Only one additional command is needed,
"Three hundred short, "fire for effect!"
Wait a minute, then you hear our guns,
Far away, closer, close, tree bursts, perfect.

The whole woods lights up like a Christmas tree!
The area is zoned, five rounds per gun.
One hundred yards range changes,
300 rounds! The destruction leaves me stunned!

    Russell L. Kelch

Chippie: A True Story

Always he was there, waiting at the gate;
He never failed, whether early or late;
His sense of timing, this forest "hippie,"
Was really phenomenal, our little "Chippie."

When we went north to visit the lake,
A little surprise we would always take;
'Twas usually some peanuts or another treat
For Chippie who stretched up on his hind feet.

His light-colored belly was clean as could be.
And his beautiful back had brown stripes, you see;
He was a gorgeous creature the color of sand,
And was so tiny he fit in a hand.

The best part of all, when he climbed like a rocket
Right up my husband's pant leg and into his pocket;
He knew a treasure awaited him there;
Then he stuffed his small pouch and came out for air.

He hid his prize and returned for more;
His sharp eyes and keen nose thought he'd found a store,
And we didn't mind, we enjoyed his soft touch,
The little Chippie whom we loved so much.

One day came a monster, a bulldozer, next door,
And it gouged out Chippie's home right down to the core.
from that time on we looked in vain
For our little Chippie who must have died in pain!

    Marguerite Popov

Holy Vision

I sneak through the ancient graveyard—barefooted,
With my friends beside me, laughing and whispering,
The thick and invisible silence affects us all equally,
While we are trying to hide our fear of unsettled spirits,
I bend my knees at a mother's tombstone—written in 1885,
And imagine her soul's rebirth beyond the horizon,
As the eggshell breaks and the earth under my knees moves,
I see two angels making love in the living grass . . .

    Daniel Pantano

Please Daddy

All day long I play as a child;
I suppress my fears, my worries are mild.
Evening draws near, I run to hide;
No one, I feel, is on my side.

I curl up behind a huge stuffed chair;
My heart beats loudly - oh! If only someone cared.
I listen for the sound of my Daddy's old car.
I'm so afraid he has been to the county bar.

I am so tired, I didn't sleep last night.
My Daddy was drinking, and caused a big fight.
Please Daddy, don't hurt my Mommy or me;
We love you very much, if you could only see.

I hear footsteps at the door, my Daddy's here;
I peek from the chair to calm my fear.
Is my Daddy drunk? Will he try to fight;
Or will things be better for us tonight?

I'll never let a child of mine;
Be abused by the actions of beer or wine.
I pray for all the Daddy's in the world.
Don't put fear into the hearts of little boys and girls.
   Jonni Eubanks

Love's Images

Crystal clear

Love's images defined timeless
In ever-changing space
Infinity solidifies into now
Showing wrinkles from sorrow
Etched through years of lessons unlearned
Seeking the key
We walked by the door many times
Never seeing it stood unlocked
We wearied
And fell asleep
A thousand years

Awakening upon an early dawn
We saw the door ajar
And entered an empty, yet crowded room
Overwhelmed by the energy emanating from within
We were confused, and fell asleep again
Alas! Perhaps,
Ten thousand years
   Elizabeth Maria Reynolds

Eternity's River

Be still and you can almost hear the water rush
So loud a roar over so soft a hush
As wide as opportunity as deep as one's emotion
With so many paths one's can change with just a notion
This river is endless; it was here before my start
This river has no true beginning; it will be here when I part
What a fool I am to have swum to shore
Could that have been my life, is there nothing more?
Or is it just this shelter I hold so dear
Knowing that change is nowhere near
I clench my fists thinking of rejoining the race
But I am frightened by its fast moving pace
A splash of cold water causes me to shiver
I think that was my call to rejoin Eternity's River
   Jason Jones

Untitled

Do you know
we are likened
to those of obese
intellect?

We are locked
rocked within
our lies.

We are crucified
by disciples
waiting for the
Antichrist.

Devouring souls
with stardust
eyes.
   Amy Pezderic

The First Of Snow

The sky forgo it is time to
leave the secure berth and
descend down...down...
A silent utterance, a feeling
of cold wonder. Oh how they
dance an innocent dance unblemished.
The mysterious sky the only
true testifier to this Waltz.
we can only observe.
A common beginning
To a common end.
   Shelley Eckberg

That Tree

It's that time of year
As I stand and watch
The shower of leaves
Rain down on the patch
Of earth under that tree.

Only a few days ago
The leaves were green
The shade they made below
Was refreshing as I leaned
Against the trunk of that tree.

Soon that tree will stand
Without its summer clothes
As through its branches bare
The winter wind blows
I see courage in that tree.

The courage I see
In that tree is also mine
As I understand God
He makes me divine
My protection's same as that tree.
   Cleo Coffin

Mystical Union

Judicious praising and confronting
Judicious urging and arguing
Judicious struggling and comforting
Judicious pushing and pulling
The myth of exclusivity
Real when acted lovingly
New unfamiliar territory
An act chosen willingly
A larger state of being
Permanently self enlarging
Work is that of listening
World becomes more blurring
A committed thoughtful decision
Concentration is love in action
Playing is also a fraction
One's individuality is a traction
A true form of courage
Romantic love does discourage
Extending one's spiritual foliage
The more loving the more homage

Carl Casteel

Heartfelt Words

Words so meaningful and poignant
    Just as a beacon of light
Touch me so deeply
    Seems at a time just right.

Difficult to describe with pen
    That place deep within my heart
Thoughts come straight and clear
    And ever tears sometime start.

Pleasure rhyming words
    Meanings going deep
Seem now to just spurt out
    Not only for me to keep.

I truly have to believe
    God takes my hand
Guides it with direction
    As he guides waves across the sand.

Please so rewarding
    Believe me—it's true
Just how much
    I never knew—until now

Shirley M. Pannell

Me

Are you sure?
I can't believe
Me
Of all people
Me
I always dreamt
of it
but I "Never" thought
it be Me!!!
She is pretty
She is nice
She could have any one
but she
picked
"Me"!!!

Robert J. DiGennaro

What A Wonderful World The Lord Has Made

What a wonderful world the Lord has made,
Let's take care so that its beauty will never fade.

The majestic mountains rising up on high,
the sun, moon and the stars sparkling in the sky.

The oceans so vast, awesome and blue,
Miles of landscape with green running through.

All sorts of colorful flowers along the way
Prompt a prayer of thanks to our Lord to say.

The desert so dry with oasis here and there,
That passing through its bleakness he does spare.

All types of creatures along the way,
An important roll they all do play.

The people we meet black, red, yellow or white,
All deserve our love and respect color despite.

Our Lord made us in his image one and all,
Let's give Him thanks for blessings large and small!

Let us respect this world with care and pride,
and with duty and love ever stand by its side!

Nancy Cacioppo

Sorry

An ocean of lonely tears...
swelling into a stormy sea.
The cries of the gulls like the cries of my heart.
I'm sorry.

Kimberly Alexis Buckley

A Warrior's Song

We entered battle unwitting warriors

Our goal was to defeat the enemy - death
Be fitting a soldier, we secured new swords
    and wrapped ourselves with strong, shiny armour for protection

Ours souls' purpose was clear and pure
Amidst their tears, we were rallied on by family,
    friends and townsmen
As we gazed at the stars, victory was ours

One mountain after another confronted us as we waged war
Still we marched on fighting the enemy
Echoes of pleading loved ones urging us ever onward
Gradually, our armour thinned and our swords dulled

Finally, we put down our weapons and spoke with our enemy —
Death
You, our loved ones, thought we had surrendered, but we did not
Death simply ceased to be our enemy

We gathered together to sing one long song and
    saluted our courage, endurance, wisdom and faith
As night swept over us, we sought our rest amidst the stars
In the years to come, as you gaze at the heavens if you hear music
It is us singing a Warrior's Song.

Kathleen R. Kearns

Sleep, The Depository Of Living

Into the deep darkness of sleep
with no chance to welcome it
Or remember that last thought
Is it Morpheus or Mors who catch us
And shade the mind from its separate reality
To float comatose in aimless searching through
Surreal cities and fields
To emerge in an eerie world of groundless animation
There entities wander, unheralded creatures of memory
Or worse
Mysterious objects acting out Delphic signs
Causes veiled in oracular depths
And signs turning gray matter into synchronic calamity,
Like leaf mold turned, exposes
The foul misdeeds performed
While a posse of crazed phantoms
Prod the hapless voyager into frenzied fleeing.
Are nightmares the sifters whose talons strain
To lay bare wounds of shame or helpless vexation.
Must the mind fail to surrender for happier ways?

R. L. Coret

Love

Love is a flame that burns
Through time and eternity,
For it is touched by a never
ending divinity.
Those who have it are blessed
beyond measure
To possess this rare treasure.
In you I see all of the above
For they are the immortal signs of love.
Your eyes are lights in our sky;
and so close to our reach
also warm and each to each
Your eyes are the lights to love!

They shine, brighter than the stars above,
Whether days are dark or fair.
Their light will always be there,
Shining through time and eternity
our love is a Heavenly thing! It is our song to sing
Wherever we maybe, on land or the deepest sea!

Charlotte J. Chambliss

The Passing Of Time History In Rhyme

In the morning the sun arrives
Creatures deep in sleep come alive
All those stars seem to fade away,
for today is here!
Only God knows what is in store.
Today is yours to make and explore.

Every person that lives on earth
has his or her choices to make
For life is precious, no matter what you say,
For tomorrow life may just fade away.
Let's make this day, a day to remember as it passes along.

I know that we cannot make that final decision,
but let's enjoy all of those precious moments we have
Do not hurry, time is yours for the sun will soon set.
It's time to close the door
for today has ended, there is no more.

Robert J. Ramp

Morning To Night

Come the morning,
  Come the sun,
Come the time
  When night is done.
Morning brings
  Another day,
To use or
  Simply throw away.
This day will pass,
  As all days do,
and how it's used
  is up to you.
So run the race
  And fight the fight,
And know the peace
  That comes with night.
The sun is gone
  You've done your best,
Now go to bed
  And get to some rest!

Sheryl Epperson

Untitled

What fools are we,
To looks at the Illusive Masquerade,
And declare the image we see;
A horse, a hare, a pig, or mule,
And complain,
Of what it does or doesn't do,
Of what it is,
Or isn't.

Sarah F. Price

Christmas Blessings

I want to wish you Merry Christmas
And share God blessings from above
I want to tell you Jesus loves you
And share with you God gift of love
A Angel spoke unto the shepherds
And told them of the savior birth
A star it was that let the wise men
Shinning brightly to the earth
Alleluia blessed savior.
Blessed redeemer Lord and King
Alleluia blessed Jesus
Christmas blessings that you bring
Mary and Joseph baby Jesus
At the manger that day in Bethlehem
The place God son become the savior
And become Jesus Alleluia
For being our savior and our King
Alleluia blessed Jesus
For the Christmas blessing that you bring

David Lee Knepp

Slowly

Slowly I see the turning of the world.
I question
Why is this so?

Kim Headley

Mon Ami

Be my friend, an Ami, sil vous plait
Be my mother, be my father
Be there to lend Votre Main, your kind hand

Be my friend, Mon Ami
Be my aunt, be my uncle
Be there to lend Votre Main when I bend

Be my friend, Un Bon Ami
Be a dog, be a cat or a pet
And never, Jamais, Jamais send me away

Be my friend, Un Ami
Be a relative, be a neighbor
Upon whom I can depend, Toujours,
Toujours.

You be what you are, Un Ami
But Lord, let me be, An Ami
To exactly those you meant me to be
Jeanne Tyson Hoover

September 10, 1995

I stare ahead
as the world melts into a cup of coffee.
The grounds of my soul
are transformed
into a aromatic blend of today and tomorrow.
So much of life
rest on the bottom
with the wasted bits of espresso,
but I can't sip it all
because the last is tepid and tasteless.
Tepid and tasteless
yet still,
settled
and hopeful for that hand to tilt it back.
A welcome escape....
another cup is brewing.
Liz Shimkus

His Gentle Touch

My guardian angel touched my arm
He gave me quite a scare
be not afraid, "He said"
you know God really cares.

Be patient, be loving and be willing
to help others if you must
I will lead the way - and
tell you who to trust.

Put away those silly dreams
forgive and forget the past
live for today - enjoy each moment
tomorrow will be gone too fast.

With his friendly smile and gentle touch
he made my body feel warm
then speaking softly with tenderness
he said, I'll keep you from all harm.
Minnie Karchinski

When Summer's Gone

When summer's gone and the days grow cool,
it's time to think of books and school.
Of autumn leaves and Indian summer nights,
of football games and bright Northern lights.
Of long hay-rides in the brisk cold air,
with your love in a corner, you ne'er worry or care.
Of popcorn and marshmallows around a bright fireplace,
the full contentment and laughter shown in each face.
the nights of bright stars in the cool, clear heaven above,
and two people bundled against the cold, think only of love,
with the full moon like a spot light shining for you.
and all the world's at peace sparkling and new.
Of soft fluffy snow hitting lightly on your face,
when walking in the soft powder at a leisurely pace.
Of turkey and sleigh bells and gift to give,
of mistletoe and holly and happiness where you live.
The seeing the old year out and ringing the new year in,
living the kind of life you want though you don't always win.
Being glad you have a good American life,
and can keep it through joy, toil and strife.
Chester H. Reeve

Face In The Crowd

You might see me as a face in the crowd.
But I see myself and I make myself proud.

I hold my head high; I hold my head tall.
I refuse to be quiet; I refuse to be small.

I know wrong from right; I do what I should.
I don't think I'm great but I know that I'm good.

I do have a voice; I have things to say.
I do what I must and I do it my way

You might think I'm odd; you might laugh or stare.
But as long as I'm happy; I don't really care.

I can't please them all, that's easy to see.
So I do what it takes just to please me.

I believe that I'm strong; there's not a thing I can't do.
And I don't believe that I'm different from you.

You'll never be just a face in the crowd.
You are your own person; so make yourself proud.
Kathleen Johnston

Last Night I Cried

Last night I cried over you, now that you're gone.
Last night I cried over you, how can I carry on?

So many words unspoken, my lively world all broken.
How can I carry on now that you're gone?

Our Lord has taken you from my sight, He needed an angel of love.
That's why He came and took you away with Him in heaven above.

My love for you still strong how can this be now that you're gone
How can I carry on?

You were my love, my life: My everything.
You were my winter, fall, summer, and spring.
How can I carry on now that you're gone?
  In loving memory of you, James Hurd
  February second, nineteen ninety six
Angelina Hurd

Early Morning Light

There! To the right! A movement!
Or could it be just the wind?

More movement - and a patch of grayish brown detaches itself
 from the trees and becomes more defined.
How can something with such a spread of antlers pass
 so easily through the low-hanging branches?

He glides smoothly and with grace in the early morning light,
 pausing now and then to sample an apple,
Bending his slender neck to nibble
 on the frost-covered fruit.

He stops, raises his head,
 and turns his nose to the wind.
Detecting no danger, he calmly continues
 on his way.

The waiting hunter - impressed by the majesty there displayed
 lowers his bow,
And continues to watch until there is nothing to be seen
 but small marks in frost-edged grass.
Joan Gallagher

Inspiration

One cannot visualize something from within one self,
so strong and laid back hidden from one's self. So
strong within one's body, like a shinning star, what
is it you ask? Inspiration! Giving off a light
unknown to many, which inspired them down a path.
Which lead many to greatness and unknowingly inspired
others including myself very rewarding. Just think
how happy one can be inspired by such a person,
remember for all times.
Clara Gange

Silent Eulogy

I long for a touching tender embrace,
And the solace of a squeezing hand.
I love to be cooed and cuddled with grace,
And lulled by lullabies to dreamland.

I like to hide in fairy tales unreal
Where life's goodness triumphs over wrong.
 I dwell in prose and poetry to seal
A placid place where I can belong.

A thrill over the house high in a tree
And playing barefoot in warm sun.
I stuff my pockets on a pebble spree
To save souvenirs of earthly fun.

I sniff the perfume of springtime flowers,
Wrap myself in autumn's sunset glow,
Chase rainbows after cool summer showers,
And brave the chill sledding winter's snow.

Truly, I've grasped no sensory delight.
I'm just a dreamer of dreamless dreams,
For dark shadows doomed my God-given right,
And aborted me midst heaven's screams.
June Nash

The Nature Of Love

You asked me once, in happier times
What was my best day in life.
I said, the very day I met you.
Ask me now, in my misery
I'll say the sad day you left me.
Loving has only tormented me,
Yet, after all these years
I still cherish it deeply,
Cause it's the best thing
That ever happened to me.
Henry A. Sarkissian

Untitled

In the life of which we lead
we can achieve
what's meant to be.
Hold strong your course a persevere
you will succeed
when you believe
Caron Farnham

Tides Of Time

A ray of light
pierced the cold dark night.

The start of a new day
quivered in its wake.

Today was the day
that my heart would break.

I closed my eyes
trying to escape.

It was just no use!
Reality wouldn't wait.

People began to arrive
to say their last goodbyes.

With each passing handshake,
there was a deeper hollow ache.

The Tides of Time roll on
with each new dawn.

Whether we make the most of it or not,
Father Time always knocks.
Annette Lynne Pentes

Luz

Luz, the lady, who lives next door,
a friend to cats, you could not ask for more.

Always, ready to help a stray,
a gracious lady, in every way.

When other people, turn them out,
and in the streets, they must run about.

To the rescue, she will come,
with medical help, and homes for some.

I know that God, always smiles her way,
every time, she helps a stray.
Richard A. Granholm

Morning Star

I wake and see my morning star,
And then I know how dear you are,
The loving way you look at me,
So deep into my heart you see,
The love that lies there tenderly.

I wake and see my morning star,
And then I know how near you are,
So near and yet so far away,
How can I start this lonely day,
How can I now that you're away.

I wake and see my morning star,
And how I wish that you could be,
Back in my arms again my love,
So very, very close to me,
To hold me, oh so tenderly.

And so I wish upon my star,
And I still know how dear you are,
Though many years have passed away,
You will be here with me someday.

Eleanore M. Rudewicz

He Called Me Friend

He called me friend and took my hand
And walked a while with me.
We talked of life and love and death
And all things that could be.

It was in the early spring
When wild flowers began to bloom,
We wandered aimlessly through fields of green
And roamed in dark forests filled with gloom.

He called me dear in summer
As through sun-drenched fields we roamed,
Our friendship had deepened into love
And at last I was not alone.

He called me sweetheart in autumn
When leaves had turned to red and gold;
But I saw a restlessness in his eyes
And felt a rush of winter cold.

He called me not at all in winter
The winds through the forests moaned,
My tears were icy upon my cheeks
For once again I was alone!

Wilda Lee Rogers

One Syllable World

I remember, I remember
when words danced tripping on my pen
lilted drolly
love was holy
oh, what a surge of writing then.

Now I fear an overstatement
delete, abstract to those which would
make it pithy
what a pity
that I'm not always understood.

Norma Ring

Life

All comes to pass, each in its turn, as the
world on its axis, goes round, Each has its own
symphony as a drummer drums. Time passes by
slowly yet glimpses are as a carousel going
round and round. Bits and pieces, some are kept
to saver on a future plane, others aren't worth
the trouble. A grain of sand, a mountain, each
has a meaning in life. Mysteries solved,
puzzles put to together. Learn, go on,
experience each new challenge, keep some memories
others pass by, History past, present, future,
all have their place in time. My existence is
part of the chain of life's events. Can't
change the future, past is just that. But we go
on, feelings, old and new emotions. Savoring
good times. Gain strength from the bad.
Counting the blessings yet reminded of the
sorrows. Looking to God to get us through it
all. Faith is the power. God is the light.
With him all things in our lifes path will be alright.

Bonnie Kaminski

Things Remembered

I gaze into the crystal balls on the festive Christmas tree—
Not looking into the future, but, rather, reflecting the past,
And my mind is brimming
With a myriad of things remembered—

Simple things—plain, beautiful:
Christmas stockings, candy canes, plum pudding, mince pie,
Christmas carolling, family gatherings, children's laughter—
Gently falling snow—

But, more significantly the essence of the season—
Angels singing, shepherds wandering,
A mother, pondering over a tiny infant in the hay.

In this world of din and noise,
Let the silent crystal balls on the festive tree
Be a simple, but lasting reminder
Of things remembered—
And the wonder and joy of the season.

Janet M. Niklaus

Believing Heart

How did you manage when your kids were young?
  I used careful planning to carry us through.
How did you cope when "home" problems arose?
  I had to be strong through some bad times, it's true.

What brought you health all those years ago
When thyroid removal revealed cancer cells?
  I had all the prayers of my family and friends,
  But belief in myself also helped make me well.

How do you make all those lovely hand crafts?
  God gave me the mind and the soul to create.
How will you conquer whatever comes now?
  I'll rely on faith and forget about fate!

You have the courage, the strength and belief
To overcome whatever life brings your way;
And though you may question the truth of this now,
These traits of the heart are still with you today!

Loraine O. Funk

It's The Place We Call Home

Growing up was miserable for everyone
Disappointments, broken promises was all he'd done
No hugs, no kisses, only a lashing of the tongue . . . but
It's the place I call home.

Cold bitter tones and cursings he would speak
Causing our emotions to play hide and go seek
Insomnia every night unable to sleep . . . but
It's the place I call home.

A house filled with hatred and untold violence
Beatings were expected, if you broke the code of silence
Every form of abuse, and dysfunctional compliance . . . but
It's the place I call home.

Now after enduring all these painful years
God's promised to wipe away all our tears
No death, no sadness, no pain, no fears . . . now
It's the place we call home.

The darkness of night dispelled by God's light
A street paved with gold, what a glorious sight
Walls made of precious stones, having great height . . . now
It's the place we call home.

Gregory Lee Proctor

Seeking

In awesome anticipation..of a majestic mountain view
A little Hindu lad observing, felt a 'presence' that he knew
The words spilled forth yea prayerfully
He could not stop from saying..
My Lord there sins have I..in humanness..
Be ye not everywhere? Yet worship I thee here?
Formless thou art, yet in these forms, I perceive thee?
Thy praise be unneedful, yet praise thee I your name?
Lord in thy mercy, heed my sin and supplication here
Neath the Dura Khaima

Doris J. Dolejs

My Intimate Foe?

What is this, that overcomes me
And now upsets my tie with the unknown?

What is this, that suddenly robs my soul
Of its peaceful reign
And yet, without shame
Insists on being my ally?

What ill habits have I acquired from old choices
That I must now confront
If only to suit
My fledging company with the present?

What varied web has my life woven
Displaying in faith all that I have been!
What spaciousness is inherent
In this peace that I crave always!

Hurray! To the dark shadows my past abode
Does cast upon my waking hours
To hold me aware of blessings
My upward journeys have brought.

Is there a foe, however intimate
Or a changed face that now sees a friend?

Bernard I. Oparah

Trials Of Faith

Faith is simply reaching
For things yet unseen,
Willing to believe in
Impossible dreams.

The task is not simple,
Uncertainties vast,
But look to the future,
Think not on the past.

Stones there to befall you,
Sticks to snag your way,
But those things will linger
Only for today.

Infernos rage boldly
To burn out desire,
Yet silver and gold are
Made pure by fire.

Patience is a virtue,
Time's not laid to waste,
For we are made stronger
Through trials of faith.

Keli Adell Killingsworth

Fathers

Fathers what can you say, they are rather unique.

Sometimes their love, although it is there, you must seek.

Their strength, quiet but strong, a glance can right your wrong.

They will provide, they will guide, and more or less with your mom they will side.

Your love for them is remarkably deep, but when they take that final sleep you try to remember every detailed memory that has been reaped.

In loving memory of my father

Angela S. Kinyon-Wilson

Drowsy Feelings

Thoughts flow unfiltered
Through an empty head
Words mumbled into phrases
Split out like sour milk
Hands like silk on my body
Nobody else in the world
Your presence runs through me
Touching my inner soul
Caressing my heart with your love
Feelings felt never before
Everlasting emotions hatch
Growing anxiety
Inside of me we are one
You feel me deep inside
You hold my heart and soul
So don't let go.

Lindsey Holmes

Kathy's Poem

God's mercy from above,
Send us a daughter to behold,
With big smiling eyes,
She curiously looked at us,
As we looked in awe,
At this gift from God,
For us to care and love,

The little girl I carried,
A woman has become,
Giving us joy,
My heart,
An album of memories hold,
She lightens our days,
With her care and love,

May she always walk in beauty,
May she always stay in God's warm light,
As she walks through the road of life,
May she have the strength to stand strong,
Through wind and storm,
And may our love she feel,
Even after we are gone.

Elizabeth L. Flores

Thoughts Are Things

The thoughts we think and will express,
Will take or give real happiness;
For someone, either there or here,
Will somehow see or feel or hear,
And will transmit to farther clime
Upon the ceaseless sea of time.

So ev'ry thought, what'er it be,
And though its motive we can't see,
Will leave its mark upon some strand,
And will give cause to fall or stand
Some hapless soul, who may not see
The restless wave, a thought set free.

Fern M. Cooper

A Place Forsaken

Beneath the limbs of a giant oak
The empty farm house stands.
The bare board walls and rusty roof
Over-see surrounding lands.

The crumbling chimney gives no hope
That it will soon be filled with smoke.
Inside the dogtrot, leaves abound
Bricks are scattered on the ground.

The fields that once grew cotton
Are all abandoned now
No furrows straight and narrow
No sign of horse and plow.

Gone the swing and rocking chair
Gone the ones who lingered there.
No curtain flutter in the wind
No fishing poles, where willows bend.

Gone the laughter, gone the tears
Gone the triumphs of those years.
In the meadow, daisies, all alone
Still try to make it look like home.

Anna K. Shoemaker

Watching The Sunset

I watched you lean against the balcony to watch the sunset.
My gaze lingered a few moments longer than usual.
You looked both young and old
with your worn out Levi's and loose flannel shirt.
I thought about how well I know you,
and yet, how I hardly know you at all.
And something about that made me smile
as I contemplated the last of my beer.

For there is so much about me that you don't know,
and yet, in some ways you know me better than anyone else.
I almost said something to you.
But instead I thrust my hand into the cooler,
enjoying the numbing effect of the ice
as I retrieved another bottle.
We watched the sunset without speaking;
there are some things we just never discuss.
And something about that made me sad.

Nycole Rochford

The Pilot

As a young boy he would look to the sky
And dream of flying a Big Plane so high.
As time went by he spent lot of his time
Studying things he knew would improve his mind.
He joined the Air Force when his country did call
But, flying the planes was no stress at all.
There was excitement yet he learned every trick
To escape any danger one had to act quick!
When he was discharged and finally got home
He took to the airways the Blue Skies to Roam.
Soon, he was captain, a job he loved more
Even trained young pilots—that wasn't a chore
When he is home he keeps in top shape
Running the miles without taking a break.
He now owns a home in beautiful Ozark Land
When he comes to relax anytime that he can.
When the pilot retires you will certainly see him
Sitting in the banks of the current dreaming happily

Norma Dotson Payne

A Bridge To Twenty-One Century

It was a day of joy, an era of a bridge
  crosses to twenty-one century.
That was on January 20, 1997, an inauguration
  of President William Clinton's second term history.

The themes and music kindled the citizens.
The leaders' oaths ensured their promises to the nation,
President's standpoints were to have whole people health care,
  to have an immaculate environment and pure air,
  to promote the high standard education,
  and to teach the tyrannies learn the Democratic solutions.

About three hundred years ago, America was a colonial land,
It has taken in freedom-lovers and hard-working immigrants,
  to fight for independent, to build a strong nation,
  and to turn the world on prospective fortune.

Time has carried generations and generations,
  to reach their victory or destruction.
The success of America isn't a magic
  it is an authentic merit,
  because she is "one nation under God, indivisible,
  with liberty and justice for all."

Diana M. P. Chang

The Box

She stares at the box, so small and
unpretentious, not knowing what lies within.
A dream fulfilled, perhaps?
Of morning candle or nighttime rust -
or something in between.

She glares at the box, almost wishing it
would spring open to divulge whatever secret
it clings to so fervently!
The death of some ancient soul - ashes now?
pale corners and crevices within this small tomb.

Her shaking hands swipe at glistened drops
on her brow, almost afraid to look at the box now!
 Robot-like fingers furiously paw the corners,
turning and rotating the box to hear
its mystery within. No sound!

 Her ear presses hard against the cube,
to jostle and shake its secrets loose, to
reveal man's darkest or brightest hopes and
dreams, it explodes sending her to her death!
Perhaps she was curious.
Jeff Harless

This Land

This is a story about laws of freedom
A Great Land wherein the tired were given,
'Tis a Country built on the blood of the fallen
And the cries of the anguished in fear—a callin'.
In the beginning, it was taken from the fold
And then the banishment of Indians bold,
The Utes, the Erie and the brave Navajo
And all other tribes of so long ago!
Then came pioneers in steady bands
Who gave their all to fight for land,
A precious commodity in the Golden West
They did seek a spot to build their nest!
Among them were men, with muscles of steel
And women that could readily lift a wheel,
A Country whereupon courage was born
And sissy boys were not average or norm!
A country wherein the best stayed alive
With hard lessons to learn just to survive,
A Country with wisdom and rightly vested
"Where men were men and women double-breasted."
Elma M. Rasor

A Buried Treasure

God isn't found in some inanimate object
He dwells in the hearts and souls of every living thing
Only man has the choice to awaken to his love
Otherwise he lives, breaths, and incarnates as any other creature
An unchosen treasure buried within
Fear, the devil's workshop, keeps God's love at bay
Love, the devil's enemy, draws him near
Whenever men gather in his name
His love flourishes and there is no greater power
For a chosen love is grandeur still
And means more to God than all the world
Mitch Gurney

Memories Of You

Some of our greatest memories
Are views we shan't forget.
So picturesque and beautiful
Your mind travels like a jet.

Mile after mile, a sandy beach
Or trees burdened heavy with snow
A vivid beauty to behold
As always a wondrous show.

A glacier mountain covered with ice
Or mountain goats without a price,
You cover miles, and yet don't move
Your mind is Rovin, yet in a groove.

Our sight is precious which we behold
Well really cherish as we grow old
A memory made like photographs
As dreams remind us of our past.
Lloyd Rexford

Starting To Believe

The sound of your heart beating
Somehow seems to relieve
The tensions I am defeating
And I am starting to believe
You are more to me than a friend
You are someone who will always be around
And I will never see the end
Of this perfect thing we have found
Connie Beard

Winter Days

Dreaming of summer breezes,
As winter winds,
Plumage through decrepit trees.
Wishing for,
warm and illuminating sunsets.
Having not seen the sun,
in what feels like an eternally.
Shades of grey,
through these long winter months.
Longing for;
Long walks on the beach,
and watching the sunset.
Being embraced,
by the warmth of the sun.
Being full of life,
and enjoying
every last minute.
Until those
long and bitter winter days return once more.
Melissa A. Bifano

To You

I'd like to be a part of your life,
Because I feel it will not be long
Until even a little of your life
Will forever and ever be gone.

I will not be here to watch what I say
Or do many things wrong I know;
I will be with Him who forgives all things;
So a part of your life will brighten mine so.
Virginia Brainard

Loneliness

Silence echoes
from the ratters of the rooms
That once resounded
with the richness of your voice;

Consciousness invades
the senses and the mind
That eagerly responded
to your loving charms;

Emptiness engulfs
the fountainhead of life
That freely flowed in streams
of happiness and love;

Solitude accentuates
the fading glow
Of summer sunsets
that we shall no longer share.

Yet, happy memories haunt
the hollows of my heart
Where your love still has power
to vanquish loneliness.

Gladys Harmon Birmingham

Black Swan

Not like those who strut
in colorful flare
Your quiet beauty is more rare
You're like a melody soft...
and lovely.
Stretching over...around
...and through me.
Refreshing and cool
like a breeze off the sea
on a deep velvet night
And I wish to wrap
you in delicate cloth
and walk by your side
Then peel it away
while gazing in your eyes
With blind hands
I find the lips
Sample the honey
losing me inside.

James Mel Brooks

Winter Wonderland

The snow is glistening
  on the trees above
Looking like a beautiful
  white dove
sitting in the branches
  up nigh
That nearly touches
  the redden sky
which reflects itself on
  the ground below
And gives the picture
  of a "Winter Wonderland"
that's all aglow.

Melita Spadafora

Living?

I feel I have no control, not even over me!
While I keep this hidden—and only deep inside
Can I scream, rage and hurt, in this confusion,
Humiliation and pain that's mine alone to bear.

Emotions so intertwined, enmeshed and twisted
Back upon each other—they spiral up and down
And around with—destroying, wreaking their
Havoc in my heart, mind, and soul—attacking sanity.

Those of us who live within this body—sharing it
And learning about one another—we try hard to
Withstand these assaults, as we keep traveling
This road from the past's hell to the present reality.

And as we try to heal the damage we endured at the
Hands of others, those who sought our mind and life—
We cling to two outside voices who listen, and care,
And cry with us, and bravely say, "I believe you!"

For they are our hope of finding our way back to
A life that we will one day want more than death.

Kathleen C. Rinker

The Day Each Of Our Children Came With Their Mate In Its Memory...

Though as your Mother I'm alone, Heaven's not far away,
And your precious Father joins with us today.

Heavenly father lets spirits to earth be sent,
When families are having a most grand event.

We can feel your dear Father's presence is here,
He has been gone so many a long, long year.

But today he joins us, we're so very glad,
He was such a kind, and loving, special Dad!

Though he worked hard, he'd still laugh, joke, and smile,
Filling our home with sunshine, and joy the while.

Neighbors, or strangers, needing help found him there,
His life was filled in easing another's care.

He's been doing great work in those realms above,
Comforting many through his kind, thoughtful love!

Today he's here with us, we give him our praise,
His life's a light, that's guided our earthly days.

Your Father, myself, and Mates of each Daughter, and Son,
Our family's together, it is true everyone!

I join with your Father, as these words we express,
This Day's brought the crowning of this Earth's Happiness!

Emma T W. S. Fuller

The Bag Lady's Cart

Hands push, possessing, moving the creaking, rusted wheels,
Grinding on their maples journey.
Revisited, unexplored, continuing under the will power of existence.
A shadow amongst shadows; bewildering gloom.

Burdened, necessary, the cart continues. Its movement steered by
grey eyes; ignored by every passing face; recognizing no one;
Only the right to salvage.

The right to someone's nothing that becomes her everything.
Smiling she bites a coin lost and pushes on.

Billy Bruns

Lost Love

Overcast skies and rain misty air
Bitter sweet memories of despair
Clothes in the closet she'll never wear
Fragrance of her perfume still hangs in the air
So many things he wanted to tell her and that he cared
Thought he had a lifetime to love and to share
Memories of precious moments in each others arms
Memories of her soft touch and her warm sweet smile
Now just painful memories of the love of his life
He still bring her flowers she used to like
Hoping she can still enjoy them from heaven above
The pain so great he feels like ending it all
But a tug on his coat brings him back to the present
The young boy never got to know the mother he lost
As they walk away the little boy waves goodbye
A ritual he's done so many times before
Not knowing the significance or the meaning of it all
Nor knowing why there is tears in dad's eyes
As the misty air leaves beads of water
On the flowers he brought to his wife that he lost
    John Hybridge

The Storm I Saw

I remember; I prefer to forget.
I was three months married.
I said to him, "God Speed."
I did not go; I wept.

He went - to Shield the Desert.
He went - to fight for oil.
He was young, happy, free.
He returned broken, turmoiled, tormented.

We struggled - we tried to understand.
We fought; his loss made him quiet, lost to himself.
We hurt, each in our own way, our own private loss.
We laughed - we cried.

I had to remove on.
I was never sent to the Storm.
I will never forget that look in his eyes.
I still see bone sticking out of shattered limb.

The loss of limb, of life
once a whole man, left broken and blighted.
So, I must ask, "What price, oil?"
You pay at the pump; He paid with his life.
    Geri Cribbs

A Memorable Sunset

I saw the sun take a handful of clouds
And scatter them over the deep blue of the skies.
Then its shot a myriad shafts of light,
And painted them all with rainbow dyes.

I stood in awe and watched the changing scene.
Where the clouds had crowded, no Light could be seen.
Huddled there together, holding each other close,
they refused the beauty of sunshine to penetrate their pause.

While those which floated aloft, in free graceful strokes,
Painted the skies with flames of crimsons, pinks and golds.
    M. Englestad

Immortal Rose

As pretty as her name
Ms. Maitland Rose
left kids only a photograph
hard knocks and blows

Simultaneously robbing
twins in belly life's wealth
togetherness with siblings
if purpose her death

Memories of them
surviving kids were denied
A void as well questions
forever truth with hide

Lacked in closure
In lieu of goodbyes
Just a red framed photograph
Why? Maitland Rose why?

Discovered among descendants
Stories, features, her ways
Also thru spirit and children
She lives! Infinite days
    Frances M. Carter

Earth

Earth is our mother
She feeds and gives us shelter
And we destroy her.

The Earth cries in pain
No one listens, it's in vain
Comes a hurricane.

The earth gives a shake
Nobody notice, seems to take
Comes a big earthquake.

Forests are cut down
Great storms begin to abound
Flooding all around.

Polluting the air
Each one contributes their share
Just ozone left there.

No one seems to care
When Earth is avid and bare
Who will be left there?
    Vincent P. Corr

An Electric Storm

Outside t'was wet with pouring rain.
  sky clearing its throat with thunder.
People scurrying down the lane,
  Trying to get to a shelter.
Lightning bolts cracked all around us.
  Burning through the sky, white and green.
Thunder rumbling continuously.
  T'was truly a sight to be seen.
The storm turned powerful and turbulent.
  Every one was consumed with fear.
Though we knew it was just nature's vehement.
  It felt like the end was soon near.
    Rose C. Devine

The Monarch

On velvet green, my life begins,
A royal bed secure;
As all around my kingdom spins,
My palace holds me sure.

Pink flowers grace the palace wall,
Their fragrance fills the air,
While fast sleep each night I fall
In a gown that's striped and fair.

A feast is e'er laid out for me
Whene'er I deign to dine;
To sup the magic milk I'll be
Invincibly divine.

Before the winter snows descend,
To my bower I'll repair,
And there in jade green splendor spend
A transforming time that's rare.

Then waking from my spell-like sleep
With a form that overwhelms,
On angel wings I'll travel deep
To lofty mountain realms.

Henry M. Ditman

Life's Mystery

In the dark of the night I awoke
With the sense that someone was near
The cats and I lived alone
Yet strangely I felt no fear.

In my mind I heard just one word
In Italian I speak but a few
It brought back a memory from childhood
And was sent by my Grandmother I knew.

She'd come back to bring me a message
For my life at the time was hell
And I still think often of her words
And I can hear her again so well.

You come into this world all alone
And alone all your life you live
For no one can walk in your footsteps
No matter how much love you give.

And when the time comes to go
And your soul once again is free
To pass through that shining gate
You'll understand at last life's mystery.

Barbara A. Dunn

Bonsai

Gnarled and withered,
Shaped by gardeners fantasies;
Branches bent as arms held akimbo,
Wired and formed,
Molded by dreamed design
And watered with idealistic desire.
And ancient appearance,
Authentic or counterfeit,
Show cased to the world.
Close your eyes and envision 'tree',
And before you it stands,
A miniature version of perfection.

Philip A. Eckerle

A Christmas Greeting

Since the Saviour was born in old Bethlehem,
The Story told over and over and over again
Is read every Christmas, and voices are heard
Retelling the wonder of God's Holy Word!
Nearly two thousands of years have passed
Since Wise Men arrived and urgently asked,
"O where is He, born King of the Jews?"
And they gladly received the Word of Good News!

The words we have written quite freely above
Just show how we dare share with those whom we love;
Not least we bespeak, and with emphases too,
Glad greetings of Christmas with love that is true!
We are bounden in faith as together we pray
That our Lord lead us always in His chosen Way!
God bless you and keep you in His gracious care
Each day of New Year: yes, this is our prayer!

Royal F. Peterson

To Joe Lawrence - Dear Night Sleeper

Dear night sleeper, who sleeps within the bed,
You made me "feel" again - my soul you fed.

As I lay upon your chest
 I think of the intellectual thoughts you speak.
So overwhelmed by your passion,
 A silent filled tear, rolled down my cheek.

My soul needed nourishment and from you that's what it got.
You made me smile in the morning, and that I appreciate a lot.

I was feeling very sad and getting too much rest.
I was dying inside - I was out right depressed.

I was feeling unwanted and a little bit rejected
Because of the love I thought I had,
 But that love got infested.

So I held you in my arms and that's all I needed
For someone to pay attention to me
And you Dear Night Sleeper succeeded.

So I'll remember this, Dear Night Sleeper
 For now and always
How you fed my soul
 Which got me out of my confused stage.

Angela Wolf

Love

Love is complete.
There is not a little love, nor a big love.
Love is, or is not.
With love, one is with God and God is a part of you.
Without love, one is nothing.
Love is meek and humble
Love can be battered and bruised.
Sneered at and reviled,
It cannot be injured
Love is an absolute.
Love is a rock
Love is indestructible and Everlasting
It is forever.
Love is . . .

Dorothy A. Newsom

The Cost Of War

Each soldier has a number upon his head.
Put there by politicians sleeping safely in their beds.

They stand making fancy speeches about keeping the peace.
While young boys called soldiers much with blisters on their feet.

They sit at big tables drinking wine and eating cheese.
While young boys in fox holes die and freeze.

They tell you about the great victories ahead.
Then go home and sleep in warm safe beds.

While out on the battlefields young men bleed and die.
While loved ones at home sit alone and cry.

They called it Korea, they called it Vietnam.
Politicians played with lives, they didn't give a damn.

As I pass these walls so shiny and black.
All these young boys won't be coming back.

Each one a hero in his own right.
They gave their greatest possession, they gave their life.
Daniel J. Gerkin

The Shore

I stroll with delight along the shore
The ocean stretches out seemingly for ever more,
Its vastness makes me seem so small
I wonder if I am noticed at all.

The millions of white grains and of sand
With multitude cover this space of and
And I'm just one, only me,
Strolling with admiration beside this enormous sea.

A sky of blue with fluffy clouds of white
Reaches heavenward, a magnificent sight,
With loving wonder, I hold out my hand
But I am so tiny in this expanse so grand.

All of these wonders are mine to treasure
The ocean, the shore and the sky without measure;
I am special and unique in God's plan
And I am grateful for His gifts to man.
Dolores M. Blessent

A Sonnet On A Spider's Web

Silently, without malevolence or desire,
The spider spun her web in evening's light,
As the August sun began to press its fire
Against the ruby lips of undraped night.
At dusk a small, uncertain suitor came.
Plucking gingerly a single, silken thread,
He sought to set her ancient needs aflame.
But she spurned him furiously and the suitor fled.
Then, when the air grew cool and wet,
She folded inward at the center of her world,
Sifting the sea of darkness with her net,
Harvesting a tremble of dewdrops as the dawn unfurled.
And the chasteness of her crystal web caught me, at least,
If not some hapless mate on which to feast.
Richard E. Cain

Heaven

There is a land far brighter
Than the one we trod today.
There is a hope far grander
Than this world could e'er display.
There is a love far more complete
Than relations here below;
For the God of Grace in Heaven
Provides mansions where blessings flow.

There is no need for sunshine.
Christ's glory will light our days.
No tears will dampen our eyelids;
On scenes of paradise we'll gaze.
Grand golden streets of glory
Lead to God's majestic throne.
Praise God for salvation that grants us
Rest in Heaven's eternal home.

So when dark days of earth are o'er
And we've seen the last setting sun,
Rejoice in the Lord of Heaven
As we meet face to face His Son!
Mary Wisham Fenstermacher

My Love

To my dream I see you
so clear, you are the holder and
provider of my love, you are the
sunshine that dries my tears, you are
my only. You're the reminder that
keeps me going; you hold my other brain.
We share the same dreams only to be
together forever; you protect me from
my fears, you are the rose that grows
by my window, the book that knows my
life, for you are my everything.
Mario E. Garcia

Final Journey

I've reached the sunset of my life
And I am standing by the shore,
Waiting for my final journey
On a ship called, "Nevermore".

I have had much joy and sorrow
On this journey we call life,
Sunny days and gray tomorrows,
Happiness and times of strife.

I would not change a single moment,
My children were my greatest joy.
Now they stand and watch me leave them
As I board the "Nevermore".

Trust my faith and trust my journey
As only heaven knows.
I can hear my children shouting,
"There she goes, there she goes".

On the distant shore my loved ones
Wait to welcome me once more.
Their smiles are like a million suns
When they shout, "Now here she comes!"
Margaret E. Kingsbury

Prayer For The Day

Heavenly Father full of grace
Bless my boyfriend's foxy face,
Bless his hair that always curls
But keep him safe from other girls,
Bless his little nose and toes.
And keep him safe wherever he goes,
Bless his hands so big and strong
But keep them Lord, where they belong,
Give him muscles, you know why.
I'll tell you now Lord, he's not shy,
Don't let him know how much I care
They call us Lord a perfect pair,
Bless the tears that I have shed
For his blessed little head,
He has faults, you know.
But bless him Lord because, he's
my Guy!
Dawnel Pettingill

La Petite Belle

The ladies floated around the room
in ball gowns of every hue.
Like flowers just burst into bloom,
on gusts of music they flew.

Roses and lilacs and daffodils,
green grass and a clear blue sky,
in a kaleidoscope of colors merged,
as the dancers waltzed gracefully by.

As I watched from my place of hiding,
a rainbow spread across the room,
And fixed in my childhood memory
was the fragrance of the dancers perfume.

Soon I too, shall come of age
and on that magical day,
I shall become one of the dancers
and take up my part in the play.

Magnolias and moonlight set the scene.
The music plays sweet and low.
All will be perfection
in the arms of my very first beau.
Linda S. Pittman

Flower

Brilliant red like the
crimson rays of the setting sun,
the flower regally sits alone
protected by its thorny guards.

It closes velvet arms
and quietly slumbers
in the silvery light
of the glowing moon.

Gently the zephyrs of the night
sing out their soothing lullabies.
As the royal flower dreams
of the coming day.

It is a special flower
that adds beauty to the world
A world that now belongs to man.
A world of concrete coldness.
Sheila B. Roark

How Lovely Life Is

How lovely life is, and the beauty that lives
From a small child's smile, what happiness it gives
From the flowers that bloom, and all things that grow
How lovely life is, in our hearts it will show
From dreams that we have, and hopes that can be
From understanding its ways, for the wonders we see
From the mountains so high, to the depths of the earth
How lovely life is, to know its full worth
From the miracles that happen, and the prayers that may
From the knowledge and wisdom, that we hear it say
From all of the wishes, it helps to come true
How lovely life is, a gift just meant for you
So treasure it always, and may you come to know
The pleasures around us, that makes our hearts glow
For the paths it has given, to show us the way
How lovely life is, so lets live it each day.
Vincent Cea

Lamp Glow

In bleak dolor and agonized tears,
Saffron lamp had dimmed.
Where raven's leer smouldered...lament.
In flight, indigo stars wept no flare.

How then the haunted specter had fled?
Dreamy dawn's flamingo eyes smiled...
Shimmered in carousel of gilded amber field, azure lake.
Tantalized satin ripples, dazzled emerald dew.
Spangled rainbow crocus medallions. Sunlit beach marsh
To caress the mallard's nestled brood.

Where willow leaf lilted, in lilac languor,
Chalices of oro buttercups chimed.
There...the preening sunburst wax wing.
There...in lantern flame: Rapture of wren song.
There...iridescent ballet... The fluttering turquoise butterfly.

How then the shrouded cape had flung its
Tattered wings to land of nevermore?
Star galaxies scintillated where
Lamp glowed in riant charisma of spun gold.
Jo Santoro Cialkowski

Goodnight Love

Lover's sweet secrets,
Blow sweetly through breezes,

Crystalline kisses sprinkle blessings,
From mutual thank you and please,

Fragrance of lover's consumed by love's calling,
Floating through treetops splendid and green,

Splashes of wine never sipped,
Dries on sleepy parched lips,

Arms entwined forever,
from ecstasies fully lived,

Diamond reflections from lovers moist skin,
Superb orgasmic memories circle within,

Velveteen pillows and blanket pulled taunt,
Holding the taste, touch and smell,
Of lover's thirst quenching drink from life's well.
Leslie Maxwell Cook

Freedom, Oh, Freedom

Freedom, oh, freedom, your price is so high;
You sons and daughters keep you in their eye;

To fight and to die for this hard won gift;
To pray and to dream gives your heart its' lift;

The Civil War and World Wars One and Two;
Korea, Vietnam, and the Persian Gulf too;

For all the bullets, bombs, and strife;
This is the cost of our land and life;

The flag that we love, may it ever hand high;
For its honor and glory, we may have to die;

The peace that we love is ever so dear;
The threat of its loss is always so near;

For, as long as men live, the freedom they love;
Is fought for and died for below and above;

But, if men are to live in peace evermore;
They must search their souls as never before;

Give up the vanity of one o'er the other;
Just learn to understand and love your brother;

Please see into his soul without looking at color;
The Glory of God outshines any other;

Judith L. Cox

Sting

I don't want to move I want to stay
quiet let it stick to me like filthy
fly paper this film is not for everyone it is dark tough
important for if you are

A recovering alcoholic it will slam
you against the wall shatter
your eyes break your bones spit on your soul butcher
your heart into bloody chunks turn you upside
down and inside out you taste
the agony smell the loss of self after awhile

You thank God you're alive and for allowing
your on-going recovery from
this dreadfully misunderstood disease

Now my Highs as the opera Sinatra a ballet most
of all the look in my grandchildren's eyes
my Kicks are a three-spooned sundae with my two
girls for I'm not "Leaving Las Vegas"

I'm sitting in Friendly's with an angel on my shoulder

Mimi Eagan

The Family

The Family is just like a tree, and its roots are
made up of you and me.
The Family is full of togetherness and strength,
and it should always stay together the way it was meant.
Let our Family grow strong and tall, and let us
follow God's lead or we shall fall.
Help us Father to be one with Thee, and to be
one with our Family, the way it's suppose to be.

Gregory Kelly

Mr. De-Cupboard
Pudderaminsky Boxnapper

Be quiet and listen
There is a Puddering
behind De-Cupboard door
Be quiet and listen
There is a Purring
in the Box on the floor
Be quiet and listen
Who was in De-Cupboard
rapping cans against the door
Be quiet and listen
Where is the puddering
The puddering is no more
Be quiet and listen
Where is the Boxnapper
who purred the purfect score
Be quiet and listen
Why he is over there
Tapping on your door
Be quiet and listen
For the cat who doesn't roar

Martha M. Rockwood

On The Nature Of Things

Virgil somewhere said, I think,
that the herd without a blow
will not to pasture go.

But then, I could be wrong
and the blame lie with a Greek.

Though most would then deny
it matters to the fact:
who claims responsibility
for what all can see
is of no consequence
for the sense to be.

And righter too are they who say
of every living thing that rushes
to the flame to be consumed:
For all love is the same.

And need, father to the dream.

Gary F. Seifert

My Little Ones

My little ones, with open minds,
look within and you will find,
all the things you want to know
are pure and gentle as the snow.

Within your smile, behind your tears,
I marvel with you and know your fears.
Forever kept within my heart,
my little ones - we'll never part.

Remind me when I start to fall,
or raise my voice above it all.
My little ones we'll never part,
forever kept - within my heart.

Donna Wood Smedley

Let Us Celebrate

Let us celebrate,
His birth.
As the kings did.
With gifts.

Let us celebrate,
His birth,
As the angels did.
With song.

Let us celebrate.
His birth
As the drummer hay did,
with music.

Let us celebrate
His birth,
As the animals did,
With sharing.

Let us celebrate
His birth,
As this father did,
with love for all.

Mattie M. Stewart

Faith Leads Its Chariot

Sweet face of Jesus, Savior of this world
Father of wonder, woe and will
The heart is fresh, though impurity deceives
in all that we wish to feel
existing simply by itself, for itself
is not our property

You are sincere, Jesus
You live and die in love

They will try to make it right
on your day, every day
they will do the best they can
the children from the many Netherlands
of darkness all are familiar
in your light, they will delight

You have lifted them out
onto a silent cloud
where hope rides harmless
and where faith leads its chariot
to your December morning

Michelle Suzette Patente

Dare

Dare to challenge the world
Dare to be different
Dare to show off your beauty
and walk the earth indefinitely
Dare to conquer your goal
Dare to make your display public
Dare to have property without harm
Dare to think you can change the world
Dare to never cross the law of any crime

Leon Hodge

A Wife's Prayer

Please help me to trust, honor and think of him first.
I wouldn't want our love ever to disperse.
Help me to remember my feelings
when we were first together,
To picture us as Grandparents,
our lives even better.
That he needs me is the most profound sensation.
He could not be the man he is,
without my support, laughter, and admiration.
Let me always remember, he is my very own.
The dearest friend and companion
that I have ever known.
Thank you for my husband
and keep us strong within our love.
Please continue to bless our union
and guide us from above.
Amen

Sharon Flath

A Date

I cleaned my teeth, washed my hair and took a shower
Hoping I looked and smelled like a fresh picked flower
Then I sprinkled on a little of this and that
And poised myself gingerly in the chair I sat
Carefully not to wrinkle the clothes I chose to wear
You had called findings sometime we could share
The lighting, the music, everything had to be just right
I had prayed and dreamed a long time for this night
The hands on the clock were moving very slow
The room is filling with smoke from the rings I blow
Nat King Cole is singing "if I give my heart to you"
It's getting later and later, I don't know what to do
My heart is beating faster each minute with fear
My mind keeps repeating the words; soon he'll be here
My hair is starting to droop; now my shoed and dress are off
You are not going to show; that realized is rough
Only a inch left on the candles, they've lost their smell
I drag off to bed, all signs gone of the romantic spell
Glad you hadn't seen how foolish I had been
Finally sleep comes, I vow, no one will hurt me again

Lucille Fritts

A Special Person

Every time I see you,
    it is a ray of sunshine at the end of a hard day.
I enjoy the unique style
    you have in getting you own way.
Although you tease a lot—your heart
    is truly genuine.
It warms my heart each time you call me angel.
When you're in pain—
    you note the good things that come from it.
You deeply touch
    each and every person you meet.
Knowing you, is to never forget Mother Teresa.
You live today-today, and look forward to tomorrow
    with an open heart and a smile.
I feel truly blessed to know you.
You can find the positive in the most insincere people.
Now everyone knows the name of the
    Special Person I call my friend!!

Brenda L. Hendricks

Adolescence

Adolescence a time when youth is
sequestered in bodies that deceive thinking.
Locked in limbo, awaiting metamorphosis
the young explore, question, experiment.
Confused, disillusioned, searching.
Adolescence, a time when youth experience
moods that swing like pendulums, bewildering adults.
High, low, blissful, alone.
Donning masks to conceal awkward,
uncertain feelings, adolescents often fool their contemporaries.
Insecure, alone, displaced.
Adolescence, a time when the young
are looking for direction, but failing to use maps,
Sincere, intense, idealistic.
Desiring affection and affirmation
adolescents often risk safety for momentary acceptance.
Daring, yearning, impulsive.
Adolescence, a time to take our young seriously.
A time for adults to be generous with their time.
A time for adults to become Heroes and Mentors.

Kathleen Kolar

Mr. Moon

Mr. Moon all shiny and bright,
you glow all through the darkest of night.
You make things look so sharp and clear,
you're far away but seem so near.

You look down at us,
when all the world is in a hush.
You're perfect white with some dark spots,
you have different faces which are a lot.

Sometimes you are orange, whether full or half,
when you are just a sliver looks like a smiling laugh.
Sometimes the clouds they cover you,
but you are always there everlasting and true.

Mr. Moon you're a comfort to me,
to watch your beauty and it's actually free.
I enjoy all the different ways that you look,
I watch you for hours from my little nook.

You are my beacon Mr. Moon,
maybe I'll visit you someday soon.
I can't visit in a rocket but who cares,
I will just use the stars for stairs.

Mary Paver

Tribute To My Parents

Be kind to thy Father,
for when thou were young,
Who loved thee so fondly as he?
He taught and caught the first accents
that feel from thy tongue,
And joined in thy innocent glee.
Be kind to thy Mother, for lo!
On her brow many traces of sorrow be seen,
Owell Maipt just thou cherish and comfort her now,
For in loving and being kind to her
now is just small gesture
in return for all she hath been to thee.
Lest God won't let you live long.

Mary V. Prisock

The Poet's Prayer

When my silent pen
Begins to speak,
I thank God
For the patience
Of my waiting times
Without words or rhymes
And the conviction,
Beyond my ken,
That in the stillness
of my heart
There is a song
Waiting to be sung.

Jane Huelster Hanson

How To Enjoy A Fuzzy Navel

We've saved a lot of lint
Rolled into a ball.
Found a bottle of Peach Schnapps
And that's not all.

We've purchased some steaks
To put on the grill,
And they y'all over
To meet old chef, Bill.

He's learned to grill steaks
From a girl of the South,
Who guarantees these steaks
Will melt in your mouth.

Old Chefs like Bill
Are real hard to find.
He'll tell you so, himself.
He's one of a kind.

William V. Rush

Fire

"Fire" - you keep burning low
You stay around and hate to go
You always leave your sparks behind
To touch my heart and hurt my mind

I thought that you were on your way
But I see you came to stay
Your flame grew dim
And won't go out
I wonder what it's all about

Don't hang around cause I won't stay
We'll be good friends one day
The passion and the flame has died
And somehow I am satisfied

"Fire" take your spark and leave
I'll never, never, have to grieve
Because of love I gave to you
The books are closed
I thought you knew

Evelyn Hayden Carter

San Diego Christmas

There is no snow on the palm trees
   nor ice on the swimming pools
One might think Mother Nature
   is playing - a Christmas April Fool.

Of course, the homes are all decorated
   twinkling Christmas lights seen everywhere
Styrofoam snowmen sitting on lawns
   in the sunshine - smiling without a care.

Bikinis are seen on our sunny beaches
   bathing beauties gracing white sand
It is no wonder the Chamber of Commerce
   calls San Diego the Promised Land.

Majestic sailboats are on our lakes
   joggers and bikers keep passing by
Picnics and soft ball games at the parks
   barbecues under the balmy sky.

'Tis hard to believe it's the yuletide
   without snow on our manicured grass
So eat your hearts out weary snow shovelers
   or join us - for a San Diego Christmas.

William Henry Jones

We Cry

You cane to me in my deepest pain
When I was needlessly insane
Twice to my rescue
When I needed you

Although we never formerly met
It hadn't been a fair bet
And you better not be dead
Or a cow, someone told me somehow

You came to me on that September day
and my mind was beck to stay
Although I never learned to pray
I'm still the prey

If one day we were to meet
My heart would surely beat
Although we don't know why
Right now we cry.
Bettey and I

Andrew M. Hunsberger

My Anchor

To you my friends
I do bid thanks,
For being the anchor
That has kept me from
Drifting into the places
Where treacherous waters
Would have ripped apart
The very seams and timbers
Which bind me together.
Yes, thanks to you,
For holding me steady
In the swirling current
Of the main stream
Where life flows so fast.

George William Ray Jr.

Memories Are Treasures

My mother, Mary Jane Lucas and father, Robert Austin Lucas
Adorn the beautiful City of Heaven.
This is comforting to me . . . and I pray that many more
Will see the wisdom and comfort I feel today.
If so, they will be able to see far away
And reap the rewards that brighten my life each day!

Each state, city, and country will realize the miracles
Bestowed upon the publisher and me!
We will all feel more serene and relaxed.
Thank you, Lord, for my two lovely children:
David — The Preacher
Lynn — The Teacher.

If and when the poem is published
   The key to opening doors of cities, states and countries . . .
Will realize "The miracles bestowed upon
   The publisher and me."

Mildred Lucas Reddoch

This Is My Prayer . . . Please

A love who will share all the work to be done,
who'll discover with me new things under the sun.
One who'll divide this attention and time.
One who'll be merciful, gracious and kind.
One who will guide me along your pure path,
Who'll make my heart sing, cause my whole soul to laugh.
One who build up a soul in despair
One who has love, warmth, a fine life to share.
One who is faithful in all of his way
To bring divine favor on us—always
A love whose been tested and approved by you,
One whose heart is faithful and true.
Could these be father one such as this
Who'll soon join my soul in a spiritual kiss?
Who can be all these things that I need so
Jehovah, Jehovah, oh please let me know!
My thoughts are always in your promised new land
To preach to the dead ones—alive through your hand.
To bring joy to you job by living your ways
To bring love to a family all our days
For the one who will finally answer this prayer
He'll be my miracle—my miracle so rare.

Elizabeth A. Rickert

Take Me Away

Take me away
   I want to go to paradise land
To a place where I can stay
   Where all my dreams and hopes are fulfilled
Just want to climb up that
   hill
Take me away
   Let me fantasize just for today
And don't let my cares and troubles get in
   the way
Because in the land of hope and happiness
   Life has new meaning
So dream when you rest
   Take me away
   To a beautiful meadow, down by the golden pond
Where robins come to sing their song
   I think I'll stay another day—so take me away

Mary Foucoult

The Voice

The voice that comes from deep inside of you,
Is the voice you should always listen to,
The voice you hear comes from deep within your soul,
It's the voice, if heard, can make you whole,
If you have deaf ears and refuse to hear the words,
Then your soul will be forever tormented and cursed,
The man who says he doesn't have an inner voice,
Is putting a severe limit on his freedom of choice,
A man who goes through life with a deaf ear,
Is a man who will live without his reliable friend near,
He will not hear the voice of knowledge of God's plans,
He will travel through life with tied hands,
Without that knowledge he will be slamming shut God's door,
And he will not find the peace and serenity he longs for,
But if you hear the voice and listen to the knowledge foretold,
You will find God's beautiful rainbow and his pot of gold,
God's pot of gold, holds many treasures just for you,
Peace, serenity, love, faith, happiness, and forgiveness too,
So listen to the voices that comes from deep within,
For it's the voice of God telling you, on him you can depend.

Marilyn Sisson

Dust From The Stars Glow Off The Moon

"Dust" from the Stars, plus "Glow" off the Moon
Shadows dance, when they cross the Lagoon

The rippling effect, sets my mind to drift
As I gaze the heavens, and forget the rift

Contentment attained, when laughter abounds
Along with the haunting, wail of the Hounds

Watching the flight, of the peaceful Dove
Now is the time, to give thanks up above

Accompanied when, the wind strokes the trees
Are some Crickets, as they cross their knees

Sounds that reveal, everything mystical
Big bugs chasing small bugs, so very typical

Clouds sail by, catching dust of the stars
Perhaps some fell, from the Planet Mars

The glow off the Moon, masked by vapors
Causing rain sounds, like rustling papers

Precipitation increases, to a "full-blown" storm
I think of dry clothes, back at the Dorm

To stop this storm, I need a trick up my sleeve
"Forget!" The tricks, it's time to pick-up and leave

Clyde Wilson

Sexual Discovery

The eternity in a minute of an epitome of silence,
The departure of confusion and chaos.
The intrusion of understanding once needed but now
Too wicked, too sinful.
A perpetual emptiness.
A silent awakening.
An innocence lost forever.
A virtue never to be regained.
This is the time of life
This is the time of death.

Angel Grooms

37

Much there is in life to do
Of which not all be true
Watch much thou should thy path
On which thou mayst find wrath
Built from thy errs done
So blindly under God's sun
For be then mindful in thy walk
And avoid such uncomely talk
As would drag the good man down
In black waters where he would drown
Note also thy business done
For greed will keep not your son
Well and live in his soul
Which that green may make cold
Want not much for our need be small
And wanting much brings soon our fall
In life may be done sure
So that the blackened soul be cured
Quite short yea it truly be
So don't waste it selfishly.

Douglas R. Brown

Baby

When you hear me say
that I love you
your whole body goes numbs
then you yell, get mad
and sometimes call me dumb.
Why can't you just say you
love me too.
Why won't you believe
my feelings are true.
When you talk to me you're mad
but if you talk to your ex you're sad.
You never seem happy
whenever I'm around
your smile is always turned
upside down.
Why don't you say you love me
Why don't you say you care
because I know the feeling are there.
Listen to what I have to say, and I'll
stay beside you each and every day!

Tandi Kilgore

Poet's Dilemma

And so... now I know
these are things of my world...
  Accept this madness -
  Accept being forever misunderstood-

Where does it ever go
when I begin to explain?
Nowhere but reeling back into insanity.
There, a hidden specter demands
that I swim against the current...
Sip nectar from her fountain...

  Accept these passions -
  Accept these raging fires -
Maybe they can burn the demon.

Roxanne C. Cunningham

The Eagle Knows

Oh God, thy forests of wild profusion.
   Now, perhaps forever lost.
To mans haste and confusion!
   The eagle flies on, strong of wing.
Nowhere seeing the sights.
   that once made his heart sing!
Ah! To fly on wings so high.
   To see and ponder from lofty sky.
The plight of mankind is revealed!
   The greatest thinker to roam the earth!
Has his fate been sealed?
   His greatest single fault!
He cared so much for power and wealth!
   he stored his common sense.
On some long forgotten shelf.
   So many animals stood on the brink.
Mankind worried about the creatures.
   But it was not they who became extinct!
His was the great intellect.
   But it was used without respect.

Ron Bunce

Reflections

As you think you travel;
As you love you attract;
You are today and will be tomorrow
Wherever those thoughts lead

As you think you gravitate
Towards what you secretly love;
You will "fall" "remain" or rise
With those thoughts
Whenever you choose to

As you think you grow
Vision, ideals and desires
become as small as the
controlling need to achieve
or as great as your dominant aspiration.

Elizabeth Sharp

To Gary Our Love Story

I want for your presence,
Thinking deeply about you,
How I love you,
More than a million times,
   Thinking of our year that we
Have been together,
So far and more years to come,
All the hardships and happiness
That we have gone through together,
Feeling all the love you have put
Inside my heart,
As you feel all the love I've put,
Inside yours.
   Thinking on to the future,
Of more happiness and hardships to come,
Of more love to share together,
Here after, forever, and always!

Jaime L. Boswell

Prelude To Love

We lie in open nakedness together
Exploring with our tongues and fingertips
Succumbing to a world of endless pleasures
And pressing close, our bodies and our lips...

There is no shame, no barriers between us
No secrets to the hunger felt inside
Our fantasies are lived, not just imagined
And nothing in our hearts is left denied...

In exactly, we cling to one another
And melt into the arms of loves' caress
We whisper words that brush against the kisses
That linger in a realm of happiness....

With every touch, emotions are awakened
With every look, comes this reality
We're everything in body, mind and spirit
That heaven's sleeping angels dream to be...
We close our eyes and smooth the sheet of blackness
While fire penetrates our every pore
Tonight is but a prelude to the moments
That lie in wait behind tomorrows door...

Helen Dodge

Dum, Taget, Clamat

From a sacred scene of lasting rest,
came again, an echo, of an order great,
of that woodsy, order, a honorable gilded crest,
whose proud members, embrace fate!
Their brotherly intent, purpose good,
once an honored great numbered lodge,
now much like a remote lonely wood;
duty honor, service, they would not dodge!
They as the ancient odd fellows old, proud,
had once, a many, many membered, tribe,
Now there's no longer, that zealous crowd;
honor proud, tradition, not drawn by Bimbe!
So I proclaim, Dum Taget Clamat,
to you whose last greetings are sent,
let your reward, good ever be that;
may the spirit, of your ways, not be spent!

Raymond Bradburn

Vanilla Pudding Days

When days are neither filled
   with sunshine or rain...
When days are seemingly ordinary
   and vanilla pudding plain...
Nothing new or exciting
   no big adventure that's inviting...
The same years old, waiting to be done again,
   chores and housework to do...
Once in a while they mutely creep in
   or softly cascade down around you.
Dry spells? Maybe it's quite simply a resting,
   preparing you for one of God's choice blessings.
Life is really a day by day adventure...
   with no perfect rehearsal to smooth the way.
But there is a Helper walking beside us each day
   One who goes with us through life's maze.
Dry spells, plain pudding days, we all have those,
   and like the pleasing, sweet dessert...
Those days can be a comfort...so I often wonder
   what God has waiting for me to discover, to know.

Sharon K. Blaker

Love? ... Yes, ... Love

Where could you be now? Is it possible to see or hear you?
Why can't I feel you when before, even in your absence,
you could touch me? Life was one long journey with you,
without you forever; but life teaches lessons whether or
not we care to learn, and understand.

Where was love? Where is love? Did it hold the promise
that it would be patient and kind? Did it re-assure that it
would not be arrogant or rude? Was it earthly love?
Was it witchcraft?

Did love bring the promise of verdant forests that were
contained in mahogany seedlings in Sitio Calinawan, and
did it dominate the serenity of Yagumgum Lake waters?

If love professed to be as constant as the cloud that
descended and settle on Mt. Talinis, and allowed itself
to be painted and photographed before drifting away,
then love was pro tempore.

But there's a painting; and there's a photograph.
For where love has been, love left marks of beauty,
  for the soul to cherish
    and for the heart to forever hold.
   Elma Diel Photikarmbumrung

Solemn Angel

An angel stands silent and still
Never a prayer shall she fulfill
Never a song shall she sing
A tiny replica, a decorative thing...

This solemn angel who stands alone
A beautiful image of marble and stone
A symbol of hope, of faith borne anew
No words for your ears, their eyes do not see you...

The forgotten angel with wings at her side
Never to unfold, never to fey
The harp you hold, you will never play
Always silent, on the shelf you stay...

Blessed angel, with kindness so rare,
Have mercy on those who forgot to care...
Send love to those who will need you when
They fall to their knees in prayer and then
They humbly acknowledge they haven't been true,
And never again will they forget about you...

Blessed angel, with your harps of golden strings...
Then what beautiful songs we'll hear you sing!
   Cathy E. Hugill

My Star

I was walking through the cold dark night alone,
I didn't know where I was going or where I'd call home.
A single star lit my way with it's clear light,
I followed the star for it was the only thing in sight.
I was scared and shivering from the black cold,
It was so lonely that I feared for my very soul.
When finally I was below that star I started to warm,
And I felt no more fear of any harm.
You stood in the star's bright glare,
And I knew I found my peace in your loving care.
  You are my star and I love you.
   Debra Billen

Music Of The Heart

Music breathes into the soul
A spirit which will rise
And bring us closer to our God
To see thru our own eyes

The glory that beholds life when
We put our faith in Him,
For God puts music in each soul
To cleanse from all earth's sin.

Music breathes within the soul
'Tis sunshine for each day,
A light to guide and guard us ... and
To brighten all life's way!

The sound of music lifts our hearts
Above earth's daily drone
And finally as we depart
Music will take us home!
   Billie F. Netterwald

Cold And Tired

Cold and tired
scroungin' the alley
a tramp
  give half of his hamburger
to the pigeons
   Charles B. Rodning

Rhythms

My aspiration to create an indelible
Rhythm challenges unproductive moods
With spontaneous attempts at original
Verse.
Engaged thoughts respond to negativism
With positive inclinations, while
Smooth desire weds idealism and the
Bounty of imagination therein.
My success of failure rests with a
Rhapsody of mind in beat with or against
The flow of selective words. Fruitful
Sensations become my key to sound
Expressions, lest depression gnaw like
A rat at the core of my sanity's
Domain.
Ah! But no course, other than the minds
Blend of realism, in entertained...no
Dreams of oblivion deter my quest...no
Stale moods drain my enthusiasm when
Delightful rhythms are the goal!
   Van Garner

The Fate Of Venus

She's
outside and
scraping the windshield

Of
her green
station wagon with

Crayons
and coloring
books in the back
   Michael Freemer

Once Upon A Shimmering

Once upon a shimmering star
Earth's castaways so many
Expendables from earth's glory.

Who feeds the sheep
Serves me.

In the oaken stable dark and lonely,
Suddenly God came to dwell.

Frankincense and myrrh
Perfumed the lonely stall.

Glorious light bathed meadowed shepherds,
Come let us see for ourselves
This love of God.

Be comforted,
To Bethlehem's stable
The journey is not far,
Only the Heart's golden store.

Hear the music
See the star!
Embrace thy brother, our Emmanuel.

Augusta Nelson

My Reasoning As To Why You're Always Happy

My reasons that you're
   always happy
Are that you're afraid to
   reveal the path that
Leads to your heart.
You don't want to show
   how depressed,
Vulnerable, angry, and lonely
   you really are inside.
You're always going to question
   yourself as well as your sanity.
The constant turmoil
   with your emotions and
Reality are slowly
   tearing you apart.
Or am I just now realizing
   a part of myself
That I didn't want
   to deal with?

Jennifer Groszewski

Darkness

The sun has set beneath the tree,
And darkness creeps along the sky.
The calm still wind becomes a breeze,
The trees begin to sigh.

The glow of a dying day is gone,
The twinkling stars catch the eye.
The legions of darkness are marching on,
Covering all that stands nearby.

The moon has risen in the east,
And lovers give a grateful sigh.
But now a cloud has passed between,
And darkness reigns supreme.

Sidney Braverman

Time, An Uncomprehensible Thing!

Time, to me is almost like the Mississippi just rolling along.
The days are coming and going and they all belong
to Father - Time, like the river He must know something.
Slowly time gives up the secrets of anything!
From the past, geographically or historically.
How earth, itself was made for fantastically!
How diamonds, rubies or sapphires were made and found!
Or how unbelievable myths were proven all around,
from under the sea-surface or the shifting dunes;
huge building-blocks, old fortresses or very old prunes!
All are proof of what had happened in a very long time!
Long long ago, never seen before, but when a silvery dime
shimmered through a rock or loose sand,
or maybe a weathered bone with a golden band,
Mummies buried in centuries old graves,
from Kings, soldiers or so called worthless slaves!
Or when scientists found dinosaurs bones or a tid-bit,
here in the America's or in faraway Mongolia or Tibet!
It is time, infinite time, running into centuries,
that molds this world and our extreme curiosities!

Johanna A. Garretson

First Love

   The first kiss
Two hearts that beat
   One out of cold-the other with heat
The first love-I do dearly miss.

   A darkened place
So quaint and secret to meet
   A passion/the lust that comes from lips so sweet
The first love-so truly a tempting treat.

   The light/a fire within your eyes
Your touch/the desire one cannot deny
   Its power to hold one so close as it may
The first love-your magnetic bond which is your way.

   If ever our paths are to drift far apart
And long is the time when we shall meet again
   I shall never forget your life force which flows within
The first love-within me and ever so dear to my heart.

Teresa Guinn-Garcia

Twinkle, Twinkle In The Sky

Twinkle, twinkle in the sky,
Was that a UFO passing by?
I've always been on my guard
Hoping one would and in my back yard.

Why do I have this terrible yearning?
About other galaxies to be learning.
I long to know what goes on afar
What happens in a sky lab on a distant star.

Are there black holes, novas, suns and moons?
In what rhythm do they sing romantic tunes?
Does gravity hold them to the planet until they die
Or can they wander in an airship in the sky?

Oh, twinkle, twinkle in the sky.
When oh when are you coming by?
To take me along into distant space
Though I want to retain earth as my home base.

June Serviss

Twister

In the middle of a twister, I stand all alone
She open's up her mouth and destroys our happy home
Her wind speeds up and entraps my very soul
Funnel arms grab on and won't let me go
The vicious attack comes when I'm unaware
There is no other Twister that could ever compare
This Twister has a tongue that's twisted to destroy
The lovely wife of her dear son, her one and only boy
The attack takes less that a minute to impart
Complete destruction upon my very heart
When the Twister is finished and the damage lies before
The on called Son, sees his wife dying on the floor
The Twister smiles and refuses yet to see
The truth of what she did and what she chose to be
The twister's son is blinded and denies her very might
He stand beside this twister as she passes through this flight
There one the floor still lies his dying Dawna
The Twister says: "Son, watch out for her! Be careful of her personal!"

Aurore Black

My 25th Birthday Today—May 13, 1997

Milestone, Mountain
  Youthful, Yearning

    25 and still alive
      trick-or-treating, turmoil
        humor, heartbreak

          Bountiful, broke
            Industrial, indigent
              Relatives, reclusive
                Trees, tears
                  Happy, haunted
                    Daydreams, depressed
                  Avenues, alley ways
                  Youngstown, Yankee

                    Today, tomorrow
                      Ohio, original
                        Days, decades
                          Altogether, alone
                            Young, yippee

Stephanie Sue Maruschak

The Sink

The small drop of water falls into the sink
Steadily plopping on the cold bottom leading to nowhere
The never-ending nuisance, continuous pace
Where does this water come from?
Where is the flow that sustains it?
It falls in pieces, spreading into a thin layer on the bottom
Until wasting away into the darkness
Sliding through tunnels without rest
Then this one little drop gradually mingles with its kind
Into a pool of pain
Each piece joining the mass
Growing more horrible with every plop
Stretching thinner and weaker on its way to the tunnel's end
Finally diminishing into nothing
The knob is turned, cutting off the flow

Angela Brunson

Night's Beauty

When I was young
I saw at night
The moon and stars above.

The moon was bright
At full moon time
It turned one's thoughts to love.

The stars which shone
Seemed oh, so near
I'd like to reach and touch.

The fresh night air
Was good to breathe
At day's end it meant much.

Now that I'm old
I still enjoy
Nights beauty in the sky.

And when I'm gone
Those heavenly lights
Will still shine from on high.

Margaret Good

Untitled

Swirling, flashing, colored lights
Confusion rules my thoughts.
Reaching towards my face I feel
My aching, swollen lips.
Blood dripping slowly down my chin
My soul no longer mine.
He slowly moves away from me
Sliding it back on his hand.
He turns to me, a whisper on his breathe,
A look in his eyes that says to me
My soul is no longer mine.

Pamela A. Dunbar

Love's Waiting

Golden moments, golden hours
Here and there touched with silver lining.
Sixty seconds, time is fleeting,
Hours come and go repeating.
Golden moments of expectations
Silvery hours, memories keeping,
Tinged with golden edges meeting,
Am I only dreaming?
Early morn 'till later on
Pleasing, gently teasing.
O' love why are you retreating?
Golden moments stolen from time,
What will it take to make you mine?
Silvery hours with golden moments
Is it worth my heart's beating?
Dreaming wishing, wishing dreaming.
Moments of gold, tinged with silver
Love is worth the waiting
If only a beginning with no ending.

DeMarias W. Brown

Guilt

Hearts pound faster and faster.
As sweat falls from his brow.
She thought they'd spend forever together.
But it all seems to be ending now.
Guilt wraps around their souls.
They can't even look in each other's eyes.
One more adds to all the holes.
As she breaks down and cries.
They swear they won't breath a word.
Of all they share together,
Yet all is heard,
And there's a stormy change of weather.
Voices like thunder roaring,
Charge across the sky.
Tears like rain come pouring,
As they scream their final good-bye.
   Valerie Cress

Showers

It drops from the heavens
Through the sky
It crashes and pounds
On the shingles of my roof

You may not be directly bombarded
But its effects are felt
The clouds combine to shut out the sun
A dreary fog lurks along the ground

But there is another
Side to the rains
It brings forth
The flowers, bees, the crows
Birds, the worms
And all the other creatures expose themselves
To gather the food

Soon the summer sun shall rise
Showing all the splendor that will be
Because of the rain
That fell from the sky.
   Steven J. Zegarelli

Soon My Love, Soon

Oh how I miss you my love
   Was I gone so long you had to
go away?
   The days were long but busy
too busy to let you know how I ached
   for the sound of your voice
that familiar laughter, the reflection
   of love in your eyes.

Was I gone too long
   were you worried and had to leave town
to hide the pain of loneliness
   from all the others?

Do your arms ache to hold me close
or do you laugh off the pain of loneliness
   and go about your comings and goings
thinking only of tomorrow?
   M. Jan Cunningham

A Message To Black America

Black America
Realize that within you lies
The power to exceed limits and
Cross boundaries no other has crossed.
It is You that will rise to succeed.
It is You that will conquer and not be conquered.
It is You that will come together as a whole, United
And let no others hold you back or bring you down.
This is not the year of oppression, but the year of Victory.
Take heed of my words, Black America, go forth and fight!
   Maisha K. Perkins

Ritual

Once our house, now mine alone,
for you lie buried cold as tone.
I sleep alone in our old double bed,
and you sleep underground with the rest of the dead.
Pieces of you lie everywhere.
They cut up my heart beyond human repair.
Fragments of memory split me apart.
Shards of hires past lacerate my heart.
Sliced into pieces, torn up deep inside;
Reduced to nothing since the moment you died.
Picking the scabs till I'm scarred deep within.
Now stitch up the wound to be opened again.
Shred up my mind, scratch away at my soul,
Till nothing is left but a big, bleeding hole.
Smash me to pieces till nothing remains.
Leave nothing intact, put an end to these pains.
   Peter Baugh

Anxiety

I hear it in the drone of the high speed engine...
Yet, it's also in the dancing echo of this passenger
   train in passing.
Now, as we approach the next station,
It's coming from the train wheels slowing on the
   iron track...
They all create those same haunting tones:
"De-onne, De-onne, De-onne, De-onne, De-onne, De-onne"
...gradually the train comes to a full stop...
The conductor calls my exit...
Then silence, except for the eerie distant murmur of
   the engine idle...
The outside terminal lights faintly filter through the
   fog in this most early morning...
As I rise from my seat and head for the exit, I think
   of all that has happened between us
The passenger doors begin to open...
Will she be here? Is De Onne here for me?
Or,....am I alone?
   James Edward Wilson III

Flight Of Fantasy

I often wish that I could fly, as Eagles soaring in the sky
their view of things is open, wide and free
unlike the ground view given me
perhaps in dreams my soul may hope to try
to join these Heavenly creatures in the sky
   Claudia Humphrey

The Optimist

An Optimist is one
Who breaks the sod
And plants the seed
Against the odds of reaping weeds.
He works long hours
Breaking his back
Before crawling into the "sack"
Just to keep creditors off his back.
Man and weather work together
To bring in a full yield
When the harvest is over
And the golden bounty is in the bin
He takes his family to church
To thank "Him".
When the future looks dim
And most find it hard to cope
The Optimist looks to his horizon
"Where forever flies the flag of faith and hope"!

Almeta Cochran

Mobile

You were brilliant primary colors,
red-blue-yellow.
I was golden breezes,
glistening—glowing—gliding.

You splashed your beautiful colors on me,
pure rubies, sapphires, and sunshine, and
with brilliant delight we dazzled we danced we sang,
like a Calder original,
we glided softly and glowed with perfection,
too wonderful not to be seen,
too perfect to ever stand still.

But, blinded by our light,
I couldn't see you taking your brilliance away from me.

Suddenly silently, I became a dark mobile
with broken parts hanging
from twisted strings
of no color, no jewels,
dull and decaying
too pitiful to be seen
too painful to ever move.

Kathleen Pappagallo

Getting An Education

It's so important to get an education,
So later in life you'll avoid humiliation.
By going to school and learning a lot,
You'll get a good job and use what you've been taught.

Being able to read and understand,
Will help you achieve something grand.
With financial support you'll be all right,
So that your budget will not be so tight.

With such an education, there is no doubt,
You'll go through life helping people out.
Some people you meet will be amazed,
Because while you were learning, they sat there dazed.

David Clarence Simon

Monarch

The mewling of young kittens
At an animal shelter
Here euthanasia kills
It sounds like Helter-Skelter

Outside the village a roar
From a lion lying in wait
Here Jim Morrison does snore
Here visions by Bonny Raitt

Peace on earth good will to all men
A Jack in the Pulpit prays
Flanders Fields all over again
Tripoli becomes the Bey

Girls and boys go together
A father and mother at peace
A letter from the Castskills
And I wish coughing would cease

Blaine A. Jones

The Dream

I dreamed of a palace,
And as queen
I stand
Looking into the eyes
Of every man.
To each face I passed
Into each eyes I seen,
A loneliness so deep,
Oh what could it mean?
My soul advised me
As I stood there within;
These souls are dying, they are
Lost in sin.
I saw the rich oppress the poor,
Felt their distress
Still even more;
I heard their cries
Against their foe.
Oh faith, your victory
Of this loneliness we know!

Linda Ann Barrows

The Finale

Alone in a darkened ballroom
Roses fall from his hand
Laughter hides behind the walls
The silence plays the band

Emotions flee the empty room
The spotlight fades away
Memories becoming clearer
Pain is there to stay

His head is there inside his hands
Tears fall at his feet
They land upon a broken heart
The finale now complete

Passion takes his living breath
As away it swiftly flies
The last dance is forever over
The romance slowly dies

Bryan C. Bowen

Seeing Beyond The Sky

What a joy it is to see,
Seeing beyond the naked eye,
In the world all around me,
Seeing beyond the sky,
Discerning between good and evil,
Not counting every bird that flies.
But seeing what is real,
Realizing your love for me,
You set my feet on high.

What a joy it is to see,
Looking beyond the sky,
As the leaves dry and fall,
You save me from it all.
What a joy it is to see,
To discern your love for me,
As the sun rises in the east,
And as it sets in the west,
You give me your very best.
Your love for me you never hide,
I can see it beyond the sky.

Barbara Dell Hobbs

His Moccasins

My friend and I
We walked along
He, in his moccasins,
I in none.

He held my hand,
  smiling timidly
searching my face
  ere' so earnest.

I bit my lip
  holding back my tears
I had walked barefoot
  for many miles.

I suppose
I didn't want him to see
the thorns in my feet
meant nothing to me.

Yet, he saw
  and spoke ever so tenderly,
"Please, wear my moccasins awhile."

Carol Chilian

Destiny

Internal soliloquy
finds me
in a sea of discontent
born of inward tears
shed through the years
from thoughts, well meant,
but, sadly, not well spent.

What's meant to be, will be.
I know, and see.
However, once...thought right,
the trip of destiny
that bears us through this
strange "life-sea"
becomes our monument.
And this, we cannot circumvent.

Babette Kaiser Cecchini

Baby Jesus

A sweet little baby asleep in the hay.
What a beautiful lovely day.
For the life of the little one, so precious, so dear.
For all of our lives He will soon shed a tear.

Time flies by, He will soon be a man.
He will give his own life, to save all that He can.
For his Father, and He, both loves us all too.
They will teach us and guide us in all that we do.

He walks and talks with us every day,
And always in a very special way.
A gentle voice, a cheerful smile.
He warms our hearts all the while.

He gives us a hug, a gentle touch,
To let us know He loves us, so very much.
Within our hearts, He hopes we will stay.
Our love for Him, and everyone each day.

Thank you dear Father, and Jesus your son.
For all that you do for each and everyone.
Which brightens our lives and loves us so.
So let us give thanks, to God and his wonderful Son.

Depthana Cunning

Guinea Fowl War Victim

I was the first one out
Stout, the lout came hulking
Hurling at the calm in my hut
A cut in my neck, ah gush!
Gushing red. And my brains
My brains, then my pipe of peace, fell
Into pieces on the ground. Following my head, my hat
A pat on my chap. He turned. Eyes aghast
An arrow crushed through
Heads, father and son, rolled
Rowing through my sea of cows
Beasts bleating and bleeding
Wailing voices
The Savannah is set ablaze
And so began the guinea fowl war
I was the first one out...
I return for nothing but my
Pipe of peace

Adams B. Bodomo

My Personal Inventory

What kind of a place
Would the whole world be,
If the whole human race
Was just like me?

As I travel down life's highway
Giving much more than I take,
Having everything my way,
Is there a difference I can make?

I've learned to love my neighbor
Hoping I'm as a good a friend as my friends are,
While earning my way with honest labor,
In the heart is where the dividends are.

Robert J. Griffin

It's Christmas

When Santa comes a callin',
And peeks around the door.
He wonders who the "tykes" are
Asleep on the living room floor.

He puts boxes and toys around the tree,
Being as quiet as he can be.
He takes a few bites of the food that was left,
Then gives his reindeer a taste of the rest.

When morning comes and all are awake,
The children wonder if Santa is real or fake.
When after all, they slept near the tree,
And thought for sure that Santa they'd see.

They slept through the night, not a sound was made,
They woke up knowing it was Christmas Day.
They were wide-eyed and full of joy,
While looking around observing the toys.

There must be a Santa to leave all these,
Toys, bikes and clothes to please.
Mom, dad, and the children got their wish,
For it's this time of year no one wants to be missed.

Virginia Schelosky

New York On A Summer's Midnight Clear

When the stars look big and bright in a lively blue of night
The constellations of the north star
Big dipper - little dipper
Orion the hunter and bull
Twinkle of glory in New York's northern sky
The milky-way shining over us in the neighborhood heights
As I look up into the moon-lit night
I can appreciate their traditional portrait of beauty
A good-night sky that's sparkling in flight
The vast glistening night that falls to me broadly in sight
Of New York on a summer's midnight clear

Jack T. Armstrong

Forget Not Dobbin's Patient Benevolences!

Horses, to many of us, are merely lost past history.
But some of us continue to remember them well.
These gainful animals provided mankind profusely
With their amazing strength and gentility.

What was their thoughts as I walked among them
In the barn as they awaited their ground barley?
They looked around, sometimes most impatiently,
And yet, they had such faith being in man's guardianship.

Horses portrayed such consistent efforts in the field
As they pulled such as plows, seeders and wagons loaded,
With absolute concentration towards man's appeal
To attain his ordained objectives and critical goals.

But alas, our faithful friends, our true achievers,
Are no longer available in our barn yards
Since alternative types of horse power is in service!
Horses have been relieved of their age-old jobs.

However, horses have long proven dependable and friendly.
They continue to be memorable of nostalgic means.
Horses have remained our friendly partners, evidently,
Even as our productive cooperation tends to cease.

Theodore R. Reich

Impressions

Whispering thunder
Shadows of the night
That different indifference
That distinct indistinct
Unique to one

We are different

Rejected acceptance
Welcomed unacceptance
Consumed in losing finding
Nothing in abyss of despair
Denial of self

Difference wishes to same

So long yet so short
As eternity unfolds
The accepted welcomed
Shadows take shape, whispers heard
And true love will find you

Stay true to self and true love will find you

Rodric Smith

After Andrew

The trees again lift their arms to pray,
The birds again greet the dawn of day,
The lawns are lush and velvet green,
The air is fresh, and oh so clean.
Mother Nature waved her magic wand,
And traces of Andrew are slowly gone.
And man has helped with his own part,
By finding deep within his heart,
To love his neighbor, and to care,
To give a helping hand, to share.
But all of this scene, that' so sublime,
Still bears the scars of the horrible crime.
It fills our streets and daily lives,
With children rampant with guns and knives.
So we must all learn to pull together,
Through crime as well as stormy weather,
And find a way to end the crime,
And make our streets safe all the time.

Mildred L. Galvin

The Mighty Pen

Poetry is like a seed,
One plants the seed of thought.
There is that chance that it may grow,
And then again, may not.
Sometimes the chance is very good,
Sometimes it's very slim.
Hang in there "Men",
With that "Mighty Pen",
And don't give up and stop.
Who knows, the next poem that you write,
May all your others top.
Poets, their harvest of thoughts,
They share, to show the world
How much they care.

Irene J. Priester

Children of the New Moon Part 3

In an everlasting current
Of stolen free will
I chant with all my lovers
Make the demons roam in some other's night
May our ecstasy be our guard
May the New Moon's darkness bless our minds
With guidance till dawn
And the air did shimmer with our words
Omnipotence did claim us all
We stood no longer blinded by ignorance
We saw our own demise
And then the beast raised a claw
Looking on in sympathy
Children of the New Moon it cried
To end your torturous sleep
I give the gift of true death
May your rest be filled with peaceful dreams
Micah Myers

The Party

Myself, along with jealousy
doubt and fear,
had all sat down
to drink some beer.
When who would you think
came stumblin' in?
T'was Satan himself
with a bottle of gin!
Well, he sang and laughed
and spoke of sins,
then thanked me kindly
for entertaining his friends.
Jack Hotchkiss

America

Though I've traveled here and there
   and found exciting things:

Russia is stern and cold
Ireland is lush and green
England has a proper Queen
And Turkey's markets, blue and gold.

Italy has its famous art
Australia has brilliant opals
Canada's folks have heart
New Zealand keep sheep on the knoll.

Scotland's sound of pipes reel
Mexico has Mayan Cities
Israel is clean with futile fields
Egypt had its Pharaoh's pity.

Greece has many sunny isles
Malta, once crusader's home
Fiji has a simple style
Tunis has a mysterious tone.

The place that's best of all
Is Red, White and Blue
America, the place I call Home!
Betty.M. Kaseman

Pristine March

Peeking the bubble beyond the edge,
Shocked, inhaling virgin grounds
Buildings fade to foggy grey,
A star shines pathetically through a small crack,
Feeling the impassioned sting of silent echoes,
tip-toeing gracefully across the glass horizon,
The waltz upon heavenly nirvana performed sarcastically,
The clowns beckon..."Peek the swollen bubble backwards",
A smile stained bucket of tears at high tide,
Pulsating bubble, smashes the crystalline horizon,
A single myopic dive, naked, blind, and exposed,
Into the murky depths of unmarked earth,
Plant destiny with a hollow pit,
To spite the torpid growth the vacuum quickly fills,
A fervent soul, arranged beautifully among the unknown soldiers
marches uniformly through the heated bubble.
Glancing, smiling, a natural phenomenon of gesticulation.
Passion personified.
The soldiers march in unvarying perfection.
Glancing forward the bubble shatters upon the crystal horizon.
An intricate collage of heart, mind, and soul, painted at sunset.
The window has opened toward the sky.
Brett Hodus

Image Reflections

Are our reflected images what and who we really are?
Or are they simply mirrored impressions to
impress others from afar.

Is there portrayal of varying types, making
an image more sociably acceptable?
Imitation or imagination breeds within us
an unknown character label.

Pendulous moods of endearment, silence, or
temper alter a sought out image.
Moods stick like a book of pages.

Presumptuous attempts are made at remaking
another's image.
The other person rebels with rage.

The all is under control image is clever.
'Off day' distractions are a never.

The self-contented image tends to suffice on its own.
Success, joy and contentment imminently fades.
Where will they have gone?

One then chooses to kneel and cry out loud.
God hears and creates a new likeness image
which makes Him proud.

Visible personal images may or may not appear to be what you see.
For within the heart, mind and soul, He knows. Agree?
Dora Low Fung

Why?

   Why me? Why did it have to happen to me?
Me, of all people. But I can't tell anyone! Not
a soul! No one will understand! No one
will care! Everyday will think I'm crazy!
But why did it have to happen to me?! Everyone
will think I'm lying! No one will believe me,
so why tell? It doesn't make sense...not even to me...
Renee Dutton

Looking Back

i take a look back to some time ago,
look back at once was tomorrow.
I think of the dreams that filled my head,
the future for me,
what will lye ahead.
But tomorrow never came
somehow my future got drowned out in the rain.
What happened to those feelings?
Where can they be found?
I've searched all through myself
all I find are traces of my past intellectual mind,
traces of my future inner peace,
I must find that locked door and try to get in,
Because as of now I'm better off deceased.
   Rita Carter

Absence

Watching the tears come to his eyes each time his job rips him away;
taking the precious time sharing thoughts on that last day.
What will be to come? What do you want me to do?
I need to know how to handle all the details for you.
Missing the smiles, tears, voices of all those he adores;
missing the feeling of love and his family even more.
Missing the changes of his son growing while he's gone.
Taking it minute by minute to make the time go on.
Helping to keep you from dwelling on what you may be missing
   while you're away,
and to keep making it through; counting down another day.
Your lives seem to stop for the time you're apart,
and when he returns you move on from yet another start.
You become more independent trying to handle what comes along.
He's wanting to be back in that life to which he belongs.
To make up for the time he has been cheated out of,
to spend as much time with all that he loves,
to see what he's missed; get back in touch,
to be home with the family he has missed so much.
He is home this time, for a while to stay,
until his job one day again rips him away.
   Julie K. G. Murphy

Christmas

That special day is finally here,
The most loving time, of all the year.
We share our gifts, and love each other,
Forget sad thoughts . . . and forgive one another.
All the presents . . . are placed 'round the tree,
Many for the kids . . . a few for me.
Lots of lights, decorate the yard,
It's been a joy . . . just the shopping was hard.
The meaning grows greater . . . as years go by,
The more we realize . . . that Jesus is why.
We're so much closer . . . than we've ever been,
Though things have been good . . . since way back when.
God truly loves us, he's been so kind,
There's no greater gift . . . a person could find,
Even if the glitter . . . and gifts weren't there,
It would be a Merry Christmas . . . with love to share.
   Darvin O. Riggs

My Farewell

To this wretched hell
Thanks to all the people,
by my side
I am happy I am gone
I am at home a last
my pain is finally numbed
I'm gonna miss all my friends
But my soul is finally, where it belongs
I will have my own star
Shining brightly over your head
visiting in your dreams
I hope for your happiness
as mine is finally here
I want you all to know
I love you and goodbye!!
   Shawn M. Kelly

Life's Truth

In youth we needed
   To be like the others
Always compared
   To sisters and brothers
To be not as smart
   Brought us to shame
to be wise is to realize
   We're not all the same

Your talents are different
   From mine as a rule
But each is important
   When used as a tool
To better mankind
   Rather than harm
When you do your best
   There's no need for alarm
   Patricia A. Munson

The Corset

She stands there
silently
putting on her binding corset
breasts exposed to the world

In her nakedness
she shows all

Why does she cinch and tighten?
Pinch and Pull?
Is she not beautiful the way she is?
Is her waistline too wide?
Are her hips too large?

Fine
Divine
A work of art

Captivating
not pinched or pulled
Bound or tightened

Glorious in her naked beauty
Alone
Sin Corset.
   Shannon Marie Duffy

The Wedding Ring

"I promise Thee", he said to her
And pledged his love to bring.
She held out her hand to him
Where he placed the wedding ring.

There were no jewels encrusted there
Just a simple silver band
But there was love inside that ring
And so it never left her hand.

She wore it more than sixty years
Through happy times and sad
And all their children knew that ring
Had bonded their Mother and Dad.

And when she died, her children took
That ring she held so dear
And placed it in a memory box
To keep her presence near.

And so it passed on down the line
Their mother as a bride,
Reminding those who kept the ring
of love that never died.

Jean Hays

When Your Heart Seems Lost

When your heart seems lost,
Which road do you choose,
Which direction shall you take;
When each path taken—
Leads to another heartache.

Pride was there,
The challenge mine to take;
Until words were spoken—
Now promises broken.
Words no longer hurt me,
My heart protected in steel;
Searching for truth—
Knowing how I feel.

When your heart seems lost,
Which road do you choose,
Which direction shall you take;
A heart protected in steel—
From yet another heartache.

Terri Lea Murray

Life

Life is what you make it
when storms are ragging high
Only God, will be the answer
and bring you home to shore.

God's love is so great
just believe His promises
Life can be so grand
sleep calmly, and embrace
His love.

When burden seems so hard to
bear, and friends, you had are gone,
Remember Jesus in your prayers,
He's always son the throne.

Ollie Bryson

Daughter

She is lovely, she is true
She can be happy or very blue
She can make your day so very bright
And can keep you up all night
When she is born you are ecstatic
Soon you wish she were locked in the attic
At times you are her confidante
Other times she will turn to her aunt
But you love her for all your life
And will worry about her throughout each night
You want for her the best
Even when she marries you do not rest
There is nothing like the love between mother and daughter
It sustains you through life; you are glad you taught her.

Donna M. Coffey

The Wondering Duck

   As the duck waddled along the ground
   Seeking food, he hoped could be found
A crust of bread, a grain of corn
They've done nothing but eat, since they were born.
   Each day they grow fatter, and slower in pace
If they could talk, they would say, were not in a race
One of these days, the owner will decide I must go
Into the oven, to roast very slow,
Then along my side, in the pan will be, corn bread dressing
And when all is done, and set on the table, then a blessing
Then carved, and each given a portion
Now to me, I have a better notion
Give me the corn, while alive and well
Then my stomach will be filled and swell
Boy if I could only talk, I'd say
Let me live another day.
   You know I'm old and tough as could be
Please turn me loose, set me free
Get yourself a ham and sweet tater
For I'm long gone, see ya'll later.

Donald L. Iannone

The Homeless Man Tastes Compassion

He walked into church, sat right beside me,
I patted his back reassuringly.
I tucked a note into his hand
With a few written words, "We care and understand."

As we walked out, I offered him a ride,
Took him home, invited him inside.

We offered him a shower, socks, clean, comfy clothes,
A beef not roast dinner, an easy chair for repose.
We kicked back and chatted all afternoon,
Shared encouraging words, invited him back soon.

We drove him away, bade him Godspeed
Knowing in some way we'd met his need.

The note given earlier had money for clothes,
To give him hope, to ease his woes.
Compassion instinctively remains aware,
With the hungry, the homeless, we know to share.

Genuine compassion commands we give care
Like a tire that needs changing, we do it then and there.

Diane R. Simon

Grace

Life is very wonderful, it's the decisions in your
everyday life that choose whether you win or lose.

If you choose God, I sought the thought that you'll
be bought by evil and its tricks. It's what you pick
that will stick, because you reap what you sow. If you
pick good you'll glow, if you pick bad you'll moan. I
believe it's all just a repeat, just like the story of
Adam and Eve, the apple and the tree. But God shouldn't
have to blow a horn to show you the right door. You'll be
seeing me dropping to my knees saying "please" and begging
for mercy. Cause God gotta let the people know what time
it is, or they'll never shine again.

You hear about murder and crime everyday; and everything I
pray to the Lord to Bless my soul and to take control.
Cause no one knows when it is time to go. There's only one
life to live and I give my all to God, but with the demons
scheming, even He knows it's hard for me to do it all.

And so He awaits for me to give Him all my love and my
compassion. For death is not sad but a passing on and
leaving behind all the bad. Moving on to a greater place
where every space is filled with love and grace.

Christopher Ramos

Ode To A Turkey

Oh, lovely young turkey, so plump and so fair
Fixed up with tenderness and basted with care
Without you, tonight, we all could not share
These feelings of love so deep and so rare

By folding our hands, God's blessings we'll ask
And plates full of stuffing and gravy we'll pass
Veggies and cranberry sauces we'll eat
And you also, dear turkey, with your white and dark meat
We'll nibble and nibble from your neck to your feet

Yes, precious young turkey, so plump and so fair
A gift sent from heaven to folks everywhere
The whole world agrees you're incredibly sweet
But personally, I'm hungry
So I declare,

Let us eat!

Heather Rogerson

Disappearing Past

Either by memory loss
or the death of someone you love.
Disappearing past.
It doesn't help in knowing that
nothing forever will last.

The past disappearing
and that makes me MAD,
and my emotions run the
gamut from happiness to sad.

The children of older parents
should make an effort and try
to listen to their stories, ask questions,
compare the now and then, tape, record, put it all
together or the past forever will die!

Denny Sternberg

Untitled

Fly by faith
Love by light
Die by day
Name by night
Fall by fate

Amanda Oberhouse

God's Grace

God's grace is sufficient
for you and me.

God's grace abounds
when we call upon him.

We must call upon him
no matter if we are at home
or in town

God's grace is all around
and can be found if we only
seek around

God's grace is for all who call
upon him

As his grace abounds
whether we are at home or in town
God's grace is sufficient
for all who call upon him.

Buna Bennefield

Brotherhood

My home is complete with love inbred.
I love the humane people black or white,
I love the people yellow, brown or red.
I look at them in shinning armor with delight.
It's trivial the God they worship overnight.
To love the peoples, I entreat the mass:
Unite!

Ignazio C. Benfante

It's Mine

In this world of doubt and change
It's my life I must arrange,
Get in order the things I must,
Look to God which is my trust.

As I go from day to day
In my hurried sort of way,
I take only from the shelf
Whatever lets me be myself.

I can't blame my faults on others
For its mine I live with daily,
And what I digest in my thinking
Are my own and for that I must atone.

My footsteps are my own
Where'er I choose to go,
But I am only human,
My creator made me so.

With the breath of life he's giv'n
And wisdom from above,
I am happy, just to be
My own self, my God and me.

Aileen Karg

Dali's Moon

Night faded into dawn.
Stars lost luster in the spawn
Of light.
The first to go
Were fireflies on the lawn.
In sequences, then,
Distant pinpoint orbs were gone
Till Venus — only Venus —
Stood her watch alone.
It was as though
She were somewhat loath to go
Away with night.

Just then the sun
Touched an electric beam
And all was done:
Venus, stars outflung,
Street lamps,
And fireflies on the lawn.

The day belongs to the rising sun,
And night was just a dream.
Louise Dodd Gerken

Eve

Adam where do you be
  you are not guarding the tree
the wicked devil must be near
  I tremble I have fear

The devil leaping talking does appear
  your partner my beautiful dear
In the back woods you know
  preparing for the big animal show

Just forget let him be
  you will learn of the honey bee
Its nectar oh so sweet
  I must repeat oh so sweet

Eve breathed God what did you say
  "Near the forbidden tree not to stay"
Your body is mine each day
  you are not the boss I do say

Poor Eve the bold woman of today
  turning away had this to say
God the maker of all.
  We women humbly before you we fall.
Larry Shields

Peace

Peace, not as a river
Only a stream,
yearning to grow mighty
Rain, flooding and yielding
a harvest of tears
Hope, dimmed by hearts and minds
bent toward the dark
Cause a filling of living water
to swell and overflow
Spill over the land
smoothing the rough places
Make gentle paths leading home
Created by ripples of love and truth
Linda Brown

Changes

My Life has been one of changes
Some mountain tops I could barely get over
Some valleys that seemed I was nearing hell
People have come and gone
Some I wanted to leave
Others I chose to keep near and safe
You were there only I rarely saw you
Was it by chance we talked one day
How did it come about we shared some time
Why did I write you to see how you were
Hoping you were happy
Wanting you to have love with someone of your choice.
Down the road five years passed
I again write you to express my sympathy
For the loss you were experiencing
Pleasant surprise when I heard from you
That letter was one of sadness
Weeks and days have passed
Each letter has brought my heart closer to yours
I thank God each day for letting me into your life
Sandy Lyle

Dusk

Dusk, time of day when it feels
as if my son came over and talked to me,
as he did, before he died.

He tells me to enjoy each day for him,
also each sunset on the water.
Which he loved.

He tells me, that he knows the children are good
and that their mother is strong,
they will make it, given time.

He tells me, that his life though short
was wonderful and that at peace
now there is no more pain.

I ask how am I doing, can I make it son?
and look up where he stood.
But he is gone.
Hedy Richfield

I Never Knew Lonely

No other Lover ever really cared
When I've reached out you were always there
Now I'm so far away and baby I'm scared
I never knew lonely till you.
You were my rock and the strength that I needed
To keep me sane in this life I lead,
Now I'm now with you and my broken heart bleeds.
I never knew lonely till you.
I never knew lonely could be so blue,
I never knew lonely could tear you in two.
And I have never loved some like I love you...
I never knew lonely till you.
I can't make up for the times I have been gone,
But I'll prove it to you, with one look in my eyes.
Because back in your arms is where I belong.
Serena Breen

Baha'u'llah

Brave and Majestic was He;
   Almighty and All-Powerful.
Also, Meek and Humble was He;
   Utter-Nothingness before His God.
His was Grace abounding and Mercy unsurpassed;
   To peoples of all lands.
All-Knowing and All-Wise was He;
   A Fountain of Both to all men.

Utter Poverty and grievous Abasement He suffered;
   An Emblem of His great Glory.

Lord of Lords and King of Kings was He;
   Lord of the Age and Lord of Hosts.
Limpid streams He made into mighty Oceans;
   By His Most Great Spirit.
Atoms He turned into Suns of unsurpassed Splendor;
   By the Power of His awesome Might.
He came among us, mere mortals, and,
   Transformed us into mighty Giants,
   By the Potency of His Holy Word;
Baha'u'llah, Most Great Name.

    A. J. Delahoussaye III

Ashleigh

Your were only three when you came into my life in love.
   Heaven shines down on you from above.
Such big blue eyes and a smile to melt my heart.
   Fate has kept us apart.
Although you are many miles away
   Ashleigh, you have a place in my heart to stay.

You have known such heartbreak for a child of nine.
   Life had been unkind.
You are a child of God, I've been told.
   A life of love is now yours to behold.

You are a lot like me, reaching for the stars in the night.
You know much about heaven and soon will find the light.

   Love must come first in all you do.
Precious Ashleigh, the Angels watch over you.
   When your heart cries, just say,
Angels help me to find the way.
   They come to you on wings of love,
With blessings and miracles too.
   Little Ashleigh, Grandma loves you.

    Mary Collins

Heaven's Gate

Hale-Bopp comet in the midst of night.
Omnipotent visions are in his sight.
Now he sits with gleeful eyes,
and with the computer his soul does cry.
That everything is meant to be,
and the pain of millions is like the endless sea.
It beckons out to the few who can hear,
like a lonely song to come be near,
and taste of the bitterness of a broken heart.
He does play a joyous part.
In this scene the joy is too great.
The final curtain is "Heavens Gate",
and when he bows good-bye,
I am freed of my role.......I bow to die.

    Michael L. Brandon

Prudence

This plateau of manhood
   that we achieve
As though today would hold no effort
   for only in us we believe.
And yet the cross is ours again
   in the why of what they leave.

Among the complacent, only,
   this plateau exists,
For minds aren't trained
   to search within, the mists,
Of those who offer the new
   from among their mold's own lists.

And yet as we discover
   their bold, brash determine,
We offer each other's "New"
   as we proceed to extermine
The layers of love's defense
   in the trusting of our learnin'!

If only to proceed...proceed...
   as though life began today!

    James M. Huffman

You Are The Flower That Blooms In God's Love

You are the flower that blooms
   in the garden of God's Love,
Bringing reality to the beauty
   and dreams from above.

Born from the seeds
   of eternal peace,
Scattered by the winds of Love
   that never cease.

Gently caressed by the dew
   or early morning rise,
Nurtured by the warmth
   of the Light's loving prize.

Feeling the warmth of your soul
   is a bit of heaven on earth,
Bringing new meaning to the
   experience of new Birth

You are the flower that blooms
   in the hearts of one and all,
For all the seasons - winter,
   spring, summer and fall.

    Paul Gray

Love

Love is beautiful, love is kind.
Love is harsh, and love is blind.
Without another it is unattainable,
Yet with your "one" heaven is gainable.
I believe it is God's great goal,
That there is "one" for each young soul.
Goodbye! Goodbye, yet before I depart;
Good luck! Good luck, on finding your heart.

    Christopher Hall

Bust

Eat it, (seat it, meat it,) feed it,
weed it,
seed it,
Smoke it, coke it, poke it,
Take it, slash it, mash it, crash it,
dash it,
cop it, pop it, drop it, swap it,
throw it, tow it, sew it,
mow it, —

Plane it, train it, car it, far it,
What ever the hell you do with it,
Get rid of it; — This is a Bust;—

Roy Rajacic

The Lovers

A hot sultry day
   A soft summer might
The breeze floats across our skin
   As we hold each other tight

Two hearts hammering away
   Beating fast and true
There's only one woman I can be
   And that's when I'm with you

It's nothing really you say
   It's nothing really you do
Each time I look in your eyes
   I melt away with you

Tell me your deepest regrets
   Show me your darkest fears
And when you listen for my voice
   Let it say, "I am still here."

Let me kiss your lips
   Let me caress your handsome face
There's no place I'd rather be
   Than within your sweet embrace

Dawn Ryan

Thanks My Love

Thanks "My Love" for this;
the beginnings of sweet bliss.
I can see; and I can feel;
It's finally becoming real.
My doubts and fears,
Have disappeared!
And my hopes and dreams,
Are becoming quite clear!
Thanks "My Love", for this;
Your tender, precious, kiss,
I've wondered many years;
Through endless, ageless, tears.
But now I can see
There's still hope for me.
Thanks "My Love" for this;
I'm becoming an optimist!
I will grow and excel;
I see the vision, so well!
So thanks, "My Love" for this;
Your sweet persistence with, that kiss.

Bonnie S. Lee

He Is Just A Little Boy

He stands at the plate
   with his heart pounding fast.
The bases are loaded,
   the die has been cast.
Mom and Dad cannot help him,
   he stands all alone.
A hit at this moment,
   would send the team home.
The ball meets the plate,
   he swings and he misses.
There's a groan from the crowd,
   with some boos and some hisses.
A thoughtless voice cries,
   strike out the bum.
Tears fill his eyes, the game's no longer fun.
So open your heart and give him a break,
For it's moments like this, a man you can make.
Please keep this in mind, when you hear someone forget.
He is just a little boy,
   and not a man yet.

Bob Fox

Are You Proud?

Would you be proud of me
My old, dear friend?
I'm not who you knew.
I've changed so much since you died.
You were suppose to be here,
Suppose to see me graduate, see me succeed.
You were suppose to be here to tell me,
What I should do now.
I have needed your wise advice so often these past years.
I've wondered so often what you'd think.
Do you approve of the choices I've made?
Am I all you thought I could be?
I stare at your picture, wishing it could talk.
I don't remember the sound of your voice.
All I remember is the love, the wisdom.
How dare you leave me to face life alone.
I wasn't ready, so much has happened to me
And what I really need now
Is to know you'd approve,
That I made you proud.

Sara M. Drake

Troy

He held the hourglass in the palm of his hand.

The last time we were together, He turned it over and let the sand begin its journey to the bottom.

As we parted, neither of us knew our goodbye was never to be followed with another hello.

He took you with no warning. He took the smile that even the stars couldn't outshine.

Through tears, I watched a cold, empty body. Too cold to house a spirit as alive as yours once was.

When I felt the soft flutter of your wing against my cheek,
I knew you lived as you were meant to. An angel on earth you always were, an angel in Heaven you became.

Amanda Salcido

Follow Your Dreams

Follow your dreams keep your goals in sight
Soar high enjoying a scenic, majestic flight
Let your passion for life map out your course
Remain unsaddled like a free, untamed horse.

Lead the way, as others follow the path you blaze
At times you'll move swiftly, other times you'll graze
Keep your sights focused on what you intend to do
Remember in this entire world there's only one you.

You're unique, there's no need to follow the crowd
There are many reasons you stand tall and proud
With a solid game plan there's no way you can fail
And nothing can ever stop you once you've set sail.

Beyond your sights are many far off beautiful places
Scenic mountains, dense forests, and wide open spaces
There's always an adventure around the next bend
Let your zest for living become your best friend.

Your dreams can be realities if you pursue them enough
Never abandon your hopes even when things get tough
Follow your dreams along the course you have set
Pretty soon you'll find your goals have been met.
Joseph J. Falco

Grandma's Quilt

Memories of other times all pieced with loving hands,
a many-colored legacy that I now understand.

T'was fashioned in her spare time of which there is no more,
a rambling riot of shapes and patterns, saved from years before.

Her color sense went wanting, but not the love that poured o're
those tiny hues of fragments and within each stitch was stored.

As age diminished eyesight and her hands would tire and ache,
each quilt would be less perfect, each one harder to create.

But it mattered not to those who snuggled, rested and content
'neath those covers of mosaic warding off Winter's lament.

Now eyes are closed and fingers still, no more to cut and patch,
fragments lie about and ponder on who will piece and match.

Journeys end as journeys will, when threads of life are severed,
and memories bring smiles and tears when moments are remembered.

Now the legacy she left is felt whenever Winter's chill
makes the quilt a source of comfort, as I know it always will.
Rosemary Herak Kohout

Journey

The journey of life was intended for saints;
The rest of us have to make do with complaints.
The maxim's the same, whether for woman or man:
Just do the best job that you possibly can.

When evening is nigh and the sun's at its setting
Don't let your thoughts fly to useless regretting.
Your agenda was long but it had your best shot,
The results were not always the ones you had sought.

But a restful night's sleep, with maybe a dream
Will set your mind thinking on a different theme,
And when morning arrives to enable your powers:
A shining new gift of twenty-four hours.
Elzie E. Futter

Ask

Ask not for treasures made of gold,
They'll not warm you, when you're cold.
Look not for diamonds for your hair,
Stones aren't memories of love and care.
Greed nought for money, wealth, and fame,
In death they're not beside your name.

Ask rather for talents of sharing love,
Passed down from sucres high above.
Let tour treasure be health, good and strong,
And the wisdom of right and wrong.

The rich and famous are like you and me,
Deep down inside, they live to be free.
So look not for trophies on a shelf,
Just be good to someone, and yourself.
Carl Hills

My Love

Your name is the sun
To which you light my day
And your love would be my moon
But yet I sit
Alone in the darkness night after night
I would use your body
As my own private protection
So never to be frightened again
But yet I stay scared each day
What I wouldn't give to be in your arms
Even just once
And have one night when it is not dark
And one day I fear nothing
I wish I could tell you
All I wish to say
But yet I'm worried that if I talk
You will not listen
Or maybe if you did you probably
Would just laugh
Angela Dane

Memories

Sitting by the window
Staring out into space
picture of you comes to my mind
and a tear rolls down my face

Thinking about what once was
is all I seem to do
but I lie, and tell the world
that I'm over you

If only it was that easy
to set aside a dream
to throw it into the river of life
and let it float downstream

Still, I know that
memories of you, memories of me
always there, they will always be
together-forever
in my memory
Janine Crumbliss

Sanity And Happiness

Leaving a smoke-filled tavern room;
traveling through foggy night darkness,
with the howl of wolves around you.
Wading across moors and feeling your way
Along a twisted rocky path, in a jagged
forest, under moonless sky, without a
hand to hold and comfort you. Where the
chilly winds blow and the misty icy rain
runs down your face, mixing with tears.
Laughter and ugly voices come from many
directions, enough to nearly drive you mad.
The esoteric of a fairy tale; it is not. But
the esoteric of many fairy tales, that expose
themselves, like a bear shows its teeth.
With your heart anchored in love and your
mind conditioned to logic, the mind seems
to work on its own, sorting out choices.
With this cunning, common sense and
patience,
you will survive. Love is the power to find
sanity and happiness, even amid chaos.

Ray O'Neal

Alone

My heart is torn in two
cause I'm missing you.
You took your love away
that keep me going on.
You have no heart or feelings
you're just as cold as ice.
You took your love away
and now I'm paying the price
I miss the hugs and kisses,
the way you touched my face,
Your arms around my waist.
Now that it's all gone I
have nothing else to say
but remember the expression
on my face.

Christan Blackman

Dynasty

Cajolery has haunted me from years past
whet my appetite with bittersweet madness
no questions asked
I am just the portraiture of all their games
towers hang from clouds
and the demigods, those fragile "toys",
call my shots and title me unduly
there are bodies bobbing in the ocean
still I am the importance of their day,
a gamin and a muse on a mission
past all the rubbish
on a new turn towards a seas daylight
ubiquitous night can't smother a savior
of sweet grace
truly their sugar will crystallize
whilst I'm stirring in my bed of thorns
maybe they're lost in finding me
this time

Andrea Bickford

My Guy

When I quit work, our beautiful future was planned
You made it happen, with patience and love
To me, you are the lionhearted of man
The joy we've had with out children, twicefold
Sweetness story ever told

Watching them grow, has been God's blessing
I've loved every minute, I'm confessing
Our dwelling you built, with your own bare hands
Years of work, you have done, with no complaint at home
You find time for all of us, together or alone

Our children are almost grown now
And where ever they may roam
I know they'll carry within their hearts
Loving thoughts of their dad
Who made a house a home

You've always carried every burden, with me
I've never had to beg
I love your compassion, your sweet gentle eyes
I love you, Richard
I'm so lucky, you're "My Guy"

Shirley LaVon Butcher

The Unwanted Child

Why should there be an unwanted child?
They are seeds from Heaven, sent to us as a blessing
In God's eyes, none purer than a child
All are different, meant to be
So why should there ever be an unwanted child?
There are people who would love to have a child.
They feel life has shortened them a bit of Heaven to shore.
Why not place a child in their arms, from those who care.
Never let a child ever feel they are unwanted or not loved.
We live in a time we need more love.
We need to care more for those who cannot care for themselves.
All packages wrapped in pretty paper, do not have the same
   contents inside.
Never let it be said, not enough love to go around.
To see a smile, or a twinkle in the eyes of a child.
Means more than all the riches of this of this world.
Love each as a precious gift, that cannot be replaced.
Many are hungry, "needs to be feel",
As none may say, I was an unwanted child.

Bertha Duff

Talking To Jesus

Talking to Jesus comes naturally, like taking a breath of air.
Even though I cannot see him, I know that he is there.
We talk about so many things, my precious Lord and I.
Topics such as ware and peace and homemade apple pie.
Sometimes we laugh together, about some private thing.
He likes to harmonize with me, each time he hears me sing.
Wen I lift my hands to praise him, he reaches down to me.
As we are joined in spirit, he tells me I am free.
Sometimes I kneel before him, and tell him of my sin.
He tells me that he loves me, and he forgiveness me once again
At times I get quite weary, while traveling down life's road.
Then Jesus says, just lean on me, and let me take your load,
Oh, blessed sweet communion, between my Lord and I.
I love to talk to Jesus and He is faithful to reply.

Hazel Enga

The Day It Turned To Night

I was there that bleak dark day
I hung there on his right
I watched the tear drops drip his eyes
The day it turned to night

I saw her sob down at his feet
Raising her arms to the heavens and moaning "why"?
I felt his pain surge through my body
The day it turned to night.

I thought of my killings, my lies and my stealing
as I listened to what he said
While all around the darkness crept
I slowly raised my head

As I strained to open my eyes
I saw him staring back
with love, not hatred, and lack of fear
while the sky above raged black

I died there next to him the day
with immortal peace like an angel in flight
Knowing I would one day see him again
from a promise he made the day it turned to night
Robin Glidden

The Age Of An Old Friend

They were two close friends back then
when Ben was just barely ten.
A friendship that was thought to never end.
As if it was kin, it was hard to comprehend.
No one knows how old the old oak tree was.
Not even Father's first brother Uncle Russ.

With the rustling of the wind the oak would sway
and without delay upon the limbs Ben would play.
Swinging from limb to limb in the old tree
and up and down the trunk like a little monkey.
In 'twenty-three Grandfather was the first to start.
The tree's bark wore the hearts of many a sweetheart.

Deep in a limb's bark the rope of a swing had left its mark
and in little Landers Park the oak had become a landmark.
That Saturday folks came in the rain to pay their last
and Ben, the last to leave with many memories of the past.
As fast as the rain came the suns rays did the same
and a woodcutter and his ax came to stake his claim.

The very next day Ben claimed his part of the past.
Counting the rings, the tree's age was known at last.
Dale R. Patchen

I Feel Sadness

I cry a tear on my face. I witness race hate.
I see young people throwing their life away
To drugs and the rest of life distasteful evils.
I see my family getting older
Since I been away
I see the gray growing all over my face
It stress at its best.
I am not at the point where I should be or can be
Please Lord deliver me
Give me the power to make each hour.
Frances C. Farmer

The Hidden Dream

Like the soft whisper of a silent wind
I keep my feelings hidden deep down inside.
Like the gentle flow of a never-ending stream
my love for you continues to grow.
If you were ever to enter my life
you shall revive my soul,
bring me to a state of happiness
where all my wishes would come true.
Yet that is a dream lost far beyond time
too far to get a grasp of.
I would give everything and a whole lot more
just to hold you in my arms,
to feel the closeness of one another.
From now until the end of time
I want to give you a part of me,
and make it a part of you.
Andrea Peda

'Let Freedom Reign'

Let freedom reign throughout this land;
Protection is the key;
Doubtful shadows cast their cunning brand,
And threaten you and me.
"Not guilty" is the fervent plea
Rendered by the wicked tongue;
Pretense flows so smooth and free,
That truth lies interred beyond.
Innocence_the blind charade_-
Coupled with guilty's facade,
Confounds the depth of truth in blind array,
And tips the balance against all odds.
Justice comes in many forms—
Sweet or malignant, the hidden design—
Man sits in a web, forlorn,
Racing with judgment's time.
Let freedom reign throughout this land;
Protection is the key;
Doubtful shadows cast their cunning brand,
And threaten you and me.
Laura J. Houston

A Blackman's Heart

Now class, now clear the air.
I have no fear.
I came to share.
We want to come clear.
To stand everywhere.
Peace was over here.
The heart and soul was in there.
Voice to listener, after voice from page.
All age on stage.
When it came grand.
Brother can you understand.
If I plan.
Achievement I can.
With knowledge in my hand.
Elevation time span.
I will stand.
Show the land.
An afro American.
Blackman
Because that's what I am
Jullian Smallwood

The Mirror

The lake, translucent and sparkling,
Is framed by verdant pines.
From its depths, images engage our eyes.
Images real or surreal,
Who's to know?
Chiaroscuro my life
Limbed in shades of grey.
Yield your images, o lake,
That I may learn your story.
What power created you?
What romances bloomed on your serene shores?
What tribute from antiquity
Left you to us, your loving children?
Susan Burroughs

The Home That Love Built

In that house you build
 is it filled
  with love, peace and joy?

Is it spiritually designed
 with love of Him in mind?

As one loves God in self and others
 one sees true beauty bloom
  with love and light and happiness
   pervading every room.

The bowl of flowers, the books, the music,
 the art upon the wall
  all echo back to you in joy
   the thoughts you now recall
 that made this home, this joy, this light
  take form behind love's door
   built by God's eternal love
    your guest for evermore.
Jeanne-Helene Wattel

The Perfect One

When Jesus was a baby dear,
His mother, Mary, held him near.
To Joseph, Jesus was a joy,
Great knowledge had while just a boy.
In wisdom and in stature grew
With God and men in favor, too.
At his baptism, to show love,
His heavenly Father sent a dove.
Disciples with the Shepherd went
To teach the crowds they must repent.
With miracles, He healed the sick
And drove the demons from the quick.
Lord Jesus prayed and taught of love,
Of faith and trust in God above.
With crown of thorns, on cross of wood,
Christ died instead of those who should;
God's Lamb, all Sinner's, souls could save,
Then rose the third day from the grave,
The Savior died to give to you
Eternal life, forgiveness, too!
Phyllis Haynes

My Mistaken Angel

My heart is like a red red dress in the sunshine-y daytime.
I whisper oh-so-silently "this is not my secret"
and I am not, you see, my own.
In time my friend, in time I will come to.
I will show up so pretty in my red red dress,
beneath the very world in which we sparkle.
Long ago these 'words of wisdom' were twinkles in the sky
to catch and cry
and my, my, my,
how quick we are to shoot each other in the backs.
 Pink is my color today.
This is not as easy to understand as one might think though.
I may have to repeat myself...
 today pink is my color.
In my red red dress I am dancing on your fingers,
spreading slowly outwards,
thinking I'm an angel.
Tate DeCaro

Judgment

Judge me not by my sketchy outer appearance,
For I still am a human being with the same emotions as the next.
Although, my looks may give off the notation that I am less
intelligent or have a lower income than you.
I still am that same person that you cannot see.
Judge me not by my appearance,
For judgement should not be the way of first perception,
For like any other individual, I have gifts and special talents,
Though hidden from the naked eye.
From across pathways judgmental eyes and thoughts
are catapulted toward my direction,
Deflecting these stigmas sent to strike me down.
Be not judgmental for untruth is at hand,
Remember, no matter how sketchy my appearance,
I still am human.
Pierre Dokes

Untitled

Born of light are a precious few
slaking their thirst on the high mountains dew
and eating till full sweet golden honey
the days they spent were warm and sunny
they spin on their looms of purest gold
threads so much finer than those bought or sold
their hair is soft, long and fair
adorned with a wreath made of flowers
plucked with fingers quick and nimble
from hidden and beauteous bowers
each of them is ilk to the other
and call each other dear sister or brother
we find these kindly folk, now only in our dreams
but once these little people were all great kings and queens
their subjects were the snails, the whippoorwill, the thrush
the swans upon the water, the rabbit in the brush
they lived their lives in peace and love
but now they've gone away
to come once more on a golden day
David Clifford

20 Lines Against The Cornflake
Bloodclot Syndrome

I say: Pinballrazorblade, hypodermicbrocade,
jailcelltimerot, showdowninkblot,
cornflakebloodclot, kiss my warm spot;
she shot semen in her veins
put Nyquil in her cereal
got...like a broken slinky...
   toothpaste
    I'm in bad taste
    sh tstain
    cl pdrip
    c ntrag
    fa hag
    sc mbag
    kerouac's a windbag
    everybody's grab-bag
    voi-la mon bag:
  I want to diatribe on the sameness;
  The routine formulaic predictability
of what you call...poetry! (But there's no sense to it)
Repetition dulls the senses repetition dulls the senses repi...

   Dorian

Untitled

The lesson plans
of an omniscient instructor
  still forces me to
review my notes
  while enjoying
the last Bon Voyage.
The Peace
  I enter
is stuffed with
the stillness of summer lakes
and the serenity of autumn's natural precipitation.
Floating
  appeared a way out
  for most
whose energies are used
for individual consumption.
My group essence
still shows
its lingering power
making the Earth
  a easy plane
to fight sin.

   Carl Ford

Value Of Names

Names given or adopted from parents,
  sacred they are, to hold with pride and respect.
A noble lady carried her name,
  in "Goodness" among hostile neighbors.
She was mocked, because
  in their language which filled,
   their mind with filth
    sounded otherwise.
Goodness shut her store
  closed her home,
   carried her package
    back to motherland.

   Shmuel Shoshani

The Two Swans In The Clock

On the wall, there they were
the swans in the clock
Swimming with grace and elegance
As the swans in the pond

An illusion, of almost faint light
Arrogance, repentance
Feeling joy and exuberance
After the sorrow of loss, came daylight

Swim on and on, awaken the soul
Which love is intent to pursue
Finding life's greatest gift of all
Recall all of your dreams come through.

Dream awake, don't miss sight
Not one moment of delight
For the soul wishes are true
Make light shine, from the dark and blue.

   Thereza C. Britton

If There Be A God

Why do we giggle and scold
the twisting worm
as we impale it on a hook?
Would we not also
writhe in pain
if upon a rod
someone pinned us?
Is it because the worm
cannot scream in agony
that we pretend not to
recognize its despair?
Does the worm curse God
for bringing it into this
blind world?
If there be a God
surely the tortured worm
will see His face
long before you and I...

   Lucia Beeler

Rings Of Time

Wild geese fly down the wind
Pilgrims to their past
Their long formations
Circling the rings of time.

I hear my father's whisper
In the slide of shovel into earth
Acorns dropping from the oak.

You draw me with a power like instinct
The rutting of blue sheep
In the Himalayan
The pairing of falcons
In the tumbling wind.

Where did the heron fly
As black clouds formed
On the western mountain?

   Peter Damm

Untitled

The rhythmic ocean proves a faith
that tides will generate a face
of snowy waves soft topped with blue
and underside of purple hue.

The surface strain projects a light
to screen the eye from sky-lit sight.
The power of water on its tour
divines a glorious sight, for sure!

May the mysteries of the holidays
bring you special blessings!
   John Finger

God Called Our Son Today

God called our son today, at
the age of ten,
To he an angel in heaven with him,
Our son has left us, but we'll
see him soon,
He'll always be in our hearts,
from year to year, from moon to moon,
In our memories, we think of his
crooked sweet smile, his smartness
and wit,
How sometimes he'd play, or
watch TV, or just think and sit,
Now to him, for now, we say goodbye,
To our wonderful, sweet little guy.
   Terry Lynn De Vore

Parenthood

Parenthood.
A word I never thought of
Until I met you.

You taught me to love.
You taught me to feel.
You gave me new emotions.

But parenthood...
That horrifying word...
Scared you away-far away.

And I am here, alone,
With no love, no feeling, no new emotions
About to become a mother.

Parenthood.
Like a nightmare unfolding
I am entering into parenthood.
   Brycie F. Klein

Sheila's Tomorrows

Sheila, lay your head down, let the
worries leave your mind.
There's always tomorrow, even if it's
borrowed time.
When you awake, the sun will shine.
Just do your best, and you'll be fine.
Life has its ways, of letting us know.
There will always be tomorrow, no matter
where we go.
   Lara Bullman

True Love

Love has existed since the conception of time,
That never ending need of making you mine,
A conveyance to recreate the mind.

I began as a child to imagine your face,
To see your beauty and encompass your grace,
I kept my heart open for the passion I'd find.

Ever since our first date,
I couldn't escape the magic of our fate,
The way I feel is hard to explain.

My body feels alive when you are near,
My mind is filled with thoughts of you here,
My soul was waiting for you to find me.

Talking to you is coming home,
Your love is so strong, I could never roam,
Your passion fires me so that I'll never be the same.

Our hearts are beating together,
I want to hold you forever,
You make me happier than I should be.

You're my true love!
   Deidre Beckley

Millennium

Is the millennium just another year or a leap of
consciousness we shouldn't fear
Is our species doomed to extinction or destined
for greatness
Can we learn from history or be imprisoned by it!
In the 60's many of us were elevated by the collective
consciousness
In the 90's we are burdened by it!
In the 60's being connected was visceral and tactile!
In the 90's being connected is isolated and cerebral.
Are we evolving or devolving!
Is the millennium just another year or a leap of
consciousness we shouldn't fear!
   Larry Steel

Snoopy And Mandy

Two very different dogs
One purebred and one 57 varieties
One silver/gray
One shades of dark brown with a silver top knot
One who never left hair around
One who always shares her hair
One selected from a breeder
One selected from the humane society
Both loyal and loving
Both noisy guard dogs
Helping me to erase memories of a nightly terror with house
Robbers
Playful
Chasing squirrels, rabbits
As well as people off their perceived space
One a memory
One growing old with me.
   Joanne Kleist

Where Do I Go From Here?

After I am done with my life,
Do I hand it to someone else?
When I have finished exploring the Earth,
Do I move to Mars?
When I have found out what cancer is caused from,
Do I treat it?
What do I do when I am done?
What do I say when there is nothing more to be said?
Where do I go when there is nowhere left to go?
After I have lived my life to the fullest,
Do I die?
When there is no more hope for me,
Do I let Satan take over my soul?
When there is no more unpolluted air left on this earth,
And when the o-zone layer has more than one hole in it,
Where do I go from here?
   Chandler E. Hinkson

Winter, Spring, Summer, And Fall

Winter is the season when people give things for no reason.
Winter is a peaceful time to relax and cuddle up very cozy.
Oh, winter, oh, winter; the season that is so lovely.

Spring is the season when birds start singing lovely songs.
It is time to smell the fresh air because the cold front has gone.
Flowers bloom and beautiful fruits grow. Oh, spring;
what a good season to know.

Summer, summer is the season for me. The plants and animals
are beautiful sights to see. Hot sun beams and big pine trees.
Oh, summer. Oh, summer. What a nice season for me.

Fall is the season to relax and be joyful, with the fun
things you can do with the rake and shovel. During the
lovely season of fall, people enjoy playing and watching
football. Oh, fall, it's time for me to have a ball.

Winter, spring, summer, and fall, the seasons we have and
enjoyed by all. No matter what the weather is and no matter
what falls, oh, seasons, oh, seasons; I love you all.
   Lisa Kamillia Simes

Refuse

Don't weep for those who find themselves alone.
They will always have themselves to talk to.
Why should you clap for those who are unknown?
They can do nothing to further you.
Do not sing for those who have no rhythm.
They will not understand your point of view.
Don't criticize those who chronically sin.
They will return your put downs with endless strife.
Show no pity on the mentally ill.
They have chosen not to face this life.
Stupidity does not deserve your time.
Your helpfulness will not be understood.
Hold onto your pennies, nickels, and dimes.
No matter what you've heard, money is good.
Turn your back on the over religious.
But be careful of the knife that they hold.
Feel free to say what you want and to cuss.
Relax and don't always do what you're told.
   Karen Amber Klassen

"Essence's"

As I stand here looking out over
the sea of misery. The windows of time
in this my mind, drifting down through
the path of a nation caught in the grip
of slavery.

Immigrants who came from afar.
"Nations these have built" slaves
and immigrants together as one
loving another. Now things of the
past has come back. Being strip and torn,
step o, and removed.

"Woo! Say he the Lord thy God"
A nation built on colors, from sea to
Shining sea must stand United within
the rim's of time. Time over time
Lapping and interlocking to create or destroy.

We cannot! We must not! Should not!
do not anything with those who have not!

"Give" gave them the gift of love.
Our nation immigrants slaves is built on the
Most high, which is "Alpha," "Omega"
The first and the last. Oh beautiful for
bless it skies God has shine its light
on thee. America, America for God is
in thee.
   Marvin Gresham

Century Farm

I cherish the acre's
My grandpa bought;
In the year of 1870,
To me, they're heavenly.

And I will tend them
The rest of my life;
Like my dad did
With joy and pride.
   Clyde W. Jontz

Easter

Have you ever noticed
How every year the weather,
Never gets nice until after Easter?

Could it be that the earth is mourning
the death of our Lord Jesus?
And rejoices his resurrection.
Then the earth again, comes to life?

Could it be, that God above is saddened
by the loss of his son,
and the early rains are his tears of grief
and the last winter snow's are the chills
of our sins to be forgiven,
His son "Jesus" died so we could go to
heaven.

Could it be, upon Christ's resurrection,
The sun warms the earth to bring
Out spring flowers in celebration of Rebirth.
   Minnie L. Besendorf

Pain

You know what happened to me in the past.
You know how I wanted this to last.
You said you'd make love to me,
But yet you never waited to see
How bad you deeply hurt me.
You looked me straight in the face,
And said I could take her place.
But you left me, I don't know why,
You'll never know how hard I cry,
While I'm burning up inside.
I loved the expression in your eyes,
Loved the smile as you told me lies.
Your child I would have loved,
Her father I would have loved also.
I never thought I could hurt so much,
Again, after both of them hurt me.
How could you hurt me so bad?
I'll get over being so sad.
But the pain of you
Will always be
In my heart.

Reese Gee

Lost Souls

The families used to be together but then
   they were suddenly torn apart.
There was no longer any laughter.
All the tears were shed.
You would turn your head in disbelief
   and look the other way.
What you did not know was that the
   pain would always be there to stay.
If you looked the other way, you would
   see the slain.
If you turned your head the other way,
   you would experience the pain.
Parents crying over their fallen children.
Children crying over their fallen parents.
Their lives were turned upside down.
Some were urged to walk on and others
   were left behind.
The pain they felt was the same
These were the people of the forgotten race.
These were the people of the Armenian race.

Ayda Panosyan

Challenger

Being deaf is my second
Challenge.
I won't let myself down.
I like being Jack-all-of-
Trades.
In spite, I'm deaf, I try
Harder.
Because I'm making so many
Accomplishments.
I correct my speech so
I make a better world.
I don't stay in the closets.
I stay as a better person when
I don't make any excuses for being
deaf.

Monica L. Bennett

My Prayers

I pray to our Lord that he leadeth me
Down the paths of assurance and divinity
I pray that he takes my warm but tired hand
To guide my way through times I do not understand.

I pray to our Lord that he nourishes my love
and that he empowers me to know I am always thought of
I pray that he gives me his fidelity and faith
and to deny the shallow of the ones that hate.

I pray to our Lord that he grants me the time
To find tranquility in my poems with harmony in rhyme
I pray that he teaches me to be true to myself
and governs me to give and to take not from anyone else.

I pray to our Lord to give strength to the weak
and to allow mother earth to inherit the meek
I pray that he protects her lands and her seas
Her mountains and valleys, her rivers and trees.

I pray to our Lord to watch over my mother
My belated father and my sisters and brothers
I pray for all my friends for whom I truly do care
and I pray that the Lord listens to all of these prayers.

Charles Muse

Velvet Morning Dream

A quiet northern misty morning,
dew glistened over the summer greens.
I awoke to the sound of a buck at play
and to the melodies of the morning bird sing.

Encircled by time that seemed to remain still,
I washed the night off my face,
listening to the warm winds blowing
with such peace, harmony, and grace.

Gazing to the sky at an eagle in flight,
smelling my cedar, sweetgrass, and sage,
I reached for the birch upon the pile,
which was ever so perfectly aged.

Watching the flames dance across my mind,
Reflected from the fires I've burned,
feeling my life and the love of living,
and of all the lessons I have learned.

There I stood on the tip of the thumb,
among such beauty as I've never seen.
Slowly I rose, then opened my eyes,
From this velvet morning dream.

Charles Muse

Reminiscing: Lost Love

In the stillness an autumn morn', I am disturbed by sounds of Indiana woods. Listen to the gentle swish and tumble of the leaves. An orchestra of chirping birds, tree frogs, and a chattering squirrel in the distance. Soothing as it seems, the breaking of silence forces my mind to reminisce of old Virginia; her innocence stirs my heart. Mammoth, rocky mountains spring forth from all around. Almost a hint of burnt embers flirt with my senses. Smells of smoky campfires on a star-lit night. Crackling wood, popping ashes and glowing hot coals tease my sight. O' melancholy, O' dreary soul, how much I miss thee; thy majestic lands. I am haunted by nature's hand. God's creation. All in Awe

Jacob W. Burke

Father's Glory

Pure as the snow, brimming with love
Unconditional is the Father above.

Forgiving, forgetting to remember no more
From east to west, from shore to shore.

Healing, praying, raising the dead
for His Father's glory is what He said.

Betrayed and beaten He was put on a cross
His blessed mother sorrowfully witnessed
His loss.

Three days the son did rise. The devil He did
surprise.

Into His kingdom He rose into the clouds
Promising someday to return to the crowds.

To judge us the living and the dead
For His Father's glory is what He said.
Mollie J. Ison

Still Heart, Calm Soul

Unknowing, uncaring, lacking a voice
Groping for the faintest light
Until beauty was found, music became
And a fragile soul took flight

Buoyed by hope, armored with belief
Buffeted by the winds of fate
A tissue butterfly tears easily
And drowns in the seas of hate

Tears fall, dreams wake
Hopes bleed away with the tide
Still they return as torn wings work
Desperately trying to glide

But tears are as diamonds which last forever
And they harden hearts with time
We see butterflies as beauty but hawks are awake
For it takes true power to fly
Patricia M. Crawford

Ellipses Of Joy

Heart wildly racing, blinding stage lights burning,
Applause still pulses loudly in my ears.
I watch black velvet curtains slowly closing
Upon a circle path that brings me here.

I move along this ring of music singing
Like on an orbit circling 'round my name.
Thus snugly into place precisely fitting,
Points destination and departure are the same.

Each one of us has energy revolving,
Fueled by the many talents we enjoy.
The past and future mem'ries are the openings
Through which we tap in the ellipses of great joy.

Alluring vistas of expression, these I see.
This is exactly where I love to be.
Fran Spears Bock

When The Earth Is At Peace

When the wind ceases to blow
and the trees no longer swerve.
All is calm and life is at peace
When birds sing songs of
melody beyond the symphony of
encores of royalties.
When snow lightly falls
and protects the earth with its
pearl of glisten.
All is calm and the earth is at
peace.
When man no longer denies
his heritage and no longer bows
his head in subservient defeat.
When one can stand straight
and walk tall and speak with
certainty.
The earth is forever more at peace.
When blood no longer flows
from the greatest hills to the
flattest valley.
When chains upon man are
forever broken and every man
is truly free, then and only then
is the earth forever at peace.
Donna Edelen

Definitions Of Love

Love is a small four letter word,
With so many meanings.

Love is unconditional.
Through bad weather and through good.

Love is strong.
It can withstand any and all things.

Love is more than just saying the words,
It is meaning them with all your heart.

Love is support.
It is problem-solving together.

Love is caring.
It is being there for one another.

Love is funny.
It is making each other laugh,
When feeling sad.

Love is stormy . . .
I Love You Stormy!!!
Charles Sapienza II

Loving You

I'm beginning to fall in love with you,
And I'm scared to death you'll hurt me too.
When I hear your voice or see your face,
It reminds me of your warm embrace.
My heart skips a beat when I hear your name,
And I sit and wonder if you feel the same.
I wish I could lay in your arms all night,
To feel you next to me holding me tight.
Maybe one day my dreams will come true,
And you'll feel the way that I feel for you.
Melinda K. Heugly

Broken Friendship

The faces that make us laugh and
the faces that make us mad.
The look of friendship? Or is it just
a thought? We build within.
Some one we put are trust into
with feelings of belief, disbelief
old times, new times joy and pain.
One's of caring, sharing! Just when
we think we know the other as
well as our self, they take a step
back while were walking ahead
and before we know, they were never
our friend "just a front"!
With not much ahead...

Lissa Cota

Deserts

Deserts are grandeur, exercising nobility
in every stretch of sand
Subliminally reaching destination
marking candid patterns born of
sun's and wind's force;
Ever barren in mind's eye
Though, hidden beneath, a mystery
of untold legacy to depict life of
centuries gone by waiting to
be unveiled in time.
Yes, deserts are grandeur
Will forever manifest its
infinite presence and divine splendor
to the eyes of its beholder.

Valerie M. Collins

And Here's To You

And here's to you, those who roam free.
I watch you through my cage.
Sometimes I see you staring in at me.
Do you want what I have, you think so.
Will think long and hard, be careful of
what you wish for.
When I see you.
When I hear your laugh.
I pretend I'm with you.
Until I remember the bars that surround me.
You look at me when you hear me cry.
There's a sad and longing look on your face.
Listen to me I'm just like you.
Wanting what I can't have.
Maybe we could be friends.
If only I were out, and you were in.

Leah Deitz

The Farmer

He laid the hay
   in a mighty way
and he had sworn
   to lay the corn
and laid the corn in a
   mighty way and
when he did it made his day!

Michael James O'Connor

The Great Seahawk

Once captain of this sailing ship,
Determined storms in summers warm are never missed.
When hurricanes just go insane, who gives them names?
They called my ship the great seahawk.
The keel was laid by restless men who just pretend,
Wood saves it strength right to the end.
But do they know this?
For sight makes time that wicked eye,
That makes those winds hold in their sins still someone dies.
When winds wear vails men's minds reveal, who makes it fats
What saved our ships was thirsty ropes that had to cope,
With lazy sails that don't reveal what must come next.
Rocks that act like locks saved the great seahawk.
That lighthouse shines but on my mind,
Remembered times won't tell me why, that wicked eye saved all
   our lives.
Is living fate just having faith, life must go on.

Peter F. Barrow

Today

In the Prism of Space
   Time and Nature evolved and created
   Majestic Mountains and Verdant Trees,
      their hues breathtaking to see;
         Species of Animals thrive,
            abundantly.
On the horizon
   far as the eye can see
      Sky and Sea merge,
         wedded to
            eternity.

Man has also contributed his expertise, exceptionally
   Molding thru the years an amazing
      World of Today;
         culminating in a phenomena
            unbelievable,
               one must agree.

Helen M. Butler

Now That We Have Freed Your Wings

We climbed the hill and reached the apex,
And saw the glory of what was beyond.
The majesty, togetherness and fun
We found in this life for just a moment,
But may know in death for ten billion years?

And as you spread your wings and took to the skies,
I heard you say "No my child, dry your eyes.
For our love is for all time, beyond reason or rhyme.
That which is white-hot will never scorch you,
But lead you on, lighting your footsteps."

And when my eyes have closed, and earthly life ceased,
I hope to awake in the Garden of Peace,
And see your face, at twenty-nine again,
And to hear you say "Welcome my friend! I have missed you so,
Wherever you are, so will I go...
So Divine were they, our blessings from above,
When in that Distant Age, we once drowned in Love."

I now understand these things, now that we have freed your wings.

Nick Tettmar

The Road To Emmaus

Our earth suits were dusty
we had long tarried in the city
now, three days roads behinds us...
some say it was as we came through that dense grove of trees
there was another
who though a stranger grew familiar
yet the matter of our concerns...
   January came in like a clothesline full a wet Mondays
   hung out on a rainy day to dry:
    'lost hope to not caring' feeling

     appeared to know not
      yet held us
     by what we could not see

till sitting at table
bread broken
eyes open
beholden
saw we
one in the other
Helen Spencer-Braden

I Am

I am the eyes that see of human kind the misery
caused by some that don't plant laughter, harvest seeds that don't
be joy, they harvest a varied and hate, cause a soul to tear.
I am the heart that grows fonder, for my people near and yonder
   who have been trampled by greedy feet, grabbed by oppressor's
   hands
that keep making a mockery of God's creation, lands God gave to
mankind to cultivate, to build, to share a like, not to destroy.
I am the hands that reach out, to alleviate the pain.
I am the balm that tries to heal the tortures grief of wounds,
brought about by, human animals without feelings of compassion
They are like a black cloud, fearing down making peace unavailance
I am the voice that screams in frustration, tears shed for ruined
earth forests, I am the vessel that tries to convey to you,
the importance of protecting the environment.
The importance of brotherhood, concern for one another,
togetherness protecting, defending the right of others
can't they hear the earth is sighing?
The sea is spilling out its eat, it could have been a true
paradise for animal and man in balance as God meant it to be.
I an wisdom of Indian knowledge.
Isabel Gallegos Byrd

The Paraclete (One Who Walks Along-Side)

Sometimes, when it seems I cannot go on
Can't take one more step down this path I've trod.
When there are no solutions to the problems I face
I lift my eyes. And—guess what??? There's God!!!

Then I realize that He's always been there,
To lift up/sustain me and keep me from harm.
And my burdens I don't need to carry alone,
Rather—thrust them into His strong, right arm.

His left arm? Why, that draws me close to His side.
And my life's path will, somehow, easier be.
'Cause I know that whatever perils I meet
We will face 'em together—my Lord and me!!
Pat Reidelberger

Good-Bye

Good-bye my child, good-bye
Let me go in peace
Don't hold me with your love
For I'm ready to fly like a dove.

I hear His voice calling
I see the heavens opening
Let me go my child
Let me go in peace.

The sky is crystal clear
The sea is very near
This boat is ready to depart
For this is when we must part.

Shed not foolish tears on my grave
But look to the heavens and be brave
For my soul seeks to be free
Let us not disagree.

We've shared an ageless love
Which was blessed by the heavens above
Fear not - for we'll meet again
Though I know not when.

Let me close my eyes and drift
And thank the Lord for this precious gift
Pray for me my child, pray for me
For that will help me cross the sea.
Inni Bawa Dhingra

On Learning Of Our Daughter's Cancer

We thought we knew life's mysteries
   And were too old to weep;
We held each other in our arms
   And cried ourselves to sleep.
Joseph Foreman

Consummation

A cold darkness surrounds me
As the lid to my coffin shuts
Silence...
Their weeping and cries of anger
Drowned out by my silk-lined madness
In my soul I am somber
But from my dead eyes
No tears...
From my still mouth
No penance...
From my wooden box
No sympathy.
I fall deeper into remorse
With every rose that is thrown
Into my pit of despair
I feel the steady thumping
Of the earth above me
Holy men chanting their benediction
Forgiving me of my sins
Ending my life in this place.
Christopher Chontos

Sanctuary

She cried.
I comforted her.
And she grew like a weed.

Lighting flashed and thunder roared.
I consoled her.
And she grew like a weed.

She laughed.
I felt the sunlight burst about me.
And she grew like a weed.

I cry.
She comforts me.
And grows like a weed.

Fears abound and darkness creeps.
She consoles me.
And grows like a weed.

I lay down in soft meadows.
Peace surrounds me as all around
Heather abounds
   Margo Halloway

A Living Hell

I know a person
nearly my age
she is a sweet person
but she is afraid,
afraid of what
you may ask

Of her mother
who takes the task
to hit and hurt her
as you can tell
this is not life
this is hell
   Wendy Geeslin

Sea

It would rain at night time
while you'd hold me near.
I can't wait for spring time
that will come next year.
I will sing you a lullaby
until you grow out of fear.
I'll sing to you
till night becomes a soft, sweet hue.
When I find you
I won't be so blue.
We'd be together
forever you and I.
I wouldn't want to
ever say goodbye.
I'd cry and cry.
Without you I'd die.
I'll stay with thee.
It would be just you and me.
Forever and ever
We'd live like the sea.
   Sarah Jane Davitian

Reflective Revelations

The world can be complex
With many people who have less
Hope may seem to be quite afar
As if to grasp a million stars

It's in the eyes of a child
Where we are see for smiles
For the innocent eyes of a child
Presents no reason to view the rich or poor
Or search for money and wanting more

It's there wide circles of magical trust
Which delight us with prisms of sparkling dust
Enjoying people of color as precious wonders
Calming the ignorance of horrendous thunders
They rain delicate teardrops of delightfulness
And keep vanity as regardless

For the meek, the sick, the one of vulnerability
The compassionate eyes of a child mirrors justice miraculously
They are the radiance of how life should be
As the reflections of God's inner beauty
To be our true destiny
   Margaret Kelly

Lazy Days

My favorite way of spending time is watching a day go by
In a frame of mind that nothing is of the utmost important
There are absolutely no calls to return or reports due
A day of reading and relaxing with both feet up on purpose
Writing notes capturing moments of days gone by
Playing with the most important people in my life
Cooking up a special treat that's nice to look at yet better to eat
To do positively nothing if my heart desire
To watch the sun rise over the lake or set in the west
Listening to some of the best music as you meditate over things
   yet to be
What some may find to be a total waste of time
Is my favorite way to relax and unwind
Lazy Days are alright by me
   Carolyn Hull

Homeless

Yes I stare during the day
   and sleep here at night

Don't glare at me that way
   what gives you the right

There was a time I had a healthy body
   and a sound mind

Everything slid down hill Amidi
   because the homeless kins

Enjoy your life and walk a straight line
My unusual behavior was surely a sign

Friend and family should not ignore
They should give support all the way

So long as you try to live life with
Ambition, morals and sensible behavior night and day

If you have family, friends and believe I'm God
You won't have to live this way
So pray for guidance, luck and morals it will pay
   Corinne Stein

Riding Home From Danbury

Autumn nights the spent land
Beneath an ivory moon rests
Deeply sleeping under the spell
Which moonbeams bequeath. On either side
Stretch the dark diversions of ghostly trees
And dimly-lit hills, a lake moves
With mists rising into the moon-gray air,
And pastures, quiet lying, are plated
With moonlight showing cornstalks stacked in rows
Bounty of the year now dying.
Florence B. Palmer

Living On The Bubble

Living on the edge
Constantly caught in a wedge
Your heart skips a beat
As you perform spectacular feats
Some are amazed
While others stare in a daze
Doing the so-called impossible
Could land you in the hospital
Living on the bubble
Will bring you to the brink of disastrous trouble
But after being given up for dead
You beat the odds and inch ahead
Disproving all the douters
Who become a bunch of pouters
Because they can't accept the fact
You were supposed to finish at the end of the pack
Somehow you get your act together
To change your outcome for the better
Sometimes it's to rise from the rubble
To prove you can survive living on the bubble.
Waylon C. Johnson

Untitled

I'll miss you when I go.
I'll think of you everyday-everyday that I don't see your face
I'll think of you.
When I'm sitting in a quiet room alone with time to think
I know that I'll think of you.
I hope you will always know that wherever I go,
you will remain a warm spot in my heart.
I'll never forget your face or your smile.
I'll never lose the memories we've shared
or forget when we talked for awhile.
You may not know it because I don't always show it,
but I will always love you.
It doesn't matter what you say or what you don't say,
because I know you are there. I will always be there for you too.
Though you will not always be right by my side or a few miles
    away,
in a sense, you'll always be with me.
I've grown to love you too much to just let you slip away.
There's so much I've always wanted to say.
So before it's too late and there's not a thing we can do,
I want you to know that I'll always, always love you.
Melissa Gunter

Blossoms

Burdock blossoms
Bloom so soon, and
Stay so short
To heighten somnia's song.
Along with witch flowers
In night's flight.
Let them stay,
Their lavender color
Stay in your memory,
Stay in sight, they remain.

Pernicious peach blossoms
Bloomed yesterday
In their own way,
They got lost
In the torrents
Of a rainstorm.
Rainmakers,
Explain why you pour
In such indifference
And make so much beauty so easily.
Ann Rhodin

Abstractions

She says She has Dancers in her head—
In Mine—the orchestra,
Vibrating through reeds and chimes
Pulsates the Heartbeat of the drum—
Beating to life a tranquil form
An Apparition rises slow—
Thrusting through its Prisoned mist—
Raising arm above head in a Force of passion,
conjuring up lustrous visions
Compelled by Destiny to swing and motion—
Winding around stricken by Death,
Escaping, merely, by a Frantic leap,
Landing solid in a whimsical Triumph,
Hands over Head, again and again—
Spinning, revolving around through the mist—
Soaring above the theatrical gaze,
Floating, fluttering down to the Stage.
Ruth Ellen Schultz

The Honor Of Red

The patter of little feet
Silent on the dirt floor
Hunger stirred
As wood fire strains
To heat adobe walls
The hum of an ancient song
Sets cadence to grinding corn
Sun greets son out the wooden door
An offspring of an elder
Down the road, another day
In search of an honorable wage
Spent months ago in Shonto
On a truck that lacks life
And a bottle long cast aside
From a toast to the moment
An escape from the bleak truth
The honor of red is lost
Somewhere between white and blue
Frank W. Bender

The Expendable Man

Robot - like he listened
to Holy Scripture read,
then asked God's forgiveness
while kneeling with white head
bowed is silent agony -
confusion lay within
his burdened soul - heavy
with guilt of imagined sin...
and when his sweet, injured,
long constrained captive bird
no longer answered
a nearby wild song heard
he let life go - no friend
to weep....child-like creature
enshrouded in a blend
of haunting notes on wind -
rendered with tender love -
a three part eulogy sung
by his caged mourning dove.
Jeannette U. Carter

Mother And Wife

These words cannot really say
  My thoughts of you each and every day.
The thoughts that fill my soul and mind,
  They're in no book of any kind.

Memory calls in retrospect,
  Your care and love I'll not forget.
The constant vigil in lonely hours,
  To each you gave in this family of ours.

When sickness came from time of birth,
  You paced and rocked them by the heart.
Many prayers for each you said,
  And by your example they were led.

With all this, you are too a wife,
  Inspiring support in your husbands life.
You may never get the badge of honor,
  But the greatest tribute - a word, Mother.
Don M. Frankie

Calla Lily

Single Calla lily
you should be my mother's present.
Because Calla lily,
I am in full bloom just as you
and I am my mothers present.
Dear Calla lily,
I also have only one petal,
just as you Calla lily
because we have been made
independent by our mother.
And she is connected to us Calla lily.
She is our root.
Dear Calla lily,
look down at your stem.
Every inch of it is like
a year to me
and every year
she has nurtured and supported me.
Nicci Peterson

They

Cherish them, guide them, shower them with love,
"They" are indeed a blessing from above.
We are given them to love, guide and to hold,
Never should we stop our love for them, to be told.
We never know in this lifetime, when it will be,
The last time, these precious being we will see.
Often times, we seem too busy to stop and say,
Hey, you know we love you and have a safe day.
To give a hug, just to do it each day,
Will brighten both you and them, as you go your way.
Days begin safe and carefree, easy to do,
Then, it can change in a hurry for you.
Never take it for grant it, there will be another day,
Cherish every moment with them, I want to say.
Even when they are grown and out on their own,
Feelings of love, should always be shown.
"They" are our children, numbering one, two or more,
Always give them lots of love galore.
Ruth Winter

Quiet

Shhhh.....
Listen....
There's a bluejay calling for his mate.
The bees are humming along collecting
honey for the queen...she only gets the best!!!
Listen...
You can hear the drops of rain from the trees
after a fresh spring rain.
Take in a deep breath...smell the freshness the rain left.
Listen...
There's no noise but, Mother Nature all around.
she moves slowly so you must remain...
Quiet!!!
Michael J. Haskins

Crossing The Tub-Ulant Sea

Sixteen men set afloat
to cross the tub in a toy boat;
The water was rough like a tidal wave
because little Johnny wouldn't behave.

He kicked up a storm sending two overboard
and his mama cried out, "My Lord!"
I guess it was a prayer for those lost at sea,
but then she turned Johnny over her knee.

The storm quickly ended and the water was calm,
til Johnny sunk that boat with some kind of bomb;
He wanted back in the water to rescue those men
but his mama said, "no", and that was the end.
Ronald E. Blacklock

Be Proud

Be proud of all the little ones
Born into our world each day
Their job will be a tough one
Please help them not to stray
The future of our world is in their tiny fingers
Please shower them with love and pride
Those affections are what lingers.
Be proud.
Susan Chiucarello

Smiles

They can cheer you up when you're down,
they can make you laugh instead of frown,
a smile can go a long, long way
when one is having a really bad day.
They can say "Hi, how are you?"
And make you feel good, too.
A smile from a friend lets
you know how much they care
and reveals the friendship that is there.
When you see someone having a gray, dreary day,
just flash a smile to brighten their way.
Suzanne Pointer

Never Forgetting

Because of the tender nights there was comfort
  Of the joy inside the nights there was love
I remember you covering me with sweet kisses
  I remember enjoying all the stars there above

And if my heart was sad in the darkness
  You would remind me of the love that's true
You would open my eyes that I'd see better
  How beautiful as you put me close to you

Never forgetting the sweet words you told me
  I always keep them inside my heart very deep
The tender nights are forever and ever my love
  The sweet tender kisses that I forever will keep
Alberto S. Felan

Everlasting Love

Our love and friendship has endured,
the storm, the calm the sunshine
and the beauty of many a day
The rewards that come from two people
in love, are worth everything
Friendship that bind you, the tears that
unite you, the closeness that hold you your love
and the years, that cement for one another
No one can take away the memories,
No one can take away the love, though
words can never express the feelings you
have for each other
Deeds express them, day after day and
what you feel will never go away
Your life will always be togetherness and the
need to be close, will last a lifetime
Otto Harris

Living Our Lives

We have to live our lives our own way,
We have to make our choices day by day.
May our choices be good and not bad,
Because it is better to be happy and not sad.

We should always be considerate of others,
And above all consider others as our brothers.
I can only speak for myself and not for others,
But may each one of us show love for each other.
Floyd W. Danley

Laburnum

She calls my name, in the shade
Walking in summer breezes
She'll caress my cheek, before the sleep
Soft as butterfly sneezes
I hold her close, she takes my hand
Whispering to my feelings
Her hair is warm, life summer wine
Passion slowly yearning

Her lips on mine, she shares a laugh
Touching each other gently
Skin is smooth, I kiss her cheek
Casing down on her slowly
A secret moon is gleaming
She shuts the light, we slip away
Quietly be start dreaming

If she cries I'll drink the tears she pours
Shining candlelight beneath the door
I'll wait for her
Until we meet in the sun
Brian J. Raineri Jr.

The Dance Of Love

We danced last night
To the music that my heart played.
My hands cupped the tears of our joy.
The smile from God
Made the stars shine brighter,
So we embraced, and continue to dance
The joy of life.
And then we became three.
Robert Gino

Ode To Life

The beating of the heart
That brings life from the start,
The birds singing in the trees
The buzzing of the bees,
The sunset setting in the sky
The busy world passing us by,
The flowers in bloom
An old lady weaving on a loom,
A child suddenly being born
A farmer planting corn,
A family full of love
Floating like a dove,
The sound of a child's laughter
During, before, and after,
Like is these many things
Life is a mighty king!
Rose Buford

Sudden Insight

Little girls with pancake faces
Too short and small
Impostors and this high school class
But hearts large, swollen with compassion,.
At last I see
What we mean:
"Created in the image of God."
Ray Brown

Through These Doors

Come walk with me
  through these doors

Then walk with me
  Along side the Lord

This house has been built
  for all may enter

For here we are equal
  no one the center

For he is in all of us
  when we open up our hearts

Within our heart
  is where it all starts

Forgiveness, acceptance
  cheating and lies

Yet through all this
  he is still at our side

Give Thanks to the Lord
    Thomas J. Hubbard II

Verity

Shall we
peek in the closet
where the skeletons live
or keep the door locked tight
with bolts and chains
as they endlessly
scream obscene truths
we cover our children's ears
and pass on the legacy
Shall we
break the chains
unlatch the bolts
open the doors wide
and let them out
Shall we
set them free
embrace them
forgive them
and ourselves
Shall we
    Lisa Marie Ransdell

The Hawk

Keen eyes in high blue skies,
Seeking below its prey.
Streaking down, down, down,
Steel claws, sleek brown body,
Frantic cries, feathers falling.
Victory to the fittest!
Molting time, new growth,
Snowy white wings clipped,
Vegetarian diet, blurred vision,
Silently pacing, days pass.
Sterile cage, human gawkers,
Hawk and war diluted,
Dove and peace saluted.
    Bonnie J. Gullick

Happiness Is . . .

Happiness is contentment, joy, a warm feeling and many things
Watching your children at play and dandelions they bring you
With smiles on their faces and a large hug saying I love you mama
A mother dog with a new litter of puppies and the puppies at play
That new colt running free for all the world to see
A busy bee in your flower garden on a warm summer day
Sitting on the back steps with your loved one at the close of day
Feeling loved and blessed by all with the joy of each other
Not as much is going on now for we are older, our love is still felt
All the good memories of the past years of growing children
Now you watch grandchildren at play and they bring dandelions
With smiles on their faces and a large hug saying I love you
As we sit on the back steps at the close of day
We wait for that bee in our garden, for life goes on
Each day brings us more happiness than the day before
    Grace K. Novak

Homunculus

Those accusing blue eyes
With their blinding chill, burn right through me

Where were you?

My throat closes
My esophagus constricts,
Involuntarily

While arctic, over vigilant eyes
Flicker dimly
I feel the undertow
Of an inextinguishable fire
Spreading furiously—

Once innocent, now forever guilty,
As fierce flames and abusive names
Envelope me.

Large nomadic hands find direction again
As they impatiently wander over my body—
In the uproar of your malevolent presence,
Under your tender-
izing touch.
    Wendi Rubinowitz

Snow Fall

The first snowflakes fell outside today
Fluttering down like the finest of fleece
Remember the story you used to be told
Mother Carey is picking her geese
They covered the ground left stark and bare
For late fall was in the air
The landscape around was dark and gray
As if God had forgotten to care
Then this wonderful happenings changed everything
As the fleecy flakes fell through the air
In millions of intricate forms and shapes
Leaving beauty everywhere
    Mildred Rex-Snyder

Hot! Hot! Hot!

Global warming is now here,
Is this something we all should fear?

Who's to blame, among us all?
It's you and me, not our earth at all.

What can we do to repair our damage?
Our atmosphere has a hole we can't manage.

Is global warming what we all feared?
Well my friends...that day is here.

It's too late now just to say we're sorry,
We must repair our earth in a hurry.

Stop our rain forests, so dear from extinction,
Reduce fossil fuel to heal our environment.

Give back something, do not just ignore,
Do we want to our earth to burn to the core?

Wake up my friends, if you wish to exist,
Have a plan and make your mental list.

Leave something behind for you children and friends,
We've taken enough...do we have time to mend?

Sue M. Gleason

Untitled

Doctor do you hear the words you say
When you speak to me?
Do you tell me words of hope
Or
Sentences of doom?
Does my diagnosis frighten you
Or
Do you want it to frighten me?
It may be or may not be the time for me
Could we wait and see?
It just could be that the spirit in me has other plans for thee.
Doctor think when you say your words to me.
Before you blow out the last candle of hope.
For in each of us a spirit dwells more powerful than
You or I can see.
So, just before you speak make sure you always leave
Some ray of hope for you, as well as, me?
This hope will make
Our journey together grow in such a special way.

Please know, I'll know the time for me the spirit will
Tell me so.

Donna Foy Jones

Rain

Rain is God's sadness that he sheds upon the earth.
Tears that fall, from his holy eyes.
Sorry for making us; sinners.
For we give him such misery.

Gray clouds are his pain.
Thunder is his frustration.
For his words we twist.
Twist them to what we think is right.
Gave us so many chances.
But we laugh in disbelief.
So God continues to cry through the rain.

April Rutherford

Lullaby And Prayer

Sleep baby, close your eyes,
it is evening now. Close your eyes.
I will pray to God above
to watch over you through the night.
Then in the morning light,
God's love will come to life
in you.

Soon the moonlight and the stars
will shine down on you and from the sky.
Their light is like the love of God
which is always with you though 'tis dark.
So though the light of day
is fading away,
He is here.

The love of a child is a miracle
so innocent and pure,
so trusting and sure
of your love.

Lord, I pray that I might have
the heart of a child.

Denise Michelle Beckman

The Game You Played

You thought you'd play a game,
You stole this heart of mine.
Then when you won in fame,
You tried to be unkind.
I played along with you,
I thought you'd see it through.
Then because of a friend,
You made the whole thing end.

Hazel L. Shuck

Our Alley

Our alley is a special place
It echoes with friendly voices,
Small boys hitting rocks with sticks
While squirrels tease cats with noises.

Tall sturdy stalks of sunflowers
Bow their cheery yellow heads
Over the white picket fence
Of my neighbors garden beds

The neighbors take the time
To enjoy small chittery-chat
And often while out walking,
We're followed by Johnson's cat.

As we move on down the alley
We note not one, but two.
Oops! There comes another -
A parade of cats following you.

My neighbor friend and I
Often chuckle on our way.
We know our alley's special.
Even cats think it's O.K.

Rue Ceil Graves

As She Cries

Her tears grew heavier
As she tried, harder and
Harder not to cry, she
Cried in fright of the
Man who kept touching
Her and touching her
With his hands, the man
Was not black he was
Not white he thought he
Could get the mother
And the daughter in the
Bed tonight, all that
Time the girl was in
Fright wondering where
Was her mother when she
Needed her to night
She lies down on the bed
And cries wondering why.

Naomi Johnson II

Resurrection's Sound

Our lives are just a foretaste,
  or perhaps a vignette.
When all comes together
  twill be a grand symphony,
  and not a minuet.

The music of the air;
  the sound, of the colors of our soul.

A crescendo of multiplicity and beauty,
  as God makes us whole.

The wonder, we know at this time;
  is just a shadow of things yet to come.

Twill all be ours at the end,
  when life's race is won.

Carol M. Powell

I

I, a raw and bitter egg
I sit mad as life
I let honey peaches blow
I fiddle in the garden
I, a red woman
I chant gorgeous, frantic, delirious language
I eat the sky
I read bare water
I pause and let the moment smear
I whisper beneath his blow
I shall shine with a symphony's spring
I am lighter than the sun
I drive through our void yet over the stare
I crush and rob the woman who is not confident
I frantically boil purple music
I fall near the shore, after the rain
I plant and grow wild flowers
I need to rust away
  our love.

Sunni L. Sheets

Stitchin'

With every stitch I give my heart
And many finished projects I don't dare part.
They each become a part of me
The memories don't leave.
It's nice to see my handiwork on display
But it tears me apart when others are put away.

Amy Johannsen

The Split Rock Mob Twenty Years Later

"And it was decreed that in the vernal or autumnal equinox, this select group would lay their cares aside, forsaking affairs of the heart and commerce. They would journey two by two, leaving the tribes of Jersey and York—to assemble by the waters of Harmony."

Thus they came—the lame, the halt and the ailing
With protective clothes on arms and legs abinding
To renew the fires of youth with jests and smiles
Bearing good tidings of food and drink besides
For the worldly goods, they knew would be found alacking
The state of Penn alas we fear is quaking.

Once assembled, mirth and fun again prevailed
And Friendships glow and warmth assailed
Our minds and hearts were full and bursting
With the joy of those here and those missing
Then prepared we for the warlike games of morrow,
With clubs of gold and tennis we own or borrow.

Alas, the time ebbs and then does sink.
One more orgy of food and drink,
Hurriedly the cabins empty
The last farewells said swiftly
Into the caravans they climb
And two by two leave all behind.

Ralph Resnick

Theatre Memories

A quiet stillness silences the air,
The screen is empty, anticipation abides;
In the faded light, I contemplate and stare.
And I wonder, what secrets do theatre walls hide;

Who are the people that dare to try?
A glimpse of life, a different way;
I guess that it's only people like you and I
Trying to escape the world for a day;

The silence helps me to proudly recall,
My joys as a child, stirred by the screen;
I was small yet with adventure, I felt tall
And when the villains appeared, I felt mean;

Waiting with expectation of cartoons to come,
My heart would laugh or maybe cry;
But I always helped the victory to be won
Or either, I wished for rainbow skies;

So here I sit, just waiting for the fun,
I love the theatre for making me proud;
Of moments spend with rain and sun
With voices soft and voices loud.

Phyllis Presley Blythe

What's Happening To My Faith

I look at myself and ask;
Am I not worthy of my faith?

Do I have to be perfect to be
According to man considered
A child of the king.

Did God not say, come unto me
Just as I am?

Thou not perfect, I strive to
Learn of the past, holding
My head up high in search for a better future.

Faith has brought me through
The reality of the world, but
Yet I feel unworthy of the blessing
Which faith has bestowed upon me.

Is not my faith intangible which
Cannot be destroyed? Though
Man may examine my past and say oh the contrary.

Why must I, a member of the Kingdom
Which was inherited temporarily on
This earth wonder what is happening to my faith.

   Joyce Dennis

Dealing With Feelings

How can we control the way we feel?
It should not be a big deal
But it is something within us
Would be great to handle without such fuss!

Sure, it would be better if it is always good
Because then it would be understood
At the same token we should not get mad if it is bad
Although sometimes that would make us very sad

As long as we try to keep peace with each other
Then we can deal with the other
Getting along is more important to our inner selves
That way we can just be ourselves!

   Gloria St. John-Moore

Dare To Dream The Impossible

I once wanted to save the world,
  but no one would listen.

I wanted to become an actress,
  but it would've never happened.

I wished I could be the first woman president,
  but only in my dreams.

I hoped that I could be,
  someone special.

I am -
  I'm myself.

You can be,
  anyone you want to be.

Just dare -
  dare to dream the impossible.

   Amanda Farnsworth

Troubles Coming

They tell me no, they slap my hands.
They tell me potty is in their plans.
They pinch my cheeks, they say I'm sweet.
They say what quite little hands and feet.
They think I should do everything
they say, but for now that's okay.
They say they love my eyes of blue,
But my times coming, I'll soon be two.

   Joyce Kempf

Rush

My lover
Runs through the field with me
Tears at my overcoat
Pulls it over my bare shoulders
Reaches through my baggy sleeves
And kisses every prickled hair on my arms
I look to the post sun sky
The pure white clouds
Slip across the vivid dark blue
And blush as they eavesdrop
My lover pushes me
To run to the river pier
I face my love
With my hair whipping behind me
And my coat collar around my elbows
We dance together in sensuality
I am chilled
But I will not leave my love
The wind.

   Desiree Bethune

Mr. Policeman

Please Mr. Policeman
Spare me your silver band
The bullets are:

Poignant silent dead, man
(Innocence, is oblivious on this dark face)
I run scared
'Cause I know the history of my race

Please, Mr. Policeman
Spare me your silver band
For I know I'm an innocent man

I run through the bushes
For the life I soon not see
The dogs hound behind me — my blood will
Not quench their thirst you, see

Please Mr. Policeman
Spare me your silver band
And change your mind about our

Black man—
For "God" knows I'm an innocent man!

   Valerie V. Cooper-Williams

The Mind

Seeking to grow
To always know
Higher, faster . . .
Better than before
A path irrepressible
Ever searching for more
Boundless energy
Fueled by love
For every obstacle
It rises above
The impossible,
Chaos of the mind
Beseeching unity
Using logic to find,
The journey never ends
A direction always new
The voyage infinite
Discovering what is true.
            Michael Seibold

To You, With Love

A cool breeze surrounds you,
As you sit silent in a chair,
The moon light glows strong,
To form a silhouette so fair.

You make no movement,
As you feelings grow strong,
I kneel down beside you,
To hold you close all night long.

With emotions you speak,
Your thoughts are so clear,
I understand every reason,
and experience every tear.

Your pain breaks free,
As I'm there by your side,
I'll never let you go,
You have nothing to hide.

I hope you'll soon feel better,
Your pain is mine,
Through every experience,
And for all time.
            Dawn J. Plenert

Haiku In Trio Martyr

A swirling snowflake
Surrendered life lovingly
On a maiden's cheek.

Hiatus
Death is a hiatus
For each of us—'tween
Time and Eternity

Bliss
Truly: Happiness
Is finding joy in being
faithful to Jesus.
        Doris Tarver Paul

Nativity

Standing near the corridor's portal, awaiting the rite
    of passage,
The birth of the child behind, the longed-for second
    birth ahead.
Not employee, child or mother, your time has come for
    maturation.
Time to create the delicate, awesome secret of woman.

You will learn to love your breasts, your heels,
    your lace.
You will enrich the glory known by your sisters.
You will wait for night impatiently,
No longer content with the glare of day.

I can give you a fortune of revelations,
I know the wealth of all that might yet be.
I will host your public worship,
I will celebrate your natal triumph.

Enjoy the feast of words, sensations orgy,
The exaltation of thought, the celebration of love.
Life will show its face of magic,
The sun will never set in your heart.
            Jack Haight

The Poet's Hand

With the reaching of the poet's hand,
to take the sword, that is a pen,
our minds will race, our hearts may chill
for what the poet's hand will tell.

Some write of love, some of hate,
some of nature, some of fate.
Some write of things of another world,
or the banners of life, floating, unfurled.

The ebb and flow from the poet's pen,
will touch your heart, through the poet's hand,
it takes you to worlds of fantasy
and brings you back to reality.

The hand will move and tell of wars,
then give you peace through other doors.
Immortal words are chiseled then,
through poet's hand and poet's pen.

As etched in granite for all mankind,
(for God has touched the poet's mind),
eternally the words will stand,
even death won't silence the poet's hand.
            G. Thom Edwards

Summer Crickets

Summer crickets call in the dusk
    another blessed day, with the Lord's special touch
Two little blessings, under my feet
    wanting to know everything, and,
    'what's to eat?'
Laughter, a tease, and a tug
    who spilled juice on the rug?
Bath time is calling, to soap and shampoo
    Prayer and reading, now what do we do
Close your eyes, rest tonight secure in His love,
    your blessings held tight.
            Brenda Fowlkes

God's Gifts

We have so much, we two.
We have a roof of stars, a lamp of moon,
A bed of grass, a pillow of flowers.

When we thirst, the babbling brook provides our drink.
When we hunger, the orchard bears fruit, dripping with nectar.

When we want mystery, the bats and owls,
Will haunt the dark places.

When we are cold, the sun will shine.
When we are warm, the snow will fall,
Covering us with a blanket of whiteness.

And when we want each other,
We are together, answering the hungry impulses
That fire within us.

Oh this is Heaven, our Heaven.

These are things that can't be bought or sold,
Traded or given away.

These are the Creations of God.

And nothing is more precious.
DeeJay Piersel

The Beach

The feel of warm sand beneath my toes,
Soothes away my cares and woes.
Looking out over the vast ocean,
Fills me with deep emotion.

The emerald tides peak and swirl,
Leaving sea shells. Will one be a pearl?
Walking along the beach's uneven shore,
Hopeful, I search its white sands once more.

Seeing the waves ripple and crest,
Always brings out my very best,
I feel as if I'm on top of the world,
Just watching nature's beauty unfurl.

Hearing the rhythm of the wind against each wave,
I on the tranquil beach, long to stay,
Just to let my imagination play,
While chirping seagulls lazily soar away.

Darkness sweeps over the seas,
Palm trees blowing in the breeze,
But tomorrow, on the sunny beach I'll lay,
Admiring the colorful sunset of another day.
Coetta Sartin

Harvest Moon

The full moon rises, pale, yellow and large.
It sits atop the refining stack,
the fumes beautifully fade the moon into the sky.
The moon evaporates into darkness,
it is overshadowed by the city lights.
The lollipop moon sits at the end of my street.
It draw my insides out,
pulls my heart into my throat, kills me.
I want to run in its bright sunshine.
Its light is my sunshine and its setting is my end.
My chance to run is coming soon and I will run until the earth sets.
Juan Cummings

Don't Blink Twice

The leaves are moving
With such ease;
In the lightly
Blowing breeze.

The flower's sweet
Tantalizing smell;
Makes you want to
Jump and yell.

Revelling in
Nature's joy;
Whether you're a girl
Or a boy.

Nature just wants
To make you think;
For everything changes
When you blink.
Nora Groth

After A Storm

The natural beauty
never ceases to amaze me.

After a storm, the new clouds
paint a picture in the sky.

The golden rays from the sun
stretch like pure gold
from heaven to our earth.

The grass seems to have
turned emerald green.

The air smells so fresh
that you wish it would last.

Sometimes you see a rainbow.
If you are lucky,
you see a double rainbow
with its radiant colors.

It is a beautiful world we live in.
Alice Piotrowska

Shades Of A River

Bursting out of the dust
And west toward the setting sun
The brilliant waters flow away
Like a song from the heavens

I savor the sun-kissed ripples
Full of lost memories
And filled with promises

I am mesmerized by its lurking waves
And quiver with fear
As it whispers softly to me

I laugh to see the trees have farewell
And in all
Its beauty I behold
Whitney K. Cornelius

My Precious Daughter

I guess I must now face the fact
That Sharon was never really mine
God blessed me so bountifully
To loan her to me for even a short time.

She's been one in a million
Always loving, cheerful, caring, sweet
This has been portrayed throughout her life
By all she came to meet.

We all just love and need her so
I can't imagine God could need her more
I have to believe that it's best for her
And we can't even fathom the riches in store.

I really feel her looking down and smiling
And saying "Mother, this is so great!
I'll watch over you till you come
And I'll meet you at the gate".

Patsy Herriage

Reflections

Do not my thoughts
Of which you've read

Secure me like
The "silver thread"

That binds me to
The world I know

Seeming never
To let me go

But needing still
A change of fate

To lead me through
A "golden gate"

Out of the dark
Into the light

So I may know
The wrong from right

Roger Jones

God's Forever Love

Friends will come and go
Sad inner feelings make me low.
Needing a special someone,
God's forever love will come.

So much I need to say.
Please God listen to me pray.
Comfort my empty heart.
Let us never drift apart.

Deep emptiness I feel.
Will any of my dreams be real?
Fighting hard to fulfill my life,
God give me faith and end my strife.

Katherine J. Chapman

Two Songs To Starting All Over

Can I gain true love without pain?
Could it rain without the clouds?
Would the brilliant twinkle of the
Stars be manifest without the
Dreary gloom of the night?
In my search for true bliss,
A miss now and then is human.
It is fine to be remiss,
after each miss.

Ready am I,
To trudge on.
Though my enthusiasm may wane,
with a pessimism that now runs deep,
having learnt to unbend a previously
unbending jocundity; I promise not to weep.
I realize I must pass through a thicket of lies
In my search for the true light, and get used to true lies.
In spite of the emotional stings, I shall not despair
or fold my wings, though my heart needs repair;
because starting all over happens to be such bitter sweetness.

Chike M. Nzerue

'Tis Midnight On Main

'Tis midnight on Main, only night owls are abroad
Traffic has slowed, dancers, music cease to applaud
A bleary eyed wastrel staggers from post to post
In the distance, sirens wail. This is the time I love
Whizzing by, lights flashing after a car comes by
Taxis take revelers home, now the bar has closed.

It's past midnight on Main, here I stand
Where chance has my meanderings landed me
A streetwalker smiles, trying to catch her a man
This unfortunately lands her in a police van
A drunk staggers by, I find that I still see
The lights from the bar that just broke me
'Tis midnight on Main, here I stand in vain
Why am I here still, after midnight on Main?

Howard A. Deaton

My Silver Bullet

I do not know what is in store
I do not know what I will endure

The silver bullet has my dates
I do not know what is my fate

As it passes thru time on earth
All I know what day is my birth

In this time will I create evil or good
And will I control the path if I could

Will I create beyond my wildest dreams
Or will I create God awful schemes

Will I destroy all earth's natural beauty
Or will I give birth to ideas as it will be my duty

Only when my silver bullet has flight no more
And my last breath and death is at my door

Only than I will know finally what life was for
And will I be loved, forgotten, or hated for evermore

Eugene Rooney

Triumphant Recognition

I stood above the world one day
And gazing down upon that silver globe, my home
Questioned my poor self again...
What is it that holds me prisoner my God from thee
What splendor have I lost; what glory
That my very essence seeks beyond the confines of this life
Craves a sweet reunion?

My soul casts back to dreams prenatal and there remembers dim
A fall thru staccato star swept vastness of forgotten space
Faces there the memory of a memory - your face!
"Patience", said a voice from deep within me
"The things you fret about are but the mooring chains
To life, to daily duty, and will be slipped as such
When comes the time' have patience now for yet a little while
The night is nearly over, the new dawning".

The light of love that flowed into my eager soul
Has in some strange mysterious fashion
Permeated barriers of time and dimension
For now I realize what I have always known
God is love and love is one, yesterday, today, forever and forever.

Blossom Blake Hammond

Through The Eyes Of An Eagle

I see through the eyes of an eagle
The wide open space of the prairie
The wind drift o'er the wings of an eagle
Home food to her babies she does carry
And then her strong body plummets to the ground
Shot by a sportsman's gun
The supply abounds
But it is soon rung
A sport many think as a thrill
Has take its toll on our world
With the collapse of us I feel a chill
Many bodies to the ground have swirled
With taking the lives of others
We have taken ours as well

Talia Dispensa

Endlessly

How long will my heart be filled with love just for you?
   "endlessly"
How long will my thoughts be centered on you?
   "eternally"
How many times will I see you in my dreams?
   "as long as there are tiny waves rippling on the seas"
how many times when I kiss you will I sigh?
   "as many times as there are stars in the night time sky"
how many times will kiss those eyes that sparkle like two jewels?
   "as many times as the red rose blooms in the month of June"
How many times will I say I love you?
   "can you count the many leaves on the trees?"
well!... that's how many times I will say I love you,
   "endlessly" "endlessly" "endlessly".

Eileen Schlaefer

Sara

The child, seeking who she is,
looking at others, emulating friends
when in reality, who she is, is who she was,
the little girl in her mom, is the person she
is, and is the woman she will become.

Donna Reihl

Piece Of Art

Grasping at straws of words:
Letters arranged for creation
Of newness in every work born;
The sweet wine of a concept
yeasts in the waiting of perfection.

Soothing the pebble of a poem,
a hand of the mind moulds
and chafes the rough word
until an artist mind nods in
satisfaction looking at the product.

Neatly, it is put on blankness
with no lines or crinkles and cuts;
Stored and looked at sometimes,
brings back a memory of that
bug that brought on a piece of art...

Mickey-Shaun Van Tonder

Untitled

She lies like a sun maiden,
still, basking in her own
peace and glory,
the warm sun's light
settling slowly
on her weathered face.
She remembers passing storms
and the ruins that were left.
Then for a moment she forgets,
in silence, scintillated.

Raquel Camelo

Surrealism Unleashed

Surrealism set free
Wild images and visions unleashed
Dancing in my mind's inner eye
Reality shatters like a broken mirror
Distorted, splintered reflections
Fragmented shards in slow motion fall.

Surrealism in action
Fevered, tortured dreams
Strange, unearthly landscapes
Alien worlds shimmer and form
Incandescent colours stun and blind
Exploding fireworks dazzling my mind.

Surrealism unbound
Flickering/strobing/twisting images
Strange sights/odours/sounds
All of them meet and rebound
While I am engulfed by pounding waves
Swept away on a surrealistic tide.

Steve Nottingham

Figure Eight

Maybe you were smiling
but I think I lost the freight
of memory's persistence
in a powdered figure eight
the band was playing softly
as we spoke against the light
and wished that you had chosen
an ordinary plight
so as you stood corrected
the instruments gave way
to sorrows long forgotten
now sadly back to stay
you wanted to be lonely
so I slipped beneath your chair
regrets in silver spoonfuls
and headed for the stairs
I went and left the shadows
to battle with the light
and while neon dimly truck you
I strode into the night
   Thomas Fisher Jr.

The Airport

As I sit here in the airport
And watch the people going by,
I wonder where they are going
When they go high up in the sky.

I look into their faces
Some are happy, some are sad,
Are they traveling for business or pleasure
Or are they going to visit Mom or Dad?

Some people are very friendly
They greet you with a smile,
They settle into their seat
They'll be traveling many a mile.

The bags they carry
Are large and small,
They have their clothes and camera
And gifts for one and all.

So when you're in the airport
Take time to look and see,
The faces of those around
One of them might be me!
   Martha D. O'Brien

Table Prayers

In deep thought
we thank thee
oh Lord
for providing us
with the nourishment
of life
we are grateful
for your love
that guides us in health
on our short journey
please give us strength
so we can faithfully
live by the laws
of your commandments
   Fred Neubacher

Procrastination

'Tis the day after Christmas and all through the house
Both cats are still stirring and I feel like a louse.
My Christmas cards sat on my desk all pre season
but write them I didn't for no rhyme nor reason.
So here are my wishes, a little bit late,
Hope your Christmas was merry, and the New Year first rate.
   Margaret Fulton

In My Mind's Eye

Looking at life through a child's eyes
So innocent, yet complex
Not understanding what they see
Yet knowing more than the next

Asking funny little questions
With the purest intentions in their heart
Wondering why we smile and giggle
Turning away dreading the day when we shall part

When they get caught, doing things
They think they do in fun
My heart and arms cry out for them
To hold them, yet to scold them, for what they have done

Yearning for their smiles,
Not wanting them to ever fear
Wanting to protect them
Forever keeping them near

I dread the day when they are ready
To go and try life out on their own
I will dread the day when my little ones
Have decided that they are grown
   Donna Jill Donaldson

Sands Mill

As a boy I'd fish at the old mill pond,
catch a pickerel now and then,
watched the hawks as they circled high,
heard the red wing's song and cries.

Those lazy summer day's I'd find,
twas hard to watch my dubber line.
My eyes would close and dream would I
about the mill and days gone by.

The sound of horses hoofs I'd hear
as they cross the old stone bridge that's near.
Twas militia men with captured spy,
they brig'd him in a born near by.

Could hear quite clear a horse's nay,
a smithy shop not far away.
Then ripping noise of a saw mill blade
as it saws the wood for the coming day.

A bawling cow from a distant farm
whose hungry calf has left the barn.
Around the bend a surrey rides,
a church bell rings as the horse breaks stride.

As I awoke from this boyhood dream,
then looked around at the changing scene,
I asked, Dear God, let me dream again,
about sands Mill as it was back them.
   Walter Ray Bell

My Magical Wooden Soldier

The night my wooden soldier came to life; it was so magical
I will never forget it for the rest of my life. I went to turn
off my light when all of a sudden I heard, "please do say
good-night!" I was feeling an overwhelming fright until
I saw my wooden soldier coming towards my light: He stood totally
still and looked so sad. I didn't dare move off my chair.
We laughed and talked for what seemed like the longest while.
He had been mine since I was a small child. He proudly
marched around my room and to my surprise he even had
a twinkle in his eyes, my wooden soldier was so very happy
now for somehow he knew I now believed he came to life just
for me. When we said good-night he proudly went back to
his place and it was as if he was a very special guest that
now went back to rest. So now when I close my light at night
my magical wooden soldier always winks good night. I know
for sure he is watching me and I will sleep with the greatest
of delight. To me, this will always be, what I believe,
was an extraordinary magical night. So for sure, for
evermore I will sleep ever so tight. Good-night!!
Esther Kogan

Mom's Special Day

What is a mother?
We often wonder just that.
They are the ones who are always there,
especially when needed and at the drop of a hat.
They are the ones we always turn to,
when the times are hard and tough.
Whether we are in our happy times,
or in our saddest moment.
They are there to help us find our way,
when we are all lost and alone.
Their love is unmatched and highly underrated,
and at times they have a heart of stone.
We can't ever give back to them,
what they have so freely given to us.
So we give them this special day,
as only a small token of our love.
So take this day into your heart,
and remember our love for all you do.
This is your special day and I only wish,
I could make it as special as you.

Happy Mother's Day
James D. Gossett

God Is Everywhere

God is everywhere!
In the blue of the sky,
In the sound of the babbling brook,
In the beauty of the bluejay,
In the perfume of the rose,
In the colors of the rainbow,
In the rustling of the leaves by a gentle breeze,
In the scent of a clover field,
In the rugged oak as it battles the wintery storms,
In the glistening snow that covers the countryside,
In the church spire that points to heaven,
In the smile of a little child as it takes its first step,
In the face of a mother as she holds her child close to her breast,
In the bark of a dog,
In the mew of a kitten,
In the beauty of the sunset when the curtain goes down on the day,
Oh, yes, God is every, but we must look and listen.
Helen Louise Busch-Gutzler

January 8th A New King Is Born

Sixty-two years ago
On this very day
A new born baby boy cries
While in his mother's arms he lay
Who could have known
The success he would achieve
Touching so many people
Fans like you and me
He started off unknown
But he gave his heart and soul
And he really earned the title
The king of rock 'n' roll
So happy birthday Elvis
Where ever you may be
You'll always be the king
From now to eternity.
Dianne Marie Smith

Nature's Song

Oft on a summer evening,
 In prairie settings rich with green,
Have I sat in blissful silence,
 Listening to Nature's song serene.

Trees bow gently, whisper softly,
 Telling stories heard before,
Heard by bold adventures like Kelsey
 When these plains were first explored.

Heard also by pioneer settlers,
 In romantic days of old.
Though the years have altered settings,
 Nature's story unchanged is told.

Though pioneer campsites may now be cities,
 And life's tempo altered pace,
Still for those who stop to listen,
 Nature's song offers solace.
Hillmen M. Holm

New Year's Day

The sun came out on New Year's Day
As the sounds, of revelry, died away.
And so, begins another year.
Yesterday's gone, to-day is here.
Our hearts now, are full of hope,
But if sorrow comes, will we cope?,
So many things we do not plan,
I guess we'll do, the best we can.
But days of joy, we'll feel the pain,
Both came last year, we still came through,
And we will live through this year too.
Into each life, there must be rain,
And then the sun will shine again.
For love will always guide our way,
The love, we feel this New Year's day.
Viola Castley

I Think Of You

As the twilight shades descend,
  Escorting daylight from view,
Sketched in the golden sunset
  Beams smiling features of you.

Tranquil calls from meadow larks,
  Rhythm from the trickling streams,
And music when quiet an soft,
  Sound your voice like echoed screams

Deafening stillness of the night,
  calmness after storms at sea,
And the void in lonely hours,
  Decry you're going from me.

Once I was a toddling babe;
  That childhood I have never missed
Those times I have never missed
  But, oh! How I pine for you.
    Rufus W. Johnson

Jacob's Ladder

Alone he climbed each step up sure,
With fear unknown and courage pure.
Behind were those who would dissent
And with restraint prevent ascent.
These he loved, and they loved him.
Still he sought a love above him.

Ever upward without rest,
Ever equal to the test,
A solemn knowledge urged his pace;
A knowing smile pursed his face.
Night or day, he gave no care.
Above! Ahead! True love was there.

And when at last he'd reached the crest,
Heart beating faster in his breast,
His beauty shone from foot to head.
And could he have he would have said,
"Look mom I've climbed the stairs alone."
Jake, you see, was six months old.
    James Perry Rhoades

An Artist's Eye

If you could see the world
Through an artist's eye,
You would see a picture
That would make you sigh.

Are those Angels or Clouds
Dancing in the sky?
Are those her wings
Spread out to fly?

The beauty of this world
Is magnified so,
You see God's beauty
Wherever you go.

Stop! See this world
Through an artists eye,
And let its beauty
Make you cry.
    Sandra Fleming

Winter Wonderland

Frosted crystal of white floating softly like feathers
Carefree children create heavenly angels upon the ground
Fresh blankets of white surround us all around
Snowballs whiz past innocent pedestrians passing by
Mitts, scarves, and hats are dub out for another season
One by one snowmen stand stout with coal black eyes, carrot
Noses, and top hats so grand
Freshly shoveled sidewalks disappear under newly fallen snow
Rosy red cheeks are seen under bundles of winter joy
Plans are made to ski, skate, and sled while cider and chocolate
Warm our insides
A polar bear's paradise and an Eskimo's sunrise
The clouds dance between the falling flakes and the sun tries to
Sneak through without success
The window fogs over as I sigh my fist breath of winter
    Tammie Boone

I Wish

My wind draws a blank as I sit here and stare.
The weeping is done — my heart is too numb.
Playing dungeons and dragons is all over now -
  for the dragon is gone and the dungeon is bare.
Piece by piece he tore me apart.
But when the end came - for we all knew - there
  seemed to be no more to despair.
Few coolness dripped from my face - my steel
  heart barely felt a trace.
And yet when all the piece fell to place
  there was nothing left but cold regrace.
Numbness came to cover the pain - but there
  was not much, there was nothing to gain.
    Kara Genoway

Mind Swept

Over and over; hypothetical dreams
Too real to dispute; never what it seems
In younger days, sleep became a slumber
Now weighted down with life; ever awake with wonder
What if? What now? What might have been?
Visions beyond the moment; sought but never gained
Wonder of what? Mind swept over me
If this is what I'm thinking; then it must be
The evening wanes; time to surmise
Fate made my own; dreading the moon rise
Innocent intensity notwithstanding
A crossover to reality beneath a bridge of understanding
Eventually overcome is the light of the night
Thoughts laid to rest but not without a fight
Instant awareness from a self awakening
Enter today, exit our motionless thinking
Focus on the time, breathe as the day before
Shadow of mine remains; the sun lays down once more
    Dave Parkins

Accountability

Silence
They move through the mountains...
Spirits of forgotten lands.
Can you feel the sound in the screams?
In the weeping children?
The souls do speak!
If you listen.
Our destruction of the native man
Was it any different than Nazi rule back when?
Was it any different than atomic power on Japan?
Silence
They move through the mountains...
Spirits of forgotten lands.
Can you feel the sound in the screams?
In the weeping children?
History does speak!
If you listen.

Jeffery L. Boss

More Than Words

Every single syllable of your voice,
holding me captive by choice,
each enticing word said,
lingering throughout my head,
entrancing me every time you speak,
my senses growing weary and weak,
except for your voice, my physical being un alert,
my body an empty vessel, lacking the power to exert.

The depth of your eyes does my soul amaze,
deeper I fall with every gaze,
Your eyes as blue as the sea,
Softly surrounding and swallowing me,
your beckoning baby blues giving a look untold,
imprisoning me with your intense lasting hold.

Your demeanor unlike anyone I've ever met,
indescribable, being why I cannot forget,
your smile complementing your perfectly handsome face,
when you move, it is the epitome of style and grace.

More than words can imply,
I am falling—there is no question why.

Misty Benedict

A Place Of Anticipated Happiness

He is just a common man, living in a promised land.
Trying to find a way to end the false promises,
in which the Government failed to keep.
He seems to think his keepers are asleep.

He is just a common man, living in a promised land.
Who is asking for a helping hand, from someone who
understands how to free him of the disappointments
spread across the land.
He is just a common man, living in a promised land.
Who is watching as his keepers, the Government
systematically comes tumbling down.
And often, he wonder when would the new ruler will
come around, to help make plans on keeping the
promised land on solid ground.
He is just a common man, living in a promised land.

Crystal Richards

Tony

Through the eyes of a baby
    a tall strong man
Through the eyes of a little girl
    a gentle man and idol
Through the eyes of a lady
    a man you could love forever
Through the eyes of a woman
    never another Daddy like Tony

Brenda M. Rivet

For Laura

Words unborn you speak to me
A gentle look my heart to move
The light of hope my soul to free
And I, once more, to dream of love

Your fleeting smile my heart to fill
A fragile trust within your eyes
And yet my heart is hungry still
While laughter oft my pain belies

Reach out for dreams and passions bold
Look beyond that I have seen
The visions bright and songs untold
I yearn for what I might have been

Fast asleep you hold my hand
A gift of glory, hope and pride
One day perhaps to understand
For you I lived, for you I cried

Sleep, my child, for I am near
A dreamful sigh my heart to move
And words unborn my soul to hear
You are my life; you are my love

Debra Polirer

God's Its Name!

When God demands
In all His Glory
That the world we know
Be set free,

No master mind
Among earthlings here
Can alter this course
Nor stop it.

The vast expanse—
The countless masses,
And all their orbits—
He controls.

In the beginning
A mighty Power
Ruled the Turbulence
That was Then.

That Force still reigns
In the realm of Time.
Call it what you may
God's Its name!

Elizabeth M. Bumgarner

Salvation By Light

Lightless for eternity.
Night evolves completely.
Trepidation and dread abound.
There is no hope to be found.
There is no such thing as sight.
In ardent and absolute night.
Suddenly, out of the nullness
Extends a light of such fullness.
Chases away all your fright.
Rescues you. This intense light
is an undescribable bright.
Encircled entirely with black
This brilliance holds shadow back.
Darkness is never the same
When interrupted by the flame
Of a candle.
Kimberly Duncan

Twilight Still

There is a time before the darkness
but it is after the days bright, when
my soul stands still.
Twilight still.

The sun, she lays down her head
still glowing through her blankets
upon the western sky. She is still
before she dreams in the shadows.
Twilight still.

The sleeping hours of the day have
been lived and have gone, they
lie still in my memory song
Twilight still

The night clouds they come,
in silent silver gown, and the
meadowlark is quiet below. I watch
as the moon races the silence over
the hill, it is now that my soul
knows it is twilight still,
twilight still—twilight still.
Kingsley Hill

Angels In Our Midst

Consider
The sweet privilege
 of knowing an angel.
 A child.
How pure, how mild.
 A smile
As bright as a starry night.
 A laugh
So sweet, it tickles your soul.
 A love,
More sure, more true
Than a shaft of light
 in a glade of trees.
 Children,
Angels in our midst.
Monica S. Palacios

Trauma At Preschool

"Ok kids it's time to go." Mel looks at me and she says, "No"
"Honey don't you want to do? "I say, "Everything will be ok"
She looks at me with great big eyes
They fill with tears and then she cries
"But Grandma," she says," I want to stay
Please don't make me go today!"
"Why not Mel? Will you please tell me?"
"Grandma, I don't want to be with Mr. Lee."
"Are you ever alone with him?", I said
She looked at me and nodded her head.
"He takes me to school in a great big van."
"Oh no!". I think, "She's alone with a man.
Isn't he always nice to you?
Does he do something you don't want him to ?"
"Yes, she says, "He does it every day.
Please, please grandma let me stay!!"
"Oh no" I think, "this can not be. I've always trusted Mr. Lee."
I look down at my little Mel, "Tell Grandma Honey, you can tell."
My mind is full. Oh such terrible things
"Oh Grandma," she says, every day, he sings!!"
Nancy Oren Kell

Afraid Of The Dark

Be not afraid of the dark. Darkness is with in. We must pass
through the tunnel of darkness to reach the light. Close your
eyes, see the darkness. Even in the light of day, darkness
exist. Afraid of the dark? Be not afraid of yourself, for
the darkness is with in. Through the tunnel of darkness there
lies in light.

"You"
Gloria A. Cooper

Just Like Me

A man at war, with someone like himself.
Fighting blindfolded, with his feelings on a shelf.

He fires his gun, through the air the bullets hiss.
His target he fired at, not a complete miss.

Down to the ground, the figure before him fell.
Smoke and fire surrounding them, men creating their own hell.

His gun still trembling, he watched the man before him cry.
As death began forming, in this strangers deep blue eyes.

He fell to his knees, and grabbed the strangers hand.
It now all seemed so wrong, human lives lost over land.

"What can I do for you", as I begged him to hang on.
"Please tell my wife I love her, and coming here was wrong".

The two of them in that moment, learned what it was to live.
Friends from now on, the enemy in each other they would forgive.

Hanging on to him, as he hung on to his life.
Blood draining from his heart, like it had been sliced with a knife.

The comfort of a friends touch, let him peacefully pass away.
Now alone one man stands, seeing life in a different way.

He was taught he was evil, but he found he shared his eyes.
He fought him as his enemy, but a friend he died.
Dawn Knotts

Eternal Mother

Radiate
the earth,
my night-covered daughter
Don't try to change or fade away.
Stand in the rain
of your ancestors and grow
Become the green you are, for it's from queens you came.

Ignore the ignorant and what they cry
Their words have new meaning in our language today
Now, happy means beautiful and Fat means fine
Full lips help develop and express your mind
The allow you to
give encouragement to the young, gain wisdom from the old
and speak volumes to all races from deep within your soul.

On the winds of my prayers you can always fly
Just remember, stand tall and hold your head high
Look at God guidance, don't put your trust in man
Take it from your mother
A eternal friend.
Adrienne Denise Turner

Screams Against The Wind

I remember the snow covered slopes of Burney Mountain
    glowing beneath a full December Moon.
I can still see the shadows clinging to the trees
    and feel the emptiness within the gloom.

No eyes stared from within the darkness then
    No tormented spirit beckoned me.
As I searched for the future on the icy sky
    and saw only the threshold of eternity.

Silently the hearse descended-
    Near the edge of that mountainous shore.
And for a moment our destinies clashed like thunder
    atop Hatchet Mountain with a terrible roar.

Sorrowfully I sang your death song-
    My screams hopeless against the wind.
From the ancient stump I removed the Tomahawk
    and chased the Rock Thrower from within.

Now sadness like an Eagle soars-
    casting shadows on Hat Creek and beyond.
To the Deer Killing Country of your Grandfathers
    Where memories like eternity, go on and on.
David A. Carrick

A Mother

A mother is a treasure God gave to every man,
With love that none can measure, and worth that none can scan.
In sacrifice unmeasured, in patience unexcelled,
In wisdom yet unfathomed, her highest worth is held.
A mother is a person whose love will see you through
Long days of toil and trial, and nights of darkness too.
Her love is like none other the world has ever known;
When other's work is finished, her work is never done,
Though through the lonely hours she toils till set of sun.
She's always there to listen; she's always there to cheer,
When problems come upon us that others will not hear.
Though there be many copies of every other thing,
We only have one mother; therefore her praise we sing!
Today the world is waiting to see what God can do
Through dedicated mothers; O, can He count on you?
Suzanne Jewers

Lost Innocence

And where has it all
    gotten us

We have created a hell
For our children
A hell from fear

To learn the truth

To learn and be
Everything around you

Somewhere along the relentless
    push
We have lost the golden age
    of childhood
Of dreams
    Lost the awareness of life's mystery

We have forgotten the beauty
From which we came

They said progress would improve our life
But they haven't bettered our world
They only created the nightmare
We live
Rudun R. Immel

Too Many Memories

Chopsticks in hand, staring blankly
at the frozen aqua vinyl
waves of adjacent booths.
Picking mindlessly at fried rice
noodles and vegetables,
probing the deepest recesses
of cauliflower, from which come
images dark and distressing,
brought to life by the
mind that recalls them.

Looking around I see no one,
the lunch buffet slipped into the past
along with my thoughts.
But I'm still picking at
cold memories with chopsticks.
Forcing the cookie open when I read:
    It is better to give one smile
    for the living, than fountains
    of tears for the dead.

Check.
Brian Jones

Untitled

I used to be able to look in people's
eyes and see only beauty
No faults
No anger
There didn't exist hate
And there was no pain
I miss that

I miss doing the things I used to
I no longer feel the way I felt
In a sense carefree
With no worries, no tears
A time I was loved
A time I was happy
Dawn Durbin

Human Spirit

Why are you still crying?
Your pain is now through.
Please forget those teardrops,
Let me take them from you
The love that you are blessed with
The world's waiting for.
So let out your heart please, please
From behind that locked door.
It's time we start smiling.
What else should we do.
With only this short time,
I'm gonna be here with you
and the tales you have taught me,
From the things that you saw,
Makes me want out your heart, please
From behind that locked door.
And if my love goes
If I'm Rich or I'm poor,
Come and let out my heart, please, please
From behind that locked door.
Dennis Hearen

Bound

Boxed daylight seeps
through minute cracks
in the old wood
Upon hearing voices
there is a new surge
of energy brought forth
And panic builds
The walls confining
appear red with
little room to maneuver
Its dark boundaries
unseen
measured solitude is felt
And panic builds
The wood box speaks
it groans with pressure
its captive still inside
The imagination teasing
on the edge, on the verge
of Nirvana
Christine Ward

When You Are Gone

What will I be
When you are gone,
Unable to hum
Or sing a song.

How can I be
Inspired to sing
When you are the wind
Beneath my wings.

I will be only a shell
When you depart
Because when you're gone
You'll have taken my heart.

I cannot visualize
How life can be
When you are gone
I'll only be me.
Marie D. Brissette

Halloween

Halloween is upon us, once again, my dear.
Tell me, what are you going to be his year?
You're much to old to talk down the street;
knock on doors and say "Trick or Treat".

But you can dress up as a witch or a ghost.
To answer the door; to be the host
for all the children dressed-up on this night,
Who come in costumes to give you a fright.

They come as Spacemen, Pirates and such,
to collect goodies from a "soft touch".
You know the voices. You've heard them before,
They giggle and laugh, as they come to the door.

When you open the door, they make such a sight
that you smile to yourself in secret delight.
Trick or treat. Which will it be
A treat for them or a trick on me?

You had out a treat. Drop on in each sack.
You hear a faint "Thank you", as each turn their back.
As they step off the porch and out of the light,
you wish them all a happy Halloween night!
Lois Bryant

Rain

Rain was falling that afternoon, caressing my skin, easing my
pain. Mother Nature herself was by my side whispering softly
through a warm breeze into my ears saying "you are not alone, you
will never be alone..." I remember that day well though the
meaning is no longer there, for my pain is strong. That night
seems so long ago.
I have forgotten why I am alive. I have forgotten why I want to
live. I have forgotten why I want to love.
She, the one I love is by my side always, but the feelings seem
to have changed. She, herself is the same. It is what is inside
of me that has changed.
I look now onto the world with different eyes. Everything seems
different from what once was. The world has taken on a new looks
familiar yet strange as though I have never been here before but
have lived here for many, many years.
As the rain slowly fades a rainbow appears filling the dark grey
skies with brilliant colors.
I know now my place in this world, beyond the rainbow and forever
in my dreams.
Kurt Hilborn

The Mystery Of Life

When the light from your sun is obscured by a cloud
And life seems so darkened and cold,
All those dreams you have dreamed,
Are not part of life's schemes,
And you feel you are missing the goal!

So what do you do, if this happens to you?
Don't fret long!
There's so much to be done!
Just glance overhead. You will find that instead.
Not that dark cloud—but—a bright ray of sun!

All that darkness has passed and the sun shines at last!
How it warms this old earth with its beams!
God has it all planned, but you must grasp His hand!
God's plans are far better than you could ever dream
Virginia Morton Ross

Where We Are

She turns to me with twinkling eyes and says hear me out, before
you reply. With interest aroused, the feeling content, I absorb
her words and revel the moment.

    My dreams and desires have finally came true, the night
that I became one with you. You make me feel like a woman
should, the way you take me, feels so damn good. When
you're inside me, I feel so fulfilled, that's when I wish,
time would stand still. The love I have for you, continues
to grow, I want you always, this you must know.

Responding with a smile, and a deep sigh, the following words
are my reply.

    As your love grows, so does mine, getting ever stronger,
with the passing of time. As we coupled, the feelings
intense, so much for our tortured suspense. So tightly
held, in more ways than one, appreciated by me, unknown
to some. We will proceed forward at a break-neck speed,
wanting always, to fulfill our needs. How easy it is,
to express to each, these feelings we thought, were beyond
our reach. To each, these feelings are like a dream come
true, no time spent better, than time spent with you.

Carl Keesler

Jake

The most memorable meaningful life experience
A day of pain and agony, then a natal emergence

The first look, A Boy! Great! Now take him away.
I'm tired, no, in my room he will not stay.
I will have him for the rest of my life
One day of absence, exchanged for parental strife
What I do I do, what about mother's intuition?
After a week of motherhood would my instinct come to fruition!

I survived, I read Dr. Spock! What a fiasco—what a shock!
Throughout the years of growing up,
I learned I read everything, never getting enough
He is now 10 years old, a product of a perfect mold
Independent, obstinate, growing so fast
I wonder how long his childhood will last

I love him more than life itself
His existence has given me unconditional wealth
He is compassionate, caring and warm.
I pray to God that he will never come to harm
I look forward to the time when he was matured
An adult, as a child loved nurtured and adored.

Deborah Patora

You And I Are Meant To Be

Imagining life without you is more than I can stand,
It hurts to think of you with someone else or holding
  another's hand.
To never again feel you body close to me, to never again
  feel your lips pressed against mine,
To never again hear your voice telling me that you'll love
  me until the end of time.
I never want to be without you, I never want for us to be apart,
For there is no one else in the world who can take your
  place in my heart.
You have become a part of me and I a part of you,
You and I are one and I hope that you can see it too.
And despite what other eyes can see,
I believe that you and I are meant to be.

Brenda L. Bolster

Ashes Of Passion Help Flowers To Grow

We were together,
until death did us part.
Our love was slowly dying,
everytime you broke my heart.

The tears that I cried,
were my souls desperate pleas.
Your final rejection,
brought me to my knees.

It seems that by accident,
or by design.
you were too often cruel,
to this fool heart of mine.

So I walk into the twilight,
to face the night alone.
The kind of love you offer,
would turn my heart to stone.

I wish you all the best,
I hope life treats you well.
As for me I'll plant a garden,
on this place where I once fell.

Ismael P. Hernandez

Jesus Is The Heart

Each precious moment
  seen through the teardrops of Morn's Dew.
Children discovering the world anew.
Touching with fragile sensitivity
  the joys of serene beauty.
Golden Moments
  blossoming like sunflowers
    in shining faces.
The angel wings of butterflies
  gentle in their souls.
Showering the glitter
  of soft rainbows.
Children tenderly cuddle teddy bears.
Gentle . . .
  like the lion lying down by the lamb.
Children
  softly walking . . .
delicately lacing reflections of love
  with Innocence.
The Soul of the Bible.

Michelle J. Murphy

Lost In A Moment

In a brief moment we touched
The softness of your skin
And the warmth of your body
Made me feel something that I had lost
Our lips touch as I pressed closer
I knew soon we would be in perfect rhythm
Moving together as one
Our bodies moist as our passions flared
Just in a brief moment in my mind

Richard G. Altmann Jr.

To Be Flushed

When the world,
Grows cold,
And the sun,
Burns your brow,
Your heart and soul,
Melt into liquid,
That fills the cup,
Of all that are corrupt.
You become devoured,
By the beast,
We call humanity,
Digested by the government,
You've sworn to protect,
Just to be flushed,
By a member of your family.

Michael R. Cousineau

The Key To Me

Just the thought of it hurts
when the thought is letting you in.

I give you the key and
you're free to roam.

You may not respects me and
you may not cherish your findings.

You may find laughter
in a place that's not funny and,

You may touch when the
sign says "don't"

You may be surprised
at what's ordinary,

And still,
you may like what you find
...Me

Joan Davenport

The Whole

My words as a person
I barely can speak
They're futile and useless
Quite often called weak.

The words in my mind
Are full of strife
They're direct and potent
They cut like a knife!

The words of my heart
Are cool and clear
They're the ones I use
To speak of those dear.

Those of my soul
Possess no hate
With patience, with love,
And time to wait.

These are the things
That make me whole
My person, my mind,
My heart, and my soul.

Elizabeth Heaton

Recurrent

When the dreamer speaks
giving voice to unseen visions
we are fearful as we listen
To sleeping eyes looking inward
How further might they see
Freed of conscious inhibitions
Worlds reshaped by whim and wishing
Without encumbering time and distance
Here lost souls may visit freely,
Reuniting in the twilight time of slumber
But are the fanciful illusion or maniacal delusions,
of hateful beasts and haunted forests
where they lumber
Beneath the mists and so enshrouded
No star to guide, the sky is clouded
Until the sun again comes peering in.
And in the hour of his waking
How much of this will be forsaken,
And how much may we really wish had been.

Joe Anthony Ellison

The Mask

I've never been good at saying what I feel,
Even though at times my heart drowns in sorrow,
It is rare that I shed even a single tear,
Even with my most trusted confidants.
In heightened moments of great anxiety
There are few that ever know the depth of my fear.

The mask that has been my ally,
That which has hidden my pain,
That which allows me to function
To work and to play without notice
That which allows me to keep my affliction personal,
It is that same ally that is also my greatest enemy,
For in wearing this mask for so long,
It has become a part of me,
Even in the most intimate and personal settings,
When it is my fondest wish to remove this cloak,
I am unable to take it off,
For the tragedy of which it hides,
Has become the glue which binds it forever in place.

Christopher Buchheit

Daddy

I try not to think of him often, for it only makes me sad
I haven't stopped loving him, this man I knew as Dad

He did his best for us, what more could he do?
I believed him to be perfect, Daddy was my glue
He made my tears disappear, put the smile on my face
His ways filled with strength, no one could take his place

But nobody is perfect, no one can do no wrong
My father was not weak, nor was he always strong
Sometimes he yelled too loud, sometimes he drank too much
He wasn't always around, but I can forgive him for such

And I wasn't perfect either, I was never expected to be
Another great thing about Daddy, he loved me just for me
He didn't always say it, though I knew it to be true
My father showed how much he cared, by the little things he'd do

I will never forget this man. He was there from the start
I try not to think of him often. Yet, Daddy never leaves my heart!

Shannon D. Mutter

Love's A Many Splintered Thing

I've felt love's jagged edges
I've known pain that cut me into wedges.
Some call it love
Yes, love's a many splintered thing.

Splinters that aim right for the heart
Splinters that pierce sharp as a dart
Splinters that slice my whole life apart
Yes, love's a many splintered thing

First my heart sang when you appeared
All of love's hope in you was mirrored
Some call it love
Yes, love's a many splintered thing.

Cupid, just keep your jagged sorrow
I'm living now the straight and narrow.
Some call it love
Yes, love's a many splintered thing.

Splinters that aim right for the heart
Splinter that pierce sharp as a dart
Splinters that slice my whole life apart
Yes, love's a many splintered thing. Splinters!

Sandra S. Bonfield

Watered In Your Love

There are many variations
to the texture of your love;
to numerous to mention,
but fit you like a glove.

Like water, you are fluid,
and giving forth the essentials to sustain life;
to moisten this parched spirit, a miracle, my wife.

As the morning mist,
drifts gently to the ground;
your touch so softly given, no evil can be found.

Your sharing of a God like love,
like ice to ease my pain.
Always with such comfort, you're a warm and gentle rain.

Water best describes you;
for it changes and adapts.
You are the key ingredient,
and fill my every crack.

Washed on you with each new day;
this steaming love affair,
and blessed beyond my wildest dreams; you are beyond compare!

W. Michael Anderton

Conquering Fog

In ghostly gray the conquering fog clung to your copper beard
As if to ask your favor in the battle just ahead.
Jealousy the defiant sun refused that night to sink
Brandishing his sword on high in wounds of violent pink.
The air grew chilled combat as I reached for your hand in fear.
Fog battalions rolled forth, the aged sun drew near.
Relentlessly the fiery sun raged on with renewed life
Fog in cool persistence cut him down with a vapory knife.
In ribbons of passionate scarlet the doomed sun cried,
"I will return tomorrow!" In one sliver of orange he died.
But fog's victory was soon forgotten, all his blustery water might
As moon's necromanic chariot won the battle of the night.

Marilyn Cory

There You Are (A Model)

As I turn the page
Shattered I was in a rage
Until I seen your face
In a braided vest

Turn to page twenty-two
Look just like I knew you
Sitting on a Harley
Looking so "dare me"

How you look so right
When dress I solid white
Lips the color of "Red wine"
Looking soft warm and fine

I want to see you dress in Lt. Blue
Sick and ratine with leather and lace
Showing to the world
Your handsome sexy face

Lillie Mae Cagle

A Chiseled Moment

October skies of blue and gray
O'er valleys laid in steel
It's here I walk on dirt and grass
And find my place to kneel
The autumn's red and yellow tide
Awakes my memory
Of times I beat my nemesis
And times it conquered me
A chiseled moment caught in time
Like Concrete Charlie's eyes
The calm before the coming storm
Of cunning, truth and lies
In bursts of anxious artistry
A story will unfold
Where fact collides with myth and lore
Where warmth collides with cold
Then what will happen after that
And what will be revealed
Is part of life that's not unlike
A game played on a field.

Daniel K. Oslin

Life's Stages

As we travel through life—
  Stage after stage,
And finally reach the wonderful
  Golden Stage—
Suddenly we feel tired, useless
  And so alone.
Lots of time to fill, pain often
  Hurting to the Bone.
To carry on sometimes is very
  Difficult to do,
Even tho this Grand Stage—
  Was looked forward to!
Past eras were laborious,
  Many obstacles to bear,
Still rewards came, accomplishments,
  And family loving care.
Thankful, we are, yet wonder why—
  And how we reached this Plateau.
Til that Great Day of Revelation—
  Will we understand all and know!

Juanita H. Butler

Seasons

Leaves falling,
Children calling,
Breezes blowing,
Not yet snowing,
Softly comes Autumn.

Frosty noses,
Cheeks with roses,
A loved one dozes,
Bare branches in old poses,
Silently comes Winter.

Birds singing,
Laughter ringing,
Flowers blooming,
Babies booming,
Swiftly comes spring.

Brutal drought,
School is out,
Dad caught trout,
Without a doubt,
Slowly comes summer.
Kimberly Norris

Untitled

On and on still to you I write
I don't want to let you go
I have searching so many worlds
You'll never know
How I looked through every bombers moon,
Meeting twelve o'clock high
Glaring suns at noon.

I knew in my heart some day
You would come along
And I would feel a different story
I would write a different song.

T'was but for a moment
And now you are gone
Your beauty in thought I won't forget
Your words will linger on

I'll look off in far and distant clouds
And meet the heights of man
But I'll search no more
For what I sought now I understand
Walter J. Frazier

Memorial Day

I visited your grave today
And, oh, the empty feeling that came over me!
Just like your grave is empty.
You are not there!
The closeness we once shared—
Is shared again when I hear music,
Songs that repeat what you used to say
Or express my feelings about you.
I always want to be alone when I hear them—
Alone to relive the memories
And let the tears come streaming down.
Somehow, I cannot wait to be reunited with you
In that distant place called Heaven.
Marie Calvey

Prejudice

With all the world's prejudice that fuels fire in us
Like kindling, smoldering pus ruining all hopes of trust
It's hard not to feel disgust over all the things unjust
It's almost like some kind of lust that will eat you away like rust
This abscess of ours must stop
Or truly we'll sink like a rock
No bandage or gesture will do
While there in the wing stands your coup
To stir up the prejudice stew
With more drive of hatred anew
What is it that we have done
To be put under prejudice gun?
Is it my skin that you feel is a sin?
Is it my hair that you feel has no flair?
Is it my eyes that you feel I must die?
Or is it my race that you feel is a waste?
This prejudice sting of a malice and lice
Must be cast to the side from all of our eyes
For then we will know why it is we're mankind
And act like God's clan with our heart and our mind
Kevin L. Parks

Poppy

My brother is kind, thoughtful, and generous,
And is known by most as Bill.
He enjoys home, family, friends, and work,
As well as reading and music.

As a boy, bill cut lawns and delivered newspapers.
During his teen years, he worked part-time in retail and textiles.
One Christmas during World War II,
He repaired, painted, and sold tricycles.

Following his graduation from high school,
Bill continued to work in textiles
Where he remained for twenty-five years,
Most of that time as a foreman.

Feeling the need for a change,
Bill resigned to pursue other work,
Which he found with a major power company.
For ten years, he was provided many opportunities.

Since his retirement, this gentle man spends time
Tending his rose and vegetable gardens and orchard,
Along with family and parent needs.
Bill is happiest with is wife and those who call him Dad and Poppy.
Dot Hutchinson Kelly

No Truer Love

I know the love that you have given to me
is truly the love of a lifetime:
I never thought anyone could love me as much as you
and for me to know and feel it so deep in my heart without question
or doubt is a feeling to never be explained
but unquestionably truer than life itself.

I need not say a word and you understand all;
as if you were a part of my very soul
experiencing all the same emotions as I.
You make all my fears vanish
by a simple but ever so powerful hug.
You wipe my tears with one wisp of a kiss
and all is well
and I know all will be, for eternity
with the everlasting love you've given to me.
Rhonda Phifer

If

If I could only capture, the joyous care-free rapture,
in her smile.
If I could discover, the reasons why I loved her,
'Twould be worthwhile.
But who can grasp quicksilver? Sunlight dancing on a river?
The twinkle in an eye?
The tinkle of her laughter, or the hug that followed after,
a heavy sigh?
When I look up at night, at a myriad of lights,
from distant spheres -
I don't think about her only, for you see I've been so lonely,
through the years.
Do we really meet again, in a world beyond all pain,
up in the sky?
Will she be waiting for me, and will she still adore me,
as in days gone by?
We must leave it to God's will, for I know He's watching still,
the human race,
And I'm sure that we will find, somewhere in His good time,
we have our place.

Donald William Dolson

Relive

Spring winds softly sway the budding trees
Rays from the sun warm my bare shoulders
I lie on a blanket and feel the quiet all around me
Clouds cover the sun...the air feels colder
Thoughts of years gone by roll through my head
I recall each moment carefully
I savor each word that you have said
Going over every line intimately
I remember how you would gently begin
And how I would willingly follow
The touch of your hands on my skin
My heart no longer hollow
I feel each kiss as I did then
My body slightly trembles
Feeling you this near again
Is more than my soul can handle
As I pull myself back to the day that is here
The feelings come rushing with it
I put my hands to my face and feel the tears
I wish again that we could relive it

Christina Green

The Dogwood's Story

The dogwood's bloom in beauty, across the countryside,
Its branches speak the story, of Christ, the Crucified.
Its body bent and twisted, speak of pain and agony,
Of the Christ who bore at Calvary, our death and set us free.

The dogwood's petals stained with blood, speak of Christ, the Lamb of God,
Crucified on Calvary's tree, the sinner's perfect plea.
Its blossoms give way to leaves of green, as nature wakes to spring,
They speak of everlasting life, that trusting Christ can bring.

Next time you see a dogwood tree, remember Christ who set you free,
Who arose and lives in Glory, who coming back you see.
Let its story speak to you, and trust Christ while you may,
And live with Him forever, in Glory's bright array.

Don C. Dickinson

Stillness

Stillness. Waiting in this pause
Listen. Spring birds call.
Silhouettes of wondrously
structured ancient trees
thicken, gradually clothing
bare winter bones with
lacy living garb.

River water flows again, fields
of ice drift slowly, ocean bound.
Slow snow melt contains the
might of rain-drowned, ice-free
flow turned roiling torrent,
sweeping all impediments in
tangled mesh of debris.

For now, spring soft air,
gentle emergence,
placid drift of might
contained, waking river
moves, slow, tamed.
For now.

L. Lindley Powers

Meaning Of The Rain

There was once a little man
Who traveled through the land
Looking for a reason
For the changing of the season
Seeking revelations in
The blowing of the wind
Trying to rack his brain
As to the meaning of the rain
He was so busy asking questions
That he never learned the lessons
He failed to see the beauty
All he saw was some vague duty
So he missed a great rare pearl
In the lands of our fair world

Kenneth D. Albert

What Is A Woman?

We're Sugar and Spice
And everything 'Nice'
But when we're mistreated
We're destructive — thrice
We're sweet and we're kind
But, don't get us riled
Because if you do
We'll behave like a child
We're kind to our children
And loving to our man
We sometimes have to 'bristle'
And take a hard stand
But, we do try to please you
We try to be true
After all — our Heavenly Father
Made us to love you
Now men, aren't you happy —
Aren't you Really quite glad
Because with all of our 'faults'
We're not "really" so bad

M. Judith Riggins

Archangel

You peer into the moonlit night
a hurting object shines so bright.
Resplendent trail of dazzling light.
Archangel swiftly taking flight
the demons of this earth to fight.
Protecting saints is his delight.

You gaze into the sunlit sky.
A cloud borne memory passes by
so vivid that you can't deny
the tears of shame that make you cry.
Archangel helps you wipe them dry
then says, "In God you must rely.

You look about while tossed at sea
and ask yourself "How can this be?"
Is this sad lot my destiny?
Will this cruel captor set me free?
Archangel speaks, "God heard thy plea,
for I have come to rescue thee."

Richard Major

Fate

If by luck or chance
Fate
Could it be fate?
A gift
Mine
Alive our's
A turn of events
Twist of fate
You came
A brand new start
Time spent
Left you behind
A brand new place
Full of love
Hope
A dream
Life.

Wendy L. Nishti

Ode To The Dandelions

Why do so many humans shun you so?
When in full bloom
in the meadows and lawns
your glorious faces rise to the sun

And we are enthralled
by the marvelous view

Then, out come the humans
to cut you down.

Your beauty to be destroyed
but the God of the dandelions
knew what to do.

As you will see next year in the morn

Olive Boyd-Bukowiecki

A Wish For A Falling Star

Meteor, meteor in the sky,
  please fall in front of my searching eye.
Show me a bright streak of fire tonight,
  let me see your brilliant red and orange light.
I lay here in darkness on this starry night,
  waiting patiently to see your glorious light.

Suddenly a swoosh from the depths of space,
  creates a warm orange glow that lights up my face!
It leaves a smoking trail in the wake of its place,
  lit by he stars from outer space!
A piece of rock tiny as a grain of sand,
  leaves a universal scene across the land!

Meteor, meteor you couldn't fly much higher,
  Thank you for showing me your burning fire.
You traveled for ages through the solar system,
  ending your journey in mystic wisdom.
I gladly saw the speed of your flaming life,
  Giving me one of the simple joys in life.

Ralph Citak

To Understand Man

What if through poetry we spoke of each man's ancient story; do you think we might all understand just what is in the hearts and minds of men? Might this be a good listening post, that would enlighten most folks? If words cannot say what we do not see, then Lord have pity on you and me.

A single nation or tribe were all of we, from the sages of long ago to the pages of history, that we now all should know! That is why God has brought us all together, to release us from his Holy tether, to see just how we could all live together! If trust is found, then mankind is sound!

How can we see from afar the hopes and dreams of other men? Theirs are the same as ours! Smiles and emotions from all faces we see, just the same as you and me. Pride of nation, family and individuality; rich in tradition and devoted to their religion. This is the love that all should see!

Prejudice, the thorn of hatred that has caused great pain, can only be counted as man's greatest shame. No gain or fame remains, of all their atrocities. Only those who opposed are honored in histories repose. That is what our souls spirit should see, thus securing man's equality through all eternity.

Bud J. Schmidt

Are We On The Same Team?

If I fall, would you catch me, or could you lighten my fall? Maybe I'll just hit solid concrete, and fall on my face. So are we on the same team? Do I have to fight these battles by myself? I need to know. Do I go solo. When you talk, I want to hear what you got to say. But when I talk you won't give me the time of day. If I'm carrying fifteen tons of hay on my back, are you going to take half, so my back won't break? Or are we on the same team? My back can handle only so much. We can climb Mount Everest only if we are...that's right, the same team. Believe me I can do it alone. But you have my back. I think. Do you? That house you want, and a nice car in the driveway. A trip to Vegas every once in a while can be ours. First, are on the same team? I'm willing to let you know my weakness, and what can destroy me. I will when I know you are on my team. Only when I know this, because I'm on your team.

Andrew W. Brinkley

My Journey

My home is somewhere in the universe
   Daughter of the sun and a rising star
A traveler in time, interlocking thoughts.
   Searching for an answer, awaiting for the sound
Of a distant signal in another world.
   The future is not ours! Not even today.
Continuing the journey that I started long ago,
   A traveler in time searching for the truth,
gathering the memories of all the lost dreams,
   Wishing to continue my mission on earth,
Hoping that tomorrow it will never end.
   Reaching for the one that will lend a hand.
In keeping the peace of all the lost souls,
   erasing the sickness, the pain and the wars.
Loving one another with brotherly love.
   Continuing the journey that started long ago,
Leaving a smile that you will remember,
   Making a difference in someone's heart.
Fulfilling the purpose of my short stay,
   Lovingly you forever when I will depart.

   Gloria Salas

I'm Lost Poem

I find myself lost, I don't know which way to go.
I'm lost, can you help me?
I'm lost there's miles of roads out there which way to go.
I'm lost there's East, West, North, South,
which way to go my life is like a road it never end,
there always a side road to turn down too.
I'm lost can you help me?
I'm caught in the middle I don't know which way to go.
I'm lost there's a future for me somewhere.
Do I dare go down that road.
There's a past I must deal with first,
can you help me?
I'm lost there a present I must conquer
before I can move forward to future cam I?
I'm lost, there's a road out there
I must take no one can help me.
But me I'm lost I must find a way to be found.
I'm lost, can you help me?

   Mary Kennedy

Why Do You Love Me?

Why do you love me so
When there's so much you don't know about me.
I'd like to tell you, but I don't know What you'll think of me.
Oh, I wonder how you can love me so?

Why do you love me so?
There's so much I'd like to show you, but
I'm afraid you'll turn tail and run.
Oh, I wonder how you can love me so?

Why do you love me so?
When there's so much we don't have in common,
that it's hard to believe that we're even together.
Oh, I wonder how you can love me so?

Why do you love me so?
They say opposites attract, I guess that's true . . .
Because I love you and I don't want to lose you.
Oh, I wonder how you can love me so?

   Christian M. Rushia

The Prowler

In a cavern deep and dreary,
Sat a rodent dark and weary,
Of running from the stalking prowler,
That chased him through the night,

In a little hole he hid,
Waiting with tearful eyes,
For the end he knew would come,
Before the sun would rise,

In it came slowly walking,
Peering all around,
For the prey he knew was there,
Hiding in the ground,

He saw the hole in which it hid,
It was over in one swift motion,
Up and then down into the prowler's stomach,
Devoured without emotion.

   Kathleen Brushett

The Dreamer

Please don't stop,
Not on my account.
Whispers are only heard by the
Souls for whom they're meant.
But when your vulnerability
Begins to prevail,
Please let me go,
But don't ask where.
Your secrets are yours and yours alone.
The silence awakens,
And yet another is born.
The unheard sounds echoing
In my ears and through my body.
But please stop me when I drift,
For only I know how far I will go,
And only you can stop me.

   Mitchell Dyck

Lustrous Splendor

A wonderful sight of opulence
Lying in the immediate foreground
Cinematic photoplay
Every desire to confront it
Over and over, a passionate caress
If only I could linger
And inevitability or blind hope
Will consummate itself
Instead I must depart
In an echo of isolation
This component arises
Immediately, repeatedly
An uncommunicative, unfeeling
and seemingly vindictive
Force of action that leads me away
With no intention or cold intention
The vision is unmoving
Ebbing to feel the flow
Dejection or a glow
Dying to know

   Bryce McNeil

Untitled

Sidewalk cracks
and
50 cents refills
tick past
my day

Loneliness breeds
loneliness
and overpopulates
courage
  as weak as
    I wish it wasn't
minutes
like soldiers
line up
and look at me
asking
with whom
I will stand

Cameron Rasmus

A Soldier's Eyes

Hup - hup - hup -
Marching on to face my death,
Rifle at my side.
Never dare to take a breath,
Eyes all blurred and wide.

Thud - thud - thud -
Soldiers falling left and right,
All our bodies twitch.
Eyes are tearing at the sight -
My mates in the ditch.

Shriek - shriek - shriek -
Bleeding bodies everywhere,
Eyes as dry as sand.
Advance! Aim! Without a care,
Rifle in my hand.

Eyes are shutting hard and tight,
Rifle at my side.
And at last, I face the night,
On my final ride.

Wilma Pidhayny

Feeding The Fire

In my self nemesistic
felonious actions
performed without foresight
the match was lit.

In your flaying
of an exactingly incompetent
tautological insight
you ignited a fire.

Neither existence of self
can we wholly comprehend
so we defend our plight
to burn eternally.

Tony Zahrebelny

On Learning Of Our Daughter's Cancer

We thought we knew life's mysteries
  And were too old to weep;
We held each other in our arms
  And cried ourselves to sleep.

Joseph Foreman

The Vacant Chair

The place is empty
By your side.
And from your grief
You cannot hide.

You reach out—
No one is there.
You glance 'cross the room.
To a vacant chair.

Your heart is breaking
The pain is so great.
You've lost your loved one—
Your soul mate.

God will bring comfort,
He says that He will.
Have patience, O heart—
Peace, be still.

Though they be gone their spirit is near.
Their mem'ries live on warm, lovely, and dear.

So hold to his promise, years soften the pain.
God always brings sunshine after the rain.

Marge Potts

The Neglected Servant

I'm here, the epitome of nothingness, the lost and deserted
of all things, left alone to rot.

Abandoned by those of whom I trust, a direct example of a failure.
Will I be remembered, will you remember, why should you?
My life dwindles away before myself, I can see it, I can feel it.
Darkness has crossed my crooked path, death lurks outside my
door.

My life is insignificant amongst all others, why spare
me...that would be a mistake.

Love doesn't exist in this world, it's just taken for
granted, a key to destruction, a password to within, never true.

Why should I try anymore, everything I know....betrayed?
Every part of me is left exposed.

I'm a target, I'm a sign that says "Come maim the innocent
and naive, come hurt the forgivers and the righteous, come
destroy the do-gooders and lovers of all", my days are numbered.

Do what you can for now.
Everything I've yearned for is gone.
I don't even exist to myself, and it's all my fault.
My punishment is deserved.
I'm the jester of all life, come kick me, I can't feel it,
I'm already dead.
I've given myself out to all, there's nothing left to be.

David R. Haldenwang

Nature's Curse

Near a small little star is the planet called Earth.
When the right mixture formed Mother Nature gave birth.
Wide varieties of life live on this paradise hearth.
Truly giving Mother Nature the real sense of worth.

All the lands were together with one continuous shore.
When giant creatures roamed that we now call dinosaurs.
Fast across the blue sky ripped a large meteor.
Striking with incredible force the land mass soon tore.

Most life dead and gone Mother Nature was shattered.
Keeping her planet alive seemed all that had mattered.
When man soon evolved, with delight she was flattered.
Spreading to all four corners, now quickly they scattered.

At first there was harmony with this self thinking breed.
Then came the severe pain of their cancerous greed.
In the name of progress on her resources they feed.
Believing, above hers, their own plans supersede.

Fighting back with disease, their onslaught won't wane.
Mother Nature wrenches with fear from this terrible strain.
Man is the sick deadly curse which causes Earth's drain.
Destroying the delicate balance nature has to maintain.

Gary D. Rick

The Solemn Man

A solemn man, the face of defeat.
No challenges left for him to meet.

No battles to fight, no wars to win.
He faces his past, and loses again.

Countless transgressions have left their mark.
Once bright and cheerful, now cold and dark.

What will it take to free his soul?
A pound of flesh? A pot of gold?
Somewhere inside there is a key.
The redemption he needs to set him free.

Judy S. Roberts

I Am Somebody Without Shame

Like a mighty river, strong as can be
I ride the waves of life like a surfer,
sometimes distressed and other times painlessly.

Black as a berry, sweet as sugar cane
I was raised to be somebody without shame.

I stand proud as an American
determined to succeed.
My forefathers fought for my freedom indeed.

My right to vote, my freedom of speech,
my constitutional rights are mine to keep.
The bigotry and ignorance that cause so much adversity
is starting to be transformed into diversity.

No longer shall I fear
my transparent brothers and sisters of society —
for all people are God's creation
not one race's condemnation.

Black as a berry, sweet as sugar cane
I am somebody without shame.

Hazel James Cole

The Float

Parades of past did so excite
Each float a fad I knew
With flowers yellow, black and white
A multitude to view

With every pass I longed for more
Then favoured only one
Whose fragrance forced my pulse to soar
And glow out-shone the sun

A second, minute, hour, day
That never crossed my mind
Of turning into years away
So happy I would find

Along the way a bloom lay dead
A squeak would catch your ear
And most would turn away their heads
But I would hold it dear

And now the float is not for show
Parades cause me to part
I know of them but do not go
For one float has my heart

Wayne Couvillon

Time

Time slips away even as
Lost dreams lie forgotten
Days turn into years
As memories drift and fade
And then time has a way of being
Standing still, awakening
In time we learn, in time we grow
And in time, we welcome changes
Our dreams emerge in time and space
To lead us past our obstacles
They may appear as fear, but wait
In time, turn around, as courage
For destiny has a way of showing
Strength renewed, alive and growing
No matter all the years in time
No matter how long forgotten
For out of all that went before
Arises who and what we are
And in that wonderment time stood still
And time has been our answer.

Joan M. Griffin

Loneliness

Sadness comes over me, many many times
My heart's been broken
I don't know why
Especially here all alone
Trying to pass the time
Wondering where my life is and why
Why does God let me cry
So many times I just don't know why
I've contemplated suicide
I decided to take a rest
And God told me he would do his best
Now I know I will get by

Jacqueline Vermette

Stellie (Epitaph)

I drown into the vast sea
Of my waking fantasy,
Where is neither thirst for life
Nor bliss, but agony and strife.

And yet I am, and dwell
Among men; I, an empty shell.

You left the warm embrace
And the flowers of Spring
Bathed in morning dew,
Then turned your white face
To catch the Angels sing
in Heaven's never ending blue.

Good-bye dear love
No, not good-bye
Smiling image floating free
Your hair lifting in the sky,
You stand before me
In all your glory.
    Lola Dunston

A Spring Dilemma

My calender proudly states
that spring is officially here,
But Mother Nature disagrees
too much snow around, I fear.

She sends her message to the birds
do not return too soon
your feet will freeze your wings will cease
you won't be able to master a tune.

She sends her message to the trees
so anxious to get in bloom,
Relax my friends or you may find
your crowning glory turned to gloom.

She sends her message to the gardener
as he contemplates his soil and seeds
keep contemplating a few more weeks
and I will help you meet your gardening needs.
    Linda Smit

Beneath The Surface

Just as the earth's inner being
burns with fiery molten,
swirling, fuming, raging,
eager to explode,
so is my soul.
Not the quiet, solid oak of strength,
nor the gentle flow of the stream.
Mine is the thunderous uproar,
seeking more,
seeking balance,
seeking souls.
Mine is the one crying.
Tears shed for a multitude of causes:
Freedom, Peace, Justice, Salvation.
And there you are with tears of your own.
Just as the rain cleanses the earth,
your blood purifies the stains of sin,
and your tears intercede for the cries within.
The turmoil is buried, but you see it all
beneath the surface.
    Leanne E. Collard

The Breath Of Winter

Looking out across the black and white and gray,
a winter so cold,
The color drained from the lands
as if the Earth's spirit has seen a ghost.

Frozen mist hangs heavy in the air
as tho the Earth Mother is trying to hug herself
and breathe life back into her frozen bones
   her summer heart

Wrapped in ice, all things fragile
bending willfully with the winds
so as not to be broken
before the spring's child
throws off its blanket of snow
and climbs gingerly from nature's bed
into the warmth of the new season
and the embrace of the Earth Mother.
    Karen Knight

Honor

What happened to "Honor"?
When a man was a man, his word was his bond
when he gave you his hand.

You needed no contract; he would do what he said.
His family would honor it even if he were dead.

His family was his pride and his good name,
not what he had gained in money and fame.

The decline of honesty is such a same,
and it's not really worth what little we gain.

I long for the day when people can see that this
"Dog Eat Dog World" was not meant to be.

God made man honest; that's the way it should be.
Not do unto others before they do me!
    Maggie Hales

Confused

That's the word I'll use
I go around and around
Til I'm bound to just break down
I've shown my sadness and used to smile
But all the while I was just confused
Do I turn here, or do I go there
People say life's not fair, so why should I care
Either way, people will say you're just confused
I can't see why I'm here today
If only I could fly away
Then nobody would know where I went
But if it was done, I'd still be confused
Why do I do what I do for who I do it for
Why can't I say, I did that for me
People will see though, that I don't need them
I've gone through life all alone but never for me
Not anymore
You'll see
But for now, I'll stay confused
    Tammy Ransom

Matthew Chapter 4

Into the wilderness Jesus was led,
Where He fasted forty days and the devil said,
"Demand these stones be turned into bread!"
For he knew He was hungry, but Jesus said,
"Man shall not live on only bread, —
But on every word from God's mouth instead."
Then the devil took Him to the temple top,
Saying, "If You're God's Son, don't even stop.
Just throw Yourself down, for You're not alone.
His angels won't let Your foot hit a stone."
Jesus answered, "That's true, but here is the rest:
You shall not put the Lord, your God to the test!"
Then the devil took Jesus to a high mountaintop
And said, "If you'll fall down and worship me without stop,
All the kingdoms of the world will be your reward."
But Jesus said, "You shall worship and serve only the Lord."
So if you're in "the wilderness" of heartache or pain,
Jesus' example for us makes it plain:
Speak out God's promises and you will see,
That through each problem you'll find victory!

Marilyn M. Snodgrass

Welcome To My World

All about me I am surrounded by darkness;
  But, the fear now is less and less.
For, in the distance I behold a light
  That seems to get closer and, oh so, bright.
As I stand near what seems to be a ledge
  My heart sings a song of love, my pledge.
Now, that the time I have longed for is near
  My hand raises instinctively to brush a tear
Welcome to my world, are the words I sense
  As you stand before me in a world so immense!
Finally, united we stand in a beautiful place
  Now all the sorrow I have felt is erased.
As we hold each other's hand ever so fast.
  Knowing we are together at long last.
Into each other's eyes we do stare
  Revealing in a love ever so rare.
Yes, my love, you do say as we gaze far and wide
  With me, for eternity, you will abide.
You, I have missed, and as the haze is unfurled
  Again, I hear you say, welcome to my world.

Phyllis M. Scott

Linen

Strong calloused hands grip the wooden rod tightly.
One powerful thrust and the rod punctures the flesh.
Water stained with crimson plunges from the moist wound.
Later a delicate linen is scattered over the gnarled flesh.
Hard, sad hands arrange the fine linen.
Soon gloom devours the linen and all is dissolute.
A coarse boulder is place in front to secure the linen and
its possession.
Upon this boulder a seal is encased.
Time darts away as if it's a lizard.
As the morning of the third day approaches the ground
grumbles and the seal shatters.
With great force the boulder is moved aside.
Sunlight smashes through the gloom, revealing the jumbled
linen lying on the floor.
Jesus has risen...

David E. Foster

Wishes

We wish for so much,
for toys and books,
for love and such -
see the wistful looks?

Christmastide,
a joyous time (for some)-
others have no guide,
eventually succumb.

Children all over the world,
some delighted, some still hoping -
here's one little girl
crying, but coping.

The holy babe must be our light,
lead us along the lonely miles -
guide us out of endless night,
turn children's tears into smiles.

Rachel Evans

Morning Has Broken

The sun breaks
through the black
of night.

The beautiful warmth
of a new day.

The deep red on black,
like a rose on satin.

The rays stretch up
to heaven.
Express ways for the
Angels.

I stand on my balcony,
savoring the beauty
of God's perfect day.

Leyla Hur-Adkins

Our Brother

Growing up was never easy
Especially for our mother
For she always told us
We have an older brother

Birthdays were the hardest
For no one more than our mother
For they would mean
Another year gone without our brother.

We often wondered
If we would meet him
Of if he looked like us
Even though the prospect looked dim

Then one spring day
Our mother called us
With excitement in her voice and said
your brother wants to meet us.

Now our family is complete
Especially for our mother
For now we can say
How much we love you brother.

Nancy M. Crowell

Another World

I saw you in the pictures,
I dreamed about your face.
Your smile did entice me,
I was living in a daze.

You were so very distant,
you were so out of reach.
I was walking in the shadows,
you were on a sunny beach.

All this fruitless dreaming,
it was, I knew, insane.
All this foolish yearning,
it was all in vain.

And as the time was passing,
and the years made us old.
The dreams was slowly fading,
and love was turning cold.

In this world we never touched,
In this world we never hugged.
In another world we might have met,
In another world we might have loved.

Curt Allan Carlson

Children In Springtime

Children outside playing,
laughing and having fun
embracing all the sun's rays
feeling freedom, feeling loved

Then, suddenly without any warning
the rain begins to fall,
Small crystal drops of water
surrounding them all

The children run and hide inside
as they listen to the thunder
then lightning starts and the
Thunder booms
and their faces fill with wonder

Can't wait for tomorrow
are the words the children quietly whisper

Bright sunny sky, green grass and toys,
are what they will encounter.

Karen Riley

The King's Juggler

Walking a foot over champagne glasses,
bleeding on crystal shards,
singing before all strangers, and
crying beside a dusty fire;
a winter's hearth,
a blind man's pyre.
A moonbeam descends,
breaking through the night,
this silvery blue light,
shines on a pale face,
illuminating grace;
breathless tears
a mountain appears,
in silhouette against the sky.

Mark Robertson

An Epitome Of Adam Algood

He died in the flowers
Fell short in hormic style
Nephrotomy bullet, incondite smile.
In dissipating blood
A short novelle reads:
"I'm just a novice."

He swallowed the soil with little protest
His last words a symptomatic death rattle
His head fell with a hollow thud upon his chest
As a commissioner sniped thru the last...
Flesh like binders of umbilical life

Guy Fawke never meant no harm.
Gut strings plucked in boyish charm
As the Son of God shed a tear on his cross

The sun rose in short stocky semblance;
Its blaze of racing chariots fell like fingers on the land.
"...in full bravely thou fleshed thou maiden sword"
Hedged in the dark courts of Labyrinth
Thy soul runs free
  Adam Algood.

Christopher Howd

No Room At The End

There sits a woman all alone
In this world
The pavement for her chair
No one to care!

Her bed at night is a dark corner
Hidden behind some walls
In a condemned old musty building

Her days are long and nights are endless
Her bones weary and fragile
Awaken by a rodent scrambling through
The home they now share
Who will care?

Morning comes only to find her searching
For food out there
Somewhere?

A garbage can even a can in her hand
Begging each passer by for a bit of change
A dollar would be nice
It would mean she could eat twice

The supermarket has a special on stale bread today!

Ruby Sheppard

God Talked To Me

God talked to me in the early morning breeze.
While the others were sleeping.
He gave me music to keep me company.
The birds in the trees who sang to me.
God talked to me that day in the mountains.
While I sat and waited for the others to drag themselves out of bed.
God was there all around me.
God talked to me in the early morning breeze.
While the others where sleeping.
God is every where not just in the mountains in the morning air.

Debra R. Cole

Illuminate

When the reverse of all begins to unfold
they navigate through a mystery curtain
leaving behind lesser lights and pale vistas
for the high ground of profuse imagery
grandly changed with enlightening themes.

Their skills deployed on the wings of prosody
these conquerors of the mind's frontiers
spring into a whirlwind of swirls
inciting a train of quickening emotions
braced into fantasia of spellbinding turns.

Masters of evocation and imprint
they breathe life into sculptures of feelings
juxtaposed against harmonized settings
and contoured by the larger passions
of the ethereal realm of the moment.

Igniting the current of their heart impulses
with the virtuostic fire of artistry
the illuminate of poetry pour into our lifted chalice
the distillation of their released visions
to offer a fantasy space for silent apotheoses.

Yseult Bayard

My Life

Sometimes the reality of life seems unfair
With nothing as to compare
It almost seems control
But I'll go on with flare
Cause that's always been my style
Forget my aching bones, I'll go that extra mile
Cast aside my grunts and groans, for I have much to do
And many miles to go before I'm through
For I have a dream
And must shine my beam
Before my last ray of life
All my struggles and strife
Become but a flickering flame
I'll have no one to blame
If I've not met my calling
And have been faltering, even falling
What I've done with my time
May not have reason and rhyme
But I've done my best
And now it's time to rest.

Carolyn Bammert Fritz

Loving

Why is love so hard to find?
I walk a cloudy path from the start.
False hopes and dreams drain my mind,
as lust and tears try to fool my heart.
And yet, the clouds begin to fade away,
and laughter fills the misty air.
I see miracles in the new day,
and find all ugliness has become fair.
The flowers dance as the winds blow,
and birds sing a glorious song.
I treasure the sunset's glow,
because I have waited for love so long.
Love makes his home in our hearts,
and who love does not touch, in darkness departs.

Eugenia Hall

Compass Rose

The petals point the way, circling,
Spiraling around to the center
Where some say is nothingness
But I say is the pure essence,
The brilliance that is unique,
aside from all others.
So, too, with people.
Stripping away, layer by layer,
All artifice, all superficiality
Until what is left is pure,
Untainted by illusion
Or self-designed images.
A special individual,
Unrivaled.

There at the core is everything.
Desires, wishes, drives,
All in plain sight.
No overtones of falseness;
Only the forces that keep the needle turning,
Finding our own True North.

D. Sean Simpson

Home Sweet Home

Edmonton — my favorite city
The place I proudly call home
With its picturesque river valley
Where once many buffalo did roam
It's known as the "City of Champions"
The famous I'll list just a few
Wayne Gretsky, Mark Messier, Paul Coffey
Ten years they lived and with us too
In July we celebrate "Klondike"
Dressing up in the costumes of old
Tourists join in the fun and excitement
Even trying at panning for gold
"Calgary" is our rival city
They boast and they brag and they chat
But we are the "Capital" fellas
So, doff them thar Stetson hats
Have I now convinced you to move here?
I'm sure you are pondering it so
"Oops" I nearly neglected to mention
We look forward to 6 months of snow.

Norma Tyler

Winter Peace

As our old world grows tired
Beds down for its winter's rest
All quilted in its many colors
From the easel of nature's best

All peoples of its many races
Will climb to its highest peaks
Exclaim with great excitement
Of the beauty for which they seek

So let us all join together
Like the quilted colors of earth
So all peoples can exclaim with excitement
Of the peace to which we gave birth

Thomas R. Bloom

Tsholofelo, My Hope

How shall I paint your portrait?
In purple, in black, in green . . .
Passionate and romantic . . .
Dancing a woman's tango.

Tsholofelo, I see you
primed in blue maid's uniform
serving hot coffee or tea
in locked executive rooms.

In construction work: Digging;
chipping boulders; sweating black;
climbing, laying hollow blocks;
looking sturdy; undaunted.

How shall I paint your bright hope?
In your womb, a child so dear;
Trapped in a world so unfair
Where diamonds are not rare.

How shall I paint your portrait?
Purple with your bleeding heart;
Black with your skin so unspoiled;
Green with your unfailing hope.
Remedios Nalundasan-Abijan

4th Dimension (Time)

Infinity rushes from reality
To a place of cool, misty grey.
Laced with salmon-colored ribbons
Endless in every way.
Floating in infinity's realm
  I sense freedom—
  But none of passing time.

At the edge of my vision I see
The hard, steel peaks of time
  Marching steady, marching on

Just then—
  Reality rushes back again.
Kim Cox

Night's Tide

Dark black waves gently stroke the shore
Caressing her long lost lover.
Sandy fingers reach out to her
Grasping, longing, desperate for her touch.

The moon is high above the shore
Waiting, but not knowing what for.
Water and land come together
Becoming one, churning turning so much.

Calm is past; the lover's want more.
Rising and falling together
She pushes deeper and deeper
Until only the rocks she can touch.

Reaching far as they can to shore
They fall away form each other.
Sandy fingers reach out to her
Grasping, longing, she strays from his touch.
Shellane Helpard

The Winter Poem

It's the time when snow falls from the sky.
Good old November is rolling by.
Sunny days have gone away.
In the wind, trees turn and sway.
It's the time when snow falls from the sky.

It's the time Christmas stories are read.
To different people nice words are said.
It's the time to laugh and play.
No time to be thinking about hot days in May.
It's the time Christmas stories are read.

It's the time when people catch a cold.
It's the time when you have a dozen cards to fold.
All the birds have gone away.
Not one bird is here to stay.
It's the time when people catch a cold.

It's the time to hang mistletoes.
It's the time of cozy fires and marshmallows.
Heavy snow covers the Evergreen.
The old house's fence is rarely seen.
It's the time to hang mistletoes.
Amanda Shareghi

The Arctic

Magnesium flares for night photography
glowing sparks flaming red at the edge of darkness
last from fleeting stars reflections
Here, feeling beauty of the artistic, sculptured plateaus
Lie naked before me—endless shapes
Moulded images form a magnificent display
Untouched, unseen, same for curious wanders.
Topography, silent, unending, quiet, absorbs,
the soul of songless wind that surrounds me.
My footsteps keep a strong rhythm, crunchy, sounding,
Pure as unwritten music played on
the tom-toms of arctic Ice
Frozen clouds of snow blow like desert sand
covering my tracks and only my shadow
knows I was here, exploring, photographing,
with my minds eye, with an insatiable appetite,
Nature's Wonderland, the Arctic.
Sandra Jeanne Myers

Ode To My Mother

She cradles me softly with a love newly found.
Guards me protects me from this world which surrounds.
Whispers of love I hear in my ear.
She wipes away gracefully each of my fears.

Some years have now passed and our love is still strong.
She cradles me softly and sing me a song.
This person I've known from the beginning of time.
Mother I call her, to me so sublime.

Life is so strange. What a merry-go-round.
Often times up and often times down.
But through it all I know in my heart.
I can count on my mother till the day that we part.
Robert Castro

Untitled

I killed a man today, he made me mad.
I killed a man today, it made me glad.
He was on his knees begging me to let him go.
I looked down the barrel of my gun, I told him no.
I probably could have let him go, but I decided to seal his fate.
He tearfully asked me why I had harbored so much hate.
I told him to be quiet, say a prayer, and just close his eyes.
I said it was nothing personal, he just had to pay for
　all those other guys.
All those other guys who screwed me and left me with
　nothing but heartache.
This poor bastard was going to be the sacrifice, the
　statement I had to make.
To let the world know this girl is nobody's fool and
　no one's gonna take her.
Mess with this one boys, and you'll be meeting your maker.
Kim Sarnoski

Raggedy Ann And Raggedy Andy

Raggedy Ann and Raggedy Andy what a beautiful
handsome pair they both were; as they sat upon
our chest-of-drawers—looking happy as can be,
at the Jack-in-the-box, Teddy Bear, Humpty-
Dumpty and other dolls and toys there.

Raggedy Ann and Raggedy Andy made such a
perfect pair with their smiling faces, they were
both all right by me, they were among one of
my comforts and joys I has as a child along with
my other toys, teddy bear and dolls.

Raggedy Ann and Raggedy Andy I'll see you both
once again soon; we have not changed much at all.

Raggedy Ann and Raggedy Andy, Raggedy Ann
and Raggedy Andy were my fun and joys.
Fay Poole

View Of The Beginning

The road we choose early in life has many bumps.
If we are lucky my making it though puberty without the mumps.
Becoming a teenager and our life is ruined because of a zit,
and homework is a job you cannot quit.
School is a mixture of musts and mights,
sometimes crushes, friends and fights.
An unplanned encounter with someone you like.
No thought to arm yourself against being told, "to take a hike,"
but somehow you know you will heal from this wound.
You will find someone else in which you are more in tuned.
Life goes on and then suddenly it's here.
The day which you though would never appear.
The day of graduation is here.
Now you face life for real.
Using all you were taught behind the school seal.
The eyes of your parents are damp with tears.
The pride in you and the memory of the difficult years.
Now you must prove to the world that you are part of it,
and place your imprint within the heart of it.
College or job, maybe both, but you will get the hang of it.
R. G. Connors

I Don't Like Tomatoes

Just who the hell are you
To tell me
What I can and can't watch,
Read or listen to
Who the hell are you
What gives you the right to decide for me
What makes you a better judge than me
Did I elect you, no
Who elected you
I am so sick of you
If you do not like what you see on T.V.
Switch it off you don't have to see
I do not like tomatoes
But it's okay with me
If you want to eat them
so you see.
What are you trying to protect me from
what is right
And who are you to decide what's wrong
Simon K. Browning

Sweet Dreams

Asleep in her bed,
The covers pulled tight.
My little sweet angel,
Is dreaming tonight.

Dreams about people,
And places she's been.
Childhood memories,
She dreams of again.

The peace in her sleep,
Is my peace too.
For my little sweet angel,
I'll always love you.
Chad Allan Mertz

Dead Love

The silent star filled night
filled me with a feeling of loneliness.

The fading moonlight matched my empty
heart.

Wishing on a shooting star
was like trying to talk to my dead love.

Standing in the twinkling light,
scared, sad and sorrowful.

For once true love dies,
it will never live again.
Kristen Bogeajis

To Fall Asleep

The pain comes so often
And runs so deep
The only way to avoid it
Is to fall asleep.

The pain still lingers
When I awake
I am forever doomed
Never to escape.
Desiree Rosenberger

Seize The Day

As we live, we die.
When we laugh, we cry.
Why do we let our lives rust?
Death is among us.
Seize the day,
Then you can say,
You gave it your all,
Despite your fall.

Nathan L. Washington

I Forgot

My mind is preoccupied
Even when I sleep it's not tame
Problems are the predators
That hunt me like a game
It's a struggle to win
When the tongue has no shame
Our world is forever changing
Yet, One remains the same

Why are my eyes blind?
And my ears have become deaf?

How do I find peace?
Can I look anywhere?
The smile of a baby
His presence is there
The babbling brook
To my ears, a sound rare
The warmth of the sun
Like the love of His heart, look there

I'm so sorry I forgot
Romans Chapter five, verse eight

Charles Eric Kingsley

Dear Father

Dear Father, now your work is done,
Your children all are grown,
And though you're sometimes lonely
You're really not alone.

For God helped you to plant the seeds
You cared for tenderly,
And from those seeds grew little sprouts,
That's how we came to be.

Then with the thread of unity
He bundled us as one,
To brave the stormy weather,
And rejoice beneath the sun.

So we can never leave your side,
Nor will you walk alone,
For we're the fragments of your soul,
The product of seeds you'd sown.

Millicent Juray-Lowry

Regrets

The tie no longer binds mother and daughter together,
Although it was meant to be forever.
Somewhere in their past the deed was done.
They can no longer be as one.
Now, in their hearts, there is a rip and a tear.
The love once shared has spread only fear.
Will son and daughter ever know each other
And live to become sister and brother?
The mother once dreamed of their lives together,
But now this will come as quick as never.

Kimberly A. Pittman

It's Your Responsibility

When you decide to marry and raise a family,
You'll soon be blessed with beautiful children;
For whom you'll, of course, provide your utmost.
It's your responsibility.

The children grow up fast and need your guidance;
To refrain them from wandering into the wrong path,
And to steer them on to the right tract.
It's your responsibility.

A good education is a must for them,
And, perhaps, a little capital to start like with,
To be able to recycle on their own.
It's your responsibility.

Right spouses do not always come along naturally,
As you may have experienced when you began.
Parental advice on their choices may be helpful.
It's your responsibility.

U. Khin

Life

I see it in the curling wave and in the placid sea,
I see it in the flight of birds passing o'er the lea,
I see it in the blade of grass, verdant, tall and proud,
I see it in the azure sky with just a lonely cloud.

I hear it in the new born babe held close to mother's breast,
I hear it in the sighing tree from root to bending crest,
I hear it in the bumble bee, pollen on its feet,
I hear it in the crowing cock, call the morning greet.

I taste it in the salty spray arching o'er the bow,
I taste it in the fresh sweet milk of the herd man's cow,
I taste it in the crisp sweet corn plucked from a tall green stalk,
I taste it in the small wild grapes found on my morning walk.

I smell it in the rain washed air, fresh, clean and pure,
I smell it in the pine wood grove the aroma a sure safe cure,
I smell it in a burned off field where seeds will be released,
I smell it in the fresh -baked bread for hunger now is ceased.

I feel it strong in farm and town where people show their kin,
I feel it in a firm handshake, by words and written pen,
I feel it in my own pulse beat, true and really strong,
I feel it in the world about, moving like a song.

Harriet Hoevet Bennett

The Protagonist

Before the great design was employed,
This vast earth was dark and void.
The Royal Builder formed a Master Plan
To complement His creation man.

The order was given, and the great light burst through;
Still the eminent architect had much to do.
The lesser glow would govern the night,
And, with the stars, form a majestic sight.

The gathering waters, those life-giving seas;
Those winged ones that soared through the air with ease;
All creeping things in this scenery so vast
Formed the great setting in which man was cast.

Man, the marvel of that Architect's features;
Dominion he was given over all other creatures.
Man, the image of that infinite sage;
Man, the protagonist, on the greatest stage.
Margarette Combs Saunders

The First Day Of Spring

To-day has been a showery rainy day.
On again, off again, windy and threatening at times,
As if winter does not want to give up.
It is raining as I step out of the door.

Dark clouds hover overhead.
The Sun peeking through, here and there,
Playing Hide and Seek with the clouds.
In the eastern sky hangs a huge rainbow!

All the colors and hues of the spectrum are there.
Its brilliance is unequaled.
A real joy to see!
The very first rainbow of Spring.

O Happy Joyful Spring!
You have not failed us.
You have returned.
As faithfully as you have always done.

Year after year since the world began.
Spring has begun!
The happy spirits will drop their mantle of cold.
The earth will be bathed in all its Springtime glory.
Sarah G. Sawyer-Shepard

A Voice

I awaken in the night startled by a voice.
All I hear is the wind.
I fall back to sleep only to be awakened again.

The wind gets louder with each awakening.
Is the wind a voice speaking to me?
Am I suppose to listen?
What is it trying to tell me?

Night after night I become more restless.
What ma I afraid of?
I struggle for nerve to confront this voice.

I walk into the night, letting the wind surround me.
I hear the voice. I listen. I feel a calm, a peace.
I begin to understand.
The voice I hear is my own.
Cheryl C. Dodson

Why Am I Here?

I can't find my place on this earthly plane
   Everything seems to go wrong
I've searched and searched, but all in vain
   And the road seems weary and long

A nomadic traveller passing through
   Seeking a place to belong
Not knowing from where, why, when, or who
   Sent me, or for how long

My soul doth lust to find its home
   And to cease its ever roaming
Is it fate that makes me comb
   This earth, forever moaning

This shell that embodies my very being
   Has become as a prison wall
It encases me and keeps me from seeing
   If there is a purpose to it all
Lois-Margaret Sullivan

My Lost Love

You were the love of my life,
   you were the light of my eyes
You were my laughter and joy
   you had the shoulder on which
   I could cry.
But suddenly you changed
   I cried and I tried
   to calm myself
But my hope, my faith and my love
   had vanished.

The star which shined at your
   name, does no more.
The flowers that danced at your
   fame do no more.
My heart that beat at your sight
   just fights with my mind,
to let me know, that
you are no more mine but hers . . .
Sonia Monica Harris Jacob

The Ravages Of Time

This is a time of unrest;
Stress, emotional trauma.
This is a time of violence;
Beatings, murders, wars.
This is a time of ignorance;
Lack of knowledge, unwillingness to learn.
This is a time of greed;
Wants, excesses, selfishness.
This is a time of technology;
Better, worse, change.
This is a time we need each other;
To mend broken fences,
To eat at the table of brotherhood,
To smoke the pipe of peace.
This is the time we need to stand together
With one voice
In the choir of human dignity.
Marcia Webb

Dear Friend

My life line
The wisdom of your thoughts
That which I cherish
Forever be mine

Words can never reveal
From lost child of innocence
Evolves this man of whole
This I do feel

So on this special day
As your aurora keeps flowing
Know that you have made
Yet another friend
To add to the list
That keeps on growing
   Daniel W. Hirtle

Childhood Lost

When childhood is denied its play
And innocence is chased away
Too soon, is there perchance a space
In heaven, some hallowed corner lot
Where childhood goes, a playground spot
Untouched by worldly care; a place
With swings and slides, gay carousels,
And pony rides and wishing wells,
Where one may freely play and run,
Build stately castles tall and grand,
And shape one's dreams in grains of sand;
This may well be, when life is done,
Yet no child should a victim be
Of childhood lost—too late for me,
I've paid the cost of play denied,
Grieved its loss, it seems forever;
And I have searched, yet I have never
Found my lost childhood on this side.
   Selina Pimblett

Essence Of Madness

Everything that I've faced
I have not had to see

Everything that I've learned
Means little to me

And all that I take
Is more than I need

Life does not satisfy
My insatiable greed

All the wisdom you can muster
Will be uttered in vain

You are merely an object
Of my perpetual disdain

Anything that can save me
Is worthless to try

I choose my disgrace
And I live my own lie.
   Tammy McCarthy

My Uncertain Mind

I have walked the wind-swept Mountains in my uncertain mind,
pining always these hours as in the reigning of time.

I've searched the wide horizon for all the signs of life,
Only to find a blackness as dark and thick as night.

Through extremes of heat and cold I struggled to find the path,
Only to stumble all the more and lose the lighted way.

I've run this gauntlet to places that I do not know,
Only to find myself in shadows of gloom and bitterness so.

The breath of this Jackal is heavy upon my throat,
taking all that was mine, my life, my hope.

Where have the rays of sunlight gone from this an empty soul,
across the wide expanse in shadows of brassy gold.

Now let the blush of life turn this way once more,
listen to the whisper for life it only can restore.

Now as I walked these mountains and felt the child of winds,
a life will not be stolen in games of selfish thrill.
   Ruth Piccola

Amity's Gone Fishin'

The little blonde girl I see each day
is not with me today. You see, she's away.
She went with her Grandma and was happy too.
I'm really glad for it's something she's wanted to do.

There's more I'll say, to the story than this
as yesterday fondly, I gave she and Boober a hug and a kiss.
Now, a fishing excursion is what's the decision,
Yep! You guessed it, Amity's gone fishin'.

If they fish from a creek there's lots to tend,
bobbers and lines and if she hooks a big fish the rod will bend,
but should they go to a river they might use a boat,
what fun it will be just to fish and float.

I hope she catches a whole lot of fish,
plus has a good two day time, that's also my wish.
What will she snare? A pike or a sunny?
A bass or a perch, I hope not an eel or that wouldn't be funny.

She's five years old and eager to do and learn.
This child and all about her is my main concern.
When she returns I'm ready to hear "listen Tai"
as to how she caught whatever fish and maybe even the one that
      got away
   Elois L. Spangler

The Walls Of Growth And Doubt

House overlooking a tree.
Heartless wind rips apart the woods.
Tearing trough the lifeless manmade void.
I wonder with gaze into the sight of green and brown.
Scraping the life from under us—killing the joker of fates.
Trusting reality to remain conscious.
Knowing the struggles that lie ahead.
Everyone's serving the sentence of a life.
Business thrives where man dies.
Make believe that all you see is all there is.
Seek the ideas of your dreams.
   Brian M. Rice

Somehow . . .

Sometimes when I look at you,
Something stirs inside me—
Something magical and mystical,
Something that I cannot describe or explain.
All I know is that
Somehow . . . you have loved me.

Somehow . . . when you kiss me and I close my eyes,
I see a beautiful place:
Where the wind blows soft against my face.
At day the sun shines down upon me.
At night the stars surround me.
And when you take me in your arms and pull me to you,
You take me to another place:
A place that I have never known
A place where reality is thrown
A place where all my hopes have gone
A place where you and I belong.

And somehow . . . as all my desires fade into me,
I feel a completeness that envelopes me, because
Somehow . . . you have loved me.

Christi Leigh Robbins

Have You Ever Watched A Babbling Brook?

The ripples of the water cascading over the well rounded stones,
that have been covered with icy mountain liquid for hundreds
of seasons.
The way the fluid laps the edges of its banks
trying desperately to leave them.
To see the mirror like substance shimmer
and dance in the sun.
Smooth and calm in its harnessed pools
between rocks, barriers and the edges of a silk
and rubble lined shore.
The laughter of the brook as it tumbles and
rolls toward a larger source is music
to the ears, heart, and soul.
So soothing that you can close your eyes and see yourself
floating as one with the ever flowing fluid.
The coolness of the wondrous liquid is life giving and
soul quenching.

Kim Martinez

A Sonnet To John

I will always remember the place where we first met
A little shabby dive between the graveyard and the park
I had not expected, nor could I ever have bet
That I would find love in a place so haunted and dark
You were not the man that I dreamed of in junior high
Your hands were rough and calloused, a wool hat over your
　disarray hair
Your eyes were sharp and stabbing, like you could see right
　through a lie
No, I did not ever think I could've found love there

But oh, the funny little tricks that life will play on a heart
By the end of that unforeseen summer, I was holding your hand
There was not a time when we were ever apart
What a precious pearl I found in someone so unplanned
Now I have found forever in your words so gentle and true
My little gardenia heart has run away from me to you

Melanie Harnage

Revealed

Mountains, mountains
so majestic, so high
horns of the earth
that gore the sky
with snowcapped peaks
and jagged ledge
piercing through the cold, crisp wind

born of fire, cut by ice
pushed from the earth toward the sky
concealing caldrons deep within
what consequences do you hold
luring mortals with veins of gold

Randy W. Johnson

Our Treasure

A Son of love our dearest joy
The treasure of our heart

With God above guarding him
Our family will never part

Though sorrows on earth
And much pain to bear

God has watched over you
Kept you in his care

Your parents arms enfolded you
In loves sublime embrace

Let mothers songs fill your heart
Like daddy's words of praise

We all were born many grew up
We multiplied and together sup

Life's journey goes on, scenes have
changed

Some were young, others old
The loved ones gone from the fold

Joys and love, heartache and tears
Have followed through the years

But given a son, and the world sharing him
Is a sure way of God's love to win

Mamie A. Breininger

Anger

Anger is red,
Which is as thick as blood.
Anger is fear,
Which moves slow and near,
Past the heart and toward the soul.
Anger is hurt,
Which never seems to go.
Anger is pain,
Which falls like tears in the rain.
Anger is fought,
To ease the pain,
But returns with every rain.
Anger is here and here to stay,
Like childhood nightmares,
Which never fade away.

Katina Edwards

Thoughts And Emotions

I've walked through valleys
   the valleys of death,
Taken a few challenges
   they've taken my breath.

Under nothin' but pain
   I have shed my flesh and blood,
Memories departing my brain
   washed away within the flood.

I've climbed big mountains
   some have burned to dust,
I've crawled to many fountains
   and found only rust.

The prose writing writer
   had lost his pen,
Sun ain't gettin' brighter
   his journey's at an end.

An old wise one once said,
   "Love becomes a cry,"
But all I could do was sit there,
   bowing my head, asking why?
      Morgan L. Post

A Bodybuilder's First Love

What a wonderful, glorious sight!
I am so sharp in this light,
And everyone knows I'm right.
With my abs all nice and tight,
The girls, they will fight,
For me and my beautiful might.

Oh my, will you look at that,
I am so pumped, not at all flat.
Great striations and low body-fat.
Really brings out my left lat.

I know that you are all gazing,
At my hot body, which is blazing.

But you cannot touch this piece of art,
Or attempt to compare, you cannot start,
For on a ten scale, I'm off the chart,
And without my shirt, you'd lose heart.

So, step out of my line of sight,
You're blocking the mirror's light.

For I am truly in love with what I see,
It's just too bad you can't be me.
   Terry Allen Richards II

Grand Autumn

Restless is Autumn
as She inquisitively
imposes upon Summer's time
casting forth Her luxurious colors
into the cool breeze
Her magnificence paints a wondrous
landscape of many hues
leaving behind Summer's majestic beauty
and ushering Her way into Winter's
wonderland
Autumn, Grand Autumn
   Rhonda L. Aquilina

Forbidden Love

If I could love you'd be the one,
   I would always love you and you alone
You remind me of a rose on a warm summers
day so lovely so free. If I was the wind and you
the rose I'd hold you forever,
   But I am not the wind and you are not the
rose so I can never hold you like the wind holds a rose.
   Stacey Dague

So Near And Yet So Far

Sprays of mist against the cheek,
distant banks of solemn gray;
Lonely chill and shore so bleak,
Splashing wavelets at their play.

Dialogue of breeze and water
murmurs softly here and there;
Dancing shadows skip and totter
across the gleam of surface glare.

Rhythmic waves with luminous sparkle
mask the cold, dim depths beneath;
Endless depths of bubbling dark will
never their own code bequeath.

Unearthly power, humble awe,
Billows silvered by the moon;
Something here not cold and raw?
Understanding, warmth attune.

This fleeting close and transient feeling
'mid such grand and endless scheme
overwhelms the soul with feeling,
Someone's with you,—it would seem.
   James Ramsey

The Hobbyist

"Sweepstakes, puzzles, crosswords and poems,
What is it about this craze? —
I sit for hours at a time,
To meet deadlines most of these days."

"Some are easy, some are tough,
It's something I like to do —
I'm always looking for challenges,
Keeps my mind active, like brand new."

"I've entered many contests,
Hoping to strike it rich —
Even if I never win,
I feel I've given it my best pitch."

"Relaxation and sheer pleasure,
And pure enjoyment I derive —
The hours spent aren't wasted,
It's contentment that keeps me alive."

"This hobby keeps me busy,
I like it more each day —
When I'll least expect it,
I've hit it big, that's what I'll say."
   Marty Rollin

The Lighthouse

It may like some time to climb these serpentine stairs
To find the narrow foot-bridge surrounding the crystal flame
Where one can stand and view the fine-line which divides
The bounded sea from a boundless sky

It will be hard for those beaten by the roaring waves
To grip the cold damp rails . . . but everyone
Everyone . . . step by step
Will overcome the slippery risers
And learn not to look back—not to look down
But to look forward and up to the far-reaching ray

Which turns slowly . . . constantly casting
Its clear compassionate eye for anyone foundering
In leaking scows over the pitch-back rollers

Inviting all in doubt to disembark
Beneath the sweep of the sharp benevolent beam
And begin a provisional journey over the rocky
Lighthouse shoal to the rust-stained door
Up into the silence of the stony inner tower
Away from the thoughtless
Swilling tide.

Randall E. Pretzer

From Dusk Till Dawn

From dusk till dawn I search the light
longing for the westward pull
taking me toward the destiny that I find
endlessly searching in the night
through my trails and triumphs He is there
finding me in careful slumber
as the days do twist through the hours
and upon the eve I fall into the night
there He cannot come to save me and there I must fight
to win the soul that I have lost
and He protects me while I rest in the light
and never shall He forsake me in the light of day
forevermore He does find my battered body
cleansing me from troubles harm and protecting
my innocence that is lost and I with it knowing
only he can be the light that saves my wretched soul
and I have let Him help me toward forgiving
those sins that He has already forgiven
and in Him I find peace.

Thomas H. Pendergest

Hag Fish

The alluring sex of navels, the scent of perfumed wrist
Full-figured bodies and well-rounded hips
Soft hands, red tongue, passionate stares
Pouty lips, warm smiles, and long curly hair
Expressions, postures, the way that they sit
Sweet laugh, long nails, the moods they can get
Attract me helpless and bound to their will
Here at dusk, gone at dawn alone I'm unfulfilled
They say there's a million fish in the sea
I've caught a hundred, but none were for me
Each day again my net is cast
Each fish I land, more fishy than last
Schooled, fun, white collar classy
Not conceited, nor spoiled, yet just a touch sassy
Is the woman I seek from my dreams that I see
Who is out there searching, and fishing for me.

Christopher Wise

Tolovana Echo

October morning
To teams guarding
Spirit of place
Silver point surprise

Harry L. Garnham

Songs Of The Night

She sits upon a hillside
Looking down upon the town.
The murmur of the city lights
Is such a soothing sound.
And in the still of darkness
She can hear a howling sound.
It's the sound of the wilderness
Flowing all around.
The wind upon the trees.
The crickets on the ground.
Frogs in a distant pond
Croaking out their songs.
No matter where you go.
No matter where you live.
Just listen to the distant hum
Of the wilderness in your head.

Veronica A. Rittel

Loving You

You have
shared my sorrows,
enjoyed my joys,
cried my pain, and
lived my expectations.

You have
explored my fantasies,
secured my emotions,
known my self, and
loved my love.

For you
I do the same and
that is love.

Dolores Repik

Life's Journey

Friends are important things,
that every person needs
Sometimes we have problems,
picking the one compatible seed
Riding that huge roller coaster,
making our own fate
Will it all be worth it
by time we reach the gate?

Time will only tell,
so live life at its best
Pretend there's no tomorrow,
and don't worry about the rest.
With a little hope.
And sharing others faith
Things will be alright,
and you will be safe.

Lisa Rizzo

A Love Like Ours

I long to touch your face,
and to feel you embrace,

Holding you as if you were mine,
hoping you'll be mine this time,

Finding it hard to speak,
as our lips softly meet,

Feelings you're trying to fight,
while magic is filling the night,

You pretend you don't love me,
open our heart and let it be,

A love ours was meant to last,
please don't force it to be our past,

My heart pounds just to hear your voice,
why have you made another choice?

Precious love I've given to you,
don't be afraid to love me too...
Zenia R. Clark

There's Only One Way

We are engaged in a very,
very, very serious
spiritual warfare

Our kids, homes, jobs families
are being attacked because,
we're not aware
of that

Satan is working overtime,
no question, he knows of
the great big sign

Has it ever occurred to
you, that man is a spirit,
possessing a soul,
living in a body? . . .

America better wake up,
before Satan gets the whole bunch
Alexi Quinones

Cammy Alexis

She speaks to me in a silent
  voice as only I can understand
Of love and life and paradise, as
  only she can.
For only her love can fill this
  giant empty hole,
That once was in my heart
  and in my soul.

For I am living, loving proof
  that dream do come true
The loving rhythm of our hearts
  when I listen
My dance after the waltz,
  the fiddler is thro.
My last sight at night, or last
  of my life, as long as
  it's her smile glisten.
Phillip Hackney

Indian Boy Looked Into My Heart

He said, "You smiled and are so friendly.
But! When I look into your eyes,
I see your heart, why is to sad?
You seem so happy on the outside."

How did you know my heart was breaking
Because of my husband's other woman.
Hurting is finally fading somewhat
After five years of being divorced.

How true was the Indian boy's look at my heart.
When you can only stand by, watching marriage go to pieces . . .
Like being on the outside, looking in.
No amount of trying to talk or work it out,
Marriage was gone.

He told me he would do what he wanted no matter who was hurt.
The hurt of watching your world crumble day by day,
Like cancer, sometimes you still lose the battle.
We all handle things differently—I put on a happy face.
No use wearing a broken heart on the outside, I display smiles.
Not many can look into my heart like the Indian boy could.
Madeline M. Queen

Thanksgiving

I once had a house but it was not a home
My Lord did not live there, much later He'd come.
This house was unhappy for all its long years;
full of sorrow and shame and so many tears.

Now my home is my castle, its humble and small,
it's not meant to dazzle, to the Lord I owe all.
I'm proud of my home and of all the things it
When visitors come, my welcome I bid them.

I don't take for granted my blessings bestowed
on this sinner who can't pay the debt I once owed.
The Lord lets me borrow these things for a while,
but quick as a wink, it could be my time.

With thanksgiving just a few days away,
I'm planning a feast and I take time to pray
and thank the good Lord for all He has given;
good food, good company and good wholesome living.
Helena Collins

Teddy Bear

To often you find there's nobody to hold,
to share your life with, nobody there.
It's nice to know you still have your teddy bear.

Your teddy bear has been with you since you were a child.
He was with you while you were sleeping, or up being wild.

Your teddy bear is so sweet, so cuddly, so warm.
Just keep him close, and he'll shelter you from harm.

When you find yourself in need of a hug.
Just pick up your teddy and hold him real snug.

You can tell him all of your secrets too.
You know he'll never betray you.

So when you need someone to count on, someone who'll care.
Always remember you can count on your teddy bear.
Glen T. Rankin Jr.

Hiroshima

It was so quiet you could hear a chopsticks fall
A clear blue sky as it was so tall
Then a blinding flash of light
It seemed so bright like the whole world was on fire
Orange, red and yellow colors filled the air
Then the buildings blasted into millions of atoms
And were blown away in despair
The earth shook everything to pieces
People were instantly vaporized
Turned into skeletons
And burned to a crisp
The houses and huts were smashed to bits
Smashed into atoms in a brisk
Radiation sickness struck these left alive
But to slowly deteriorate to death
An inch at a time
And the horrors of war should come to an end
Never should this weapon be used again
Norman Sadler

Reason To Live

I try to love, to hope, to feel
But there's nothing inside - nothing real.
I cry and wish to be saved from the despair
That engulfs my mind and thickens the air
All around me as I try to hear
The voice of my soul whispering softly in my ear
But the sounds are too muffled to comprehend
And I know those low moans are just a beckoning to descend
The depths of the forest anxiously awaiting me
Sneering, jeering, entrapping - I want to be set free.
To feel the sunshine on my face
To ride the wind and win the race -
There must be more to my life
Some reason to live, to put down the knife
That shiningly begs for my firm, careful grip
To guide its blade and begin the final drip
Of life from this body so numb and cold
I want to cry out for someone to hold
Me and show me that life isn't only
A place of unyielding pain, so dark and lonely.
Jennifer Brown

Frankly, My Dear

As I write these ditties of rhyme and verse,
I think of you, with imagination, that's my curse.

Though I would not be the one to deny,
that sex is on my list, lustfully high.

It's not that all men are the same.
I just hate these silly dating games.

I wrote this verse that rhymes for you,
To show that my intentions are true.

   Roses are Red
   Violets are Blue
   If I could taste your dew
   I would dip my wick too.

As you can see my visions are clear,
It's your body I want, my dear.
Kay Keiser

True Love

At the thought of mentioning your name
My heart burns inside, an eternal flame.
While I ponder on our love,
I know it was sent from up above.

In the middle of the sea,
My dreams are of you and I think of me.
As time passes and goes on by,
I look up to heaven and I often sigh.

Through the thunder in the night,
I see in you a wondrous light.
Through the passing of the day,
I think on you and what you would say.

How I love to be with you,
Knowing that our love is true.
And once again it comes along,
Another day, a beautiful dawn.
Darlene R. Hall

Ama

Ama, of a loss for words
   For the love I shared with you
   Longing, a silent justice
   I wait for you

Ama, a love possessed
   As if a mythical telling
   Remembered by its movie ending
   Farewell kiss in close-up

Ama, the ways of lovers separating
   She said I was in her heart
   Forever, my life spent walking
   in the rain or sitting in the park

Ama, Goddess of Poetry, your beauty sinister
   Beneath a moonlight serenade
   Naked tango on a balcony with Lynsander
   Instead of love she spins escapades

Ama, a silence so deep
   Sensuous, but invisible
   Quite of speech and incomplete
   Infinite, but censurable.
Miguel A. Pagan

Camping

The trees the butterflies
the birds and the bees.
The sounds and sights of
the canyons, I hear and see.

The campfire crackling and
popping. In the forest the
wildlife hopping.
The smoke hanging over in a
haze; into the campfire
of burnt wood I gaze.

The smell of coffee perking
in the morning. A new day
   awakening and adorning.
Mitchell S. Payne

Basket Of Life

The shrill urgency of the doorbell
Brought me to my feet.
To the door I leaped.
No one was there!
I peered into the night-silence.
As I started to close the door,
A tiny whimper escalated
Into a piercing squeal.
Then I saw the basket
With the tattered blue blanket.
There was a crumpled note
Pinned to the squirming blanket.
It read:
"Please give me life.
You have so much.

I am so little.

Give me a small piece of your heart
And I will give you all my love."
I took her in my arms and gave her
All my love and all my heart!

Lois A. Pratte

Time's End

The day began calm and serene.
Alarm clocks ended nights of dreams.
A cup of coffee ... A glass of milk...
Hip riding blue jeans... A blouse of silk.
Newspaper headlines screamed of wars,
Drugs and hate, death gore.
The sky grew dim. The wind stood still.
Shivers greeted the morning chill.
Highways crowded with trucks and cars ...
No one noticed the shaking stars.
Tempers flared, screeching brakes,
Blaring horns, curses raked
Drivers who were slow to start...
No one saw the heavens part.
Two men crossing a dew we lawn
Paused to chat, and one was gone.
One by one, without a tear,
People began to disappear...
Clocks counted minutes, one by one
Never knowing that time was done.

Dorothy V. Blakeman

Morning Walk

This morning the woods are brilliant
In vibrant red and gold;
I can only walk and marvel
At the glory to behold.

I walk with keen awareness
Of summer's flaming end,
Amidst the shimmering trees
As autumn's colors blend.

I can hear the geese, honk, honk,
And see their V so high,
As warm winds gently blow
Across the autumn sky.

Ethel-Lee Osborn

Angel Of Light

Darkness is all around us, but the angel of light is not
far away.
The morning sun's rays brighten the windows of life.
The world see the light and reflects upon it.
Darkness is all around us, but the angel of light is not
far away.

Poet Canavan

My Father

My Father, in heaven, you hear my every word
Your eyes are upon your child here in this world

You hear my deepest cry
My Father there in the sky

You answer each and every time that I call
Many times with a blessing greater than I could ever recall

You knit me together in my mother's womb
I think about this as I touch my hair with my comb

Oh, God, my Father, I love you so much
Your hand I wish I could touch

You made the universe
I know, it is here in Genesis, the first verse

I want to praise you in your might strength
I lean on you to the last length

Your ways are far beyond my understanding
As I stand forgiven and my day of reckoning

My lord I pray that you will not look at my dirty rags of sin
I know that these are covered by the atoning blood of your son.

I wish that I had known you many years ago
Oh, the hurt that I caused would not be so

The greatest command of all
I pray that I can stand that all

To love as you loved me
Today will be my greatest plea

Linda C. Brown

Seasoned

She is well seasoned with vines.
Her eyes, clear as the sky, glisten through
The Rose pedals that surround her face.

The fields of her youth; once held her
spiritual study.
Have now become the deserted halls of her life;
with mincing steps side by side.

At the end, to the right.
Is her room, so bright.
Album walls portray the biography of her life.

Now, resting in her chair.
Her prayers are whispered in the air,
"Lord, take care of my children; they're all I need."

Solitude, except her telephone,
"Mama, Mama", "How are you, today?"
"Oh, a little tired, just tired," she replies
As raindrops cloud the sky.

Brenda Kay

Katrina

He brought her love unpromised many years ago
Two hearts, three lives divided within their own.
Was it Gods infinite wisdom
A bonding unclearly seen
A vision, unraveled and scattered
Or a dream?

Of what became those moments
She stood alone to understand.
An angel so pure and gentle eagerly grasped her hand.
They carried each other like warriors.
Defending their honor and youth,
Heart and hand, face to face, truth to truth.

She gave her life, she brought her love,
She gave her wings to fly above
A flicker of light, that fills the sky
And pales all that passes by.
She reaches out, as I reach in
Looking back from where we've been.
   Jill D. Ahmann-Smith

Broke But Not Beat

You say, you only, have fifty bucks, left.
You are out of a job, and you're broke
Why son, if I ever got fifty bucks,
I'd think it, some kind of a joke,

So sing me more, of your sad songs.
Tell me no tale's of woe,
For I've climbed that same, old mountain,
A long long time ago.

My pockets are empty all the time.
Despair! I've been in that well
My stomach ache's, met up with my backbone,
More often, than I care to tell

I've been down on my buck, for so darned long,
I don't know, if I should cause or give thanks.
Why! If I walked out, with a nickel,
I'd loose it, on the way to the bank.

My cheque book! It's so dammed out dated,
I can't even enter the time.
And, if I were to try and call, someone who cares,
I couldn't come up with a dime.

But! You're not broke, till you've nothing.
Not one coin, in those tattered, old jeans,
Then, if you still have good health, body and mind,
You are still, a man of means.
   Hazel Bean

Grandmother

Grandmother you were so dear to me
your smile, laughter, a joy to see
the rocking chair that I know so well
still rocks when the wind blows
letting me know you are still with me
the thought of your loving embrace
comforts me when I think of your smiling face
the sweet songs of lullabies
are with me through sunrise
Grandmother, you will remain in my heart forever
   Charlotte Burke

Ghost

While driving after dust on an old deserted Georgia back road. From the trees came Beverly, she was young about 23. Dressed in a white old fashion evening dress. With long flowing red hair and eyes as blue as the sea. She said to me can she take a ride near Eagle Rock and Broken Tree. I was from out of town on military leave. All I say was wait and see, after conservations ranging from A to Z I heard that this was a sight of old civil war victories. As we neared Eagle Rock and Broken Tree. She said pull over and let me be. With my car lights on High Beans Beverly disappeared right in front of me. At the cemetery named Eagle Rock and Broken Tree. Well that's my story it's up to you to believe.
   Charles Frazier

New Beginnings

This day marks the beginning
Of the rest of our lives
You as my husband
And I as your bride

To have and to hold
To love and adore
Our love is forever
Until time is no more

For God has anointed
The bond of us two
He pours down his blessings
When we say "I do"

No greater happiness we've known
Before Christ entered our lives
His love has made all the difference
Bonding two souls—yours and mine

Totally devoted
I surrender all my love to you
This day we will cherish
A day when dreams come true
   Pat Schulz

Oh, The Pain!

Reluctant to experience this game,
I caved in to its loud, resounding claim
That I would grow to love its thrilling aim
  For pain.

I heard the crack, and then my victim's cry.
I saw the scars...Could not imagine why
I'd do such harm, and thinking "How can I
  Cause pain?"

I - trying harder - felt my lip get wet
And wiped across my brow to clear the sweat.
Could I be ready for my Love to get
  The pain?

I take a breath; now, carefully, I throw
My soul into it, never letting go
Of this new joy - my newfound pleasure.
  Oh, the pain!
   Cindy DeDanaan

The Answer?

The seed of hate needs no special soil
to nurture its dread fruit
And though its first born is rotten and
decayed it still proliferates
You are fortunate who find its very form
repulsive and turn away
For those who linger in morbid fascination
are tempted and fall prey

The antidote is near at hand for the
flower of love abounds
But you must wear it in your heart don't
pin it on your jacket or gown
Let it grow deep inside until it
finds your soul
Let its warmth heal your and make
your body whole

Ellwood F. Saxton

A Winter Night

Snowflakes glistening like diamonds
falling to the ground.
Covering in a blanket white
everything around.
The moon up in the evening sky
shining clear and bright.
Shining down upon the ground
with a silent eerie light.
Majestically the pine tree stands there
dancing in the breeze.
While the Aspen seems to shiver
naked of its leaves.
The silence is only broken
by the sound of a mournful howl.
A song sung by a pack of wolves
as they begin to prowl.
Yes, an eerie silence fills the air
on a winter night.
When everything is covered
by a blanket white.

Carl G. Clark

The Storm Has Passed

The clouds have broke.
The sun is shining through.
I can see the rainbow.
With its brilliant yellows, reds and blues.

The storm has ended.
The rolling thunder has ceased.
The skies turn to blue,
With pearly white clouds
That exude with peace.

The fragile flowers
Bent and beat from the rain
Now lift their precious petals
To the sun, forever to reign!

Judi Bishop

Life Reflections In A Window

Across the lawn the window reflects all that lights the day.
It mourns for those who slipped slyly by and
lie three miles away.

Closure must be an errant child hiding in a bush enclave,
Clothed in deep velvet warmth but cool as a mountain cave.

Pray look! The bewigged missionary appears, weighs
evil as pounds of Good.

Trashes our three generations advance, enlightened
truth never understood.

Oh fie! Abhor the thief of fathers, reflects credit
for children bereft.

Receives the prize allotted for compassion's deliberate theft.

Sow and reap, sun dims and twilight emerges,
image fade on the window's pane.

Now only the shine of the Creator's humor
is a reflection that will sustain.

Nathalie Ellman

Ultimate Weapon

Calculated strategically
Worse yet
Attacking impulsively.

Invisible and odorless
Irreparable damage, similar to a cold war
But infinitely more toxic by far.

A weapon so powerful, yet so minuscule
So effective, so efficient.

Only a superficial wound
When set on low.

But amped to full blast
Slow torture unmasked.

Accessible to the young and old alike
Illuminating dangerously as a sharp gleaming knife.

Artillery of the strongest degree
Threatening ominous agony.

Echoes reverberate in your mind
Of what you once heard.

The profound intensity
In the painfully paralyzing word.

Vaive Estam

Autumn

Autumn is a flag, a waving banner fraught with color
A riot of smells, so tart and sweet and sharp
Autumn is an end to the long, golden days of summer
The promise of icy winds and chattering teeth
My footfalls through the forest crisply tell my love I'm near
I pray he's getting ready to light the fire
The chilly air quickens my step, puts roses in my cheeks
The sun sinks swiftly, earlier each day
The squirrel's stored his acorns and the fox has dug his den
And any birds with brains have all gone south.

Gina Daidone

Parted Clouds

Oh dear mother of mine,
If only we had more time.
I think often of the past,
and always wonder why love will never last.
I can no feel all your sorrow and pain,
and see now how much we are the same.
I prayed your depression and addiction would go away,
and cried fro you many a night and day.
I now know you are finally in peace,
and now pray my own depression would cease.
Your calling came early that cold and dreary day in January,
My own fall came when they locked the door behind me late that
    February.
The day you took your last breath,
I never really mourned your death.
I mourned what should have been,
You know I always felt I was a sin.
I know you did your best to be a better mother,
even if it was with a bottle in one hand and pills in the other.
Life can be so cruel, but I will always love you.
The clouds have parted and now I see,
The Day Has Come To Love Me.
  Eileen Fischetti

Albedrio

Did you not know you never make a choice?
Have you not learned your acts are not your own,
and all you do is at some higher voice
you must obey, although to you unknown?
Some smirking universal dramatist
hath writ your lines, for you to act and be,
your speeches fit the plot, or would desist;
Pierrot, you dance for them to laugh to see.

When you laughed yester eve, it was not you,
yours was a mirth ages ere then decreed,
and your regret, ordained too, had no need.
You were the spinning leaf the long wind blew.

Yet do not cease to cling, since you must fall.
That leaf best spins which waits. This is your all.
  J. Kellogg Burnham

Someday

I walk with you in my dreams.
We hold hands, we dance.
Just like when you were here.
It seems like just yesterday
That you were taken from me.
I will never forget that night
The sound of times screeching
The sound of your voice screaming
The headlights were so bright
We couldn't see a thing
As the car hit us, everything went black.
I lied there with her, in that smoking car.
She squeezed my hand tight, then her grip began to loosen
It was hard for me let go of her
But I know we'll meet again.
I know in my heart I'll find a way
A way to see my true love
Love will unite us, somehow, someway.
We'll be together, someday
  Wayne Bailey

This Gift

From whence did it come,
With its trial and error—
At times so without sum,
At times full of terror?

Some moments—grand wonder,
Great thrill in it all.
Surely one might ponder,
So much does enthrall.

Be there any glad reply
To this haunt, this ample quest?
On which response will one rely,
And if so, at whose behest?

Is it really of consequence
From whence it came—
Why such insistence
To give it a name?

Accept what can be oh such joy,
Void of commensurate pitch or strife,
Take this gift, its wonders employ;
Take this gift, this gift called life.
  Legora M. Norwood

Les Miserables

I've run away from God
and run away from man.
I've run away so long!
Can I begin again . . .

. . . To see the sun behind the clouds
. . . the beauty in the beast?
Can I look back and find some joy
  in the darkness that I see?

Can I still hope for friendship
when love cannot be seen,
or have I run from Truth
  and Everlasting Spring?
  Mary Ryk

Love Survived

Here we are together
After all the years have passed,
Still close friends and lovers;
What magic makes it last?

What secret do we share
That keeps our love alive?
Is it something deep with us
Or a goal for which we strive?

No matter what the reason
This relationship survives,
It becomes more precious daily
As our golden years arrive.
  Patricia Cibula

Abandoned

The desert is cold at night-
There's nothing but wind and stone;
The desert is where he died;
The sand turns to ashes
  around
    his bone.

It's hard to be cold alone-
It coils like a snake, the sky-
It's hard to get up and die;
Where the sand meets the clouds,
  the landscape
    is shaped

How easily this desert fits
Inside of this cardboard home,
The desert where he now sits -
A roamer
  with no place
    to roam.
(Nothing is more restricting than emptiness.)

Alexander Stessin

Shoestrings

As the slinky
  fell from her
    tiny hand
      and
bounced down the
  carpeted stairs,
    she watched with
      blank expression.

Her eyes, cold as her heart.

"What is death?" she
  asked the pup
    gnawing on her shoestrings.

"Will Mommie still tuck me in
  at night and
    tell me stories
      and
place Teddy in my arms
  when I saw my prayers?"

Shirley Conrad

One Thousand Pictures

Family pictures hang on my walls so proudly
Sitting, peeking, wondering.
All start with why.
Moments, so few, are remembered.
Still, smiling faces stare back at me
As if to say, "We love you!"
All start with why.
Why hide pain?
Why make it fake in portrait? To strangers?
Always more strife.
Never ending release.
All start with why.
Three such power!
Why hold so tight to family?
Because family is what holds you?

When no one else wants to!

Danielle R. Imhoff

Bag Lady Of Alltowns, U.S.A.

Torn and tattered she roams the streets
Accepting alms from strangers she meets
Pushing a store cart which holds all her things.
How does she maintain a heart that sings?
Frail and needy of body and bone
A happy spirit, but quite alone.
Very quietly, she hums and sings,
In fluttering sounds, like angels wings.
She wanders until she can walk no more
Longingly gazes at the bakery store.
The window reflects her eyes, so huge
Her cheeks as red as though wearing rouge,
She feasts her eyes on the visions there.
Already knowing, they won't be her fare!
Then weary of body and cold to the bone
She now looks to sleep, 'neath a box she calls home.
In a tattered coat and one threadbare glove
A smile on her face, a heart full of love
Tomorrow she'll rise and again start to roam
'Midst millions of people, and still be alone!

D. LaBianco

Inspiration's Master

Poems, poems flooding the shores from human emotion.
Yet it's the crest of the experience itself,
that powers its mighty churn toward another new
landing. Like an explorer for land, so too are those
who claim by moving quill another kindred bond,
from a land we've all stepped onto. Yet
these claim not for gain nor crown. Their quest,
the nod of understanding — the smile that heralds,
"I too have lived that moment" — that single tear
of comradery or companionship — or that gaze of
remembrance. Yes these are the treasures for which
they sail, the breeze that blows
them as they chart, the winds of change.
To wit they shall with each so
gentle stirring, give helms place to
"Inspiration's Master"
as they themselves behold the gift once more
again, to what cometh from above...

G. Michael McGarel H.S

Bonding

When I became your daughter, you named me.
When I was a baby, you sang to me.
When I was three, you put me on your knee.
When I was 13, you made a dress for me.
When I became 16, you sat in the front seat of the car with me.

When I became a mother of one, you were there for me.
When our family moved away, you visited me.
When I became divorced, you were sympathetic to me.

When my later birthdays came, you remembered me.
When I became older, you became older with me.
When I remember the older days, you try to remember them with me.

When I cook for us, you try to cook with me.
When I'm not with you, you try to take care of yourself.
When I must leave you, you try not to cry, and so do I.

So now I must tell you Mother Dear, you do not have to Try Not To Cry anymore, because I will be there for you, every day in everyway. As you were there for me.

Flavia V. Smith

The Maiden

Grandfather, hear my prayer
Have you seen the maiden,
A white feather in her hair?

Was it the wind I heard last night,
Or the sound of her laugh, is she still in flight?

On her journey, she will take the path
from me, back to your care.

You will know her Grandfather,
for few are so fair,
As our beautiful maiden,
a white feather in her hair.

A woman will walk beside her, face
wet with morning dew,
Grandfather, hear my prayer.

For I am the daughter of the woman,
and mother of the maiden, who walks
the path from me to you.

Lynda DeMarco

They Have Gray Snow, Don't Ya Know

They have gray snow, don't ya know.
Its on the sidewalks near the tall buildings.
Stacked high in mounds on the city curbs.
As wet gray slush in the busy city streets.
That sometimes splashes on shoes and clothes.

They have gray snow, don't ya know.
Even though it doesn't fall that way.
It falls white like cotton before it's dyed.
It falls in white flakes!
Not gray mounds or gray slush that's found in the city.

They have gray snow, don't ya know.
In the city it changes color.
To match the concrete sidewalks.
The blue road salt doesn't mar its hue.
The traffic does change its pigment.

They have gray snow, don't ya know.
The heavy city traffic hustling and bustling.
City streets crammed with cars, trucks and buses.
The dirt from the tires and the exhaust fumes
transfer the snow to a dirty gray.

Hope Brien

For Only A Short While

Dedicated to my love, Chad Ata

For the last six months you've been mine,
And I wish it to last for all time.
But now the time is going away,
And how I wish you could stay.

You're leaving me for a reason that's good,
I hope you know I understood.
Away to college is where your path takes you,
While I'm still here to finish high school.

To be with you forever is what I pray,
But I know back to me you'll find your way.
So as my heart cries and my mind says to smile,
I know we're apart for only a short while.

Sarah Waeyenbergh

For You

For it was you—I was thinking of,
As I traded my throne—
For a vessel of flesh—a vessel,
that soon would be beaten and torn;
In the garden of Gethsemane,
I prayed for strength—to endure,
and there did my tears-flow,
for upon my shoulders—salvation,
Of the world—I did hold;
I would be betrayed by a kiss,
And my friends—me—they would deny;
So unto the hands of my enemies,
I delivered myself—and no pleas,
For mercy—would I cry;
My hands and feet were pierced—from
My side the blood flowed—the hand
Of death I faced—alone;
Out of my love for you—my life,
I did not spare—for you I gave,
The utmost sacrifice-I gave—myself.

Cherie Springfield

Stars

Our paths cross like the waves on the sand,
in the great blue sea.
Although I've only seen you once,
I now know my destiny.
I'm not sure how I'll get there,
but I know how it will be.
There will be lots of beautiful rainbows
and you standing next to me.
While lying beneath the moon-lit sky,
we see a falling star.
We make a wish and then you leave,
but I know you won't go far.
Because on that night the wish I made,
was for you to stay with me,
today, tomorrow, the rest of our lives,
or through eternity.

Heather N. Post

The Intangible

That which pours through
raw fingers into
a void named reality;
Tumbles, falling like the
apathetic rain through
the mist of society.

Plummets to an end that can
never be achieved . . .
only desired,
Screaming in all dialects
"I am love, and you shall
feel none higher."

Distinct yet intangible again
it pours through
my ever failing grip;
Desperately I reach to hold the
pain that pales
the sharpness of the rapier's tip.

Mike Pulin

Do Not Bury Me

Do not bury me when I'm
  dead and gone.
I do not wish to be put into
  a cold dark hole.
It is too lonely. There is no
  happiness or laughter
Do cremate me let not my ashes,
  My last remains be left in a jar, like
some Genie awaiting a rescuer.
  But sprinkle me into the air, to travel
To places I long to be or have never seen.
  Set me free to roam as I please.
No headstone, no plaques to tie me down,
  Just remember that I was here and
now I'm gone.

Frank Seerattan

Always Waiting

You bring joy to life
You bring end to strife
If only we depend on you
To do what only you can do

You shoulder our load
When we think we'll explode
You share our joy
When we shout "Oh boy!"

You are always there, waiting
Always waiting
For us turn to you
For what only you can do

Only you can carry our burden
When we are heavily-laden
Only you can wipe our tears
When we have great fears

You walk hand in hand
When we stumble in the sand
On the shores of life
You share all our strife

Deborah Miller

Falling In Silence

The snow—descends in
  unequalled splendor,
Its finite crystals covering the
  barrenness of writer,
swirling in a cloud of white
  fire and ice.

Almost Holy, their tiny bodies
  a swift sacrifice
  unfailing in beauty
  unfailing in purity
  falling in silence.

Bonnie Lee Ridgely

A Wise Woman

As it is said, into each life some rain must fall,
  This is a certainty for one and for all,
Don't sit there docilely on a shelf,
  Learn how to live and grow for yourself.

Choose to be all that you can be, to live life,
  To be a strong lady, not a weak wife.
No man is strong enough too lean on for very long,
  To lean too heavily, on him, is wrong.

Don't be afraid to walk alone, to seek your own way,
  Branch out a little more, day by day.
Step out with courage, listen to your inner voice,
  Yes, my friend, you do have a choice.

Men, too, need to lean from time to time,
  A strong woman is an asset, not a crime.
You'll respect yourself more and be better able to handle life,
  So have courage, be strong, it will help you be a better wife.

Walk tall, by his side, together, hand in hand, heads held high,
  Look up, step out, give it a try.
Work together toward common goals, have fun along the way,
  Create, learn, and grow some each day.

Jackolyn M. Hill

Your Honor

Eyes directed at the door as you ingressed into the room.
The guests were amazed by your gallantry.
Blushed did the bride and groom, as they received
  your honor with a complacency above all else.

The men conjectured that you were a man of conceit.
Of course, they are fastidious according to their manners.
Your attendance at the party wasn't a plan of deceit;
Instead, a state of propriety for the occasional felicity.

Mother's effusions for a wealthy gallant fellow to relieve
  them of their daughter's passion was directed toward you
  as an ostentation.

From your civility, you accosted complaisance.
Over all, you gave one heck of a presentation.

Lisa Baker

Help

Life is a symphony of worn-out shoes.
Blindly waltzing to the tune — repeat offenders.
Unfortunate dancers, having scarcely a clue,
Scream out for help — no answer.
"Will work for food," the bewildered, destitute cry.
Homeless humans sit wearily on abandoned sidewalks.
Orphans, needing assistance to find a home, scream out for
  hope.
Help, stripped to the bone.
"Who will hear us?" Voices echo, delirious in need.
"I will!" Shouts a woman pushing forward.
"This is my obligation," she said. "It is our responsibility!"
The mammoth crowd suddenly awakens.
Astonished upon hearing her devastating words,
The piper's flute — still in hand — plummets from his lips.
His explosive symphony abruptly ended, momentarily silenced,
With just one voluntary offer of help.

Tamara Wireman

In Those Little Three Inch Cars

        It was the perfect setting for
a parent and child
a panorama of fantasy zones
        driving all the cars
        they had not yet
in this lifetime
feeling in control of the situation
        parking those cars
        opening garage doors
and following roads together
        in those little three inch cars
    Christine Birben

Black Man, White Man, Red Man Too
These Are The Emotions I Read...

You look at his skin and you look at your skin,
but never do you look at the skin of your kin.
You make these labels for all to wear,
but does the God of creation seem to care.
It's the path of God's ministry he likes you to tread,
not the love of God's adversary spewing from your head.
The anger, the hatred, the demeaning lies,
are all spoken in the name of 'racial ties.'
How can you take these dark seeds to heart
When God's truth, the Bible, states to take no part.
Listen to the voices of those who've been burned,
as they scream the 'racial slurs' you force them to learn.
O you may mean no harm in the words that you speak,
but to stumble another is the last thing to seek,
for the love of our brother our neighbor our child,
we should ponder our views of the human race and all its
beguiles.
    Kris Schultz

Upon The Horizon

The setting sun in rays of gold
set clouds of the Western sky on fire.
Like your shining eyes and your kiss so bold
alight my passion and my heart's desire.

The rising moon is shimmering silver
herald the coming of ebony night.
The twilight air carries the scent of flowers
and send love upon its wings a flight.

My body yearns for your caressing touch
as I search for your shadow here beside me.
My eyes close when loneliness becomes too much,
and I feel your embrace deep inside me.

It seemed that beside me, you suddenly appear,
and I feel hope burn in the depth of my heart.
For Fate is a musician of a millennia of years,
and our love is the masterpiece of all Her art.

I believe that we'll always be together,
through all the sadness and unending sorrow.
Just hold me against you and love me forever,
and I'll always be beside you each tomorrow.
    Albert Nguyen

Feelings

In your arms I feel security
from your touch I have ecstasy,
In your eyes I see the key,
to the door of complete happiness.
What would I give in exchange
for you devotion,
Where could I go to experience
a deeper emotion.
How should I show how intense
are my feelings,
When did I ever find someone
more appealing.
Trust me, trust my sincerity
Doubt me, doubt my dependability,
Love me, love my honesty
Hold me, hold my liberty.
Have faith in my ability
To love without changing,
To honor without falsity
To cherish without manipulation.
    Lenora M. Corbett

The Choice

Leave it alone, you're such a mess,
Little by little, torn such as flesh.
Stand it not once, your power is strong.
Never forgiven, forever so wrong.
Dig deep within, yet never touch,
Running astray, needing so much.
Evil does lurk, you see no fear,
Walking the line, year after year.
End it it's done, you are aware,
Time to let go, you're never fair.
You made The Choice, close up your eyes,
Fold up those arms, tell all your lies.
It's all over now, enough has been said.
You made The Choice, lay still in your bed.
    Tammy Bradley

Waiting

In the days of future's past,
Sits a lone man like me,
Trying to keep his hopes alive,
Trying to remain free,
All the world is thin and pale,
Time is but a dream,
But time is true and real,
And will be the end of me,
Constant watching,
Constant waiting,
For something I don't know,
Time is no friend of mine,
But I cannot let him go,
When my heart beats,
Its secret rhythm slow,
And my dreams, realities,
Maybe then I'll go,
If the world,
Ceases then,
Silently, will I go.
    Phillip M. Ballard

Untitled

I longed for us to meet again
And start our life anew,
My life has been so empty
Since I said good-bye to you,

We loved each other with a passion
From deep within our hearts
Oh! How it hurt deep down inside
When you said that we must part,

We held each other very close
We spoke no word it's true,
And as I waved good-bye that day
I whispered 'I Love You'

So lets cherish all the time we have
Now that we're back together
For we both know this love of ours
Is sure to last forever!

Teresa Wyatt

To The Group, There's Life Here, Just A Different Earth

I'm a Hippie without drugs
A Drunkard without booze
Every Thursday afternoon
God and Nancy come through

We watch a great movie
Listen to a great tape
Earth is very fast moving
There's very little or no escape

We take on that challenge
With Group support
We sort through our difficulties
And yes Nancy always reports

A little of this
A little of that
I like those two lines
Like the bald spot under my hat

Meaning life doesn't go away
Even after death
Some Buddies will say
What a great guest

Charlie J. McIntyre

Thirteen Years With You

Thirteen years have come out way
thirteen years until this special day
But a special day is nothing new
that's all I've had being with you

Marina, I love you so much
My life is made sweeter by your touch
I love the touch of your soft sweet hand
to hold as we walk across the sand

Together, as we walk across the sands of time
I am so happy to find your hand in mine
A treasure I've found from across the sea
How blessed I am, to have you with me

Gerald W. Brooks

A Dream Remembered

I stepped into the realm of her grace,
we sat and talked as time raced.
Her obscure presence cast such a spell,
with just a face, hiding in the mist.

I dined in the warmth of her smile,
and was completely mesmerized for quite a while.
Helplessly enchanted by her charm, and yet,
I was so glad we finally met.

What treasures thought I, to compare,
with the richness of her dark brown hair?
Her hand with silk like touch,
filled me with such life, so much!

Our thoughts, plans and fears,
we shared with happiness and tears.
Standing among the shadows, embracing and set,
her tender lips I had barely met...

Awakened! Awakened suddenly with loss and despair,
for the woman, the woman so alluring and rare.
If reality, induced our paths to cross once more,
to recreate, a dream, remembered.

Clifford Foster

A Death From Within

The sand never stopped flowing,
just slowed to a threatening trickle.
Simultaneously the sun blackened,
the moon and the stars disappeared my family was dealing
but, no cards were dealt.
Eventually.
The sun could be seen, but none to bright.
A partial stir, in artificial light.
Hopes in tact, but no land in sight.
Like a ship without oars,
just floating within sight.
It's sunny, but I can not see.
A hardening crust, just around me.
The sky is clearer, but only barely for me.
My drive may have died, but not me.
It's frightening to survive,
still alone without thee,
living with the painful loss within me.
But hey, I'm still alive,
even if all my brain did not survive!!!!

Scott D. Hasenmiller

Searching

Searching everywhere — I find — I'm missing something —
Peace of Mind!
Where to find this elusive treasure —
The importance of which you cannot measure
I've searched here and I've searched there —
In fact, I searched most everywhere.
Not a thing you can hold in your hand, or really even
    understand.
It slips through my fingers like grains of sand.
'Shape up' I said, 'To find what's missing — have you forgot
    your dear Lord's blessing?'
So search again, and you will find —
Peace of Soul brings Peace of Mind.

Tacey M. Hoban

Mistress Kingbridge

I'm not sure of what I feel? What I felt? This can't be real.
It's your head! You can be kill, yet ode to Sir Henry I plead
with my soul, an oath . . . my lips be sealed, just a love
contemporary, why should I worry? Is it much less than a love
sought, why don't I learn from hearts desires, unknown to love
true essence, love is it not taught? Your love takes me
higher, burning like fire, as time pass my heart pondering
still, a lust, passion, that enhance longing for your dance, a
royal choice, the last chance, I, your Queen, like a bird in a
cage, forgetting the one, in whom he's engaged, I kneel at my
Lord, my King, with a lust enraged, our aching hearts, that my
womb be filled, remaining in silence, caring about? You and I
swearing? Two people simply sharing my Lord, I've found love
to be as a theft, never minding if one's caught, like the wind,
at God's command, commanding the send. Heaven knows
when . . . when my Lord? Sometime at the gate, the Ole
Kingsbridge! Hurry! Don't be late! Hoping unsaid! Holding
on to what's faith. I'll be waiting Kingsbridge.

Janette Fletcher

MarchT Aux Puces a Paris (Flea Market In Paris)

Greasy, glamorous folks amble through the avenue,
Bodies press together, drifting past bone bracelets,
Silken scarves, and pipes —
Intricate instruments of inhalation, carved
Into hollow faces, dancing dragons —
He-llo, hi, les vendeurs cry: a special price for you!
An ashtray, cupped, supplicating hand of clay or
Better — leather jackets fleece-lined, flea-ridden, ready
To hug your back in style.

As the labyrinth relaxes, the rows wind round to
Where the booths start thinning.
There, grinning Ghana transplants offer
African drums, caressed by callused thumbs and
Thumped, calling forth the round, rich sound of ritual.
Wearing waves of yellow, red and green
A man looms, leering, entreating you to want his wares.
Quelquechose pour la jolie jeune-fille, he asks,
But you quickly shake your creamy head no.
He grabs your wrist and twists and
Tries: Or would you like to have a coffee with me?

Haley Whipple

United States Of America Women Of War

Let us help you in times of war
Let us stand with you all over the world
Let us wipe away your tears
And help you in times of pain.

Let us go in our ships, tanks and planes
Let us be with you on all battle fields
Let us be what we would like to be
And you will see what a comfort we will be.

Let us salute our USA Women of War
Who stood with us throughout all wars
A special thanks to women of the Vietnam War
And to all women who fight on life's battle fields.

O' Lord, comfort the mothers who lost children in war.

Charles Harvey

Sibling

A fly on the wall
Like wallpaper,
She does not
Exist.
Mouth opens
Words come,
Nobody responds
To the sounds.
Her words float
In her head.
They stare there
Like crying, I am a
Person — hear me.
Denial is such,
That siblings
Hand it back,
To hurt, not
Understanding, why.

Ilka Suarez

Windows

World defined — the window's view,
To some it may seem small.
From color stained to filthy glass,
This room contains them all.

What future vision lies behind
The one through which you stare?
Do angels light the path of truth,
Or can't you see them anywhere?

As longing gazes set with dusk
You'll find you cannot see
All aspirations left behind
For what has come to be.

Retrieve your faith in God above
And cling to what is good
When things do not appear
As once you thought they should.

Don't press your head against the pane
As if to get a better view,
Search the windows of your soul
And choose another to look through.

Heather E. Yopp

Untitled

Mist encircled the icy waters.
Sun streaked through the sky.
Trees wept into the ground;
My body strained to fly.

He perched above a silver rock.
His eyes burning deep red.
Their fangs ripped into my body.
My soul fought and fled.

Rain fell soft into this place,
Washing crimson through the sand.
Shadows caught my tortured screams
Silencing this darkened land.

Mist swallowed me into the waters.
His eyes became my sun.
They ate my blood, my tears, my life.
Within the mist, we became one.

Jenn Borlee

I Love You

To say to someone "I Love You"
Is an expression that should come
from the heart.
An expression that's real,
An expression you feel,
An expression from all others apart

Those beautiful words "I Love You,"
Are not words of endearment alone,
But words of a magnitude,
of devotion and strength,
And as solid as a well rounded stone.

To utter these words without meaning,
Is blasphemous right from the heart,
to desecrate an expression so beautiful,
Is more deceiving than words
can impart.

So express these words with discretion,
make sure they are honest and true,
Let your heart do the talking,
From your inner most soul
when you utter those words,
"I Love You."

Hal H. A. Lasky

Mother Of Joy

My mother is a symbol of
Love and joy,
Happiness and sadness,
Laughing and crying

But most of all she really Cares,
Cares about life
Cares about a live person, "Me"!

Jennifer Alicia Fooks

Cape Buffalo

I went to Fortress Ikoma
on Africa's Mara plain
to visit the Garden of Eden.
I'll never be the same!

I saw Tommy, Topi, Zebra,
Wildebeest far as the sky.
Early one morn in the long grass
I looked death in the eye.

Black, big and belligerent, his eyes
seared through to my soul.
Only a step or two further, this story
would never be told.

He vanished into the long grass
and left me alone in peace,
but those eyes will ever haunt me.
My dreams will never cease.

Yes, I'll remember the Serengetti
Until I draw my last breath.
'Cause early one morn in the long grass
I saw the eyes of death.

Joseph C. Greenfield Jr.

Time To Break The Chain

It's been repeating itself for decades,
Echoing explosions, as if grenades.
A mothers instinct is the first to know,
Having only suspicion to bestow.
Melancholy, and yes in denial,
Nerves of fire, just one thought, unearth the bile.
"Why?" you ask yourself, never saying no.
They have not a reason, for such sorrow,
All grown up now, and still just a child . . .
With nothing "broken" and everything filed,
Guilty are free, and innocent; hurting.
So uncompassionate with their wording,
Those barbarians, in our so called law,
Supposedly our gate, I'm still in awe.
Nights aren't easy, always feeling distraught,
This action we're dealing with, was one taught.
These memories will always stay with them,
Our children; more precious than a rare gem.
Those perpetrators are insane and vain,
Definitely, it's time to break the chain!

Ronnie K. Endre

You Can Be An Angel

An angel is sometimes someone right next to you,
they show their love by the things they say and do.
Some you can't touch or see,
they make things as nice as can be.
Help you walk through the door,
maybe with a walk across the floor.
You can be an angel if you try,
do your best and don't ask why.
Angels don't always have wings,
they are sweet and gentle, songs softly sings.
I want to be an angel every day,
helping the ones who need me, all the way.
The Lord said I don't need wings for what I do,
he put me here to help every one, even you.

Elsie J. Vermuele

Sensuality

Unseen sprites quietly moving with ease
Whisper secrets giving voice to the breeze.
Moonlight filters through their frail phantom wings
Sheer curtains flutter; softly a sprite sings.

She holds him gently in her loving arms
Protesting bedsprings give remote alarms.
Bearing his weight, his body comes to rest
As his warm moist breath caresses her breast.

Her hand guides his head toward its desire
So his soft parted lips thus can acquire
The love, the life that she'll selflessly give,
The essence of which all men need to live.

Gliding fingers o'er the curves of his back
Hung'ring needs sated, his body goes slack.
Content in slumber, atop her he rests
Head nestled securely between soft breasts.

Her heart says sleep now; her mind says instead
To carry her sleeping babe to his bed.
The sprite ceases singing, her song now through
She stands watching o'er babe and sleeping mom, too.

Robert M. Rowe

Never Again

Late at night, as I'm snuggled down in my bed,
I close my eyes and think of what you said.

These salty tears that stream down my face,
are remembering words that my mind can not erase.

You found it so easy, to hurt me in every way,
I hoped things'd get better, knew that tomorrow's another day.

Black magic is the spell you so deeply put me under,
but no matter where I ran, I could never seek some cover.

I told you that it was over, and wasn't meant to be.
Yeah, you were listening, but just not hearing me.

My mind is always telling me, that I should just let go.
My heart wants to love you, but my soul says no.

The light you once saw, deep in my eyes,
is gone along, with the tears that I cried.

I was a prisoner of love, always trying to break free.
I'm taking back my heart, you'll no longer hold the key.

Somehow missing you, is not what I plan,
I'm going to forget about you, the best that I can.

I'm doing the right thing, and saying goodbye forever.
You will always be a memory, but never again my lover.

Dee Dee Smith

High On The Hilltop

Oh! What a breathtaking view
Beautiful sunrise and skies so blue.
Beyond the horizon cloud-capped palaces
Stolidly safeguard their domains.

Miles of woodland to be found
With trails of beauty all year round.
Streams cascade out of their royal homes
Reduce to a slow dance on the rocks below.

Mountain laurel bushes and flowers abound
Snuggled under hemlocks and pines on shady ground.
Their leaves sprayed by the gentle mist
Which rainbows in the sunlight and pirouettes in the breeze.

The gorgeous sunset is now out of sight;
Wild birds chirp wearily before the night.
Sorrowful singing barely heard
Echoes from cloud-capped palaces.

Kay Wood

Those Moments

I love those moments
  those moments when you look that way.
It's not your clothes
  or your hair
  or anything else.
It's just the way you look
  the way you look at me.
You radiate beauty.
It is in those moments, arriving always unexpectedly, in which
I can see your love for me so clearly - that it reveals your soul.
  And then I understand...and know...and everything is right.
In those moments, when you look that way.

Robert Daum

Life Of Nature

Weeping flower
in its space, alone
sprawling ivy
bold, over grown
oak tree strong
climbing high
lily bloom wrinkled
brown and dry
the sun, the fire
the heat so bright
shimmering stars,
crisp light of night
mother nature's
display of life,
loneliness success
glamour and strife

Nicol Agelastos

I Run . . .

With the pulling of my muscles,
with my ankle when it sprains,
with exhaustion in my legs,
with my stomach when in pain . . .

With the hours of practice,
with the weights I must lift,
with the hard work and sweat,
that comes with this gift . . .

For the glory of victory,
for the agony of defeat,
for the thrill of the race,
for that rush you can't beat . . .

For the love of the sport,
just for the fun,
for happiness,
for myself . . . I run.

Elizabeth Gorecki

Granny

It was a shadowy dark day
  No one had very much to say
Tears were shed by the sky
  Wetness soaked every eye
Black cars stretched for miles
  Sadness stole our smiles
She looked at us from above
  She looked at us sharing our love
She was forever long gone
  Then they played her favorite song
The one that breaks our hearts
  Tears our very souls apart
The wind blew threw my soul
  The void left, the gaping hole
The emptiness of your death
  You've taken your final breath
Your spirit forever unbound
  While your smiles hide underground.

Troy R. Vars

Daddy

Daddy, Daddy, Daddy
The careful manipulated prose
of tomorrow will culminate
into a burgeoning enterprise
known as—Mason's market
It will be in honor of the late
   Nathaniel Joseph Mason
My immaculate father
who has raised me in an
inherently positive, good manner
that has and will develop me into
a great writer and song writer
for eons to come . . .

Michael J. Mason

The Test

The word sears into my brain, burns my ears.
My head aches, throbs, yet the word continues
to echo over and over until I become dizzy and weak.
Suddenly the test changes while the word
stays the same; it becomes soothing and melodic.
The word tests my strength, endurance as well as
my abilities to survive. The word is thrown at me
again and I am left reeling in pain, confusion, tears.
Now I hear it for the hundredth time today and it
leaves me feeling happy, excited, and satisfied.
One minute I deserve to be associated with this word;
the next I feel overwhelmed, incompetent, alone.
Do all Mommies relive this test everyday?
I am tested to the extreme of my patience, but I shall
endure the bittersweet word for the love in his eyes.

Amy Ratto

Untitled

Love is not what the story books say
All love, all hate and no shades of gray.
Love is pain and love is sorrow
Love is wondering where you will be
   tomorrow
Yet knowing, somehow knowing
No matter what tomorrow brings
You'll be together through it all
No matter what you'll stand brave and tall.
To face the challenges that may come
And still say dear you're the only one.
I love you as much as I did that day
When you said dear will you be mine
And I said yes 'till the end of time

Elizabeth Staley

Summer's Exit

Making its exit, summer growls,
Forlorn and spent, like weary wolves,
The wind howls round
My windows
Down —
Screeching, pounding
To and fro,
Like haunted hearts, thrashing in hollow chambers —
Loud, loUD, LOUD
And LOUDER it grew,
Until my deafened ears,
Withdrew.
And searching skies, both east and west and north and south
And fearing, leSt the sun won't shine,
I best embrace the chills that bind —
That beckon vigilantes of my soul
To search my calendar — an empty page,
As winter licks its dreary haze,
And trashes all my fun filled days.

Jean V. Hayden

Thoughts Of A Libertarian

"What happened to America,
can you tell me Daddy please?"
"They turned their backs on Jesus Christ
and quit praying on their knees."

"What can we do for America,
to try and keep it free?"
"We have to try and organize
the Christians for liberty."

"What will happen to America,
do you think it will survive?"
"As long as we do Christ's written will
and keep his love alive."

"What happened to our Bill of rights,
our justice, and universities?"
"They became tools for unrighteous men,
to spread their blasphemies."

"Where is the republic for which it stands,
the light God shed on thee?"
"Evil men destroyed it
and gave us democracy!"

Jeffrey Allen Cady

For Beverly A. Little

In a minutes time you captivated my emotions
held them tight in the palm of your graceful hand
swirled them with delight and enchantment
that engulfed me like a tempest
crashing into my heart happiness like no other
and of course I stand amazed at your presence
the way you are simply over flows the realm
of my reality facing tomorrow is easier
after you touched the very heartbeat inside
tearing down my nervousness with the softness
of your voice as it spoke to the very life of me
breathing in confidence without a single doubt
I've fallen into the madness happily
not afraid of the outcome of this encounter
between two familiar strangers here and now.

Clint Harding Ballard

From The Inside Looking Out:
A Praise Through Darkness

Black thunder clouds roll across the sky,
Lightning stabs the ground in my mind.

A desolate land where I kept misery,
Yet through afflictions, God gave me peace.

From a cold, black, heart of steel,
To soft, warm affections for others I now feel.

For the devil took his toll on my soul,
But, my soul, the Lord wouldn't let him hold.

Through gratefulness I write these words,
For the Lord saving my soul, I write them bold!

   Praise be, to God almighty!
      Dondi Springer

Granny's Day!

Hi! Grandmother! I'm your grandson "Patrick Joe".
Please hold my tiny body in your loving arms
Close to your ear.
While I'm in your arms of love and we're so close,
If only for this special moment. I knew how to talk,
This is what you would hear.

Grandmother, I sure love you, and it grows,
More and more, every single day.
I love you for your acts of love, and
The words you say, you often show
In a very loving way.

So!
Grandmother, before you start crying, reach down
And take me from my daddy's knee.
Hold my tiny body in your loving grandmother arms,
Close to your ear.

While we're embraced in the arms of love,
I know you feel these words I will one day say to you.
And pray to God in heaven, you'll be able to hear.
"Happy grandmothers day, granny"!
I love you, so much.
I'm your grandson!
      Patrick Joe Peery

Uncle Allen's Journey

I heard you'd be leaving soon,
To travel with the stars, beyond the moon!
Nothing I can say can make you stay,
Though it hurts to watch you going away.
I'd help you get ready for a hundred more years.
As you prepare to go, I can only hide my tears.
So much left to do and say!
More than can be done in just one day.
Just one more joke, one more story —
For us to share, before you depart for glory!
Thanks for the smiles, and the times you cared;
For all the memories of good times we shared.
The clock is ticking; the time is here!
I know you're ready and have no fear.
As you go, I'll try for you, to smile —
I'll even laugh again in a while.
You'll live forever within my heart;
Tucked away safe, we'll never part!
      E. Renae Boyd

Gentle Rain

Gentle rain pattering down,
calm me with your lullaby song.
Heal my wounds and ease my pain.
Cleanse my world, oh gentle rain.
Softly fall on a melancholy day.
Gentle rain, take my troubles away.
      Jo Dell Smith

Untitled

In a place I did dwell,
I met a man I loved so well.
He came and took his love from me,
and sat a strange girl on his knee.
Home I went,
cried on my bed.
Not a word to mom was said.
Dad came home late that night,
searched for me left to right.
Up the stairs the door he broke,
and found me hanging from a rope.
On my jeans this note was found:
"Dig a grave, dig it deep.
Make it wide from head to feet.
And on my grave place
a dove to show the world that
I died for love."
      Jodi Hill

Under Water

Trapped in the seat belt underwater
their mother knew but not their father.
Though she said someone else did it
she's the primary dimwit.
The love triangle reaches the climax
good or bad the police just want the facts.
The unfit mother drove her boys off the end
into a situation they could not defend.
Trapped in the seat belt underwater
their mother knew but not their father.
Alex and Micheal, heaven-bound
never to utter another peep or sound.
Why she did it no one knows
crying in tears, her emotion shows.
Brothers they are and brothers they were
laid together where nothing will stir.
Their mother knew but not their father.
      Missy Lloyd

Take Me

Take me. Take me. Take me home.
Take me where my loved ones roam.
Take me to a higher land,
Where there is no mortal man.
Take me to a land of Kings.
Take me where the angels sing.
Take me off this wretched earth.
Take me for what life is worth.
Take me and my blessed loved,
To the Holy. Up above.
      Liz Bosanko

Fly Away

Fly away my love.
Spread your wings and soar.
Never faltering. Never slowing down.
Looking back only to see your future,
never to see regrets,
fly away.

The universe is yours my love,
indulge your mind with the
depths of its existence,
change what you must.
Fly away.

Come home my love.
Rest peacefully in my arms.
Knowing this haven will always be yours.
Now, fly away.
    Pamela J. Helms

I'm Long In The Tooth

I'm long in the tooth
and short on the spoof
so if you need proof,
live under my roof.
You'll get to know me
you'll not remain aloof —
So I'll tell you what is it
I need you to come and visit.
You'll find out I'm a card,
if you pull into my yard.

When deep in thought
times seem for nought
I listen to mountain streams —
There is a feeling benign
so gentle and kind
which sings in this gentle sea.
I try hard to grasp
a song that will last,
but like the wind it goes past
like a leap year song.
    John G. Willis

Love

Who needs love
when it makes you lie?
Who needs love
when it makes you cry?
Love tears your world apart.
It leaves you
with nowhere to start.
True love is hard to find.
And it's in the heart,
not only the mind.
I don't know about you.
Who needs love?
I do.
    Jennifer Dykema

Being Special

God made me very special, when he put me on this earth.
My duties were already given to me,
At the moment of my birth.
He must have known how much strife,
In my lifetime I could take.
Because he gave me one great mountain,
Whose climb not many others could make.
I've seen a lot of sorrow, I've seen a lot of tears.
I've climbed a lot of mountains,
Through many weary years.
He gave me a sense of humor,
To replace the sadness in my life.
So I can laugh off the heartaches,
And the very unbearable strife.
Yes, I know I'm very special,
Because many others could not take.
The loneliness and helplessness,
That I must always fake.
So when it's time for me to go,
My heart will be set free.
My soul will go to heaven, where I will live eternally.
    Helen Genovesi

Second

For the second time I'm waiting.
The first time was enough — too much.
I'm going to be sick.
Surrounded by people I've known all my life,
they are garbed in sorrow.
We have nothing to say, we just stare at each other
our hands, the door, the coffin.
I cough and everyone stares at me.
The sweet air smells putrid, too many flowers.
The lights are dim, I note,
but one shines brightly on her face.
The deafening silence continues; it roars in my ears.
I'm suffocating, dying like she did,
my breath being cut.
This time of closure: a time of moving on,
is taking too long.
    Matthew B. Krajewski

A Beautiful Wife

Drudgery, amidst harshness, a day's work.
A beautiful wife appeases the mind.
Home coming, pace hastens with anticipation.

A beautiful wife to cherish, an angel silhouette
yonder in perfect beauty, in the glare of the
evening sun, my bliss of inspiration in gentle
comfort relief.

Background echoes, softer rhythm of laughters,
children's play, my threshold to life's strength
embraces my delight to venture.

A beautiful wife, her warm loving arms assures.
My harbor to a lost ship, my light to a whirling
darkness, my hope to grasp when life's unworthy.

A beautiful wife, God's creation made perfect.
A woman liberated. She's everything I stood for.
My life's perfect blend. She's my wife my love,
my only world, and she's my beauty...to behold!
    Francis Taylor

Gone Forever

So confused, so alone.
So many questions running through my head,
Sometimes I wish I was just dead.
It hurts so bad to feel this way.
How can I turn away and return to stay?
If I were to stay, what would change?
Nothing, there would still be a house full of hate!
I can't stand it and they can't stand me.
What can I do to set myself free?
I just want to be out of here.
Gone forever without any pain.
Everything I do turns out wrong anyway.
Why stay strong if I'm only going to get pulled right back down.
Scared to make a move or even speak the slightest words.
Nothing I show would make their heads turn.
I can't run away, I can't disappear.
Sometimes I wonder "Why am I even here!?"
Say goodbye and good riddance to everybody.
No regrets and no tears, just a simple goodbye...
And now I will disappear!

Cari Lee Nakamura

My Eulogy At A Funeral

How do you describe a truly good man?
I'm talking about the leader of your clan.
His virtues were endless, to list them would take hours;
His abilities to charm were like mystical powers.
His sweetness, his kindness enraptured us all;
His world seemed so full, for him 'twas a ball.
His good face lit up whenever he spoke;
Like in the commercial, life was a smile and a "Coke".
We'll miss him like crazy, he was our favorite guy;
Too bad he left us, and only God knows why.
But his warmth and his way will always be with us;
Having had him around was a fabulous plus.
The body may have left, but his spirit lives on;
In no way will we consider him gone.
So, family and friends, please be of good cheer;
He's gone for awhile, he's just visiting his peer.
So forget him not and remember him well;
For forever and a day, we'll remain under his spell.

Joe Nadell

What True Love Is

I have seen you pull strength from within
and look back at where you've been.
Sometimes you were homeless, living on the streets
not knowing what you'd do or who you might meet.
There were times you'd try to call a friend on the telephone.
When no one answered is the moment you realized that
you were all alone.
Then you think I have to do this for me.
And I'm the only one who holds the key.
That will let me break free.
Then I realize I have to love myself in my heart.
If I ever want to keep my life from falling all apart.
You picked up an addiction along the way.
That I have to cope and fight with every day
I must conquer this to straighten my life out.
Then I can know what true love is all about.
For I have to love me.
Only then can I look in the future and see what
is meant to be.

Shannon L. Brown

Forest Tears

Do not deny my right to speak
Though compared to you my stature's weak
I can not step to run or walk
Do not deny my right to talk

I've stood on earth many years
In sun and rain without fears
I bore my own and lived with God
And only at the force of wind—did nod

You have trespassed on my land
With iron and steel your force at hand
You cut me down and made me fall
With God in me—I curse you all

Is there nothing you can learn
As you set my limbs to burn
This is not mist or dew you see
It is tears—I shed for thee

So be it if this is what you choose
And time will tell it's you who lose
Man what shall come of thee
When your last breath—is my next tree

Thomas John Norbeck

Beauty

I saw the most beautiful sight the other day.
  Friends
Sitting on a park bench.
  Looking
Laughing at the people walking by.
  Talking
Then I saw a spark.
  Bright
I knew, as they did, what it was.
  Burning
Their laughter changed, their looks
changed.
  Subtle
Anyone walking by could tell.
  Smiling
I saw the most beautiful sight the other day.
  Love

Karie Scoughton

Dale Ann

There are no fitting words to describe
The most precious gift God
Blessed me with.

Her little mouth and dainty fingers
Will always last, and always linger
In my mind as I reflect
Upon my precious heavenly gift.

How wise he was
I realize,
As I gaze into those hazel eyes,

It was she that taught me
How to be
Strong, and steady all the while.

And now she walks down the isle,
My one and only,
Godly child.

Janet D. Reeps

Love

I plant the seed with care
and water it every day
on it I lay a prayer
hoping forever it will stay

Soon I can see something
something begins to grow
pure beauty it soon brings
its flower begins to show

I reach out to grab this rose
my hand turns instantly red
everybody already knows
that thorns a rose does shed

Ross W. Kindler

Reality

I searched to see what I could see
But what I saw just couldn't be
Fantastic sights and dreams that came
Across my mind, frame by frame.

What do I do with visions bright
That come on starry, moonlit nights
Do I dismiss this wondrous view
Just so I can be like you?

I walked along the streets of time
Both friend and foe intertwined
Someone said, "How can this be
It doesn't match reality.

In the world of paradox
One must first remove the clocks
For clocks are tools that set the tone
Of either this or that alone.

But there's a place, eternity
With different rules, reality
Is seen and felt through different eyes
One sees truth, the other lies.

John F. Sullivan

Far Away

How do you know who you really are
Your history has blown away so far
So much to discover
Who was your mother
In that distant life you used to live
Maybe they're out there
Trying to spare
That big part of their heart
That you once filled
But if they find you
The real secret will still remain
Why finding you
Also caused great pain

Kerri Conrad

The Question

A suspicion of man's intention alive in the skin
   He asks, "Where did I begin?"
I build and save
   Counted days gone by, I age writing each one, by and by

My weightless spirit waiting to arrive
   The soul inside taking all these pictures to hold inside

Leaving the body behind, my being is in transition
   In love without cognition

In love we hold all that lives and forever do we attend
   Just some thing we've never been

Light leading us through
   The road just bends, so see, there is no end

Love leads the only path for divine quarters
   In living for man's orders
     You'll never find what holds past life's borders

The investigation of man's inventions
   Building crumble, for mothers wrath in quakes

Ye forms of love move men for
   Miles upwards . . .

Heidi MacDonald

Rhapsody

I never knew what love could do
'Til you came to me

I heard a song when you came along
'Twas a rhapsody

I want to be with you wherever you are
'Cause when I'm near you, you're my caviar

And so I've found there's love all around
If one only looks

Our love affair can only compare
To the story books

I feel such bliss with each tender kiss
I know that our love came from heaven above

So please tell me dear what I long to hear
That our love has grown

Say we'll never part 'cause you've taken my heart
For your very own

June C. Dean

The Light

My Son, I held your hand expressing all my love.
Saying goodbye and follow the Light to Heaven above.
You were loaned to me for awhile, yet I wonder why.
With all your sweetness and love, you had to die.

I will always love you and miss you each day.
Your wisdom and guidance is needed in so many ways.
I visualize your face and whisper your name.
My life without you will never be the same.

I often feel sad and the emptiness won't go away.
But I can look forward to that glorious day.
When my span of life is over then I will see.
You, my Son, waiting at the end of the Light for me.

Etta R. Floyd

Sands Of Time

Silently the sands of time are passing by,
Memories of laughter and of tears left in
the sands of yesterday years,
Echoing in this heart of mine...
Silently and swiftly passing the sands of time.

Times together...and then apart...
Always your memory lingering in my heart.
The warmth of your embrace...
Memories of you that time cannot erase.

Silently, silently the sands of time pass by.
A God, who knows the answer of my hearts cry
A God who cares, a Father who sees
The depth of love that flows through me.

Ever watching all knowing, is this
Father of mine.
The keeper of my heart, the Creator of time.
Silently, silently the sands of time pass by,
Sands of time silently drifting,
and passing my way...
...Silently beginning and ending each day.
Diana Lynn Rogers

The Stork's Eye View

The stork says to you, at the times of your birth
What kind of a place do you think this is?
You wiggle and stretch with thumb in your mouth,
And feel that you've found worldly bliss.

Months roll along; you're contented with life
You're the pride of the family, the apple of the eye
You've plenty of food, fresh air and clean clothes
With a future, so bright by and by

As years come and go, you're developing skills
With which to encounter the problems of life;
So from youth on through old age you could really be
Prepared for perpetual strife

Engrossed in your job and events of the day
Trying to gain some respect and renown;
You find that the skills you thought would suffice
Fall short of the goals you'd set down.

So your child or your grandchild may hear the stork say"
What kind of a place do you think this is?
You'll squirm and writhe in anguish to see;
The new life confronted by this.
Lulu Peiffer

Evening Showers

In the splendor of the cloud draped falling sun
  I can see your loving face
In the swish of raindrops on the window,
  Hear God's seedlings saying grace.

In the distant roll of thunder
  I sense Your awesome power,
Held in check to cherish
  A small exquisite flower.

In the brilliance of the rainbow's colors
  Lies the promise from above
God the Son and Holy Spirit
  Tell of God's eternal love.
Leola Davis

The Ignored

Surface beauty is so common place
To gaze upon a lovely face
Prompts fantasies to arise

   Though . . .

No one stares into the eyes
Or hears the painful cries
Of the one so desolate

   And . . .

Lest another should forget
Their darkened times, albeit
They think little of us.
Elizabeth Kelso-Davila

Visualize A Picture

Visualize a picture of my strength,
that seems so weak.
Thinking about the problems,
I have left to overcome and seek.
Yet everyday is a struggle,
I'm fighting day by day.
Something is there inside of me,
standing in my way.
A voice, a person, an image,
it's all to hard to say.
I am left here thinking,
will there ever be a way?
I want to tell you listen,
I'm not the one to blame.
But who are you to look at me,
and curse me with all shame?
I'm looking at you for answers,
I need you to understand.
It's not who you are looking at,
I'm no longer in command.
Jessica Dunbar

Let Go

The vengeance you feel
will turn on you
like a dog that turns
on his master
the anger you hide
will haunt like a ghost
and will tear you to pieces inside
the past you live
will spin your head
like a top spins until
it falls down
the hate that you bare
will hold like a trap
and eat up the love you would share
give up the vengeance
learn to forgive
turn the anger to something worth more
the love that you sew
will teach others trust
and you'll find it's the hate you let go.
Ursula Pike

Heart In The Highlands

My heart is in the highlands,
Perhaps you've seen its signs;
It colors up the flowers
And sweetens up the pines.
It captivates the sunbeams
And strews them 'round with care;
And after all the showers,
So freshens up the air,
It brightens up its bowers
Just to prove it's there.

D. J. Kennedy

What About Me

What about me,
I sleep where the alley cats play,
eating the food that's thrown away,
watching the people pass everyday,
staring and smirking with nothing to say,
slowly watching my body decay.
What about me,
I search every inch scrounging for heat,
pacing the alley with no shoes for my feet,
no cushions for my back just hard concrete,
I search for a blanket, a cover, a sheet,
day by day I'm facing defeat.
What about me,
I need a sense of security,
I want to feel safe and live peacefully,
I'm ashamed to live in this obscenity,
What about us, what about we,
what about you, what about me.

Richard J. Shepherd

Beautiful Lady In Black

Blonde hair, blue eyes,
sizzles, unforgiving skies.
She does not wail
beneath the veil,
does not cry
both eyes are dry.
Beautiful Lady in Black

Tents and high-rise,
caravans to the sea.
Franchise and Bazaar,
shining stars on motor cars,
stepping carefully.
Beautiful Lady in Black

Western gem, now settled in.
Fragile petal on the sands,
ancient script on henned hands.
ummm saleh,
  "prayer in the desert."
Beautiful Lady in Black

Rabia Al-Adawiyya

If I Could Stop The Sun...

I wish I could pull a lever
or push a button
to stop the sun from going down
I wish I could hang the sun
just above the horizon
so it could shine on me forever...

And the edge of the earth would always be bathed in pink and
    peach
the pale moon would always be poised in a baby blue sky
the silver-lined clouds would forever float below twinkling white
    stars
the tranquil current would always reflect a shimmering orange
the autumn trees would forever be shadowed in silhouette black

And my ears would always be attune to the crickets' song
my nose would forever inhale the scent of damp pine needles
my skin would forever feel the caress of the wind
my hand would always taste your gentle touch
my heart would always see your deepest affection
my mind would always be at ease
and my soul would forever be at rest

If I could only stop the sun...

John Lindauer

My Inner Peace

   The sun shines over flowers of its everyday
bloom, in the grasp of the earth's atmosphere.
   It is the season where leaves fall, birds
wistfully fly and buds magically appear.
   The rays of each color leap in every
direction, of possible reach and possession.
   What could cause a normal being to
write of this obsession?
   Because the day is clear, the sun is
hot, and the blooms grow radiantly stronger.
   But the sun grows weak and its power
has left, so the flowers may not hold up much longer.
   In a flash, forceful rain will plunder
the surface, possibly drawing the flowers.
   It will end in a storm, after building and
building from more less a wee little shower.
   The sun returns just serene as can be
not disheartened for any main reason.
   It has happened before of that she
is sure, that it happens no matter what season.

Krystal Freeman

Timothy

You lay sleeping while ringlets of Cranberry light
reach through the curtains to taste your flesh.
In the fading light you look as though you are made
Of honey and butter and cream.
You turn your face and offer me eyes wet with
secrets,
and I give you my soul in return.
I slide across you,
Our fingers intertwining like vines of ivy
as I welcome you in again.
Your body draws me into safety as I watch mulberries
drop from the heavens,
and settle on the windowsill outside . . .

Celia Adamczyk-Marker

Wondering, Wandering

Wondering, wandering around and around,
walking up and down the streets of town.
Sights, sounds, scents, and feelings you sense,
staggering forward but thinking in the past tense.
What do I think or believe; what do I seek;
why am I focusing on a rusty door creak?
Out of the corner of my eye, I feel a stare;
what does it all mean, do I even dare?
The flow of a stream, the light from above,
all things I remember that fit like a glove.
In the background I concentrate on her step,
suddenly stopping, forcing me to turn and check.
Whose world is this and why does it all seem clear;
this is where I learned about who and what to fear.
So as I head for home where a pen and paper wait,
I pass by knowing I've left my mark on Christy's gates.

Benjamin W. Landis

Poetry In Me

What is poetry?
What is poetry in me?
It's using words in such a way that what they say is real.
It's how every situation looks and each emotion feels.
It is how I look at you
and have a name for everything observed.
I take my point of view
and mold it into countless words.
It's got clear and Holy power
nestled right within the text.
it can make me laugh for hours
It can turn my spirit vexed.
It's a lighthouse built atop a rock
that saved a many ship at sea
by casting out a trillion watts
of luminosity.
It's a bridge connecting God's domain
to this ungodly place.
It's a snapshot view of me, when sane,
in caps and lower case.

Warren K. Madden

A Vague Wonder

A vague wonder to me tis death
It calls my name
It roars like thunder
Yet, why am I to blame?

I am frightened
They all laugh
They say they're enlightened
But deep inside I see their fear
To me tis so crystal clear
It may be small
But tis there
They just don't care

They don't listen
As my soft tears glisten
They don't understand but neither do I
We will have to wait for this vague wonder to
pass us by, but we'll have to wait until we die!!

Shelby Chlopak

Gardens Of God

I just love to go to the country
Far away from the rules and the rod
To escape the city's noise and toil
and stroll through the "Gardens of God"

It's so peaceful and quiet in the country
As I tread o'er the fresh, soft sod
Or just gaze at a field of clover
Out there, in the "Gardens of God"

There is so much beauty around me
And I feel free as the golden rod
As they sway in the soft, warm breezes
out there, in the "Gardens of God"

Charlotte C. Odell

Abandon Cove

No words are spoken
As we walk the soft white sand,
Oceans waves chasing our bare feet;
The clouds and moon
Play peak-a-boo
We are wrapped in summer's night;
You reach out,
Take my hand,
A simple, caring motion,
Then you wrap me in your arms
Where I am locked forever
In the memory of your kiss.

Diana Shilkett Jamison

Just One More Time

Tears flowed freely when I told him,
　Our hunting days are near at end.
A body not young as it once was,
　Old legs that pain as they bend.
Many trails we've explored together,
　Many mountains we've climbed to the rim.
God's great beauty always around us,
　Fond memories that will never dim.
The years crept down upon me,
　Like thieves in the still of night.
Oh Lord, I do not question you,
　Still the end just doesn't seem right.
Father and son we've shared together
　The thrill of the great outdoors,
Companionship few will ever know,
　Partners, camaraderie, love and more.
Son, you saw the tears flow from me
　When I said this might be the end.
Please God, just one more time
　To us may you be willing to lend.

Virgil A. Ruckdaschel

Silence

I am sitting under an Oak tree,
silently wishing
silently dreaming.

A leaf falls in my lap,
silently crying out for help
dry and fragile,
I crush it, quietly it follows the wind.

Leaning my head against the trees,
I listen, wondering, why it is so quiet?

So, I scream at the top of my lungs
birds fly, dogs bark, my heartbeat pounds
in my head.

Slowly,
Everything goes silent,
And I wonder,

Should I scream, again?

Mary L. Beyer

Positive Thinking

As I look around me
I realize how lucky I am
to have all of my favorite
things around me. They brighten
up each day with hope
and guide me on my
journey through life.
I live each day
to the fullest and take
it one day at a time.
I know that someday
I will find true love
and my soul mate for life.

Jennifer Lloyd

That Is What I See

An angel shining
A sky as the lining
Golden beams surround

The ocean he's sailing
Winds are prevailing
So she whispers a sound

His dreams they swell
No longer they dwell
On happiness they agree

Their love is real
That's what they feel
That is what I see.

Michael Quinn Williamson

The Shadow Walker Legacy

Moonlight washes over a stream and a man
He looks like he finally came out of the dark.
It looks like he didn't think he could back then
But if you look close you can see a new spark.
Exuding a confidence that's new and amazing
His smile reflects off of a nearby pool.
Stars shine over his head in a fluorescent praising
Paying homage to a man who won a life long duel.
In an instant it was over before my very eyes
The shadows seemed to wrap round him as he stepped back
I stand there coming out of a strange state of surprise
Not sure what I just saw as I picked up my pack.
Perhaps one day I'll be the one in his place
Hopefully the test of time will allow me to see.
As I walk a spark hits my eyes and a smile shows on my face
A torch had just been passed in the shadow walker legacy.

Richard A. Gramlich

Salt Grain Melodies

Don't rely on everything that your ears take in
Often times you will hear what others do not mean.

Look carefully with your eyes and see the picture whole
You might be surprised to discover what you didn't know.

Keep your mouth to yourself unless you need to say
Because everything that one says can be told another way.

Try and not clench your fists with the anger that's inside
Instead find a trustworthy friend in whom you can confide

Do not let your exposed feet take you where they want to go
They may lead you through a patch of glass, broken in the road.

But let your heart control how you act today
And share it tomorrow with the friends along your way.

Katy Stangland

Morning Aftertastes

Lightly scented musk wafts through me
Mellowing the sensuous aftertastes
Still lingering.

Stretched gazes calm my assurance
That I am here under warm blankets
Still very safe and secure.

Softly shaded curtains host the new seeking sun
For my pores to kiss, my hair to heat.

I yawn my limbs longingly outward
Stroking long relaxed legs
Waiting to be touched again.

Simulating his touch and sighs of contentment
I pause and see his towel, taut and wet.

Relaxing the coffee aside my bed I raise my blankets
And stretch out to his towel and yank.

Falling beside me we laugh loudly shrouding our
Nakedness nuzzling together again.

Heavenly scented musk wafts through us
As our sensuous tastes seal fresh
Within the blankets.

Deron Dahlke

The Death Of A Tree

Our old apple tree stood ravaged by time.
Its limbs all gnarled with age.
The boughs once laden with luscious red fruit
Now droop with disease and decay.

I remember when it stood stately and tall,
Strong limbs stretching up to the sun.
An array of pink blossoms in springtime,
Snow frosted when winter comes.

We took of its bounty year after year
Rosy apples so juicy and sweet.
But the winds of time have taken their toll
Now it bows its head in defeat.

I watched as the saw bit deep in its side
There's a lump in my throat and a tear I can't
hide slides slowly down my cheek.

The old tree trembled and with a crashing sound
All shattered and broken it fell to the ground.
Now all that's left is just a pile of wood,
Where once a stately apple tree stood.
   How sad is the death of a tree.

Audrey Burnett

Pinnacles — P.R. For U.S.A.

Goin' down to valleys, hear high winds blow.
Angels from heaven, let songs sing aglow.

F.B.I. files, they have known and transcribed.
Citizens, employers and applicants:
Need falsified statements be verified?
Will officials be granted innocence?

Promote respect or public relations.
Accentuate the productive as proof.
GNP growth is not from addictions.
Community service amends each goof.

Who benefits from fear propaganda?
who profits from teen drug abuse babies?
What matter's 3 R's? Or Phenomena?
Who honors privacy in Bill of Rights?

Military industrial "soles?"
We're all heaven sent — clouds before rainbows?

Jacklyn L. Shaw

Footprints Of An Angel

As I awoke this morn with footprints on my sheet
I touched it carefully I could feel its heat
she had no shoes upon her tiny feet
for she was an angel there was no need
She watched me as I lay sleeping
I could feel her presence as I lay dreaming
She watches over the ill and low
I could feel the radiance of her golden halo
She stays with you till you're well and reborn
then she floats off to another in a different form
You really must believe in heaven and thunder
because angels are real and they are truly a wonder.

Dale Forrest

Laughter And Tears

Circus life is not my style
All that travelling across the long miles
Dealing with the stubborn animals
Is like dealing with realism and life
Training ornery business men
To relieve your own strife
Balancing high on the tightrope
Dealing after a fight and how to cope
Flying around on the trapeze
Enjoying all life's fun with complete ease
Cleaning up after the mess
Taking on a shrink to relieve stress
Feeding the people of the shows
Growing how no one knows
The cotton candy, peanuts, and such
The simple pleasures in life, not much
The little moonless and small day
The worries of every normal day
To travel on through out the years
To bring adults and children
   laughter and tears

Tina Marie Racut

The Little Things

Thinking, thinking, thinking,
About life, about troubles,
Trying to get my thoughts in order
As I sit here alone.

A single leaf catches my eye
As it breaks away from the tree
I'm sitting under, and I realize
The significant changes a leaf
Goes through as its first born
On a branch, bright and green,
Then as it ages, turns colors,
Becomes stale, and falls to its death.

As it hits the ground, I realize
Nature is much like our own lives,
Struggling to survive, just to die in the end,
But while they are here, they add
A special beauty to the world,
Making everything whole,
And I see just how important
The little things in life really are.

Jennifer Leigh Rasor

Children Of Yesterdays

Does anyone know the answers,
to the questions that I ask.
To know about the future,
to think about the past.
Remember all the things,
that I forgot to do.
Now that all the old things,
are blocked out by the new.
You know it's so depressing,
that everything will change.
Whatever I see before me now,
will never be the same.

Steven Horner

Grown And Gone Away

Children are a gift from God
or the devil you may say.
Their noise and pranks near drive you mad
but — too soon they'll go away.

Will he call? Will she write?
How did they get so tall?
I know my children well you say
but — you don't really know them at all.

We all have hopes for our children
no matter our station or race,
we pray their lives will be better
without the problems we had to face.

Teach them well the love of God,
To love their country too,
respect for their elders,
and that bad attitudes will not do.

So — young parents I plead with you,
spend time with your children today,
thank God that you have them,
too soon - they're grown and gone away.

Reba Crooks

Untitled

so . . . i hate the way yoU look at me
eyes pick-ing prOb-ing play-ing
with mY mind (i wished on a star
that you would go blind and lEave
my brain alone).

sometimes . . . i always neVer hate it
when you touch me your hands (like
snakes) no me so well my blOod
starts to singanddance — shh — (don't tell)

maybe . . . i hate the way you make me
feel so happy like life Loves to laughandcry
angetmadansad.

then again . . . i hate the way you make me
believe in y(moonstarsun)ou

but . . . most of all I hate it when . . .

Nicole Giustino

For Patty J.

A sinewy kitten crept from the fallen body.
Smoke-colored and thin;
She leapt through glass onto the ledge.
Pelting rain, like tears or spittle
Ran down the ghostly figure that
Shivered after the punishment was done.
The ritual stripped her of what she was.
Of what she could become.

The cat crept from useless flesh
Fleeing through shattered glass.
Tender pads touched cold, unyielding stone
As onyx eyes glowed in yellow-diamond
Orbs of light.
Diamonds lit a path to the earth.
I stood behind her in silhouette.
She prayed for a happy ending.
I prayed for her life.

Y. Regina Whitmore

Desperate Dreamer

Lay me down on the bed of fire
Surrounded by black lace
Your hate is my ill desire
To stare in your astonished face
Tie me down and leave me burning
Let my existence melt away
While I'm escaping, I'm just now learning
You should've taught me how to pray...
Glance deeper into my sinful eyes
Discover unknown to me truth
You and I are slaves in disguise
Forgotten mistakes are protecting our youth...
Watch my patience roll down my face
Reluctantly shatter as it hits your lips
My dreams contaminate reality with haze
Once your empty smile drops on my fingertips...
Free my soul of my desperate emotions
They only cause unforgiving pain
I need to discover forbidden secrets of oceans
How to stay calm and at once be insane..

Julie Pastron

Filtered Light

Sunlight lies like salt sprinkled on the leaves,
While pea-size bits skylight filter through the trees.
This is where my love walked with me,
Through dense, green forested floors.
But now, no more.
Time has passed.
Days are gone.
Memories only are these
Of walks,
Love,
Leaves.
Only the green remains
For other lovers;
And the sunlight is salt sprinkled on the leaves.

Susan A. Leonard

Down By The River

Down by the river, to a park where I go
I sit there and think of a woman I know
I think of the memories, the times that we shared
I hope that she knows that I really do care
Down by the river, you can feel the wind blow
I can hear children's laughter as I sit there alone
Through the trees there's an echo of a voice I once knew
I turned around to look, to see if it was you
Down by the river, memories rush in so fast
I think of our future, the present, and past
I remember the days and nights we had shared
I feel so empty, alone, and scared
Down by the river, I wait there for you
Hoping you know my love is special and true
Waiting for the day you come back to me
Listening to the wind blow through the trees

Shannon Barrett

On A Day Like This

It's a raw, thin weather world this day.
The wind is high and shrill, crying through
the tree silhouettes against the smudgy gray sky.
There will be no warmth today . . .
But it goes deeper than the skin.
Sometimes it goes through the soul and passed time.
This lack of warmth . . .
Sometimes this feeling has nothing to do
with this day and age . . . and wants no
connection with them.
This shiver that runs across the shoulders,
and through the heart, has nothing to
do with what is transpiring now.
I suppose there is no explaining it . . .
There's no one left to explain it to . . .
The ones who would understand have
all gone . . . on a day like this.
H. Gwinn Peck

The Future

The world turns 'round slowing down then it stops, starts
 going down.

Down down down into the ground till the world's no longer
 round, not a soul can be found.

Do not look underground.
Karen H. Deal

Obsession Of Love (The Flower That Lies In Your Hair)

A night of cries my sweet child
Dry your eyes for the love is truly within your heart
the obsession of love and lust are those that are separate
An I the obsession of love will open the gateway
"Follow me"
Follow me in to the love of all in the paradise of truth
For that flower will shine in your hair,
And the kingdom will rain love down upon those that care

"Oh see"
see what I see,
For this I want in the name of love
"oh" shine like the sun my sweet child
Shine like the flower that lies in your hair
Daniel J. Ramaglia

Testimony Of Faith

From my hill high above all
I gaze in awe at that which I see
In the valley below.
Nestled serenely, mountain protected,
The pure white spire of God's home
Beckons me, and nourishes me.
Inner peace comes, my fears are now calmed
As I focus inward and draw strength.
As the mountains are sentinels
Protecting the valley and all therein,
My God, my faith, my church
Envelop me, love me, protect me in that same way.
Thank you for giving me
Your staff to lean on.
Joann H. Proud

A Journey In The Life Of . . .

Leaves of enjoyment
Fluttering past me today
Like a huge doorway.

Voices running wild
Watching the minds of others
Nothing can change me.

Engulfing happiness
Nothing can restrain me now
Like a hawk in flight.

Visions diminished
Like trying to see but can't
Dark's and lights swirling.

Strolling through the mind
Unleashed within a death zone
Wishing freedom near.

Entering the ramp
Decisions are everywhere
The ride beginning.
Nicole Gould

The Tiny Bronzed Boots

The tiny bronzed boots
once filled with my little round boy
size one and a half
they stand near me on a table
across the room

Long ago filled with
childhood's hope, purpose and sturdiness
then abandoned
in life's wondrous rhythm
its progression into a larger size
a larger tomorrow

My little round cowboy
in these then leather boots
growing healthy and strong
leaving his first boots behind
for me to bronze, to cherish
as a joyous keepsake

A reminder today of death, of despair
of dreams turned to darkness
of my little boy, grown, gone to ashes
Patricia Zoch Ferguson

In Loss, Man's Best Friend

He will forever,
be a part of me.

I have pictures,
so that others can "see."

I'm thankful for the years,
that we spent together.

For that part of my life,
I will always treasure.
Michael C. Libertini

A Gift Received

I have a son, so soft so sweet
Shining blue eyes, and tiny feet.

I am a father, miracle of life
Thanks to my Lord, thanks to my wife.

To carry on, the name I hear
Is why men love, a son so dear.

I think that this, is true of me
My name to last, eternally.

My tiny son, this precious gift
Grow strong my boy, be sure be swift.

And when you Don, a grown man's shoe
Be straight my son, always speak true.

For from your words, grow doubt, or trust
Speak steel my son, for lies are dust.

Be fair with all, that you should deal
Speak not a lie, and never steal.

The name I leave you, bears no mark
Only the sign, of love's soft spark.

So grow my son, and in this land
To all the weak, offer your hand.
Bill Wilkins

Dabney Hill

I stood on the hill top
This evening and felt
The first cool November
winds on my brow.
A crystal night with
pine trees silhouetted
against the sky;
Like birth pains she
came slowly out of
The north slipping
quietly and building
to a crescendo to become
The first frost of the season.
Turning aside, thoughts
of another night when
Two lovers strolled
down a pine strewed
lane on a night such
as this
Janice Rayburn

Tomorrow's Adventure

No blue snow fine achievement
vibrant health fine bank balance
income growth luxury and leisure
real progress a beautiful tomorrow
gains new green pastures
more social life be yourself
present need met new from
abroad power and prestige
great adventure luck is
with you.
Lois Bell

There Is A Purpose In The World

Some people tell us that the world lacks purpose
"Life has evolved through blind chance," they say
Random mutations account for natural selection
Produced by adaptation to an ever changing earth

In their myopia they view "the selfish gene"
As the supreme monarch of all things alive
The single-minded monarch gives but this command
"Survive, increase, spread me across the earth."

Let us not believe that we know all there is
About purpose in the universe, but we can ask
"Could it be that with the advent of human life
The universe found purpose that some fail to see?"

Where is the scientific evidence for purpose?
It lies unrecognized within that very question
Purpose is found in our asking who we are
Where are we going and what can we accomplish?

With humankind a purpose for the world was born
To banish random chance and replace it with justice
And to rebel against the rule of selfish genes
To sing, and dance, to play, and to create beauty
Theodore C. Kent

If

A collage of memories I've managed to gather,
Protected within the walls of my being,
They shall forever exist.
For your continuous flow of positive energy
Awakened me from my cynical slumber.
Saving me with deliberate acts of kindness
I no longer inhale polluted thoughts of rejection.
Untainted treasure so memorable you'll never vanish.
Even within time, recollections of you will just grow stronger.
For I was in search of a pure communion
When the heavens directed your wings towards me.
A ray of light I was able to capture
As my eyes first encountered a glimpse of you hypnotizing smile
But now I must accept
Time had an appointment with you and felt it fit not to delay,
Rather arrive and give no notice to us who are left in dismay.
Thoughts which were unspoken but definitely felt,
Will be carried with great regret,
For you were never told all I needed to express.
So with this beloved William I bid my farewell.
Heidy Hernandez a.k.a. Pipil

Untitled

It began as a joke
But, I'm not laughing anymore
The farce has quickly evolved into truth

Thoughts of you
Wander aimlessly through my consciousness
I am comforted by your presence in my mind

There is an image of you - your eyes and your smile
And like a soft blanket, I want to wrap myself in you
To feel and experience your warmth

And I want so badly
To paint you in vivid, breathtaking colors
Across the canvas which is my life
Jessica L. Salyers

The Essence Of Time

Yesterday is held in today.
Tomorrow is on its way.
Forever is a relative term.
Never has lately come.
Goodbyes have been said.
In a cycle we are led.
Tangents lead us astray.
Soon again to find our way.
Hopes are held high.
The children are made to cry.
The future seems, to them, gay.
They are confident that they will find their way.
We see the children's future as bleak.
We can only hope they find what they seek.
Yesterday is gone tomorrow.
Today is filled with sorrow.
Tomorrow holds hope.
Making us able to cope.
Forever will creep upon us soon.
Never was yesterday gone.

Mary Jo Foley

Expression

I walk alone in a desperate search for an answer but only finding myself crossed between two roads;

My choice can be as simple or as difficult as I make it.

It is a matter of how I view myself and knowing what I can and cannot live with;

I have yet to learn about myself and how far I am willing to go but it's finding a way to discover my soul is what torments me;

Escaping through my poems as I express my innermost feelings I, then, feel my spirit lifted to a level where joy is found.

Is a way of escaping from a world of pain and sorrow and walking into a new dimension where happiness is a virtue of reality;

My true feelings are what I employ in my poems for they are spoken words from the bottom of my soul and the depth of my spirit;

Reading my poems is giving you the key to my heart!

Rosa Torres

Fishing For Salmon On The Little Wasilla

In The Arctic North
Under my feet I see the silver flash
racing up the crystal river.
Like a dance of anger fighting the frothing current,
they swim exhausted from the open sea
towards ancient spawning grounds.

A northern gale hastens the journey.

From the corner of my eye I catch
the glistening sands of the blackened riverbed,
and see several fish flopping, gasping their last breaths
in a race against time.

I step back and observe how the river claims it own,
and how the turbulent journeys through life,
also claim those who struggle against it.

I will be sorely missed . . .

Cynthia Ashton

Lullaby

I cried.
And a single.
Silent tear.
Rolled off my flesh.
Then splashed into a millennia
of pieces, for the earth
could not cradle it.

And I fell.
To the same cold.
barren, ball of dirt.
that could neither hold
nor cradle
me.

Just like you.

Laurie L. Brabec

Autaugaville

In spiral decentation
She wrote me forever,
letters . . . Stained
with his love,
from underground —
somewhere in Autaugaville
belatedly,
if that is the word she used
on that evening,
when we grew tired,
disregarding topics
I cared not to discuss,
Inducted to pursuits
of her dreams of him,
and never diminishing
her belief in it all,
which happened to be . . .
our mistake.

Jannice Brooks

Reflection Without A World

Absolutely nothing changed in
civilization since beginning to
utilize fire,
Trying to contain and master
burning desires.
Mixed feelings for thoughts, ideas
someone or something else
brought.
An open door lingers just out of
reach of entering, sounds wash
away eluding reasons for being
human.
Still the mighty scorn the weak,
greed subdues the middle and
poor becomes easier to expect,
Lifting our heads in pride, another
millennium may pass before
we comprehend our world into
which we all reflect.

M. J. Andrew

Froth

A secret ideology
For self awareness by decree.
Uncertainty, imposed suspense,
Illusive words to make no sense.
A tune sneaks through that would entrance,
"That sinful beat ain't got a chance"
Short lived? Suppressed? Unnatural death,
By Nay, amen, by "Shibboleth"
With rhythmic cycles so despised.
Recursive waves anathematized.
Useful meaning information
Summed in bits for limitation.
Trivia to confound the thought,
With transitory dogma taught.
Remember Nature? It's still here
Beneath the hate; beneath the fear.

Michael A. Pereira

Goodbye, My Love

Can you touch a cloud?
Can you pull a voice from a stone?
Can you climb a stairway of moonlight
   To whisper to the stars?

You need only your voice
   To reach the distant mist.
You need only your smile
   To hear the silent rock.
You need only your hand
   To talk with the night sky.

You have made this man of granite
Sing like a free bird long ago,
But now rain begins to fall
From the mist at my eyes
As I hear again the word
"Goodbye"
Ring from your lips.

Climb the stairway and whisper,
Even if it costs you a stamp,
And I'll meet you at the stars.

Joseph F. Bohan

The Blinding Light Of Truth

Thought, which ponders, analyzes,
Keeps inquiring, never rests,
Constitutes its own last problem,
Everlasting, final quest.

   In a puzzling disharmony
   Between concept and percept,
   Unconcealment, through concealment,
   Brings to light its frightful depth.

We are doomed to chase in darkness
Tiny streaks of sunshine bright,
But the truth continues hiding
In a blinding flood of light.

Rostyslaw Pawlowych

Birth Of A Song

The worst of the war was on its way,
for the British attacked Washington on this day.
Baltimore was next to feel the British power,
but at Fort McHenry America would not cower.
A new flag was ordered to fly over the fort,
one that could be seen by the British ships in port.
The war raged on all through the night,
but for new found freedom America would fight.
By daylight September 14th the fighting had ceased,
and those who fought knew the meaning of peace.
In the morning the British fleet got underway,
and moved down river and into the bay.
A prisoner wrote about a flag that was tattered and torn,
and on an evening in 1814 our National Anthem was born.

Christal Brooks-Smith

October 31

A knock knock knock at the door. There was more.
A coffin lid opened and out popped a
Cornucopia of mischief. Zombies
Dancing wildly across the zig-zag tombstones
To the monotone of haunting drones. Witches
Rode by on snorting dinosaurs waving
Their brooms in the black clouds. Voices shrieked out
Above the blast of lightening: "Watch out!
We witches will get ya! Ha Ha Ha Ha!"
Watchful grinning pumpkins in drab windows
Of gray spider webs joined the parade
Of charades into a weird broom closet
To be opened - another year - another day...

Geri Dyer

Blind These Eyes

Blind these eyes that see only discontent
Pleading with dust in a pit of sand
Bury me if I cannot again be innocent

Timeless groves whisper eternal laments
Glory is never touched in Charon's land
Blind these eyes that see only discontent

I believe I climb while I continue descent
With honey and milk death's speech I command
Bury me if I cannot again be innocent

The Stygian mire pulls with powerful torments
The Furies nigh, for corruption is at hand
Blind these eyes that see only discontent

Cationic creatures wait hungry, malevolent
Sounding their fury with insistent demand
Bury me if I cannot again be innocent

I have nothing to hold amidst this pestilence
a desiccated husk Hecate commands
Blind these eyes that see only discontent
Bury me if I cannot again be innocent

Nina Garcia

A Horrid Spring Day

If only you could see the view from my window
In the spring. The buds of a thousand trees
Outside
Leave a blanket of putrid lime green
Mixed with brown bark and gray sky
Outside my window today.
If only you could hear the birds from my window
In the spring. The young screeching
Outside
For the freedom of flight
That has not yet been granted their wings
Outside my window today.
If only I could leave the confinement of my window
In the spring. To roam and live
Outside
The Confinement of my body to have my soul know freedom
Away from the screeching green grayness
Outside my window today.
Meghan Elaine Plumb

Winter

Tensions tighten as the snow falls,
Seems Mr. Depression is on call.

Days are dreary without end,
And wintertime has just to begin.

The birds all flutter from tree to tree,
As if to say, "Where are the seeds, you promised me."

Feed the birds, take out the trash,
Heard a noise, sounds like a crash.

My thoughts are wandering not too far,
As I proceed to scrape ice from the car.

Brew some coffee or maybe a cup of tea,
That will soothe the nerves of me.

Spring please hurry and show your face,
Hope winter doesn't leave a trace.

Tensions loosen, Mr. Depression hide,
Then I can spend some time outside.

Watch the flowers, bud and bloom,
So move over winter and make more room.

So winter hurry, please don't stay,
Come back again, but not my way.
Yvonne T. Huls

The Tunnel

I yearn for a light beyond this tunnel
Trapped within its destructive tunnel
All interests lost, deep within the nothingness
Searching to find, to suffice the loneliness
Engulfed within, all distance lost
Desertion, confusion, paid all cost
Distracted only by sounds among shadow
Unable to discern above and below
Time escapes or ceases to exist
Indulgence in fantasy persist
Life continues without knowing the abyss
Until the light receives my kiss.
Debra Phillips

Before The Beginning

As yet I look from a distance,
But feel too close for an instance.
If only I could come forward
And bring your heart and hand toward
A brave change for us tomorrow
And all the bright days that follow.
But now is not the time for Spring,
'Tis just before the beginning.
Gary R. Wehrle

Parting

Our thoughts go back over the years
Floating from one to the next.
Reminding each other of the time when . . .
   the place where . . .
   the person who . . .

Parting is not sweet sorrow — only sorrow.
As in death, only one must leave.
Each bearing a portion
   of their sadness,
   of their madness.

Forcing a smile, we keep our distance,
Letting the other know that we are strong.
All the while, we want to reach out,
   to touch, to hold,
   and not let go.

The balm of time will heal.
Until then, we can only hope,
To keep our thoughts fixed
   upon each other
   and our hearts soft.
W. James Metzger

Mess, Mediocre, Masterpiece

What will your life be when you grow up?
Will it be a mess?
Will it be mediocre?
Will it be a masterpiece?
God gave you a brain.
Will you fill it with trash?
Or will you study and seek diligently
What is worthwhile?
You can wreak havoc,
Or just get by in an ordinary way,
Or use your talents wisely
And become a masterpiece.
It's all up to you.
Edna Zimmerman Prentis

Summer

Summer days are fun;
Soaking up rays in the sun.
Playing in the park;
You get to stay up till dark.
Having picnics and going to fairs;
Eating watermelon, plums and pears.
Playing in the pool;
And trying to keep cool.
So don't forget this summer day;
While in the heat you play.
Lorraine Muse

A Song Of Trees

Trees grow tallest when the sun
Deals gently with them; one by one
The precious days, with measured length
Increase their strength.

The winds come from the stately hills;
Low whispering, their singing fills
The branches with a symphony;
The rains in sudden ecstasy
Of freedom pour their bounty there —
Contrive to make the trees more fair.

The wind, the rain, the sun, all these
Comprise the majesty of trees.
Virginia Nedrow

Faith

It is not come by easily.
Faith is a verb rather than a noun.

You can't buy Faith—
You can't have Faith
or
Obtain Faith.

You can only practice Faith.
By setting your intent,
Placing yourself in alignment
with God's Principles
This sets your attitudes
Which will sustain you.

Remember Faith is not obtainable
as it is not a product.
Faith is a Process.
Jherrie Rubeyiat

If I Could

If I could sell the diamonds
That glitter on the snow
I would be as rich as Croesus
And could put on quite a show

I could build myself a mansion
And a library or two
And out do Mr. Carnegie
And make him fret and stew.

I could help the poor and needy
To put bread upon their tables
Create jobs for all the jobless
Who are willing, strong and able.

Build churches for the righteous ones
Who turn up their pious noses
At lesser ones with pick and hoe
Who cultivate the roses

If I could buy the wonder
In a child's inquiring eyes
I could pay for it in diamonds
Newly fallen from the skies.
Lula Rud

Try God Praise Him - God

Praise be to God most high, who said, "seek
my face, for I am the first and the last"
Give him a try and he will lead you to the most
ultimate fast.
He will lift you up when you are down.
Just humble yourself and bow toward the ground.
God is worthy to be praised; he will not let you down.
When all your friends are gone, he will still be around.
He will lift you up on high, when you are feeling low.
Praise God, give reverence and he will show
you which way to go.
Try God, praise him and he will be around;
with a flicker of an eye or even a frown.
Praise him in the morning, noon or night; put him
to the test.
I guarantee, he will make everything alright.
No matter what you problem is, you can take
it through Jesus.
God will answer you regardless of the reason.
Nola Grace Holder

The Passing Of A Mentor
In Memory of J. F. Merritt Jr. (My Dad)

The passing of a mentor, what a tragic bell to ring
the one who taught you right from wrong
to be strong never weak, for a weak person falls for
anything, therefore stands for nothing.

The passing of a mentor how could it be
the passing of his knowledge is it yet complete?

The passing of a mentor who teaches the enjoyment of life's,
down as well as ups,
not only keeps us young, but thirsting from life's
endless cup

Only thru adventure can one truly live,
If he is not walking among the living,
is he walking among the dead?
The mentor says come on boys let go to bed.
Jeffrey L. Merritt

Have You Ever?

Have you ever heard the butterfly's wings
or a hummingbird's cry?
Do you smell the clouds as they go rolling by
or taste a snowflake as it falls?
When you stand in a rainbow do you change colors
or twinkle like a star?
As a snail goes crawling do you hear him laugh,
or see the stars in his eyes?
Can you hear a daffodil unfurl its petals
or turn its face to the sun and smile?
Have you ever watched a fish sleep
only to see him smile at his dreams?
And there's the honeybee all sticky and gooey
tending its golden sea.
Turn around; they're stars no bigger than a minute;
where life, beauty and time abound,
And we're in it.
Danni Hudson

Burgundy Velvet

I love the feel of burgundy velvet.
Dark and rich like hot chocolate in your favorite cup,
When you drink down the sweet, hot treat to ward off the cool of late autumn.
Soft and soothing like bubble bath and jazz after a long day.

Burgundy velvet

My grandmother made a quilt of velvet scraps once.
I would stand on tiptoe to see the top of her tall iron bed,
adorned by the beloved velvet quilt.
To touch ever so gently the one burgundy scrap.
I was only six then.

Burgundy velvet

Soft gentle memories of childhood wrapped in burgundy velvet.
I am grown now.
I rush daily to tend to job, home, things important.

But even so I still stop to admire to an old velvet quilt.

To drink hot chocolate
To listen to soft jazz.
And remember burgundy velvet.

Beryl Imboden

Who Am I?

I am who I am, this very moment
Let the moment leave, then . . . Who am I?
Someone's mom, a loving wife,
a caring responsible person, then . . .
Who am I?

Darkness falls, secrets arise
Anger comes to the surface, then . . . Who am I?
Let the anger come, let it explode
Finally wipe the slate clean, then . . .
Who am I?

Scared and alone, and frightened to death
At the mercy of an angressor, then . . . Who am I?
A defenseless child, hoping for help that does not come
Someone knows, but does not respond, then . . .
Who am I?

A child trapped in a grownup's body
Longing, longing for release, aching for love, then . . .
Who am I?
Who am I?
I am who I am, this very moment.

Mary Joanna E. Grady

For The Soldiers In Saudi Arabia

The stench of death hangs over a city, so far from home.
Too many brave souls unable to kiss their wives one last time.
Fathers are many, not hearing their children's prayers.
A nation outraged from the diabolical acts of the wicked.
Rubble and distraction over cast the summer sunshine.
The screams of fear and utter content brush off the singing of the birds.
Why—such a little word
Why—a powerful question
Why our Fathers, husbands, sons and brothers?
Tell us why!

Staci L. Row

Untitled

You leave me behind with no regret
alone in a world of injustice. You,
yourself the Queen presiding over this
desolate land. Looking down can you
not see my love deep within for my Queen
or the continuous pain you caused me?
Am I just another servant among many?
Love must mean nothing for mine own
has not yet touched your cold heart
forever longing the warmth of another.
I love you. Why can you not understand
and accept what I've placed before you?
Love is the greatest gift and yet you refuse.

Dawn M. Ramirez

Echoing

As tears fill up in my eyes I
realize I better say my last goodbyes 'cause
I think this is gonna be the day, the day
   that he dies

So I'm holding him tight but I
don't know what to do cause he's
lying in my arms bleeding through several
   bullet wounds

As I'm wishing it was a dream but,
I know it's true 'cause the sound
of the gun fire keeps
   echoing through.

Medhan Morris Moreno

Destiny

I look into your eyes, what
   is it that I see?

A simple gesture of kindness
   given from you to me

I have no explanations for
   the way our lives unfold

I only know that eyes are
   the windows to one's soul

So speak not a word, touch me
   with your mind

The love I see within feels
   so intense and wild

Let me taste of it, share
   this with me

For as I watch you now
   I know you are my destiny . . .

Carolyn L. Avila

Clouds

On the ground I lie,
Gazing into the sky.
What is that I see,
Could it be a picture of me?
This has to be a trick of the
imagination,
But it seems like a real situation.
At first glance it is a cloud,
But in the sky when I look around
I see flowers, trees, and
bumblebees,
Cars, trains, and airplanes.
Not a puffy white mass,
But things that change shape so
fast.
When I look way up there
I can imagine anything I dare!

F. Michelle Allen

Forgotten Knowledge

Deep blue.
Bodies of light flash past me
Their paths chosen and in progress.
I call out—Stop! Please talk to me!
I'm so sad and weary, I need to rest.
I want to hold ancient wisdom and peace
In my heart and I'm sure you know the way
To happiness that I can't find
In my simpleness, on this earth, on my own.
Pause and speak to me! Shed some light
Into this hopeless whirlwind of my heart!
Whisper my purpose on this planet of futility!
I am so tired of searching in the dark!

Sherrie Wakeland

Rare Jewels

Dug from
　the innermost depths of the earth
red diamonds and ice emeralds are
　only ugly deformed rocks at birth!
cut, polished,
　and buffed . . .
　　they shine in all
　　　their glory!

Holding all
　eyes in hypnotic stare . . . In awe
　of their splendor
Flawless in
　their shape . . .
Perfection to
　the trained eye.
　they do adore!
Transformed from
　ordinary rocks to masterpieces . . .
　what a story!!!

Mitchel A. Phelps-Wiley

The Final Amazing Grace

I look to the horizon; there is a very bright light.
And there, is an outstretched hand and a golden gate.
He reaches out to me with; "I'll escort you that night."
"But it's not the time, not just yet, and you must wait."

It's time to reflect on what's to come, and what has been.
Did I take the time to help a friend in difficult places?
Did I reach my goals, did I accomplish? Did I mend?
I wonder, and I look at you all, into your sea of faces.

Now my long and endearing love, he is very close at hand.
Through trial and error and loss, heartache and separation;
We have come full cycle, now together in death, we stand.
Oh don't cry, do not feel alone, it is only preparation.

Please don't let my thoughts overflow and overwhelm me.
Don't let me get lost in the slowly shifting of the sand.
Look out and know it's like my love of the beautiful sea.
Reach out to me dear family and friends, and take my hand.

I'm sailing a tall ship to the small islands in the sun.
I'm hoisting my sails, preparing for this my final race.
My long journey into death, has only just now begun.
Because cancer is taking me to my final . . . "amazing grace."

Beverly I. Schillinger

I Lost

I worked my hardest I lost a lot of rest
not much left to say except I did my best,
but I tired and I lost — failure the ultimate
cost, no one can say I didn't care or that I
didn't give a damn no one can say I gave up or
that I didn't give it all that I am. Because I
did my best I don't feel I owe anyone an
explanation, no one can blame it on procrastination.
Life is kinda a game, until the end if you're not
truly happy you can't win. I've been living by
a certain aspect that no one has come to
respect, but for them people I just have to
say this is a game I'm not going to throw away
no one's going to say well she tried, they're going
to say well she failed she couldn't hang on
to what she wanted and had held. I did my
best and I'll do the same when life gives me
another one of its many tests, I'm going to have to
live by the decisions I make and the life that I
choose I never gave up, so did I really lose?

Rachelle Aughinbaugh

Child Of My Dreams

You have lived with me throughout my life,
residing in my soul, my mind and heart.
An as yet unreachable piece of myself
waiting for your moment to be.
Then came a delicious pain to translate
imagination into reality and fiction to fact.
There was a soul and given wings it became you.
And now I hold you in my arms,
your eyes searching mine as I seek to find
the words I cannot speak.
I revel in your newness, you're unashamed love
and know you are the best part of
who I was meant to be.

Karen Kennedy

Bonding With Love On Your Wedding Day

"Crystal and Byron, yours in a Disney story of love,
Pouring down from the Sovereign Father above.
Cinderella and Prince Charming . . . such a romance!
Crystal and Byron just desire to sing and dance.

Father, earnestly we pray for their success sign:
Power unending, that becomes truly divine!
Love from you outpours in all your pleasing ways.
Prosperity is received through all your light rays.

That prosperity is not just their earthly wealth . . .
But gifts of the Spirit also, with grace and good health.
Byron, strive to be diligent all of your life.
Crystal, strive to be a prudent and loving wife.

Life, with all of its confusions, bright joys, and care,
Happens to meet this inspired, newly-wedded pair,
Who bind their true hearts, walking in sunsets of love;
Bonding with gold and enduring far from above.

Blessings of that love, peace and joy are sent their way,
Joined they have been, in wedlock, on this special day!
As through many years, they will stand every test,
Forever, may this dear couple be greatly blessed!"

Charita Schneider

True Love

Hold me gentle
Wrap your arms around me
Like a cool breeze on a hot day.
I know what we are doing may not be right.
But that does not matter to me
All I need is your love to carry me
Through the everlasting kaleidoscope.
Colorful twisted ways of life changing
With every choice and decision we make,
Looking past tomorrow hoping that
Someday we will devote ourself to one
Of life's beautiful colors of the kaleidoscope.
The perfect unity of two people who
Love so deeply
It makes each day a constant battle,
Because I know my heart will never
let you go.

Jennifer Lynn Sanderson

The Prison Of Pain

I lock myself away in a prison of pain.
It's a game that should have never been played.
The bars that lock my heart from the outside world
Were created by me.
Now my heart begs to be free.
I hide in my prison of pain,
like a mouse after a chase.
I'm frightened by each snarl that crosses your face.
You win the game, you caught the bait.
I'm the wounded mouse full of hate.
I'm the one locked in a prison of pain.
When you're trapped, you gain strength,
And that's just what I've done.
I'm breaking free, taking a new look at reality.
I refuse to be trapped in a prison I have created.
I am free from my prison of pain,
and you are a fading memory.

JoDee Watson

Moments From The Heart

I remember fresh baked bread.
   And the wonder fragrance
   that made your mouth water.
I remember her favorite games.
   And learning how to play them,
   while she sometimes let me win.
I remember my first cup of coffee.
   And how she taught me to dunk,
   so the cinnamon roll didn't fall apart.
I remember doilies on chair arms.
   And crochet hooks in a basket,
   and beds piled with homemade quilts.
I remember cheek kisses.
   And hugs that would infold you,
   and make you smile.
I remember the warmth of love.
   And I miss her so,
   my Grandma — (Gram).

Rita J. Toovey

On A Carousel Of Dreams

On a Carousel of Dreams
All our life's may turn.
Some of us don't seem
To know and others never learn
Just what it is that we
Must be.
Sometimes it is hard for
Us to see
Just which path we
Must take
And all the choices we
Must make.
But on yourself you must
Depend
And it is the way that it
Will end.
For there is nothing given free
And that's the way that it
will be.

W. Jerome Blackwell

A Simple Thank You

I've loved you
a thousand times
in my mind.
A slow gentle love,
over and over.
I look at you,
and I feel like
I can see
into your soul.
It calls to me,
as if it were my own
You so gently touch me,
not only with your body,
but also with your mind.
You give me so much.
   You are my comfort.
     You are my peace.
      Thank you.

Heather R. Elliott

To Soar

I look up and wonder,
what it would be like
to soar, to fly,
where the birds float on air.
Through the clouds dancing
'round our lively sphere.
To connect the stars and bathe
in their twinkling glow.
I could reach and touch the edge
of the universe, if there is one.
Dream in the bed of heaven
and be cradled in the arms of love.
To look down and view this vast world
of blue and green.
Stroll the sidewalks in the sky,
with the sun and moon to guide me.
If only I had wings, to carry me to the
never-ending realms of wonder.
To experience the freedom and excitement
of the fantasies dwelling in my mind.
Cynthia Zdanczyk

Before

She's not pretty enough
or thin enough
or popular enough
She's not right for you.
They told you stories of this and that
did you ask her if they were true?
Did you tell her you are sorry
in your life your friends must rule.
Do you know how much you hurt her?
How sad she must be
you hurt her for your friends
where do your feelings come in?
Apparently
You are not the person you appear to be
Because before you did not care
if she was pretty enough
or thin enough
or popular enough
She was right for you.
Karen Sullivan

Knees And Tabletops

Come down here and sit with me,
And see the things all day I see,
It's mostly knees and table tops,
And an endless flow of no's and stop.
Things like "oh! To be a kid again,"
While I just long to be a man
And when I'm tall and all grownup.
I'll sit on the floor and share my cup.
With little guys who just can't see,
Above the tabletops and knees.
And try to make him understand,
That some day he will be a man.
And maybe he will show concern,
For all that grown ups have to learn.
About the needs of little tots,
Who dwell down under table tops.
Mildred Hyatt McLoud

Out on a Limb

On each side of the worn path,
they give us the breath of life.
We strip them of their roots -
killing them and ourselves.
They stand in solace - watching our every move.
"It's getting warmer out there"
Thought a lumberjack.
He sought shade from the next Goliath on his list.
Wiping the sweat from his brow - he felt a movement.
A long branch grabbed his collar.
Suddenly above the green canopy - he is looking at a large hole,
The sun burning his face.
"If you can't stand the heat - get out of the forest!!"
Bellowed a thunderous voice from the tree.
The lumberjack woke up in a cold sweat.
Feeling for the safety of the ground 'neath him,
He put his saw away and left the forest.
One has to ponder -
Can you hear the voices of the falling trees...
If you're in the forest...
Carol Ocampo

Life's Song

The melody began as soft as the sunrise.
The harmony added with the beauty of the stars.
Each day began a new concerto
each moment a new measure.
The music built upon itself until
it was all that could be heard.
Jumbled, confused, boisterous...

...And then it stopped...the music lost.
It seemed an eternity of silence.
The stars disappeared.
The sun didn't rise.
Death filled the world...
The son returns one day in the eyes of a friend..
The heart of a friend.

The melody begins as soft as the sunrise.
The harmony added in the beauty of the stars.
The kindness of the gentle sound returned...
The music started again.
The orchestra begins in each new day.
Life begins again.
Katherine Johnson

Twinkle Little Star

In Loving Memory of Harold Weatherly

My mother once told me when I was afraid, to look up at the
stars in the sky.
She said they were angels watching over me and not to cry.
There was someone special in my life.
He taught me what was wrong and what was right.
I was his favorite little one.
He always smiled at me with a twinkle in his eye.
Now I know my Grandpa is a twinkling star in the sky.
He is my angel, watching over his little dove.
Twinkle little star, I'll always remember you with great love.
Shawna DeMeulemeester

Brad, The Smoke Jumper

Was there ever a better lad—he is one to make his family glad.
He's a clown of reknown—the best in the town
The grin of the great, not too late he makes his own fate.
We live and we learn, we get what we earn
Brad knows the score, his tales of great love
His job is away from home—but he isn't all alone
His mom's as close as the phone, then he's not all alone
Brad is just quite a guy—say all the girls with a sigh.
Gloria Haugh

Sun Rise, Sun Set, Must Remember To Forget

Sun rise, crest the skies
Then settle toward the West.

Without Love, who would bless, the journey of the day?

Sun rise, sun set;
I must remember to forget;
The pain along the way.
No not forget the lesson learned.
But hold fast to that which has been burned, into the soul.

Through tears, through pain;
It would be so easy to complain;
The dwell on lost instead of gain.

So when the rain falls on my face;
I must remember the soft embrace, of the day.

As I travel along my way;
I must smell the rose, and watch the children play.

Sun rise sun set;
I must remember to forget.

And as it travels along its way; and settles toward the West;
May it confess, not contest;
But confess, that I have blessed the day.
Rose L. Marsh

Sing Of Chi's Forest Door

(In memory of the 1st Sec. of Defense James Vincent Forrestal)
Beware of footsteps in the *Forest,*
A trail of earthen Bear tracks,
Since their "Holy Trinity" is blest,
By Heaven's historical almanac,

A SAN of Salmon, Bears, and Trees,
In a blackjacked prison of iron,
Where Remington bees,
Know the cataracts of Byron,

Computed beyond God's trust,
Into Dante's *Divine Comedy,*
Where the suicide of lust,
Rules souls by Pound's poetic "Eddy,"

Capitalism for sir Richard's Storey of *Pulp Fiction,*
Yet the Truth shall make them free,
To "The String of Pearls" that's spun,
For De Lange's Grizzly decree,

The linguistics of Nobel Peace,
Which Wars against masterminds,
So Wilderness will cease,
To protect the spirit of mankind!
Deboarh Ann Bruce

Rain

Tonight the rain is falling
On city streets and walks,
Its soothing voice is calling,
To me it ever talks.

Like tender hand upon my brow,
While on my bed I lie,
My fevered brain it cools now,
I will no longer cry.

Thank God, for sending rain tonight,
I need its soothing grace,
To help me in my hardest fight,
And what I have to face.

I close my ears to other sound,
And listen to the rain,
I pray to God, to bring me peace
To give me faith again.

When my prayer is ended,
The rain still softly beats
My broken heart is mended
And clean are city streets
Ruth S. Ozanich

Today

In our haste for Tomorrow
We forget the lessons of the past,
So we repeat the mistakes
of yesterday.

In our foolishness,
We ignore the warnings of the Past,
So the future creeps in
with a stamp of chaotic reality.

In our indolence,
We neglect the duties of Today,
So Tomorrow comes
to find us unprepared.

In our peevishness,
We strain for Tomorrow.
So Today ebbs with a soft cry
of dissatisfaction.

Be wise!
Learn from the past,
Fulfill the needs of today,
And hope for tomorrow.
O. Satty Joshua

Old Age

Despair takes root at very center;
The tendrils move quickly in silence
Tightening 'round the nerve ends
Embracing them passionately
Until the body screams without sound.
The tears wash empty the eyes
As the soul closes the door
and disappears.
Flo Perry

Identification

Our blessed Lord and Savior came
His life to give for man,
To purchase who would come to Him —
'Twas God the Father's plan.

In shame He died upon a tree,
They laid Him in a tomb,
His Spirit went to lowest Hell
To lead the captives home.

"I've gone to make a place for you
The Great I Am sent Me.
Though you might think of brick and stone,
New light I'd have you see.

That you would have a home in God,
In Spirit there below.
When I shall take you up with Me
You'll see and hear and know.

So walk by faith and not by sight,
Act that it might be real.
Now let Me order all your steps —
On you I've set My Seal."

Melvin A. Ludvigson

Heart's Truth

There's a brown-eyed haze
That clouds your sky,
And you cannot where I lie.
My arms reach out
But the dark of youth
Never hears the heart sigh truth.

Ego's cancer
And fear, it's lust.
Together, they embody your forbidden trust.
My soul drinks anger
Of constant neglect
and binds me with its controlling effect.
Your insecure secrets
Are the ropes of death,
Restricting my freedom, my life-giving
breath.

I cannot live in the shadows of trust,
Without love, it's a facade of lust.

Christina Pagano

The Moon Is Always There

I'm lying in my bed awake,
looking at the moon,
hoping someone far away
is looking at it too.
And I travel in my mind
to a place I've been before,
where smiles are sweet, the touch is warm,
and I long for nothing more.
Then I'm lying in my bed again,
thinking, if I dare,
those days are gone
and life goes on,
but the moon is always there.

Amy Elizabeth

A Chosen Few

My crippled body works no more,
I'm always hot, swollen, and sore.
I no longer look like I used to,
Except to a special, chosen few.

These people don't look at the outside of me,
The twisted body, the swollen knee.
They don't see the scars, the scrapes, the sores,
They sometimes wonder why I closed the doors.

Folks who don't know me stop and stare,
With curious eyes, not with care.
They whisper to their children, "Let the lady through,"
"She can't do the things we do."

I've found out how much my family cares,
Thought it's hard to see the pain they bear.
They accept me for who I am right now,
They accept my whats and whys and hows.

I can't say inside, I'm still the same,
To be that person is to play a game.
We all have to come to grips,
I have a broken body, and wider hips.

Carolyn Gingrich

Time That Slipped By

While listening to the radio alone with my thoughts,
I think of the past and some of my old haunts.
A certain sound buzzing within my head -
brings back memories of where I was bread.

This haunting melody of time back to then
is cherished with fondness of those few men.
We gathered at street corners to while away time
and talk about women that were in their prime.

The emotion that flows excessively deep -
is triggered with music which we tend to keep.
This fondness of memories that soothes the soul
shall repeat through the years till it takes its toll.

An eerie feeling that we always sustain,
will stay dormant and forever remain.
So with the drumbeat of life gone awry-
we try to capture our "Time That Slipped By."

Edward R. Williams

Pop

Pop was a man of very few words
He could sing tenor higher than birds,
Always loved to pick and sing,
with a talent that made the Heaven's Ring,
Pop was a very big family man,
Raising seven sons with very strong hands,
Showing them the right way to go,
Telling them the things they needed to know.
Leading them down life's road making them see,
All the turns a life can take, saying you can always count on me,
He took them to church and they all joined in,
Playing music and singing the Hymns,
One day together they stood by his side
Singing and playing, He was filled with Great Pride.
Pop now sings in Heaven a wonderful place.
I wish I could see the bright joy in his face.
We miss him dearly since he has gone,
Listen carefully, Pop's singing a brand new song!

Kathryn Morgan

Memories Of Home

As I sat and looked at the old photos
The memories came flooding back.
I was there on the farm, a young child again,
With Mom and Dad, my sisters, and brother Jack.

I could still see the old farm as it used to be,
In those days before World War Two,
Three rooms, a porch, a garage with a lean,
An old outhouse, and skies of azure blue.

One rickety old henhouse, a ramshackled barn,
And barbed wire fences long unkempt.
To look at this place a real farmer might think,
What the Hell! But to dad it was heaven sent.

Outside the back door sat a rusty well pump
But the water was pure, clean, and cold.
To sip from this spa on those hot summer days,
One might think he was rolling in gold.

Not many good things could be said for this place,
Except that which is undoubtedly the best,
It was the home we knew for all our young lives,
And in every way, it beat all the rest.

Frank P. Murphy

Memories

Though I have not wealth nor worldly fame,
Though I have not riches, nor jewels possess,
I have a storehouse of priceless treasures.
Gems that time cannot tarnish or fade.
Memories.

Memories of laughter and sunny days;
Of gentle words and kind deeds.
A rose hidden years ago,
Whose petals have wilted and lost their fragrant scent.
A song of love.

Memories of sorrow and tears that were shed.
Of a broken heart.
A day when there was no laughter.

Memories of springtime,
When the earth was fresh and new
And our thoughts turned to love.

Memories of a bright full moon;
Of wishing on a star.
And dreams we've seen some come true.

Memories of you.

Carolyn D. Dorsey

No Tomorrows

When the pain is too much to bare
Happiness is so rare.
Demons from the past standing there
Hovering as if to wear.
Thoughts that no one seems to care
Fills the mind and the air.
No one to cry out to;
anxieties kept within.
Cannot live with your sin.
You hope your loved ones understand your sorrows
End it today, they'll be no tomorrows.

Joseph R. Ciciless II

Desert Night

Boundless scope of sand and sky,
Lit by countless stars on high;
Vastness in whose baffling size
Haughty self-importance dies;
Silence, dreadful and complete,
Yet in essence strangely sweet;
Loneliness beyond compare,
Yet so comforting to bear;
Gentle breeze too light for sound
Sifting over dip and mound;
Bringing with it scenes of yore,
Faces too we see no more,
as in memory we relive
Joys that only love can give,
Soothing present grief and care,
Calling us to silent prayer,
As it healing timeless pace
Cleanses us in its embrace.

Vernon Stucky

Home From Florida

I followed Spring across the land,
She offered feasts on every hand
Spread farther than the eye could see.
She ran ahead enticing me.

Soft pastel shades of every hue
Were spread on fields for me to view.
Pale chartreuse green of willow tree
And white of cherry were offered free.

The vivid lavender of peach,
The mint-green shoots of mighty beech.
The drift-clouds white of dogwood stand
So on I followed as she ran.

Light hearted spring played fancy-free
And kept right on beguiling me.
Then, in a fit of pique, she flung
White snowflakes, feather-light that hung
On every bush and leaf and flower,
While drifts grew higher every hour!

Spring is a wanton I now know,
Because she really told me so!

Margaret A. Barger

Love Remembered

I saw him last with moonlight
Upon his handsome face, as he
brushed away a tear and said goodbye
so long ago in another time and
place. I wonder where he is today
and if life has been kind to him
along the way.
Sometimes I see a face in a crowd
who looks so much like he, but
I know that it could never be, but
still I wonder if in his heart he
remembers and sometimes thinks of me

Alice Chaussee

Drips

Champagne was in our glasses
Love was in our eyes
We lit the tapered candles
Wax dripped down the sides.

The milk had made a puddle
You came through the door
I left the child forgotten
Milk dripped to the floor.

I try to hide my fear by
Saying it's the rain
That keeps you out so late.
It drips down window panes.

Alone now, I'm without you.
Should have faced the facts
Before; my tears keep dripping
Just like drops of wax.

Katy Arensen

Dream

I fear I will awaken from this dream
to find you a mere shadow in the mist
disappearing from my sight,
And again, my heart will be empty
and my soul in half
because the one who has made me whole
is not real, but a creation,
a notion really;
a spectre in my mind's eye
taunting me,
whispering to me,
making me believe in its truth,
its being,
its reality,
its all consuming beauty.
But I am here, and you are here
holding me,
touching me,
loving me,
and I shall never awaken.

Gwendolyn M. Sullivan

Yearning

The nights are cool when you're not here
Dreams cannot replace my tears.
A pillow soaked with tears I've shed
A blanket warm — but never spread,

My love grows on through days and nights
Shines through all the brightest lights.
Though we both have worlds our own
Someday we'll meet upon a stone.

A stone — a rock as is our love
Cannot be broken from above.
Be calm — be sure, but never fret
We'll be together on that parapet.

Through children, work and worries dear
Quiet longing through the years.

Vivian M. Lawrence

Seventh Heaven

The heels she wore were a little too high
She wobbled a little as she went by
Threw back her shoulders let her hips sway
As she flipped past me in an alluring way

Her lips all painted a rosy red
Her hair hung in curls off the top of her head
Her polished nails were badly chipped
She looked back at me and nearly tripped

Regaining her composure looked back with a smile
I could easily see she was a lady with style
She giggled a little and I could plainly see
That this sweet young thing was flirting with me

I held out my arms and she rushed right in
She gave me a kiss on the side of the chin
Whispered I love you I said I love you too
I looked into her eyes and saw love that was true

Her arms wrapped around me she gave me a hug
My heart went to pounding as I felt her tug
In that moment I was in seventh heaven
As I held my grand daughter who was not yet seven

Lynn Beasley Sr.

The Great Abyss

Guilt, ridicule of one's self,
Tears being sucked into a great whirlpool
Of undefined magnitude
Unknown dimension.

A giant hole with no escape,
Too much fear to make the climb
Or understand the passing of time.
A beautiful garden awaits,
a line one cannot cross,
lack of vision to find.

Not good, not bad, just what is-
This illness of Depression.

Exercise, meditation and many a prayer,
Some do succeed for themselves.
For those who suffer, it's not that rare
To take the gun in hand
With that decision for life not to spare.

It's true, not at all fair,
Unless help is secured, the malady will not cease
For one lonely soul their right to a life.

James A. Pennington

Wrongful Confiding

Confine and forget.
. . . Dismiss all of me.
Chase away the indelible memories.
Indulge yourself to conceive my hurt.
Suffer and relinquish.
. . . Dissipate all objects of significance.
Dissolve away the undeniable feelings.
Fight your heart and close your eyes.
Cry and confess.
. . . Determine your repressed emotions.
Speak to me of the unbearable pain that surrounds.
Trust me to understand and help.

Holli Steinmann

Rain

Rain . . .
How it just falls from the sky.
Some say it is the angels crying.
Some say it is God's tears.
I see it as a cleansing of the Earth.
The opportunity to wash away our problems
   under the anointment of heaven.
Rain . . .
So many interpretations for it.
Many Hate it and wish for it to go away.
Several Love it and just want to play.
It darkens the sky.
It makes people feel gloomy and depressed.
As for me, I Love the smell of the freshness in the air.
Rain . . .
Tears from Heaven.
A shower to cleanse.
Hot cocoa by the fire together with loved ones.
Days of rain, but when it stops . . .
The sun shines bright to begin a fresh new day
   where people are happy and the sky is blue
   and the birds come back to sing.

Cristita Mae Sanchez

A Cry For Help

Am I submerged in water? Am I caught in a whirlpool? I can feel myself being sucked under. I can feel my body being thrashed as I fight to reach the top.

My lungs are burning, they feel as if they're going to burst. I feel lightheaded, my brain give the command, you must fight to reach the top, you must get some air.

I send out a silent prayer, God, have mercy, Is there anyone there? I know the answer as my body is sucked back. My strength is gone, I have lost this fight.

I am loosing consciousness, I imagine myself in a tightly sealed bottle. I am trapped and there's no way out. My eyes are slowly closing, I accept my fate. I am all alone, oh, how my soul aches.

I see a hand cover the bottle. I can feel it being cast to the floor. The bottle is broken, the glass is shattered as it impacts.

Air penetrates my lungs, it engulfs my body, I can breathe. My brain sighs with relief. I am finally free.

Wait! I can hear the sound, I can feel the pull of the whirlpool. Oh, God, here I go again . . .

Mary Tolbert Coy

Untitled

I look at the pictures of you and me,
I look at our expressions,
   happy, silly or serious.
And I think of the days gone by;
When we would have done anything for each other.
You were my man and I was your lady.
We could just look at each others faces,
and know exactly what we were thinking.
And now we can't even look at each other.
   What happened to us?
Why did it have to end this way?

Lisa Sommerville

Flight

For the Flying Chaplain
Ribboned runway slips beneath
Like quick caress of silken sheath.
Breath abates as lift occurs,
While wheels encase with clomps and
   purrs!

Lifting higher o'er the land
Doll house cities shrink beneath us.
Quaint designs of furrowed sod
Spread like antique quilts bequeathed us.

Silent corridors embrace us.
Time stands still, and yet we hasten
With a skill still new to man
Though ages old to winged creation.

No quasi destination ours.
This small craft bespeaks our climb,
For as we lift and bank and soar,
We join the Architect of Time.

Yahweh, God of cloud and sky,
Past and present, earth and sea,
Grant us as we onward fly
Enlightenment, and peace, with Thee.

Netta Sue McKnight

A Dream

Oh winds that blow
please blows real slow
and go and catch my dream
you can swirl around the world
unseen.

Margie Maggard

Untitled

   I loved him once in a dream,
and then sadly I awoke.
I've been looking so long to find him,
trying hard not to give up hope.

   I laid awake for many nights,
wondering where he were.
Hoping by someone,
my prayers would be heard.

   Without his love I was nothing,
I had no stable mind.
If I didn't find him soon enough.
I knew I'd surely die.

   Wishing to be near him,
and hold him in my arms.
To feel the warmth of his body,
and every beat of his heart.

   To gaze into his eyes,
and softly kiss his lips.
To do this just once,
would be my last request.

Kristina Milligan

Snow

There are things that make me wonder,
There are things I surely know,
And one of the wonders of winter,
Are Cardinals in the snow.

Their bright red coats against the white,
Warm the heart and cheer the soul,
And somehow with each cheery chirp,
They keep away the cold.

So clean and fresh, and free of slush,
It is at break of day,
Except for tiny rabbit tracks,
It waits for kids to come and play.

They pull their sleds up and down,
Wherever hills are found,
They ride headfirst down the slope,
Faster than the speed of sound.

The snow, the cardinals, the rabbit tracks,
The children's, precious laughter,
The beauty of this winter day,
In memory kept forever after.
    Betty Ann McKenzie

Life

Another born on to me
To carry our love forever
Part of us that will never die.

A family we have now
Together we make it work
A life that has been promised.

A home
New challenges
Our responsibility.

Nothing as it was
Never to be again
Forever changing.

To realize our dreams
as a family,
To achieve our goals
as a person,

Two different lives
One on hold for the other.
Only to meet too late in the future.
    Tracie L. E. Perreault

Separation

Hard to believe it,
Only the thief was there,
    And with his lies he took
    from me my innocence
    and now I am like this.

A stranger,
    A stranger with a different face.
    Marilyn Lenzen

A Person Proud Of Me

Measures of me sadly reveal — truth — but not as I will
Arrogant, impatient, imperfect and phony
How lacking, God knows only
But inside the depth of me, can you sense the integrity
For which I reach and almost clasp not quite yet within my grasp
The person I want to be — a person proud of me

To the world I present a face which seems to claim its place
Recently I've come to know; in reality its only show
God within I affirm this day, asking Him to show the way
Let Jesus the perfect guide help the unwanted in me subside
Show me how to conduct my life, lead me from conflict and strife
Revealing the person I want to be — a person proud of me

On life's path I'm not alone, God provides the stepping stone
Across my doubt and tribulation to understanding and jubilation
Opens my heart and sings to me — a child of God I'm proud to
God's child has obligation to tell individual and nation
Positive thoughts to hold in prayer, God within always there
With His help we'll soon see — a person truly proud of me
    Selma Emerson

One More Time

Once surrounded with a white light of warmth,
    a cadence so enticing, no longer exists . . .
Hardened by betrayal and deceit,
    now stands an abandoned well.
Encased in ice,
    wanting no commitments . . .
No attachments . . . or allowances for mistakes.

Unexpected . . . unwanted,
    through the darkness,
    a minute ray of light stirs confusion.
Sweet seduction
    to welcome this embrace wars within.

Weary, yet not despondent, in this defeat . . .
No longer stands a battle-worn warrior,
    instead emerges
    the hope of healing.
    Carolyn M. Amano

Until Eternity

My mind is a scrap book of our time together,
The images painted there forever.
The love songs we've danced to, I still hear,
My arms still reach out to pull you near.

The words you've whispered still race across my mind,
And the letters you've sent have made my heart blind.
Picture perfect memories are stilled in time,
And the bells that rang so long ago, still chime.

My heart yearns to stand up and tell you today,
That the kind of love we share doesn't go away.
So many wonderful miracles we've seen,
There are so many ways to say what we mean.

When we're together, nothing else seems to matter,
The problems on my mind instantly shatter.
That's the way it will be forever between you and me,
In love always, for an eternity.
    Erin R. Bielefeldt

Too Much To Drink

I couldn't walk straight, I barely stood
And take advantage, I knew you would
You took me home, and that's when I knew
There was really nothing, that I could do

Too much to drink, couldn't say "No"
And that's when you offered, to take me home
I let you take me, because I knew in my mind
Wouldn't make it by myself, if I can't walk a straight line

I woke up, you were gone
My money missing, my brain shut down
I tried to remember, who you were
What we did, and if you played fair

Everything blank, what time is it?
What happened last night? My head ahead
My heart throbbing, my heart pounding
I fell for the trap when you called me darling

It's been two years, since that day
But I remember it, like yesterday
You took away my life, that night you got laid
You might not know, it but you gave me AIDS

October A. Pawlik

Sketching Squares In A Circle Of Guilt

With fingernails in full froth, she scratches silly clown
Shaped multiples in the soil,

But anyone looking from the outside in can read the pain
Between her crooked lines.
Her attempts are to reinvent the times, but taken her Mathematical
impurities, she achieves only the invention of mental lies . . .

Some myriad psycadelicopterpus with 10 and 20 eyes.
And in this her self-induced dementia, so she whispers . . .

Gain hold of his tongue, for it is leathery . . . wherein viscous
salivate. Thorny barbs will lather to knobs. So stake a foot hold
if you can, cause sometimes . . . just sometimes my love. To fly
amongst angels, upon the backs of demons you must stroll.
I whispered back . . . it is the guilt that does all your erasing,
Won't be long, till it erases you.

Eugene Broussard

Eternity

Eternal in your mind, eternal in your soul.
Eternal in your thoughts, for you keep me whole.
Forget all others, love me as I am.
With all my thoughts, as strong as you can.

Eternity with me, decide with all your heart.
Or push me away from the start.
While pain constricts, within my very self.
Love me forever, or let me off this shelf.

I promise to always hold you.
Eternally to love you.
To do everything you please.
Just don't do this, it isn't just a tease.

I am so very vulnerable.
Yet at the same time hopeful.
So needing you to see.
That I need you now, and for eternity.

Tara Bower

My Memorable Trip

The Lord my wish did grant
To the Holy Land I went,
With wheelchair in hand
I traveled by air and by land.

Jerusalem, Nazareth, and Bethlehem,
Mt. Carmel and Mt. of Olives.
What a privilege to see them
And be a part of their lives.

La Vía Dolorosa we did climb
Where Jesus suffered so.
Unexplainable awe.
Inexplicable woe.

The Great Sea will always be
A treasure I thought I would never see.
The Sea of Galilee
A beautiful peaceful water undoubtedly.

Dear heavenly Father, thank you
For granted prayer and pleasure,
For being able to see Your Son's milieu,
And for the safety You did ensure.

Isis Norma Lopez

Talk About People

I really don't like it
When people talk about other people
I just hate the way they sound;
As if they are so superior.

It really burns me
When people talk about other people
And they slur their innuendoes
With their all-knowing expressions.

But it really hurts
When people talk about other people
And they talk about me with a wink,
Or they roll their eyes in exaggeration.

Are you listening to me?
If you are really listening,
Maybe you shouldn't be,
Otherwise we are gossiping too!

Ronald J. Anderson

Sooth Me

Soothe and console me
Put me to sleep
Lay me down gently
At Jesus' dear feet

He will sustain me
And comfort my soul
His love hovers o'er me
As ocean waves roll

Peace and contentment
From pain and from strife
Love everlasting
Sweetens my life

John W. Roach

Child Of The Wind

The Moon is mysterious,
The Sea is sly,
But I am a child of the Wind.

A warm meadow breeze;
A fierce driving gale;
Stiff seaborne gusts
To billow the sail.

It moans among the treetops,
It rustles through the leaves,
It waves the flowers in the fields,
And makes the sea to heave.

They whisper through my hair
And whistle past my ears
The strains of the Windsong
I like to think I hear.

The Moon is mysterious,
The Sea is sly,
But I am a child of the Wind.
Dianne Wierenga

Word Weaving

This is my secret world
where I gather
my woolly thoughts
spin them into yarns
Matted magic
stretched and pulled
into patterns, pretty
complicated
knotted and smooth
Intricate ideas
twisted webs of me
flowing on in the
noisy silence
where I chose to be.
Lee O'Keefe-Hardy

Who's To Say

Who's to say what you are?
Who's to say where you go?
Who's to say what you think?
Who's to say what you know?

Who's to say what your future will hold?
Who's to say what life will bring?
Who's to say who'll get the pot of gold?
Who's to say anything?

Who's to say how old you'll live to be?
Who's to say what memories you'll keep?
Who's to say what you'll see?
Who's to say what lessons you'll reap?

Who's to say when you'll feel pain?
Who's to say what you will do?
Who's to say what friendships will remain?
No one except you!
Crissy Cole

Colin Jacob Stevens

As you watch over us, our little angel boy
fulfilling our hearts with love and joy

We remember your beautiful, precious face
full of happiness, love and grace
your tiny fingers to grasp our love
now you're in heaven soaring high above

We yearn for your love and touch
wanting to show, we love you so much
wishing we had a lot more time
but knowing you will always be mine

Knowing your soul is so perfect and pure
allowing you to gain wings and soar
only needing to show
how much we love you so

As you watch over us, our little angel boy
fulfilling our hearts with love and joy

Although we'll never hold you, in our arms again
you will forever remain in our hearts and souls
we shall cherish memories of your short times
Forever in our hearts, and always on our minds
Candice L. Stevens

Remember When...

We were family and friend.
Joyful gatherings for special occasions
Family reunions.
See the smiles on our faces.
They were genuine then, and so we were.
Now...strangers and foe lost in the shuffle
No where to go.
Someday in this picture there'll only be one
The remainder left with the burden of regret.
With a heavy heart, tears of sorrow, and the memories of...
Remember when...
Who put that wedge between us
Making it impossible to live, love, in harmony
Who placed the distance, and miles of anger in our souls
We did!
Don't wait for the inevitable when our existence is not.
Find it in your heart to cherish this "gift of amends."
And every so often recall the memories of...
Remember when...
Lois Lydia Friskey

Divine Inspiration

Sitting at his desk, sipping coffee
God comes to him like a blaze of fire
The shining light of God's radiance blinds him

"Who are you?
What do you want?" he asks
The emaciated man listens in perfect silence.
"I am the way, the light, the truth
You are My child; I have come to help you
in this troubled time."
The old man's tired eyes start to shine like new-bought
emerald stones glittering in the sunlight.
The man began to smile and glow, a white light
enshrouding his shriveled form.
His virtue was fulfilled; he could complete his song
Preeti Samtani

Change

As I sit under the willow tree wondering what to do,
I hear a lovely melody come shining through.
And the melody moves the leaves and the hair upon my head,
Then it steals all feelings of fright and dread.
Next it digs into my soul
And plants a very tiny thing which seems to make me whole.
After that I feel a change in me,
But through appearance you cannot see.
This change has brought me closer yet,
To a change that someday I shall not forget.
    Nicole A. Nelson

A Piece Of Me

I could have gone out and bought a gift, or maybe
made something especially for you, but I thought
that this would be better. My gift to you is a
piece of me, but don't think of it as a farewell
gift — how can it be?: It is a piece of me.
Wherever you are in this great big world, you will
always carry this with you. It will not hurt you;
it will not break. It will not grow old and it will
not die. I give you a piece of me. This peace is
not an object and you may not be able to see it, hear,
or touch it, but it will always be with you. No
matter how far we may drift apart from each other,
physically or sometimes mentally, you will always
have a piece of me. You cannot throw this away or
discard it in any way. This piece will always be
near you. As we go into this wonderful world, we
will never guess what lies ahead of us; but as we
move on, you will always carry a piece of me and it
will never drift away. If you are sometimes scared,
or lost and alone, remember — you have a piece of me.
A piece of me is all I can give you. I would do
anything for you — climb any mountain or swim any
ocean. I would even give the world to you if I
could. But all I can give to you is a piece of
myself, a piece of my heart.
    Paola De Bartolo

The Greatest Gift

Tiny feet, ears and hands
Their laughter's heard across the land
Eyes full of wonder, trust and love
As Guardian Angels watch them from above
This most precious gift of ours
Their hearts so innocent and lite
They try to do everything right
But sometimes these little beings blunder
And begin to fear the thunder
Yet with an Angelic voice soft but clear
"I'm sorry" is said as their eyes fill with tears
Your heart begins to melt
When they wrap their little arms around you
You know their love is never untrue
With a gentle kiss upon your cheek
At times you find it hard to speak
For they give their love unselfishly
That is when you begin to understand
The greatest gift given to any woman or man
Is ... a child.
    Amanda M. Hale

Double Minded

You see, there are two of me, or so it seems
One you see, one inside of me
Which is real? Which is me?
I don't know which you see
And I don't know which is me
    Dawn A. Kepple

Infertile Ground

Black, inky mud
  trapping, slurping, sucking,
    deep, deep into the bowels
      of evil.

Black, inky mud
  trapping, slurping, sucking,
    deep, deep into the roots
      of my family.

Mud running through my veins
  coloring all that I do,
    coloring all that I am,
      coloring all that I want to be
        black, inky black.

Black, muddy blood
  still stagnates
    without moving
      yet slurping, sucking, trapping.
    Stacy K. Larson

Somewhere

A smile
A glance
Souls of chance
Passing through the vapors hue
Endless time and space review
Ever ever I pursue
  Somewhere
    There's you
    Jeanette Herring

I Am Just Fine

There is nothing
Whatever's the
matter with me; I'm just
as healthy as I can be.
I have arthritis
in both of my knees,
when I talk I talk
with a wheeze.
My pulse is weak
and my blood
is thin, but I am
very well for the
shape that I am in.
I think my liver and kidneys
are out of whack,
I have a pain going up and down my back.
The way I stagger, it is sure a crime,
I am likely to fall on my face at any time.
My hearing is poor,
but I am really quite well.
    Algahagan

Airborne

Butterflies,
   in mourning cloaks
   as delicate as smoke
Upfold their fragile wings
   and let themselves
   be borne to the tip top
   of wind stirred trees.
They drift
   aloft upon some vagrant breeze
   to unknown destinations
   without a show of fear
   just float away—ephemeral as
   our souls' most wistful dreams.

      Ellen V. M. Carden

May In Missouri

O, they are here again!
Wondrous days for me!
May in Missouri
Where I chanced to be.

Their promises I sing
And my luck to see
Earth's here beautiful
Regularity.

I more than sensing
The sounds of bird life,
Blossoms in the trees
And scents nice and rife.

I feel goods to be
In the days of May
Feel fulness of living
A crest in earth's way

A lyric of lives
A great song of cares
A pattern for man
When all love he dares.

      Ralph Gregory

Recital One

She takes the stage
The center part
And dances there
With all her heart!
Our little ballerina.

Did e'er a child look more lovely?
So polished, poised and sweet
As our little ballerina
Dancing on with lightning feet?

Her leaps are gazelle graceful.
Her runs like a sylph o'er grass
Her little arms are arched just so.
All other's talent does hers surpass.

She takes the stage.
The center part
And dances there
With all her heart!
Our little ballerina.

      Mimi Schilling

Genesis

Galaxies drift like iridescent fish
within the onyx sea of space.
While caught in nets of chaos,
the gypsy stars escape the eye of God
and fragile lights of yesterday send enigmatic messages.

      Ann Linsey

The Magic Touch

Like a runaway train, I hurried through the night.
A heart full of anger, and teaching with fright.

Eyes full of sorrow, the nose—foul stench.
In the safety of dreams, were my quiet tears quenched.

In this journey of darkness, a light appeared.
To give peace to my anger, and give chase to my fears.

Her golden hair glistened, like the street after night rain.
In her blue diamond eyes, I saw hiding pain

Her smile struck like lightening, into the fabric of my soul.
With her kind, gentle words, my aching heart paid a toll.

Then ever so light, she touched my shivering hand.
As softly as the sea, runs over the sand.

Her kiss left me trembling, when it magic was done.
Filled with the white hot intensity, of ten thousand suns.

A simple wink from her, could make an angel sigh.
One single tear from her, could make the mountains cry.

      Bradley Koch

Marion Chornobrywy

Marion Chornobrywy, born July 1, 1933,
In Belfast, Northern Ireland. She studied
Art at the Belfast Technical College and
Window design in Scotland. She then took
Charge of interior and window display for four stores in Ireland.

In 1959, Marion moved to Canada and studied
Under various Canadian landscape artists.
She also attended and was guest teacher
At the Schneider school of fine arts in Ontario
Where she obtained first prize in watercolors
1983 and 1984.

She has taught art for 30 years, in Ireland
and Canada. Owned and operated an art gallery
for 8 years in Montreal.

Marion has had a number of one-man shows in
Montreal, Ottawa, New York State and Ireland.
Her paintings can be found as far away as
Australia, Germany, United Kingdom and the
United States, as well as across Canada. Marion
Is a member of the Lakeshore Association of
Artists, Montreal. She has also written and
Illustrated 3 books, published poems in Canada
England, U.S.A., Ireland.

A graduate of fine arts at John Abbot College,
And a bachelor of fine arts Concordia
University, MA Interior Design De Montfort
University England.

Marion is continually exploring various media and striving to
Give a new dimension to the world of art.

      Marion Chornobrywy

The Holy Spirit

Today the Holy Spirit tested me
As I went to be baptized
He'd often heard me say, "I'd come up kicking and cussing
if anyone dunked me like that."
Well today was the day!
The Holy Spirit would find out who would have their way
As they led me down into the baptismal font
I was ready! Even though afraid of the water
Everything started out fine
I went under or so I thought
But not enough for my sins to be lost
We'll have to do you again came the reply
Oh No! I sighed, but yes here we go
Bend your knees, put your feet against the wall
When I came up the Holy Spirit laughed and said
"Welcome to our church! Your sins are dead
Come abide with your Lord, for you'll have no cause to sin anymore
Your life may have its ups and downs
But you'll always feel the love of Christ all around

Connie Rose

Sores Of Wars

Once upon a time, I saw a life fluttering ever so.
It fluttered like a butterfly,
But on the ground, not in flight. Its eyes stared at me.
I heard it please; yet, it didn't speak.

Though its screams echoed in my head,
And I caught the sores the body wore,
I couldn't extend a helping hand.

Swollen knees and sore feet,
Held only by flesh and bones, struggled to get up once more;
Wobbling underneath its frame,
Home to scores of sycophant.

Steps were taken going nowhere.
And though no tears showed,
A mother's love no longer was. Her sprawled body,
Feet from him, stricken down by guns of wars.

Aghast people ran about, heedless of the little boy
Staring at faces in the crowd.

Dressed in pity, I viewed the tube
Displaying visions of the war. I watched, unable to help.
Then I saw him trip and fall, fluttering forevermore.

Maria A. Ortiz

Good Characteristics

Some say it's the sparkle in my eyes,
while others claim it's my bow-legged walk.
School mates say he lingers in my voice
when I feel the urge to talk.

My city-born wife swears it's my easy-going nature
that easily gives him away.
My co-workers say it is obvious . . .,
"You must be a Cowboy, as much as you listen to George Strait."

Not one to argue much,
I'd like to think it's the way I carry myself.
Courteous, Respectful and Thankful
That's what makes me a Cowboy,
different from everyone else.

Rodney C. Wallace

Shadow Catcher

Soul bends as willow
To the whims
Of mankind's capricious breeze
Without love's centering force
Spirit is disconnected
A leaf captured by the whirlwind
Soul becomes a shadow

Aho! Aho!
Creator
Catch it
Bring spirit back to center-place
That You might seize the shadow
Hold it in Your love
That it may love unconditionally

Ronald D. Rudy

A Decision

To decide; to choose;
to leave the comfortable blanket
of the known perhaps to lose.
To follow your wandering heart
or allow your controlled mind to guide.
Why must I decide?

Darrell A. Evans

Stand

Stand firm against the storm.
It beats against the flesh
While tossing those things
That are held so dear.

Homes go as swirling winds
Carry away things saved.
Things that bring to mind
Of times past and loved.

Trees bend and crack.
The land itself is moved
By some liquid scrapper;
Pushing all that is dear.

Against this storm. Stand firm!
Its passage, a wake of sadness,
Leaves the land barren
And clear of our possessions.

Take heart! The land is reborn!
Though valuables have disappeared,
In thought, what will be lost?
What could you have taken in death?

Emerson Wilson

Heartbreak

To know the torment of despair
Too deep for tears to bring relief,
To be familiar with the pain,
The throbbing ache, of bitter grief,
To suffer until life seems death
And death itself would hold allure,
To yearn to die, and yet to live:
This triumph is for the mature.

Halina Piotrowski

Outspoken

Echoes in my heart and soul
Are welling up inside
My breath is being sucked away.
As I taste the tears I've cried

Forgetful thoughts will drift away
As I glimpse into my heart
To feel the aches of every day
Why do I play this part?

A puppet show of never-ending
Hopes out of my reach
It all goes right but oh so wrong
And I can't find what I seek

I thrive on somewhere out there
While surviving on who I am
I pretend that I still have my soul
And that I have not yet been damned

The truth will hurt too bad to face
While I sit here in distress
Wondering why I'm stuck to be
Always chosen second best
   Tricia King

Panhandler

Standing near your corner,
Most any time of the day
I've become an importuner
Seeking handouts through dismay

Trapped at the edge of penury
Now transient as can be
Some who pass; berate me as scenery,
While others choose to flee

Facing those who stand to gape
I'll always find some gain
A buck to help me into shape
Or temporarily relieve some pain

As a Panhandler I'm now astute
For, habit's become my will
Without a job, I must compute
Standing a corner means a daily meal.
   Robert Louis Perkins

Always A Friend Who Cares

With the hands that you are dealt
through life's uncertain paths
there will always be someone
to lend a helping hand

When things turn into problems
or the tears just keep on falling
this special certain someone
knows when to start calling

If you'd like to talk for hours
or just a minute or two
this person doesn't mind
they'll listen through and through

When you don't know where to go
or exactly what to say
a friend you never knew was there
will guide you on your way!
   Sara Hanyzewski

Battle Of Wills

Computer, computer, you're as strong willed as I!
I can't seem to beat you, so why do I try?
You make me angry and cause me such stress;
But I'll keep on trying 'cause I'm stubborn, I guess!

You cluck like a chicken—you chirp like a cricket
You make me so mad, I could tell you to stick it.
I rant and I rave; I plot and I scheme;
To master you someday's my greatest dream.

Computer, computer, I've studied real hard.
We've come a long way from the old punch cards.
Programming now is done on keyboards
Instead of wiring those big, heavy boards.

No narrow age bracket is using you now.
Children, teens, senior citizens learn how.
But why at strategic times must you crash?
With a heavy brick your screen I could bash.

You run our banks, hospitals, grocery stores!
Even the credit for space flights is yours.
You do incredible things; you even speak!
But, boy, when you go down, what havoc you wreak!
   N. A. Hammontree

My Faithful Pet

The best friend to have has four feet
A dog or a cat, they listen and understand,
They are always there whether you're sad or happy
The wag of a tail,
The purr of a cat —
They will lay next to you,
Sometimes with a hug or a nudge.
They are always there,
Faithful to their owner
You can tell them anything,
They won't repair it.
They sometimes will answer by voice,
Or in their own way.
A dog or cat will never turn away and leave you.
So the best friend you can have has four feet
Never a person have I seen,
So true as my faithful pet.
   Ann Marie B. Charron

God Help The Girl

She was disowned by her family, by her own Mom and Dad,
She can't even remember any good times they had,
But sometimes in her dreams, she remembers them still,
May God help the girl, cause no one else will,

She lost her husband, whom she held so dear,
She dreams of the child, whose cry she'll never hear,
But she keep on trying, she has no time to kill,
May God help the girl, cause no one else will.

She has no friends, she spends her time all alone,
She has nothing she can call her own,
She has no home and never eats her fill,
May God help the girl, cause no one else will.

But she keeps on trying and being so brave,
And she will till she goes to her grave,
Then she'll have no tears and nothing will be hid,
Cause then God will help her, cause no one else did.
   Dean Sellers

Opening Day

Many things come to mind
In the game of baseball you will find:

The smell of hot-dogs and the taste of beer
on opening day the fourth month of the year
and the greatest fans are here today
for the greatest players are here to play

The field is groomed, what a beautiful site!
with Knuckles in left, and Lefty in right
A nine man field, a perfect machine
All tall, all proud, all strong and lean

I sit in my seat and start to dream
of me being the best anyone has seen
Right away I'm "The Home-Run King"
with the Golden glove, and a World Series Ring

I step to the plate and take a strike outside
I thought it was out, but I let it slide
The next pitch comes, I hit it back to the wall!
suddenly I'm awoke by the sound Play Ball!
Christopher M. Cooke

Squall

Waves of ocean water,
Waves of driving rain,
Whitecaps rushing into shore.
Clouds roll in grey upon grey
   until the overcast is complete.

Heavy, fat raindrops explode on the hard surface of the
   ground, then faster and faster.

Calmness has suddenly become rage
   in a swirling, chaotic blend of elements.

Now the window is drenched with water,
   impairing vision.

The sky lights up, grumbling for a moment,
   but it is silenced by the endless sound of Shhh!

Looking out from the sanctity of a safe, dry room,
   exciting inspiring feelings unfold;

Open a door and the deluge descends upon you—
   attacking and dangerous!
Charleen Harris McKenne

Rain Forest

As days go by, and the sun comes and goes
More of you disappears, more than people ever know
Your leaves will never shake in the wind
Your animals will never growl
You will never see another tiger or owl on the prowl
Your home will turn into farmland
Cows will eat your grass
Your wood will turn into furniture
For people of a different class
Your land will be burnt
More every year
No one can hear your cries for help
Or see your streaming tears
And soon only dust will blow in the wind
Where a kingdom once reigned high
And then there will be the final day
When all the world will cry
Rachel Fernandez

INRI

"I'm thirsty"

The saying only makes wind —
Chapped lips crack swollen
Grit-laden tongue scratching
A long already parched walls

The sky around me grows
Dark pleas with muttered hope
Phantom figures surround me
Pass into undistinguished forms

Fastened ropes no longer burn
Cold as nails in my hands
And feet no longer feel
Ground no longer at my soul

Soured wine still bittersweet
Offered now to satisfy my desire
For forgiveness requested from
My God
"My God, why
Have you forsaken me?"
D. R. Spellman

The Navigators

To greater horizons
our 'Mentor Spirits' deftly soar . . .
Entrusting 'the traverse'
of souls . . . left traveling
(the wrong roads),
To We, who, have not yet,
found the path.
Lindy Atkinson-Matalone

The Middle East

Donkey carts and ziggurats,
Prayer calls from minarets,
Stone walls with parapets,

Men smoking cigarettes,
Clinking, clanking castanets,
Even women suffragettes.
Poppe

Greed Doesn't Pay

This story must be told
Little brother and little sister
Had a pig, which they sold
To the grocery store they went
Bought a cake and ate their fill
But the rest, they wouldn't take home
Didn't want to share it
With their brother and their sisters
"They'll eat it all, yes they will!

"Let's hide it in the ditch
By the railroad track
Then we can have it another day
When we come back".
The next day came, they couldn't hardly wait
To have some more of that good cake
They went to where they'd left it
But they soon found, greed doesn't pay
For there it was, covered with ants.
Helen Myrtle Stoddard

Infinite Poetry

Poetry's everywhere anyone looks.
Poetry's found in more places than books.
Poetry lives in the heads of its authors.
It's in the birth of a son or a daughter.
It's in the sky, in the soil and the sea.
It's in all creatures that ever could be.
It's in the country and it's in the city.
It's in the smooth as well as the gritty.
It's within labor and it's within rest.
It's in the worst as well as the best.
It's in your happiness and in your sorrow.
Poetry's yesterday and it's tomorrow.
        Keith Kirouac

A Daughter's Love

No more hugs
No more love
No more a mother does

My mother has gone away
But I know I will see her
Again in Heaven some day

My heart is broken and
I am blue, I love you Mom.
And God does too
        Tammy Flanigan

Rose

This Rose I have carried
for the longest time.
The petals may have withered.
But there's still much love inside.

This Rose has seen many miles
across this great land.
The journey has been a grand one,
now I place it in your hand.

One thing I need to tell you
how special this Rose is.
I have held it close,
praying for certain things -

   A wish for complete happiness
   that our lives would be complete,

   A wish for an everlasting love
   to last all through time,

   A wish for someone to share forever with,
   someone like you.
        Becky Welch

The Stranger

Children playing
shrieks of happiness
suddenly stop.
Silence falls
like the blanket of night.
The stranger
rounds the corner,
and the game starts again.
        Tania Tzelnic

Love Satire

Love must be the meat and drink of devils,
For its fruits are only good feelings.
It's never the source of that which dishevels,
So hate must serve the Gods in their dealings.

For the game they've begun is one of pain,
For which the only cure is this thing called love.
And is it not true that the Gods must be sane,
For the Bible says they're in heaven above?

Love is but folly, for pain will persist.
How can one settle for anesthesia
When one has a human imagination,
So strongly desires a panacea?

Apathy is superior to love
Because hateful ambivalence yields pain,
And it's true that love and life are hand and glove,
And that lovelessness defines the insane.

True love requires faith, so it's taking a chance,
But the alternative is risker still.
without love, we'd be less than marching ants.
See now, isn't love the bitterest of pill?
        Eric A. Million

Bitter Memoirs That Blight My Mind

Is there any simple reason
Behind the treason of the season
While in solitude we beg
Searching through the moving faster
For the master everlaster
But alas we hang our futures on an old forgotten peg

Is the guerdon any better
Read the letter lock your fetter
There is no prize that's worth the cost
Play your hand at fortunes lotto
In your grotto find your motto
See the distance of your life that life is gone and all is lost

She was always such a looker
But I mistook her she's a hooker
I said my love would always last
But I could not give her a throne
I can't atone now I'm alone
I can never find a future for a worthless piece of past
        Daniel Shane Erwin

A Tribute To My Mom

   This is a poem to my mom to whom I owe my life,
whose overwhelming forgiveness and support have made
this life's road less bumpy, lonely, scary and frustrating.
   Lonely, scared, and frustrated was I, but she was always
there - patiently listening, giving encouraging words,
bringing optimism and hope to all of life's moments,
   I didn't know she knew of my once darkened world-
she did- but, with all a mother's unconditional love and
constraint that she could muster, she never said
a word against my darkened world, only encouraging,
praying, and letting me make decisions along the way.
   After awhile, as I questioned, she listened and presented
options - never encouraging one over another, so
   I write this for listening, challenging, encouraging,
for letting go, for forgiving and the unconditional love
you give, for you mom, my one and only cherished MOM!
        Deborah L. Scheerer

The South-Side Super Heroes

The crowd was dull, not one fan did cheer
After the Sox missed the play-offs again last year
Hopes were down and tears did stream
Even loyal fans lost faith in their team
Their once powerful order was going weak
Too many times had they turned the other cheek
They needed a savior and needed him fast
If he didn't show, they might finish last
"You stink!" cried the fans, "Get outta' here!
You always lose year after year!"
But then out of Cleveland came a man named Belle
And he promised that things would go well
That man called Belle, he did as he said
He revived the Sox who seemed to be dead
In the championship they rolled over the Mets
And when they flew home in their two private jets
The celebrated magician said "Never fear,
I like Chicago, I'll stay for next year!"

Greg Segal

My Mother, Eleanor

A brand new mother, like no other
Yet, she is not my mother
She came to me when I was nine
Our father's bride, I thought her mine

To our family she brought class
Which fork to use and how to pass
Mimi singing La Boheme
Silk stockings with a straight seam

Her passionate heart began far away
Suffering genes, hard put to play
Wandering across the Russian steppe
Her father's sperm was getting set

That Russian winter is in her soul
a minimalist appetite in her bowl
Her passion is for children, baseball, every flower
a push for truth her enduring power

With ample breast, legs long and lean
a serious person, a mind that's keen
My mother Eleanor is quite a lady
Always has been, especially now at eighty

Mollie Odell Bourne

Turpan Love Song

A desolate desert, dry and poor, my heart used to be.
Your love was the melted-snow water from the Tian mountain.
which moistened and enriched my soul;
so that the grapes cultivated
in the garden of my heart
have become very sweet.
Oh! Love is like sweet grapes;
smooth and lovely, beautiful and glistening.
It makes me forget the roaring wind
and swirling sand of the desert.
It makes me forget the merciless sun
that sends scorching heat.
Because I have your love in my heart
and love is as sweet as grapes.

Flora Chen

Roseleaf

Yet green, the roseleaf
graces the bronze stalk
with spring's voice
as winter hugs a prairie.

Yet green, the roseleaf
speaks her promise
to the woman curled
within her hidden bloom;
both hear the pledge,
the troth, the vow unsaid,
one woman and the hidden rose.

Virginia Lee Mathews

Fishing In Montana

Fishing is not really fishing
But a course in philosophy
See how fish congregate in the deepest parts,
In the calmest parts, where food is carried in
   on a swift current and is released as
   the water slows

See how bigger fish, and older
Move yet deeper and into calmer waters
   not hurrying
Fishing offers much advice
Simply by being and living

Go deep into the water of sustenance
Seek the safety of calm places
Trust that nourishment will come in those
   places calm and deep.

No need to move,
trust, be ready,
Don't bite at tempting morsels
floating unrealistically at the surface.

Ellen Brownig

Good Bye

I see and feel a tear
So little time to say how I feel

I talk to you and wonder
How it could have been
Time always moves on

Tears come
Feelings hurt
To love is to hurt
Admitting was hard to do
But why do I love you so?

Thoughts come and go of you
Thoughts of kindness
Thoughts of pain
Thoughts of happiness
All thoughts of you

Time will pass and you'll forget me
But my heart will never....
Forget you

Christopher Zeller

Jonathan Swiney

You are the stars in my sky
   and the wind through my trees
The soft spoken words
   sung with such ease.

You are the bearer of love
   and all I hold dear
You fill me with peace
   and take away my fear.

My heart is so open
   for you to posses
I love you forever
   so easily I confess.

Your intelligence I respect
   and all that you do
All that I've wished
   you've made come true.

Anything you ask
   you know I'll be there
I love you forever
   I'll be forever in your care.
Sara D. Tohlen

Exhausted

Everyday that I live my life, a
   Blundering 84 year old dame,
I'm amazed that I ever considered
   That one day I'd be brought to fame.
While I was younger, I was able
   To find poems coming free from my mind.
But now, my life has changed greatly —
   It is almost as if I were blind!
Nevertheless, I still love poetry —
   And when I can express what is true,
And feel that it is worthwhile to send out
   I shall gladly mail it to you.
Beulah E. Jenkins

Bewildered Vision

You dance across my dreams.
Aqua blue suit and you,
like a feather falling from the sky.
Do you remember being here
while I sleep?
Is it really you beating out a rhythm
on the Congo drum?
Waves of sweat wash over you
and your pinstripe piles.
You bellow —
hands in the air pursuing me,
chasing me,
through strange worlds and orange skies.
I run before you,
I chase after you;
you disappear from my sight.
Jennifer Bartlett

Betty's Journey

This world has lost a beautiful being,
The angels won't believe their eyes
   at what they're seeing.
They'll know they got the best of all,
when Betty Smalley come to call.
She fought to the end with an iron fist,
her new life started with big chuck's last kiss.
The journey will be a memorable one,
with thoughts of her husband, daughter and sons.
When she gets there, we'll all know,
the sun will shine, and the heavens will glow.
She'll think of the future but never,
   ever forget the past,
when she gets to the end of her journey at last.
If you're feeling greedy or selfish or blue,
remember, she's looking down on you.
So, look to the heavens, and you will see,
a beautiful angel named, Betty.
Ronnie Keirs

This Star Is An African

Be my Star, O' you Brightest Star.
O' you Brightest Star, I can see myself in your wonderful light.

Please be my Star, and let my life be as bright as your light.
O' you Brightest Star, You, the brightest and loveliest haven
Please be my Star amongst the stars of the heaven.

My spirit bears me witness
That you're my Star of Greatness.
Just as you're brighter than all other stars
So let my life be brighter than all other lives.
You've always stayed straight up above my bed
Watching me all night long, to know how I've slept
And I've woken up to find that you've not departed.
You're always up there, and above me here
In the Land of Africa.

O' you Brightest Star, please keep my World alive,
Oversee my activity and direct my destiny here in my
   Precious Land of Africa.
O' you Brightest Star, there's no doubt you're an African
Just as I'm, of course, an African.
And You're my African Star.
You are my Brightest Day and Night Star.
Joe Osamwonyi

Dreams Come True

A faceless stranger with your aura
   tip-toed through my dreams.

His genuineness intoxicated me
   as I drank in his essence.

Every pore inhaled the silhouette of his form.

Breathing deeply of the rugged angles of his face,
   softened by the gentleness of his nature,
   I once again become hungry.

Awakened by the longing for the reality
   of his gentle caresses,
   I come to realize . . .
     you are my dream come true.
Maureen Smith Annand

No Time For Grandma

She spends her days trying to stay busy.
Working in her home as she has always done.
Cooking, dusting, sweeping the floor.
Always listening for a knock on her door.

But; the knock never comes and as night settles in.
The longing, the loneliness and the tears all begin.
For all of the years that have gone before.
When every day brought a knock on her door.

When laughter and love filled most of her day.
Her heart filled with joy watching grandchildren play.
Wiping noses, healing hurts with soft tender kisses.
Those are the days that grandma now misses.

Cleaning house doesn't take the place of soft loving arms.
Or the smile of a child with sweet special charms.
Nor little blue eyes revealing trust beyond measure.
Those special things that all grandmas treasure.

Loneliness is her companion now.
Nothing is like it was before.
The children are grown, busy living lives of their own.
They don't have time for grandma anymore.
June L. McNeely

Reflection

You found your reflection
In a love that was true
The mirror reflected the beauty inside you
The love was so deep
The heart overflowed
A long empty life, finally fulfilled you

You gave yourself over
To the love, endlessly
The warmth that received you, brought passions to flame
You know there was risk
In devoting your heart
The reflection could vanish as quick as it came

Now you face your worst nightmare
As you wake from the dream come true
The reflection is gone, but the image reminds you
You embraced the divine
All that's left is profane
The reflection, a light that once burned inside you
Bill Gibson

The Heart Of A Rose

Have you ever peered into the heart of a rose—
A velvet rose of deepest hue?
Plucked it gently in the early dew,
And found life's answers all anew
As the exquisite perfume drugged you?
Where beauty is, like a diadem, so
The noble rose
In gracious rose,
On delicately chiselled and verdant stem.
Lifting its petalled bowl up high
In homage to an azure sky, then
With a floricultural sigh
Disintegrates: (like human kind).
A coloured cascade caught by wind;
And when, of petals all bereft
Its constant heart is always left.
Winifred Moyle

Unknown

I have salt water in my veins.
Shells as my nails.
The sun is my strength.
No problems or pains.
To surf with dolphins and whales.
How can nature be so simple
and powerful at the same time?
There is nothing as awesome
as to be at the mercy
of the sea.
Brendan Sullivan

My Babies

My little babies
Are very special to me;
You have Keila and Caylee,
And Logan makes three

Keila is three
And quite a big handful;
Caylee and Logan are twins,
To watch it's delightful

They are my biggest joys in life
Watching them grow;
Sometimes they're rowdy,
One day I'll have to let them go

For now they're just little
Full of happiness and vigor;
Every days a new day,
Watching them get bigger
Lori A. Sargent

Love

My darling
It is not my wish
That things are the way they were.
I have always wanted to remain the same
Holding your hand forever.

For fifty years,
I have taken all that it took
Loyal, kind, helpful, faithful and loving.
Needless to say, my strengths and
weaknesses.

For the past several weeks,
And today.
I want to serve the same.
My strength, my love and heart
But I cannot.

This damn weakness
Has left me hopeless and numb.
Little can I do that I want
My rights and freedom gone
Still my heart yearns for love.
Nyambane T. K.

Sarasota Bay

Here is heaven at sarasota bay
A special place God's protegee
It is a place for one to see
Into the heart of eternity

Sarasota bay is friendly and warm
Relaxing and resting are the norm
The dolphins fly and the pelicans sail
Peace happiness and goodwill prevail

The bay breeze it washes away
Any unhappiness of yesterday
It lifts the spirit it buoys the mind
Sarasota bay is a gift to all mankind.

Jack Lichter

The Staircase

I place one foot upon a step,
That no one should ever dare,
As I begin my slow descent,
Down the staircase of despair.

Behind me lurk abundantly,
Lost hopes, and broken dreams,
With no guard rail there to guide me,
I'm on my own, it seems.

I stumble blindly forward,
Only to slip and fall,
My soul is left in tatters,
While my spirit can barely crawl.

This blackness fills my being,
With not a single sound,
My mind enveloped indignantly,
With a cruelty most profound.

Amidst these cracks and crevices,
There must be some escape.
Perhaps, a dream that's long forgotten,
Or trapped in the web, of life's red tape.

Dina Bettis

Object Of Question

I found a heart
  so broken in two
that words can not express
  the depth of a soul so blue.
It was so ugly that
  I could hardly bare to touch.
I abused it
  I hated it so much.
I began to feel pity
  for such beastly misery
So, I picked it up
  and took it home with one.
I looked at every night
  until the disgust subsided.
I touched and held the pieces
  and beside me they always resided.
Then one day I put them together
  from off of the shelf
And was amazed to realize
  the reflection of myself.

Melisa Hayes

The Dance Of The Crystal Clouds

Earth is but a round word in naked space,
A blue and white ghost amid the stars,
An illusion, as transitory
As the fading flesh of its brief tenants.
What specious plea its siren shore purveys,
Blind truth to stale and tired stone, leaving
Silence as the loud echo at the end
Of the deepest voids in human hearts.
Far from a harvest of willing seasons,
Earth is the womb of eternity,
When the ancient cage of heavy bones will
Open like a flower to set the spirit free —
Free to fly as a shadow of the wind,
To sing a song with a breathless voice, to see
The light of Infinite Love engulf a timeless
Landscape with a veil of gold, to feel the boundless
Joy uplifting crystal clouds to dance as though
With wings in their endless celebration of being.
For then, the smile from the very heart of God
Will greet the soul at last emptied of its Self.

Donald G. Shanahan Jr.

No One Allowed

Sometimes I just sit here and cry
Wishing I could forget you or lie down and die.
You made it past the barrier protecting my heart
You taught me to love then tore my world apart.

The touch of your fingers tracing the curve of my face
My skin quivering and my heart starting to race.
Your scent lingering upon my clothes
Tantalizing and tickling my nose.

Tasting your sensuous lips covered in wine
The heat of your body pulsating against mine.
The echo of your sexy voice in my ear
Whispering, "I could never live without you, dear!"

I put my complete trust and faith in your hands
I loved you for who you were without any demands.
How could I be so blind and allow you in?
Now I have to pick up the pieces and start over again.

My soul was ripped from my chest the night I saw
The two of you in a passionate embrace down the hall.
Time healed the wounds and the barrier was replaced
Standing rock-solid until I saw your smiling face.

Shirley Mae Arens

Ship Lights

Lights shine from a place just beyond my reach.
I sense their energy as it travels across the darkness,
On its journey to my soul.
Nothing more than ship lights on the ocean.
One by one they unite,
A barrier that provides a sense of security.
Is my energy strong enough to be felt by them?
Do they sense my fear at not being heard?
Surely they do.
For as they sparkle from one realm of brightness to the next,
A single voice echoes in my mind.
And I feel their pain.

Matthew A. Walker

Waiting For The Moon

The sun reminds me of you
hitting me without asking
burning me with the rope.
The rope of rage.

I need a shadow
A big tree to hide from you
Ugly sun! Don't burn me.
My eyes get watery every time you get close to me.

Now I am sitting at the beach.
I hide under the palms from the sun
I am waiting for the sun to go away.
It's gone, now I can go into the water.

It's like Daddy and me
He is like the water in the beach
every time the evil sun is not looking
I have fun with the water.

When she was around no one could have fun
She didn't like to see other people laughing
Why would they be happy
when she is burning inside?

Olga Renta

The Storm At Sea

The waves rolled in with their white foam crests
an awesome see
Perhaps they were so long ago on the
sea of Galilee.
Yet those were subdued by three small words
As Christ said "Peace be still",
The wind obeyed, the sea became calm,
In obedience to his will.
The storms of life can also be stilled
of we turn them over to God,
and trust in His power
and leave it with Him
and believe in His world.

Carrie Mulhern

Divorce

Going through notions
Directed by lawyers
Closing and opening doors
To endless foyers
Feeling two-sided
One holding the heart
And the other the pride
This divorce rips us apart
We become petty
Change our minds
Confused and distraught.
From varied signals and signs
We rush into things
Don't sort them out
Making rash decisions.
Then there's that wonder and doubt.
Using reason and logic we forget about the caring
That held Us Together. And taught us about sharing.
But we know we have deeply hurt each other
And we wonder if—we will ever trust another.

Hallette C. Dawson

Presence

I hear Jesus whispering
Hear Him as the wind goes by
Swishing the leaves soar high
Gently hushing in the breeze
As the whispering willows droop to call
Out my name in the dying fall

I hear flowers rustling
In the forest in early spring
Hear the birds with a flutter of wings
Fill my heart with joyful song
A rabbit patters softly into his home
And I heard Him calling in the rushing
stream
Gently gushing out my name.

Rainey Howarth

Winter Memories

No matter how cold the winter's may be
Visions of what might have been
Or still be, brings back the
Warmth of your being to me
The memories of you to me
Are so kind
They bring back the joy that
I've left behind
And some how I still find
You're inside my heart and inside
my mind.

Dexter M. Johnson

Don't Forget

Don't forget,
to always have
a dream.

Don't forget,
the friendly
smiles you've seen.

Don't forget,
the plans
you have.

Don't forget,
if you're lonely,
only you can change.

Don't forget, the victories you've
won, or the mistakes
you've done.

The biggest don't forget is,
you must never feel defeated!

Because as soon as you do,
all you've worked for will soon be gone.

Debby S. Lamothe

Birth Of A Poem

The pain is great
The words aren't there
Then you rack your brain
And lay your soul to bare.

The struggle is mighty
The reward is small
You pour out your heart
And give it your all.

Then you see a tear or a smile
As your poem is being read,
You know from their face
And nothing has to be said.

You feel tired and lonely
As if you have given birth,
You have created something,
The only one on this earth.

You are finally done
Now you have filled a need,
Your soul is still bleeding
But you have planted a seed.

William "Frosty" Dryden

Gourmet

"Brother Coyote"
Intently pursuing
Dinner
At the "Roadside
Diner"
Oblivious to traffic
And mankind
Whizzing by
Almost within
"Touching distance"
Good hunting
Little brother!
A window
On "Yesterday"
"Tomorrow"
And, hopefully
"Forever"!

Amie Trout

Forever Yours

Floating on top of a world,
Looking down upon the darkness
Grasping life by the hand.

Then walking step by step,
Through the wet water...
The blistering heat....
Shivering snow and the calm cool breeze.

The darkness is cold and blinding,
But yet you can see
Warmth of your hand
Grasping life so tenderly.
Stepping as one...
Floating forever...together

Diane M. Black

A Little Light Music

Ah the tintinnabulation, the chiming and rhyming
of the brazen bells, how it illumined the curving rows
of listeners that Sunday afternoon. The audience caught
the radiance the flashing sound emanating from the chancel
with its row of music-makers and their handfuls of bells.

Though this was not the only radiance, for the scene
was lit from above, the waning December sunlight
refracted, scattered, made golden
by the hundred-year-old west window
now shining like a star.

Caught unawares by harmonizing waves of light and sound,
an observer glances at window and ringers. Stirred by a harmony
transcending physical laws, he sees program notes
(black figures on a golden ground) blur and fade.
So he closes his eyes to attend to this light music,
this music of the spheres.

W. Eugene Davis

I Want To Live

In the moment of passion, my life had begun.
Now when you know it was I, You do not want me to see the sun.

Oh if You could remember the love,
when your mom carried you inside.
She didn't say I want my rights!
She carried you with dignity and pride.

She chose life, you are here,
it was the most beautiful gift she could give.
Many of us will not have that chance,
please hear my voice, I want to live!!

My heart will give You love, my arms will give You warm embrace.
My eyes will be glad to see You,
I will touch You, and always remember Your face.

But if my life will be washed away, you will think of me every day.
And at the end of Your journey You will meet the great judge,
what will you say dear mama, what will you say?

Oh remember You were where I am now!
Remember I want to live!
Remember there is a God!
Remember You have a life to give!

Mary Fumic

Life's Mission

Be more concerned with character than reputation.
Be more demanding of your most charitable traits.
Be more ambitious in achieving your untold dreams.
Be more patient in the rush to your eternity.
Be wary of any easily acquired treasure.

But . . .

Be realistic in personal expectations.
Be more forgiving of your human imperfections.
Be more understanding of emotional pressures.

Most of all . . .

Be satisfied in the mold you have cut for yourself
Because the world is in need of more people like you.

Catherine E. Mitchell

Which Road Shall We Take?

As we travel down the road of life,
Some may travel alone, without a wife.
One road goes to the left, the other to the right,
Did we make the right choice? Or just go out of sight?
So many things in life, that we all have to ponder,
But we are reassured, by the "Good Man" up yonder.
Certain people travel through life, and find it a bore,
But they should watch Mother Nature, with her blessings galore.
The leaves, in full colours, when we get into the fall,
The water, and the mountains, put there for us all.
In the winter, the sleet that will cover each and every tree,
Makes a real winter wonderland, just for you and for me.
In spring, the robins come to let us all know,
That winter is over, and there will be no more snow.
To see new spring lambs, running and jumping around,
I'm sure it would make the hardest of hearts, to start in to pound.
With new kittens and puppies, and children at their play,
Gives us a new lease on life, as we watch them each day.
Which road shall we take? Now here are just a few,
Be a friend to all people, whatever else you do.
Albert M. Cruikshank

His Lonely, Human Tears

Man sits on sequestered shoulders
Yet will he find the answer to his dreams?
His heart feels like it's being crushed by boulders
He's giving up on love or so it seems

He asks himself if there will ever be
A time to drive away his loathsome pain
In silence he won't thrive, he can't be free
His lonely, human tears fall down like rain

Society feels he is not the same
Because they know his lover is a man
Closed-minded people shower him in shame
In the way that only heartless humans can

His only wish is that one day he'll see
A place where all may live in harmony
Old stigmas thrown aside; replaced by peace
Differences forgot make hatred cease

We all must try to end this kind of hate
By being who we are we'll change our fate
And someday soon I pray we shall be free
To live our lives together openly
Luke Fillion

Summer Shower

Our mutual memory, a summer shower,
With time into oblivion it went.
The rain beating down with passionate power,
Upon the stretched raincoat—our protective tent.

Within: a tightly closed world is reigning,
Our own, embracing only ourselves.
A few minutes—eternity feigning,
But eternity is only a moment's shelf!

Limited time in limited stance
Human drama, within breathing distance
Played upon four pupils reflexion score.

But blown away are summer showers
Flown away are tents of makeshift power
Upon reality's water-washed shores!
Alexander Kristof

The Moon-Shine Fairy

The moon-shine fairy . . .
  Oozing from the moon,
  It Percolates beauteous.

The moon-shine fairy . . .
  Decking with milky garment,
  It bruises darkness

The moon-shine fairy . . .
  Tossing up the ocean,
  It lights the affairs of life.

The moon-shine fairy . . .
  Gazing from the moony balcony,
  It conceals under blanket of darkness.

The moon-shine fairy . . .
  Raining the delights to the Earth,
  It flutters the wings world to world.

The moon-shine fairy . . .
  Pouring the nectar of smile,
  It grips the Sweet heart.
P. B. Patel-Das

Silhouette

She stands in the window
looking out at the lake
The wind is blowing strong
the waves cover a boat's wake.

She's a young lady
just past eighteen
Something's on her mind
it's so easy to see.

She's too shy to talk
her mind's a closed book
You ask her what she wants
she just gives you a look.

I'd love to make contact
just to see a spark in her eye
But whenever I see her
I feel I'm wasting my time.

Brandy is her name
she's important to me
Someone so young
not to be trouble free.
Thomas Buckmaster

Time

Tick tock, tick tock
Says the clock
Old time is dying
Seconds and minutes are flying
The days of youth are passing
Hours of beauty unlasting
Month by month is gliding away
Leaving nothing but memories that stay
The years are rolling by
As one by one they die
Yes, old time is flying
So let the year go cheerfully
While they're dying.
Grace Riffle

Finally!

I have an image, vague as yet,
But existent none-the-less
It is mine, all mine,
Unable to be touched or corrupted,
As it is still only an image
Within my mind
Crucial steps to be taken, taken now
Transforming this image into something
Tangible
Yet, I'm still in the dark
Only my instinct to guide me
Now it is time, my time, to do what I must
To allow myself to reach for all I want
To live for me, my dreams
To retrieve my sanity,
Ever lost in this labyrinth we call life
Rediscovering myself, all of me
Revealing all I once buried
All desires set free . . . finally!

Julie Adams

I'm A Poet!

When I tell I am a poet,
I feel terribly meek.
I wonder if there's wonder
at what kind of attention I seek?
Yes,
one of each.
But poetry also gives me reach
for freedom from dogma,
so that who I am
cannot be statistically verified
with norms and means,
and such averaging liens.
I want license to be
different,
free,
and me.

No matter how it's always been done,
or said,
I beg the liberty
to pose an instead.

Janie Kent

Prayers

A prayer can be answered
In many different ways
Regardless what we ask for
No matter what the day.

We ask for peace and bounty
And thus it did come
When we counted our blessings
Twas quite a large sum.

He granted us our wishes
Made no real demand
Sent us a lovely rainbow
Thus peace comes to our lands.

Pamila Jasmine Fuller

Ancestral Pride

In this time of indoubtful deeds,
what reason does my flesh 'n blood
have in my route of happiness?
I will not, by any reason marry
to whom I do not Love.
Should I marry to justify my place of birth
or shall I not.
To listen to my heart and not do what
others of time propose.
Without love, I shall not marry,
no matter what my family proceeds to be valued.
I the second eldest was chosen,
for my sister was to be so called wed.
I do not choose to wed;
without my value of love.
No matter what pride is deemed to dissolve.

Christal Linnard

Undying Love

You and I met in the month of September,
A minuscule spark, became a burning ember,

Magical colours of harvest gold,
The sweet scents of autumn,
Surrounding our abodes.

A sparkling angel arrived on a feather,
Bringing the gift of love,
Which can't be measured.

We have no riches, money, or fancy car,
But the bond in our hearts, A valued treasure by far,

The trials and tribulations,
Our love has surpassed,
Proves how our union is meant to last.

Someday our time will come to rise above,
And with our souls, will go our love,
For within the heaven's,
We shall be placed side by side,
Caring and always surviving the tide.

Ours is truly an . . . Undying love.

Mike J. Malloy

Sleep

Surrendered to unconsciousness we are.
Now sent to be seduced by our sweet dreams . . .
Nightmarish screams may leave some deep-dug scar,
That hounds and rips at our sides' shiv'ring seams.
In our mind's eye some monstrous red eye gleams.
Alone we'll face these unrealities!
These images look real or so it seems.
The serpent will demand his terror fees,
As "he" unlocks our fear with skel'ton keys.
A childish practice to be gripped in fear,
But grown-up also may get knocking knees.
As nightmares cloud eyes with a lonely tear . . .
No one knows what our mind's subconscious seeks
And yet, each night on us it horror wreaks!

Kim Ingrid Mattheson

Abode Of God

Undulating emanations enfolding waves of
glorious hues comes the breath of God! His
voice of music! His love,
It comes through spiralled radial powers to
inspire us from above.
With all the answers to prayers with knowledge
verse and song,
With wisdom and forgiveness! For wrong.
With blessings and guidance with beauty warmth-
and glory! In reflection,
With prayer and comfort! With touch! Wit!
Sufferance! Purity and all in perfection.
Les't ye' be a paragon! For all is glory-
Then thou' must be glorious! There is no-
other way to reach attainment or abode of
God! The summit cannot curtain the-
impure of kind.
    In the heaven of the mind.
    Agnes Burns Lawson

From Darkness To Light

The darkness of my life began to engulf me,
and the end of my rope became crystal clear.
When I thought that all hope was lost,
an angel wrapped me in comfort
and said that my journey must begin.
The angel that guided me through the loneliness
and past the despair,
forced upon my face a smile,
and a feeling of warmth overwhelmed me.
The black became grey and the gray became
an illuminating force waking every fibre of my being.
My angel set me back on a path of happiness,
paved by love and rose petals,
and cleared the obstacles that would slow my progress
to the future before me.
For the first time since the darkness took over,
I can see the light and hope is within my reach.
I now know that the angel that led me, is you,
and I will never lose sight of the light again,
as long as my angel walks with me.
    Julie Wall

Brian

You are regal, you're majestic.
You're the air I breathe, every breath I take.
The sounds I hear, a voice carried near.
You're the sights I see, a vision of need.
The feelings awaken, a desire forsaken.
You're the steps I take, the voyage I'll make.
The hand that caresses, you've touched my senses.
You're the wings of the night, in a dream you'll hold me tight.
The hands of time, close in with every rhyme.
Within this poem I offer you, verses of wisdom and truth.
I'm lost inside the labyrinth walls.
I ask of you to guide me through.
Will you?
    Xenia Santowski

Only Love!

Love, is only what I know.
Love, only lets us grow.
Forgiveness, a bright light to show,
Love's the only seed to sow!

Love is only what can free,
Without it, now one can see.
Love's our divine right to be,
We are in thine sight, Love—we!

Love exists to heal.
Love lets us feel
Love's a might that reveals,
Yes, it is quite very real!

Love cannot be anything but.
Love truly is wealth, so strut!
Cause in love, there is no fraud
For this love, simply is God!

Love, is the choice to live.
Love, is the voice—the gift.
Love is only love,
Is only—Love!
    Shawn Hoffman

Snow

Falling fine and fast,
  or
Flaky and feathery,
Weighing down remaining leaves
From near-barren trees.
Boisterous, cheering children,
Building great big snowmen.
Some go merrily coasting,
Others choose swiftly skiing.
Enjoyable scenes like these,
Leave me feeling
Happy as you please!
    Lois M. Steele

The Answer

A tree in the garden of life
One branch was burning bright
Some thought it was a fright
But for all, it lit up the night

Can you see it happening
Can you interpret the code
I thought that maybe I could
But some would remain untold

I shouted it aloud one day
Someone heard my words
They agreed, we all could see
We all had found the way

At last there is an answer
We can't forsake the truth
The awesome power of Love and Respect
Must be ingrained in our youth!
    Nancy Lynn Naquin-Pope

Oasis

Restlessness has become
a part of my life now

And the strength in me longs
to explode wide open!

The fight is so inevitable
that I want to lock the doors

With the keys I've lost so long
ago.
If they were found
I could smile again

And feel the sunshine
Which would free the mind of my
soul
Little child am I trapped in
this body

How long has it been since
I sang my song of
Freedom and danced in
the sands of my
oasis.
Darling Stone

A Better Place

We long to see a better place
No confusion, no pain, no fear
To be a part of that better place
We must leave what we have here.

The journey to that better place
For some, can be short and sweet
The only price — eternal happiness
As our Father we stand ready to meet.

We go through life hoping and praying
That all we've done is forgiven
And He will stand ready to welcome us
To a better home waiting in heaven.

Venus has gone to that better place
But — her legacy can be carried on
By Four "Living" generations
And a part of her lives in them all.
Cheryl Holmes-Williams

Blessed Are The Seekers

Blessed are the seekers,
They will find the answers.
Let love color the conclusions.
And the rainbow appears
To be drawn on for life's purpose.
Colors form vibrations
That speak to the heart.
And the display of all colors
Confirms infinite possibilities are possible,
In nature as well as in the realm of forever.
The seekers rejoice as the heavenly symbol
Forms ribbons of brilliant acknowledgement.
Blessed are the seekers
Their focus remains above the mundane.
Beverly A. Kane

God Made The World

They tell us God made the world in six days,
He took some water and earth
and molded it into a ball,
Then he suspended it in air.

Then he made the sun and moon
so there would be day and night,
He made the stars, so shiny and bright,
To add magic to the night.

He planted trees to make the forests,
He planted flowers to make a garden,
He planted things for food,
Then he planted grass to make a carpet.

Then he took some clay and made Adam and Eve,
He breathed life into them, and gave them a brain,
He gave them choices of good and evil,
and they gave birth, for generations to come.

He made the world for you and me,
He gave us love and laughter.
He taught us the way, and gave us the will,
and he did all this in only six days.
Grace Long

December

December is here, and the old year is dying.
The wind in the willows, are gently sighing.
The evening sky is a joy to behold
Showing purple and green and crimson and gold
No flowers to greet us, as we go on our way
But holly a plenty with red berries so gay.
The moon sailing high in a start studded sky.
The lake looks like glass in the forest nearby.

The lanterns are beaming across the white snow
Shedding long Fingers of gold on our way as we go
The Christmas tree sparkles, what a lovely sight
And carol singers voices help gladden the night.

The Christmas bells are ringing their echoes near and far
They're calling us to worship led by the Christmas star.
The Christmas table is groaning with lots of Christmas fare
The children pulling crackers, there's laughter everywhere.

Santa Clause has come and gone, and everyone is jolly
'Neath garlands bright and candlelight,
And mistletoe and holly.
The log fires burning on the earth casting a rosy glow
The dog is sleeping on the mat, outside the ground is white
with snow.
Olive Wylie

Lisa

Remember her smile as she ran through the years
Taking time for her children as she spared their tears
Her heart was so deep as she gave her love to you
Leaving you a memory of her love so true
Remember the love she gave as she gives herself a rest
Take the time to prove to her yourself at its best
Her heart is open to you if you need to shed a tear
She leaves with us a memory of her love so dear
Michelle Connolly

Soliloquy in Journey

Splendor's desire cannot be bridled
for the grasping of life is in its loins.

A trickling bloom is what entices
And a folding of its petals is what causes possession.

A newly erected tower set upon voluminous boulders is full of
stamina, but is supplanted by a mere blossom.

The towers army comes rushing forth only to be captured.

Its inhabitants are imprisoned.

The cannon booms and its effects echoes indefinitely.

The enemy urges it to reload.

Your artillery makes me strong. Keep firing. As your ammunition
dwindles, I am reinforced. Attack! Attack, oh majestic one. I
welcome you with open arms and will exult triumphantly for I lay
upon fertile ground and it is I you will bless eternally.
Julie Szabo

A Western Australian Summer

The visitor that rattles the door
Has breath from the east that breathes fire.
It circles an abode like a prowler out to score.
Spreading dust and dry leaves in a shower

The heat that ensues, radiates on the ground,
Leaving all life debilitated and stale.
No creature has the energy to fight or growl,
Granting truces to hide in dark veils

Cyclones threaten as they loom off the coast.
Massive storms of destruction and power.
Surveying with malevolence the jagged host,
Before pouncing with a passion to devour.

Yet nature not always has the upper hand
With those who dwell in the regions.
She's tough but this teaches to understand
To survive with rehearsed preparation.

Australians adjust with versatility
To extract pleasure from the harsh conditions.
Respite with rituals of social iniquity
Are practised to deny natures proposition.
Peta Rossiter

Pilgrim Vision

Joy, like a fragrant flower wafting from heaven,
Blossoms brightly tonight
Shining through earth's darkest sorrow
Like misty petals in the early morning light.
Hope wells in the hearts of millions
Filled with heavy dread,
Soothes the frightened masses
Crying for their daily bread,
Guides the weary travellers
Wherever they may roam,
Lights their plodding footsteps
Searching for refuge and home.
Marianne Ruth Hartmann

The Beauty Of This Land

Oh man of this earth,
that cannot see the beauty of this land,
for they seem to close their eyes,
as if they are asleep,
when they walk all over this land,
and miss all the beauty
that God gave to you and me.
They seem to be walking,
as if they are in a deep sleep
and miss all this beautiful land,
as far as one's eyes can see.

Oh man of this earth,
just why can't you open your eyes
to see all this beautiful land,
that only God could give to all mankind
on this earth to see.
For I fear to close my eyes each night,
afraid of missing all the beauty
that God put into my sight.
Eunice Arnold

Love Is The Paradox Of Life

Love is ever sustaining
Love is ever building
Love is ever lasting.

   Love ever renews
   Love ever rebuilds
   Love is elastic.

Love multiplies
Love manifests
Love replenishes.

   Love is life
   Love is freedom
   Love is Joy.

Love is Holy
Love is Wholesome
Love is Fulfilling.

Without Love Life is futile.
I NOW meet my Love.
Violet Young Kalust

Angel On Earth

Some say they don't exist
Angels... from above,
But I know they are here
Sharing all their love.

They're always right beside us
Through good times and through bad,
They guide us and they know
When we're happy or we're sad.

They seem to know what's best for us
And will be there if we call,
They'll comfort and support us
They'll catch us when we fall.

I know myself that they are real
And I believe they have much worth,
For you, my friend, are what I call
"An angel here on earth".
Michele Marie Janes

The Winter Of My Hope

The mountains capped in ermine robes,
Trimmed in forest winter-gray,
Dormant, patient, endless waiting,
The Winter of my life portray.

Fond memories of tender shoots,
Yellow-green of early Springs,
Autumn hues and dropping leaves,
And Summer's fragrant blossomings

Are memories to warm the soul —
   though wounded —
To shelter, to protect, until the
   thaw begins to grow
And Winter melts away to Spring
To form new rivulets to flow.
Eleanor B. Crowther

Mother

Mother, kindness and dear
so many years
  it's been
   since you've nurtured me
   coddled me
so many years
  since I've said how much
  I've missed
   your kind and gentle touch

That touch
  which guided me
  reminded me
   that someone cares
And that no matter what
  you'd always be there

One thing shall always be
one thing always to share
Always there
  for you and me

Love Eternity.
Bryan Brunzell

Molehill

Day is done, eyes close;
  darkness falls, descending
  over a cemetery of homes.

Flaunting the eternal pitch
  a grave light comes on,
  kept repaired forever.

A gilded epitaph shimmers,
  enshrined in perpetuity
  by its impious trustor.

"My sight is gone;
  but others will come
  seeking illumination,
  and new ager carnations."
Patrick R. Penland

The Clear Scent of Love

Oh you, deep in verdant shadows of spring,
smile of violets on the shores of the rivers of waiting!
Oh you, dance of happiness in the vein of solitude
  tender lyric in the tightness of the heart!
Call me to the caress of your hands
  and to the kindness of your flaming glance.
I want to die with love
  I want to die in love
   I want to die of love.
Parviz Pisheh-Ehsan (Warenavich)

Chagrin and Shells

What have you learned on this orbiting earth?
Have you learned a core lesson of meaning or worth?
As the pendulum swings 'tween the joy and the strife,
Tell me what have you learned on your journey through life?

I've learned about tears—how they fall for a reason,
How sand-dunes are lonely no matter the season,
That sea gulls and starfish won't talk about love,
That pools mirror clouds upon faces above,
That cliffs pull like magnets, and waves are like pain:
How they rise, then they fall, then they rise up again.
I've learned that the warmth I so cherish and need
Can be snatched by cold winds like the wild tumbleweed.
I know the dark depths like a lone deep-sea diver,
And the nightmares and scars of a shipwreck survivor.
I'm a scholar of chagrin and shells and felled pride
And feelings of driftwood washed up by the tide.

So what have I learned on this orbiting earth?
Engraved on my heart—a moral sans mirth.
I've learned that some dreams fall like fireworks to dust.
That love is a traitor. I have learned not to trust.
Beverly Cole Earney

Shades of Singapore

The broad and easy sweep
Of brightly coloured houses on the river front
Stands in the shadow
Of the phallic and monochrome towers
Which straddle the city and seek to contain it
Making it conform to a man-made aesthetic
Of pure and prominent lines.
They rise upward to meet the longed-for future
And cast off the gravitational and earth-bound pull
Of history.
Colonialism and ethnicity
Both fallen to the modern God of technology;
A culture sanitized and money-based.
In this new world, reality is virtual,
Insubstantial.
Small wonder then that ghosts abound
And wander restless through the streets
In search of offerings large or small
On which to feed their blighted spirits
And save their hungry souls.
Fiona J. Doloughan

Sweet Dreams

I meander down a pathway of shadows and light,
   That twists and turns into morning and night.
I stand alone in the forest and breathe the quiet air,
   As the free wind gently blows through my hair.
There is a world above me, there is a world beneath.
   I close my eyes and float to the earth like an autumn leaf.
I lie in the cool dewy forget-me-nots at twilight
   And dream of warmth into the night.
Not the warmth that filters down from the sun,
   But the kind that is born in the hearts of everyone.
I dream of voices whispering kind words . . .
   The sweetest sounds I have ever heard.
I dream of splashing childishly where the sand
   meets the sea,
I dream of dancing in the moonlight next to a heart that
   beats for me.
I dream of a world where there is nothing to fear.
I dream that I have already cried my last tear.
I dream until tranquility washes over me,
   And I will rise to face the world again, merrily.

    Cynthia Hamilton

Somebody Other Than Me

Ever notice how cold it is . . .
   when you sit alone?
Or how loud the music plays . . .
   when it's quiet?
How still the air is . . .
   when nothing moves,
And how feelings are evoked.
See how dark it is . . .
   when lights are out?
And sleep is disturbed . . .
   cause no one said good night.
Words on a page are only words . . .
   thoughts invade instead.
Day dreams are a pastime . . . Dreams an escape,
Yet they both seem real.
Feelings get in the way . . .
   emotions are a handicap.
Sleep becomes addictive . . . So close to death.
Ever notice how life became
   a well known fear . . . As you live your daily life?

    Bronwyn Quilliam

Prayer of Thanks to God Our Father

My Lord and my God, how generous and good you are to me.
From my weak sinful self and the Power of Darkness.
You have rescued and redeemed me, unworthy though I am.
On my own account I know I do not merit.
The love and Compassion you so lovingly bestowed.
Yet in your infinite mercy you deemed it fit.
To shower me with your grace of salvation.
My grateful thanks I express to you unreservedly.

Praise be to you Father all powerful.
You have opened my eyes to the reality of truth and sin.
You have shown me that your love is without limit.
Not only for me but all my brothers and sisters on earth.
Henceforth strengthen and help us all.
Through the power of the Holy Spirit.
To adhere to the teachings of your Divine Son Jesus.
Who died for our sins and opened the gates of Heaven.

    Wilfred Pierre

The Homeless

She came into a world unleashed
A painful birth, a punish—breached!
Hungry, cold, unwanted, too—
Remained alone, like bastards do.

She lived her life, and did it well.
This forsaken soul from hell.
Tired, twisted in a "Home"
She laid there dying—all alone.

Before she closed her eyes in death
A voice boomed out—and caught her breath
She thought demented, she must be
Until she heard—my child, it's me!

I watched you from the day of birth
I knew your heart, I knew your worth!
Although this world was not too kind
I've come to take you "Home," you're mine.

    Monica Sanchez Rilling

Some People

Some people have memories
of happy, smiling faces
some people have dreams
of seeing far-off places
some people think
of what they'll someday do
some people follow
what they know is true
some people are givers
giving from the start
some people are lovers
they have a big heart
some people try to fix
the hurt they always see
someday, somewhere
a somebody, I will be.

    Amanda Radandt

At The Beginning

When the world was young and life began
God saw fit to walk with man
and like the wind in a burning bush
man stood by as the earth He shook.

God put each creature to the test
yet in his heart he loved man best
In him he placed a living soul
and even time can't make it old.

So pleased was man with God's master plan
That he multiplied and life's race ran
God taught him how to live it right
And in prayer blessed him, day and night.

God is still mindful of man's days
and pours moral graces on his highways
let's humbly kneel and return this love
that flows unconditionally from above.

Many men have walked this path we trod
and have proudly returned to live with God
at the end with Him in that placed divine
much love and rest we all shall find.

    Vera Lightsey

Oceanside

Like the shell seeker
I comb the barren winter sands
of my mind
searching for the perfect memory of you

One that, when I hold it to my ear
will whisper
of your beautiful body
cascading into me
again and again

Like the tide returning
my thoughts of you
brush the beaches of time past
flowing and building
to that stormy crescendo
breaking
and easing onto the shores of your
shoulders
silhouetted against my frothy form

   The passionate volatile sea
   coming finally to rest
   against the silent sand
        Lorilynn

Color Me Blue

   Color me Blue, . . .
'Cause I'm missin' you!

   Color me Blue, . . .
'Cause I was you wife, and
   you threw me out of your life.

   Oh, Color me Blue, . . .
'Cause I'm missin' you!

   Color me Blue, . . .
'Cause I was faithful and true.

   Color me Blue, . . .
'Cause I'm missin' you!
        Karen McCulley

The Present Eternal

You rowed me to your island
Through silver watery waves,
And there you fed me
With some unearthly magic.
You crushed me with your passion
So hard that I thought I could fly.
You sank into my pores
And breathed gold into my secrets.
My soul grew in your arms.
We drifted back in the dark
While you spoke of time,
And it all passed like a strange dream.
But my soul feels heavy now—
I cannot deny that your touch was real.
        Windy D. Cooke

Love Is

Love is a force
it can't be broken
the links are stronger than steel
you can not fight with the state of love
it squeezes you and holds you tight
you try to get away but it pulls with more might
you hang by a thread and your muscles get all brawn
I will never forget the way she left me
she broken of all my thorns . . .
        Jason Anthony John Vena

Opened Unto Thee

Beneath the carbon rib it's been, since Adam through the ages
and bears the matter to this day, and wisdom to the sages.
What is life? What is life? Echoes the refrain,
till prostrate lies the sparkless form, and then but dust remains.

Beneath the carbon rib there is a doorway to beyond,
that opened unto thee bestows the Home where we belong
but ownership commands the day and this doorway to beyond
is witness to our serving self but seldom knocked upon.

Within this rhythmic beating core, this propulsion to the morrow,
since "go forth and multiply" and its resulting sorrow,
seldom seen for what it is, yes flesh and blood, but more,
it is bearer of the mysteries, this rhythmic beating core.

Beneath the carbon rib there is a hot-line to the one
Creative mind of the universe, to some it's God above
Good behavior grants us light, reward to help our seeing,
when darkness finally leaves for good, awareness fills our being.

Beneath the carbon rib it's been, since Adam before the Fall
the First Truth, from which there springs, the oneness of us all
For God has lived us, every one, with nature He doeth weave,
The final truth, with carbon rib, this Adam before Eve.

Then Man will know a better day, and goodness will abound,
In every heart that nature makes, no darkness will be found,
And peace will be upon us.
        Gary Richard Ferguson

Ice And Snow

In land where, ice and snow, command
   And polar winds
Do sculptor icy shapes
   As by, like, some gigantic hidden hand
And glaciers curve and heave!
   So as they will!
And tear the rocks beneath
   Like some grinding, turning lathe
Awaiting, looking, quiet and still
   Where just a few, of human feet
Do venture forth
   To meet the fury, of polars angry wroth.
There are no roads, no paths nor track
   Just steps of foot
And they are gone If you do turn your back!

You layman - who know not such of this
And dwell in city fair! Your rain or sleet!
Upon streets, do sometimes fall such fuss make you
   If snow upon, your garden wall an inch or so
Perhaps you may recall
        Michael F. Sofer

Mysterious Pasts

In our time,
We have many mysteries of the past,
That we try to decipher,

The rise and fall of Atlantis,
what led to its destruction?
Though its location is unknown.

The great Anisazy,
Just vanished,
All that's left is wood and stone,

The architectural Egyptians,
How did they move the gigantic stones?
They shaped pyramids in patterns of stars of night.

The statues of Easter Island,
Who built them?
And so strange to the sight,

We try to find an explanation,
We might, we might not,
Maybe some things were meant to stay a mystery.

Cecilia Irvine

Above All

With God's help be strong
And let your heart take
Courage in all things.
Desiring right over wrong
So then it shall be done!
Acceptance of one's fate
With grace participate...
Pride answers each call
With every assigned task
However great or small.
It helps to know his most
Precious love will prevail
With each new passing day
Through our daily prayers
All's left in His care...
Receiving his blessings somehow we find our way.
His great love expressed
Reminds us all, we're here
Strictly on borrowed time
As his most honorable guests.

Georgina Grace Gorman

John Cabot's New Founde Lande

John Cabot was sailing in his ship called "The Matthew,"
he was looking for land, days through and through.
He sailed his ship through storms and rain,
he kept up his voyage despite the tears and the pain.
Finally one day in the year 1497,
he discovered Bonavista and thought he was in Heaven.
The air was fresh and the grass was green,
it was the most beautiful place he had ever seen.
John Cabot sent word of his New Founde Lande
and of all the fish that couldn't be caught by just one man.
The people in England, oh how they started to talk,
about all the fish off the coast of this "Great Rock."
They jumped in their ships both woman and man
and this is how the settlement of our province began.
Five hundred years later we celebrate the founding of this land
and we owe our thanks to one brave man—John Cabot.

Neil Dean

Gizmos To The Rescue

On gizmos we sustain,
Our daily life to maintain.
Tons of gadgets we make,
To give ourselves a big break.

Oh timer, oh timer,
A ring-a-ling you falter.
Oh hail you smoke alarm,
It's just burned bacon, no harm.

Oh you crazy car crank,
Now, we must go to the bank.
"Oh hi teller machine,
Just eat my card and be mean."

Oh shopping cart do turn,
Wheels jammed and squeal, my ears churn.
Oh blue pen do your job,
Sign my name, oh dear, a blob.

Dear Father lend an ear,
I ask my prayer, please do hear.
On You ever sustain,
My daily life to maintain.

Dawn Marie McCandless

Remission

There was never anything as beautiful
as a sinner saved by grace.
When he looks among the stormy clouds
and sees his saviors face.

No longer does he have
the feeling of doubt.
but the feeling of security
that remission brought about.

So when you look upon beauty
as though a scenic place.
There will never be anything more beautiful
Than a sinner saved by grace.

Robert L. Bray Sr.

Baby Girl

The smile you possess
You share so generously
Sweet sounds and laughter
Flow freely from your lips
Eyes staring with warmth
With love
Knowing who I am
And how much you mean
To me
The kiss I give you
Will last forever
Holding you in my arms
Never wanting to let you go
My baby girl
Never forget
I will be here for you
Always

Jocelyn R. Flojo

Standing Alone In A Crowd

When the wind storm of life
makes our eyes swell with tears
At times the cold that is our loneliness
makes our teeth chatter
The sand from the dessert which is our fear
clouds our vision
Or when the ocean that is our past
washes salt into our wounds
Those times we approach the oasis
which is our replenishment
The one time we know we are not
standing alone is
When we let the sunshine that is love
heat up our hearts
only then, we stand with many friends.

Kathie Moore

Memories

As I sit among the trees
And smell the country air,
I can feel the summer breeze
And haven't a single care.

It reminds me of the past,
When I was young and free.
Though the time went by so fast,
Wouldn't even pause for me.

Those good ol' days back then,
Are like gold today -
I'd relive them all again,
If I could have my way.

By the river we would go
To escape reality -
It was so simple though
With no responsibility.

Back then I never thought
I'd cherish all those days -
But the memories they've brought
Will be with me always.

Kelly Lynn Brooks

The Woman In Doubt

The woman who thinks she's not
In doubt
Thinking she's not a woman yet
Being a woman sometimes she regrets
Living her life strange as it may seem
The beginning of her life cycle
Sometimes make her mean

She's trying to cope with the world abroad
Hoping someday she'll pull the right chord
Woman!
You are visible as the sun
Not invisible as you think
Being invisible is for a lonely crank

Live life woman as you see
For someday life will cease
God created woman that's what man claims
God created man to bring you fame
So be a woman and not ashamed

Freddie Leslie Sr.

Rainbows

The colors of the rainbow flash through the skies, reflecting
sad memories of harsh good-byes. Red, yellow and purple are
what people have seen, but for me black and blue are what they
have been. My life once so full of light, ended with the first
fist fight. I should have left that cold and brutal day, but he said
sorry and begged me to stay. Every day when I come home, an
empty bottle's by the phone. The bedroom door is always shut so
tight, I try not to wake him for another fight. The bedroom
door hits the wall, as he's yelling down the hall. He grabs me
by my auburn hair, as he asks me where I've been, he glares.
His hand hits my cheek with a blow, and to the floor is where
I go. His feet hit my ribs until they break, I now realize my
life's at stake. He jumps in the truck and roars down the
street, I'm just starting to rise to my feet. The blood runs
from my mouth and my nose, my memory fresh with hard right
blows. I crawl to the bathroom and look in the mirror, as my
tender black eyes begin to tear. I decide to leave this hell
right now! I will go far away, this I vow! The front door slams
and I stand still. Maybe, just maybe, someday I will.

Melissa Hutchings

The Curse Of Hell

"The curse of hell"
The soldier cries,
with no arms, no legs,
and tear filled eyes.
With nothing in him
But a voice that moans,
to think of days when he was home.
The fresh baked bread,
The morning kiss,
The pretty town girl that he would miss.
All lost on the day when the tolling bell
Called all young men "To the curse of hell."

The tolling bell rang loud and clear.
All the men quickly downed their beer.
They said goodbyes and cleared their slates
and marched along unsure of their fate.

They marched even though they knew war was wrong.
They marched in rhythm, rhyme and song
They marched to the sound of the tolling bell.
That called all young men "To the curse of hell."

Cindy Patterson

Reminiscing

Today I went on a journey—a journey down memory lane;
Walked down a country roadway and smelled the new cut grain.
We walked in mud in the springtime and a crocus began to grow
Burned in the blazing sunshine, then waded through the snow!

But mostly we talked, or giggled, perhaps of the night before
A dance? A meeting? A concert and the song we had performed?
Or maybe we looked to the future, and spoke about how we'd go
And leave these farms behind us—get into the city 'glow'!

So we traveled that dusty highway but it never crossed our minds
How years would change the picture of all we'd leave behind!
But today I am reminded, one thing that never ends
Is the joy of having a visit with my everlasting friend!

Audrey K. Thompson

Little Amy

Our little Amy
What a beautiful girl
Blue eyed and blond
She dances and whirls

Little arms hug her Gramma
She sure makes my day
She calls to her Papa, let's go get the sleigh
Her and her Papa build snowmen with pride
Then they get out the sleigh and Amy goes for a ride
Then she tells her ol' gramma with so much delight
I think me and Mommy will stay overnight
We must play with Barbie, her favorite toy
Then read bedtime stories of girls and boys
Then our little Amy, her beauty so rare
Sleeps like an angel
I'm so glad she's here
She's my ray of sunshine
In this cold ol' world
I love you dear Amy
Gramma's sweet little girl
   Mona Bochar

Soul Of Heaven And Hell

Grave of dust, you've awakened
and taken my dreams to replace
them with fears, not of mine but of others:
   You wait in silence 'till
I awaken to feel you near
I see your shadows come near
and feel no fear yet you disappear into the night.
   Grave of dust, you move my
soul that bleeds at night,
A higher grace of power still
fights for my trust and soul,
though it seems at times you've won.
   I pray to my higher grace
for his power yet I fall onto
your power, grave of dust.
Now I pray for any answer
from both strengths as to why;
why is the grave of dust and the grace of higher power
at war for my thoughts, my trust, my soul,
have I a power of great neither have . . .
   Evelyn Theoharis

Surfing On Silicon

Deprivation, salivation, Surfing On Silicon,
Staring on screen, desperate digits wearing to the bone,
Sending snippets of sincerity down the optic fiber,
Searching over sound bites, secrets of pseudo name cyber,
Sentinels of security shielding our hearts holes,
Wielding monstrous megahertz which are siphoning our souls,
Staving off sunlight, praying for electric salvation,
Stuck on sensation and digital gratification,
Seized in a web, we seek out synthetic social contact,
Securing our shackles in this paradoxical act,
Seekers of soul mates upon their multimedia perch,
Intimate alienation sabotages our search.
   Loring Miles Lascu

Someone To Love Me

I want someone to love me,
   (I don't mean to share my bed)
Someone who can make me laugh
   Put happy thoughts in my head:
One who can make conversation
   (Whose limits aren't sports on T.V.)
One who'd share love of music
   and who actually likes poetry.

I want to feel arms around me
   Breathe in the scent of cologne,
Taste the sweetness of a kiss
   (that awakens feelings long gone!)
I want someone to love me
   Weary and maimed tho' I be,
I long to feel loved and pampered,
   Need his strength to nourish me.

I need to know, could someone love me?
   Love me for what's deep within?
O where is that someone who'd love me
   And bring me to life again!
   Lily Neilson

Family

First there is the wedding
Forming family foundation.
Often follows, joining
The couple, tiny new creation.

During this special year,
Whether a precious girl or boy;
For parents and family,
They are always their pride and joy.

Third year they prefer
To play side by side, but all alone.
Still reluctant to share
The numerous toys that they own.

Second year they learn to share
And like to play with a new friend.
Fourth year brings less conflict,
Usually have a special friend.

Fifth and following years
Their interest, friends will increase.
Now more independent
Time with their family will decrease.
   Ella A. Olson

To Declare Love . . .

To declare love . . .
What does it mean?
Is it like spring,
Where everything blooms and comes to life?
Is it like summer,
Where playful time is spent together?
Is it like fall,
Where leaves fall and colors change the world?
Is it like winter,
Where the warmth of one, warms another?
Maybe it's all year . . .
Time spent together is an endless season.
   Matt Hiu

The Poet's Prize

I write a lot of poetry,
It's mostly silly rhymes.
So far all my earnings
Don't add up to a dime.

I like to write the silly stuff
And funny nonsense rhymes;
My friends all smile and chuckle,
It brightens up their lives.

The poems I send to contests
Have never won a prize,
For those who do the judging
Have minds so very wise.

My hopes were high — My poem might win!
But I've already won
The love and fun and friendship
Of all the folk back home.

It would be nice to win some cash
And catch the judge's eye,
But I'm rewarded all the time —
My friends joy is my prize.

Juliette Phair

Book Dreams

Alone in silence,
words no longer comfort me.
I can't escape . . . into their reality.

Worlds of thieves, wizards, dragons,
of Unicorns bringing light.
This day passes slowly,
into an eternal night.

With dawn comes a new day.
The words focus and characters come into play.
Now I can enter into the world in my mind.
I open the door . . . what wonders I find.
So many dreams are now mine.

I can be the hero or a sage wise.
Perhaps the falcon that soars the skies.
All I have to do is imagine . . . .
Fantasize.

Ruth Hammond

Heart's Desire

Lord set me free.
With your chosen man I want to be.

Wake me from deep within.
Show me the many pleasures I will be given.

I want to experience love at first hand.
Provide me a bond to be sealed with a band.

Comfort me until this day.
All these things in your name I pray.

If never to be loved on this earth I roam,
Please spare me the grief and take me home.

Joanne Cavanagh

Ursula's Puppets

In preparation, the puppeteer manipulates,
　though child-like in her way.

Casting players for that narrow stage which we all call . . .
　today!

The music starts and strings are taunted:
　The play begins at early dawn.

All puppets dance to false illusions, until the strings break,
　one and all.

The one last strand, like love imprisoned,
　slowly peels with grace and falls . . .

Emotions lacking: the play suffers;
　along with multitudes of lookers-on.

Leaving the performance incomplete,
　the Puppeteer astounded
　　and love in tearful gasp.

Michael Sidorenko

The Teen Tune

Boys 'n girls they keep
Each other happy with the
Way they rock n roll, unlike
the mum's and dad's whose minds
a regular worry well I guess
that's just been old. Check how
they walk and talk wearing the
latest fashion and the hair
it's so control, they live their
lives asking nothing from
tomorrow as right now good
times they will always follow
Get up and move to the teen tune just for satisfaction,
start a new toy reaction, get down and groove
to the teen tune, now you're
in the mood, looking and feeling so good.
Say, from those car's and phones money sure ain't much
trouble this world's such fun luck's crown they own and
as day and night yeah they're both meant for living,
making plans a pretty nice non-stop 24 hr late show.

J. Sirghoyd Dubarry

Superstarved

I have lived the life of luxury and never was ashamed
Never hesitated even once to consummate my fame
I'm a superstar in Hollywood known all over the nation
But tonight I'm going to call it quits and take a long vacation.

I need something more to satisfy me - this is not enough
I'm so hungry for a better life and maybe even love
I know all my life is spent in metaphors of happiness
But I'm empty on the inside and I can't handle the stress.

If I died tonight
I never would have even lived at all
I just play the parts they pay me for
This life seems oh so small.

Will there ever be an answer
To the thoughts that plague my mind?
I keep searching I'm still hoping
But I cannot seem to find.

Jason Paul Hill

A Symbol Of Birds

Death had reached my friend. We had planned to visit again
but her time had come to an end, alas.
So we planned her memorial mass
for a wonderful woman gone, of whom so many were fond.
With her we had a special bond.
As we read of her virtuous day
in her home parish place, two birds flew in that way;
in harmony with our commemoration,
to the wonder of the congregation,
The soloist halted her sweet song.
But the birds had still not gone . . .
The priest continued his oration and lo and behold
one bird lit upon her coffin amid flowers at her feet.
It was shocking yet touching, really quite a feat
unlikely to repeat.
There it joined us in song, unusual but nothing wrong
Cecile loved life and nature.
This seemed a symbolic gesture.
We saw such a gift of love
sent to us from above.
Carmel Despins-Klassen

My New Found Love

When nights are sleepless and days drag on,
I wonder where the hours have gone.
It isn't hard to figure what has happened to me,
cause a special gal has become my lady.
There's much to say about her beautiful smile
that keeps me closer all the while.
Her skin is as soft as new fallen snow.
Her eyes meet mine, and I'm all aglow.
Her lips tell me just how she feels.
When kissing mine, they set me on my heels.
With musical talents that have no end,
I felt very special just to be her friend.
But the friendship has grown to something much more.
She's become the lover that I adore.
Soon she will become my loving wife,
and we can start a brand new life.
A truer love I've never known.
That's why I want her to be my own.
Church bells will ring to express our joy.
With God's help we'll be as girl and boy.
William R. Leimkuhler

Firemen

I'm gonna be a fireman, he said as he danced around with glee
Those big red trucks and uniforms were made for me
I want to save that house or barn
Or just be there to help when someone turns on the alarm
Little fellow now but he'll probably be
Because that's something that stays with a boy you see
All grown up and marching with the band
Listening to the judge from the grandstand
Having a chicken barbecue to raise funds
Or dancing with your lady at a square dance for fun
Yet when those red trucks have to roll
You wonder and wait not knowing what may be the toll
As brave men band together to win a fight
Against wind, electric, gas and fumes far into the night
Or hold back their emotions as a neighbor's house burns
Never knowing when it may be their turn
It's one of those jobs that has to be done
Thank goodness for little boys, who men have become
Faith Sherman

The Cherry Tree

Can computers grow a cherry
Or all other kids of berry?
Can all the answers in a chip
Give a refreshing ocean dip?

I marvel at the cherry tree
First comes the bloom for all to see;
Then the cherry with crimson tone
Quickly appears with inner stone.

Nature, with all its magic ways
Still takes first place for loudest praise;
And all the works that humans do
Must give to nature credit due.

The flowing stream and forest green,
The sunrise and the sunset scene,
The waves that break upon the shore
Shows our short life holds much, much more.

And I, in my old fashioned mood
Still keep going on nature's food.
Computers answer in a blink —
But will we lose our power to think?
Edward W. Britt

The Way Up

Step by step, is the way to go
Start from the bottom
And work your way to the top.

Set yourself a goal, you ever know
You may get lucky and score a goal.

Life is full of ups and downs
Not knowing which way to fall.
The grass is always greener on
The other side.

For sure someone is looking
To see how green your grass is.

To make the grass grow
You have to look after it
Treat it well, it will respond to you.

It's strange how we can relate
To something we take for granted
It can still die just like we do

Believe in yourself, and things around you
In the end you'll see the top.
The only way is up.
Amanda Evans

A Mother's Prayer To My Children

I can't begin to tell you
How much you mean to me
And just how proud I am
To have you for my family

The road of life's been rocky
Many wrong turns I did take
If I could do it over
Lots of changes I would make

But each and every one of you
Has made my life so blessed
That joy I'll keep within my heart
When I am laid to rest

Don't ever doubt my love for you
Though sometimes I don't call
I'll write this little poem for you
To hang upon your wall

And when you stop to read it
You'll know that I am near
And that I hold you in my heart
To me you're all so dear
   Wanda Rowland

Weather Report

For long months now a silence deep
Has hung upon the morning air,
The birch bough has been cold and bare
Save when the heathen starlings keep
A sanctimonious meeting there
Outside the window where I sleep.

My senses, winter sere and numb,
Have grown resigned, I quite forgot
In snow-strewn field and mud-choked plot,
That dawdling spring would ever come.
I'd slept this morning like as not,
Had I not heard spring's woodwinds hum.

I woke to those first gentle notes
The birch bough wafted on my dream,
Then with the sun's swift warming beam
Spring's choristers in Easter coats
Spilled through my window stream on stream
Glad music from a thousand throats!

I reached the window on the run
While heartbeats snapped their winter ties,
And there before my wond'ring eyes,
A tapestry by magic spun
Spring laid and with a sweet surprise
I smile back at the smiling sun!
   Frank MacGregor Caswell

Where?

Where are people rushing
Eating like an upright squirrel gnawing a nut
Whose shiny tiny eyes are already busy
Searching for another nuts?

Where are people going
Running like a tense car racer staring the front
With fiery eyes, and
Pressing the accelerator with all their energy?

What are people doing
In the cell of monstrous buildings
Making their faces like a pale blue ghost's
Coming out from a shadowy tombstone?

Why are people in a hurry
Climbing the mountain like a combat soldier
Whose mission is only to occupy the peak?

Where are people rushing
Without having time to enjoy
The emerald sky, the green trees, and the conversation
With a good friend over a cup of hot coffee?

Is that a so-called advanced modern life?
   Ok-Gyung Kim

Lucid

On a rainy rainy Saturday
In a car driving, I
The sense of me
Became it all
Time and space and Jane and Bill and this and that and
War and peace and light and dark and music and flowers
Noah's Ark and all to come
Existed in my familiar ever present sense of I
Unburdened by my temple walls
Untethered, weightless, infinite, completely free
Of person, of role, place or thought, friend or no
Lights, no bells, no love, no bliss, no emotion
No human state or sense
Solely and wholly Conscious I became
Conscious . . .
And conscious of Conscious . . .
While Conscious . . .
   Ginger Y. Covalt

Running With A Shadow

With eyes closed and palms froze,
   I look as though I've seen a ghost.
   As I run through dark towers
   of green.

A shaggy, black-eyed beast,
   screaming at me in unfamiliar
   voice.

He sounds his mournful howls of animosity;
   as I am pale; so once was he.

He screams and cries and softly sighs.
Running between towers that break but don't bend.
Running with a shadow, that never seems to end.
   Mykel Wiseman

When Summer's Over

Sitting in the swing one day, I looked around
Everywhere I looked, not a soul was to be found
Nobody is in the tree house
No one is in the pool
No one is on the trampoline
They've all gone back to school
Up early each morning with a little fuss
Better hurry up or you're gonna miss the bus
Grab a glass of milk and a bite to eat
No time for eggs and bacon, just something sweet
You study hard, late into the night
The answers, you hope they are right
You have a teacher, one that's quite concerned
Explaining your lessons, hoping they get learned
To get along in life you must be really smart
School is the place, where you get your start
So no one is in the tree house
And no one is in the pool
Better study long and hard
If you don't want to be a fool

Donald H. Elfreich

Changes In Me

Change what's inside of me, so that others may see,
That I am living for thee.
Change my mind and way of thought,
Then I will realize that the answers were always there,
That I have so often sought.

Change my eyes and the way that I view others,
Then I will know that I have no opinion,
Other than that of myself,
And if I concentrate on changing me,
Then there is no opinion left.

Change my heart,
Fill it with forgiveness for my enemies,
Yet . . . I am thankful,
For they keep me on my knees.

Change my walk,
Although, I could never fill your shoes,
But walk closely beside you,
With hope that your light will shine through.

Mold me into what you would have me to be,
I am less than perfect, change all of me.

Jeanette Thomas-House

Home Journey

There are no dark corners in this house
As my soul seeks its familiar reverie of peace
The face of your memory kisses my heart
With the setting of an early winter sun
Oh, who is it that I cry out to in the dark
When only the lightness of love surrounds me
At moonrise comforting is the wordless grace
Encompassing my eerie breath
Who art thou who art me?
Even my cat meows knowing by whom it is loved
The intelligence of the growing leaf leaves me with one truth
I am of the life which has made me so self evident
Who can dispute the beauty of this?

Georgia Kathleen Connor

Thoughts On My Eightieth Birthday

The years pass swiftly
As a bird in flight,
The Seasons come and go,
Day follows night.

Time has a way
Of healing all our pain,
Sad memories fade,
Only the good remain.

Small miracles unfold
Each day for me,
A flower blooms,
A bird sings in the tree.

Pleasure in household tasks
I still perform,
The smell of baking bread,
Fragrant and warm.

Blessings abound, and
Like a song unsung,
Somewhere inside
We are forever young.

Joyce V. Coles

Mary's Little Lamb

Mary's Little Lamb was born
One night a long time ago
What we didn't know about the Lord
The Lamb was sure to know.
Mary gave birth to her Little Lamb
Under a star so bright
And the glory of the Lord shone 'round
The lowly cave that night
Mary's Little Lamb,
A King someday He'd be.
To reign over all the earth,
Especially you and me.
Mary had a Little Lamb,
Not knowing the extent of His fame
How everyone, for years to come,
Would somehow know His name.
Mary had a Little Lamb
Our first Christmas night
So He could come into the world
And be our Guiding Light.

Heather Sullivan

Thank You Mark

Thank you Mark for all you've done
You have made my life a special one
I can never picture you not there
because I know you will always care
I feel so blessed with you by my side
My love for you will never subside
You are the only one for me and
I hope together we will always be
You're constantly there to see me through
There wasn't a time I couldn't find you
You found the key to my heart and
now life has a fresh new start
So thank you Mark for being you
You really are a dream come true

Gina M. Costa

Memories of My Younger Days

The sun is hot,
the grass is warm upon my back,
as I watch the fleecy clouds
drift across the azure sky and
I dream.

The water is crystal clear
as it ripples over the gravel bottom and
along the grassy banks.
The trout are hungry and rise to my fly.
"What a joy!"

It is July,
the water in the old swimming hole is warm,
we frolic in the pool and
bask in the mid-day sun.
"What happy days!"

We are newly married,
we wander through the woods,
across the fields and along the brook,
then lie together in a sunlit glade.
"What wonderful memories!"

George M. Blakney

Christel Sweet Sixteen

You wouldn't believe how thrilled
I was when you said you'd stay
So many years it seemed since
you were taken away
A chance at last to be close
I waited for so long ago in old Sweden

Please know have much I've missed
you Christel
And how you are dearly loved
I have not been able to live near

With my other family here

But in my heart I love
I've always been near

Love always
Mommy

C. Loraine Judge Young

Lost and Found

Searching for mail,
I found none.
I came across an almost
empty vial of coke instead.
It reminded me so much of you.
Out of place, among all my
childhood memories.
Only a few remained,
just a few, of course.
Those particles of the white fool
still inside the vial-trapped
and clinging,
helplessly to the inside of the glass.
Again, a memory of you flashed by.
A white fool.
Always the fool.
Still trapped and clinging.

Rhonda K. Baughman

Taylor Ansley

Taylor Ansley, my little one,
Taupe hair glistening in the sun,

Peaceful in the arms of your nursing mother,
Laughing at the antics of your brother,

Your father dancing you to sleep,
Your brother whispering secrets to keep,

Determination bursting into rage,
Fascination with each new discovery and sound you make,

The reflection grows clearer day by day,
In your actions, in your ways,

A beautiful princess to be crowned,
A brilliant mind, world renowned,

The dreams I have left unfilled,
I leave for you to build.

Beverly Vigil

Looking Through The Hour Glass

Looking through the hour glass, I see a broken
mixed up past, and from this view it can be seen, a
peaceful untouched field of green

In these years of human range, the earth and life
Have gone through change, things have been that
never should, and we've done things we never could

Past cliches a present lie, for I have seen a true love
die, elder wisdom plead and cry, to change our path,
why do they try?

They left a path too long ago, have we learned what
they don't know? Are we on the trodden path?
So will we face our Mother's wrath?

Ahead the answer soon may lie, our doom could meet
us eye to eye

Unless we hold the future rest, if we postpone the
knowledge quest, turn back the page where it began,
we flip the piece, reset the sand, the answer missed us
at the past, I found it through the hour glass.

Byran Puls

The Labyrinthine Brain

The brain, and all we know of it; is to many,
to you and I, so much the wonder that it is,
for all purposes of discussion, self-contained,
a separate unit, uninhibited, extroverted,
but different and unique to each in many ways.
From what we can discover, it can do miracles, almost;
for we have known that it is like the brain to think
before the body has the chance to act, and react—all
responses to any form of stimulation, from sunshine to
coffee, is a good enough reason for action, and to put on
the thinking cap and to love nature. But, from what we know,
kept secreted in the mind, to what we aren't sure of: the
relationship of emotion and thought, or the cause of love and
fear: it is the mind/heart connection that stays strong.
The labyrinthine brain: the chances to be what we like, even as
the emotions are the gears of how we feel, to tell it the way that
I see it does feel good. From all of the ability we have to have,
there are but the spaces and places left to discover, to begin
to change the world around, for the better.

Robert L. Cassidy

Rhodesia? — Before Heaven's Retire?

There's never been a question
  as to "what" I was to be;
It seems my family saw a nurse
  when I was only two or three.

Thus so — through natural manner,
  and raised in Christian ways —
I fell right in with what they'd seen, and
  became that nurse of prediction days.

Through many years, a cherished dream
  kept beating in my heart; —
But through life's circumstances
  there was naught to fan the spark.

A medical missionary I'd hoped for some day —
  but guessed no more 'twould be . . .
And I settled down to raising my boys —
  This "mission field" enough for me!

But now, at this late date of my life,
  God's picked up that dormant desire —
And wrapped in layers of blessings . . .
  Asks, "Rhodesia? — before Heaven's retire"?

Mildred L. Goldthwaite

His Name Was Whitey

Dedicated to a friend
    Ya know — He used to catch
      grapes in his mouth
A beautiful black mouth;
Shy and innocent
    He loved us — I loved him;
    Now nothing I say can help
I could tell you more but why must I?
    · I held him as an infant
    · His first snow encounter was a laugh
    · He died in an instant — careless, car-i-cide act
I'm so, so sorry — you didn't need to die;
But you and I had a great ride

Clement A. Skirpan

The Old House Analogy

Many of us are like an old house...
tired, weary and weather worn,
  like an old house, that has sustained heavy storm,
    in the living room a supportive wall has been
      torn away, moving to another part of the
        old house, in the bedroom, apart of the
          ceiling and roof are missing, torn/
            blown away by the raging storm...

Can an Old House be repaired? Some can, others, cannot...
  You renovate an old house, slowly and by removing all
    the damage you can without further compromising its
    structure....you get rid of all the debris,
      then you plan and start the rebuilding
        process, putting in new and better things....

Can damaged storm lives be made new?
  Absolutely, by getting rid of All of the old mess...
    and putting in new and better things and
      by a people's heart and mind willing
      and ready to do their part,
        then an old house will be restored.

B. H. Frey

So Smile!

A smile will always win the day,

So never mind what others say;
Make others happy, in grand style,
In giving them a lovely smile,
Love does it all in full details,
Encourages the one that fails;

With tenderness repair the rift.
Instill in them that lovely gift,
Love, that gracious impetus,
Love that freely flows from us.

Will fill their hearts with tenderness,
In helping others in distress,
Never mind the ups and downs.

Smiles are ups, and frowns are downs;
On and on with constant flow.

Smiling onward as you go,
Making every moment count;
In climbing upward to the mount,
Love will plant a memory,
Ever smiling, a smile is the key.

Maurice A. Mallory

Silhouette

I saw the Eagle
Silhouetted against the morning sky
A sentinel exuding power and respect
Oblivious to life around
Unmoved by human presence

Below lay a carnage
Abandoned bodies of ocean life
Barnacled stones lay glassy eyed
Starring nowhere in raped stupor

As eagle eyed and visionary
This majestic creature
Proclaimed its presence in silence
It looked at me as if I too
Was part of the carnage below

God had made the one as the other
Death without life
As life without death
Seems so meaningless

Jacob Eric Dyck

You Were There

Today I asked if You were there,
You shook the earth . . .
It snowed, it rained, and the sun shone.

Today I asked if You heard my prayer,
You brought me people to love and to share.

Today I asked if You would speak to me,
The birds sang of Your glory,
Creation shouted Your praise,
I heard You in the silence.

Today I asked if You were there,
There came no answer,
But Your Love.

Jane Unsworth

Gee Mom, I'm Glad You're Home

Mommy, Mommy, you've come back!
O gee I'm glad you're home!
D'you know it snowed all night last night
and covered all the ground?

I got up in the dark to see
how everything gets white;
Dad came and put me back to bed
And said to sleep 'til light.

Tip chased a squirrel and teased the cat
Sue took me for a walk;
I prayed last night you'd come today,
So we could sit and talk.

I like the weekends without school
There's so much things for fun;
But this weekend was kind of sad . . .
Gee Mom, I'd glad you're home.

Esther Crandall

In A Hundred Years . . .

In a hundred years no one will care
    What troubles us today.
In a hundred year, not you nor I
    Will have one word to say!
Friends and enemies, rich and poor,
    Will be reduced to dust;
Their houses crumbled, tumbled down,
    And cars long turned to rust;
Our hard-earned money dwindled away
    To dross in strangers' hands;
And offspring blown like thistledown
    To settle in distant lands.
Time soothes the passage of all things,
    Of spirit, heart and mind;
Yet others will inherit problems
    We must leave behind.
In a hundred years this restless Earth
    Like a child's top still will spin;
And her children still play tug-of-war
    With Innocence and Sin.

Valerie J. Palmer

Frailty

Dark and cold, before the dawn,
Eyes see across a frozen land,
Giving testament, and truth
To the frailty of man.

Natural things, upon this scene
Need no computered heat,
No sweater on their backs,
Or slippers on their feet.

Sleeping forest, trees don't care.
Their slumber is their underwear.
Grieve they, though, for their lost friends.
That made homes for man to dwell.

Man, you see, cannot survive.
In his natural form.
The elements would take away
Each and every man today.

Richard K. Doey

A Sensing Of Nature

    Come ye, oh whispering winds, even like
unto times ancient, for your fragrance gives
life, for all to breathe, even so, for those after me.
    And come, oh mighty sun, ruler from on
high, for your power is light and of never knowing
darkness, and to give life, beauty, for all eyes to see.
    And listen, for the birds do sing, alive with
harmony and flights of majesty, pray always,
that no man will ever fall deaf, to the magic in our skies.
    And from the heavens, comes rain, so drink
ol' dry earth, to nourish your rivers, even so as
to quench man from dust, lest he drinks not, and dies.
    So carry on, oh sacred mother, for in your
nature lies mysteries, for feeble man is weak
and has no answers, for he only knows what he
can touch, and only then, does he feel.
    We must realize, nature is burdened, almost
to her end, so take heed and have wisdom,
to pray our senses won't pass and
understand, together, we all have the power to heal.

Ernie Bell Jr.

The Shoe

Wading in the ocean one day,
The tide came in and took it away.
The plastic sandals she so loved to wear,
Were no longer a complete pair.
Packing in haste, there is only one more,
Her too small dress shoes to the funeral she wore.
Though crying and frantic, their search in vain,
The trio returned, Michelle in much pain.
Not from the sun, the surf, or the sand,
Nor for the sad time at hand.
Not for the tangles in her long brown hair,
But for the shoe she could no longer wear.
To calm her fears and dry her tears,
These words I said to her tiny ears.
I can buy another shoe,
I can't buy another you.

Mary Linda Ellis Donley

Russian Poets

Russian poetry Maiakovskii, Mandelshtam also Pasternak
Yevtushenko too very powerful poets so charismatic
Russian Revolution Reds and Whites
Reconstruction, revitalization
Repression follows—decrees, KGB stress suicides Maiakovski
Sclerotic Stalin Frowns on Zhivago's Pasternak
Who then chides iconic Mandelshtam
"You now got an apartment now you can write."
Mandelshtam's Ode to Stalin fails to melt the man of steel
Jewish writers, Jewish doctors cultural genocide
Luminous Mandelshtam one of century's finest poets
Exiled, tortured in Siberian gulag Younger Yevtushenko's
Elegiac memorial poem: "No monument stands over Babii Yar
A drop sheer as a crude gravestone I am afraid
    Today I am as old in years
As all the Jewish people now I seem to be a Jew."

    A monument was erected.

Sacred and moral—
    Power of poets survive
      In boundless archives.

Ben Siegel

The Ride

The pat of the wipers make a cheerful song
As in the rain you go riding along
And in the twilight so quiet and still
You get a feeling of hope, peace and goodwill.

The sway of the car as it rounds the curve
Seems to rock and soothe your nerves
And the thrill of wandering what's over the next hill
Would it be an angry town or one of goodwill.

How long to live and how soon to die
You wonder if you really care why;
Because in an insignificant normal day
One million lives can pass away.

Born to live and yet you die
The tears of the soul are a soundless cry.
The cycle of life is an endless chain
Set in the cry of the nights lonely refrain.

Robert H. Goode

Voices In The Dark

   I hear voices in the dark,
And I daydream in class . . .
   So tell me dear friend whose
At the impasse, the words of this
Rhyme may not make much sense,
But if you look close you'll see
Through my mask.
   The mask that is there to keep
Out all eyes, that would pry into what's
Hiding deep down in side, where no one
Can go, not even myself.
   Who knows what it is that hiding
Down there. Is it my darkness, my hate,
And my spite? Is it my dreams, my hopes,
And delight? Is it a part of me that never comes
Out or is it the part that's writing this now?

Shaina Hansen Edmondson

Lonely Dove's Cry

For the twilight of life is upon me.
Alone, I sit motionless by the window and
   Stare at raindrops that dance like tiny
Ballerinas on the pavement below.

Oh, oh, how my heart aches to run from this
   Room; to run barefoot through the rain;
To run free.

My eyes look in earnest toward the heavens.
The hour, totally unknown to me, has been
   Betrayed by the sun falling off the horizon.

As the room darkens
My pillow beckons me to sleep, sleep
   An opportunity removed from the face of
   Reality, will sustain my sanity.
A sweet sleep, I pray, will open the doors to
   A place where the impossible becomes
   Possible

The rain has stopped.
Silence prevails.
I close my eyes, freedom is at hand.

G. Frances Duffy

Fred, A Tabby Cat

He gazes at his own reflection
Much longer than modesty allows,
Looking into his eyes with wonder
Was he Narcissus I inquired,
Seeing into his own dreamy pools of vision
Beautiful he may be, but not Adonis
Although he thought Venus had beckoned him

The head turns and he regards himself
From a different attitude,
Then moved his head to stare at me,
Disdainfully as though I were beneath thought.

Is he distressed that I caused him
To lose his masculinity?
Later, I ask him as we meet in the garden
Walking between the lilac lanterns where,
We speak, I ask the questions he answers
In a throaty, reassuring tone
And we are at peace among blossoms.

Rose Mary Hooper

The Gift

It hid in me, like a mountain pond
Silent, still and deep.
Many years flew, so much to do,
And still this pool did sleep.

I felt it there, and knew somewhere;
I'd let the floodgate free,
And never dam it up again,
Although it may drown me.

One magic day, (it was in May),
With brush and palette in hand
I began to dabble and dab away,
To paint this beautiful land.

I could not eat, nor could I sleep;
With the surging power free;
To touch, to taste, to feel its flow;
Inundated, me.

Like a luminous kiss, of radiant bliss,
I'm being born, anew
Cascading visions stream through me,
And I share this joy with you.

Terry Lee Erickson

Prayer

An assembly of body, mind and spirit
we in prayer can achieve
faith grounded in knowledge
ask and we shall receive.

A journey of our soul to grace
supplying power in our daily lives
but prayer must become a habit
the most powerful energy one can make.

No prayer ever goes unanswered
God speak to us throughout the day
we can pray everywhere
no definite time, place or way.

Olivia Carpenter-Gibson

The Snowstorm

Cold and damp,
Close and binding,
Winter folds
About us winding,
Looking soft,
And landing lighter,
Making all
About us whiter.

'Neath the white
The edge is sharp.
The wind is strong
Enough to warp
The landscape,
Leaving all in chaos,
Evincing not
But sense of loss.

Elva Haggarty

What Did It Cost?

What was the price of the Dogwood tree,
From which they made the cross?
I could not find a "bill of sale,"
Stating what that tree had cost.

The nails that were driven in His hands,
What did they pay for those?
And the spears that pierced His precious side
Was not free, I don't suppose.

What about the crown of thorns He wore?
It was not a gift, given free.
They pressed it down upon His brow
And He bore it, for you and me.

I can't imagine the price of a tomb,
That wasn't His to occupy,
But what a price He paid for us
As He, the Lamb, had to die.

If dollars and cents could pay for His love,
If money could set you free;
What would you give, just to hear Him say,
"Dear child, Come unto me?"

Bessa McKaye

Mary

Mary is my girlfriend
My girlfriend of yore
She has a nice fur coat
I just don't see her anymore
She did not like my style
It was too self confident
Now I'm being stalked so to speak
By another Mary
Who waits on us here she is nice and pudgy
And I was always nice to her
I'm still nice to her
But I'd prefer to be calling the tune
And now maybe that's what I'm doing
And what is this Mary doing?
She rang me up one night
And I thought it was the older Mary
So I gave her the old oh, hello — Mary
And that got things under way
And now things are all in order.

Deamus Kelly

Visions Delight

In the sleepy, misty, charred darkness,
there appeared a flickering light.
Looking like God's lovely angel,
with fluttering wings and halo bright.

Overlooking the rippling lake,
sparkling diamonds in the night.
With images of gemstone's reflections,
creating brilliant colors of glorious sight.

The pale yellow moon peeked through the horizon,
casting warm shadows of great delight.
With rainbows of glittering colors,
red, blue, orange, yellow, purple not white.

In the picturesque distance lingered,
honking sounds of Canadian geese in flight.
Flying against the blistering wind,
and gaining endless feet of heights.

Rosie Scharschmidt

Mirrored Image

She stands apart, clutching at her neckline
amidst the seven she bore, and the farmer she wed.
I smile faintly at my reflection, flickering in her auburn eyes,
and the mimicry of my motions, so in time with hers.
There's a fragile purpose to our unwilled walls
that needy fingers cannot grasp, nor deep sorrows demean.

Her grace strikes me across childhood,
bearing down upon me as I suffer the unstilled room;
loud again with raised voices.
The old house, and a mother's heart
familiared by the fullness . . . Yet strayed
by inner sanctums so few are privy to.

It is an age old song; the melody of mothers and daughters.
We dance with naked movements
to symmetry, now made legacy.

My nervous hands flutter gracefully;
a sparrow's wings stirred with a kindred glance.
The mystery of my birth stands beside me,
staring back at me;
hiding shyly . . . yet perversely revealed.

Kelly Carrick

A Fever In The Heart

The heart, the main flagship of every human being,
having the power in moving you from here to eternity.
The commander's voice nicely heard, but unable to be seen,
a command of love, keeping us in complete unity.

An orchestrated and loving vessel beating on request,
giving generously and always willing to share with the rest.
A sweetheart, a heartthrob, and a charmer's 'tis often called,
at peace with a happy spirit, it sincerely cares for all.

A truthful portrait beaming with absolutely no hate,
forever lightning His footsteps towards the pearly gates.
In the end you win as it has always truly shown,
where life begins anew in our newly prepared home.

Paul J. Rheaume

Mother

You are like a ruby, so shiny and bright
You are like a star that shines in the night.
You are like a rose, without any thorns,
You are like the sunshine after it storms.
You are like an angel but without the wings,
And your words of wisdom have taught me many things.
You are a great teacher, wife and guide, and I
know it's because you have Jesus by your side.
You're a great housekeeper, mother and friend
and my love for you will never, never end,
You are one of a kind, a true diamond for sure
through all of life's troubles you have stood strong, you endure.
You are a blessing sent from above,
you're also as gentle and mild as a dove.
There's no one anywhere who could take your place,
with that kind, understanding look that is always upon your face.
You are beautiful, sweet and rare, and
I thank God, through your example you've taught me to trust in prayer.
   Lisa Ann Panzino-DiNunzio

With Me

Weary, but not torn,
By His love, I am ever drawn.

When I feel defeated, disappointed even misunderstood,
Why can't I see that in this there is good?

Although endless nights I cry, I know He loves me,
With me, He said He will always be.

Through tribulations my faith is sometimes shaken,
When I feel so all alone, I know I am not forsaken.

Shattered, but not broken,
At times, my tears have no end.

Through tired eyes, I no longer see,
With me, He said He will always be.

As I rejoice as victory is met,
I know there is greater yet.

Above my circumstances, I rise,
I soar above obstacles, without compromise.

Through His triumphs, I am free,
With me, He said He will always be.
   Angela Ragin-McNeil

What Therapy Has Done For Me

I fly thru the air on gossamer wings
I float free and easy my whole being sings
why oh why did I wait so long
maybe before I couldn't be strong
I'm free - I'm so free
I hear the universe whisper to me
my child, my dear, my wonderful one
look at the sun - see all the stars
you're up there too - past Venus and Mars
I say to myself - what does all this mean
It means you are free to pursue all your dreams
you finally are yourself
your destiny is fulfilled
   Judy Teubert

One Plus One

Warm, languid days
by the hazy sea,
Curved fishes
served for me.
Walnut trees giving
restful shade.
Spirit one, yet not
amazed.

Gentle mountains, friendly seas,
Two and one or is it threes?
Blue carpeted earth
through flowers breathes.
And cold castle walls
echo enlightened years.

Autumn mists and
the spirit fades.
But through passing time
the song pervades.
One plus one
is surely two.
But now I am a part of you.
   Moira Fraser Juliebo

Clay Pots

You remind me
of clay pots
pretty to look at
appearing substantial
empty

Everything relating to you
is a clay pot
large ones, small ones
each relationship a clay pot
empty

Our relationship
is a broken clay pot
nothing to hold it together
never filled
empty

A life full
of clay pots
life blood of love
never touching them
empty
   Heather Vis

My Dream Ship

A fearful dream came welling up.
It took me for a ride.
A sail upon a clipper ship
across the rolling tide.
I looked down on the waves below
in panic and despair,
they rolled and tossed, and gnashed their teeth, where'd end this bleak nightmare?
Then calm at last the ocean grew
and golden shone the light.
My dreadful fear had disappeared
lost cargo in the night.
   Vernelia B. Jobe

Origin

What is there to love
In this harsh and bitter life?
How can one drink from the Fountain of
Youth
If one grows weary
Before finding the Untrammeled Truth?

Will not the ancient, pristine place
Be found in Holy Artistry,
Brushed upon the morning light,
Pale hush of eve,
Lavender wings in flight?

One may spend a lifetime
Enmeshed in a frail embrace.
Dewdrops sing sweet harmonies,
Yet the Symphony of Grace
Pervades all centuries.

When at last beholding life
With a quietly awe struck heart,
We tap the source of all activity,
Ever old yet ever new, its origin abiding:
Exquisite Calm in God's Tranquility!

Susan F. Rose

Swampnight

Ghostly tendrils of shifting fog
  Embrace the night of land and bog
Silent wings dart to and fro
  Seeking prey in faint moons glow
Distant lightening dances round
  Signals reaching, cloud to ground
Silken web of woven might
  Holds intruders deadly tight
Rustling fronds in the breeze
  Hiding bullfrogs on their knees
Rippling water, oh so slight
  Swims the croc, in all his might
On horizon dawn comes creeping
  Slowly, yet surely, as all lay sleeping
Stealing, stealing — just over the top
  Then suddenly!
    Springing!
With visual delight!
  Repelling the remnants
Of shadowy night.

Steve D. Maney

The Sea

The sea shows no fear
When the tempests arise,
Nor does it shiver when
The icy storms near.

It does not know when
Men live or men die,
Nor does it quiver when
Evil men lie in a watery grave.

Nature goes its own way,
Unknowing and uncaring,
Blind to the coming and the going
Of time or men's lives.

Yolande Bullock

A Cry For Love

Money is the root of all evil, you say
Nonsense! Say I - its lack of love
Behind our friendly mask is hidden
Our anger and our jealousy.

Those planes that crashed - the floods that came
Earthquakes - tornados - hurricanes
Ships that sank and trains derailed
Battered wives and rapists reigned
   Was volcanic hate erupting.

Hatred is a cry for love without which we'll expire
If we only have love, chaos would cease
No suicide - no murders - no disease increase.

If the fuss we make over a crumb on a table
A hole in a stocking or the price of sable
Could be truly made over the lonely and depressed
Reaching out in kindness - caring - and sympathy
Trying to understand each other's plight and misery
Love would travel from sea to sea
   The whole world needs a cry for Love.

Maureen Fitzpatrick

Rainbow Child

   Rainbows come after a stormy day, when
one's hopes have gone astray . . .
   But God gave me a Rainbow Bright before
the storms were ever in sight . . . He didn't
wait till I was tossed in fear to enjoy my
Granddaughter dear!
   Her Bright Blue eyes as fair as the sky
and lovely Red Hair like Molten fire . . .
Sometimes so meek in her Childish Charm,
gives me strength from all Life's storms . . .
   Never a Rainbow after a storm has passed,
could be more beautiful than her cheerful laugh . . .
She's unpredictable just like the weather, which
makes me love her all the better!!
   My child like the Rainbow shall fade
someday but the memories of her are in my
heart to stay . . .

Ruth E. Light

A Change Of Season

Tall and long, mighty and mean
She froze in horror at such a scene

It was an accident she couldn't explain
It just sort of happened, "You're a Killer!" they proclaimed

The knife dropped, she couldn't remember
Just how he died that day in December

They zipped him up, drove her away
His life taken from him like hers on her 1st birthday

The case was clean cut, she was guilty and scared
For she paid her due for being a pair

They let her go for obvious reasons
It was his time to die, like the change of a season

She bid a thank you for breaking the chain
Her childhood memories now healed - no more pain

Diana L. Sir Louis

Pour La Femme Latine Qui J'aime

You look upset, sad,
you think you are going insane, mad,
you are upset with your lover,
and you miss ardently your dad.

Many years ago he protected you,
and nobody dared to touch you,
your feelings candidly rejected that too,
but the safety valve, again, nested you.

Now he is gone, and you feel free, vulnerable,
he taught you well; you don't like men that look at you desirable,
you don't like to feel you are the main dish at the table,
you want your dad again with you, to keep alive the fable.

Your dad protected you, and damaged your mind,
because to him, you were close to God,
and no man was worth a dime,
because he knew you were weak, and men will use you;
and toss you in a nick of time.

Now, in your forties, you must grow,
you must fulfill all your life and grow tall,
you no longer can't deny your desires in the dance ball,
you like to look a million, sexy, happy woman,
and your dad is gone!
Oscar Chao

A Smile

Your mischievous, chaotic grin tells the world
Just who you are.
Keep relying on that smile
That doesn't take you very far.

Another cycle of lies with all the trouble it buys
Leads you to that place you despise.
The place where hope is lost
From all the people you've crossed.
A place you long to be
The place you'll never find me.

I flee from your face
From your life of disgrace.
All the things you've done
You can never erase.

But still there's that grin, that back-stabbing grin
It makes you so happy to live in your sin.
That black, twisted smile
In the world you defile
Will keep you trapped in a web of denial.
Deny all you want but you know it's true,
There will be another as worthless as you.
Jake Trimm

Golden Streets And Heaven's Shore

Her little hands were wrinkled, her hair had begun to gray.
Gone were the times she worked in her kitchen all day.
The sparkle in her eyes was no longer there.
Only memories remained of the laughter we once shared.
Sometime long ago her age began to show.
Then on Sunday morning God softly said, "It's time to go."
He needed a special angel - He chose my beautiful Mother
To go to a place that compares to no other.
And He promised she would suffer no more
For now she walks golden streets and Heaven's shore.
Wanda H. Goff

Rite of Passage

A friend to the universe
Has now passed

Into the wind
A spirit is cast

With life and light
And intent gazes

Upon open trails
A brave man blazes

He peers
He listens
He hears a cry

A warrior is saying
'This is a good day to die.'
Theresa A. Drew

No Touching

Certain zealots have decreed
That touching is forbidden
"Verboten" is the encircling arm
And kissing must be hidden.

Thou shalt not touch a little child
Nor touch a female either,
No matter if they like the touch
You must touch neither.

The Sistine ceiling shows a touching
Sending forth a bolt of life,
And Jesus touched a prostitute
Blessing not just man and wife.

Touching comes with every species
Natural as every breath
Bonding every living being
A touch of life delaying death.
Harold Putnam

Castles Of Crystal

I dreamed of a day
not so long ago
Not so far away
I lived in a land
full of castles made
of crystal
I rode a white horse
of glistening white
While my long auburn
Hair, danced in the night
Across hills and valleys
The gravity was there
In search of a prince
my long-awaited knight.
Patricia Ann Rosemarie O'Hare

Catch A Fallen Star

Deep in a dream one night
   I ran with horses in evening glow.
We chased the stars as they fell
   making ribbons of shining light.

We raced over clouds of fluffy white,
   these magic horses and I
Stood in the moon's silver song,
   A beautiful vision so bright.

All night long we ran so bold
   until we came to the dawn;
prancing and pawing in morning mist
   my horses faded in pools of gold.

They disappeared one by one,
   stars on the wind they flew.
Sparkles and lights heaven bound,
   vanished when night was done.

These enchanted horses I long to see
   when shadows start to fall.
They'll come again in a dream
   knowing they'll run with me.

Carol Pfankucken

Father

Father's are wonderful people
   too little understood,
And we do not sing their praises
   as often as we should...
For, somehow, Father's seem to be
   the man who pays the bills,
While mother binds up little hurts
   and nurses all our ills..
And perhaps that is the reason
   we sometimes get the notion
That father's are not subject
   to the thing we call emotion,
But, if you look inside Dad's heart,
   where no one else can see,
You'll find he's sentimental
   and as soft as he can be....
And like our Heavenly Father,
   He's guardian and a guide,
Someone we can count on
   to be always on our side.

Cynthia Granger

In My Flower Garden

As I walk among the flowers,
The wondrous beauty unfolds,
of each and every petal,
that sets me all aglow.
The colors are so radiant,
Against the foliage green.
As I look upon the flowers,
Created by God above,
I know He made the flowers,
To symbolize His love.
So perfect are the details
Of each and every one,
that I thank the Lord above me,
For the wonders that He has done.

Mary Morris Parnell

Dog Days Of Adulthood

Into my mouth, I pour poison
I sometimes hate my life, I wish I could recreate it!
Let's get drunk and go for a ride
Ride like the wind, forget the rules of decency
Adulthood sometimes corrupts my sensibilities
Why do I still have to believe in fear?
I want to cry
Like a little boy left standing in the rain
Life is nothing but a crazy monkey's dream
Trapped, confused, hungry,
Every time when you're free of responsibility
Pain and anger taps you on your shoulder
Don't worry about being so numb,
It comes with the territory.
Oh to play kickball, just one more time!
I wish I was eight years old for just one more day
Good night little boy, hide under your blankets
Sweet dreams big man, Time to meet your destiny!

James Stoffel

A Day Of Wonder

For some reason, today, I feel good!
The way I should!
It's nothing for me to ponder,
or wonder,
it's just a day that I should honor!
I feel good about my accomplishments this week,
I realize that these days are rare!
Today I feel good, and not quiet and meek!
I don't even care if people stare!
Today is a day, I just don't have a care!
For some reason, I feel happy and satisfied!
Because I know it's a day that I have tried!
Today is a day I appreciate!
No matter what is my fate!

Paula Patterson-Stevenson

Speak To My Heart

Oh Lord, it is my prayer that You speak to my heart.
For without Your Grace in my life, I can't even start.
The things that I do on my own seem to fail.
But Your promise says to walk with You and prevail.
I started a business, promised to be a new trend.
But the world did not notice and my business did end.
So, I thought, get a job to put food on my table . . .
Even with this simple task, I just wasn't able.
It seems with all my trying my ends still never meet.
Oh Lord, speak to my heart. I'm admitting defeat.
What a turn of events, what incredible relief!
My trust lies in You and in You my belief.
It's been years now my Friend, with You guiding my life.
'Twas an end to my failure, my misery and strife.
Keep me strong by Your strength, and faithfully true.
On my own I am nothing, I can't do without You.
I know that You love me, this I know without thought.
My enemies You've beaten, my battles You've fought.
In my walk with You, Lord, I've had peace in my heart,
an answer to a prayer and a life with a start. Amen

Patrice Meyer

House By The Sea

The House by the Sea is where I want to be,
   Hearing only the sound of Ocean Waves crashing on the
   shore, where Love began once before.

How perfect it would be if we spent time together in the
   House by the Sea.

We could be free to rekindle the Love we once knew.
   Time has turned our Love cold.

Let not the glow of the fire and passion we once knew grow
   dim and leave us in despair,
   Let's not become victims of the trouble we share.

The House By The Sea is where we need to be,
   Where we first found Love and I knew you were right for me!

Let's go back to the House By The Sea where Love began for
   you and me.

     Harry E. Keller

Jesus Was There

I took a look behind me today.
What I saw was such a mess.
But Jesus was there with me all the way,
There was never a time Jesus missed.

When my heart was sad and aching.
I could go to Jesus in prayer.
When storm clouds where dark and stormy,
Jesus found ways to show His care.

Life has been lovely and hard at times.
God had no Rose Garden on His mind.
God only promised to go with us all the way,
With arms stretched out with love so kind.

I never could have made it this far.
Had I walked alone on the rough and stormy path.
I knew Jesus was always there beside me.
Arms outstretched protected me from Satan's wrath.

I'm looking up for Jesus is coming back.
I'll welcome Him, He's my best friend.
No more will I travel rough and stormy roads.
Jesus promised to be with me to the end.

     Harriet Plummer

Adolescence

He stands alone, bewildered at the conflict that he feels,
Not understanding why that this should be;
His deep desire to reach the stature of a man
At war with giving up a lad's security.
Reluctant to reject the carefree pleasures of a boy,
To put aside the happy hours he has known;
Yet he yearns for independence of a man,
The right to make decisions of his own.
I watch him, feeling fear and pride and joy,
The same emotions moms have had since time began,
And pray for all the wisdom and the strength required
To help my little boy become a man!

     Patricia Gustafson

I've Learned

All this time alone I've learned
can I please have one more turn

I can't breathe without you
I can't see without you

Everything's out of focus
please don't leave me alone and hopeless

I've always loved you
But realized how much when it was too late
I constantly cry about you
Let's start over 'cause I know we are fate

Let's stop being lonely
I know you still have feelings for me

We can rekindle the romance
But only if you give me a chance.

My love still burns
So believe me when I say I've learned.

     James Miscioscia

A Stranger

With the death of a loved one
Came the appearance of a stranger
To shelter and protect me.
With skin as soft as a marshmallow
Browned by a roasting fire,
With a voice as charming as a lark
Singing its song of praise,
With a face as honest as a child
Knowing not the concept of wrong,
And a heart as caring as the loved one
Gone to a better place,
This stranger came in from her world
And helped me through
The harsh realities of mine.
With the death of a loved one
Came a miracle
In the form of a stranger.
She said she had no name
Yet called herself my angel.

     Marie-Catheline Jean-Francois

The Troubadour

Troubadour by moonlight
A roving path she travels
She follows only a mind filled sight
And image she often ravels
With impressioned fright
From a time before castles
She struggles to enlighten
The mysterious baffle
With fiery pen she writes
Images without gavel
Poems of a soulful plight
Her heart heavy with gravel
A mind in full flight
A spectacular dazzle
For it was this night
She was born in lyrical jest
     . . . The Troubadour

     Kim C. Teachout

Shadows

Shadows in the moonlight
Shadows in the sunlight
Shadows are almost everywhere
Even on the thoroughfare.

Some shadows are big
and some are small
Some are short and some are tall.

Some shadows are on the floor
Some come in the door
Some shadows are dim and dreary
Others are clear and cheery.

Shadows are of two kinds
Those that are the result of light
and those which are of the mind.

Probably the best shadows are
Those which are in your mind and of the past
For these are the ones
That last and last and last.

When I look out a window many times it seems
I can see a past shadow.

R. Adams

My Beloved

If we had lived in days of yore,
   would thou have loved thee more?

Would thy heart have spoken
   words of love and passion,
expressed in a different fashion?

Oh! I long for thy loving caress,
   and thy head upon thy breast,
Thy tender kisses and loving arms,
   keeping thee safe from harm,

Thou pledged thy troth to thee,
   and man and wife were we,
Thy children followed numbering three
   a daughter and two sons resembling thee,

Our lives took on more meaning,
   as father and mother,
Sometimes overshadowing our love
   for one another,

Alas, those days didn't last,
   all too soon thy life passed,
Now I can only remember thee,
   and pray thou knowest I cherished thee.

Sandy "O"

Sometime

Come with me sometime when we can be,
So close that words become an excess thing.
Come then take my hand and we can watch
The stars slide through their lonely arcs.
We may be young then, our minds still quick
Our eyes alive to see our own two fates.
A thing that could not be, and now to late?
The skin wrinkled on your outstretched hand,
As on mine, so now we find
The years of difference dissolved,
And still your kiss is sweet

Edward A. Ellis Jr.

Have Faith, God Knows

I do not know what tomorrow may bring
   Nor, beyond today's thoughts may ring.
I do not know everything about love,
   Nor, to understand everything above.

I do not know what pleasure or pain,
   Nor, the falling of sunshine or rain.
I do not know if I shall be wise,
   Nor, may be tomorrow, I'll rise.
I do not know every great thing,
   Nor, every secret to know.

I do not know, if I should rejoice on the work that is done,
   Nor, to know that I have won.
I do not know the breathe of life which gives you power,
   Nor the lovely flowers.

I Do Know, having faith in God, He will prevail,
   While remembering God's word, that he will never fail.

I Do Know, you are never alone with the Spirit of God,
   With the rock of salvation, as my rod.

I Do Know, just to be cherished, as thy child,
   And to be guided, wherever I go.

Susan R. Tucker

The Abbe' Prevost

Prevost papa's going the word or no bread.
Yes papa use two sticks, yes papa use two sticks,
The word and beat is all you'll ever need.

Prevost be no fool sticks no turn to bread.
Yes papa use two sticks yes papa use two sticks,
The world and beat is all you'll ever need.

Prevost what's that dance a Cajun two sticks.
Yes papa use two sticks, yes papa use two sticks,
The word and beat is all you'll ever need.

Prevost what! Lock elbow, lock knee, lock . . .
Yes papa use two sticks, yes papa use two sticks
The word and beat is all you'll ever need.

Prevost what's that cover coming over me.
Yes papa use two sticks, yes papa use two sticks
The word and beat is all you'll ever need.

Frederic Joseph Prevost

A Note From André

A christening is a special time
   I'm glad that you could come to mine.
Salt and oil and water pure,
   I'm really blessed, oh!, that's for sure
Snow white clothes and candle light
   make a precious, lovely sight.
I'm God's dear child and that's so great
   now it's time to celebrate.
I made some noises,
   were you listening?
They meant "Thanks for coming to my christening."

Carol DeConto

Never Captive

Yearning with drifting leaves of autumn dancing
to their death, I cried,
"Time takes beauty and crumbles it to powdery bits
between her jealous fingers,
Scattering what remains on sudden breath of wind.
I'll take my brush to record her on canvas and use
my pen for poems against ravages of time."

Beauty herself with mocking smile only said, "Fret not.
Speeding hours nor rolling patterns of stars in Universe,
Nor rough gray of hulking cliff along the mountain side
confine me for a moment.
I will not die nor be destroyed, nor live
by poem or picture.

Quick dissolving is a sunset
Yet each new twilight comes on wings of gold.
I only seem to die in narrow bounds of confinement.
As silent Phoenix, I never perch above my ashes,
But startle the beholder from jeweled branch
of some new tree."

Louise M. Morgan

America

America is a hypocrite behind a mask she hides.
Her appearance is as truth but her real identity lies.
She kills people across the world,
while the Black race she silence.
Killing people in Kuwait over oil
She ironically screams "Non-violence!!"
In the name of Christianity she labeled slavery just.
Slaughtering individuals and on her money . . . "In God We Trust."
She refuses to express the truth
But her bubble will have to burst.
She claims the pilgrims founded her
I'm sorry but Africans first.
She stated she disliked Hitler for his racist Nazi stance.
Black men are isolated from society in jails.
Now can you see the resemblance.

If you look deep into America, what you'll find will surprising
Evil lurking deep in her soul made fresh by false advertising.

Zelma Weaver

Whatever

I try to grasp at straws from time to time
But even they elude me, I know not why.
My attitude just now is far from sublime.
Most of my thoughts bring a huge sigh.

However, one thing remains constant
My faith in God and Christ never waivers
It's there like a solid rock, I'm content.
Yet, in the depths lingers something that pesters.

That bit isn't really bad, more unsettling to say the least.
Dare it be brought to the fore, imagination ever an active thing.
It seems almost like a holiday feast.
A person can easily be sated - but hold, forget it, just be glad
   and yes, let freedom ring

Whatever it be, time passes and those troubles will surely wane
To the very end, followed by a soft and gentle rain.

Donald A. Richards

Skol (The Old Man's Toast)

I welcome death, the challenger
   to my ancient sailing across

Old seas with new horizons,
   cool comfort of its breath

Gives soft compassion
   for my heart

I share the voyage,
   Valhalla opens eternity to life.

Now is the sunset
   where there was sunrise

Brilliance of Northern Crown
   a proud Valeyrie greets my passage

The open waters of tomorrow
   whisper with assurance.

My canvas sail snaps full

   Skol!

Leif Greneforst Olson

Fleeting Moments

The rain it falls upon me
Its grip a subtle strong,
But as I walk into the sun
Its loving grip is gone.

So now the sun it warms me
It warms me to the bone,
And though I've lost my loving rain
Somehow I feel I've grown.

But now the sun is setting
It's giving way to night,
And as that night now holds me
I start to shake in fright.

For life's a fleeting moment
Like the coming of the moon,
And like the setting of the sun
Our lives end all to soon.

Christopher R. Wills

The Wrong Path

In the mist of nothing he lay looking
   for his body.
A itchy flock of fire flies calling him
   to his eternity.
Remembered feelings of all the things
   that made him such a creature.
And each one stopping only to hit his
   soul with every terrible sin.
He walks forever, yet gets nowhere.
He drinks to quench, yet stays thirsty.
He sleeps on nails and bathes in mud
   and finds no dust of pleasure.
High above who shows no pity and
   locks the key to that man's destiny.
This place is hell where he belongs.
The Lord will show no mercy.

Chris Steinkraus

I Held An Angel

I held an angel close to me;
sweet and innocent, so tiny.
Its care entrusted to me alone.
This beautiful baby of my own.

Born in a world of trouble and strife;
its mother a child who's no one's wife.
Conceived in love and a moment's passion.
Judged by a world with no compassion.

But God in his own inevitable way,
decided this little one could not stay.
Now harsh cruel words from her peers,
have often reduced his mother to tears

I held an angel in my arms,
tried to shield it from all harm.
A candle of love, this little life.
We bask for a moment in his light.

I've heard it said and believe it to be so;
The brightest light is the first to go.

Joyce Stiles Spencer

Vengeance Of God

His eyes rolled white
His heart beat its last beat
He slipped into the night
To sleep the eternal sleep
With His life behind Him
He faces the future with open eyes
For the third day
He began to rise
An eye for an eye from the Pentateuch
The Word made law from the depth of a book
Contradictory laws from a merciless God
Domination of a man born from sod
Opportunities given and choices made
The unfortunate first disobeyed
Divinity tainted with sin
Lay His hand to let the anger begin
Drown the earth with a soul hungry flood
Turn His homemade puppets form dirt to mud
Destruction of a maze constructed from sand
Vengeance from a God with an iron hand

Justin McClain

As We Hold Hands

Two alone and in each other's company
Married for life we vowed.
A love that surpasses all.
A life of wedded bliss.

Now we sit, holding hands,
Unable to remember our loved one's names.
But all does not fail, in love again.
A new love emerges as memory fails.

A life together, a love so strong.
With memories failed, love hangs on.

Husband and wife till death do us part.
No lack of memory will keep us apart.
As we hold hands, our love anew.
My mind has failed, but I love you.

Shirley Tsosie

I'm Beginning To Wonder

I'm beginning to wonder just where in blue thunder you are?
You promised to hurry; your friend says don't worry,
you couldn't have gone that far. "She went to the fountain."
"But where? On a mountain? I'll bet she took off in my car!"
She said, "You must trust her!"
I said, "Oh, I trust her but don't even ask me how far."
She took my hand, said "I do understand;
you are angry and hurt and confused.
But watch this play, it's so funny, they say."
(I'm not even slightly amused.)
It wasn't long after, I joined in the laughter
and even before the end of the final act (and this is a fact!),
I'd fallen in love with your friend!
We finally found you, a guy's arms around you
(I can't say it was a surprise).
You laughed up a riot and then you were quiet;
you saw the look in my eyes.
"You think it's so funny? I'll take my ring, honey!
I don't give a hang what you do!"
At last it's all over! I feel I'm in clover!
I won't have to wonder about you.

Marjorie M. Watchek

The Unexpected

I can still remember the day I met you
I was nervous, and I almost think you knew
  Never sure of what we'd eventually find
Only knowing what was farthest from our minds
  With you being in the navy, it should have
Been easy to let you go on your way
  Now my only thought is to say
I love you in the worst way
  I've been through the stages of saying why and why now?
Through these past 2 months love has found us somehow
  So many things I've learned about you
Numerous places to go and things to do
  Our time together can't come too soon
Then time will be ours beneath the sun and moon
  Until then I'll think of you always
Rest assured your heart is where my love stays

Alicia Dennee

A Hectic Life For Mom Is Me

A hectic life for Mom is me.
  I feel so frazzled and unwoven.
Two school-aged children to drive me nuts!
  Constant fighting and messes a must!
Gum and Jello, who knew?!
  Could stick to anything just like glue!
A spastic dog who tends to bite,
  And tries to rule with all her might.
Two hamsters always on the run,
  Chasing them down, isn't much fun.
One goldfish won at a county fair,
  That mom has fed, watered and cared.
A husband who works night and day,
  Trying to earn that bigger pay.
Money is something of the past.
  Unlike the Energizer Bunny, it doesn't last!
A wife who yearns for rest and peace,
  Just doesn't have time to even sleep.
Oh what would life be like, with out all these?
  A mother's life is the life for me!

Jennifer L. Miano

Untitled

He saw the great big limousine
Pull up inside his block.
Those people had lots of money
They didn't have to walk.
He saw a lady fold their clothes,
That she pulled down from the line.
She cleaned and scrubbed around the house
Each day it looked just fine,
He wished his life could be that way
Someone to do his chores.
His mother would never be tired
From cleaning and scrubbing floors.
His mother said, "When I'm done, I feel good.
It's a great feeling inside when I work like I should.
Those people will never know this feeling I get
Of discipline and accomplishment I'm sure they haven't yet.
So always be thankful for all the things you have got
Instead of dwelling on have you have not."
   Bonnie Valihora Robledo

True Love

They say love is blind, who are they to say what love is
True love is not blind, true love is immeasurably sightless
As deep as the heart can feel, as far as the eyes can see,
As infinitely wise as the mind can free two souls to be
As inspiring as sunlight, as soothing as moonlight,
As passionate as when night meets day and day meets night
As intense as the ocean resting herself on the shore,
As profound as the shore sustaining life forever more
As serene and composed as a cloud in absolute silence,
As peaceful as a snowfall about to commence
Snowflakes gently falling, as softly falling in love,
The clouds quietly gathering to liberate the waters above
The rain that fills the land and overflows into a stream,
A stream breaking the shore into the ocean into a dream
Day dreams or evening dreams where true lovers live,
To awake with the wisdom to release all their lives have to give
To exchange, to deliver and to unite into a perfect fuse,
And true love is so much more than this poetic muse
True love begins when two feel eternal bliss,
All those who profess love is blind know not what true love is.
   Milton Daniel Rios

Soothing Words

I feel as though a spider is wrapping its web around me,
Choking the breath right out of me.

I know this feeling well, have it quite often,
The everyday pressures of life,
Working its way into my mind, body and soul.

If I close my eye's and pray, soon, I'm not alone.
The Lord is right inside of me, whispering His soothing words.
His love engulfs me, His vision implore's me.
I am in the awe, that His love and goodness,
Can cast the web off me.
I can breathe again,
And as He fades out of my mind He smiles and say's,
You will be O.K., for tomorrow is another day.
   Katherine Altmeier

Faceless

What am I?
A spirit floating aimlessly, a distant light?
Am I a shadow, a glimpse of darkness?
Or am I?
Am I one or many?

For what is it that I am here?
Not to save, but yet I do.
Change directions, from destruction to dawn.
Not to die, but yet I do?
Imbedded deep into my heart,
dull with the stains of past.

Not to create, but yet I do.
Images of the day, colors of the night.
Not to love, but yet I do.
Selfishly taking, relentlessly giving.

I am one of many, born of light,
shaped by shadows, grasping for destiny.
And yet,
Am I?
   Lyssa Allison

The Butterfly

Oh loveliness that God has made
Shimmering in yon woodsy glade
Flitting in and out of view
Sipping crystal drops of dew.
Your iridescent colors vie
With the rainbows in the sky
Such brilliant raiment surely must
Be mingled with the angel dust
That fell from silver angel wings
When God created all these things.
   Mary Alleracht

Precious Sounds

The precious sounds of a child's
laughter, that only a parent
could learn.
A special hug and smile
that only a parent could
earn.
A world of memorable
feelings only a
family could share.
Scraped knees, when walking
the first time.
First word, first tooth,
first picture at school.
The precious sounds of a child
trying to learn to play an instrument
or a sport.
Oh those sounds of growing up
are what you hear the most.
Precious as they seem, they'll
never disappear.
They'll grow, and grow.
   Laurie Butler

So Long Ago

The night you met me at the dance
It was so long ago
The night you followed me back home
In all the drifting snow.

I was afraid and frightened
My friend left me alone
And when I went to look for her
She left to go back home

I'm glad you followed me that night
It was the very start
The beginning of romance
You came and won my heart.

And after all those many years
I remember our first date
We saw the movie "Picnic"
And married in Fifty Eight.

Our wedding rings, still on our hands
They sparkle all the same
The way our love remains Today
Since the day I took your name.

Louise DePino

For The Sake Of The Children

A marriage full of hurt,
No longer filled with love.
You wonder why you stay,
As tender touches turn to shoves.

You say, "For the sake of the children,
I must stay and endure this pain.
Or else everything I have worked for,
Will all have been in vain."

I beg you to consider,
As they fall asleep at night,
How much pain the children feel,
As they listen to you fight.

You have worked so very hard,
Fulfilling their needs has been your goal.
But to free them from the anger,
Would be the gift to save their souls.

To leave them feels as if,
Your heart has been ripped from your chest.
But for the sake of the children,
In the end you'll find it's best.

Pamela K. Berkhiem

My Creed

Dear God, I wish to thank you
For the blessings that brought me here.
For you were there on every turn.
The blessings that I have today
Are the ones you bid me earn.

My only prayer for future acts
Is that you put me in the proper place
And make the instructions clear
That I may know your master plan
And make my works adhere.

Edward W. Morey

Essence Of Death

Father, mother, friends and lover
Cemented my sense of perfect cover,
A bulwark strong against the winds
Of hopeless change, unsure life's trends.

Father strong, he passed away
In coma deep for many a day;
But mother still a granite rock
Was always there to help and talk.

One day she left for retirement home
Abandoned all she left alone
Myself, and friends heartbroken deep;
Just fleeting memories ours to keep.

The day forlorn came to call
Just hours before the funeral pall,
Her raging sepsis very brief
A final gasp—empty relief.

I grieved, I watched them all the bulwark fall;
But the final death the worst of all
As my lover's life inched away
All essence of life with joy—ashes away.

James C. Rymer

Black Orchid

Black orchid, jungle flower,
　Petals from paradise,
Beautiful woman, full of power,
　Only you, could please my eyes.

Black diamond, precious stone,
　Borne from vulcan earth.
Never a man could leave you alone
　and your value is beyond worth.
Black pearl, wondrous gem,
　from a grain of sand you had to start
You could fulfill every man's whim
　but me? You've stolen my heart.
Black oil, Raw earth power,
　for you men are fighting wars,
They'll need you, keep you, 'til the last hour,
　but it's you they actually adore.
Black orchid, precious one,
　you're the one to please.
Beautiful woman, bright as the sun
　you've brought this man to his knees

George Vine

Love Poem

A love poem should be round and soft
mauve colored and perfumed
a love poem should be whispered
through darkness or the rosy glow of candlelight
no mention of old sneakers,
worn sweatshirts,
Monday mornings,
or tv dinners
but without these things
a love (poem) is incomplete

Samantha Chaifetz

A Flower's Dream

A flower's dream is to look glamorous and wonderful,
like the prettiest thing in the world.

A flower's dream is to be picked
and put in a lovely room.

A flower's dream is to be treated carefully
and not to get stomped on.

A flower's dream is to fly and soar
through the air like a bird.

A flower's dream is to travel around the world
and not stay in one spot.

A flower's dream is to have someone smell her
wonderful smell.
That is a flower's dream.

Stephanie Meyers

Scarecrow

Straw man tied upon his throne,
   Empty-headed horror, scaring all the crows.
Living day to day, doing nothing more,
   Standing in the fields watching the eagles soar.

He wants to fly, but he doesn't have his wings.
And so he cries, but his tears are bits of leaves.
He standing by, hearing the church bell ring.
Looking to the sky, to his hopes he still clings.

Strong Man nailed upon His throne,
   True and faithful servant saving all His foes.
Going man-to-man, their pain He had bore,
   Dying on the hill - they've crucified my Lord!

He had to die though didn't commit a sin
And still He cried, "My Father - forgive them!"
He paid the price to set the captives free;
No more sacrifice, He says, "Come and follow Me."

Distraught man praying to the Lord,
   "Give me the wings of eagles. Let your child soar."
Flying through the clouds, praising His name,
   Jesus and distraught man flying home today.

John C. Little

Grandfather

I follow the six sturdy men
all dressed generously in black
Loud rifles shot into the air in harmony
Then the lone trumpet cry's to the heavens above
His silver casket is slowly laid in its place
The red, white and blue cloth is draped over the top.

A Father to a daughter and two wonderful sons
A Grandfather to five beautiful grandchildren
A veteran who fought for his country
But he will rest now with his only true love

In time the leaves that fall will be replaced
In the spring, new grass will grow, bringing new life.

Lori Ann Comnick

Waterhouse Retreat

Dawn with icy winds cut deep,
November crisp the leaves give call,
Clear water caresses yonder creek,
Quietly we watch the snow fall,
For years I have asked him to come along,
Today he has accomplished me,
anticipation seizes this early dawn,
As we stare into the trees,
Somewhere waits the majestic buck,
We envision him on his flight,
I doubt we will have any luck,
Yet somehow it all seems right,
Though the icy winds do cut deep,
I spent time beside my father,
In the woods called waterhouse retreat,
It seemed worth all the bother.

Kerrick D. Caldwell

Frozen Heart

The cold winds of October
chill me to the inner-most depths
of my soul
the days become shorter
nights become agonizing
my frozen heart
no emotions, no feelings
expressionless gaze
stare into nothingness
lifeless eyes
no more love inside
too tough to cry
too sad to smile
A world of hopes shattered
dreams broken
a struggle to face each day
all meaningless to me now
Once you were there
now only memories
remaining to break the heart

Michael Anthony Putignano

Music Am I

No life could be more full,
   nor more empty.
Tears wasted, hours fade,
   life gone before lived.
Love is only lust,
   justified,
Only music fills the depth of sadness,
   such lovely sadness.
How we revel in its depths,
   a lonely shell clings round.
Its meaning life or hell,
   no music rings within.
Just sweet, sweet sadness.
Huddled in the midst am I,
   sweet sadness, life, love, music,
Music and loneliness.

Karen Ann Brown

The Mountain

The mountain standing so tall and bold
Beyond the shadowy sky;
Not knowing what the weather unfolds;
The mountain reaches high.
The mountain so mysteriously glows;
With all its snowy peaks,
To captivate each and every soul
While forever they seek.
The mountain so beautiful during the day,
And romantic during the night;
Attracting tourists from so far away
To camp, adventure and even hike.
The mountain intriguingly awaits
During stormy weather by ocean or sea,
While nature seductively a baits,
The mountain forever will be.
The mountain stands courageously
Even when nature call,
Winter, spring, summer and fall,
The mountain still standing through it all.

Deloris White

It Is The Day

When peace arrives and comes for you,
there's nothing left for you to do,
but be prepared. You can't delay.
When peace is here, it is the day.

I'm sitting here beside the bed,
and wishing you were home instead,
and doing things we used to do.
But that's a wish that won't come true.

I cannot help but see the strain.
I know you're in a lot of pain.
I know you've lost a lot of weight,
more than your life can tolerate.

I know you've lived a lot of years,
and that you've shed a lot of tears,
and that your life is in your past,
and that you need to rest, at last.

I love you, Mom. I understand.
I'll get up close and hold your hand.
Now close your eyes. It is the day
for peace to take the pain away.

A. R. Milkes

Of Me I Speak

A light, a vision,
My eyes' true seeing,
I look at my world, it is me I see.
I look at myself, my world I see.
A universe unfolds:
My eyes' true vision,
awash in emotion—deep in reverie,
searching for something inside of me,
So we live,
　So we die,
　　So we exist forever.
A light, a vision,
My soul does dance upon these molecules,
and play the mental tones so musically . . .
for here am I, a sparkle within the whole.

Edward Merrill

Escape From A Banshee

One night late, the fog rolled in.
I suddenly felt a chill from within.
All at once, the leaves began to rustle.
Quickly inside, I decided to hustle.

The wind began to make an eerie sound.
Harder and harder my heart began to pound.
What could this strange noise be?
I realized then, it's the cry of a banshee.

Who does she want? Why is she here?
Her sudden presence, I thought, was queer.
She reached out and cried, "Come to me.
Together we can live through eternity."

Her beauty was certainly one to behold.
She cried, "Come with me and never grow old."
I went to her, dazzled by her charm.
I started to grasp her outstretched arm.

Where I found the courage to go, I can't tell.
She turned and said, "We'll spend eternity in hell."
I ran back to the house and dropped to my knees.
I cried, "Dear Lord, from this evil, deliver me, please."

Marshall C. Wilder Sr.

Life Cycles

Where are the flowers of yesterday?
The frost came and took their beauty away —
It was cruel and unkind
To leave only the shriveled petals and stems behind —
But, the roots are still alive
Buried deeply underground,
Giving birth to new shoots,
When Spring comes around —
The same cycle is repeated year after year,
Some flowers fall into their eternal sleep,
But, in their place new ones appear —
We humans also meet a similar fate —
We bloom for awhile,
And then gradually we disintegrate —
Generations come and go
Life is moving to and fro —

Magda Herzberger

Teenie Weenie Religion

Is "Teenie Weenie" the faith you call yours?
Just enough to get by, not the kind that pours?
Do you skimp on the time you should take to pray?
Do you forget God, at the ending of day?
Is there time in your day to pass out a smile?
Or do you find other things more worthwhile?
Examine yourself — see your reflection
In this mirror called life, in the right direction.
Today is the time to do greater things.
Forget "Teenie Weenie" and try out your wings!

Virginia Null Miles

The Voice Within

I listen in hopes that I may hear
Something, almost anything that would tell me I'm
   near the voice within.
I'm still, yet all I hear is thoughts dancing in and out
   Some soft, some shout.
Listen, just listen, oh yes it's hard.
As I listen, I'm aware that there is something there,
With practice, I'm beginning to feel
Oh yes, the voice is real
I can hear it clear
It saying I am always here.
You ignore me, put me aside
Then cry when your life goes awry.
Pay attention! The voice is God speaking
I'm guiding you, loving you, telling you how, oh so dear,
You are my creation, my prize
Hear me, hear me, open your eyes.
I speak softly in your ear
Hoping this time you'll hear
   The voice within.
I'm listening, I hear
As I go into the closet of my mind
I know this time I'll find the voice within.

Peggy Shella Moody

Twilight

If each star in the sky holds the soul of a great man passed on
When I look up at the brilliant night sky
How will I know which soul is yours
Is it that star that burns bright
Or the faded one that dances across the sky
How will I know which one to look to
At times when I need your wisdom
Your advice
Is it just one star
Or was your soul too great
That it had to be spread
Shared among the twilight
Or can I just look up
Face turned towards the heavens
And know that no matter where your soul lies
My voice reaches you
And your everlasting light
Will always shine upon me.

Barbara Shaffer

In Love

When you love someone and need to tell them and can't,
it eats up inside but until you can tell them and
hope that they feel the same way. If they don't, what
do you do with your heart? You pick up the pieces and keep
going or hope they would say I love you. Being in love
with someone; it hurts. But to me love is a
great feeling if you know what you are looking
for in that person. I look on the inside
and I take that part and look at it very slowly.
And you will find the thing
that makes that person so great so if you
are alone and crying and need someone to hold
you think of why you are in love with that
person and hold on to that with
all your heart.

Angeline Showers

Techno-Mage

I type quickly on my keyboard
   my password to log-on
First I check my e-mail
   and to some I will respond

When I use an on-line service
   and open my web page
It's the Internet I'm surfing
   I am a Techno-Mage

I spend hours searching web-sites
   my mouse is on the go
I gather bits of knowledge
   my files just grow and grow

To surf the world-wide-web
   is now the newest rage
I've learned the latest techniques
   I am a Techno-Mage

Donald M. Woodward

For Tom, In Trying And Sincerity

I feel you
Sometimes,
   when I will look away.

Your eyes remain
on me
Fixed
and deep.

I feel your strength,
   your desire to know.

Do you see me?
   Know me?
   Share me?
Can we,
know each other?
Fully?

In trying and sincerity...
   no bounds has our love.

Mindy Duncan

I Want To Come Home

A Navy medical discharge
Got his mother on the phone.
From a Virginia hospital bed he said,
"I want to come home."

His Oregon mother commandeered
The family van.
She informed her bedridden son,
"I'll come as fast as I can."

"I want to come home,"
Flowed from a lonely heart.
From a man wanting to be
Where his roots got their start.

Home is a way-station
As you traverse eternity.
When ill winds blow
It's the place you want to be.

Kleon Kerr

A Gathering Of Crows

A trembling oak braces
Earth below is stranded
Remember today before it has past
A gathering of crows has landed

Feathers ruffled and tattered
Black from the corridor of hell
Marbled eyes of emptiness
Stories they will never tell

Cackled cries of warning
The air is whisper thin
Among us to complete their deed
Judgment of all our sin

Orbs dark and sullen search downward
Subjects beneath are lost
Ignoring signs of nature
Soon to learn the cost

A gathering of crows has landed
Be sure to say your prayers
When heaven and earth collide
We will know who truly cares

James Lawrence Ore

Nancy, My Wife, My Friend

To be with you is a wonderful treat
So kind, so gentle, oh so sweet
Hair of blond, with eyes true blue
Skin so soft and five foot two

A heart of gold, a smile so bold
Tender hands, a joy to hold
Your radiant voice and happy face
Reminds us of heaven and all its grace

You talk to the animals, admire the trees
Chase the butterflies and run from the bees
As full of fun, as the morning sun
You brighten the day for its course to run

Not only my wife, but my best friend
From across the way, a kiss you would send
The love you've shared throughout these years
Would even bring God, to shed a few tears

The day you were born, the church bells rang
An entire chorus of angels sang
For never again on this earth would be
Another like you, for the world to see

Lloyd W. Balaque

Ocean

As I walk across the sand
It's the ocean as far as I can see

Foamy, with just a cap of white,
Rolling over and over again

Ripples of waves
As it slams against the sand

And then as a quiet calm
it rolls out again

As far as I can see.

Velda R. Townsend

Angel In A Cul De Sac

Pools of shadow settled in the contours of her face
and suggested that flesh, not a day-dream,
occupied her space.
But when I stepped toward her,
to touch that face and prove its depth,
she turned her head quickly to me
and took one cautious step away,
As birds often do, a gesture that demands distance.
I lifted my foot to approach her,
to prove her that she wanted me to touch her,
and she fluttered, anxious for flight.
Then she left, upward
and spread herself against the sky.

I could feel her urgency, a divine gale,
playing in my hair as she arched to the sun.

I waited for a rain of wax
and burning feathers.

Ryan Mitstifer

Time

"Some other time" is often said,
When the doing is not so convenient.
"Some other time," you may come to dread,
As time is not really that lenient.

Time must be used as it passes your way,
And in passing, it should always be tasted.
Make each minute count of each living day,
Or you will regret what you wasted.

Use your time wisely as you endeavor
To live a full life on this earth.
For when time is wasted it's gone forever,
And your time is limited at birth.

Time is with us and will never stop,
It brings happiness, troubles, and care.
All pails of time are not filled to the top,
Yet some with the short pails still share.

Whats done today, needs no doing tomorrow.
This leaves time just for your pleasure.
Putting things off, will just bring you sorrow,
For time, you can't keep like a treasure.

William G. Jenings

Life's Changes Arrive...

Changes sought . . .
   improvements welcomed, excitement invited,
   self-preservation realized . . . ecstasy and joy awaited.
A glimmer of happiness shines.
   Calm, Gradual and Steady.

Changes feared . . .
   contempt took hold, disappointment ensued,
   expectations crumbled, destruction construed.
A blinding shade of sadness darkens.
   Abrupt, Angry and Harsh.

A special blend of temperament, a balance of emotions,
   overwhelmingness subsides, shown in feelings in our eyes.
Adjustment to our lives anew,
   for lives have changed . . .
   Continued.

Jack T. Wright

Waiters' Table

A table near, far from here
Cozy set in secluded way
The wine makes own, a special few
Gardenia's center scent

Memorized to the sound of a violin concerto
Candles dance to streaks of light in sway
My goodness has arrived to dine this day

A floral flume showers in mist
She is everything I could have list

Mademoiselle, you're lovely, your eyes, your lips, your hair
Please be sealed here, close and near
Let us pour the wine with cheer
Laugh, giggle, and whisper sweet . . .

Larry! Larry! Brakes over!

Your customers are ready to order
Larry Spaulding

Our Cloud

Once upon a time
There was this cloud in the sky,
And on it sat a woman and a guy.
They shared the same dream,
But, lost hope of ever finding it, it seemed.
Looking out in opposite directions,
For someone to share their undying affections.
Neither realize what could be found,
If they would only turn around.
They looked everywhere for the love they thought they'd
    never find,
But, no one ever matched their kind.
Then one day, they turned around,
And were so delighted with what they found.
Now they have their lifetime soul mate,
And realized being together was always their fate.
They fell in love and all was right,
Now they lay in each other arms on their cloud at night.
Kimberly Farkas

The Poets, The Thinkers

Time stands still in a small part of the world.
A place with exotic plants and gardens,
And cures for all humankind.
A place with iridescent animals,
That would make your eyes thunder and glow.
A place with the tallest trees for the greatest forest,
That may hold the key to the history of the world.
A place with all the enchanting colors of the earth,
For one to paint the most perfect sunset fantasized.
A place were one can lose himself,
And find all the secrets once lost.
A place where love is born,
And undeniable passions create indivisible relationships.
A pace for all the individuals of the world,
Regardless of the differences and conflicts between them.
A place where joy and innocence are plentiful,
and where all the true treasures of the world can be discovered.
This is my imagination, my hope, my desire.
A place where we are all poets, a place where we are all thinkers.
Margaret Anne McCants

First Love

I see her rising golden red
to join the night of stars ahead.
Beyond the tree, so softly now,
I dream of her the night she fled.

I laughed and sang and asked her how
to leap so high above my bow,
and take her hand in mine tonight
so I could pledge an eternal vow.

It stings me still to watch the night
and see my love so far from sight.
Across the sky and away she fled
to laugh and sing with bright starlight.

But for a time below the tree
I ran as fast as love could be
and knelt with her of golden red,
holding her close with words I said.
D. W. Brooks

Husband To Be

I can't help but wonder
what it would be like today
if I didn't have the one I love
with me each step of the way.

My knight in shining armor
who's made my dreams come true,
the only one I truly love
and have given my heart to.

The one who holds me when I sleep.
The one who holds my treasures for keep.
The one who accepts me for just who I am.
He's mine, forever, and truly a man.

He picks me up when I fall.
He's there with me to stand proud and tall.
He celebrates my joys
and helps me through my sorrows.
This is the man I want to be with
when there is no tomorrow.
Layla Davidson

Silhouettes

I glimpsed my children's children
Darting among trees
Silhouettes on mountain heights
More than illusion
Less than factual
Or was it a dream
A fantasy
Their arms reach for me
Surely this I see
Hair of iridescent sheen
I must have seen
Rosebuds, pearls and eyes
The blue of summer skies
This must be
Reality
Opal F. Adkins

Thanks For The Memories

It was Christmas of seventy
and Vietnam so near.
When we looked to the stage,
for some hope to appear.

He brought dancers and singers;
he himself, told jokes.
We all laughed till we cried,
and then I . . . thought of my folks.

Together we watched
his special each year.
Never dreaming one day . . .
he'd be bringing me cheer.

Thanks, Bob, thanks . . .
for all the memories you made.
You brought our troops hope . . .
and told faith . . . don't fade!

No dry eye could be found
on our base that day.
As we sang silent night . . .
and then Bob . . . flew away.
    D. H. Nuske

Hopelessness

I am the Knight that you await for,
The only thing,
    my horse is blue,
It is not white as they describe it,
Yet, my love for you, is always true.

I know that never,
    will we be together,
You are a rising star,
    while I am a fool,
A fool to love,
    someone so lovely,
Knowing the distance,
    I am from you.

Nevertheless, I am the Knight you wait for,
Forevermore, I will love you.
And hope someday,
    if your love is conquered,
I will be down the aisle,
    waiting for you . . .
    Marcelo R. Ortiz

Crazy For You

No greater statement was ever true
Than the statement, "I'm crazy for you"
I'm crazy for the love we share
I'm crazy about the way you do your hair
I love the way you primp and fuss
I have always loved you so very much
Not health, wealth, family or whatever
Will ever keep us from being always together
I love all the little things you do
And know I couldn't live without you
Some people say that I'm crazy, and it's true
Because I will always be, crazy for you
    Barry Wickund

Transition

Our seed sown, so spiritually ago;
    my chrysalis shed, drying wings 'neath our dawn,
    teetering on the rim of flight.
Why those defenses rise, those trip-wires in disguise,
    like a flock of startled birds in frenzy . . .
    in all honesty, I don't know?
This regression from progression baffles me;
    when I take the time to think.
    Like a turtle/totem, a sensate snail,
reverting to my shell, my solitary cell,
    withdrawing towards my abandoned womb . . .
    trying to assume, some vague illusion of safety.
I guess transition exposes inhibition;
    magnifying the menace of dangling doubts.
    This was never of you . . . this festered solely in me.
But final strands I now sever, from this umbilical tether,
    the heart of my mind, the eyes of my soul still see,
    the tranquility, the ultimacy of intuition.
Your touch compels the positive conviction . . .
    as I bask in the birth of our transition.
    Merlin J. McMinn

My Breath

I exhale the freezing cold air
And watch my cloud of breath disappear.
Despite the blackness of the night,
My cloud glows brightly.
I think of a happiness I once knew
As I walked my way to a stream
Which was not frozen.
The sky shone blue
Not black
And the breath I breathed was warm.
I looked up at the sky and saw the face
Of my lover disguised as a cloud
And almost instantly, his lips were upon mine.
I pulled away, looked into his eyes,
Surrounded myself in the warm brown.
He was my love,
My only love
Which faded away like a dream.
I inhale the freezing cold air
And exhale, watching my cloud of breath disappear.
    Katrina W. Robinson

Lost And All Alone

I'm here at work, it's a hot, humid day
Thinking what else I'm able to say
I feel drained from head to toe
We all go through depression, on some it won't slow
When we hit bottom the world seems to stop
We look at ourselves and see we're not on top
Our lives are filled with mountains of stress
Our brains become cluttered and filled with a mess
We think nothing of the world that's around us
Then thank God to the ones that found us
I thank Nancy who's a friend indeed
For saving my life, in my time of need
I thank you and bless you, for seeing the sign
A friendship I will treasure till the end of time
    Maurice A. Routier

The Wings Of The Dove

High above the clouds, he glides.
His wings carry the wind.
He is at peace soaring upward
The clouds his escape.
Higher and higher he soars alone.
Reach upwards with your hands and feel the peace.
He is there above the clouds.
The sky and universe await his flight.
I have seen him before.
I have felt his presence;
I have seen his peace;
Yet, I have not been able to reach it.
Slowly, I reach for his wings
Gently, he allows me to touch him
Suddenly, I am in his peace.
The clouds bow in respect.
I reach out and touch his wings
Slowly, he brings my hand upwards.
I too am now above the clouds
I reach out and touch His hand.

William E. Cooper Jr.

Fresh Snow

Fresh snow—glistening bright,
Whether in the sunlight or moonlight.
It can be seen as pretty after it falls
On many things short or tall.
But it can be dangerous,
Making traveling rough.
Children delight in snowfall—
They use it to make snow people and build a fortress small
Fortified with many ready-to-throw balls.
They can groan when they hear the call,
The call to come in out of the cold.
But soon, they are back out in it—the snow has got a hold,
A hold of the fun and play side
Of them—they soon return outside,
Trying not to throw or get hit
By a snowball that has ice in or on it,
Which does not feel at all good,
And can change the fun mood.
Be sure to be careful with fresh snow,
Whether with fun or work, at home or away, or on the go.

Carol Lee Ammons

Jesus

From the hills of Galilee a voice reverberates
Into every nook and corner of the world.
For two thousand years, its echo travels
Through time and will pierce eternity.
Words heard by all people from all races,
But not all understand —
Words spoken by one Golden Tongue
In a language purer that pure,
In the voice of Truth!

Arise from thy sleep, listen well, open thine heart,
So that thy spirit may be uplifted, thy pains cured,
Thy doubts illuminated, thy life rejuvenated,
Thy soul tread upon a Glorious path.
Let His words fall upon sensible ears
And be like the flowers of the water lily
Which rise above the water to its life giving sunshine
With welcoming reverence!

Ramon G. Palanca

Stoned

A hidden feeling
a hopeless love
a heart stoned cold

A warm touch
a warm smile
a heart stoned cold

A gently stair
a caring gesture
a heart stoned cold

Feelings revealed
love aroused
a heart stoned cold

A lost soul
a found way
a heart filled whole

Summer Stover

A Beautiful Dove

One day I saw a beautiful dove
up in a tree staring out at me

Her coat it was as white as snow
she stood so proud and yet so bold

Beside that tree there was a path
that most kids took to get home fast

As I approached she flapped her wings
and cried so loud it frightened me

She wouldn't let me pass her by
her screams so loud I wouldn't try

I was frightened and filled with fear
for I knew not what trouble was near

I turned and walked the other way
to gramma's house where I'd be safe

I feel that dove protected me
from harm that was beneath that tree

So now when I see a beautiful dove
it reminds me of God's protective love.

Thomasine Fant Smith

When A Woman Loves A Man

When a woman loves a man
  The love is deep
  The love is true.
When a woman loves a man
  The world is a better place.
  The sky is bluer
  The air is warmer
  The hills are greener.
When a woman loves a man
  Birds sing
  Flowers bloom
  Rainbows abound.
When a woman loves a man
  She opens her heart and soul
  To the man she loves.

Sonja Ann Zofrea

Marble

I love to look at marble
Because in it, you see,
Are strange and most fantastic things
A lookin' back at me.

A child, a bird, a face, a cloud
Are strangely hidden there:
Amidst the mottled shades and hues,
Imagined, fancied, rare.

The stone is cold and silent
Yet in its heart I find
A gentle warmth, a vibrancy,
An elegance designed.

A form of endless beauty,
Majestic in its might;
Its pleasure-giving surface begs
My touch of pure delight.

Kay Schenk

I Love You

"I love you" are three simple words
    That mean so many things
"I love you" is a simple phrase;
    And yet, it's so extreme.

You can say it to your sweet Mom
    Who loves you most of all,
And no matter what the season brings
    We'll catch you when you fall.

You can say it to your friend Joe
    When stumbling on life's road.
For that's what makes the greatest friend
    That anyone has known.

And then there is that special love,
    That only two can share
The kind that sends warm feelings
    To let you know he cares.

These words go to my special Love
    "I love you in such a way,
It grows stronger with each moment
    And stronger, with each day."

Jennifer Thornton

Ivyside

A boy leans his bicycle
against an arthritic tree
that stretches and bends
steadfast
behind the faded red barn
of a dead man

And as he casts his eyes
over the fields towards
the burnished horizon
the sun sets
unpolished
sinking into the husk of the earth
without a sound

DM Fleming

Where Do The Birds Go

Where do the birds go when they die
do they fall, do they rise;
rise transformed in thrall
light years above the sky
do the clouds cry
does the wind catch its breath
or wonder why
these are two less wings to ride

Does heaven mark a bare place
hear no less song to dawn
feel one heart gone
do the voices of the world still
is the eternal symmetry of space less full
do the trees mourn a tenant
does the branch choir sing a lament
are the leaves of less joy
do the angels account, paint another flower and sigh

Does the sun send one more ray
does heaven sum one more immortal light
one more star to mark
the fall of night

Norman Wayne Sedelmarer

Heal Our Hearts

You know this world would be more appealing,
If we had more peace and a lot less killing.
If we would just think before we react;
Instead of arguing who is better, the "Whites" or the "Blacks."

We could go forward instead of falling back
And concentrate on our lives being focused and in tact.
Let us all join together to help plant the seed;
Not worrying about one's race, color or their creed.
We need to learn everyone does have sensitive feelings.
So now, stop the hate and let's begin the healing.

Let us put our pride aside, then try to help each other out.
Together sharing love is what it's all about.
If we'd look inside one's heart instead of looking at one's face;
What really counts is what's inside, not his income nor his race.

It was King's dream to walk hand in hand.
Let's all unite, Side by Side, the way that he had planned.
Sometimes we have to forgive others
And sometimes we just tolerate;
But in order to live in peace,
We must first **ERASE THE HATE!!!**

Pamela Faye Yancey

Destiny

Is she my Destiny, the one of whom I dream
she is my vision, my heart, so it seems
it is her that I long for, her that I need
it is her that my heart truly wants to please
for when I am lost she shows me the way
and brings hope like the sunshine to each and every day
so I search my dreams
and know them well, for my soul has fallen to her spell
I have no questions, no doubts in my mind
that she is my destiny
and shall be through time.

John Chetuck

Sweet Pete

The game of life, I can no longer play
   I dug my ditches, plowed my rows
I must go. I cannot stay
   To reap, God says, if I sow.

The ditches were deep, the row long
   the mules, I followed, that pulled the plow
So weak, I feel, no strength to be strong
   would make another field, but how?

My feet are tired — legs refuse to remove
   The shoulders, once strong, are bent
The heart that sang is no longer in the groove
   pain, my body has rent.

Weak, weary, and worn the eyes
   That beheld God's wonderful world
The sky of blue, the birds that fly
   The dawn of a new day — unfurl.

Inside this old head, visions of God's world whirl
   Mansions and glory — I dream
Streets of gold, gates of pearl
   Rainbows are the color scheme.
     Alma Ann Williams

A Funeral Goodbye

Canvass-pressed eyelids cover her shine.
Her cold, stiffened hands still shaped like mine.
Wiry, gray hair—a fake display,
A head-turning grin now stretched away.
The porcelain skin that wrinkled too young
(All because she corroded her lung).
Rounded, dry cheeks were once moisture christened,
An ever-bent ear ceases now to listen.
A petite and frail body rests in that box
Evidence of mortality, eternity knocked.
Love that so loved me now makes me cry.
Time demands me to tell her goodbye.
   Amy E. Walls

Once We Were Warriors

Once we had meaning
Once we were proud
Once we were men
Once we were warriors
   We live on the land
   We live off the seas
   We once were free
   We once were warriors
Once my people had manta
Once my people had pride
Once my people had life
Once we were warriors
   The land where I once laid
   Is not the land where I will die
   This is our land that you so cheaply destroy
The men you killed
The men I knew
The men I loved
The men for which you will die
For now, we are warriors once again
   Steve Mazur

Mother And Child

Heaven's tears twist and turn about us
Thrown aimlessly about by skies breath
they proceed downward, relentless
to a fated junction below.

We are reminded of the red monster.
Whose thirst is quenched only by that
which now ravishes the ground.

Windowless buildings rise and fall
and from their green chimneys
wet, white smoke climbs
upwards towards furious firmament.

Mother earth comforts her heavenly one
causing light to pierce the pitch.
Leaving nothing behind except
a maternal cheek streaked with tears.
   Melinda Stone

A Friend

A friend is a precious jewel
Truly one of a kind.
Hold on tight to them,
They're very hard to find.

A friend you can talk to,
When no one else will listen.
Enjoying the get together's,
And all the friendly visits.

A friend can soothe your heartaches,
Share your joys and sorrows.
Helping you get thru
To face another tomorrow.

A friend I hope I can be,
To share with them the precious time
My friend has given me.

The days and years go by so fast,
We lose so many friends.
But I will never forget the one,
Who cared and was my good friend
   Muriel Hoell

Leaves

Yellow, orange, brown, and red,
Autumn colors dancing in my head.
Enjoy these colors at their peak,
For they will be gone in about a week.

As they let go of the tree,
They float down like feathers to see me.
But if a strong wind decides to blow,
They all let loose like a blizzard of snow.

Great huge piles they start to make,
Where on earth did I put my rake?
Although raking can be great fun,
I give a sigh of relief when it is done.

Soon all the trees will be bare,
And there will be a crisp breeze in the air.
Dig out your sweaters, coats, and hats.
Autumn is over, and that is that.
   Jacklyn D. Kiefer

An Aquarian's Thoughts

Where to start?
Where to go?
Where to be?
Where to begin?
Where to finish?
What to walk?
Should it be
Beneath the burning sun
Not by the shimmering moon
Does one follow the beating heart
The pulsing blood
Endless pounding river
Walk among the clouds
Dance within stars
Frolic in swaying grass
Skip through towering trees
Run with life, sing with death
Where to end?
   Rachel Wilson

Ode To 362nd

I am a fighter pilot, said he . . .
   As he gazed upon his portrait
      Donned in helmet and dungarees.

I am a fighter pilot, said he . . .
   Looking upon his medals
   Hung so auspiciously.

I am a fighter pilot, said he . . .
   Remembering the past, the thrilling dogfights,
   Hoping for a victory.

I am a fighter pilot, said he . . .
   Brought down amongst the enemy,
Imprisoned, and awaiting liberty.

I am a fighter pilot, said he . . .
   The war, now over, and starting a family.

   I am fighter pilot, said he . . .
His years now past, wrinkled,
   And hanging on to memories.

I am a fighter pilot, said he . . .
   But now, he too is gone, and all his history.
   Joseph McCleary

Dream

I see things no one else sees,
I hear thing no one else hears,
I know things no one else knows.
Your eyes, sweetfully seductive, met mine.
Your voice, sexy and calm, called out my name.
Blood rushed to my face as you held me close.
My arms yearned for your embrace, as you
whispered sweet nothings in my ear.
Nothing in the world could compare to our love
when we are together.
I looked up at your eyes and...
And, I woke up.
Well, it as good while it lasted.
Till next time.
   Jennifer Smith

The Night Before, The Morning After

I always regret the night before, the morning after.

The night before seemed a rollicking good time,
but the morning after I can't remember what was so much fun.

The night before I laughed and danced and drank and flirted,
but the morning after all I want to do is stay in bed,
in a dark room, with the covers over my head!

The night before the music was lively and gay and so was I,
but the morning after, if anyone turns on a radio,
I'll lose what's left on my mind.

The night before the wine was sweet and I felt seductive,
but the morning after, the wine has a sting
and I feel like death warmed over.

The night before I tell my self I won't drink too much
or play too hard, but the morning after
I know I've done what I said I wouldn't do.

The night before, I don't remember the morning after,
so I find myself the morning after
wishing I'd never had the night before.
   Vicki L. Dawson

Tapestry Of Life

Cloth and colorful strands,
Vividly cover every wall of the room.
Each picture carefully depicting, with particularity,
Varying degrees of inner growth.

Some suggest an emergence, or beginning,
Full of anticipation, wonder, and courage.
Brilliant hues alive with newness and possibility.

Others have been completed through deliberate reflection,
By inherently sifting through trial and triumph concurrently,
For theme and form.
A representation of times and seasons
Etched indelibly upon hearts and minds.
Places and feelings that have been timelessly revisited,
Or time-worn and forgotten by neglect.

As I near the end of the display,
An incomplete picture captures my attention.
Only when I realize it is my last masterpiece,
Do I cross through a doorway
To cast the finishing stitches,
And eagerly embark into eternity.
   Eva Hinckley

Summer

I love summer
It's not a real bummer.
It's fun to jump in a nice cold pool.
You can have fun knowing there's no school.
The sun is bright
And that's quite all right.
The flowers are blooming
And bees are zooming.
Bike riding is fun.
You can play until the day is done.
Campfires are nice
And you can play outside more than once or twice.
   Haley M. Covol

Diamonds

We're born like diamonds in the rough
Taken from birth to be shaped, sized, made
sturdy and tough
Growing ever so slowly until we reach the
appropriate age
Then given all necessary material on how to
love, create, and behave
We head out into the world to command and
conquer our dreams
The things we do sometimes goes to the extreme
Each of us our families most valuable and
precious treasure
Even when we think our lives are dim and doesn't
add up or measure
A diamond never loses its gleam or shine
And the best examples of our life we leave
Will never disappear not even in the darkest hour
of time

Linda Nelson

Once Upon A Child

Once upon a child
Crawling quietly then quickly,
Lower lip fluttering in frantic fantasy,
Crying for comfort: I am innocent!

Standing shakily then steadily,
Eyes ever-searching and seeking security,
Reaching for reminders: I am excited!

Running rapidly then in rhythm,
Legs leading in strong, sinuous strides,
Urging our understanding: I am independent!

Walking wisely yet willfully,
Minds mastered by years of yearning and learning,
Sighing in serenity: I am content!

Once upon a child,
Then face-to-face: A Man!

Thomas L. Tinker

Surrounded By Love

I can picture us running in a wide-open field
with nothing existing to which we should yield.
Smiling and laughing and twirling around . . .
his hand in mine, his voice in my ear, surrounded by love.

I can picture a picnic underneath old oak trees
with him stroking my hair as it blows in the breeze.
Grinning and gazing into each other's eyes . . .
whispering softly, twinkling eyes, surrounded by love.

I can hear our favorite song in the distance so clear
while we dance so close as the evening draws near.
And summer stars slowly appear . . .
his arms cuddling me, my head on his shoulder,
surrounded by love.

I can think how I'd feel if I saw him today.
My heart would say "run to him" and I would obey.
And I'd run and he'd pick me up and swing me around . . .
his smile would embrace me, obvious soul mates,
Surrounded by love.

Allison Davidson

Untitled

He made out like a bandit.
He preyed on your sympathy just like
  a bandit would.
He took all your money pretending to
  be so friendly
He wanted to learn all your trade
He made out like a bandit for your
  weakness overpowered your goodness.
He made out like a bandit, but
  you used up his time,
He taught you the ways of the evil and God.
He preyed on your weakness as long
  as you let him.
He did not know that good overpowers
  the bad all the time.
He was a bandit that preyed on your
  weakness and good.
He was a bandit and stole anything
He could.

Mary De Lozier

Finding The Light

When skies are grey,
no sun in sight,

When you just can't seem
to find the light

Knowing man has failed your trust,
having to get through you must.

Even though God has been betrayed,
you can keep your trust in his way.

Through sadness and loss,
your life be tossed in
the sea of life.

Through all the strife we find in life,
remember we all live in God's sight.

Keep your soul calm,
because like that psalm,
the troubled waters will fade.

And as in before your soul
will then soar through
the lessons each day God has made.

Rebecca J. Denardo

My Prayer

Let me live every day in a peaceful way,
Let me have a smile for a neighbor or friend,
Or an understanding word if that will surface,
Let me be one who cares, just plain nice.

Let me be a safe driver, always aware
That the highways and by ways are to share.
Keep me cautions and ever alert
For accident can happen and hurt.

Let me be patient, loving and giving,
For those virtues make life worth living.
Let me give credit where credit is due,
Let me think less of me and more of you.

Beatrice Brewer

Tahitian Nights

Tahitian Nights, I knew them
they were so exciting
they gave my worried, stressed out mind
blissful rest and peaceful quitting

The essence or exotic
straying from the beaten path
adventure without danger
no fear, discord or wrath

When I held a sweet young body
whose desire was just to please
I knew of giving pleasure
the same as given me

I felt a sense of freedom's wonder
and guess I always will
oh, those wondrous Tahitian Nights
nothing seems to dim the thrill

But that was long ago
and although youth has taken flight
my mind's still young and it's still a thrill
to recall those warm Tahitian Nights

F. D. Skeeters

Ashes

Choking dust in a snuff box home
spirit tucked away in a drawer
Michael's crumbled bones
no more than a momento
captured in sealed tin
crying again
not in pain for lost time
for missed chances
just the dances with death he couldn't win
in the riverbed brush with poison'd strangers
   a last rush with unknown men
   a fatal mistake of lust for love
   a belief he was above such danger.
Cast my ashes back by the shore,
he begs me now
to open the door of this sad past
to wash it away and begin.

Thomasina Duckworth

Christmas Day

Christmas is a time to remember
of the babe in Bethlehem,
Who gave great peace, love, and joy
to every living man.

Christmas is a time to come together
with friends and loved ones far and near,
and a time to thank the one who made
this special day of the year.

It is time we shared our gifts
let us bow our heads to pray,
and give thanks to the Lord our
savior for this special Christmas day.

Victoria J. Bredeweg

August

In cotton dreams a silent angel sleeps in summer haze
Alone at peace she shines with love that echoes through the days

The liquid pulse of heaven escapes her lips and frees the heart
A sleeping angel dreaming of a love not torn apart

Inside the gold of morning nestled soft inside the dawn
Our hopes provide the pillow that she lays her head upon

The eyes of Venus fall in tattered ashes at her feet
This silent sleeping angel that makes my world complete

Lawrence E. Parlier

She Ain't My Baby No Mo'

I'd call her on the phone, I'd listen to her talk,
I held her hand, when together we'd walk,
I was her man, and I called her "my sweetness",
When she was my sweetness...
But she ain't my sweetness no mo'.

I'd drive south on Wyoming, east on Montgomery,
Then south on Juan Tabo, is how I used to go,
To see my baby,
When she was my baby...
Now she ain't my baby no mo'.

We'd go to the movies, then home to her son,
She'd put him to bed, so we could have our own fun
I made love with my Nikki,
When she was my Nikki...
But she ain't my Nikki no mo'.

I saw the light in her face, saw my future in her eyes,
I look back now, and it's no real surprise,
I was falling in love with my baby,
When she was my baby...
Now she ain't my baby no mo'.

Gary A. Wright

For Kenna

You were two weeks old when,
Your Daddy and I brought you home.
Not from the hospital, the maternity ward,
But from the adoption agency.

"Oh," they say. "You're not her real parents?"
"She's not," they nod with new understanding, "your real daughter?"
Is love, nurturing, love, guidance, love, discipline, not real?
Are we fake parents?

Is the strength of biology more powerful,
Than the strength of the soul, the spirit, the heart?
For some, I guess it is.
For me, "real" is just a four letter word.

It is love that is the true power and miracle of life.
Kenna Marie, you do not have our DNA.
But you will, forever,
Have our Souls.

Ann Elizabeth Smith

My Grandpa

As all little girls look up to a very special person who they call
  Grandpa,
As a little girl you watched me grow, as I watched you grow.
You taught me as much, as I taught you.
I started loving horses, just like you,
Cattle was our specialty for you taught me a lot.
You always told me your hair was silver, not gray;
When Grandma moved on, we were sad together;
When you move on, I'll be sad, but I'll try to be glad
'Cause you and grandma will have another chance
To be together, in a new life, at a new place
A place where you'll be together forever.
I'll join you one of these days
Where there will be so much love and we'll be one big family
  again.
'Til that day I want to say, I love you in a special way.

Diane R. Stouwie

Widow Maker

He paused atop the riders' chute, his hands were cold and wet
Although the sun was boiling down; his body drenched in sweat,
The words of many other men, were ringing in his ears:
"The Widow Maker boils your blood and stirs up ancient fears."
When numbers had been drawn last night, for this day's rodeo
He'd hoped like all the others hands, to keep his ticket low
But when he turned the little square, his face grew ashen white
The Widow Maker; Old Thirteen, flashed in the dusky light.
He'd spent wee hours in the night, alone there by his bed
To give his soul to God above, with all the prayers he said
A vicious snort from inside the stall, caused him to be aware
That he must slip down on the back, of widow maker bare
The well worn oaken rails were hard, with hell behind the gate
There all of Satan's grim revenge, pawed dust and dirt in hate
The beast was blowing molten spit, his eyes were huge and red
His awful horns; long, sharp and black
Struck mounting fear and dread
The roar was great, with screams for blood, when 13 darted wide
Then Widow Maker swung his horns ... and ended one more ride.

Aaron Greywolf

Summer Afternoon

Atop the hill we stand,
cool blades of grass tickle our toes.
We sit, lay down,
cross our arms over our chest,
close out eyes and shout
1, 2, 3, Go!

Slowly, we roll then faster and faster we go.
Reaching the bottom, we lay there
like snow angels as the sky and ground
spin around us. We close our eyes and
wait for the feeling to pass.

A gentle breeze caresses our grass, covered skin,
as we watch the clouds drift by.
They look like cookies on a cookie sheet.
Flat on the bottom and fluffy on top.

We sit up.
Mom, let's do it again!

Dianna Kirkpatrick

Coop Eternal

He is my life,
I am his breath,
He is my soul,
I am his death.

We've danced for centuries,
We've known all along,
We'll love forever with a love so strong.

With our hearts melting,
Our minds melding,
Our souls exploding,
But eternally together.

Reaching across the ages
We've regained a love lost,
A love that has failed
  through many a host.

To describe our love, it can't be done,
Except to simply say
  We have always been one.

Holly KISr Heatherly-Cooper

Love

  Love is Cement!
It can heal and it can bind,
It can bring enemies together
In God's love sublime!
It can mend broken hearts
It can give strength to doubt,
It can forgive the unforgiven
And turn lives about!
It can bring peace to nations,
To families and to friends!
It's the precious jewel of Calvary
God's first and last command!

Cora M. Van Der Zee

The Shadow

Cast your eyes on the shadow on the wall
Can you see what you cannot here,
Can you hear what you cannot see
Can you feel the pain of another,
Can another feel your pain,
If you are willing to help them,
You will be the one to gain.

Can you see the shadow move now,
Is it coming closer or drifting away,
It all depends what you say to it,
It all depends how you play to it.

Remember that once you were a child,
Pure of mind and full of innocence,
Not a worry in the world to speak of,
Full of fun and games, no pestilence

Now you're grown up and worried,
Every day has its own concern,
You're always searching for a meaning
As the shadow beckons you with every turn.

John Edward Cleary Jr.

You and Me

There's a fine line between
darkness and dawn.
There's a fine line between
life and death.
There's a fine line between
you and me,
and our love can make us as one.
There's a fire building in my heart
and I hope that it remains.
When I look back in twenty years
I hope we feel the same.
As I glance toward the future
and look at our past
I get the feeling our love
is going to last.
I hope you feel the same as me,
and we'll see our dream
turn into reality.
Brad David Buckley

The Dream

Dream incarnate beckons me
   From distant lands and sultry seas
Of passion formed from deep within
   My soul of discontent and sin.

Her eyes of pure cerulean
   Whose depths I can not fathom,
have drawn me nigh to certain death,
   A dark, primeval chasm.

Yet chance I fate and yet proceed
   Through her enchanted night,
And find that I have spent myself,
   My dignity and might.

Her words like ancient siren's song
   Enthralled and held me fast;
Until I, weak with mirth and wine,
   Gave in and acquiesced.

Her hair like summer corn-silk flowed
   As waterfalls of sunlit gold
Upon my cheeks, across my breast;
   Alas, my heart hath found its rest.
Wesley K. Curtis

In A Dream's Day

Songs come free
moment's fore slumber
dreams awaken
with the dawning of each new sun
everything I thought
I knew
was living in a dream
once before and now again
back and forth between mind and man
in and out we float
through this life
and then
darkness falls upon us
music begins again
Jennifer L. Wagner

My Prayer At Springtime

O give me the faith of a crocus, Lord
   The trust to push forth without any fear.
In a world of discord, let me be a note of cheer:
   Let my countenance prove that you are near.

Let me show peace like a pond, Dear Lord.
   Reflecting to all, my bond with Thee.
A resource of life to those around me
   So that they too may be totally free.

Let me be awed by your creatures, Lord.
   The egg in the nest, the miracle of birth
Every creeping, crawling thing of the earth
   Proclaiming to all your omnipotent worth.

Grant me endurance — like a stream, Dear Lord.
   Mirroring freshness and purity of heart,
Gathering momentum from the very start,
   Laboring endlessly your love to impart.
Neysa E. Seed

The Magic Of Her Presence

I hear her whisper in the moonlit eve while all alone
I sit beside the fire whose fading light
Is chasing shadows through the room.
I see her in my mind as she prepares to come to me.
I sense the soft and gentle rustling of the satin as
She climbs the stairs and lets it fall upon the floor.
I sense her stirring in the room as if
She really walked upon the faded carpet there.
I smell her fragrance as it fills the room and
Touches all my feelings — waiting as her presence
Stirs the passion in my blood — taking me to soul-filling moments
Gone, I know — a lonely night before.
I feel the joy and peace that marked her time within my life.
And once again I know within my soul
That such a one can never leave the places
Where she walked, or loved, or whispered sad goodbyes.
The magic of her presence fills my life — half slipped away —
And half still waiting in the loneliness of night.
Julian Craig MacNachtan

The Birth Of Spring

As I ride down a valley,
I see pictures before me.
Some show up bold and bright,
Others are hidden, only shown at night.
They are signs of the coming season,
A doe with her fawn,
Or a trickle of water running out of a pond.
The flowers are almost blooming,
While the owls are busy hooting.
Winter is almost over and soon it will all change,
As new life pops up everywhere,
Spring is almost here.
With all the beautiful things I see,
It makes me appreciate what spring really means to me.
Missy Mraz-Holmes

A New Child

The beautiful boy was one year old
at the beginning of '97
In November of 1995 when he was born
He was Grandchild #11

He joined a big sister who was 10 years old
and they soon become good friends
She wanted a brother and he fit the bill
The mutual love seems like it will not end

A "sturdy little boy" are good words to use
to describe this neat little guy
His attitude of well being and content you can see
when you look in his pretty hazel eyes

Meghan likes to take him to play in her room,
to Walker, that's a special treat
He is welcome where ever she is
they make each other's life complete

Looking at this from a grandmother's view,
to watch them play together,
Even though they were born 10 years apart
Their love will last forever.

June Crafton

Football Times . . .

I can clearly see the grass with lines that are neat.
Big players, small players, some on one knee.
Parents and fans cheering on my team.
Helmets on each side of me.
It's hot and humid,
someone smells like wet feet.
Players are dripping sweat from
Their heads to their knees.
Whistles blowing while the huddle sets.
My quarterback calling the play.
We break the huddle getting
closer to the end zone.
Remembering the snap count on 2 not 3.
Sweat burning my eyes,
my eyes blurring.
The sound of the hut hut!
I snap the ball.
My quarterback drops back, throws,
a touchdown in scored.
We Won!!

John Urdialez

Why?

A whisper, a small voice becomes more and louder.
People talk
But they don't listen.
Why aren't I accepted?
Why do I hide behind this mask?
Why am I scared of people who just
Don't want to understand?
I just don't know.
Why?
Why do I care?
Why can't I be me?
The Real me.
Why do people laugh just because they don't understand me?
I want to be me for myself not for anyone else!

Christianna Morea

My Spirit Dances

Oooh enchant me with your
Smile and make me dream
forever.
Caress me with your heart so
I will know no other.
Begone tears of loneliness take
leave, as wind through rain
does part.
You are my song, my unbounding
joy, my breath of life.

B.A. Mitchell

The Real Mastermind

Willows and twilight
Permeate the snow.
A bull moose in my windowpane
About an hour ago.

Antlers and snowflakes
(enemies benign)
Consolidate the oenomel
Eternity and time.

Leisure and nature
Synonymize crevasse.
They quaff the mixture drunkenly,
Then, in turn, crack my glass.

Mountains and rivers:
Creators sublime.
But midnight in my windowpane
The real mastermind.

Nothing subtotaled.
The bull moose is gone.
The dark night in my windowpane
Defraudation due dawn.

Bill Hymas

Dreaming Aloud

   I muse of days gone by,
Of friends, kin and beloved ones.
   Then, end with a sigh.
They are gone, as water that runs.

   So much has been lived
And now is in the past.
   Today and tomorrow are ahead,
Yet only the past will last.

   Thank heaven for memories,
I can think only for the good.
   The bad recedes into a darkness
That is there, and now understood.

   To look ahead to a life fulfilled,
Overlooking the mishaps that could befall,
   And hoping for guidance
For one, yet for all.

   And so, I turn to heaven above
To fulfill cherished dreams.
   Happy days with fond friends,
Utopia, or so it seems.

L. Ryder-Park

Soul

The soul of a man is an interesting place,
where nothing we do can be erased.

It's like a piece of celluloid tape,
keeping track of things,
as they really were,
with pictures that will never blur.

It has no opinions,
and right and wrong,
are not in its dominion.

Beware of what is taken there!
It is the part that transcends the heart,
and leaves a mark of who we are.

And you will see it all again after the end!!!

Donna J. Andrews

Half A Year

Oh give me love for half a year
and lie sweet woos upon my ear.
For although brief, our love is true.
Much dearer than those less than you.
For though they offer years of life
they pale to six months as your wife.
So take my hand, ignite your flame.
Burn fast the candle of your fame.
And as death lays its wicked hold,
I welcome years of bitter cold,
to warm beside your flame my dear,
and love you though but half a year.

Kimberly Hipps

Memories

The sweetness of September,
Memories of days gone by:
The colors of the autumn trees,
The bright blue autumn sky.

I walk the way to yesteryear
As leaves come tumbling down.
They make a soft and lovely path
Of yellow, red and brown.

My heart rejoices, young and free,
As childhood dreams unfold
And fill my autumn days and nights
With treasures of pure gold.

Sister Alice Mary Glennon

Noel

No gift of gold
From wealth untold,
But just a candle,
Burning.
That through the night,
This tiny light,
May greet the child's
Returning.

Mary M. Gaylord

Christmas Thoughts

The seasons come, The seasons go,
   This year is almost past
The Yuletide season approaches, I know
   In a short while, Christmas, at last

Yes, We look forward to the activity then
   These hustling, bustling days
These moments we cherish with family and friends
   In so many wonderful ways

Amid our merriment, laughter and play
   Let us pause in serious thought
And remember our Saviour this day
   And the change in our life he has wrought

So praises to the Saviour above
   To him be The Honor and Glory forever
How wonderful to feel secure in His Love
   And know from His Love we cannot be severed.

David C. Beasley Jr.

The Spirit Within

From infancy to adulthood,
   the mechanics are the same.
The heart pounds, the blood flows,
   the being is bestowed a name.
Smiling then seeing, walking then talking,
   motions that embark on a lifelong journey.
Then comes love, followed by compassion and anxiety,
   becoming the influential sources of energy.
This kinetic resource, bornes the passion,
   empowering one's very own adrenalin.
Its negative effect, encumbers a hurting,
   and its positive effect, promotes a healing.
So that life force which creates one's own vision,
   turning energy into matter, is out sourced —
   by the spirit within . . .

Roseann M. DePinto Naber

The Quest — The Credence

The horse rides on . . . untamed and pulsing
through deepest night of unknown passage
stark, companion only, sounds of hoof and breath
rouse memory echo — ventures past resounding

the horse rides on . . . wind sharp and pressing
through shards of rain cold, piercing, pain
to withers, heaving breast and nostril wide, breathe deep
the quest of journey, alert, vast chasm eyes of flame
choose lone light destiny of path and turning

the horse rides on . . . road cruel and twisting
dark-steep-upward-harsh-places-unforgiving-bleak
black rock cracking — shatter spark and spilling
under hoof-stride strong and rhythmic

the horse rides challenge on . . . and churning
to master not, with faltering shod,
a summit met in low sun shining
though few and swift the joys of warmth,
linger fierce the moment bless, credence of life giving
tender soul in body fearless strength protect, reluctant turns —
majestic the horse rides on . . .

Barbara Jean White

My Special List

When I feel down and get depressed,
I quickly reach for "Mt. Special List"
Of all the things with which I am grateful and blessed.
As soon as I see them, I feel less depressed.
Here are but a few from that wonderful list.
My wife ABD my children are all in good health.
The rest of my family, and also myself.
Food on the table and a roof overhead.
The wisdom to pray before I go to bed.
Family and friends who help me along,
Trust in God that I am never along
My wife and my children with whom I am truly blessed
Knowing they know where my heart rest.
While gazing at this wonderful list
Suddenly I realize I'm no longer depressed
So when things are not going as well as I wish
I quickly reach for "my special list"

Scott A. Louque

Friends

To all my friends that
have since passed gone I
sometimes wonder why you
left me alone. Rebecca,
Randy, Jennifer, Jeff, Carlos.
Mandy, Barbra and Michael, I
feel as if you left me
stranded, the lives you
lived no longer exist but
as for your souls I can feel are stronger, you were
all taken by the force man on earth could never
understand, I see your footprints in the sand
I hear your voice still
With the band, I feel your warmth with every
chill, I wait still for
answers that you may never revile,
but friends will always stay together even it
one has to find her own way...

Jennifer Peavy

One Wish . . .

One night an angel came to me,
and reflected her light down my bed . . .
she asked for a wish,
and then gently kissed my head.
I didn't want to wish for luck,
and I didn't want to wish for gold,
I only wanted one wish,
and it was for a family of my own.
I was tired of feeling empty,
and I was hurt for them rejecting me . . .
I only wanted to ask my angel,
for a relationship with my family.
But my angel said she couldn't grant my wish,
for my parents refused to abide,
I was crushed and deeply disappointed,
by my parents' traditions and pride.
So I had to live with the reality,
of being alone and forced to be without family,
because I can't wish for them . . .
if they never wanted to love me.

Cheryl Ocampo

Devotion

You rise in the east
Strong and bold
You've set in the west
Since days of old
Your strength and your warmth
Are worshiped by all
Through winter and spring
Through summer and fall
You make the buds bloom
You make all life grow
You bring us the spring
By melting the snow
You warm spring into summer
And summer to fall
By shedding your light
And your warmth on us all

Russell Villingham

Almost Lost

Go back to before
Go back to once more
Look into that secret place
Where you bolted the door
Unlock those memories
Unchain your heart
See if you could only
Get a fresh new start
Go back to it's easy
Go back to find your spot
It's simple to impart
With one pleasant thought
Go back to remember
Go back to forgiving
An act of human living
Is worth a moment mending
In a special place where
One wish could make you feel
Going backwards is as
Gentle as a warm breeze

Mildred C. Buncom

Ebbing Memories

I walk along the sea each evening
Walk beside the lonely sea
Listen to the sea birds crying
Wondering where you can be.

When I feel the tear drops falling
And the heartache none can see
Only time can ease the sadness
as I walk along the sea.

I walk along, walk along
Watch children play in the sand.
Walk along, remembering,
all the tomorrow we planned.

Washed away by the tide
gone forever from me
I'll walk along the sea this evening
There beside the lonely sea.

Bernadino L. Betz

The Love That Twas

You said I love you,
You said you are thee,
You said we would be,
We would be together; forever!

I said I love you,
I said now we are one,
We said let's not be fools,
Let us use our tools,
Our tools of love, and trust.

But one drowsy Monday, I said Hi,
And you said, good-bye,
The note that you slammed down,
Down into, on my hand,
Banned me from your heart,
We were now apart.

It was not us,
I felt like a bus had slammed in,
Head on, with my heart,
The part of my heart that was love,
Is now gone.

Jason Schachter

You Captured My Soul

You brought out the best in me
Because
I never knew someone like you
So quiet, unnoticeable
— in the crowd
Not seeming to care
Nor wanting to share a life with one
Could capture my inner-soul
I come so alive not caring
"Just wanting you."
For you've brought out a longing in me
That only you could foresee

Catherine E. Adams

Just A Call Away

How long has it been since you called
Home?
How long has He waited to hear?
The line is open night and day
And any time of year!
There is no number needed
And neither is the phone -
So why not get on
That long distance line
And place a call to Home?

I often find I'm on the line
On just a moment's whim
To let my Heavenly Father know
My thoughts are there with Him...
Oh, I'm sure He knows I love Him;
Still, it's always nice to hear -
It was He who designed
The prayer line
To keep His family near.

Elsie Hagberg Jensen

Don't Stray Little Lamb

To My Son (In Memory of Karsten)
Don't stray little lamb from the flock you were born,
It's much to soon for your loved ones to mourn.
Don't stray just because temptation you meet,
there are so many dangers in these meadows called streets.
Stay within your fold where you're protected from strife.
And if you're lucky, real lucky, you can have a great life.
For when you are born there's no guarantees,
just wishes, and dreams, yes there's plenty of these.
But it's up to you dear lamb which path you must take,
A decision that's hard but it's one you must make.
Don't be lured by promises of green pastures by fools,
There are many crooked games, and most with no rules.
Don't be charmed my lamb by every beauty you see,
for it may be the wolf in his shroud of deceit.
Learn to earn respect and give it in return,
Then later in life there's no bridges to burn.
So little lamb stay close to the flock as you graze.
And you'll be protected from the wolves, and dangers you'll face.

Johnny De Loatch

The Blue Heron

Who would have told me when I woke up this morn,
That I would see a Blue Heron eating our goldfish,
Standing, in the middle of our stamp-sized pond,
And eating his favourite dish!

Goldfish seemed pleasing to the Heron
Helping himself to what he didn't own,
Twas a way of life, he inherited from long ago
And was taught how to survive, by mother nature.

All of a sudden Mr. Blue became aware of my presence.
Regretfully, he decided to run.
He threw his head as far back as he could
And just by magic, his neck became, ess-shaped!

I was standing in the middle of the garden,
Instead of running away, the Heron changed his mind
And flew over where I stood, instead.
Looking like a modern dinosaur with his outstretched six foot
 span wings!

Fro where I stood, the Heron seemed suspended in mid air,
Immobile, like a white cloud, with so much grandeur and majesty
He looked like a celestial apparition, its underbelly pure white
This was but a miracle that ended when the Heron, flew in thin
 air.

Paula S. Kendros

The Key

This cure springs forth from thy disease,
What maketh me stand has sent me to my very knees;
For the wound she opened only she can heal,
Deadened small things I used to feel.

She is the sun in the world she made dark,
In her labyrinth she is the mark;
I bid her 'O heal thy pain your wounds given,
'Before I am mad driven'.

This cure springs forth from thy disease,
What maketh me stand has sent me to my knees;
She has the key that might set me free,
Or does that appertain to me?

Evan R. Law

Crying: The Art Of Temporary Denial

The night's hand graces the day.
They have shattered lives, yet the children play.
Rapture, excitement, ecstasy . . .
we live, yet none of us is free.
Give it up, put your hand down, there is no point in trying.
Follow the lines, see the words.
Like animals they are shuffled away in herds.
Cover your eyes, land on your feet.
I can't calm down, I'm crying.

Perhaps you're wise and I the fool but I can't sit back and be
   your tool.
Not, not any longer.
But, then again, I can't compete.
You. The strong and I, the weak.
I can't help you now, I'm much to busy dying.

They drop their toys, they run inside,
On their face they cannot hide their fears.

Look into my eyes and see . . .
I belong to you and you to me, stop crying!
I am the master and the tool, the wise man and the fool.
I am everyone inside of me. Stop hiding.

Catherine Fisher

A Good Life

At night I'd dream in bed alone,
Of painting the walls in our new home.

I'd put away all the things,
We've saved throughout the years;
I look back at the memories,
Look back at the fears.

I am a woman now,
My own chores I foresee;
I must do for my children,
The way my mother did for me.

As years pass, I look in the mirror,
What did I see?
But the teaching of my parents,
Staring right back at me!

My husband has long passed on,
The kids grew up and moved away;
As I sit here alone in my favorite chair,
I remember that painting day!

Life's too short before you are old,
Tell stories of when was you, sometimes they're the best told.

Maggie Green

Best Wishes

Bread and butter on the table
   eggs and jelly, when you're able . . .
Santa to bring everyone a gift,
   That Turkey at thanksgiving would not be an if.
Weariness taken away from all toilers.
Inking out from us a: Of the spoilers:
Seven league boots for every step up we want in life,
orses an carriages and maybe a wife:
   Employment for all the able bofied
so much and yet so little, in the space allotted.

Elnorist E. Dial

Melting

spring comes round like ancient memories
the overflow along the river
like the melting edges of our childhood dreams
the grey sky of our hidden wishes
broken in places by sunlit clouds
reminders of the things there are to do
the fading dreams are tempered
by the need for care & workmanship
i pull on my wet weather boots
to slog through melting snow
& melting visions of unreal sweetness
to undertake the tasks at hand
store the sled, prepare the boat
check the kicker & the nets
prime the pump for summer flow
the dreamer lives the dream & so
the dreamer soon forgets.

Nils P. Sara

Love Usually

Sweet touch and soft eyes.
Forbidden feelings followed by lies.
Lost love and a new found heart.
An awful ending and a beautiful start.

Blind, but can see.
Deaf but can hear.
Lost, yet know direction.
Everything has connection.

Style, but yet no class.
Pieced together like broken glass.
Too many thoughts,
Yet no time.

Confused mentally, but a strong mind.
Assumptions and doubts.
Worries and fears.
Love usually ends in tears.

Richard A. Moyle

My Sister's Walk

Walking in the beautiful fields with Jesus
Is where my sister soon will be
No more sadness
No more pain
Only joy will be hers
Beautiful starry nights
Beautiful sunny days
All so clear and bright
The color of the flowers
Nothing can compare
Grass so green
Mountains so deep blue
Oceans glistening in the light
I will miss you my sister
Yet I'll rest assured
In your delight

Judy K. Strawderman

Love Expecting

Unborn child, my love divine,
I am yours and you are mine.
Enshrouded in my body still,
until the day we meet, until . . .

Two souls at once in love entwined,
I am yours and you are mine.
Your life my child depends on me.
My heart, my blood I lend to thee.

Safe from harm while you take form,
within my womb so dark and warm.
I am yours and you are mine.
My life, a stepping stone for thine.

Long the days I wait for you,
to feel your breath, to hear your coo.
When Spring-time wakes the daffodil,
then we shall meet. I wait, until . . .

Mary Jo Galente

Roses

Stale, withered roses
Sitting in garbage
awaiting their Final Fate
Trapped within other's perceptions
Hear the hollow howl of loneliness
Scream within you
A shrill, striking soprano
Fading within your soul
Warm, clutching touch
The smell of youth
Lost among the city streets
In an unfamiliar town
Licking sweet suppliance
Danger around the corner
If you cannot let go of yesterday
How can you live for today?

Ethan Molnar

For Dino, On New Years Eve

Let me tell you of my need
silent, it's a desperate thing
ferocious, it waits to unleash
and wraps around each word I speak.

But, oh . . . the words you leave unspoken
knowing I won't miss a thing
you etch the silence like a master . . .
breathing life in broken dreams

Each conversation is a mine field
designed to go off within
but I'm still in past explosions
the likes of which I've never seen

Even though the dust has settled
one call stirs it up again
I pay in time and consequences
This . . . sacrificial suffering . . .

Sheila Stone

Satan's Tomb

No eyes have seen what mine have seen;
unless; they too were a wayward child of gloom.
I saw first hand the depths of satan's tomb.
There, I wish, I could hang a sign to boldly say,
"Beware, stay away!"
To save my brothers and sisters the depths of pain,
I fell into, when too close I came down the path to
Satan's tomb;
The entrance to hell!

Doris A. Ray Surratt

Through The Years

Through The Years an acquaintance of mine,
Our friendship enjoyable, gracious kind.
Right explanation say,
Follow suggestion without delay.
Careful consideration, ability guide,
Assurance know, dependable pride.
Hand extended, "How are you?
Friendly smile make life worth-while, true.
Friends, wish you to meet, Donald Knarr M.D.
He is the best Doctor in the land, believe me.
Let me explain a thing or two,
When you are sick, right thing to do.
Confide about the illness best you can,
Make sure the Doctor does understand.
Helping the sick made well, know medicine to take,
Kind word spoken, Hope to the Hopeless right path make.
Man of courage, Donald Knarr M.D.
Has God given talent, helping those in need.
Miracles still happen in the world today,
Assurance to know, God planned it this way.

Edith Mae Payne

BIRTHDAY BLOW-OUT

Dedicated To My Dad
On October 18th, 1944
The 21st birthday for this young bombardier

In a Flying Fortress called a B-17
The 390th bomb group did try to endure

In the Silver Meteor as commonly called
Climbing 20,000 feet yet destined to fall

No candles no cake merely enemy fire
Now shot down in Germany sadly few survive

The parachute opened an attempt to escape
Only flames and explosions his birthday must wait

Surrender and capture for this bombardier
Gives rise to a power his strength deep inside

He does not give up the will to survive
Although unaware of the future in store

Three children he'll sire and pass on to them
A gift of forever a gift which is him

On October 18th in the year '44
His day to remember a day we acclaim

No treasures nor riches worth more than our Dad
Our Dad and our hero the young bombardier

Shelley Love

As My Ship Goes

The Master walks the upper deck,
His eyes upon the sea.
To try and fathom what is next,
In this vast array of mystery.
The green, the blue, the gold and brown,
A world of colors and all with sound.
Some fish fly high and find the deck.
Others swim by the laboring wreck.
Who would dare to tempt the gods?
To fling a challenge in their teeth.
To smash the seas with a devil's wreath.
The world stands still:
As she climbs the Matterhorn.
Failing: She crashes back,
Broken and forlorn.
The sounds of trembling mount, the cymbals pound.
The seas climb.
The seas crash down.
The Master clings to the crumbling ship.
The Master goes still being the whip.

Ken Flanders

Those You Left Behind

If I listen closely, I can still hear your voice
reciting words of wisdom
reminding me just who I am and what I should do
And I can still see your smile
like an eternal image frozen in my memory
and with it, I can feel your touch
remembering when my small hand slid gently into yours
How strange it is that I sometimes find it difficult to recall the
   details of yesterday
yet I can relive a moment spent in your presence so vividly,
even those we shared many years ago
How I long to have just one last moment
to tell you all that I never took the time to say
and to hold you as I feel you hold me
But I know that simple request cannot be answered
So I celebrate the most precious gift you ever gave me
Yourself
and share that with those you left behind

Elizabeth Judge

You

Your entrance into my life was an intrusion
at a time when my thoughts were adolescent in nature
and responsibility was merely a repulsive word.
I gave you away to a better place
where you would have the love you deserved.
Try as I might, I cannot erase your memory.
As the years pass, I age,
and my desire to forget you strengthens.
Yet you always penetrate the invisible barricade
I have placed between us.
You haunt me, taunting me with all of your
would'ves, could'ves, should'ves.
Though my determination to erase you increases,
you remain,
as though the cold, hard steel of shackles bound us.
And I know that I will never forget,
for you always return,
just as December unceasingly appears.

Angie Foreman

The Green Room

Water drips mercilessly
They file out the door.
A sagging mattress with no stuffing
Is slumped in a corner;
A cross on the wall
Tilted, about to fall.
Paint, peeling and cracked
The light bulb goes out
All is dark
Pain intensely pounding
And building...and then
A flower sprouts
The sunlight breaks free,
And leaps out the window
To its freedom.

Amanda Fawver

Something More

Bright hits of glass in a woman's window
Glad notes of color in an other wise
Bleak scene during white winter days.

But there can be unseen jewels
Shining like the glorious rainbow
Wherever the 'love of truth' and really is.

Truth is more than a law - a Spirit
Which lives and forever sings
In the hearts of those whom Jah has taught
Making a people more kindly wise.

More than that - but what words can
explain the wonderful Essence of splendor
shining down from high heaven?

In a window bright colors that
please the eyes;
But give a blessing, one may know
There is Something More which
hears small children's cries!

Elisabeth B. Constable

The Scar Remains

From the Coast of Africa we came,
Without our language, not even our name.
Our feet were held together with chains,
Until this day the scar remains.
Without our consent we were brought here,
But of bondage we had no fear.
For weeks we stayed in a crouched position,
Many could not stand this condition.
For this reason many died
With their eyes opened wide.
But we made it by God's grace
Mama, Daddy and Baby Face.
When in Florida the boat did dock,
Dad was put on a slave block.
To the highest bidder he did go,
I never saw my Dad anymore.

Dorothy Douglas Gilbert

Tiny Little Baby In The Manger

A host of Heavenly choir
Sung in sweet accord
For the little tiny baby in the manger
Was Jesus Christ our Lord
The little tiny baby in a manger
Born a king, a savior and a friend
His kingdom would go on forever
His raiment would have on end
The little tiny baby in the manger
Was Mary and Joseph pride and joy
Mary and Joseph really loved Him
They loved this special little baby boy
The tiny little baby in the manger
The son of God who brought peace to earth
He was the greatest gift ever given
The moment of his birth
The tiny little baby in the manger
Makes our Christmas day
Happy birthday Jesus, I love you.
Thank you for coming our way

David Lee Knepp

All Is Not Well In The Valley

Where apples grow
and orchards sleep.

Came the prophecy.
Twenty on from
a bi-century mark.

All that was
will not.

And from strange lands
they will pour.

Displacing all the
native lore.

And from the Apple
came this worm.

Germinating in
strongest terms.

That was one sows,
one reaps.

Bradley S. Tice

My Lady Night

Shadowed winds the road
along a jewelled pool
nestling in the hollow
at the throat of Night.
Climbing steeply to soft shoulders
we are stopped, struck breathless:
Precious ropes of neon gems lie,
loose-strung and brilliant;
opera-length strands
along soft, midnight velvet swells
beneath a snood of myriad silver stars
through which escape with joyous grace
moonlit wisps of cloud tresses.

Linda C. Himes

Loneliness

Have you ever felt lonely, well so have I,
It's a strong empty feeling that makes you cry.
Loneliness is such a sad thing.
No one there to talk too, no love for them to bring.
You have no body who even cares,
about all your chances all your dares.
Loneliness is a strong empty feeling inside,
you will bury it deep, you will try to hide,
You talk to God please bless my heart,
for my body and soul are drifting apart.
As darkness falls over me,
I feel as though I will never be free.
As I hold on trying not to fade,
wanting and wishing to be where happiness is made.
I need someone to hold my hand tight,
Help me win this endless fight.
Tell me everything will be okay,
Sit beside me help me pray.
Take the emptiness away from me,
And I will be strong I will be free.

Christine Perkins

Time Darkens

"I don't care" does not take the hurt away.
"I don't care" does not ease the passions of the day.

We live in dreams of longing which cannot be fulfilled.
We drink the nectar from the cup and pray it will not spill.

Reality seeps through and eyes are opened to its light.
We say, "Too bright, too bright, give us back the night."

Our hopes and satisfactions are never quite attained
And we build walls around ourselves and hope to ease the pain.

Loreene Ray

The Sheath

The sheath you wear is your scarlet letter.
In our times of love, it is ever constant.
As bright as the sun.
Waving and screaming of your tainted love.

And it is I, who loves you that wants it to stop,
Or better yet, to have never been.
Stop the memories, stop the pain.
But the waving and screaming never ceases, nor does the pain.

Your tainted love applied the sheath.
Yet, it is you that complains of your diminished sensation.
Tonight, if your will only the sheath would be shed,
And your pleasures excel.

By my will only we wait.
Is this because I rock the cradle and you spear the ram?
Stop the memories, stop the pain.
The wait is finished, your fluids are pure.

The real touch awaits us as seconds go by.
Remove the sheath and pierce! There is fire in my belly.
And it is I that loves you,
That can feel you no more.

Patty Stiles DeJarnette

Fantasy

When I sit at home alone, my mind begins to wonder,
I dream of things, like ancient kings, of pirates and their plunder.
When I am here and you are there, life can be quite dull,
So I journey to lost Atlantis and visit with King Kull.

At other times, when nothing rhymes, I sing a song of sorts,
It speaks of ancient Babylon, or ladies in their courts.
I counsel Sir Lancelot, King Arthur and his minions,
Advise them how to win the war, they heed my wise opinions.

I pirouette with Antoinette at balls and castle dances,
I charge beside the Light Brigade with sabers, guns and lances.
You've heard of Homer's Iliad? Well I was there of course,
I fought for Greece and hid inside the famous Trojan Horse.

But all my wars and conquests are in my mind you see,
Immortal hero of Fantasy, in reality, just me.

Michael D. Schaefer

My Enemy

Why is it my brother you chose to ignore
Our bloodline, our friendship, and all the more

Need I tell you again, blood is thicker than water
For you I once would have died a faithful martyr

Tell me who did you trust and play with as a kid
Then who protected you and fought for you as I did

It's something to think about, it's a critical time
Because the love I once had for you I can no longer find

You knew she was my wife, yet, you uncovered her fountain
Now between us lies an insurmountable mountain

I know one cannot turn back the hands of time
Nor can one trust the words of a brother like mine

For an act like yours, there are no gains
How I regret my blood runs through your veins

Did it affect you the way it affected me
Why haven't you at least offered an apology

A wicked thing you did to your only brother
It hurts badly and I pray my life won't go further

Pain dwells as I reconcile, just who is he
The man once my brother is now my enemy

Reginald Redrick

The Earthquake

The earthquake hit in Frisco Bay,
The Oakland Bridge began to sway
The buildings shook for miles around
And the shaking and breaking made an awful sound
And the people were running around and around.

It was time to pray or was it too late?
The ones the Lord called had already passed through the gate,
All of this was God plowing again warning people of their sin,
So in the future before these things start,
At times when the Spirit is shaking your heart,
Don't shake your head, just answer His call,
Then at times like these your worries will be small.

And in the future when God starts plowing,
Let's say a prayer and thank Him again for sending His Son the Saviour of men.

F. L. Jayroe

Thank You God!

Occupied womb — happy heart
   Excitement, anxiety — constant companion
   Sudden pain - bloody end
   Oh God, why?!
   Worst fears — realized
Vacant womb — sad heart
   Dead, empty inside — alone
   Crying, praying, grieving
   Lost dreams — memories never to be
   Loving Husband — supportive
   time passes — healing — acceptance
   A heavenly meeting — someday
Occupied womb — happy heart
   Tentative, scared, anxious
   Healthy heartbeat — praise God!
   Excited — joyful — thankful
   Beautiful baby boy
   Happy, fulfilled, blessed
   Dream come true,
   Thank you God!

Kimberly S. McCright

The Divine Heart

Hear the Divine Heart
   As it beats for thee...

"O, to bring freedom
   Be in Divine agreement
   To bring good GOD Will
   Into every heart."

Hear the Divine Heart
   As it beats for thee...

"O, to bring freedom
   Say: "YES" have Mercy on us,
   And on the whole world...
   Let us be forever free."

Hear the Divine Heart
   as it beats for thee...
   "How Great Thou Art."

Shana MaKuRa

Precious Friend

   You'll always be the flame,
   That sets the fire to the ember in my heart.
   You were my friend then
   You were my friend when
That was an eternity ago.
   If you were put on this earth for such a reason
   To be my friend for all seasons,
   Your worth would not be measured by any amount of money.
And although I haven't seen you for so long;
   Your love will
   always be
"A melody to me".

Marylin Cynamon

People

Only the foolish and unwise
would allow someone else's opinion
to become their own, without
doing their own judging and forming
their own conclusions, or opinions.
Paul E. King

My Rude Awakening

I woke up this morning
and realized
You weren't beside me
I'm in a cell
All alone
No, I am not
afraid of this place
My fear is
knowing that
you'll never again
be there for me
Loneliness...a
hell all of its own
BJ Murphy

Trust

Be silent, listen inward
I AM the one who said
The heart is a muscle
it cannot break.
While counting your best friends
did you forget about you?
Words cannot harm you
Only the way you feel them.
The most precious gift you
have to give is you.
Take the journey
Your secret is safe with me.
Gilbert G. Gordon-Hall

Voyage

I was sailing on a misty cloud
The sail was full of wind
Height was in my view
Smooth voyage through the dew

Sparkling raindrops formed rainbows
Distorting visions in the sky
Slipping into dream
Filled my open eyes

Fields of waving tulips
Mirages set against the sun
Sensing images of change
Reality is within range

Sailing deep within my thoughts
Clearly navigating through the eyes
Relaxed and carefree ways
Is a day within my gaze . . .
Kenneth David Pollans

Speaking Of Love (A Love Letter)

...And speaking of love;
I apologize for any wrong I've done.
I realize sometimes it seems I don't care,
but never you worry,
I will always be there.

Also, speaking of love.
Those times when I cause you anger,
which leads to you being sad.
Please know that's not my intent.
My aim is to keep you happy and ensure you're glad.

Yes my dear, I'm speaking of love.
So be proud in knowing for you only
my deepest, heart-filled devotion will be.
Because I'm definitely proud to have you as my lady
for this entire world to see.

Understand that I'm speaking of love.
We both know it's not perfect,
but we can continue to do our best.
For as long as we stand together,
we can pass all of life's tests.
Michael L. Sullivan

Waking Up

   The sun shines gently through the morning mist.
Frost lay heavily on the brown grass of winter. With
the greatest of anticipation of spring that will come,
bringing flowers to bloom, and birds twittering in the
soon to be green leaves of summer.
   The world stretches mighty waking from a long
winter's nap. As mother nature looks on from her
mysterious place around us. Showing us another
spectacular first act.
   Looking on with wonder, love, hate and despair.
As the gentlest of rain, rumbling of thunder, all sounding
out her magnificent fury. Love of the seasons we all
greatly share as we sit back and watch her in all her
majestic glory.
Linda Bennett

Burn

Fire-dance.
Flame-tongue.
Prophetic embers
Rallying against darkness,
Feeding on wood and fuel,
Giving birth to flame.

Love burns, too. -hadn't you realized?
It consumes the soul with a
Flame so hot that it vaporizes whatever it touches,
And leaves behind an empty husk
That once was a person.

Burn me burn me burn me burn me burn me burn me burn me

Christ, that raging tiger, knew love, was crucified for it,
And arose three days later unscathed.
If only we were so lucky.
Robert Jump

Rhonda

It was a late evening in November,
when my life was changed forever.
She did not have to say anything,
her soul and inner spirit spoke for itself.
In a time of my life of such despair,
she gave me a reason to look forward.
Our friendship has developed into something
that transcends explanation.
Her words envelop me
and her personality has always enraptured me.
She accepts me for who I am
and doesn't judge me for who I'm not.
In turn, I ask nothing of her,
I'm grateful she's my friend.
I'm not the lucky one though,
that honor goes to her three young people.
In a time of negatives and bad influences
they have a light of hope that will never flicker.
To Ashley, A.J. and Darian,
you could not have a better role model.
Joshua C. Sandlin

Laura Dee Ann Owen

From A Baby To A Lady — Head For My Hand
From a baby, to a lady
My little Laura Dee Ann
The years have passed so quickly
Since I heard her say, "Mama, head for my Hand"

From blue jeans to a suit of navy blue
From a ballerina lunch box to a leather attache
From white sneakers to high heel shoes
From ribbons and bows to pearls and antique lace

From Van Buren to Dallas
From my arms to the great big world
From Eleventh Street to New York and Paris
From Southwestern Bell to GE Capital

Where ever she goes, in what ever season
Whoever she loves and why
Whatever she does, for whatever reason
She's still my baby, "the light of my life"

However high up her ladder of success
This she will always understand
When she is feeling sad, lonely or just a little stressed
Her mama will always "head for her hand"
Martha Anne Holt Nichols

Sapling

On the grass filled plain the stately Oak tree held its ground.
Along the river's edge the regimented Willows
Steadfastly banked their course.
Deep within the forest there stood upon a rise
A strong and sturdy sapling reaching for the sky.

Yon Beach, Maple, Oak and Ash,
All Conifers, Walnuts, Hickories and Sassafras
Take heed of that sapling growing strong.
The time will come when all will whisper to the wind
That once what was a sapling rooted there
Has become a straight trunked tree with majestic spreading limbs.
David R. Chaffee

Sadness

Sometimes we forget,
   the feel of delight.
From a smile of a friend,
   or a hand that's held tight.

Sometimes we misplace,
   good memories we know.
And change them for sadness,
   of seeds that won't grow.

Our hearts should be like flowers,
   that open to the sun.
Not closed as in darkness,
   Oh! Where did we go wrong?

If we would open up our eyes,
   to love, friendship, and song.
God's beauty all around us,
   our burdens would be gone.

We should look up to heaven,
   and feel God's warming rays.
He didn't mean for us to have,
   this sadness all our days.
Nema Maxine Fender

Fear

The constant fear I have
Of what you're going to say
When I tell you what I have to say
It's meant to bring you closer
But I fear it'll push you away
There is so much I want to say
The words form on my tongue
And there they stay
That constant fear I have
Of what you're going to say
When I, if ever
tell you what I have to say
I want you to say the things
That I need to hear
I want to know what's on your mind
Maybe then it'll be easier for me
To tell you what I have to say
Maybe then my fear will go away
When I tell you what I have to say
Missy McBreairty

My Story

God, I wish not to complain,
but, understand your art.
I've seen pools from the rain,
and felt the cold of the dark.

Help me understand what it is—
You—a mystery in the sky.
Watching our lives go in a whiz,
yet always standing close by.

The mystery of darkness below,
has covered the beauty with scars.
God, I wish not to complain, but know
the art of understanding your land and stars.
Judy Pierce

11:35

I dreamt I woke and it seemed to me
that I rose in another's dream
For all the things that make no sense
Did then and there all commence

And played on the horizon
Down the winding road
And I caught a glimpse
Of friends and foes

It was then you drifted toward me,
A familiar sight to behold,
With stealth and strangled silence
Like the beautiful shadow of smoke

I looked at your face
And I saw it change twice
Your words all came out backwards
It was then I realized

If nothing in this morbid place
Had cause to come to view
The dreamer must be dreaming me
And the dreamer must be you

Jonathan D. Ford

Our Way Of Living

The ocean is our house
The mountain is our friend
How big our house is
How strong our friend is
Life is suffering
But we cannot give up
Love is our strength
Faith is our light
Let's keep forward
Everything is waiting for us
Everyone needs us
There are things we should know:
Living in Peace
Loving in Peace
And struggling for Peace

Tri Duc Ta

Time Out

I sit in the darkness wondering.
Wondering what to do next.
Wondering what God has in store for me.
Wondering what tomorrow holds.
I sit fantasizing about my future.
Imagining who I will meet.
Imagining what I'll be doing.
Imagining who I'll be with.
I sit thinking about many people.
Thinking about who is where.
Thinking about what they are doing.
Thinking about if they are happy
I sit and pray to my God.
I pray for my future to be happy.
I pray for His protection against evil.
I pray for the goodness of the world.
One day I'll have answers.
One day I'll see all of my loved ones again.
One day I'll know what to do.
One day I won't have to wonder.

Misty L. Crawford

Friendship Found

A quiet little bird sits outside my window.
Gazing at the snowy scene before it.
Such a small bird all alone
Quietly trembling in the cold
Its past is left untold
Its dream and hopes left unknown
The curious eyes turn to mine
And all I can hear is its small trembling body
Gazing back into its eyes, leading to its soul
I raise my hand to the latch and bid the bird come in
With something of a smile
And a quick graceful move
The bird lands upon my finger
And lowers its head into its soft fluffed feathers
A bird no longer trembling with cold
But serenely sleeping in the warmth

Amy Weger

Déjá Vú

The children are coming home tonight for Christmas —
flying in from those places they now call "home."
The chatter at dinner will drown out
the stock market averages,
and the day's latest reports on Bosnia
(may God bless those peoples!).
So, the silver has been polished,
and the copper pans shine like those in the stores.
Beds freshly made; candles on the dining room table.
My roses in the little cut glass bud vases.

The evening is finally finished —
like childhood, and life, and mother's chores.

As sleep comes softly to close my eyes
I realize that we have talked (not of cabbages and kings)
only of Scout meetings and camp-outs,
and Christmases in other lands, other years;
and the rainy days, when we waded barefoot
in the street gutters,
sailing little paper boats.
And about college days, at Christmastime.

Pearl Webb Hammerle

The End Of A Life

A bird,
flying high and freely in the wide blue sky,
overlooking the ground below,
gleefully chirps a song.

    The bird,
    suddenly finds itself falling, (reluctantly)
    onto the earth,
    down below.

The bird,
now mourning and groaning,
instead of humming a joyful tune;
tries to hold its last and final breath.

    The life of this innocent bird,
    ended by the vicious weapon
    of an envious hunter,
    just...a single shot.

Kevin Yeo Soon Leng

A Whisper From The Past

A whisper, a small sigh total silence fill the rooms.
Small echoes from the past appear as tears on the walls.

So many tears, then so much laughter
once filled these rooms called home.
Family secrets hidden like blood stains on the walls.
Cob webs of old memories linger in every crook and cranny.
My first Teddy bear lay dry rotten on the floor.
I can still faintly hear the screams from the basement and
joyful laughter when the family gathered.

Severely dysfunctional, then as normal as we perceived home
  to be.
A whisper, a small sigh, total silence filled the rooms.
Small echoes from the past appear as tears on the walls.

A burial in silence of a life not fully understood.
Then the acceptance of peace within.
Survival, only to become the over achiever.
Successful in every endeavor.
Our bonding love drew us closer.
Just a whisper and a small sigh left from the past.
      Terry A. Harrison-Duke

The Realities Of Evening

I like to travel at night in my own company
Watching other people's lives.
The passerby with eyes downcast,
The occasional free thinker
Outside, in cultural rebellion.
The pools of light that flood out
Drawing me in,
Demanding my attention.
Perhaps the bright facade of the corner store,
The emanating yellow light.
Or the child watching me pass
Inventing my history and purpose.
More interesting, no doubt, than the one that I created.
The glass surface of every Promethean arch
Displays a miniature movie,
One solitary moment.
And in every movie,
Scripted people gaze out windows;
Authors of their world.
      Chris Dennett

Flowers

Depression, a weed, creeps through this soil,
requires, demands, my conscious . . . it foils.
Damp and double it spreads and grows,
juxtaposes life, care-free odes.

Strong as a gust, or a bull from the chute,
only colours in flower can topple this boot.
Purple, Red, Orange an amiable haze,
betwixt black omens, respite - reprieve.

Today's dark, doleful. Tomorrow incandescent.
This floral array captures the cape, it's bliss.
Sunshine fosters blossoms, burning roots to despair.
      Peter Svensson Couch

Natural Peace

  The firelight flickers
on a calm summer's night.
The stars twinkle and shine,
like diamonds so bright.
  By the rippling stream
small creatures sing their song.
The chirping of the cricket,
the croaking of the frog.
  Out in the distance
a lonely wolf howls.
Above in the tree,
sits a wise, old owl.
  Peace is what nature brings
to people like you and me.
Leave the city toil behind,
see what life was meant to be.
      Laura Larson

Betrayal

Deep down in my soul the hurt reaches
Depths of despair, melancholy felt intensively
Holding on to my last strand of life
Not knowing where I've been or going
Yesterday is nothing but a vague picture
Tomorrow can't be comprehend
My strength hurriedly slipping away
Will power disappearing
Calling out for help with no one there
Battles fought in the darkness of my room
Tears rushing from my eyes
Frightened and trembling I sit
Rocking myself for comfort
Pulling at my hair I scream
Begging for him to go away
But he's not really there
Only his smell, touch and his betrayal
      Shelia Harvey

Days Gone By

A walk along the water's edge
Brings back days gone long ago
Days of happiness and joy
A quiet peacefulness in my soul

Days of tossing stones in this water
And watching the mighty river flow
Running as a child with you
Making sure I was never alone

Thinking of hours and hours of play
Games we knew and ones we made
At the park I was swinging high
Reaching out for the beauty of day

Sitting in your lap to hear a story
You didn't mind reading it again to me
I sat mesmerized by your voice
Until we both fell fast asleep

Yes, those days are long gone now
My children have become the child I once was
Running and playing at the water's edge
My soul and yours now becoming one
      C. Jonell Layton

Delusions

Self inflicted glances of pain
Improvise with the dawn
Impersonating heroes
In a demon's dream

Jan Stephens

A Glance Away

Amidst enduring disarray
Pause a chance to glance away
Time concise, the years depart
Nurture thee, your craving heart

Fetch a smile while it is worn
Hinder fleeting seconds come
Cradle children's essence near
Capture images so dear

Falling petals to the ground
Moments pass, the world goes 'round
Rushing waves upon the shore
Growing children leave the door

Nocturnal sleep, till dawn's new light
Jubilant, the morning bright
Bliss-filled hearts bequeath from them
Gratitude bestowed within

Sally Ann Zaccone Graffeo

At Death's Door

Tonight I look up at the sky,
And think about my life gone by.
I wonder what my life was for,
To live and then be at death's door.
I think about my family,
And wonder what they'll do without me.
Will people miss me when I'm gone?
Can they find the strength to carry on?
And then the world becomes so clear,
As I look back across the years,
And I know that it was all worthwhile,
And so as I die, I start to smile.

Ashly Raiti

Innocence

Look at them in their childlike play
  Look at them may their innocence stay
Wander away from the good
  Not everyone thinks you should
Stay away from the dark
  But fancy thy minds amidst the lark
Age creeps up in a wondrous haze
  The innocence once known set a blaze
Where did the child go
  Or did evil over throw
What visions fancy in thy minds
  Visions of warped world mankind
Child like play no longer know
  Happy emotions turned to stone.

Elizabeth A. Gallegos

Autumn's Dance

Earth colors present in the air
Red, yellow, orange, everywhere

Trees dressed out, ready to dance
Waiting for the wind to present the chance

Wind comes singing to nature's arms
Branches move gently with grace and charm

Leaves come free to fall to the ground
Tumbling and spinning around and around

Each performs a dance, sprightly and gay
Showing their inner joy in a special way

Landing on the earth, clothing it all in color
To keep the seedlings warm, to make cold's bite duller

Ground is covered over, the trees are all bare
Autumn's dance is over, winter's in the air

Thomas W. Calabro

The Bulls In The Rogues' Gallery

I'm sure you've heard of a bull in a china shop;
Well, I've met a few I've wanted to bop:
When we moved into our first house,
A door jamb was scarred by an imbibing louse;
On another occasion a plumber defaced my bedroom door
On his way to settle a basement score;
Another plumber fixed my toilet tank,
Which no longer parallels the wall — many thanks!
Solder stains on my basement carpeting remind me
Of an overhead repair that I can't put behind me.
A visit from a window repair man on the loose
Deprived my front lawn of a favorite painted-wood
  Canadian goose.
Now all the people from the foregoing "Rogues' Gallery"
Expect me also to add my bill to their salaries;
So is it any wonder that I lay claim to whatever tools
They carelessly leave lying around, poor fools!

J. Farrell Griffin

Pulse

I've opened a window into my soul
  The words pour through the wound
Each one hurts, and tears start to form
  It hurts and the words still come
I've tried to staunch the flow and it never stops
  An open wound, that bleeds words freely
To stop it would kill me, and to continue futile
  It takes over my mind and body and pours forth
Onto the blank page, like blood on a white sheet
  Stark on the pale pages, with the same meaning
Both causing a kind of pain, but only one heals
  I constantly write and it doesn't stop
Poetry's the blood that throbs through my heart
  Passionate to the last beat
Constant and rhythmic, always pulsing
  A gift and a curse to be in my veins
Forever there and made to be my life-line
  It's my life, my passion, and my pleasure
For as long as it flows from my heart, through the wound,
  and onto the page

Sara Jayne Hoadley

A Special Friend

Silently, the all-encompassing approach is made;
Covering, hiding, causing things to fade.
Lighting is nebulous; outlines are faint,
The mysterious becomes, there is a taint
Of uncertainty and fear, the unknown is there!
Relentless is its arrival from the mere:
My subtle friend—the fog.

William E. MacDonald

Three White Doves

There's an imaginary window in the sky
Through which the white doves did comply

Graciously fluttering wings unfold
They dart in precision formation bold

Our eyes beheld the three, as if in jest
Symbolically our Lord sent His very best

Twinkling stars in the coolness of the evening
Hovering above we could almost hear them sing

Words of wisdom, words of authority, yet unspoken
These words meant to be received by us as His token

A time to put aside past hurts to rise above the shame
A time to assume command and stop passing on the blame

Our engagement a souvenir keepsake we'd always treasure
Remembrance of the three white doves gives us pleasure

Sitting there clinging ever so close, as if in a trance
Condoning our decision to love and for taking a chance

And now, standing on the threshold of our faith
Accepting the challenges and living the truth

And through our imaginary window in the sky
God retrieved the doves, vanished, before our eye

Martha Warden Mass

Books

Books can be so much fun;
when the road to imagination has begun.

A mystery can make you feel like you're there;
trying to solve it if you dare.

There are books about people in different lands;
how they lived and how they began.

How about one on how to cook;
and give your meals a special look.

Here's one that will make you sad;
the boy looking for his dad.

Ghost stories are a real treat;
They'll leave you sitting on the edge of your seat.

Open this book and you will flee;
to the mystic land of make believe.

Need to know more on different sports;
or how about our U.S. Ports?

Well here is a book that tells no lies;
the encyclopedia which is known world wide.

So just pick up a book and you will see;
how much fun reading can be.

Jeanette A. Wright

With A Joy

I sing with joy
In my heart
To know of a place
Where we are all free
Where one can find
Their hope and their dreams
Where dreams never die
Where hope is alive
Where I shall go
To this place
Where I always see
Beautiful souls
Singing in harmony
Where all can come
If they only, let go
Of all their hate
And see with understanding
Of what we are always to be

Ronald Hight

Drive Away

Would you drive a person away, who wants to become a saint?
Would you drive a person away, who wants to find God?
Would you drive a person away, who wants to be fulfilled?
Would you drive a person away, who wants to be enlightened?
Would you drive a person away, who wants to be free?
Would you drive a person away, who wants to be his/her own self?
Would you drive a person away, who wants to be a gift for others?
Would you drive away, the God who loves you and wants you to be all that you can be?
Would you drive a person — away?

Cletus M. S. Watson, T.O.R.
Franciscan

Sweeter Wrought Pearl

Sweeter wrought pearl ne'er envisioned rhyme
A symbol of the joy of paradise,
From deepness to reach a mightier stage.
And rise with a glow to the desire.

For the joy in the gain of sacrifice
Harken to cry from those in need, and
Show goodness and power to satisfy;
Blessed peace of soul for the mind to know.

See now the luster on this sphere of light
Spread though patterns of faith that illumine
The vision in strains of tenderness, and
Break in showers of gold upon this dawn!

Amelie Doombadge

Who Owns Whom?

My house is not a lonely one
Though I live alone, 'tis true;
Five furry friends are company
And tell me what to do.

There's Zachary, whose eyes are blue,
And Lucas, up in years,
Miss Mary Ann, Rebecca too,
And Cherie — all are dears.

"Give me a drink!!" "Give me my lunch!!"
"Give me a lap!!" — You see
I've never owned my cats at all —
Instead, they all own me.

Marie T. Harris

A Mother's Lament

The wonder of your heartbeat
pulsating in my womb
filled my every hour.

Stillness invaded my soul,
shattered my dreams.
Your heart beat no more.

You never felt the warmth
of sunshine, softly falling rain,
or my embrace.

I never held you to my breast,
cradled you in my arms,
smothered you with kisses,
wiped your tears away
or held your hand.

Joseph,
my son, my little one,
in my heart
you live forever.

Patricia A. Leposa

Suburban Preferred

You may have the crowded city
With its hurry and its noise;
People showing little pity
For the struggling news boys.

Where independence is merely a word,
Relaxation a thing of the past;
Silence nowhere can be heard.
Motors and people moving too fast.

The only substance imparting leisure
Is smoke from chimney flues,
Which robs us of the quiet pleasure
Of viewing azure hues.

I'll take the life of a farmer
(Though his days are full of toil);
Still, he needs no coat of armor
To protect him from the soil.

Georgianna N. Rios

Child Of God

You had a sparkle in your eyes when you were born
that could only come from a child of God.
I loved to hold and cherish you when you were one
because you were a golden child; a child of God.
I watched you learn to walk, then run
and at two I saw you smile and nod
as we started teaching you the ways of God.

At three I knew you were in God's grace
when I looked at you and that great smiling face.
And when you were five I began to see
what God had in store for you and what you were meant to be.
At eleven he began to test your will
and by thirteen you were defiantly fighting him still.

By fifteen you were beginning to apparently see
you were a child of God and it was meant to be.
By eighteen you were turning into a young man
who was trying to find himself and take a stand.
At nineteen you realized what life had in store
that you were a still a child of God:
   as you knelt to the floor.

Norman R. Fugate

Memory Lane

Take a stroll with me, down memory lane.

Where I wander often, but not in vain.

I remember times of yesteryear,
   where people did not complain.

If only I could have captured life, made it stand still,
   what would I have gained.

I wouldn't be able to look back,
   instead be in the hall of fame.

But I'll take life as it has been,
   with all my memories and my name.

God has let me write about it,
   the gentleness and the tame.

In the mountains of Kentucky,
   in a little county called Wayne.

F. Carolyn Bennett

Living A Christian Life

Embrace me, Lord, in your arms so strong . . .
Help me to see that when I do wrong
as hard as I try, the commandments, I can't keep
But don't let me fall in the doldrums so deep.

Make it known to all if they do their best,
In our father's home, they'll have eternal rest.
He will grant us comfort and heavenly peace,
When, for his mercies, we so desperately reach.

Give me the courage to face each day
Helping our brothers in every way . . .
To live their days in a Christian manner
and wave none higher than God's loving banner.

Barb Williams

Love Hurt

A twist of evil in the dark night hour
Fog rolled in across the myre
The sun had sunk low, and the moon rose high
There was a glimpse of madness in the hunter's eye

A strong cold wind blew in from the north
The one he'd been seeking had stepped forth
The hunter spoke out in a loud, clear voice
The hunted stayed calm, he had made his choice

"You stole her away from me, now you must die."
"So it shall be, at least I know why."
There was a thrust, a scream, a stab, and much pain
The hunted's body lay limp, he'd quickly been slain

The hunter walked off, blood covered blade in hand
In his twisted mind he'd proven himself a man
As rain poured down upon his windshield
He sadly stared out at the blood soaked field

He knew he must kill all that she'd been with
He counted out loud, that had been the fifth
He hoped that one day his devotion she'd see
But for now did she even know that the hunter...was me?

Jay Shadix

My Child

Looking down upon you, I see a tiny being . . .
with breath unburdened.

Looking into your eyes, I see a tiny soul . . .
yet marked by poor choices.

Seeing my child full of trust, yet tested . . .
sensing contentment, not yet challenged.

Seeing your development
As my greatest task,
My greatest morality test.

I must clear from my life . . .
All hatred, bigotry, shame,
Resentment and disrespect.

Reaching out to you . . .
In faith, love, care,
Encouragement and respect

Ever vigilant, circumspect,
valorous.

Thus, I offer to you . . . my child
basis for your book,
your life.

Dorothy L. Campbell

To Make It Big In Business You Gotta Think

Johnny Wad, whose nickname was "Tight,"
stayed up all day and most of one night
to figure a way he could reduce the cost
at his cafe where minor profits were lost.
His hamburgers and fries were already small
so there was no way he could reduce them at all.
But suddenly he came up with an ingenious plan
to stop use of napkins by every woman and man.
He had stamped on each napkin he'd issue,
"This napkin was recycled from used toilet tissue."

Bob Moore

Darrel's Lament

I got to seeing double
And I knew I was in trouble,
So I went to see my doctor right away.
He said you'll soon be hearing voices
Which are telling you your choices.
#1 is to give up driving right away.
Now, I'd rather lose my hearing
Or my hair, I know it's nearing,
Than to lose the ease of driving near or far.
But the thing that hurt the most
Was to hear the dealer boast,
"I can't give you very much for your car."

Darrel C. Maxson

Traditions

In the shadows of the past
This old cowboy still roams
Some call him an outcast
For the mountains are still his home

He still works the land
Where his folks made their place
He does the best he can
In this modern technological race

I learned many a lesson
From this old gent
Thought I'd just tell him
How much it meant

Into the future I cannot foresee
But maybe someday such a man
Will become of me

Keith Duncan

Mother's Day

We have set a day for mother.
She's so special to you and me.
We shall tip our hats for mama
She's as cute as she can be.

She's the mom, the cook, the driver
Takes me everywhere I go.
She's the best known world survivor
At work, at play, at home.

To mother dear we wish good cheer,
Baking, making, all we need.
Honor, love and help Thy mother
Thank her for her every deed.

Yes, we'll honor our dear mother
Not forgetting grandma too.
They're important. Oh yes, Brother.
Their love to us is always true.

Now hold hands with your dear mama
Daughters, grandmas, sisters too.
Pledge your love and act no drama,
For she will always love you too!

Madeleine Msarsa Hoss

Vengeance

You see vengeance
In my bloody lips

Vengeance in my
Hateful eyes, full of tears and anguish

Vengeance in my
Scar filled body

Vengeance in my
Wicked smile that I smile up at you

Vengeance in everything
I say and do

Vengeance as I
calmly watch you die!
J. D. Rueben

Words Never Spoken

You looked at me as I looked at you.
All those rumors you heard were true,
That I had been crying,
Yes, over you.
I thought you were my friend,
But your hand you did not lend,
The advice you didn't give,
The friendship we didn't live.
It's gone away,
As I stare down where you lay.
I tried to love you,
But you had lied,
But that's no excuse why you died
Julie Ann Lademan

Labor Of Love

With great anticipation, she waits
The coming of the life within

With a special love, her labor begins
Such intense pain brings new fear
And the struggle between confidence and doubt

Can she bear the burden now given?
Will her dignity be intact?
Will the life within be whole
And bring the joy others have foretold?

The moisture upon her lips
Her self totally spent
Her long journey at last at end
And justly rewarded the gift of life!
Larry C. Gilstrap III

A Little Sorrow Nested

A little sorrow nested
In the bosom of her soul;
She almost clipped its wings —
It brought a measure of console.

New rejection bode a sting
Feared more than that to her befell
When the scope of Cupid's arrow
Proved imprecise compared to Tell's
Jan Olson

Yielding To Manhood

Puberty is nothing that can't be overcome
The months turn into decades while you struggle for each crumb
And down the road a toll booth waits for yet another token
You pay the fee and continue on, no words of thanks are spoken

The creeping hands of father time know only one direction
Around and 'round and 'round in circles, changing your reflection
You have no choice, so age in peace, enjoy the times ahead
Don't work so hard, don't sleep too late, get your body out of bed

Your bones will creak, your back will ache before you realize
Your best years are before you now, man eats, he sleeps, he dies
And speaking of death, not long ago came a day I cried and cried
For the day that I became a man was the day my father died
Dennis M. Mele

My Sister's Spirit

I'll stand by my sister hand in hand
I'll be my sister's strength and she'll be mine
As we stand.
I will not talk about my sister, instead I'll lift
Up her name.
When my sister is weak, I'll make her strong and let
God lead us on.
When my sister is hurting, I will heal her hurt.
When my sister cries, I will wipe away her tears.
When my sister is going through trials and tribulations.
I will not knock her down, but pick her up with my prayers.
When I open my mouth to talk about my sister, I will
Think first, for she may be talking about me.
I will look into my soul, so what comes out of my mouth
Will not be harshly cold.
I am my sister's spirit, word, thought and deed.
I hope she is my spirit as lives and read.
Louise J. Nunn-Walton

Innocent Faults

Waiting for something that shall never be
To let it go is the only choice — I now see
Another chance I was willing to give
But with my decision I must learn to live
The final chapter of a book left unfinished
Now itself has written, these dreams diminished
Nothing I've done should I feel shame for
No wrong done, no need to wonder anymore
In the silence and distance, the answers speak clear
Though in my heart, the past shall remain dear
Friends, still we will always be
Speaking with a smile, if each other we see
This path once left behind, I have now traveled
Now smoothly paved, once bumpy and graveled
Peace of mind, yes I now possess
Pick-up the pieces of this so-called mess
In the present and future, I can now focus my thoughts
For finally, I have dealt with the greatest of
My heart's innocent faults!
Deana Spears

Untitled

The words I speak have lost their meaning;
garbled messages of transgressions long since past.
Old lovers holding on; new ones barely given a chance
for seduction.
Sadness surrounding my mind, clouding the thoughts that
create my desire;
Ambiguous lines that must bear the responsibility for pain.
Where is the door that I have entered?
What has happened to the essence of love?
   Stephanie L. Hanson

A Keystone Of Turns

Lukewarm wind dapples my face
"Typhoon is coming!" I heard the bells proclaim in a rusty,
salt-air voice
"Alleluia!" my ancestors ring—
  'O' wondrous night, my precious child.
  You shall stun earth boiling in your kindness.
  Do not leave me, not here, not yet,
  Do not go where the bells are tolling.
  Stay away from the long waves reigning.
  The curtain draws back from my arrow.
  The flags are pouncing for you and for me.
  For the realm of the sun, the stars, and sea
  is far beyond grace of many mortal hearts.
  Ever as yet, listen to the breeze.
  It tells you of life, of soul happiness.
  Be in calm, or face the starless night.
  Speed away from the backdrop forest.
  The ridgeless mountain you must climb.
  Ever as yet, the angel guide you.
   Jacquelyn Clark

Those Shoes!!!

A year ago I had the blues,
So I went out and bought new shoes.
They were in style
'Cause they were in the news
I walked tall and felt proud being
able to afford such expensive shoes.

I was young and felt fine,
as the admirers and compliments received
made me feel extra proud:
being able to afford such expensive shoes.

One year has passed since I bought my shoes:
Now they are old, I have no use for them
they are under the bed swizzled and gathering dust.

This reminds me of Mary Jane:
she was young and attractive
now she is old and feeble, can't care for herself
no one looks in her direction
She is never in the news! Only when
she is robbed, beaten and dies alone

Let's not forget the aged
Remember they were once like those shoes!
   Muriel Waterman

A Lonely Child

I saw a child today
She didn't smile or anything
I watched her for awhile
to see what she would do
I looked at her
she looked at me
What a lonely child I see
   Sandra Cerritos

My Love For You

Rick and Sean my love for you
no one can explain,
but since you've gone away from me
my heart feels the pain,
for my heart you filled with happiness
and my tears you took away,
but now that you're up in heaven
I know I'll see you someday,
I hope you'll always remember me
for who I am inside,
I'll never forget who you were
my love for you won't hide!
   Jamie Slichter

When I Cast My Eyes

When I cast my eyes upon you,
all else seems to fall away.
With eyes that are truly
a mirror to your soul,
you have also to quality of mystery
surrounding you.
I thought I might never love again
but that strange sensation
has crept into my heart once more
and filled it with a happiness that penetrates
to the very core of my soul.
   Jennifer Goldberg

The Darkness

The world is a vortex of pain,
A black sphere of corruption,
   a corona of hope.
A hundred thousand minds,
   poisoned, twisted, black.
The plague that is war,
   streaks the surface in blood.
The outburst of pestilence,
   shreds the night with screams.
The spread of famine,
   tortures the appetite of the planet.
The Horseman of Death,
   spreads over the Earth.
Harbinger of the dead, tormentor of souls,
   the Angel of Death is pleased.
The savior is born once again,
   his life is brief, meaningful.
With his death the planet grows darker.
The corona grows dim, dim, black.
   Matthew Robinson

All We Have Is Now!

One moment
One second
One minute
One hour
One day
Today
Live now while you can
Breathe
See
Hear
Talk
Think
Touch
Smell
Taste
All we have is now!

Sandra Moreno

Growing Pains

I wish there was some way I could
　help you grow.
　　You know that your mercurial
　　　moods are a fleeting thing,
and yet they hurt you so much.

　They disappoint you in yourself.

You think they hurt me too
　and they do,
　　but not in the way you think.

They hurt me because I see
　how hard they make you
　　on yourself

You have to remember, dear,
　I was once fourteen, too.

Lorrie Serrao

Pearled Wisdom

Enter my heart
　And dance with me
　　Our cosmic union rejoined!
Bless me with the touch of remembrance
　Of Divine,
　　Our origin,
And speak to me your pearled wisdom,
　Born of tumultuous oceans.
I will hear your inner voice
　With love's understanding
　And wear your sacred pearls
　　Around my neck . . .
So will we speak the same truths
　And dance the same dance
　　In heartbeat with Divine.

GuruPrem Kaur Khalsa

It's My Hand You Hold

It's My Hand You Hold whenever you're near,
removing all doubt and all other fear.

I feel the beat of your heart when you're holding me near,
the words never spoken but the message is clear.

When I'm feeling down I suddenly hear
the sound of your voice whispering clear.

As I lay my eyes upon your face,
I'm filled with a joy that can't be erased.

Your love touches me in such a special way,
my heart feels words that you never say.

Your love pierced deep within my soul,
I'll never forget . . . It's My Hand You Hold.

Angela M. Johnson

Heaven Or Hell

Is God's Heaven this once cared for Earth?
How destructive we've been since its birth.

Do people make their own Hell,
destroying space where they dwell?

Must today's morals bring disgrace,
Make a mockery of this place?

Aren't science, religion two parts of one
from the time of conception, earth first begun?

Now is the hour to set things straight.
All nations need to participate.

Dictionary descriptions; Heaven, supreme happiness,
Earth, our planet paradise, a pleasure ground, state of bliss.

Let's bring back our heaven, all its glory,
show we care, not forced by duty.

Once again all folks will recognize
God's Heaven on Earth, our paradise.

Margaret Story Myers

Trust

Has your heart been broken so many times
That it's held together with ice?
Do you think you're all alone in this world
And you got there by paying a price?

It was not God's intention for us
To bear all our burdens alone.
It never was His purpose for us,
To harden our hearts as a stone.

God knows of your every heartache,
He knows when there are tears that have cried.
He's aware of your successes and failures,
He knows of how hard you have tried.

If you can't find the courage to reach out your hand,
'cause you did and you felt sacrificed.
Don't be afraid to try one more time.
Reach out again, and touch Christ.

Bask in the love He shines on you,
Don't question, don't ask yourself why.
Trust that He is there with you,
'Til that day when you meet, in the sky.

Joyce Miller Hardeman

Undone

A picture of alone can be drawn,
seldom on canvas or paper as in
the being, within a you, they, or
me, who so desires it to flee.

Found by some, not much more than one, in
circumstances (unexpected) and so strange
as to exhaust inquiries to and from.
An act done to appease apparent taunting of
thoughts that ingrain injurious ideas (don't think,
they've won).

Of woe and blind, rationale is
undermined, (it's underneath and upside down) until
we find ourselves without all (who still surround) and
yet amazingly unknown, no desire for more,
wonder nothing less, (unachievable).

Lawrence H. Black

Upper Gauley River, West Virginia

Fog hides the river in a giant web of mist.
Obscures our future. I am left-front in our raft
where I lean over to gaze into green tension.

A crescendo begins like some unreachable itch.
Our guide barks orders, as we stroke into
white noise where the current captures us.
Beyond sound, a deafening silence.

I look ahead into blinding spray as I look back,
into my teammates' eyes and the stoic crowd
one autumn day along lakeshore in Chicago.
I am left-wing off scrum as

a rugby ball descends from gray clouds.
Beyond silence, a motionless object
leads a muddy wall racing towards me
one chill autumn day.

In the calm between rapids I lay the oar on my knee
like I can balance thrill and death.
Why it is we're on white water where we're just debris
we choose to keen our souls in free fall epiphany.

Tim Frye

Untitled

I'm trapped inside a tiny box, I want to be let out.
Who holds the golden key? The box has four walls, a
top and a bottom. It's an ordinary box with me stuck
inside. One wall shows a picture of fear - a tiny
child hiding from someone who wants to hurt him.
The second wall shows a picture of depression - a girl
sits alone with tears streaming down her face. The
third wall shows death - a corpse who died a tragic
death. The last wall shows a picture of hate - a man
threatening to kill someone because he's filled with
rage and hated. Could the key holder please unlock the box and let me out? I need to see happiness
again.

Megan Langfitt

Live—Love—Learn

When life is new and love unknown,
We live to learn and learn to love.
While many learn to love and give;
Others blindly learn a selfish love;
Teaching anger, hate, pain, fear or fury.
So choose your pathway carefully, my child,
As you alone unfold your living story.
We live and learn to love more still,
Confidence bringing strength to choose.
While Master Luck may guide our fate,
Madame Chance boasts only of success.
Then we learn some may win as others lose.
First know yourself, then love another,
Strive for peace, then teach your brothers.
Guide the children through fear and sorrow;
Help your sisters see their worth.
Learn to love and live in harmony,
Together exploring unknown joys,
Dreaming still, of future loves;
Living only in tomorrow . . . .

Farr North West

Monet In Alaska

Cold slides through the valley
Weighed down with night so deep
It cannot leave the hollow and
It breathes the barren branches
White around the cabin;
A narrow crescent moon
Spangles the snow with stars.

Traveler new to the country
Lit with frosted fire
Kindled at his feet, he stops for a moment
Frames the window glass, touches the pane
With asters, wheat, forget-me-nots, daisies
Waiting for the cold to ebb from the garden
And spring to color the blooms again.

Donald S. Mulder

My Fathers Forgiveness

Oh Lord up in heaven
that shineth on me
I offer my life
and I'm down on my knees

I'm begging forgiveness
for life now and then
I'm asking my father
I'm asking my friend

So please won't you guide me
down life's empty roads
cause I know you love me
that's what I've been told

I thank you my father
It's good to be home
Life's hills are no bother
cause I'm no longer alone.

Donna A. Kirkness

Unspoken

Everywhere you look around
There are children full of rage
Locked within their anger and
Hatred as their cage.

What is this world coming to
When no one seems to care
That our kids are slowly dying
While we just blankly stare.

With ears that do not listen
We demand that they obey
Telling them they shouldn't do
The things we do each day.

So why then, are we taken back
By the way things are today
When we're the ones who showed
Them, by the words we didn't say.

Deborah Russell

Jivah Jivasya Jivanam
(One Life Is Another's Living)

The fig ripened, from pale green to purple,
under a shroud that scattered the birds,
and the squirrels that watched from afar.
How were they to know the enemy lived within?
When they sliced it open, he rose, a filament
sinewy and supple, in a joyous dance.

His karma persevered
in a game of random chance.
Didn't he belong where he came from
to live or die on his own?
They left him under the tree
turning, tumbling in his velvet confine.

Now watch the bird carry him aloft,
a pink and blue quiver,
against the clear light of the day.
Haven't the scriptures said,
jivah jivasya jivanam:
One life is another's living?

Padma Desai

Sand Castles

Solid like a rock, or so I thought
  My castle built for two
It was a union of love blessed by God above
  And called "marriage" by most of you

My castle of sand slowly washed away
  By the waves of change...and time
So young was she, compared to me
  Since then, I've not been fine

I cried from sorrow and thought I'd die
  My castle, gone fore
My heart was broken by the words she'd spoken
  Build another castle? Never!

I'm bitter, it's true; in time I'll heal
  Sand castle come and go
My dreams were strong, maybe it was wrong
  But how I loved her so!

Stephen A. Crews

Mortal I Am

When we're young we want to be old,
"Take a bath and do as you're told!"
Kids say grown ups don't understand.
Our teen years we start to explore,
We see the world and yearn for more,
Again we're told which things are banned.

Mortal I am, mortal we are, we live and we die.
And in death there is life reborn once again.

As we grow old we value life,
The laughs, the tears and all the strife.
Once we thought we couldn't be hurt.
I realize we live to die,
No matter what time passes by.
In the end we're buried in dirt.

Mortal I am, mortal we are, we live and we die.
And in death there is life reborn again and again.

Mark Brannan

Stars On The Lake

There were stars on the lake this morning.
The sun, as it caught the prisms
Of ice crystals strewn on glass surface,
Twinkled with warmth and welcome
Though temperatures frigid rebuffed us,
Denied the apparent cordiality
And made wise the choice to stay sheltered,
Cosy by fire amber-glowing.
Gazing on star-strewn vista.

There were stars on the lake this morning —
Appeared there quite without warning,
Descended from heaven on alabaster wing,
Fluttered down silently, no one noticed a thing,
Till the sun appeared and sensing their charm
Gave illumination, a light though not warm
Sensationally beautiful, awesome to view
On yon frozen lake, a gift to you
Of crystalline magic, not often seen.
Then a whisk of wind, no sign they'd been,
Swept capriciously from my sight,
To be seen again displayed by night
Where we're accustomed to seeing them shine.
But that magical moment on the lake, they were mine.

Patricia Lawhorn

Heaven On A Tired Day

Sometimes, on a tired day, Heaven will show herself
As the sun glides through an unshaded window
And lands on a dried flower petal,
or an aging picture of a memory nearly forgotten,
To remind us that beauty is ever-present in our lives,
But only noticed when for a second we can grasp the
Life flow within ourselves, and our heart shudders
With the realization of perfection and love.
And often upon this realization, we are so enlightened
That our hearts at once yearn to spread the loving glow
That has a lighted upon our heart.
This is where we find God,
At the crossroads of understanding his union with
Our mind, body, and soul,
And we will achieve the truest of loves,
When we embrace our own heart.

Mike Murphy

Exploded Bottle

As I go from emotion to emotion
I wonder where each one will lead,
Where it will begin,
Where it will end.
As I try to hold in everything bottled up
It slowly begins to make way to the top
I try not to let it go
But yet it seems to build strength upon strength
Draining my every power, my every pride
My every will to hide.
The bottle burst
Everything came out
Not one emotion, all emotions ever felt.
Emotions from years ago, to emotions I come to know.
Rage tremendous,
Anger enormous,
Hurt overbearing,
Pain overwhelming,
Love never known
Sacrificing a heart, now stone.

Kim McBriar

Riches Of The Heart

Times are hard
And the moneys tight
Day to day we fight that fight
God says good things come to those who wait
I guess we'll have to wait and see . . .
Right now it's the little things that get us by
But something tells me we'll survive
Steady through the highs and lows
We can't get by no matter how hard we try
We're getting good at barely getting by
Bill collectors at our door
Wanting money but we got no more
Sometimes we feel so poor
We still have each other though
Steady through the highs and lows
Riches of the heart that's what we've got.

Patti Kostiou

It Isn't You

When you are down and out and feeling sad,
Nothing goes right, "life" just treats you so bad.
The boss and your creditors won't give you any slack,
Just when you're down they kick you in the back.
When you think things just can't get any worse,
And finally, tired of fighting, into tears you burst.

Take a walk through a Children's Hospital ICU,
You'll see who has it bad—it isn't you!
Watch the news—a child is killed for his shoes,
You'll see who has it bad—it isn't you!
Read about the homes and lives lost in Hurricane Andrew,
You'll see who has it bad—it isn't you!

So no matter how low and down in the dumps you get,
Hold your head up, take a big breath and don't give up yet.
There is always someone with things a little worse than you,
And a prayer of thanks would be a nice thing to do.
You might find how much better you feel for a while,
If you can shrug off the blues and put on a smile.

Lucinda Hanson

Rebirth

I knelt among the empty pews
And blessed myself and prayed.
The tears about my cheeks were few
I knew I'd been betrayed.

I drew my dagger from my purse
And held it near my breast,
My life had grown so quickly worse
I longed for endless rest.

As I began to end my strife
I drew in a long breath,
But I no longer held a knife
For I should not have death.

In my hands I held a rose
As red as blood, and warm.
I reconsidered and I chose
To live and be reborn.

My purity to God I vowed
His passage I did mourn,
The rose I added to his brow,
His kingly crown of thorns.

Autumn Raniere

Caprice

She frolics in the dewy morn
As free and gay as dreams unborn.
A simple life and mind has she,
Fulfills a simple destiny.

A noble nose and sincere eyes
Bedight a wisdom on her guise.
Delightful ears flop up and down
Not more than inches from the ground.

A new plaything to gnaw and chew
Is all she needs, or wants to do.
Old, knotted socks or leather balls
She champs between incessant jaws.

Intrepid bones compose her frame,
But in her heart there burns a flame
Of loyalty and love for me,
Of innate joy for revelry.

She spends her daytime bantering,
Reclines at night recovering.
Endeared to me is my Caprice
Of noble nose and blackened fleece.

R. Larry Grayson

Silence

I caught a silent moonbeam
And took a silent ride.
Inside the silent light it gave
I found a silent joy.
The silence of its wisdom
Filled me silently
Until my silent mind rejoiced
In silent splendor rare.
And when my silent ride was done,
I silently returned
To a noisy world
I knew was silence in disguise.

Kat Bergstrom

Hope

Hope came,
Hoping to stay
Close to the one she loved.
Hope lingered,
Hoping to hold the one she thought
She might get to keep.
Hope lost.
She should have known better
After being hurt,
So many times.
Hope has aged.
Hope is lost forever.
Hope.
Gone?
Yes.
My name is Hope.

Ramona Cole

A Patch Of Prairie

I am a titan
as I walk through this microcosm
   treading on ant villages
   and beetle cities
each step taking untold lives—
   a Godzilla of destruction.
The crack of a branch was
   just before that
   a bridge for an ant
or a shortcut on his long journey home
   now broken by careless curiosity.

I am a God
as I walk through this microcosm
   deciding which will live
   and which has crawled its last
knowing that I, too,
am merely another life form
   whose fate
   has yet to be decided.

Janie Koos

The Well

It seems as though I fell
Into an eternal well.
My heart wants to see
All the love left in me.
It stays out of sight
For fear of eternal fright.
I can't eat, sleep or dance
For I've lost my true romance.
Mind you it's not for forever
But only a short little lever.
My heart won't stop
Until time takes an eternal drop.
Deep down into my well
In which I shall cast a spell.
Till then my heart shall lurk
Protecting all its valued work.

Stormy Mehlhoff

Anticipation

He walks with me in the early hours of the dawn
He carries me when I cannot travel on.
It is then I hear my master gently say
Turn not to the left, or to the right
And always keep my word in sight.

He instructs me in the path of righteousness
So my thoughts won't go astray
The burdens and the problems of life
All quickly melt away.

He gives the strength that is needed
To ascend the mountain top
And there the faith is added
To make us the cream of the crop.

The promise of eternal life
In the celestial city of god
Is given to every son of man
Who believes and lives according to His plan.

Don't walk away from this plan of God
The blessings are rich and deep.
The promise of eternal life
Is something you want to keep.

Wanda V. Griswold

Waterway

Atlantic and Pacific, they were to a new begin, as sometimes in birth, oceans among the meetings — to others waters with an end; Mediterranean and some seas, flowing steadily, wavey, and rapidly, of some these did feed. Two bands as the transcurrents, as like two revolving eye — because of its vastness in boundary, other nations shared an oar, at times the cosmics can be heard from them among the gentle sky. Oh! To see the tidals and
   wonders
to its intricates, what makes the winds which roars across it, does tell us he's not just of the sky. As the two have met at the American Gulf Gate — some Isles are amidst, shall we take the time to remember the splendors of waterways.

Beauford Johnson

It Was Only A Dream

Suffocation, I cannot escape it.
It closes around me; writhing; binding.
Falling into a deep, dark pit.
Never to be free again.
In one last effort I reach out.
A strange hand entwines mine.
Locked.
To never be torn apart.
A strange, unknown feeling.
The sound of rushing water as I'm being pulled out.
I see his face; dark, brown eyes.
Warmth.
His suffocation; I cannot escape him.
He closes around me, writhing; binding.
Falling into a deep, dark pit.
Never to be free again.
No struggle, no fear...
I wake to find
   it was only a dream.

Tammy Sue Poynter

The Ocean From A Sailboat

The ocean is peaceful,
Blue waters surrounding,
White birds fly above,
Jagged rocks go by slowly,
Sister boats are heading to their destination.

Seagulls squawking,
Fish jump out of the water,
Waves splash the bow,
The faint sound of the radio below deck,
competes with the whistling wind,
Buzzing motors whiz by.

The rocking back and forth; back and forth . . .
moving up and down; up and down . . .
Never getting anywhere . . .
Sea sick.

Sheri A. Jalbert

The Streets Of Yesterday

There were streets of yesterday, alley ways
   which never reached the sun.
Ox carts ground the cobblestones.
All these, paved over and gone.
There were streets of yesterday, avenues
   where shaking shadows spun.
On silver leaves the gas lamps shown.
All these, grown over and gone.
There were streets of yesterday,
   twisting lanes with brambles over run
   where crickets chirped in undertones
   and these are faded and gone.
I found a road of yesterday on ruts and
   rocks which ancient shadows cast.
I followed it. On either end it faded out and
   led into the past. Onto that winding road
I'll stray, that hidden way where ends are
never seen, but lead to a million yesterdays
on silent moon paths which lie there
   peaceful   undisturbed   serene.

T. H. Owen Knight

Our First Meeting

You walked into my life, on a warm summer night.
With eyes sparkling like the morning sun light.
Shining with warmth and tenderness as you talked.
Class and dignity followed you where ever you walked.
Your hair shone as pretty as a winter rose.
With lips gently moistened as by the first winter snow.

Gentleness of angels flows from your smile.
We popped a beer and then talked for a while.
It seems we enjoy the same things you and me.
You're a very special woman it's plain to see.
Full of love, life, and so much energy.

I feel a special bond of trust between the two of us.
Just by your respect and the way our friendship has touch.
There's grace and kindness in everything from you I have
   ever heard.
You're a real lady in every meaning of the word.
Lifting up my spirit with your smile.
Sharing your warmth and friendship all the while.

Jeffrey J. Shuda

"What..."

i stared at my hands
and the coffee they clutched for warmth
his words like thunder, distantly rumbled
as the fog of my breath clouded my vision
i didn't feel his hand upon my shoulder
or see him walk away

thomas j. madigan

The Freshmen

As the wind brushes her face,
And her hair begins to dance;
The smell of summer mixes with her smile.
The touch of a hand that warms the heart —
The eyes that seem to flow from within,
The sky casts a shadow of her silhouette,
But the green chases the darkness away.
As the trees gaze, they seem proud to be alive
When love is blown through the air —
It could have been a thought,
Or it could have been a dream;
Because reality hides the truth
When we were merely freshmen.

Charles Batcher

Do, Don't

All the work, All my life
And all the sorrow, All the strife
And all the friends, And all the pain
Yet still I'm not as I have claimed

Not alone as I've claimed to be
Or maybe more than I can see
I am alone
Perhaps I'm not as I have thought
My thoughts and feelings on this page
Feelings of pain, immortal rage

Do I feel the mockery
Of the world outside me
I think I do, Yet still I don't

Someday I will
I know I won't

David Hentzel

History

I felt such intense emotion
You pretended total devotion.
A deliberate lie—an unreal ecstasy
Another abuse—perverted fantasy
Violence filtered through the seams
Scarring my heart—also my dreams.
In an innocence of youth
I couldn't begin to imagine the truth
Of a mind so crazy and twisted
which wisdom would have resisted.
I have developed the faculty
Of mentally blocking out reality.
Forgiving—denying—gaining tranquility
This silence holds the mystery
Of a past permanently sealed in history.

Anna Frances Lipinski

Dream

I often dream how it would be
for everyone throughout
the world if we could all agree
what greed is all about
and just because you're black or white
or red or pink or blue
the one thing we should keep in sight
is what we all should do
is treat your fellow man the same
as you would want then to
treat you throughout this mortal game
and surely would ensue
a place where all are free to live
where no one is repressed
a place where everyone would give
their very, very best
our children would not learn to hate
or prejudiced to be
would surely help to set the fate
of you, yourself and me
Jeffrey A. Lundstrom

The Stranger Within Me

Under the tall, tall maple tree,
With leaves of red and gold,
I stood and wondered about the stranger,
That lived within my soul.

The stranger that lived within me,
A person that I did not know,
Was it really a stranger,
Or someone I had known before.

I thought about the stranger,
I wanted to know its name,
What did it really look like,
And the place from whence it came.

I looked and looked around me,
And held out my weary hand,
The spirit of peace came to me,
The ruler of all the land.

The stranger that lives within me,
Is God's everlasting love,
It is that stranger within me,
That brings peace from up above.
Vashti J. Hopkins

Valentine Day

Instead of sending love notes
That "one day" of the year
Try daily spreading love words,
To those you hold so dear.

Time moves so swiftly,
The present becomes the past.
May it never be too late
To share memories that forever last.

God gives His love so freely
Everyday that we live
So share a smile, a hug, each day
And all the love you can give . . .
Elsie M. Elmore

God's Gift

What a gift to be born in the USA;
To be able to worship each and every Sunday
To be able to pray any time and anywhere.

I thank the Lord for my family,
Who has respect for the Lord; His majesty.

Though some don't search Him like they should
Deep in my heart I wish they would.

For to have Christ in your life is a great gift;
And knowing the Lord;
Can really give your heart a lift.
Carla Shawn Quisenberry

Blessings

My life is rough and tumble, my house is never neat;
there are hand prints on my windows,
the floor decorated by muddy feet.
My living room is a jungle gym complete with a wrestling mat.
No cuddly kittens in our home;
only turtles, bugs, and rats!
Baseball cards, chewing gum, lots and lots of blue;
pockets filled with nature's treasures
and other sorts of goo!
Dirty faces, banged-up shins,
chubby hands clutching bouquets of weeds,
slobbery kisses, mischievous grins . . .
The Lord Sure Knows My Needs!!!
Fishing, racing, climbing trees-energy galore!
Fixing things with Daddy
waging brotherly war . . .
Random acts of kindness, angelic faces fast asleep,
Yes, my life is rough and tumble,
but, oh, the blessings that I reap!!!
Candi Mathews Wynn

American Indian

I did not walk in your shoes so long ago,
So I really cannot know.
If I could have traded places with you for only a day,
Then perhaps I could have understood your way.

So proud and humble are the Indians and the way they live,
A spiritual quality that only God can give.
You wanted to live in perfect harmony in this abundant land,
But it was just too hard to understand.

Though I cannot communicate with you as your people do,
Nor can I feel the hurt and deep emotions inside you.
But I do extend my hand as a gesture to you
Of my love and friendship so true.

For love is the key to our sacred heart
And will connect us though we're worlds apart.
We are one with God, the great spirit, you see,
Perfect love, brothers and sisters through all eternity.
Jeannette Raff

Hands And Feet

Little hands and little feet, He's crying for his mother.
Come to Him and hold Him tight, for there will never be another.
Growing hands and growing feet, busy working for His Father,
Teaching in the temple, telling of the living water.
Working hands and working feet, going to and fro,
Telling others of God's love, of which they did not know.
Nail pierced hands and nail pierced feet, blood is pouring down.
The cries of pain and anguish are nowhere to be found,
The hands, the feet, the pain He has inside,
He's crying out for mercy, mercy for you and I.
The hands the feet went willingly to the cross,
His cries for mercy not for himself but only for the lost.
So bring your hands in fervent prayer, your feet for his service.
Repent of all your sinful ways and make yourself his servant.
So when you meet upon that day and put your hand in His,
Your feet will follow in His steps, so Heaven you do not miss.

Sandra Elaine Schlessman Yung

Faith In Me

There once was a time I thought my world end.
There once was a time when all the colors started to blend.
There was a time I didn't see the light.
There was a time things did not seem right.
That time has past and gone away.
For God has my soul and it's there to stay.
I feel his touch in a tender breeze.
I feel his presence in the dying leaves.
He will help me through it all.
Stand by my side through thick and tall.
Nothing will go wrong.
For God will make me strong.
He will make it right.
He will make me fight.
Before it's over, my fate will turn.
Before it's over, I will have learned.
Nothing can be wrong - you see.
For God has faith - in me.

Amy Jo Czarnecki

My Swing

My swing was the highest swing in the world,
And below me great wonders of the earth were unfurled.
I soared as I swung out over green trees,
Reaching my apogee above the bluest of seas;
How free was my thought, how exempt, like a bird,
To float on the air with motion unheard.
Thus, filled with marvel, and yet noticed by all,
What I took to be freedom, I found was my thrall,
For the heavens were empty and meaningless too,
Now void of fancy, now vulgar to view.
For I was alone, and 'midst all certainty
High on a swing filled only with me.
I slowed my great motion, returned to earth's floor
With no recognition of what life held in store.
Lone soaring is futile, the most specious of flight,
It lacks love in its wonder; my swing was too light.
Then with no hesitation you climbed upon my swing,
You gave new meaning to dreams, and those dreams took wing.
Now with you at my side toward the heavens we are hurled,
And our swing is the highest swing in the world.

Vincent P. Russo Jr.

Futility

I've sent you pretty flowers
With lovely, lovely scent
And written to you, poems
With sweetest sentiment

Perfume, yes—by the gallon
Enough to fill a lake
And gladly more I'd give you
If that's what it would take

But though I am persistent
And try, and try, and try
Your heart remains resistant
It almost makes me cry

Your heart still I'm pursuing
Though little I succeed
Continuing my efforts
Encouragement I need

You are so sweet and lovely
But is your heart of stone?
I wish that I could soften
And claim it for my own

John Sunday Jr.

The Bowhunter J.D.

Ever so quiet—his footsteps
    As he slowly slips through the forest
His movements only a whisper
    As he searches the shadows for game.
Sharp eyes miss no movement
    As he watches the animal feed.
Slowly, fluidly, draws his bow
    His eyes never leaving his prey
At full draw—he floats like a cloud
    As the animal begins to move.
With precision release—the arrow flies
    Perfect aim guides the shaft to its mark.
The deer taken—the hunt rewarded
    With meat for dinner and the winter.

Cheryl Warren Williams

Sun, Moon And Stars

Morning sees changes
brought by the sun.
Shadows sneak away like thieves
and the sun begins to warm the earth
bringing life to everything
it touches.

Shadows creep back with the night
deep and dark, in limbo
waiting for the moon
the pale translucent light edges up
and dazzles a small lake
in diamonds.

Millions of stars splash across the sky
twinkling, winking and trying
to out do each other.
The milky way becomes lost in infinity
as the Big Dipper pours
its way through the night.

Regina Cook Williams

Cycle

Rainbow skies splintered,
littered with tangled wires.
Geometric shadows loom
where we survive.

Golden rose moonbeams,
from steel trees grow.
Blistered, painted barricades
shelter creatures below.

Hours later sunburst,
glistening beneath our feet.
Sharp, jagged beauty,
imperfection we greet.

Ravaged thoughts roll,
free as synthetic tumbleweed.
Toxic fumes swell
making reality complete.

Rainbow skies splintered . . .
Michele J. Chamberlain-Hale

The Cry Within

Who cares for me when my feet are cold?
Cried the women living on the street,
Who will give me a hot cup of coffee?
Will it be a stranger or a Priest?

Where is love that I heard about?
Has it gone away with the lonely years?
Where are the children I cared for?
As on my pillow I shed these tears.

Does Jesus love the poor and hurting?
That has drifted and lost their way,
If someone would just come by
Shake my hand, sing a Hymn or pray.

Once again I want to hear lovely music,
The Beautiful words of "Amazing Grace,"
And find the true love of Jesus,
If only, someone would come by my way.
Nancy Mineer

The Driver

It's only natural that we wonder
With all the wrongs we see.
Why people gain materially
By not obeying the moral laws.

But do not let that sway you
From the Creators rightful path
For the rewards given here
Are not the ones that last

Remember to live by the spiritual laws
That bring everlasting peace.
And if depressed and lonely.
And the world seems all down hill
That on a dark and desolate road
In the middle of the night
You do not see the face
Of the driver.
For whom you blink your lights.
Ron Easton

Earth

Earth and Heaven around us.
Roll us with love and faith in God.
No matter, how hardship, that we overcome,
Like thunderstorm, tornados, or earthquakes or
Wars of all nations. We are still divided in true love
in our own heart. So even the Winds, the rains, and the Brighties
Sunshines, The flowers, the trees, the Birds that flying by.
The eagles look like sparrows in the eyes of GOD. He is
always there up above the sky. To grand our wishes
like a million stars. When it comes to money the root of all evil.
Jesus Christ our Lord the Savior of mankind!
Letty F. Mendoza

Mother

She's dipping a needle
with meaty farm fingers
into the softness of my wedding quilt
Her thimble bounces on the pretty girls with umbrellas
"That Leslie" she says of One Life To Live
"She's always sleeping with this one or that
That's all it is anymore"

In the limp light
I see the silver start in her hair
the way japanese beetles gnaw at a bean field
in unwanted patches
"My poem was published," I say
her thimble taps a needle sliding along a yellow skirt
The tap slams into the dank basement air

"Oh Rita's pregnant did I tell you"
she says turning the quilt and
dipping another needle through the softness
"You'd be surprised how much
I can get done on this in one day" she says
Carol J. Stratman

Silence

Forever in solace I cannot defy,
This faltered world and its lies,
No one ever finds the truth,
It can be in your grasp only once,
As it slips through the fingers of all you've known,
Forever in penance I've been misled,
This wicked life seems so sacred,
There's always an answer hidden so deep,
But it can never, ever be seen,
It makes its way into confusion,
My mistakes in life leave their abrasions,
Forever in silence I will not deny,
With my mistakes I've lost my pride,
No one can ever replace what's missing,
Cause something is missing in man's heart,
With one man's quest towards atrocity,
He doesn't want your apology,
Just the silence is all he needs,
Just the silence,
And he'll descend so happily.
Jimmy Mills

Be Aware

I lie in bed beside you, your body next to mine
It gives me so much pleasure you send chills up my spine!
Your eyes look down upon me with
  Such gentleness and care . . .
I look back up into your eyes . . .
Can you really be aware?

Of how much you really thrill me,
  When you turn to me at night.
And look over at me it
Your eyes twinkling so bright.
Of how the whole room lights up,
  Just because you are there . . .
It really turns me on inside . . .
Could you really be aware?

Of how you do excite me, reaching out to touch my face
With hands so strong but gentle,
The memory cannot be erased!
Of how with your arms around me, I feel beautiful and rare
You make me feel like heaven!
Are you possibly aware!

Barbara Cole

The House Of Faith

Blisters over the winding night skies
The flower could have been a butterfly
Flung off the crotch of petals in some strange birth
Or a skunk on the run through starbrush and pine
Slipping through the net of nights
With an inward eye toward the unseen
A festooned clock, perpetually fingering
in the circle for more time
Shedding flames like tears
Leaves me hang, supine and loose
In the seaweed of my mind
While the barnacles of time
breathe warmly through me
And red light silvered your eyes
With arms outspread
I felt the mind tearing, clinging closer
Soaked with the promise of rain. Soon
We walked as if all naked—swearing
The aphorism of hard endurance—circling
The roads surrounding the house of Faith

Kerstyn Porsch

The Solution

You say you can't live with me anymore.
You've not given a hint of this before.
We're not only lovers, you're my best friend.
Our life is so perfect, why do you want it to end?

You say when you're with me, time passes too fast.
You want to do something to make the time last.

If you have so little time left
Isn't there just a small doubt
Your life would be better with me
Than to be without?

I think that the answer to get over this shock,
Is stay on together but throw out the clock.

Betty Jeanne Buckey

Crossroads

I'm approaching the crossroads,
to choose a path for me to travel,
for I must adapt to life's changes
and evolve, before I unravel.

For better or for worse,
I'll never be the same again,
the person I was last year
isn't who I am now, my friend;
and where I'm going will be better
than where I was, in the end.

I'm still running against the wind,
fighting this blow on my own,
for it's the only way I know
how to deal with this ghostly foe.

When the time comes,
I'll spread my wings and go;
'til then, I'll be like a rock,
going against the flow.
As I approach the crossroads
and a destiny that I don't know.

James Porter

To The Artist In You

You paint life's picture
With myriads of emotion.
You started work
With an object in mind.
Unaware, unknowingly
You've portrayed your persona
In colours of feeling
And sentiments
That filtered through
Your mind
While you were at work.
That extra stroke . . .
. . . that excess shade
Reeks of you
As the words you speak
Don't
And perhaps will never do.

Chering Tenzing

Smiles

A smile is like a wave,
Rippling and spreading
From one to another.
It may start,
Almost imperceptibly,
In the eyes of one person,
Often caused by a reason
Seemingly trivial.
It brightens the face
Like a sun;
Suddenly appearing
From behind the clouds,
Spreading to people nearby;
Until the whole area
Is illuminated
By the gentle beauty
Of a smile.

Verina Shaffer

The Eagle With Two Heads

They merge with echoes
And thin searing eyes;
They conserve with magician's spells
To claim forbidden fruit:
Picasso and Cocteau knew the secret
And became masters in their own right,
With stars and angels
And codes of being true to the Brotherhood.

Yet the prophetic vision
Is always there,
To be peeled away,
To break moulds of fashion,
To conquer new territory.

Life is beauty and the beast
And we must accept both,
The harvest-time and the winter.
But only within intimate relations
With powerful connections,
Can you find that space
Between the eagle with two heads.

Peter Corbett

Untitled

Away you go. Loch Nessie Beastie.
Into fathom. No one can Reachie.
A phantom fancy. You travel still
Across, some minds of men.
Where shadows dance, and call to them.
Upon the Loch, you're seen to glide.
In your wake, your beastie hide.
No one can tell, if you are real.
Where from the depths.
You choose to steal, away men's minds.
Upon the Loch, where wait the charmed.
In kilted frock.

Phillip D. Jude

A Winter Evening

The moonlight casts a subtle glow
Upon the freshly fallen snow,
And glances over drift and crust,
Which scintillate like diamond dust.

A snow-clad cottage, seen nearby,
Stands black against a starless sky,
Offset by room-lit windowpane,
That casts a gleam on white terrain.

Billowing smoke from chimney flues,
The lucid evening sky imbues,
Creating patterns bold and free,
Of ever changing fantasy.

And trees of most inspired design,
Encased in ice, look crystalline.
No image either brushed or penned,
Can to their beauty justice lend.

A strong environmental rapture,
Are words that best define and capture
The peacefulness and sense of bliss,
Experienced on nights like this.

John-Allan Champion

Realized Love

When there is darkness and nothing left to see
Life seems as it's at its end
Emotions running rapidly
What has all of this even given me?

An empty heart with broken dreams
Clouded skies with rainy days
Another day with unspoken words
That last forever—as though it seems

Another tear slowly falls from my eye
Trying to just walk away
But not knowing which direction to go
All my heart really knows is to cry

The journey was short but with extended dreams
With love and happiness
As one would ever desire
Shattered in moments—as it all would seems

Another day continues no without you
Still with lingering anguish
Not one tear do I cry
But realizing now that I fell in love with you . . .

Jennifer Sile

We Will Miss You Papa

You were rough and tough, as a big old bear
But when it came to loving us you did it with
Warmth and loving care.

You spoke the truth, at times we didn't want to hear
But somehow, you made us face all our fears.

You were there to help and guide us through it all
The one we could count on, on troubled times to call.

Although, you have left us all behind,
You have left us with memories of laughter and love in our
Minds.

So rest now papa, you did your job very well,
For all of us we can go on by sharing your love and
To others we will tell,

Of the man you were, and how you touched so many lives
Along the way,
You are missed and loved, on each passing day . . .

P. Diane Martin-Sims

They Ask

Pets: they ask for so little.
They don't ask for much, just a nice, soft bed.
and to have a drink and be well fed.
They don't answer back, and if they don't get a treat
they don't lose their temper and stamp their feet.
An encouraging word and a gentle touch,
to us seems small, to them means much
and what do they give us in return?
They give us love, when no one else seems to care.
They are a companion, when there's no one else there.
They are clowns when you're feeling low.
When you're down, they are your get up and go.
They are all these things and much, much more.
And all they ask of us, is to be safe and secure.

Marion I. Goodwin

My Little Princess

My 'little princess' with coal black hair,
skipping thru my door without a care.

My 'little princess' with eyes of blue . . .
wearing white anklets but only one shoe.

My 'little princess' pretty as can be,
looking at me . . . hoping that I see

All the little capers she happens to do,
knowing so much, tho she's only two.

My 'little princess' in her braces and glasses
going to school then to dance classes.

Learning new things like new steps and math,
how important girls things are . . . like a bath.

My 'little princess' in her cap and gown . . .
out of high school and leaving this old town.

Now my 'little princess' is all grown up . . .
dating guys who wear jeans and tucks.

My 'little princess' in her bridal veils,
walking down the aisle . . . hearing church bells.

Looking at her husband the new love of her life . . .
but still my 'little princess' tho she is a wife.

Joy Lockhart Black

Yesterday's Table

Three of us is all I can imagine,
reaching into the distant past, groping for your face.
A shadow is the most that can be conjured.
Blood ties, yet even your voice has thinned,
an echo I can live with.
The hand, still poised to strike, is safely buried,
your lips finally sealed.
The beating that did not raise welts, raised questions
you will never answer, and shame, your only legacy,
has faded. Even that.
Three of us only sit at yesterday's table,
spooning the just desert you always missed,
watching the evening light through nylon curtains,
a delicacy, an elegance, a memory fragile as a woman's wrist.
Mother, daughter, sister, all of your women, grown
We have outlived the need for explanations,
outgrown your noise, your little tyranny.
The chair at the head of the table now is vacant,
three of us sit here, only three.

Patricia Kelley

Friends

Just a little parting gift from two real nutty friends
One is always known as George the other one as Den.
And every time you use it, it may remind you too
Of the happy hours we had, what fun in knowing you.
Smoked you out of house and home and still you asked us back,
We came and ate your baking, played games upon the mat.
Someday I hope you'll visit, to Canada you'll come
Brian can bring his trombone, we'll have a lot of fun.
Farewell to you at present, I hope our paths will cross
Nice to keep in touch with friends; I'd hate if you got lost.
So once again I thank you for all you've done for us
Thought you needed more to do, here's something else to dust.

Denys B. McLaughlin

Country Road

There is a winding country road
Beside a lilting stream
Where in our youth we loved to roam
And laugh and talk and dream.

At eventide when chores were done
We walked there hand in hand
Into a world of sweet romance,
Enchanted Fairyland!

This road is our sweet memory lane
Down by the winding stream
Here, hand in hand, we love to roam
And reminisce and dream.

John Hornfjord

I Believe In Angels

I believe in Angels,
I believe they're everywhere,
They are God's messengers,
Who show us our Lord, love and cares.

They watch us every day and night,
They're in with us always.
They ensure our life stays in tune
with God us, our Lord, who loves and cares.

It's easy to know an Angel,
For one must love themselves,
And love others too,
For without this, no angel can help you.

Always put your faith in God,
and his holy word.
For an angel is God's messenger,
for this the Angel heard.

And when we are in trouble,
or have problems we can't solve.
There's an Angel watching,
that will help and become involved

Stephen D. Pommer

Silenced By The Gunshot

Silenced by the gunshot
Misty waters shudder cold
And rippling fields to attention
Bloody as a vampire flock

Silenced by the war-wound
A young doe and her spindly fawn
Framed by conifer clearing
In a painting far too dear to see

Silenced by surrender
See the flowers slowly creep toward
The boundary line
The forest edge

Opposing land
A soil of bloodshed
Fertilise opposing crops

Tamsin Douglas

Counting The Beats

In the shadows, my heart beats.
I listen to its rhythm.
I count the beats 101, 102, 103.
Holding my breath 104, 105, 106.
And wishing I couldn't count at all.
I'm still scared to death.
It's not helping 107, 108, 109.
I want to scream and scream and scream.
Instead, I silently count 110, 111.
The seconds become a lifetime
Of counting, of screaming, of shadows.
So I count the beats 112, 113, 114.
Still trying to forget.

Judith Winchel

Love's Shadow

From my window
 nature grows.
  Trees
   sway in the wind
and clouds float by.
 They do not
  recognize me
   For who am I?
But I know them
 for I am as they,
  flowing and free, but
   full of the earth's tears
For the struggles
 and the sadness.
  From my window
   I see all there is
and shed a tear
 for that which will never be.
  From my window,
   Love's shadow

Nancy Brown

Oh! Ah!

In the middle of the ocean,
Now I am floating
between two lips of the sky and the ocean
that are kissing together to be one
with all their ends.

To the sky
with the light of life
with the blue of the deep and the clear
with the silence of forever,

The ocean
is kissing endlessly
digesting its own longing,
calmly and quietly
with the passion of the wave.

When has this kissing been started?

Now I lost my time and my space
as a little earth throwing up all in me,
and see myself fading away
saying, Oh! Ah!

Chong Yum Park

To A Friend That Means So Much

People like you are hard to come by.
You're like an angel that was sent from the sky.
I know you're a friend I can trust,
Because you seem to care so much.
I know if I need someone to talk to
You will be there to help me make it through.
You've already helped me out in a lot of ways,
And when I'm sad you've helped me have a good day.
It's nice to know a person who cares so much.
Friends can always well when you need a hug or that
 gentle touch.
I really look up to you and the wonderful things you do.
There is a lot of very good qualities that I've found in you.
Friends stick together through thick and thin,
And when you fall they're picking you up again.
I know I'm not the only one that feels this way.
You are always smiling and,
Trying to have a good day.
You are very wonderful at all the things you do.
I couldn't have picked a better friend, and that's what
I have found in you.

Amy Barnes

Best Wishes

Thank you for your interest—Regret to inform you
Must regretfully inform you—We are sorry to inform you
Sorry to tell you—After serious consideration
Committee has reviewed and is unable—We are unable to offer
Careful consideration was given, however
After careful consideration, We regret—selection difficult
Competition is keen—Highest number of applications
Highly competitive—Number of spaces—unable to accommodate
Thorough review was given, however—Selection is difficult
Committee has established a minimum index
3,300 applications for 260 spaces—More than 3800 applicants
Applicants compete for 280 spaces
Admission standards have increased—Must deny many
 with interest
Best wishes for your future—wish you success—Wish you well
Good luck in future endeavors—Wish you the best
Wish you well in attaining your goals—We wish you well
Best wishes—Best wishes for your study at another institution
Appreciate your interest, thank you, best wishes.

Cliff Kayser

Utah

I've finally left the city for a place I know I'll love
There the air is crisp and clean and the sky is clear above.
The mountains to the East and West capped with pure
 white snow,
And everything is so serene in the valley that lies below.
A quiet town, a tree lined street,
Mountains and valleys and lakes all meet.
A smile, a hello and a friendly face,
All these things combined make this place
What I want to and now do call my home.
I am quite sure I will not again roam
Just in case you're wondering, this place is Utah. Where
I've found such peace and beauty made with God's loving care.
Yes, I'm glad I left the city where things all move too fast,
To live in this beautiful valley, I've found my peace at last.

Carole A. Adamitis

The Bottle

A cry for help, a plea from within.
A longing from deep inside.
For someone to help, and to protect.
Yet she choose to hide.

She can't understand the feelings she feels
or where in life she went wrong.
So many people say not to give up.
But how will she ever be strong.

So many memories collide in her heart.
Many so hurtful and filled with pain.
What is it like to smile she asks
To make the sun shine through the rain

Maybe some day her life will change
And happiness she'll feel again
She prays each night that she'll never wake up.
But she knows these feelings will end.

Terri Needle

My Kelly

Survival smile
moved me closer
in joyful acquiescence . . .
to stare into beautiful blue tranquil luminosity
blessed with heavenly ecstasy
the day my grandma died.

Indemnifying spirit,
Embracing affiance,
Respect your tender responsive kisses
when we met; silent unspoken courage,
did metaphorically erase and heal past abuses . . .
Fortitude, now frightened?

New breaths together in tropical sunshine,
warm, passionate moments filled with adventure . . .
Survival, not love
moved you to remember forgotten hurts;
Strength's paradoxical rebirth
clouded you from me.

My brave warrior, reclaiming our peaceful surrender
Happy "survival smiling" beyond survival's pit!

Daniel B. Hanewich

Lovely, In Spring Time

My mother's satin dress, I thought, was like
the grass of Spring: cool, soft, shimmery green.
Through the grass I ran, happy to be
on bare feet loosed from winter shoes and free.
My father's pocket-watch was old, and like
Spring's warm gold sun. Under sun we'd go
where we knew tiny violets must be
among the moss, beneath the big oak tree.

Winter's child was in Spring time conceived
by their love joined. So Spring and I began
that year together. And I seem somehow
entwined with warm gold sun, cool soft green
and violets, when now remembering
that once their child-to-be was new as Spring.

Lucy Means

Pass To Silverton

Pale puffs of powder fade
into damp drops on
the dark path
Hairpins hang
far above
crystallized rivers
beginning to flow
Icicles weep
trickling tears
down deep powder
Snow dust
blows in the chilled wind
over the jagged mountains
settling in white trees
before moving on

Donna S. Savage

My Coupon Clippin' Mama

She's my "Coupon Clippin' Mama,"
You bet your life she is!
A discountin', sales rackin',
Money savin' whiz!

She's happiest when she's shoppin',
For a sale or bargain item,
Searchin' for the best deal
And you know she's gonna find 'em!

My "Coupon Clippin' Mama" —
Cost cuttin' and gettin' one free,
But one thing she's never discounted
Is the love she's shown to me!

She's always there for anyone
Who needs a shoulder or feeling lost,
And all of this she gives quiet freely
Without any obligation or cost!

So, when she gets to heaven,
God will smile at her and state:
"I'm glad you finally made it,
'Cause you're due a Big Rebate!"

Betty Northcut

A Child Made Of Hell

Pass through these eyes of flesh
does thou see as man see
willow with the rest
we're down on bended knee

Our eyes are the windows to our soul
does thou feel as man feel
I see you now as a whole
our lives spin as a wheel

We are the same
but unlike others
we are untamed
you wish we were another

You see me as a child made of hell
does thou hear as man hear
all our feelings we force to dwell
you all have something now to fear

Heather Dodds

One Last Goodbye...

To die in my heart,
if you only knew.
I'd change the past,
but I'd still love you.

If I could say goodbye,
before you left.
I would be at peace with myself,
but not with your death.

Often I wonder,
why it was you?
Was your time really up?
No one really knew.

God gave you a goal,
you achieved what you could.
The love that you gave,
has now dwindled away.

But now that you are gone,
will we meet again?
I guess when it is my time,
I will see you my friend.

Temple Turner

That Special Night

Why do you think is the end?
   The night we cuddled on the gym floor
   eyes met
   hands touched
   bodies warm

   The night we used each other as blankets
   thoughts exchanged
   ideas raised
   questions answered—except one

I though it was a beginning
Yet I must ask again
Why do you think this is the end?

Lyle L. Schmerz

Golden Times

In golden youth lavishly leaf
Came flaking from the bough,
Bathing us all with brilliance brief
And happiness enow.

Lavishness lessens with passing time,
Tho' leaf comes flecking from the bough,
Bathing us now with mellow rime
And happiness still somehow.

Bobbie Bobo-Hennecy

A Memory Of Elise

The memory of her was sweet smelling
like that of perfume
An if you could drink in the smell
than that's what you did
An you let it linger in your nostrils
till it vanished
into a memory
An with each inhale
to smell you over and over again.

Jennifer Kerezsi

Creation

An Awe inspiring aura of originality by Our Father.
Spectacular Splendor Everywhere.
Breathless Beauty beyond compare —
Bold, Brilliant, Colorfulness; No other's
Work could dare.
His crowning act - His image - Man.
From Man — Woman.
He created them.
Authentication, Perfectness.
Forever Only! Forever Rare!

Kelvy Buck

Foretold

Tired eyes straining to see ahead
Eyelids are swollen from tears they shed

Deep lines have made a home on that face
the mouth was once strong and spoke words of grace

The shoulders now rounded and weak
long gone their squareness from the height of their peak

The frail frame of the body not so long ago
was its master's pride
now after years of living it's losing its fight

So now he walks slowly, step by step
thinking of the long hard road ahead

He comes to a stop in the middle softly he can hear their giggle
he looks at the children and folds his hands to pray
to thank the Lord for their youthful way

But he is ready to go to the end of the road
his body looks it he has been foretold

And humbly he whispers oh Lord please bless me
I am ready to repent send down your angel to take my hand

And there it lies in the middle of the road
the old man's body it had been foretold.

Marga Eich-Collins

Full Circle A Case Of Deja Vu

Just got off the phone just got the news
My girl is fourteen years old now heard she's starting to lose it
Not here to make excuse for my absence not here to explain
About losing touch with reality oblivious to my responsibility
Just hoping for a second chance to make her smile
Gone without a trace no letters or cards
Never realized your mother and you were hiding out in
   my backyard
But I guess I really didn't look too hard
Pain from being all alone the empty feelings after leaving home
The memories although faded thinking of you
The pain from your father not being there
Where nothing matters and no one cares
Reminds me how often fate can be so cruel
Full circle a case of deja vu
Now I'm not talking miracles for a can never right the wrong
I promise you I'll be there for you when you're not feeling strong
If you reach that fork in life wondering what road to travel on
I'll be there to lend a guiding hand if you will only let me belong
Believe me when I say I wish...I'd never gone
Believe me when I say I wish I'd never gone.

Peter Thorburn

Home

Home is a place I like to be
Where a natural simplicity fills the air
And a feeling of peace comes over me

Here in this personal space of familiarity
I am surrounded by subtle reminders of who I am
Everything from simple joys to
Representations of values and responsibilities

As I embrace the sense of warmth and love within
Home provides an atmosphere of rejuvenation
It becomes a source of strength as it gently reveals the
Importance of loved ones for motivation

The expression of contentment in a smiling face
Supports the ease for which it stands
I take comfort in the friendly energy of welcoming arms
And the generosity of helping hands
Clearly without expectations, without demands

I can always count on home to keep me in touch with
Where I've been and where I'm going
It is everything that really matters
And truly a place worth knowing
    Diane Farrell

Retrospect (Young Impatience)

Wrapped in the fire of all of fifteen years,
When everything is felt, acute, unsure,
O'ercoming thoughtful act and reason pure,
Then is the time we judge with eye severe
And take harsh stand 'gainst those we love most dear,
Who seem so unaware of our censure
Of inept words, of looks we long to cure
And of recurring flaws to us most clear.

And yet our youthful eye has failed to see
The understanding, years of life may give
To those who came before us in their time.

Their diff'rent voice and diff'rent look will be
Our mindful joy when they no longer live,
And can no more offend our youthful prime.
    John F. Petrie

Time Is Not An Enemy

Long ago, alone was I
Noting but that the days gone by
Solitude my companion, loneliness my friend
All of my life was but a way to the end
The calendar bore the scars of Time's gentle touch
Nothing but my wounded heart could hurt so much
Wounds inflicted from battles not attended
Hurting still from loves coldly ended
And I blamed Time for it all . . .

Without warning you struck with such speed
Nothing could have prepared me for the fulfillment of need
The darkness of my life had been lifted
And with sweet endearment I was gifted
Each day that passes makes me hope for many more
Every gentle touch gives me love to endure
My life has been filled by your charm
You have saved me from my solitude's harm
And I thank Time for making me wait for it all.
    Philip D. Mann

The Force Within

White hot pain
Searing thru my senses
Moist red lips
Leaving no defenses
Good and evil share your soul
Pain and pleasure make you whole
If I could tame the force within
What passions await in your bed of sin
You lead me on until I'm lost
Only now I learn the cost
You take the heart I gladly give
But leave me not the will to live
The dreams I had you made come true
And ecstasy I never knew
Than you showed your darker side
Treacherous Goddess with selfish pride
What power have you to tempt me still
Your satisfaction received from the kill
I turn to flee while I'm still sane
And lose myself beneath the rain
    Teresa M. Warnick

Pinch Me

Is he real? Am I asleep;
Nestled in his arms so deep?
So I whisper; to be sure;
"Touch me, pinch me, kiss me more".

Is this life or fantasy?
A dream or new reality?
Pinch me softly, so I'll know;
Pinch me gently, nice and slow.

Let me see your candlelight,
Between the flickers of my life.
Hold me; take away the fright,
Of those long, cold, stormy nights.

Is she real? Am I asleep;
Lost within her eyes so deep;
Kiss me softly; make me sure,
Pinch me slowly; just once more.

Let me feel your shining light,
Between the shadows of my life,
Hold me; take away the fright,
Of those long, cold, lonely nights.
    Christopher W. Boyden

Sonnet To My Valentine

I pledge my true love to thee forever,
Inspiring vision of my lifelong dream;
And sweetheart to part from thee I'll never,
So long as love eternal reigns supreme.
Mem'ries of your home life that I admired,
Bring back the happy hours I shared with thee
Who made my manhood even more inspired;
Thus to be worthy I'll strive to be.
Let us my love entrust ourselves to God,
Our hope for happiness, our faith and vows;
Unmindful of society's changing fad;
So as to reach the goal which God bestows,
To loving hearts that only beat as one,
In wedlock that unites woman and man!
    Filomeno L. Pacis

Callings

Sister spider,
tucked warmly
in a dark, damp corner
of the little bathroom,
how carefully you weave
your web
from shadowed walls
to the edge
of light at window's sill,

while I
so callously
and clean
will use my broom to sweep away
the dust,
your silk,
and all our children's whispers
singing
in your strings.

Donna M. Marbach

To Doubt Is Treason

Thou shall love thy neighbor
The scriptures clearly say
And follow the Lord's way
Holding high thee saber

Do not question why
Just worship His name
Play the holy game
And ignore the lie

He is all merciful
But do not cross His path
For He has quite a wrath
Can be just as vengeful

No rhyme no reason
Bow to His power
Or face His glower
To doubt is treason

Melanie Winters

Affections Of Love

What is love?
Love is the affection of
Two people, who share one
Life and who give to each other.

They share the joys and wonders
From the gifts of life
They cry and do not surrender
When there is pain and strife.

Together they plan for their tomorrows
And look back at the past.
The love and affections they have made
Let's them see, that life is not easy.
Gift's are not free, we pay for
Our time on earth, but it is much, easier
when you are with me

So I share it with you, since you
Came into my life, I have love, and
I give all my affection to you, this
Is love, true love shared by one
Another life through, till forever

Janet E. Gendron

As We Live Together

As we live together,
Life gets better and better.
because neither one of us is a Hater
We work together and play together
Our Old ages of 84 and 88 Never make a difference
At our age, we have learned to Love and Play.
And our Love is strengthened Day by Day.

George S. Knapp

What Else In 1996?

The deplorable state of the human condition in 1996.
Where cultures, values and behaviors intermingle or intermix.

Where religion's influence is in a fix;
Because subculture's belief contagiously tricks!
The New Age, stones, candles lit and psychics are the rage.
Personal conceptions, computers to learn you just turn the page.
Personal hygiene, perfection set the stage:
E-coli, Aids came when herpes left.

Sexual frankness and numerous experiences of,
Knowledge and learning;
Brought back celibate practices and aims of urgency to
Remain aloof, than be a goof.
Marriage was retroactive; whereas always babies
brought many a couple to the altar.
J F K's Zero population growth did falter.
Now the world is overrun by hungry 3rd World people
Spreading like disease.
Water use is causing World self ruin,
And will be rationed as everything else.
Where will this over growth as Cancer end?

Ilene A. Evans

Butterfly

I dreamt of being a butterfly for it was freedom that I yearned

Only to discover the perils
   Of life and the stones yet unturned

We trap ourselves in our fears and doubts
   And worries that have never been

For freedom is in the hearts and minds
   Of all those who believe in Him

We live in a cocoon, reaching out,
   Struggling from our infant birth

We try to imagine life beyond sheltered now while we live
   on earth

We must reach beyond the walls so thin
   Where our senses won't let us go

Letting reason of the eternal world
   Make our spirits begin to flow
Like all the phases of our earth-bound lives
   Experience unfolds each turn
So can our belief in Him shine light
   On the knowledge we've yet to learn
One day I will be that butterfly
   Reaching out I'll shine in His light
As a flicker to the world beyond, He'll guide me to His
   Kingdom bright

Allysan Drew

For Sam

I love the way you look at me, you see into my soul
You see what's inside of me, not what I put on show.
I love the way you talk to me, each word is a caress
Every time I hear your voice, I'm filled with happiness
I love the way you hear me when I don't say a word
You hear what I want to say, though it goes unheard.
I love the way you touch me, your hands against my skin
There are no words yet to describe the joy I feel within.
I love the way you love me, my senses running wild
I lose myself within your arms, you hold me like a child,
But most of all I love you just for being near
I know that with you around, I have nothing to fear.
    Krystal Brown

Pebbles In The Sea

Now that we know we shall not abide
as long as the sun moon and stars that
survive and mourn each of us in turn
Now that we have seen mortal bodies waste
and wane crumbling into ash and dust under
the ruthless heels of the sure wheels of fate
that crush and grind mortals in turn

Like waves from a pebble flung into the sea that
stir for a while and return to sea as if nothing
has changed so our days scratch the endless stretch of time
Which memories abide
Which legacies are alive
They are the fountains that are hewn from all
the rocks around and along the ways which
water the seeds and mature the harvests of posterity
Forget not that the paths we now trod have been walked by
countless mortals now into oblivion but the fountains
they cracked and the pebbles they threw in that have
continued to stir the waves of time.
    Augustine Ogbunugun

Behind The Curtain Of Liberty

Upon the Plymouth Rock, anchored they their weary souls,
Our Fathers of the Pilgrimage, mingled shame with glory!
The fear of never ending journey has just ended!
Fleeing for freedom, which, forever not be ours,
An aftermath of faith yet to be decided by future!

"And so why did our fathers flee home?"
Poor Usa asked grandpa, just before the horizon darkens!
"Oh small boys are young," he lamented,
"Small boys are young, indeed!"

"God has been our integral life!
The old great Eagle had brooded us under her wings!
Until the old enemy flooded in unawares!
Seeing our Washingtons and Lincolns have left for their day,
And leadership has become a privilege, and not a responsibility,
Snuck he in, with a disguise holly name of wood!
And began he, sacrificing our daughters to striptease Baalim!"

"Boy, it has taken over ever since, ruling with a snare in mind!
And today we are left squatting on our principles of Liberty!
Old grandpa has finished his sayings, cleared his throat, "hmm!"
"We have far drifted toward Gomorrah zones—Good night!"
    Robert Van-Earl Danso

Poor Man's Prayer

Looking out the window
I watch our four year old
Playing in the yard
And I start to wonder
What lies ahead for him

So innocent and young now
He knows nothing of hate and war
Knows nothing of poverty and hunger
He's just an innocent child
Without a single care now

So my dear Lord
If you happen to hear
This poor man's prayer
Take this child by the hand
Don't let him stray

Won't you watch over him
He's so innocent and young now
Won't you take him by the hand
And don't let him stray

So my Dear Lord . . .
    Terry Neal Albin

Days

Days of old,
Days of new.
Slowly coming,
Speedily being renewed.

Yesterday was honest,
Today has been false.
Day before testy,
Tomorrow will be just.

Someday I'll be free,
Possibly for evermore.
Waiting for these days,
Till I wait,.....no more.
    Marcia M. True

Airborne

Breathless in the morning sun,
High on the rocky hill I stand,
Gazing down the path I climbed,
Viewing this rugged mountain land.

Below, a glider, tether-free,
Floating like a great white bird,
Catching a flash of sunlight now,
All round the valley moves unheard.

Pilot and glider without constraint,
Rising weightless as they pass,
Borne over fields on wings of air,
Drop ghostly shadow on the grass.

As that glider, one day free,
My soul no longer body pent,
On morning's airy wings may fly,
Soaring upward, heaven bent.
    Memory Lane

Free Spirit

Fly high, fly free
the way a spirit ought to be.
Do not threat, nor dismay
let your spirit soar far and away.

The day will come for it to land,
hold it gently in your hand.
Do not force that spirit to stay,
for it will only go astray.

Love it, nurture it, let it roam.
Your spirit will always come back . . .
it knows its home.

Never let your spirit die.
Kimberly Carroll

It Is Here

It is here.
The birds are flirting
  and singing.

The bugs are hatching
  and chomping.

The flowers are painting
  the landscape anew.

The sun and rain are
  playing their games.

My heart is light
  and feeling young.

It is here
  It is Spring!
Judy Turner

Two Poems

The organ in the center of my chest
Pours out a wilting song
My muscles heave a tired sigh
Everything feels so wrong
My surrounding are familiar
Friends and family, still the same
But beep within these chambers
I'm viewing different frame
I can't get you out of my head
My heart and brain are pounding
On the window of my thoughts
The scram of a new day sounding
It's almost frightening, what I feel
Your face is in my dreams
We bond like sand and water . . .
Chrisanna L. Hibbitts

Rain

   The rain, it comes to wash the earth of
dust and scorn, it comes to wake the dying
leaves and drench the drowsy morn.
   It brings the mist, the driving sleet that
on our window panes will beat.
   It brings the sadness and the light
and refreshment in the night.
   A gift of God to men on earth, the gentle
rain, the flowers' birth.
Edna Laffin

A Promise

Shoulders shrouded with hair of gold,
  Lurking behind, deep fields of blue,
    Speckled with tints of yellow.
      A promise, as of yet unfulfilled.

Feelings of unknown origins and yearnings not fully understood,
  A faint blush from becoming cognizant of others,
    one of whom will be chosen.

Her feelings and yearnings only partially understood,
  Thoughts not on the one she has her arm linked to,
    As she half steps, toe to heel,
      Heel to toe down a decorated aisle,
        Cheeks suffused with the full bloom of a red rose.

As her arm is transferred,
  To be linked with the one she has chosen,
    After the vows have been exchanged,
      A promise faithfully kept will soon be fulfilled.
Daniel W. Manosh

Independence Lost

I have eyes, but you say I do not see
I have ears, you say I choose not to hear
It is not of ignorance or of calculated action,
but perhaps a miscommunication on my behalf

My fears seem to have a hold on me these days
I can't seem to grasp the answers
that I know must lie within my own mind

I have certain goals in mind for my own
personal gain, and some for us as we
share a life together

I want to be and do all of the things
that I am afraid of, but how?
How do I overcome all of my fears and
inhibitions? I only have one solution;

To once again be the person you fell in love with
and regain my Independence Lost
Sara A. Marro

Such A Cold Feeling . . .

Such a cold feeling, the line of headlights
wrapping down the lane
beyond the tree line and into the fog
thick like a demon's breath
your tears lost on your dress
your hair wild, strange.

I felt you flinch as they lowered the coffin
I felt you shiver with cold sweat
As you stared somewhere past the empty
Spot of earth, past me
as I looked into your face with a worried sigh
I wish he could live once more
though all of that is behind us

Just lost is all we remember of him,
just lost is all we remember of ourselves anyway
with a longing to be where he's at
And taste the earth as you only could once
buried, and mildly forgotten.
Benjamin Skiles

Untitled

You kiss the morning passionately
And grasp the earth tenderly.
Your outstretched arms reach for me seductively.
   Holding you close;
   Intoxicating aroma,
   Beauty beyond compare:
    The rose
   Terri Lazzaretti

Beyond The Fog

A whispering wind soothes on by
A murmur of gulls, break the lull,
Thoughts of fear, and visions of delight
Seem to canter about — yet nothings in sight.

An endless stretch of water like a dark blanket adrift,
Lays affront out there — a path of reminisce
Of far out secrets beyond the mists.

The harbors of life come into view
And out there is calm, and serenity too
Yet — the dark blanket shrouds the path of day,
And shuns the right of way.

Too many days of utter despair,
With only time left for helpless thoughts appear
The blanket ahead — further enhances its wrath,
By strengthening its cover — playing totally unfair.

We the ships that pass through these fogs,
Must smoothly and slowly direct out course
Avoiding the dangerous logs when entering the harbors
   of remorse.

The final mooring — secured further in the twilight hours,
Anchors the peepholes of fears and tears —
As we pass through, and beyond the misty fog of years.
   Joseph L. Reho Sr.

Betrayal

Where have you gone among the fields in bloom?
Were the hands too cold that greeted you?
Whose warm embrace gives you shelter now?
Outside the meadow, the rains pour down.

Your eyes peer out from the picture tube;
A promise we let slip away too soon.
Your image, a parade we nightly endure;
The failure our lessons continually ensure.

The same graves bury killers and they're dead:
The same children of promises unkept.
Do you play with one another, alone no more?
You and the child never spoken for?

Betrayal was a mobile that hung overhead,
Twisting and turning and twirling it sped.
Round and round with dizzying speed,
Capsizing your crib, drowning your dreams.

Can you smell the flowers that lay by your head?
Does it matter to you that they're given instead?
The memory of you fills our rooms
Within these hearts, forever entombed.
   Kyle Wadsworth

Meant To Be?

Hand in hand
Half-accidentally
I saw in her eyes
What is meant to be

Eye to Eye
Most innocently
I see myself
As I wish to be

Face to face
Wholeheartedly
I see her smile
As no one sees

Lips to lips
But in a dream
I feel her kiss—
It's meant to be
   William Patterson

Sybilant Whispers Of Ecstasy

A moment of ecstatic complexity
within a dynamic essence of revery . . .
these muses echoing in the spheres
confound and excite my mortal ears.

Worlds of wonder and extravagance
willing me into a marvelous dance.
Soul-fires and grand subtleties,
wily whispers in emerald trees.

Soul-moves and pyrotechnics
in spirit groves swoop swoons ecstatic.
Ethereal fires in colors cold
wash ambient treasures of old.

Sybilant calls from delphic mystery
are echoes of ecstatic tranquilities.
Muses singing choirs untold,
weaving tapestries of spectral gold.
   Jesse S. Hammel

The Full Moon Night

Night fell and the moon rose.
The two lovers
met on the twin towers.
He was in a black velvet robe;
she was in a yellow silk dress.
How excited they were
after a separation of
the whole month!
Trying to calm down, softly
she moved her steps,
gazed at him,
quietly, no words.
No words,
better than a thousand words!
Her shying beauty
reflected in the golden spots;
His gentle caresses
rippled with the blue waves.
   Tina Hao

On Illness

Of pain and suffering
One can only surmise

Of the hurt and fears
and virgin thoughts
beyond those hollowed eyes.

Who can qualify as expert
in this particular field,
until they feel the surgeons
knife and wonder, "Will I be healed?"

And what can be said
of the unseen scars
Long after the wound has closed
Must it remain, to
finally become
open and exposed to scorn.

Can the hurt, the fears,
the unaccustomed tears
upset the troubled calm
Not if love and understanding
interact to form a balm
for man's chasm of hurt.

Louis E. Martin Sr.

Stand And Believe

We sometimes have bad habits
striking our lives with mistakes.
Think positive to correct all pain,
believe with our hearts, cast the aches.

We sometimes know not who we are,
disguised against our dreams.
Results of our goals seem to fade
and are not always what they seem.

We can all live up to achievements,
goals we have set to call.
If we believe in ourselves
and believe in our Father,
for he will never let us fall.

We cannot go wrong with honest living,
learn and create with pride.
God loves all and his fellow creators,
and for this he will remain at our sides.

James E. Dunham

Rainbows

Legends are told
that at the end of every rainbow
there is a pot of gold.

When you see a rainbow
truthfully look inside.....
At that time
the rainbow will touch you
and a blessing will arise.

Only your heart will know the treasures
that the rainbow has released,
it's to which way you use this gold
that fulfillment will be reached.

Twister

Lost In Your Eyes

Today I looked behind your cute smile
I saw a wonderful world I had never seen before
And I got lost in the circle of your exquisite eyes
I heard the echo of your pleasant voice fading into the heavens
My body was before you
But my soul was inside you
Listening to the delightful music of your heartbeat

These eyes have seen beauty but not like yours
Every curve every contour every pinnacle
Every valley was created to perfection
A butterfly in the garden is beautiful to behold
But in you I saw the splendor of the rainbow with its pot of gold
The sunset at day's end is picturesque
But before me stood a precious picture-perfect princess

Suddenly I drifted back to reality
As I left your presence I smiled
For today I looked behind your cute smile
And I got lost in the beauty of your eyes

Roy Watson

A Smart Mouse

Have you ever heard of a smarty mouse?
   We had one in the basement of our house.
For almost a month the master of the house
   Had set a trap for an elusive mouse.

Every night he set a trap with some cheese.
   (To catch a dumb mouse should be a mere breeze.)
Each day he went down to the basement to see
   Who was the smarter . . . the mouse or he.
Each morn he returned with a face quite sad.
   "The trap was sprung. There's no mouse to be had.
What kind of a creature can outwit me,
   An educated man with a Ph.D.?
I'll reset the trap with new bait," he said.
   "This time the trap will have some nice white bread."

Next morning down to the basement he went, but
   There was no mouse and the bread was spent.
"I'll catch that rodent with a smell," he said.
   "This time it calls for some bacon instead."

It's been a month and there's still no mouse, but
   There is a humbled master of the house.

Bonnie A. Schmidt

Shades Of Tomorrow

   The grayness of her body the light shade
in which most do not see. The way in which her smile goes
   further and further away every day. Causes
me to see the flashes of the credits of her life. The flashes
   send a freezing bolt of stillness through my
body. For if she continues to get closer and closer to the
   credits. I also get near the end for she is what
makes me continue my existence in this universe and yet
   I feel more hopeless for I realize that there is
nothing to do as my insides are gradually ripped from my
   body. The pain is so extreme I may not think
again for I fear of what may come tomorrow

Bryan Huls

Wedding Day

Dedicated to Stacy and Bill

From this day forward your lives become one.
You have many goals, dreams, and aspirations,
  as ride off into the setting sun.
Times are tough...I'm sure we will all agree...
In most all our lives, each of us has suffered
  some pain, strife, or agony.

It's for these times, let me make it clear...
This will be a day you will always hold dear.
I want you to take a moment...to look around,
At the family, friends and sincere Love that abounds.

So in the years to come, when life deals what it may...
You can recall all the feelings you had...on this your
  Wedding Day.
Drawing strength to overcome any fears and doubts...
Working harder than ever to, "Work it out!"

Lynn E. G. Strauman

The Flowering Rose Buds Of Eden

The flowering rose buds of Eden.
A quiescent flowery; floriferous, in a copious
Of ecstasy; a pictorial image. The art of
incantation: an infinite pro fluent of an amethyst of
  Crowned jewels
  A fulfilled ethereal.

The flowering rose buds of eden.
A rosed, and clover filled panacea with artemis in
Acme, a flowering utopia where cerise plums grow,
In an orchard of dulcet blooms; and where budding
  Roses are flowering
  In this genteel, a society
  Of panacean.

The flowering rose buds of eden.
Where dreams are inevitable; and laughters are exuberant;
and a lucid eclogue that's enchanting for
Engager and enthraller; there, ebullience is the
Norm; fresh air is as tasty as esculent to dinner
  And wine: and elongated
  Is an extension of
  Mellifluence.

J. David Thomas Jr.

Rain Washing

From a stuffy bus, we stepped to cobbled streets
Of a small citta' —a temporary stay.
And heading home, a calm summer rain began.
The smell of dust disturbed breathed deep in the mind,
A silent rhythm played an exclusive song;
Our heads titled skyward and clothes matted tight.
A drop on the tongue, a drip to a trickle—
In the eye, down an arm, they race to the ground
Where the stones reveal colors, bleed off the dust.
And immersed in the water, with arms stretched wide,
My mind jumps on the wall and shouts "Do You Feel?"
"Feel the rain?" — "Understand the life?" feel the rain
But the audience was empty streets—foregone.
The afternoon bustle escaped the weather
Under eaves, packed doorways, faces behind glass;
They watch the rain, plug the leads—protect the dust.
A shelf of figures in a history class
Dug up beneath layers; fossilized in clay.

Curt Morris

There Was A Time

There was a time no matter what you said
I believed you, but not now
There was a time I trusted everything
You did, but not now
There was a time I followed every plan
You designed without question, but not now
As I look around me I see the shambles
of those empty words that defied my trust.
And the plans are just a design on paper
that have disintegrated along with all
my broken dreams.
There was a time I would have done
almost anything for you, but not now
There was a time I was in love with
you, but not now.
Because I know who and what you are.

Annette Maria

The Dance Of The Rose

The most beautiful flower
in the spring and summer
is the red rose
when you first see it
it is a small bud
when it rains
the raindrops nourish.
And moisten the bud
the petals of the rose
begin to open in the rays
of the dancing sunbeams
soon, it will be in full bloom
then, you can smell
the scent in the air
of the wonderful,
enchanting,
red rose
perfume.

Yvonne B. Canfield

Our Space

To Bill—My Husband

You and I with each new day
Enjoy the world in this "our space."
We live our lives in our own way
We touch . . . within our soul's place.
What joy! What delight to touch you
To see the warmth upon your face.
At times we hear, without speech
As one soul to the other will reach,
The essence of all peace.
The freedom from all worry
Lies pure, embedded deep within
We know love, as each day begins.
The world—we need not conquer it
Nor change the minds of those we meet
Together, with Jesus, do we create
All peace and beauty anyone could seek.
And here, alone—within "our space."
We build through God's love from above
Our sacred bonds, our special love.

Diane Turmaine Leslie

O Jewel Of Stone

O priceless jewel of stone
You have no flesh, no blood, no bone
You stand and stand alone

Sheer cliff like walls
With colorfully stained and painted glass
Have seen a thousand knights

Laughing gargoyle faces
That leer — in unchanged time
Have seen a thousand years!

The arch — of your entrance
Frozen — in eternal sleep
Has seen a thousand kings

And the very vesper chambers
Where Quasimodo the bell ringer lurked
Have seen a thousand ghosts

And if your walls — a story could tell
It would tell it to us well

Of you — o' Notre Dame
Priceless jewel of stone
Who will stand and stand alone

William L. Snead

Impossible!

Today I died; and then your face
I saw with disembodied eyes.
Your sprightly charm, your youthful grace
Could almost make my body rise.

My airy fingers could not clasp
Your sprightly hand of swarthy hue.
My spirit arms could scarcely grasp
Your slender form as fresh as dew.

The joys of life we could not share.
We lived in worlds that never meet.
I gazed at you in deep despair
And longed to kiss at least your feet.

I reached in vain; you could not see
My insubstantial fingers grope;
My happiness was not to be;
I entered here, abandoned hope.

Daniel Zimmermann

Decisions That Plague

Why must we make decisions
About others—life or death?
Decisions once made

Are rashes on memory
Time doesn't alter or heal
It cuts with a blade!

Chemotherapy or not?
Start intravenous or not?
Tell or not? Afraid!

Using law to justify
Fight, argue and insist? Watch
Pain-filled eyes, hopes fade

Or heed their plea, "Let me die"
Either way, "Why didn't I?"

Alice Lambert

Shaba Shalom

Today I said at last; "Good by!
I turned my back and walked away.
Behind were you and the memories;
But with one step forward; one more away;
Was that the last good by?

My darling child got lost.
She tried it all, she will never come
And time has taught me to forgive.
Now all is just a ghost
For she will never have for me a love.

My prayers I left at God's hands
And I pushed under his robe so holy
All my children and all their demands
And I said whispering "Oh Lord thanks!"

Everything has fallen into place;
My white hair and my wrinkles
My arthritis and wisdom; only my children stay out of place.

My heart has felt the good and the evil.
It's just too tired to feel alive;
But it is enough alive to heal, for this surely is my last good by.

Sabrina Sewell

Children Of Sadness

What is it that makes childhood different for some —
some children see happy, carefree years
while other see violence and fears.

It seems to me that kids are kids
and yet, kids are different as different can be,
I wonder what makes a young life
turn violent, as we all know and see.

Is it the home, the friends, the church, or school
who are so busy and unaware until it's too late,
this child was screaming for help — maybe silently —
enduring a horrible fate.

Who is at fault when kids turn violent
it's hard to understand that shame,
so, let us just think a minute —
Aren't we all a little to blame?

Take a moment and get concerned
about a child's life,
Remember, that minute of interest and care
could turn a child from many years of strife!

Shirley Sorensen Hinz

A Love Sonnet

I sat me down a love sonnet to write,
But who will be the subject of my rhyme?
The kid who taught me how to fly a kite,
Or the teen who kissed me that first time?
Or should I ode the man who with me wed
Who cared enough to give up being free —
Who introduced my innocence to bed
And made a latent libertine of me?
Or should I versify on him whose brain
Piqued me to worship, idolize, adore —
Or, lately, he whose eyes live wistful pain?
Or... but then, I think of many more.
This poem can never be complete and whole
Till I am buried deep — or else — too old.

Mary Ann Blakely Wagner, Ph.D.

Repent

The holy road of righteousness beneath my feet,
still cursing the unknown with fear,
but why still praise a carved piece of wood?
Boggled my mind with mystical myths.
The golden street was covered with soot,
I have not yet to acknowledged the spirit of heaven.
Frantically panting, hoping to catch my breath,
fright took on meaning within my soul.
Denying myself a world still undiscovered,
not once seen by thine eyes even now.
Search for me, dear Lord, I'm here waiting.
But for the misery and unbearable sorrow
I've created out of spite rituals.
Plunge my heart with not a blink.
I beg fearing Thee for mercy, beyond my grave.

Anna Oberst

Give Him A Day

Take a boy and give him a bike
   a way to catch the fish that bite
a gun that shoots a watery stream
   a rubber ball or anything
like colored marbles in a bag
   a puppy with a tail to wag
a great big box of modeling clay
   but don't forget to give him a day.

A day when he can be alone
   to do things on his very own
like wading 'til his clothing's wet
   knowing you won't be upset
and when he's grown into a man
   he'll take his own boy by the hand
and from sweet memories he'll say,
   "Son . . . here's a gift, your very own day."

Precious and few are the moments we live,
   remember . . . you only get when you give . . . .

R. Douglas Veer

Mom

You gave me life one autumn's day
you loved and cared for me in each and every way.
As a kid afraid of the dark, you'd stay with me
until the sun came up to brighten the new day.
I'm a teenager now with new questions and fears.
You'll turn to me and give the motherly advice as only you can do.
You'll be with me throughout the years
To comfort, and soothe, and wipe away my tears.
Your little girl is growing up, and she needs you near.
Before you know it, college will be here
and yet I'll have again new questions and fears,
And still you'll be there, waiting for a hug and itching to
once again, share that motherly advice as only you can give.
Mom, you're always there for me, and I know you'll never stray,
even when I make mistakes, I know you'll never go away.
I thank the Lord for you a million times a day.
So mom, just remember, your baby is always near,
even when I'm far away, my love will still be here.
This is one of my ways of saying "I love you, mom and
I'm thankful that you're here!"

Lindie Beth Van Antwerp

Love Is

Some talk of love as if it were
A toy to throw around.
When happy they will play with it,
When bored they put it down.

Some people think it is a myth,
A theory to beset.
Conveniently they use it and
Conveniently forget.

Some don't believe in love at all
And do not give it thought.
They try to run and hide from it,
But they will all be caught.

Some say love is a mystery
Which they can not explain.
When good it brings them happiness,
When bad it brings them pain.

You ask me what I think love is?
Perhaps I do not know,
But I say love is you and me,
And where we want to go.

Ronald D. Aitchison

Two And Twenty

Two and twenty, she had taken plenty.
Pretending everything in her life was fine.
Her style showed; no color in the stark
black lines. Her strokes were sharp and
clean as a surgeon's scalpel. As she
painted, all the hurt and anger she
suppressed. Her theme was of torment,
pain, misery, and despair.

Until she could no longer take it there.

Packing her bags and fleeing for her life;
left into the dead of the night. Never daring
to look back.

Nancy L. Figgins

Uncertainty

Uncertainty is the feeling
   Which now overwhelms me,
For what was once so certain
   Is no longer what seemed to be.

As time goes by,
   People seem to grow together.
Alas, not with us,
   We even disagree about the weather.

There was a time that of the future
   Was all of our dreams.
Now I cannot believe how long ago
   All of that seems.

What was once so
   Solidly agreed upon,
Instead of being a building block,
   It too, seems to have gone.

So what I am left with
   Is the worst one that could be
And that is this painful feeling
   On uncertainty.

Paul S. Bresko

Faded Memories

My body goes numb
when remembering is tried
something should be there
yet I'm empty inside

The memories are gone
both good and bad
and I can't even hold on to
something I might have had.

I built a wall
so strong in my head
that times from my past
might as well be dead.

I want to break through
yet I'm so scared
that what I'll remember
will be too awful to bear.

So until that day comes
they'll stay locked deep inside
and when the time is right
they'll be easy to find.

Deborah L. Hicks

Flames

I saw the red blazing across the sky,
the amber flying by
all clear and bright,
hot as the fireplace
going farther and higher,
flaring brighter but yet getting darker.

Soaring this way
than the other,
through the door
covering the floor,
cowering beneath
failing to see
the exit out.

Screaming and crying
again and again,
minute after minute
hour upon hour....
Power under thee.

Maria D. Berry

Blessed

With all the wonders in this
world,
And all the famous places,
There are no wonders quite like
you two,
With your bright and smiling
faces,
The Lord has blessed our little
home,
With the feeling of a palace,
So we give our hearts and all
our love,
To our daughter Marissa,
And our son Dallas.

Drew Murrieta

My Children

When both of you are away, I yearn for you;
and my little abode becomes large and lonely.
But when both of you are home, I care for you;
and my modest dwelling becomes small and homely.
As both of you are away at this minute,
I listen for the sound of your absence and hear silence.

When both of you are away, time seems to stop;
and silence and your memories are my only companions.
But when both of you are home, time passes by;
and silence dissolves into a symphony of your voices.
As both of you are away at this hour,
I gather the memories and endure the silence.

When both of you are away, night follows day;
and my lonely nights seem to be too long.
But when both of you are home, day follows night;
and our days together seem to be too short.
As both of you are away on this day,
I shall cherish the memories rather than curse the silence.

Anthony A. Ikaiddi

Autumn Song

The days grow short as the wind blows cold.
Leaves on bending boughs sings a plaintiff tune.
The earth moves into its quieting phase,
as hints of winter is but a thought away.
I, too, approach the winter of my life.
The seasons of awakening, ripening and mellowing
have passed by.
In nature's bosom I would gladly take my place,
but one last thought haunts me before I'm laid away.
Have I repaid earth's bounty in an equitable way?

Jack K. Wakamatsu & Ellen Wachtershauser

A Marine And His Wife

Your enemy is not foreign nor is he unknown.
Your enemy has been identified much closer to home.

He does not care that your brass shines bright, nor
about your cover, which you wear straight and tight.

His artillery is his mouth which he feels he has the
right, to spout, never really caring what harmful
words he might spill out.
The same five words your enemy spouts in your face,
for missing that social event in their day.
The life you have chosen, is not foreseen by me as a
dishonorable phrase, nor was it delivered by a grenade.

Unfortunately, your enemy has no respect for your way of
life, nor have they shown any for your lady, your wife.
In my eyes, as your wife, I see no shame, I cherish
the pride you have instilled in our name.

Surrender is not an option, nor is retreat on your
mind, for duty is your plight and honor is your life.
Together we go forth in our own path of life,
known only to others as a Marine and his wife.

Dana Diamond

Sweet Slumber

Blistering remembrances obscured
Immaculate mercy implored
Dying dreams exist in daylight
Awaiting dismal shadows of night
Sweet delusions dance across cerebral plains
Blocking out guilt and shame
Drowning essence of bitter tears
Collections of childhood fears
Words abusing mentally
Will haunt with age eventually
When the conscience is unconscious and the Id is down
Only the music of the Spheres will sound
Fantasies frolic in dreamland
Evil blowing away like crystal sand
With reality gone and life so far away
We forget the scarring maledictions of the day
Reality blurs in existing flashes
Down to Earth the body crashes
When sadness comes it is sleep I pray for
I long forever to hide behind Sweet Slumber's door.

Lisa Marie Mehalik

The Despair Flood

Raindrops gently pitter-pattering in puddles on pavement
Ripples of water and gasoline, iridescent memories appearing
  through dense fog
Rhythmically flowing downpour unites with the beat of my heart
Filtering through my mind like water through my veins
As the drops roll down my face
I close my eyes and tilt my head towards heaven
Wishing that with the rain will come new found hope
The solution to all my turmoil
Living in layers within my soul
The rain pounds down, bruising my body
Eyes black like my tears
And I, choking on lungs filled with watery hatred
I swallow it as it swallows me
The rain pours down, stinging and burning my skin
Life fiery sunlight in August heat
Skin melting, blood boiling, heart drowning
As the despair flood washes away my dirty soul.

Jennifer Johnstone

I Need To Be Free

Don't stare at me. I need to be free.
Those eyes say far too much,
Your smile is translucent,
and your thoughts clear.
Your love is too strong,
your words too calm,
you say it can only be me,
But what brought us here?
Was it destiny
or the walls pushing us together?
Will we ever know why?
Don't stare at me. I need to be free.
Lost is the key,
Locked up tight the door, it creeks.
Over and over the record it plays
reminding me of my yesterdays.
Can I open my eyes and look into your baby blues
without having to close them once again?
Will it ever be ok and serene?
Don't stare at me. I need to be free.

Patricia G. Pond

For I Am Man

I am the real, the unexpected
  the extreme
I am my mind's only wonder
My choices are unending
Yet my soul is complete
I can be the wind if I want to
Or a tiny spot on the moon
Even the deepest place in the sea
For I am man.

Kevin S. Amstead

My Special Rose

Jesus is my Rose, my beautiful Rose,
Sent from Eternity's Garden,
He gave His best, nothing less,
Than His sweetness of life,
With peace and pardon.

Nothing can compare with this flower,
In His perfection, or His power.
He never wilted, or faded, or stayed
  buried away,
But re-bloomed more beautiful
  with each new day.

Many hold this Rose,
And the petals fall all around
Never to depart,
They just bloom and grow in
each loving heart.

Truly my heart shall always be
A place of fragrant tranquility.

My Rose, my special Flower,
The precious Rose of Sharon,
The flower of all Earth, and Heaven.

Pauline Noland

Love Is Like A Pot Of Gold

Happy is he who finds his love,
Soaring like a bird above.
Into his heart opened wide,
And walking by him side by side.

Love is cold, if not true,
A winter's storm through and through.
Love, it's treasured as fine as gold,
And grows more strong by growing old.

Love lights the face in its fairest hour,
Shining bright like a golden flower.
Love, it is kisses that linger long,
Binds to the heart when growing strong.

When love, its light blossoms over,
The man who finds it, like a four leaf clover.
How lucky is he, his pot of gold,
Walking together and growing old.

Daniel J. Fernandes

As Cold As The Stone Which I Lay Beneath

The world is full of hate
and mistrust in one another,
   Trying hard to create
a simple peace within each other.

   A place of war, disease
and poverty which destroys
making it hard to keep it safe
for our little girls and boys.
   People so ready to shoot,
stab and to kill.
Not always for the money
sometimes just for the sick thrill.
   My life had been taken
all for a misunderstanding of belief.
   The world as we know it;
as cold as the stone which I lay beneath.

Carriann MacDonald

Mourning Ground

Circling — Circling,
Round and round ov'r the hill,
The hawk surveys his morning kill!
He Drops . . .
With alarming shriek — to snare,
The foe beneath his feet.

The struggle begins with writhing pain,
As he rips and tears — again and again!
He Stops . . .
Slowly rising, circling —
Round and round,
He re-surveys the mourning ground.

Alan Wilcox

Discovery Of Love

With you I feel,
content.
So why is it that I'm so,
unhappy?

With you I feel,
secure.
So why is it that I'm so,
frightened?

When you speak of your love for me,
Why do I hesitate to respond?

When you fail to repeat it,
Why do I ache deep in my soul?

Why, when I begin to think,
I may love you,
do I want to turn and,
run?

Chantele Stovin

The Spirit Of Life

The spirit of life
Is such a treasure to me,
It's full of promises and joy
And of weddings to be.

Life is like a trunk full of treasures
Locked at the end with a key,
Waiting for the right moment
To flourish very surprisingly.

The spirit of life
Is like the wings of a dove,
It's very smooth sailing
Across the world above.

The "Cupid of Love" may shoot a heart your way,
To give you a special someone
To celebrate the spirit of life each day.

The "Rainbow of Love"
Now has filled your hearts,
The spirit of life will help you to soar onward
And there in the world of love,
You will never, ever depart.

Jenny L. McClease

My Bible And I

We travel together
   my Bible and I,
   through all kinds of weather
   with smiles or a sigh.
In sorrow or sunshine,
   in tempest or calm,
   its friendship unchanging,
   my lamp and my Psalm.

We've traveled together
   my Bible and I,
   when life has grown weary
   and death e'en was nigh.
Yet through all the darkness
   of mist or of wrong,
   I found it a solace,
   a prayer and a song!

So now who shall part us, my Bible and I?
Thou sword of the Spirit, bid error to fly.
And still through life's journey until my last sigh,
We'll travel together, my Bible and I.

Luetta G. Werner

Today's Women

Today's women are smart, capable and the very best at
   what they do.
The price is sometimes high to become an important "Who."
Competition is here to stay. They say!!!
So, look for us. We're on our way.
To climb the ladder to the top,
Not because of what we've got.
But what we do
To become a "Who."
So, stay in school and
Heed the golden rule.
"Can't" is not a word for you
If you desire to be a "Who."

Dorlene Bressan

Nancy E. Starr

To the special woman I call my adopted Mom
Who in every storm was my port of calm
To the special woman who was always there
Showing love and concern, kindness and care.

To the special woman I truly admire
Always lifting my spirits so I could soar higher
To the special woman who mended my life
So full of confusion, chaos and strife.

To the special woman, who with a whispered word
The heart aches and worries, had always endured
I can't begin to say how very grateful I am
Along life's passage way you have always been there.

Her understanding could not be measured, not by any length
And though she will soon depart
I will thank her each day, with all of my heart.

Robert T. Cohen

Essence

There you are
Do you know where I am?
Wandering in exile from the destination I seem to reach;
Roaming with certainty of where I've been;
Running from the face I long to see;
Here—in the midst of my dream.

There you are
Do you know who I am?
A porcelain bell, brailling her ancient tune;
An apple, to bear the harvest of her knowledge;
A dove, fluttering but always still.

Life is but an illusion of the greater life within,
a chaos, a confusion, a fisted hand;
Shadows dance within our life that lie within our path
And the paths we create are the dreams that we follow—
and the dreams that breathe are dreams within dreams . . .

Sarabeth Stockmal

. . . Ending In Death

An abyssal malice to my dismay
has struck her dead where she lay.
My heart hath given way to compunction
for the complacency I have done.
Error done in delectable ecstasy;
A deed done by mere cajolery.
Ah, what fools God can create!
Oh how well I ingratiate!
You must think me arrogant the way I boast.
Of all the profound juveniles, she hits nadirs the most.
Should I feel remorse for the human I damn?
You may see her as an unguarded lamb, but I
have seen her true soul.
She is devious; out of control.
I may be devious for the things I've done her, but
when she crosses my mind; to the devil I refer.
I write to warn, she may deceive you as she did me.
But I ended the potential suffering, as I made her
recite "To be or not to be."

Nicola Nellams

Grieving my life

Stuck in insanity,
In a place that I hate,
All of these sacrifices,
To be with my mate.

A life full of anger,
Of unexpressed rage,
I hold to many responsibilities,
For someone of my age.

I want to be free,
To run with the pack,
To tell all of them,
I've got my life back.

Instead I sit here,
And let life go by,
I sit in my house,
I watch them and cry.

Jackelyn Helmer

The Flame

The flame,
Symbol of my desire to learn
Burns within me—
As a candle will burn
When you light it.

A candle can come alive
When ignited by a match,
A human being can come alive—
When inspired by a mentor.

The flame can come to both—
From the same hand.

Josephine B. Chase-Jennings

Heaven

Ask Saint Peter please to wait
Before he locks the pearly gate
That I may enter safe within
Forgiven of all earthly sin.

If need, I'll try to earn my keep;
Perhaps the stardust I might sweep;
Perhaps I'll clean around the table
Where the Record's kept, if able;

Or I could polish the golden street,
Those walking there I'd gladly greet;
And if I'm permitted near the Throne,
I'll dust the footstool on my own,

And gather fallen angel feathers
Into a bouquet all together,
And try to please my Maker dear,
So glad to be with him up there.

Bobbie Bobo Hennecy

Hawaii

Nature serenades me:
The songs of the birds
Ring through the palms
As the waves crash upon the shore
And the rain drums upon the tin roof.

The twang of the ukulele
Fills the air
And my ears
As the wet heat hits my body
In passionate waves.

The drums beat
In honor of Pele
The woman of fire
The woman of the volcano
My heart beats
In honor of my love:
Hawaii.
Lynda Durante

The Missing Cue

I don't want to visit the future;
I'd rather go back to the past.
Since I didn't know,
The scenario,
I may have been miscast.

I'm not ready to tackle tomorrow;
I'm not finished with yesterday.
I'd like to go back,
And straighten the track,
That curves along the way.

I really must learn about progress;
I have never known where to begin.
I wasn't aware,
Of the tortoise and hare,
And how to play to win.

If the past was life's rehearsal,
My entrance was wrong from the start.
Just show me the way,
To my yesterday,
So I can learn my part.
Norma Morris Rozmyn

My Hero

In Thee is my wholeness
I give you all my fear and you
Transform it into faith
Through you all things are
Possible if I but receive
your strength

Lord, I've been knocked down that
your sufficiency may be
seen through my transparency

Break me o'er and o'er that
the pieces of my body may
be multiplied to all in need

Wound me that this river of
love may flow from sea to sea!
Fenella Schaeffer

As The Cross Came Down

As the Cross came down my life was sought,
As the Cross came down my life was bought,
When Jesus died He tore the gown,
Bringing God to me as the Cross came down.

Life has been different since that day,
When His blood was shed to pay my way,
I now have a redeemer who knows my strife,
Who died on a cross to save my life.

God called my name as He has called yours.
He paid the price through His blood stained sores,
You He called for, as He spoke "It is done",
And gave up His life, God's only Son.

Then, as the Cross came down your life was sought,
And as the Cross came down your life was bought,
Jesus died and rose up with a Crown,
Giving salvation to you as the Cross came down.
Chris Losh

The Massacre Of Summers Flowers

Valiantly, I tried to save them from their doom,
The beautiful summer bloom of potplants in the yard,
With scissors, quickly I cut each gorgeous bloom,
Placing in watered vases, inside, so I could guard.

If they could only adjust to their watery new home,
And put out roots aplenty, 'tween now and Spring,
Come Spring, I'd plant again in sandy loam,
They'd live to smile again, at Insects on the wing.

To feel the joy of new life and sunny skies,
The delicate touch of a kitten's tiny nose,
Tender shoots probing upward, free to rise,
What thoughts do flowers think? Only God knows!!!

If left in gorgeous bloom, under Autumn trees,
Unaware of falling leaves and nippy air,
If abandoned and forgotten, till first freeze,
Like innocent newborn babies, with no one to care.

Forgotten and neglected, they died in vain,
As beautiful pink, red and orange blooms,
Grew colder and colder, falling over in great pain,
God took them to Heaven, once more to bloom.
Lavonda Eastup Chambliss

Songlines Of Her Smile

Harmony — in cousinage with joy —
Can couple forces,
Can weave in varied hues
And referee a tug-of-war by our opposing teams,
Drawn from both sides of Fourteenth Street.
That peaceful energy
Unflinchingly embraces me
Along my roughest edges,
With no fear of hug-abrasions
On its tender upper arms;
But sweet harmony does not ignore
This woman's brightness, her distinctive ways.
It sits at the confluence
Of our individualities,
Blending songlines of her smile
With the rhythms of our dancing feet.
L. Barry Barrington

Within

When I use my imagination, I think of us as the ocean
and everything that lives within the still waters is the life
and love of our great foundation together.

I often render deep in the forest, finding only you my dear
with eyes of sapphire which reflects the scenery of the
ocean and rich green forest, oh, such beauty that
surrounds you.

When I think of how bright you are, I compare you with
such things like the moon, stars all combined as one
knowing I would be in complete darkness without you.

When I think of loyalty it reminds me of us united as one
therefore, you are my shadow and I am yours combined
and equally yoke.

This love I have for you passes my knowledge, I can't
understand or even explain. There are my emotions and
thoughts of you an answer to my prayer, a gift so Divine
that I can't even thank the Lord enough for such passion I
have within.

Robert Whitheod Jr.

Delivered

A broken heart needed a mend,
You were the first to be a true friend.
Dying inside—just wanted to be there,
You escorted my being out of tender loving care.
Afraid of the endless journey to make all alone,
You spread your angelic wings beckoning—Climb on!
Pampered and delivered to that safe, warm bed,
With a strong beautiful arm to lay my weary head.
Generated were memories that will last a life long,
A crushed heart was touched through a dedicated song.
God smiled with stunning weather to enjoy and have fun,
Frolic and play in the warm sun.
New experiences were conquered on our behalf,
Nourished—sheltered like a herd of prize calves.
Time had no mercy for it quickly moved on,
Tossing a fragile heart from its peaceful throne.
Good-byes filled with an ocean of tears,
I Love You—Be Safe, we dispensed over the jamming of gears.
Removed once again from my security,
Blessed to have traveled with your purity.

Valerie Lisa Blankenship Cassady

Neighbors

Strange creatures in rainbow light
Cat eyes that love the night
Little people green, brown or gray
Sometimes seen in light of day
Imagination or fact
Dreamer, schemer or quack
Forces beyond comprehension
From Space without dimension
In discs, globes and triangles beyond invention
Roaming the world without convention
What part we play in their plan
Friend of foe or survival of man
Socorro and Roswell our admonition
Ignorance and complacence our submission
A trip to Mars and beyond, our transition
To meet neighbors created beyond cognition
Keyhoe, Hynek and Mantell redeemed.

Austin Thomas

Friend

Sometimes in life there is a day
When someone special comes your way
The mix is such a perfect blend
You come to call that person friend

And then you share your hopes and plans
You lend each other helping hands
You laugh together sometimes cry
But never do you say good-bye

Exchanging thoughts and gifts a card
It somehow makes each quest less hard
Just knowing that you can depend
On that someone that you call friend

And through the years it stays the same
No matter what you do
You are always there for them
And they are there for you

There's many treasures in this world
Their value has an end
But priceless is the one that's called
A true and faithful friend

Joann Taylor

Song For The Devas

All of us,
the living and the walking dead,
rolling stones,
and road dust,
slake our thirst with birdsong.

All of us,
solitary red rocks and
minuscule crystals
on the flanks of anthills,
are star seeds.

All of us,
blood running without rest
under skin, over earth,
under bark and through flesh,
are woven of lustral waters.

All of us,
mirrors dancing the wheel,
are unique, and yet one,
each an arrow of light.

Martine Racine

This I Know

Jesus loves me, this I know,
He said He'd never leave me,
And I believe it's so.

He died and rose again for me,
And returned to Heaven for me too;
He said he'd prepare a place for me,
And this is true, I know.

Jesus loves me, this I know,
I may never be sure of another thing;
But this much, I know.

Esther G. Buckner

Then There Was One

One life
One heart
One soul
One lonely existence mirroring another
Upon our empty lives
Fate chose to shine
"We" came to be
Souls forever intertwined
When you whispered
Please be mine
Two lives
Two hearts
Two souls
Building our life
Making our way
One day we awoke

One then there was one.
Meg Lundy-Brinster

A Prayer For God Only

"The void within us all must
be filled by sex, drugs,
alcohol and selfish desires,
please, Lord, let our
void be filled with truth,
beauty, understanding and a
love for our fellow man;
who we must share our
wealth with—otherwise,
God can never live within
our hearts and the
perfect circle of oneness
with God will never be achieved.
Make this circle of oneness
within us all, so we may
achieve perfection in our unity
with God, who lives in the
hearts of all mankind; therefore
Perfection is ours!
And the circle is complete."
Georgia Mindes

Oh What A Pain

I've been in pain for oh so long
It just does not seem to go away
Pain makes me feel none too strong
For it is a different pain each day

Sometimes my disability gets out of hand
And when it does I know not why
Sometimes it ties my stomach in knots
This pain of nerves gone awry.

Some pain is caused by the simplest of words
Spoken by my friends most dear
For they know not their words cut deep
Wounds that take time to heal

There are many ways people cover pain up
From alcohol to drugs that they deal
We all struggle with things that need change
And change is the pain that is most real
Gary R. May

Vermont On A Winter's Night

Standing on a secluded Vermont mountain top,
the full moon glows through the flurrying snow.
An oval and long frozen pond is in front of me.
Reflections off the glassy surface attracts my attention.
A formation, an artificial radiation of brilliant colors,
a canvas of ice with a portrait of a most beautiful face.

In has a partially rounded structure with high cheek bones.
A slightly tanned complexion with rosy cheeks
Long wavy hair, auburn covered with snow flakes.
Her glassy eyes with sparkling opal pupils
seem to steal the star's brilliance from the heavens.
A pleasing smile and glistening white teeth.
Such beauty is unsurpassed and untouched.

As I pull out my camera to remember the moment,
the image fades away into the darkness.
A voice of the night says "Please don't take my picture!"
I look up to this beautiful young woman and
ask her "Isn't Vermont a lovely place?"
Mordy Naftaly

The Treachery of the European Peace
Process in Former Yugoslavia

Jingle bells all over the ocean
travestying time by the behaviour
of the orchestrating traitors to humanity
baking the European peace bread
celebrated by all and the mighty
in the nick of time.

All the peace talk is irrelevant evil
in the dog-done early tomorrow
ripping through the dawn sun and sky
faulty as all hell,
raping and torturing the flesh and blood
of civilian men, women and children
murdered
by converging trajectories of the peace babble.

What has been said and done
is now travelling through the annals of time
switched on by the insidious false beams of traitor lawyers;
exonerating their awful deeds of hate to their fellow humans
for justice will soon win out, and they will fry in hell
no, be it when the day of judgement comes.
Paul C. Sandison

Waiting

The days slip by as I wait for you,
The nights seem endless, midnight is blue

It is said eternity never ends,
My wait is not over, it just begins

I lived in a dream that became real,
I learned the truth of love and how it feels.

Will you return to me one day?
Will you end my wait with words to say?

I am waiting and waiting for words so dear,
That you will have me forever, I long to hear.
Jil Thompson

War Wraiths

On each Remembrance day's eleventh hour
As soft rains start to fall and dark clouds lour
The dear graves open and from heavens womb
Our glorious dead return - the war wraiths come.

The silver bugles summon, drums implore
Bringing our dead from many a far-off shore
Though sadly gathered, close they stand yet dumb
To our memorial thoughts - the war wraiths come.

While pipes lament and trumpets "Last Post" call
Tears streaming down the cheeks of comrades fall
As blinking cleans their blurred vision, some
May see, through gathering mist - our war wraiths come.

Warriors far-flung, land and sea and air
Clad in their battle shrouds, they muster there
To see if we remember and to plumb
The good their deaths have wrought - the war wraiths come.

God, may we keep their memories evergreen
Telling their tale to young who have not seen.
Finding us here, alert to war's dread drum,
May the poppies prove our love - when war wraiths come.

James W. Beetham

Untitled

The wick is short of light,
Torpid by my plight.
With every artery engaged in dark,
How shall I fuel my spark.

My soul does thunder, grimly frightening,
Such invasion of brutality strikes as lightening.
Swarmed in woe I begin to cry,
Knowing but few of the reasons why.

What love I cherished is now in mutiny,
From the moment loves suitor abandoned loves dignity.
And viewed honor on plaque or crest,
Upon a mantle where it displays best.

He set morality aside to decay,
Whilst mocking the existence of our sacred day.
Then without a spoken word named our son Bastard,
Embalming my soul to my own backyard.

Now barren of spirit is my heart,
I grieve for all who must part.
And warn the daring who may rise to ignite,
The wick is short of light.

Lerna Chadwick

Unknown Guardian

No place is there for him to dwell,
He goes where he is needed well.
No loved ones are with him because of danger,
All see him as a passing stranger.
From his code of chivalry he will not waver,
He fights injustice; there is none braver.
No one for him has he adored,
For his love is his sword.
Destiny declares he protect the meek,
Since he has never been one of the weak.
A traveller and vagabond that's home without,
His mission is peril to seek out.

Aaron Bernal

Heart And Soul II

Through the hatred they once saw
In one another's eyes
And the time they've spent together
their friendship must defy
The distance they've uncovered
on this lonely ride
Their heart and soul once torn apart
now, stand side by side.
Though they've travelled separate paths
they never left their sides.
Cause in their heart and soul
they knew they could confide
and each uncertain of the other
Deep feelings they shall hide
Cause with this bond between them
True friendship shall not die.
An uneasiness fades to pass
their futures thrown to fate
Through kindness they shall see
understanding dissolves the hate.
Their bond forever strong . . .
And forgiveness, none too late.

Carrianne Shortt

Love

Love is the center of creation
Love is the indwelling of our existence
Love is our protection against evil
Love is pure and simple
Love defends injustices
Love seeks goodness and fairness
Love brings us closer to our Creator
Love is the desire to see the face of God
Love changes hearts to kind and peaceful
Love reflects the Heart of God

Doris L. Rock

Who Speaks

In the calmness of the dark,
Breathing whispers in my heart.
In the silence of my mind,
Echo voices of divine.
Who speaks in silence, in the dark?
Who sings the answers in my heart?
In the sacred deep inside,
There's a hush that clouds my mind.
In the deepest great within,
There's a warmth of knowing when.
Who speaks in darkness, and in light?
Who tells me of all that is right?
In the shadows of my soul,
Like a child takes control.
Feel the breath against my skin,
Who speaks to me in the great within?
In that blackness of my thoughts,
There are dreams left to be caught.
Who speaks in silence, plays hide and seek?
In the darkness, I know who speaks.

Heather Adamkiewicz

All That I Am

I see through the Universe
and see all there is to see,
only because He allows me.
I am, all that I am
because He is,
I Am.
Sandra L. Galletly

Peace

Where does it lead?
Who does it feed?
You wander confused.
Are you user or used?
Looking for truth,
Till long in the tooth.
You ponder the trick,
Until worried and sick.
You look near and far.
You wish on a star.
You think it's out there.
You cry it's not fair.
But out there it's not.
It's something you've got.
The foundation of you,
Known only to few.
Peace from inside,
Beyond troubles or pride,
To a place always still,
And a peace that is real.
John Carl Van Houten

Little Star

Little star of the night, can you
Tell me why you shine so bright?
Can you tell me please, if you know,
Why a flower doesn't grow?
Does the seed we plant all at once,
Turn bad? Or was it the sun light,
That it never had?

Can you tell me why the season's change,
From ice cold winter's into warm
Spring rains? Can you tell me, where
Do lovers go when they lose the love,
That made them whole?
Do they travel far and start over again?
Or stay behind and remember when?

Oh little star that shines so bright,
Aloft in the distant summer's night
Can you tell me why it's her I love and
Why it's her I always think of?
Please make haste with your reply,
For you see, the sun is rising,
In the eastern sky, and soon now
You'll have to leave, along with
The answers to which I need...
Tim Barrett

Untitled

May your heart be warm with kindness;
your future unknown to tears.
How thoughtful when someone remind us
love will carry us through the years.

There's a spirit that captures our senses
bringing comfort to those near and far,
discarding our common pretenses
and accepting us as we are
Gary W. Smith

Crime Of Love

Dark and gloomy was the night
She had put up quite a fight
But the man was far too strong
To him it seemed he did no wrong
He loved the girl really a lot
Eventhough he had treated her like she was bought
Each time the knife went through her back
He had evil thoughts towards her loving Jack
For Jack was her gracious boyfriend
Who's life would too soon come to an end
The murderer was a mean and spiteful man
Although he was the young girl's number one fan
She was very gifted with her song
Which made her famous all life long
He always wrote to her but she did not even call
Killing her was away to take her from all
The murderer thought too much Jack knew
So Jack went to his grave with his love too.
He never got caught for his awful crime
However her thoughts were with him all the time.
Diana Elliott

Corpses Of My Former Self

With yet another backward glance, I cast you off,
relentless corpses of my former self.
Time escapes, ticking, clanging, echoing in my empty head.

Stalking shadows, increase their pulse if I slow my pace.
Clockwise circle, spirit, body, I defy the corpses
to try and catch me.

Shadows without earthly profile, hover, prodding me along.
They sometimes soar and swoop and drag my carcass
back to where I began.

Corpses are indifferent to the direction they will follow.
And follow still, for as long as I will let them come.
They are hobbled corpses, be assured,
a crutch for zombies living dead.

I refute my boundaries, self-imposed, to stand
and face the intimidating fear of challenge.
Backward glances waste my time, counter nothing corpses did.

With a forward glance I cast you off,
old hobbled corpses of my former self.
You and your splintered crutches, stalk me nevermore,
as my zombie eyes awake, I live.
Lorie M. Vincent

Nostalgia

The oldest things that take me back,
No sound or smell, nor taste I lack.
Things were sweet, the odors drift,
Sounds seemed cheery, Mama's needles swift.
The taste of life was simple then.
Sometimes I long for those times again . . .
For sounds of Daddy chopping wood,
For Mama's stove to cook our food.
Of oatmeal in the early morn,
Though all I had for it was scorn!!
The smell of fresh bread was the best.
A small loaf made besides the rest,
To tear apart for brother and me,
Hot, fresh, buttered, so deliciously.
Wrigley's gum came wrapped in pink.
No imitations then to stink!
It is ironic all these things
Bring thoughts so clear, my memory stings.
I catch myself here in December,
Doing — for our children to remember.
Sharon A. Norton

The Atheists

I've met some pretty outspoken folks
    who think creation's just a hoax.
Wonder how they got that way.
    Perhaps they just differed, as anyone may.

They said life began with just one cell
    Had no sex, but what the hell.
The cell grew until it became
    more than one, not the same.

I can't imagine what they see,
    how one hundred plus elements
Can somehow work together
    and come up with an eyeball
Or an elephant or a flea.

Don't they realize that all that happens
    takes much planning...don't they see?

These folks talked about taking a cruise
    perhaps to spread their special views.
I saw them off, despite our diff...
    on a ship, aptly named, Das Narrenschiff.
John Susmuth

The Cross

It hovered in the air,
    just left of the cracked pole
Silver and lifelike,
Only I could see it,
    my sign of life.
It was sent,
    for me to see
For me to know,
    he was there.
He let me know,
    that he cared.
He loves me,
    as he spared my life.
Now I believe —
Now I love,
thou Jesus.
Derek Nelson

Life's Reflections

As I walked along the desolate ocean
feeling the misty winds of the ocean upon my
face,
hair windswept back,
I can't help but look back at the past moments
of my life.
As I look out into the ocean,
watching the heavenly body of water come back
to shore,
within the waves my reflection stands out.
The reflection of a man,
a man standing alone but yet not a lonely man.
A compassionate man,
a man with great desires and much love.
A man that has seen pain along with promise.
A man that has seen many a dream rise and fall.
A man that has known heartbreak,
along with the greatest love of all.
For I found within this reflection,
that life is within me,
and I am within life.
Joseph Tancordo

The Reason

The reason for the season is Jesus has risen.
So clap your hands way up in the sky and
praise the Lord up on high.

Jesus gave His life to save us strife,
and died that day to give us eternal life.

I praise his name His Holy name and
know my Lord is always the same.

No matter the problem no matter the pain,
Thru God's love I'm sure to gain.

So thank you Lord for carrying me thru
those trials in life when I tested you.

So I praise you Lord for all that you do.
Without you our dreams would never come true.

    So praise His name His holy name and
    know my Lord is always the same.

Without a second look
I want my name in the book

Now browsing thru those, pages they'll find me there
and the gate will open and visions I'll see which nothing can
compare.
Rosalee Dyer

Amber Skies Left Me Alone To Forge Together The Black Smith

Transparent memories of a girl I love, six years past to know her no longer
She left me the other way around to share my birth without her
Her friend, my lover, never knew the end our union would bring
Glimpse the eyes of hers so few times long sent by me
I sit alone here away trying to see her flash of face—
    —last our eyes met
Repeating rhythms of drums fill our ears each other fill our eyes so brief
Each year my birth renewed I celebrate hers giving no gift I try
No dream too short to taste my love for her we love together
My rib she wears under her breast, too young we were to remember
Is she were I left her or gone to the worlds unknown
I'm late maybe too soon we will meet again I will always need her
Jason Mekrut

Letters To My Love

So much I want to write
So much I want to tell
So much I want to say
If only I could do it well

So much of my heart
I want to spread
But only to you
I want it read

For you are my inspiration
For you I write
So it has been
For most of my life

Before I only knew the emotion
Of the love and the pain
Now I can understand
Of how I much I gain

The letters to my love
That I wrote
Fill my existence
With want, desire and hope

Steve Gowan

Forever Gray

It was a cold gray day
As he looked at me . . .
We knew we had to
take that drive . . .
It was then we knew . . .
He no longer would be
by my side . . .
When days of gray come . . .
He'll always be forever
by my side . . .

Elinor Gallup

Brief Career

I found it
lying atop
the tin cave
of the mailbox:
A generous
one-inch
snowflake
that must
have fallen
a mile
landing
ever so
gently
and lying
there waiting
patiently
to be noticed
and honored.

Terrence C. Wright

For You Now That Time Has Freed Its Bounds

Through the eyes of a child not quite blue as your own
I gazed lovingly up with esteem.
Years gone now, since grown, my heart still in awe
of your ever inspiring deeds.

Although silent your dignity stays with me still,
I was never to know of your pain.
With anger unjust, my heart left behind
strains to tear at its mortal restraint.

So much that we lift to the highest import,
so far from the truth we oft stray.
In the purest and deepest of soul-searching act,
how little we know to be real.

How I love to think you unfettered beyond
life's peculiar ironic retorts.
Run free, noble spirit, soar onward with joy,
keep wisdom to tell next we meet.

Until such a time that our paths shall converge,
may the first glimpse of dawn
from the highest of peaks kiss the wind
to keep pace by your side.

Cornelia Santschi-Haywood

You Are My Heaven

At times I refer to You as Mother Nature
when going gets tough I blame You for my troubles
if I want to masquerade as a sophisticate
I refer to You as Master Time
although I realize that every creature
in Your sun-veiled valleys is unique

If I but challenge one of Your humblest stars
countless others adorn Your dark space with lights
from here to the end of time
too distant for a man to reach
and You remain unknown for what You are

There isn't anything that's nothing, only what's mean to be
developing and growing on You authority
We look for our beginnings far and wide
yet our own brain can call us blind
Only in life's still moments I somehow sense Your presence
in every inch and atom of this mysterious universe
Indeed I sense You are my Heaven
You are my Earth

Veneranda Ciemins

A Soldier's Cry

Now I want to go home but it ain't no use, Uncle Sam won't turn me loose.
Hound Dog sitting down by the Rail Road track, waiting for this boy to come back.
Opossum up a Sweet Bum Tree waiting for that old hound dog and me.
Maw got some busquite in a pan, she can bake them up as fast as anyone can.
Opossum on a rack, sweet tater pie, well all I can say is a me oh my.
For I still want to go home but it ain't no use Uncle Sam won't turn me loose.

Warren N. Whitworth

Make Me Yours

Hold me, take me off my stem and make me yours.
I shall be your spring
and your lips will blossom kisses that
slept in the paleness of the years.
Hold me, I am yours. I have no keeper.
I grew wild, under the light of the moon,
full of wonders in the night for your tenderness.
Hold me, take me in your warm hands,
so that you may feel the caresses
of my soft petals.
I have waited centuries in the
crossing of your path, moistened with dew.
Hold me and take me into your strange world.
I shall give you my joys, the whispers of my breeze,
the sweet nectar of my love,
that I have saved only for you.
Drink my calmness and pacify your fever.
Drink me, hold me, take me . . .
And make me yours . . . Only yours . . .
For your tenderness . . .

Marianela Puebla

God Cares

There is, so very much to do;
But my heart's like lead;
And my feet are too;
If only, he cared, and said so!

Perhaps, the tasks would be quickly done;
And the heart would sing,
As I did each one,
If only, he would care, and say so!

I could not make it on my own;
I am so glad I'm not alone;
I'm in my heavenly Father's care,
Although there seems unanswered prayer . . .

His Word gives strength beyond my own:
For me, His own Son, hurt and groaned,
And I will look to God on high,
Though I know not here the answer why!

Naomi Floyde

Coming Home

Please Dear God, come lift us up,
All we need is a drink from your cup.

A cup of kindness, peace and love,
to let us know, there's a friend up above.

We search for answers, but questions remain
what was our purpose, did we fight in vain?

We were called to duty, and did our best,
now our soul troubled, we find no rest.

We'll sort it out one day I guess.
Until then the whole things a mess.

Feeling dejected, tears down my face
torn by the memories from a horrible place.

South East Asia, just leave me alone.
The War is over, and I want to come Home.

Charles R. Hampton

President Clinton

O letter trivial and cold!
How can you read
Gladly these fruitless lines,
When your countrymen exceed
Caressing your sweet name with love.

America! center of equal races,
All, all alike, law and love;
Honeycombed from top to toe,
Epical presentation of democracy,
You give the best best culture for Americans

Lo soul, this retrospect brings to me
The idioms and beliefs of your values
That brought lasting peace in Europe;
Change, change in Haiti
Come forth, break the solitude of Middle East

O president! drive out the wolf,
With rocky fangs agrin for Middle East
O daring joy of the world,
Atoms still packed dense;
Bring peace, peace, peace.

Rashmi Roy

Rosebud

His "rosebud" was a sled
Kane's wisdom shined
through the tyranny
of power and wealth.

My "rosebud"
is a child
whose infectious laughter
echoes through
the halls of heaven.

Dorothy F. Parente

Prayer For The Lost

We offer it up, this prayer for the lost,
Never once considering the priceless cost,
Of all they suffer day in, day out,
Of nightmared evenings filled with doubt . . .
Their silent screams echo deep within,
We don't realize we could be one of them,
We dress up in our Sunday best,
And expect someone else to do the rest . . .
We walk on by those helpless ones,
Thinking that our part is done,
When we repeat those sacred prayers,
Without faith to take them anywhere . . .
"We must do more," my conscience screams,
I see their faces in my dreams,
The ones who've been abused and tossed,
So I offer this prayer for the lost . . .
God, help me be more like your Son,
To work until the last task is done,
To comfort and to bear the cross,
More than just a prayer for the lost . . .

Elizabeth A. Gordon

The Room Of Stature

Her death prolifically showed a woman of substance
Upon walking into her room, awards of honor, merit, and letters
Lined the walls like pictures, poetry telling a story of sorts
Polite reciprocations, from those in power expressed sympathy
While others acknowledged her work on issues affecting us all

One wondered as you looked around at pictures of her loved ones
Why she bothered to defend our liberties, protect us from crime,
She had lived such a comfortable life by all standards
Perhaps her comfort motivated her to defend others' rights
The right for others less fortunate to live free without crime.

Her artistry was apparent in the dusty guitar that lay silently
Well worn with creative tunes that entertained the others
Her poem published by the Library of Congress, "Truthseeker"
Tells of her unwavering hand in getting to justice tenaciously
All such selfless acts of humanity in a world where it was rare

Her dedication to all she believed in from family and friends
To her country and mankind, reflect a woman undaunted
Who was enriched by life's experiences like no other
But rather used them to help humanity in this room of stature.

Cheryl Houston-Jones

Aftermath

The aftermath is the result of being an abused child. With it comes silence-silence is not being able to share your pain and anguish with anyone so you begin to act out what is being done to you, but no one notices. People are blind, so you begin to turn that pain and anguish inward and that is when the self destruction begins. You start drinking, trying drugs being tough while at the same time being silly. The tougher things became at home the sillier you became away from home while keeping a tough exterior.
You start becoming the person the abusers abused you into believing you are. Which is a totally incompetent untrustworthy person.

Deanna Noel

Why These Children? (Why These Wains?)

Wee laddies and lassies in the tranquil village of Dunblane,
beautiful wee wains, were frolicking and playing
amongst their field of protection with delight and abandon,
their laughter and usual clamor filled the air for all to hear.

Simplicity of innocence was transfigured in an instant!
These wee wains stricken with horror shielded their companions
with each other's fragile frames, with each other's spilled blood!
Their teacher and friend, shielded them with her very marrow!
Quintessence spirits became forever laid silent...

Anger and insanity both made of the devil, a maniac out of control,
Satan guiding and commanding him...slew these angels of God!
OH GOD! WHY THESE CHILDREN? Why these beautiful wee wains,
your laddies and lassies slain in spite of Your might?

Why in the stillness of the heather, in the lowlands of Scotland?
Now silent processions, one-by-one, past rows of fragrant bouquets,
of passion on paper, of stuffed animals crying out to be held.

In this tranquil village of Dunblane, innocence now lost,
its future victimized, its idyllic image forever humbled!
Mourners, hand-in-hand, neighbors embracing sorrow and pain,
enshrined these beautiful wee wains from Dunblane.

Dan Lewis

Child Of Fate

The marker of death
was void of a name.
The child that laid there
was hurt and ashamed.

The life of this child
was lonely and sad.
The world that ignored it
made it bitter and sad.

Its childhood was stolen
by the system of fate.
It forgot how to love
and learned how to hate.

This child should remind us
of all that is lost,
And teach us to give
no matter the cost.

Jonna Reagan

Depression Of Love

Peering through distorted view
my only thoughts are of you
Thoughts of the past
circle very fast
The taste of your kiss
I will most miss
The love thought once had
has become out with fad
Hurting is rather traumatic
but not as bad for a nomadic
I can't begin to think
without considering a drink
I need to drench my pain,
perhaps tap my veins,
But all would be wrong,
life is meant to be long
Loneliness is a fear
that signals quite clear
With the absence of space,
does love have a place?

Daniel Norton

Just Dreaming

What do you dream of
when asleep at night?
Do you dream of me
holding you tight?
Do you dream of me smiling
only for you?
My main goal in life
to make your dreams come true.
Do you dream of us
sharing the sunset alone
thinking only of us
and letting our hearts roam?
Do you dream of us together
till the end of time
our hearts beating as one
in that special rhyme?
I pray this is the dream
you've been wishing come true
cause that's how I've
been dreaming of you.

Rhonda Culmer

Filthy Lucre

Money buys pomp and power
Demolishes anything—it encounters
The rich always want to be richer
The poor trodden down and under

Dollars, Francs, Yens or Shekels
Have men bound, in mental shackles
Caught in a world, stricken with poverty
Haves controlling all their liberty

Many a man has met his death
In trying to guard his life-long wealth
Earned at times without any heed
And hoarded sans his neighbour's need

When death strikes now or later
Where does it go, the filthy lucre?
In the hands of a clueless progeny
With neither direction, nor destiny

Will man ever learn to share
His wealth with those who need solace and care
Bring light to those in darkness
With nothing even to hide their starkness.

Fredrick V. Balasingham

History

Down through the annals of time
Rumbles the history of human kind;
Heaps of dust blown in the sands of time.

With wondrous intellect and reasoning minds,
Why the ruins, crumbled arches
And earthen covered remnants behind?

Where is any lasting peace to reign?
Why does civilization expire in vain?
Why must the huddled masses lie repressed,
Again and again, in the blowing dunes unrest?

How long before human suffering can cease?
How long must a people live
Before they can find peace?

The answers lie in crumbled broken stones,
Trampled by desecration's storms;
Left blown and scattered by barren norms
Of hissing, venomous greed and lust,
Imbued etched in the blowing dust.

Only when the desecrating hisses are crushed
Will the tragedies of history be hushed.

Lorin C. Saunders

Untitled

Somewhere on a dimly lit street corner a 13 year old girl sells her
body in the hopes of find warmth and love . . .
And the world keeps spinning 'round and 'round.

A 12 year old boy finds his father's gun and takes in to school,
hoping to scare away the bigger kid that keeps bullying him.
Instead of scaring him, in retaliation, he shoots him dead . . .
And the world keeps spinning 'round and 'round.

A young couple filled with lust, joins together in the back of his
car. Their needs are satisfied, but in the air lurks a hidden
danger that won't show itself for at least 10 more years . . .
And the world keeps spinning 'round and 'round.

In a small rural county, a once loving couple argues over who gets
the dishes, the furniture, the house and the dog . . .
And the world keeps spinning 'round and 'round.

On a hill, high above the city, in a large house, a woman sticks a
needle in her arm, closes her eyes and tilts her had back as the
liquid ecstasy rushes through her bloodstream
leaving her in a state of euphoric bliss . . .
And the world keeps spinning 'round and 'round.

On a small form, a family sits down to dinner and holds each others
hands as they prepare to say grace, unknowing of what's going on
around them . . .
And the world keeps spinning 'round and 'round.

Patricia Ross

Christmas In Wales

Snow grew arms and hands
from the whitewash bodies of trees
and swam overnight on the sky,
settled on the moss roofs of grandfather postman
like that same daft Christmas drifted.
   Nik Morgan

Saving Snow Leopards

We snow leopards jump along mountains wide,
Grip rocks with front paws to climb the rough side.
Muscular bodies and long tail
Help keep our balance so climbing won't fail.
Huge lungs and strong chests
Help us breathe easily climbing mountains' crests.
Heavily padded front paws
Protect us in climbing, and we use our claws.
Hunters try to kill me for my layered, winter fur.
When my friend attacks flocks, farmers shoot at her.
Protect my fellow leopards by giving them a place,
A special habitat with food and living space.
   Mary Anne Simon

In My Father's Hands

The uncertainty of tomorrow holds the basis of our fears,
Searching for the answers as the day gives way to years.
Discovering in our striving the loss of yesterday,
Venturing out to meet with life and learning on the way!

As bygone days grew littered with the fragments of my quest,
And expectation quietly yielding to misgiving and regrets,
I despaired that life is trifle more than what we say and do,
And questions only lead some on or just see others through.

We cannot know the many ways God reaches fallen man,
For me the anguish struggle was integral to His plan.
The desire to find my purpose led to the object of my search;
Suffice to say that He found me on my knees inside a church!

As Christ's disciples, I hear but one burden in my heart:
To all the earth declare God's love, the Gospel to impart.
For though a man may gain the world, he might pay a dreadful cost:
Without God's saving grace, his soul will eternally be lost.

To demonstrate His love for us, God sent His son to earth,
That we might be restored to Him through spiritual rebirth.
More than a teacher sent from God: He is God who comes to touch,
Jesus' death joined God and now; His cross repaired the breach!
   Jon Plumb

Enigma

The golden hawk glides softly through the mirrored walls of introspection,
And floats, without conceit or graft, upon the longing of the soul for peace.
It tilts it head in graceful calm inflection,
To see beyond the artless constructs of a clangorous world.

Its wings inscribe a breathless sigh
   inside the arching phrase of incandescent ecstasy.
Weightless feathers sweep the clouds,
   and climb the unseen thermal mountains of the mind;
Then ride the gentle pulses of tranquility,
To celebrate the silence of the sand.

Laser eyes burn deep into the world beneath
The fragile camouflage, sensing lust and greed,
And savouring the agitated rhythms of another day.
Stiletto talons tingle at the rippling thrill of death,
And plunge to earth to seize the game on which to feed
The hungry hope of peaceful thoughts within a hurtful frame.

The song purveys the contours of the restless heart,
Enticing threads of hope to weave the chords of majesty.
Strings play warmly on the timbered bridge of time,
Exploring shadowed crypts of love and catacombs of fear,
Where lonely souls swim vainly through the mirror maze of poverty
And breathe laments for days of glory long since spent.
   C. B. Pascoe

Love In Working Gloves

Father, I look around me at the business of every day
the hustle and bustle of life as people go their way;
to an office here, a marketplace there, hurrying busily by
the needs of many staring back, barely catching the eye.

But yet a few have heard your call to go and teach all nations;
they reach with willing hands to peoples of all stations;
to the homeless here, the hungry there, faithfully giving care
for the needs of some gazing back, with grateful loving stare.

The Master's call to go and preach didn't mean merely sit in a pew;
to do so would be to only reach so little and so few.
Instead the call is to roll up your sleeves arm yourself with love!
The task at hand is true labor — it's love in working gloves!

So my Father, my prayer today is for more laborers to work
who see needs of those around, the task they will not shirk.
So when at last you come again, to bring God's ultimate saving love
may we be found busily sharing your love in working gloves!
   Nickie Linder

My Child

My child has grown up makes for a soul to cry out.
Seeing what lies ahead for the youth of ourselves.
Hoping it will see what it means to you, and me.
Knowing that they are a reflection of a loving past.
If by chance they grow up to become a good woman or man we can rest
assured we done our best.
Even with this in mind we have fear of future time.
The troubles, and good times that face the youth of mine.
So with love in our hearts we know it's time to let them depart.
So good luck my child in your life's road bearing in mind you will
always be a part of our soul.
   Glyn Stewart

Angel

Beautiful, beyond all belief
Magical, to say the least
Loving her? Need no relief

She is sent from the heavens, no doubt
Her merit and greatness I must tout
Gaze into her eyes and you shall see what she is all about

Angel is there through thick and thin
Her vigorous spirit unparalleled amongst all men
Laughing and joking; you can't help but grin

There might be times when you think she is gone, but have no fear
She will remind you dear,
That she loves you and will always be near

Do I deserve this being who is as graceful as a dove?
What of my wrongs? She can surely see I am not like thee
That is when she reminds me; her heart is full of love

Tenderness, joy, and compassion she gives with heart
These are things all men want a part
They are all enough to make one happy, if he is smart

And yet, there is one key to this happiness I cannot flee
The letter 'a' is the key
For if an 'a' added to the end of Angel one shall see
The secret love that dwells within me
   Joseph W. Clements

Shalom

Peace talks—summit meetings
World leaders talk more about peace now than ever before.
This is the focus—Peace in the Holy land—in the Middle East
But when have they ever had less peace?
The final curtain call. It is about to fall.
The Prince of Peace, Jesus Christ, is soon to break the Eastern sky
Will you go with the Church of Jesus Christ?
Only those who are ready—whose sins are under the blood of Christ
Who have their tickets and documents ready so to speak will go
Those who have repented of their sins
Who have asked Jesus Christ into their hearts
Only those who have a personal relationship with Jesus Christ
Will go and have perfect peace in their hearts
The peace that passeth all understanding
He is Jehovah, Shalom, the God of Peace—the Prince of Peace.

Make Him your Saviour and Lord of your life today
Certainly I know He'll give you peace way down in your soul
Peace that passeth all understanding
In the midst of trouble, trials, tests, temptation

Jesus loves you.
  Kristin Bethell

God's Bouquet

A balloon flows up from a young man's hand and goes floating towards the sky,
He points and jumps to catch the string and then he starts to cry.
His mother tries to soothe his tears, as all the times before,
When these colored orbs of air, would get away and soar.
Now she bends to pull him close and mend his wounded heart.
She tells him not to worry, that balloons are never lost,
They float and jump and bob around and to heaven they are tossed.
Where waits the hand of Jesus, who gathers them around
and takes a string of silver and wraps them till they're bound.
Then gives them to Saint Peter to hold, to keep them safe.
and when God says the time is right, and you're standing at the gate
Well! Then you'll be greeted by a big balloon Bouquet.
  Mari E. Lewter

Is There Justice In The End?

What is happening at this time on earth?
I think it is safe to say "a curse."
You are taught what is right and wrong.
Then you encounter what is considered the law.
You are to pay your fair share of taxes
With new ones always emerging.
But it is never enough because something new always comes up.
I don't believe what they say, especially with all their secrets
  hidden away.
Yes, we want good services and to help all people.
So we pay, so they can mismanage it all away.
I think this is a sin when the government is always out to win!
They hire their friends who own the big businesses.
They soak you for everything and then ask for more.
So they can retire and then hire more!
What can we do but just budget and work
They keep you so busy you're too tired to look.
We are the ones who suffer among small business, family and friends
The one we keep telling, "do good, do right, we can still win
  the fight."
Justice in the end. When???? . . . .
  Diane Delveaux

What It Means To Be A Trooper?
In Memory of Jim Jones

One man's dream and legacy is another's memory and experience.
It takes special people to make this all happen.
For being a Trooper stands for dedication, loyalty and commitment.
Not all of us but most will feel the joy and excitement after each show.
For a Trooper's job is to entertain their audience.
After we bring the crowd to their feet our job is only half done.
Then one goal is set and that is to be the best.
The memories flow though us year after year until one ages out.
Through the memories will always be kept in their heart.
The fans and the audience fill us with stories and excitement.
From an eleven-year-old's perspective it was hard work and challenging.
But in the end it was all worth it.
Not everyone can say I marched with the Troopers.
One man's dream and legacy is another's memory and experience.

Erika Schmidt

Gentle Spirit

Gentle Spirit knocked at the door of my soul.
The door unlocked, giving way to Gentle Spirit's light
that brightened my immaterial essence.
It was an illumination star burst with colorful and fruity flavors
for my soul to taste.
I savored every morsel for there was none to waste.

Gentle Spirit gracefully floated out the door,
leaving me with calm and peace.
Pure love was released into the atmosphere
that erased all fear while reaching an existence beyond earthly life.
In that second it removed from consciousness misery and strife.

Gentle Spirit has become one with the Infinite
yet having no material body or form.
Blissful in the Infinite Gentle Spirit has become.
Happiness and Joy were reunited that day.
Gentle Spirit gracefully floated away.
I shall wait for Gentle Spirit to come again
and knock at the door of my soul.

Joyce Cave Parker

Aunt Mattie's Quilt

My Aunt Mattie had a quilt, a magical quilt.
This quilt was full of memories, because it had so many people in it.
There is a block of Uncle Joe's shirt. Grandma Mae had an apron of
this print. There is a piece of a skirt that was mine when I was ten.

Aunt Mattie's quilt could take me on a fantasy ride,
the horse print was from brother John's pajamas.
The block with stars from Grandpa's handkerchief.
I could fly away on Aunt Mattie's magic quilt.
There was even food for me. That piece in the corner looks like rice
pudding and I count the raisins.

Oh, there is some of Mom's blouse and Dad's old blue chambray shirt,
Look, there's a piece of Jayne's Halloween costume,
and some from a Christmas napkin.

This magic quilt becomes the earth for indoor picnics, or a tent on a
rainy day. A security quilt when I was sad or afraid,
to protect me from the dark.
A magic quilt and a child to make the magic real.

LuJuan Bartlett

Untitled

Why is there the Mad Trucker
Driving down the road
Why do we walk these painted Lines
What is there For me to Find here
Why the hell was I created
Sometimes I Just hate the whole point of my existence
We have these electric Lights and TV sets
These shiny cars and schools
But why was it all here?
What in Gods name compelled the Forces
To create themselves and invent Life
Why do we Fight and have death in the world
And why were we born to begin with
These questions without answers are driving me insane
And my own mind on its quest
For the creating and the reason behind its walls
  which we can't see
Is Frizzling out on its knowledge
The lights before me are calling out
Beckoning me to Follow
But where do they want me to go?
  D. Waters

The Journey To Destiny

As I look across the blinding
  barrier I see him
As my heart and soul tie together
  in a cringing bond
As my heart grows wings and flies
  to the heaven's
The rain clouds appear like a sheet
  of dark gray
As his deep set eyes fix a long
  gaze
As my soul departs my body
Like an angel seeking its wings
Like a crime blinded with expectations
Like a baby searching for its mother
Like a deep hole, cold and damp
Or like a lost soul searching for the candle
Looking for the piece that fits the puzzle
Like a warm fire place, crackling
  sparks, furious flames
Like a warm sort of peace straight from heaven
Like a dream destined to be fate
  Marie Palmer

The Extraterrestial Syndrome

Determined abreaction - deferred rabbit of rabes - I form'd a pair of
coordinating stop light-eyes, crumbling in result - spasmic melt-down
metallic miserability - lukewarm lies - and stray assault massages
the milk-flowing matter in the corridors of response - refracting
neglect - unsignatured signs of growing off - a slow flicker and it's tomorrow,
  all squirm'd up the worm-mould of grey brain-matter - a
ladder down to withdrawal, on a sheep-sided scope - on an
extraterrestrial edge - leaping before they kill me - leaping before
lost respect - before I'm drawn, all over again
  Michael Black

Jake's Song

You were such a lovely boy, when I saw you smile, playing with your toys,
You were such a lovely boy, when I saw you smile at me.

Hey, Jake! Time goes by, so we laugh and cry.
Hey, Jake! Time goes by, time goes by too fast!

You say— "Hi there, good old Dad, it's nice to see you, I'm so glad!"
You say — "Hi there, good old Dad, it's nice to see you, again!"

Love is patient, and love is kind, love's not jealous, nor rude at anytime.
Love enemies, and loves friends, Jake, love never ends!

Years went by and I saw you again, handsome, strong and wise young man;
Years went by and I saw you again, saying — "God bless you, Jake!"

We had trials, and I was sick, seven years went by so quick;
We had trials, and I was sick, I'm sorry, I missed you a lot!

Hey, Jake! Time goes by, so we laugh, more laugh than cry.
Hey, Jake! Time goes by, life goes by too fast!

You'd say — "Hi there, my dear Dad, it's nice to see you, I am so glad!"
You'd say — "Hi there, my dear Dad, it's nice to see you again

God is patient, God is kind, He's not jealous, nor rude at anytime.
He loves enemies, and loves friends, Jake, God's love never ends!

Years went by and talked to you again, handsome, strong and wise young man;
Years went by and I talked to you again, saying — "God bless you, Jake!"
  David B. Protivnak

Turning My Back

Filled with anger, pain, and lots of confusion.
I look on, as you turn your back on me once again.
As a child, I saw your pain as you were abused,
swearing to help, to get you out.
You were never liked, considered dumb and retarded.
No one understood or ever really cared.
I stood in front of you attempting to shield.
Feeling guilty and ashamed, not wanting others to know we were sisters.
Graduating, running as far away as possible, I knew I'd come back for you.
Grown up now in motherhood, I had done what I swore to and more,
though every time she beckons, you run back for more.
I stand here watching you, knowing you have never matured.
Still experiencing the ever lasting pain and confusions of yesterdays.
I took responsibility not only of a sister and a friend,
but attempted to be your mom, which I could never be.
So many times you have ran to me, holding my arms out, pulling you to me.
I can't be your mother though I wish I could have been.
I would have never abused and caused the terror that lies so deep within.
Now, my dear sister, I close our book. I turn my back, also, just as
you have, to start another without you.
    Renee L. Salnave

From Mother To Daughter

From childhood, to womanhood, to motherhood, and widowhood, the flame
of life is consumed
Scars of old and wounds unhealed etch a heart
where youth once bloomed

As mortality before me, my eyes can clearly see
the reality of what I am - and what'll never be

In the soul of the woman that is,
only a ghost of the girl that was remains

I gave you all I learned from life, and now I pass the flame

The road is long before you, lead on daughter, lead on,
lean against the wind
    Sandra A. Heffington

Zaz Arc

The silence was broken with a thunderous roar
The clouds were forming beneath the floor
Tears were shed, words were thrown like spears
The time has come, God bless these virgin ears
Light from high above will shine once again
Leaves will always struggle, against the blowing wind
No matter how hard to we try, the clock will tick on
I may have lost the battle, but the war she has won
Throwing flowers in the dark, lust in the summers heat
Fingertips across my lips, look kisses are so sweet
Starring into the eyes of evil, while kissing an angels cheek
Walking along the shore all alone, silence is what makes me weak
Caught in the middle, up is to ear away
The moon is not laughing, since being burned by the day
Winter's heat is so intense, I long for summers past
Nights are so cold and lonely, I pray for days to last
Nothing can mend this bleeding heart, the candle has burned out
there once was a time I questioned our love, now there is no doubt
The name which onced graced my lips, is now tucked away
I've been put back into my place before, this time I'm there to stay
Tears of laughter run down my cheeks, my face behind no sin
Words cannot describe the pain I feel, that's why I lay down my pen
    Shane A. Beavers

The Time I Spent With You

Here I sit all by myself,
Dreaming of a life I knew,
When nothing seemed to matter,
But the time I spend with you.

Your smile, your laugh, your tender words,
Your gentle strength and pleasing will,
Your happiness and zest for life,
Your kind sweet nature haunts me still.

You gave me the sincerity I yearned for in a man.
You filled me with serenity, like no one else can.

Together we were like one being, sharing all our
    thoughts and goals,
Nature bearing witness to the blending of our souls.

But now, alas, you've found another,
And I wish I could discover,
What it is that tore apart,
The feelings we had at the start.

Why did God take you away,
And leave me here alone to pray,
That someone come and fill the hole,
You dug within my very soul.
    Rachel Rubel

The Millennium

Arise, arise my departed friend, said to me
For I speak of air, land and sea
The millennium is close at hand
Now we want the world, to understand.
Fear not, for I was purchased long ago.
To crush the serpent's head, and lay him low.

Your fatal air crash, just off Dartmouth shore.
March 1949, you came in spirit; you when no more.
Still you came in the midst of night
To leave a message with me, your wings so white.
You told me all about outer space;
That you had been chosen to save the human race
Then with one sad last kiss goodbye
I saw you rise into the sky.

That fall my mother simply said;
There's a letter on the buffet, I've just read.
I read her letter and I read it well
What a story it had to tell.
Jim's Mother told us with tenderness
About her stay in the wilderness
How the lake overflowed, they had to run.
That's in Rev. Chapter XII
  I'll show you Mum.
    Zylpha Swan

Just A Tired Old Man

His eyes were bleak yet watchful, ragged stubble marred his chin, and
tension seemed to crowd the room the moment he walked in. His clothes
were worn and grimy, tattered patches webbed his knees, as he sidled
to a counter seat, muttered, "cuppa coffee please."

I turned to fill his order and I feel ashamed to say, that as I did I
wondered if he'd have the cash to pay. His hands were trembling on
the cup and he gave a shaky sigh, saying "Lord I'd sell my soul for
just a piece of that there pie."

Just then my boss came walking up with a hard look on his face,
saying, "Buddy drain your cup and go, we don't want burns in this
place." The old man ducked his head down as my boss frowned me away,
and I bit my tongue to hold inside the words I longed to say.

But as the tears welled in my heart, I said "Mister, you can stay.
There's a dinner special with that pie, and I'll buy your soul today."
I watched him as he ate the meal, while I searched for words to
say. Then he smiled at me in gratitude, and I whispered, "Dad, please stay."

His eyes grew bleak yet watchful, like they were when he came in, but
I recalled them long ago; framed in my Dad's friendly grin. Stark
recognition filled his eyes, and he turned his head away, while my
words trembled between us, holding long, lost years, at bay. Then he

smiled and said, "Why thank you child, that's a lovely thing to say,
and if you were mine then I know I'd have to settle down and stay.
I'm not your dad, though I'd be real glad if I could make that claim."
Then with renewed step, and head held high...he went out the way he came.
    Karen K. Blamey

I Surrendered!

Three times I surrendered children back to you Lord "As Angels," and of my other four,
Almost surrendered three more, and those four I love always with all my heart!!
Their not even small anymore, they went and reached the age of grown,
Like the blinking of an eye it seemed they had gone from babies to full grown.
Before I knew it Lord, you made me a "Happy Grandmother",
As you blessed three of mine with children of their own,
Then we surrendered several grandchildren as "Angels" again at the start!
I learned from you Lord, to surrender my children, and grandchildren to you,
So in your hands you could mold them your way in life, and your will, will be done.
For they're "All Gifts" from you, and it had to be done that's true,
Because right from the beginning of their life they've "All Belonged To You"!

As for me my children were not grown when it "Broke my Heart" to see them walk out the doors.
I wanted to keep on "Protecting Them," to "Shelter Them" daily from life's harms,
Then you showed me another way to care - it was yours!
But it didn't stop me from wanting them to keep needing my arms!
Even though "My Heart Was Breaking", you assured me it would mend,
Somehow I didn't want to believe, oh how you know us better than we!
For my "Mending of my Heart" really began the moment I surrendered each child,
Into your "Wonderful" and "Loving Arms", is where I did send!
For in the life we all must be surrendered to Thee!

Angela J. Hicks

Eulogy

Slumbering in the depths of the infinite sleep, I find that my
whispers do not stir you;
Emotionless facial cast looks up at all, but the memories simpers
and sniggers fill my mind;
Stone-still is a body that use to flow free with life, that bucked me
as a child on the lap at rest;
Tears trickle down the cheeks of all in remembrance of a friend lost
and an added angel above.
Medley of feelings shower the chamber - sorrow, gratitude, mirth,
and void;
Given my God, taken by God; the gift of you will always be
engraved in my heart.

Bethany Dobrzykowski

Sequel To Miss Holy Life's Destruction (The Great Battle Obedience...)

The Great battle of the age is about to begin. Between obedience and sin.
As Miss Holy Life's Destruction encounters her foe. Who by her will not be taken in.
Miss Holy Life's Destruction is about to encounter her rightful fate.
For Miss Holy Life's Destruction has returned to deliver God's people from this Demon of hate.

On this calm dooms day night beneath a waning waxen silvery sphere.
The 2 foe will engage in time worn battle one last time to make God's message clear.
That peace and love will reign supreme and evil will be conquer and returned to hell in a fiery blaze.
And Miss Holy Life's Destruction will be cast from earth forever. With all her satanic ways.

Miss Holy Life's Destruction on a golden cloud arrives dawning peace through azure eyes.
Dressed in sandless and white linen, long dark hair and truth not lies
The angelic warrior of peace is armed with life and goddy love.
Sent from the almighty father God in heaven up above.

Miss Holy Life's Destruction wears a crown of pure aureate light.
Carries a staff be jeweled with blessed powers of God's own eternal might.
Miss Holy Life's Destruction has the image and the aura of rotting decay.
With eyes of fire and tears of blood with the slyness of the wolf she stalks her prey.

Miss Holy Life's Destruction from Satan of darkness she is sent.
To fight and win for evil sin. To possess all souls for Satan. On this mission she's hell bent.
The battle it is out raged as God's angelic warrior of peace points her all powerful staff.
Bringing down the evil she devil. And returning her to hell forever. By God's own mighty wrath.

Carla Jean Laglia Esely

Together Forever

This planet earth constantly rolls traveling in orbit around the sun
Turning to high light the surface from one side around the other one
Around and around I'm in a whirl admiring the one whom my heart loves
For her my heart throbs my being yearns yes cries out and even shoves

As a ball spins around a roulette wheel searching to select the winner
My love surrounds her being hurriedly with the excitement of a beginner
True love is a mighty force it is continual like sun light from the sun
Cause he hear is molded in love and sweetness she is the choice one

Her love sends my heart into an orbit to the highest high I've known
My woman my love as beautiful as a vision attractive as a birthstone
From on high her love is a guiding beacon sharp as the morning star
She is altogether lovely haunting to my being like strums on a guitar

Her voice is sweet her face is lovely and love radiates from her eyes
In my heart she stirs feelings that helps me keep in view the prize
Should my being sleep my heart stays awake yes wide awake even smart
How beautiful is her love she is the treasure in the midst of my heart

Pulled by gravitation I' drawn to her being she is my aim my goal
Matched mates established forever close as a midday shadow to a pole
Softly touching like a passing breeze with a love as strong as death
Our beings wrapped in tender love together forever as close as breath
Roy N. Green

The Life Of A Son

Life often seems unfair, this is not the way it should be,
and you're always tempted to say, "It should've never happened to me."
Now, I need courage and strength for more than one,
it's important for me and the life of a son.

There are days when you think, I have nothing left to give,
so you say, "God please help me and help him to live!"
When there's no other choice, you do what needs to be done,
anything that will save the life of a son.

The courage, love, and strength you have shown,
for the life of a child you call your own.
It's truly amazing what you have done,
and it was all done for the life of a son.
Pat Kennedy

The Perfect World

The perfect world to me would be, fun and safe, full of tranquility.
There would be no fighting, no yelling, no child abuse.
Just carefree laughter, love and peace.
There would be no crime, no killing, no evil, no hate.
Just kindness, respect and unity.
There would be no wars, no guns, no knives, no bombs.
Just happiness, playfulness and harmony.
This would be the perfect world, you see!
With no name calling, no cross burning, no bigotry.
Just compassion and trust and equality.
There would be no pain, no suffering, no cancer, no AIDS
Just dignantly dying, when our time came, having done all we could for humanity.
No sorrow, no mourning, just gladness for thee, who sits at God's table, so Heavenly.
There would be no poverty, hunger or homelessness, only sharing, to bring all happiness.
Though not a perfect world, to date, does not mean we cannot change our fate!
We must take the initiative to turn this world 'round!
For if we continue on this destructive path of hatred, ignorance and ambivalence,
We will destroy ourselves and be sucked into the abyss of eternal hopelessness.
So let us all live by that one "Golden Rule",
And "Do unto others, as you would have them do unto you!"
Jennifer R. Bradley

Waiting

As she looked in the mirror, All she was a shell...
A shell of a lonely woman.
Who has never know the true feeling of love.
Who has let it fall lightly from her lips,
Like the leaves fall gently from the trees.
Always knowing that it was not true.
That her heart said other wise...
Her soul cried for more, cried for another.
She knew that true love was waiting for her,
Beyond the sunrise and wishing on the same star.
She will know the day she sees him, she will see it deep in his eye's..
The same look she has, the same cry from his soul, as from hers.
The fear that most overwhelmed her, was the waiting!
The fear of blowing away with the wind, becoming the dust that blows
    thru the air...
As the sand runs thru your fingers...
As the waves crash against the shore...
And as the sun fades and the stars rise and set.
But, with this fear, came peace.
The peace of knowing that he was there not so far out of reach...
Waiting for her like she's waiting for him!

Yvette K. Dorn

She

He read the letter that said she loves him and that she was his
girl. So with dreams and prayers he left his home and went to her.
For awhile everything was like he hoped it would be. He loved her and
she loved him. Then for reasons he can't understand her love started
to fade. No matter how hard he tried to please her or what he did.
Her love still fades.
    He traveled eight hundred miles just to be with her, just because
he cares. He wants her for his wife and she says one day they might.
She said to give her time that she's been hurt before and she's
not ready to make a commitment. She says she doesn't want to hurt him
and not to give up hope. He says he understands, that he's been hurt
before too. But his heart aches to be held by her. His lips want to
be kissed by her. But no matter how much it hurts no matter how long
it takes he'll try to hold on to those two words. (They might.)
    So he prays every night that her love will return and he cries
every night that it doesn't. But with the good Lord's help they will
make it together.

Stephen Cox

Mother's Day

Can you take time for mother on this her special day
and let her know you love her in a special kind of way?
Could you take her to a beauty shop and let them fix her hair
or take her out to dinner, just to show her that you care?

Just spare a little time for her, she is your very own
but when her time on earth has passed your tears cannot atone,
so use the time you have with her, her comfort to insure
and show her you appreciate her love that is so very pure.

Take mother home with you today and treat her very kind,
show her how much you love her, it will give her peace of mind.
So if you really love her, which surely you must do,
please tell her while there still is time, she'd do the same for you.

She gave you life so special, she did her very best.
She gave her all for you my friend, I'm sure you know the rest.
Your mother's love is special, for you she would have died
So show her that you really care and don't push her aside.

James W. Fox

If Asked

If asked what I would be tomorrow, the answer is only a thought away.
If asked what I would be tomorrow, myself is what I would have to say.
If asked what I would be tomorrow, I'd be serious but full of joy,
I would cautiously react being sometimes certain, sometimes coy.

I would speak what I felt, giving heed to my soul . . .
I would relax in my head sending fears out in the cold.
I would ask more questions fulfilling the needs of the day
And would answer with replies that made plain what I had to say.

If asked what I would be tomorrow I'd say yes to yes and no to no.
A sense of dependence would not dictate where I might go.
I'd give time to my Lord and listen upon every word
Giving heed to His voice no matter what I heard.

If asked what I would be tomorrow the answer just rolls away.
For why put off tomorrow what I could do today?
The gravity of my life would seem to be a hold on each day.
When asked what I would be tomorrow, myself is what I have to say.

Barbara Barrow

Untitled

Searching our souls, combing our depths we delve
We must prove nothing to anybody but ourselves
We are always more afraid than we wish to be
Yet we can always be braver than we expect to see
Our strength and weaknesses are the sum total of what our life represents
The difference we made in how we used them and for what pretense
We are our own judge and measurement of our success
Treat others with patience and compassion you will earn respect and admiration I confess
What we are is good enough if only we would be it freely
We cannot lose what we do not have and we create our own fears really
People resist change because discomfort is a by product of development and growth
The result of what we have thought is all that we are by my oath
A persons doubts and fears are his worst enemies
They limit and cripple you they are no friend to me
See your life as you desire it to be
If you put your will to work you'll have what you want try it you'll see

Joseph Ivacic

My Winter

All the while I'm growing older, I find that I am growing bolder;
growing bolder, growing colder, with the passing of each new year.

Seasons changing, spring's behind me; greeting strangers who remind
me winter's chill will sweep beside me, chilling all that I hold dear.

Coping with my own mortality, hardly just a mere formality; desperate
as some dark Greek tragedy, exposing flaws, exposing fears.

Dawn to dusk, the sun is setting; you won't find me here forgetting,
you won't find me shaking, sweating; but , instead, I persevere.

Evening shade, I see it coming; winter's frost, it has me running,
hiding, fleeing, darting, dashing anywhere away from here.

Yes, I know soon it will take me. No, I know it won't forsake me;
but never, never will it break me. Not heaven, hell or anywhere.

My spirit lives, and never dies. And when I'm gone it grows more
wise; subsisting still in any guise; it lives, it breathes, it will
be spared.
It thrives, it triumphs - everywhere.

Jennifer Liguori

Honored With Praise

Fire trucks with red lights flashing
sirens screaming policeman's whistle blowing
direct the traffic that's coming, pedestrians no crossing
no slowing down with intense speed keep moving on straight ahead
with the switch of traffic lights, they remain all in red

Up the ladder to the sky, flames blazed near my eyes
ax in hand, chopping when I can, I see billows of smoke
flames singed near my coat, lest they forget we save their lives
within short time our fire crew arrives, escorted with hoses of forceful water
pouring to put out the flames, only cinders and black soot remains

Impact of roof top falls to charcoal black, colored timber
a praise in time is like a souvenir with a satisfied mind, honors
from the chief we're courageous and brave, one believing time is essential
bringing bravery at hand they are dangerously attempted to give all they can
resting in his arms doing his best, little girl Jane rescued from her
bed in her night dress

The bed and mattress disintegrate into a bed of fire, It's a shame
finding her dolly smoldering into a mass of ashes of blue flame
locked in with window panes, and door combustion of flames in fire red glow
continuing winds blowing and snowing freezing underfoot of ice, sliding and
heavy hoses, with muscle holding, firemen honored with praise
Irez Kobus

I'm Free

Am I not beautiful enough for you! Why must you ignore me when I speak? Could it be my high intellectual peak or my undeveloped physique? If beauty is only skin deep, why must your eyes judge my shape and size? Am I not beautiful enough for you? Why must you ignore me when I dance? Are you afraid of romance? If only you could see how beautiful you are to me. I dream a dream, when you speak like a gentleman, you flatter because it matters, you respectfully bow before a dance and ask for my hand...and ask for my hand, can you understand? I see beauty that only time will allow, as I dream a dream and capture all kinds of things, like a monarch flying free on a journey unbeknownst to me, in my garden it landed, allowing me to touch its beautiful wings without a care, it seemed. The monarch continued its trip leaving behind colorful traces on my finger tips, a beauty lost forever, yet shared so unselfishly. Am I not beautiful enough for your touch? Why must I hurt so much? Could it be the lies I ignored, by men who pretend? As I open my eyes I realized all the beauty I have inside, with chin held high I grin proud faces, taking trips to many places, leaving colorful traces of me for the world to see... I'm free!
Francine Donley

As The Morning

As the morning sun peeks through the darkness and shines in the window
It surrounds you like an aura of an angel
As I lie there next to you and look at you
I see just how beautiful you are
Your beauty astounds me
Your hair is like softly spun silken threads
Your skin is as soft and as smooth as a beautiful rose petal
I slide closer to you and gently caress you
You slowly awake and smile at me
And with that sweet smile it ignites a fire within me
As we embrace that feeling of love comes over us
We kiss and that kiss is as wonderful as the first one we ever shared
The two of us in love with each other not caring what the world holds for us
For two people have found LOVE
James D. Brader-Sims

The Past And The Future

Today I walked familiar paths, the ones I walked for years.
And as I tread across this ground, my eyes would fill with tears.

I saw the field, now covered in snow, where my sons did play.
As well as houses I'd come to know, as I passed again their way.

My eyes beheld so many things, while memories touched my heart.
For as I walked this path again, I knew we soon must part.

My sons are grown, the lives we shared, are now part of the past.
And while I grasp sweet memories, these days must end at last.

The house that's been my home for years, is filled with memories.
And as I stand before it, I touch again the keys.

Oh those pumpkins that played at my feet, and tugged so at my heart.
Have left those boyhood days behind, for new lives they must start.

My house is sold and I'll move on, for life begins anew.
But at this moment, for one last time, I grasp the past it's true.

David G. Turner

God Can Make It Better

Miracles can happen when you're filled with grief and pain
Just talk to God and share your fears; he can make things right again
He can lift your heart, take away your grief, take away any blame you have
He can turn your life completely around, make your spirit soar again
For God loves you, he knows your needs, even before you ask
He's planned your life, knows what's best for you, all you have to do
  is trust and hold fast
When you feel you're losing yourself, and your dreams are fading away,
You're low and out of sorts, it's time to kneel down and pray
You'll feel much better, your pain will be less, when you turn your problems
  over to him
Touch base with God everyday, you'll feel refreshed and renewed again

Joan Pleasant

Visions, A Stairway To Heaven

My visions began, I was a child about seven; with my sister one day,
we saw together, in the sky, the stairway to heaven above, in the sky
so very high, we saw a cross, so bright. This cross was incredible,
intense, it lighted up the sky, a beautiful sight, may it last forever. My sister and I were so excited, at that
moment, we knew we had seen the glorious loving light. What we had seen in the bright sky was
the Lord God; we witnessed it with our own eyes. It was not believed or recognized by others, what we had
seen was truly sent from heaven above. I am searching for the meaning of this true vision, bright, light, incredible
sight, in the skies. Three decades, that cross still illuminates my mind, heart, soul; we need this love. In my
dreams, I see this glorious cross again, as I walked the stairway, clouds high,
I continued to walk, I see bright colors, a glorious rainbow, outlined in silver and gold. I see flowers every shade,
color, above the luster of flowers, I see all kinds of birds fly, as I continue to walk, clouds disappearing, I hear
angels sing, before, I felt cold, I wipe away my fears, I feel peace, harmony, I never knew existed, up high in the
sky. I found the true meaning of love, from above, I have learned the truth, to me, was told. My God!, I know you
heard my crying, suffering, pain, why, then did I want to die?
Forgive me, I have no right to choose the time—I believe in you, my
heart, soul can't be sold. Intense thunder lighted up the sky, a
strong voice said unto me, "you have been tested for love, a calling,
I have for you, your work on earth, is not over." At my best, I
finished, God's goal. My faith recognized, judged, witnessed by the
Lord, my vision, love, no denial from above. God opened heaven's
gates above, I pray for all, everlasting love, faith, truth, shared, told.

Charlene E. Nichiniello

Rebirth

Deep within the evergreen forest stands a symbol of eternal life. An old oak tree stands still in the cool spring breeze. Vigorous and full of life its beauty enchants the animals of the forest as they bathe in the rays of the morning sun that glisten between it branches and dance upon the ground; they join in a ritual praise as they here the echo of shining needlepoints of sound. The animals sing all through the day, and laugh out loud as they work and play. Alas it's time to rest form their busy day, as the sun sets on the horizon they take their places under the shadow of the old oak and quietly drift off to sleep dreaming of tomorrow and the fun they will have beneath the old oak where they lay. As the years go by and as time starts to pass the old oak withers away and perishes for its time had come at last. Time stands still in the evergreen forest and a sigh of woe is heard in the land, joy no longer fills the hearts of those that once dwelled within the midst of the giant oak, hope is all but gone, and has dried up and died, nothing is left but sadness. Now the animals dwell in the clefts and the caves where they take shelter from the cold bitter days, here in this place they shiver in silence as they fall off to sleep; it seems theres a storm on the way. The smell of the fresh morning dew their faces shimmer with pure joy and galore; for the once forgotten old oak has been born again: (And behold; a joyful song is heard throughout the enchanted forest once more!)

Brian C. Gordon

A Proud Face

The sun is nice.
I like the way its warm, golden light shines on me.
But the sun always has to have everything and be first all the time.
I like the moon better.
For the moon doesn't mind being second.
And the moon doesn't care that its light isn't warm like the sun's.
The moon likes having silver light for the light is its own unique light.
It's nobody elses, not even the sun's.
The sun thinks it has everything, but it doesn't:
The moon has something more than the sun.
A proud face.

Julia Handel

Symphony

He spreads the pages wide to see the product of his work. As she unfolds before his eyes, he reaches for the instrument of his possession. The instrument is played so well, his hands moving across the body so fine - he is truly master of the score.

His hands move across the instrument well-tuned to respond perfectly to his every touch, creating a symphony of sound so sweet. Intoxicating resonance. She rises above the music so and looks upon the masterpiece that lies beneath his hands. Indulgently, he drinks this life, astonished by his very creation. Sliding her hand behind the neck of the instrument of her desire, she touches the face of her creator.

His fingers caress the velvet skin, and trace the curves and folds of flesh. A rousingly, a veil so thin can slice right through the heart.

The mist ensues, the rhythms rise; hands caress the neck so fine, resonating sighs throughout the night. The smell of sound so powerful, so sweet, emanates from the players flesh.

The heated dew of passions breath - a mist that makes the skin so moist - crescendoing waves of musical score carry the height to passions' end.

The music flies throughout the room, lifted on immortal sighs, flying into pleasure's lap where it never dies.
Rhythmically, the audience's cries are drowned in the moaning sighs of pleasure between the maestro - and his work.

Deborah Stambaugh

The Affair

Of lavish, strange, black tie affairs, I recall the night foremost,
She'd sneaked me up the spiral stairs—to the horror of our host.
'Twas dark, that upper dressing room on New York's East River's coast.
I touched a snifter to her lips—a salute, and proper toast.

She queried me in whispered tones, whether any'd seen us leave.
I reached for her to draw her close, though entangling some cloak's sleeve.
We fell through garments neatly hung—the best of clothier's weave.
"Fear not, Madam," I then replied. "Many saw what few'd believe."

With smoothest brandy splashed about on cashmere and silken cloth,
On the finest, crump'ed apparel ever spared by man from moth,
With no regard for eyebrows raised, nor the ire of housemaid worth,
I kissed her without given oath to soon wed or, e'er betroth.

I drew a finger down her nape and along her form, indeed,
Aghast, to find the lady's skin quite resembled English tweed.
I'd battled sev'ral button loops, when I shuddered to concede:
"'Twas not a woman's garb at all—but, an empty vest I'd freed."

[With cummerbund and gown intact, we had made discreet descent
To festive throngs with royalty, who'd attended the event.
"Dear countess," greeted I one guest, "Your grace exceeds the sky."
"Beautiful creature," she replied. Then, "Dahling, fix your tie."
   Stephen Paul Schulz

Breathe

Clutching desperately trying to grasp the understanding of nothingness
The incredible vastness of that realization engulfs me
Weighing heavily on my heart like a crushing weight
My breath escapes me like a drifting fog into a fathomless pit
Leaving me nauseated and forlorn
Struggling to suck in a breath to no apparent avail
I limply fall back onto the cold, hard earth
Laying there dazed my tearful eyes drift heavenward
White fluffy clouds roll aimlessly by with no apparent destination
Their lack of urgency and concern stills the rapid pounding of my heart
Like the gentle rustling of the leaves in a nearby tree
A smile touches my lips and reassuring breath escapes me.
   Carolyn Tedder

My Grannie Was Love

You know what was at my Grannie's house? There was love tucked into every corner.
There were play things that other children never dreamed of. There
was an old orchard with trees and vines everywhere.
There was a cellar to get cool in when it got too hot outside. There
were stairs to climb and to slide down on your bottom.
If you were a little bored, Grannie you take you to the attic to see
   what lurked there.
She knew how to make a rainy day fun and exciting.
Oh my, what treasures she had! To others they probably meant nothing
but to her grandchildren and great-grandchildren they were so special
   and they were Grannie's.
Nobody had courage like Grannie; she always kept going no matter what.
She cared for everyone and she knew no stranger.
She believed in people and they believed in her, she was feisty and
spunky; she was opinionated and unafraid to stand up for her own beliefs.
She sang as she worked or whistled a funny little whistle under her
   breath; she laughed and cried from deep inside.
She love was inside and out. She loved to talk and she was willing to listen.
She always remembered special little things that many would have forgotten.
I want to be like my Grannie! I want my home to be filled with love
   like my grannies.
I want to live my life to the fullest as she did.
   Shirley Christian

Betrayal

A bouquet of love awaits his arms, as I stride through the long
hallway the lights under the door sparkle and dance . . . Drawing me near.
As my twisted reality appears . . . My heart stops and my stomach falls
I see the lust in his eyes, the light sweat of his neck . . . Showing
the desire I used to know
She looks through me, yet crushes me . . . Leaving me desperate for air.
My fingers tremble as the vase shatters . . . Filling the room with silence.
My eyes turn gray as all color is drained from view
I see only the red of her lace . . . The tool of entrapment . . . The art of deceit.
I cringe at the attempt of a calming word . . . I'm losing air;
someone's taking my breath.
All vision is blurred . . . Patterns fading together
Rage fills within . . . I want to run, scream, punch
Bottles get in the way . . . Crashing, breaking . . . pieces scatter.
The glass tears into my flesh and I can't even feel the pain.
At this moment I can hear everything—babies crying, parents fighting,
sirens, bells, cheering . . . Laughter
I slowly collapse on the ground . . . Sliding down further and further
and blankly stare into his plastic eyes
As all things are said all things become tarnished
and I laugh at his feeble attempt of sincerity.
    Laura Lee Revercomb

Down The Drain

I woke up this morning and thought,
"Oh, it's my day off and I've got all the time in the world."
I stumble into the shower and turn to pick up the shampoo.
Looking at my hand on the bottle, I freeze, and my eyes fill up with tears.
"My God, it seems that I just did this ten minutes ago not a day ago.
I had never realized that there was thousands of days gone by like this!"
How silly I was to want to cry over such a thing. I thought "you must be depressed."
Another part of me answered, "Now way!
A really depressed person wouldn't care to wash their hair everyday!"
I laugh to myself and I figure out that I am just as fortunate one.
I'm lucky enough that from time to time, I am reminded
How truly fleeting life is.
Life flies by
Like water down the drain.
    Michelle K. Woddell

What? Where? When? Who? And Why?

Inconceivable is the age of the Universe—no beginning, no beyond.
And our planet in it? A mass of fire cast from the sun,
   theories posit it had been. If fire, whence and how emanated
   the waters comprising its greater self? And God separated
   land from the waters, doctrine states.

Inconceivable is the age of man—homogeneity, Homo Erectus,
   Homo Sapiens—enigmas prevail. Did not God create man on
   earth already a mind intelligent?

And paradise: Where on earth was it? Some say here, some say   there. Why guess? Many times cata-
clysms reformed mountains   and covered lands by seas and ice in different locations since its   concept.

Life in other planets? Multitudes of soul-Spirits whose feet
   walked on our earth are now on the Above in various ethereal   planes of consciousness. Estimated ages
of only some are known.
   One Being is King Jupiter, who reigns not only over planet Jupiter—   his domain in the cosmos, but is at
present assisting in the cleansing
   Earth—Terra of effluvia caused by Satan and his cohorts for
   millenniums.
And Merku, from planet Alcor, is also close to our earth, a volunteer.

The Earth is the Lord's and all there—verity is.
Heaven on earth—not hell on earth, it must be.
    Marie Pilny

Last Lunar Eclipse

Autumn came in mild and sweet, the Harvest Moon was due,
   I sat beside an open window, until it came into view.

A soft breeze played across my face, like zephyrs from Angel's Wings.
   The stars shone brightly in the sky, bright, Heavenly, Cosmic Things.

The moon, majestically on high, rose over mountains yonder,
   And filled the valley with its light, my heart o'erflowed with wonder.

The Big Dipper shone so brightly, anticipating, it seems,
   That it would fill its ladle, with liquid silver moon beams.

Then Mother Earth did her own thing, she covered moon, stars and cloud,
   Like some great, living creature, being covered by a shroud.

The Moon was round and reddish, like a ripe peach in the sky,
   Still great, in all its glory, it seemed to make Earth sigh.

Then the lonely Harvest Moon, came to us once again.
   The last eclipse of this century, this enigma, so witnessed by man.

   Gloria M. Huntington

Bumps In The Road

Awakened by bumps in the road to the dawning of the past.
Which part the trip we travel? Which signpost did we pass last?

The further down the road one goes, the deeper the holes become.
When we've all been wakened up, our souls will all be one.

First conscious man, Adam, attempted to shine a light.
Something about a grand plan and how they got their sight.

A story from the garden becomes a lesson to be learned.
We continue to pass it on but what's to be discerned?

The big bang is life in the perfect tense and civilization is Adam's
   desire to tell.
One a reflection of what is and the other a man made hell.

Man is the echo of Adam, the little boy who peaked.
Was existence changed forever, condemning all to a life of seek?

   Raymond Isco

W2

Fantasy came to visit me last night . . . again
I closed my eyes and I could feel the warmth of her touch that penetrates to the heart
Her voice telling me to never forget that she loves me.

I see her before me standing in the dim light
She comes to me and I hold the dreams of a lifetime in my arms
Her skin so soft and alive as I touch her we move as one, breathe as
one, we are one.

When sleep becomes inevitable I lie awake watching her silent beauty
as the moon peeks
through the window Wanting to again drink from her fountain, to absorb her to the deepest
regions of my soul that only she has navigated

Sleep overtakes me with her in my arms, her body fitting the contour of mine
We breathe in time, dream in time, this is our time I long for morning
to see the light in her eyes, to spend hours in bed talking, touching,
loving but . . .

Reality was waiting with the light of day
The pain of her loss overpowers me as outside the winter wind blows
I scramble to retain her warmth to shelter me from the cold
My arms are once again empty, she has another to hold

Will she hear me whisper her name when dark overtakes the light
Will she come back to be with me in my dreams tonight
Where we breathe in time, dream in time, this is our time
Will this ever again be reality, not just the fantasy of my mind

   Michael Keeterle

Grand, Grandchildren

Eight grandchildren! All of them grand.
They're cute, they're nice, they show me they care.
We can get together anywhere.
My children, you're a flower, a gift of love.
Heaven knows I'm thankful for that joy from above.
You talked to the Father when you were very very small.
And now that you've grown, that isn't all.
You like to share your pictures, or a story that you've made.
They're nice to look at, nice to read. To me they're works of jade.
There's a little bit of heaven in the smiles these children give;
a little bit of heaven in the way they like to live.
They know they must live each precious hour the best that they can be.
Their parents and their Lord made riches they could see.
The wonders of the universe showed them God is great!
The sunlight arching through the mists, the promises of hope and faith
are the rainbows we await.
Just as a tender sapling's bent, we know that this is so,
God has bent us just the way he wanted us to grow.
Heaven knows I'm thankful every day and night
for this gift of love, a flower for delight.

Mary Becker

Gifts Unopened

In my heart is a gift, a treasure, a gem, a locket of my love so dear.
Feelings of the past, the present the future, intimacy I'd like to share.
Of you I've expressed my honest conviction, the laughter, the pain, the grief.
True love is such a wondrous thing, it makes anger so very brief.
On that first day, the day we met, you loved me right from the start.
Forgetting it all for your ambition exactly why you want us apart.
And while you're doing that thing that you do, feeling the rise, the fall.
Remember life's briefness if nothing else, remember that too is your call.
In the light of the truth of which we are, are chances for wisdom, to soar.
For the time in which we know each other, turn to months, to years, to more.
Your absence brewed a horrible thing, I was lonely, anguished, depressed.
Feeling as if I could not go on, clutching my heart, distressed.
It wasn't till later I began to learn, my pain was truly a gift.
The sorrow, the tears, so much to mourn, my spirit began to shift.
I long for those words, you know the ones, please tell me again so I'll hear them.
Come closer now, you're far away, there's little time to share them.
If nothing else I'll send best wishes, my friendship, my warmest regards.
Perhaps someday you'll respond to my letters, my poems, my phone calls my cards.

Christine Grace

Life's Highways

While traveling along life's highways we formed the patterns of your
past. Somehow when we were much younger, these intense feelings
didn't last! At the age of two you started to learn the most basic things in your life. Like tying shoes, using a spoon and things that
never caused any strife. At the age of four you got on your way,
looking for everything new. It was a simple thing but at that age,
your life changed, isn't that true? When you grew older to the age of
five all of your senses came fully alive. You noticed the things that
you never saw before, like a little girl of five! At the age of ten, do you remember when your emotions caught on fire. Your life was on
the move, you know, with all of your passion and desire! At the age of seventeen, the girl you knew was now the prom night queen. Other boys were after her, but she had your heart, and that was easily seen! At the age of nineteen, you married, you know, and she became your mate. Of course this was always destined to be and it had nothing to do with fate! At the age of thirty your love had stayed, which wasn't common in those days. As man and wife you had a good life and you understood each other's ways! In later years you both had some fears about the rest of your elderly lives. We worried about health and things, not knowing which one would survive! God above showed all his love by letting us both go into his promised land. We made mistakes in our lives, but we both knew, God would understand!

Thomas C. Rupert

To The Many Poets Of Our Time

To those picturesque writers who paint clear visions of favorite pets,
To those whose words paint intricate details of animals caught in nets.
To those through war their lives changed forever to a different state of mind,
To those who tell our future by aligning stars an planets and objects various kinds.
To those who have or lack understanding writing with or without diction,
To those whose hardness and coldness of heart do not show feeling or conviction.
To those who misuse their abilities, talents and skills to take a life without reason,
To those whose ultimate purpose in life is giving to help the needy in every season.
To those who paint delicate, intricate qualities as if being there in the flesh,
To those who show the innermost feelings of the mind like being stuck in the mesh.
To those who show different kinds of patterns of thought,
To those encouraging the weak giving strength so often sought.
To those who very existence gives us hope to see through the sorrow,
To those who share their dreams giving us for a better tomorrow.
To those who through sincerity and truth with depth show love to me and you,
To those who care for one another, grandparents and children too!
To those who have love for one another, themselves and their God,
May you all be held someday in esteem for the direction in life which you have trod.

David P. King

My Childhood Home

Things have changed, progress has come, but in all the hurry, I would like to go back to my childhood home.

Home meant mother, she was always there, she didn't drive or work outside the home but was always doing her fair share.

Life was peaceful, no radio blaring all day, no TV to get in your way. You could swing for hours on the front porch swing just wondering what life might bring.

Daddy worked hard every day at the mill and some days he worked some more in the field.

Those good ole days and have gone but in my mind, they linger on. When life gets too much and I can't cope, my mind goes back to the place I love the most, to a little country home at the foot of the hills, where life was always peaceful and still.

Bonnie Watson Jolly

The First Yesterday

Within a rabbit's eye-blink, a pronounced, intense, immense explosion,
The Big Bang, celestial dynamics, spawned ages of violent evolution,

This universe consisted of dense, rapidly expanding matter, fish air
bladder, not the familiar, not the homey stuff that surrounds us now, but as batter,

Sedately composed of quasi-atoms, a strange and exotic
particle-swarms, such as gluons, quarks, and bosons, neutrinos, pi-masons, and gravitons

Impossibly dense, impossibly hot, the universe expanded and commence
cooling, which wrought changes to this ancient matter, like water to leather tooling,

One change followed another, like fawn to deer, continuing to fulfill,
Within a mouse's shiver, quiver, our universe had frozen three times, until

A Flea's hop, an ants antic, it is becoming relatively familiar,
spectacular, exotic particles, combining, decaying, producing organized, recognized, matter,

Within a worm's squirm, the important fourth freezing occurred,
quarks, gluons, came together forming more familiar, other particles, protons, neutrons,

Till they existed in the nuclei of atoms, but the temperature was
still high, no nucleus could remain intact, the temperature would destroy all atoms nigh,

Causing collisions of the particles, also, too violent for anything
complex, within a quail song, it did dropped to a point where nuclei of atoms, simplex,

Swarmed in a sea of loose electrons mixed with hot, left-over
radiation, to their last forms, as we now know, the building blocks of naturalization!

John C. Flores

A Dream Of Flight

I look up to the sky and watch the dark clouds moving in. A storm is
on its way.
   I feel light drops of water splash onto my cheek as the eagles
across my vision. I imagine every time I see an eagle I'll be
reminded of him, and his dream to fly.
   The rain falls violently now, falling in a pattern to that of my
tears. My clothing clings to my shivering body as they are soaked
through, yet I refuse to acknowledge the cold. I have chosen to deny
a number of my emotions as so I may protect from further harm.
   The eagles swoops down through the canyon then up again towards the
clouds. The rain doesn't seem to bother him either.
   I am suddenly aware of his sad sharp gaze. The eagle is watching
me now as a rat of sunlight stretches out from behind the mountain.
I lay back on the wet grass to let the warm sun dry me and I close my
eyes. Here, within my heart, I can imagine him, my father, holding
me as he used to do. I can once again feel safe within his strong
arms, but only for a brief moment. My heart aches more than ever
before as I say to him the last words he'll ever hear, "I'll forever
be awaiting the day I may fly along with you."

    Caitlin Bernstein

Passion

The Stars are showing me their glory on this wondrous night.
I use not only my eyes but my heart to see the light.
I get a feeling inside that almost causes a fright.
Why oh why, must I gaze upon the stars alone.
For you, nor I know not why, but this is thy fate for you and I.
To thee I plead my pain for love, as you possess the cure for my pain.
I wait to see the light from this wondrous night with the
one who will cure my love and fright.
For you, nor I know not why, but this is thy fate for you and I...

    Steve Chavez

Without You

I remember the day you said you were ill- many heads were bowed, eyes
were full of tears: The day seemed to stand so very still, I
cried...and hopelessly thought...

What would I do without you?

Do I continue to stay or do I just walk away? Do I stop? Do I put a
hold on everything or just let it drop? Would I remain in God's word,
if someone else spoke the truth?

What would I do without you?

I would remember that you were a Pastor, a man who lead God's people
with wisdom and understanding. I thought that way three years ago,
but here you are this very day, Uncle John, I'm proud to have a chance to say:

You are a Pastor, a man leading God's people with wisdom and understanding.
A man who has the ability to detect, to recognize,
To perceive beyond what is said, you know what's best.

Reading between the lines you have that ability,
You can size up any situation or a person accurately.

You are a man who can sense truth and good. Spotting evil lurking in
the dark. You love people, you have a compassionate heart.

Your words are deliberate and profound, you are quiet and sound.

What would I do without you?

In you this is what I see, I'd like to emulate this life you have set before me;
Wise Discernment, Sound Wisdom, Common Sense, Tact, Finesse, Diplomacy

I love you

    Whittonia M. Hobson

Hidden Desire

The answer to my happiness is not within reach. Hidden deep
down in my heart lies a secret that will not give me any peace.
When you are gone hunger fills my soul. When you are near
loneliness is still there. I wish for an answer that will make me
whole. Many things hurt, most without a name. It is best to carry
them in silence, that way there will not be any shame. In my many
lonely moments my tongue is burning to tell you the beauty I feel and
dream but in your presence my thoughts keep turning. You and only
you are one and all of my dreams. How I want to share my thoughts
and desires but that would not be justified, so it seems. I want to
awaken the warmth and the tenderness that fills your heart and
precious soul. To be the one that fills your eyes with joy, God bless.
My beloved one, I would like to take you to a height where the earth
is burning under melting ice and where the brightness of the stars
lights up the night. You will leave, and nothing of this will I have
given you. I will never reach the place where your soul lay bare.
You will leave and I will be on my way too. So my secret will be
hidden deep down in my heart. The thought of you will always
bring a smile to my face and in my dreams we will never part.

Britt Heymann

Margaret

She sat at the table next to mine in the small cafe,
Though we'd never met, we talked like old friends that day.
She wore her lipstick like an aging actress, thick and smeared and
red, and a blond wig, askew on her head.

She told me her husband had left her for a woman half her age,
as she tore up crusts of bread and piled them by her plate.
She stifled her wheezing, casually mentioning the cancer in her lungs.
In what seemed like only minutes she was gone.

Outside, she threw up her arms toward the sky,
like someone hailing a passer-by.
Crumbs of bread flew from her fingers,
to the grateful birds swooping around her.

I look for her whenever I pass that little cafe,
with the candle flickering on the empty table by the window,
and the expectant wrens sitting under the eaves in a row,
and I look toward the heavens and ask,
for just a little of her grace.

Linda S. Colon

Share A Smile

Finding time to share a smile is almost hard to do.
With spiteful tongues and raging hearts, this task seem but a doom.

To share a thoughtful word or few of comfort, love, and joy,
is but an ancient gesture that ties the tongue in two.

When such a sweet expression is given like a smile,
however gloom the day may seem,
a strange yet fixed impression is left upon the mind

A thought or few of joy renewed comes flowing through the night.
The heart is melted, the spirit lifted, and that which was beat is now sweet.

Remember all those sweet expressions?
Perhaps you had but few.
It captured all those puffed-up ways and bid them all adieu.

Yes! A smile is kind and it wears no guile, so be careful what you do.
When you can't see a smile don't detest give a smile,
and it is sure to come back to you.

Sharon E. Spencer

Auto

Our love is
   nestled
in the rumble seat

A kiss
   wrapped
in an empty box

    H. Lee Williams

Boredom, What Is It?

What is boredom?
Well I should know.
I was probably bored half my life,
Seems even longer to me.
Boredom I think,
Is like emptiness.
Like holes in your life.
When Boredom empties me,
Days seem to pass like years,
Especially,
When I'm waiting for something to fill me,
Something to fill up the hole Boredom has dug.
But when the day has passed,
Over time it seems as only a moment.
Then, it all starts over.
Boredom crawls back and digs its burrow.
Boredom is a part of my life,
And will be.
Unless, And I will
Find a way to fill myself up with something,
Something that Boredom can not eat away.

    Steve Menyhart

Sunshine Coast Memories Down By The Sea

I thought of you.
   Because someone had asked me yesterday
About you.
   Your charisma still prevail this place;
I remember; remember.

So the other day I went down to the sea,
   Seeking where she used to be.
The sun was bright on sea and sand,
   Thinking she would take my hand.
Her golden hair and eyes so bright;
   But only a memory was in sight.
The waves gently kissed the shore,
   Each one whispered her name once more;
Quietly to me, beside the sea.

The sea gulls cried as I left the shore,
   "If you could love her just once more!"

And now I live with dreams so fine,
   They stay with me all the time;
Close by where she used to be,
   West of the pier down by the sea!
Down by the sea!

    Robert B. Grimsdick

The Beast Within

What is the nature of the beast within?
It drives me to unthinkable sins.
It strikes in lunar phase.
My actions become a darkened haze.
I weep for the victims of this treacherous thing.
Torn limb from limb by the cruelty I bring.
They scream for help and then they pray.
These marks on my soul, I can't break away.

The beast he gives a wolfish howl.
A cry of anger for a life gone foul.
Damned to this life of moonlight feast,
I am the man who walks beside the beast.
God take me before I strike again.
For this is the nature of the beast within.

Knowing no love, but only pain, don't let this
   nightmare begin again.
To search for flesh that cannot flee, Lord take
   this evil lust from me
I try to fight this transformation,
Knowing only eternal damnation.
It's a looser's game I'm trying to play.
These marks on my soul I can't break away.

    C. Scott Gallaher

Greatest Love

Dedicated to My Husband, Christopher J. C-S

He glares at me with those warm, gentle eyes
With a love so strong
As if it were brand new
Like the sun that rises on a whole new day
Giving the sky its powerful blue colour

He sings to me with his soft, loving voice
With words so strong
That they have so much meaning
Like the birds that sing in harmony
Creating the harmonic music
During the summer season

He caresses me with his warm, tender touches
With hands so immaculate
That they send tears to my eyes
Like the leaves that grow on empty branches
Giving the tree its gracious beauty

He hears me with his warm, caring ears
With speakers so loud
That they absorb every word I say
Like the earth that listens to the wind
Giving the wind a chance to raise its voice

He holds me in his arms of warmth
With the greatest love
That it sends a happiness through my veins
Like the stars that dance in the darkened sky
Being, un-expecting, the greatest man I know.

    Sandra M. Cacilhas Sampogna

A Chance of Heart

You just looked at me with such hurt in your eyes,
That I felt as if I would burst for telling you so many lies.
I said that I felt trapped, and that I wanted for us to be through,
I said that I felt like time and time again, all I ever did was hurt you.
I said that you deserved better, and that you should find somebody new
Somebody that would be more caring, honest, and true.
I said that I felt as if we had stayed together for way too long,
Despite knowing that thing's had started to go terribly wrong.
But now a chance of heart has come over me, I now see the light,
I know that I acted like a fool, and I want to make thing's right.
I only said those words out of total ignorance and insecurity,
I was wrong to say them, and I want a new beginning for you and me.
I never felt trapped, I never wanted for us to be through,
I never wanted for you to leave, or find somebody new.
I never wanted to hurt your feeling's in any way,
It's you that I want to be with, and forever stay.
You are the only one that's in my heart,
It's you that I truly love, and I never want for us to be apart.
So, if you will, listen to my desperate plea,
Please forgive those thing's that I said, please come back to me.
   Stephanie 6A. Hatton

Impressions

Time rushes by in the blink of an eye,
we live in the present, remembering the past for tomorrow is another day.

A week, a month, a year go by, so many scenes clouding the eye,
the memories sometimes fade, but the impression remains.

Forged in our minds in the sands of time, altered by the wind,
the shapes loose form, but the impression remains, though slightly rearranged.
A few are lost, but more are found, they blend together in sight and sound.
A spark, a flash, a cloud of pain, the impressions will always remain.

All the joy and every pain, every pleasure and all the games.
Childhood memories, teenage tragedies, times while growing older,
and maybe getting boulder.

In truth and in lies, and years gone by,
The details have changed, while events remain the same,
and the impressions will always remain.
   Henry E. Garrison Jr.

Look Up, Little Children, And Live

Look up little children, black, white and brown
For the future is before you and opportunities are all around:
Don't hang your head in shame as though life would pass you by,
For God has planned your future and the limit is the sky.

Look up, little children, hold your candles up high
For there are others following you whose dreams are about to die:
You have the stuff within you to help make your dreams come true
And whether your little light gets to shine is really up to you.

Look up, little children, and feel the glow inside,
Of life aglow and things to know and songs of eventide.

For you have the gift of living and giving that no one can take away,
And this gift is to share with whomever you dare, so why not start today?

Look up, little children, black, white and brown,
Claim your star wherever you are and nothing turn you around;
For the gold ring is there for you to grasp and claim your prize in This life,
Because God has declared and you must believe that life's pleasures
Will outweigh its strife
   Anna R. Curtis

Summer Needs

I feel so tired,

I wanna lay on a hammock and sleep in the breeze.
I wanna drink lemonade and look over at the sea.
I wanna smell the ocean, warm and salty,
    feeling the wind blow through my hair.
I have no cares.
I wanna feel him love me until my soul swells with harmony.
I wanna smile for a while and laugh until I cry.
I wanna dance to the sweet beat of his heart.
I wanna swim with the fish and wish my only wish.
I wanna sparkle and glow and put on a show.
I wanna run free and wild and act like a child.
I wanna feel his kiss, gentle, warm and soft, as dew kisses a flower.
I wanna have him hold me, stare deep into the depths of my very   being and say that I'm the only one.
I wanna hear the seagulls, the rain and his voice cry my name.
I wanna feel his arms envelop my passion and burst into flames.
I wanna play in the sand and have him hold my hand.
I wanna feel the heat of the sun, bronzing and burning,
    oh, his love of hot.
I wanna sing a song that makes me feel wonderful and right.
I wanna scream my love for him, the whole world can hear me now,   let my light shine in!

    Debra T. Pollock

Dreamer

Lying on my bed, my naked body cooling down from the hot summers day.
The warm breeze whispers through the open window.
Silken curtains, dance with a slow ripple.
As the sweet smell of evening air blows into my bedroom.
Closing my eyes, letting my mind wander freely, I feel like I
am floating above flowers, they smell so clean!
My body continues to enjoy the freedom, drifting onward
Over the stream my body soaks up moisture with great thirst,
cooling and soothing me.
I am floating faster now through the billowy softness of the
clouds, "I see a light!" Gently drifting towards it. "It's the
sun"!. I feel so warm secure touched from the beauty of it all.
I wake now from my dream.

    Jean Marie Smith

New Millennium

Six billion members depending on mother—on earth,
hoping she will sustain all—to bring forth new birth.
A time for sharing—old and young loved ones caring,
with time quickening, each hoping, expecting . . . Daring.

Mysteries of lifes may reveal—by: An alien, God, friend?
It's in our power to study, to explore, on us all goals depend.
Ways of the past found answers revealed, written alone by men.
Today, with challenges a new, most can be done by both: Men/women!

Years just four away, we'll see earth-made on planets both near—afar, vehicles designed to search with star,
traveling in water, in air, land—by car.
Technology, with our best to guide us, utilized people, machine and
religion, a few, a score, then thousands more, will travel here and there remote with vision.

Countries, militaries, and world-wide cooperation,
to get their in the years two thousand way beyond,
will take each and all giving to achieve new age goals.

Harvesting, the fruit, grain, and what abundant land provides, is possible on the farms, achievable in the varied cities and factories,
if each one and all puts forth each and every day a full day's worth.

Volunteer help across the land help here your leaders, your horizons
to expand, to win a battle ahead of us, we need but climb, take one step with, or Head the band.

    Robert C. Sandness

Untitled

Life! Occasionally "sweet" . . . often "sour" . . . usually "in-between"
Seedlings play a vital role in this "action" known as "life" . . .
You began as a "seedling"; transferred from "man to woman";
Were "conceived," took "shape and form"; "grew" and were "born"
For the purpose and reason, to "live!"

Adam was "self-contained"; until that is, he was purposefully
"Split" . . . to introduce his "other half," woman! Woman; created
On that very "Eve" of God's chosen day of rest!

Then followed the "disobedience"; the plucking of "Forbidden
Fruit." A tree of knowledge overflowing with "spices," much
Too "dangerous" to be consumed. However, humanity [via woman]
Consumed them in accordance with an over-all plan holding
Definite purpose and reason!

What purpose and reason? You cannot "get up" without first
"falling-down!" A "simple plan" but one very difficult to
Achieve, without the proper knowledge gained.

Life, folks, is your personal opportunity to learn how to be:
Your very own "Best Friend" (or) "Worst Enemy"! Amen!
Betty J. Sambo

Man's Useless Chatter

Think upon this when birds of a flock are disturbed, they will scatter,
It is the same with many words, known as "man's useless chatter."

It's well known, that with our mouths, we speak life or death,
Now reflect on past words you've spoken, then hold your breath.

If we had the ability to control our tongues, and we do not,
Except with God's spirit in us, to prevent us from saying a lot.

We would then speak the words of life that truly and really matter,
And not say those things that hurt, coming from "man's useless chatter."

Only if I could speak those words of love and eloquence,
Those who listen with their hearts will know that it all makes sense.

Many times in our anger, words of love we do not seek,
For God has said, "from the well spring of the heart man will speak."

So in my life, may I always speak loving words that flatter,
And not make the mistake, so simply speaking with "man's useless chatter."
Wilkie L. Sanders Sr.

Forgotten Love

Hateful words spun vengefully, an intricate design of false hope.
Entwined in lost desire, left for us to cope.
We used to be best friends, like earth signs eternally bound.
Our love became a romantic hymn of a majestic mythical sound.

You the water that nourished me, and I the land that kept your form.
Deep within my crusted heart, your liquid was my core.
The music that our love made, was like celestial harps in tune.
Adding symmetry to our lives, like Summer days in June.

Now those strings that chimed sweet tones, have stretched beyond
repair. Like weeping willows that feel winter's icky kiss, of frost
within the air. The cold way that we treat ourselves, has left only
bitter regrets. Revengeful, spiteful, memories... this is not the
way we met!

No longer do we have strong lines, of trust to attach the delicate
strains. Just a portrait of forgotten love that holds two wedding
bands.
Rose Ann Haeussler

The Hill-From The Window

I walked day and night to find the way to the hill,
It was still there—silent and dark as the night—I was alone when I
reached the top,
And looking back on my childhood I thought of my father.
He was like an angel in my early years and made my little world appear
bright, Happy I was when he used to walk with me to Eden's hill.
I remember feeling that we were close to the stars one night
when I felt the misery of his cry.
Tears were in his eyes, but I didn't understand why; I was only five.
Oh, how silent was that night!
Father, I was very little when you closed your doors,
And for ten years I've dreaded the days after night,
Because I knew I would find myself staring out the window,
Waiting for someone who would never come.
Now that you're gone, may I say that I finally understand you?
Your hurt then was the same as mine now.
I wonder sometimes, when I look up into the blue sky and see your
eyes, and trace the furrows of old age on the hill,
If there will ever be anyone who can make time stand still,
And open the doors to those waiting children at the window.
Clothes they can do without, a hug will keep them warm,
But the glow of love keeps them from harm.
I walk alone down the hill now. The stars say nothing and the wind is
still, and when I get home there is not one face but four at the
window to take my place.

Ida Maria Bentley

The Pages Turn

Where has the time gone the old man asked, from the side of the road,
I used to run fast, be quick on my feet, but now I look like a toad.
Not long ago I could stand up straight and bend and touch my toes,
But now my back is stiff, my eyes are weak, and that's not all my
    woes.

I can't remember where I went or what I did as short as yesterday,
But from thirty years ago I can recall, where I went to play.
It don't seem right that just, when you have the time to spare,
The mind goes blank, the body wears out, and you've lost your hair.

But some things always function, without regard of the time,
The sun sets, the moon comes up, and poets write rhyme.
So never mind if the pages turn, and things ye know are withered,
Remember only life's beautiful things, and leave your mind untithered.

Russell L. Case

The Silence of Success

Through prayer and all people, regardless of race, creed, color, and religion,
learning to live and coexist with each other, will put an end to useless murder and ultimate peace.
   Unless human beings of all ages put away their conspiratorial plots
to reach goals the world among us has no future. But there is hope
if everybody binds together. Strong words will do nothing. Action
does "wonders." These wonders will put the world back together.
Action, without violence, will help people who feel inferior to others
understand and accept other people. In order to live in a world that
"works" everybody has to learn to live with each other. How else can
people live and get along in a world that has a "wall" between it?
That "wall" has to be taken into and then the inhabitants can start
opening-up to each other's feelings. Then there will be a "silence of success."
   This is why I want to go to law school. I want to get a legal
education so I can, eventually, help college students who went through the same problems that many students in
college campuses all over the country, including myself, went through. Life is made stronger when an abun-
dance of obstacles are first known and finally broken and are changes into successes. This is the silence of
success!

Larry B. Rubin

Learn To Appreciate, My Child

Thank God for all your blessings, from the good Lord up above
Your home, your special friendships, and your caring family's love.
When you look at things too closely, at times you do not see,
As sometimes people do not see the forest for the trees.
Step back and count your blessings, my child so young and fair,
For surely you would miss them, if they were no longer there.
It's hard for you to understand, not being a parent yet,
But someday you may see how hard this parenting can get.
At the risk of appearing foolish, a parent will shield and protect,
The most precious possession it will ever hold dear-the offspring from its nest.
And, even when unwittingly, your mendacity hurts and stings,
A parent knows its transference of anger from other things.
To forgive and forget is a virtue, and parents know it well.
They have no ulterior motive - just pure love of their child, they tell.
So start to be more grateful, and start to appreciate,
What a wonderful life you really have, compared to the less fortunate.
The things you take for granted, some others do without,
Especially during catastrophes, with widespread tragedy throughout.
Now paradise is before your eyes, but blindness clouds its view,
so clear your heart of heaviness, and happiness will come to you.

Irene Andrighetti Dietz

A Fighting Survivor

My Enemy has returned—though conquered once some thirty years ago.
More vicious now, sneaking up, invading places I didn't know.
Until this demon eat away inside me until with pain I'm forced to run
For help and doctors cut this enemy away—my fighting has begun.
My mind and heart and faith will heal this body—life will go on,
The dreams of happy times to come will fade the scars the demon done.
Life has so many kinds of trials and hurts for all mankind—
Each has to overcome the flaws and better days they'll find.
So I'll find the courage to blot out the hurts, remembering the good.
My Lord will help me do so if I trust Him as He said He would.
So friend, hang on, believe and trust, look forth to better days.
Remember our God works miracles, His own mysterious ways.
The big "C" so dreaded, also stands for Christ, Courage, Caring, too.
So, fight back, have faith and know, God will take care of you.

Ruby H. Hubbard

Uneven Exchange

Once upon a long time ago, when I was six years old,
I got word of a fairy who traded teeth for money, or so I had been told.

Falling out of the first tooth said to be a passage,
A big step to the becoming of a grown-up age.
But to me the story seemed dubious in nature, as my
Logical thinking told me, it sounded too ridiculous and strange.

Mother claimed every child had done business with the fairy,
And heartily suggested that I'd be wise to do the same.
After all me having no use for it, and her a buyer,
It did seem to be a fair exchange.

Again at bedtime mother smiled and assured me, it truly was no ruse.
So, tired of her constant urging, I decided to go along,
And make the trade with this fairy too.

Next morning I looked to see, and the item to be purchased was gone.
But I'd been swindled, there was no money! I knew then I'd been conned.

I'd been robbed, horns waggled, just a pawn in some duplicitous game.
All I found was a note the thief in my mother's hand had written,
For on the bottom was signed the Tooth Fairy name; just saying,
Dear Connie, I'll catch you tomorrow,
Last night I was out of change.

Consiwella R. Ray

Jagged Blame

"Will work for food", the sign said, I never looked to see the face.
   I never thought that someday I'd be standing in their place.
The hand reached out for pennies, I just quickened up my pace,
   Never thought I'd reach for pennies with tears upon my face.

"How pitiful the prideless ones, how sad they just let go.
   Why can't they stand on their own feet, how could they sink so low?
One never thinks, as one walks by, of their too human woe,
   Their story isn't their design, their tale is not a show.

How easy it is to turn one's head, to look the other way,
   Until one finds himself sitting there, without the means to pay.
How easy to say they don't exist, they should just go away,
   Until you are yourself too weak to move, you can only stay.

Do not cast the blame my way, do not turn your back,
   Until you know for sure that Life will never you attack.
Life is not fair to all her babes, be they white or red or black,
   Life cares not for your worldly toil, or the feelings that you lack.

Or for the heart and blood that flows within your worldly frame,
   Or for the tears your children cry, or for the cold and rain.
Winter's bite can never cause the grief or chilling pain,
   As men who turn their face away, and cast sharp, jagged blame.

   Barbara Deacon

The Rose

To have kissed the delicate blossoms of life, and dabbled in the
depths of the flower: To have experienced a few moments of happiness,
that gave way to the hours:

To have enchantingly beheld the beauty of its bloom and caressed its stem with love:
Is a joy that one cannot express, for the heart taketh wings like a dove.

But to find that rose is covered with thorns, and its beauty a means of deceit:
And the flower is open to the passing bees, to enjoy at their own discreet:

Is a hurt that can be never endured, no matter how hard its tried:
For like the subjective beauty of the rose, love will have withered and died.

   Joseph N. Smith

If You Need Me

After they said their wedding vows, He still treated her nice and kind
And he has said these same words to her so many times.

If ever you need me, just call me and I will be there,
He always would tell her this if he was leaving her to go some where.

So every time he would leave her to go to work for sure,
He would tell her these same words so gentle, with care.

Each and every night he would hold her so tight,
And always say these words just right.

He had told her these words so much that she knew he cared,
If ever you need me, just call me and I will be there.

He never left her that these same words he did not say,
But now the Good Lord has called him away.

So as her pain of loosing him, she can not hardly bare,
She remember is words, if ever you need me, just call me
and I will be there.

Some how time goes on even though he is not around,
But it has helped her to remember his words, she has found.

When the nights are so dark and there is no one to care,
She tries to remember his words, if ever you need me, just
call me and I will be there.

   Clara Baugus

The Old Man And The Sea

Said the Old Man to the Ragging Sea, his lips now quivering from the cold
Forever and a day you have held tight, the fate of my life in your hands
And for this I am eternally grateful, but it is no longer my life, that you hold
Please take me home, for my lover awaits, in the warmth of the sands
Understand that my youth has left me, and now I am nothing, but old

Said the Ragging Sea to the Old Man, as her waters lie still from the pain
Yes forever and a day I have held tight, the fate of your life in my hands
True indeed Old Man, but by going home, you will have nothing to gain
I've fooled your heart, for she no longer waits, in the warmth of the sands
The time away, that you have taken, has driven your sad lover insane

To this day you can stand by the waters, where the Old Man's spirits lies
And you will hear if you listen closely, a sorry man's desperate cries
And if you look real close you might see, a sorry man's wave of good-byes
But it is most important my friend to know, the answer to all of his why's

There once was a man who sang a song, it was a love song,
And it was sweet, it was as sweet, as it was pure
Who could it have been, 'that he sang about, I am really not so sure
But the song he sang I do believe, I believe this to be true
Was a memory of, a long lost love, it was a lady awaiting in blue

Said the Old Man to the Ragging Sea...
Debbie Sinclair

Have You Ever

Have you ever spoken words that you knew were not true?
Have you ever made a promise that you knew you could not do?
Have you ever learned a lesson that you vowed you would never forget?
Have you ever fallen in love with someone that you knew you could not get?
Have you ever had the feeling that you had lost a great friend?
Have you ever said things that you regretted in the end?
Have you ever made peace with someone you had always hated?
Have you ever had such patience for a person you had long awaited?
These are questions that come and go.
Will they ever be answered?
Only you will know.
Jaclyn Zapanta

His Shirttail

I can see you walking in front of me, with Your shirttail in my hand.
I know in my heart, this is where You want me,
But a part of me does not understand.

Why it turned out like this? Why is my heart so weak?
I want to live for You and only You,
But I walk behind You, dragging my feet.

I see Your cloak of angelic white, as I pull it close to my face and hide.
I am still stumbling in Your holy light,
As I am assured You would never leave me far behind.

I want to walk beside You, wavering, I tag along instead,
Holding on to Your shirttail so I don't lose You,
But like a child, I wander so close to the edge.

Tempting the fate of falling down to my death,
But having the security in my hand, a shirttail soft and sturdy,
And Your tolerant reach to pull me back in.

I know You suffered without hesitation for me, while my weaknesses
take my Redeemer in vain, you still allow me to hold on to Your
shirttail, to guide me away from my guilt and shame.

You always give me a choice to live in the manner of who I chose to be
But I chose to not let go of Your shirttail, Lord because of Your
suffering on My cross,Your strength and mercy is all I need.
DeeDee Hamm

Soul Withering Downward

Staggering alone in the shadows, heart full of loss.
I have come to this place to penetrate my wall.
My dreams and hopes have faded with the setting of the sun.
Darkness engulfs my heart as tears fall embittered to the frigid ground.

I hammer bloody fists against the wall, only succeeding in crumbling my faith.
Even hope cannot placate my mind; troubled by my interrupted dreams.
Resolution and endurance fade.
I fall into the all encompassing void, chilled and afraid.

Tell me what to do, soothe the pain from my torn breast.
I cannot cry anymore, for tears only aggravate thoughts that won't heal.
Help me find myself, before it is too late.

I feel myself slip from my shell, torn and tattered.
Soul withering downward to emptiness.
Soul withering downward to despair.
Soul withering downward, like a dead leaf in the cold Autumn wind.
Soul withering downward . . .

Christopher J. Chung

Metamorphosis

I am a brand new person because of Jesus Christ.
Ever since I met him there's been a great change in my life.

He found me when I had sunk as low as I could go,
yet he showered me with a love I thought I'd never know.

His mighty arms engulfed me as I broke down and I cried,
then he took the time to introduce me to my completely different side.

He said he'd never leave me since I asked him to come in,
he'd take up residence in my heart and cleanse me from all sin.

Through toils and trials he said I'd go when I am being tried,
he'd be my source of comfort as he smooths the bumpy ride.

I know that I can trust him and that makes me feel so nice,
for I am a different person, and it's because of Jesus Christ.

M. J. Glover

The Loss

The night was cold and icy, and the snow lay on the ground.
The moon lit up the countryside, there was very little sound.
The trees stood motionless and still, linked by the spider's weave,
Which glistened in the moonlight, for it was Christmas Eve.

She lost control of the car that night, it skidded in the snow,
And plunged into the river deep, one hundred feet below.
On her way to the sitter to collect her son, she'd bought presents
for Christmas Day.
Found dead in the wreck, hours later, by a rescue team, they say.

They said my mommy had to go, but they never told me why,
They just said that she had to go, but she never said goodbye,
And his little eyes well up with tears, each time he thinks of her,
As he holds his teddy near his breast, and his vision starts to blur.

Did Santa take mommy, I really want to know,
She said she'd always love me, why did she have to go?
Was I really that bad, I thought I was being good,
Will I ever see my mom again, I wish, I wish I could.

He would kneel and pray beside his bed, like when is mom was here,
He'd say, "God bless my mommy, God", as he wiped away a tear.
And then he'd say in a crying voice, a voice that held much pain,
"I'll swap my teddy with you God, to have mommy back again".

Jerry Treacy

The Golden Fishing Pole

The contest rules were simple: "One golden fishing pole
 to the first to catch the ten-pound bass in Simpson's Fishing Hole."
The people came from miles around, with fancy rods and reels;
 and boats and trailers filled the banks, and often filled the fields.

Now Daddy was an angler; the best in our whole town;
 and his old pole caught many a hit when he cast his sinker down.
I often went down with him, to sit upon the banks;
 to feel the lines taut in our hands and to sometimes just give thanks.

Through the years, no prize was claimed by those who came and went;
 despite the time and effort, and the money that was spent.
And I became more puzzled, as I watched my Daddy cast
 - and catch, and smile, and toss back in, that sought for ten-pound bass.

The days were growing shorter; the winter took its toll;
 and Daddy sighed and then hung up his worn and weathered pole.
He met St. Peter at the Gates; and joy filled up his soul;
 for with his name, beside the Book, was a Golden Fishing Pole.

Bette A. Conrad

The Class Of '97

We used to laugh about the nuns who tried to teach us right from
wrong. We'd roll our eyes and share a glance when their sermons go
too long. What use was their wisdom? They didn't know a thing about
the world that we were living in. It was a time of chance, it was a
time of war. It was a time when we didn't know what we were fighting
for. We knew we wanted peace and love and to be left alone to live
our own way in our own times. We knew more than our parents, our
teachers were all fools. What they were teaching us couldn't possibly
be worth all the time we spent in school. Our hair, our clothes, the
way we talked were cause for confrontation. But we were good enough
to die to save some never heard of nation. When I look back upon the
'sixties I find it hard to see that now my kids are growing up and
they're really just like me. They want their freedom from the rules,
they have their own plans. They don't want to fight our wars for us
in far off eastern lands. It is a time of change, it is a time of war.
It is a time when they don't know just what they're fighting for.
They know that they want peace and love and to be left alone.
To live their own way in their own times.

Karen A. Huffman

Sleep

As he stood staring open eyes he asked, so tell me why does he sleep that way?
She smiled and turned toward him and asked, some more tea?
As she poured the tea she added, Now you've got to listen carefully.
It happened a long time ago, when his sister was three.
His baby sister was always ill and finished her life shortly.
And for the first week she was gone, he slept in her bed soft and soundly.
His last sentence revealed, Mom, I don't know why my nose don't work so good.
So I try to remember he smell, thought this would help.

And as for the position he sleeps, with his rump in the air and his head on the pillow,
Arms and legs underneath and securely curled. Well that one's easy.
That's exactly the way she slept. And most nights face to face with her comfortably on his chest.
Me and Harold used to watch from the hall, until the sleep in her eyes would finally fall.

I remember the first month she was gone, his tongue revealed no more words save but one.
And as I look back at time, for the life of me, I could not understand why it was 'sleep'.
But I found the answer while I was trying not forget her:
Like the first step she took, like the first word she said.

And once I made the connection, it all seemed so clear to me now.
The first word she said was 'sleep' and I began to weep.
For I knew somehow, they were together.
And this is, I think, how.

Christopher Danowski

Pain

You call but receive no answer. Still you call. In every bit of air you lurk.
Where ever I turn you're there. You love me. I do not share this love.

No matter where I roam you're with me, thus making no me with out
you. As much as you hurt me I can not leave you. You have fused
yourself deep into my soul, wiping any memory of life with out you
away.

And still you call to me. You ring out louder than happiness. So
loud you dull all other feelings until only you are heard. You call
steadily, day after day; night after night.

You roar louder and louder until I have no choice but to answer.
I know I must leave you but am afraid. Afraid to be alone. With out
you who would I become. Would I recognize myself in a crowded room?

I must find out who I am without you. Loneliness and your
company is starting to rate the same. Your will is no match for mine
and are relationship is coming to its end. Your passion is strong,
but fate is stronger as now, finally, we start to drift apart.

Benjamin Seymour

Ocate

Pines, stickin' straight up, green, dark green, darkest green
zig-zag dirt road - dry and dusty and ochre
blown greens, powdery and grey
pitted old rusty putty charcoal boulders
leaves like coins hang off the aspens, they blow in circles
deep rich loam, dead wood and forest leavings.
Yellow (who knows what they are) bluebells, rosy lilacs, fierce foxtails
lots of buzzing, dragonflies, flies - buzzing bugs - transparent wings

Huffing, puffing, going up, cockeyed foot grips, pushing legs down
to make them go up, sweating, water, water stop sprawl
breathe, breathe, breathe this thin delicious air peaceful,
some blue in the sky mostly pale white and softest grey

Humanity roars in on a fighter jet

Jill C. Klein

Life's Telescope

I enter at the brink of darkness, I sit and look up at the sky.
I study the order and reach for answers, because the starts will never lie.

I see one star above. This is my heart, the star of love.
I spread around sight of this star, still many want to make it scar.

Not far behind, the star of fear. I push away this star of tears.
Regardless of how hard I push, this star is near, it will appear.

I spot the star called generosity. "Give from your heart" this star tells me.
Give what you have, what others lack! And satisfaction you'll get back!

Far to my right I see the star of greed, many grab this star indeed.
Happiness is not about possessions. Greed is sour, it breeds aggression.

The northern star, the star of dreams! This is the biggest star it seems.
This star's the basket of people's goals, the bank of people's future roles.
Some will succeed and some will fail, stick with this star and you'll prevail!

In clear view, the star of pain, the star that everyone will taste.
The star that enter's every person, overcome this star, your soul will reign.

The star of peace and grief are one. This double star will cling together.
Society will always grieve for peace. This cycle will rotate forever.

Love, peace, fear, grief, greed, dreams, pain,
without these stars, life's not the same.

Anton Shufutinsky

Away With The Angels

In an instant it all changed from a joyful picture to a tearful one.
A mother's child has been taken and her heart is breaking.
Tears of sadness and of fear not knowing what tomorrow brings.

In this picture his father sits wondering what will come next.
A playful child he called his own and then came tomorrow and it was all gone.

Another picture to behold is his grandparents.
His mamaw is crying and watching things go.
While his papaw is trying to be bold.
Each in their own way to be hold the wonderful moments of their grandson.

Next in the picture is his brother and sisters.
How they watch their family grieve and trying to keep it all in peace.

The picture is almost complete except the piece that is unable to see.
Away with him the angels he sees and hopes that soon his family he'll see.
Away with the angels no pain will he see and his love grows greater.
What more will he see?
Heather M. Bowser

Sunrise By The Bay

Darkness lies against the hill, silver streams touch waters still;
seagulls squawk as they fly by, silhouettes against the sky,
egret stalks, with bill so bent, on his breakfast, eyes intent;
swallows swoop, dart here and there, to and fro without a care.

Seaweed strewn from tide before, oyster leases by the score;
periwinkle, black sea snail leaves behind a slender trail.
Puffs of grey float, touched with pink. He man ceased to sit and think?
Soft orange blaze, than light so bright, finally dispels the night.

Sun comes out, man is about to enjoy his day, no doubt,
shattering in motor boat scenes that shroud like overcoat;
revving motors spew their fumes—stark contrast with nature's tunes.
See, a touch of blue comes through, boy with dog completes the view.
Grace V. Knight

Where Am I?

Almighty God, how do I find my way through the forest of confusion
when all paths look alike?

My child, only the straightest path will carry you out of the forest.
For confusion is built on twisted paths the carry you nowhere.

Almighty God, how do I find the warm light of truth when the trees
canopy shadows upon my thoughts and reasoning?

My child, the light is found within, in which no shadows can be cast.
For truth is pure and bright and warm.

Almighty God, how do I forsake pleasure when the flowers smell so
sweet and their beauty lures me into its bed with lies?

My child, the sweet smell of flowers do not last past the first breath
For pleasure only seduces those who are willingly lured into a bed of thorns.

Almighty god, how do I find strength by dipping into the pool that is
overgrown with reeds, when it mars my reflection at the mere touch,
and ripples away from me?

My child, the pool only ripples at the surface and reflects a new
image. For strength is only found within the depths, and you must
swim through its darkness alone to find it.

Almighty God, how do I find my way through the forest of confusion
when all paths look alike?

My child, only the straightest path will carry you out of the forest.
For this path has no shadows cast upon it, no flowers worth smelling,
and in itself, will bathe you in strength to complete your journey into the light.
Rhonda K. Fleming

No Time To Listen

Through those long, tough years I needed you there,
I would sit in that window and watch for you.
I wondered if you really cared.
From trying times to sad times I just learned to face them on my own.
I was just a kid, how could I have known that you would never
Be home.
Many times I would throw my ball into the wind.
Not once were you there to catch that ball.
All I needed was for you to be my friend.
As I grew to be a young man I could easily see that someone was
Missing from my life.
There was no one there to share my life with.
No one there to help me sharpen my pocket knife.
I guess I will never know what joy I could have experienced if
Only you would have been there to carry me through.
I could never answer the question that keeps going through my mind,
Daddy, where were you?

    Christopher S. Poore

Family

God has personally selected each of us to be a member of this family.
He designed our distinctions to compliment and support one another
and our similarities so we can appear as one.

Mom and Dad shared all their wisdom to enable us to cope with come what may.
No one is right or wrong or any better than another, we each have a specific role to fulfill.

All of us are full of love and some have grace overflowing.
One of us designed the way we walk, another the way we talk.
Someone else spreads about tenderness and joy to make us all
feel better, while another beings the inspiration and is always there
when someone is in need. There are several around pretty thick.
Due to the size of the configuration several were required just for
coordination.

So as you look around the family remember God selected us to be
together for our specialties. God's plan works very well you know,
from any view it is very clear to see. Look how he created
Our Awesome Family.

    Karen Royster

Life's Journey: An Interpretation

The never-ending road to...where?
It keeps going and going, never stopping for a breath or even a gasp of air.
Over hills and around bends, continuing on an endless voyage too. Where?
With many bumps and turns, the adventure just begins, no sight is seen twice.
The road is the guide, taking control of the car's wheels, forcing
them to follow on the destinationless path to...where?
Though signs may give directions, they are not the key to unlocking
the wheels from the road's tricky hold.
But the road is too clever and forces them to crash and even die.
This evil, hellish, demon-like road to...where?
A smokey fog moves in capturing the road as its prisoner and then
controlling the weak and tortured car as it is pulled into the cloudy
mist, on the horrible, hazardous, hangover highway to...where?
The cloudy sky turns black, lightening hits a tree and it falls, just
missing the imprisoned car.
Suddenly, the rain falls and abuses the car, taking the car and
sliding it from side to side like in the game air hockey,
Continuing for what seems to be forever on the never-ending road to...
Where?

    Julie Lissner

A Mother's Love
Dedicated to my children
The time is nearing for me to go and there are some things that you need to know.
I love you all, there is no doubt, through sometimes I don't know what you're all about.
You are grew up so very far apart but each had with you a piece of my heart.

My darling son, with his soft brown eyes, taken away at eight much to his surprise.
This latest Daddy his Mommy did make was more than his little mind could take.
Stepfather's abuse, this sealed his fate, love and trust for his Mommy turned to hate.
Counseling taught new ways to communicate, but for my little boy it came too late.
Cruelty to animals and to school a gun he did take. To protect him from harm, Mommy gave him to the State.

One little angel left so quiet at home, keeping her fears inside, so all alone.
She lived with her Mommy all her young life, she learned right from wrong and had a good life.
Then her stepfather thought she should act like a wife, he kissed her and touched her saying don't tell his wife.
Told her Mama wouldn't believe her and they'd have a big fight so she fought off his advances and kept her lips
 sealed tight.
When she got older, his advances got stronger. She ran off and married so she'd live there no longer.

Now you're all grown and out on your own, into fine young adults you all have grown.
Too late in this life your Mom has taken a man not like the others from which she ran.
He's honest and moral with a love of the purest kind, he's the step father for you she was a searching to find.
Open your hearts and let his love in, for against you, his stepchildren, he did not sin.
My time is growing short and I want you to know that you'll have a real father when it's my time to go.
   Judy Ferguson

My Love—My Jacquilu
Where, in timeless wedded majesty, the river becomes the ocean, and the water lilies grow. Drawn back across the bridge of time, my
love, my Jacquilu. Unwavering, are my lingering thoughts of long
ago and you. Gracefully then, the long brown tresses of your fourteen years your beauty declared, When, fate pledged us true love, our heritage for always revered. Where, in timeless wedded majesty, the river becomes the ocean and the water lilies grow God's sunshine sustains all our love—magnifies the dreams of youth.
Fifty years—a golden time—memories blooming in infinite truth.
Undaunted through life's valleys of despair, humbly accepting—
mountains of hope and blessings. In harmony—our happiness
multiplied—our trust—our friendship—forever sings. Like in timeless wedded majesty—the river becomes the ocean, and the water lilies grow. Now our life's fulfillment nears, together we're walking the descending side.
Contented—together we've shared the greatest gift, true love multiplied. Soon comes the time—by God's design, deaths temporal shadow our lives o'er flows. In celestial love embraced, our new beginnings, where life immortal grows. Where, in timeless wedded majesty—the river becomes the ocean and the water lilies grow.
   George Edward Snow

My Soul
   I close my eyes and within their cover rises an evilness, turning its stout body, looking at me down a long, crooked witch's nose with an almost smile that belies innocence.
   A ring of gray, lined with pink on either side, glowing within,
rose in concentric circles up its body.
   Eyes, that smiled knowingly, looked back at me with something that
one could perceive as friendliness. Yet, deep inside me a twinge of
fear sprouted, responding to something in its smile, some knowledge in its presence, to some slant of its nose.
   With this came a sure knowledge, unequivocal awareness that my soul looked back at me, mirroring to my innocent, naive, disbelieving eyes what I really am: A shining demon that knows no wrong, has no faults, and believes in its own purity as a standard of morality. In its
arrogance is the certain knowledge of death, of its death.
   The fear that sprouted within me was the of an unwilling, unaccepting knowledge of my own culpability of its blackened
existence. A gleaming blackness that shined with pristine elegance in
the darkness of my eyelids; jewels, that light randomly reflects from,
and honored by their wearer.
   Denford L. Owens

My Brother

My brother wants equality
But don't want to work.
My brother wants to justice.
But don't want to work.
My brother wants a better life
But don't want to work.

My brother, my brother
My brother, we must work for

My mother needs help
My sister needs help
My daughter needs help

For this reason we must work until
Our feet ache, our backs break and
Our minds explode

Because our queens are calling out
For strong kings, my brother!
Frederick L. Brown

Hamartia

The mortality of my soul
Directed by this fatal mistake

I have missed the mark
Killed the spark

Drowned the flame
Forgotten her name

The path has twisted
And my road reinvented

The angels are grieving
The loss of this brilliant being

The demons are awaiting
The moment they will feast upon
  my frame

I am escorted to the underground
The ceremony has begun

I reluctantly take my place
On the altar of no grace
Lisa Zavaletta

A Tear Falls Upon My Face

A tear falls upon my face,
For I am lost once again
Lost and alone

A tear falls upon my face;
I know not what I do
I can't hang on
Love leaves my soul

A tear falls down upon my face,
I try to work it out
It's another one I will miss

A tear falls upon my face
Alone is what I am
It is to be my fate
Jason Van Hoose

An Ordinary Stone

I've found all that glitters is not necessarily gold
Sometimes it takes a jolt for these truths to unfold
That the sparkle of a rhinestone's not a diamond's glare
and true love can't be found just anywhere

I had a real true gem, he was a perfect stone
I had everything in life that I could want to own
I didn't know the value of this gem I owned
'Till I exchanged my gem for an ordinary stone

Ordinary stones can be found anywhere
but real true gems are hard to find
in fact they're rare
I didn't know the value of this gem I owned
Till I exchange my gem, for an ordinary stone

So if you have a perfect gem hang onto him there's
   fools gold all around to make you stray, and then
you'll realize too late this perfect gem you owned
Was not just an ordinary stone
Viola Maxine Basham

Happiness

Happiness is peace of mind that's tranquil with desire
Calmness of emotions clear and free that will inspire

Happiness is music that needs to be sung
Whole notes of melody that has rhythm to run

Happiness is feelings of peace while you're still
Moments wrapped in sensuous thoughts
That leave you with a chill

Always keep the thought in mind
That true love won't be hard to find
It's seldom there when you're in need
But time will allow it to proceed
So don't feel down withdrawn with fear
Keep yourself ready everyday of the year

Happiness is a gift of the mind
That won't be denied its time
Sheron E. Regular

Morning's Fog

Creeping across the morning's grass on silent cat's feet
Making the heaven's clouds and the earth seem to meet
Impairing your vision with its cool and damp mist
Clutching the land in its vaporous moisture laden fist
It shrouds the trees in its soft and white loving arms
Obscuring the countryside and all the surrounding farms
It glides over the land being directed by the gentle breeze
Vague are the outlines of the meadows, the hilltops and the trees
This translucent moist vapor envelopes us in its cool gentle fingers
Resisting the early sunshine warmth as it struggles and lingers
Reluctant to surrender its grip from the land that it shrouds
Reduced to vapors by the sun's heat it ascends to the clouds
It leaves no visible trace except the memories your eyes have seen
And the sweet fragrance that hangs in the air of a land scrubbed clean
It came from out of the darkness on a cool and damp night
It always arrives in the early hours before the morning's first light
When the earth is warm but the air is damp and cold
Once more it comes forth on cat's feet, silent and bold
Henry Jeffs

House For Sale

I had to put my house up for sale: it was in desperate need of care;
More than half of the windows were broken, each room in need of repair.
The minor things turned major, for I had not the means:
And I knew not how to repair the hinges, nor all the other things.

The roof was missing some shingles, the hardwood floors, some wood;
I wanted to fix it up someday: For I knew its possibilities were good.
I finally gave up the idea that I could repair what was broken:
So I put my house up for sale, and prayed for someone with a token.

It wasn't long, I got a knock upon my poor cracked door:
He said he wanted to buy "the place," and the price, he could afford.
I was quite honest with him, as I told him the need for repairs;
The man looked at me compassionately,
He said, "you have had many cares!"

"I do not need the house" he said, "I only want the site;
I can tear down, and rebuild a home that I like.
Don't be sad to leave it, for you will be very pleased:
When you see a Castle in its place,
Then your heart and mind will be eased!"

Dawn R. Gwin

The Poet's Eye

The poet's eye, it's often said, sees things that others dread to see,
or cannot!

It isn't that he wishes to, but that he can't avoid it; he must know,
in his heart of hearts, just how he can exploit the thing that others
cannot see, or will not!

Should he tell them what it is to know that thing they dread? Is it
only right to tell them "The fear is in your head?" Or would they
laugh and say to him, "How could you know what fears have I?

The poet's eye, my friend, The poet's eye.

Walter E. Sinclair

The Love Between Us

I became a wheelbarrow
While he held my feet,
Running on my hands
Around the room we'd fleet.

He carved out goony birds
And marionettes too,
The alphabet and numbers,
Then showed me what to do.

He held up money
A nickel and a dime,
"Which one would you rather have?"
The right choice took time.

He spent time talking with me
And made me feel so good,
His loving voice is in my heart
On my special memory chart.

I wrote this poem about grandpa
It's a good idea I thought,
Lots of things I know now
Are things that grandpa taught.

Mary Anne Simon

Nothing Happens

Nothing happens. Nothing will ever happen.   Ever.

As the sun goes down I build for you my monument of darkness—
the black rose that once bled red withers away and with it the childhood of mine

Childhood's end . . . and again, a dead God in my way
dead promises fill in the blanks and spaces,
and in the distance heavy clouds build up only heavy rains—
though nothing ever, ever happens.   Nothing will ever happen?

Nothing, but Continuum. Ad infinitum, only
stray condoms and condominiums . . . and nothing, nothing, to ever happen.

Like I still stay alive and alone
(but loneliness is rudimentary)
on the day of birth, of death, and of death-like love—
I still survive to somehow love, to laugh at the shadows of you that fill up my room
            and O, Banquo's ghost, you're back again?

For nothing to happen, for nothing to live or to die
and simply for nothing I stay cocooned for the rest of my life.

Nothing ever happens to the darkness of these days
Nothing, nothing happens, until someday
I obit   and quit
  and then Nothing is complete.

Niladri Sarker

Ellie G.

She seems ok to everyone she knows; people pass her, wave and go.
She's surrounded by people who really do care.
She feels so alone, like nobody's there.
People think she does little wrong, but she sings off-key in life's little song.
She lets out a helpless sigh; deep inside her heart cries.
People pass her, but they just glance; She really never had a chance.
No one understands her, she seems so out of touch.
People just can't see she hurts so very much.
She's the life of the party; she's the class clown.
She makes people laugh, but she wears a frown.
She doesn't understand the confusion of life.
She lives each day in utter strife.
She cries herself to sleep each night;
She stays in the dark when she turns on the light.
With her head buried in her hands and her mind wondering so fast,
Every step she takes, she wishes it were her last.
With a gun to her head and a tear in her eye,
She smiles, pulls the trigger, says good-by.
People pass her, cry and pout.
In life she was a whisper, but in death, she's a mighty shout.

Virginia Keeton

Please Don't Stop

Please don't you stop smiling, though inside you may want to frown.
For that smile someone is seeing, may lift them up if they are down.

Please don't you stop giving, although tough as it may be.
The more you give to others, you'll be blessed, don't give to receive.

Please don't you stop encouraging, and giving those pats on the back.
For you're giving someone hope and confidence, that they may sometimes lack.

Please don't you stop praying, keep the faith and just believe.
For you're a source of power and strength, comes by staying on your knees.

Please don't you stop loving, and caring for your fellow man.
For that love that you are showing, will defeat hates demands.

So please don't you stop doing, all that you can do. For you never know who you'll be helping, with the little things that you do.

Derek L. Braxton

One More Reason ... To Live

I have suicidal thoughts.
My fear of living used to keep me alive; and the knowledge that
   God can't forgive me.
My mind kept me going, while my body took the pain.
I would write things out as I'm doing now to get me through the
   pain somehow.
It's five years later and things have changed.
My husband comes first, with his kind and gentle ways, showing me
   a love I've never known.
My young children come next; through their eyes, I see a world
   I've never seen before.
I am seeing that I am a mother first, and they come before an
   outside job so they'll be the best they can be.
I see more romance in a quiet talk with my loved one.
I am amazed when my child starts understanding this world we live in.
I respect life and death more, seeing its shape in so many forms.
Although I still get the feelings, I sit back and look at all I've
   got and life starts to look more pleasant.
I love my husband and children, and pray for my family's well —
   being; and I thank the Lord, for one more reason to live.

Becky Thrush

Wishful Thinking

I remember having several incredible childhood dreams. My favorite,
occurred soon after my Mother had tucked me snugly into bed, and
tenderly whispered "I love you, sweet dreams!" And now its debut
unfolds...I'm wandering about aimlessly in a beautiful, enticing,
enchanted paradise. Feeling young and carefree, I stopped to pick a
big bouquet of lush, velvet like, deep purple flowers, that grew wild
everywhere. I'm intrigued by many different, brightly feathered
exotic birds, flying all around me. I then walked nonchalantly along
a winding, never ending path. Pausing, I viewed "a spectacular, deep
amber colored, shimmering lake, sparkling, with flecks of gold."
While basking in its beauty, my eyes fell upon a floating, peculiar
looking, crystal clear object. With my little girl's keen sense of
curiosity, I plucked it out, as quickly as the blink of an eye.
Holding it towards the sun's light, like magic, it started radiating
"the most brilliant colors of a rainbow!" Fascinated by this colorful
display, I didn't see the "big" gleaming object that was slowly moving
toward me. Suddenly, it captured my full attention! Almost
instantly, my mouth flew open, and my eyes were popping out, as I
feasted upon "the shiniest, 5' tall, gold piggy bank, spewing large
gold coins from its snout!"

Carol R. Cameron

Mother Dear

Mother Dear, gives birth to life, to situations that comes her way.
Embracing decisions that can mold generations everyday.

Mother Dear, not perfect, but wish she could be.
Teaching the time of world respect, harmony, and spirituality.

Mother Dear, the twinkle in your eyes tells the voice of your heart.
Wisdom and love comes from God, the substance that will never part.

Mother Dear, times get hard, trials you face.
Look into the future of hope and grace.

Mother Dear, God will give perfect security.
Take the hand of the journey that leads to eternity.

April Joan Robinson Yokley

Of Diamonds And Children

In our world of rapid changes some believe that like clay,
children can be molded.
Others believe that like a flower, the warmth of love
will allow a child's petals to become unfolded.

Although seeing some wisdom in these two views,
there is yet a better way to view a young child.
It's the lasting strength and beauty of a jewel called the diamond
that best describes our small gems, as they travel down life's road, mile upon mile.

Mother Nature formed diamonds in eons of time and fiery heat,
and children in brief moments of fiery passion.
Both priceless gems enter this world with roughness of edges, smoothness
of touch, innocently awaiting their changes, yet to be fashioned.

Flaws are in all things that come from nature, but it's through time and
tender hands of special people that bring that hidden sparkle into view.
Those with vision know the true worth of nature's gems only increases,
for it's not so much "What They Are..." but "What They Can Be Made In To."

The purity of diamonds and children are of the hardest elements to be shaped,
yet, you polished and added facets, brightening their life
with the time you shared, but for a while.
In the reflection of tomorrow's light your work can be seen in years to come,
and it is because of "You" that they sparkle, this precious gem called a child.

Bill Zinke

You Don't Know

You say you understand my pain, my anger and my fear.
You don't know how if feels to be ripped of your dignity and self respect.
You don't know what it feels like to have your family taken away from you.

You don't know how it feels to be taken away from your home.
You don't know how it feels to have your birth name taken away from
   you and replaced with the name of another.

You don't know it feels not to be able to speak your native language.
You don't know how it feels not to be able to speak of your past.
You don't know the feelings of anger that passes through you when
   another man takes your wife for himself.

You don't know how the stings of some horses whip feels as it tears into your flesh.
You don't know the fear that overcomes you as your child endures
   another beating from the master's wife and there is nothing you can do about it.

So don't tell me you understand my pain, my fear, and my anger because you don't.
You have never experienced these feelings and I hope you never will.

Cori Lynn Dorsey

Oh Mother

Suddenly, I am aware of myself.
I am going through the motions exactly as you would.
The mirror reflects your familiar face
and assorted emotions kiss my nerves when I notice the striking resemblance.

The comfort of detachment battles the longing for union.

Visions of the distraught Goddess comfort me in the lost time of night.
The gray mist devours her. I can see her, but I cannot reach her.

The chill she carries is comfortable for her, but her cold eyes lead me to ice.
I am left alone, to fend for myself, with no instructions on how to melt.

In that moment I awoke to the seeker in me,
and during my diligent search for truth I discovered the sun.
The tears fell from my eyes as the ice around my heart began to melt.

Suddenly, I am aware of my connection to the Mother of us all and I am love.
"Create the love you have found," were the only instructions left by Our Mother.

Sugar cookie anyone? I made them myself.

Tonia Erin

I Am Another Animal

You wanted me to be a tender handy cat to live in your boudoir
to take your stress away so flexible so ready for endearment
   but I am another animal
I want to hear all the rustles of the night grove in autumn
I want to catch all the smells of the morning valley in spring
   I am another animal

You wanted me to be a grateful rabbit to live in a made-for-me-cage
so obedient and so indifferent and chewing what-I-had-been-given
   but I am another animal
I want to get drunk with the aroma of wild flowers from a meadow
I want to jump and run the head over my paws on the bank of a creek
   I am another animal

You wanted me to be an undemanding dog to live in your back yard
so fearless and so faithful and obeying the orders straight away
   but I am another animal
I want to explore the amazing world around me in all its diversity
I want to be right and to be wrong and to choose and not to feel a constraint
   I am another animal
   I am another animal
   I am just another animal.

Alexander Celebrowski

Great Men
(Happy 70th Birthday Grandpa Joe)
Throughout history there have been many stories written and told of great men,
Men who were great artist like Michelangelo, or great inventors like Da Vinci
And men of great minds like Albert Einstein and William Shakespeare,
Or men of great courage like Martin Luther King and Jackie Robinson.

I know of a great man who was there to see me struggle to take my first steps
And he was there when I cried as I walked into class for the very first time;
He clipped and saved the honor rolls from the papers that my name sometimes graced,
And he was there with me through every challenging step I took to get my degree.

Although I did not know him in the days that they use to call him "Joltin' Joe"
And I wasn't around to see him run and play in a single game, he was always,
Rain or shine, found in the stands cheering 'til the last second ticked off the clock
Or every time I stood at the plate and knocked the dirt from my cleats with a bat.

In everything he has done and continues to do, he teaches me to take pride in who I am,
About having courage and believing that I can accomplish every goal my mind sets,
He teaches me the importance of a close family and the gift of giving of myself.
This he has taught me was not from taken from a book, but from experience and love.

So the world can keep adding to its lists of Albert Einsteins, Da Vincis and Michelangelos
And all the many other stories of these great men throughout history and time,
But no list of great men will be complete if it does not show a man of all great qualities
And there is a such a great man, with a great heart, and I love and know him as my Grandpa Joe.

Jason T. Trafny

Memories
Cryptic troves of treasures, insanity masked by dark and cold,
Indulged with sweet keepsakes of the past untold.
Often inflamed by the breath of a word,
The sting suffocated to remain unheard.

Feign the moment, avow resurrection, shake away the lamented past.
Brevity of peace will betray loyalty, cowardly succumbing fast.
HabituT summoned, an enslaved armour, to return like a secret friend,
Joy, regret, delight, sorrow; like a grave unknown it has no end.

A soul embittered, fed on remembrance, held captive from within,
The torment that smolders a reckless love rekindled by time and again.
Thundering through the halls of emotion inside a cumbered chest,
Enlarged by images and intimate bouquets, the fragrance of memories
   that once were the best.

Karen B. Hindman

The Mysterious Traveler
Alone man travels from place to place. Mystery and knowledge
etched on his face. Eyes so dark, skin so tan, rugged good looks. My God, what a man. He is searching for
something, to find out the plan,
the one made for him, this Mysterious Man. The one true in heart,
the one who will back him from finish to start. The one who will love him and hold his hand, she will walk by the
side of This Mysterious Man.
Stars guide his travels by night and sunshine by day. A soft voice will beckon him and show him the way. He will
know when he sees her if she is the plan. Her smile will tell all to this Mysterious Man.
As he looks in her eyes, his search comes to an end. He will see all that shines there and it be then, his past will
cease haunting him. She knows it all now. She wants to be with him, what she loved is now.
My Mysterious Traveler has found peace at last and happiness in life he thought he'd long passed. A partner to
share with, a friend when in need, a lover to fly high with, a soulmate indeed. They travel side by side. They
travel hand in hand, he has found what he's longed for. He has found out the plan. The love he's been
searching for is here holding his hand. She came out of no where and found love with this man or perhaps he
found her. Who knows about fate?
They have both come full circle. They no longer wait.

Pamela Witt

On This Our Wedding Day

Stay with me - hold my hand, as I will yours - allow us to be one
Our journey through life - One in Heart, Mind, Body and Emotion
Striving for the best in understanding and communication
Together always - a joyous entity - sharing life being ourselves
To do our own thing - yet belong to each other - in areas that count
Because love is something that must grow - with faith and trust
Giving more than taking - On This Our Wedding Day!

Come with me - like two children at play - fantazise for awhile
Make the world go away - because today is a very Special Day
No one will ever know - just you and me - this is the way it will be
Two hearts beating as one - no need to verbalize because our love is
Greater than life - be my love forever - on this beautiful day
The first day of our Best Years together - to live in unity and bliss
Mutual sweet ecstasy - On This Our Wedding Day!
    Louise Medulan Froehlich

America's Boot Hill

There once was a loose woman who lived in a boot.
She had a lot of children and didn't give a hoot.

Third child was to Henry, forth and fifth was to George,
several were to traveling salesmen when their stale condoms surged.

Where the rest of those kids come from, we really don't know.
Seemed every time the weather changed the number would grow.

"We breed 'em — you feed 'em", read a sign on the wall.
Welfare checks coming and food stamps rolled in
    as the taxpayers money grew very thin.

Soon, these hand-out children grew up in a misguided way,
no help from their fathers from the very first day.

Some went on welfare to keep up their tradition,
while others burdened society by no set ambitions.

The welfare roll got bigger, the jails came jam-packed,
porn pushers, druggies and many gang packs.

The rules of the land became, kill or be killed
and if you must, be a fool in your folly and don't give a cuss.

So as we walk the streets of this very fine land,
don't rob us for trying to lend you a hand.

Pray, if you must for more love and kindness,
but wouldn't it be great to leave welfare behind us.
    Robert M. Dively

Dreamers

Dreamers, a different way
  a different style
  Optimistic opposition

Dreamers, outgoing and passionate
  risking and vulnerable
  outrageous expectations

Dreamers, intense and talented
  committed and versatile
  anti "other"

An experienced dreamer lies in wait . . .
With those credentials, life becomes an intense battle
Dreamers can't hide—they are always in pursuit . . .
Running in hazardous conditions, clouded by thinking, trampled by
pain, seized by the moment—unconditionally—

Why won't they read the warning signs?
Those dreams will be the death of each of them.

But from the vision of the dreamer, life always has another "dazzle".
And if not, there must be something beyond the darkness.
Maybe a dreamer's hideaway . . .
But, whatever, the dream is still there.
    Juanita Fernandez

God's Signature

Framed by an azure sky and a tree lined shore
A rippling gurgling stream flows, contentedly in its moist bed.
Its wavelets, scurrying happily along with the tide, forming
   a mass of liquid glory.
An unseen breeze sweeps the stream, rhythmically, in a
   tender embrace.
As the morning sun rises mystically, from its eastern cradle
It sends out penetrating rays, which excitedly diffuse the ripples
Molding them into sparkling dancing jewels.
Surely God has sprinkled the surface with the spontaneous
brilliance of His glory!
Never, have human eyes, witnessed a more breathtaking,
   majestic and awesome view
As this jewel studded stream
Along the shore line, the sun's rays quivered among the trees
Reflecting the movement of the tiny waves
Unveiling a continuous wave pattern, creating interest and excitement
   and arousing imagination.
As I watched, I was overcome, with the evidence of God's greatness
and the manifestation of His glorious handwork, His creation
This mystic stream deposited its gentle kiss of damp spray
on my cheek
And then flowed into a larger body of water and on into
   the sea.
Exuberantly enriching the depths of God's magnificent work.
Filling my soul with wonder and joy and peace
Brought about by this lovely display of God's "Signature!"
   Frankie "Dee" Rice

Mother's Day... Personally!

My mother is gone on to be with God, you see
And I some times look back and remember how it use to be.
I think about the times she wiped my nose.
And changed my dirty little clothes.
And taught me how to tie my shoes.
And when I was wrong, she gave me the blues.
She told me what was bad and good . . . she left it up to me to choose.
But warned me if I chose the bad, I would surely lose.
All the things she said came to be true,
I some times today wish I had her around to tell me what to do.
So this is for the mothers today . . . personal salute to you!
For all the things we as children tend to put you through!
   Jerome Sterling

Place In Time

I really don't understand,
How I got to this nowhere land
I've never seen this place in time
Puzzles and riddles and nursery rhymes
I guess the end will never come, I'll never feel my work is done
I tread the dirt beneath my soles hoping to reach an invisible goal
I guess that I will never learn, when I get to the end there's another turn
For every question is an answer
For every musician there is a dancer
So why can't I find my place in life?
Does my existence dull the knife?
People tell me forget the past, but remembrance will always last
Will tomorrow be better than today, or is it best to throw away
My hopes and dreams come in-between
My feelings go up and down like the swings, in the park, in the dark
Thinking of things that life brings
Just give me strength for another motion
And send my soul out to the ocean
Until I figure out this rhyme-give me hope,
I have a place in time
   Lisa Rawlings

Lost But Not Forgotten

Here I sit alone again,
   another night's about to end,
I pass the time with letters
   and my dreams are my only friends.
Remember dreams we used to share
   our forbidden love, we didn't care.
Time slips by slowly all the tears I have cried,
   young love lost forever no chance to survive.
Remember how we need so tight,
   the hours passed from day to night.
Lost but not forgotten bits and pieces still remain,
   pieces of my love are lost, it will never be the same.
Letters I still carry, and memorized each one,
   words are all just whispers, promises of love undone.
Your picture's old and faded, but in it I see our past
   memories I kept forever, somehow dreaming it would last,
Remember how we said goodbye
   to feel "in love," the tears I cried,
And here I sit alone again
   another night's about to end
Now my dreams are my only friends.
   Lori Prickett

A Poem

A poem is all the sadness and the happiness together
is all the feelings, is a dream, is happiness, is an illusion
is a disappointment, a tear, a injury, a leaf felt, a river, a friend,
a love,
a route of a lot of ways, a cross of millions of ways
a close circle, a hide treasure
millions of stars and only one Moon.
A poem lock in a treasure, keep a feeling, hide a passion
full of life, is a waste of time.
You are a poem, I'm life is poem, the life who bring us,
a poem is a mother, is a son
a poem is everything and is nothing,
more than words over a paper
are brushes of an author, are a metaphor made of clouds
are expressions without sense, but with a lot of feelings.
A poem is nothing and is everything for different's persons.
A poem is my life, yours, in the way that you want
with the rhyme that you want, free, metered, broken
as you wish, is only a poem
from the petal of a rose until the universe
a poem only depends of the person who had write.
   Claudia R. Villanueva

Kill the Pain

Don't look at me and say that I don't know pain; I met Mr. Pain a long
time ago. I see him steal, kill and destroy a heart, yes, he knows
where to hit the most wounded part. I saw him in my eyes when I
wasn't very outspoken; he stole my dreams and left me shattered and
broken. I saw Mr. Pain laugh when my child was hungry and cold when
another happy party was destroyed and stolen. He sat between my marriage
   and urged on a fight; he lied and cheated and stole him
all night. So don't look at me and say I don't know pain; I felt the
extreme hurt and tears fell like rain. It hurt so bad that I wanted
to die, I almost listened to Mr. Pain's lies.

The scars of his damage are almost gone. He tends to sneak in when
I forget to pray. I may look happy and full of joy when Mr. Pain
is nowhere in sight, because he found nowhere to linger, to hide
and to stay all night. I can relate to what you're going through,
I know how it is to cry and give up too. I want to help you fight
Mr. Pain, it's the Blood of Jesus that will take away even the stain.
I found the only way to destroy Mr. Pain is to tell him to be bound
in Jesus's name. Mr. Pain cannot linger long because Jesus destroys
him with a song. Just totally surrender to the Lord; Mr. Pain will
have no place to be stored. Jesus Christ is the only way, in His
presence I bid you to stay.
   Vera Tourangeau

The Sad Song Of The Forgotten One: Lady Helen

Oh, sweet gnarled woman exiled in the ivory towers
Of the nursing home at Salem Hills,
Vanished from her rose gilded cottage
Feeling hopeless in bondage.
She hunger for family warmth while her mind play tricks.
At ninety-two, she fights demons in white uniforms, climbs
Icy mountains, and walks alone on torturous roads in silent rage,
Waiting for her dashing son, and grandchildren of tender age.

While cultivating a small garden on her window sill
A flower spoke and said her name was Jill,
Alas she can't remember her name, her memory fails,
Like a cerebral vacuum cleaner cruelly assails.
Her gloomy roommate for years, died, she did not know her well,
Her grief was wallpapered on the sterile walls that tell.
Many times an angel came and whispered, "Helen, sing with me,
And I'll bring your only child and his second wife to be."

Now, her empty world is slipping slowly by her,
While her pained heart people daily tear.
Softly she crooned, "Let thoughtless and loveless souls be wrung
Contemplating my unbearable life sentence" . . . Silently dies the song.

Cynthia Monique M. von Uthemann Dorsey

My Son; Your Son

Somehow I knew you would be different as I carried you thru month
number nine, you were anxious to make your entrance into this world
even before it was time.
You were the youngest and would be the last, and like your sibling's
you grew up way too fast.

Your love for life showed, thru your mischievous grin and joking
around, some thought you were trouble, never serious and a little bold.

You were big in stature and in heart, and she was trouble from the
start, but you married her and gave her baby your name and you loved
him all the same, when this came to an end, you were to see him again.

Your young life was snuffed out before you knew you had a son on
the way. I believed he was not your own until I saw him that heart
wrenching day. I knew you had left a legacy and some would say
'What a pity, you never knew' but I believe you are looking down
from heaven, and you do.

Shirley Davis

How Must I Return Thine Alluring Gaze?

How must I return thine alluring gaze, when over our eyes lingers this misty
haze of two hearts entwined with another's love, though all the while I seek thine eyes.
Of what is thine enchanting presence comprised? Thy compelling gaze draws me inside, and its force is beyond
my comprehension. To shut out the
world around us is my longing, when captured by thine eyes—I could but
drown in them. Thy thoughts, thine heart, I scarce can tell, but thine alluring
gaze I know so well! Thou seekest mine eyes and regardeth my being, and
when thou findest me, we share moments of eternity. Yet, in the polite look
away, we are strangers. The delight of our engaging eyes ignites my trembling
heart. To whisper thy name in these brief moments rendereth my body limp, and my thoughts awhirl.
When shall these tantalizing rendez vous end? Thine ardent gaze entangleth my thoughts with dreams. To
resist thy face, to turn away, could tear
my trepid heart in two. Yet, that which I know to be good and true I must
obey, lest my dreams turn upon my soul;
Ah-yes, turn I must, for indeed I am enticed by thine alluring gaze,
and I
long for freedom . . .

Janel Loomis

Sands Of Time

The hourglass turns over eternally
The sands of time fall gentle like a gentle winter's snow
Slipping through my fingers, time passes me by
Floating amidst a swirling chaos of colors and faces
Loved ones and hated ones alike fly by
But I alone remain untouched
The pain and grief of time's passage leave their marks
Scars unhealed burn from the salty sting of my tears
Tears shed for faces forgotten, faces lost
All a jumble in my memory, nothing to remember them by
By and by the sands of time fall past
I alone float above it all
Pondering existence, my existence
Fragile threads of life bound me to the hourglass of time
Oft' in days and ages past have I considered severing those threads
The burning ache in my heart drawing knife to strand
Strands of colour, strands of beauty
New faces come and go trying to fill the emptiness inside me
Crying for the only emotion I feel, can feel, is sadness
The sands of time pass me by, leaving me alone to gaze upon the colors
of my life
   Charles A. Massoglia

What Does Father Mean To Me

F is for "Friendship" a father has with his children.
A is for the "Arms" always open to welcome a child home.
T is for the "Tears" he sheds when one of his children is in pain.
H is for the "Hands and Head" he used to support his children.
E is for the "Eyes and Ears" he used to watch over and listen out for his children.
R is for the "Rough Times" he goes through while raising his children.

   That is what Father means to me
      Catherine St. Cyr

The Third Oracle Thee Host To The House Of David

Thee Messiah is Thee eternal light host to the house of David. Hear
O' Israel tree of everlasting fruit. I thee elected lady did witness
thee tree of fruit abundantly transforming the bare branches to seeds
of everlasting fruit to feed God's will the chosen sought after people
I was showered with thee light and the fruit of the tree. The seeds I
could not count there were so many. But I felt the dappling beauty of
the Holy Soil of Glory beneath my feet to be watered forever in the
land of the Holy. Thee voice of the firmament did speak a truth "Evil
will not reach my soil of truth. I your Lord have a foundation on
High!" At this point thee light over took me only to be enlightened
by thee trance of awakening in thee holiest of holies as pure as can
be and transformed my being into the love of loves seas. I wallowed
in the light no darkness to be. And my thoughts were transformed for
you and for me and where we all shall be. My Lord was behind me and
spoke to the cast of the holy angels and the men in cloaks standing
with staffs, praising God the father and Israel below in the purest of
his light. His people naked, garments with sparks, ready for the
coming of Moshiach arrayed the eternal glow, ready are the people of
the book said the cast, Lord of hosts worthy is the raiment we have
affirmed your eternal look. Crowned with the stars of David I stood
before Moshiach that shall come in my womb for I helped prepare by
being deep in the fields of meadows pure light. The gatherer of the
sparks that shall weave the flesh garment of eternal light, who beheld
the stars that bejeweled the eternal night. Thee host to the star of
David.
   Kathyann Morse

The Train Station

Sometimes late at night alone, I muse, of the clamoring place I was before
Reminiscing about a bygone era, a way of life that will come no more.

I recall the ceaseless clatter of the wheels on the old train track,
As one train would leave the yard, another one would be coming back.

I was a hubbub of continual activity, noisy and bustling with constant commotion;
Passengers rushing and racing around; loud piercing whistles of a locomotion.

You know—they call it progress, but me—well, I think it's sad,
When I recall the echoing laughter, and all the good times that we had.

People from every walk of life were in my midst in the dark of the night;
There is a number of stories I could tell, for I have seen many a strange sight.

Throngs crowded within my walls, gathered round the old wood stove;
Others warming up with a little sip, while concealed in a small alcove.

Beleaguered parents with crying babies, older children excited about a train ride;
While the train crews only smiled, and very calmly, took it all in stride.

The harried station master hoping the train would not be late,
For he didn't want to tell these people, they would have a two-hour wait.

But, I have outlived my usefulness, that's why I've been torn down;
Now, I am nothing but a memory in the hearts and minds of a railroad town.

Elaine Baskey-Hales

No One To Love

Nobody to care about, no one to love. No need for loving, anyway.
   I'll just walk away.
No need to take that walk to clear my head, my head's already clear.
Now that I'm away from you, I've come to feel real and sincere.
You used to make me feel that way, now that's just a blur.
Life with you was for the birds.
I couldn't tell you what made me see, I didn't need to find you,
   I need to find me!
I wish it all were clear to me, why it was, you just couldn't see.
You knew my ways, my strengths and woes, yet still, you couldn't me go.
Your love for me was never real, so why the fear of being free?
You'll come to see, in a week or two, that what's right for me,
   will be right for you.

Gloria Mullavey

The Old Man

The old man waits in anticipation, wondering when the phone will ring
He longs to hear a friendly voice, or get a letter the postman might bring
He can't remember ever feeling so lonely since his wife died and left him behind
He hopes for a visit with his children, but they have not called for some time

His memories drift back to the old days, he was a strong and healthy young lad
They didn't have much in the beginning, still, they felt blessed for all that they had
Farming had been such a hard life, so in to the city they went
A new home in a quiet neighborhood, surrounded by a white picket fence

He worked in the mill and she in their home, together, six children they raised
Now in his little room as he sits all alone, he recollects the love and laughter of those days
A nurse arrives with his medication, another woman, his room she will clean
He's impatient with intruding strangers, they've interrupted his precious daydreams.

Your son has sent a message, he'll be coming by today
He said that you should pack your bags, his family wants you to stay
He's concerned about your happiness, he fears you're feeling all alone
It's your comfort and health they're worried about, so they would like
you to live in their home

The old man's prayers had been answered, he knew that someone still cared
Quickly, he gathered his clothes and mementos, then sat by the window prepared
Later, that's where they found him, his smile was hard to describe
First the pain, then his wife was calling, in his happiest moment he had died

Lin Dressler

From My Heart

Although she spoke very few words, Her heart spoke loud and clear
The laughter of joy in songs she sang, Filled hearts when she was near!
Softness in her gesture, Kindness in her heart, A truly special lady
    One who played a special part!
A part of her stays with us, while she goes on to be
The one who has been chosen, at this time
    To Be With Thee!
Through her eyes you see her smiling, What's in her mind you may not know
From her lips she'd say "Jesus Loves Me—For the Bible Tells Me So."
Sometimes words need not be spoken, Yet the sounds ring in your ear
Shh . . . take a moment to listen, What's in the heart you need to hear!
The heart is how we are judged, by the Lord who sits on high
We all must go before Him, Not one of us will He pass by
        Mother's heart was very full
    With Love she would forever share!
"Know" that she is still with us
    A Mother's Love is always there!!!
Shhh . . . take a moment to listen
    What's in the heart you need to hear!!!
    Eva M. Matthews

My Apache Ancestors

My Apache Ancestors once moved like the wind
Through sun and rain - through snow and sleet
They loved the land - it was their's indeed!

How lovely how great were the mountains and rivers
The deserts were quiet the heavens were bright
Nature provided and gave them light.

It was so perfect - why did it fall?
When intruders came - what happened to all?
Greed possessed them to take it all.

The Intruder Forces were many and armed
The Army with guns - The Government with laws
The Apaches knew it - thus they were warned.

Victorio led them with all his might
They moved and waited and then did fight
Brave to the end by day and night - Victorio led them and it was right.

Extermination was the plan - No more Savages to spoil the land!
All were Exiled in the Land Of The Free
What will be the End is left to See!
    Mercedes Conner

The Poet's Words

Read my words, for words are all I have
to tell the world the way it looks to me.
Turn the page and there I am, sometimes happy . . . sometimes sad,
For poets are creatures of mood and whim,
They walk alone for no one understands
their world, woven with fragile, silken dreams,
seen through rosy-tinted glass.
Where reality entering, rends the threads apart
and floods with blinding tears.
Read my words, find Me between the lines,
The things I do not say, shout my dearest heart's desire,
It was not written in the lines, it drifted on a sunset cloud,
It walked along the rainbow's rim, and sung a plaintive melody.
Tell me, did I touch your heart today
with a gentle word or a tender thought?
Did you find me, feel my heartbeat in lines upon the page?
Do I linger with a little touch of sadness as you close the book again?
For it is words that weave my dreams and place
my heart upon the world-wide viewing screen.
My words are Me, all that I am, all that I shall ever be.
    Anne Kaye

Umpire Time

I once had time to spend with you, but I found other things to do.

Weekend parties; out with friends.
Now you're gone I can't make amends.
Grandpa, I loved you; Grandpa I miss you . . . strike 1!

I spent some time with you, but not a lot
Didn't tell you my feelings; I had time or so I thought.
I wrote you a poem you took to heart.
Now the cancer has taken you and we're apart.
Terri-Lynn I loved you; Terri-Lynn I miss you . . . strike 2!

I met you and we married way to soon. I pretended to be as
   happy as a loon.
We had two sons and lost another one.
Now our marriage is over and all but done.
Garrett and Wes I miss you; Cathy I don't want you . . . ball 3!

Now as I step into the box for one last pitch,
My hands are sweating; my lip starts to twitch.
Friendship throws a curve, love a fast ball; hard to judge,
   not expected at all.
Do I strike? Do I walk? Time is throwing one last ball.
Jackie I love you; Jackie we have time, let's not take it for granted.
Time is too short to waste; I want to give life another taste
   . . . play ball!

   Don J. Meek

Over The Rainbow

When I was a little girl, many long years ago,
My mother took me to this wonderful "picture show"!
The "Wizard of Oz" was the name of that very special movie,
And I can never tell you how very special it is to me.
'Cause years later along came my lil' angel, Jennifer,
And this lucky Meemaw got to watch that movie with her!
So, my little "Dorothy," I wanted to let you know,
That I'm so glad we shared that trip "over the rainbow."
You're six years old today — and, my goodness, how time has flown,
You must always remember how to click your heels and say
"There's no place like home"!
So Happy Birthday, Lil' Angel, and don't forget to "Wish upon a star" . . .
May your troubles always "melt like lemondrops" and you stay
as sweet as you are!

   E. Nell Johnson

His Laughter Drifts Away

The memories of him surround me his cologne is in my hair
The last time I saw him he had that evil grin

He dances in the icy water where we once danced as lovers
His laughter drifts away, his laughter drifts away

His body so divine and strong ways wasted and ever so limp
The icy water covers the traces which hides our secret forever

He dances in the icy waters
Where we once danced as lovers
His laughter fades away, his laughter fades away

The wind whispers our secrets, his blood stains deep beneath my skin
As a switchblade runs so red
Buried in the sand where we made love

He dances in the icy waters where we once danced as lovers
His laughter fades away his, laughter fades away

The wind carries your whispers of love, fears and betrayal
I will love you forever beyond the tides of time

He dances in the icy waters where once we danced as lovers
His laughter drifts away, his laughter drifts away

   Flora Carde

Shades Of Feelings

Shadows of pain pass over me and touches the heart,
Recalling memories that were thought long gone.
Why have you chosen to return at this time,
Didn't I face you and release you long ago?

Shadows of pain pass over me and touches the mind,
Dredging up thoughts and visions of past experiences.
Why am I being reminded of these long forgotten memories,
Have I failed to remember the lessons that I thought I had learned?

Shadows of pain pass over me and touches a nerve,
For I am being insincere about my growth, and I don't like it!
Why have you tested me with pain when you know it will hurt?
I know it gets me to listen, and to listen is also to grow.

Shadows of pain pass over me and touches my mended heart,
A smile surfaces, as I realize the memory is pain free.
"Why must I make life so difficult?" I ask.
And then a shadow of pain passed over me as a new lesson was created.

    So Be It
Sue T.

Setbacks

My heart's only desire
is to create something of beauty, using both my hands and mind,
A pattern uniquely defining brightness, softness and warmth.
Once again, I happen to find my needles for knitting, tips broken
and my yarn of fine wool in such disarray, intermingled, intertwined.
I dare not pull, the silken hairlike strands on the surface,
lest I tighten every knot that lies within.
Before my eyes, all that I see, often resembles, my mind's own confusion.
With both, I must be patient and gently work to untangle, that
which is my endless struggle.
To do this, my own will, wills to once again begin.
Please help me work through this My Dearest Friend.
I pay a debt of guilt for,
more then, that, which is my sin.

Elizabeth Ann Moritz

Story Of The Elusive Soul

Creamy petals on the floor, champagne coloured roses, cufflinks, silken tie;
Crinkled linen, delicate lace, strand of pearls all carelessly tossed aside.
If but a sigh falls all their exquisiteness will be disturbed . . .
Perfume, aftershave, mingles intimately in wisps of a fragrance yet uncaptured.
Your newly awakened smile — softly persuasive — lingers on my mind.
And still, I wish time would stand still so I could seek out realms unknown;
To where I can find the key that unlocks the secrets of an elusive soul.
Candle lights have died; morning light filters through casting long shadows on the wall.
Love poems, re-read, re-captivates my mind before they are allowed to fall,
To lay among crushed petals and half-emptied goblets of wine . . .
Like linen and lace, are tangled and shaped into an intriguing work of art
That will retain a decorative charm until they are packed away and stored.
And still, I wish time would stand still . . . to read the story of your elusive soul . . .
Endless love, dreams, tangled webs of fantasies woven like an intricate tapestry
Heart, mind, body and soul, re-acquainted all sensuously blended . . .
Last night's adventure follows morning's glory in a hauntingly familiar afterglow.
Morning lethargy sweeps in, hints of something unspoken something undisclosed.
Your gentle kiss upon the brow your softly persuasive touch lingers a while.
With nothing left un-explored, still early morning promises of more . . .
And still, I wish time would stand still . . . to touch the sweetness of our elusive soul . . .

    Jamie C. Mangal

Brian's Story

I look to the hand before me. The ring just sparkles—like her
eyes. I hear the happiness in her voice. I see the bounce in her
step. Time passes, it still seems so new—still full of life and love.

I hear the promises made before God, friends, family—promises made
to each other of a love to stand the test of time, to cherish and
honor through times of good and bad, to be at each other's side in
sickness and health, until death do they part.

Words and promises meant at the time, who was to know of the distance
a heart could roam. Who was to know the ring would find a new home
in a box. Who was to know of the pain a lost love could bring. Who
was to know the shine would fade.

Broken promises, lies, hurt—small faces of a love gone, confused.
Not understanding why Mommy and Daddy aren't together in their house.
Small face with tear-streaked cheeks. Now unsure of forever. Trust
has been broken for more than just the two of you. The small hearts
suffer also.

The ring seems so dull of its glimmering life. Life that has been
put to a box. A love that has been put to rest.
    Carol L. Hill

Thoughts

Thoughts racing, mind wandering focus on one or maybe two, like a
building being built, a nest for the young being built by a bird or a child.

Growing to an uncontrollable surge, built up inside and nowhere to go.
Can they go here or there, no one really know they just fade one at a
time and yet a few stick like glue, or taped onto your mind, heart
or soul like a patch, or a scar forever there 'til death do you part.

It truly a wonder for the thoughts cannot be controlled but my fade
or stay. Like memories. We live once and die one, the time is here and now.

Stand up for your mind, thoughts, feeling or love. You may never
have a second chance for one really never has a second chance at life
it just changes and goes day by day, do it or die trying, keep the
faith, do yourself right and be strong, survive now, try now . . .
    Adam Estrada

All The Same

Nefarious sky, fills my eye, questions of the dawn
Will it be long, will it be strong, will casualties be drawn?

Acceptance spent, feel contempt, couldn't help but note its colour
Eyes aghast, I look on past, its soul different than any other

Persuaded on que, by its dusky hue, evil lay round the bend
Threatened loud by darkened clouds, forebodes an ominous end

Protect my castle, prepare to wrestle, gather children from the storm
Avert their eyes, from blackened skies, keep them always from harm

Hold my wife, for dear life, thickly the cast did darken
Turn my back, await attack, whilst reason silently harkens

Fear the cost, sure of loss, demon color never sated
Came the morn, feel forlorn, but . . . depraved sky had abated

The evil rave, it did not rage, just a changing of the day
Fear so great, this angst of hate, etched bloody marks along the way

Fleshed out scars, or iron bars both colored in ever different hues
To shamefully deride the man inside, denies us all our due

My tempest ride a master guide, xenophobia: the ignorance within
To judge on sight, to avoid the light, blinds us to our kin

Sky once rabid, now its tepid, changes brash to tame
While heaven abounds, full of clouds, all different and all the same
    Luke Jackson

I Wonder How God Felt

As We come upon this sacred time, I wonder how our God,
Feels about the sacrifice, His only Son had Trod,
Our God had given a heavy load, and we know how Jesus Felt,
As in the garden he did pray, and on His knees He knelt.

His Sweat became as blood they say, and the burden not so light,
Then on the cross He suffered shame, as the day was turned to night
Our Holy God had turned His back, not on His Son, as thought—
but on the sin our Jesus bore, For Salvation that He bought!

I Wonder how our God had felt, as Jesus cried like rain,
My God, have you forsaken me? and then He died in pain—
Bur first God's Son, His only Son, asked forgiveness for them all—
They who tortured, beat and scorned, for them who on Him call.

I Wonder how our Mighty God, had felt on that dreadful day,
The day that Jesus, His begotten Son, In love, gave His life away?
Could I, if put in that same place, say yes, i'll send my son—
for all the world to see such love, and do as He had done?

So We, The blest, the Saints, The Redeemed, On Easter morn' can praise,
The One True God, and Jesus Christ—
Whom the Holy Ghost did raise!!

Ruby N. O'Haver

Help Them

My friends are in trouble; their lives are going down.
I try to help them out, but when I need them they're not around.
Drugs, lies, and murder are affecting my peers.
If they could only see themselves, they would have some fears.
At the rate they're going, they won't be here for long.
Their lives aren't suppose to be this way; everything's gone wrong.
Please, someone help them, before they've too far gone.
If they don't get help soon, then their lives are gone.
Don't think all is hopeless, for there is always a way.
All that you have to do is find something to say.
There are some good ones who will really change the world,
But don't let them get in, it would be better for Earth to stand still
So if you want to help them, hurry. Do all that you can.
They are not all gone, yet. So help the ones left to win.

Kristopher Clark

Jill (As No Material Could Symbolize) The Passion In Her Whispering...

Blown away in the daring drift, my body begins to sway and shift
Watching her glide, passing by - blinding my naked, dilated eyes
Rubbing them slowly, softly still; the girl flew past - her name was Jill

Jill's pure love could always sift, procuring the elements of
forgotten myth, Quickly spreading her wings over all, holding their
call from a narrowing fall, As she loves to soar above and sing,
while the bells begin to ring and ring

But on one she keeps a sharp keen eyes, so his love will never wither
and die, She always walks him along his path, helping him to heal and
cry and laugh, Until the day when he joined her light, sailing away
and over the night, Never feeling so loving and free, they dove down
into the shimmering sea
To swim with the sharks, and dance with the nymphs
To run through the caverns, and explore the lost ships

Then to the land, under the sun; skipping and hopping - just having
fun, Conferring with snails and otters and birds, bereft of the need
for useless words and running away with the elk and the deer, the
boy was so happy he felt his first tear

Jill was the one, his only true love; she was the girl who cooed
like a dove, Jill was his angel, to hold his hurt and hand; she was
the joy overwhelming his land And Jill loved this boy with all of
her might, she was the one who forgave his first fright

James A. Bruce III

Remember

You were herded like cattle in crowded box cars
Sent to factories and camps for the crime of innocence
You became numbers, stamped for all to see
Striped of humility, made to stand naked in the cold
Your lives were no longer filled with promise-only shades of despair
Together you lived and died for your nation.

You gallantly walked to your execution
Coming upon the smoldering smoke stacks of humans being vaporized
They led you past the pits filled with mother and child
Your tired eyes fell upon a tiny babe still clutching a soft white daisy
    Was it then that you became afraid?
Your innocence lost, your fate written in stone
No, you were courageous until the end
Until your last breath was taken
It was then you were quieted by the *wind* . . .

Hundreds, thousands, millions were mercilessly slaughtered
All in the name of one soulless man
It is years of sacrifice never to be forgotten
Long life to you, the courageous, who fought until the battle won
For your struggle, whether in life or death, is more precious than any on earth.
    Jane Marie Osgood

Good People

Who are we???
We are what we want to be, Good people . . .
We are hard to find
People take advantage of us.
We get lied to, trampled on, and tossed around like a rubber ball.
But we get back up, and we find what it was that made us good to begin with.
We remember the kindness we give out to each of you!
We remember the love you take from us
We remember the smiles we put on your face.
We remember the caring we shared together!
We remember all the good we do for you, and we want nothing in return.
We just want to be there for you and take care of you, and share our love with you.
You get a piece of our heart and we get the satisfaction of knowing that once again,
We have been and will always be, good people!!
    Joan B. White

The Forgotten People

Don't gaze too hard, it could be you stumbling around with nothing to do.
My hair is smelly and matted with dirt, I walk everywhere on bunions which hurt.

When you see me, don't curse in despair then stick your nose up in the air.
It's more my air cause you're not here, you go home and find good cheer.

Home is where we lay our head in noisy subways, malls, and parks.
We pray for our safety when it turns dark.

We look like packed pickles in a tiny jar. Our things are stuffed in broken-down cars.
Food is so scarce in my poverty, even the rats take scraps from me.

Some are smart or have degrees. Being over-qualified is a problem, you see.
We should groan when thrown a bone, we are still people so sadly alone.

Give us a chance to turn our lives around, the frowns will blossom
and we won't let you down.
We're put out of neighborhoods for looking unkept, but you're not mean when we are clean.

We might be someone you know, so don't act cruel shouting silly rules.
We need help and you have nothing to lose. There was a home, a job, and family—now we have none—This just can't be . . .
    Jewelene Ivory

Life

A wonderful new day has again risen
The world is still here —
The sky is blue with billowy clouds
And life is very dear.

My perspective has changed —
My thoughts follow another path
Everyday happenings are so special
More wonderful than the last.

My dreams will continue on
My hopes will emerge and become realities in life's tumultuous rage
The circumference of my life will come full circle
And will be adventurous at every stage.

If only I could convey to others
The thrills that life has to offer in its simplistic ways
If only all could appreciate and cherish each and every day.

It's sad sometimes that we can't just clutch to our hearts
All that is availed to us in measure
But must experience a crisis point to realize what we really treasure

So let's take another look all you children, husbands and wives
And make the most of every second for this dear heart is life.
    Laraine M. Huneke

Beijing On Eva's Arid Garden

Save Eva's garden for it's a wasteland

Eva and fellows took up the call
To save the land from a chaotic fall
To Beijing they went in an ardent quest
Like the questing Knight
In the Grail legend of the West
Aridity in the garden must be dispelled
To Beijing they went
Knowing well their time and efforts
Would be well spent
Surely when they went,
They knew well who They Were
They knew well Treasures to pursue.
They knew well too, Who to rescue
Thanks to Eva and fellows, for this preliminary major breakthrough
Before Eva and fellows sit back and say
Hey please, horn us tunes of triumphs
All deaths that hover over them must be conquered
All The Wrought Chaos must be undone.

Save Eva's garden for it's a wasteland, on goes, the fertility call.
    Helen Apolo Ocaya

Con//science-Stricken

How do I right my wrongs dear God? Others I have hurt
Help me correct them like a man not dragging another in my dirt.

My guilt is oh so difficult my behavior is to blame
Help me God to deal with this letting my guilt not turn to shame.

Knowing I can never erase the choices I did make
Having to confront the dreaded my conscience did awake.

It's a con that swindles a victim after gaining his confidence first.
Science is a branch of knowledge pushing us forward with a thirst.

Let me live the science part and not the con I plead
Using my gift of discernment sowing some fruitful seeds.

This load is oh so heavy on my conscience it does lie
Did my victims feel this heavy load when my con I tried to hide?

Wanting to confront my load sooner the con got in my way
The science never left me the clouds just covered the rays.

My conscience was way off center only one side I wanted to show
Displaying my logical knowledge the weeds continued to grow.

This garden is not so pretty the weeds have an unruly way
My work is staring at me requiring more than a day.

Although I'm Con/science-Stricken I shall ultimately see,
The science was always dominate, the con never hidden,
  not even from me!
    Paula Ortago

Clandestine Enchantment

Be it untenable but parallel to August sentiment
Cursed sweet affliction! Shackled my chest does burn
To taste and beguile . . . you refuse to shame me
only to taunt and blame me.
To reject? To protect? What of the reason?
Not I of you—you did the leaving
Quite like that of November gales
Soaring, wailing—but with much purpose . . . to be supposed.
To feign trite trepidation may eradicate its integrity
Eminent coyness marks felicity's sufferance.
A torture to thine that is created
Hindering, vexing with shrouded dole
Truth your nightmare, my shield! Much that of sunlight to a vampire.

May I; shall—prick gently the juices of your mind?
Adorn the altar—the celestial pedestal of our domain
I with grace beseech you, to probe and reach you
To taste of the preserve, lest it fall soft and rotten
You oft desired to tame me; to prick and sting me.
Woe! Clandestine enchantment—take me, complete me.
Release me.
Shelly Bridges

Mr. Tattooed Devil Man

Arms big and gruff
Right shoulder carries a ferocious fire breathing dragon
On left a deadly skull
Mouth with a smile like the Grinch
Eyes translucent emanating a red glow
Back covered by a pentagram
Walks with his head high — smoked with marijuana,
    buzzed with alcohol
He's my tattooed devil man
He is not a devil to me you see
To me he is a show
For I'd not be friends with a devil nor an associate or an
acquaintance
He is mentally erect by my charm
He is sexually flaccid by my innocence
I fell into his eyes and kissed his soul
He is not a devil man
He just tries to be.
Espree Devora Kessler

What's Up With My World

Today I turned my head only for a moment. While distracted my
world got up and walked away. Took its clothes, filled up its bags,
and wandered out the door. I was only gone a second, not even a
blink. And when I returned the world was gone.
With it went my friends, what family that I knew, and the only love I
had ever known. No warning, no reason, no excuses, or explanations,
just gone. Suddenly I was so alone. No one to talk to. No one to hear.
Today I took a short pause, and while I was away, my world took
its suitcase. Grabbed my dog and left. Walked out and left the key.
Only problem was, it also took my car, my wallet, my money and
an earring from a friend of old. Left me standing in an empty door.
Nowhere to go, no place to turn. No up, no down, just emptiness.
I don't get it. What did I do? Why did it leave me? Not even the
chance to say wait. Just zip and away! Nothing.
So I took a deep breath, a heavy gasp of air.
Reached deep into my pocket, found paper
and pencil, and I wrote my world a letter. I asked it why it deserted
me. Just how it would explain. I made it a quite a long one.
Let it know my total disdain. When finally I had it finished, I folded up my paper
and sealed it with a kiss. And when I went to mail it something was amiss.
Darn world it took my mailbox.
N. Todd Carnine

My Flight

I can't remember when it was we started out to climb,
The mountain that would represent this wondrous life of mine.
It was a journey meant for me, but I didn't go alone,
You both were there to guide the way, and uncover the unknown.
Hand in hand, and side by side, we started on our way
You planted deep the roots for me that I'd need to grow one day.
"Trust in God and tell the truth." Are footholds you gave me.
"Think of others and always work hard, 'cuz nothing in life is free."
The bottom of that mountain gave ease to tiny feet,
It served as preparation for the obstacles I'd meet.
My journey became more difficult the higher up we'd climb,
I'd soon be forced to test those roots with each passing day of time.
Those roots became the anchor that held fast when strong winds blew
The stumbling rocks that were pitfalls for me, you pulled me safely through.
Along the way I'd grown my wings—I was close to my journey's end,
You were so much more than just Mom and Dad, I also called you "friend."
Then finally, I could see the top, just a few more steps to take,
Those last few conquering steps, you said, were mine alone to make.
As I stood at the top and looked around, I beheld a wondrous view,
You walked up beside me and gave me a push, then watched me as I flew.

Krissandra Gatz

Bended Knees

On bended knees he came to me, with love and promises for all eternity.

On bended knees he reached for his child and promised to always love.

With a father's pride he held his hand to guide his child through life.

On bended knees, beside my bed, his strength he gave to me. Years of love and friendship he never wavered from me.

On bended knees I wept for the man who always loved me. Headstone cold, flowers upon his grave, on bended knees I pray.

A simple man of the greatest heights, my love on bended knees.

Deloris B. Mathes

Atlasphere of Care

Through the night there was a light, misty rain
    that made the next morning so wonderful to begin without
        any strain

That very lite movement of air filled with such refreshments
    of amazing scents in a coolness to wake me up with no resentments

The sky being a little bit hazy but really rather clear
    as the sun shined brightly, those trees placed me in some shade
        so dear

While nature with the animals' orchestra altogether made an
    enjoyable song
as faithfully I sang hymns of worship of praise unto our Father
    through Jesus unto whom I do belong

Christ is the one who enables me to notice, to take part in
    such amazing occasions of many
Jesus is my all in all, I can do nothing righteously without Him
    guiding me through the rough roads of plenty

That is why I truly do enjoy every moment of every day
    through Jesus, even the times of testing that are allowed to
        happen brings on no dismay

While taking time to study the Bible, being constant in prayer
places joy in all occasions through my Saviour Lord Jesus enabling me to know
    how much God does truly care!

Anthony L. Surratt

Requiem For A World And Universe

The wise voices inside my brain say, "The world's and universe's
citizens have failed to care about one another".

"Any world and universe based upon illegal, unlawful, sinful, and evil
brainwashing, slavery, physical and psychological control, segmented
and compartmentalized brains and nervous systems, cut brains such that
the victims possess multiple consciousness and multiple personality,
shrunken bodies, radio and cameras implanted, beatings, torture,
and mind control are far worse than the Roman coliseum and by the
inner nature of their illegality, unlawfulness, sinfulness, and evil
lead to the destruction of families, social groups, cities, nations,
worlds, and universes, and lead to world and universal war and mass
murder and mass destruction.

"The only hope of the world and universe is to honestly care about one
another and honestly respect one another, assuming almost everyone
and everybody will use this wisdom and this wiseness of caring and
respect as a big lie, con, hustle, and fraud, to stab their brothers
and sisters and fellow world and universal citizens in the
back — therefore, setting in motion the destruction of the world,
galaxies, and universes and ensuring the destruction of themselves.
of the world, galaxies, and universe and ensuring the destruction of
—Be wise as a serpent and try to be gentle as a dove".

Leslie S. Amison

Butterfly Wings!

Walking through the garden of hope. Feeling under the weather.
Not knowing where I'll find the strength to go on another day.
Feeling amiss in such a beautiful place. Seeing the flowers of
all different colors illuminating the day. I just wanted to end this day.
Turning to leave. I spotted the splendor of the day, such a tiny
butterfly in all of its glory. Oh, so beautiful are the wings! Going
from flower to flower, then flying up towards the sky.
So delicate are the wings but yet so strong to soar into the wind
Pondering this vision I just seen. Where is the strength in such
delicate wings?
Quietly my Lord speaks to me. "For the strength you see in such a
delicate vessel, is within the soul of every living creature."
"For I live within you. Call upon me every day. And the joy of
the Lord is your Strength!"
And you are my precious tiny butterfly!
Delicate but yet so strong as the butterfly wings!

Jacqueline L. Greek

Heart Speech

I thank the Lord who returned my soul the morning in the body,
It took me five years to realize his major importance,
so here's my story:
I awoke perfectly well rested,
Numbness slowly evacuating from the sleep it infested.
Suddenly the eye lids bursted wide open,
Insignificant thoughts overpowered; and by the strong rays of sunshine broken.
I stepped outside my captivity today,
And the air smelt so fresh, even the sky above was clear from gray,
Met a few teenagers on the way. Who rejected my open arms, without regret.
On the other side of the street, parents and cops discuss how to fix
society's debt.
We can spend a lifetime on arguing what's normal,
Although it only takes a glare, to agree on the weird or immoral.
Tender minds persuaded how to think, and to resist fail.
Entertaining their opinions with drugs, so they could face betrayal.
Delaying the nervousness of time, with a wide grin.
Endless strange uncertainties, keep them on the billboard of sanity,
with the strength of a pin
Rescue yourself before this chaos drowns all your love inside it.

Ethan Shalom

Washington Town

Along the glamourous curvature of the grandeur of the curvature of the
grandeur along the Potomac river, sights.
Looking South, from the grand capital heights.
Is the pyramid of the spiral Washington's monument height.
To the left and sound, with the grandeur of the Potomac basin, lee of its rise.
A glimpse of its lee, and the outstretched sound.
The clink of the deciduous tree line, alike in, lee and gathered around
To the right, the statute of Jefferson's monument, to the right and
out of the spiral sphere.
With its grandeur, of round dome, and Roman columns, of white marble tile.
The strut, out of its pose, on the Potomac basin lip.
With the tread of its grandeur, to back of the modern, high road bride,
to the right and back.
And the conform of tree line, right and around, this dome spiral
sphere historic nature.
With the basin of blue, brown, black and grey, waters to the east, with its wide bayet.
The preview of yesteryear, of a long, old, historic span.
The monument of Freedom, of Colonial renown.
The adage of freedom of 1776.
Washington town.

Ramond Draghi

Everwords

"Whenever"
How can one word mean any yesterdays, any todays, or any tomorrows?

"Whatever"
How can one word mean so very much, yet mean so very little?

"Whyever"
How can one word be the question to so many answers?

"However"
How can one word mean so many ifs, ands, buts, yet be so persuasive?

"Whoever"
How can one word mean you or me, him or her, and them or us?

"Wherever"
How can one word be so near, yet be so far away?

"Forever"
How can one word effect our lives for now and for all time?

Gary L. Clark

My Gallant Knight

In all good stories where Kings and Princes rule,
there are lovers in the plot.
Delilah had Samson, maid Marian had Robin Hood
and Gweneviere had Lancelot.

These gallant men on trusted steeds did all the dragons slay.
And when the deed was done, the dragon at their ladies' feet did lay.

These men wore honor as a vest and courage as a second skin.
So loyalty and integrity were without a doubt within.

No incantation or witches smoke could make them traitors be.
When their gallantry and goodness could only to victory lead.

Like a knight in shining armor riding on a pure white steed,
You are my Merlin to work your magic whenever I shall need.

When the seas threaten to rise and the sky comes crashing down.
You part the seas and find the sun to see that I don't drown.

The knights of old no longer reign, we can't turn back the clock.
You are a man of the 20th century, a gentleman, a paradox.

If a choice I were given — choose an armored knight or thee.
They had no lights, no microwaves, so it's the 20th century for me.

Linda Dismukes

Eternal Day

As life's raging fire dies, a Phoenix new and infant-eyed
rises from his cold, cold ashes, casts off years in bolts and flashes,
then leaps to the sky and flies.

Flies through skies he's never known to shores that life had never
shown through dulcet chords of songs just sung and rainbowed clouds
in worlds just hung, and wisps of breath just blown.

On wings of deepest, velvet black, he sees the timeless ages back
and into eons yet to come warmed by pristine, ancient suns
and forgets to fear attack.

Forgets, as well, the pain he felt from the days when he clawed and
dwelt among the race of petty men, who choked upon the word "Amen"
and never, ever knelt.

He spies a distant, shimmering, land, where many other Phoenix stand
before a wondrous, living throne that calls his name and pleads,
"Come home to the One who understands."

Alighting in the astral hue, he hears a voice, deep and true.
"Death and tears are passed away. Now! Begin! Eternal Day,
in which all things are new."
Rusty Grainger

Aspirations

How can we expect the world to ever change if we continue
to remain the same, when hope seems lost consumed by empty
thoughts, then it's time to make some decisions built on brand new
visions, the earth will still revolve as we continue to evolve into
greater aspirations, trying to avoid our greatest temptations, it's a
shame that life can be so strange at times, forever rearranging like
the tides, so I close my eyes and realize where I've been, so that I
can understand what direction I'm headed in, to know the truth of
where you from, is the key to unlock the mysteries of where you
want to be, now thoughts become sporadic running wild at infinite
speeds headed in separate directions, yet they seem destined to
coincide with one intersection, now ask yourself what's it worth, to
just survive on the Devil's earth, trying to avoid his work, and how
can we become a person of grace if we can't find our place, I find
that my only crime committed, was with my birth sent here on
earth to die, can you understand why?
Matthew Enterline

If Only I Knew

I won't forget those heart filled eyes as you lay there still in bed.
A bed where many people have laid before.
Daddy sat there by your side as much as he could, everyday and every night.

I went to school that day thinking everything was fine.
When I returned home that day I was told what had happened to you.
My dearest mother, I couldn't believe what I was hearing.

Oh mother, if only I knew the truth about you.
I hated seeing you in that weird bed, in that weird environment.
I'm telling you now, if only I knew. I would have visited you more often.

I was only in kindergarten, how was I to know the truth about you?
Daddy kept on telling me that you were fine and would be home soon.
How was I to know that day was the last day I'd ever see you?

Oh mother, if only I knew. I wouldn't be able to change your
situation, but I could have visited you more often in that weird environment.
Now I'm resenting the fact that I didn't visit you more often like
I should have.

Mother, I'm doing the best I can to follow in your footsteps
I won't be able to follow them all because I'm not you. I'm me, my own person.
Mother I'm sorry. I'm not perfect, but if only I knew.
Rebecca Boles

Trying

Here in the pit, descending damp darkness blocks all light, but I
need not light to see. The darkness' safety fills my soul with eerie
dread. Grasping rocks, gripping, praying that I don't fall, I now
watch. Protected in the dampness, alone, watching others seeking
others seeking safety. But, I know what they don't, there is not any
safety here with others! People pass me by, sometimes up, most times
down. We do not talk, haunted eyes speak volumes, hollowed faces tell
the truth. Once I too used to move. I started low, not near bottom,
no where near top. Rocks pierced cold hands and stubbed tired toes.
Times became ruff and I fell, not far, but enough. That is when I
began to watch. Alone with tear streaked cheeks, I thought about
falling all the way. Others and done it, I had seen. But, I
disregarded that notion at once, and dreamed about going up. Today
is the day that I start to move up. Fears of falling threaten new
born courage. Rocks once again are thorns, and no one helps. Now I
can see the top, and people peering in at me. Now no one passes
me on the way down. They smile and reach helpful arms down to me.
I strive to reach them and wonder if they are my own imagination.
They pull me up. Now I am not alone. I have found safety. It is
not in the pit, as I always thought. It is here.
   Michleene Johnson

A Country Dawn

The frosty chill from a dew covered morn embraces the breath-taking air.
A gentle, wobbly-legged foal of silken coat just born to the family mare.
The dapper rooster screeches out a familiar call to the sight,
Of the sun with dandelion color shutting out the peaceful night.

A gray cat purring in deep slumber curls upon a bale of brittle hay.
Grunting piglets satisfy appetites as their portly mother silently lay.
Wide-eyed, cud-chewing cows to give milk, anxiously wait.
Unsuspecting ole' Tom turkey gobbles near the front gate.

Intently watching, a shabby rat steals tasty grain from a sack.
Woolly sheep warmly covered with fleece of white or black.
The blaring light against the barn of deep red,
Peaking through glistening windows of those in bed.

Delicious aromas of crisp, sizzling bacon, buttery hot grits in bowls.
Steaming clouds of coffee, and Grandma's famous cinnamon nut rolls,
Sneaking beyond, sending sweet messages underneath the doors,
Awaking innocent sleepers to do their morning chores.
   Jennifer M. Cossaboom

The Northern Flicker

As I lay fast asleep in the early morning hour,
dreaming dreams, planning schemes, before time to take a shower.
I was suddenly awakened by a staccato on the roof.
Invaded by a wily bird and the noise I had as proof.
It was that blasted Flicker, a handsome bird is he,
He mistakes my chimney flue, for a bug infested tree.
He picks the dawn to begin his quest, a rat a tat tat he goes.
There's many trees in the woods and yet it seems he chose,
A metal insert in my chimney; it was never a home for bugs,
He likes the music and the rhythm of his insistent drilling for slugs.
He sits upon a branch all puffed up and so proud,
announcing his challenge in a voice clear and loud.
Who can we wake next, come and we'll see,
we'll hammer and drill on this condo's chimney.
I like the Red Flicker, he's one handsome bird;
but my patience is waning his lack of sense is absurd.
I'd like to dissuade him from summering here.
Perhaps a wee slingshot to his derriere.
will drive him further on to some far distant tree,
just riddled with juicy bugs, and in quiet and peace leave me.
   Deidre Simpson

My Mother My Rock

Like an Island in the sun standing tall
Shading your waters and doing it all
I admired you Big, Black, Beautiful woman. You are my mother
Mother, I admired your strength as you moved throughout this world
Without staying down when you fall
No matter what, you always stand tall

Like an Island in the sun standing tall
Your presence is like the cool breeze that blows in the early morning
at the beach
Through the breeze echoes the strong sweet voice of your concern
because you deeply care
You are really like my star through the night

Mother of great wisdom, the strength of your caring helps me to
understand my weakness
Mother, your showing of your love are greater than words
I am so lucky to have a mother like you
So many things about you always make me proud to have you as my mother
Even sometimes when you fuss and mutter without fear
I know is just because you care

I love you my mother
You smart, creative, courageous woman
You are my mother, you are my rock
With love from your pebble.

Luanne L. Thorpe

On Being Middle Aged: A Response To Young Friends

Look forward to the middle age with fear; yet fear not the passing of life as much as its fulfillment. Fear, instead, the kind of days you may become.

I am the loving heat you can not find; and yes, it is prolonged, committed to the squinting glare and scalding streets; consistent warmth, I am a living beaded

Sweat that passes salty into eyes, running across a cheek to fall below an ear, dampening a pillow, the slippery balm that hides between your breasts, I slide the

Muggy nights away breathless, without a breeze to flirt with curtains sheer, hems lifted to the window rods, a prayer that air might pass across the screen.

I am tangled roses, vines that snake around the trees to abandoned nests where breeding sparrows sang, complex green that took direction from risen limbs,

A web of knots and thorns, with flowers bravely fully open.

I am all of summer's breeze: One that cools to warn you of a storm, one that barely moves a drooping leaf, one that will seduce you to a lazy day at the beach;

I am also he that tears at sails, naked masts and brass bells, he that then soils hanging sheets that fly to garden gates. I am sleepless storms, thunder, cats

And dogs, neglected gardens filled with splashing pools that drain off floating petals, swirling into gutters filled with dark green leaves; windows shatter as branches

Torn away sail through; I am the heat and hopes of April come alive.

Your cherished youth is merely buds in May, fickle days, splashly rain impotent winds and flowers fearful that the winter will return. A summer's days you will, we hope, become.

G. B. LaFleur

The Storm

    In the distance a woman appeared. Dressed strangely in black and
gray she seemed to hover gloomily with each step she took. My eyes
became fixated for her strange beauty made me stare in awe. As she
approached, her presence filled the air and everything began to stir.
Changing an uncomfortable moment into a cool, cozy numbing feeling.
She noticed my staring and turned to my direction. Taunting as she
strode, she flashed her flaming white teeth from her twisted smile.
As she ground them together in a teasing way a monolith of sound
danced through my soul, shaking my very being.
    She came even closer and her perfume filled my lungs for it was
a fresh and cool smell. Her hair flourished and blanketed out all
light allowing only darkness the freedom, the roam and play. Then she
began to pass me slowly with her movements taking on a violent peace
with each and every footstep.
    Her laughter echoed and struck like a million grains of sand being
thrown by spiteful children which covered the ground with a thin,
smooth surface as that of glass.
    Her departure was slower than her abrupt approach but through
all the irony she left a gift. Sacrificing peacefulness in the
beginning only to return it with a greater sense of serenity.
    Christopher J. Rich

Copper Dreams, Ghetto Scenes

We all have copper dreams, it seems, which help break-up our daily schemes;
But while we're dreaming our dreams, we interrupt our process of means
by which we're to accomplish our dreams.
Sometimes it's so hard to continue living in the reality of our
ghetto scenes, that so often it's very easy for our attentions to
be diverted; distracted' disconnected.
Eventually some people get pushed over the edge, then we label them crazy.
Many others just lose all perspective and in dreaming they ignore
the achieving, then we label them spacey or lazy.
So if we keep a level-head before we all go to bed, you can have
copper dreams within ghetto scenes;
Just remember not to try to shine and clean your copper dreams until they gleam.
You can't get gold, you'll only get old.
It takes hard work, hope, and love of life, which make all dreams
accomplished goals.
    Benjamin D. Loudermilk

Lower Bogue's Calamity

The July 1928 morn was calm, fair and crystal clear,
And no Bogueman 'bout hurricane warnings did hear.
So about their fishing/farming chores they did go,
While eyeing the weather for signs that could spell "woe".

When of a sudden the sea raged and howling winds blew high,
And across the sky darkened clouds did fly.
Beating rain, like angry bees, the Boguemen's feet did sting
While these people to houses on the hill, some food and themselves did bring.

Later through battened windows their eyes popped wide,
For gone was all the water from the bay and all the weather commotion died.
Then like happy children, Boguemen over dry sea bottom walked,
And under clear skies 'bout the bad weather, they laughed and talked.

Then suddenly in the southeast a prodigious black cloud appeared,
And the big black sea rose like a monster, the people it scared.
Bogueman ran to hillside houses, themselves to save,
But the sea-chase gave their farm animals a watery grave.

Then off with Steadman's house roof, him to kill and drown,
And with a stick, James to stab, his entrails ran on the ground.
After the hurricane was over, my uncle James was dead!
Many Bogueman had bodily injuries, including great grandma Sara's head.
    Carmelina M. Burrows

Knowledge of Power

To search for the entirety of eternity traversing the universe from
end to end looking for all the answers to questions unimaginable and
when finally the light of realization dawns brilliant and searing into
the soul to scream the soundless scream of the understanding of forces
never meant to be seen let alone for any one being to comprehend
unreality coalesces with what was thought to be the constant and all
constants are found to be false chaos is found and lost and barriers
never meant to be crossed are crossed and burned and crossed again and
then there is nothing left nothing to gain and nothing to lose alone
and together apart and close free inside of chains breathless inside
of air knowing everything is found to be the curse of knowing what is
not meant to be known or understood or comprehended or realized or
remembered or forgotten or breaking or lasting or reacting or lonely
or even forsaking of everything the search ends but the loss remains
and nothing is lost and nothing is gained and nothing found out that
wasn't already known to the universe and the universe alone and with
the mistake of wanting to know behind to slink homeward lesser for
the more of the travels.

S. R. Parke

You See Me

You see me Hurting, you see me crying, you see me drowning
in my tears, while I lay at night
Lord, I know your children loves thee
Lord, I know the children still cares
It's the drugs, that has taken so many lives away
It's the drugs, that they may now love instead
It has left so many lives in shambles
It has left so many children futures so gray
I don't think they're gonna see another blue sky
Only darkness, along with gruesome rainy days
Lord for you I kneel and pray

Because that devil, he's months ahead
While I weep, he creeps, he never sleeps
And he's always in the streets
You see my hurting, you see me crying' you see me
Tasting my tears, while I lay at night
You see me praying you see me hoping you see me
Trying not to worry, cause my hair is turning gray
The love I have for you is everlasting
The faith I have in you is rare.

Wade Tapp Jr

Fireflies

Fireflies and feelings,
fragile and fleeting,
glowing brightly, gleaming briefly,
gliding softly on inconstant breezes
that whistle strongly, then whisper gently.
A moment's gust, a change of course;
drifting aimlessly over unknown fields and dark, thick forest;
lost at times in unfamiliar places
furiously flying buffeting, battering winds;
then a moment's calm reprieve and a gentle landing,
peaceful ponderings of where one now might be,
only to once again be caught in updrafts of uncertain direction and duration.

One night's adventure beyond the telling —
a firefly has no language to describe its travels and the beauty it has seen,
no way to answer the why's of its existence and perceptions.
It is what it is. And no one asks that it explain itself.

Could it possibly feel as I? Wanting to sing and share the songs
inside with another,
yet knowing, even the most precise lyrics and music cannot express the fleeting
interpretations of a reality so mercurial and unique that it has
already changed and grown
from what it was only nebulous moments before.

D. Anne Ufford

Rage

In anger and in burning rage,
Bring forth your sword unto the stage.
We fight until the day is done, until the resting of
  the sun.
The rules are set, now we must fight.
I swing my sword with all my might.
He who wins has passed a test,
And with this note, I strike your chest.
You grasp your chest and try to breathe;
I turn my back and start to leave.
Then in a voice timid and low I hear you say,
  "You cannot go."
"Think back unto the rules," you cry,
  "You can not leave until I die.
Take my heart with my father's knife,
Then give my heart to my loving wife."
A shot was then heard through out the air.
We both died right then and there.
What was the purpose of all the pain;
To die in love or to die in vain!?
So, in anger and in burning rage,
Bring forth your sword unto the stage.
And throw it down as I have done; in my mind,
  we both have won.

Mandy Grover

Joy

Joy is looking into your eyes
while my heart is aglow with love.
Joy is being near you
like the stars and moon above!
Joy is holding your hand
and feeling the warmth of your smile.
Joy is the feeling of happiness
when your heart is stirred
with tenderness.
Joy is Oneness, when we are together,
Joy is saying; I'll love you forever!

Naomi J. Hall

Destiny

Pounding in my head I must heed
Hoofbeats of the messenger's steed

Tugging at my sleeve
The child says I cannot stray

The knots in my stomach beckon
Upon this road I must reckon

The road is paved with will and strength
Pieces of rock and stone from days since passed

Yet there are holes not filled
Holes of fear, anguish and hate

And upon my travels I may too find a hill or chasm too
  heavy to climb
To make the journey challenge

The obstacles will be met with vigor and dream
They shall not hold me back

As I feel the messenger approach I prepare for my
  destiny
To great it with open arms and see it to its home

Christopher J. Ruske

Always Thinking of You

It's like floating softly,
Into misty clouds, caressed by the sun . . .
Relaxed, and gently lost of every thought, but one . . .

I feel the lost happiness,
Flow through me . . . every time, you're on my mind . . .
Oh Lisa, you're so beautiful, so special, so kind.

Through the day and days . . .
Through the silent nights and night . . .
I'll be thinking of you.
Drifting slowly, toward a sereneness moon light.

If there was a wish to be made . . .
It would be for you and me . . . To be . . .
Oh, Lisa . . . The things I would do for you.
Here and now, and over sea.

There are no words . . . that can explain the feeling,
I feel . . . When I hold you . . . in my arms.
It's like fairy tale, it's like I'm dreaming.

Every day . . . every night . . .
My mind is floating . . . thinking of you,
Lisa . . . Oh Lisa Parisi . . . I am so deeply in love . . .
  with you.

Ben Innamorato

Never Allowed Inside

As a puppy, brought to a prairie home.
And never allowed inside.

Facing our home, wistfully resting on my
Paws, hearing music and laughter and
A tree "growing" in the house with
Twinkling lights!

My three legged friend triptik and I,
Happily roamed the prairie, she could out run
Me and all creatures, but after we returned
she "lived" in her home.

One day this gentle lady came, taking me
For a last good-bye to my friend and then
Started our long journey home.

I woke to see white mountains, sparkling
White trees, paths and house covered
In fairy land white with a tree growing
Inside with sparkling lights!

Near the glowing fire place, and under the tree lay
  two friendly dogs,
I snuggled between them as the gentle lady smiled,
  stroked my head
and sang. You will always be allowed inside...

Gertrude Yeager

Biographies of Poets

ADAMS, R. DEVERLE
[b.] March 20, 1923, Claypool, IN; [p.] Noah and Edith Adams; [m.] Donna Adams, July 3, 1952; [ch.] Robin, Tom, (Sandra/Deceased), Connie; [ed.] High School - Claypool, High School La Salle University Extension - Chicago, Ill. - 2 yrs. Accounting; [occ.] Retired from Management; [hon.] Lettered in High School Basketball, Publisher's Merit Award; [oth. writ.] Poem - The Great Designer wrote High School basketball column for local newspaper in the 1950 say titled "How They Rate"; [pers.] High School teacher - Mary Keever stated that my poems were very good and someday could be published.; [a.] Warsaw, IN

ADKINS, LEYLA
[pen.] Leyla Hur; [b.] May 6, 1973, London, England; [p.] Ibrahim and Marlene Hur; [m.] Stephen Adkins, June 10, 1995; [ed.] Shatin College (Hong Kong), Taylor's College (Melbourne, Australia), Carleton University (Ottawa, Canada), Willis College of Bus. and Tech. (Kanata, Canada); [occ.] Housewife, Sunday School Teacher; [memb.] Member in Good Standing (International Society of Poets" 1995-1996; [hon.] Latter-Day Saint - "Young Woman of Progress" Award 1994 "Editor's Choice Award" - National Library of Poetry; [oth. writ.] "After The Storm", "Daybreak On The Land".; [pers.] Goals and dreams can be reached and achieved by pursuing your dream and realizing your own potential.; [a.] Nepean, ON

AGELASTOS, NICOL
[pen.] Niki Agelastos; [b.] August 6, 1965, Detroit, MI; [p.] Milton Agelastos, Catharine Freeman; [ed.] Shadow Mountain High School, Paradise Valley Community College; [occ.] Medical Secretary; [hon.] Dean's List Paradise Valley Community College, Honorable Mention Poetry Writing for Local Newspaper; [pers.] An extension of thought that stimulates emotions is an ultimate gift shared by beings and is the highest asset one could ever own.; [a.] Scottsdale, AZ

AHMED, SHAH SALIM
[b.] Calcutta; [p.] Dr Wali Ahmed & Marium Ahmed; [ch.] Shah Fahim Ahmed; [ed.] Islamia High School, Calcutta, Quaid-E-Azam College, Dhaka, Long Island University, New York; [occ.] Real Estate Sales in New York City; [memb.] General Secretary, Pakistanis' Well Wishers Association, U.S.A., D.M. in International Society of Poets, Maryland; [hon.] Award of Merits received from Chief Justice of Pakistan in Columbia University, N.Y.C. in 1992; [oth. writ.] "Ehsaas-E-Zian" A great book in Urdu got published from Jung Publications, Lahore, Pakistan, in 1992. Poems: "Cloud", "Childrens' Equal Rights To Parents", "Stigma on Human Faces", "The Formation", "My Friend, If You Can" and many more.; [pers.] This world can become a heavenly planet to live in, if "Law and Morality", "Rights and Duties" imply together. [a.] New York, NY

AL-ADAWIYYA, RABIA
[pen.] Hallie-Ruth Murray and Umm Hilema; [b.] September 29, 1944, California; [ch.] Cathryn M. Murray, Ayn Murray, Michelle (Hilema) Artman, John C. Ashford; [ed.] Lane Community College, University of Oregon, Diablo Valley College, Los Medonas College, Islamic Studies, Berkeley, CA, Arabic Sciences; [occ.] Writer, Artist, Lecturer, Vice President, Global Teen Club International; [memb.] Vice President, Global Teen Club International, International Image, Spokesperson, U.N. Assn. for world peace, Bay Area Poets Coalition, Chronic Fatigue Immune Deficiency Syndrome, American Assn. Walnut Creek Poets Communique, Intl. Society of Poets; [hon.] Certificate of Award, African-American studies, "Woman of the year Award, 1994", Alden Foundation, Award for International Community Service, 1995, Global Teen Club International, Editor's Choice Award, 1996, National Library of Poetry, Certificate 1994-95, Intl. Society of Poets; [oth. writ.] Periodical poetry, Intl. periodical Islamic Articles, poems published National Library of Poetry, "Songs on the wind".; [pers.] The Prophet Muhammed (Sallallahn Alayhe wa Sallam) asked his companions, "Who are those that are truly knowledgeable?" They responded, "Those who practice what they know."; [a.] Walnut Creek, CA

ALDAPE, YOLANDA
[b.] El Paso, TX; [ch.] Three sons; [occ.] Attendance Technician at Chualar Elementary School; [memb.] Loyal Woman of the Moose, Iglesia Ni Cristo; [oth. writ.] I've had short stories and poems in The Monterey County Post, Salinas Californian and the Monterey Bay Monarch published.; [pers.] If I ever pass on, I'd like to be remembered not only by relatives and friends, but by those I've inspired by my poems and stories.; [a.] Salinas, CA

ALLEN, F. MICHELLE
[b.] October 4, 1982, Florence, SC; [p.] Frankie D. and Kimberly H. Allen; [ed.] Hudgens Academy and The Carolina Academy; [occ.] Student; [memb.] Beta Club and FCA Club; [hon.] All American Scholar, The National Honor Roll, U.S. Leadership Merit Award, Presidents Award for Educational Excellence, George Grice Eight Grade Scholar Award, Math Meet Award 1995 and 96, Music Festival Award

AMISON, LESLIE
[pen.] Les Amison [b.] March 12,1945, New York City [p.] Mr.and Mrs. Samuel Amison [ed.] Cornwell,Morvian Col.N.C.C. (Dean's list)Allentown College, Hutztown Univ. [occ.] Prisoner/writer/inventor-in other words slave [memb.] International Soc.of Poets,National Space Soc.planetary society. [hon.] Nominated poet of the year,1996; Editor's choice,Golden Poet; Best Poems of the 1990's; 1993 St.Prison Comp. Winner. [oth.writ.] Cinder Earth, The Buck and selected poems, published in anthologies, new papers and literary magazines. [pers.] Christ's new commandment, "care about one another," Is the solution to all human hate's social problems. Try to be direct. ; [a.] Bellefonte, PA

ANDERSON, TAMMY
[pen.] Twister; [b.] March 12, 1961, Wisconsin; [p.] Gerald Anderson and Nancy Marzahl; [ch.] Ryan, Chad and April; [occ.] Bookkeeper, Holder Pallet, Dexter, MO; [memb.] International Society of Poets; [oth. writ.] Published in several anthologies.; [pers.] Don't get caught up in life, let life live in you and enjoy every moment your here.; [a.] Dexter, MO

ANDERSON, VIOLET HENSON
[b.] June 8, 1931, Knoxville, TN; [p.] J. Cline Henson & Lena Simmons Henson; [m.] Charles A. Anderson, Jr., August 1953; [ch.] Susie A. Lowry, Nancy A. Lashbrook, James Arnold A.; [ed.] Graduated Knoxville High School, 1949, University of Tennessee, Knoxville, 1953 with BS in Education for PE and Art; [occ.] Professional Artist, Retired Teacher; [memb.] International Society of Poets, Stones River Womans Club, Alpha Delta Kappa—Educational Sorority, Delta Zeta Sorority, TN Art Leaguel TN Watercolor Society, Donelson Chamber of Commerce; Cumberland Valley Girl Scouts; [hon.] Poet of Merit Award, Golden Poet, '89, '92, Silver Poet, '91. Who's Who in Poetry, 2nd place award for poem from TN Federation of Womens Clubs, Merit Award from International Society of Poets. Best Poems of the '90's, Best Poems of the '96; [oth. writ.] Iris Dreams & Orchid Memories, "Best New Poets", 1988, "Great Poets of the Western World": "World Treasury of Great Poems"; "Distinguished Poets of America" "Dancing on the Horizon".; [per.] Poetry has become a very important part of my life, for I love to write poems about Nature, Family, and my closeness to

God & Christ. All of these items are an intergral part of my life. I am so fortunate to have been acknowledged as a Poet in many ways!; [a.] Nashville, TN

ANDREW, MICHAEL JAMES
[pen.] Michael J. Andrew; [b.] May 23, 1955, Utah; [p.] William and Lillie Estella Andrew; [m.] Elizabeth Ann Andrew, October 22, 1988; [ch.] Step-children - 3; [ed.] South High, Glendale Jr.; [occ.] Restoration, Auto Body and Painting; [memb.] Idiom Clearwater Clan; [hon.] Auto Restoration #1 in Concourse: Music and recognized in the 25th Annual Utah Library and poetry Arts Council; [oth. writ.] Have never been published. I have approx. over three thousands written poems and essays. Currently finishing a book of poetry, hoping to publish; [pers.] I search for truth. I study nature and mysticism. I have been performing and playing music for over 32 years. A master in percussion.; [a.] Salt Lake City, UT

ANDREWS, DONNA JOY
[b.] August 22, 1946; [p.] Alfred and Bernadine Smith; [ch.] Shawna, Pamela and Charles; [ed.] B.S. at Univ. of San Francisco M.S. at U.S.F., and Ph.D. at S.F. School of Psychology; [occ.] Director of Therapy Research at Andrews/Reiter Epilepsy Research Institute, Santa Rosa, CA; [memb.] Orthopsychiatric Association, American, American Psychological Association, Physicians for Social Responsibility; [hon.] Recipient of five Editor's Choice Awards from the National Library of Poetry, the Carroll Lunt award, Distinguished member and Poet of Merit of the International Society of Poets; [oth. writ.] (Co-author) "Taking Control of Your Epilepsy", Other poems published by International Society of Poets, Contemporary Poets of America and Britain, Sparrowgrass and Arcadia include the following titles: Trees in the Wind, Cold, Cold Sea, My little son, Ebb and Tide, Every Day an Adventure, The I Want Blues, The Seers, The Art of Sharing, End of A Season, Heart and Soul.; [pers.] "Spem Successus Alit" Success nourishes hope.; [a.] Middletown, CA

AQUILINA, RHONDA
[b.] November 28, 1969, San Francisco; [p.] Thomas and Jean Aquilina; [m.] Gary Saballos; [ed.] H. S. Some University of College Education; [occ.] Court Reporter; [oth. writ.] Poem entitled "If Only"

BALAQUE, LLOYD W.
[b.] April 1, 1940, Swanton, OH; [m.] Nancy E. Balaque, September 12, 1975; [ed.] Swanton High School (1958) Swanton, Ohio; [memb.] Marine Corps League; [oth. writ.] Amongst The Heather, The Kilt, The Love We Share, The Chester Barber, The Old Man Next Door, My Hometown; [a.] Cleveland, OH

BARKS, MICHELE MARIE
[b.] May 22, 1965, Pontiac, MI; [p.] Ken and Jeanette Barks; [ed.] Clarkston High School; [occ.] Paint Operating Technician for the Saturn/GM car company in Spring Hill, TN; [oth. writ.] "A Shadow of Heart" published in the voice within '96"; [pers.] "The real beauty of a poem is seen by the writer. And like a photograph, the beauty is shared by its viewers". Early influenced by Edgar A. Guest.

BARRETT, TIMOTHY
[b.] November 2,1961, Kansas City, MO. ;[p.] Margaret Ramsley (mother) ;[occ.] Warehouse manager ;[hon.] Two editors choice awards 1996-1997 from the National Library of Poetry ;[oth.wri.] Falling Star, Red, Yellow, or Blue, Both published by (National Library of Poetry) He Wear's a smile, Her Little Box, Angels Among Her, Secrets ;[pers.] Inspiration comes from my music and my past personal experiences. ; [a.] Kansas City, Missouri.

BARRINGTON, L. BARRY
[pen.] Brendan McGurn, Nadetta Glennon; [b.] Ninnesah Valley, KS; [m.] Sharyn Marie Carlson, 1975; [ed.] De Paul Univ., Univ. of Chicago (Ph.D.-Biochemistry); [occ.] Technology Consultant Writer; [memb.] Irish Institute of Chemistry, Chicago Literary Club, Technology Transfer Society; [hon.] Sigma Xi Honor Society "Dean of the Directors" (see attachm't) National Silver Senator (See Att'd Card); [oth. writ.] Collected Poems: "Bound To Rain", and "The Tilt Before Time Began" plus short stories and features in local newspapers, and Historical Novel - "Feasting with the Deacon"; [pers.] I am a push-over for bright and beautiful females of all ages, and have been pushed over several times.; [a.] Arlington Heights, IL

BARROW, PETER F.
[pen.] Peter F. Barrow; [b.] May 23, 1925, New York, NY; [p.] Mrs. Gladys Nye; [m.] Wanda M. Barrow, February 23, 1953; [ed.] Self Taught in the real world we live, if your a poet; [occ.] Retired; [memb.] American Legion; [hon.] The National Library of Poetry, Hill Top Records Inc. Library's where I read my poems and play my songs; [oth. writ.] In your books and American Legion Magazine: When The Next Battle Comes, 2 Pretty Flower, 3 The Great Seahawk, thousands of short poems, songs - I specialize in classical tango, country, rock, etc.; [pers.] You are the best my goal is to hold back my knowledge in other poems until I get orders say 10 million payed in advance. For one poem it will cost you a dollar. Monopoly I call it, if you love my poems?; [a.] Philadelphia, PA

BARROWS, LINDA ANN
[b.] August 7, 1961, Southern California; [p.] Portuguese Immigrants; [ed.] Southern California Schools; [occ.] Business Owner; [memb.] Detroit Chamber of Commerce; [oth. writ.] Include messages of hope, faith, love understanding and forgiveness.; [pers.] I believe that the Bible is simple enough for a child to read, and much too deep for any scholar to master, so when I feel hopeless I look to the God of Hope, Faith and Love.; [a.] Detroit, MI

BARTLETT, JENNIFER
[pen.] Jennifer Tidball; [b.] November 23, 1973; [p.] Dr. and Mrs. J. Scott Tidball; [m.] Mr. Douglas Bartlett, May 19, 1996; [ed.] High School - Naples American High School, Naples, Italy 1988 - 1992 1 yr. University of Iowa 1992 - 1993 B.A in Studio Art and Many Washington College Fredericksburg, Virginia 1993 - 1996; [occ.] Housewife/Red Cross Volunteer; [hon.] Honorable Mention - Sculpture 1995 and 1996 Mary Washington College student Art Show.; [oth. writ.] "Do You Remember Me?" in Fields of Gold

BASHAM, VIOLA M.
[b.] September 9, 1926, Lodiburg, KY; [p.] Samuel E. Tindall, Patricia Bradstreet Tindall; [m.] Wilbert O. Basham, March 20, 1945; [ch.] Five; [ed.] High School; [occ.] Retired; [memb.] Nashville Song Writers Assn.; [oth. writ.] Numerous unpublished poetry and songs.; [pers.] Don't know much about music or poetry, nor have I studied the art but ever since a tiny child I've written from my heart. Thoughts and words would come so quickly that I hardly had the time to write the words and melodies running through my mind I'd write of truth, imagination, dreams and fascination, of love and faith and tenderness and even my frustrations I thought a melody was needed to go with every rhyme of all the only saved the poems I've written in my time. The many pitched into the trash whose melodies I couldn't find.; [a.] Louisville, KY

BAUGH, PETER
[pen.] Duane; [b.] June 12, 1979, Hanover, PA; [p.] Perry and Stella Baugh; [occ.] Illustrator; [memb.] International

Society of Poetry; [oth. writ.] Burned, Voices, Never, Never Land; [pers.] Special thanks to Brian Warner.; [a.] Peabody, MA

BAUGH, PETER
[pen.] Duane; [b.] June 12, 1979, Hanover, PA; [p.] Perry and Stella Baugh; [occ.] Illustrator; [memb.] International Society of Poetry; [oth. writ.] Burned, Voices, Never, Never Land; [pers.] Special thanks to Brian Warner.; [a.] Peabody, MA

BAVAFA, PARVIN
[pen.] Parvin Bavafa; [b.] January 7, 1946, Tehran, Iran; [p.] Mohamad Embrahim Bavafa Tehrani, Bhodsi Vaghefi; [ch.] Arezou and Elham; [ed.] Received her highschool diploma in Persian Literature, she started to study as a full time student in several colleges in different fields. Up to 1987 she received three degrees in Fine Arts: Music, Studio Arts and Art History from University of California, Student at UCI; [occ.] Artist, Poet and Writer; [memb.] Member of Association of Iranian Writers in Exile Member of Iranian Art Foundation in America Member of International Society of Poets in America; [hon.] Dean Honors; [oth. writ.] Her articles, poetries, sketches and paintings were published in valuable Persian magazines and periodical publications in United States. Such as, Javanan, Tamasha, Payam-e-Ashena, Zan, Simorth, Sobh-e-Iran, the Persian book review, Cyrus the great and Asheghaneh. Her two poetry collections by the name of "The Veil of Light" and "The Trace of Women", has been published in 1995. Her most profound compositions and lyrics has bene two national anthems. "The Coralation" 1992 and "The Human Rights" 1993 which has been published and admired worldwild, by Iranian medias, political parties Cultural centers and was played in one of the United Nation's Human Rights conference in Austria, Vienna 1993.; [pers.] In painting, Parvin has created her own technique and style inspired by Persian ancient Carving and relief

BAVE, EMELIA L.
[pen.] Emelia L. Bave; [b.] September 17, 1910, Salt Lake City, UT; [p.] Gustav Wm. Wurzbach, Karola (Schlatter); [m.] Milton Marsh Bave (Deceased 1984), June 10, 1945; [ch.] Peter Marsh (Brent, Marsha Lorene, drowned age 4); [ed.] 7 yrs. Grade School, 2 Jr. High, 2 High. A lot working as Stock Girl in Hosiery, later as Head Timekeeper in same store) as Tool Leader at Douglas Aircraft. Most of all as Spar in C.G during WWII; [occ.] Housewife (widow living alone) children and families in Utah; [memb.] Church of Jesus Christ of Latter-Day Saints. (Many past and Cultural Memberships but now Honorary Member), years of Illness prevent participation.; [hon.] When younger, many in sports, Ballroom Dancing, Ballet, Establishing Cultural and Creative Arts on Island...Several for Poetry! In 1959. Preserving Unique History with Plays and Pageants and now have my Own, Museum displays to preserve History.; [oth. writ.] Biographical, Plays, History, real life experiences, children stories.; [pers.] Was taught to always look into doing good, to help others..use our God given talents and encourage others to do so.

BAYARD, YSEULT
[p.] Scherer Craan - Engineer, Francine Craan - Educator; [ch.] Victoria Bayard, Lawyer; [ed.] College; [hon.] Editor's Choice Award for Outstanding Achievement in Poetry NLP, 1996; [oth. writ.] Poetry published in the anthology "Amidst the Splendor", NLP; [pers.] My writings tend to capture the igniting feelings visiting man's soul in his yearning for oneness with his universe and to celebrate these intangible which often act as a catalyst for his transformation.; [a.] New York, NY

BEAVERS, SHANE A.
[b.] February 20, 1973, Topeka, KS; [p.] Daniel Beavers and Pamela Lilley; [ed.] Shawnee Heights H.S. (Tecumseh, KS), Kansas University (Lawrence, KS), Allen County Community College (Burlingame); [occ.] Large Die Cut Scrapper Hallmark Cards Inc.; [oth. writ.] "To Be With You", "A Voice Within"; [pers.] "Remember when you point a finger to blame, there are always three fingers pointing back at you".; [a.] Topeka, KS

BEELER, LUCIA
[occ.] Nature Preserve Monitor; [memb.] Central Ky. Art Guild, North American Vegetarian Society, Greenspace Autobon Society, Earthsave, Peta, Fund for Animals, KY Native Plant Society; [hon.] Editor's Choice Award in 1994, 1995 and 1996 for Earler Submissions of Poems. Have also received numerous awards for my photography; [pers.] Happy are those who dream dreams and are willing to pay the price to see them come true.

BELL, LOIS
[pen.] Paige C. Fisher; [b.] May 8, 1947, Ava, MO; [p.] Mr. and Mrs. Harvey J. Bell, (both deceased); [ed.] Volunteer at Public Library; [occ.] Consumer Vol. Support Services; [memb.] A.R.C., People First, M.D.S. Family Counsel and Community Employment Class; [hon.] Ribbons through special Olympic Basketball Certificates through United Way; [oth. writ.] Better Than Medicine.; [pers.] Mission to improve educational support services in the county. Motto: Believe in your mission as you sail life's seas.; [a.] Grand Junction, CO

BELL, WALTER
[pen.] Walt Ray Bell; [b.] October 30, 1920, Portchester, NY; [p.] Walter R. and Mildred L. Bell; [m.] Divorced, December 1, 1944; [ch.] Gail B. Malloy; [ed.] Graduate 4 years Pleasantville High, Pleasantville NM., served 5 years US Marine Corp WW II; [occ.] Retired from 30 years Reader's Digest, Pleasantville, NY; [memb.] American Legion, Post #1097 N.Y., (Life Mem), Armonk, NY, West Chester County Marine Corp League, (Life Mem), Second Marine Division Ass., (Life Member), Disabled American Veterans Ass., (Life Member), Nature's Conservancy, North Castle Historical Soc., Hudson Valley Raptor Center, St. Stephens Episcopal Church; [hon.] USMC-Asiatic Pacific Theater WW II, Two Purple Heart, my poem "Tarawa" was microfilmed and place in a time capsule under the second Marine Div Monument on the Island of Batio in The Gilbert Island, to be opened and read the years 2043. (November 20, 1943 year of our landing); [oth. writ.] Forty two poems, several published in local papers, news letters, and magazines.; [pers.] Walter Bell a native of Armonk, New York having moved as a young boy in 1928 from the neighboring town of Port Chester NY. He is 75. He served in the Marine Corps from 1941-1945 and participated in the landing of the Eastern Solomon's Guadalcanal, Tarawa and Saipan. After 30 years of employment with the Readers Digest in Pleasantville, New York, Walt's retirement years began his poetic expression. A self-taught naturalist, botanist and ornithologist, he spends much of his time studying and enjoying wildlife and all of God's creation. He is known for his love and kindness to all living things.; [a.] Armonk, NY

BELL JR., ERNIE
[b.] March 9, 1964, Beloit, WI; [p.] Ernest, Julie Bell; [m.] Melanie Fregeau; [ch.] Nathaniel Fregeau; [ed.] Beloit Memorial High School; [occ.] Frozen Food Manager (Logli's); [memb.] North American Hunting Club, B.A.S.S.; [oth. writ.] A Poem "Faith" in Forever And A Day Anthology; [pers.] I feel man must change, together, or we will see nature cease. It is for the betterment of all societies, after all there is but only

one earth!; [a.] Beloit, WI

BENFANTE, IGNAZIO
[pen.] Ben Fante; [b.] January 30, 1914, Bronx, NY; [p.] Ludwig, Lillian; [m.] Julia Audino, 1945; [ch.] Ludwig; [ed.] Masters of Education BA; [occ.] Retired; [memb.] ASCAP; [hon.] Honors awards I take my award in 1955 song in "Why My Break My Heart", "Until We Kiss Again" the later jubilee and the former silver leaf; [oth. writ.] I had a poems publish, 20 pages in acrostic form a letter "Janice" following the "Janice"; [pers.] I take all people I known better.; [a.] Boynton Beach, FL

BENNETT, F. CAROLYN SMITH
[b.] December 24, 1937, Mount Pisgah, KY; [p.] Everett Smith and Jinnie Burnnett-Smith; [m.] Steve Bennett, May 27, 1972; [ch.] John Young, Carol Hubbard and Perry Young; [ed.] Wayne County High School; [occ.] Homemaker; [memb.] International Society of Poets; [oth. writ.] Over 125 poems of childhood memories in the Kentucky (Wayne County), reflections of Mt. Pisgah, KY today and poems of my husband.; [pers.] Since 1993, I have written to share the true memories of the simplicity and happiness of life in a remote mountain community and the love of family and friends.; [a.] Decatur, IL

BENNETT, HARRIET HOEVET
[pen.] Harriet Hoevet Bennett; [b.] May 19, 1930, Lowell, IN; [p.] Edward and Bernice Hoevet; [m.] Divorced, March 5, 1949; [ch.] Daniel Charles; [ed.] BA Mus Ed-Olivet Nazarene Univ., MA Mus Ed-Univ. of Illinois; [occ.] Retired Teacher; [memb.] International Society of Poets, National Audubon Society, National Wildlife Assn., AARP, United Church of Christ, Honorary's, Alpha Tau Delta, Indiana Girls' State; [hon.] "Joy", "Shall I Tell You", musical pieces, "Rosettes" a craft project in New Generations, poems "Flowers" and "Kindness"; [pers.] We are on this Earth to help one another. Stretch your potential!; [a.] Hodgkins, IL

BENNETT, MONICA L.
[pen.] Monico; [b.] March 1, 1967, Thomasville, GA; [p.] Loette Kennedy and Earl H. Bennett; [ed.] Model Secondary School for the deaf, North Florida Junior College; [occ.] Sign language teacher, adult Education Program; [memb.] Taekwondo America, Democratic head quarters, writer's digest subscriber International Society of poets; [hon.] Honor rolls, government and history award, deaf woman of the year, black belt, best poets for years, no nominate ports of the years for years; [oth. writ.] On and Out Moon, my Favorite Emotion, Rain, and working on a novels, writing more poetries. What a beautiful color. Life worth it.; [pers.] I have the passion to write. I also believe that my deafness has nothing to bother my accomplishments. I believe not to be afraid of anything. I want to write more poetry and show others.; [a.] Knoxville, TN

BENTLEY, IDA MARIA
[b.] September 20, 1935, Italy; [p.] Enrico and Giulia Catalini; [ch.] Patricia, Vincent, Justin, Yvette; [ed.] Phoenix College, Arizona State University; [occ.] Director, Children's Academy; [memb.] National Law Enforcement Officers Memorial Fund, National Association of Police Organizations, AZ Child Care Assoc.; [hon.] Certificate of Merit from AZ Child Care Assoc. Certificate of recognition from strive program of North High School and Arcadia High School. Certificate of Merit from "Association of Police Memorial Fund"; [oth. writ.] From a child point of view newspaper "Tempo" Italy - Poem to you and you The National Library of Poetry - book "Tomorrow Never Knows"; [pers.] I believe the most important thing in life is the family.; [a.] Phoenix, AZ

BETHELL, KRISTIN SUSAN
[pen.] Crystal; [b.] November 20, 1958, Nassau, Bahamas; [p.] Mr. and Mrs. C.W.F. Bethell; [ed.] Le Rosey - 11, 12 grade High School Diploma, University of Miami - Miami, Fla., Franklin College 1 year College Bahamas Host Tourist training 10 weeks; [occ.] Self Employed, Selling Natural Herbal Products; [memb.] Bahamas National Trust, Basra - Rescue of Boats; [hon.] Special Honors in 2 Bible Courses, Editor's Choice Awards (poetry); [oth. writ.] "Precious Treasures" better than Silver and Gold. (My first book published.); [pers.] The worse tragedy in life is having been given a great talent or gift (ability) and never using it. The Creator of the universe surely would be insulted. I keep writing and using this precious gift in appreciation to Him. God is so good. (And I thank Him for it.); [a.] Nassau, Bahamas

BILLEN, DEBRA
[b.] November 28, 1965, Chicago, IL; [p.] Mary Bragg Kelly, Fred Bragg, and Step Father Jerry Kelly; [m.] Dan Billen, June 17, 1995; [ch.] Joshua Chambers, Greg Chambers and Cheryl Chambers; [oth. writ.] I Remember and The Life of A Child published by National Library of Poetry; [pers.] I write mostly about my feelings about my life experiences. I find that writing about them helps to sort out the many phases, both good and bad. It's like a kind of therapy and a release for me that I enjoy.; [a.] Kenosha, WI

BLACK, AURORE
[b.] February 23, 1945, Brockton, MA; [p.] Emile Chartier, Aurore Paquette; [m.] Walter J. Black, October 8, 1977; [ch.] Daniel E. Buck, Dawna Vassalotti; [ed.] Graduate 1963 Mansfield High School, Mansfield, MA; [occ.] Day care provider; [oth. writ.] Wind Of Happiness Brings Release, published in anthology, "Where Dawn Lingers", poem also included upon "The Sound of Poetry", Rain Within My Heart: Published in, "Best Poems of the '90s. Several un-published poems.; [pers.] My poems reflect my thoughts, my feelings, or those of the people I love, or touch my life.; [a.] Norton, MA

BLACK, DIANE M.
[b.] February 5, 1972, Wmspt; [p.] Mr. and Mrs. Donald Black; [m.] Mr. Nathan Smith, June 15, 1996; [ed.] Williamsport Area High School, Pennsylvania College of Technology Associate degree in Human Services; [occ.] Residence Manager for Hope Enterprises Inc.; [memb.] Trinity United Methodist Church; [oth. writ.] Poem published in creative writing.; [pers.] I love all poems because each poem is seen differently through everyone's eyes.; [a.] Williamsport, PA

BLACK, JOY
[pen.] B. J. Hart; [b.] June 13, 1943, Baton Rouge, LA; [p.] Quinton and Jewel Lockhart; [m.] Jay Black, June 30, 1963; [ch.] Lynne Black-Wall, Greta Black, Jara Black-Miller; [ed.] Graduate Humphrey High School Humphrey, AR., U of A at Montecello Phillips Community College; [occ.] Housewife, Farmer; [memb.] Corinth Baptist Church, AAAW; [hon.] Creative Writing Grand Prairie Best of Show, 1st place Cross Stitch - G.P. Art Council, An State Cross Stitch, International Poet of Merit award; [oth. writ.] Poem and prose appeared in Ag-pilot International The Arkansas Gazette, AP, Ag-Air Update, Threshold of a Dream, The Coming of Dawn, Outstanding Poets of 1994, "A Crop Duster" Prose limited edition distributed in 22 states.; [a.] Humphrey, AR

BLACKMAN, CHRISTAN
[b.] May 19, 1981, Birmingham, AL; [p.] William Blackman Jr., Cindy Glenn; [ed.] Pinson Valley High School 10th grader; [memb.] Creative writers Club for 2 years at PVHS; [oth. writ.] Been published in 2 other national Library of Poetry books and at age 10 published in "Anthology of Poetry by

young Americans"; [pers.] "No matter what keep your head up high, stay strong, and never give up no matter how bad things get in life. It all works out at the end."; [a.] Birmingham, AL

BLACKWELL, W. JEROME
[pen.] W. Jerome Blackwell; [b.] February 7, 1950, Collensville, AL; [p.] Robert F. and Ruth Blackwell; [m.] Widowed; [ch.] Dana, Michael and Connie; [ed.] Ut. Chattanooga; [occ.] Owner of Maxi Muffler Slup

BLAKEMAN, DOROTHY V.
[b.] March 25, 1928, Renovo, PA; [p.] James and Martha English; [m.] Leonard Blakeman, December 8, 1973; [ch.] Duane Bratz; [ed.] Renovo High School, Renovo, PA The Williamsport Hosp. School of Nursing, Syracuse University Syracuse, NY; [occ.] Retired from the Visiting Nurse Assoc. of C. NY; [memb.] Lafayette Ave. United Methodist Church, Choir Member, National League of Nurses, V.I.P. Seniors Group, Arthritis Assoc.; [oth. writ.] "Stars" 1996 Anthology The National Library of Poetry Several Poems Published in the Church Newspaper.; [pers.] Most of my writings reveal my faith in God and His influence in my life, also life experiences and the beauty of the world around me.; [a.] Syracuse, NY

BLAND, BERNADETTE
[b.] October 22, 1942, Westerly, RI; [p.] James P. and A. Jessie Smith; [m.] James F. Bland II, March 3, 1970; [ch.] Chris, Lori, Lisa, Therese, Tom, Derry, James III, Patrick; [ed.] Stonington High, Schenectady Cnty. Comm. Coll., Writer's Institute; [occ.] Writer/Paralegal; [memb.] Intn'l Society of Poets, Women's Writers Guild, (NALA) Nat'l Paralegal Assoc. and a Local Poetry Group - Sponsored by Border's Book Store; [hon.] Letters of Commendation and Appreciation, Honorable Mentions, Editor's Choice Awards and a Literary Medal of Honor; [oth. writ.] Newspaper stories, editorials, business and historical features, essays, and short stories; [pers.] The opportunity that has allowed me to creatively express my thoughts and feelings,... without the factual restrictions... has been a soul - stirring experience - an uplifting of my spirit.; [a.] Louisburg, NC

BODOMO, ADAMS B.
[pen.] Veng Veng Naa; [b.] May 6, 1959, Tirapa, Ghana; [p.] Yinye and A-uree Bodomo; [m.] Mary Bodomo, September 8, 1987; [ch.] Naana, Yelvilaa and Nuotoma; [ed.] Ph.D. NTNU-Norway 97, M. Phil Univ. of Trondheim, Norway 93, M.A Univ. of Ghana 89, B.A. Univ. of Ghana 85; [occ.] Research Fellow; [memb.] African Studies Association International Society of Poets; [oth. writ.] Book: The Structure of Dagaare to be published by CSLI, Stanford Univ. Article numerous technical English article in journal. Also general article in newspapers. My heart speaks - unpublished collection of poems.; [pers.] To help make the world a better place to live.; [a.] Troudheim, Norway

BOETTCHER, ALBERT P.
[b.] March 23, 1936, Lackawanna, NY; [p.] Albert W. and Georganna; [m.] Rosemary Boettcher, July 21, 1962; [ch.] William, Joseph, John and James; [ed.] Bishop Timon High School, Carisius College, BA (Latin), '57, M.S. Ed. '62, 60 graduate hours in Spanish, Latin, English; [occ.] Retired Latin, Teacher from the Buffalo Board of Ed.; [memb.] Buffalo Diocesan prayer warriors, Legion of Mary, Perpetual Adoration Society (Diocese of Buffalo and St. Catherine of Sienaparish...); [hon.] Honor Society of Carisius College, Recognition by the State Education Department of New York State for a Latin word root course of Excellence; [oth. writ.] To date, I've written over sixty poems on a wide variety of topics. I've also authored a satiric essay titled, "The Parable of The Smoo Sheep".; [pers.] My faith experience and spiritual beliefs have provided me with an invaluable source of inspiration: Favorite poets include Ezra Pound, T.S. Eliot and Robert Frost; [a.] West Seneca, NY

BOHAN, JOSEPH F.
[b.] February 7, 1977, New Haven, CT; [p.] John G. and Mary Bridget Bohan; [ed.] Notre Dame of West Haven High School; [occ.] United States Air Force Electronic Analyst, Holloman AFB, NM; [oth. writ.] My Date With An Angel; [a.] Holloman AFB, NM

BONFIELD, SANDRA S.
[b.] October 26, 1953, Shawnee Mission, KS; [p.] Ralph P. and Helen G. (Payer) Bonfield; [m.] Divorced, May 28, 1983; [ch.] Liana Caitlin, August 30, 1984; [ed.] Shawnee Mission North H.S. '71 SM, KS John Brown University, Siloam Springs, Ark. Central Missouri State University, Warrensburg, MO; [occ.] In-home Daycare; [memb.] National Honor Society, Quilland Scroll, Journalism Honor Society, College Church of the Nazarene; [hon.] President Sigma Tau Delta 1982-83, C.M.S.U. - Warrensburg, MO, Dean's List 4.0 1980-83 Central Missouri State University; [oth. writ.] "Final Thought" published in Rippling Waters, Fall 1995, earned Editor's Choice Award.; [pers.] It is during the times of deepest emotional pain that my creativity is expressed through songs and poetry.; [a.] Olathe, KS

BOONE, TAMMIE
[b.] October 21, 1960, Wessington Springs, SD; [p.] Elmer and Nancy Peterson; [m.] Terry L. Boone, May 30, 1985; [ch.] Tyler, Todd and Tara Boone; [ed.] Graduate of Washington High School in Sioux Falls, SD and Augustana College Graduate with a BA in Education; [occ.] Teacher at Sheldon Middle School Sheldon, Iowa; [memb.] National Education Association Middle Level Education Association, American Red Cross, Sheldon United Methodist Church, Quill and Scroll, and Mission to Russia Group.; [hon.] Past member and Award winner in Quilland Scroll. I have written and received grants for my school.; [oth. writ.] I have written many poems and short stories. I have had several teaching ideas published in the mailbox magazine; [pers.] when the spoken word comes difficult the written word flows from your heart and soul with meaning and love.; [a.] Sheldon, IA

BOSANKO, LIZ
[b.] February 24, 1981; [p.] Paula Bosanko, Randy Bosanko; [ed.] Argo Community High School; [memb.] Smyrna Missionary Baptist Church, International Society of Poets; [hon.] Editor's Choice Award for All You Had; [oth. writ.] Several unpublished works and one poem in Lyrical Heritage.; [pers.] I deeply thank all those who influenced and encouraged me. And I thank God for everything he's done in my life.; [a.] IL

BOSS, JEFFERY L.
[b.] October 21, 1971, Seymoor, IN; [p.] Debbie Crowe, Jerry Boss; [ed.] S.H.S. Scottsburg, Indiana, S.L.C.C. at Meramec, St. Louis Mo.; [occ.] Factory Worker; [memb.] International Society of Poets, Human Race; [hon.] Montage Journalism Award St. Louis Community College at Meramec; [oth. writ.] Planet Death, she called my name, Dawn, Oceanic God; [pers.] This poem is dedicated to John Crowe my stepfather. You are a wonderful person.; [a.] Scottsburg, IN

BOSWELL, JAIME LYNN
[b.] September 27, 1977, Cheverly, MD; [p.] Claire and Ronnie Boswell; [m.] Gary Roland Broome II (Fiancee); [ed.] I went to Calvert High for 3 1/2 years. Completed my GED and I have a Diploma in Cobol programming.; [occ.] A beauty Advisor at Pebbles Dept. Store.; [memb.] Member of the Emmanuel Methodist Church in Dr. Frederick Maryland.;

[hon.] I received an Editor's Choice Award for "Outstanding Achievement" in Poetry and An Award "Honorable Mention" for a poem I have written.; [oth. writ.] All these writings were published: An "Untitled" one, "The Darkened Cold", "The Invisible Tear", and "Wind".; [pers.] I believe poetry comes from the heart and the mind. Whether it may be love, hardships, or other thoughts. But it's something you cannot makeup. It has to be true from the heart.; [a.] Huntingtown, MD

BOURNE, MOLLIE ODELL
[b.] November 20, 1932, Pasco, WA; [p.] Ned and Eleanor Odell; [m.] Jim Bourne, February 6, 1963; [ch.] John, Dawn, Leslie, C.J.; [ed.] West Seattle High, University of Washington; [occ.] Golf Sales Rep., Restaurant owner (Bay House), Freelance Writer; [pers.] "No tears in the writer, no tears in the reader." Robert Frost. Good thought and good deeds bring me good fortune.; [a.] Tacoma, WA

BOWEN, BRYAN
[b.] May 21, 1973, Erie, PA; [p.] Karen and Donald Schuez; [occ.] Waiter; [oth. writ.] Published in Across the Universe; [pers.] To my mom and dad thanks for the patience, the guidance and making me who I am today.; [a.] Erie, PA

BOYD, VERLEY LLOYD
[pen.] Rev. VB; [b.] February 20, 1951, Jamaica, WI; [p.] Deceased; [m.] Algerita Boyd, September 7, 1996; [ed.] Jones Town Primary, Kingston College, Jamaica Police Academy; [occ.] Loss Prevention Officer; [oth. writ.] Mother - published in "Windows of the Soul" This poem was written as a card for my wife on Mother's Day 1995.; [pers.] I am still being influenced by that same woman who has now become my loving wife.; [a.] Jamaica, Queens, NY

BREDEWEG, VICTORIA J.
[b.] February 17, 1968, Monroe County, IN; [p.] Robert W. and Phyllis Drake; [m.] David D. W. Bredeweg, March 1, 1996; [ch.] Chantel and Kaylah Suter; [ed.] I went to School at Eastern -Thunderbirds, K-12; [occ.] Housewife and Mother, Brownie Co-leader and Head-Start Vice President; [memb.] Saron United Church of Christ; [hon.] I received an F.H.A. pen my Freshman year of School.; [oth. writ.] I have written 5 poems in the last 1 1/2 years; it takes a lot of time and effort.; [pers.] I work really hard at what I write. I've worked and put a lot of my time in the things I write, and I hope someday that people all around the world will like my work.; [a.] Worthington, IN

BREHM, PAT
[b.] March 3, 1938, Hamilton, OH; [p.] John and Mae Leatherman; [m.] H. Gene Brehm, November 29, 1958; [ch.] Shawn and Brian Brehm; [ed.] Hamilton High - Class of '56; [occ.] Certified Coach/Judge; [memb.] Twirling Unlimited, United States Twirling Assn., National Baton Twirling Assn., Zion Lutheran Church, National Wildlife Federation, National, Audubon Society, International Society of Poets, and local animal charities; [hon.] 2 Editorss Choice Awards; [oth. writ.] Tomorrow's Dream, Across the Universe, Best Poems of the '90s, Morning Song, The Best Poems of 1997, Silence of Yesterday; [pers.] My love for the great outdoors and nature inspires me to write.; [a.] Lexington, KY

BRESSAN, DORLENE
[b.] January 13, 1925, Ophiem, MT; [p.] Olaf and Selma Eliason; [m.] Angelo Bressan, December 29, 1948; [ch.] Five; [ed.] 1-12; [occ.] Retired, from Valley Medical Center; [memb.] Children's Hosp. Guild Renton Museum Society; [hon.] For 20 years Service at V.M.C. Hosp. and for outstanding employee in Dietary Service; [oth. writ.] Editor's Choice Awards (4) Life Time member of The National Library of Poetry; [pers.] Been writing 10 years for enjoyment of family and friends.; [a.] Renton, WA

BRINKLEY, ANDREW W.
[b.] May 23, 1960, Norfolk, VA; [p.] Mr. Carl and Audrey Brinkley; [ch.] Trina (13); [ed.] 2 years of College - Courses in Philosophy and Psychology; [occ.] ABQ Public Schools; [hon.] I was awarded good conduct medal in the Air Force July 10, 1983; [oth. writ.] "I Poet" Books of my poems I've written. I'm Not King Without My Queen" Published in a book called "Forever In A Day"; [pers.] It's important to express how you feel at all times, but putting on paper it will last forever.; [a.] Albuquerque, NM

BRISSETTE, MARIE D.
[pen.] Marie D. Brissette; [b.] March 6, 1934, Holyoke, MA; [p.] Marie and Odeas Desjardins; [m.] Robert A. Brissette, June 20, 1953; [ch.] Gail - Gary - Cynthia - Paul; [ed.] Graduate of South Hadley High School, 1952, and Business Education Institute in 1975; [occ.] Am now Retired; [hon.] Poem, "Life" in Amidst the Splendor; [oth. writ.] "Life" in Amidst the Splendor; [pers.] Always loved writing poems as a child, my family has encouraged me to continue composing poetry. I retired Sept., '96 and am spending a bit more time in composing. I received a beautiful Italian leather book to keep my poems for my children and grandchildren.; [a.] South Hadley, MA

BRITT, EDWARD W.
[b.] March 23, 1930, Glace Bay, N.S., Can.; [p.] Ed. and Ada Britt (Deceased); [m.] Barbara, September 20, 1958; [ch.] Edward and Donald; [ed.] New Aberdeen Public to grade nine, then machinist trade.; [occ.] Retired; [memb.] Glace Bay Historical Society, Senior's skating club, Social Action-helping seniors.; [hon.] An honor to be chosen to submit a poem for your anthology Best Poems of 1997.; [pers.] "In my poetry, I wish to express if modern technology is better for the human race than old time thinking. Can we replaced by robots-and is it wise? Are we losing the human element?"; [a.] Glace Bay, New Scotia, Canada

BROWN, LINDA R.
[b.] June 19, 1937, PA; [p.] Roy and Lucille Reed; [m.] Walter Eugene Brown, June 20, 1959; [ch.] Four children, ten grandchildren; [ed.] Queens College, Charlotte, N.C.; [occ.] ETV Endowment of South Carolina; [memb.] First Baptist Church, Teach Sunday School to 80 year old ladies; [oth. writ.] I have written close to 100 poems - have not tried to have any published. I wrote one in college that was read in a poetry Jazz concert.; [pers.] I write for enjoyment to express my love for God, family and nature.; [a.] Spartanburg, SC

BROWN, NANCY
[b.] January 13, 1949, Chicago; [p.] Herschel, Corinne; [m.] Mark, April 28, 1968; [ch.] Jess, Tracy; [ed.] Sullivan High - Roosevelt University - Priv. Art School; [occ.] Self Employed; [memb.] Florida State Poets Assn., Wisconsin Fellowship of Poets, National Fed. of State Poetry Societies, Poetry Society of America, International Society of Poets; [oth. writ.] Candlelight Poetry Journal, Ember (The Fire Of Love), Fire And Ice.; [pers.] I wish to touch others with imagery and passion in my writing.; [a.] Skokie, IL

BROWN, RAY
[pen.] S. A. Carter; [b.] September 13, 1947, Poughkeepsie, NY; [p.] Murray F. Brown, Emma Jean Brown; [ed.] Syracuse University (NY), SUNY at New Paltz (NY), California State University at Fullerton; [occ.] English Teacher, Cerritos High School, Cerritos, California; [memb.] American Life League, Saint John of God Catholic Church, International Society of Poets; [hon.] Honorary Columbus Cr. D. Awards, Who's Who Among America's Teachers; [oth. writ.] Several

articles and short stories published, several poems also including one in Recollections of Yesterday.; [pers.] My mother was my greatest influence. She encouraged me with every moment of her life. Gentle and loving, she entertained me when I was a child with truly original stories. These imaginative tales have inspired my own.; [a.] Norwalk, CA

BROWNING, SIMON K.
[pen.] Tethodii; [b.] March 2, 1971, Southampton, England; [p.] Keith and Yvonne Browning; [ed.] Very little; [oth. writ.] 1) 1993 'Magic Man' published in 'Gentlemen of Television', 2) 1994 'Untitled' published in 'The Space Between' (Editor's Choice Award), 3) 1995 'The Mountain Top of Stability' published in 'Best Poems of 1995', 4) 1996 'I Hate (Part I)' published in Best Poems of 1996. (Editor's Choice Award), 5) 1996 'Judgmental' published in 'Footprints in Time', 6) 1997 'The Point of War' published in 'Daybreak on the Land'; [pers.] I also dislike cabbage! Thank you for letting me speak my obviously overcrowded and evil mind.; [a.] Southampton, England

BRUNS, BILLY
[pen.] Billy Bruns; [b.] January 29, 1952, Oak, CA; [ch.] Three all boys; [ed.] Life and education of 13 yrs. Reading, looking and sometimes seeing and feeling.; [occ.] Construction Masonary Artist; [memb.] The Human Race and more; [hon.] Father, lover friend, brother and a bonafide member of the Human Race; [oth. writ.] Hundreds in boxes and drawers and closets. Many more forgotten before I could find paper and pen.; [pers.] Life is in itself the dwelling place of human beings returning to the spirit of love, but, why wait.; [a.] Jay, FL

BRUNSON, ANGELA MICHELLE
[b.] December 5, 1979, Goldsboro, NC; [p.] Cecil H. and Jean Brunson; [ed.] Junior at Germantown High School, Germantown, Tenn; [occ.] Student; [memb.] Thespians; [hon.] Who's Who Among Amer. High School Students, Beta Club, All American Scholar, National Leadership and Service Award, US National Speech and Drama Award, U.S. Achievement Academy, Tenn. Miss National Teen-Ager (Top 10 and Community Service Award, National Foreign Language Award, All-State Chorus; [oth. writ.] "The Wall"; [a.] Germantown, TN

BRUNZELL, BRYAN
[b.] February 5, 1952, Moscow, IA; [p.] Bryan and Margaret Brunzell; [ed.] Boise State University Boise, ID, College of Idaho, Caldwell, ID, Rogue Community College, Medford, OR; [hon.] Phi Theta Kappa, winner of "Women's Association of the First Presbyterian Church, Lake Forest, Illinois Perpetual poem award"; [oth. writ.] Published in "Veterans Voices" and "Seasons to Come," an Anthology.; [a.] Central Point, OR

BRYANT, LOIS
[pen.] L. E. Bryant, Lois Baker; [b.] April 30, 1949, Coos Bay, OR; [p.] Victor Baker, Marilyn Baker; [m.] Michael H. Bryant, August 15, 1967; [ch.] Angela E. (Bake) Michael E. Bryant; [ed.] Marshfield Sr. High Coos Bay, Oregon; [occ.] Home maker, Grandmother; [hon.] Editor's Choice Award; [oth. writ.] Challengers, several other poems that have not been published.; [pers.] I write poetry as a way to express my feelings and life experience.; [a.] Idanha, OR

BUCKEY, BETTY JEANNE
[pen.] Bee Jay Buckey; [b.] June 28, 1925, Pennsylvania; [p.] Dale and Ruth Houk; [m.] Divorced; [ch.] Dale, Shawn, Brett, grandchildren Corbin, Brieanne, Morgan; [ed.] A.A. Stephens College, Columbia, Missouri, B.A. Soc. University of Pittsburgh, Pennsylvania, B.S. Ed. University Slippery Rock, Pennsylvania Kappa Alpha Theta; [occ.] Retired,

Kgn. teacher, 1st grade teacher, college teacher, Sociology Ass't. Spvsr. Bldgs and Grnds for six schools, Fort Lee, New Jersey; [pers.] I love to write poems for anyone who asks, for any occasion, for friends who are most encouraging and for my own enjoyment. I especially love to write humorous poems for children.; [a.] Lake Wylie, SC

BUCKLEY, BRAD DAVID
[b.] August 8, 1956, Pasadena, CA; [p.] David L. Buckley - Pauline Hadley; [ed.] Mt. 1 College, Citrus College; [memb.] American Liver Foundation; [hon.] Member Alpha Gamma Sigma - Honor Society, Dean's List; [oth. writ.] "Springtime Sunshine" in Silence of Yesterday; [pers.] I am a liver transplant recipient and know what a gift life is.; [a.] Solana Beach, CA

BUMGARNER, ELIZABETH MOTLEY
[b.] September 14, 1916, Sheva, VA; [p.] Pinkie S. and William George Motley; [m.] Charles Simpson Bumgarner Jr., October 19, 1946; [ch.] Mary Ann B. McKinnon; [ed.] B.S. Mary Washington College, Fredericksburg, VA, Advanced study at N.C. State College, College of William and Mary, and University of VA.; [occ.] Retired. Former teacher of H.S. Hist. and Soc. Sciences, English, Chemistry, Physics, and Biology, and Librarian.; [memb.] Honor Societies - H.S. through College, Science clubs and Literary clubs, Mill Creek Baptist Church, and Teacher's Organizations.; [hon.] Chatham H.S. Valedictorian, Averett College Valedictorian, Dean's List throughout College Scholarship for Masters Degree at U.N.C. Scholarship for six month's study in each of U.S. Gov't. Departments, with guaranteed job to follow.; [oth. writ.] Poems and editorials published in local newspapers.; [pers.] Nothing cannot produce something. Therefore, something had to exist in the beginning, and, whatever that something was, was God.; [a.] Danville, VA

BUNCOM, MILDRED C.
[b.] February 24, 1947, Saint Louis, MO; [p.] Willie and Mildred Morris; [m.] James C. Buncom, October 21, 1967; [ch.] Derek, Cornel, Mildred, Nicole and Lesa

BURKE, CHARLOTTE
[b.] January 25, 1924, Astoria, NY; [p.] Thomas and Charlotte Winkel; [m.] Jerome, June 28, 1947; [ch.] John, Robert, Paul, Michael, Thomas, Rosemary; [ed.] Bryant High School; [occ.] Retired; [memb.] International Society of Poets, Notre Dame Choir, Herricks Community Playhouse; [hon.] New York University Goodwife Award A poet and Musician wrote a song in my honor; [oth. writ.] Poems published in various anthologies and newspapers; [pers.] I get inspiration from music, photographs and looking at scenery.; [a.] New Hyde Park, NY

BURNHAM, J. KELLOGG
[b.] November 22, 1916, Portland, OR; [p.] Jay and Edith Castle Burnham; [m.] Alicia, April 9, 1941; [ch.] Mary Alice, James Kellogg, Herbert Russell, Cynthia Robin; [ed.] Berkeley BA '39 Belmont Hi, LA, M. Keyes, Teacher 1934; [occ.] Merchant, so to speak; [a.] Chula Vista, CA

BURROUGHS, SUSAN
[b.] December 2, 1918, Bpt., CT; [p.] Caroline and Henry Burroughs; [ed.] Private Grade Schools Bpt. University of Bridgeport, BA 1964, Middlebury College, School of Spanish, MA 1969; [occ.] Nada Madrid-Lecturas de Entreambesaguas 1969; [oth. writ.] Radioscripts for Columbia Records; [pers.] Personal love for poets - Verlaine Baudelaire Machado, Frayheir de Leon Lorea, Keats Poe, Wylie Shelley, Frost

BUTLER, LAURIA A.
[b.] April 13, 1962, Southington, CT; [p.] Mr. and Mrs. Louis H. Guolet; [m.] Thomas L. Butler, November 1, 1986; [ch.]

Amanda, Stacy, Marcy, Michael; [ed.] North Attleboro High School Deca Business; [occ.] Mother of four; [memb.] PTA Thalia Elementary Fund Raisen Committee; [hon.] Awards Special Ed, Poetry, Outstanding achievement with children; [oth. writ.] Poems published in Hometown Paper, poetry Corner Sun Chronicle, Attleborn.; [pers.] All my writing comes from my life's happenings. I feel every world I write, they come from within.; [a.] Virginia Beach, VA

BUTLER, LAURIA A.
[b.] April 13, 1962, Southington, CT; [p.] Mr. and Mrs. Louis H. Guolet; [m.] Thomas L. Butler, November 1, 1986; [ch.] Amanda, Stacy, Marcy, Michael; [ed.] North Attleboro High School Deca Business; [occ.] Mother of four; [memb.] PTA Thalia Elementary Fund Raisen Committee; [hon.] Awards Special Ed, Poetry, Outstanding achievement with children; [oth. writ.] Poems published in Hometown Paper, poetry Corner Sun Chronicle, Attleborn.; [pers.] All my writing comes from my life's happenings. I feel every world I write, they come from within.; [a.] Virginia Beach, VA

BYRD, ISABEL GALLEGOS
[pen.] Chavele; [b.] November 19, 1925, Mamassa, CO; [p.] Antonio Abade Lyon Gallegos, Manuela Gonzales LeBlanc; [m.] Widow; [ch.] Joel Manuel-Samuel, Carla, Bertina, Connie, Gregory; [ed.] 11th gr/Nurses tranining Fort Garland, Certified Practical Colo Elementary and Nursing per NYA Denver, Colo High School and St. Monica Hosp. Phoenix, Ariz.,; [occ.] Retired - Writer of Nurse Books and poetry. Cultural presentations schools and colleges; [memb.] Tempo dela Cruz drama team played mother OF main character of none ritual filmed in Oakland, CA, Community Activities for last 20 yrs - Ludha PA singing group Latin of theater; [hon.] American Cancer so reach to recovery 15 yrs. Cert. Cert. of service Luren Eden School Street Evangel is M-amazing Grace Ch, Oak.; [oth. writ.] Unpublished Adobe Heart #1 Book of poetry autobiography Adobe Heart #2 Los Manitos Book titled Life Health Miracles.; [pers.] I was inspired to write by my maternal gr. father and my paternal grand mother. Eugenio Vigil Le Blanc and Margarita Archuteta Lyon. Spoken words are blown away by the wind. Written words last a lifetime, perhaps forever.; [a.] Oakland, CA

CACIOPPO, NANCY
[b.] March 25, 1914, Italy; [p.] Frank and Rosa Martucci; [m.] Gaspar F. Cacioppo, June 18, 1948; [ch.] One daughter; [ed.] Had to leave 8th grade when I turned 15 to go to work and help support a family of 12 children.; [occ.] Retired; [memb.] Seniors Citizens in Long Island and also here in CA; [pers.] I learned much just by living life and the people I met along the way. I am an avid reader. My husband has passed away. I now live with my daughter, an only child (adopted) great son-in-law and three beautiful grandchildren.; [a.] Burnleigh Chase, GA

CALDWELL, KERRICK D.
[b.] December 7, 1970, Tyrone, PA; [p.] Harold and Cynthia Caldwell; [m.] Kerri A. Caldwell, September 1993; [ed.] BA in Administration of Justice and Minor in Psychology - The Pennsylvania State University, Municipal Police Academy - Mercyhurst McAuley Division; [occ.] Patrolman for the City of Titusville Police Dept. in Titusville, PA; [memb.] Faternal order of Police; [oth. writ.] "A Days Worth" which was submitted for "Recollections of Yesterday" in 1996. Numerous personal works for my own enjoyment.; [pers.] Powerful words: Words enlighten and touch, they sooth and encourage, they are a release and an expression, they lead when one is lost and explain when one is confused, and then can prevent a war or cure a dreary day.; [a.] Titusville, PA

CAPLOW, FLOYD
[b.] January 19, 1934, Cleveland, OH; [m.] Toni Ross, July 4, 1976; [ch.] Irving, Julie, Randi, Lisa; [ed.] M.S.W. (1961); [occ.] Licensed Clinical Social Worker; [hon.] Second Place Winner in the National Library of Poetry's Best Poems of the '90's Poetry Contest ("The First 20 Lines of Fruition"); [oth. writ.] Limericks, sci-fi poetry, a 749 word palindrome, you name it, I've probably written about it. Longest poem: 13,811 words ("Kettledrum"). Shortest poem: Zero words ("And form the Title Alone Shall Ye Know the contests"), 13th year as feature columnist for the Sanrobles Traveling Nudist Club monthly newsletter.; [pers.] From poem #194: "Wilst mir... Wilst mir nisht... Ich bin doh! (You want me... You want me not... I am here!); [a.] Vacaville, CA

CARDE, FLORA
[pen.] Ziggy; [b.] May 18, 1967, Sackville, NB; [p.] Herb and Elizabeth Carde; [ch.] Tyler Ace Carde; [ed.] River Hebert District Highly cosmetology springhill/practical and Applied Psychology and Abnormal Psychology at Granton Institute of Technology Toroto, Ontario; [occ.] Student in Psychology; [hon.] Certificate of Editors Choice award by the National Library of Poetry; [oth. writ.] Beyond Reality and My Lord, My Savior published in two anthologies by the National Library of Poetry; [pers.] I give thanks to the Lord for the inspirations and my parents for always having faith in me.; [a.] River Hebert East, Nova Scotia, Canada

CARTER, EVELYN HAYDEN
[b.] August 17, 1917, Boston, MA; [p.] Charles and Gertrude Hayden; [m.] James E. Carter, June 15, 1955; [ed.] High School - Nursing School art School; [occ.] Retiree; [memb.] A. Phillip Randolph Senior Center of N.Y.C. and Seniors helping Seniors Organization of N.Y.C.; [hon.] Care givers - 1985 RSVP - 1985 Certificate of Appreciation RSVP - 1985. D.C. 37 Union Certificate Office Training and Psychology Certificate Senior Teaching Seniors - Brookdale Inst. - Award from C.C.N Y for Computer Intro. Course. I write poetry for my Center's paper "The Challenge"; [oth. writ.] National Library of Poetry 1994 and 1995. Poem in quill book of Poetry 1993. "All My Tomorrows", "The Peoples Bible" book, my poem also included.; [pers.] Writing poetry is like using my other self as a friend to whom I am speaking or who understands what I mean.; [a.] New York, NY

CARTER, RITA
[b.] May 20, 1971, New Jersey; [p.] Jennifer and David; [occ.] Accounting Manager at Mannequin Company; [oth. writ.] "Birds View" and "Some Say"; [pers.] "Time has a way of playing hide and seek with your dreams."; [a.] New York, NY

CASSADY, VALERIE LISA BLANKENSHIP
[pen.] Valerie Lisa Blankenship; [b.] February 22, 1964, Martinsville, VA; [p.] Henry and June Blankenship; [ch.] Rena Shiann Cassady; [ed.] Candidate for diploma in Computer Aided Drafting and Design, May, 1977 from Patrick Henry Community College; [occ.] Engineer Design Dept. CAD Clerk; [memb.] Phi Theta Kappa, National Honor Society; [hon.] Honor's List, Editor's Choice Award for poem "Jealousy"; [oth. writ.] Poems - "Hurt", "Lonely", "Ultimatums", "Pretend Friends" and lots more.; [pers.] I strive to be a good influence on my 5 year old daughter. Rena Shiann. I want to provide a good quality life for her while teaching the blessing of nature and God. Poetry is my release of stress and emotions.; [a.] Ridgeway, VA

CASTLEY, VIOLA
[b.] March 30, 1919, Sydney, Australia; [p.] William West and Dorris Lee; [m.] Deceased, 1st marriage May 28, 1940, 2nd m. January 22, 1971; [ch.] Robert, Noel, (Deceased) Garry,

Christopher and Sharron; [ed.] Intermediate Certificate at Crown St Girls High School Sydney; [occ.] Retired; [hon.] I had a poem printed in "Portraits of Life" Last year; [oth. writ.] I have been writing poems all my life, for family and friends and events, I write them on Birthday, Xmas and Wedding Cards, and also try to write a little poem of comfort on a sympathy Card "They are mostly personal; [pers.] Why is it, when it rains we are sad, yet when the sun shines we are glad. Why should we only love the sun, when we can't live without either one. No flower would grow, no bird would fly, and there would be no you or I.; [a.] Sydney, Australia

CASTRO, ROBERT
[b.] April 6, 1972, Santa Clara, CA; [p.] Alfonso M. Castro, Carmen Castro; [ed.] Santa Clara High, West Valley College; [occ.] Sales; [hon.] Editor's Choice Award for "Confusion" as published in "Memories of Tomorrow"; [oth. writ.] Confusion, published by The National Library of Poetry.; [a.] Santa Clara, CA

CEA, VINCENT
[pen.] James Vincent, Vincent James; [b.] October 14, 1947, New York; [p.] Vincent and Rose Cea; [ch.] Vincent James, Joseph Paul, Nicholas Anthony, Samantha Lynn; [memb.] Distinguish member of International Society of Poets, famous poets society; [hon.] Several Editors Choice Awards - 1995 and 1996.; [oth. writ.] Several poem already published.; [pers.] Life is like the four seasons we look back to our past for answers: we stand pat when it is necessary, we change when we have to, and we go forward to secure our future.; [a.] Selden, NY

CECCHINI, BABETTE KAISER
[pen.] Babette Kaiser Cecchini; [b.] February 11, New Jersey; [p.] Babette H. and Bernard C. Kaiser; [m.] Albert L. Cecchini, June 13, 1954; [ch.] One son, Dr. Albert B. P. Cecchini; [ed.] H.S., Business College, and accumulated credits in psychology, philosophy, education, religion, real estate, commercial law, sociology, and the greatest education of all, in Life itself, and the people I have known. You learn most by observation and communication.; [occ.] I am self-employed.; [memb.] Past and present: - International Platform Association, Concerned Women for America, W.C. Humane Society, W.C. Historical Soc. Eagles Club, (Crystal Cathedral), Crippled Children Committee of Warren Co., Family Motor Coach Assoc., Honorary Sheriff, on board of the Salvation Army, and the very Best, a member of The International Society of Poets! Distinguished Member, Poet of Merit.; [hon.] The International Society of Poet's award of Distinguished Member, The International Society of Poet's Poet of Merit Award, and the Editor's Choice Award of The National Library of Poetry! I also consider it an award by being published in The National Library anthologies, and now to be printed in The Best Poems of 1997! My one poem being read to music in "The Sound of Poetry is an "award" I cherish greatly. Thank You.; [oth. writ.] I have had my poetry printed in education publications (schools I attended), some in newspapers, and I am in the process now of publishing a book of poetry, and hope, after this, to publish more of the poetry I have written, along with the poetry I continue to write. What a Great gift! To be able to Enjoy poetry!; [pers.] If you love good poetry, (and what poetry isn't good if it comes from the heart) you understand and feel all the beauty in the world. Even heartache can be the creator of beauty. Poetry is the music of the soul.; [a.] Warren, PA

CHAIFETZ, SAMANTHA-LEE
[pen.] Samantha-Lee Chaifetz; [b.] June 22, 1978, New York; [p.] Leonard and Maryalice Chaifetz; [ed.] Clarkstown North High School, Harvard University (Freshman); [memb.] Harvard Ballroom Dance Team, Harvard Intramural Hockey Team; [hon.] Salutatorian of Clarkstown North High School Senior Class of 1996, Rockland Westchester Debate Team Champion; [a.] New City, NY

CHAMBLISS, CHARLOTTE J.
[b.] March 6, 1910, East Feliciano, LA; [p.] Mr. and Mrs. Henry Jackson; [m.] Robert F. Chambliss, February; [ed.] B.A., M.A. and Doctor of Education Art, English; [occ.] Retired but Writing and Multi Works in Art and Literature; [memb.] Beth Eden Baptist Church, Zeta Phi Beta Sorority, Women in the Arts, Alum Association - Mills College Alumnae Association, WN of Cal.; [oth. writ.] "Poetry - The Inner Me In an Outer World, 1976," Now Let Us Pray-Prayer In-Reach and Outreach - 1982, Deep South When - Novel 1979, Pencil Points - Poetry -1989.; [pers.] There is so much to be done in the world no matter how much one works, but one should find Himself for herself, busy with some thing worthwhile.; [a.] Oakland, CA

CHAMBLISS, LAVONDA JO
[pen.] LaVonda Greer Eastup; [b.] August 29, 1931, Valdasta, TX; [p.] Ira Albert and Maxine L. Box Greer; [m.] A.C. Eastup, Jr. (1st husband), December 12, 1948, (Divorced October 29, 1985), Married J.C. Chambliss, Jan 16, 1993 Hunt Co., TX; [ch.] Lana K. Reggie Dale, Allen Ray, and Debra Darlene Eastup; [ed.] McKinney High School, grad. May 1948, age 16, McKinney, TX, Collin Country; [occ.] Retired, love travel, writing poetry, going walking, dancing, growing flowers and cats; [memb.] Hunt County Little Black Book Society. Have 7 grandchildren. I have had a book published in 1982, about my son, Reggie, who was killed in a terrible traffic accident in 1975, entitled, Two Wheels To Glory, The Gentle Giant. I am currently writing on my life story. I have had my poetry published in many books and Anthologies; [hon.] I won the Golden Poet Award for my poetry in 1988, 1989, 1990, and 1991. Had 4 poems released as songs in 1991, by the Rainbow Record Co. in Hollywood, CA. I have received many awards and plaques. I've had poetry published in Purpose magazine, Scottsdale, AZ; In The Farmer Stockman magazine in Oklahoma, in the Hunt Co. Right To Life magazine of Greenville, TX. I have been a guest Radio speaker several times over KGVL Radio station in Greenville, TX and have been spoken in Plano, TX, too.; [oth. writ.] Biographical data has been published for several years in the book: Who's Who in The South and Southwest, by Marquis Pub. Co. of New Jersey.; [pers.] "Writing is such a noble and worthwhile occupation that even God wrote a Book The Holy Bible." I try to live by the Golden Rule.

CHAMP, ROBERT
[pen.] Bob Champ; [b.] November 24, 1914, Indiana; [p.] Luva Larve and Ralph Champ; [m.] June Hester, 1937; [ch.] Four Boys, Bob, Steve, Kurt, Richard; [ed.] High School, North Side - Ft. Wayne, Ind., 3 yrs. college - Ath. Specialist - U.S. Navy Graduate American Academy of Art Chicago - 1 yr. College - Shell Oil Co.; [occ.] Commercial Artist and Designed (Los Angeles); [memb.] Foreign Correspondents Club - Boy Scouts - Art Institute - Y.M.C.A. Official - Breakfast Club; [oth. writ.] Published - Life of Johnny Appleseed - various poems in local papers.; [pers.] Favorite poet - James Whitcomb Riley (Indiana Poet), to rhyme words, is a challenge - a challenge fosters happiness.; [a.] Hollywood, CA

CHANG, JANICE MAY
[b.] May 24, 1970, Loma Linda, CA; [p.] Belden Shiu-Wah Chang, and Sylvia Tan Chang; [ed.] B.A in Liberal Studies, CA State Univ., San Bernardino, 1990, Certificate in creative writing, CSUSB, 1990, Certificate in Creative Writing, CSUSB, 1991, J.D. La Salle Univ., 1993, N.D., the Clayton School of Natural Healing, 1993, Ph.D. in Psychology, International

University, 1994, D.O., Anglo-American Institute of Drugless Therapy, 1994.; [occ.] General Counsel, JMC enterprises, Inc., 1993-present, Adjunct professor, La Salle Univ., 1994-present.; [memb.] American Psychological Association, Association of Trial Lawyers of America, American Naturopathic Medical Association, American Society of Law, Medicine, and Ethics, Delta Theta Phi Law Fraternity.; [hon.] Poet of Merit Award, American Poetry Association, 1989, Golden poet Award, World of Poetry, 1989, Publisher's Choice Award, Watermark Press, 1990, Presidents Award for Literary Excellence, Iliad Press, 1995, 1996, Editors Choice Award, The National Library of Poetry, 199-1996.; [oth. writ.] American Poetry Anthology, American Poetry Association, 1987-1990, The Pacific Review, CA State Univ., San Bernardino, 1991, The Piquant, CSUSB, 1991, American Poetry Annual, The Amherst Society, 1996, Interludes, The Wexford Poetry Society, 1996, Perspectives, Iliad Press, 1996, meditations, Iliad press,1996.; [pers.] Poetry is one of the most expressive forms of revealing ourselves. It speaks truthfully about our world. Poets create their expenses of life's joy, sorrows, trials, and triumph through the universal language of poetry.; [a.] Loma Linda, CA

CHAPMAN, KATHERINE J.
[pen.] Kathy Ex; [b.] June 1, 1956, Inglewood, CA; [p.] Ronald Jerome Ex, Donna Alice Ex; [m.] Thomas Mirl Chapman, May 3, 1975; [ch.] Ages 20, Matthew Chapman, 10 Luke Andrew Chapman; [ed.] Graduate from Chino High School; [occ.] Co-Owner of Chapman Equine Arts of Foster City, Cal.; [memb.] Audubon Parent Teacher Association Golden State Tae Kwondo, Race Track Chaplaincy of America, Boy Scouts of America; [hon.] American Soccer Organization San Mateo County Special Olympics; [oth. writ.] The National Library of Poetry published "Little Hand", book title, "Of Sunshine And Day-Dreams" several poems written for family and friends.; [pers.] In my 40 years of living if I had only one chance to give all readers of this book a world of wisdom, it wold be no matter what tribulations we all go through, always be your own best friend. God Loves you.; [a.] Foster City, CA

CHIUCARELLO, SUSAN
[pen.] Sue; [b.] August 15, 1959, Waterbury, CT; [p.] Mario and Georgie Cantamessa; [m.] Albert Chiucarello, April 4, 1992; [ch.] 1 son, A.J.; [ed.] College Graduate; [occ.] Mommy and homemaker; [memb.] International Society of Poets; [hon.] Editor's Choice Award for poem entitled "Joy child" awarded by National Library of Poetry.; [oth. writ.] Book Entitled "Thoughts Of..." due out in publication in midwinter, 1997.; [pers.] I just have to make sure I thank our Lord daily for our precious son, A.J. is who inspires me all the time. I hope he'll be very proud of his Mom when he is older. I am already very proud of him in every way.; [a.] Waterbury, CT

CHONTOS, CHRISTOPHER
[b.] September 27, 1976, Colorado Springs; [m.] Lisa Chontos, March 15, 1996; [ch.] David T., Nathan C.; [ed.] Studying for Associates degree in Art. Future career in Editing; [memb.] Member of International Society of Poets; [hon.] High school newspaper Meritorious Service Award, National Library of Poetry, Editor's Choice Award; [oth. writ.] "Sunshine" published in "Through the Hourglass".; [pers.] I'd like to thank my wife for encouraging me to make something of myself and my poetry.; [a.] Colorado Springs, CO

CHORNOBRYWY, MARION
[pen.] Chorno; [b.] July 1, Belfast, NI; [p.] Mary Agnew, Robert Agnew; [m.] Amil (Deceased), 25 October 1961; [ch.] 2 Dennis and Lynn; [ed.] Whitehouse P. Es. Belfast Technical College Schneider School of Fine Arts BFA Concordia U. John Abbott College Dec. Du. Montfort University in England; [occ.] MA. Interior Designer Artist - Restorer - Lecturer; [memb.] Lakeshore Assoc. of Artists a Member of Beaconsfield United Church; [hon.] Schneider School of F.A. first prize 1983 and 1984 for water colors, summer school; [oth. writ.] "Wishing Upon A Star" premier Press Burnaby B.C. "Poetry Now" Northern Ireland Published in England "write to the core" by Greenway Women's Press Belfast; [pers.] My life is reflected in my art which is often (combined) with my poetry. Music also plays an important part in my life.; [a.] Montreal, Canada

CHUNG, CHRISTOPHER J.
[b.] October 25, 1973, Madison, WI; [p.] Joe and Nancy Chung; [ed.] Sun Prairie Senior High School, University of Wisconsin, Whitewater; [occ.] Student at the University of Wisconsin, Whitewater; [hon.] Editor's Choice Award for poem published in The Rippling Waters.; [oth. writ.] Poem published in previous poetry anthology, The Rippling Waters; [pers.] This is for Eithne Ni Bhraonain (Enya), who's music healed my broken soul, and all those in Cats National II, for bringing me back into the light. Thank you for saving me.; [a.] Whitewater, WI

CHYATTE, ELI
[b.] November 30, 1930, Brooklyn, NY; [p.] Max and Ida Chyatte; [m.] Frances Eve Chyatte, August 20, 1961; [ch.] Michael Arthur Chyatte, Dr. Franklin Jeffrey Chyatte; [ed.] Univ. of MD, B.A., George Washington Univ., B.S., Univ. of Pennsylvania, D.D.S.; [occ.] Retired; [oth. writ.] Volumes: "Come, Walk With Me", "Frozen Forever", "The Wall", "Thoughts I Ponder", "The Bridge"; [pers.] In my poem "The Road We Traveled", I wrote - "It's strange to have the feeling what I write will reach many eyes of people, I will new know from words, I hope you will know me", this is the reason that write.; [a.] Laurel, MD

CIERI III, JOSEPH N.
[b.] January 2,1947, Norwalk, CT. ;[p.] Joseph and Grace Ciere ; [ed.] High School graduate ; [occ.] confined to an extended care facility brain injured in accident -1979 ; [hon.] awards only given The National Library of Poetry ; [oth.writ.] Many poems written between 1967-1978. This will be the 4th submitted to the National Library of Poetry. ; [pers.] Poems written about my ears as a flower child, drugs, misc.women in my life my years away from home, (at an early age) hold the lies that tried to explain my life my life then. ; [a.] Old Lyme, CT.

CLARK, BARBARA
[b.] April 3, 1941, Lancaster, PA; [p.] Foster Child; [m.] Claude J. Clark, August 29, 1963; [ch.] Kathy, Penny, Claude III-Deceased; [ed.] 10th grade; [occ.] Factory worker; [oth. writ.] One poem in Tomorrow's Dream. I wrote it for our son who was killed in 1995. One poem in best poems of the 90's. Also written for our son.; [a.] Lititz, PA

CLEARY JR., JOHN EDWARD
[b.] December 9, 1953, Philadelphia; [p.] John and Catherine Cleary; [ed.] Cardinal Dougherty H.S. Phila., Charles Morris Prize School for Advertising and Journalism, Philadelphia Wireless School of Electronics; [occ.] Security Shift Supervisor at Frankford Hospital Phila. PA; [oth. writ.] Published in "The Cardinal", a high school book of poetry in 1972 or '71. Have had poem accepted in up coming print of anthology this June.; [pers.] I give in to inspiration. Whether it be comedy, tragedy, truth or fiction. Whatever my mind tells my hand which holds the pen to write on the paper, that is what I write. That is the best way I can describe it. It is my release, it makes me happy.; [a.] Philadelphia, PA

CLEMENTS, JOSEPH W.
[b.] September 19, 1974, Atlanta, GA; [p.] George and Linda Clements; [ed.] Brookwood High School, currently attending Georgia State University; [occ.] Full-time student; [oth. writ.] "Growing In The Fields Of Love" published in the book Etches In Time; [pers.] "Angel", as well as my other poems, would not have been made possible if I had not met a truly extraordinary young lady named Angela Trimmer. She has listened when no one else would listen, and in turn, pushed me to succeed. Angela, you truly are in inspiration. I thank you!; [a.] Lilburn, GA

CLIFFORD, DAVID
[b.] December 9, 1981, Manhattan, NY; [ed.] 10th grade education Ward Melville H.S.; [occ.] Student, Transcendental Meditation, Traditional Wu Shu, Kung Fu; [oth. writ.] Many poems, some published works.

COFFEY, DONNA M.
[b.] April 30, 1946, Lowell, MA; [p.] Patrick J., Margaret E. (Ralls) Finneral; [m.] Dennis P. Coffey, August 16, 1969; [ch.] Sarah Elizabeth; [ed.] BS in Ed Lowell State College, Masters of Ed Lowell State College; [occ.] Educator - Lowell School System; [memb.] Spindle City Garden Club American Def, of Teachers Immaculate Church; [oth. writ.] Essay published in an Anthology of Essays Edited work for publication in the Boston Globe published in Lowell San Newspaper and National Library of Poetry.; [pers.] I believe that having time to oneself to reflect on life and its happenings is important.; [a.] Lowell, MA

COLE, DEBRA R.
[b.] April 10, 1963, Torrington; [p.] Sam and Alice Davis; [m.] Eugene (Gene) Cole, February 5, 1983; [ch.] Amy and Kimberly Cole; [ed.] Torrington High School; [occ.] Clean houses, and part time free smoke and water rester with captich clean; [memb.] Member of the First Church of The Nazarene; [hon.] Editor's Choice Award, for Take My Hand; [oth. writ.] Take My Hand published in Amidst the Splendor (anthology).; [pers.] I want to help any one in need. I want people to see God in my life and I hope to help them find God too. I love to wright.; [a.] Torrington, WY

COLE, HAZEL JAMES
[pen.] H. James Cole; [b.] December 26, 1964, Abbeville, MS; [m.] Elvert, September 25, 1982; [ch.] Kimberly and Sterling; [ed.] Lafayette High, University of Southern Miss B.S. and M.A. in Journalism/Mass Communication; [occ.] Marketing and Public Relations Practitioner; [memb.] American Advertising Federation, Sales and Marketing Executives American Association of University Women National Council of Negro Women Public Relations Association of Mississippi; [hon.] 1996 Editor's Choice Award with National Library of Poetry. Won numerous awards for Leadership; [oth. writ.] Author of two children's books, published numerous articles in trade publications and newspapers.; [pers.] I write because it makes me happy. My writing allows others to look into the window of my world.; [a.] Hattiesburg, MS

COLE III, JAMES W.
[b.] August 1, 1947, Baytown, TX; [p.] Bill and Colleen Cole; [ed.] B.A., English Lit. University of Houston; [occ.] Mill Worker, Paper Mill; [pers.] The pressure against individual liberty mounts daily, and this nation's media is no friend of truth.; [a.] Baytown, TX

COLES, JOYCE V.
[b.] February 10, 1916, Musgravetown, Newfoundland, Canada; [p.] Eli Greening, Sandra Greening; [m.] Maxwell Coles, (Deceased), July 25, 1939; [ch.] Maxine William; [occ.] Retired Postmistress; [hon.] Two Editor's Choice awards from National Library of Poetry; [oth. writ.] Two poems published in anthologies Thankful Today and How Many Days?, Several poems for my own private collection also personal memoirs; [pers.] Retirement is a time to enjoy the things we have missed in earlier years. A time to remember only the good. A time when nature appears more beautiful and bird song is sweeter. The later years are often the best.; [a.] Steady Brook, Newfoundland, Canada

COLLINS, HELENA
[pen.] Alexandra Linke Wassmann; [b.] April 26, 1940, Coburg, Germany; [p.] Gisela Linke, Egon Wassmann; [ch.] 3 Daughters; [ed.] G.E.D., 2 yrs. College; [occ.] Retired former, Bookkeeper, Office Manager; [memb.] A.A.R.P. Arthritis Foundations, Mt. Olive Lutheran Church; [hon.] 1st published poem 1996; [oth. writ.] Many started, need help on translation on some plays, songs as yet unpublished.; [pers.] Living one day at a time with the Grace of God. Hoping to devote more time to finishing projects rather than scattering my limited energy going off on tangents.; [a.] Seattle, WA

CONNOR, GEORGIA KATHLEEN
[pen.] "Something From Grace"; [b.] November 20, 1949, Columbus, OH; [p.] Dr. and Mrs. Nolen and Grace Connor; [ed.] Certified EEG Neuro Feed Back Trainer, Honorary Phi Beta Kappa, Wislow Michigan University (1969), B.F.A. Magna Cum Laude 1973, MA Summa Cum Laude 1974, The Ohio State University; [occ.] Peak Performance in Biofeedback and Founder President of `Possibility Kids Non-profit'; [memb.] SRG, AFTRA; [hon.] Grad. fellow the Ohio State University 1973-74, Who's Who Women In Entertainment 1992 2nd Edition; [oth. writ.] Mind Moves - The Accelerated Learning Formula, various poems, articles on biofeedback and acceluated learning, children's stories.; [pers.] My aim is nothing short of global lynchrony - uniting heart and mind toward states of transcendent awareness - there is no wound on earth which can not be healed when united with the will of heaven.; [a.] Carmel, CA

CONNORS, R. G.
[b.] July 4, 1933, Butler Tonwship, PA; [p.] Leo and Reginia Connors; [m.] Constance, December 31, 1955; [ch.] Geri Anne, Timothy, Brian and Joseph; [ed.] High School, Marine Corps and a student of life; [occ.] Retired Airline Worker after 41 years of service; [memb.] AARP, the Nat'l. Assn. of Watch and Clock Collectors Inc., The Int'l. Poetry Hall of Fame; [hon.] Web Page in The Int'l Poetry Hall of Fame, Awards of Merit from United Airlines; [oth. writ.] Published in "At Water's Edge," "Memories of Tomorrow," "The Ebbing Tide" and "The Best Poems of 1996."; [pers.] Poetry is a chance to make a statement that will live long after you do. So choose your words as if you were speaking to those many people of the future.; [a.] Wenonah, NJ

CONRAD, KERRI N.
[b.] February 14, 1985, Topeka, KS; [p.] John and Tammy Conrad; [ed.] 6th Grade at Knob Noster Middle School; [occ.] Student; [memb.] Junior Optimists, Student Council Representative, Puppeteer Club; [hon.] 1996 Dare Essay Winner, Year Book Cover Winner for 1994, Presidents Achievement Award 1996, 1995 Young Authors Winner, Honor Roll 1991 - 1996, 1993 Reflections "Honorary Mention, 1994 Reflections" Best of Show"; [oth. writ.] "Imagine That" published in Seasons To Come, "Night" published in 1995 Young Authors Edition, "If I Could Give The World A Gift, Reflections Winner; [a.] Knob Noster, MO

CONRAD, SHIRLEY
[ed.] Bachelor of Arts in writing from Southern Oregon State College; [occ.] Computer Network Specialist; [hon.] Editor's Choice Award 1996, Earth Day Award for Poetry 1996; [oth. writ.] Published poems in several Pacific NW Anthologies,

COOK, LESLIE MAXWELL
[pen.] Blue Gums; [b.] May 9, 1958, Detroit, MI; [p.] Carrie B. Maxwell; [m.] Tim Cook, April 30, 1994; [ch.] none; [ed.] Mumford High School, University of Michigan, Laney College of Cosmetology, Computer Learning Center, Diablo Valley College - College/Environmental Engineering Dept.; [occ.] Environmental Engineering, & Poet; [memb.] Glide Methodist Episeopal Church, SECA; National Cosmetology Ass.;

COSTA, GINA MARIE
[b.] April 10, 1971, Smithtown, NY; [p.] Joseph Costa and Bobbie McGuire; [ed.] BA - Adelphi University; MA - New York Institute of Technology; [occ.] Assistant Editor at Parents Magazine; [oth. writ.] 2nd poem published, various other articles published in local newspapers and magazines.; [pers.] This poem is dedicated to my partner and best friend, Mark Schrunter. He is my inspiration.; [a.] New York, NY

COTTONHAM, MAUREEN H.
[b.] April 22, 1930, Homer, LA; [p.] Wesley H. and Mattie Pace Harper; [m.] Ernest L. Cottonham, June 13, 1982; [ch.] Anthony, Cedric and Greta; [ed.] BA in Sociology - some courses from grumbling state, graduated from Chicago State University Retired L.P.N.; [occ.] Retired; [memb.] Mt. Earia C Me Church Lifetime member ESP NAACP Various Community Activities; [hon.] Poet of merit award ISP, poet of merit medal (ISP) editor's choice wards (2) ISP. Poet of merit for lyrics from Jeff Roberts Publishing Co. Profiled in full issue of poet's corner magazine; [oth. writ.] Author of 1 poetry book entitled "Songs of Life". Poetry published in local newspapers, published in two anthologies by The National Library of Poetry.; [pers.] I thank God for the gift and opportunity to write poetry. It is an opportunity to put my thoughts on paper instead of keeping them in and building up pressure. It soothes the soul.; [a.] Jonesboro, LA

COUSINEAU, MICHAEL RICHARD
[b.] May 11, 1971, San Francisco; [p.] Donna and Robert Cousineau; [m.] Marci Anna Loftus, July 30, 1994; [ch.] Chance Michael; [ed.] Monte Vista High School, U.S. Army, Military Police Academy; [occ.] Security Supervisor Black Hawk Country Club, Danville, CA; [hon.] Certificate of Special Congressional Recognition, Certificate of Appreciation from San Ramon Valley Fire Protection District; [oth. writ.] "The Blade Of Life" in, Amidst The Splendor, several unpublished poems.; [pers.] Poems are expression of the mind and soul translated to paper through feelings and emotions.; [a.] Concord, CA

COUVILLON, WAYNE LEO
[b.] December 30, 1948, Windsor, Ontario, Canada; [p.] Leo Couvillon, May Rickert; [m.] Sheila Ann Lock, October 22, 1971; [ch.] Tammy Jean, John Wayne, Rebecca May, Rachel Ann; [ed.] Marlborough Public, Forster Collegiate, University of Windsor; [occ.] Owner/Operator Vid-care Electronic Home Service; [memb.] Legion Branch #143, Airforce Club Wing #412, Airforce Association; [oth. writ.] "Blossom", "Elusion", "The Flood", "The Shadow"; [pers.] If there's a will there's a Wayne.; [a.] Windsor, Ontario, Canada

COVALT, GINGER Y.
[b.] July 3, 1943, Honolulu, HI; [p.] Francis Gordon Yates and Annabelle Johnson Yates; [m.] Wendell L. Covalt; [ch.] Erika and Leif Bradly; [ed.] Undergraduate studies: U. of Nevada Las Vegas, Columbia NY, Cornell NY, Dental Hygiene Degree North Western Chicago, IL, Post graduate studies Gurndeu Siddha Perth, India; [occ.] Dental Hygienist; [pers.] In my journey to realize and live in the truth. Writing poetry crystallizes my ever expanding awareness. Sometimes to see and often to mark a transforming, lucid shift in awareness.; [a.] Redondo Beach, CA

COX, JUDITH L.
[pen.] Rusty Cox; [b.] April 9, 1935, Los Angeles, CA; [p.] "Doc" and Mabel Goodwin; [ch.] 3 daughters, 10 grandchildren, 1 great grandchildren; [ed.] Cal-Poly-Pomona, CA 1977 Catherine College - 1993; [occ.] Transcriptionist; [hon.] Int'l Poetry Hall of Fame Catherine College - Adm. Asst. Student of the year 1992/93; [oth. writ.] Time of Fall, Christmas Time, Hearts and Flowers, Wearin' O' The Green, etc.; [pers.] I am pleased to be included in this Special publication. Our Flag has been one of my greatest inspirations, and of course, Mother Nature provides a neverending supply of her charms to choose from.; [a.] Black Mountain, NC

CRIBBS, GERI
[b.] March 27, 1970, Longbeach, CA; [p.] Charles and Geri Cribbs; [m.] Andreas Cribbs, June 14, 1996; [ed.] BA English, Univ. Alaska Anchorage; [occ.] Teacher Austrian American Society, Winter; [oth. writ.] Poetry published, Technical Manuals.; [pers.] Life is an eternal blinking eye from which I see all and nothing.; [a.] Saint Aegydam Neuwalde, Austria

CROOKS, REBA JEAN
[pen.] Reba J. Snow; [b.] October 1, 1932, Thayer, MO; [p.] Bertha Ethel McKeel and John Harrison Miller; [m.] Paul Faith Crooks Sr., September 22, 1962; [ch.] Seven; [ed.] A.A. degree - Goal was M.A. in Body Therapy and Phd. in Psychology but illness prevented my completion of BA - Psych. Tech. - Med. Tech.; [occ.] Retired; [memb.] Lifetime - Alpha Gamma Sigma Honor Society (Miramar College, San Diego), Womens Missionary Union, Pulaski Fine Arts Assoc.; [hon.] Scholarship National University San Diego, CA 1985, I feel honored that I've helped raise 7 children I'm proud of. We have lots of grandchildren and one great-grandson; [oth. writ.] "Precious Memories", "I Wonder Where You Are Tonight", "Do You Know Him?", "Memories Are Roads"; [pers.] We must teach our children to honor God and country. I try to always look at the sunny side of any event. I pray a lot we have been greatly blessed.; [a.] Waynesville, MO

CROWELL, NANCY M.
[b.] February 28, 1970, Halifax, NS; [p.] Karoly and Nancy Czagala; [m.] Larry Crowell, November 18, 1988; [ch.] Emily-Anne, Samantha, Victoria; [ed.] Cole Harbour District High School; [occ.] Jewellery Sales Clerk; [oth. writ.] One poem published in Sparkles in the Sand; [pers.] My writings usually involve family and love. This poem was dedicated to my brother Donald.; [a.] Dartmouth, Nova Scotia, Canada

CUMMINGS, JUAN
[b.] October 31, 1980, Houston, TX; [p.] John and Maria Cummings; [ed.] High School Student; [memb.] St. Dominic's Youth Group, Boy Scouts; [oth. writ.] "Our Pain Within" printed in another library of poetry book; [pers.] The words only sound write when they have my music to accompany them.; [a.] Benicia, CA

CUNNINGHAM, ROXANNE C.
[b.] October 14, 1954, Nashville, TN; [p.] Anna and Robert Caughey; [m.] Divorced; [ch.] Daniel, Michelle and Kristina; [ed.] High School, Commercial Art (some), Writer Workshops; [occ.] Gardener, Landscaping; [memb.] International Society of Poets, Master Gardener of Tennessee Agricultural Society; [hon.] I was interviewed on 'Poetry Today' and one

of my poems was also read over the air. It was quite an honor to be heard by so many people.; [oth. writ.] Years ago printed by World of Poetry, some recent magazine and newsletter printings; [pers.] Anne Sexton, one of my absolute favorites, once said that 'A woman who writes feels too much.' I thinks she's right.; [a.] Nashville, TN

CURTIS, ANNA R.
[b.] January 13, 1936, Houston, TX; [p.] Joseph and Florence Washington; [m.] Theodore Nathaniel Curtis, January 17, 1964; [ch.] Stephanie; [ed.] Wheatley High School, TSU University B.A. Degree Social Work (Magna Cum Laude); [occ.] OCC: Center Administrator Houston Health and Human Services Kashmere Multi-Service Center; [memb.] American Heart Association, American American Red Cross, Mental Health Association, Fifth Ward Community Redevelopment Association Board of Directors, Interfaith Ministries RSVP Program, Volunteers in Public Schools.; [hon.] Sam Houston Area Council Scouting Award, VIPS 20 Year Service Pen, Woman of the Year XI Chapter Eta Phi Beta Sorority, Inc., Outstanding Contribution to Youth Award- Community Volunteer Youth Council, Success By Six Shaping the Future Award, Dare to make a Difference Award, - Top Ladies of Distinction.; [pers.] It is not the great things that we do that count but the little things that make life worth living for those around us.; [a.] Houston, TX

DANE, ANGELA
[b.] November 17, 1980, Coving, CA; [p.] Cecil and Diane Dane; [ed.] Currently attending Azusa High School; [occ.] Student; [memb.] I am a member of CSF, NHS, FBLA, Colorguard and French Club.; [hon.] Editor's Choice Award, 2 Presidential Academic Awards; [oth. writ.] Dead love from the anthology A Far Off Place.; [pers.] The best things throughout life are the things you love. It is the key to happiness.; [a.] Azusa, CA

DAVENPORT, JOAN
[b.] December 7, 1957, Brooklyn, NY; [p.] David Jefferson and Mary Louise; [m.] Davenport (Deceased); [ed.] Fort Hamilton H.S., VA. Union University, Marymount Manhattan College; [occ.] Bookkeeper, Catholic Charities, Diocese of Brooklyn; [hon.] DA Citation of Honor Outstanding Young Woman of America DC1707 Local 207 Service Award; [oth. writ.] Anchor - H.S. Literary Magazine; [pers.] "I have always been a learner and am grateful to everyone who has been my teacher, the Lord gave me a gift for words, and I have used it in his praise". Sirach 51:17, 22; [a.] Brooklyn, NY

DAVIDSON, ALLISON
[b.] November 8, 1976, Shreveport, LA; [p.] Robert and Linda Davidson; [ed.] North DeSoto High (Stonewall, LA); [occ.] Senior journalism major at Louisiana Tech University (Ruston, LA); [memb.] Kappa Delta Sorority, Liberal Arts Senator (SGA), Omicron Delta Kappa Honor Society, Gamma Beta Phi Honor Society, The Tech Talk, Society of Professional Journalists, Southside Baptist Church; [hon.] Vice President - Society of Professional Journalists, Associate Editor - The Tech Talk, Journalism Scholarship; [oth. writ.] Published in: The Space Between, The Best Poems of 1995, The Best Poems of 1996, The Ruston Daily Leader, The Tech Talk, The Mansfield Enterprise, General Electric Newsletter; [pers.] I like to express my thoughts on Christ, love, family and life — things people can relate to, learn from, or both.; [a.] Mansfield, LA

DAVILA, ELIZABETH KELSO
[pen.] Elizabeth Kelso; [b.] June 16, 1967, New York; [p.] Jesse and Mary Kelso; [ch.] Marcos Davila III; [ed.] Harry S. Truman High School, John Jay College of Criminal Justice; [occ.] Investment Banking Secretary; [memb.] Distinguished Member ISP; [hon.] Editor's Choice Award - NLP, Merit Award - ISP; [oth. writ.] Various publications in National poetry journals. Previous NLP Anthologies.; [a.] Bronx, NY

DAVIS, W. EUGENE
[b.] September 30, 1934, Toledo, OH; [p.] George A., Grace N. Davis; [m.] Shirley M., July 7, 1962; [ch.] Thomas, Rebecca; [ed.] BA Journalism, Bowling Green, OH, MA English, Bowling Green, OH, Ph.D. English, Western Reserve Univ. Cleveland, OH; [occ.] Professor of English Purdue Univ. W. Lafayette, IN; [memb.] Midwest MLA, Southern MLA; [hon.] Fulbright to Univ. of Freiburg, Germany, 1969-70; [oth. writ.] Several essays on Thomas Hardy and other Late-Victorian authors, a very few poems in local journals.; [pers.] Credo in unum Deum, as man and writer. My poetic subject is my personal experience, compounded as I see it of the everyday and the numinous.; [a.] Alexandria, VA

DAWSON, HALLETTE
[b.] July 22, 1947, Atlanta, GA; [p.] Harris and Evelyn Dawson; [m.] Divorced from Mr. Day; [ch.] Emily Juliana Dawson; [ed.] Frankfort American High School Class 1967, Gulf Park College 1967-68, Shillar College 1968-69; [occ.] Mother and Poet; [memb.] Dunnsville United Methodist Church; [oth. writ.] One poem in Windows of the Soul page 121 - Untitled; [a.] Herndon, VA

DAWSON, VICKI L.
[pen.] Victoria Scott Dawson; [b.] September 16, 1951, Magnolia, AR; [p.] E. L. Scott, Trixie Scott; [m.] Gilbert W. Dawson, January 28, 1995; [ch.] Rachel, Daniel, Ashley; [ed.] Jennings High, Jennings, La Houston Community College; [occ.] Owner and President of Administrative Assistance; [memb.] Romance Writers of Am., Golden Triangle Writer's Guild; [hon.] Texas Wide Writer's Competition - Corpus Christi Byliners, Golden Triangle Writer's Guild for Poetry; [oth. writ.] Heart Songs — A Poetic Journey of Truth, Shadow's Heart, Wind Chase, poetry published in literary journals.; [pers.] Life is meant to be lived fully - but in living my life I try to go forth and do no harm. I want my legacy to be wisdom and love.; [a.] Houston, TX

DE PINO, LOUISE
[pen.] Lou; [b.] May 25, 1932, New Haven, CT; [p.] Joseph and Fortuna Cimmino; [m.] Robert F. De Pino, September 6, 1958; [ch.] Four; [ed.] Columbus Elementary School, Wilbur Cross High, Eli Whitney Tech. (memb) St. Maria Della Virginia Society, St. Michael's Church Wooster Pl. New Haven, Conn.; [occ.] Housewife; [memb.] St. Maria Della Virginia Society St. Francis Parish Society; [oth. writ.] I've written poetry for other literary anthologies and I'm waiting for another book with my poems from another publishing Co.; [pers.] I enjoy poetry and find great enjoyment, to express in words, the feelings in my heart. May others also find mutual enjoyment in verses and rhymes.; [a.] New Haven, CT

DE RODRIGUEZ, ARLENE F.
[b.] September 8, 1935, Guayanilla, PR; [p.] Francisco A. Frank, Celina Rodriguez; [m.] Carlos R. Rodriguez, May 10, 1957; [ch.] Carlos F., Rafael A., Carlos R. Jr., and Javier A. Rodriguez; [ed.] BS - Font Bonne College, St Louis, MO, Catholic U, English major, Education minor-California State U, master of Arts - Concentration, Literature; [occ.] English Professor at Colegio Universitario del Este - Cabo Rojo P.R.; [memb.] T.E.S.O.L, Sigma Tau Delta - English Fraternity Catholic U., International Society of Poets; [hon.] Advance English Placement Seminars, T.E.S.O.L-P.R. Seminar Human Resources St. Croix U.S.V.I. Seminar Colegio Universitorio

del Este; [oth. writ.] Thesis published 1995, The Novels of Charles Dickens, Poem: Silver Anniversary 1995, Poem: Vanity of Vanities 1996.; [pers.] I strive to reflect Christian concepts exalting Jesus Christ as our Redeemer and Savior - I have been greatly influence by the life of Jesus Christ - what He has done in my life.; [a.] Cabo Rajo, PR

DEAL, KAREN H.
[pen.] Karen Deal; [b.] August 14, 1948, NC; [p.] (F) Aubrey M. Helms; [m.] Jesse M. Deal

DEJARNETTE, PATTY STILES
[b.] October 15, 1950, Kentucky; [p.] Gale and Ruth Stiles; [ch.] Ashley, Jason, Linze; [ed.] Associate Degree in Nursing Western, Kentucky University; [occ.] Registered Nurse Director Nursing Information Systems; [hon.] Who's Who's in American Nursing; [oth. writ.] In Process: Book of Poetry, Novel; [pers.] Writings began for personal therapy. Now writings are geared toward awareness for women.; [a.] Bowling Green, KY

DELAHOUSSAY III, A. J.
[b.] April 4, 1942, Washington, DC; [p.] Leona Marie Andry, Althemus Joseph Delahoussay Jr.; [ed.] B.A. in Zoology from U.C.L.A. one years graduate work in nutrition at U.C.L.A. and one trimester at Cleveland Chiropractic College; [occ.] Writer of Poetry; [memb.] International Society of Poets, the Bahai Faith, American Legion, Veterans of Foreign Wars and The Disabled American Veterans; [hon.] Graduated with Honors from Mt. Carmel High School. 1960, Received Commission to 2nd Lieutenant in Army - 1965, Editor's Choice Award, National Library of Poetry, 1996.; [oth. writ.] Poems in other National Library of Poetry Anthologies 1996, 1994, and 1993.; [pers.] I strive, in my poems and other writings, to impart that mystical aroma derived from reading the Bahai, Sacred scripture and other Holy books, to my works. I try to practice what I read to the fullest extent possible, for that is an essential requisite of the mystic path.; [a.] Los Angeles, CA

DELOATCH, JOHNNY
[b.] March 4, 1954, Tarboro, NC; [p.] Chester and Maude DeLoatch; [m.] Margie; [ch.] Johnny II, Michelle, Dana, Lamonica; [ed.] Conetoe High School, Conetoe North Carolina, Robertson Elem. School N.C., Speed School, N.C.; [occ.] School Bus Operator, Bronx, NY; [memb.] World Vision Sponsor since 1988, 1181 A.T.U.; [hon.] Citations from City Council of N.Y. Award from Bronx Assembly Mans Office.; [oth. writ.] The Signs Are There, To Go Back; [pers.] I've always been a believer in Martin Luther King, and the fight for rights that he stood for. But now I question, if he were here to see some of the results of his labor (would he really be impressed?); [a.] Bronx, NY

DEMARCO, LYNDA
[b.] June 9, 1945, Lexington, VA; [p.] Beatrice, Hugh Davis Jr.; [m.] Dennis DeMarco; [ch.] Robert, Den-ise, Samantha, Debra, Denise; [occ.] Rest.-Bar owner; [hon.] Two Editor's Choice Awards from the National Library of Poetry; [oth. writ.] The Apache, Life's Storm; [pers.] I write what is in my heart. This poem is for my mom Bea and my daughter Denise I will always remember you - Love You Forever.; [a.] West Milford, NJ

DEPINO, LOUISE
[pen.] Lou; [b.] May 25, 1932, New Haven, CT; [p.] Joseph and Fortuna Cimmino; [m.] Robert F. De Pino, September 6, 1958; [ch.] Four; [ed.] Columbus Elementary School, Wilbur Cross High, Eli Whitney Tech. (memb) St. Maria Della Virginia Society, St. Michael's Church Wooster Pl. New Haven, Conn.; [occ.] Housewife; [memb.] St. Maria Della Virginia Society St. Francis Parish Society; [oth. writ.] I've written poetry for other literary anthologies and I'm waiting for another book with my poems from another publishing Co.; [pers.] I enjoy poetry and find great enjoyment, to express in words, the feelings in my heart. May others also find mutual enjoyment in verses and rhymes.; [a.] New Haven, CT

DEPOYAN, VAMAKEN
[b.] September 21, 1977, Beirut, Lebanon; [ed.] A waste of precious time except for a few Allen Ginsberg poems Jim Morrison poems and 3rd grade writing grammer classes; [occ.] A gemologist at the master jeweler; [memb.] National Organization of the Reform of Marijuana Laws (NORML); [pers.] "I got my tribe it's my own right and I don't have to tell you why. It's been like that from the start sepultura in our hearts, can't take away, these roots will always remain Sepultura"; [a.] Pasadena, CA

DIAMOND, DANA
[b.] December 4, 1963, Burlington, VT; [m.] Michael W Diamond, July 3, 1987; [ed.] Piscataway High School; [occ.] Marine Corps. Wife; [oth. writ.] The National Library of Poetry; [a.] Clifton Park, NY

DICKINSON, DON C.
[pen.] Don C. Dickinson; [b.] September 28, 1943, Double Springs, AL; [p.] Joel S. and Gladys M. Dickinson; [m.] Jo May 9, 1964; [ch.] Craig, Dwain; [ed.] Winston County High School, Draughon's Business College, Lasalle Extensior University; [occ.] Public Accountant Lavonia, GA; [memb. National Beta Club, Hon. Order of Kentucky Colonels, Grace Baptist Church, Toccoa, GA; [hon.] Ordained Baptist Deacon, 1974; [oth. writ.] Poem "Daydreams" published 1996 "Portraits and Life". Over 100 unpublished poems, most of which tell a story, highlight a scripture passage or have a particular message to share; [pers.] Poetry is my way to reminisce the past tell a story, or to record a thought about a scripture passage. I attempt to communicate the goodness of God, the love of Christ and to drawn the reader to the scripture, The Holy Bible.; [a.] Toccoa, GA

DIVELY, ROBERT M.
[pen.] Bob; [b.] July 8, 1936, Bedford, PA; [p.] Mr. and Mrs Harper Dively; [m.] Shirley J. Dively, September 27, 1969 [ch.] Barry, Paul, Jill; [ed.] Graduate - Bedford High School, Graduate - Penn. College attended Penn. State University, completed many courses through correspondence; [occ.] Retired from Penn. State University, Retired from U.S. Air Force and PA Air National Guard; [memb.] PA. A.R. National Guard, Past Emergency Medical Technician, Past Member Air Force Association, Past Member of YMCA, worked with American Red Cross and the special Olympics Programs; [hon.] 3 Freedom Foundation Awards, Airman of the Year Award, Air Force Association Citation, Rep Legion of Merit Award, 30 Military Awards, USAF-ANG Inducted into Republican Hall of Honor; [oth. writ.] "A free Ballot-A free Country", "I Am Your Flag", "Are We", "Be Not A Dreamer", Have written many letters to the editor (Newspapers).; [pers.] Well-written poetry can give us great insight and wisdom in a few short paragraphs. It can enrich our lives and bring greater meaning to our shortcomings and also any success that may come into our life, be it today or tomorrow.; [a.] Port Matilda, PA

DOEY, RICHARD K.
[pen.] Rick Doey; [b.] February 7, 1949, Ontario, Canada; [p.] Frank and Salme Doey; [m.] Joyce M. Doey; [ch.] Two; [ed.] Gr. 12 Equivalent; [occ.] Mechanic and Roofer; [pers.] All the harms of this world, will stop, when we learn, to love a lot.

DOLOUGHAN, FIONA J.
[b.] February 14, 1960, Newtownards, N. Ireland; [p.] Phyllis and James Doloughan; [ed.] (1982) BA. (honr.) 2:1 French and European Literature, University of Warwick, England, (1985) MA, (1989) Ph.D Comparative Literature, UNC - CH, USA; [occ.] Lecturer in English for non-native speakers, U of Buckingham; [memb.] British Comparative Literature Association, Modern language Association of America; [pers.] I am a great admirer of the contemporary British Novelist, Jeanette Winterson.

DOLSON, DONALD
[b.] March 28, 1926, York Co., Ontario, Canada; [p.] John A. and Emma D. Dolson (Nee Hall) died Emma 16, 1965; [m.] 1st Mary A. Dolson (Nee Berrie), August 11, 1951, 2nd Ruth E. Dolson (Nee Holloway), May 20, 1978; [ch.] Donna A. Dolson, Gail J. May; [ed.] 14 years Auto body repair and spray painting. Past T.V. Technician exams at Radio Electronic Television School 1957. Air conditioning, oil burner servicing and Appliance repair, aprox. 1959 at Standard Engineering School Toronto.; [occ.] Retired-Write Poetry, Tinker with fixing electrical things, and take Photos for a hobby; [memb.] Ennerdale Baptist Church Inc. Federal and Provincial Member of Liberal Party. Voice of Canadians, Evangelical Fellowship of Canada. C.S.N.P. (Canadians in Solidarity With Native People, Knox Adult Fellowship Life Member International Society of Poets.; [hon.] Editor's Choice - Library of Poetry 1997 Parkdale High Park - Liberal of the year, 1990; [oth. writ.] Fact, Fancy and Philosophy, 1970. Heart Talk, 1972. Satire Sentiment and Humour, 1974. Let There be Love! 1980. In The Shadow of His Cross, Feelings! 1993, and 1997. Editions self published, Ranging from over 50 poems and 750 copies. 1970. To 50 copies and 24-60 poems in later years.; [pers.] I write to express my love and respect for God and His People, and share the inspiration He gives me, hoping to help not only our youth, but also the aged, the lonely and dispossessed of all races and colors and beliefs. Love is a universal language!; [a.] Toronto, Ontario, Canada

DONALDSON, DONNA JILL
[pen.] "Jill Donaldson"; [b.] August 19, 1965; [p.] Gail Wesley and Helen Kay Sigman Wilson; [m.] Phillip Michael Donaldson, November 7, 1979; [ch.] Michael Ray Donaldson and Phillip Wesley Donaldson; [ed.] Webster Co. High School, Cowen, W.VA; [occ.] Receiving Manager, Wal-Mart; [hon.] My greatest honor was being published in "Recollections of Yesterday".; [oth. writ.] "Ode To Dad" wrote "The Holler" small hometown newsletter "The Window"; [pers.] "I thank my husband and my sons, for their endurance and faith in me during my times of writing, and having to listen to all my poems. I would also like to thank fellow co-workers for reading and giving their opinion on my poem. And my sister-in-law Delta W. and Barb S., Dina G., Michelle I., Chris F., Tecka V., Jackie E., Sherwin S., Glen C., Eric S., Darla A., Sherri S., Angie G., Julie H., Jessie C. and Becky Ho. Thank You All! God Bless!; [a.] Ashland, OH

DONLEY, FRANCINE DENISE
[b.] January 26, Chicago, IL; [p.] Daisy Mae Donley, Norman Marshall; [m.] (GP) Mattie Mae Jeffries; [ed.] Manierre School, Waller High, Loop Community Col., Illinois School of commerce, Dean's List.; [occ.] Public relations, interior design; [oth. writ.] Poem published in beneath the harvest moon by Anthology the National Library of Poetry - titled 'Our Children'.; [pers.] Always try to treat people with respect, whether they deserve it or not, who knows?, it's not for me to say... I know to receive it can brighten your spirit, even your day. Inspired by Maya Angelou and Nikki Giovanni.; [a.] Chicago, IL

DORSEY, CAROLYN D.
[b.] October 7, 1955, Arkansas; [p.] Mr. and Mrs. Mack McClure; [m.] Rev. Randy Dorsey (Deceased); [ch.] Cary Rene' (16) and Lara Michelle (11); [ed.] Claremore HS - Claremore, OK, Claremore Jr. College - Claremore, OK, Southwestern Assemblies of God University - Waxahachi, TX; [occ.] Missionary to Cambodia - Pastor of International Christian Assembly in Phnom Penh, Cambodia; [memb.] Numerous Community Service activities and other charitable work.; [oth. writ.] In addition to poetry, have written numerous articles for publication in various magazines and periodicals.; [pers.] I find great enjoyment from all types of literature and desire that any of my writing will inspire the same type of enjoyment.; [a.] Claremore, OK

DORSEY, CORI LYNN
[b.] April 23, 1978, East Chicago, IN; [ed.] East Chicago Central High School, Ivy Tech State College (currently).; [occ.] Student (Nursing); [hon.] The National Library of Poetry Editor's Choice Award; [oth. writ.] One published poem, "The After Effect" and several other unpublished poems; [pers.] If you can visualize it, and believe if you can do it. I have been greatly influenced by my love of African-American history, and I try to reflect this in my writing.; [a.] East Chicago, IN

DORSEY, JANETTE F.
[pen.] Janette Fletcher; [b.] September 14, 1958, Austin, TX; [p.] James and Angeline Fletcher; [m.] Donald Dorsey, May 1; [ch.] Glen Markeith Fletcher, J'reem, Le'shar, Reimar Fletcher, Leticia Quishon Fletcher; [ed.] Reagan High School at Austin, TX; [occ.] Dallas Area Rapid Transit; [memb.] Texas Film Com. Zacary Scott Theater; [oth. writ.] The Ebbing Tide, anthology "Sir James"; [pers.] Life consist of so much beauty. With my instrument, I can share on paper, my thoughts wonder into places, most imaginative, a gifted hand that create beauty, drama, lived and shared, with all others a pen, an instrument that no boundaries an invisible power words rested upon what's written.

DRESSLER, LIN
[b.] October 8, 1950, Edmonton, Alberta; [p.] Lorraine Sowpal and Ken Nobbs; [m.] Jacob Christopher, August 30, 1986; [ch.] Jodi, Michael, Cheryl, Carolyn and Kelly; [ed.] Social Service Worker Executive Director for a Society that assists abused women and children; [occ.] Retired, owing to disability - Post Polio Syndrome; [memb.] Post Polio Society; [hon.] Nominated "Poet of the Year 1995", National Institute of Poetry; [oth. writ.] Published Medallion Winner for A Fair Weather Friend, Poetry Institute of Canada, Just another Dream - "A Moment in Time", National Library of Poetry 1995, An Angel's Kiss - "Sparkles in the Sand", National Library of Poetry - 1995; [pers.] Many things in life inspire me to write poetry. It is gratifying to know I am leaving a legacy for my grandchildren sot hey will remember who I was and what was most precious to me.; [a.] Surrey, British Columbia, Canada

DRYDEN, WILLIAM J.
[pen.] Frosty; [b.] November 15, 1952, Kountze, TX; [p.] E. D. and Willie Mae Drydon; [m.] Dolly, December 4, 1971 (25 years); [ch.] Jason, John, Shawn; [ed.] High School; [occ.] Paper Maker; [pers.] Poetry is my way of opening up my most deep dark inner secrets. I write a lot of poems for special occasions and it is my way of expressing my self.

DUBANNY, AAROW J. E.
[pen.] Sirshoyd; [b.] December 30, 1947, Montserrat; [occ.] Driver; [memb.] Life time member of The International Society of Poets; [hon.] Elected to the International Poetry Hall of Fame Museum on the Internet's World Wide Web; [pers.]

Don't demand promotion promote demand.

DUFFY, G. FRANCES
[b.] August 6, 1953, Bronx, NY; [p.] Antonietta, Michele Colombo; [m.] William Duffy, March 7, 1987; [ch.] Richard, Joseph Lombardo; [ed.] Graduate Holyoke Community College, attend American International College.; [occ.] Buyer - Tubed Products Incorporated; [memb.] National Association of Purchasing Management, The International Society of Poets; [hon.] Editor's Choice Award, Phi Theta Kappa, Dean's List; [oth. writ.] Reflections; [a.] East Hampton, MA

DUNBAR, JESSICA
[b.] August 3, 1977, Grande Prairie, AB, Canada; [p.] Susan and Gordon Duncan; [ed.] Graduated Lake Gibson High School in Lakeland, Fl.; [occ.] Salesperson in a clothing store; [oth. writ.] I have always been able to express my feelings through my writing. I am also writing a book.; [pers.] I am proud to be accepted by the National Library of Poetry. It has given me the boost needed to keep on with my writing.; [a.] Lakeland, FL

DUNCAN, MINDY
[b.] April 24, 1968, Atlanta, GA; [p.] Dr. and Mrs. Claude D. Duncan; [ed.] Westminster Elementary through High School - graduate, University of Georgia - BFA in Photography - working on Masters of Communication at Georgia State University; [occ.] Production Coordinator for Veranda Magazine

DURANTE, LYNDA
[b.] March 2, 1981, San Diego; [p.] Karen Finneran and Patrick Durante; [ed.] Good Shepherd Elementary and Jr. High School, Currently enrolled in the Academy of Our Lady of Peace High School, class of 1999; [occ.] Student, bus girl at Capriccio's Italian Restaurant; [memb.] OLP Academic League member, CSF, OLP Literary Magazine Staff; [hon.] OLP Honors at Entrance, Principal's Honor Roll, 1st and 2nd honors at OLP, Citizenship award upon graduation from Good Shepherd; [oth. writ.] Other poems, both unpublished or published by The National Library of Poetry.; [pers.] If you tell it like it is and try to change things, maybe someone will follow suit. Never change or hide your true self, or you'll be miserable. Appreciate nature, and she'll appreciate you.; [a.] San Diego, CA

DURKIN, KEVIN T.
[b.] July 14, 1956, Evergreen Park, IL; [p.] Anthony and Margeret Durkin; [m.] Bradley F. Carlson, November 23, 1991; [ed.] Brother Rice H.S. 4 yr. University of I C. 1976 Columbia 1977; [occ.] Retired; [memb.] International Society of Poetry National Arbor Foundation Garfield Park Conservatory Chicago Architecture Foundation; [hon.] National Library of Poetry Third place award 1996; [oth. writ.] To share a life with someone else please I'm thinking how our love will change I keep wondering where love goes when it dies.

DYCK, JAKE E.
[pen.] Eric; [b.] October 8, 1941, Portage La Prairie; [p.] Abram & Johanna Dyck; [m.] Eleanor Dyck, August 17, 1991; [ch.] Tamara Bowman & Shane Tholenaer; [ed.] Grade 11, U of Man - agriculture Diploma, Winhler Bible School ETTA Olds College - Com. floriculture; [occ.] Manager of a Training Centre; [oth. writ.] 30 plus other poems; [pers.] I believe in life, love and happiness. The rigours of life have been devsatating but they have made me a more complete person.; [a.] Morden, MAnitoba, CANADA

DYCK, MITCHELL
[b.] October 13, 1979, Sparwood, BC; [p.] Teresa and Darrell Dyck; [ed.] Currently in grade 12 and will graduate in June of '97. Will attend the Trebas Institute in October of '97 to further my education in Audio Engineering.; [occ.] Currently employed part-time as a service clerk at our local grocery store; [memb.] Editor of the school yearbook; [oth. writ.] Several published poems in local papers, school yearbook, and by The National Library of Poetry.; [pers.] I write about personal experiences and of things I've witnessed and feel strongly about. I find my inspiration in the works of such artists as Stephen Scott, Mike Smith, Jason Archibald, Glen Ballard, and Madonna; [a.] Elkford, BC

EAGAN, MIMI
[b.] August 28, 1926, Syracuse, NY; [p.] Leo T. and Eleanor Eagan; [ch.] Margot Papworth, Muffie Wilson, Chris Cheney and nine (9) grandchildren; [ed.] B.A. Georgian Court College; [occ.] Retired; [memb.] Distinguished Member, International Society of Poetry, 1995; [hon.] Elected to International Poetry Hall of Fame, 1994; Guest on "Poetry Today" on Public radio, NY City, 1996; Awarded Editor's Choice for Poetry, 1994; International Poet of Merit Award, 1995; Editor's Choice Award for Poetry in 1996 by National Library of Poetry; [oth. writ.] Bittersweet - book of poetry, published 1995; [pers.] "I write about everyone and everything I love, as well as about the wasteland of war. I've been lucky to live in many parts of the U.S. and in Saudi Arabia, which has given me the courage to write."; [a.] Fayetteville, NY

ECKBERG, SHELLEY
[b.] August 31, 1964, Clearfield, PA; [p.] Joseph and Rose Holenchik; [m.] Randall Eckberg, November 12, 1983; [ch.] Ronald J. and Heather R.; [oth. writ.] My poem 'The Lost Season' was published in Spirit of the Age (National Library of Poetry) and my poem as November Sing's published in Admist the Splendor (National Library of Poetry.); [pers.] Even on the warmest of Summer days, I long for a tiny piece of winter, if only for a little while, to grasp in my hands, that cold exhilarating mystery.; [a.] Madera, PA

EDELEN, DONNA
[b.] South Bend, IN; [p.] Margaret and Kenneth Brown; [ch.] Barbara, Wendy, Edward, Derrick, Jeffery and Penney Edelen; [ed.] Nursing degree, Psychology degree Business Certificate; [occ.] Medical and Business Consultant, Poet; [memb.] NABCW - Founder and President, Member American Red Cross; [hon.] Deans Honor List; [oth. writ.] Several poems published in various local newspaper, poem published in Sea of Treasure; [pers.] I'm a political poet, I speak for those unheard. Special dedicated to my five grandchildren Justin and Edward Edelen, Michael and Tiffney and Whitney McPherson Friends-Veinie and Rhoda Campbell, Tommy Davis.; [a.] San Diego, CA

EDWARDS, G. THOM
[b.] July 27, 1948, Farmington, NM; [p.] Billy T. Edwards, Leila Mae Edwards; [m.] Terri F. Edwards, April 23, 1995; [ch.] Jeremy Duane, Kyle Mitchell, Shari Dawn; [ed.] Mustang High School, Rose State College (OK), Community College of Bakersfield (CA); [occ.] Paralegal, Albuquerque, NM, Poet/Song Lyricist; [memb.] New Mexico State Bar Association, Legal Assistant Division, Ridgecrest Christian Church; [hon.] Honors graduate, Dean's List, 7 other poetry awards; [oth. writ.] Numerous published in 3 other books.; [pers.] In my poetry I try to pull out the feelings of the reader, feelings, thoughts or experiences they too have had.; [a.] Albuquerque, NM

EDWARDS, KATINA
[pen.] Kat; [b.] January 31, 1980, Greenville, OH; [p.] Ron and Marianna Edwards; [ed.] Junior at Greenville High School; [memb.] Greenville FHA, Greenville, BPA, Greenville Greenwave Color Guard; [oth. writ.] "Help" published in

Windows of the Soul.; [a.] Greenville, OH

EHLERS, FLORENCE RAUSH
[pen.] Flora June; [b.] March 20, 1925, Brooklyn, NY; [p.] (Deceased) Pauline and Philip Raush; [m.] Divorced, March, 1945; [ch.] Allen Richard, Phillis (Chris), Donna, Anita and 6 grandchildren; [ed.] A.A. (Theetre Arts) A.S. (Psychiatric Tech.) Additional Studies in Music Theater, Psychology, Voice, Piano Actress (Drama and comedy - over 45 plays); [occ.] Retired Psychiatric Technician (Musical/Playwright); [memb.] Actress (Community Theater), Senior Citizen Assoc., Writer's Club (Ceal Beach, Ca Leisure World, Democratic Club, Yorbalinda/Placenta; [hon.] Music and Arts Assoc. from Choral Group as founder the (Whittier Women's Chorus and Note-a-belles), certificates/Poetic Achievement American Poetry Assoc. Internet'l Poetry Assoc. Award as Community Leader and Noteworthy American, listed in International Bibliographical Editions and Marquis, Who's Who Editions; [oth. writ.] Much Poetry, Songs (separate and included in musical/plays in my name (Drama Autumn Promise and Comedic Animation Critter Chatter) newspaper articles as weekly reporter (3 newspapers) (310)-430-0921; [pers.] I believe each person is endowed with some gift, the trick is to find it and use it as an aid towards peaceful and humanitarian purpose with open heart and word and deed. Poetry owns this ability in so many varied forms of expression.; [a.] Seal Beach, CA

ELFREICH, DONALD H.
[b.] July 19, 1924, Evansville, IN:; [p.] Herbert and Catherine Elfreich; [m.] Margaret M. Elfreich, January 19, 1943; [ch.] David A. Elfriech, Donna E. Henning; [ed.] 1 year college, incomplete; [occ.] Retired plumbing contractor; [memb.] Veterans of Foreign Wars Post 2953; [hon.] Service Award from Local 136 Plumbers Union for Labor and material contribution for Evansville School Corporation Survive Alive Building; [pers.] I believe we should always help others less fortunate than ourselves and, in cases of emergency, give up pleasure to help others.

ELLIS JR., EDWARD R.
[pen.] Ed Ellis; [b.] November 26, 1943, Melrose, MA; [p.] Edward Ellis, Phyllis Ellis; [m.] Elaine Amass, November 26, 1977; [ch.] Karen, Kristine; [ed.] Reading Memorial High - Reading, Mass, Tufts University - Medford, Mass, BS- Engineering; [occ.] Sales Representative Avon Corrugated Co. - Miami, FL; [memb.] American Society of Mechanical Engineers; [oth. writ.] Poems published in through the hourglass, poems and articles published in local papers; [pers.] Our lives are enriched by the variety of our experiences and the people we meet.; [a.] Sarasota, FL

ELLIS SR., EDWARD A.
[pen.] Ed Ellis ; [b.] November 26,1943, Melrose ;[p.] Edward A. Ellis and Phyllis ; [m.] Elaine ; [ch.] Karen, Kristine ;[ed.] BS- Mechanical Engineering Tufts University -Medford, Mass.- Reading Memorial High School, Readine, Mass. ;[occ.] Sales Representative Avon Corrugated Co. ; [memb.] American Society of Mechanical Engineers ; [oth.writ.] Poem published in Through the Hourglass, Poems and short articals published in Local papers ;[pers.] Our lives are enriched by the variety of our experiences and the people we meet. ; [a.] Sarasota, FL.

ELLISON, JOE ANTHONY
[b.] October 10, 1968, Greenville, SC; [p.] Joe Gary and Kathey Darlene Ellison; [m.] Crystal Marie Kuykendall, Engaged (April 1, 1997); [ch.] Jeremiah Layne Ellison; [ed.] Palmetto High; [occ.] Lead Singer/Songwriter for Rock Band "Aesop's Fools".; [hon.] U.S. Navy - Battle Efficiency Ribbon, Sea Service Deployment Ribbon Editor's Choice Award - The National Library of Poetry and 3rd place in 1996 Open Poetry National Competition.; [oth. writ.] "Hands Across Time", A short story appearing in the Palmettonian, and "Enigmatic" - A poem appearing in "The Rippling Waters". Published by The National Library of Poetry; [pers.] I really miss going to Rainbow Family Gatherings since I've been on this recluse trip, so if any brothers or sisters are reading. Please write to us at this address: 1951 Reedy Fork Rd., Pelzer SC, 29669. Have Music, will travel.; [a.] Pelzer, SC

ENGA, HAZEL
[b.] February 10, 1935, Robinsdale, MN; [p.] Orlin and Mae Underdahl; [m.] Robert Enga, May 9, 1953; [ch.] Deborah, Bonita, Robert Jr., Tamara, Paul, Jennifer; [ed.] High School - some random college classes - on going Foster Parent Training; [occ.] Homemaker/Foster Parent; [memb.] Assembly of God Church; [oth. writ.] "Morning Light" (Published in "Our World's Favorite Gold and Silver Poems" world of poetry press 1991), many more unpublished poems "Mother's Knee" (Published in National Library of Poetry 1996 "Memories of Tomorrow"; [pers.] My writing reflects what I am feeling at the time that I am writing. My inspiration comes from the Lord, my family, and my friends.; [a.] Princeton, MN

ENSOR, REBECCA M.
[b.] October 5, 1916, Glenco, Balto. Co, MD; [p.] George and Effie Ensor; [ed.] Sparks, Md. for High School Nurses Training for Three Years at Franklin Square Hospital - a registered nurse; [occ.] Retired RN; [memb.] Victory Villa Church International Society of Poets; [hon.] Award for highest marks in my class when I graduated from nurses, Training, An honored guest at The 1996 ISP convention; [oth. writ.] Children's stories in a course I am taking Family history articles.; [pers.] I have been writing poetry since I was in high school, I am retired, but still caring for friends and relatives.; [a.] Baltimore, MD

ERICKSON, TERRY LEE
[pen.] Terry Lee Erickson; [b.] December 2, 1933, Vancouver, BC, Canada; [m.] Divorced; [ch.] Four; [occ.] Wildlife Artist; [hon.] First poem published in "The Vancouver Sun" at age 13 - several others in newspapers all over Canada; [pers.] When I paint, my works reflect the intricate details of nature. When I write I paint the nature of mankind.

ESELY, CARLA JEAN LAGLIA
[b.] February 20, 1954, Findlay, OH; [p.] Domenick Laglia and Nellie G. Oman Laglia; [m.] William C. Esely, April 10, 1982; [ed.] "Graduate" - Findlay Senior High School in 1972 was in High School "Chorus and Drama" or (Thespians).; [occ.] Housewife, Poetic Writer. I also raise registered AKC Keeshondens for pets.; [memb.] The American Kennel Club, Women in Military Service For America, San Antonio Catholic Church & Distinguished Member of the International Society of Poets.; [hon.] 1969 - President & Jr. Chairman - Ralph D. Cole Post Unit 3 American Legion Jr. Auxiliary - Both parents - Honorably Discharged Naval Veterans (WWII & Korea). 1995-1996 - International Society of Poets Recognition. The National Library of Poetry, 3 Editors Choice Awards - 2 in 1996, 1 1997 For Outstanding Achievement in Poetry.; [oth. writ.] Several unsubmitted. 1 Song poem published through Columbine Records Defend your Lord Stolen. 3 poems published 1 A Quiet Repose, 2 Freedom Cries & 3 The Desert In Spring by National Library of Poetry. And 1 Getting Ready for Publication The Sequel to Miss Holy Life's Destruction (The Great Battle Obedience Versus sin) by N.L.P.; [pers.] I am a firm believer of God & Country. I have been greatly influenced in my writing by my parents & my grandparents Mr. & Mrs. Elmer Royoman who raised me with love, honor,

discipline, understanding & support. and by my loving supportive husband William Co Esely & also by the splendid beauty of God's creations.; [a.] McIntosh, NM

ESTRADA, ADAM
[b.] December 21,1965, Boswell, NM. ;[p.] Mr. and Mrs. Raul Estrada ;[m.] Dawn Ann Valentine Estrada, February 21,1997 ;[ch.] Adam Odiam Powell/Estrada ;[ed.] Eastern New Mex. Univ.-Electronics Technology Engineering Studies Southwest Acad of Technology- Assoc. of Arts and Sciences (Computer Aid Drafting) Drafting and Design ;[occ.] Walgreens Healthcare plus order production personnel ;[hon.] Ribbons for Art work along with boy scout badges etc. Promotion to order entry technican at Walgreens Healthcare Plus. ;[oth.writ.] Faith among several others. ;[pers.] I thank our dear Lord heavenly Father for all my blessings with a wonderful family and friends. I thank him most of all for the opportunity to share my artistic work with everyone through this company. ; [a.] Chandler, AZ.

EVANS, AMANDA
[pen.] Evans; [b.] January 10, 1972, Harpenden; [p.] David Evans and Janice Evans; [ed.] Abbots Hill School, Hemel Hempstead, Hertfordshire; [occ.] D.J at "Capital Radio Cafe"; [memb.] Tennis Club; [hon.] National Champion Double "Great Britain"; [oth. writ.] The last National Library of Poetry.; [pers.] I'm somebody who wants to be happy and do my best in my life.; [a.] Harpenden, Herts

EVANS, ILENE ANN
[pen.] Ilene Ann Evans; [b.] July 28, 1942, Portland, OR; [p.] Lily Osterback and James L. Evans; [ch.] Allan Lyle and Gina Mae Gerking; [ed.] Lincoln H.S. and Roosevelt H.S. Seattle, WA. Highline Community College 1975, AA Degree University of Puget Sound, Tacoma, WA. '78 B.A. Double Bachelor Degree in Art and Sociology, Delta Kappa Sociology Honors Society; [occ.] Writer/Artist, trying to get 3-300 page manuscripts published of non-fiction; [memb.] Kappa Delta-Sociology honors. Pacific N.W. Aleut Council - member CAPS Child Abuse Prevention Council/Fed.Way; [hon.] Phi Beta Kappa '72 '73,-'75 at Highline Comm. College Writing and Art. Delta Kappa Soc. Honors Society 1978 at University of Puget Sound, Tacoma, WA. Delta Kappa Sociology Honors; [oth. writ.] Lonnie Kaneko writing instructor there/ Des Moines, WA., Article I wrote on "Art Museum Membership" was in the Tacoma News Tribune and is used by Art teacher to teach students. I wrote, researched and self published 2 booklets, "Toxicity How Personal Is It? of "(Lead, Cadmium, Arsenic)" and "The Toxicity of Schizophrenia Victims and Psychosis" 1988 and 1990 sold 370 of 400.; [pers.] "To be a good writer you must experience life, as we add years, experiences, we have more to write about." "To get published it takes tenacity and knowing a publishers, I suspect..." I have 3 completed non fiction manuscripts 100 pages each long sent out to Publishers for 2 yrs. now.; [a.] Federal Way, WA

FALCO, JOSEPH
[b.] November 28, 1955, Passaic, NJ; [p.] Alice, Joseph; [ed.] William Paterson College, Wayne, NJ, BA History 1984; [occ.] Teacher of Social Studies; [memb.] NJEA; [hon.] 1988-Award of Excellence Senator Bill Bradley's Geography Awareness Contest, 1991-Selected to appear in Who's Who Among America's Teachers, 1996-Selected to appear in Who's Who Among America's Teachers; [oth. writ.] Wrote three books of poetry: Sacred Ground (1992), A Man of My Words (1993), Chasing Sunsets (1994). Books published by: Weir Here Productions Saddle Brook, NJ; [pers.] I strive to reflect my many interests in my writings. My hobbies include: reading, conservation, music, native American culture, photography, etc.; [a.] Saddle Brook, NJ

FARMON, FRANCES C .
[pen.] Scoop Morale ;[b.] August 21,1958, Cleveland,OH ;[p.]Beverly Farmon and Gontry Farmon ;[ed.] Jane Addam Vocational High, Cleveland,OH, June 10,1977, Excoliso spring job corp- 1981. Lincoln University BS-Radio-TV-199 ;[occ.] Residential Advisor at Exculison Spring Job Corp ;[memb.] Sigma Gamma RNO Soronity Inc, Audio Consul ant First world communications president NJCAA exclusio spring NJAA exculison spring Cnapton, Member Spark Bureau ;[hon.] most flexiable R/A, from Job Corp 199 Oustanding Award TN Cleaniness of both Dorm 1994 to radio announcer, 1983 ;[oth.writ.] Just recently recieve m copy-right lincense for my books of poems. The best of scoo morale the best of Fran Farmon. ;[pers.] I believe in myse and my talent. You can suceed through struggles and har knocks. If you don't go down that road again. Gladstone,MC

FARNHAM, CARON
[b.] October 29, 1962, Australia; [p.] Joy and Jim Farnham [ed.] Palm Beach - Currumbin High; [occ.] Retired Commer cial Fisherman: Traveller/Surfer; [memb.] In Classica R.A.D. Ballet and Women's Olympic Gymnastics; [hon. "International poet of Merit" for 1996 "Editor's Choice Award for 1996 by "The National Library of Poetry"; [oth. writ.] M writings have appeared within the following books: "A Muse To Follow", "The Best Poems of The '90's", "The Bes Poems of 1997", published by the National Library of Poetry "Famous Poems Of The Twentieth century" published by the Famous Poets Society. My words are available on audio cassette "The Sound Of Poetry" recorded by the Nationa Library of poetry: And aired on "Poetry Today" broadcasted by New York City; [pers.] Keep life simply there lies withir beauty and truth.; [a.] Haleiwa, HI

FELAN, ALBERTO S.
[b.] July 31, 1949, Robstown, TX; [p.] Guadalupe Felan anc Petra Salazar; [m.] (Ex Wife) Paula Gallardo, January 4 1971; [ch.] Seven; [ed.] Three weeks into the fourth grade [a.] Lone Wolf, OK

FENSTERMACHER, MARY WISHAM
[b.] April 11, 1952, Bridgeton, NJ; [p.] Charles D. Wisham and Mildred W. Wisham; [m.] Todd Edward Fenstermacher September 2, 1972; [ch.] April Dawn, Angela Marie, Abigai May, Aaron matthew, Arik David; [ed.] Bridgeton High School (N.J.) 1970, Catawba College (N.C.) 1970-72, Kutztown State University, B.S. in El. Ed. '95; [occ.] Elem. Education - substitute, teaching piano lessons, Home schooling; [memb. Home start Home school Support Group, Member portfolio review committee; [hon.] N. J. Girls State Delegate '69, Babe Ruth Sportsmanship Award '70 (H.S.) Ellsworth J. C. Flexer Scholarship '75 and '76, Magna Cum Laude (KSU), Editor's Choice Award from National Library of Poetry, May '96, Elected to International Poetry Hall of Fame, Oct. 1, 1996.; [oth. writ.] Nine poems scheduled for publication in the National Library of Poetry Anthology series, 1996 and 1997 eight other poems have been purchased by Lillenas Publishing Co. articles and stories for Institute of Children's Literature Writing Course.; [pers.] Language is a special gift from the Lord. It is my desire to use this gift to bring on understanding of God's salvation, love, and hope to others.; [a.] West Peru, ME

FERNANDEZ, RACHEL
[b.] June 25, 1980, Rene, NV; [p.] Dianne Fernandez and Alex Fernandez; [ed.] Attending Reed High School in Sparks, NV. Graduate in 1998; [occ.] Student; [pers.] Thanks to my friends and family for supporting my writing. I think that the human race communicates, quietly, through poetry, and maybe it will help us understand one another more and finally bring long-awaited peace.; [a.] Sparks, NV

FIFE, CHARLOTTE A.
[b.] March 24, 1943, Hamilton Co., IN; [p.] Ralph and Thelma (McRoberts) Padgett; [m.] James E. Fife, December 4, 1983; [ch.] Lisa L. (Anderson) Saulmon, James L. Anderson Jr. and Shelly C. Anderson; [ed.] Lebanon High and Indiana Vocational Technical College; [occ.] Retired (Volunteer Work); [memb.] Otterbein United Methodist Church, Sheridan Order of Eastern Star, Literacy Action Group of Boone County; [hon.] Editor's Choice Awards, (Previous Publications); [oth. writ.] Several poems published in local newspapers and the poem "Home" in the book The Rainbow's End as well as the poem "My Friend" in the collection "The Best Poems of the '90's".; [pers.] The poem included in this collection is one I wrote for my youngest daughter, Shelly when she and her husband, Tim were married. I enjoy writing about events which are important to me, my family, and my friends.; [a.] Lebanon, IN

FILLION, LUKE
[b.] October 16, 1978, Hamilton, ON, Canada; [p.] David and Janis Fillion; [ed.] Westdale Secondary School, Hamilton, Ontario; [memb.] The Bach Elgar Choral Society's Vox Nouveau, I.S.P., The Gay, Lesbian and Bi-sexual Alliance at McMaster (GLBAM); [hon.] Academic Proficiency Award - 1996 Westdale Secondary School, Editor's Choice Award (1995 NLP); [oth. writ.] Two poems published by the N.L.P., many unpublished poems; [pers.] The world could be a much better place if we would learn to love one another regardless of physical, social or emotional differences.; [a.] Hamilton, Ontario, Canada

FINGER, JOHN
[b.] June 14, 1919, Wyomissing, PA; [p.] Mabel and Carl Finger; [m.] Virginia H., June 16, 1945; [ch.] Five (3 boys and 2 girls); [ed.] B.S. in Mechanical Eng.; [occ.] Trying to recuperate from bone and lung cancer; [memb.] ASME, ASMA Phi Kappa Sigma; [oth. writ.] Same as last year NLOP; [pers.] Operate Art Gallery of 200 oil paintings in Beresford S.D.; [a.] Beresford, SD

FITZPATRICK, MAUREEN
[b.] August 25, 1936, British, Guiana; [p.] Deceased (Van Sertima of dutch descent); [m.] Divorced, June 8, 1963; [ch.] Three; [ed.] Diploma in Public Communication University of Guyana, Diploma Executive Secretary Canada College; [occ.] Freelance Writer; [memb.] Writers Group, Markham, ON, Canada; [hon.] First Prize Poetry, second prize short story National Newspapers Guyana; [oth. writ.] "Peace" (poem) "Adieu" (short story) Several articles published in House Journal in Guyana.; [pers.] Others going through adversity should know they are not alone - also where there is life, there is hope. Love music especially Chopin, Beethoven, Schuman.; [a.] Richmond Hill, NY

FLANIGAN, TAMMY
[b.] November 19, 1971, Arkansas Pass, TX; [p.] Buster and Linda Flanigan; [ed.] First grade to the 9th grade; [hon.] Editor's Choice Award for Outstanding Achievement in Poetry; [oth. writ.] Four of my other poems are published in four different books.; [pers.] This poem is dedicated to the only woman I ever loved. This poem is dedicated to the memory of my mother whom I love with all my heart. God take care of her for me.; [a.] Ingleside, TX

FLEMING, DAVID MCADAM
[pen.] D. M. Fleming; [b.] May 13, 1971, Boston; [ed.] BA, Wheaton College; [oth. writ.] Two poems: Landscape" and "Wide Iris", unpublished collection in progress; [pers.] Thanks for taking the time to care coffee's on me.; [a.] Boston, MA

FLEMING, RHONDA
[b.] September 13, 1962, Windsor, MO; [p.] Larry and Mary Fleming; [ed.] University of Texas at Arlington School of Nursing; [occ.] Nurse; [memb.] Association of Operating Room Nurses; [oth. writ.] Several poems published in youth magazines, high school and college publications, and in "Amidst the Splendor" and "Essence of a Dream" by the National Library of Poetry; [pers.] A wise woman builds her own home, but with her own hands, the foolish one tears hers down, Proverbs 14:1; [a.] Irving, TX

FLEMING, SANDRA
[b.] April 22, 1952, Chippewa Falls, WS; [p.] Ray and Marty Masopust; [m.] Mike Fleming, April 20, 1974; [ch.] Michelle, Jon; [ed.] St. Joseph High School; [hon.] Editor's Choice Award presented by the National Library of Poetry; [oth. writ.] Take My Hand published in "Portraits of Life"; [pers.] My work reflects who I am my feelings, what's in my heart people who read my poems, probably know me better than anyone.; [a.] Madison, MS

FLORES, ELIZABETH L.
[b.] Sanderson, TX; [p.] Simon and Gloria Lopez; [m.] Adolfo Flores, November 22, 1959; [ch.] Michael Anthony Flores and Kathryn Marie Flores, grandchildern: Gabriel Simon and Brooke Ashley Iverson; [ed.] BA Early Childhood/Special Ed. from Arizona State University, Arizona State University, Education, Bilingual/ESL; [occ.] Clint ISD, Desert Hills Elem.; [hon.] Graduated "cum laude" from Arizona State University. Award of Scholastic Excellence by the faculty of the Department of Education at Arizona State Univ., Selected by TEA (Texas Education Agency) and the Departmento de Educacion y Ciencia de Madrid to participate in the III Summer Institute on Children's Literature at the Universidad Complutense in Madrid, Spain. Who's Who Among Hispanic Americans 1992-93.; [oth. writ.] "La Tortilla Hulda" (The Runaway Tortilla), 1981 published by Donor's Production, "Poema de Amor a Papa," 1988, Father's Day, Today's Catholic. "From Civil War Archives," a story of Hispanic valor, Vista Magazine, 1990. Poem "A Daughter's Gift" published by the National Library of Poetry, 1995, in East of the Sunrise. Poem "Godspeed, Little Baby, Godspeed," published by the National Library of Poetry, 1995, in At Water's Edge.; [pers.] Reason I write, when something or someone touches that inner core in my very being, I write. I am in the process of writing some children's stories and a children's book of poems, some in Spanish, some in England. My students are the best critics and very "honest".

FORD, CARL
[b.] August 22, 1973, Boston, MA; [p.] Susan Batson (Mother); [ed.] B.A. in Political Science took creative writing courses at N.Y.U.; [occ.] Production Assistant Filmmaker; [oth. writ.] Just The Two of Us (screenplay); [pers.] Cultural expression, and the honest side of humanity as my forte.; [a.] New York City, NY

FOSTER, DAVID E.
[b.] May 16, 1977; [p.] Cecil and Nancy Foster; [ed.] Armherst County High School; [occ.] Foster's Septic and Excavating; [memb.] International Society of Poets; [hon.] Editor's Choice Award presented by Editor The National Library of Poetry; [oth. writ.] Poem Dancers published in Admist The Splendor; [pers.] I just enjoy writing poems.; [a.] Monroe, VA

FOUCAULT, MARY FRANCIS FAITH
[b.] March 23, 1951, Everett, WA; [p.] Deceased; [ch.] Chas age 21; [ed.] High School; [memb.] Lifetime Member of Songwriters Club of America; this has nothing to do with writing, but I also am a member of the Humane Society of the

United States; [hon.] Awards from Jeff Roberts Publishing Company, NCA Records National Library of Poetry; [oth. writ.] I have been published several times, and sold a couple of children's poems, wrote songs on records and tapes.; [pers.] I like to bring people joy their my poems; I hope they enjoy reading them as much as I'm enjoyed writing them.; [a.] Seattle, WA

FOWLKES, BRENDA D.
[hon.] 1st Place in Essay Contest, Drawings in School Publications.; [oth. writ.] A poem in Through The Hourglass; [a.] Meadow Grove, NE

FRAVEL, KEVIN D.
[pen.] D. W. Brooks; [b.] April 29, 1968, Waverly, NY; [ed.] Temple University; [occ.] Software Engineer; [oth. writ.] Many, many poems and stories. (Unpublished).; [pers.] So many words, so little ink.; [a.] Bristol, PA

FRAZIER, MR. CHARLES
[b.] December 29, 1953, Greensboro, GA; [p.] Mrs. Eulon Gray; [ed.] Boggs Academy Keysville, Georgia - Class 1972 Seton Hull U. South Orange, NB class 1985 Essex county College CAC Councillor; [occ.] Laid off Security Person Due to being sick too long; [memb.] American Legion Post 22 West Orange, MT, Democratic National Committee 1996 Contributions member, East Orange UT, American Red Cross Citations Tech Volunteer; [hon.] Rookie of the Year, Cable Visions 1989-1994 Volunteer TV production - 32 and 1 year Comcast same company new name; [oth. writ.] Poems Bomb one plus one two plus c/o written five star music masters - of Boston 1. Fire Forgotten love (2) I got to find peace of mind (3) On For The Love Of You; [pers.] Love of God, Love of Nation, Love of Family, Love of Women's, Love of New Life, Love of home; [a.] Orange, NJ

FRECHETTE, DANIEL STEPHEN
[b.] February 9, 1979, Farmington Hills, MI; [p.] Daniel C. Frechette, Teresa M. Frechette; [ed.] Edsel B. Ford High School, future plans to attend Western Michigan University in fall of 1997; [memb.] Michigan Democratic Party, Medical Explorers, Drama Club, Edsel Ford high school band and Orchestra, swing chorus, science olympiad; [hon.] Honor Roll, 1st chair in band and Orchestra tenor 1 in swing chorus, rank leader in Marching band, Co-Editor of the Edsel Ford High School Literary Magazine; [oth. writ.] Many poems published in the Edsel Ford High School Literary Magazines and a short story published in the magazine.; [pers.] My poems express my feelings towards egotistical and selfish individuals. My goal is to coerce my readers into a state of catharsis. I have been influenced by E. A. Poe.; [a.] Dearborn, MI

FREEMAN, KRYSTAL
[b.] February 18, 1985, New York City; [p.] Charisse Collier; [ed.] PS 201, PS 24, PS 169, PS 214, now attending PS 214 (Alpha Program for Gifted Children); [hon.] Yearly honor roll (1st-5th grade), Brotherhood Poster Contest, Artistry Exhibited in Sotheby's, and Lever House, poetry published in school newspapers.; [oth. writ.] "Our United Colors", "The World At Our Hands"; [a.] Flushing, Queens, NY

FREEMER, MICHAEL
[pen.] Robert Henry Malraux; [b.] March 15, 1972, Groton, CT; [p.] Raymond and Linda Freemer (Divorced); [ed.] Three Rivers Community College, Community College of Rhode Island, University of Rhode Island; [occ.] Discharge Operator, APC America Inc., Undergraduate student at URI; [memb.] International Society of Poets; [hon.] Dean's List; [oth. writ.] Several poems published by The National Library of Poetry and numerous stories in progress.; [pers.] I am, quite gradually, going deaf.; [a.] Westerly, RI

FRIEBEN, KERRY
[pen.] J. B. Quinn; [b.] April 1, 1972, Madison, WI; [p.] B. and Lynn Frieben; [m.] Angela Frieben, August 21, 199?; [ch.] Savannah; [ed.] BA Psychology, MSW Clinical Socia Work; [occ.] Therapist; [memb.] NASW; [oth. writ.] Octobe Breeze, Contemporary Insanity, Behind the Hall, Ocean c Sand; [a.] Wayland, MI

FRITZ, CAROLYN
[pen.] Carolyn Bammert Fritz; [b.] December 1, 1944 Menomonie, WI; [p.] Rupert Bammert and Jeannette Tibbett Bammert; [ch.] Gregory Michael, Ronald James, Jeremia Aaron, Isaac Benjamin, Carrie Jeannette, six grandchildre - 4 boys and 2 girls - and another on the way; [hon.] Editor' Choice Award thanks, National Library of Poetry 1996; [oth writ.] Poetry and children's stories, two poems published i Anthologies 1994 and 1996.; [pers.] This poem is dedicate to Nico Demus. In my poetry I write what I feel and abou life. Hopefully others can relate and find my words touch then too.; [a.] Shepherd, MT

FUMIC, MARY
[pen.] Maria Fumic; [b.] April 1, 1940, Dalmatia, Croatia; [p. Marko and Marica Samardzic; [m.] Vjekoslav Fumic, Janu ary 20, 1968; [ed.] Grammar School; [occ.] Housewife [memb.] Tamburitza - Dance Group "Croatian Vines", Ange Guardian Catholic Church, 700 Club; [hon.] Honored by th Lerner Neighborhood newspaper as a Person of the Month [oth. writ.] You are My Guiding Light, It was Only a Dream My Meado; [pers.] Life is like a big test at school. You knov it's hard, but you have to do it, if you fail cheer up. For toda you learn how to past the test for a better tomorrow. To giv up it's so easy.; [a.] Chicago, IL

FURR, AUDREY T.
[b.] April 16, 1928, Charlotte, NC; [p.] James T. Tarlton an Annie M. Carpenter; [m.] Colen L. Furr (Deceased), Octobe 19, 1946; [ch.] Joy F. Tucker and Linda F. Mullis; [ed. Peachland High School; [occ.] Retired; [memb.] VIP Suppor Group; [hon.] An Editor's Choice Award in "A Break in th Clouds" and nominated for "Poet of the Year 1995"; [oth. writ Published in "Best Poems of 1996", "A Break in the Clouds" and "Outstanding Poets of 1994", poetry printed in loca newspapers, many pieces written for the VIP Support Group friends and family who inspire me, and poetry written fo social affairs and occasions.; [pers.] My writing fills a voi in my life brought on by my impaired vision and brain tumor My writing is a source of inspiration and strength to me.; [a. Stanfield, NC

FUTTER, ELZIE ELIECE
[pen.] E F '96 Ft. Bragg Ca; [b.] Houston, TX; [p.] Walter anc Frances Alton; [m.] Irvin C. Futter, Ed.D, February 1948 [ch.] Six; [ed.] R.N. Registered Nurse, specialty - surgery [occ.] Retired R.N.; [memb.] San Francisco State University Women's Auxiliary; [hon.] Honorary Member of Trumar Society. I loved that man!; [oth. writ.] Usual types of shor articles while being Editor of Tuberculosis Sanatorium news paper weekly in the 1930.; [pers.] I believe that true strength lies in being gentle and getting away with it.; [a.] Fort Bragg CA

GAKEN, LINDSAY RAE
[b.] June 1, 1977, Ann Arbor, MI; [p.] Lawrence and Mary Gaken; [ed.] Graduated from Chelsea High, currently a Sophomore at Washtenaw Community College.; [occ.] Asst Manager at a fast food restaurant; [hon.] Several literary awards and honorable mentions.; [oth. writ.] Short stories, songs and book ideas.; [pers.] Believe in yourself and you can achieve anything!; [a.] Chelsea, MI

GALLETLY, SANDRA L.
[b.] May 22, 1947, Klamath Falls, OR; [p.] Chester O. Brown and Mary L. Brown; [ch.] Christy Lynn, Tessie Kay, Carrlie Marie; [ed.] Graduate of Wyandotte High School; [occ.] President, Founder and Owner of National and International Research and Development.; [memb.] Sterling Member of Sterling Who's Who, Member of the Research Board of Advisors of the American Biographical Institute, Inc.; [hon.] 1995 Honoree International Who's Who of Professional and Business Women Fourth Edition, The International Poetry Hall of Fame; [oth. writ.] Previous poems published through the national library of poetry.; [pers.] I strive to achieve all that I can so others may also prosper.; [a.] Leavenworth, KS

GALVIN, MILDRED L.
[b.] September 24,1917, Natick, MA. ;[p.] Mary Jane and Fred Griffin ;[m.] Irving H. Galvin, May 20,1939 ;[ch.] Joan, Bob, Barry, Judy, Tim, Brian, David ;[ed.]High school ;[occ.] housewife ;[hon.] Blessed with a wonderful marriage and seven wonderful children. I consider this lifes highest honor and award ;[pers.] I find it easier to express my thoughts abour special things in poetry. ; [a.] Miami, FL.

GARCIA, MARIO
[b.] February 4, 1979, Pueblo, CO; [p.] Eloy and Tina Garcia; [ed.] Centennial High School; [occ.] Student, Senior; [memb.] R.O.T.C. (Centennial); [hon.] 3rd Place in State Wide Science projects. Several 2nd place ribbons in Wood Caving at age four and five.; [oth. writ.] Poems published in Mile High Society of Poetry 3 times in The National Library of Poetry.; [pers.] Strive everyday for time is virtuous.; [a.] Pueblo, CO

GARRETSON, JOHANNA A.
[b.] January 14, 1917, Java Dutch, E. Indies; [p.] Jan and Fien Van Haastert; [m.] John Garretson Dutch American, May 4, 1954; [ch.] Two sons; [ed.] Junior College in Indonesia and Assistant Librarian; [occ.] Retired house - wife (I'm 80 years old); [memb.] The National Library of Poetry; [hon.] 15 Yrs. as a volunteer at Palomar Hospital in Escondido, CA; [oth. writ.] None just poems since 1994; [pers.] I love nature and the God, who created it.; [a.] San Dimas, CA

GARVIN, ANNETTE VESSEY
[b.] September 22, 1944, Seattle, WA; [p.] Lydia Starkel Vessey, Russell Melvold Vessey,; [m.] Marrion Edwin Garvin, June 14, 1980; [ch.] Lenora F. Davis, Deborah A. Laux; [ed.] Rona, Mt. High School, Computer School, Mat-Su College, Palmer, Alaska, International Bible Student, Watchtower Society, NY; [occ.] Management of Rural Development/WA, CAHR Housing; [memb.] International Bible Student, Watchtower Society of NYC, NY; [hon.] Computer Course Achievement, Star FMHA (CAHR) Management; [oth. writ.] Poetry, Research of Genealogy support writings for "Vessey" book.; [pers.] The privilege of proclaiming the `Restoration of Peace' upon the earth by our powerful creator.; [a.] Anacortes, WA

GEESLIN, WENDY ELAINE
[b.] April 28, 1982, Ashburn, GA; [p.] Lela Layfield and Fred Geeslin; [ed.] Wilcox County High; [memb.] Beta Club, SGA - Student Government Association, Pleasant View Baptist Church; [hon.] A average Honor Roll, T.T.B.S. Math Award, Science Award, P.E. Award; [oth. writ.] Poems called "Love" and "Fear".; [pers.] I try to do my best and live life to the fullest.; [a.] Rochelle, GA

GIBSON, OLIVIA CARPENTER
[pen.] Olivia Carpenter-Gibson; [b.] August 18, 1952, Atlanta, GA; [p.] Robert E. and Mildred D. Carpenter; [ch.] Mark Davis Gibson; [ed.] Decatur High School, Young Harris College. Georgia Baptist School of Nursing; [oth. writ.] "We Are Never Alone" pub. In Dappled Sunlight; [a.] Lothonia, GA

GIBSON, WILLIAM ARTHUR
[ed.] Bachelor of Music in Instrumental Performance, California State University, Los Angeles; [occ.] Songwriter, Guitarist, Vocalist, Producer; [memb.] Golden Key National Honor Society, National Academy of Songwriters, ASCAP; [hon.] Honorable Mention Awards and Semi-Finalist Awards in the Billboard Song Contest and the Mid-Atlantic Song Contest

GILLEY, KAREN
[pen.] Lilly Gilley; [b.] April 22, 1949, Chicago, IL; [p.] Philip Gilley, (Dr.) Jean Pearson Gilley; [ed.] Had 12 years of schooling, received High School Diploma, 2 yrs. of Jr. College, got Cert. of Completion, for College, have taken classes at night.; [occ.] Have a wide variety of skills, was in food serv. - 25 yrs. as a dishwasher.; [memb.] I am a member of the Smithsonian Ins. and Lit. Foc. of Poetry for the past 1 year, also, have been asked to be member in The Int. Soc. of Poetry's Hall of Fame.; [hon.] Have received 4 Editor's Choice Awards, Have lots of Credits, was in Outstanding Poet and many others. I enjoy the importance we all share.; [oth. writ.] Over 6 years, I've had a lot of poems published in anthologies. Cader and the Int. Soc. of Poetry. Am almost done re-writing my first book, Heartfelt Emotions - Also have done art but want to re-write them.; [pers.] In life, there are many things a person feels; poetry for everyone will help promote peace, while bringing enjoyment and fulfillment to others. So I feel if a person believes in something, they should follow their heart and conscience.; [a.] Leominster, MA

GLENNON, SISTER ALICE MARY
[b.] September 4, 1927, Laurel, MT; [p.] Leo and Laura Glennon; [ed.] B.S. in Education L.P.W.; [occ.] Retired; [oth. writ.] Book of Poetry, Walk With Wonder; [pers.] Poetry, nature sources of inspiration, Poetry and nature have always been sources of inspiration in my life so it comes naturally for me to combine them. My love of nature seems to be expressed best in poetry. It makes me happy inside when I am able to put into words the beauty I see just as I'm sure an artist must feel when putting such beauty into a picture or a statue. This is a gift I've been given, and no one is more aware of this than I am. When I read what I have written, I'm amazed to think that I really wrote those words. If I can give pleasure to others when they read what I have written, then I feel I am using my gift as God intends that I should. He will know, then, how grateful I am.; [a.] Billings, MT

GLOVER, M. J.
[pen.] M.J. Glover; [b.] January 27, 1939, Pittsburgh, PA; [p.] John and Arabella Collington; [m.] Charles Glover, January 5, 1986; [ch.] Edward, Frederick, Charles, Michelle, Nicole; [ed.] 2 yrs. college (assoc. degree program), Temple U. 1977; [occ.] Housewife, poet, songwriter; [memb.] Covenant Community Tabernacle Church (expediter), and hospitality coordinator; [hon.] Honorary doctoral degree — University of Pittsburgh; Meld Program 1991; [oth. writ.] "Mother's Day of Rest" a short story; "Jeffie" a short story used to teach metamorphosis to very young children; "Black and a Woman" poem turned song; [pers.] My joy comes from seeing others happy.; [a.] Philadelphia, PA

GOLDTHWAITE, MILDRED H.
[b.] November 2, 1912, Tonawanda, NY; [p.] Deceased (Gustav); [m.] Deceased, July 25, 1939; [ch.] Four sons, Roger, Richard, Arnold, Ronald; [ed.] Genesee Hospital School of Nursing, Rochester NY, Clinical Lab. Course, S.F. Calif., Med, Steno Course Palo Alto, CA, Several Bible Correspondence Courses; [occ.] Retired RN and Missionary Emeritus of Los Gatos Christian Church, Los Gatos, CA. Volunteer grader of Bible Correspondence Lessons to prison inmates for A.R.M. (American Rehabilitation Ministry);

[memb.] Los Gatos Christian Church - 4th years active all Church activities, other Christian areas, Camps, Bay Area, Calif., etc; [hon.] Untold blessings from the Lord throughout my fruitful years, which no human award could measure up to...although praise has been given for poem dedication of 3 churches - one in Africa.; [oth. writ.] "Bless The Lord O My Soul" (poems). "Once In The Blood" - Nursing article. Stories (XI years) of missionary work for "Central Africa Story" (Central Africa Mission).; [pers.] "In his time when all is ready, it will come to pass"...prayer (even heart desire) answered...I know! - when at age 58 ("I'm too old Lord") He led me to Rhodesia, Africa, where for 21 years I was closer to being in Heaven than hoped for, dreamt, or imagined, and I would not trade, change, alter any of it! "Thanks Lord, But...how old is old?"; [a.] Joplin, MO

GOOD, MARGARET
[b.] February 4, 1933, New Mexico; [p.] Claude and Bertha Brown; [m.] Paul W. Good, 1962; [ch.] Three; [ed.] Two years college; [occ.] Retired Secretary; [memb.] Word runners (writing group) ISP, Genealogy Club, Gem and Mineral Club; [hon.] Scholarship to Harding University Girls State Rep. - High School; [oth. writ.] Published in High School Poetry Anthologies, College Poetry Anthologies, NLP Anthologies, several Local Newspapers, 2 religious papers my own book "Wings of Flight".; [pers.] I write about things with which I am familiar, nature, religion, specific events. My 6th grade teacher got me started writing poetry in 1945.; [a.] Stephenville, TX

GOODE, ROBERT H.
[b.] December 12, 1935, Elkins, WV; [p.] Arley Wesley Goode, Goldia (Hartsaw) Goode; [m.] Mary L. (Coberly) Goode - Deceased, December 24, 1953; [ch.] Robert Wesley Goode, Pamela L. (Morgan) Goode; [ed.] High School Graduate 1953; [occ.] Meat Cutter; [memb.] Local 347 - Union Methodist Church VFW; [oth. writ.] Poetry that has never been published working on a book the title "The High Hills Of God".; [pers.] Life is a dream and when you awake you realize it is the beginning of a new day.; [a.] Elkins, WV

GORDON, BRIAN
[pen.] Jacob Casey; [b.] June 20, 1970, Chicago; [p.] Bill and Rena Schoon; [ed.] Locke Elementary, Lane Tech, Wilber Wright College; [occ.] Upholstery, Woodwork, Construction; [memb.] Writers Digest Book Club, Shepherds Chapel; [hon.] Editor's Choice Award for Outstanding Achievement in Poetry; [oth. writ.] The Man's Battle, The Child's Triumph, Silent Stalker Of The Night. I Shed My Last Tear. The Knowledge Of Time, Rainy Days, Changes.; [a.] Chicago, IL

GORMAN, GEORGINA GRACE
[pen.] "Three G,G,G's"; [b.] Aquarian, London; [ch.] Three; [oth. writ.] Since 1979, I have written approx 70 poems, which I hope to eventually publish. Subjects varied. Nature, love, compassion, humility, and "Things of Beauty".; [pers.] Without choice: Regardless it's subject always prepared with the knowledge that poems of true worth, contain a required substance, which ultimately, upon completion include along the way, through some mysterious enclosure the giving and taking of a piece of one's heart and soul.; [a.] Toronto, Ontario, Canada

GOSSETT, JAMES D.
[pen.] Jim; [b.] August 13, 1986, Los Angeles, CA; [p.] Bobby G. Gossett (Deceased) and Donna Anderson; [ed.] Pelham High School; [occ.] Industrial Electrical and Waiter; [oth. writ.] Several poems published in local newspapers.; [pers.] I write what I feel inside at certain times in my life and from others expenses.; [a.] Thomasville, GA

GRAFFEO, SALLY ANN ZACCONE
[b.] December 11, 1959, Brooklyn, NY; [p.] Serafino and Anna Marie Zaccone; [m.] Giuseppe Graffeo, June 1980; [ch.] Michael, Salvatore, Rita Maria, Anna Marie, and Christina; [ed.] Christ The King Regional H.S. Middle Village, NY; [oth. writ.] Moments In Time, published in Portraits of Life.; [pers.] Dedicated to my children, who are always an inspiration in my life.; [a.] Queens, NY

GRAINGER, RUSTY
[b.] September 8, 1949, Toronto, Ontario; [p.] William and Kathleen Dunlop; [m.] Nancy Grainger, March 22, 1975; [ch.] Yvonne Nancy, Andrea Leah, Elaine Frances, Justin Lee; [ed.] Eastern High School of Commerce, George Brown College of Applied Arts and Technology, The Institute of Children Literature; [occ.] Owner of N and R Services Plus A Janitorial Services Company; [memb.] Merrill Wolfe Leadership Program, Distinguished Member - Int. Society of Poets; [hon.] Award of Merit - United Way Award of Distinction - United Way Editor's Choice Award, National Library of Poetry, Citation of Community Service United Way; [oth. writ.] Numerous poems, article published in Edmonton Journal, Human Resource Manual, Article for Trade Journal, Children's Stories; [pers.] "Eternal Day" is written in the memory of my son, Justin (09-27-85 to 09-08-94) He is the Phoenix! Though my youngest child, he has taken the ultimate journey.; [a.] Sherwood Park, Alberta, Canada

GRAMLICH, RICHARD A.
[b.] August 30, 1973, Veterans Memorial Wanton, IO; [p.] Robert and Diane Gramlich; [ed.] High School graduate, Ree High, Lansing; [occ.] Factory worker; [hon.] Outstanding Speech Student Plaque; [oth. writ.] Two poems previously published by the National Library of Poetry and a regular entertainment column in my school paper until I graduated.; [pers.] I strive to write from the heart with the intention of touching every soul I can. Live life as an exclamation, not an explanation.; [a.] Lansing, IA

GRAVES, RUE CEIL
[pen.] Rue Ceil Graves; [b.] May 10, 1924, Boone, IA; [p.] Glenn Ross and Bess Ross; [m.] Charles C. Graves, June 23, 1949; [ch.] Melani Gwen, Marcilu; [ed.] Boone High, Drake Un. (Elem Ed) Des Moines, IA, Clover Park Tech (Day Care Spec.) Tacoma, WA; [occ.] Retired (was owner of Roto Rooter) now work with foreign students (was sec. to Teen Life Intn'l); [memb.] DAR, Peninsula Christian, Fellowship Church, Intn'l Soc. of Poets; [hon.] Letter for cheerleader with identical twin sister for: High school, Jr. High, Jr. College and Drake Un in Des Moines, IA "Editors Choice Award" from the Nat'l Lib. of Poetry for 1996 in "Recollections of Yesterday"; [oth. writ.] Poems in church monthly newspaper, also for Birthdays, funerals, D.A.R. etc. and Intn'l. Soc. of Poets; [pers.] My desire is to reflect God's love in my poems, and bring glory to His name.; [a.] Tacoma, WA

GREEN, CHRISTINA
[pen.] Tina; [b.] August 27, 1960, California; [p.] Willie and Carole Chapman; [m.] Carl Green; [ch.] Jennifer, Dylan and Dustin; [occ.] At home mother; [oth. writ.] M.I.A. in of Sunshine and Day Dreams 1996; [a.] Manassas, VA

GRESHAM, MARVIN
[pen.] "Watcher"; [b.] January 9, 1956, Chicago; [p.] Willie and Florence Gresham; [m.] Diana, January 22, 1992; [ch.] Seven - 5 girls and 2 boys; [ed.] Bowen High School; [occ.] Business Owner and Construction Worker; [hon.] Previous winner of Editor's Choice Awards; [oth. writ.] Presently working on a book of poetry to be publish.; [pers.] We should all love one another. For with love the world will grow and flourish.; [a.] Chicago, IL

GRIFFIN, JOAN M.
[b.] September 17, 1932, Toronto, Ont., Canada; [p.] Herbert and Sarah Rose; [m.] D.J. Griffin (Deceased Feb. 5/92), September 29, 1950; [ch.] Donald and Brenda, grandchildren - Shawn, Trevor and Sherisse Sequeira; [memb.] Life-time member: Church of Universal Love; [hon.] National Library of Poetry, "The Sound of Poetry" selected four times, 4 Editor's Choice Awards; [oth. writ.] Book of poetry published 1977 "Thy Nature So Deep", Articles and Poetry - Church of Universal Love's News Letters.; [pers.] I believe the focus in creative constructive energy and bringing forward that expression helps to serve within the growth of one personally, further helping within the welfare of mankind and of our world.; [a.] Toronto, Ontario, Canada

GRIFFIN, ROBERT
[pen.] Mr. Arrgee; [b.] October 19, 1918, Danby, MO; [p.] Tom and Stella Griffin; [m.] Helene Griffin, March 19, 1944; [ch.] Jeff Griffin; [ed.] 2 yr. College GED; [occ.] Retired; [memb.] American Military Society. Fleet Reserve Association. National Family Caregivers Association. Well Spouse Foundation. Multiple Sclerosis Society of America.; [hon.] Just military awards for 20 years under the sea on submarines. My old home and I went to hell and back together many times in 1942 and '43, and she's still on patrol at the bottom of the Pacific. I miss her very much, because a part of me is still down there with her.; [oth. writ.] Just the wit and wisdom of "Mr. Arrgee Says"; [pers.] I have fought our Wars, and now I find it's very sad that our once great Nation is in the throes of the rise and fall of the Roman Empire re-visited. At my age, however, I have no more mountains to climb - I'm already on the other side of the mountain, and, Hurray, the rest of the way is all down hill, on my way to rest of the way is all down hill, on my way to a far better place. There is always "Good" and "Bad" in everything. Take Today for example - one thing Bad about Today is that I'll never again be as young as I was yesterday. But the Good part reminds me that Today I'm one day closer to Heaven than I was yesterday.; [a.] Keystone Heights, FL

GRISWOLD, WANDA V.
[b.] November 9, 1920, Harrisburg, IL; [p.] Otto Wilson, Evah Wilson; [m.] John L. Griswold, November 6, 1937; [ch.] Judith Gaye, Lestalee, Toni Gail; [ed.] High School; [occ.] Retired; [memb.] First Southern Baptist Church Roranna, IL; [hon.] My award is the blessing of having been a housewife and mother and raised three wonderful daughters, who today know the Lord and live in His will.; [oth. writ.] Have written poems over the years, but just as enjoyment for myself and my family.; [pers.] These poem have been written only as I have been inspired by God to put on paper what I am feeling in my heart.; [a.] Wood River, IL

HAEUSSLER, MRS. ROSE ANN
[b.] May 20, 1961, Windsor; [p.] Florence and James Ferguson; [m.] Richard Haeussler, June 26, 1982; [ch.] Jenifer, Adam, Emily, Charles and Eric; [ed.] Walkerville High, St. Clair College; [occ.] Housewife; [memb.] Women Writers of Windsor; [hon.] Two Editors Choice Awards for 1995 (The National Library Of Poetry) for poems Communication, and Embracing the Light. Two Editor's Choice Awards for 1996 poems, Fences, Our Love; Published in Best Poems Of the '90s, A Sensuous Love; [oth. writ.] Communication pub. - Sparkles In The Sand, Embracing The Light pub. - The Path Not Taken, Fences pub. - Shadows and Light, The Birth Of An Idea pub. - Believe In Yourself, And A Little Miracle pub. in The Ebbing Tide, Our Love - pub. Portraits Of Life.; [pers.] Write from the heart, let all your true feelings out.

HALDENWANG, DAVID R.
[b.] September 11, 1978, West Islip, NY; [p.] Albert and Deborah Haldenwang; [ed.] West Brook Elementary, Beach Street Junior High, West Islip High School, Nassau Community College; [occ.] Grand Union Associate; [oth. writ.] Poems: Emotions, Paradise, Marijuana, Illusions Disarrayed. Stories: Childhood Playgrounds. Some of my other works are published in the West Islip High School "Spectrum"; [pers.] Connect your emotions to your writing and use their power to help you create an awesome piece of work.; [a.] West Islip, NY

HALES, ELAINE
[pen.] Elaine Baskey-Hales; [b.] October 18, 1947, Parry Sound, Ont.; [p.] Moses and Eva Baskey; [m.] George Hales, October 23, 1965; [ch.] Debra, Dan, Ronda; [ed.] B.A., C.G.A.; [occ.] College Professor

HALL, CHRISTOPHER
[b.] May 12, 1980, San Bernardino, CA; [p.] James and Glinda Hall; [ed.] Collierville High School (Junior); [memb.] Key Club, Beta Club, Junior Classical League; [hon.] President's Award for Academics, poem published in local newspapers and in earlier edition of River of Dreams, editor of a top yearbook staff.; [oth. writ.] "Dreams"; [pers.] Literature is an art not to be forced, but used to express one's feelings in times of great emotion.; [a.] Collierville, TN

HAMMERLE, PEARL WEBB
[pen.] Pearl Webb Hammerle; [b.] December 7, 1918, Weesatche, TX; [p.] John L. Webb and Elizabeth Hohn Webb; [m.] Col. (USAF Ret) Clarence B. Hammerle, May 29, 1941; [ch.] George Bernard (5-15-44), Holly Ann (12-22-45); [ed.] Univ. of Maryland O'Seas Campus - in Germany No. Va. Community College in Leesburg, Va. Univ. of Alabama (Montgomery Campus) in Montgomery, Alabama; [occ.] Housewife/Homemaker and Traveler; [memb.] Military & Civilian: Service-Oriented Girl Scouts USA-Germany/American Red Cross - USA & Germany— Air Force Officers Wives Clubs-O'Seas State Dept. Clubs-Japanese/American Clubs in Wash., DC-Texas Historical Society; [hon.] 1984- poem in "Amer. Poetry Anthology", 1995 - First Prize, Poetry in Tahsa (Texas Assn of Homes and Services for the Aging) Art Contest and Exhibition, 1995 - "The Garden of Life", Pub. by Nat'l Library of Poetry", 1996 - Best Poems of the '90', National Library of Poetry, 1989 - Publisher's Choice: Selected poets of the new Era, Pub. American Poetry Assn. "Poet Laureate of Air Force Village II"; [oth. writ.] In preparation for publishing: 1. Seed Pearls - personal poetry, 2. A Ring From Tiffany's - family genealogy, 3. Let The Rose Lose Their Bright Colors - a translation of Gr-Gr-Grandmother's Friendship Book Circa 1945 - Germany to New York; [pers.] Please use the personal write-up used in "Best Poems of the '90's (Your publication).; [a.] San Antonio, TX

HAMMONTREE, NANCY A.
[pen.] Nancy Gibbs; [b.] August 5, 1944, Newport, VT; [p.] Gordon L. & Theresa E. Alexander; [ch.] 2: Scott & Melissa; [ed.] 1 yr. college - Palm Beach Community College, LK Worth, FL; [occ.] Admin. Assist./Office Mgr., Environ. Serv., Bethesda Mem. Hops., Boynton Bch, FL; [memb.] The International Society of Poets; [oth. writ.] Poems pub. in church Lent booklet, 1978; poems in Our World's Most Treasured Poems, 1991, World of Poetry Press; poem in "Frost At Midnight, 1996, The National Library of Poery; [pers.] My self expression is in music and poetry. I hope to encourage and inspie others through them. [a.] Delray Beach, FL

HAMPTON, CHARLES R.
[b.] February 5, 1949, Lebanon Junction, KY; [p.] Herbert and Mary Hampton; [m.] Belinda Lyon Hampton, September 25, 1970; [ch.] Charles R. Hampton II; [ed.] Shepherdsville High School, Locksmith Degree, Small Engine Repair Degree, Various Engineering Courses; [occ.] Disabled Veteran; [memb.] 1st Cav Div. Assn., American Legion, DAV, National Poets Society; [hon.] 2 Bronze Stars with "V" and Oakleaf Cluster Air Medal, American and Vietnamese Commendation Medals; [oth. writ.] Poems published in "A View From The Edge", "Outstanding Poets of 1994", "Distinguished Poets of America", "Best Poems of 1995", "Best Poems of 1996". Articles in Pioneer News and Courier Journal Newspapers.; [pers.] Poetry is my form of therapy and a way of dealing with my experiences from the Vietnam War.; [a.] Louisville, KY

HANYZEWSKI, SARA
[b.] February 18, 1981, Calumet City, IL; [p.] Geralyn and William Hanyzewski; [ed.] Sophomore in High School; [occ.] Part-time job at Munster Animal Hospital; [memb.] I'm in the Lake Central Band, I play basketball, soccer, and softball; [hon.] Honor Roll, Academic Honors, Citizenship Awards; [oth. writ.] Write poems in my free time, one of my other poems published in another anthology.; [pers.] I once saw a movie and one of the actors quoted, "We write poetry not because it's cute or fun, but because we are the human race and poetry is what's inside us." I write every poem and think of that because my poems reflect my feelings.; [a.] Saint John, IN

HARDEMAN, JOYCE MILLER
[pen.] Joyce Louise; [b.] November 22, 1950, Greenwood, SC; [ed.] Tallulah Falls, H.S., Clayton State, Morrow, GA., Waubonsie, Aurora, IL; [oth. writ.] Poetry in The Voice Within.; [pers.] My compassion and empathy for people who have experienced injustice, and my faith in my religion, are reflected in my writing.; [a.] Between, GA

HARP, MELISSA DIANE
[b.] June 27, 1965, Frederick, MD; [p.] Bernard Andrew Keeney Sr. and Nickie Diane (Stine) Keeney; [m.] Gregory John Harp (Deceased), November 26, 1989; [ed.] Walkersville High School (79-83) General Studies Walkersville, MD, Frederick County Vo-Tech (82-83) Business and Management Frederick, MD, Abbie Business Institute (1993) Computerized Accounting Frederick, MD; [occ.] Manager, Financial and Data Processing Services for Network Communications in Ijamsville, MD. Employer, T. Susan Hill Rozynek; [hon.] National Library of Poetry - Editors Choice Award (9 times), Abbie Business Institute-Presidents Counsel List, Abbie Business Institute-Accounting Student of the Year, Neoterik Health Technologies-Employee of the Month Frederick County Vo-Tech-Certificate of Achievement; [oth. writ.] Your Eyes Whispers In The Wind Country etc., Press (1993), Long Lonely Path At Day's End National Library of Poetry (1994), I Am No Poet Song On The Wind National Library of Poetry (1994), When Your love Dies Quest Of A Dream Pacific Rim Publications (1994), Always My Love Best Poems of 1995 National Library of Poetry (1995), Bodies Like A Sponge Best New Poems Poet's Guild (1995), The Walking Dead Mist of Enchantment National Library of Poetry (1995), Clear Blood of the Soul Best Poems of 1996 National Library of Poetry (1996), You Are The One Best Poems of the 90's National Library of Poetry (1996), Paradise Best Poems of 1997 National Library of Poetry (1997); [pers.] It is nice to have friends, but sometimes they just don't understand. Sometimes the best friends are strangers who have shared your experiences. I want to remember those of whom inspire my poetry. Steven A. Harp (Brother-in-law) 1988, Bernard A. Keeney, Jr. (Brother) 1988, Annie V. Stine (Grandmother) 1989, Cindy Dayhoff (Friend) 1991, Gregory John Harp (Husband) 1992, Marie Keeney (Nanny) 1992, Helen Hatfield (Aunt) 1994.; [a.] Woodsboro, MD

HARRIS, OTTO
[pen.] Otto Harris; [b.] January 3, 1920; [p.] Ben Harris and Louise Beale; [m.] Ann Harris, October 22, 1947; [ch.] Six children; [ed.] High School graduate; [occ.] Retired; [memb.] Elk's V.F.W. American Legion and Humane Society; [hon.] Have received, the Golden the Silver, honorable mention from the World of Poetry, California 3 bottle stars W.W.II, and Medal of Freedom; [pers.] I only go through this world once, let me treat each individual, with kindness and respect, le me never forget, we are hear for a short time and let every day be enjoyed and nourished, with charity and a love for my fellow human beings.; [a.] Rotonda West, FL

HARRISON, LAURA
[b.] April 28, 1975, Sacramento, CA; [p.] Jane and Tom Harrison; [ed.] University of Kansas Majors Business and Accounting; [occ.] Full-time student; [memb.] Delta Sigma Pi business fraternity, Delta Delta Delta Sorority; [oth. writ.] "Joyride", "Titles", "A Lunous Thing, Love".; [a.] Woodbury MN

HARRISON - DUKE, TERRY A.
[pen.] Terry A. Harrison ; [b.] October 25,1960, Cleveland, OH. ; [p.] Clarence and Essie Mae ; [m.] Herschel D. Duke II, May 13,1995 ; [ch.] Christopher Duke ; [ed.] BA Family Life education. B.A. Human Resource Management, Spring Arbor College., M.S.A. Master of Science in Administration Central Michigan Univ. Arbor College ; [occ.] Corrections Administrator ; [memb.] Union M.B. Church. Deans list at Spring Arbor College ; [hon.] Won honorable mention for poetry in the National Library of Poetry and the Iliad Press Poetry competitions, several times. ; [oth.writ.] over thirty five published pieces in various anthologies in the U.S. ; pers.] I hope that my writing touch the hearts and souls of children in the world. I have been greatly influenced by the poet Maya Angelo. ; [a.] Lansing, MI.

HASKINS, MICHAEL JOSHUA
[b.] March 13, 1967, Lorain, OH; [ed.] Shupe Elementary, Nord Junior High, Marion L Steele High, Academy Pacific, Pierce College; [occ.] Retired; [oth. writ.] Long time companion, rainbows.; [pers.] "Life is a bowl of cherries.... so eat em' while ya' can".; [a.] Los Angeles, CA

HATTON, STEPHANIE A.
[b.] December 29, 1968, Findlay, OH; [p.] Mary Ann Boehler, Michael Hatton; [ed.] Associates Degree in Law Enforcement Police Science; [occ.] Police Officer; [memb.] Poets Guild; [oth. writ.] "My Beloved Louis", "It's Times Like These", "A Change of Heart", "Without A Warning"; [pers.] My poetry not only reflects personal pains and tragedies from my past, but it also touches on the experiences, feelings, and emotions that everyone has been through at one time or another.; [a.] Brandon, FL

HAUGH, GLORIA FIALA
[pen.] Gloria Haugh; [b.] May 28, 1938, Dayton, OH; [p.] Ralph and Bea Fiala; [m.] Richard Haugh, January 9, 1960; [ch.] Shari and Ted; [ed.] Dayton Holy Family, Bellevue High OH, grad., Nursing Grad. 2 yrs Tiffin, Grad. at Sandusky Fehont, Grad. of Sandusky School of Nsg., Grad. Business School, Dayton, OH, Grad. of Findlay O, High W. Findlay, Mercy Student, L.P.N. Nurse; [occ.] Future worker, Poet and Writer for papers, Telephone Marketeer; [memb.] Ohio Practical Nurse Assn. Dept 20 yrs, Seneca Co. Sr. Cit. 4 yrs. V. P. and Ritz Honorary Theatre, Tiffin, OH, Scy. Right To Life, Chinn, Writer for Healthy Eating Recipes for 20 yrs., St. Patrick Church, Bascom, OH; [hon.] Who's Who Women of

World, 1994, 1995 last and current edition, Alumna Bussn. Fro. Women of America, Lt. Col. Bah McDonald Award from Merit Island, Fla, Space Center - The Award from Nat'l. Machinery Found.; [oth. writ.] Two other poems published someday in 4-6 newspapers, write for 4 newspapers, Courier - Findley, OH, Bellevue Crozette, Bellevue, OH, News Messenger, Fremont, OH, Advertisers - Tribune - Tiffin, OH, Helburn Meadows Gardens, monthly, Tiffin, OH; [pers.] I love humanity, children and elderly downtrodden, expecting to be an ambassador to Australia later. Prince Kevin gave me honorary citizenship Stutt River Province and award for service to humanity world.; [a.] Tiffin, OH

HAWKS, MICHAEL J.
[b.] May 9, 1968, Hantford, CT; [p.] John Hawks, Rena Bielitz; [ed.] East Windsor High, CT.; [occ.] Security Guard; [memb.] Star Trek Fun Club, U.S.S. York Town, Rock Hill Chapter; [hon.] Editors Choice Award from The National Library of Poetry nominated for Poet Of The Year 1996 (did not win) inducted into the International Society of poetry museum nominated for induction into The International Society of Poets.; [oth. writ.] Three poems published by the National Library of Poetry include in Best Poems of the 90's.; [pers.] I write about man's search for God. In that search I try to answer the unanswerable question. Did God create man simply for enjoyment or did man create the image of God to explain his existence; [a.] Rockhill, SC

HEDGES, BOBETTE L.
[b.] August 12, 1959, Glendale, CA; [p.] Robert L. Newman and Charolette J. Garris; [m.] Jesse H. Stubblefield, February 2, 1997; [ch.] Michael - 15 and Matthew Hedges - 14; [ed.] Indian River Community College Business; [occ.] Business Administrator, Corporate Director; [memb.] Business Advisory Council, Abundant Blessings - Assembly of God; [hon.] 1976 Miss Alaska National Teenager, 1997 Who's Who in the South and Southwest - 25th Silver Edition; [oth. writ.] "Because of You" published in Shadows and Light, 1986. "Elihu's Wall" published in Best Poems of the 90's, 1996.; [pers.] My husband and I believe a person should seek first to understand. When we do this, it is easy to understand that "hurting people hurt people.; [a.] Okeechobee, FL

HELMER, JACKELYN
[b.] October 24, 1975, Petersburg, AK; [p.] Kimberley Bell, Kevin Bell; [m.] Lynn A. Helmer, June 18, 1993; [ch.] Renee Marie, Ryan Michael; [oth. writ.] Renee, My Baby, published in Fields Of Gold Anthology; [pers.] Joseph Agassiz Lyons was born on June 6, 1996 and died August 6, 1996. Gone but not forgotten. Rest in peace, little angel.; [a.] Petersburg, AK

HENDRIX, LOUISE BUTTS
[pen.] Louise Butts Hendrix; [b.] June 16, 1911, Portland, TN; [p.] Luther and Johnnie Butts; [m.] Edwin Alonzo Hendrix Sr., August 1, 1934; [ch.] Lynette Green, Ed Hendrix Jr.; [ed.] AB Chico State University, Graduate Study-College of Pacific Sacramento State, University Southern California; [occ.] Retired Teacher, News Correspondent Marysville, Oroville, Retired Teachers Assoc. of Calif; [memb.] Save Sutter Butts, Pres., Yuba City Women's Club, Pres., Marysville Art Club; [hon.] Sierra Club Northern Calif. Conservation Awardee, Kuba Sutter Conservation Committee my husband built the cabin of the poem; [oth. writ.] "Suttee Buttes, Land of Histum Yani (6th printing) "Squawman" (Novel), "Petals and Blossoms" (Poetry), "Better Readin' and writin' with Journalism" (Textbook); [pers.] 85 yrs. "Young", Legally Blind, read and write with a Telesonic machine, Widow Afre 57 1/2 wonderful marriage, blind 7 yrs. for writing please excuse!

HENNECY, BOBBIE BOBO
[pen.] Bobbie Bobo-Hennecy, Glyn Marsh; [b.] August 11, 1922, Tignall, GA; [p.] John Ebb Bobo, Lois Helen Gulledge Bobo, (Deceased); [m.] James Howell Hennecy, (Deceased), December 28, 1963; [ch.] Erin, Michele Vanglaive, Mrs. Max Vanglaive, grandchildren: Vladimir, Valour, Maxi and Iain; [ed.] Att'd. Wesleyan Conservatory, A.B. Summa Cum Laude, Mercer University, Post grad. ESU School, Oxford University, Eng., M.A. NDEA Fellow Emory University, Postgrad. with grant from MU, Cambridge University, Eng.; [occ.] Emeritus Associate Professor, and Adjunct Prof., Merce University, Research, and writing poetry; [memb.] AAUP, AAUW, MLA, SAMLA, So., Am., Int'l Comparative Lit. Assoc. GA. and Nat'l Assoc. Tchrs., Eng., Eng. Spk-Union, LWV, Collegiate Press (adv. bd.) Amer. Acad. Poets, Soc. of Am. Poets, Hereditary Register, Magna Charta, Col. Dames XVII C, DAC, Des. Col. Clergy, Jamestown Soc., DAR, UDC, 1812, Col. Order of Crown, Amer. Royal Desc., Soc. Genealogists, London, Ala, Ga, S.C. Hist. Soc., Chi Omega Frat.; [hon.] Scholarship named in her honor at Tattnal Sq. Academy and at Mercer Un., Phi Kappa Phi. Alpha Psi Omega, STD, Sigma Mu, Cardinal Key, Named "Oustanding Psi Gamma Chi Omega, Listed: Who's Who of Am. Women, Who's Who in S & SW, Who's Who in Am. Ed., Who's Who of Women in the World, Int'l. Who's Who of Bus. Prof. Women., Dict. Int'l Biography, Two Thousand Notable Am. Wom., Foremost Women of the Twentieth Century, Who's Who in GA, Personalities of the South, Community Leaders; [oth. writ.] Modernization of the Famous Histories of Sir Thomas Wyatt by Dekker and Webster (1607) (unpub.), Tot's Miscellany, Book of Poems, (desk top pub.) mystic thesis on Variations of Hamlet, other poetry and papers.; [pers.] I seek to explore and reinforce the bond between God and man. I am strongly influenced by 17th poet. Romantic and Victorian poetry, and somewhat by early American poets, as well as the King James Version of the Bible.; [a.] Macon, GA

HERRIAGE, PATSY
[b.] September 20, 1931, Emory, TX; [occ.] Retired; [hon.] Have received several "Honorary Certificates" for poetry; [pers.] In loving memory of Sharon Harvey Fuller, who lost her battle with cancer January 9, 1997.; [a.] Sulphur Springs, TX

HERZBERGER, MAGDA
[b.] February 20, 1926, Cluj, Romania; [p.] Herman Mozes, died 1944 in Holocaust, Serena Vinacour, died March 25, 1994; [m.] Eugene E. Herzberger, November 21, 1946; [ch.] Monica Riekoff and Henry Herzberger; [ed.] Bachelor's of Science Degree, one year medical school at King Ferdinand University, 1946-1947 in Cluj, Romania; [occ.] Poet, Lecturer, Composer; [memb.] Distinguished Member of the International Society of Poets, Member of Women's Club and Kiwanis Club in Fountain Hills, Arizona; [hon.] Featured in the Encyclopedia 1991, Dubuque, Iowa, Personalities of West and Midwest Award, 1977-78-82, three poetry grants, 1977-80-85, Who is Who in Poetry 5th Edition, Cambridge, England, 1977-78, Poet of Merit Award, International Society of Poets, 1993, The National Library of Poetry, Editor's Choice Award, 1994-95-96, and 2nd prize winner of 1994 National Library of Poetry Competition, The International Who is Who of Intellectuals, Cambridge, England, 1978-79-82, Elected into the International Poetry Hall of Fame and for my poetry exhibit to be in the Fame's Museum on the Internet's World Wide Web, 1997; [oth. writ.] Books: Will You Still Love Me?, The Waltz Of The Shadows, Songs Of Life, Eyewitness To Holocaust, and 300 independent poems published, one short story, two narratives (poetic), one children's book, one book on the Holocaust in the making, inspirational poetry book

recently completed.; [pers.] Being a survivor of the Camps, my goal is to keep the memory of the Holocaust alive through my writings and music and to instill a love of poetry in the hearts of all the people. I'm also a hiker, skier and marathon runner.; [a.] Fountain Hills, AZ

HESTING, VINCENT SHANE
[pen.] White Tornado, Bear Oaks; [b.] July 27, 1967, Smith Center, KS; [p.] Paul August and Ruby Joy Hesting; [ed.] White Rock High (1986), Emporia State University (BS 1990), Emporia State University (MS Pending); [occ.] Private Naturalist and Fish/Wildlife Specialist Seasonal Kansas and Montana Fisheries Fieldworker; [memb.] Bear Oaks Big Bass Fishing Team; [hon.] Emporia State University Honor Roll (Several Semesters), Magna Cum Laude 1990, Four Consecutive Certificates of Appreciation from Division of Biological Science, Emporia State University 1986-1990, Kansas Northern Largemouth Bass Master Angler 1986 and 1996, Director of Annual Bear Oaks Bonfire; [oth. writ.] Graduate paper, "Abiotic Correlates of Fish Assemblage Structure in Melvern Reservoir, U.S.A." (Pending), Poems include "Upon Morning's Dew" (Spirit of the Age, 1995) and "Will" (Lyrical Heritage, 1996), Original News releases in Newspapers (1993), Several Unpublished Poems; [pers.] The struggle for life in a world checked by death is a beautifully balanced oscillation on Earth. Along a desolate backroad, you hit an animal crossing in front. Immediately after impact, you wondered whether you killed it or just wounded it, leaving it to crawl off alone and die somewhere unknown. for a moment you looked through the lies and deception of civilization to see your own animal face, reflecting from the rearview mirror. Then all was forgotten, and you drove back to civilization, where there is a right and wrong.; [a.] Ezbon, KS

HIBBITTS, CHRISANNA LYNN
[pen.] C. L. Hibbitts; [b.] December 22, 1977, Fort Worth, TX; [p.] Judy Ann and Donald Hibbitts; [ed.] Pantego Christian Academy - 6 yrs. Bailey Jr. High School - 3 yrs.; [occ.] Subway Sandwich Artist, Student; [memb.] First Baptist Church, Arlington, TX, Golds Gym, Arlington, TX, Member of National Honors Society; [hon.] 1st Place in music Comp. division in City Wide Cultural Arts contest '92, Outstanding Veteran Camp '95, Graduate with Honor, Principals Award, National Honors Society Member '96. Editor's Choice Award for poem "In Dappled Sunlight" '97. Graduated with honors from AHS '96 principal's award for Student Leadership; [oth. writ.] "Luminescence" published in the National Library of Poetry's "In Dappled Sunlight" '97. Also 6 years worth of personally written poems and songs in a big notebook at home!; [pers.] Poetry is my soul. It has opened my eyes to the beauty of expression through words and has enabled me to stare directly into the face of some of my greatest insecurities I give full credit to Jesus Christ my Lord and Savior.; [a.] Arlington, TX

HICKS, ANGELA JOSEPHINE
[b.] September 9, 1948, Wirral, England; [p.] Josephine Mary Violet Ferguson and Ronald Norman Hawkins; [m.] John Henry Hicks, July 22, 1994; [ch.] Lisa Anne Betts, Robert Alan Stickler II, Michelle Renee Barkley, Ronald Charles Barkley; [ed.] Central High School, La Salle Extension University, various Bible Correspondence Courses; [occ.] Riding the highways with my 18 wheeler trucker husband, caring for him and the truck, and writing.; [hon.] Bowling Award, numerous honor certificates from U.S. Navy (As a navy wife), U.S. Navy Award for Yard of the Month, Honorable Mention from World of Poetry, two Editor's Choice Awards (1996) - Nat'l. Library of Poetry, 1996 Nomination for Poet of the Year; [oth. writ.] Short articles (non-published), several songs be-written (non-published); [pers.] To always keep God as my head, and my inspiration, in all aspects of my life, no matter what life may hand out, He is the answer to all life's burdens!; [a.] South Bend, IN

HIGGINS, CHARLOTTE
[b.] September 20, 1915, Blanton, TX; [p.] MM J.E., Montgomery; [m.] Virgil W. Higgins, September 16, 1933; [ch.] Eight; [ed.] 10th High School, if my poem is going to be in the next book, I want one; [occ.] Housewife; [hon.] 2 in World Book of Poetry, (Eddie Lou) Cole Editor, 2 in National Library of Poetry (Caroline Sullivan); [oth. writ.] I have an Album, my daughter typed for me and dozens I have written by hand.; [pers.] I am 81 years of age, mother of 8.

HIGGS, JOYCE L.
[b.] April 27, 1965, Martins Ferry, OH; [p.] Robert (Deceased) and Hazel Higgs; [ed.] High School; [occ.] None taking care of a very sick mother. She has cancer etc.; [hon.] Two Editor's Choice Awards from the National Library of Poetry; [oth. writ.] Just Believe In Me, My Father Would My Father Still Part II and III of whatever God Grants Us Today which the first part was published in "Tomorrow's Dream" etc.; [pers.] I really like writing from my heart and soul. God and I write together. My gift and strengths are from Him.; [a.] Martins Ferry, OH

HILBORN, KURT
[b.] July 13, 1973, Long Island, NY; [p.] Robert and Shirley Hilborn; [ed.] Johnson and Wales University, University at Montana, Front Range Community College; [occ.] Sign Language Interpreter; [memb.] Colorado Registry at Interpreters for the Deaf; [oth. writ.] Personal files filled with stories, poems, pros. never tried no publish them.; [pers.] Life is poetry and poetry is life.; [a.] Boulder, CO

HILL, JACKOLYN M.
[pen.] Charleigh Douglas; [b.] April 12, 1940, Lansing, MI; [p.] Maurice and Thelma Brundige; [ch.] Charles D. Grondine (Deceased); [ed.] Associate Liberal Arts - NMC - Traverse City, MI. Medical Unit Manager - MGCCC - Gaufier, Miss.; [occ.] Cashier; [memb.] AARP; [hon.] Editors Award from National Library of Poetry, President List at MGCCC.; [oth. writ.] When The Alarm Rings - 1995; [a.] Suttons Bay, MI

HILL, KINGSLEY
[b.] August 16, 1960, Swansea, South Wales; [p.] Roger and Joy Hill; [m.] Raymonde Hill, May 5, 1989; [ch.] Samantha Franses, Johnathan Samuel; [ed.] Pennard Primary School, Goverton Grammer School. Camosun College; [occ.] Recreational Therapist; [memb.] Saanichton Bible Fellowship; [hon.] Publication of Poems in (path not taken, Best Poems of the 90's, Editor's Choice Award for poem published in (OTV. Writ) and poem published in Best Poems of 1997; [oth. writ.] Presently working on my first book (my best friend), and also a book of poetry (Golden Leaves from the Autumn Mist); [pers.] I like to write about my experience of God. Getting to know his person. And appreciating his awesome creation. He is very "Great".; [a.] Victoria, British Columbia, Canada

HILLS, CARL
[pen.] Carl Hills; [b.] March 6, 1947, Georgetown, MA; [p.] Deceased; [m.] Sally Hills, September 1, 1980; [ch.] Canhace, Robert, Lisa and Michelle; [ed.] Business School - Associate degree in Managerial Accounting and one year Nursing School; [occ.] Self Employed; [memb.] New England Theater Conference; [hon.] International Library of Poetry Editors Choice Award 1994, Best Poems of 1995, Best Poems of 1996, injected Int. poetry hall of fame October 1996, and Best poems 1997; [oth. writ.] Newspaper article of human interest and investigative style, short story collections, mystery novels, and children's looks.; [pers.] Reading is the key to

education. And education is the key to reading without either, mankind stays locked in halls of his own mind.; [a.] Seabrook, NH

HINCKLEY, EVA
[pen.] Eva Hinckley; [b.] February 11, 1960, Price, UT; [p.] Tharon and Barbara Hinckley; [ed.] Kearns High School, Kearns, UT Ricks College-Rexburg, ID BYU-Hawaii -Laie, HI Life; [occ.] Teacher, Kaaawa, HI, Elementary School; [memb.] Church of Jesus Christ of Latter-Day Saints, Hawaii State Teachers Association; [oth. writ.] "Secret Chambers of the Heart", "In Dappled Sunlight" several poems for weddings and special events, special people; [pers.] Quite the optimist, I love putting words that creative a visual image on paper. My love for my family and belief in God have always sustained me.; [a.] Hauula, HI

HINDMAN, KAREN B.
[b.] March 24, 1957, Huntsville, AL; [p.] James and Mary Hindman; [ed.] Bachelor of Science from Lee College - Cleveland, Tenn.; [occ.] Free Lance Writer, Technical Writer and Quality Coordinator.; [memb.] International Society of Poets; [hon.] Editor's Choice Award from The National Library of Poetry.; [oth. writ.] Memphis Midnight, Secret Sins, A Christmas Message.; [pers.] Words have meanings, place them carefully, those who comprehend, have read your soul's existence.; [a.] Ruckersville, VA

HOBAN, TACEY M.
[b.] May 4, 1926, Nebraska City, NE; [p.] Bertha and Charles Lewis (Deceased); [m.] Louis T. Hoban (Deceased), November 4, 1952; [ch.] Avis, Paula, Virginia, David and Tom; [ed.] 12th grade Omaha, NE, Business School Omaha, NE; [occ.] Retired Widow, Office Mngr.; [memb.] Served on Council in Butte Falls, OR, Friends of Library, President - Butte Falls Historical Society - President Lioness - B.F., OR; [oth. writ.] Poems and short stories; none submitted for publication.; [pers.] I feel poetry comes from the heart and I can only express myself and my innermost feelings from my life experiences.; [a.] Stockton, CA

HOBBS, BARBARA DELL
[b.] October 27, 1943, Hubbard, TX; [p.] Mr. and Mrs. Ellie Hue Hobbs; [ch.] Dexter L. Hall; [ed.] High School Graduate, Texas, A.A. degree, Los Angeles Metropolitan College, BA degree, California State University, Dominguez Hills; [occ.] Administrative Secretary, LA City College; [memb.] Member, West LA Church of God in Christ, Member, Walet Literacy Group; [hon.] Outstanding employee, 1993, Editor's Choice Award, National Library of Poetry 1996, Acknowledgement from President Clinton of poetry written in August, 1996; [oth. writ.] Published work in anthologies, "A Gift They Can't Take", Across the Universe, "Givers and Takers", Essence Of A Dream, "Atlanta 1996 Olympics", A Moment to Reflect, Chief Editor, LACC Employees News Letter, Former Staff Writer, Dominguez Hills News.; [pers.] I'm usually inspired to write poetry that will be an inspiration to the world in general, especially for young adults and teenagers.; [a.] Gardena, CA

HOBSON, WHITTONIA M.
[pen.] Whittie; [b.] February 18, 1955, St. Louis, MI; [p.] Whittonia Evans; [occ.] Computer Technologist; [memb.] Rose of Sharon MBC, Agape Christian Retreat and Conference Center, Agape Homeless Shelter, Richstone Family Center; [oth. writ.] Several short plays written and performed, poetry journal, poem published in 1994 edition of Dance On The Horizon and The Best Poems of 1996.; [pers.] To delight, encourage, uplift and inspire. No matter how difficult a time still I rise. Encouraged by my mentor Maya Angelo.; [a.] Los Angeles, CA

HODGE, LEON
[pen.] The Kid Who Wonder ;[b.] February 14, 1950, Valdosta. ;[p.] Walter and Catherine Hodge ;[ed.] I completed school ;[occ.] Pigdmont Hospital, Housekeeping ;[oth.writ.] The only other writing is other poetry and tried to write a story that I called A Guy Of A Different Sex. But it was too short so I'm writing it over but I've written my life story and send it out now. ;[pers.] I am a primal donal for words I like putting them together and I will continue to do so whether you like it or not. But if I can make my feeling different. ; [a.] Atlanta,GA.

HODSON, ERNEST F.
[pen.] Ernie Hodson; [b.] May 14, 1929, Detroit, MI; [p.] Francis Hodson, Agnes Hodson; [m.] Margaret D. Hodson, February 6, 1965; [ch.] Stephen, Ann, Robert, Carol James, John, Thomas; [ed.] Stratford High School, Creative Writing: Sacred Heart University; [occ.] Commercial Real Estate Broker, semi-retired; [oth. writ.] Several poems published in the Sacred Heart University Journal "Horizons" and a self published booklet of poems entitled "Insights"; [pers.] My poetry covers a variety of everyday subjects and situational matters wherein I attempt to express some deeper, perhaps unfelt, meaning or perspective.; [a.] Trumbull, CT

HOHN, EVERTON LLEWELLYN
[pen.] Everton Llewellyn Hohn; [b.] May 4, 1953, Saint Ann., Jamaica, West Indies; [p.] George and Siclyn Hohn; [m.] Angela Yvonne Hohn, July 26, 1980; [ch.] Kristopha, Melonie, Alex; [ed.] High School Diploma - Lauder Hill GED Centre, Aboukir Institute, St. Ann Jamaica. Certified Patient Care Assistant. Licensed Security off.; [occ.] Patient Care Assistant; [memb.] Distinguished and Honorary Member of International Society of Poets; [hon.] Certificates and Honorary Mention - International Society of Poets 94-95. Peace Awards - International Society of Poets; [oth. writ.] Publication of poetry in news letter - in Stavenel, Plantation FL. Stand Up And Be Counted, It Will Be Better World's best poets 1992, Go Tell The World - songs on the NLOP with 1995 - Someone Lost A Dream best poems of the 90's - NLOP 1996. Song nothings gonna stop me now.; [pers.] It is my personal intention that my writings in still hope in the hopeless, courage to those who are discouraged and challenge to those that need to be challenged I strive to reach the top of the mountain - Mt. Success.; [a.] Lauder Hill, FL

HOLLOWAY, MARGO
[b.] May 25, 1941, Philadelphia; [p.] Robert and Eula Green; [ch.] Donna, Cecil, Heather; [ed.] BS Univ of PA, the Wharton School; [memb.] Oxford Presbyterian church; [hon.] Four Chaplains Legion of honor membership; [oth. writ.] Wanderings, senses, the Last Dance, Resolved, Noise, Life Is, Chances, The Mother of Sons, Sisterhood, The Price of Sorrow; [pers.] Touch one another for only in touching one another do we touch the face of God.; [a.] Philadelphia, PA

HOLM, HILLMEN MAURICE
[b.] July 3, 1918, Watrous, Saskatchewan, Canada; [p.] Christian and Emma Holm; [m.] Jean Marion Holm, February 26, 1945; [ch.] Marjorie, Myrene, Clifford, Howard; [ed.] Graduate, Moose Jaw, Sask, Normal School Graduate, University of Saskatchewan without Bachelor of Science Degree in Agriculture and a Master of Science Degree in Soil Science; [occ.] Retired, (for 33 years Formerly soil conservationist for Saskatchewan Department of Agriculture.); [memb.] Saskatchewan Agricultural Graduates Association. Saskatchewan Government Superanwater Association. Saskatchewan Vegetable Growers Association.; [hon.] Received Bachelor of Science Degree with Distinction. Awarded Honorary Life Membership in the Saskatchewan Vegetable Growers Association.; [oth. writ.] I have had several agricultural booklets published including "Save the

Soil a study in soil conservation and Erosion Control." "Soil Salinity -a study in crop tolerance pad cropping practices" "Understanding salt affected soils" co-authored with prof. J. L. Henry univ of Sask. Non-published poems: "Nature's song", "Winter Storm", "Ode to Morning" published poem "Autumn". National Library of Poetry; [pers.] I have a great affection for nature. My professional career as a soil conservationist allowed me to commune with nature and brought me into close association with farmers, scientists, administrators across the prairie provinces of canada and the Northern Great Plains States of USA. Wordsworth poem "Tinlern Abbey" was an inspiration to me in my youth. I am always particularly impressed by his thought that "Nature never did betray the hear that loved her".; [a.] Penticton, British Columbia, Canada

HOLMAN, BONNIE LEE
[b.] July 2, 1925, Kiowa, KS; [p.] Raymond Lee and Jewel Dixon; [m.] Charles E. Morris, March 29, 1945, Arthur J. Holman, February 24, 1996; [ch.] Ken La Rocque, Todd E. Morris, Candace Morris Nicholas; [ed.] High school graduate - grd 12, 1 year college in Childhood Education; [occ.] Retired; [memb.] Old Age Pensioners Assoc; [hon.] The National Library of Poetry, Christian Writers; [oth. writ.] Many poems, novel "Silver Creek Valley", novel "The Sparrows Nest", commentary "The 108 Resort Women's Institute of Canada Pioneer Story"; [pers.] I have been a born again Christian since age 13. I have been influenced to want to help others by Gospel songs.; [a.] Chase, British Columbia, Canada

HOOVER, JEANNE TYSON
[b.] July 18, 1914, PA; [p.] Maurice Frederick Tyson, Eva Lucinda Shiffert Tyson; [m.] Ray F. Hoover, May 7, 1938; [ch.] Sandra Claire, Marley Shiffert; [ed.] H.S. Hosp. Un. Penna. Phila., R.N. Degree Phn Un. Md., World Traveler; [occ.] Retired R.N. - full time care-giver for husband Ray Conservatrix Dav. Sandy etc.-etc.; [oth. writ.] 3-4 poems published Nat. Library Poetry.; [pers.] Special note: It is really uncanny - my twin, Claire Tyson Murray died of cancer on the same day I wrote and finished Ithaka. She helped me write it. Really being a twin has always been very special. Claire too, was an RN - a special one. She too wrote poetry - wonderful poetry of the Universe.; [a.] Phoenix, AR

HOPKINS, DR. VASHTI JOHNSON
[p.] Late Rev. Louis Tenner and Matilda Robinson Johnson; [m.] Haywood H. Hopkins Sr.; [ch.] Haywood Jr., Yvonne Andrews, and three grandchildren; [ed.] She attended the Harrison Elementary and graduated with honors from the Lucy Addison High School in Roanoke, Va. She received a Bachelor of Science from Virginia Seminary and College, a Bachelor of Science in Elementary Education from Saint Paul's College in Lawrenceville, a Master of Education Degree and a Doctor of Philosophy in Education from the University of Virginia.; [occ.] She is a retired Lynchburg Public School Teacher and taught Literature and English at the Virginia Seminary and College.; [memb.] She is a member of the Phi Delta Kappa Fraternity in Education and served as Vice-President of Membership. She is a life member of the University of Virginia Alumni Association, and is listed in the Directory from 1980-1995. She is a member of the Saint Paul's College Alumni Century Club. A life member of the Lynchburg Retired Teacher's Association. and served as President and Treasurer, a life member of District F. Retired Teacher's Association and served as President and Treasurer. She is a life member of the Virginia Retired Teacher's Association and serves as Vice-President. She is a member of the Y.M.C.A., N.A.A.C.P., and the Zeta Beta Sorority. She has served as a Past Loyal Ruler Golden Circle, a member of the Daughters of Isis, a Past Worthy Matron of the Order of the Eastern Star, and a Past Grand Deputy Organizer of District No. 10 in Virginia. She is serving as officers in three Social Clubs in Lynchburg. She is a member of the Grace Memorial Episcopal Church, a Past President of the Episcopal Church Women, Past Advisor to the Youth Department, and has served as Director of the Church's Vocation Bible School. She is a member of the Prayer Band, visits the sick and shut-ins, and drives for Meals on Wheels.; [hon.] She is listed in the Marquis Who's Who of American Women, the Who's Who Among Black Americans, and in the Zeta Phi Beta Sorority. She has won the Golden Poet Award from the National Library of Poetry from 1896-1995.; [oth. writ.] She paints landscapes and writes poetry. Many of her poems have been published, and her book of poetry is being made ready for publishing.; [pers.] She has traveled in the Virgin Islands, Bermuda, Puerto, Hawaii and Saint Thomas. She has toured England, France, Belgium, Switzerland, Germany, Holland, Austria and Italy. But above all she is a Christian and she Loves People All People.

HOUSE, JEANETTE THOMAS
[pen.] Jeanette Thomas House; [b.] January 14, 1954, LaCrosse, VA; [p.] John L. "Peter" Thomas, Jeanette C. Thomas; [m.] Sam House Jr., November 17, 1984; [ch.] Stephanie LaTara, Travis Samuel; [ed.] Park View High; [memb.] Meherrin Baptist Church; [oth. writ.] "Riding On A Cloud" - published in the 1996 edition of "Recollections of Yesterday". Have numerous other writings.; [pers.] I am truly the writer of these words, but Jesus Christ is the author. I am merely the vessel from which His words flow. And I thank Him.; [a.] Brodnax, VA

HOUSTON-JONES, CHERYL
[pen.] Cheryl Houston-Jones; [b.] October 27, Dallas, TX; [p.] Roy Monrow Houston and Ruth Lee Houston; [ed.] Weschester High School, El Camino College-Grad in English Cal. State Dominguez Hills - U.C.L.A. School of Dentistry-Cerritos College Dental Hygiene School Blair College Med. and Dental Assist. - Certified in Dental Asst/x-ray license - Extension Courses U.S.C. and U.C.L.A. in Dentistry-Certified io Code Blue 33 CPR and HIV-Cross Contamination; [occ.] Dental Consultant-Administration and Assisting, Written of poems and working on Screenplay, Charity Work, Worked on Presidential Campaign with White House Staff Office, Work on educating general population on health issues; [memb.] Writer's Guild of America-West, Member of President's Second Term Committee Nat'l Assoc. Former Intelligence Officers, Founding Member American Air Museum in Britain, Member of Nat'l Resources Defense Council, Member Democratic Nat'l committee, Member of ACLU, and Brass Ring Benefit Horse, Show for Handicapped Children and International Society of Poets; [hon.] Citation of Merit - from Sir John Grandy and Lord Bramall for American Air Museum in Britain Award from President and Vice President for work on Presidential Campaign Made "Hononary Member" Presidential Second Term Committee and Editor's Choice Award Nat'l Library of Poetry; [oth. writ.] "Truthseeker" Nat'l Library of Poetry - Working on screenplay poem in local paper - "Live and Play In Marina Del Rey" - Press release for dental office.; [pers.] This poem reflects the pride of my family in all the work I have done for humanity and the awards etc. that I have received from the President to the awards from the United Kingdom in which we have directly descended, from the Royal Family.; [a.] Marina Del Rey, CA

HOWD, CHRISTOPHER
[pen.] OMT, NM Classifications; [b.] April 23, 1977, Atlanta, GA; [p.] Bonnie and Mike Howd; [m.] Shannon Howd, August 23, 1997; [ed.] Dacula High; [occ.] Manager McDonald's; [memb.] Hebron Baptist Church, Green Leaf Company,

Lighthouse Friends; [hon.] Excellence Award - Mosaic Writing Contest, Editor's Choice - Admist The Splendor, Barry Patch Award; [oth. writ.] "The Falling" Admist The Splendor; [pers.] Thank God for my best friend and wife, who I love and cherish. 1 John 4:16 "God Is Love."; [a.] Dacula, GA

HUBBARD II, THOMAS J.
[b.] February 12, 1963, Libertyville, IL; [p.] Joy Vargas and Thomas Hubbard; [ch.] Jessica E. Albertson; [ed.] Irvine High School; [occ.] Air Conditioning Service Tech.; [memb.] Local Union 250; [oth. writ.] Time With Old Mon in Recollections of Yesterday.; [pers.] I strive to help all those I can with the time I have been granted here in that's lifetime.; [a.] Huntington Beach, CA

HUGILL, CATHY E.
[b.] July 7, 1950, Oklahoma; [p.] Wilson and LaRue Cantwell; [m.] Richard R. Hugill Jr., September 21, 1984; [ch.] Seven; [ed.] Truman High School, Graduated - 1968 (Independence, Mo.); [occ.] Own my own business; [memb.] Community Christian Church, B.S. Chamber of Commerce; [hon.] Published poems in high school paper, community papers, NLP Editor's Choice Award, NLP Best Poems 1997, Published poems in Sherwood Community Paper; [oth. writ.] Short stories, over 100 poems, songs; [pers.] I believe words can be inspiring. They can make you laugh or cry. They can paint beautiful pictures, while they tell you a story. With my poetry, I try to do all of these things. I am inspired by life everyday, and the love of our Lord.; [a.] Blue Springs, MO

HULL, CAROLYN
[b.] September 10, 1955, Chicago; [p.] William and Essie Fullilove; [m.] Lester Hull, December 23, 1980; [ch.] Jeremy Lemont, Jasmine Watress; [ed.] Wendell Phillips High, Roosevelt University; [occ.] Senior Operation Clerk; [memb.] Alpha Missionary Baptist Church, The Alliance of Black Telecommunication Employees Inc.; [oth. writ.] Several poems published in The Alliance Local Chapters Newsletter, others published by The National Library of Poetry; [pers.] My prayer is that my poems reach the hearts of some and reunite others with their personal feelings. I find that Maya Angelou has influenced me greatly.; [a.] Bolingbrook, IL

HUMPHREY, CLAUDIA
[pen.] Claudia Humphrey; [b.] February 3, 1939, Duluth, MN; [p.] George and Geneva Bennison; [m.] Kinsey H. Humphrey, March 8, 1958; [ch.] Steven Dean and Wendy Jean; [ed.] 2 yrs. college; [occ.] Homemaker; [memb.] Friends of E. County Arts, Inc. Foothills United Methodist Church; [oth. writ.] Several other poems that I've sent you - Through Children's Eyes - and Flight of Fantasy.; [pers.] I'm moved by the written word, look my country, my God are my family just a very ordinary homemaker who loves life immensely.; [a.] El Cajon, CA

HUNEKE, LARAINE M.
[pen.] Laraine M. Huneke; [b.] April 6, 1941, Newark, NJ; [p.] Edward and Louise Korczowski; [m.] Arthur, May 5, 1962; [ch.] Gregory Arthur, Russell Edward; [ed.] High School - "Business Student of The Year Awards" National Honor Society - Business Honor Society; [occ.] Beauty Consultant with Mary Kay Cosmetics, Inc.; [hon.] National Honor Society Business Honor Society; [oth. writ.] Poem published in "A Voyage To Remember" - Editor's Choice Award for this writing - poem published in "Best Poems of the 90's Editor's Choice Award for the writing.; [pers.] I strive to bring forth my deepest feeling through my writing - my hobby art/my greatest support.; [a.] Fairfield, NJ

HUNTER, ISABELLE
[pen.] Isbelle; [b.] February 16, 1927, Dayetteville, PA; [p.] Lucu I., Alex Jackson; [ed.] Student University College; [occ.] Retired; [memb.] Boston Public Library Life Mystic Valley Rail Road Life, Museum of Science; [hon.] Hall of fame the International Poetry Communication Certificate; [oth. writ.] Basic obvious skies.; [pers.] Live from day to day.; [a.] Boston, MA

HUNTINGTON, GLORIA M.
[b.] August 20, 1927, Calais, ME; [p.] Mary Davida and George McKay; [m.] Earl H. Huntington, September 22, 1945; [ch.] One Daughter Dianne; [ed.] Graduated from Calais Academy, 1944; [occ.] Homemaker; [memb.] Lifetime Member VFW Aux, DAV Aux. International Society of Poetry, NMEA, AARP; [hon.] 4th prize, world of poetry, Poet Numerous Honorable Mentions, 5 Golden Poet Awards, Who's Who In Poetry, second place in The National Library of Poetry, 1993; [oth. writ.] Published in Calais Advertiser, and Hot Springs Herald, Numerous poems Published in World of Poetry, American Poetry Asso. and The National Library of Poetry. Phone interview and poem read on F.M. Station in Metropolitan N.Y. in March of 1996.; [pers.] First, be true unto yourself. The rest of life will be a challenge you can deal with ever so much easier.; [a.] Truth or Consequences, NM

IANNONE, DONALD
[b.] January 1, 1922, Benwood, WV; [p.] Vito, Rhea Iannone; [m.] Geraldine, March 19, 1994; [ch.] Donald Diana Douglas; [ed.] 10 grade GED; [occ.] Retired; [memb.] Lions International; [oth. writ.] Several unpublished most longer than 20 lines.; [a.] Tupelo, MS

IMMEL, RUDUN R.
[b.] December 3, 1959, Los Angeles, CA; [p.] James Robert Immel, Angela Morales; [m.] Dawn Greeley (Fiancee); [ch.] Michelle Rena, Jamie Lee Ann; [ed.] H.S. grad., U.S.N. Class 'A' School, 2 yrs. F.C.C.; [occ.] Carpenter; [oth. writ.] Untitled poem published in "Of Sunshine and Daydreams"; [pers.] Fear not the evil in the night. The dawn bring new light.; [a.] Fresno, CA

ISCO, RAY
[b.] March 17, 1950, Sharon, PA; [ch.] Phillip and Benjamin; [ed.] College of Wooster, Wooster Ohio Pol. Sci; [occ.] Teacher; [a.] Warren, OH

JANES, MICHELE MARIE
[pen.] Shell, Shelly Janes; [b.] October 12, 1969, Batavia, NY; [p.] Ralph and Mary Leigh Johnson Janes; [ch.] 4 Godson Steven Shaw, Nicholas Bailey, Gabriel Shults and Ryan Wisniewski; [ed.] Attica Senior High - Grad. 1987 Genesee Community College - Grad. 1989 Institute of Children's Literature - Grad. 1992; [memb.] International Society of Poets, Trinity Methodist Church, Attica, NY; [hon.] Golden Poet Award, Silver Poet Award, World of Poetry. Editor's Choice Award - National Library of Poetry, Numerous Art Awards; [oth. writ.] 4 Poems published by Quill Books - Dreams Come True, Never Say Good-Bye, My Love For You and The Only Sound In The World!, Also "Dreams Come True" - World of Poetry and EPS Publishing and Batavia Daily News. Also A Memorial - National Library of Poetry; [pers.] Whatever your dream may be never give up and always believe in yourself. Most importantly, always believe in God. Your dreams can come true.; [a.] Attica, NY

JENKINS, ROSE
[b.] March 28, 1943, Washington, DC; [p.] Mary Elizabeth and Alfred Dintino; [m.] Franklin Marvin Jenkins, March 27, 1961; [ch.] Franklin, Anthony, Renatta, Christian, John, and Jimmy; [ed.] Suitland High School, graduated 1961 - six years of dance "L&S Willer"; [occ.] Homemaker, Mother,

Wife, Grandmother; [memb.] Our Lady help Christians Catholic Church; [hon.] Dance on "Brooke Farm Show" channel 5 - Made Steel Pier Audition - Atlantic City New Jersey, danced in line; [oth. writ.] "Chloe" Reflection of Light, 1995 "Joshua" Tomorrow Never Knows, 1994 "Happily Married" Songs on the Wind, 1995 "Pete" Poetic Voices of America, 1996 "Sneaking" Shadows and Light, 1996 "Sneaking" famous poems of Twentieth Century 1997 "Mama" Reflections of the Soul; [pers.] The personal opinions of my thinking, as I live each day. The many bottled up stories and memories I want to express - and the everyday daily happenings.; [a.] Waldorf, MD

JEWERS, SUZANNE
[b.] February 27, 1933, Nassau, Bahamas; [p.] Cecil Jewers, Berdie Jewers (Deceased); [ed.] Queen's College (Nassau, Bahamas), Trinity College of Music (London, England), Moody Bible Institute (Chicago, Ill.-one year), Commonwealth Bible College (Nassau, Bahamas, three years); [occ.] Retired - Writing in spare time, charity work; [hon.] Eliza Young Prize for Proficiency during last year of high school (Queen's College, Nassau). Award for most outstanding overall student (Commonwealth Bible College, Nassau, Bahamas); [oth. writ.] Tributes to deceased family members and friends. Articles and song published in the local newspapers. These include poems for Christmas, Easter, and other special occasions. I have had Articles published as well.; [pers.] I love people which has driven me to write many tributes to people of all walks of life. I have made many friends through my poetry, and am encouraged to continue writing poetry to express my love of life, people and places. Poetry is the true language of love which will never lose its charm and beauty.; [a.] Nassau, Bahamas

JOBE, VERNELIA B.
[b.] January 7, 1926, Cardova, MN; [p.] Sherman and Orsie Preble; [m.] Walter F. Jobe, June 25, 1945; [ch.] Ten; [ed.] Grade school - High School - 1 yr. Teacher's Training; [occ.] Housewife; [memb.] Neenah Valley Homemakers, St. John's Ladies Aid; [hon.] Published in "Country Woman", World of Poetry - Golden Poet Award; [oth. writ.] Mostly Poetry; [pers.] I have always enjoyed poetry. Try to find the best in every day life. Enjoy bird watching.; [a.] Endeavor, WI

JOHNSON, KATHERINE
[b.] June 9, 1976, Omaha, NE; [p.] Jerome and Cheryll Velehradsky; [m.] Jeremiah L. Johnson, November 25, 1995; [ch.] Michael Raistlin Johnson; [ed.] Mercy High, very little college; [occ.] Dry Cleaning; [memb.] American Legion Auxilliary, New Renaissance Fighters; [hon.] Motherhood; [oth. writ.] "Where Are You?" published by the National Library of Poetry.; [pers.] I want only to love my family and to revive the glory and granduer of my dream....My Camelot.; [a.] Omaha, NE

JOHNSON, RUFUS W.
[b.] May 1, 1911, Montgomery County, MD; [p.] Charles L. Johnson Sr. and Margret (Smith) Johnson; [m.] Vaunda L., May 29, 1971; [ch.] Three stepdaughters and two stepsons; [ed.] Howard Univ., Wash. D.C. 1930-39, 1. Under Grad. School, 1930-34, A.B. Degree, 2. Graduate School, 1934-36, 3. Law School, 1936-39, LL. B Degree, 4. Four yrs. ROTC Commission 2nd Lt. Infantry ORC 1934; [occ.] 1. Retired Lt. Col. USAR, 2. Semi retired Atty at Law; [memb.] Member of the Bar: US Supreme Court, Supreme Court of South Korea, D.C. Ct. of Appeals for D.C., D.C. District Ct., Supreme Ct of CA, Supreme Ct. of Arkansas, Federal Cts. in Ca., and Ark., Member: American Dudicature Society, American Academy of Political and Social Science, 32nd Degree Mason, 5th Degree Black Belt, Shorin-Ryu Karate, Life Member: American Legion, Vets. of Foreign Wars, Military Order of the Purple Heart; [hon.] Army: Combat Infantry Badge, Purple Heart, Bronze Star, Special Unit Citation for Bravery. First Black Officer to serve as staff judge advocate for a military base in the U.S. Ft. McArthur, Calif. 1952, Civilian. Appears in first Edition of "Who's Who in American Law," 1979-78, College: Captain Football Team in Sr. year, CIAA Co-Champion in the Pole Vault, 1934, CIAA Lightheavy Weight Inter Collegiate Wrestling Champion, 1934; [oth. writ.] Others poems none published; [pers.] As an outstanding College Athlete my theme was: "No celebrating in victory and no alibis in defeat" taken from Rudyard Kipling's If to meet: "If you can meet with triumph and disaster and treat both those impostors just the same."; [a.] Mason, TX

JOHNSON, WAYLON CROSBY
[b.] August 10, 1977, Louisville, KY; [p.] Alise Johnson and the late Thurman E. Crosby; [ed.] University of Louisville (Freshman), Louisville Male Traditional High School, Jefferson County Traditional Middle, Benjamen Franklin Elementary, Whitney M. Young, Jr. Elementary; [occ.] Student; [memb.] Kentucky Alliance Against Racism and Political Oppression; [hon.] National Alliance Against Racism and Political Oppression (Kentucky Branch) award for hard work and Dedication is The Struggle for Freedom and Justice, Editor's Choice Award for Outstanding Achievement in Poetry Presented by The National Library of Poetry; [oth. writ.] "Unloving Soul" published in Sparkles In The Sand; [pers.] Everyone deserves a second chance in life. WCP.; [a.] Louisville, KY

JOHNSON II, NAOMI R.
[pen.] Nana, Snoopy, Lil Snoop; [b.] August 7, 1996, Oakland, CA; [p.] Naomi Johnson I, Delmer Johnson I; [ed.] 7th Grade; [occ.] Student; [hon.] Math trophy's, medals, and plaques. Science plaques.; [oth. writ.] My Aunt is gone and Aaron Kelly's bones.; [a.] Oakland, CA

JONES, KAY
[pen.] Brenda Kay; [b.] July 28, 1947, Cairo, IL; [p.] Helen and Burley D. Watson; [m.] Ralph Jones, October 18, 1985; [ch.] Ricky, Randy and Ben; [ed.] Wondruff High School, IL. Central Jr. College, Southeast Jr. College; [occ.] Semi Truck Owner/Operator Jones Trucking; [memb.] Truckstop Ministries, Feed the children; [oth. writ.] Children's stories, poem published in the lyrical heritage.; [pers.] My mother is the inspiration for this poem, she lives in a nursing home in another state, she deserves recognition for her years of 91. It saddens me, not to be near her. She is responsible for my love of life.; [a.] Hermitage, MO

JONES, KIM KINGSBAKER
[b.] November 12, 1955, Pittsburgh, PA; [p.] C. Louis and Sue Kingsbaker; [m.] Edward M. Jones, October 3, 1993; [ed.] Taylor Allderdice High School. The Pennsylvania State University B.S. Education Mathematics, Suma Cum Laude; [occ.] Avon Salesperson. Medically Disabled.; [memb.] International Society of Poets, American Society of Adults with Pseudo Obstruction, Inc. (ASAP), The Society for Neuromuscular Diseases of the Gastrointestinal Tract, Southwest Christian Church - Choir; [hon.] Poems published by The National Library of Poetry, Quill Books, and ASAP.; [oth. writ.] I am currently compiling a "Chap" book of my poetry, approximately thirty poems, to raise money for ASAP. My poems that have been published to date are: "Twist of Fate", "Forgiveness," and "Life."; [pers.] I started writing poetry as an outlet from the stresses of chronic illness. Many of my poems express the rawest of my emotions, while some are humorous. I have written about my family, finding love, and about the preciousness of life. Singing in the church of choir has added a spiritual dimension to my poetry. My poetry has been compared to that of Emily Dickinson. I hope to have more than seven poems published in my lifetime! As a

member of ASAP, I tentatively shared my poems with the other members. With encouragement, the first poem I submitted to The National Library of Poetry was published. Now, my poetry adorns our walls. My wish for 1997 is to become healthier so that I can keep on writing!; [a.] Norcross, GA

JONES, MR. BLAINE ALAN
[b.] February 3, 1951, Paris, IL; [p.] Ernest Blaine and Virginia Joy Jones; [ed.] Homewood-Flossmoor High School (1969), EIU, SIU, Prairie State College; [memb.] Author's Registry; [hon.] 9 Editor's Choices and 1 honorable mention from the National Library of Poetry, two honorable, mentions from Iliad Press.; [oth. writ.] A chapbook and numerous collated books.; [pers.] I wish that everybody would be happy in their lives, marriages, churches, work places, and singles particularly say a prayer for the person you're dating - they might end up married to you!; [a.] Homewood, IL

JONES, WILLIAM H.
[pen.] Captain J., Bill Jones, William Henry Jones, W. H. Jones; [b.] April 1, 1924, Black Diamond, WA; [p.] Helenor Jones (Father Deceased); [m.] Barbara A. Jones, May 17, 1960; [ch.] Robert Jeffery Jones, Denise Lynn Williams; [ed.] B.A. San Diego State Naval School of Hospital Administration; [occ.] Captain, U.S. Navy (Ret); [memb.] (1) Federal Health Care Executives (2) Fleet Reserve Association (3) Distinguished Member International Society of Poets; [hon.] Legion of Merit (Navy) Numerous Service Medals and Awards, Graduated with honors 5 military schools, Advanced from Apprentice Seaman to Captain during Naval Career. Editor's Choice Awards (12) The International Poetry Hall of Fame; [oth. writ.] Endless Thought Treasured Poems of America April 1996, In His Wisdom We Must Trust Poetic Voices of America June 1996, Charlie Treasured Poems of America August 1996, A Humble Apology Poetic Voices of America Oct. 1996, The Window of His Soul Treasured Poems of America Dec. 1996, How Sad Memorial Day Poetic Voices of America Feb. 1997, Shared Dreams Treasured Poems of America April 1997, Just Desserts Poetic Voices of America June 1997, Songs Unsung Beyond the Stars Fall 1996, Catacombs of the Night Best Poems of 1996 Summer 1996, Please Another chance Across the Universe Fall 1996, Embers Of Sunshine and Daydreams August 1996, Lonely Is The Poet Lyrical Heritage Winter 1996, In Love With Love The Colors of thought Winter 1997, The Joy of Poetry Whispers at Dusk Winter 1996, Grim Reaper A Moment to Reflect Summer 1997, All God's Creatures, In Dappled Sunlight Spring 1997; [pers.] I believe in personal achievement, inspiring others to fulfill their dreams, at peace with self and others, all with a sense of humor, dedication and perspective.; [a.] Lake San Marcos, CA

JOSHUA, MR. SATTY
[pen.] Josh; [b.] February 19, 1955, Nigeria; [p.] Joshua Amopho and Mary Joshua-Amopho; [m.] Rita Benjamin-Joshua; [ch.] Abigail, Kitoye, Atanah, Kebin and Eella; [ed.] Morrisville College - NY, City University of New York, Pace University, NY; [occ.] Engineer - Lucent Technologies, Warren, NJ; [memb.] IEEE, ACM, ISP and Norsed; [hon.] Copyright Awarded by The Library of Congress, Editor's Choice Award, 1995 and 1996 by the National Library of Poetry; [oth. writ.] Several poems published by World of Poetry Press, Several Poems Contracted by Record Companies as Lyrics, Author of Visions - Collection of Poems recorded by the National Library of Poetry; [pers.] Our greatest victories in life are thoses we gain over ourselves.; [a.] Montclair, NJ

JUDE, PHILLIP DANIEL
[b.] May 17, 1938, Westminser; [p.] William Jude (Deceased 1944); [m.] (Deceased 1979) July 7, 1962; [ch.] Two boy - girl, Phillip, Angela; [ed.] Sec Mod. School, and Enfield Technical College; [occ.] Driver at the moment Engineer by Trade; [hon.] City and Guilds for Engineering; [oth. writ.] Just three poems submitted to N.L.P., and other poems I have but as yet unpublished.; [pers.] Beyond the veil, lies wisdom's font beyond the pale, is one's own want. Beyond one's reach, is one's own grasp. Beyond all reason, one's truth at last.; [a.] London

JUDGE, ELIZABETH
[b.] May 17, 1977, San Mateo, CA; [p.] William and Carol Judge; [ed.] Indio High School, College of the Desert; [hon.] Scholarship from Palm Springs Women's Press Club, Dean's List; [oth. writ.] One poem published in Poetic Voices of America, several poems published in the annual publication of student writing, and a poem published in Etches in Time.; [a.] Indio, CA

JULIEBO, MOIRA FRASER
[b.] September 15, 1943, Glasgow, Scotland; [p.] Joan and John Aird; [ch.] Ruth and Martin; [ed.] M.Sc. University of Pennsylvania, 1968, Ph.D., University of Alberta, 1985; [occ.] Professor, Faculty of Education, University of Alberta; [hon.] 1967 Thouron Scholarship, 1994 Faculty Award for Excellence in Teaching, 1995 University of Alberta, AC Rutherford Award for Excellence in Undergraduate Teaching; [oth. writ.] Numerous Research articles and the Read-More series for young children.; [pers.] In my working life my passion is to help young children experiencing language difficulties. In my other life I paint.; [a.] Edmonton, Alberta, Canada

KALUST, VIOLET YOUNG
[pen.] Violet Young; [b.] February 10, 1918, Saint Cloud, MN; [p.] August, Cecelia (Deceased); [m.] Pierre (Deceased), July 12, 1990; [ed.] High School, Part College, Cosmetologist, Artist, Author, Speaker, Spiritual Science Minister and Teacher, W.A.V.E. SK 2/C W. War II; [occ.] Spiritual Counselor, retired; [memb.] Cosmic Light Center, CA - Founder, Universal Harmony Foundation, Florida - Spiritual Science Researcher; [hon.] Aura Light Counselor and Healing Ministry, Society of Spiritual Verities, California. Appeared on radio and TV by invitation, Hair Design Award, Permanent Wave Teaching. Descendent of Carl Jung, Swiss Psychologist; [oth. writ.] Mystic Chords - Golden Age Principles, Keys To Unlock The Kingdom In The Here And Now. Poems, articles, newspaper report on meetings of school, etc.; [pers.] Align your outer self with your inner self and express your whole self to express all facets of life and living - thus success comes automatically. "Find a need and fill it."; [a.] Sun City, CA

KAMINSKI, BONNIE
[pen.] Bonnie Seefeldt Kaminski; [b.] February 24, 1950, Marinnette; [p.] Lawrence, Adeline; [m.] Donald, October 3, 1970; [ch.] Corre, Tirsa; [ed.] NWTC Green Bay, WI; [occ.] LPN; [memb.] International Society of Poets; [hon.] Editor's Choice Awards 1996 for after all child I'm only Human, 1996, Time, 1996 Don't Weep for me'; [oth. writ.] Time, in a muse to follow also on tape. After all child I'm only Human, in a Tapestry of colors, also on tape. Don't weep for me in poets of the nineties. Crimson Cathedral in whispers at Dusk and also in of moonlight and wishes, also on tape. Seeing in the colors of thoughts on tape also all by National Library of Poetry. Crimson Cathedral in whispers in the Garden by the poetry guild. M is for the moments bought by Blue Mt. Arts Visions of Boulder, Co. My name as author is on back of greeting card. They own poem. 2nd printing. Collection of poems in Essentials of Mental of Health Care. Planning and Interventions 1986 WB Sanders Co.; [pers.] I thank God for his gift of my poetry it has given me the joy of helping others

handle their grief because of God's words often an answer to my prayers.; [a.] Coleman, WI

KARG, THELMA AILEEN
[pen.] Tackarg; [b.] June 30, 1918, Montgomery, CO; [p.] Fred and Orpha (Stewart) Crow; [m.] Henry Herbert Karg (Deceased), August 18, 1944; [ch.] Susan Marie Chrysler and Karen Weiss; [ed.] Graduate-Crawfordsville High School, BS Taylor University-Upland, IN, MS Indiana State-Terre Haute, IN, Oregon Law and History-Oregon St.; [occ.] Retired Teacher, United Methodist Minister's Widow; [memb.] Christian Writers, IRTA, UMW, AARP, Republican Committee; [hon.] Editor's Choice Award, several from Poet's Organizations Listed in Who's Who in the Midwest 1996-97, others DAR award in H.S. on George Washington; [oth. writ.] Newspaper Articles - Scripture Press, Nazarene Materials, Music Materials, Government Concerns (Communications); [pers.] I loved teaching. Along with Albert Schweitzer it is well to say that the best way in teaching children is by, example, example, example.; [a.] Crawfordsville, IN

KASEMAN, BETTY M.
[b.] November 11, 1930, Sebastopol, CA; [p.] Dolly Dean Middleton and Marlin Wesley Kaseman; [ed.] BA from San Jose State; [occ.] Retired, Occupational Therapist; [memb.] American Occupational Therapy Association; [hon.] From American legion Aux-for long term service to veterans, VA-for excellent service, Migos for outstanding service, Quadradic Soc. for dedicated service, carnation co. for distinguished volunteer service to community, project fire for outstanding volunteers service to community; [oth. writ.] 9-self-published booklets of poetry re: Family events - 12 childrens stories for family - 2 newspaper articles. 2 professional articles, quoted in two books by other authors.; [pers.] Kindness, a helping hand and a smile goes a long way.; [a.] San Diego, CA

KEETON, VIRGINIA
[b.] March 7, 1978, Florence, AL; [p.] Mr. and Mrs. Allen Keeton; [ed.] Freshman at North West Shoals Community College; [oth. writ.] Several poems published in local newspapers.; [pers.] I am not a poet by choice. God gave the talent and desire. Teachers and family gave me the encouragement to make the most of them.; [a.] Florence, AL

KELCH, RUSSELL
[pen.] Russell Kelch; [b.] September 17, 1913, Kansas; [p.] Harry and Alma Kelch (Deceased); [m.] Clara L. Kelch (Deceased), November 2, 1941, (2nd marriage) Mary Margaret, June 4, 1994; [ch.] One boy (Deceased), one girl; [ed.] Grad. HS. 1931, NCO 1940, grad. OCS Ft Sill, Nov. 1942, Grad. Assc C and GS Course 1960, Grad. Arty Signal School 1950; [occ.] Retired; [memb.] Retired Army Officers, 33 years active duty, Member McConnel AF Base Officers Club, OCS. grad. in 1941, C and GS Associate course 1960; [hon.] Honor Society in High School, ETO ribbon with 5 Battle Stars got ashore on Utah Beach, Morning of D + 6; [oth. writ.] You Know Fear 1995 NLP, Only 2 Rows Of Ribbons 1995 NLP, Miracles Do Happen 1996 NLP, Easy Lesson Winter of 1943, 1996 SPE The L4 Observation Plane 1996 NLP, Total of 25 on WW II 8 others on civilian Subjects; [pers.] I am a great admirer of Rudyard Kipling. I try to make my poems realistic, like many of his. I tell it like it was.; [a.] Derby, KS

KELLY, DEAMUS
[b.] May 8, 1933, W. Mayo, Eire; [p.] Ellen and Thomas Kelly; [ed.] B.A., U.C.D.; [occ.] Security Officer; [hon.] Editor's Choice Award the National Library of Poetry; [oth. writ.] Poems in the local newspaper.; [pers.] Having a purpose in life gives stability and stability. My purpose in life is to help myself and others.; [a.] Dublin, Ireland

KELLY, DOT HUTCHINSON
[b.] Clover, SC; [p.] D. N. and Margaret P. Platt; [m.] Lawrence J. Kelly, October 8, 1994; [ch.] Karen Hutchinson McRae, R. Eric Hutchinson; [ed.] Education Specialist in Administration 1986, Winthrop University, Rock Hill, SC, Master of Arts in Teaching 1972, Winthrop University, Rock Hill, SC, Bachelor of Science in Elementary Education 1964, Winthrop University, Rock Hill, SC, Rock Hill High School, Rock Hill, SC - Diploma 1950, South Carolina Certification Areas: Elementary Principal, Elementary Teacher, Elementary Supervisor, Media Specialist; [occ.] Temporary Instructor (EDU 449) 8/1995 - present, Winthrop University, Rock Hill, SC - Also serve as Winthrop Area Coordinator for Interns; [memb.] South Carolina Association of School Administrators, South Carolina Elementary and Middle School Principals, Palmetto Reading Council, Association for supervision and Curriculum Development, First Presbyterian Church, Rock Hill, SC; [oth. writ.] Poetry: 1) "Rear View Mirror" (In Sunshine and Daydreams), 2) "Celebration" (The Colors of Thoughts), 3) "Life's Gems" (In Dappled Sunlight), 4) Have just completed a children's fiction book.; [pers.] Given the background interest, imagination, recollections, desire and motivation to write, thoughts and ideas can be organized in a form that provides for great personal satisfaction.; [a.] Rock Hill, SC

KELLY, GREGORY
[pen.] Gregg Kelly; [b.] June 17, 1951, Memphis, TN; [p.] Lon and Mary Kelly; [m.] Leona Kelly, October 21, 1994; [ch.] Latoria, Gregory Juan, Gregg Martel and Sherrell; [ed.] 12th grade; [occ.] Warehouse manager for (Fleming, Furn Co.); [memb.] Norris Rd, Church of Christ; [hon.] Employee of the year, for 1985 and 1986, I'm a member of the President's Club of Fleming Furn, for being a 10 year employee; [oth. writ.] I write spiritual poems, for people that are trying to find God. And I also write love poems to my wife.; [pers.] I live only to serve and do the will of God in everything I do. And to bring the lost to Christ and His Church.; [a.] Memphis, TN

KELLY, MARGARET F.
[b.] March 12, 1959, Rockville Centre, NY; [p.] William and Dorothy McCulloh; [m.] Thomas Kelly, August 14, 1982; [ch.] Daniel, Michael and Lisa-Marie; [ed.] Master of Arts-Long Island University, B.S. St. John's University, A.A.S. Nassau Community College; [occ.] Adjunct Professor of English as a Second Language (E.S.L.); [memb.] Reading and Writing Committee, Suffolk Community College, PTA Smithtown Elementary School; [hon.] Deans List - St. John's University; [oth. writ.] Two other poems published by The National Library of Poetry.; [pers.] I attempt to sensitive people to unfortunate lives and the purpose of our lives.; [a.] Smithtown, NY

KEMPF, JOYCE
[b.] September 26, 1943, Canton, OH; [p.] Evelyn Rolston, Clifford Stage; [m.] Kermit Kempf, January 12, 1968; [ch.] Kimberly Diane; [ed.] Attended Timken H.S. Horace Mann Elementary; [occ.] Housewife; [oth. writ.] Mortal Man, My Love, The Resting Place; [pers.] Life is only as good as you make it.

KENNEDY, DONALD J.
[pen.] D. J. Kennedy; [b.] April 16, 1918, Coleite, MI; [p.] Joseph A. Kennedy and Myrtle M. Stewart; [m.] Divorced, July 29, 1942; [ch.] Terry, Cindy, Philip, Liz and Mary Jane; [ed.] Bachelor of Arts, CSTC - Mt. Pleasant Mich., MA - CSULA, Los Angeles, California; [occ.] Retired; [oth. writ.] Poems and essays in various College, School and Institutional papers; [pers.] Words are symbols and the meaning is in the aura that surrounds them; [a.] Highland, CA

KENT, THEODORE C.
[p.] Samuel and Julia; [m.] Shirley Kent, June 7, 1948; [ch.] Donald, Susan, Steven; [ed.] B.A., Yale, M.A. Columbia Ph.D. Univ. S. Calif. SC, D. Johannes Gutenberg University (Germany); [occ.] Writer - was clinical psychologist; [memb.] Am. Psychol. Ass'n. Am. Psych. Society Am. Ass'n. for Advancement of Science, Unitarian Fellowship. Former President of the International Society for the Study of Symbols; [hon.] Listed in Who's Who in America Outstanding Professor, Univ. S. Colo. (1997) Superior Performance Award, Indian Health Service (1986); [oth. writ.] The following are books: Behind the Therapists Notes, Conflict Resolution, Mapping the Human Genome, Genetic Engineering - Yes, No, or Maybe, A Psychologist Answers Your Questions; [pers.] The Universe consists of Potentialities. A unique potentiality of humans is morality and justice. Meaning in human life is created when we activate this potentiality.; [a.] San Diego, CA

KERR, KLEON HARDING
[b.] April 26, 1911, Plain City, UT; [p.] William A. and Rosemond (Harding) K.; [m.] Katherine Abbott, March 15, 1941; [ch.] Kathleen, William A., Rebecca Rae; [ed.] AS, Weber Coll., 1936, BA, George Washington U., 1939, MS, Utah State U., Logan, 1946; [occ.] Tchr., Bear River High Sch., Tremonton, Utah, 1940-56, prin. jr. high sch., 1956-60, prin. Bear River High Sch., 1960-71, city justice Tremonton, 1941-46, sec. to Senator Arthur V. Watkins, 1947. Mayor, Tremonton City, 1948-53, former state senator, educator; [memb.] Utah Local Govt. Survey Commn., 1954-55, Utah Ho. of Reps., 1953-56, Utah State Senate, 1957-64, chmn. appropriation com., 1959—, majority leader, 1963, Utah Legis Council, NEA, Utah, Box Elder edn, assns., Nat., Utah secondary schs. prins. assns., Bear River Valley. C. of C. (sec., mgr., 1955-58), Lions Kiwanis, Phi Delta Kappa, Ch. of Jesus Christ of Latter-Day Saints; [hon.] Dist. dir. vocat. end. Box Elder Sch. Dist. Recipient Alpha Delta Kappa Award for outstanding contbn. to edn., 1982, award for outstanding contbrs. to edn. and govt., Theta Chpt. Alpha Beta Kappa, 1982, Excellence Achieved in Promotion of Tourism Award, Allied Category Award Utah Travel Counc., 1988, Merit Award, 1993, Andy Rytting Community Svc. Award, 1991, named Tourism Ambassador of Month, 1986, Honorary Member of Utah Sherriff's Association, 1996 and 1997; [oth. writ.] (Poetry) Open My Eyes - 1983, We Remember - 1983, Trouble In The Amen Corner - 1985, Past Imperfect - 1988, A Helping Hand - 1990, Sound Of Silence - 1991, Power Behind The Throne - 1992, Unreachable Goal? - 1993, The Only Difference - 1994, Please Boss - 1995, Beach Comber - 1995, (History) Those Who Served Box Elder County - 1984, Those Who Served Tremonton City - 1985, Diamond In The Rough - 1987, Facts Of Life - 1987, Gettin' And Givin' - 1989; [a.] Tremonton, UT

KESSLER, ESPREE DEVORA
[pen.] Espree Devora; [b.] March 2, 1979, Los Angeles, CA; [p.] Joseph Kessler, Hermine Hilton (Kessler); [ed.] Warner Elementary, Emerson Jr. High, University High, Malibu High; [occ.] High School, Intern at Management Agency; [memb.] Writer's Boot Camp (Screen Play Writing), Amnesty International, Red Cross; [hon.] California Scholastic Press Association Award, Certificate of Achievement from the American University of Paris, Principal's Award Contest Illustrator of parent/child book "Tongue Ticklers for Toddults"; [oth. writ.] Feature Editor of High School Newspapers "The Warrior" and "The Current", literary editor for annual magazine "Indian Ink".; [pers.] "Run with your heart or don't run at all."; [a.] Los Angeles, CA

KHALSA, GURU PREM KAUR
[b.] March 6, 1951, Chicago, IL; [p.] Mr. Louis A. Ule and Mary Ule; [m.] Dr. Vip B. Short, DC aka Wahe Guru Singh, June 22, 1997; [ch.] Adi Shakti Kaur; [memb.] I have been a Sikh and a teacher of Kundalini Yoga for 27 years. I am a member of the International Kundalini Yoga Teachers Association, and a Sikh Minister; [pers.] "Pearled Wisdom" September 28, 1996, in response to the request of my childhood friend, Vip Short, for me to give him a poem from my heart. We were resuming letter writing after a silence of 27 years. "Pearled Wisdom" is a love song to come full circle, returning to our sacredness and innocence without the burden of sharing painful life stories. Instead the poem is loving, blessing him to transmute his life's pains into pearls, and so to embrace, is a gift from God. We will be married June 22nd, 1997.

KHIN, U.
[b.] April 21, 1911, Pegu, Burma; [p.] U. Ba Thein and Daw Hla Thin; [m.] Mrs. Yvonne M. Khin, August 25, 1945; [ed.] Bachelor of Science, University of Rangoon, Burma; [occ.] Retired (As a Language Teacher from the US Department of State, Washington, D.C.); [oth. writ.] Spoken Burmese published by the State Department, Quilt articles in various Quilt Magazines.; [pers.] I try to reveal in good qualities in mankind.; [a.] Rocky Ridge, MD

KIEFER, JACKI
[b.] June 9, 1980, Brazil, IN; [p.] Frank and Catherine Kiefer; [ed.] Northview High School; [occ.] Student; [memb.] I am a member of the Tennis and Volleyball Teams at my High School and am a member of student council; [hon.] I have been featured in who's Who Among American High School Students; [a.] Brazil, IN

KILGORE, TANDI
[pen.] Tandi Kilgore; [b.] June 6, 1982, Lamesa; [p.] Bob and Hope Kilgore; [ch.] family: Brandi, Tandi, Randi and Andy; [ed.] Freshman at Klondike High School; [occ.] Student; [memb.] NAR - National Author's Registry; [hon.] 2 Poems published; invitation to convention in Washington, DC.; Editor's Choice Award; [oth. writ.] Short stories and lots of poetry; [pers.] I want to thank all of those who have influenced me to keep writing and not give up, especially my parents.; [a.] Lamesa, TX

KING, DAVID P.
[b.] January 26, 1954, Bakersfield, CA; [p.] Joyce A. King and Betty C. King; [m.] Marcia A. Bucchianeri King, June 29, 1986; [ed.] South High - 1972, Bakersfield, CA, Pasadena City College, CA, 81-82, ITT - Trade Technical School - Van Nuys, CA, 1996; [occ.] Custodian Lead Supv. and Stock Room Manager; [memb.] American Red Cross, Neighborhood Watch Coordinator, North American Chess Champion Club, Worldwide Church of God; [hon.] First and 2nd Place Ribbons in High School in Poetry; [oth. writ.] Many unpublished poems, song poems, fiction and non-fiction unpublished books.; [pers.] I express to you the best I can give of myself so that you may glean from me useful helps to inculcate into your life and be perceived greater than me. Life is in the words and heart of poets.; [a.] Los Angeles, CA

KINGSLEY, CHARLES ERIC
[pen.] Roivas; [b.] March 17, 1975, Warren, PA; [p.] Charles Breaton, Lorraine Anne Kingsley (Divorced); [ed.] One year of Grove City College, PA. one and one-half years at Slippery Rock University PA and currently enrolled; [memb.] National Honor Society, Sigma Alpha Sigma; [hon.] Dean's List, Service Award; [oth. writ.] Poem published in Watermark; [pers.] You can't go wrong when you have Jesus on the brain.; [a.] New Castle, PA

KLEIST, JOANNE
[b.] Reedsburg, WI; [p.] Edward and Alice Brunhoefer; [ch.] Daughter, Marie, Son-in-law, Keith, Grandchildren, Lauren and Christopher; [ed.] B.S. Concordia Teachers College, M.A. Michigan State University, Specialist in Administrative Leadership University of Wisconsin-Milwaukee; [occ.] Assistant Superintendent of Curriculum and Instruction, School District of Waukesha, Waukesha, WI; [memb.] American Association of School Administrators, Association for Supervision and Curriculum Development, Phi Delta Kappa, Ducks Unlimited; [hon.] Selected to be member of State Commission on Schools for the 21st Century, participated in Wisconsin German Studies Program including two weeks in Germany, poems selected to be published by The National Library of Poetry; [oth. writ.] Poems published in Songs on the Wind, Best Poems of 1996, Best Poems of 1990s, articles for professional magazines.; [pers.] The opportunity to have my poetry published is one of the major highlights of my life.; [a.] Waukesha, WI

KNEPP, DAVID LEE
[pen.] David Lee Knepp; [b.] October 3, 1938, Mineral Springs, PA; [p.] Dorthy and Fredrick Knepp; [m.] Shirley Ann Knepp, October 20, 1961; [ch.] Gary Lee Knepp his wife time, three grandchildren Gary David, Gregory, Tyler; [ed.] 10th grade I got my GED 1995 Clearfield High School; [occ.] TAFCO TMP Hide City Clearfield; [memb.] Glad Tidings Assembly of God Church, Goldenrod Clearfield, PA; [hon.] Scout Master Volunteer of year award Community Group of year award, Three National Library of Poetry, Best Friend Award; [oth. writ.] "Go Land Four Seasons" National Library Book, Coming of Dawn American Dreams" Dance of the Arison National Library Book of Congress "Best Poems of 90's and others; [pers.] I thank God for my salvation and for the talent to play Mandoline- Fiddle Guitar and Banjo and talent for writing song's and poems I thank God for my family and for National Library of Poetry for helping achieve poetry.; [a.] Clearfield, PA

KNIGHT, GRACE V.
[b.] November 3, 1931, Sydney, NSW, Australia; [p.] Matilda and Axeli Northby; [m.] Mervyn W. Knight, September 11, 1954; [ch.] 2 sons and 1 daughter; [ed.] Leaving certificate I wanted to teach English and Art. However, I learned Ticketwriting and Advertising, also Silk Screen Printing I had a wonderful job using these skills; [occ.] Wife of Australian Director of Voice Of The Martyrs ...I'm 'General Backstop!'; [memb.] Baptist Church also Choir, we arrived in America to work with Voice Of The Martyrs in Bartlesville, January 12. I am still finding my feet!; [hon.] English Honors for Leaving Certificate, Floral Art (flower arranging) Art (pencil drawing - teenage years) I turned to writing poems after whiplash and spinal injuries; [oth. writ.] Several poems in Christian Woman - "The Way Ahead", "Mourning", "Morning Prayer", these read on also On Being - Article on Serving - after breaking a bone in my foot, I spent 12 weeks on crutches, and needed help!; [pers.] My faith in God and His love is strong. Born in the 'Depression', I was taken from my own home, because of family Breakdown. I thank God for His love and protection throughout many sad days. 'Do unto others what you would have them do unto you'. We live in a needy world.; [a.] Bartlesville, OK

KNIGHT, KAREN A.
[b.] December 11, 1961, Philadelphia, PA; [m.] Joseph Knight, September 19, 1987; [ch.] Nicole, Joshua, Anthony and Kelly; [occ.] Legal Administrator, Librarian, Free-Lance Artist and Arts Instructor; [memb.] New Jersey Arts Alliance AfterImage Writing Group, Linwood Summer Enrichment Program-Coordinator and Arts Instructor, Linwood Library-Children's Poetry Program Instructor; [hon.] Editor's Choice Award, Portraits of Life Anthology 1996, Finalist, Atl. County Secretary of the Year Contest, Lite 96.9 Radio, 1990; [pers.] Find release and reward in my writing and have been doing so for nearly 20 years, I owe my inspiration to Wm. Hamilton, H.S. English Teacher and James Pulvino, H.S. Art Instructor.; [a.] Linwood, NJ

KNIGHT, THOMAS HOWERTON OWEN
[pen.] TH Owen Knight, Owen Knight; [b.] 1928, Sandy Spring, MD; [p.] TH Owen Knight, Katharine Studley Knight; [ed.] Washington Col. BA Univ. of Maryland, 2nd Inf. NCO Academy; [occ.] Music Producer; [memb.] Izaak Walton League, Nature Conservancy, Rainforest Alliance, Green Dome Temple; [oth. writ.] Moonlight Snow - song and recitations to be published by black moon publishing.

KNOLL, D. J.
[b.] May 14, 1934, Salida, CO; [p.] Russell and Leone Peck; [m.] Robert E. Knoll, February 12, 1954; [ch.] Deborah, Robin, Scott, Dawn, Bobbie; [ed.] High School College credits in Oil Painting - 3 Courses; [occ.] Rancher; [memb.] Mt. Zion Baptist Church, Cancer Support Groups - 2, Reach to Recovery Volunteer; [oth. writ.] Published in Tapestry Of Thought; [pers.] I give the credit for my poetry, to the Lord Jesus Christ.; [a.] Washburn, MO

KOSTIOU, PATTI
[pen.] Babe; [b.] April 12, 1964, Beaver County, PA; [p.] Richard and Elsie Scarsellone; [m.] Nicholas Kostiou, May 16, 1989; [ch.] Tom, Amber, Melissa; [ed.] High School graduate 1982; [occ.] Housewife, mother, writer; [memb.] International Society of Poets. Member of Saint Joseph Roman Catholic Church. Virginia PTA Thaila School Virginia Beach; [hon.] Who's Who Among American High School Students 1981-1982 Volume; [oth. writ.] "Whispers To A Friend" 1995 Anthology East of Sunrise "Capture A Moment" anthology at Waters Edge 1995 "We're They" Best Poems of 1996 "Once Friends" published 1997 anthology of Moonlight and Wishes.; [pers.] This poem is dedicated to my 3 children: Tom White age 11, Amber Kostiou age 6 Melissa Kostiou age 4; [a.] Virginia Beach, VA

LADEMAN, JULIE
[b.] December 30, 1981, Lansing, MI; [p.] Steven and Beverly Lademan; [ed.] High School - I'm a freshman; [occ.] Student; [memb.] Okemos Varsity Dance Team

LANGFITT, MEGAN
[b.] September 13, 1978, Clarion, IA; [p.] John and Lynda Langfitt; [ed.] Graduated in 1996 from Eldora - New Providence High School. Freshman at Kirkwood Community College in Cedar Rapids, IA; [memb.] Lifetime member of the International Society of Poets; [hon.] Editor's Choice Awards 3 yrs. in a row; [oth. writ.] Poems published in 3 other books. Wrote two poems for senior class, published in the yearbook.

LASKY, HAL H. A.
[pen.] Hal H. A. Lasky; [b.] June 15, 1914, Philadelphia, PA; [p.] Kate and Jack Lasky; [m.] Ruth (Deceased 1970), March 12; [ch.] Jerald Lasky and Barbara Lasky Kimsey; [ed.] Limited; [occ.] Retired; [memb.] AARP. Senior Citizen Council, Senior Friends of GA., Jewish Sr. Resource Center, Two Masonic Lodges, Adas. Yeshurun Synogogue; [hon.] GA. Eye Bank, Donor Producer of the Year, Interview on GA. T.V. Station, Pictured and Write up in GA "Health Scope Magazine the Senior Citizen Council 1994", Senior Achievement Medallion Award, Credit Merchant (PA.), Man Of The Year Award Association in 1994, The Georgia Eye Bank gave me a write up my picture and my poem, "The Best Should Be Today" the poem is in the 1996 "Through The Hourglass" poetry book at the time I had obtained 26 eye donors and was told no individual had ever turned in that

many. This past June (1996) I was give a Certificate entitled, "Donor Producer of the Year," at this time I now have 53 Donors.; [oth. writ.] (Poems written up in a few publications) "The Best Should Be Today", What Is A Man?, "Thoughtfulness", "I'll Do It A Bit Later", "Life is A Ball Game", "Be A Volunteer", (plus others); [pers.] Your tip for the day: "Yesterday is history, tomorrow is a mystery, today is a gift from the good Lord, that's why they call it the present."; [a.] Augusta, GA

LAWRENCE, VIVIAN M.
[b.] June 17, 1929, Sheboygan Falls, WI; [p.] Mr. and Mrs. James Rhines; [m.] Philip G. Lawrence, April 7, 1973; [ch.] David, Richard, Sharon, Steven, Sandra, Scott, Bruce (Deceased); [ed.] 12 yrs. Sheb. Fall H.S., Business College; [occ.] Homemaker - Retired: 30 yrs. - Shaws Supermarkets; [memb.] Sacred Heart Church Smithsonian Inst. Extension Group Library of Congress; [hon.] Plaques for years of work at Shaws.; [oth. writ.] US -World of Poetry Sunshine and Love - National Library Feelings - National Library Love Letter - National Library; [pers.] Great pleasures come to me through giving people food for thought.; [a.] Eustis, ME

LAZZARETTI, TERRI
[b.] January 27, 1974, South Carolina; [m.] Tony Lazzaretti, July 29, 1996; [ed.] Carrabelle High, Mitchell's Hairstyling Academy; [occ.] United States Navy; [memb.] Distinguished member of The International Society of Poets; [hon.] Editor's Choice Award by The National Library of Poetry 1996; [oth. writ.] "Shadows" (Poetic Voices of America-Spring 1996), "Tomorrow" (The Ebbing Tide) and Poetic Voices of America-Fall '96; [pers.] "Poetry is how we perceive the world around us."; [a.] Naples, Italy

LENG, KEVIN YEO SOON
[pen.] Leonardo, Aspen; [b.] June 7, 1980, Malaysia; [p.] Yeo Kee Seng, Christine Yeo; [ed.] St. James Primary School, Sabah Tshung Tsin Secondary School, Beaverton High School; [occ.] Student (Optional); [pers.] "The End of a Life" is dedicated to everyone of all ages, occupations etc.; never put your focus on worldly things, material, for they are perishable! Instead, put your focus on God, learn more about Him and use your life to serve Him. You never know when the time for you to go is coming.; [a.] Beaverton, OR

LENZEN, MARILYN S.
[m.] Louis C. Lenzen; [ed.] Northwestern University, B.A. English and Art History, Art Institute of Chicago Fine Arts Painting; [occ.] Poet, Watercolorist, Balletomane; [oth. writ.] Poetry and prose essays; recently I have had published some dance criticism; [pers.] Writing, like painting, is a descent into yourself which brings forth a vision, hopefully, of shared human experience. It is about the soul's search for its own identity.; [a.] Belvedere, CA

LEPOSA, PATRICIA A.
[pen.] Pat Leposa; [b.] April 9, 1934, Rutland, VT; [p.] Walter and Catherine Cendroski; [m.] Ernest F. Leposa, October 11, 1958; [ch.] John, married to Jessica, Maryanne married to Patrick Craft; [ed.] St. Patrick, High School, Georgian Court College, The Upper Room Spiritual Center; [occ.] Spiritual Director, St. Matthias Parish, Spiritual Directors International; [memb.] Associate-Sisters of Mercy of America, Regional Community of N.J.; [oth. writ.] Reality, War, Love, a Roller Coaster Ride, previously published poetry anthologies.; [pers.] In the traveling of this journey called life we need not be alone. Writing and sharing poetry enables me to share, share my truth, to connect. I then become, become a part of you and you in turn through your writing become a part of me. For this I thank you.

LESLIE, DIANE
[b.] August 28, 1941, Clinton, MA; [p.] Dr. Jeanie Roffe & Leon Turmaine; [m.] William H. Leslie, January 16, 1988; [ch.] Lance Bradley-son, Billie Ann Bradley-granddaughter; [ed.] Business, Fine arts, Journalism and Medical Science; [occ.] Journalist, retired medical professional, poetess; [memb.] past president of "National League of American Pen Women" Washington, D.C. - Las Vegas Branch, Poetry Guild - New York, American Cancer Society of Palm Springs, CA, others to benefit mankind and animals.; [hon.] I have been on the "Board of Directors" of Nike House, Las Vegas, NE, Teenagers in Trouble and also received honors from the family abuse center, Las Vegas, NE, a Battered Womans Shelter and Re-education program to help them to a new life; [oth. writ.] Several poems published, and columns in various publications across the country.; [pers.] If a poem I write can touch another soul to soul - then it is worthwhile, and each poem is a gift from God. I have written poetry since I was a child. If I can help another human being I am doing what God wants us all to do.; [a.] Thousand Palms, CA

LEWIS, DAN
[pen.] MacLeod; [b.] September 19, 1949, Berkeley, CA; [p.] Dan and Laverne Lewis; [m.] Pamela Kay Groshart Lewis, June 29, 1975; [ch.] Dan Charles, Robert Patrick, Darcie Jeanne, Samuel Alexander Ford; [ed.] Champaign Senior High School - Parkland College-Champaign, IL Boise State University B.B.A Behavior Business Management, B.B.A Aviation Management Boise, ID; [occ.] Transportation Consultant Northwest Freight Consultants, Inc. President and C.E.O; [memb.] Delta Nu Alpha/Transportation Fraternity, First Presbyterian Church, Photographic Historian-Boise, ID, Bench Logistics-Borah High School, Basketball Program-Founder-Boise, ID; [hon.] Several poems published in small town newspapers, the V.A. Medical Center News Letters, World's Greatest Father bestowed by my children. photographic awards received at Idaho State Fairs, Photographer for Miss Idaho U.S.A in 1986 and 1989, Honored member of Who's Who in Business-1994, poem "Life in Continuum" in Recollections of Yesterday, 1996 and "Changes", in Amidst the Splendor, 1996, both published by the National Library of Poetry; [oth. writ.] I have written a collection of poetry about various subjects, but always of the heart and soul.; [pers.] I visualize and create stories in poetry form, each contains either a reflection of my heritage, my friendships, my sorrow, my loneliness, and or my thoughts. I have been influenced by the writings and style of John Donne and Marguerite Duras ("The Lover"). Poetry is the window by which my soul can visualize reality.; [a.] Boise, ID

LEWTER, MARY E.
[pen.] M. E. L.; [b.] August 2, 1949, Indiana; [p.] Deceased; [m.] Jerry K. Lewter, March 11, 1971; [ch.] Three; [ed.] High School (and Life); [occ.] Waitress - Mother/Grandmother; [hon.] Golden Poet awards for 1981-82-85, Honorable Mentions (many); [oth. writ.] Many (unpublished) as well as many that are; [pers.] While we try to teach our children all about life, our children teach us what life is all about.; [a.] Chicago, IL

LIGHTSEY, VERA
[pen.] Bobby Doyle Lightsey; [b.] June 17, 1933, Canada; [p.] Lyra and Michael Doyle; [m.] Vernon Lightsey - Deceased; [ch.] Son - Wayne, grandsons - Dyllan, Logan and Cody, Stepdaughter - Sandra Beth, granddaughter - Jessica of Colorado; [occ.] Retired Secretary; [pers.] The Lord eternal reigns!

LINDAUER III, JOHN W.
[b.] September 6, 1967, Yonkers, NY; [p.] Joan and John; [ed.] BFA Film and Television Production from New York

University; [occ.] Segment Producer for CNBC Television; [oth. writ.] Recently published in a past National Library of Poetry Publication: "Since My Last Confession".; [pers.] Inspired by long walks on the beach, train rides, sunsets, cityscapes, mountain ranges and rainstorms. My work is all very personal and reflects the connection I feel with nature.; [a.] Croton, NY

LITTLE, JOHN C.
[b.] September 15, 1973, Amherst, OH; [p.] Larry and Linda Little; [ed.] Marion L. Steele High School (1992), Navy Nuclear Propulsion Program; [occ.] Nuclear Machinist Mate Second Class (E-5); [memb.] Amherst Church of the Nazarene; [hon.] Good Conduct Award, Enlisted Surface Warfare Specialist Sailor of the Quarter, Battle Efficiency, Editor's Choice Award from Nat'l Library of Poetry.; [oth. writ.] Half Shut Eye: The Rippling Waters; [pers.] All things work for the glory of God.; [a.] Newport News, VA

LLOYD, JENNIFER
[b.] August 24, 1970, Hawaii; [p.] Lynn Lloyd, Richard Lloyd; [ed.] Metcalf Middle School, Ponaganset High School, Creative Writing Scituite High School (night school); [occ.] Cleaner; [hon.] Metcalf Parents Council Award-June 1984, Journal-Bulletin Scholastic Award-1988 (Ponaganset High School); [oth. writ.] All Love Is Lost, published in the poetry book, Walk Through Paradise; [pers.] I write my poems from personal experience. I wish to get my poems published one day and to have my own poetry book someday.; [a.] Warwick, RI

LOPEZ, ISIS NORMA
[b.] July 7, 1931, Los Angeles, CA; [p.] Luis and Amelia Marichalar; [ch.] Clarissa A. Lopez, Rachel A. Laurn; [ed.] Seattle Community College, Seattle, Washington, A.A. Degree in Office Management/Executive Secretary; [occ.] Retired on disability; [hon.] National Honor Society, Typing, Dean's List at Seattle Community College; [oth. writ.] Poems: Clarissa, My Memorable Trip, It is Your Turn Now, Jacquetta, and other personal poems and manuscripts.; [pers.] I write only when inspired by God and it is usually about family and friends.; [a.] Phoenix, AZ

MAJOR JR., RICHARD L.
[pen.] Dick Mason; [hon.] Distinguished member - International Society of Poets: Editor's Choice Award - National Library of Poetry "Forever and a Day" (anthology) poem "There Is"; [oth. writ.] Poetry for magazines, bulletins and loved ones. I have also composed several spiritual songs that I pray many others will sing and be blessed by someday soon.; [pers.] My quest in life is "To be and to seem". This can only be accomplished by daily submitting my will to Christ. By doing this I not only "seem" to be a good person to man, but more importantly, God can see the light of his son reflecting in my life - and therefore I am.; [a.] Gaithersburg, MD

MALLOY, MIKE J.
[b.] July 15, 1963, Ottawa, Ontario; [p.] James Malloy and Theresa Malloy; [m.] Cathy Moffett (Girlfriend), Forthcoming; [ch.] Casey James Malloy, Stephanie and Shane MacMillan; [ed.] High School of Commerce, Ottawa (Vocational Art/Business), Algonquin College Course, Ottawa, (Professional Loss Control); [occ.] Business Admin.; [memb.] Centretown Citizen's Community Association; [hon.] Editor's Award (Nat'l Library of Poetry), 1996 Poet of the Year Nominee (Int'l. Poets Society), 1996 Elected into (Int'l. Poetry Hall of Fame), Nov. 1, 1996; [oth. writ.] Passing Death (Published in "The Paths Not Taken") Nat'l. Library of Poetry, 1996.; [pers.] I trust in morals, truth, honesty and God. Everyone has a guardian angel watching over them, listen to his whisper and the path is clear. Treat others as you want to be treated.; [a.] Ottawa, Ontario, Canada

MANOSH, DANIEL W.
[b.] July 27, 1922, Sheldon Springs, Vermont; [ed.] Graduated from Towle High School, Newport, New Hampshire in June of 1941; [occ.] Radio Operator, N.C.O.I.C., 606th Air-Craft Control Warning Squadron, Kimpo Air Base, Korea PACFC, N.C.O.I.C. for point to point communications at Kunsan Air Base, Kunsan, Korea. For P.A.C.A.F. Logistical Services for Okinawa and Japan, also served overseas in Newfoundland, Greenland and Morocco as a Channel and Technical Supervisor, and concluded his career with the 2130 Communications Squadron, Air Force Communications Service, R.A.F. Croughton, England.; [hon.] Air Force Good Conduct Medal with 1 Bronze Oak Leaf Cluster, Good Conduct Medal with 5 Bronze Loops, Distinguished Unit Citation with 1 Oak Leaf Cluster, Word War II Victory Medal, American Campaign Medal, European-African-Middle Eastern Campaign Medal 8 Bronze Service Stars, Korean Service Medal, United Nation Service Medal, Republic of Korea Presidential with 1 Bronze Service Star Air Force Defense Service Medal with 1 Bronze Service Star, Air Force Longevity Service Award Ribbon with 4 Bronze Oak Leaf Cluster, Small Arms Expert Marksmanship Ribbon.

MARBACH, DONNA M.
[b.] December 9, 1948, King City, CA; [p.] Wm. E. Marbach and Elfriede H. Maurer; [m.] Joseph P. Brennan, September 6, 1980; [ch.] Brian, Erin, Shannon, Kevin and Colin; [ed.] MS - Univ of Penn, BA - Univ of Calif, Santa Cruz; [occ.] Freelance Writer, Painter; [memb.] Writers and Books International Women's Writing Guild, Nat'l Museum of Women, Institute of Children's Writers Arts and Cultural Council of Greater Rochester, Internat'l Society of Poets; [oth. writ.] Several poems, articles, and some fiction published in newspapers magazines, journals and anthologies.; [pers.] Currently on temporary assignment in Guadalajara, Mexico; [a.] Rochester, NY

MARIA, ANNETTE
[pen.] Annette Maria; [b.] April 22, 1944, Irvington, NJ; [p.] Rose Marie and Charles Stevens; [m.] Annulment, July 18, 1964; [ch.] Thomas E. Buccine Damian J. Buccine Scott J. Buccine; [ed.] Ann Street Grammer, East Side High, Northamton Community College; [occ.] Entrepreneur of "The Ace of Cups" Ancient Wisdom; [memb.] M.A.G.I.C. "Merchants Association for Good in the Community"; [hon.] President of M.A.G.I.C.; [oth. writ.] Hello Child, I Am, In the Silence, There was a Time; [pers.] There is one slave but the one you make of yourself.; [a.] Bangor, PA

MARKER, CELIA ANN ADAMCZYK
[pen.] Cessy Adamczyk; [b.] June 15, 1977, Lewiston, NY; [p.] Leon and Dorothy Adamczyk; [m.] Timothy Marker, January 4, 1997; [ed.] Niagara Falls High School, Niagara County Comm. College; [occ.] Writing poetry and studying the work and lives of Poe and Hawthorne; [memb.] Phi Theta Kappa; [hon.] Phi Theta Kappa Honor Society, Alpha Pi Beta Chapter, Dean's List throughout career at N.C.C.C./Who's Who Among American Students during High School; [oth. writ.] Perspectives 1995; [pers.] My writing reflects my view that people should take pride in and relish all of their emotions. Sorrow can be as fulfilling and empowering as joy.; [a.] Norfolk, VA

MASON, MICHAEL S.
[pen.] Mickle Vern Electron; [b.] July 24, 1961, Perry, FL; [p.] Nathaniel S. Mason and Verlyn E. T. Mason; [ed.] Five years post secondary education and always continuing education - since life is an education long pursuit.; [occ.]

Writer, manipulator, store supervisor; [memb.] Lifetime member of International Society and Poets, Washington, DC; [hon.] Editor's Choice Award Several Honors for Poetry; [oth. writ.] (1) "Prosperity On The Rise" a self written expression about life in Steinhatchee, FL and Interests Worldwide. (2) Poetic Verses, (3) Other Writings.; [pers.] The poem and my life in general and specific means is in honor of father - age 62 a honesty stable and sincere man who has many great values and endearments for (his Word) Perpetuality.; [a.] Steinhatchee, FL

MASSOGLIA, CHARLES A.
[pen.] Tony Massoglia, The Traveler; [b.] June 24, Lansing, MI; [hon.] Honors is Singing and Photography.; [oth. writ.] Poems: Alone, A Lashing, Rain, Silence, short story: Dreams; [pers.] Life is a chaotic river, we are the leaves that float upon it.; [a.] Mason, MI

MATHES, DELORIS B.
[b.] November 25, 1948, Bartlesville, OK. ;[p.] Nadine Moore and Cecil Bailey ;[m] Richard L. Mathes, August 8,1966 ;[ch.] John Mathes, David Mathes and Ronnie Mathes ;[ed] high school ;[occ.]Business Owner-Design Tile ;[hon.] Recipient of the Golden Rule Award-Jacksonville, FL. Recieved honors for my work with the Guardian Ad Litem Program. Boy Scouts, P.T.A. and the Association for Retarded Citizens ;[oth.writ.] Several poems published in local newspapers, published in Fields of Gold anthology, first honorable mention poets roundtable of Ar. ;[pers.] In all my poems I strive to write about our daily lives and write so that all can relate to the feelings of the poem. My love for my indian heritage and the enviroment are also very much a part of my poems. ; [a.] Barling, AR.

MATHEWS, VIRGINIA LEE
[b.] September 25, 1940, Syracuse, KS; [p.] George Baird and Edith Myra Mathews; [ed.] Double major in English/Journalism with a minor in social science as well as physical science. There was a special emphasis on folklore and the West in American Literature. While formal education was obtained Kansas University and Fort Hays Kansas State University, the ability to write creatively, to write constantly birthed itself in circumstance similar to Thoreau's Walden when I lived on $50 a month or less while caring for an elderly mother. After her death in 1991, my income was even less and I found myself living as the pioneers lived with oil lamps, cooking in my fireplace and hauling water. Since I also have a heart disability, I have learned that adversity breeds the desire to savour life, that in pain one can find beauty and that real love wins and that richness is in who one becomes not what one possesses. Even in adversity, I pace myself and look for that which is covered with light. In tears there is a sparkle of laughter.; [occ.] My current occupation is writer/artist. I have had 11 one-man art shows in mixed media and pen and ink sketches, and two shows of comforter sculpture (cloth). My renewed teaching certificate is valid in English/Journalism, social and physical science.; [memb.] I am a member of the Sandhills Art Association, the Hutchinson Art Association, the Kansas Press Association, the American Academy of Poets, the International Society of Poets, the Irish Writers Center. I have taken special course in Dublin in 1995.; [hon.] I received both literary and speech awards in high school. State I's and league I's and II's. My feature writing ranked, if I remember correctly, second place. I have also received honorable mentions in various contests. I was elected a national Poet of Merit by the International Society of Poets and Irish writers classify my work with Walt Whitman and William Blake. My poetry varies in length from 20 pages to three lines. I live to create to capture a bit of that true beauty that keeps the heart going.; [oth. writ.] Seasons, Harbour, Sam, the Leprechaun (a short story for children). I have 50 Journals of poetry, some published some not. Some unpublished but copyrighted Titles include Love, No Ordinary Pathway, Wisdom, Short Stories for Two, plus, Children Walking, Tracings. Other poetry published included: "As the Lute Whistles to the Meadowlark", "Child", "White Rain", "Twentieth Century Christmas", "The Spirits of Christmas." Numerous feature stories, profiles, regular new stories and several series.; [pers.] My first book of poetry was written at the age of eight, complete with illustrations. I composed my first musical compositions at six. The piano teacher terminated the lessons because she could not handle that so I taught myself to play the piano. I also sing (at one time professionally with the Voices of Faith in Tulsa) and play the French horn. I love gardening, flowers-herb-trees. My home lots can hardly be seen for the hedging and the trees, a bit of Ireland built on the prairie.

MCCLAIN, JUSTIN
[pen.] Jud; [b.] January 7, 1978, Paducah; [p.] Ronnie and Donna McClain; [ed.] High School Diploma, Graves Co., High School; [occ.] Parts Salesman Wheeler-McClain Ford, Mayfield, KY; [oth. writ.] A collection of original writings and songs. A poem (Concrete Rose) published in The National Library of Poetry - Windows Of The Soul and Local Newspaper.; [pers.] Knowledge brings power. Too much power corrupts the mind. A corrupt mind is useless.; [a.] Mayfield, KY

MCCRIGHT, KIMBERLY S.
[b.] May 24, 1970, Oklahoma, OK; [p.] Greg and Christy Dahlgren; [m.] Matthew J. McCright, July 2, 1993; [ch.] David Andrew McCright; [ed.] Houston Community College, Sierra Community College, University of Oklahoma; [occ.] Homemaker and Image Consultant; [oth. writ.] Various poems, essays, and short stories, weekly fashion column published in local paper, poem published in "Forst At Midnight".; [pers.] My life was richly blessed with the birth of my son, David. I thank God for him everyday.; [a.] Yukon, OK

MCCULLEY, KAREN
[pen.]Karen; [b.] Lincoln, NE; [p.] (The Late) Albert Oldenburg, Moreen Pomajzl; [ed.] Lincoln High, Moorpark College; [occ.] Businesswoman, Specialty Cards and Gifts (Original); [hon.] Editor's Choice Award from The National Library of Poetry (1994); [oth. writ.] Published poetry, "Wonderin'," "Our Hope/Our God", and "A Time To...". An article/piece for The San Diego Union Tribune.; [pers.] The supreme work to which we need to address ourselves in this world is to learn love. As commanded in the greatest two commandments of God, which are: You shalt love the Lord thy God with all thy heart, and with all thy soul, and with all thy mind. And you shalt love thy neighbor as yourself. To become Christ/Y'shua is the only thing in the world worth caring for.; [a.] Encinitas, CA

MCKENNE, CHARLEEN
[b.] November 2, 1944, New York City; [m.] William, August 28, 1981; [ed.] H.S. Music and Art, NYC B. of Sci Music fr. Hunter College NYC studied piano Juilliard School of Music; [occ.] Piano Teacher and Artist. Have business printing custom ordered silk scarnes; [memb.] Greene Countrie Garden Club; [hon.] Blue and Gold for Best of Show arrangement for Phila. flower Show and 2nd Prize for large Flower Garden for the Phila. City Gardens Contest; [oth. writ.] Lyrics for a original Opera.; [pers.] I endeavour to create beauty everywhere and have been greatly influenced by poets Shelley, Keats and Longfellow.; [a.] Philadelphia, PA

MEANS, LUCY MARIE
[b.] November 26, 1925, Abbeville, SC; [p.] Clarence Harvey and Allie M. (Power) Pennell; [m.] David Harold Means, November 27, 1970; [ed.] Schools of Abbeville County, S.C. and Senior High School year near Atlanta, GA, B.A. Erskine College, Due West, S.C., M.A. Presbyterian School of Christian Education, Richmond, VA; [occ.] Homemaker; [oth. writ.] Curriculum writings, including 2 books for children, for The Presbyterian Church, U.S. (now P.C.U.S.A.), freelance, poems and stories, mostly for children, in Church paper, The Christian Observer, published in Mananass, VA.; [pers.] It is my conviction that God gives to human creatures the capability to create, "secondarily" and out of God's Creation. I hope that my writing reflects my "variation" on this theme.; [a.] Lake City, FL

MELE, DENNIS
[b.] October 19, 1960, New Jersey; [m.] Wendy, July 13, 1991; [ch.] Olivia Rae; [ed.] Bachelor of Architecture, New York Institute of Technology; [occ.] Architect; [pers.] Hopefully you will see me as a poet, as one who displays imaginative beauty and power of thought and language, and not as a writer of mediocre verse.; [a.] Centre Island, NY

MENDOZA, LETTY F.
[pen.] Letty Mendoza; [b.] October 21, 1945; [p.] Lucia and Benigno Ferrer; [m.] (Deceased 1981), January 12, 1975; [ch.] Carol, Edwin and Earl; [ed.] Home Economic Teacher, in Tailoring Dressmaking; [occ.] Care-giver to elderly people in Home care; [memb.] American Heart Association; [hon.] Your Award, which you have giving to me in my poem. Until - kind hearted; [pers.] God is my strength in all my trial and He is my survivor in my life, the answers in all my predicaments!

MERRITT, JEFFREY L.
[pen.] Jeff Merritt; [b.] October 1, 1962, Winchester, TN; [p.] J. F. Merritt Jr. Louise G. Merritt; [ed.] Franklin Co. High; [occ.] Bill Collector; [memb.] Franklin Co. Republicans, Franklin Co. Friends of the Library; [oth. writ.] Had my poem "Life Is" published in The Ebbing Tide by the National Library of Poetry; [a.] Decherd, TN

MEYERS, STEPHANIE ALICE
[b.] May 5,1987, Santa Barbara ; [p.] Mary and Keith Meyers ; [ed.] Fourth grade ; [occ.] student ; [oth.writ.] Poems and one book.

MIANO, JENNIFER L.
[b.] August 7, 1969, Minneapolis, MN; [p.] Karen Branham; [m.] Mike Miano, December 22, 1989; [ch.] Jessica (8 yrs), Michael (6 yrs); [ed.] Berkmar High School Graduate; [occ.] Housewife; [oth. writ.] "Change" - In Dappled Sunlight, "These Walls" - Treasured Poems of America, "Inner-Sole" - Revolutions Of The Sole. All poems will be published by Fall '97.; [pers.] Writing poetry is a wonderful way to express my feelings and attitudes towards the ever-changing emotions of everyday life.; [a.] Chillicothe, OH

MILES, VIRGINIA
[pen.] Virginia Null Miles; [b.] April 29, 1918, Bethany, OH; [p.] Charles W. Null-Blanch H.; [m.] February 24, 1951; [ch.] Eight; [ed.] High School Springboro, OH Lee Miles School of Real Estate Sale Carnegie Course; [occ.] Registrar Lee Miles School of Real Estate; [memb.] South Park United Methodist Church, Toastmasters International Kentuck Colonels, International Society of Poets; [hon.] Ten years advisor 4H Dale Carnegie International Speech Contest, - Toast Masters International Speech Contest. Finalist in several poetry, contests; [oth. writ.] Five songs, many children's stories, and over 100 poems, short stories; [pers.] I have taught cooking classes, volunteer public speaking at nursing homes and schools, collect antiques. I like to spread good cheer every where I go.; [a.] Dayton, OH

MILKES, ART R.
[p.] Bernice Milkes; [m.] G. Ann Milkes, February 17, 1979; [ch.] Crystal, Ardi, Lisa; [ed.] B. S. Degree, University of Oregon, Minor in Creative Writing; [memb.] International Society of Authors and Artists; [oth. writ.] One Act Comedies presented in Grade Schools, a short story published in Safety Magazine, and The Last Dance, a poem to published in Etches In Time (Summer of 1997); [pers.] I start writing a poem with an idea, not a formal outline, and let the poem develop and pull me along. Therefore, when I get to the ending, it is as exciting to me as I hope it is to the reader. I have discovered, since I started writing poetry in May 1996, that it is a wonderful way in which to communicate.; [a.] Gaithersburg, MD

MILLS, JIMMY
[b.] August 13, 1973, Rogers, AR; [p.] Jerry and Sue Mills; [ed.] Pea Ridge High School, Northwest Arkansas Community College; [occ.] Computer Technician; [oth. writ.] Compilation of poems and lyrics. Non published; [pers.] My influence generally comes from the anti-transcendentalist view. E.A. Poe had an extremely large affect on my style of writing, along with modern gothic music.; [a.] Bentonville, AR

MINDES, GEORGIA
[pen.] Georgia O. ;[b.] April 28,1932, Des Moines, Iowa. ;[p.]Thalas and Cleo Thalas ;[m.] Arthur Mindes, January 30,1964 ;[ch.] Alexander and Rachel ;[ed.] I did not finish at the University of New Mexico, in Albuquerque, New Mexico. Achieved 3 1/2 years and was a senior when I left for Miami Beach, Florida to have my son, Alexander in August, 1964 and Rachel in 1962. ;[pers.] My personal "A prayer for God Only" says it all. ; [a.] Surfside, Florida.

MITCHELL, CATHERINE E.
[pen.] Sam; [b.] June 16, 1957, Kitchener, ON, Canada; [p.] Joan Stroh, Bruce Mank; [m.] Stewart, March 26, 1982; [ch.] Lee, Matthew, Sandy, Corey; [occ.] Insurance Broker; [memb.] Insurance Institute of Canada, R.I.B.O.; [hon.] C.A.I.B., A.I.I.C.; [pers.] It is my wish to leave everything I touch better than I found it.; [a.] Ottawa, Ontario, Canada

MOLNAR, ETHAN
[b.] January 28, 1978, Cleveland, OH; [p.] Edward and Ellen Molnar; [ed.] University School, Ohio University; [occ.] Student; [oth. writ.] Poems published by the Poet's Guild and Quill Books; [pers.] "This is the strangest life I've ever known" - JDM.; [a.] Northfield Center, OH

MORENO, SANDRA
[b.] July 15, 1953; [p.] Angelo and Adriana Moreno; [m.] Ron Green Esq., 1973, May 1990 Divorced; [ch.] Rashaad and Reinaldo Green; [ed.] PHD Equivalent Kean College of New Jersey, M.A. Kean College of New Jersey, B.A. Lehman College of New York; [occ.] Teacher/Bilingual Needs Assessment Coordinator; [memb.] Puerto Rican Educators Association, Parent Teacher Association; [hon.] Teacher of the Year awarded at Vailsburg Middle School May 4, 1993, Diamond Homer Trophy, Famous Poets Society, Sept. 1996; [oth. writ.] Public Speaking and the Adult ESL Learner. Cooperative Learning and the ESL Adult Learner. Published Essays NJ TESOL; [pers.] Just do it. Always do your personal best.; [a.] West Orange, NJ

MORGAN, NIK
[b.] March 31, 1962, Norwich; [ed.] University of Wales, English B.A. (Hons), University of Wales, English M.A.; [occ.] Artist and Poet; [hon.] Exhibitions of painting and

poetry: St. David's Hall, Cardiff, 1991. Freuds, London and Oxford, 1993. Edinburgh Festival, 1994. International Festivals of Humour and Satire, 1993, 1995, Gabrovo, Bulgaria; [oth. writ.] Small press magazines. Poems and illustrations published in "Grandchildren of Albion" contemporary poetry anthology, 1992.; [pers.] In my work I am attempting to rediscover a sense of the magical. I have been influenced mainly by surrealism, Dylan Thomas, and Mervyn Peake.; [a.] Cardiff, Wales, UK

MORRELL, JUDY
[pen.] Hope Brien; [b.] March 21, 1956, Pittsburgh, PA; [ed.] Keystone Oaks High School, Clairion State, University of Pennsylvania - B.S. in Elementary Education; [hon.] Award for helping the homeless in Pittsburgh PA; [oth. writ.] Windows of The Soul - a poem, writing in high school, worked on a presentation of women's poetry.; [pers.] My writing and poetry are a reflection of my life. A mirror of my thoughts and feelings. They are aids in many ways to me. A small view of a world shared by many.; [a.] Pittsburgh, PA

MORRIS, CURT W.
[pen.] Curt Morris; [b.] October 9, 1966, Salt Lake City; [p.] Craig and Karen Morris; [m.] Tamara Bentley, December 28, 1988; [ch.] Cassidy Morris (Daughter); [ed.] B.A. Brigham Young University, J.D. Gonzaga Law School, Major: English, Minor: Italian.; [occ.] Attorney; [memb.] Utah State Bar; [pers.] Favorite authors: John Donne, John Milton, Dante

MULDER, DONALD S.
[b.] January 17, 1949, Grand Rapids, MI; [p.] Irving and Marguerite Mulder; [ed.] Calvin College, Grand Rapids, MI A.B., English, University of Alaska Anchorage, M.F.A., Creative Writing; [occ.] Process Auditor; [pers.] A work of art reflects a perspective on life back to the beholder.; [a.] Grand Rapids, MI

MULHERN, CARRIE L.
[b.] March 24, 1905, Wiscasset, ME; [p.] Jame and Zulietta Clark; [m.] John D. Mulhern, (Deceased), August 5, 1936; [ed.] Grammer and High School. Training in Hospital to become a nurse; [occ.] Retired Nurse; [memb.] First Baptist Church, Maine General Alumni; [a.] Portland, ME

MUNSON, PATRICIA A.
[b.] January 5, 1946, Dowagiac, MI; [p.] Muriel Adams and L.C. "D.D." Adams; [m.] Raymond M. Munson, May 29, 1963; [ch.] Lovette Freeland, R.L. Munson, Starla Apodaca, Nathan Munson; [ed.] NSG, NMSU, CCT, RN; [occ.] Retired RN; [memb.] Humane Society; [hon.] Meritorious graduate NMSU Golden Poet Awards, Editor's Choice Awards; [oth. writ.] Poems included in: Best Poems of The 90's, Best Poems of 1996, Best Poems of 1995, Outstanding Ooets of 1994, The Coming Of Dawn, Poems That Will Live Forever, Word Poetry Anthology, Our Western World's Greatest Poems; [pers.] The worth of a person has nothing to do with looks, wealth, race or social standing. We all face the same evaluation. It is the worth and health of our souls, I pray for the wisdom to see that part of people.; [a.] Carlsbad, NM

MURPHY, JULIE K. G.
[pen.] Julie Gianakas; [b.] April 1, 1973, Florida; [p.] Christopher and Sherry Gianakas; [m.] David Alan Murphy, December 19, 1992; [ch.] Whestley Murphy; [ed.] Hudson Senior High School (1991 - Graduate); [oth. writ.] Friendship, Changes, some other poems in high school year books.; [pers.] Don't ever take the time you have with your loved ones for granted. make every moment as precious as it could possibly be. Absence - dedicated to my husband David.; [a.] Kingsland, GA

MUSE, CHARLES
[pen.] Charles Muse; [b.] August 18, 1966, Detroit, MI; [p.] John L. Muse and Lenora E. Muse; [ed.] Robichaud 4/5 DBN. Hgts. Mich Class 1984; [occ.] Maintenance Tech.; [memb.] International Society of Poets; [hon.] Editor's Choice Award for The Poem believe published in the East of the sunrise also received an Editors Choice Award for the Poem The Owls Name published in the Best Poems of 1996; [oth. writ.] Believe - East of the Sunrise The Owls Name - Best Poems of 1996 (Believe was recorded on Cassette Tape Titled The Sound of Poetry 1995).; [pers.] The poem my prayers is exclusively Dedicated To a very special person whom I love very much. Not only is this person my very best friend she is my mother, Lenora E. Muse I love you mom, Charles Muse; [a.] Dearborn Heights, MI

MUSE, LORRAINE
[pen.] Lorraine Muse; [b.] December 15, 1971, Bridgeton; [p.] Lawrence and Pat Muse; [ed.] Alloway School, Woodstown High, Schalick High School and Salem County VoTech.; [occ.] Unemployed; [hon.] National Honor Society and 2nd place Conservation Essay Award.; [oth. writ.] 2nd place conservation Essay Award.; [pers.] A poem creates imagination.; [a.] Elmer, NJ

MUSHINSKI, ANN MARIE
[b.] November 28, 1956, Burlington, CO; [p.] Shirley and Joseph Mushinski; [ch.] Katie Elizabeth; [ed.] Hainesport Elem., Meadow View Elem., Rancocas Valley Regional H.S., University of Mass.; [occ.] Medical Billing and Collection Rep. - Orthopaedics; [memb.] Mt. Holly SDA Church, Motherhood; [hon.] 3 Editor's Choice Award by the National Library of Poetry; [oth. writ.] Article for a Teen Magazine - Black Secrets; [pers.] Love life! Embrace it, touch it, and cherish it. Thank God for each day. Have a smile ready for everyone. And carry love and laughter in your heart.; [a.] Mount Holly, NJ

MYERS, MICAH GRANT
[b.] October 7, 1979, Blytheville, AR; [p.] Harry Grant Myers III, Debby Myers; [ed.] GED, currently attending Mississippi Delta Community College; [occ.] Student and Part Time Employee of Irvin Industries; [memb.] Greenwood Country Club, Twin Rivers Recreational Center, FBC (First Baptist Church); [hon.] Several Art Awards, chosen by Duke University to take The ACT in 7th grade (made 21 composite score), He was in Eggstra (Encouraging Greater Greenwood Students to Reach Ahead) a program for gifted children.; [oth. writ.] The poem pursuit published in In Dappled Sunlight.; [pers.] I see the cause of the degeneration of man being the lack of individual thinking. My wish is that one day everyone will become virtual bargain bins of their own ideas and opinions.; [a.] Greenwood, MS

NABER, ROSEANN M. DEPINTO
[pen.] Roseann M. DePinto Naber; [b.] December 27, 1953, Bronx, NY; [p.] James and Claire DePinto; [m.] Awni Naber, October 24, 1976; [ch.] Dina Marie and Anthony James; [ed.] High School Graduate - Roosevelt, Yonkers, NY, 2 year course - Inst. of Children's Literature, Long Ridge, CT, Certified - Travel Agent - Bocestech, Yorktown, Certified and Licensed NY's realtor - Bocestech; [occ.] NY's Commissioned Notary Public Administrative Asst., Coldwell Banker Realty; [memb.] American Society of Notaries, American Biographic Institute, Nat'l Assn. of Female Executives; [hon.] Award: 2000 Notable Women Award by American Biographic Institute. Honored: Internat'l poetry Hall of Fame for my Poem, "Simply Heavenly" published: Honored: Who's Who In New Poets 1996 for my verse, "The Silent Revolution"; [oth. writ.] "The Silent Revolution", "Simply Heavenly" both published; [pers.] God has blessed me with a wonderful,

loving family whom I cherish very much. This love has inspired my writing to share my innermost convictions with others my motto to live by: Live, love and laugh much!; [a.] Peekskill, NY

NEILSON, LILY KALLIS
[pen.] Brande Denis; [b.] October 10, 1923, Redcliff, Alberta, Canada; [p.] Julius and Adeline Kallis; [ch.] 2 sons - 1 daughter; [ed.] Public School grades 1 thru 4 in Medicine Hat, Alberta-then moved to Sundre, Alberta-walked 3 miles to and from School (1 room) for next 4 years; [occ.] Live a quiet retired life in Calgary, Alberta. Wrote very first poem at age 12 while walking to school; [oth. writ.] 1 children's story published. Poem published in 7 anthologies. My favorite poets are: Robert Service and Edgar Guest. The latter seems to express my own own opinions so well. I enjoy the down to earth, simple stories his poems tell.

NELSON, DEREK M.
[b.] February 23, 1970, South Haven, MI; [p.] Martin Nelson and Judith Nelson; [ed.] Green Run High, Florida Keys College, Old Dominion Univ.; [occ.] Network Engineer; [hon.] CNE 3.X, CNE 4.X, CNI; [oth. writ.] 'Together with Age', in The Ebbing Tide; [pers.] This poems reflects my view on how my guardian angel made me aware of the presence of the Lord and how he saved my life.; [a.] Chattanooga, TN

NESS, EVA ANNE
[pen.] Vannie; [b.] April 5, 1942, Bagley, MI; [p.] Edward, Anne Baker; [m.] Gordon T. Ness, December 27, 1958; [ch.] Tammy, Todd, Timothy, Lisa, Linda; [ed.] High School; [occ.] Self employed; [memb.] Women in Arts; [hon.] Nothing Formal; [oth. writ.] Poetry short stories family fun things; [pers.] I would like to go back to school - and get to be a better writer. I want to sell something! I love to write and pour out my emotions.; [a.] Kenosha, WI

NETTERWALD, BILLIE F.
[b.] June 17, 1932, Marcellus, MI; [p.] Ruth Eleanor Cornisb Forbes and Howard Forbes; [m.] C. Edw. Smith Jr. 1951, Frederick G. Netterwald Sr., 1981; [ch.] Karen Elaine Johnson, Mark Edward Smith; [ed.] B.S. and M.A. Western Michigan University of Kalamazoo Michigan Emeritus Teacher of Michigan Music Teachers Assoc., Music Teachers National; [occ.] Private Piano Instructor; [memb.] KOS - Kalamazoo Oratior Society and Concert tours, 1989, 1991, 1995, 1997 NGPT - National Guild of Piano Teachers - in NGPT Hall of Fame - International Composition Chairman 1993-1995, Judge 1989-1995, MFMC - Michigan Federation of Music Clubs, NFMC - National Federation of Music Clubs, MFMC - 1996 Michigan Chairman - composition contest, (KAMTA) Active Member Kalamazoo Area Teacher Assoc., (MMTA) Active Member Michigan Music Teachers Assoc., (MTNA) Active Member Music Teahers National Assoc., (SAA) Active Member Suzaki Association of Americas; [hon.] 1951 Western State High School Salutorian Hall of Fame in National guild is a lifetime award in Music Teaching, Have been International Judge of Music Contest for American Music Scholarship Assoc. of Cincinnati, Ohio Students of mine placed First in International Composition Contest in 1983, 1993, and 1996 Many First Place winners from Elementary. Thru Collegiate in MTNA - MMTA Composition Contests from 1983-1993, MFMC-NFMC- 1996 First Place Elementary Michigan and Regional Composition Winner; [oth. writ.] 1989 Copyright Book "Desiring More Music" 1993-1995 Author of Music Articles in Piano Guild Notes, official Magazine of National Guild of Piano Teachers, 1996 Poem entitled "Hope" in Where Dawn Lingers" published by the National Library of Poetry, 1997 Poem entitled "When" in The Best Poems of the 1990, published by the National Library of Poetry 1995-1996 Article in Compositionfor Michigan Teacher Bulletin, Composer of Music Entitled: 1989 Oh Papa! Come Dance with me, 1989 Twins: A Fughetta, 1990 Twins and A Fughetta, 1990 A Rose Randeau, 1991 Suite Seasons, 1993 How Do I Love Thee!, 1996 Caring!; [pers.] The poem Music of the Heart was composed as a legacy to my "Four Musical Granddaughters," Kervie Lynn, Erin Rebecca, Caitliu Elizabeth and Andrea Lauren Johnson. Children and music are the hope of the future we can make it a better world thru our children and a love of music! The gift of grandchildren and all children is a treasure.; [a.] Kalamazoo, MI

NEUBACHER, FRED
[b.] March 19, 1937, Australia; [p.] Neubacher Elsa and Roman; [m.] Valerie Taller, June 2, 1995; [ch.] Roman Manny, Jacqueline and Joshua; [ed.] Public School, High School, Art School; [occ.] Professional Artist (High Realism Painter); [memb.] Several Art Clubs; [hon.] Many Awards in the fields of Art, Editor's Choice Award (Nat'l Library of Poetry); [pers.] I write what I feel, what I feel is life.; [a.] Kanata, Ontario, Canada

NICHINIELLO, CHARLENE
[pen.] Char, Nicki; [b.] February 24, 1951, Lynn, MA; [p.] Charles W. Joslin, Adrienne G. Burrell Joslin; [m.] Joseph R. Nichiniello Sr., November 26, 1967; [ch.] Denise M. Nichiniello, Manns, Joseph R. Nichiniello Jr., James T. Nichiniello; [ed.] High School Diploma, Accounting Business Seminars; [occ.] Bookkeeper, 25 years (Family Business. J. N. Appliances Co. Owners Joseph E. Charlene Nichiniello) Entrepreneur, Husband Wife.; [memb.] Concerns: Heart Fund, Cancer Fund Substance Addictions, Emotional Stress. Our American Soldiers and the American Dream, Health Care for all love, peace, freedom; [hon.] International Society of Poets Received 2 Editor Awards Distinguished Member. Poem published (Where Dawn Lingers) 1996 The International Poet of Merit Award. 1996 Invited to (read) ISP Symposium, D.C. 1997 Poem accepted, for best poems 1997.; [oth. writ.] (Dad, I Hear Your Voice, Guide Me Through Life) (Visions, A Stairway To Heaven) (My Loving Strong Ship) (My Journey To Heaven) (Higher Power Love, My Son) not sent in yet (plus more poems).; [pers.] I love the art of poetry, the rhythm of creative writing, my inner thoughts, ideas, dreams, poems of love, life and spiritual visions, shared with others.; [a.] Georgetown, MA

NICHOLS, MARTHA ANNE HOLT
[pen.] Martha Anne Holt; [b.] July 28, 1938, Rogers, AR; [p.] Howard H. Holt, Alpha Haskins Holt; [m.] Edward Orlin Nichols, November 6, 1994; [ch.] Laura Dee Ann Owen, Kenneth Eugene Poague; [ed.] Van Buren High School, West Ark College; [occ.] Administrator - Western Arkansas Employment Development, Inc.; [memb.] Alexander Christian Church Ark. Employment-Trng. Assoc. - Western Ark. School to Work Council - Board of Directors - Van Buren Chamber of Commerce Board of Dirs. - National Assoc- Trng.-Emplymnt., Professionals - National Assoc. of Counties; [hon.] Woman of The Year - Gamma Beta - Boss of The Year - Jr. Chamber of Commerce - Outstanding Citizen - GFWC - Women's League Outstanding Citizen - State of Arkansas for Public Service - Who's Who Among Outstanding Business Executives - Elected Official - Crawford County Democratic Central Committee; [oth. writ.] Forty Years - The Guitar Man - Linda Louisa - My Only Son The Lady - Polly Jane Holt - Daddy, Did You Know? - My Hero - From A Baby To A Lady - Queen Of Hearts - Ode To Laura Dee Queen Of The Road - Leo Trio; [pers.] All writings inspired by the beautiful people who have influenced my life. God gave me love and He gives me the words to describe my love and appreciation.; [a.] Van Buren, AR

NIKLAUS, JANET M.
[b.] Septebe 14,1930, Fall River, Mass. ;[p.] Roy and Jessie McIlwaine ;[m.] Robert L. Niklaus, August 16,1958 ;[ch.] Karen Rovito, Erica Butler, Judy Poferl ;[ed.] High School, United College of Barrington and Gordon- Boston, MA School of Tropical Medicine Antwerp Belgium ;[occ.] RN- Hospice Nurse (Pikes Peak Hospice) ;[memb.] Front Range Alliance Church Colorado Springs Symphony ;[hon.] 5 year award: Pikes Peak Hospice, Nursing Award- The nurse I would choose If I were ill. ;[oth.writ.]" What Hospice Means To Me"" Alton Bay at Evening" ;[pers.] Born Sept.14,1930, Fall River, MA. Husband Robert L. Niklaus: High schood Gardon Barrington College, Truesdale Hosp. Sch. Nurshing School of Tropical Med- Anbinerp Belgium. ; [a.] Colorado Springs,CO.

NOEL, DEANNA
[b.] September 6, 1962, Concord, CA; [p.] Howard and Roberta Bisek; [ed.] Pinole Valley High, A.A. degree from Contra Costa College; [occ.] Student, Currently Studying for B.S. Degree at California State University Hayward (CSUH); [memb.] Rollingwood Baptist Church, San Pablo, CA; [oth. writ.] One poem published in Memories of Tomorrow put out by National Library of Poetry.; [pers.] The world would be a much nicer and better place if human beings would show more tender, loving care for one another.; [a.] San Pablo, CA

NORRIS, KIMBERLY
[b.] May 4, 1970, Victoria, TX; [p.] Olan and Alice Hunter; [m.] Kenneth Wayne Norris, June 8, 1991; [ch.] Tawny Rebecca Norris; [ed.] Bachelor of Science, degree in Psychology and English from Liberty University (1992) Klein High School Graduate (1988); [occ.] Homemaker, Mother, Writer; [memb.] Officer's Wive's Club, Squadron Wive's Club, Member of Midland Park Baptist Church. OWC Scholarship Committee.; [hon.] Texas A and M University Distinguished Student Award (1990) Outstanding Young Women Of America (1991) Outstanding Volunteer CAFB (1996) Outstanding First Baptist Service Award ('93-'94) Honorary Pilot Award (1992) Phoenix Spouse "The lady who stands beside the silver wings" Award (1996); [oth. writ.] (1987) "Time To Write On Houston" Essay Contest Winner. Column in "Airmates" - CAFB Wive's Newspaper. Clippings and Advertisements for Base Newspaper. (1996); [pers.] I enjoy writing about nature in my work. English literature and Shakesperean Sonnets influence my pieces, and I endeavor to write about pleasant topics.; [a.] Charleston AFB, SC

NORTHCUTT, BETTY
[pen.] Betty; [b.] July 12, 1957, Texarkana, TX; [p.] H. V. Green and Dorothy Green; [m.] Carroll E. Northcutt, March 17, 1986; [ch.] Christopher William Northcutt; [ed.] Linden - Kildare High School, Linden, Texas; [occ.] Security Guard, Texas Eastman, Longview, Texas; [hon.] Two Editor's Choice Awards from the National Library of Poetry for previous poems published.; [oth. writ.] Published poems: "My Family" in The Voice Within and "Stop And Smell The Roses" in Best poems of The 90's other poems written and given to family and friends.; [pers.] Thank you, Mama for your support and encouragement. Without you this would not have been possible.; [a.] Beckville, TX

NORTON, DANIEL
[b.] September 4, 1978, Elmhurst, IL; [p.] Diane, Daniel; [ed.] Waubonsie Valley High School, 2 semesters at College of DuPage; [occ.] Marshalls Sales Associate; [hon.] Published in National Library of Poetry's "A Muse to Follow"; [oth. writ.] "Expression" from A Muse to Follow; [pers.] I believe that poetry is indeed an art form, without restrictions, it is a medium to release any emotions.; [a.] Naperville, IL

NORWOOD, LEGORA M.
[b.] March 26, 1938, Mound Bayou, MS; [p.] Isaac and Eldra Peterson; [m.] Willie Edward Norwood Sr.; [ch.] Joseph Dudley and Marcus Dalton; [ed.] Philander Smith College, Little Rock, AR, Delta State Univ. Cleveland, MS, Mound Bayou Public Schl. Sys.; [occ.] Elementary Principal; [memb.] Alpha Kappa Alpha Sorority, Inc., MS Assoc. of Educators, Nat'l Education Assoc. (NEA); [hon.] Who's Who in American Colleges and Universities, Who's Who in American Education; [pers.] Human beings are ends within themselves, not means to an end.; [a.] Mound Bayou, MS

NUNN-WALTON, LOUISE
[pen.] Weszi; [b.] April 14, 1960, Detroit, MI; [p.] Frank and Patricia Patrick; [m.] Michael, July 19, 1984; [ch.] Mycal and La Ishia; [ed.] U. of D., Mercy College, B.S. MSW, William Tynsdale Bible College; [occ.] Director/Child Care - Vernor Elementary School, Det. MI; [memb.] Trinity Miss. Baptist Church, New Day Church of Deliverance (Radio Broadcast Dir.); [oth. writ.] Several poems published in area newspapers. Women's day speeches on file. At different churches.; [pers.] I keep a spiritual vision, for God holds the key to my future. I was truly inspired by my late Grandmother, Louise J. Armstrong!; [a.] Southfield, MI

NZERUE, MD. CHIKE MAGNUS
[pen.] Pawa; [b.] June 23, 1963, Nigeria; [p.] Godfrey and Grace Nzerue; [occ.] Assistant Professor of Medicine Morehouse School of Medicine, Atlanta; [memb.] Association of Physician Poets American College of Physicians; [pers.] I emphasize the joys and travails of the human condition in my poems.; [a.] Avondale, GA

O'BRIEN, MARTHA D.
[b.] February 10, 1933, Kansas City, MO; [p.] Milton and Berenice Doyle; [m.] James E. O'Brien (Jim), February 6, 1982; [ed.] Holy Names High School, Oakland, CA, Holy Names College, Oakland, CA; [occ.] Coordinator of Religious, Education in Assumption Parish San Leandro, CA; [memb.] International Society of Poets, Holy Names College Alumni Association; [hon.] Outstanding Alumni Award from Holy Names College, Diocesan Award for years of teaching religious education.; [pers.] I strive to have people realize the goodness in our world, to live in peace and harmony.; [a.] San Leandro, CA

O'CONNOR, MICHAEL J.
[b.] August 27, 1985, Boston, MA; [p.] Mark and Karen O'Connor; [ed.] Thomas Blake Middle School; [occ.] Student; [hon.] Editor's Choice Award for "Spring" in Recollections of Yesterday, 1996; [oth. writ.] "Spring" in Recollections of Yesterday.; [pers.] I like poetry because it is short and dramatic.; [a.] Medfield, MA

O'HARE, PATRICIA ANN
[pen.] Patricia A. R. O'Hare; [b.] February 4, 1965, Bayshore, NY; [p.] Sgt. Raymond R. O'Hare, Elizabeth Theresa O'Hare; [ed.] Central Islip - High School "84"; Suffolk County Community College "87"; Moody Bible Institute; The Laural School of Health Careers and Prof. Sccy.'; [occ.] Literature Sales, Freelance Writer, Model, Crafter.; [memb.] The International Society of Poets, A.A.M.A., Seventh-Day Adventist Church, Central Islip Community Patrol.; [hon.] Four year High School Music Award, Freshman Class Vice - President, Sophomore Class Secy., Town of Islip Senior Citizen Volunteer Award, Future Bus. Leaders of America, Student Librarian; [oth. writ.] The Rapier - High School Paper. The National Library of Poetry - Of Moonlight and Wishes, Best Poems of 1997, and the Sound of Poetry (Selections on tape).; [pers.] Writing is an expression of self. I love to write poems for others, as an influence to their life experience. I

thank God for my special gift of expression.; [a.] Central Islip, NY

O'HAVER, RUBY
[b.] January 15, 1945, Keyser, WV; [p.] Nina Mary (McVicker) and Olyn Elzworth Tichnell; [m.] Rev. William A. O'Haver, Jr., June 16, 1973; [ch.] April, Nina & Olyn (O'Haver); [ed.] Barton Elem. School, Valley High School - Lonaconing, MD., Catherman's Business School - Cumberland, MD; [occ.] Homemaker and Ministry in music; [memb.] Ordained Minister with Fellowship Evangelism, Inc., DDAL, Inc., HSUS, Inc., PETA, Inc., Nat'l. Comm. for the preservation of Soc. Security, International Society of Poets, The National Library of Poetry and The International Poetry Hall of Fame; [hon.] Certificate of Ordination License, The President's Athletic Award, Editor's Choice Award for outstanding achievements in poetry, 1995 and 1996.; [oth. writ.] Several poems published in local newspapers. I've written Easter plays, a christmas play. Two poems have been published by The National Library of Poetry in "A Delicate Balance", "Recollection of Yesterday", and "The Best Poems of the '90s".; [pers.] I wish to bring honor and glory to almighty God and His son Jesus Christ thru my poetry. Thru His inspiration, and the encouragement of my husband, children & parents. I wish to show others that there is a reason to live, and joy to be had.; [a.] Cabins, WV

OGBUNUGWU, AUGUSTINE IBOODINMA
[b.] September 15, 1952, Agulu, Nigeria; [p.] Okeke X Gloria Ogbunugwu; [m.] Catherine C. Ogbunugwu; October 4, 1982; [ch.] Chioma X Uchenna Ogbunugwu; [ed.] BSC (Hons) Ed. Biology University of Nigeria Nsukka, Dip Th, Trinity Union Theological College, Umuahia, School of Nursing, Houston Baptist University; [occ.] Pastor - Church of the Epiphany Houston, student college of Nursing Houston Baptist University; [mem.] House of clergy, Giscopal Diocese of Texas, House of the clergy, Diocese on hte Niger, Province of Nigeria; [hon.] First place in poetry, Danny Lee Lawrence creative writing award 1995; [oth. writ.] Unpublished novels - Dance of the Queen, Echoes of Victory and many other poems, news commentorries for Anambra Broadcasting Corporation, Nigeria; [per.] Unless your seeds are sown, no fruits can be expected; [a.] Houston, TX

ORE, JAMES LAWRENCE
[b.] January 30, 1961, Pueblo, CO; [p.] James and Ida Ore; [m.] Sharon Ore, August 4, 1981; [ch.] Tiffany Ann-Marie, James Lawrence II; [ed.] Rocky Mountain H.S., Big Bend Community College, Military Leadership Courses, Correspondence Course - Institute of Children's Lit.; [occ.] Pool/Spa Service Mgr.; [hon.] Numerous Military Awards over nine years of service; [oth. writ.] Four published poems to date, several unsolicited poems and shorts written.; [pers.] The world is already too full of trivia. I keep searching for profound in my writing. Perhaps someday I will.; [a.] Loveland, CO

ORTIZ, MARCELO R.
[b.] April 27, 1930, Puerto Rico; [p.] Herminia and Sinforoso R. Ortiz; [m.] Magdalena, June 23, 1957; [ch.] Maggi, Elizabeth, Genesis; [ed.] Passarell High, R. Rico Nycc; [occ.] Retired substance abuse counselor; [memb.] International Society of Poets. Revista Kofresi (Hispanic); [hon.] Certificate of Merit 1987, Golden Poet Award 1988 and Silver Poet Award 1990 all World of Poetry; [oth. writ.] Spanish poems, published in Revista Kofresi of New York. Short Stories and plays used at work as educational tools as well as recreational.; [pers.] In my poetry I try to follow the philosophy of Theodore Roethke of seeking his essential self by expressing all feelings and emotions to the point of nakedness.; [a.] Bridgeport, CT

OSAMWONYI, JOE
[pen.] Joseph Iyobosa Osamwonyi; [b.] February 28, 1959, Nigeria; [p.] Mr. Ben Osamwonyi and Mrs. Margaret Osamwonyi; [m.] Eleanor LaVerne Osamwonyi, November 9, 1990; [ch.] Adesuwa Osamwonyi, Precious Burke, and Gibril Kuyateh; [ed.] Law Student, LaSalle University, BS and MA, John Fay College of Criminal Justice, Diplomas in Paralegal Studies and Civil Litigation, School of Paralegal Studies; [occ.] Adjunct Lecturer, Hampton University, and President of Lyobosa Limousines; [memb.] 1) American Society of Composers, Authors, and Publishers (A.S.C.A.P.), 2) Nu Gamma Sigma, 3) Who's Who Among Students in American Universities and Colleges, 4) Law Society, 5) JJC Alumni President's Club, 6) World of Poetry, 7) African Student's Association; [hon.] 1) Outstanding Leadership Award, 2) Distinguished Service Award, 3) Thematic Studies Award, 4) Leadership Excellence Award, 5) Outstanding Service Award, 6) Dean's List JJC, 7) National Dean's List, 8) Africademics (ASA's highest Awards for Outstanding Contribution), 9) Golden Poet, 10) Editor's Choice Award, 11) Employee of the Year Scholarship Award, 12) Belle Zeller Scholarship Honorary Mention; [oth. writ.] Computer Conquest, Mr. Pen, My Good Friend, Africanism, My Heart Is In Inferno, Love You Dearly, Give Peace A Chance, Stealing In The Name Of The Lord, Utopia, I've Been There, Midday Darkness, Unusual Kind of War, etc.; [pers.] I have come a long way and have a long way to go. Life hasn't been easy, but well-deserved successes have been achieved.; [a.] Williamsburg, VA

OSBORNE, JAMES R.
[b.] January 31, 1943, Lenior, NC; [p.] Ray and Opal Osborne; [m.] Janet L. Osborne, May 25, 1973; [ch.] Sherry Osborne Burns and Jimmy and Rachel (both deceased in infancy); [ed.] Attended Happy Valley High School in Lenior, North Carolina, Toledo Academy of Police Officer Training, Certification as an Associate Death Educator and Counselor; [occ.] Disabled; [memb.] Association of Death Educators and Counselors, Member and Co-founder of the Remember Me, Support Group for Newborn Death and Pregnancy Loss, Member of the International Society of Poets; [hon.] Chosen as Father of the year from the Remember Me Support Group; [oth. writ.] Bittersweet Hello.....Goodbye poems published, several poems published in various bereavement books and magazines.; [pers.] Coping with grief and the feelings of parents lasts a lifetime and in my poetic messages I strive to convey my innermost thoughts of emotional and spiritual healing.; [a.] Northwood, OH

OSGOOD, JANE MARIE
[b.] August 22, 1977, Park Ridge, IL; [p.] Richard and Penny Osgood; [ed.] St. Cecilia Academy Indiana University (Currently); [occ.] Student; [oth. writ.] Article published in local newspaper, writings for school paper, poem published in Memories of Tomorrow (The National Library of Poetry); [pers.] The world is continually changing all around me, always offering a surprise. It is best to grab hold now while the moment is ripe!; [a.] Nashville, TN

PAGANO, CHRISTINA
[b.] October 27, 1971, Edmonds, WA; [p.] Robert Pagano, Francia Parson; [ed.] MBA - Univ of Chicago's Graduate School of Business, current, Middlebury College '94 (Dean's List) English Major, Univ. of Washington '91, Honors Program; [occ.] Industrial Manager/Professional Basketball Player; [hon.] Published poem "The Dove Bled Red" - winner of the Editor's Choice Award. Professional Basketball player in Brisbane, Australia - voted MVP '96; back to back conference championship '95 - 96, All-American '94; graduated Dean's list with High Honors in English; [oth. writ.] Published in The Ebbing Tide - "The Dove Bled Red."

Currently being reviewed for publication: "Amour Wait Omnia" (Romance novel) and "Playing with my Heart" (Romance novel). Published the copy text to "Bedouin Faces," a Historical Coffee-table book recounting the lives of the Bedouin people.; [pers.] The quest to love and be loved is the greatest journey of our lives. Stop - savor the sunsets, the hugs from mom and dad, and do everything in your power to keep romance alive! My family is my inspiration. Peace, love, and laughter.; [a.] Edmonds, WA

PALANCA, RAMON G.
[pen.] R.G.P.; [b.] June 23, 1928, Manila; [p.] Carlos Palanca Sr., Rosa Gonzales Palanca; [m.] Janice Y. Palanca, June 5, 1967; [ch.] Ramon Jr. and Mathew; [ed.] B.C.S.; [memb.] Manila Polo Club, Manila Yatch Club; [hon.] Poet of Merit Award, 8 Editor's Choice Awards; [oth. writ.] 180 other poems, Layman's Meditation, Blending Crucible; [pers.] Try your best always; God is within all; [a.] Las Vegas, NV

PALMER, FLORENCE B.
[pen.] Bereckenridge Palmer; [b.] September 8, 1908, Winsted, CT; [p.] Allison Palmer, Louise Palmer; [ed.] The Gilbert High School, Winsted Ct Elmira College, Elmira, NY, BA 1931; [occ.] Writer; [memb.] American Association of University Women, First Congregational, Unite Church of Christ, Elgin, IL; [hon.] AAVW Educational Foundation Named Grant, Elgin Branch; [oth. writ.] "A Taste of Poetry", "The Agenda Poems", "Seasonings", "Seraphic Observations", "A Lake for all Seasons"; [pers.] I write for my pleasure, hoping it will bring pleasure to others, using Edmund Stedman's Book of Lectures: "The Nature and Elements of Poetry's", for inspiration; [a.] Elgin, IL

PALMER, MARIE
[b.] September 10, 1980, Baltimore, MD; [p.] Anne Palmer and Ed Palmer; [ed.] Centennial High School (Sophomore year); [occ.] Student; [hon.] Been chosen for three anthologist, tape read by professional poet, Minerva B. Campbell award for literary ability; [oth. writ.] "What Is Love?"; [pers.] I've always looked to writing poetry as voicing my inner self. It has always been a confidant and my best friend, writing is my soul and my future dreams.; [a.] Ellicott City, MD

PANTANO, DANIEL
[pen.] Jordache; [b.] February 10, 1976, Langenthal, BE Switzerland; [p.] Gluseppe Pantano, Katharina Wiest; [ed.] Secondary School Kreuzfeld, Langenthal Switzerland, Palmer College Preparatory School Tampa, Florida; [occ.] Student/Poet; [memb.] International Society of Poets, Ancient Astronaut Society; [oth. writ.] Several poems published in different anthologies and magazines. Poems published by "The National Library of Poetry".; [pers.] To my one and only love. Nicole, I love you. "United we are in the faith of falling ball. Bouncing around within Heaven's hall!".; [a.] Langenthal, BE, Switzerland

PAPWORTH, ROBIN MARIE
[pen.] Robbie; [b.] December 23, 1947, Albuquerque, NM; [p.] Mr. Bryant R. and Eleanor Jane Papworth; [ch.] Vaughn Richard Park Stroud, Meredith Culver Stroud, Keith Douglas Wayne Stroud; [ed.] I am a student of "Fine Arts" at the University of Utah; [occ.] Daytime Security guard at Brasher's Salt Lake Auto Auction; [memb.] I am a member of DAR (Daughters of American Colonists); [hon.] I learned early on in elementary had the ability to write and create stories! But I did not earn any awards...friends just liked my work.; [oth. writ.] My poem "Rules" that was published in the "Windows of the Soul" and "School" my second poem published in "through the hourglass".; [pers.] I enjoy talking to people about what they've done in their lives or are currently doing.; [a.] Salt Lake City, UT

PARKE, S. R.
[b.] May 17, 1978, Chicago, IL; [ed.] Pending Decisions; [hon.] Charter Member Dist. 149 NJHS, #1 Female Chess Player Southern Suburban High School Conference 1995; [oth. writ.] Published in 1993, '94, '95, and '96 Thornwood High School Kaleidoscope Literary Magazine, Poetry and short stories (Poetry Editor in '96), "A Delicate Balance" (Top 3 % of entries) "Best Poems of the 90's"; [a.] Calumet City, IL

PARKINS, DAVE
[b.] August 5, 1967, Lancaster, WI; [p.] Maurice and Carol Parkins; [ed.] Bloomington High, Southwest Wisconsin Technical College; [occ.] Farmer/Student; [memb.] National Rifle Association; [hon.] "Editor's Choice-Award" 1996 North American Open Poetry Contest (National Library of Poetry), High Honors; [oth. writ.] "A Look Back At Hope"; [pers.] Walk forward not backward so you can see what's coming.; [a.] Glen Haven, WI

PARLIER, LAWRENCE EMORY
[b.] January 7, 1972, Georgetown, OH; [p.] Charles and Brenda Parlier; [ch.] Keagan Tyler 6, Kenan Thomas 5; [ed.] Bethel-Tate High School, Class of "90"; [occ.] Farm Equipment Fabricator; [oth. writ.] Currently working on science fiction novella, Quest for Enolis. Also working on long form poem, The Walk.

PATENTE, MICHELLE SUZETTE
[pen.] Naigret - Jensin; [b.] February 21, 1949, Philadelphia; [p.] Rose and Robert Marcel Patente; [ed.] George Washington High School, The Jay Dash School of Dance (Certificate of Teaching), The Community College of Philadelphia (Associates Degree in Library Science); [occ.] Story-writer and Performing Artist; [memb.] Twenty - seven year member of Nichiren Sheshu of America, a Buddist organization for value creation and human revolution.; [hon.] Royalties are for drug and alcohol rehabilitation in America, esp. street alcoholism, prism system reconstruction, child prostitution, teen run aways and lastly the shelter and protection of street prostitutes; [oth. writ.] Umbrians Poetica: Poetry and Lyric Myth, The Guards Of Matilde, selected poems, My Father Was A Frenchman: Mystical short-story and mime, The Lollipop Man: Selected short-stories mystical and mimes; [pers.] My work is dedicated to social reform - for the recognition of the continuation of social system (social services) for the poor and under priveledged I have lived my poetry and short-stories with fervor and great mission and look forward to the royalties graces (Note: Royalties).; [a.] Philadelphia, PA

PATORA, DEBORAH
[b.] November 14, 1957, Brooklyn, NY; [p.] Sam and Virginia; [ch.] Jake; [ed.] BS - Music Theory and Composition State University of New York at New Paltz, Magna Cum Laude; [occ.] Equipment Sales Manager; [memb.] National Wildlfife Federation: ASPCA; [hon.] Best Salesperson of 1993, 1994, 1996, Gold Medal Products 100 Club 1993, 1994, 1995, 1996 for Sales Excellence; [oth. writ.] Good-Bye, Creation Sonnet, Obsession, Dancing With His Mistress, Composition for Piano: Woodwind Trio; [pers.] I have evolved spiritually within the last 10 years. I have learned to forgive people for their short comings. Life's hardships have great learning and healing capabilities.; [a.] La Habra, CA

PAVER, MARY
[pen.] Kandy Reed; [b.] January 15, 1956, Erie, PA; [p.] Walter and Alice Reed; [m.] Paul A. Paver Jr., August 20, 1993; [ch.] William, Stephen, Thomasina; [ed.] Harborcreek Central School, Harbor Creek High School; [occ.] Housewife,

Mother; [memb.] Distinguished Member of International Society of Poets; [hon.] Poet of Merit, Two Editor's Choice Award (Don't know if those count); [oth. writ.] Four poems published 4 short stories written (not published yet). Working on a horror novel.; [pers.] I've been writing poetry since 1969 because I've always felt the opinions and need to express my feelings about life, love, religion, nature, and the world we live in.; [a.] Union City, PA

PAYNE, NORMA DOTSON
[b.] January 22, 1918, Forrest, IL; [p.] Mr. and Mrs. E. L. Dotson; [m.] Jess Willard Payne, March 3, 1948; [ch.] Teri Ann Payne Nunnally; [ed.] Attended Millikin U - Teachers certificate B.S. at Northwestern Univ. at Evanston, IL - Masters at U of Illinois also attended Chicago University - taking social works.; [occ.] Retired Educator; [memb.] International Society of Poets, Axon - Women's Study Club inducted in The International Poetry Hall of Fame from October 1996; [hon.] Who's Who in the World of Women Outstanding American - Who's Who in World of Women. Outstanding American, Leader of American Secondary Ed. in 1971 - Who's Who In Missouri Ed, Personalities of Mid West 1977-78 Who's Who in Child Development 1986 - served in an Red Cross W.W II - Certificate from President Truman for Services - International Hall of Fame for Poetry 1996.; [oth. writ.] Just poems published by National Poetry Society and in local newspapers.; [pers.] I love to share my thoughts with my friends also, to write poems for special occasions.; [a.] Van Buren, MO

PECK, HARRY G.
[pen.] H. Gwinn Peck; [b.] April 16, 1962, Montgomery, WV; [p.] Betty Newton Peck, Harry Peck; [ed.] Two Masters Degrees in Health and Counseling. Studied art at Concord College in Athens WV; [occ.] Counselor/Health Professional/Short Stories; [memb.] Phi Kappa Phi National Honor Society; [oth. writ.] Some Other Day, A Taste Of Home, Sometime Gone, and other poems, prose and short stories.; [pers.] I enjoy the time spent on exploring thoughts and feelings, and writing them dawn. It's the love, and memories of others, that prompt me to share the writing.; [a.] Morgantown, WV

PEERY, MR. PATRICK H.
[pen.] Patrick Peery; [b.] June 5, 1948, Liberal, KS; [p.] Amos and Ruth Peery; [m.] Betty Peery, ("Ex-Spouse"), October 5, 1981; [ch.] Patrick Joe Peery and Angie Walden; [ed.] High School; [occ.] Retired; [memb.] American Legion and Baptist Church; [hon.] Two - Golden Poet Awards 1990 and 1991 2 - Award of Merit Certificates - 1990, 1 Editors Choice Award 1995, 1 Who's Who in American Poetry Wall Plaque.; [oth. writ.] "Take Two" poem published in best poems of 1995, National Library of Poetry" Book, "Our World's Favorite Poems Who's Who in Poetry" - Book.

PEIFFER, LULU
[pen.] Lu Peiffer; [b.] February 18, 1913, Pepin County, WI; [p.] Dr. R. S. Rawson, Mrs. Kate Rawson; [m.] Carl Rudyard Williams, October 30, 1933, Leonard Peiffer, October 19, 1973; [ch.] Neal, Nancy Lous, Carol, Allan, Larry, Vicky; [ed.] High School, College prep. for teaching; [occ.] Retired School Teacher; [oth. writ.] Wrote for papers at Longville, Mn., wrote articles for the Pine River Journal Mn., "Northwoods Horizon" using my pen name, inserted a few poems from time to time.; [pers.] I have always been interested in small children.

PENLAND, PATRICK R.
[occ.] Information Consultant; [pers.] As an Information Consultant, Patrick R. Penland has been involved with movements promoting universal knowledge production and utilization. His name has appeared in various biographical listings. He has served on the editorial boards of professional journals. Recognizing the age in which we live, one cannot help celebrating the blessed advances of electronic technology. Yet it would be foolhardy not to preserve one's own, and others', fully functioning behavioral freedom by helping to offset the era's humanistic liabilities. Emerging Direction: The creative endeavor of my dedication aims to present existential moments of truth in poetry and narrative episodes of proactive personality in various novels already published. Release from the bubble-brained addiction of virtual reality, so prevalent in an internetted and mediated environment, can be obtained in all of these dramatic works.; [a.] Bellingham, WA

PENNINGTON, JAMES ALLEN
[pen.] Penning; [b.] June 29, 1949, Rhode Island; [p.] Vanis and Margaret Pennington; [m.] Nancy L. Pennington, May 6, 1989; [ch.] Wesley Alan Saxton Pennington; [ed.] Undergraduate Degree in Social Work; [occ.] Student; [memb.] Episcopal Church of the Epiphany, Phi Kappa National Honor Society; [hon.] Two awards from the National Library of Poetry, Student Support Services Award for Academic Excellence; [oth. writ.] Include shorts stories, poems and research papers involving adolescent delinquency.; [pers.] The Quest for truth is beyond a day, A question asked of one does sometimes cause a casual offense because of its intent, But the truth goes on an on, A question of a question is the only way. To find the Shallow Truths we Bare, To find Ourselves If We Dare, The truth Isn't really Fare or just, Its all there is for us.; [a.] Flagstaff, AZ

PEREIRA, MICHAEL A.
[pen.] Mike O'Dan the Snakeman; [b.] November 12, 1944, Boston, MA; [p.] Deceased; [m.] Divorced, December 23, 1989; [ed.] Graduate of Milton High School. Self educated in every branch of science engineering, and superstition; [occ.] 100% Disabled Veteran; [memb.] American Civil Liberties Union, Amnesty International, The Hemlock Society, People for the American Way, Coalition Against Censorship, Americans United for Separation of Church and State; [hon.] Wanted for blasphemy in Massachusetts, fugitive from the Massachusetts Mental Health System, considerable FBI, CIA and NSA records, for tour behind the old "Iron Curtain" for visiting and complaining to my family there; [oth. writ.] "Pluralism Knocks" (36 lines), "Flowing Eridana", "Liberation", "Inflation", "Know Thyself", "Krystate", "Crapity Crypity", "Ubiquity", "The Emerald Tablet of Hermes", "Ad Hunc Modem" and "Rauga", an epic poem of 124 lines.; [pers.] Pain is evil, relief is good, there is no other morality. Actions bring reactions that return with equal worth, there is no other justice. Zero equals minus one plus one, therefore, minus one plus one equals zero, there is no other God.; [a.] Groveland, CA

PERKINS, MAISHA K.
[b.] April 16, 1979, Bellflower, CA; [p.] Charles and Barbara Perkins; [ed.] Graduate of Crenshaw High School - class of 1996; Freshman at Howard University; [occ.] Student; [memb.] Proficiency in English ; Oratorical Contest (1st place), Society of Women Engineers Essay Contest (3rd place); Optimist Club Oritorical Contest (1st runner-up); [oth. writ.] Colorblind (Poetry form Where Dawn Lingers); Jazz (Poetry from Best Poems of the 90's); [a.] Los ANgeles, CA

PERRY, FLO
[b.] August 3, 1924, Boston, MA; [p.] Marion and Warren Lutz; [m.] Robert B. Perry, May 29, 1949; [ch.] Stephen, Laurel, David (Dec) Robyn; [ed.] Boston University BA Sociology Philosophy, University of Redlands M. Ed; [occ.] Retired School Teacher and Administrator director of music in several churches; [memb.] P. Lambda Theta; United Methodist Church; [pers.] I write poetry as therapy. To me, poetry

is art.

PETERSON, ROYAL F.
[b.] August 22, 1910, Olsburg, KS; [p.] Oscar and Nathalia (Haff) Peterson; [m.] Hanna Helene (Nelson) Peterson, July 7, 1937; [ch.] James Lownell, Miriam Helene and Lois Elizabeth; [ed.] Bethany College, Lindsborg, Kansas, '33 MA, Augusta Seminary, Rock Island, IL, 37 B of Div., Lutheran School of Divinity, Chicago, Master of Divinity '72 (Granted on previous work at Augustana); [occ.] Retired; [memb.] First Ev. Lutheran Church, Lincoln, NY, Evangelical Lutheran Church in America, International Society of Poets!!!; [hon.] Awards for 30, 35, 40, 45 and 50 yrs. as pastor from ELCA. Also awards from four Congregations served.; [pers.] My hope and prayer has been and is that my witness by life, and by spoken or written word, may assist others to know the Saviour, Jesus Christ, King of Kings and Lord of Lords.; [a.] Lincoln, NE

PHAIR, JULIETTE
[b.] N. Ireland; [m.] Stan; [ch.] Sharon and Dave; [ed.] In N. Ireland State Registered Nurse; [occ.] Travelling and Church Activities Reading Poetry to Groups and Friends; [memb.] Several Local Groups; [oth. writ.] Many poems, some published; [pers.] Thank God for all his blessings, and The Gift of Poetry. Through life's sorrows and its joys he's always been with me.; [a.] Alton, Ontario, Canada

PHOTIKARMBUMRUNG, ELMA DIEL
[b.] February 26, Philippines; [p.] Alfredo D. Diel and Concepcion D. Diel; [m.] Sam Photikarmbumrung, October 14; [ch.] Nate, Nick and Neil; [ed.] Dumangas High School, Iloilo, P.I., University of the Philippines, Silliman University; [occ.] Lecturer in Biology, Office Assistant; [memb.] Presbyterian Women's Association, Delta Lambda Sorority, Silliman Alumni Association, The Dumangasanons/Midwest; [hon.] Class Salutatorian, College Scholar; [oth. writ.] "It Pays To Be Alone At Times", "The Wanton Trail", "Daydreams '94", "Musings '95", "Alternatives At Daybreak", "Makajawan", "The Awakening '93", "Eternal Fires", "The River Kwai '96"; [pers.] "Writing is where I find my true self, I believe in a very strong faith in God where there is nothing impossible to achieve. Faith can and does move mountains, a strong faith overcomes man's limitations."; [a.] Palatine, IL

PIERCE, GORDON C.
[b.] October 27, 1918, Atlanta, GA; [p.] Dr. Carl F. and May S. Pierce; [ed.] Graduate, Greensburg, PA High School, Graduate, College of Architecture, Carnegie-Mellon University (Degree: B. Arch.); [occ.] Retired (practiced architecture in Greensburg for 40 years (1953-1993); [memb.] Emeritus member: The American Institute of Architects, Pennsylvania Society of Architects, National Trust for Historic Preservation, Greensburg Art Club, Life Member: First United Methodist Church, Greensburg.; [hon.] Charles McKenna Lynch Award, 1936, Eternity Emaille Award, 1953, Redstone Highlands Award 1995.; [oth. writ.] Articles on religious architecture in architectural journals such as the Journal of The American Society for Church Architecture, and in regional Penn'a, newspapers. Poetry in 12 national anthologies.; [pers.] Writings based on personal experiences thru travel in 57 countries worldwide. Also on childhood memories and observations of nature and the world we live in; [a.] Scottdale, PA

PILNY, MARIE
[b.] Central Europe;emigrated to U.S. at an early age with my mother and syblings, joining my father who had been in this country for several years without us. [ch.] one daughter [ed.] H.S.,Business School, and various college courses. [occ.] Retired Sr.citizen. [hon.] Editor's Choice awards for Outstanding Achievement in Poetry for 1993,1995.1996 from he National Library of Poetry. [oth.writ.] Have ready for publication a non-fiction book covering a historical subject and am in the process of preparing a sequel to it. [pers.] Have found it more interesting to read literature based on truths rather than fiction. My hobbies for many years have been writing and painting.In music I enjoy classicals and operas.; [a.] Baltimore, MD

PITTMAN, KIMBERLY A.
[b.] March 24, 1958, Belleville, IL; [ch.] Marie Josefsen, Christopher Lewis; [ed.] Homer High School and a Degree in Criminal Justice from Santa Barbara City College; [occ.] Security Dispatcher for the Hughes Corp.; [oth. writ.] Dreamland, previously published in Memories of Tomorrow, and other poems not yet published.; [pers.] Regrets was written to my daughter, Marie. Since the day you were born our lives have been shakey and we've spent 20 years apart, but I've never stopped loving, or thinking of you.; [a.] Goleta, CA

PLEASANT, SANDRA JOAN
[pen.] Joan Pleasant; [b.] February 19, 1941, Jacksonville, FL; [p.] Lindsay E. Cameron and Pearl D. Cameron; [m.] Jerry H. Pleasant, January 20, 1962; [ch.] Paul D. and Rodney G. Pleasant; [ed.] High School Graduate, Jax. Fl., Business School, Jax. Fl.; [occ.] Poet, Song Writer, Singer, and Home Maker; [memb.] Garden Club, Book Club, Church of God, Tyler, TX; [oth. writ.] "Rainbows and Promises", "You Are My Everything", "The Candle", all published. I have written twenty four songs, have made two Gospel albums and I am currently working on a third album. My Gospel albums are on the Cherubim label.; [pers.] I write from the heart. My writings deal with life, people and nature. Some of which come from personal experience. In my writings, I strive to reach a person's heart, make them feel good about themselves, give them hope and peace and bring them closer to God. I believe in living life to the fullest by sharing, giving and loving others. I try to live my life by doing unto others as I would have them do unto me.; [a.] Flint, TX

PLUMB, MEGHAN ELAINE
[b.] August 8, 1979, Columbia, SC; [p.] Nina and James Plumb; [ed.] Norwich Free Academy, and eventually Australian School of Environmental Science in Brisbane; [occ.] Assistant Vetinary Tech, Life Guard, High School Student; [oth. writ.] Book of poetry compiled with friends as a high school graduation present to ourselves.; [pers.] My poetry is a reflection of the repressed feelings I bury inside so that I may function within society's confining boundaries. Does this make me insane? Most likely.; [a.] Voluntown, CT

POLIRER, DEBRA
[b.] June 13, 1962, Mount Kisco, NY; [p.] Dr. Frank Gasthalter, Cynthia Gasthalter; [m.] Peter Polirer, June 26, 1988; [ch.] Laura Judith; [ed.] Mercy College: BS Accounting Summa Cum Laude Georgetown University: Linguistics; [occ.] Accountant on leave to raise family; [memb.] Delta Mu Delta, Institute of Management Accountants, International Society of poets; [hon.] First Prize: International year of the child poetry competition, Eleanor Prouty Creative writing scholarship, Who's Who of American Women 1995/96, Dean's List; [oth. writ.] Poetry has been published in local newspapers, literary magazines, and poetry anthologies. Currently working on a book of poetry to be published in 1977. Also a writer of short fiction.; [pers.] Using a sharp, direct style and vivid imagery, I seek to excavate and illuminate the deepest conflicts of the human heart, mind and soul.; [a.] Poughkeepsie, NY

POLLOCK, DEBRA THERESA
[pen.] Theresa Rose; [b.] May 5, 1975, Philadelphia; [p.] Dennis and Louise Pollock; [ed.] Archbishop Ryan High School, Hahnemann University (Associates Degree); [occ.] Adm. Asst. for a Securities Broker/Dealer; [memb.] "American Society for Clinical Laboratory Science", "Investment Women's Club of Philadelphia", "Business Philadelphia"; [hon.] Distinguished and Notable Honors, The Irish Society Award, Editor's Choice Award; [oth. writ.] I write articles for "Silent News" which is the world's most popular newspaper for the deaf and hearing impaired.; [pers.] My favorite quote is "The world is never the same once a good poem has been added to it." Dylan Thomas; [a.] Philadelphia, PA

POMMER, STEPHEN D.
[b.] April 10, 1939, Brooklyn, NY; [p.] Louis and Mae Pommer; [m.] Apolinaria A. "Nellie" Pommer, March 21, 1986; [ch.] John H. Pommer, Kenneth L. Pommer, Laura M. (Pommer) Dawdy, Mary Ann (Pommer), Chandler, Patricia E. Pommer; [ed.] (BA) St Leo College, St Leo FL (84), (Received at Homestead Air Force Base, FL), Institute of Children Literature Redding Ridge, CT (83), Assorted Military School (Personnel/Administration/Career Counseling (1956-1974)); [occ.] (Retired) Military, (Retired) Federal Civil Service; [memb.] DAV; [hon.] Military: Purple Heart, Arcom (2010), VNCR, VNSM, Meriterous Unit Comm, General (5 awards) No Civilian Honors; [oth. writ.] Several songs, poems, in early stabbs of possible commercial release; [pers.] Enjoy writing poetry, that captures a person's emotions and feelings, towards themselves and others.; [a.] Quezon City, Philippines

POOLE, FAY
[b.] August 28, 1951; [ed.] Hempstead Public School System, Prairie View A and M University, University of North Texas, Texas Southern University; [occ.] Sales Associate, Taco Bell Restaurant, Corp, Austin, TX; [memb.] The International Society of Poets, distinguished Member, Cystic Febusui Foundation, National Ostroprosis Foundation; [hon.] Editor's choice award, Certificate of Achievement song writer; [oth. writ.] I have several poems published and songs recorded and produced; [pers.] I attempt to relate my philosophy of life in my writings.; [a.] Austin, TX

POPE, NANCY LYNN NAQUIN
[pen.] Mother Pope; [b.] September 20, 1959, Houston, TX; [m.] Divorced; [ch.] Daniel - 13, Estelle - 5; [ed.] High School graduate 1978, J. Frank Dobie, spent several years in Restaurant Management; [occ.] I am on a work Sabbatical, the last 4 years have been devoted to children and writing; [memb.] PTA, International Society of Poets; [hon.] My poem: A Mother's Prayer has been published and won an Editor's Choice Award in 1994; [oth. writ.] Poems by Mother Pope and Before copyright - 1996, #TXU 753-353, Proverbs 2000 - Solomon's Wisdom Reborn copyright 1994 #TXU 641-428; [pers.] I love the old wisdom - Confucious, Socrates, Nostradamus, Jesus Christ, etc...I believe we need to teach the children a new set of 3R's with a new class added to our schools. The art of being Right, Responsible, Respectful.; [a.] Houston, TX

PRATTE, LOIS A.
[b.] February 3, 1933, Calais; [p.] J. Earle Pike and Addie Pike; [ed.] Graduated from Cabot High attended Midwestern UN. Witchita Falls, Tex. Received B.S. Degree in Human Services from New Hampshire College of Human Services; [occ.] Homehealth Aide VNA Community Health Care Inc.; [oth. writ.] Summer published in Dance on the Horizon, The Piano Is Silent published in Dark Side of the Moon, Utter Despair published in Best Poems of 1995, That Rascal Jack Frost published in East of the Sunrise and others; [pers.] I like to write about the beauty of nature, family and feelings from within my heart. My Christian faith and compassion faith and compassion is reflected in my writing.; [a.] East Haven, CT

PRENTIS, EDNA ZIMMERMAN
[b.] November 15, 1915, Welcome, NC; [p.] Emanuel Jackson and Beatrice Craver Zimmerman; [m.] Rev. Robert Brown Prentis, a Methodist minister, (Deceased); [ch.] Linda; [ed.] Graduated from Welcome High School, attended Duke University two years. Continued study of art and music.; [occ.] Artist (I enjoy working in oils, watercolors, acrylics, pastels and colored pencils.), News Columnist, Piano Teacher, Poet.; [hon.] Recipient twice "The Citizen of the Year" from Welcome Civitan Club. Honorable Mention of Jefferson Award from Winston-Salem. Both awards for Community Service.; [pers.] To make the world better and more beautiful. That includes safety and environment.

PRETZER, RANDALL E.
[b.] July 15, 1944, Kalamazoo, MI; [p.] Raymond E. and Eleanor M. Pretzer; [m.] Rosalyn D. Pretzer, January 27, 1968; [ch.] Randall W. and Daniel C. Pretzer; [ed.] B.A. (English) and J.D. (Law), U. of Houston, Houston, TX; [occ.] Private practice of law; [pers.] Never be resentful, never look back.; [a.] Corpus Christi, TX

PRISOCK, MARY V.
[b.] December 6, 1943, Hot Springs, AR; [p.] Steven (Deceased) and Estelle O. (Ross) Vander Ziel; [m.] Stephen O. Prisock, September 21, 1991; [ch.] Steven John Callahan and Tonia Lynn Prisock; [ed.] B.S. in Nursing and B.A. in Ed.; [occ.] Hospice Sitter; [memb.] Ret. Teacher, A.N.A. Amer. Cancer Assn. Amer. Daibetic Assn., Girl Scouts of Amer.; [hon.] Sigma, Chi, Kappa Delta (KAY), Poets Guild, and Lendon Players.; [oth. writ.] Several poems published in local new paper, magazines (literary) and in my church's bulletin.; [pers.] I try to reflect my deep feelings of peace, love and unity and brotherhood in my poetry while perusing other great romantic, philosophical, and Christian poets past and present in order and let others to learn from so they can go and do like wise so this world will be a better place in which to live, work and play in as a village.; [a.] Pearl, MS

PROTIVNAK, DAVID B.
[b.] April 14, 1954, Vydran-Slovakia; [p.] John Protivnak and Mary Burcin Protivnak; [m.] Natalie Protivnak, March 29, 1975; [ch.] Jake John, Joel John, Peter John; [ed.] Took College courses at the University of Pittsburgh and Clarion University, (English, Singing, Engineering) also got Associate Degree in Mechanical Drafting from Triangle Institute of Technology; [occ.] Self-employed, Home Assembly Business; [memb.] Twenty year member of the Worldwide Church of God, it's Spokesman Club Member and Graduate; [hon.] Awarded a cash prize for a Mechanical Drawing Done by me in ink. Which I entered in a drafting contest. Drawing award, not writing award); [oth. writ.] My first poem "Years And Years Without The End" was published in a poetry book called "A Time To Be Free", put out by the Quill Book Publishing Company, also my writings were included in the NLP Mists of Enchantment and in the Treasured Poems of America winter 1996 published by Sparrow Grass Poetry Form, Inc.; [pers.] I believe that ultimately this 6 word statement "With God All Things Are Possible" is the answer to all the answer and questions. It's a direct quote from Matthew 19:26 what awesome possibilities! What unlimited opportunities!; [a.] Pittsburgh, PA

PROUT, JOANN H.
[b.] December 20, 1943, Manchester, VT; [p.] Kenneth F. and Lois G. Hill; [m.] Thomas P. Prout Jr., November 26, 1988; [ch.] Julia MacDonald, Brian Scott Oakley; [ed.] Burr and

Burton Seminary, Manchester, VT, (high school) Catawba College, Salisbury, NC; [occ.] Teacher (Semi-retired); [memb.] 1st Congregational Church, Robert Tadd Lincoln's "Hildene", Southern VT Art Center, Ekwanok Country Club; [oth. writ.] A notebook of unpublished (but hope to be published) poems from the 1960's to now.; [pers.] My writings express my love for my surroundings and the recognition of God's hand in creating them.; [a.] East Dorset, VT

QUEEN, MADELINE M.
[pen.] Madeline M. Queen; [b.] March 31, 1935, Nicut, WV; [p.] Clawson and Arminda Queen; [m.] Divorced; [ch.] One Tony Becker (son); [ed.] High School -Some college, Vocational school for sever things; [occ.] I do private duty Nurse Aide; [memb.] Several Poetry Clubs (Women Club NAFE) Round table of Ar., Poets Northwest Ar.; [hon.] Had a poem published in a national college book, won a Diamond Homer Award of Hollywood for a poem last year. Lots of my poems have been published in The Grove Sun Newspaper, Grove, Ok. Been published in several different anthologies; [oth. writ.] Won third place in tall tell's contest. (I write mostly poems) Won honorable mention in comp. 6# of American song feast.; [pers.] I strive to have positive outlook in life and my writing.

RACINE, MARTINE
[b.] September 6, 1943, Rabat (Morocco); [ch.] IsaJelle, Xariez; [ed.] B.A., M.A., MBA; [occ.] Jungian Psycho Analyst; [oth. writ.] Several poems published in French newspaper and magazine 1 volume of collected poems published in 1983 (Paris Le Cherche Midi Ed..); [pers.] Currently a citizen of France living in the U.S. I began to write in English in 1983; [a.] Potomac, MD

RAINERI JR., BRIAN JOHN
[pen.] B.J. Raineri Jr.; [b.] April 26, 1971, Lawrence, MA; [p.] Mr. and Mrs. Henri J. Seymour; [ed.] Greater Lawrence Voc. Tech., Berklee College of Music; [occ.] Woodwright, Mason and Hamlin Piano Co.; [pers.] "Love looks not with the eyes, but with the mind, and therefore is wing'd cupid painted blind" (William Shakespeare, A Mid Summer Night's Dream); [a.] Lawrence, MA

RAMOS, CHRISTOPHER
[b.] March 21, 1981, Oakland, CA; [p.] Rufino and Catalina Ramos; [ed.] Currently a sophomore at Alameda High School; [memb.] Alameda Babe Ruth, Alameda Soccer Club, Bay Isle Judo Juijitsu School, Karate and the United States Judo Federation; [hon.] Honor Roll student, 3 times nominated as an All-Star in Alameda Baseball, awarded first place in local state tournaments in Judo and Karate, distinguished member of the International Society of Poets, Editor's Choice Award for Outstanding Achievement in Poetry; [oth. writ.] Several books which I donated to local children's hospitals. In 5th grade I entered one of my writings in a state contest which took 3rd place.; [pers.] As a teenager I am aware and see the struggles of teenagers today. Through my poetry I hope to reach them and enable them to see the light in a world they see so dark.; [a.] Alameda, CA

RANIERE, AUTUMN
[b.] May 29, 1982, Bethlehem, PA; [p.] Frank Raniere, Eva Raniere; [pers.] Poetry is a Science. You experiment with it for years until it's absolutely perfect, and you gain knowledge about the world. Only, in poetry, you also gain knowledge about yourself.; [a.] Bethlehem, PA

RAYBURN, JANICE
[pen.] M. J. Rayburn; [b.] July 26, 1932, Columbia, MS; [p.] John Rayburn; [ch.] Danny, Mark, Perry, Don, Melanie; [ed.] Associate Degree Marketing Nichols University, Rhibodeaux, LA; [occ.] Self-employed Grey Wing Ltd. - Inventor; [memb.] ABWA - American Business Woman Assoc., Pine Beit Devel Corp. (Chamber of Commerce) Hattiesburg MS. South MS. Art Association; [hon.] Involved in fine arts for thirty-three years with master artist Henry Hensche. Workshops within continental vs. Europe, Mexico, Hawaii and Portugal.; [oth. writ.] New poems, "My Light Source", "Memories of Last Autumn", "Dabney Hill", "The Runners", "Wall of Many Colors", "Thanks-Giving Day"!; [pers.] Every dreaming child needs to know - that no horizon is so far that you cannot get above it or beyond it.; [a.] Hattiesburg, MS

REDDOCH, MILDRED
[b.] March 1, 1916, Texarkana, AR; [p.] Mr. and Mrs. R. A. Lucas; [m.] Mr. E. D. Reddoch; [ch.] Ada Lynn R. and Elbert D. Reddoch; [ed.] College Degree, Sam Houston State Teachers; [occ.] Retired Educator; [memb.] National League of American Pen Women/Second Christian Church, National Republican Senatorial Committee; [hon.] American Biographical Institute: "The Decree of International Letters for Cultural Achievement". (An Honorary Appointment); [oth. writ.] I have been published in their book and recommended a few. So White Lilies book of my poems (a few - too many to send); [a.] Raleigh, NC

REDING, EUNICE ABBY
[b.] January 13, 1918, McKees Rocks, PA; [p.] William Henry and Eunice Wyres Ward; [m.] Richard Wallace Reding, August 28, 1937; [ch.] Barbara Ann and Richard William; [ed.] Warren G. Harding High; [occ.] Reading, corresponding, enjoying my Grandchildren, Great and Great Greatgrands; [memb.] St. John United Church of Christ Philatelist, US Coastguard Auxiliary American Diabetes Association, AARP, National Wildlife Association, Retired Cinema Manager; [hon.] Being accepted by the National Library of Poetry and receiving the Editor's Choice awards plus the thrill of seeing my poetry in the Anthologys.; [oth. writ.] Invisible Enigma, What's Good What's Not, Lasting Happiness, Travel Dreamer, 'Sno Fun; [pers.] Memories of the past make me appreciate the present time and hope for the future.

REDRICK, REGINALD
[b.] December 28, Detroit, MI; [p.] Charles Redrick, Evelyn Redrick; [ed.] Eastern Michigan University, California State University, Cooley High, Detroit, MI; [occ.] Financial Mgr.; [oth. writ.] Multitude of all occasion poems, near completion of first novel, "The Broken Rainbow"; [pers.] Everyone is not a leader. So, lead or be led, but, go in a positive direction.; [a.] North Hollywood, CA

REGULAR, SHERON
[b.] September 1915, Sawter, SC; [p.] John C. Boone and Bloneva Boone; [ch.] Deneen and Davida; [occ.] Asst Mgr. of Credit and Collections K-III Directory Corp.; [memb.] International Society of Poets; [hon.] Professional Entertainer Golden Crost Cabey, Soldier Boy I'm Sorry (Lead Singer), Atlantic Recording Label - Gee Baby, The Drifters Under The Boardwalk (Back Ground With Group), The Name of Group Mortells, changed to the Pussycats and then changed again to The Witches and Warlock.; [oth. writ.] Silence of Yesterday (poem) I Love You.; [pers.] My inspiration of writing comes from the beauty of love, the experiences of life and the miracles of living.; [a.] Brooklyn, NY

REIHL, DONNA
[b.] October 5, 1951, York, PA; [p.] John Wanda Ensor; [m.] Tim, June 19, 1982; [ch.] Sara; [ed.] Phd. Southern California University; [occ.] Director; [memb.] AGR, NRPA, NRPA; [hon.] 1993 National Dottie Muller Arts and Humanities

Award; [oth. writ.] Molasses, Feathers, and Eggshells; [pers.] Don't look back.; [a.] Baltimore, MD

REILLY, JESSICA
[b.] June 24, 1982, Freehold, NJ; [p.] Patricia and Glenn Reilly; [ed.] Howell High School, 9th Grade; [memb.] Journalism club, Latin Club; [hon.] Honor role, modeling and taekwando trophies, Editor's Choice Award in Mists of Enchantment, book of poems, Academic Certificates; [oth. writ.] Winter Wonderland, (1995); [pers.] Try your hardest in all that you do, and never give up hope.; [a.] Howell, NJ

RENTA, OLGA
[b.] April 6, 1975, Santurce, PR; [p.] Santiago Renta, Olga Esteva; [ed.] The College of Insurance BBA, NY Pace University-Literature Studies, Poetry/Essay Writing Concentration; [occ.] Student; [oth. writ.] Collection of personal poetry - "June Being In Water" published in Memories of Tomorrow.; [pers.] The world is full of people that want to burn you. Our just has be strong just has be strong and become a big sunblock bottle. It helps when other people get in your bottle and make it stronger.; [a.] New York, NY

REPIK, DOLORES
[b.] November 13, 1939, Bosque, NM; [p.] Alfredo and Seferina Chavez; [m.] John Repik, March 20, 1971; [ch.] Ed, Waid, Eric and Jason; [ed.] 2 1/2 yrs. College of St. Joseph, Albuquerque, NM; [occ.] Executive Office Mgr and Artist (Paint in Oils); [hon.] 4 Yr. Scholarship to College of St Joseph, Albuq. NM - Pres. of Soph Class; [oth. writ.] Several unpublished poetry (writing since 1969); [pers.] It is always wise to stop wishing for things long enough to enjoy the fragrance of those now flowering.; [a.] Ridgecrest, CA

RESNICK, RALPH
[b.] June 15, 1920, Brooklyn, NY; [p.] Bessie - Jacob Resnick; [m.] Caroline Resnick, May 29, 1951; [ch.] Jane - Robert; [ed.] BBA - College of City of N.Y., LLB - Brooklyn Law School, JD - Brooklyn Law School; [occ.] Retired CPA - Attorney; [memb.] Crohn's - Colitis Foundation of America (CCFA) - Volunteer in UNC Hospitals. UNA/USA Treasurer United Nations Association - Acting in Drama Groups - Active in Local Political Groups; [hon.] Law Review Editor 1st scholarship prize; [oth. writ.] Poems published in New York Post - Letters to the Editor in local papers. Favorite poets: Wordsworth.; [a.] Pittsboro, NC

REYNOLDS, ELIZABETH MARIA
[b.] March 3, 1953, Jamaica, WI; [p.] Mallica Reynolds and Caroline Haynes; [m.] Divorced; [ch.] Michael, Michele, Clarissa and Malesha; [ed.] Thomas Jefferson High School, New York University; [occ.] Poet, Writer, Playwright, Speaker, Bridge and Tunnel Officer; [memb.] Black Women in Publishing, American Black Book Writers Assn., International Society of Poets, Kiwanis International. Bright Star Chapter 84; [hon.] Barnard College, Columbia University, Department of English Editors Choice Award, The National Library of Poetry; [oth. writ.] Book of Poetry "The Circles of Time Survive Where Memories Dwell". Play "Africa's Children" Several poems published in Anthologies.; [pers.] To love, to share, to heal, to educate and elevate to a level of communication which transcends, race, and color, and focuses of humanity as a miracle of life.; [a.] Elmont, NY

RHEAUME, PAUL J.
[b.] July 2, 1949, Saint Albans, VT; [p.] Mitchell and Jeannette Rheaume; [m.] Imelda Rheaume, April 19, 1975; [ch.] Melissa - 20, Joseph - 19 and John - 17; [ed.] St. Annes Academy, Swanton, VT (6 yrs.) Highgate High - Highgate Center, VT (6 yrs.) Univ. of Arizona (1 yr.) Univ. of Vermont Night Schooling; [occ.] Career in the post office - White River Junction, VT, mail handler craft 12 yrs. to go till retirement;

[memb.] Sacred Heart League, Bowling Leagues, AFL-CIO Local 301 member, Best Loading Crew on the F4C Aircraft in Thailand During the entire year of 1970; [hon.] (Three) U.S Postal Special Achievement Awards in Recognition of Notable and Exceptional {erformance with monetary inclusions in the years of 1992, 1993 and 1996; [oth. writ.] Four published poems in the National Library of Poetry books - in the books titled as follows, "Between the Raindrops", "Across the Universe", "Best Poems of 1996", "Best Poems of the '90s".; [pers.] Read poetry - for it will tell you many hidden secrets of many people's hearts, as it is written and more probably than not, will never be said I verbally enjoy!; [a.] Bradford, VT

RICE, FRANKIE J.
[pen.] Frankie "Dee"; [b.] December 7, 1917, Valdosta, GA; [p.] Jasper J. and Hattie B. Bonnell; [m.] Joel N. Rice, October 25, 1935; [ch.] Three; [ed.] My whole life is an Education I finished High School and have taken College courses and studied much of my years including Bible Study; [occ.] Retired; [memb.] Herb Society, Church AARP, NARFE. in past years I've her active in Civic Organizations I enjoy working with the elderly, the ill, the lonely and the lovely; [hon.] Mother, grandmother, greatgrandmother, Poem in your book in 1995, I've done nothing of great fame now awards; [oth. writ.] None published but an assortment at my house including short stories. Am currently embarking on a book have my children about my life.; [pers.] I live in a house by a rippling creek. Nature is all around me - I glory in my pen for out of my flows a never ending desire to write words that will inspire and bring good into the world.; [a.] Jacksonville, FL

RICHARDS II, TERRY ALLEN
[b.] Hartford, CT; [p.] Terry and Gloria Richards; [m.] Lisa Ann Richards, May 18, 1991; [ch.] Christopher Timothy Ashlee; [ed.] Recently transferred to University of NC at Asheville to finish degree in Literature; [occ.] Writer/Student; [memb.] National College Honor Society International Society of poets; [hon.] Dean and Presidents Lists, Editors Choice Award for nation "African American Haiku; [oth. writ.] Out of the Ashes to Gehenna and Back; [pers.] Psalms 49; [a.] Asheville, NC

RICKERT, ELIZABETH A.
[b.] December 19, 1930, Bloomfield, NJ; [p.] Marion and Douglas Austin; [m.] Hugh Stanley Rickert, June 19, 1949, Divorced April 1990; [ch.] Stephen Douglas, Scott Austin, Donna Louise, parent of Kerry Christopher and Darian Douglas; [occ.] A Tired and retired homemaker; [hon.] After raising my 3 children I had the honor of inheriting my 2 grandchildren, Kerry and Darian, in 1976 when their mother died. In 1984 Darian was killed in an auto accident. Regardless of tragic losses, Jehovah my God, has awarded me with joy, strength, friendship and love; [oth. writ.] A Moment In Time, Tools Gold A Walk Through Paradise, the prize Best Poems of 1997, this is my prayer...please Best Poems of 1996, House Guest a Tapestry of Thoughts, The Ice Age, Best Poems of 1990's, Little Cacti all published by the International Library of Poetry.; [pers.] I am a self-taught piano player and a self taught artist.; [a.] Cedar Grove, NJ

RIDGLEY, BONNIE LEE
[pen.] Bonnie Lee - Bonnie Harrell; [b.] October 22, 1949, Washington, D.C.; [p.] Ivon K. Harrell & Vivian A. Harrell; [ed.] M.B.S. University of Maryland; [occ.] Retired Educational Diagnostocoan Special Education, Montgomery County, MD.; [memb.] Soloist Cedar Brook Church Member; [hon.] Sigma Alpha Iota (National Music Society), Volunteer Docent Glenview Farm Mansion; [oth. writ.] "Up The Path To Calvary" published in Silence of Yesterday; Numerous

contempory, religious songs; [per.] I am greatly influenced by the teaching of my Lord, His/power to hal and my love of His music. [a.] Germantown, MD

RIFFLE, GRACE
[b.] November 14, 1911, Davidson County; [p.] Joseph and Pena Willard Siceloff; [m.] Ralph Leonard Riffle, October 16, 1943; [ch.] Charles Riffle; [ed.] High School graduated of a class of 1929; [occ.] Homemaker; [memb.] I am a charter member of Bethany United Church of Christ; [hon.] I was published in the Worlds Faith. Anthology of verse I have been published in numerous anthologies in New York California, I have won an Award in Art and have had my Art in Museum I love the nature and the beauty of the world.; [oth. writ.] Written songs.; [pers.] Writings poetry helps me focus on the beauty of simple things, and the good things of life.; [a.] Winston-Salem, NC

RINKER, KATHLEEN C.
[b.] July 6, 1951, Reading, PA; [ch.] Nephews - James and Jeremy; [ed.] Reading High School, The Reading Hospital School of Nursing-1972; [occ.] Registered Nurse in Psychiatric Nursing - over 20 years; [pers.] I write about my feelings and where they come from, as a recovering sexual and ritual abuse survivor. I hope that I can break some of the isolation survivors feel, and enlighten and demystify things like Multiple Personality Disorder, and other emotional/mental illness caused by the abuse of innocents.; [a.] Reading, PA

RIOS, GEORGIANNA N.
[pen.] Ann Rios-Ann Soir; [b.] October 30, 1923, Seville, OH; [p.] Cora Lucille Dunham Neasse, Myron Dalrymple Neasse; [m.] Restituto Rios, July 26, 1956; [ed.] 1 year Business College, 2 years College Journalism Correspondence Courses Creative writing courses; [occ.] Retired Executive Secretary; [memb.] Lions Club International, Mayflower Society, Colonial Dames, XVII Century, Berkley Plantation Chapter, National Society Daughters of the American Revolution, Magna Charta Dames, Presbyterian Church, Friends of the Library, Historical Society, held offices in above organizations, Guest speaker Mayflower Society, Safety Harbor Library and Colonial Dames XVII Century; [oth. writ.] Children's Stories, one book published, several poems and articles; [pers.] I have religious faith and believe in beautiful thoughts to make the world a beautiful place. I believe in the golden rule and helping others.; [a.] DeBary, FL

RIOS, MILTON DANIEL
[b.] November 17, 1966, New York City, NY; [p.] Felix Junior Rios, Carmen Milagros Rios; [ed.] Life; [occ.] Auto Technician by Trade, Poet by Heart; [oth. writ.] Battling Doubts, From Myself-For Yourself, A Child Dancing In the Wind, All three published in previous anthologies.; [pers.] I am in the process of releasing a book with the words to assist all in search for a soul, for the future, for the well-being of earth and all the creatures that dwell among this planet.; [a.] New York, NY

RIVET, BRENDA M.
[b.] April 2, 1955, Providence; [p.] Antonio, Victoria Viscione; [m.] Raymond, May 26, 1996; [ch.] David and Josh-Raymond; [ed.] High School Completed Hairdressing School; [occ.] Own a VCR Repair Shop; [memb.] Literacy Volunteers - Northern Rhode Island; [hon.] Editor's Choice Award 1996; [oth. writ.] Short story titled Searching For The Book Life, Isn't Just A Panic poem: Life for of Sunshines and Dreams, poem: Our Romance; [pers.] I write from the heart.; [a.] Cumberland, RI

RIZZO, LIZA ANN
[b.] January 15, 1980, Baltimore, MD; [p.] Phillip and Theresa Rizzo; [ed.] Queen Anne's County High School Junior; [memb.] SGA, Peer Counselor/Tutor, Varsity Club, Varsity Volleyball, Basketball, Softball, ASA Fastpitch Softball; [hon.] National Honor Society, All Mid-Shore Sports, minds in motion (4.0 grade average); [oth. writ.] Poem published in Memories of Tomorrow and others recognized through school.; [pers.] Truth exists, only falsehood has to be invented.; [a.] Stevensville, MD

ROACH, JOHN W.
[b.] October 19, 1917, Thompson Falls, MI; [p.] Moses and Dona B. Ballet Roach; [m.] February 14, 1952; [ch.] John Jr., David, Edith; [ed.] Sonora Union High School, Polytechnic College of Engineering, Draftsman, Delta College, AA Poly, Scie. and History; [occ.] 45 Years Retired Sheet metal worker; [memb.] I have worked with Teen Missions, The Christianville Foundation, The City of Hope and skills applied for Evangelism; [hon.] My poem "Prayer" in 1996 won "Best Poems of 1996" was recently published in the local and was very well received.; [pers.] When I was in grammar school my teacher had me memorize poetry for an hour a day for my 7th and 8th grades. It became almost a second language, I never until 1992 tried to have any published. I try to express my love of God and His care for humankind as well as my love for others while observing the world around me.; [a.] Sonora, CA

ROBBINS, CHRISTI LEIGH
[b.] January 19, 1975, Wichita, KS; [p.] Allen and Lila Robbins; [ed.] Arlington Heights High School, Bachelor of Music Education from University of Texas at Arlington - will graduate Spring of 1998; [occ.] Private Flute Teacher; [memb.] Texas Music Educators Association, National Federation Interscholastic Music Association, Tau Beta Sigma, Golden Key National Honor Society; [hon.] Who's Who Among Students in American Universities and Colleges, UTA Honor Roll, Earl D. Irons/Tau Beta Sigma Award; [oth. writ.] Several poems published in anthologies.; [a.] Arlington, TX

ROBERTSON, MARK ALLEN
[b.] May 28, 1968, Los Angeles; [p.] Geary Lee and Mary Lou Runnels; [ed.] Williams High School; [memb.] Lamp of Hope: Anti Death Penalty, Anthroposophical Society of America; [hon.] National Library of Poetry's: "Outstanding Poetry" Award 1995; [oth. writ.] Poems published in the following books: "Out of the Night" (poem: So Many Times), "Seasons to Come" (poem: Incommoded), "The Ebbing Tide" (poem: Abraded Hope), "The Nightfall of Diamonds" (poem: His Choice); [pers.] I wrote this poem for my wonderful friend, Doris Jordi, whose love is a vessel of hope. Du fandest mich in diesem Alter, meine liebste, In dem nachsten Zeitalter finde inch Dich gerne. Vielleicht I'm Russland...; [a.] Huntsville, TX

ROBINSON, CALVIN
[b.] June 14, 1935, Braddock, PA; [m.] Gracie Robinson, January 12, 1967; [ch.] Sarnia, Kelvin, Calvin II; [ed.] Detroit Institute of Technology, Detroit Engineering Institute, Detroit Institute of Musical Art, Univ. of Washington; [occ.] Jazz Musician; [memb.] Detroit Writer's Guild, International Society of Poets Society of Jazz Musicians; [hon.] Inducting in to the graystone Jazz, Museum, Editor's Choice Award, for 1995-96 The National Library of Poetry, Short Story Award, Detroit Writer's Guild; [oth. writ.] Short story's that have been published in different novels.; [pers.] That quality should dormant the center, of all of your artistic work.; [a.] Detroit, MI

ROBINSON, KATRINA W.
[b.] October 4, 1982, Gastonia, NC; [p.] Rick and Carolyn Robinson; [ed.] Halfway through Swansboro High School;

[occ.] Waitress, cook, etc. at a small 50's and 60's restaurant; [oth. writ.] Two poems published in other anthologies.; [pers.] Poetry is the written form of deep thoughts and feelings. If everyone gave up on poetry, there'd be no spirit in any written word. Greatly influenced by nature and somewhat by T.S. Eliot.; [a.] Emerald Isle, NC

ROBLEDO, BRENDA VALIHORA
[pen.] Bonnie Valihora Robledo; [b.] November 6, 1960, Canada; [p.] Lee and Mike Valihora; [m.] Richard Robledo; [ch.] David; [ed.] High School, Some College; [occ.] Market Research Specialist; [memb.] Thespians (Drama Society); [oth. writ.] Learn for Life, my latest poem: He Saw the Great Big Limousine, Pull Up Inside His Block, Those People Had Lots Of Money, They Didn't Have to Walk, He Saw A Lady Fold Their Clothes, That She Pulled Down From the Line, She Cleaned and Scrubbed Around the House, Each Day It Looked Just Fine, He Wished His Life Could Be That Way, Someone To Do His Chores, His Mother Would Never Be Tired, From Cleaning and Scrubbing Floors, His Mother Said "When I'm Done, I Feel Good, It's A Great Feeling Inside When I Work Like I Should, Those People Will Never Know This Feeling I get, Of Discipline and Accomplishment I'm Sure They Haven't Yet., So Always Be Thankful For All The Things You Have Got, Instead Of Dwelling On What You Have Not"; [pers.] It would be a lot more peaceful existence if we thought of each other as God's children, and always had consideration for others. My poetry reflects my own experiences well as my observations of human interaction.; [a.] Tustin, CA

ROCKWOOD, MARTHA MARGARET
[b.] May 6, 1947, Bremmerton, WA; [p.] George Emmett Rockwood and Martha Margaret Farrell; [ch.] Troy Allen Cates, Kathryn Elizabeth Cates, Louanne Islene Cates and Kwametasha Craig Rockwood; [ed.] Whitecliff Elementary and Ketchikan High School, Ketchikan, Alaska, Southwest School of Medical Assistance Laboratory Technician, San Antonio, Texas, Pioneer Ministry School for Jehovah's Witnesses, Pacific Beach, California; [occ.] Minister: Caretaker for In Home Support Services, San Diego, California; [memb.] Jehovah's Witnesses: Coordinator for the Linda Vista Village Citizens Patrol San Diego, California; [hon.] 1996 Editors Choice Award for Outstanding achievement in poetry by The National Library of Poetry; [oth. writ.] Poem, The God Called "Video Games" published in 1996 by The National Library of poetry Anthology "Tapestry Of Thoughts" copyright 1996, ISBN1-5755-064-3; [pers.] Some year ago I was given a beautiful male Flame Point Persian Cat. This poem I wrote for this anthology of poetry is about that cat. His name is Mr. De Cupboard Pudderaminsky Boxnapper, AKA "Pudder". I wrote this poem to express my appreciation for the Breeder 106658, the Parents, Sire Zeekers and Dam Ninotscha Elena Baryshnikat, and the gift giver, a male nurse name Darren. He is a very elegant, dignified, talented, extraordinary gentleman type Persian and a great credit to his breed. He has brought a lot of joy and laughter.; [a.] San Diego, CA

ROGERS, DIANA LYNN
[pen.] Diana Lynn Rogers; [b.] May 7, 1947, Kokomo, IN; [ch.] Michelle, Jarrett; [ed.] Western High School; [occ.] F.E.M.A.; [memb.] International Poetry Society; [hon.] Editor's Choice Awards; [oth. writ.] Modern Poetry Society/ Mirrors Of The Soul - Nat'l. Lib. of Poetry/East Of The Sunrise/ Best Poems of 1996, The Rippling Waters, Best Poems of The 90's Song Release Until Then (album - The Light Of The World/Gospel Songbook rel. Until Then (Book Sing Hallelujah).; [pers.] My desire through the pen in my hand is to reflect the love of God shed abroad in my life, giving hope to the hopeless and light to those who sit in darkness.; [a.] Denton, TX

ROLLIN, MARTY
[b.] August 28, 1909, Philadelphia, PA; [p.] Betty Rollin and Rubin Rollin (Both Deceased); [m.] Dorothy Rollin, July 20, 1946; [ch.] Stephen Rollin and Esther LaKen; [ed.] Central High School, Phila, PA, Graduation Diploma - Baronian School of Watch making and Watch Repairing; [occ.] Retired in 1977, from the U.S.P.O. with 36 years of service; [memb.] Life member #148 - Local #77, A.F. of M., A.A.R.P., NARFE, Chapter 1212, Philo., PA. and Wash., D.C. National Office, I am a remember in good standing, certified by the International Society of Poets - 1994-5-6, and the National Library of Poetry, Distinguished Member of I.S.P. 1995-6; [hon.] Award of Merit Certificate Certifying that Marty Rollin has been awarded special mention in the free poetry content sponsored by Hollywood's Famous Poets Society for my Poem, "Beauty In The Sky". I received the Editor's Choice Award for outstanding achievement in poetry 1994-5-6, presented by the National Library of Poetry. I received a Plague from the International Society of Poets on becoming a Distinguished Member. To date, 27 of my poems have been selected to be published in various Anthologies by I.S.P. and N.L.P.; [oth. writ.] I've written over 350 poems relating to my profession as an Orchestra Leader, my family and friend, every day events, interesting subjects, etc. all for my own enjoyment. I plan to continue writing poems as long as I am able.; [pers.] My poems are not fancy or too deep to used understand. I try to give my subjects a fair shake. I try not to be unkind in expressing my thoughts.; [a.] Philadelphia, PA

ROONEY, EUGENE A.
[b.] October 31, 1940, Brooklyn, NY; [m.] Carol Graf Rooney, 1945-1995; [ed.] BA Florida State University 1968; [occ.] Owner-Victorian Manor Jewelry New Market, MD; [memb.] Estate and Antique Jewelry; [pers.] Strive to reflect human relationships.

ROSS, VIRGINIA MORTON
[b.] April 29, 1927, Petersburg, IN; [p.] Clyde and Merle (Hale) Morton; [m.] Adrian Eugene Ross, September 21, 1946; [ch.] Adrian Dewayne Ross; [ed.] Petersburg High School; [occ.] Author, Wife and Mother; [memb.] Attend Petersburg Free Methodist Church, the National Library of Poetry and County and State Art Exhibitor; [hon.] Around 70 Art Ribbons, Poetry Awards; [oth. writ.] Author of two poem books: Just Beyond The Bend and Thru Sunshine And Shadow.; [pers.] If my writing can encourage someone who is down, alone and about to give up, then I feel that is the highest award that I can ever receive in this life!; [a.] Petersburg, IN

ROW, STACI
[pen.] S. L. Row; [b.] April 27, 1970, Kentucky; [p.] Gary Ogden and Barbara Dunn; [m.] Brad Row, May 1992; [ch.] Lindsey and Haley; [ed.] Sierra High School Colorado Springs, CO; [occ.] Vice Pres. Elite Programming; [memb.] Harvest Fellowship Church; [oth. writ.] Several poems, children stories and short stories; [pers.] I believe that God has brought me to where I am. He gave me the gift of writing and I pray that I can use it for his will.; [a.] Jacksonville, AR

RUBEYIAT, JHERRIE
[b.] October 5, 1934, Det., MI; [p.] Jean and Ben Ribiat; [m.] David Zander, May 30, 1960, May 30, 1976; [ch.] Karen and Karl Zander; [ed.] Bross BS M. ED, Dr. Metaphisias Reiki Master, Jore Practishier; [occ.] Retired, Commander of Flotilla 19, US Coast Guard Auxiliary in Hilo, Hi, Bd of UN Women; [memb.] Ex-president of League of women voters of Hilo, Hi, Ex-president of AAUW; [hon.] Volunteer Hawaiian Paradise Park award '96. U.S. Coast Guard Auxiliary:

"Group Action award for superior performance" Certificates of advancement for, Instructor and crew rescue; [oth. writ.] Renderings of the Heart; [pers.] We are one in spirit when we act and care like one - we shall improve the world. We now realize that the only thing necessary for the triumph of evil is for all the good caring people to do nothing.; [a.] Keaau, HI

RUBIN, LARRY BRUCE
[b.] April 5, 1958, Chicago, IL; [p.] Philip and Helen Rubin; [ed.] B.A. Journalism, Roosevelt University Chicago, IL. (1983); [occ.] Free-Prance Writer; [memb.] Pi Delta Epsilon a Journalism "Fraternity", In Jewish - Groups; [hon.] In Who's Who, "Best Poems Writer" "Among other"; [oth. writ.] "Wrote a books called "The Silence of Success". Numerous investigative type articles and poems in local newspapers.; [pers.] People must learn to get along, instead of hating.; [a.] Chicago, IL

RUBINOWITZ, WENDI N.
[b.] March 27, 1973, NYC, NY; [ed.] Univ. of Rochester - BS in the School in Nursing; [occ.] Surgical, RN; [oth. writ.] Possess a ten of unpublished work - anyone know of a good, semi-kind Editor! Have yet to find one (except here of course).

RUCKDASHEL, VIRGIL A.
[b.] May 28, 1923, Rockford, IA; [p.] Mr. and Mrs. J. A. Ruckdashel; [m.] Betty Lou (Huntley) Ruckdashel, March 28, 1959; [ch.] James and Daniel (Deceased) Glenn; [ed.] B. A. Journ, Univ. of MT; [occ.] Retired; [memb.] Lions (active) AARP, Elks - VFW - Amer. Leg. (Past Member), City Park Board Member (past); [oth. writ.] Many, widely varied - news articles - life history - short stories - a Ruckdashel Gen. Book and Poetry (my favorite).; [pers.] My writing comes from the heart. It often reflects past incidents in my life. I feel God has given me the gift of writing for a reason. May it in some small way help someone - someway.; [a.] Polson, MT

RUDY, RONALD D.
[pen.] Ron Rudy; [b.] November 29, 1947, Colby, KS; [p.] Earl L. Rudy, Francis Irene Rudy; [m.] Deborah A. (Newby) Rudy, May 18, 1974; [ch.] Hilary Rose, Alicia Aileen, Garth Ian (Dec); [ed.] Jefferson High, Western State Col.; [occ.] Disabled, Retired; [memb.] American Legion, Disabled American Veterans, Vietnam Veterans of America, Nat'l Rifle Assn., NRA - second Amendment Task Force, Numerous Wildlife, Civic, and other memberships.; [hon.] D.V.O.P. of the year from Colo. Dept. V.F.W. 1985. Some poems published in "Veterans Voices" received awards; [oth. writ.] Several poems published in College and local papers. Articles written for local papers.; [pers.] Writing has always been a therapeutic way of dealing with problems or issues. The most memorable comment that I read! "You don't choose poetry, it chooses you, then you are obsessed the rest of your life".; [a.] Olathe, CO

RUPERT, THOMAS C.
[pen.] Tom; [b.] February 17, 1933, Akron, OH; [p.] Agnes V. (Rupert)-Strole, Deceased, Step-Father Ray A. Strole; [ch.] 2 children Tom Jr. and Terri; [ed.] High School Graduate - Long Beach CA. Jordan High, United States Air Force Institute College Equivalency Editors: Cats Purr-Long Beach, Jordan High School CA. Newspaper, High School Sport writer - Long Beach Independent/Press Telegram; [occ.] Trans World Airlines as fleet services lead and occasional Chauffeur to Howard Hughes. Left TWA to work for Southwest Airlines as Assistant Manager at Los Angeles Airport. Owned and Operated three Travel Agencies, Space Age Travel, Torrance, CA., Bay Chalet Travel, Hermosa Beach, Ca., Leonard's Travel Service, El Segundo, CA.; [memb.] Occupied the position of Acting California State Treasurer under Former State Treasurer, Jess Unrush until his death. Served as a member of the Board of Directors, California League of Cities along with Pete Wilson, now California State Governor, Diane Feinstein, now United States Senator and Tom Brandley, former Mayor, City of Los Angeles. I also served as Chief administrative Aid and Confidant to CA. Lt Governor and retired congressman, Glenn M. Anderson, (now deceased) for a period of six years. Pass President of the International Treasurers Association, 1971-72.; [hon.] Enlisted, U.S. Air Force. Served 4 years during the Korean conflict as an Air Operations Specialist attached to California and Wyoming National Guard Fighter/Interceptor Squadrons as a Base Operations Specialist and Control Tower Operator. At the age of nineteen I become a worked class archer. Finished ninth in the U.S.A.; [oth. writ.] Prolific Author and Writer - Published front cover featured articles for Motor Boat and Sailing magazine, Treasure magazine and Pennant Magazines. Currently writing poems and sonnets - average 3 per week.; [pers.] I was fortunate to be good friends of Bob Baker, Chief Test Pilot, North American Aviation, along with Scott Crossfield, First man to fly into space, as pilot of the X15, Buz Aldrin, John Glenn and numerous others including famous Aviatrix, Pancho Barnes. I am now retired and at Canyon Country Club in Palm Springs CA for six years, practising my lives hobby, "Archeology." Since the age of sixteen I became a gatherer and finder, during this period I became a serious collector of pre-historic artifacts. I am considered by me peers and friends to be an expert in this area. My code is now, as it was then to be: "Gather whenever you see a thing that really shouldn't be there." Oh yes, I'm a typical "Aquarian!"

RUSH, WILLIAM V.
[b.] September 21, 1914, Washington, PA; [p.] Harry & Izetta (Deceased); [m.] Deceased; [ch.] Gary & Donna; [ed.] High School - James Madison in Brooklyn; [occ.] Retired; [memb.] AARP, 2 Senior bowling leagues, Member of "Internatinal Society of Poets"; [hon.] $150.00 from bowling magazine & $50.00 from "Society of Poets."; [oth. writ.] Two articles in Bowling Magazine several years ago. [pers.] "Nothing ventured nothing gained."; [a.] Stone Mt., GA

RUSKE, CHRISTOPHER
[b.] August 29, 1969, Bridgeton, NJ; [p.] Roger and Margaret; [ed.] University of Delaware - BS Agriculture; [occ.] Owner - Cumberland Nurseries; [memb.] New Jersey Farm Bureau, New Jersey Agricultural Society, NJAES - Board of Managers, New Jersey Agricultural Leadership Development Program; [oth. writ.] Several poems for the National Library of Poetry, numerous articles and papers for professional organizations.; [pers.] Words are the seeds that give rise to change.; [a.] Millville, NJ

RUSSELL, RHONDA
[b.] February 3, 1962, Amherst, OH; [p.] Emily Phillips, James Phillips; [ch.] Tiffany and Mandi Russell; [occ.] Restaurant Manager (Burger King) 9 years; [hon.] Too many to list.; [oth. writ.] Thankful power in the book Voice Within. I sit in the book Best Poems of the 90's.; [pers.] Life is good!; [a.] Sunrise, FL

RUSSO, VINCENT P.
[pen.] V. P. Russo Jr.; [b.] January 3, 1930, Washington, DC; [m.] Nancy Ann Ivone, September 15, 1990; [ed.] B.A. University of Maryland; [occ.] Food Service Administrator, New York City Department of Correction; [oth. writ.] Former columnist, The Mid-Atlantic Food Service News, former columnist, the Baltimore Chronicle, feature writer, the Baltimore Review, poetry published in the Little Patuxent Re-

view, two books of poetry, Is Ugly Then The Rose and Love And Marigolds.; [pers.] Youth is in one's perspective, and in the friends one keeps. Youth is still embracing hope at sixty, as it was embraced at six and with the same enthusiasm.; [a.] Sunnyside, NY

RYAN, DAWN
[pen.] Dawn Ryan ;[b.] November 19,1972, Springfield, IL. ;[p.] Larry and Susan Byrd ;[m.] Jeff Kruger; March 21,1992 ;[ch.]Marissa Katherine, November 10,1994 ;[ed.] Springfield College of IL. major=music ;[occ.] make-up artist ;[pers.]So often society will limit love to a physical experience. I believe true love is the complete embrace of a persons Dody, soul, and heart. ; [a.] Springfield, IL.

RYK, MARY ANN
[pen.] Mar; [b.] December 12, 1943, Chicago, IL; [p.] Mr. and Mrs. Anthony P. Mishor; [m.] Jan Ryk, April 20, 1963; [ch.] Laurens, Julie, Joseph, Jon, Anthony, Jacques and Adrian; [ed.] Graduate of Depaul School for New Learning (SNL) 1940 Chicago, IL; [occ.] Retired Choplorn, Bethlehem Words Ret. Living Ctr, Labrange, IL; [memb.] St. Mary of Gosryn - Choir, Post Member, Ellinois poetry Society; [hon.] Published by Nat. Lib. of Poetry, in three anthologies present vol, three Volumes of published poems under title of "Peotry of the Soul" Lyncol Heritage, Dance on the Horizon, The Coming of Dawn and the Best Poems of 1997 also published Sparrowgrass Poetry Forum's Anthology-poetry voices in America winner of Nat. Lib. of poetry's Editor's Choice Award; [oth. writ.] Materials for Inspirational Group and retreat materials.; [pers.] Through my poetry I seek to convey the common experiences of faith, life and love. It is God's gift to me (to write), I want to share it with others many of my poems are similar to the psalms of scripture.; [a.] Downers Grove, IL

SAFFRIN, MARY
[b.] November 26, 1980, Evanston Hospital; [p.] Carole and Dennis; [ed.] Graduating from High School (Libertyville) in 1998; [occ.] Student; [memb.] Distinguished Member; [hon.] Editors Choice, Poet of Merit; [oth. writ.] Rivers of emotion, Indecision, Silhouette, Ridolence and many others; [pers.] In my heart I don't want to be alone...but in my eyes I do. For my eyes see all, and what I see crushes my soul and eats my heart alive.; [a.] Vernon Hills, IL

SALAS, MS. GLORIA
[b.] June 4, 1931, Bayamon, PR; [hon.] The "Editor's Choice Award" from The National Library of Poetry

SAMBO, BETTY J.
[pen.] B. J. Mos; [b.] December 17, 1925, St. Louis, MO; [p.] Clara and Albert Marston; [m.] Divorced, June 26, 1946; [ch.] Donna and Michael; [ed.] High School, University City, MO; [occ.] Retired; [hon.] Personal satisfaction from writing - a very unique "Award" when anything I write (poems or stories) have been accepted.; [oth. writ.] Not a well-known or published" writer poetry and short stories with one novel under consideration!; [pers.] Honest and decency are my guidelines cannot/will not tolerate "Lying/Cheating" in any way, shape or form! "Life", to me, is an obligation - not to be misused.; [a.] Union Star, MO

SAMTANI, PREETI RAJ
[b.] October 25, 1980, New York; [p.] Raj and Pushma Samtani; [ed.] Saint Mary's Elementary School, The Holton-Arms School; [memb.] The National Poet's Society, Model United Nations, Scribbler Newspaper, The Dram Club; [hon.] Most Improved Tennis Player of 1996, Poetry Award for 1996; [oth. writ.] Poem in "The Desert Sun", articles in the Scribbler Newspaper, various poems published in Scroll Literary Magazine.; [pers.] "There is a fountain of youth, it is your mind, your talents, the creativity you bring to your life."; [a.] Potomac, MD

SANCHEZ, CRISTITA
[b.] March 7, 1972, Aurora, CO; [p.] Feladelfio Sanchez, Wilma Sue Acor; [ed.] Burlingame High, College of Notre Dame; [oth. writ.] A few poems publish in my High School literary magazine, poem published in Across the Universe - Poetry anthology; [pers.] The world seen through the eyes of a child may seem exciting and new, but when it's seen through the eyes of a hurt child, it may seem dark and threatening...my sights and experiences are my own seen through my eyes, but many have influenced me for the better and for the worse, which made who I am.; [a.] Belmont, CA

SANDLIN, JOSHUA C.
[b.] December 6, 1974, Portsmouth, VA; [p.] James and Susan Sandlin; [ed.] Graduated Fletcher High School in 1993; [occ.] Currently Employed at an answering service; [oth. writ.] A Poem "It was..." appeared in National Library of Poetry's anthology "In Dappled Sunlight"; [pers.] If you wish to know more about me, please write to: 791 Assissi Lane # 1509, Atlantic Beach, FL 32233 all letters received will get response! This address will never expire! Special, special thanks to "Rhonda".; [a.] Jacksonville, FL

SANDNESS, ROBERT C.
[pen.] Bob; [b.] February 28, 1936, Chicago, Cook Co, IL; [m.] Divorced; [ch.] Erin Arlene, June 1, 1969, Erik Andrew, April 28, 1973; [ed.] 18 years. Three years Electronics, two years university study abroad and in the United States - Business Administration, Engineering, Journalism, specialized military and government on assignments, along with continuing university and correspondence study to update needs.; [occ.] Volunteer: Valley Hospital - Emergency Room, Medicare ICA Program, Maryville Academy, Zelza K Shrine, Scottish Rite, Masons, Political Candidates - National and Local, ASC-NAB, Lions, Moose, Safe Teens, and Bike Patrol; [memb.] U.S. Naval Institute, Air Force Association; [hon.] Meritorious Honor Award - Department of State, American Embassy Tehran, Feb. 1966, by Armin H. Myer, Ambassador, Zelzah Temple Oct. 1987, Valley Hospital May, 1995; [oth. writ.] Edit and ghost plays and books of Las Vegas Celebrities, Tea Concepts U.S.A., Showbiz Magazine, Las Vegas Sun, Federal Laboratories/ Breeze Corp. Staff Writer - Blue book, Hose Clamp book, Plus: Poetry, Corporate Awareness Guide, Cost Accounting Reference Guide, Manuals, Articles in many papers. Self-publishing Books: Spy Development 1985, Variety of books made with copies sent to Foreign Governments and U.S. Politicians. Books in works include: Alien Force, The Battle - The War, Iraq - Trouble in the Middle East, Alternative for Nuclear Waste Repositories, Heroes I Have Known, Nutrition and Life; [pers.] Love and understanding should be a basic tenet of Man-Humankind, if however, your faced with hate and or aggression directed at yourself and family - remove it from your path with dispatch!; [a.] Las Vegas, NV

SARA, NILS P.
[pen.] Nils P. Sara; [b.] November 19, 1947, Bethel, AK; [p.] Clement N. and Martha Sara; [m.] Divorced, 1983; [ch.] Rebecca Matilda Sara; [ed.] High School; [occ.] Subsistence Fisherman; [hon.] Award from the National Library of Poetry; [oth. writ.] Poems in various Alaska publications and 2 National Library of Poetry books; [pers.] I believe that people should live as simply and naturally as possible, growing food in gardens and harvesting fish and game for heat.; [a.] Bethel, AK

SARKISSIAN, HENRY
[b.] 1922, Tehran, Iran; [m.] Annik, 1948; [ch.] (Sons) Armen and Vahe; [ed.] Self-Taught, English is my fourth language;

[occ.] I.R.S. Enrolled Agent; [oth. writ.] "Tales of 1,001 Iranian Days" St. Bk #533-04476-6 Lib. Coug. 79-67512

SARNOSKI, KIM
[b.] July 23, 1975, Philadelphia, PA; [p.] William and Patricia Betzler; [ed.] Lacey Township High School Ocean County College; [occ.] Receptionist, Ocean County Eye Associates, Bayville; [hon.] Honorable Mention in Essay Contest, Editor's Choice Award, Nat'l Library Poetry; [oth. writ.] Published in School Literary Magazine, Essay published in travel brochure, poem published in National Library of Poetry's last compilation.; [pers.] I started writing to work out stresses or problems that I would have in my life and it really helped me. I realized the written word is a very powerful tool and perhaps others would benefit from my writings.; [a.] Forked River, NJ

SAVAGE, DONNA S.
[b.] October 29, 1970, Birmingham, AL; [p.] Don and Joan Smith; [m.] Hunter Savage, September 10, 1994; [ed.] B.A. English/Creative Writing Randolph - Macon Woman's College - M.A. Secondary Education - University of Alabama at Birmingham; [occ.] 7th grade Language Arts Teacher; [memb.] Galveston Junior League, Resiterns, Houston Museum of Fine Arts; [oth. writ.] Other poems published by The National Library of Poetry.; [pers.] For my grandfather Donald Bratton Bickerstaff who always loved new places.; [a.] Galveston, TX

SCHAEFFER, FENELLA
[b.] June 4,1935, Houston, Texas ;[p.] Mr. and Mrs. Haymand Teplow ;[m.] Vernon Schaefer, 1975 ;[ch.] 4 grown men by previous marriage ;[ed.] M.O. University of TX. medical branch Galveston, TX. ;[occ.] Retired ; [a.] Coleman, TX.

SCHARSCHMIDT, ROSIE
[b.] August 27, 1946, Oakfield, WI; [p.] Theodore and Erna Strook; [m.] Michael Scharschmidt, October 1, 1977; [ch.] Cherie Ann and April Jean; [ed.] Brandon High School; [occ.] Housewife and childcare; [memb.] International Society of Poets; [hon.] Editor's Choice Award; [oth. writ.] "Loves' Rose" poem published in "Indappled Sunlight"; [pers.] Writing about members of my family in past and present times brings love, joy and much happiness in my poetry writings. Poems are the love of my life.; [a.] Markesan, WI

SCHILLINGER, BEVERLY
[pen.] Beverlee Benson; [b.] March 31, 1935, Rochester, NY; [m.] Robert Schillinger, April 25, 1959; [ch.] Sherry, Terry, Vicky and Wayne; [ed.] Degree in Marketing several travel courses and accomplishments.; [occ.] Travel Consultant and Free-Lance Writer; [memb.] Scottish Heritage Society of Rochester; [hon.] Holland Travel Professional Award, several travel certificates, Licentiate Minister of Spiritualism, Secretary of Scottish Heritage Society of Rochester; [oth. writ.] Poems published by The National Library of Poetry. Wrote travel articles for "Singles Magazine". Articles published in newspapers and various publications.; [pers.] As an incurable romantic, I believe in hope, dreams and decency, tenderness and kindness. These things, I try to reflect in my writings. I have incurable cancer and I'm grateful for the opportunity to write at least once more.; [a.] Scottsville, NY

SCHLAEFER, EILEEN
[b.] February 2, 1913, Caffage Patch; [p.] Momma Patch and Daddy Patch; [ch.] Two little Brussel Sprouts; [ed.] School of Earth's Knowledge; [occ.] Dreamer!; [memb.] Last but not least! God gave a sense of humor; [hon.] If I win any of that $3,500.00 dollars - please take the money out for the book for 1997 - Thank you!; [oth. writ.] Poems published at times in the "Buonnille Herald" newspaper, NY; [pers.] Think good, say good! Do good, like good and last but not least, act good - good - good.; [a.] Staten Island, NY

SCHMIDT, BONNIE ALLEN
[b.] September 27, 1917, Trinidad, CO; [p.] Fred D. and Ruth Allen; [m.] Marvin O. Schmidt, May 30, 1942; [ch.] M. Allen and Fred P. Schmidt; [ed.] B.A. at Missouri Baptist College, St. Louis, Degree in Music Education, Graduated Magna Cum Laude; [occ.] Retired; [memb.] Southwest Baptist Church, St. Louis; [oth. writ.] Amateur composer of vocal music.; [pers.] Most of my poetry centers around nature.; [a.] Fenton, MO

SCHULZ, PAT
[b.] May 21, 1960, Brooklyn, NY; [ed.] University of N.C. at Greensboro B.S. Business Administration; [occ.] Accounting Manager in the Insurance Industry; [memb.] N.C. Writers Network, International Society of Poets, America Business Women's Assoc.; [oth. writ.] Metamorphosis - A Life Journey Oct. 1996 Released (Self Published Collection), "Our Knowing" - Memories of Tomorrow published by the National Library of Poetry, "Our Knowing" - Sounds of Poetry Audio Series - published by Nat'l. Library of Poetry.; [pers.] Literary Influences: Emily Dickinson, Langston Hughes, Nikki Giovanni, Maya Angelou, Helen Steiner Rice; [a.] Charlotte, NC

SCHULZ, STEPHEN PAUL
[pen.] Stephen Paul Schulz; [b.] June 24, 1955, Cape May, NJ; [p.] Carl Alfred and Lillian H. Schulz; [ch.] Charlene Yvette Schulz (daughter); [oth. writ.] "Reflections of Pearls and Swine" (hardcover book of poetry - Vantage Press Inc.), "Thrown From Within - A Battle Fro Possession" (unpublished autobiography), "Le Poete - 'Twixt The Laurel And Quill" (unpublished poetry book), seven anthology publishings.; [pers.] Influenced by Rudyard Kipling and Edgar Allan Poe.; [a.] Crystal Beach, FL

SCIARETTA, DANIELLE
[b.] March 11, 1980, Morristown, NJ; [p.] Donald and Regina; [ed.] Villa Walsh Academy; [occ.] College Prep. Student; [memb.] International Society of Poets 1994-1995; [hon.] Nat. Library 1995, Editor's Choice Award; [oth. writ.] "Thumbprints" Magazine, "Create", "Poet", Poetic voices of America 1995 "Golden Fields", Songs on the Wind, "A Walk in the Woods"; [pers.] Far away distant lands that I have once known, The familiarness has made me happy, The Familiarness has made them home.; [a.] Far Hills, NJ

SEGAL, GREGORY LYONS
[b.] June 13, 1984, New York; [p.] Monica and Rick Segal; [ed.] Rye Country Day School, Rye, NY, class of 2002; [occ.] Student, 7th grade; [oth. writ.] "It Was More Than A Key," Through the Hourglass, National Library of Poetry; [a.] Rye, NY

SERRAO, LORRIE
[b.] December 1, 1956, Oneonta, NY; [p.] Manuel and Lydia Serrao; [ch.] Ben Serrao; [ed.] Franklin Central School, Franklin, NY, State University College, Oneonta, NY, Tompkins Cortland and Community College, Dryden, NY; [occ.] Information Services Associate; [memb.] Dryden PTA, NYSEG ITHACA Employees Association, National Honor Society, International Society of Poets; [hon.] Lyons best all around student, NYS Regents Scholarship, MVP - Cheerleading, Editors Choice Awards, The National Library of Poetry; [oth. writ.] Short story in Catskill Review, poetry in B-D review, enrolled in the Institute of Children's Literature, poetry in a Tapestry of Thoughts, the National Library of Poetry, Best Poems of the 90's, the National Library of Poetry, Footsteps in the Sand, The Poetry Guild.; [pers.] I have

always had a love of words and enjoy expressing myself through poetry.; [a.] Harford, NY

SFORZO, KRISTIN
[pen.] Kris; [b.] September 30, 1983, Oceanside, NY; [p.] Judy and Peter Sforzo; [ed.] St. Mary's Middle School; [memb.] Basketball, Softball, and Girl Scouts; [hon.] Editor's Merit Award for Poetry; [oth. writ.] Reminiscing Meadow, By the Scheming Fire, and The Poet published in other volumes.; [pers.] Everybody has a Romeo.; [a.] Parlin, NJ

SHADIX, JASON P.
[pen.] Jay Shadix; [b.] June 13, 1977, Toledo, OH; [p.] Nancy Wilson, Dave Shadix; [m.] Brenna M. Shadix, November 23, 1996; [ch.] Amber Leigh Shadix; [ed.] Graduated Goose Creek High School in Goose Creek, S. Carolina in 1995; [occ.] Artilleryman in the U.S. Army; [memb.] American Legion; [hon.] National Defense Award, NATO Award, Army Achievement Medal, Presidential Citation, National Service Medal; [oth. writ.] Sunshine Enemas; [pers.] There have been new loves, broken hearts, friendships came and went. Births, deaths, happiness and remorse. There were illegal acts, broken bones family, wins and losses, fun, excitement and boredom.; [a.] Goose Creek, SC

SHAFER, JOYCE E.
[b.] August 3, 1928, Wisner, LA; [p.] J. L. and Alva Cupit Evans; [m.] Deceased; [ch.] Charles Davis, Lynn D. Wallace, and Albert Davis; [occ.] Retired, writing children's book; [memb.] First United Methodist Church, God's Recycled Angels, Windowed Persons Counselor TOPS International; [hon.] Teacher of the year 1966, International Poetry Hall of Fame, World Wide Web Internet; [oth. writ.] Reflections of Light, Best Poems of 1996, Daybreak on the Lord, Dance Upon the Shore and several other anthologies and local papers and children's news letter.; [pers.] My goal is to share my faith with others, especially children, and reach out to those in need of a friend and encourage. I want to make a difference in a troubled world to be a good mother, grandmother and friend.; [a.] Pineville, LA

SHAREGHI, AMANDA
[b.] December 18, 1986, Houston, TX; [p.] Hoang-Anh Pham and Hassan Shareghi; [ed.] 5th Grader, Popper Keizer Advanced Elementary School and Maintaining The Highest Honor Grade and Completing Algebra 10 yrs. old; [occ.] Student; [hon.] The Santa Cruz Spga 1994 first place award winning in the "Be Kind To Animals Weeks" essay contest. Second place in National Geography Bee at her school 1997 at award gold medal of a 5th grader; [oth. writ.] Article for San Jose Mercury News "My Best Friend, Fur Better Or Worse", "The Autumn Poem" in The National Library of Poetry Amidst The Splendor.; [pers.] I like to write poems about nature and seasons and holidays.; [a.] Santa Cruz, CA

SHAW, JACKLYN LAUCHLAND
[pen.] "Samuella Clemency"; [b.] Lodi, CA; [p.] J. and C. Lauchland; [ed.] B.A. University of California, M.Ed. University of Nevada, Pd.D. (Pend.), California Coast University, Multi-credentialed (K 12 and College), Real Estate; [occ.] Consultant, Professor-Author, Founder of Program Design in Communications; [memb.] Choir, alum, other associations (for professional, civic, and community services); [hon.] World Trade and Tourism Honors, "Correspondents Log" Founder (COC Historian), Research Advisory Boards (Biographical Journalism), IBC-England and ABI-USA, Distinguished Leadership (IBC); [oth. writ.] Port-Folios TM (Research, ETC), Careers "Tricathlon" TM program with organizers. Research and Thesis Writing (skills text.). Afghanistan article, co-credits by Dr. L. Dupree, American University Fieldstaff Reports, design for learning game.; [pers.] Poetry Note (By Limerick): Writing Verse — is both work and play. It's a service or Word to pray, rhythmical and reasoned, embraced and emboldened. It's truth from our hearts each day.; [a.] Santa Ana, CA

SHEETS, SUNNI L.
[pen.] Juliette Brandon; [b.] March 27, 1979, Wellington, KS; [p.] Daryle Jon Sheets and Cathy Lynn; [ed.] Belle Plaine High School, plans beyond college are located at the University of Kansas, others South Haven and Hill Crest Bible Baptist Academy.; [occ.] Personal assistant at J.P. Weigand Suburban, Belle Plaine.; [memb.] First Baptist Church, Belle Plaine, various School Organizations; [hon.] Honor Roll, Yearbook Ad Director, Editor; [oth. writ.] I have many, many other poems under lock and key and I also write a little everyday. At this point I still only have one poem published "Stardust" can be found in the Rippling Waters.; [pers.] I would be no where without my parents and grandparents who showed me God's love and taught me how to live pleasing to him. However, my poetry stems from vented emotions and the wonderful techniques that my English and Creative Writing teacher Lynne E. Hewes taught me. Clearly, my poetry is based on all the wonderful people in my life and the experiences we have shared, without the numerous blessings of friendship and love in my life, I wouldn't have poetic words to record. This poem, "I" is based on a woman who I believe I know very well, but try to get to know more and more with every new situation in life.

SHELDON, ROSE L.
[pen.] R. L. Coret; [b.] July 21, 1931, Eastlyme, CT; [p.] Peter Coret and Victoria Sofia Pastor; [m.] Henry Sheldon, June 4, 1978; [ch.] Rochelle Elaine, Roxanne, Marie and Rose; [ed.] Housatonic Community College, St John's River College St Augustine Technical School Universal Life Seminary; [occ.] Retired Pastor and Case Worker; [memb.] International Society of Poets, The National Library of Poetry, several other Poetry Associations; [hon.] Who's Who in American Jr. Colleges, 5 Departmental Awards, 2 College Scholarships, Dean's Community Services Award, Pres. of Student Senate; [oth. writ.] Many poems in Newspapers, Newspaper Journalist.; [pers.] As we are in the world let's get to know it.; [a.] Saint Augustine, FL

SHEPARD, SARAH SAWYER
[b.] October 28, 1919, New Bedford, MA; [p.] Florence and Frederick J. Sawyer; [m.] Walter Owen Shepard, October 28, 1939; [ch.] Brenda G. Waltero Jr., Faith-Ann Webster all Married - Spangler Shepard; [ed.] New Bedford Vocational High School, Dimian Vocational School of Nursing; [occ.] Retired Nurse; [memb.] Past Pres. St. Luke's Retirees, Member Bierstadt Art Society; [hon.] Thanks Badge - Girl Scout Leadership, 4 Painting Art Award, Citation from Mass. State Senate for Distinguished service for service to retirees several "Editor's Choice Awards" National Library of Poetry; [oth. writ.] Published poems, Quiet Place, Cry Loudly, An Cry Storm, Sadness in National Library Poetry Books, Numerous unpublished writings - A Family Cookbook/family stories poem published in local newspaper.; [pers.] I write for personal satisfaction, writing helps me cope with physical chronic pain. I hope my writings will help some one to cope with pain for one more day or even an hour, to help forget pain and enjoy happy thoughts.; [a.] New Bedford, MA

SHERMAN, FAITH D.
[b.] June 2, 1926; [p.] Edmund and Mildred Conklin; [m.] Morrell Sherman, January 7, 1943; [ch.] Millie, Billy, Richie, Dixie and Rocky; [ed.] Graduated High School Afton, NY when I was 43 was on paper in school, won award, did book cover; [occ.] Housewife do Woodcrafts, Bird houses, etc.,

[memb.] Was active firemens auxiliary, also member UFW Auxiliary; [oth. writ.] Have poems published local paper tri-town news, Sidney NY Pageant of Poetry, The International Poetry Hall of Fame; [pers.] Fill my time with poetry, painting and Woodcrafts, have a shop for this called "Fay's Daze".; [a.] Nineveh, NY

SHONK, JOAN ABIGAIL
[b.] February 1, 1935, Honolulu, HI; [p.] Harvey and Mary Nobriga; [ed.] Roosevelt High School; [occ.] Retired; [hon.] National Library of Poetry Editors Choice Awards for "The Silence" in "Shades of Gold"; [oth. writ.] "The Silence" anthology The Voice Within, "Shades of Gold" Anthology Best Poems of the '90, "Jungle Rain" anthology the nightfall of Diamonds; [pers.] I am struck by the goodness extended by the "good samaritan" (The Bible Luke 10:33-35) it has lead me to do a lot of self-examination how wonderful 'twould be if we all walked in the shadow of the "Good samaritan" and cast the same shadow.

SHOSHANI, SHMUEL
[pen.] Shaham; [b.] March 8, 1926, Jerusalem; [p.] Haviv and Monavar; [m.] Farukh, December 31, 1947; [ch.] Ilana, Edna and Amir; [ed.] College; [occ.] Writing Poetry and Translating Persian Poetry; [memb.] Dix Hill Jewish Center, Ritual & Education Committies, Volunteer of British Royal Air Force, & Haganah, Jewish Defence Forces (Israel Palestine), Special Tasks; [hon.] National Library of Poetry, Int. Soc. of Poets.; [oth. writ.] "The Jasmine Fragrance" to "The Persian Nightingale In Cage" translations of selected Diaspora Persian Poetry, Post Islamic Revolution in Iran into Hebrew and English.; [pers.] Be proud of your heritage, enjoy your traditions and pass both to your children. Learn other nations languages to have better understanding.; [a.] Huntington, NY

SHUCK, HAZEL L.
[b.] March 22, 1929, Benton Harber, MI; [p.] Floyd Austin and Thelma Austin; [m.] John N. Shuck, July 4, 1947; [ch.] Roger, Patricia, Justin, Keith, Laura and Harry; [ed.] High School Grad. Kokomo, IN; [occ.] Retired reupholsterer self employed of 43 yrs. owned my business.; [memb.] Phi Beta Psi - Sorority Pres. Tri Add Club Home Extension, Indiana Club Pres. and County Pres.

SHUDA, JEFFREY J.
[pen.] J.J.; [b.] September 3, 1951, LaCrosse; [p.] John and Rose Mary Shuda; [m.] Theresa A. Shuda, September 5, 1970; [ch.] Jeffrey, Michelle, Kristy, Katie, John; [ed.] St. John's School, Aquinas HS W. W.T.C. Training School; [occ.] Sand Mullor Operator; [memb.] Eagles Club, Local 437 GMP Union; [pers.] I strive to write true feeling and actual things that have happened to me.; [a.] LaCrosse, WI

SIMES, LISA
[pen.] Lee-Lee; [b.] April 15, 1978, Durham, NC; [p.] Pamela and Jasper Southerland; [ed.] Warren County High; [occ.] College Student; [memb.] International Society of Poets; [hon.] International Society of Poets (Poet of the Year), National Public Speaking Award; [oth. writ.] Several poems published in local newspapers, school newspapers and poem was selected to be in the USA Today magazines for "The Largest Poem Ever".; [pers.] I strive to continue the goodness of my writings, and I have been blessed with the talent and hope to accomplish my goal to the fullest.; [a.] Warrenton, NC

SIMPSON, DEIDRE
[b.] September 21, 1936, Winnipeg, Manitoba, Canada; [p.] Iris McMillan and Horace Buley; [m.] John Simpson, March, 1957; [ch.] Shaun Lori, Brett Aubrey and Marit Lynne; [ed.] Kelvin High, U of Man., BScHec, U of N. Mex. Teachers Cert.; [occ.] Direct Sales, vitamins, cosmetics, home products; [hon.] Citizenship high school, Freshie Queen University; [oth. writ.] Poem published in local newspaper, several submitted to magazines. Hope to have my poems published as a book.; [pers.] I write to inspire people to live out of their hearts and not their heads, to do what they know in themselves is a dream, and to have the courage to be all they can.; [a.] Kelowna, British Columbia, Canada

SIMS, P. DIANE MARTIN
[pen.] Di; [b.] August 31, 1952, Dallas, TX; [p.] Joe G. and Gerandine Freeman; [m.] Edwin C. Sims, March 23, 1996; [ch.] Jason, Jimmy, Makyla; [ed.] R. L. Turner (1970), Irving Beauty Academy (Cosmetologist), University of Maryland; [occ.] Secretary - Air Force Village II, San Antonio, Texas; [oth. writ.] The Ebbing Tide (Tears), Personal Book of Poems; [pers.] I am proud to be asked to submit another of my poems. This one is special and for my dad, who encouraged me to always follow my dreams, and what I had to say was important; to write from my heart and put my feelings on paper to share with others.; [a.] San Antonio, TX

SINCLAIR, DEBBIE
[pen.] Denise Crane; [b.] April 13, 1957, Mansfield; [p.] Mr. and Mrs. James Crane; [ch.] Monica Lee and Scott Allen; [ed.] Madison Adult Education, Certified in Creative Writing; [occ.] Molding General Assembly; [hon.] An award given by The National Library of Poetry; [oth. writ.] Several articles written for wheels/smart shopper, a local paper free to the public.; [pers.] "Life has taught me well, we have only the words to be written, for the story has already been told.; [a.] Mansfield, OH

SLASTEN, GUENNADI
[pen.] Gene Nicholas Slaston, Slagen; [b.] May 4, 1957, Kegichevka, Ukraine; [p.] Nikolai Slaston, Vera Boiko-Slaston; [ch.] Marina Slasten; [ed.] B.A./M.A. at Kishinev, State University (Moldova), Moscow Institute of Information (Russia); [occ.] Free-lance Songwriter, Poet, Philologist, Teacher, Translator; [memb.] Distinguished member of the International Society of Poets, International Poetry Hall of Fame.; [hon] Editor's Choice Award (1995, 1996, 1997) by the National Library of Poetry, International Poet of Merit Award (1995) and Nomination as Poet of the Year (1995, 1996, 1997) by the International Society of Poets.; [oth. writ.] Three dozen of songs and poems in English and in Russian some of them published in 'A Moment in Time', 'The Rainbow's End', 'Best Poems of the 90's by the National Library of Poetry', in 'Best New Poems' by the Poet's Guild, et cetera.; [pers.] My beloved readers, now is your time to support the idea of creation of a truly common auxiliary language to be spoken by all and everyone. Interlinguistic can help people in creating such a universal language of peace and cooperation for the whole mankind.; [a.] Brooklyn, NY

SLASTEN, GUENNADI
[pen.] Gene Nicholas Slaston, Slagen; [b.] May 4, 1957, Kegichevka, Ukraine; [p.] Nikolai Slaston, Vera Boiko-Slaston; [ch.] Marina Slasten; [ed.] B.A./M.A. at Kishinev, State University (Moldova), Moscow Institute of Information (Russia); [occ.] Free-lance Songwriter, Poet, Philologist, Teacher, Translator; [memb.] Distinguished member of the International Society of Poets, International Poetry Hall of Fame.; [hon] Editor's Choice Award (1995, 1996, 1997) by the National Library of Poetry, International Poet of Merit Award (1995) and Nomination as Poet of the Year (1995, 1996, 1997) by the International Society of Poets.; [oth. writ.] Three dozen of songs and poems in English and in Russian some of them published in 'A Moment in Time', 'The Rainbow's End', 'Best Poems of the 90's by the National Library of Poetry', in 'Best New Poems' by the Poet's Guild,

et cetera.; [pers.] My beloved readers, now is your time to support the idea of creation of a truly common auxiliary language to be spoken by all and everyone. Interlinguistic can help people in creating such a universal language of peace and cooperation for the whole mankind.; [a.] Brooklyn, NY

SMEDLEY, DONNA WOOD
[b.] February 22, 1958, Syracuse, NY; [p.] Don and Lucille Wood; [m.] Johnny Smedley Jr., September 10, 1988; [ch.] Amanda and Emily; [ed.] Grad 76 from R.J. Reynolds, Winston-Salem, NC; [occ.] Mother, P.T., Bookkeeping; [memb.] NC Van, Arbor Day Foundation, PTA; [hon.] Being blessed with 2 beautiful, healthy children; [oth. writ.] Call Me From Heaven, Angel Wings, Angel David - published by National Library of Poetry.; [pers.] Life is so precious and should never be taken for granted. I count my blessings daily and am thankful for them.; [a.] Raleigh, NC

SMITH, CELESTINE H.
[pen.] Celestine - Sassy; [b.] August 31, 1938, San Francisco, CA; [p.] Frances Blake - Celestine Hourtal; [ch.] Tami Ann - Carla Tenese, James Finley, Scott Jerome; [ed.] Holy Names Academy - Seattle, WN; [occ.] Independent Contractor; [hon.] Editor's Choice Award from National Library of Poetry 1995 and 1996; [oth. writ.] Work In Process - poems published in "A Delicate Balance" and "Best Poems of 90's" through National Library of Poetry; [pers.] Let all strive to work through our own subtlefuge - a must need to tail this sail, cultivating against hate. Let all maximize essential truth to attain our goal. Only then well we reach our true status as a Nation of Universal Soul.; [a.] Wilsonville, OR

SMITH, CHARLES RAY
[pen.] Charles R. Smith ; [b.] November 25,1946, Littleton, NC ; [p.] Ray and Jane Smith ; [ch.] Charles Capieron Smith ; [ed.] Aurelian Springs High, Wilson Community College, Nash Community College, Halifax Community College ; [occ.] Continuing Academic Studies ; [memb.] Good News Baptist Church of the World, NRA. ; [hon.] Graduated with honors A.A.S. Degree Nash Community College - Diplomas and certificates in several fields of study ; [oth. writ.] "Point of View" pulished in Carvings In Stone, several other poems and short stories. ; [pers.] I have always strived to convey humanly attitudes and feelings sometimes with a blending of Nature and it's surrounding beauty. ; [a.] Nashville, NC.

SMITH, DEE DEE
[b.] January 11, 1973, Fallschurch, VA; [p.] Jim and Caroll Smith; [m.] Greg Yeck, October 14, 1995; [ed.] Falls Church High School 1991 Washington Business School 1992; [occ.] Human Resources Administrator; [oth. writ.] "The Honeymoon" published in At Water's Edge, "Letting Go" and "Courage" to be published in Keepsakes in February 1997, "Letting Go" to be published in Best New Poems inspiring of 1997.; [pers.] I love writing! It's away of expressing myself and saying things I couldn't even tell my best friend. I want to thank my family for believing and supporting me. Especially my husband! I love you all with all my heart!

SMITH, JANICE
[b.] July 15, 1981; [p.] Danny and Rosemary Smith; [ed.] High School Student at Immaculate Conception; [occ.] Student - 9th Grade; [hon.] Creative writing awards for 4 years in a row; [oth. writ.] Several poems published in other books.; [pers.] If you are not ready for the responsibilities of drinking then Don't Drink!; [a.] Rochelle Park, NJ

SMITH, JEAN MARIE
[b.] June 2, 1950, Lewiston, MN; [p.] Rene and June Gagnon; [m.] Robert Atmar Smith, November 5, 1994; [ch.] Cynthia, Kelli, Trudy, Daniel, Robert; [ed.] Lewiston High School, Attended CMVTC for Nursing, Activities Director, CMT, CNA, Medication Tech.; [occ.] Homemaker at present time; [memb.] The National Library of Poetry; [hon.] Editor's Choice Award the biggest honor in my life is being a mother and enjoy my beautiful children and 4 grandchildren Lacie, John, Steven, Bayley, they are the joy of my life; [oth. writ.] "My Patient's", Peacefulness, Understanding, "Touching You Deeply", "Empty Soul", "Autumn", Mother; [pers.] My patient's has been published in Nursing home flyers, read to nursing students. I write to express my feelings to people so they understand how they feel. My dream is to go back to collage to be a social worker.; [a.] Virginia Beach, VA

SMITH, JOSEPH N.
[b.] February 17, 1944, Virginia; [p.] Cleophas and Eva C. Smith; [m.] Marion B., November 3, 1967; [ed.] High School; [occ.] DAV; [pers.] In trading, He that let the desire of his eyes cloud the mind of his reason, maketh himself a prey to the seller.; [a.] Upper Marlboro, MD

SMITH, KRISTY
[b.] November 9, 1979, Albuquerque, NM; [p.] Paul and Carol Smith; [ed.] Junior at Los Lunas High School; [occ.] Student; [memb.] New Mexico Motor Racing Association, Pythian Sunshine Girls, Nat'l Honor Society; [hon.] Nat'l Honor Society Member - Student of the week - 3 times; [oth. writ.] Poems in "A Delicate Balance" and "Best Poets of the 90's."; [pers.] Everything I write comes from my heart.; [a.] Bosque Farms, NM

SMITH, RODRIC S.
[occ.] Cadet at the USAFA; [memb.] International Poets Society; [oth. writ.] "Envision" in Across The Universe.; [pers.] You will only find true love if you share your true self with others. Sarah Rehm, Alice Laeger, Julie Guertin, Jacque O'Mealey, Quentin Cox, Phil Dillingham, Vince Kendrick, John Baria, Michael Lyle, Glenn Gonzalas, thanks for the love you've shown me through our friendship! Love all ya'll.

SNODGRASS, MARILYN MCCOY
[b.] October 22, 1944, Pittsburgh, PA; [p.] Kenyon and Ruth Cook McCoy; [m.] Robert B. Snodgrass, November 29, 1968; [ch.] Beth Ellen McCreary and Amy Fae Dietrich; [ed.] Gateway Sr. High Graduate 1962 June 2, 1/2 yrs. College in Music Education 9/62-8/64, Counselling Classes 1992-93 for 1 1/2 years, Organ Lessons 1993 to Present; [occ.] Homemaker; [memb.] Grace United Methodist Church Contemporary Worship Team Member, Playing Flute; [oth. writ.] "Valentine's Day" published in National Library of Poetry's Anthology called "Amidst The Splendor", have had poems published in church and nursing home newsletters. I've written over sixty poems and non-fiction stories, Bible studies, as well as one fiction story with titles, including: "The Two-Way Door", "A Good Memory", and "Communion Miracle". My book, which will be published in 1997, is entitled "Peace Through The Storm"; [pers.] I really enjoy helping people find wholeness, freedom, and peace in their lives, through a personal relationship with Jesus Christ. I hope this freedom, wholeness, and peace will be found through my writing.; [a.] Indiana, PA

SNYDER, MILDRED E.
[pen.] Mildred Rex Snyder; [b.] March 28, 1912, Syracuse, IN; [p.] Walter and Jessie Warble Rex; [m.] Richard E. Snyder (Deceased), January 1, 1933; [ch.] Richard Rex and Mary Gail; [ed.] Salutatorian of high school graduating class of Avilla, Ind. Graduate of International Business College Ft. Wayne, IN; [occ.] Retired; [memb.] National Library of Poetry, Distinguished Member International Society of Poets, Resident Council of Concord Village; [hon.] Many for being a pianist and organist. Published poems in 12 anthologies

including "Best Poems of the '90s" and "The Best Poems of 1997". Poet of Merit 1995 and 4 Editor's Choice Awards.; [oth. writ.] Poem "Introspect" for autobiography of relative to be published soon; [pers.] My family has a history of musicians, artists and poets. Laughter and positive attitude are everything; learn to laugh at yourself. It will make you and everyone else feel better.; [a.] Fort Wayne, IN

SOPER, M. F.
[b.] June 1926, Middlesex, UK; [p.] both deceased; [m.] Eileen, January 1951; [ch.] Two - son and daughter; [ed.] College standard to 17 years Seale Hayne Farming Devon; [occ.] Retired; [oth. writ.] Excess of 500 poems and 50 children stories, articles in local newspaper in Hertfordshire, UK Poems written for local schools also full length musical show; [pers.] I have been an admirer of the great poet Tennyson who my Grandfather knew. I wish to let my verses mold and guide the youth of all the nations of the earth.; [a.] Hertfordshire, England, UK

SPANGLER, ELOIS L.
[pen.] Lorene; [b.] February 23, 1928, Washington, DC; [p.] Boyd and Mabel Shaffer; [m.] Charles (Deceased), February 8, 1946; [ch.] Randall, Lucinda and Valerie; [ed.] High School, 1944 grad.; [occ.] Retired and live alone except for great granddaughter visits; [hon.] Beautiful things from I.S.P.; [oth. writ.] One in Shadow and Light. Four more poems and three already in anthologies and sixteen ready for approval all by I.S.P.; [pers.] Good poetry touches the heart and tells a story. It thrills and entices. I am understood. Longfellow, Sarett, Spargur, Wilcox, Rose, McCray, Lillard, Field and the every great E. A. guest to me are great.; [a.] Wellsville, PA

SPENCER, JOYCE STILES
[b.] Wynneewood, OK; [p.] D. G. and Hester McKinley; [m.] James Spencer, April 16, 1994; [ch.] Rick, Stan and Ronnie Stiles, Susan Campbell, and Rhonda Wisely; [occ.] Early Retirement from Tinker Air Force Base; [memb.] International Society of Poets, Tinker Arts Alliances, The International Poetry Hall of Fame; [hon.] 1995 and 1996 Nominee for International Poet of the Year, Two Editor's Choice Awards, voted into The International Poetry Hall of Fame November 1, 1996.; [oth. writ.] Remember Papaw, My Ship Has Sailed, A Friend, Children's Art, Everything Is Quiet, Never Alone, Widow, Rancher's Wife, Life Has Been Good To Me.; [pers.] I have written poetry most of my life. Thru poetry I am able to express my inner most thoughts and feelings. I hope this open window to my heart will aid someone else in dealing with life.; [a.] Tecumseh, OK

SPENCER, SHARON E.
[b.] October 1, 1969, St. Croix, V.I.; [p.] Valren Andrews; [ed.] Augusta State University; [occ.] Counselor/Teacher; [memb.] First Assembly of God Church; [hon.] Cross-country running; [oth. writ.] Seasonal articles for the women Ministry at the Assembly of God - church in Augusta, Georgia; [per.] I strive to reflect the goodness of God through nature.; [a.] Augusta, GA

SPRINGER, DONDI
[b.] May 26, 1976, Marion, IN; [p.] Annie M. Whitfield; [occ.] Personal Advisor to a select group of friends; [hon.] This is my first accomplishment, though I've been writing poetry for the last five (5) years; [oth. writ.] "Life Everlasting" only the other one published.; [pers.] I feel that since I left home at 13 yrs. of age alot of what I write comes from that experience of hard times, and now knowing that God is always there in the face of adversity to lead me through to victory! Also greatly influenced by music.; [a.] Marion, IN

ST. CYR, JACKIE
[b.] March 27, 1931, Houston, TX; [p.] Louis G. and Irene (Marcovich) St. Cyr; [m.] Steve C. Campbell 1949, Divorced 1969; [ch.] Steven B. Campbell, Sharon K. Page, grandchildren - Stephanie Renee Page, Shannon Christine Page, Louis Martin Campbell; [ed.] S.F. Austin High, University of Houston; [occ.] Southwestern Bell Telephone Co. (Retired - 1991); [memb.] Poets of T.C., Ft. Worth, TX, Pantry Raiders Kitchen Band of Watauga, TX (Drummer) Telephone Pioneers Of America; [hon.] Graduated with Honors (1949), Nat'l Honor Society, Place 1st, 2nd and 3rd in Poetry and Art Contest in Sr. Citizens Services, Pantry Raiders Kitchen Band placed 2nd in Group Competition at the Texas State Fair, Oct., 1996; [oth. writ.] Several poems published and a couple of short letters published in local newspapers.; [pers.] I enjoy writing children's poetry. "Candyland for Louis" published in this book is dedicated to my only grandson, Louis Martin Campbell, Louis (5 yrs) loves "Fantasy!"; [a.] Watauga, TX

STEEL, LARRY
[b.] March 7, 1948, Long Island; [p.] Nathan and Lillian; [m.] Betti Hey Steel, June 1, 1987; [ch.] Jesse Harrison; [ed.] B.S. Business Administration, Travelling with Ani cycle Basketball Company; [occ.] Import/Export Textile Company-Owner, Eduction (continued), Fatherhood, Marriage; [oth. writ.] "The Millennium Ball" - Co-Authored, "Uni-Ball" Athlete; [pers.] "It is hell on earth to live Without Passion" and to pass this emptiness on to your offspring."; [a.] New York, NY

STEIN, CORINNE
[b.] April 20, 1921; [p.] Rose and Phillip Leader ; [m.] Dr. Seymour Stein, September 14,1954 ; [ch.] Paul and Emily ; [ed.] Boston U. School of Ed. ; [occ.] at home ; [memb.] many in medical causes ; [oth.writ.] Free Lancing with poetry ; [pers.] I live my life strictly by the 10 Commandments ; [a.] McCutom, Mass.

STEINMANN, HOLLI R.
[b.] November 4, 1977, Portland, OR; [p.] Wilfred Steinmann, Kathleen Naliiekia; [ed.] Chaparral High School 1995 Graduate.; [occ.] Accounts Receivable Billing Clerk; [hon.] Honor Roll, Dean's List, Student of the month, Creative Writer of the year in Creative Writing Class.; [oth. writ.] Poem published in the book Morning Song, many poems published in the School Literary Magazine.; [pers.] Goals are to be reached when there's a road block, make all efforts to go around it. Most importantly, never give up striving for what you want most.; [a.] Las Vegas, NV

STERLING, JEROME
[pen.] Bro. Jerome; [b.] December 18, 1949, Torance, CA; [p.] Deceased; [ch.] Four; [ed.] 10th Grade; [occ.] Barber; [memb.] The Bible Covenant Church; [oth. writ.] Working on a book.; [pers.] God is good.; [a.] Los Angeles, CA

STERNBERG, DENNY
[pen.] Denny Sternberg; [b.] June 23, 1924, Chicago, IL; [m.] Arnold C. Sternberg, January 21; [ch.] 7 - 12 grandchild; [ed.] High School- 2 years Secretarial School; [oth. writ.] 6 self published books for children, grand kids and friends.; [pers.] I write, so, the past will not disappear!; [a.] Santa Rosa, CA

STEVENSON, PAULA PATTERSON
[pen.] Diane L.B.; [b.] January 25, 1951, Gowanda, NY; [p.] Sally and Robert Patterson; [m.] Terry Robert Stevenson, July 31, 1971; [ch.] Jodi Diane, Tammara Dawn, Tara Denise; [ed.] Troy Area Schools, Troy, Pennsylvania, East Forest School, Marienville, Pennsylvania. Graduated: May 29, 1969. Duff's Business Institute, Pittsburgh, PA. Graduated: April, 1971.; [occ.] Clerk Typist for a Job Training Consortium/Part-time Waitress; [memb.] First Presbyterian

Church, Marienville, PA, MACA (Marienville Area Civic Assoc.), Marienville, PA, Golf Membership - Highlevel Golf Course; [hon.] Salutatorian - Class of 1969. East Forest School, Marienville, Pennsylvania; [oth. writ.] Poem published by: EPA, Book - "Reflections of Life"; National Library of Poetry, Books: "Tomorrow's Dream", "Where Dawn Lingers", "Best of the '90s", "Frost at Midnight", "The Best Poems of 1997"; [pers.] My poems are written from my feelings. Also writing poetry is self-healing for me.; [a.] Marienville, PA

SULLIVAN, HEATHER
[b.] October 12, 1961, Saint John, NB, Canada; [p.] Patrick and Sandra; [ed.] High School, grade 12 (Saint John High), typing course; [occ.] Unemployed; [memb.] Member of Nerepis United Baptist Church. I am a teacher a leader of Youth Group and pre-school group.; [hon.] Writings in local paper, Editor's Choice Award from the National Library of Poetry 1994.; [oth. writ.] Writings in local paper. A poems in Library of Poetry Anthologies ("Signs" - "In The Desert Sun" and "Natures Expressions" - "Tears of Fire", plus many unpublished works.; [pers.] I look around and write about what I see, and how I feel about what I see. I see things through my heart's eyes, and that's how I write about them.; [a.] Westfield, New Bruswick, Canada

SULLIVAN, MICHAEL L.
[b.] February 8, 1969, Woodbine, GA; [p.] Homer and Luberta Sullivan; [ed.] Camden County High School, St Mary's, GA; [occ.] Information Management Technician (US Air Force); [pers.] Since perfection is humanly unattainable, we should all strive to be exceptional.; [a.] Tampa, FL

SURRATT, DORIS A.
[pen.] Doris A. Ray Surratt; [b.] November 24, 1954, Lincoln, IL; [p.] Avery and Emma Ray; [ch.] Michael and Brandy Surratt; [ed.] High School Graduate; [occ.] Motel/Office and Independent Interpreter for the deaf; [memb.] Street Ministry/Individually; [hon.] Speaker for homelessness, Speaker for epilepsy, for prostitutes to give up their way of life and better themselves to become God's army of messengers,Speaker against gangs and violence.; [oth. writ.] Worthy of the Gospel, Homelessness and Lord Jesus Knew, The National Library of Poetry, A Valentine For You; [pers.] I've lived, Literally, in a life of hell on the streets belonging to satan, and survived to testify to the ones who live there now, and all I can pray for is my words, coming from the spirit of God, will help those who I meet, too.; [a.] Peoria, IL

SUSMUTH, JOHN
[b.] September 21, 1923, Bridgeport, CT; [p.] John and Felicia Susmuth; [ch.] Dawn Kennedy; [ed.] Grammar - Madonna, Ft. Lee, N.J., High - De La Salle Mil. Acad., Toronto Univ., Northwestern U. 1948, U.S.A.A.F. Pilot Training 1943-44; [occ.] Retired; [memb.] Sigma Nu; [hon.] Distinguished Flying Cross Air Medals and Other Military; [oth. writ.] I have attempted to influence Map Makers to Re-do their thinking as to what the world's Land Areas really look like. So far, no success. My World picture is called "Terralae" meaning from Latin, Earth Wings.; [pers.] Always look back...what you learn will help you in gaining.

TENZING, DR. CHERING
[b.] November 6, 1971, Mangan, Sikkim; [p.] Mr. Nima Tenzing, Mrs. S. M. Tenzing; [ed.] Higher Sec. Tashi Nameyal Academy, Gangtok, Sikkim, M.B.B.S - B.S.M.C. Bankura, Weset Bengal, D.N.B - C.F.H., O.D.C. Tamil Nadu; [occ.] Doctor (D.N.B Trainee); [oth. writ.] Several poems published in several poetry journals (SN India) and National Library of Poetry's Anthologies. ; [pers.] I would like to thank Mr. Pinsoom Tenzing, (University of Hawaii) whose gift of 40 made this possible!!; [a.] Tamil Nadu, India

TEUBERT, JUDY
[b.] October 3, 1933, Viola, WI; [p.] Marvin and Adah Buros; [m.] Ronald Teubert; [ch.] Ronald, Jeffrey, Leanne Dale, Kathy and Julie; [ed.] Viola High School; [oth. writ.] I had a poem published in The National Library of Poetry Anthology "Amidst The Splendor"; [pers.] I've been writing poetry for many years it makes me feel lighter and really clears my mind which helps me find peace and tranquility.; [a.] Edgerton, WI

THEOHARIS, EVELYN
[b.] March 9, 1976; [p.] Vicky and Peter Theoharis; [ed.] L.H.A. High, College April Fortier, Travel Agent.; [memb.] AVET Club of MODEERF; [hon.] Honor of being part of another publication of the National Library of Poetry; [pers.] When you write a poem write with your heart and soul, not with your mind. For the writing with Heart Will win the Heart of a stranger, written by mind would be like Blank Paper.; [a.] Montreal, Province of Quebec, Canada

THOMAS JR., JOHN DAVID
[pen.] J. David Thomas; [b.] February 7, 1931, Dixie, GA; [p.] Mr. and Mrs. Hattie M. and John D. Thomas; [m.] Ida Thomas, May 1989; [ch.] Two daughters and two sons; [ed.] Attended Dekalb Coll.; [occ.] Retired U.S. Navy, also retired Fed. Service Employee; [hon.] Four Good Conduct Medals, service connected; [oth. writ.] 2 book of poetry - 2 published books, I love writing poetry, it's very engaging, relaxing to me. It's irrefutable creative imaginable work, of great awe art with every fulgent inenarrable meanings.; [pers.] I'm a retired military man. I've travel world - wide, I had lots of time to think about writing. But, most of it started at an early age.; [a.] Lithonia, GA

THOMPSON, SUE
[pen.] Sue T. ; [b.] November 21,1944, Jacksonville, IL. ; [p.] Marshall Fulton and Marcella Fulton (deceased) ; [m.] divorced ; [ch.] Jeffrey (29) Eric (26) ; [ed.] Grade school and High school at Pow Pow, Illinois, Copley Memorial Hospital-Diploma School of Nursing ; [occ.] Registered Nurse, Salem Memorial Hospital ; [hon.] Editors Choice award, for poem-entered for "Frost at Midnight" ; [oth.writ.] "A Circle of Friends", Found in Frost At Midnight" Random Poems through life were written to others on a personal basis. Two years ago I began my path towards my reawakening, "Spirit", from me. My struggles of growth are expressed through my poetry and I give my teacher friend Jessica Firewalker credit for inspiring me to write and share with others my good and bad times. [a.] Keizer, OR.

THORNTON, JENNIFER
[b.] October 4, 1972, Provo, UT; [p.] Brent Sperry, Judy Wilcox; [m.] Terry Thornton, July 3, 1992; [ch.] Skyler James; [ed.] Trabuco Hills HS, Ricks College; [occ.] Housewife; [oth. writ.] Inner Strength (unpublished), Wisdom From A Child (pub.), Familiar Face (unpub.).; [pers.] I write things of a spiritual nature, as well as things close to my heart.; [a.] Idaho Falls, ID

TREACY, JERRY
[b.] February 5, 1946; [p.] Martin Treacy, Julie Treacy; [m.] Avril Treacy, October 26, 1968; [ch.] Marie, Loretta, Sean; [ed.] Caherline National School, County Limerick, Republic of Ireland, Christian Brothers School, Limerick City, Republic of Ireland; [occ.] Police Officer, South Australia Police; [memb.] Gaelic Athletic Association, South Australia; [hon.] Editor's Choice Award 1996, International Society of Poets; [oth. writ.] My Love, City of Courage, Where Eagles Fly, Mountains of the Mind, 1916 - The Dawn of Freedom, Solitary Place from a Place to a Nation, Partner in Time, Footsteps

of Brian Boru, The Balance, Logical Reality, River Lady, Despair to Hope, Thoughts of a Refugee, The Homecoming; [pers.] There is much more to our existence than that which is locked between the boundaries of conception and death. It would be easier for all of us to be believers, if all that we should believe in, had to contradictions.; [a.] Adelaide, South Australia, Australia

TUCKER, SUE RICHARDSON
[pen.] Susan; [p.] Sam and Sarah Richardson; [m.] John R. Tucker, June 30, 1984; [ed.] Bethlehem Industrial Academy, Alabama State University, York College, City of New York, Univ. of PA. ICS - Master Art; [occ.] Retired; [memb.] St. Luke Baptist Church, St. Luke Deaconess Board, St Luke Economic Development, St. Luke Missionary Society, Telephone Pioneers of America, International Society of Poets; [hon.] Outstanding Award Performance from AT&T, Outstanding Award as Family Historian from President Bill Clinton, Outstanding award from the Dale Carnegie Institute, Outstanding Editor's Choice from the National Library of Poetry, Proclamation from Governor Fob James Jr., State of Alabama, as family historian; [oth. writ.] Poems published - St. Luke Gazette Periodical, Lyrical Heritage, Fall 1996 Edition, Books published: "How To Control Blood Sugar", "Fast Food, Killer of the Nation", "New Day, Now"; [pers.] I strive for the betterment of family, personal and spiritual values, in my writings, I have been gratefully influenced by the poet Mayo Angelou.; [a.] Jamaica Estates, NY

TURNER, JUDY
[pen.] Judy Wilkinson; [b.] October 18, 1955, La Grande, OR; [p.] Buddy and Reola Glenn; [m.] Randy Turner, November 9, 1996; [ch.] David Wilkinson; [ed.] Imbler High School Western Business College; [occ.] Power plant Operator U.S. Army Corps of Engineers; [hon.] Editor's Choice Award for "The Playful Sun" published in "A Tapestry Of Thoughts" and Editor's Choice Award for "Best Poems of the '90s"; [oth. writ.] Poems published in "Tapestry Of Thoughts" and "Best Poems Of The '90s"; [a.] Daytona, WA

TZELNIC, TANIA
[b.] April 6, 1981, Boston, MA; [p.] Mori, Percy Tzelnic; [ed.] Currently a sophomore at Concord-Carslile High School in Massachusetts; [a.] Concord, MA

VAN ANTWERP, LINDIE BETH
[b.] November 18, 1982, Shawnee, OK; [p.] Sherries Vernon Houck and Mike Van Antwerp; [ed.] 8th Grade student attending North Rock Creek, Shawnee, OK; [occ.] Student; [memb.] Aydelotte Bapt. Church National Honor Society N.R.C. Cheerleader Academic Team; [hon.] President N.R.C. Honor Society; [pers.] Poetry and writing is a way of expressing my love and encouragement to others.; [a.] Shawnee, OK

VAN DER ZEE, CORA
[b.] April 26, 1913, Kansas; [m.] Charles Van Der Zee, June 19, 1942; [ch.] Joanne Marie; [ed.] Beloit High 1931, Wisconsin, U.B.S. 1935 U. of S. California MA 1941, McKendree College 1935-42 Ill.; [occ.] Housewife 1942-1997; [memb.] While Teaching, Pi Kappa Delta (Hon. Forensic Altha Psi Omega Chat. Dramatic Fraternity); Riverside Church of God; American Bible Society; [hon.] High School Nat. Honor Society Pins Letters for Athletics and Leadership - 3rd in Cottage Grove's News Poetry; [oth. writ.] Several poems published in local newspapers articles for church papers. Poems in the Family Treasury of Great Poems, Eddie-Lou Cole, Our 20th Century's Greatest Poems, John Campbell; [pers.] I strive to reflect the beauty of God's creation in nature and have written many poems while travelling and enjoying "God's Handiwork!"; [a.] Cottage Grove, OR

VAN TONDER, MICKEY
[pen.] Mickey/Mackey/Kiewiet; [b.] August 6, 1972, Windhoek; [p.] Magda and Marinus Van Tonder; [ed.] Matric. Baker, Confectioner, Chef/Cook, course in law and order. Because of severe back in jury, I am a full-time writer now, as I cannot stand or sit for long; [occ.] Full-time writer, and poet; [memb.] Nucleus Gym, Writer's Corner (Namibia), poets of Namibia, Association for Afrikaans Writers, International Society of Poets (ISP); [hon.] Editor's Choice Award for poem in "Shadows and Light" National Library of Poetry is the first organization that I submitted my poetry to.; [oth. writ.] Poem published in "Shadows and Light", "Complete magical book of Dreams". Several short stories, two erotic novels, a book about poets and poetry, a book of spiritual poems, "Christmas Is Paradise". Written over 700 poems!; [pers.] I create a world for others to live in and realize that there is someone out there who knows exactly what they're going through or has been through. My talent is a great gift of God...; [a.] Windhoek, Namibia

VARS, TROY RAYMOND
[pen.] Amric Starr; [b.] April 12, 1976, Aurora, CO; [p.] Paula R. Kavan, Raymond J. Vars; [m.] Lindsay Joelle Mercell Vars, September 13, 1996; [ch.] Jefferey Raymond Xavier Mercell Vars; [ed.] Iver C. Ranum High, Naval Nuclear Power School; [hon.] Graduated with honors from high school, honor man NNPS; [oth. writ.] Untitled work in Forever and a Day, currently writing a fantasy novel.; [pers.] I believe that poetry is an expression of emotions and ideas originating from the depths of our souls. In every human being is a poet waiting to escape. As long as a person writes from their heart and uses their mind all their poetry will be good.; [a.] Old Fort, NC

VENA, JASON ANTHONY JOHN
[pen.] Jason Vena; [b.] March 9, 1980, New York; [p.] Carolyn Vena and James Vena; [ed.] Albany Ave. School, Lindenhurst Junior High, Congress Middle School, and Congress GED program; [oth. writ.] Several poems and short stories that have not yet been published.; [pers.] My poems are based on things that have happened in my life. I think poetry is one of the most beautiful talents anyone can possess. Poetry is a art that will be around for millions of years. It also shows emotion, pain, hurt, love, anger, depression, and talent. So try to put your feelings down in a poem if you can.; [a.] Boynton Beach, FL

VINE, WILLIAM GEORGE
[b.] July 16, 1952, Placerville, CA; [m.] Mistress Theresa Vine, June 6, 1996; [ed.] Full time student SMC transfer to Cal-state LA. to pursue career in education; [occ.] Educational Dacent UCLA, ODC. (Volunteer); [memb.] Lifetime member Alpha Gamma Sigma honor Society Callegians, SMC. Director of Alumni Development and Student Outreach, (Associated Student SMC); [hon.] Former Vice President, President, and Pariamsatarian of Alpha Gamma sigma honor Society James and Lucille Cayton Award SMC; [oth. writ.] Foxx, published in Journey of the Mind by NLP; [pers.] If a day has passed and you didn't learn from it, that day was wasted.; [a.] Los Angeles, CA

VON UTHEMANN DORSEY, MONIQUE CYNTHIA
[pen.] Monique Dorsey, Victor Silva Velasquez, Charles Ogilvy-Saunders, Jacques D'Orleans; [b.] December 16, 1954, VA; [p.] Lt. Gen. Ted Sagayadan I., Dr. Nestora Elayda del Fierro Sagayadan; [m.] Marquis, Michael von Uthemann-Voukitchevitch, at St. Patrick's Cathedral; [ch.] Tatiana Cynthia Vera, Nadia Gilda, Alexandra Nestora, Georgi

Mihailo, Franz Theodore; [ed.] St. Paul's, Ateneo Graduate School for Law and Business, Cornell University, New York School of Interior Design, Escuela Oficial de Idiomas, in Spain, University of St. Thomas International Dance School of Carnegie Hall Studio, and Juilliard (piano under Profs. Emma Tiongson and Classical guitar under elena Valdi; [occ.] Director, International Division of the Guggenheim, Dorsey and Von Uthemann Management Associates, Founder and Director of the American Ballet Company in Spain and the French Caribbean, National Arts Club, Royal Yacht Club of Spain, American Society of Interior Designers, The English Speaking Union Clug (Spain); [hon.] Magna Cum Laude, Dean's List, First Prize in Poetry of the Miguel Hernandez Literary Competition, First Prize in poetry of the Southeast Asian Literary Competition; [oth. writ.] Journalistic articles written for the London Times, and Times Magazine, poems published in the Marymount Manhattan Review and St. Gregory's Magazine, all essays, editorials, stories and reviews written as Editor-in-Chief of E.O.I. Forum, International Newspaper published in Europe, the UST Law Review, and IMPETUS Literary Quarterly, novels, "Paradise Revisited", "Rangoon Run", "The Caribbean Triangle", and "Collection of Poetry in Modern Languages". (To be auctioned to publishers); [pers.] My profoundest thanks to my parents as inspiration, my husband for his constancy, my children for their radiance, Philip, his children and mother, Helen, for their affection, and Rev. Fr. Carmelo Amangtegui, S.J., Rev. Fr. Lorenzo Ma. Guerrero, S.J., Rev. Fr. Angel Perez and Rev. Fr. Kenneth Murphy for their guidance. My literary works reflect society's glorious past and present decadence.; [a.] New York, NY

WADDELL, MICHELLE
[b.] September 10, 1964, Buffalo, NY; [p.] James and Margaret Kearney; [m.] James, February 28, 1987; [ed.] AAS in Nursing Studied Music also; [occ.] R.N. Orthopedics; [memb.] PETA, WWF, International Society of Poets; [oth. writ.] "Your Song" published 1995 The National Library of Poetry; [pers.] I have smothered my creative side in the eleven years I have lived the practice of Nursing. I feel like a butterfly now and hope I can develop my creative side as my brother the poet Lawrence Kearney and former sister-in-law I did.; [a.] Westminster, CO

WADSWORTH, KYLE
[b.] December 29, 1967, Pocatello, ID; [p.] William B. Wadsworth, Martha N. Wadsworth; [m.] Sanaa Tbeileh Wadsworth, October 11, 1996; [ed.] Glen A. Wilson H.S., Occidental College; [occ.] Editor, Leisure Publications Inc., Los Angeles; [hon.] The National Library of Poetry, Editor's Choice Award for Outstanding Achievement in Poetry 1996, 1995, Leisure Publications Inc., Award for Outstanding Performance 1993; [oth. writ.] Published poems, as well as magazine articles, columns and news stories.; [pers.] "Betrayal" was written for abused children. It represents our broken promise of a fulfilling life free from physical, psychological or emotional scars, and the death that occurs, whether physical or otherwise, as a consequence of that betrayal. It high lights our responsibility.; [a.] Santa Monica, CA

WALKER, MATTHEW A.
[pen.] Mason Waters; [b.] September 29, 1971, Pawhuska, OK; [p.] Jack and Hazel Walker; [ed.] B.S. in Marine Biology from Texas A&M, Barnsdall High School; [occ.] Marine Biologist/Aquarist; [memb.] Texas Marine Mammal Stranding Network, Phi Gamma Delta; [hon.] Phi Eta Sigma, Dean's List; [oth. writ.] Poems published in college journals at Oklahoma State and Texas A&M.; [pers.] My writing is a beautiful reminder of the interesting company I keep.; [a.] Austin, TX

WASHINGTON, NATHAN L.
[b.] March 13, 1976, Birmingham, AL; [p.] Charles and Kathy Smith, Jack and Barbara Washington; [ed.] Graduated 1994 from L.V. Berkner High School Richardson, TX, attend Missouri Western State College; [occ.] Student-Athlete, football and baseball; [memb.] Fellowship of Christian Athletes Football team, Baseball team; [oth. writ.] I had work published in 1995 by National Library of Poetry. I am currently in the process of writing my first book. Wrote sports articles for school newspaper as Sports Editor.; [pers.] Never quiet, always be perfectly persistent, and believe in yourself and others will believe in you. Keep faith in God.; [a.] Saint Joseph, MO

WATERMAN, MURIEL
[pen.] Kay; [b.] June 10, London, England; [p.] Deceased; [m.] Divorced, December 26, 1959; [ch.] Two sons, Wayne and Andre; [ed.] Public School, Westham College, Cambridge College, Medger Evers; [occ.] Medical Surgical Tech.; [memb.] Disabled Veterans, Covenant House, Mays Missions Care, AARP and Brooklyn Tab; [hon.] Leadership at work, Beauty Culture from Wilfred Academy, Commercial Medical Field; [oth. writ.] Writing poems for Health and Hospital focus also in my spare time and to my friends.; [pers.] I strive to show love and to encourage each other to reach out - I'm inspired by great writers.; [a.] Brooklyn, NY

WATSON, JODEE
[b.] March 29, 1978, Tipton, IN; [p.] Jim and Judy Watson; [ed.] Student at Marantha Baptist Bible College, Studying Elementary Education; graduate of Tipton High School; [occ.] Student; [memb.] First Baptist Church, Kings Kids, Church Choir, Band; [hon.] Who's Who Among High School students; [oth. writ.] Poem published in the Rainbow's End.; [pers.] I try to communicate my feelings in hope that they will impact someone's life. My writing comes from personal experiences I have had.

WEEKS, MRS. A.
[pen.] Agnes Burns Lawson; [b.] December 29, 1919, Fifeshire, Scotland; [p.] James, Margaret Lawson; [m.] Desmond E. Weeks, February 22, 1946; [ch.] Three; [ed.] Council - Secondary; [occ.] Housewife; [memb.] Just The Poets Society; [oth. Writ.] "Poetic Mythology", Theoretic Theosophy. Children's Stories, Love Stories, Spiritual Progressive Teaching. Six Manuscripts, "Gods in the Making, " 1st One, Lyrics. Humorous Poems, Romantic Poems, "Verses" Proverbs Citations Epitaphs. I Tape Back Proud Music Towards Ever Rap; [pers.] It is better to be wise than clever. For 'tis often clever to be wise.; [a.] Hillingdon Heath, Middlesex, UK

WEGER, AMY D. C.
[pen.] Amy Compton; [b.] November 1, 1973, California; [p.] Celeste and James Hoffman; [m.] Travis Weger, December 15, 1996; [ed.] Federal Way High, Highline Community College, Central Washington University; [occ.] Art Student; [oth. writ.] Poem titled "Sleep" published in Daybreak on the Land.; [pers.] I don't find subjects to write on, they find me. I attempt to capture my feelings and thoughts in those brief moments, a poem is created.; [a.] Federal Way, WA

WELCH, BECKY
[pen.] Emerson; [b.] February 25, 1967, Wash., DC; [p.] Nancy Ratcliff and Bob Welch; [ed.] Valencia, Orland, FL; [occ.] Bartender, Westin Hotel; [hon.] FL Jaycees, (Writing and Speaking); [oth. writ.] "Someone", several upcoming novels and screen plays; [pers.] I like to think life throws us curves just to see if we can handle the waves. There are too many negatives in the world. Lost remember the positives.; [a.] Cincinnati, OH

WHITE, BARBARA JEAN
[pen.] Barbara; [b.] May 26, 1943, Des Moines, IA; [p.] Jean and Raymond McCarty; [ch.] Thomas Christopher Redfern, James Gregory Redfern; [ed.] Graduate of Long Beach Poly High School; [occ.] Graphics Supervisor/Designer; [memb.] Honorary Phi Beta Kappa on Graduation from High school - Graduating in the Top 2% Member/President Phi Gamma Chi; [hon.] Several One-Woman Art Show Exhibits, Owner: Barbara Ink - Wholesale Greeting Card Company; [oth. writ.] "Volumes" of poetry - verse etc. I am most honored to be part of the National Library of Poetry Publications.; [pers.] "The living of this life is the catalyst to creativity."; [a.] Long Beach, CA

WHITE, JOAN B.
[pen.] Joan B. White; [b.] February 13, 1952, Atlanta, GA; [p.] A. Lois McCleskey and Harry L. McCleskey; [m.] Divorced; [ch.] Stephanie Joan Sheridan - 24; [ed.] Cross Keys High School (70) 1 year typing, work - waitress, Bookkeeper, Teller A.V.P., Branch Manager and Loan Officer (12 yrs. banking); [occ.] New Car and New Trucks Selesperson for Jim Ellis Chevrolet - Chamblee, GA, 2 yrs. Cookie Chairman; [memb.] Girl Scout Leader 7 years GA Legion of Leaders for Chevrolet and Truck Honors (1995); [hon.] 1st poem published in national anthology in book title "Through the Hourglass" by The National Library of Poetry, the poem entitled "Mom This Love Is For You" 1996, Member of International Society of Poets 1995-1996; [oth. writ.] Book "What About Me", completed in spring 97, "Letting Go", "Love Is", "Dating", "My Eyes Have Seen", "My Friend", "Older Sisters", "Good People", - this poem is dedicated to very special people in my life that has been and will always be "Good people" Carolyn Jackson, Sandy Brookshire, Peggie Brotcher, BJ Cordell, Deann Seagraves, Jim Sims, John Busby, Susan Aylsworth, Linda Davis, Darla Booher, Joey Crowe, Cecil Brannon, Sharon Statham, Louise Banks, Judy Kensington, Val and Anita Valentine, Robert Weathers, and my dearest family, God Bless and thank you all. I enjoy writing, all my work comes from my heart, my soul and my own experiences.; [a.] Smyrna, GA

WHITEHEAD, JR, ROBERT
[b.] December 28, 1964, Chicago, IL; [p.] Robert & Alice Whitehead; [ch.] Brittany, Joshua, & Robert III; [ed.] Morgan Park High School; [oth. writ.] Currently working on an inspirational book of poems, which shows my expressions of thoughts I have written. [per.] I am thankful that God has blessed me with such talent, I have been writing poems all my life. I hope that my poems will inspire and capture the hearts of many.; [a.] Chicago, IL

WILCOX, ALAN
[b.] October 24, 1934, Toronto, Ontario; [p.] Horace and Beatrice; [m.] Pamela Ann, March 6, 1957; [ch.] Glenn, Wayne, Sharon and Gail; [ed.] B. Architecture U of T, graduated 1961; [occ.] Architect - Private Practice - Lindsay, Ontario, Canada; [memb.] Ontario Assoc. of Architects Royal Architectural Institute of Canada; [oth. writ.] Sparkles in the sand.; [pers.] Poetry is my expression of a kind of inner-sanctum of the mind!; [a.] Lindsay, Ontario, Canada

WILLIAMS, CHERYL HOLMES
[b.] January 3, 1963, Los Angeles, CA; [p.] Mrs. Ronald Higgins, Harold R. Holmes; [m.] Jack Williams, April 6, 1996; [ch.] Trinell Williams; [ed.] Crenshaw High School, CSU Long Beach, Watterson College, Pasadena, CA; [occ.] Sr. Cust. SVC. Representative, for Fedex, Glendale, CA; [hon.] Dean's List - Crenshaw High School, Certificate of Completion in Paralegal Work; [oth. writ.] "Your Civic Duty" publ. by National Lib. of Poetry Anthology. An essay publ. in company newsletter, 1st poem publ. in High School Advanced English Class Anthology.; [pers.] This poem is dedicated to my great grandmother who I feel privileged to have known. Our family is rich in history and I have enough inspiration to last a lifetime. I also have a short story in the works that I would eventually like to have published. I love you daddy!; [a.] Monrovia, CA

WILSON, EMERSON
[b.] December 13, 1931, New York, NY; [p.] Helen and James Wilson; [ed.] BS and MS in Education, State University of New York at Oneonta; [occ.] Retired/Sales Associate Wal-Mart Stores; [hon.] From Famous Poets Society, CA, from World of Poetry, CA, from Fla State Poets Ass., FL, from National Library of Poetry, MD; [oth. writ.] Short children's stories, "Travels with Uncle Emy".; [a.] Flagler Beach, FL

WINTERS, MELANIE
[b.] July 8,1967, Hartford, Ct. ;[p.] Harold and Judy Flanagan ;[ed.] Marist College- BA in Communication Arts ;[occ.] Staff writer for Woodshop News, a national trade magazine in Essex, CT.; [a.] Clinton, CT

WRIGHT, JACK T.
[b.] April 22, 1961, Steubenville, OH; [p.] Robert N. Wright, Wanetta L. Lamp; [ed.] Weir Sr. High School, West Virginia Northern Community College, Roanoke College; [occ.] Office Administration; [hon.] Who's Who Among High School Students, Who's Who Among American College Students, Dean's List, National Dean's List, Phi Theta Kappa Honorary Fraternity; [oth. writ.] Several writings in various publications. Cover story for V Magazine. Calendar Editor, Entertainment Magazine.; [pers.] I write on my raw emotions, those that rule humankind. I do my best to treat every person with respect and as an individual.; [a.] Whittier, CA

WYNN, CANDI MATHEWS
[pen.] (Candice) Candi Mathews, Candi M. Doezema; [b.] October 11, 1972, Corydon, IN; [p.] Halleck III, and Diana Mathews; [m.] Brian Wynn, December 31, 1993; [ch.] Leon and Justin; [ed.] New Middletown Grade School, Corydon Central H.S., Faulkner State; [memb.] Daphne United Methodist Church; [hon.] Editor's Choice Award - NLP 1997, Golden Poet 1987 World of Poetry; [oth. writ.] "I Walk Alone On Unsteady Ground..." A Moment To Reflect; [pers.] "Do not look for the end of the tunnel look for a way to light it"; [a.] Fairhope, AL

YOKLEY, APRIL JOAN
[b.] March 13, 1954, Chicago, IL; [p.] Dolores and Emmett Dozier; [ch.] Dyron N. Yokley and Samuel K. Robinson; [ed.] Holy Angels Grade School, Chgo. IL, St. Stanislaus High, Chgo. IL, Daley College, Chgo. IL; [occ.] Now on disability; [memb.] Boys and Girls Club, Boy Scouts of America; [hon.] Boy Scouts of America Awards; [oth. writ.] Have written other poems.; [pers.] Jesus is my joy, God is my hope and salvation, holy spirit is my inspiration.; [a.] Pulaski, TN

YOUNG, C. LORRAINE JUDGE
[pen.] Carolle Loraine; [b.] May 8, 1948, Toronto; [p.] Dr. Ray Judge & Ella Louise Judge; [m.] Ronald Gary Young, July 9, 1994; [ch.] Derek age 24, Christel age 22, Jonathan age 15, Justin age 5; [ed.] Achieved grade 12 diploma, Branksome Hall, Toronto, , Acting and Drama Canadian Academy of Talent, Supporting Actor and extra certification; [occ.] Homemaker and mother, Telemarketer Sears Clean Air Services, Self employed distributor; [hon.] Editor's Choice Award for outstanding Achievement in Poetry presented by The National Library of Poetry 1995, Amarey Sponsoring achievement pin awarded 1988; [oth. writ.] Tranquility in the North in a national anthology 1995, name of book "Walk Through Paradise". Poem published as a child for Wee wisdom a unity church childrens magazine; [pers.] Christel is my only daughter. I have three boys as well.

Christel went to live with her father at age 12 yrs. Poem was written on her 22 years birthday. She knows about the poem being sent in. Christel came to stay with us at age 16 from Spring till the Fall, this poem I wanted to express my feelings of happiness of having missed her, to tell her I still love her, as her mother. I will always feel close even though I live far away.

ZDANCZYK, CYNTHIA
[b.] October 31, 1979; [ed.] Willowbrook High School; [hon.] National Honor Society, Mu Alpha Theta; [oth. writ.] Poems published in Windows of the Soul, Anthology; [pers.] My goal is to live life to the fullest and strive for what I want.; [a.] Villa Park, IL

ZOFREA, SONJA ANN
[b.] December 18, 1969, Chicago, IL; [p.] Frank and Mara Keserica; [m.] Peter Zofrea, June 10, 1995; [ch.] Stefanie; [ed.] Fairfax High School Santa Monica College; [occ.] Floral Designer, Crafter; [oth. writ.] "Deception," "Uncertainty," "Remembrance," published by the National Library of Poetry.; [pers.] My writings are based on personal experiences that have had a profound and moving emotional impact on my recent marriage.; [a.] La Habra, CA

Index of Poets

A

Adamczyk-Marker, Celia 149
Adamitis, Carole A. 259
Adamkiewicz, Heather 278
Adams, Catherine E. 231
Adams, Julie 185
Adams, R. 209
Adkins, Opal F. 218
Agelastos, Nicol 142
Ahmann-Smith, Jill D. 132
Ahmed, Shah Salim 17
Aitchison, Ronald D. 270
Al-Adawiyya, Rabia 149
Albert, Kenneth D. 112
Albin, Terry Neal 264
Aldape, Yolanda 22
Algahagan 172
Allen, David Edwards Jr. 11
Allen, F. Michelle 161
Alleracht, Mary 212
Allison, Lyssa 212
Altmann, Richard G. Jr. 108
Altmeier, Katherine 212
Amano, Carolyn M. 169
Amison, Leslie S. 341
Ammons, Carol Lee 220
Amstead, Kevin S. 272
Anderson, Ronald J. 170
Anderson, Violet Henson 17
Anderton, W. Michael 110
Andrew, M. J. 156
Andrews, Donna J. 229
Annand, Maureen Smith 179
Aquilina, Rhonda L. 127
Arens, Shirley Mae 181
Arensen, Katy 167
Armstrong, Jack T. 70
Arnold, Eunice 188
Ashton, Cynthia 156
Atkins, Marguerite H. 16
Atkinson-Matalone, Lindy 16, 176
Aughinbaugh, Rachelle 161
Avery, Ruth Sigler 12
Avila, Carolyn L. 160

B

Bailey, Wayne 134
Baker, Lisa 137
Balaque, Lloyd W. 217
Balasingham, Fredrick V. 284
Ballard, Clint Harding 143
Ballard, Phillip M. 138
Barger, Margaret A. 166
Barks, Michele 41
Barnes, Amy 259
Barrett, Shannon 153
Barrett, Tim 279
Barrington, L. Barry 275
Barron, Gloria R. 24
Barrow, Barbara 295
Barrow, Peter E. 40
Barrow, Peter F. 87
Barrows, Linda Ann 68
Bartlett, Jennifer 179
Bartlett, LuJuan 288

Bartow, Barbara J. 28
Basham, Viola Maxine 320
Baskey-Hales, Elaine 331
Bastien, Dianna 40
Batcher, Charles 252
Battis, Jesse 7
Baugh, Peter 67
Baughman, Rhonda K. 199
Baugus, Clara 312
Bavafa, Parvin 39
Bave, Emelia L. 21
Baxter, Vera 8
Bayard, Yseult 120
Bean, Hazel 132
Beard, Connie 52
Beasley, David C. Jr. 229
Beasley, Lynn Sr. 167
Beavers, Shane A. 290
Becker, Mary 302
Beckley, Deidre 83
Beckman, Denise Michelle 94
Beeler, Lucia 82
Beetham, James W. 278
Behrens, Phyllis I. 3
Bell, Ernie Jr. 201
Bell, Lois 155
Bell, Walter Ray 101
Bender, Frank W. 90
Benedict, Misty 104
Benfante, Ignazio C. 74
Bennefield, Buna 74
Bennett, F. Carolyn 243
Bennett, Harriet Hoevet 123
Bennett, Linda 237
Bennett, Monica L. 85
Bentley, Ida Maria 310
Bergstrom, Kat 250
Berkhiem, Pamela K. 213
Bernal, Aaron 278
Bernstein, Caitlin 304
Berry, Maria D. 271
Besendorf, Minnie L. 84
Besetzny, Corene K. 24
Bethell, Kristin 287
Bethune, Desiree 96
Bettis, Dina 181
Betz, Bernadino L. 230
Beyer, Mary L. 151
Bickford, Andrea 79
Bielefeldt, Erin R. 169
Bifano, Melissa A. 52
Billen, Debra 64
Birben, Christine 138
Birmingham, Gladys Harmon 53
Bishop, Judi 133
Black, Aurore 66
Black, Diane M. 183
Black, Joy Lockhart 258
Black, Lawrence H. 248
Black, Michael 289
Blacklock, Ronald E. 91
Blackman, Christan 79
Blackwell, W. Jerome 162
Blakeman, Dorothy V. 131
Blaker, Sharon K. 63
Blakney, George M. 199

Blamey, Karen K. 291
Bland, Bernadette M. 32
Blessent, Dolores M. 56
Bloom, Thomas R. 120
Blundell, Dorothy L. 8
Blythe, Phyllis Presley 95
Bobo-Hennecy, Bobbie 261
Bochar, Mona 194
Bock, Fran Spears 86
Bodomo, Adams B. 69
Boettcher, Albert P. 28
Boettcher, Beth A. 14
Bogeajis, Kristen 122
Bohan, Joseph F. 157
Boles, Rebecca 343
Bolster, Brenda L. 108
Bonfield, Sandra S. 110
Boone, Tammie 103
Bordner, Pat 27
Borlee, Jenn 140
Bosanko, Liz 144
Bosiljevac, Jim 15
Boss, Jeffery L. 104
Boswell, Jaime L. 63
Bourne, Mollie Odell 178
Bowen, Bryan C. 68
Bower, Tara 170
Bowser, Heather M. 317
Boyd, E. Renae 144
Boyd, Verley Lloyd 25
Boyd-Bukowiecki, Olive 113
Boyden, Christopher W. 262
Boyle, Frances 10
Brabec, Laurie L. 156
Bradburn, Raymond 63
Brader-Sims, James D. 296
Bradley, Jennifer R. 293
Bradley, Tammy 138
Brainard, Virginia 52
Brandon, Michael L. 76
Brannan, Mark 249
Braverman, Sidney 65
Braxton, Derek L. 322
Bray, Robert L. Sr. 192
Bredeweg, Victoria J. 225
Breen, Serena 75
Brehm, Pat 31
Breininger, Mamie A. 126
Bresko, Paul S. 270
Bressan, Dorlene 273
Brett Hodus 71
Brewer, Beatrice 224
Brewer, Doris Hartsell 34
Bridges, Shelly 339
Brien, Hope 136
Brinkley, Andrew W. 113
Brissette, Marie D. 107
Britt, Edward W. 196
Britton, Thereza C. 82
Brooker, Barbara>Rose 14
Brooks, D. W. 218
Brooks, Gerald W. 139
Brooks, James Mel 53
Brooks, Jannice 156
Brooks, Kelly Lynn 193
Brooks-Smith, Christal 157

Broussard, Eugene 170
Brown, DeMarias W. 66
Brown, Douglas R. 62
Brown, Frederick L. 320
Brown, Jennifer 130
Brown, Karen Ann 214
Brown, Krystal 264
Brown, Linda 75
Brown, Linda C. 131
Brown, Nancy 259
Brown, Ray 92
Brown, Shannon L. 146
Brownig, Ellen 178
Browning, Simon K. 122
Bruce, Deboarh Ann 164
Bruce, James A. III 336
Bruce, Tania 5
Bruns, Billy 53
Brunson, Angela 66
Brunzell, Bryan 189
Brushett, Kathleen 114
Bryant, Lois 107
Bryson, Ollie 73
Buchheit, Christopher 109
Buck, Kelvy 261
Buckey, Betty Jeanne 256
Buckley, Brad David 227
Buckley, Kimberly Alexis 45
Buckmaster, Thomas 184
Buckner, Esther G. 276
Buford, Rose 92
Bullman, Lara 83
Bullock, Yolande 205
Bumgarner, Elizabeth M. 104
Bunce, Ron 63
Buncom, Mildred C. 230
Burke, Charlotte 132
Burke, Jacob W. 85
Burnett, Audrey 152
Burnham, J. Kellogg 134
Burrier, Paulette A. 41
Burroughs, Susan 81
Burrows, Carmelina M. 346
Burrows, Evelyn N. 26
Busch-Gutzler, Helen Louise 102
Butcher, Shirley LaVon 79
Butler, Helen M. 87
Butler, Juanita H. 110
Butler, Laurie 212
Butterstein, Howard P. 30
Byrd, Isabel Gallegos 88

C

Cacilhas Sampogna, Sandra M. 306
Cacioppo, Nancy 45
Cady, Jeffrey Allen 143
Cagle, Lillie Mae 110
Cain, Richard E. 56
Calabro, Thomas W. 241
Calain, Mary A. 43
Caldwell, Kerrick D. 214
Calvey, Marie 111
Camelo, Raquel 100
Cameron, Carol R. 323
Campbell, Dorothy L. 244
Canavan, Poet 131

Canfield, Yvonne B. 268
Caplow, Floyd 38
Carde, Flora 333
Carden, Ellen V. M. 173
Carlson, Curt Allan 119
Carnine, N. Todd 339
Carpenter-Gibson, Olivia 202
Carr, Christine Taylor 17
Carrick, David A. 106
Carrick, Kelly 203
Carroll, Kimberly 265
Carter, Evelyn Hayden 60
Carter, Frances M. 54
Carter, Jeannette U. 91
Carter, Mary V. 42
Carter, Rita 72
Case, Russell L. 310
Cassady, Valerie L. Blankenship 276
Cassidy, Robert L. 199
Casteel, Carl 45
Castley, Viola 102
Castro, Robert 121
Caswell, Frank MacGregor 197
Cavanagh, Joanne 195
Cea, Vincent 57
Cecchini, Babette Kaiser 69
Celebrowski, Alexander 324
Cerritos, Sandra 246
Chadwick, Lerna 278
Chaffee, David R. 238
Chaifetz, Samantha 213
Chamberlain-Hale, Michele J. 255
Chambliss, Charlotte J. 46
Champ, Robert 21
Champion, John-Allan 257
Chang, Diana M. P. 51
Chang, Janice M. 24
Chao, Oscar 206
Chapman, Katherine J. 99
Chapman, Mary Elizabeth 29
Chase-Jennings, Josephine B. 274
Chaussee, Alice 166
Chavez, Steve 304
Chen, Flora 178
Chetuck, John 221
Childs, Wilbur J. 33
Chilian, Carol 69
Chiucarello, Susan 91
Chlopak, Shelby 150
Chontos, Christopher 88
Chornobrywy, Marion 173
Christian, Billy 42
Christian, Shirley 299
Chung, Christopher J. 314
Cialkowski, Jo Santoro 57
Cibula, Patricia 134
Ciciless, Joseph R. II 166
Ciemins, Veneranda 281
Citak, Ralph 113
Clark, Barbara 39
Clark, Carl G. 133
Clark, Gary L. 342
Clark, Jacquelyn 246
Clark, Kristopher 336
Clark, Zenia R. 129
Cleary Jr., John Edward 226

Clements, Joseph W. 286
Clifford, David 81
Cochran, Almeta 68
Coffey, Donna M. 73
Coffin, Cleo 44
Cohen, Robert T. 274
Cole, Barbara 256
Cole, Crissy 171
Cole, Debra R. 119
Cole, Hazel James 116
Cole, James W. III 18
Cole, Jan Carroll 16
Cole, Lois E. 29
Cole, Ramona 251
Coles, Joyce V. 198
Collard, Leanne E. 117
Collins, Helena 129
Collins, Mary 76
Collins, Valerie M. 87
Colon, Linda S. 305
Comnick, Lori Ann 214
Conner, Mercedes 332
Connolly, Michelle 187
Connor, Georgia Kathleen 198
Connors, R. G. 122
Conrad, Bette A. 315
Conrad, Kerri 147
Conrad, Shirley 135
Constable, Elisabeth B. 234
Conway, Michael Sean 6
Cook, Leslie Maxwell 57
Cooke, Christopher M. 176
Cooke, Windy D. 191
Cooper, Fern M. 51
Cooper, Gloria A. 105
Cooper, William E. Jr. 220
Cooper-Williams, Valerie V. 96
Corbett, Lenora M. 138
Corbett, Peter 257
Coret, R. L. 46
Corey, Harold 25
Cornelius, Whitney K. 98
Corr, Vincent P. 54
Cory, Marilyn 110
Cossaboom, Jennifer M. 344
Costa, Gina M. 198
Cota, Lissa 87
Cottonham, Maureen H. 21
Couch, Peter Svensson 240
Cousineau, Michael R. 109
Couvillon, Wayne 116
Covalt, Ginger Y. 197
Covol, Haley M. 223
Cox, Judith L. 58
Cox, Kim 121
Cox, Stephen 294
Coy, Mary Tolbert 168
Crafton, June 228
Crandall, Esther 201
Crawford, Misty L. 239
Crawford, Patricia M. 86
Cress, Valerie 67
Crews, Stephen A. 249
Cribbs, Geri 54
Crooks, Reba 153
Crowe, Roberta J. 36

Crowell, Nancy M.   118
Crowther, Eleanor B.   189
Cruikshank, Albert M.   184
Crumbliss, Janine   78
Culmer, Rhonda   283
Cummings, Juan   98
Cummins, Sarah   19
Cunning, Depthana   69
Cunningham, M. Jan   67
Cunningham, Roxanne C.   62
Curtis, Anna R.   307
Curtis, Wesley K.   227
Cynamon, Marylin   236
Cyr, Jackie St.   28
Czarnecki, Amy Jo   254

D

Dague, Stacey   127
Dahlke, Deron   151
Daidone, Gina   133
Damm, Peter   82
Dane, Angela   78
Danley, Floyd W.   92
Danowski, Christopher   315
Daum, Robert   142
Davenport, Joan   109
Davidson, Allison   224
Davidson, Layla   218
Davis, Leola   148
Davis, Shirley   329
Davis, W. Eugene   183
Davitian, Sarah Jane   89
Dawson, Hallette C.   182
Dawson, Vicki L.   223
Day, Eric   7
De Bartolo, Paola   172
De Loatch, Johnny   231
De Lozier, Mary   224
De, Terry Lynn Vore   83
Deacon, Barbara   312
Deal, Karen H.   154
Dean, June C.   147
Dean, Neil   192
Deaton, Howard A.   99
DeCaro, Tate   81
DeConto, Carol   209
DeDanaan, Cindy   132
Deitz, Leah   87
DeJarnette, Patty Stiles   235
Delahoussaye, A. J. III   76
Delveaux, Diane   287
DeMarco, Lynda   136
DeMeulemeester, Shawna   163
Denardo, Rebecca J.   224
Dennee, Alicia   211
Dennett, Chris   240
Dennis, Joyce   96
DePino, Louise   213
DePinto Naber, Roseann M.   229
Depoyan, Vahaken   18
Desai, Padma   249
Despins-Klassen, Carmel   196
Devine, Rose C.   54
Dhingra, Inni Bawa   88
Dial, Elnorist E.   232
Diamond, Dana   271

Dickinson, Don C.   112
Dietz, Irene Andrighetti   311
DiGennaro, Robert J.   45
Dismukes, Linda   342
Dispensa, Talia   100
Ditman, Henry M.   55
Dively, Robert M.   326
Dobbs, Martha   19
Dobrzykowski, Bethany   292
Dodds, Heather   260
Dodge, Helen   63
Dodson, Cheryl C.   124
Doey, Richard K.   201
Dokes, Pierre   81
Dolejs, Doris J.   50
Doloughan, Fiona J.   189
Dolson, Donald William   112
Donaldson, Donna Jill   101
Donley, Francine   296
Donley, Mary Linda Ellis   201
Doombadge, Amelie   242
Dorian   82
Dorn, Yvette K.   294
Dorsey, Carolyn D.   166
Dorsey, Cori Lynn   324
Douglas, Tamsin   258
Downs, Jay Warren   39
Draghi, Ramond   342
Drake, Rodney   22
Drake, Sara M.   77
Dressler, Lin   331
Drew, Allysan   263
Drew, Theresa A.   206
Dryden, William "Frosty"   183
Dubarry, J. Sirghoyd   195
Duckworth, Thomasina   225
Duff, Bertha   79
Duffy, G. Frances   202
Duffy, Shannon Marie   72
Dunbar, Jessica   148
Dunbar, Pamela A.   66
Duncan, James W.   22
Duncan, Keith   244
Duncan, Kimberly   105
Duncan, Mindy   216
Dunham, James E.   267
Dunn, Barbara A.   55
Dunston, Lola   117
Durante, Lynda   275
Durbin, Dawn   106
Durkin, Kevin T.   32
Dutton, Renee   71
Dyck, Jacob Eric   200
Dyck, Mitchell   114
Dyer, Geri   157
Dyer, Rosalee   280
Dykema, Jennifer   145

E

Eagan, Mimi   58
Earney, Beverly Cole   189
Easley, Alonzo D. Sr.   35
Easton, Ron   255
Eastup Chambliss, Lavonda   275
Eckberg, Shelley   44
Eckerle, Philip A.   55

Edelen, Donna   86
Edmondson, Shaina Hansen   202
Edwards, G. Thom   97
Edwards, Katina   126
Ehlers, Florence Raush   34
Eich-Collins, Marga   261
Eichman, Richard   1
Elfreich, Donald H.   198
Elizabeth, Amy   165
Elliott, Diana   279
Elliott, Heather R.   162
Ellis, Edward A. Jr.   209
Ellison, Joe Anthony   109
Ellman, Nathalie   133
Elmore, Elsie M.   253
Emerson, Selma   169
Endre, Ronnie K.   141
Enga, Hazel   79
Englestad, M.   54
Ennis, Loren Bill   37
Enterline, Matthew   343
Epperson, Sheryl   46
Erickson, Terry Lee   202
Erin, Tonia   324
Erwin, Daniel Shane   177
Esely, Carla Jean Laglia   292
Estam, Vaive   133
Estep, Patsy   9
Estrada, Adam   335
Eubanks, Jonni   44
Evans, Amanda   196
Evans, Darrell A.   174
Evans, Ilene A.   263
Evans, Rachel   118

F

Fahey, Jack   9
Falco, Joseph J.   78
Farkas, Kimberly   218
Farmer, Frances C.   80
Farnham, Caron   48
Farnsworth, Amanda   96
Farrell, Diane   262
Fawver, Amanda   234
Felan, Alberto S.   92
Fender, Nema Maxine   238
Fenstermacher, Mary Wisham   56
Ferguson, Judy   319
Ferguson, Patricia Zoch   154
Fernandes, Daniel J.   272
Fernandez, Juanita   326
Fernandez, Rachel   176
Fiegelman, Rich   5
Fife, Charlotte A.   32
Figgins, Nancy L.   270
Fillion, Luke   184
Finger, John   83
Fink, Essie   31
Fiorini, Roland J.   30
Fischetti, Eileen   134
Fisher, Catherine   232
Fisher, Thomas Jr.   101
Fitzpatrick, Maureen   205
Flanders, Ken   234
Flanigan, Tammy   177
Flath, Sharon   59

Fleming, DM 221
Fleming, Rhonda K. 317
Fleming, Sandra 103
Fletcher, Janette 140
Flojo, Jocelyn R. 192
Flores, Elizabeth L. 51
Flores, John C. 303
Floyd, Etta R. 147
Floyde, Naomi 282
Foley, Mary Jo 156
Fooks, Jennifer Alicia 141
Ford, Carl 82
Ford, Jonathan D. 239
Foreman, Angie 234
Foreman, Joseph 88, 115
Forrest, Dale 152
Foster, Clifford 139
Foster, David E. 118
Foucoult, Mary 61
Fowlkes, Brenda 97
Fox, Bob 77
Fox, James W. 294
Frankie, Don M. 91
Frazier, Charles 132
Frazier, Walter J. 111
Frechette, Daniel Stephen 41
Freeman, Krystal 149
Freemer, Michael 64
Frey, B. H. 200
Frieben, Kerry 31
Friskey, Lois Lydia 171
Fritts, Lucille 59
Fritz, Carolyn Bammert 120
Froehlich, Louise Medulan 326
Frye, Tim 248
Fugate, Norman R. 243
Fuller, Emma T W. S. 53
Fuller, Pamila Jasmine 185
Fullerton, Richard 3
Fulton, Margaret 101
Fumic, Mary 183
Fung, Dora Low 71
Funk, Loraine O. 49
Furr, Audrey T. 20
Futter, Elzie E. 78

G

Gaken, Lindsay 18
Gale, Bree 11
Galente, Mary Jo 233
Gallagher, Joan 48
Gallaher, C. Scott 306
Gallegos, Elizabeth A. 241
Galletly, Sandra L. 279
Gallup, Elinor 281
Galvin, Mildred L. 70
Gange, Clara 48
Ganley, Virginia L. 20
Garcia, Mario E. 56
Garcia, Nina 157
Garner, Van 64
Garnham, Harry L. 128
Garretson, Johanna A. 65
Garrison, Henry E. Jr. 307
Garvin, Annette Vessey 27
Garza, Ludema M. 21

Gatz, Krissandra 340
Gaylord, Mary M. 229
Gee, Reese 85
Geeslin, Wendy 89
Gendron, Janet E. 263
Genovesi, Helen 145
Genoway, Kara 103
Gerardi, Dave 6
Gerken, Louise Dodd 75
Gerkin, Daniel J. 56
Gibson, Bill 180
Gifford, Dave 11
Gilbert, Dorothy Douglas 234
Gilley, Karen P. 24
Gilstrap III, Larry C. 245
Gingrich, Carolyn 165
Gino, Robert 92
Ginsburg, Seth L. 9
Giustino, Nicole 153
Gleason, Sue M. 94
Glennon, Sister Alice Mary 229
Glidden, Robin 80
Glover, M. J. 314
Goeglein, Matthew 8
Goff, Wanda H. 206
Goldberg, Jennifer 246
Goldthwaite, Mildred L. 200
Gomoll, Mildred 10
Good, Margaret 66
Goode, Robert H. 202
Goodwin, Marion I. 257
Gordon, Brian C. 298
Gordon, Elizabeth A. 282
Gordon-Hall, Gilbert G. 237
Gorecki, Elizabeth 142
Gorman, Georgina Grace 192
Gossett, James D. 102
Gould, Nicole 154
Gowan, Steve 281
Grace, Christine 302
Grady, Mary Joanna E. 160
Graffeo, Sally Ann Zaccone 241
Grainger, Rusty 343
Gramlich, Richard A. 151
Granger, Cynthia 207
Granholm, Richard A. 48
Graves, Rue Ceil 94
Gray, Paul 76
Grayson, R. Larry 250
Greek, Jacqueline L. 341
Green, Christina 112
Green, Maggie 232
Green, Roy N. 293
Greenfield, Joseph C. Jr. 141
Gregory, Ralph 173
Gresham, Marvin 84
Greywolf, Aaron 226
Griffin, J. Farrell 241
Griffin, Joan M. 116
Griffin, Robert J. 69
Grimes, Ralph E. 23
Grimsdick, Robert B. 306
Griswold, Wanda V. 251
Grooms, Angel 62
Groover, Kristina M. 42
Groszewski, Jennifer 65

Groth, Nora 98
Grover, Mandy 348
Guinn-Garcia, Teresa 65
Gullick, Bonnie J. 93
Gunter, Melissa 90
Gurney, Mitch 52
Gustafson, Patricia 208
Gwin, Dawn R. 321

H

Hackney, Phillip 129
Haeussler, Rose Ann 309
Haggarty, Elva 203
Haight, Jack 97
Haldenwang, David R. 115
Hale, Amanda M. 172
Hales, Maggie 117
Hall, Christopher 76
Hall, Darlene R. 130
Hall, Eugenia 120
Hall, Naomi J. 348
Haller, Gretchen 15
Hallet, Marian 43
Halloway, Margo 89
Hamilton, Cynthia 190
Hamm, DeeDee 313
Hammel, Jesse S. 266
Hammerle, Pearl Webb 239
Hammond, Blossom Blake 100
Hammond, Ruth 195
Hammontree, N. A. 175
Hampton, Charles R. 282
Handel, Julia 298
Handley, Steve 4
Hanemann, Michael Eric 42
Hanewich, Daniel B. 260
Hanff, Traci 32
Hansell, Lola I. 29
Hanson, Jane Huelster 60
Hanson, Lucinda 250
Hanson, Stephanie L. 246
Hanyzewski, Sara 175
Hao, Tina 266
Hardeman, Joyce Miller 247
Harless, Jeff 52
Harnage, Melanie 126
Harp, Melissa 30
Harris, Lee 23
Harris, Marie T. 243
Harris, Otto 92
Harris, Ted 32
Harrison, Laura 42
Harrison, Scott C. 36
Harrison-Duke, Terry A. 240
Hartman, Carl 17
Hartmann, Marianne Ruth 188
Harvey, Charles 140
Harvey, Jesse F. 30
Harvey, Shelia 240
Hasenmiller, Scott D. 139
Haskins, Michael J. 91
Hastings, Helen 28
Hatton, Stephanie 6A. 307
Haugh, Gloria 164
Hawks, Michael J. 34
Hayden, Jean V. 143

Hayes, Melisa 181
Haynes, Phyllis 81
Hays, Jean 73
Headley, Kim 46
Heard, LeAnna 36
Hearen, Dennis 107
Heatherly-Cooper, Holly KlSr 226
Heaton, Elizabeth 109
Hedges, Bobette L. 35
Heffington, Sandra A. 290
Helmer, Jackelyn 274
Helms, Pamela J. 145
Helpard, Shellane 121
Henderson, Matthew 5
Hendricks, Brenda L. 59
Hendrix, Louise Butts 19
Hennecy, Bobbie Bobo 274
Hensel, Rita 40
Hentzel, David 252
Hermann, Edna May 23
Hernandez a.k.a. Pipil, Heidy 155
Hernandez, Ismael P. 108
Herriage, Patsy 99
Herring, Jeanette 172
Herzberger, Magda 215
Hesting, Vincent Shane 38
Heugly, Melinda K. 86
Heymann, Britt 305
Hibbitts, Chrisanna L. 265
Hicks, Angela J. 292
Hicks, Deborah L. 271
Hicks, Irene 18
Higgins, Charlotte 38
Higgs, Joyce L. 35
Hight, Ronald 242
Hilborn, Kurt 107
Hill, Carol L. 335
Hill, Jackolyn M. 137
Hill, Jason Paul 195
Hill, Jodi 144
Hill, Kingsley 105
Hills, Carl 78
Himes, Linda C. 235
Hinckley, Eva 223
Hindman, Karen B. 325
Hinkson, Chandler E. 84
Hinz, Shirley Sorensen 269
Hipps, Kimberly 229
Hirtle, Daniel W. 125
Hiu, Matt 194
Hoadley, Sara Jayne 241
Hoban, Tacey M. 139
Hobbs, Barbara Dell 69
Hobson, Whittonia M. 304
Hodge, Leon 59
Hodson, Ernest 29
Hoell, Muriel 222
Hoffman, Shawn 186
Hohn, Everton L. 32
Holder, Nola Grace 159
Holm, Hillmen M. 102
Holmes, Lindsey 50
Holmes-Williams, Cheryl 187
Hooper, Rose Mary 202
Hoover, Jeanne Tyson 47

Hopkins, Vashti J. 253
Horner, Steven 152
Hornfjord, John 258
Hoss, Madeleine Msarsa 244
Hotchkiss, Jack 71
Houston, Laura J. 80
Houston-Jones, Cheryl 283
Howard, Cynthia 37
Howarth, Rainey 182
Howd, Christopher 119
Hubbard, Ruby H. 311
Hubbard, Thomas J. II 93
Huddleston, Nell 43
Huddy, Mary Ellen 13
Hudgins, Sandra 20
Hudson, Danni 159
Huffman, James M. 76
Huffman, Karen A. 315
Hugill, Cathy E. 64
Hull, Carolyn 89
Huls, Bryan 267
Huls, Yvonne T. 158
Humphrey, Claudia 67
Huneke, Laraine M. 338
Hunsberger, Andrew M. 61
Hunter, Isabelle 20
Huntington, Gloria M. 301
Hur-Adkins, Leyla 118
Hurd, Angelina 47
Hutchings, Melissa 193
Hutchison, Kathy 37
Hybridge, John 54
Hymas, Bill 228

I

Iannone, Donald L. 73
Ikaiddi, Anthony A. 271
Imboden, Beryl 160
Imhoff, Danielle R. 135
Immel, Rudun R. 106
Ingram, Thom 15
Innamorato, Ben 348
Irvine, Cecilia 192
Isaac, Eli Chyatte 19
Isco, Raymond 301
Ison, Mollie J. 86
Ivacic, Joseph 295
Ivory, Jewelene 337

J

Jackson, Luke 335
Jackson, Tom 10
Jacob, Sonia Monica Harris 124
Jacobsen, Linda Lee 14
Jalbert, Sheri A. 252
Jamison, Diana Shilkett 150
Janes, Michele Marie 188
Jayroe, F. L. 236
Jean-Francois, Marie-Catheline 208
Jeffs, Henry 320
Jenings, William G. 217
Jenkins, Beulah E. 179
Jenkins, Rose 35
Jensen, Elsie Hagberg 231
Jewers, Suzanne 106

Joan Robinson, April Yokley 323
Jobe, Vernelia B. 204
Johannsen, Amy 95
John-Moore, Gloria St. 96
Johnson, Angela M. 247
Johnson, Beauford 251
Johnson, Dexter M. 182
Johnson, E. Nell 333
Johnson, Katherine 163
Johnson, Michleene 344
Johnson, Naomi II 95
Johnson, Randy W. 126
Johnson, Rufus W. 103
Johnson, Waylon C. 90
Johnston, Kathleen 47
Johnstone, Jennifer 272
Jolly, Bonnie Watson 303
Jones, Blaine A. 68
Jones, Brian 106
Jones, Donna Foy 94
Jones, Jason 44
Jones, Kim Kingsbaker 18
Jones, Roger 99
Jones, William Henry 61
Jontz, Clyde W. 84
Joshua, O. Satty 164
Jr., Robert Whitheod 276
Jude, Phillip D. 257
Judge, Elizabeth 234
Judge Young, C. Loraine 199
Juliebo, Moira Fraser 204
Jump, Robert 237
Juray-Lowry, Millicent 123

K

K., Nyambane T. 180
Kachelriess, Audrey R. 22
Kain, Magali Gueits 4
Kalust, Violet Young 188
Kaminski, Bonnie 49
Kane, Beverly A. 187
Kao, Patricia 25
Karchinski, Minnie 47
Karg, Aileen 74
Karsten, Mary 6
Kaseman, Betty.M. 71
Kay, Brenda 131
Kaye, Anne 332
Kayganich, Nicholas J. 30
Kayser, Cliff 259
Kearns, Kathleen R. 45
Keesler, Carl 108
Keeterle, Michael 301
Keeton, Virginia 322
Keirs, Ronnie 179
Keiser, Kay 130
Kelch, Russell L. 43
Kell, Nancy Oren 105
Keller, Harry E. 208
Kellerman, Mary 11
Kelley, Patricia 258
Kelly, Deamus 203
Kelly, Dot Hutchinson 111
Kelly, Elizabeth 7
Kelly, Gregory 58

Kelly Hibbard   36
Kelly, Jeff   14
Kelly, Margaret   89
Kelly, Patricia   3
Kelly, Shawn M.   72
Kelso, Elaine E.   31
Kelso-Davila, Elizabeth   148
Kempf, Joyce   96
Kendros, Paula S.   231
Kennedy, D. J.   149
Kennedy, Karen   161
Kennedy, Mary   114
Kennedy, Pat   293
Kent, Janie   185
Kent, Theodore C.   155
Kepple, Dawn A.   172
Kerezsi, Jennifer   261
Kerr, Kleon   216
Kessler, Espree Devora   339
Khalsa, GuruPrem Kaur   247
Khin, U.   123
Kiefer, Jacklyn D.   222
Kilgore, Tandi   62
Killingsworth, Keli Adell   50
Kim, Ok-Gyung   197
Kinch, Carol   23
Kindler, Ross W.   147
King, David P.   303
King, Paul E.   237
King, Tricia   175
Kingsbury, Margaret E.   56
Kingsley, Charles Eric   123
Kinyon-Wilson, Angela S.   50
Kirkness, Donna A.   248
Kirkpatrick, Dianna   226
Kirouac, Keith   177
Kiwi, Wolfgang Bleached   39
Klassen, Karen Amber   84
Klein, Brycie F.   83
Klein, Jill C.   316
Kleist, Joanne   83
Klien, Angelika   14
Klotzbach, Lucas   13
Knapp, George S.   263
Knepp, David Lee   46, 235
Knight, Grace V.   317
Knight, Karen   117
Knight, T. H. Owen   252
Knoll, D. J.   39
Knotts, Dawn   105
Kobus, Irez   296
Koch, Bradley   173
Kogan, Esther   102
Kohout, Rosemary Herak   78
Kolar, Kathleen   60
Kondo, Esaku   13
Koos, Janie   251
Kostiou, Patti   250
Krajewski, Matthew B.   145
Kristof, Alexander   184

L

LaBianco, D.   135
Lademan, Julie Ann   245
Laffin, Edna   265

LaFleur, G. B.   345
Lambert, Alice   269
Lamothe, Debby S.   182
Landis, Benjamin W.   150
Lane, Memory   264
Langfitt, Megan   248
Larson, Laura   240
Larson, Stacy K.   172
Lascu, Loring Miles   194
Lasky, Hal H. A.   141
Lautsu, Edward C.   318
Law, Evan R.   231
Lawhorn, Patricia   249
Lawrence, Vivian M.   167
Lawson, Agnes Burns   186
Layton, C. Jonell   240
Lazzaretti, Terri   266
Lee, Bonnie S.   77
Leeber, Toni   10
Leimkuhler, William R.   196
Leng, Kevin Yeo Soon   239
Lenzen, Marilyn   169
Leonard, Susan A.   153
Leposa, Patricia A.   243
Leppo, William C.   33
Leslie, Diane Turmaine   268
Leslie, Freddie Sr.   193
Lewis, Dan   283
Lewter, Mari E.   287
Libertini, Michael C.   154
Lichter, Jack   181
Light, Ruth E.   205
Lightsey, Vera   190
Liguori, Jennifer   295
Lin, Austin   12
Lindauer, John   149
Linder, Nickie   286
Linnard, Christal   185
Linsey, Ann   173
Lipinski, Anna Frances   252
Lissner, Julie   318
Little, John C.   214
Lloyd, Jennifer   151
Lloyd, Missy   144
Long, Grace   187
Loomis, Janel   329
Lopez, Isis Norma   170
Lorilynn   191
Losh, Chris   275
Loudermilk, Benjamin D.   346
Louque, Scott A.   230
Love, Shelley   233
Ludvigson, Melvin A.   165
Lundstrom, Jeffrey A.   253
Lundy-Brinster, Meg   277
Lyle, Sandy   75

M

MacDonald, Carriann   273
MacDonald, Heidi   147
MacDonald, William E.   242
MacNachtan, Julian Craig   227
Madden, Warren K.   150
madigan, thomas j.   252
Maggard, Margie   168

Major, Richard   113
MaKuRa, Shana   236
Mallory, Maurice A.   200
Malloy, Mike J.   185
Maney, Steve D.   205
Mangal, Jamie C.   334
Mann, Harold W.   12
Mann, Philip D.   262
Manosh, Daniel W.   265
Marbach, Donna M.   263
Marcus, Raymond   4
Maria, Annette   268
Marie B., Ann Charron   175
Marro, Sara A.   265
Marsh, Ginny   11
Marsh, Rose L.   164
Martin Sr., Louis E.   267
Martin-Sims, P. Diane   257
Martinez, Kim   126
Maruschak, Stephanie Sue   66
Mason, Michael J.   143
Mass, Martha Warden   242
Massoglia, Charles A.   330
Mathes, Deloris B.   340
Mathews, Virginia Lee   178
Mattheson, Kim Ingrid   185
Matthews, Eva M.   332
Maxson, Darrel C.   244
May, Gary R.   277
Mays, William E.   5
Mazur, Steve   222
McBreairty, Missy   238
McBriar, Kim   250
McCandless, Dawn Marie   192
McCants, Margaret Anne   218
McCarthy, Tammy   125
McClain, Justin   211
McCleary, Joseph   223
McClease, Jenny L.   273
McCright, Kimberly S.   236
McCulley, Karen   191
McCulley, Rhonda   21
McGarel, G. Michael H.S   135
McIntyre, Charlie J.   139
McKaye, Bessa   203
McKenne, Charleen Harris   176
McKenzie, Betty Ann   169
McKenzie, Tracy Lynn   38
McKnight, Netta Sue   168
McLaughlin, Denys B.   258
McLoud, Mildred Hyatt   163
McMillan, Michelle   14
McMinn, Merlin J.   219
McNeely, June L.   180
McNeil, Bryce   114
Means, Lucy   260
Meek, Don J.   333
Mehalik, Lisa Marie   272
Mehlhoff, Stormy   251
Mekrut, Jason   280
Mele, Dennis M.   245
Mendoza, Letty F.   255
Menyhart, Steve   306
Merrill, Edward   215
Merritt, Jeffrey L.   159

Mertz, Chad Allan 122
Metzger, W. James 158
Meyer, Patrice 207
Meyers, Stephanie 214
Miano, Jennifer L. 211
Miles, Virginia Null 215
Milkes, A. R. 215
Miller, Deborah 137
Milligan, Kristina 168
Million, Eric A. 177
Mills, Jimmy 255
Mindes, Georgia 277
Mineer, Nancy 255
Miscioscia, James 208
Mitchell, B .A. 228
Mitchell, Catherine E. 183
Mitstifer, Ryan 217
Molnar, Ethan 233
Moody, Peggy Shella 216
Moore, Bob 244
Moore, Kathie 193
Morea, Christianna 228
Moreno, Medhan Morris 160
Moreno, Sandra 247
Morey, Edward W. 213
Morgan, Kathryn 165
Morgan, Louise M. 210
Morgan, Nik 285
Moritz, Elizabeth Ann 334
Morris, Curt 268
Morse, Kathyann 330
Moyer, Barbara 9
Moyle, Richard A. 232
Moyle, Winifred 180
Mraz-Holmes, Missy 227
Mulder, Donald S. 248
Mulhern, Carrie 182
Mullavey, Gloria 331
Munson, Patricia A. 72
Murphy, BJ 237
Murphy, Frank P. 166
Murphy, Julie K. G. 72
Murphy, Michelle J. 108
Murphy, Mike 249
Murray, Terri Lea 73
Murrieta, Drew 271
Muse, Charles 85
Muse, Lorraine 158
Mushinski, Ann Marie 34
Mutter, Shannon D. 109
Myers, Margaret Story 247
Myers, Micah 71
Myers, Sandra Jeanne 121

N

Nadeau, Therese 41
Nadell, Joe 146
Naftaly, Mordy 277
Nakamura, Cari Lee 146
Naponelli, Jill 8
Naquin-Pope, Nancy Lynn 186
Nash, June 48
Nedrow, Virginia 159
Needle, Terri 260
Neilson, Lily 194

Nellams, Nicola 274
Nelson, Augusta 65
Nelson, Derek 280
Nelson, Linda 224
Nelson, Nicole A. 172
Ness, Eva A. 25
Netterwald, Billie F. 64
Neubacher, Fred 101
Newsom, Dorothy A. 55
Nguyen, Albert 138
Nicely, Ron 26
Nichiniello, Charlene E. 297
Nichol, Keith John 24
Nichols, Martha Anne Holt 238
Nielson, Alyce M. 23
Niklaus, Janet M. 49
Nishti, Wendy L. 113
Noel, Deanna 283
Noland, Pauline 272
Norbeck, Thomas John 146
Norris, Kimberly 111
Northcut, Betty 260
Norton, Daniel 283
Norton, Sharon A. 280
Norwood, Legora M. 134
Nottingham, Steve 100
Novak, Grace K. 93
Nunn-Walton, Louise J. 245
Nuske, D. H. 219
Nye, Diane Bishop 9
Nzerue, Chike M. 99

O

Oberhouse, Amanda 74
Oberst, Anna 270
O'Brien, Martha D. 101
Ocampo, Carol 163
Ocampo, Cheryl 230
Ocaya, Helen Apolo 338
O'Connor, Michael James 87
Odell, Charlotte C. 150
Ogbunugun, Augustine 264
O'Hare, Patricia A. Rosemarie 206
O'Haver, Ruby N. 336
O'Keefe-Hardy, Lee 171
Olson, Ella A. 194
Olson, Jan 245
Olson, Leif Greneforst 210
O'Neal, Ray 79
Oparah, Bernard I. 50
Ore, James Lawrence 217
Orejola, Wilmo C. 6
Ortago, Paula 338
Ortiz, Marcelo R. 219
Ortiz, Maria A. 174
Osamwonyi, Joe 179
Osborn, Ethel-Lee 131
Osborne, James R. 38
Osgood, Jane Marie 337
Oslin, Daniel K. 110
Owens, Denford L. 319
Ozanich, Ruth S. 164

P

Pacis, Filomeno L. 262

Pagan, Miguel A. 130
Pagano, Christina 165
Pakele, Edna 16
Palacios, Monica S. 105
Palanca, Ramon G. 220
Palmer, Florence B. 90
Palmer, Marie 289
Palmer, Valerie J. 201
Palumbo, Liudmilla 19
Pannell, Shirley M. 45
Panosyan, Ayda 85
Pantano, Daniel 43
Panzino-DiNunzio, Lisa Ann 204
Pappagallo, Kathleen 68
Parente, Dorothy F. 282
Park, Chong Yum 259
Parke, S. R. 347
Parker, Joyce Cave 288
Parkins, Dave 103
Parks, Kevin L. 111
Parlier, Lawrence E. 225
Parnell, Mary Morris 207
Pascoe, C. B. 285
Pastron, Julie 153
Patchen, Dale R. 80
Patel-Das, P. B. 184
Patente, Michelle Suzette 59
Patora, Deborah 108
Patterson, Cindy 193
Patterson, William 266
Patterson-Stevenson, Paula 38, 207
Paul, Doris Tarver 97
Paver, Mary 60
Pawlik, October A. 170
Pawlowych, Rostyslaw 157
Payne, Edith Mae 233
Payne, Mitchell S. 130
Payne, Norma Dotson 51
Pazhedath, Glenda M. 17
Peavy, Jennifer 230
Peay, Jesse D. Jr. 20
Peck, H. Gwinn 154
Peda, Andrea 80
Peery, Patrick Joe 144
Peiffer, Lulu 148
Pendergest, Thomas H. 128
Pendergraph, Millard G. 35
Penland, Patrick R. 189
Pennington, James A. 167
Pentes, Annette Lynne 43
Pereira, Michael A. 157
Perkins, Christine 235
Perkins, Maisha K. 67
Perkins, Robert Louis 175
Perreault, Tracie L. E. 169
Perry, Dollyna K. 16
Perry, Flo 164
Peters, Elizabeth 41
Peterson, Nicci 91
Peterson, Royal F. 55
Petrie, John F. 262
Pettingill, Dawnel 57
Pezderic, Amy 44
Pfankucken, Carol 207
Phair, Juliette 195

Phelps-Wiley, Mitchel A. 161
Phifer, Rhonda 111
Phillips, Agnes M. 17
Phillips, Debra 158
Phillips, Susan Stowe 27
Photikarmbumrung, Elma Diel 64
Picardy, Allan 40
Piccola, Ruth 125
Pidhayny, Wilma 115
Pierce, Gordon 42
Pierce, Judy 238
Pierre, Wilfred 190
Piersel, DeeJay 98
Pike, Ursula 148
Pilny, Marie 300
Pimblett, Selina 125
Piotrowska, Alice 98
Piotrowski, Halina 174
Pisheh-Ehsan, Parviz 189
Pittman, Kimberly A. 123
Pittman, Linda S. 57
Pleasant, Joan 297
Plenert, Dawn J. 97
Plumb, Jon 285
Plumb, Meghan Elaine 158
Plumley, Constance 6
Plummer, Harriet 208
Plummer, Rebekkah 27
Pointer, Suzanne 92
Polirer, Debra 104
Pollans, Kenneth David 237
Pollock, Debra T. 308
Pommer, Stephen D. 258
Pond, Patricia G. 272
Poole, Fay 122
Poore, Christopher S. 318
Popov, Marguerite 43
Poppe 176
Porsch, Kerstyn 256
Porter, James 256
Post, Heather N. 136
Post, Morgan L. 127
Potts, Marge 115
Powell, Carol M. 95
Powers, L. Lindley 112
Poynter, Tammy Sue 251
Pratte, Lois A. 131
Pretzer, Randall E. 128
Prevost, Frederic Joseph 209
Price, Melanie R. 33
Price, Sarah F. 46
Prickett, Lori 328
Priester, Irene J. 70
Prisock, Mary V. 60
Probasco, Pattye 22
Proctor, Gregory Lee 50
Protivnak, David B. 289
Proud, Joann H. 154
Puebla, Marianela 282
Pulin, Mike 136
Puls, Byran 199
Putignano, Michael Anthony 214
Putnam, Harold 206

Q

Queen, Madeline M. 129
Quentin, Edna May 10
Quilliam, Bronwyn 190
Quinones, Alexi 129
Quisenberry, Carla Shawn 253

R

Racine, Martine 276
Racut, Tina Marie 152
Radandt, Amanda 190
Radloff, Druscilla L. 33
Raff, Jeannette 253
Ragin-McNeil, Angela 204
Raineri, Brian J. Jr. 92
Rains, Susan 36
Raiti, Ashly 241
Rajacic, Roy 77
Ramaglia, Daniel J. 154
Ramirez, Dawn M. 160
Ramos, Christopher 74
Ramp, Robert J. 46
Ramsey, James 127
Raniere, Autumn 250
Rankin, Glen T. Jr. 129
Ransdell, Lisa Marie 93
Ransom, Tammy 117
Rasmus, Cameron 115
Rasor, Elma M. 52
Rasor, Jennifer Leigh 152
Ratto, Amy 143
Rawlings, Lisa 327
Ray, Consiwella R. 311
Ray, George William Jr. 61
Ray, Loreene 235
Rayburn, Janice 155
Reagan, Jonna 283
Rebecca Ensor 36
Reddoch, Mildred Lucas 61
Reding, Eunice Abby 37
Redrick, Reginald 236
Reeps, Janet D. 146
Reeve, Chester H. 47
Regular, Sheron E. 320
Reho, Joseph L. Sr. 266
Reich, Theodore R. 70
Reidelberger, Pat 88
Reihl, Donna 100
Reilly, Jessica 22
Rembecki, Robert 5
Remedios Nalundasan-Abijan 121
Renta, Olga 182
Repik, Dolores 128
Resnick, Ralph 95
Revercomb, Laura Lee 300
Rex-Snyder, Mildred 93
Rexford, Lloyd 52
Reynolds, Elizabeth Maria 44
Rheaume, Paul J. 203
Rhoades, James Perry 103
Rhodin, Ann 90
Rice, Brian M. 125
Rice, Daniel L. 35
Rice, Frankie "Dee" 327
Rich, Christopher J. 346

Richard, Gary Ferguson 191
Richards, Crystal 104
Richards, Donald A. 210
Richards, Terry Allen II 127
Richfield, Hedy 75
Rick, Gary D. 116
Rickert, Elizabeth A. 61
Ridgely, Bonnie Lee 137
Riffle, Grace 184
Riggins, M. Judith 112
Riggs, Darvin O. 72
Riley, Karen 119
Rilling, Monica Sanchez 190
Ring, Norma 49
Rinker, Kathleen C. 53
Rios, Georgianna N. 243
Rios, Milton Daniel 212
Rittel, Veronica A. 128
Rivet, Brenda M. 104
Rizzo, Lisa 128
Roach, Janice 30
Roach, John W. 170
Roark, Sheila B. 57
Robbins, Christi Leigh 126
Roberts, Judy S. 116
Robertson, Christopher S. 22
Robertson, Mark 119
Robinson, Calvin 29
Robinson, Katrina W. 219
Robinson, Matthew 246
Robledo, Bonnie Valihora 212
Rochford, Nycole 51
Rock, Doris L. 278
Rockwood, Martha M. 58
Rodning, Charles B. 64
Rodriguez, Arlene F. De 26
Rogers, Diana Lynn 148
Rogers, Wilda Lee 49
Rogerson, Heather 74
Rollin, Marty 127
Rooney, Eugene 99
Rose, Connie 174
Rose, Susan F. 205
Rosenberger, Desiree 122
Ross, Patricia 284
Ross, Virginia Morton 107
Rossiter, Peta 188
Routier, Maurice A. 219
Row, Staci L. 160
Rowe, Robert M. 141
Rowland, Wanda 197
Roy, Margaret 37
Roy, Rashmi 282
Royster, Karen 318
Rozmyn, Norma Morris 275
Rozsman, Mev Borso 15
Rubel, Rachel 291
Rubeyiat, Jherrie 159
Rubin, Larry B. 310
Rubinowitz, Wendi 93
Ruckdaschel, Virgil A. 150
Rud, Lula 159
Rudewicz, Eleanore M. 49
Ruding, Karol 3
Rudy, Ronald D. 174

Rueben, J. D.   245
Rupert, Thomas C.   302
Rush, William V.   60
Rushia, Christian M.   114
Ruske, Christopher J.   348
Russell, Deborah   249
Russell, Rhonda   40
Russo Jr., Vincent P.   254
Rutherford, April   94
Ryan, Dawn   77
Ryder-Park, L.   228
Ryk, Mary   134
Rymer, James C.   213

S

Sadler, Norman   130
Saffrin, Mary   21
Salas, Gloria   114
Salcido, Amanda   77
Saldana, Aida Ophelia   28
Salnave, Renee L.   290
Salyers, Jessica L.   155
Sambo, Betty J.   309
Samtani, Preeti   171
Sanchez, Cristita Mae   168
Sanchez, John   26
Sanders, Marilyn   15
Sanders, Wilkie L. Sr.   309
Sanderson, Jennifer Lynn   162
Sandison, Paul C.   277
Sandlin, Joshua C.   238
Sandness, Robert C.   308
Sandy "O"   209
Santos, William   8
Santowski, Xenia   186
Santschi-Haywood, Cornelia   281
Saphier, Patricia   4
Sapienza, Charles II   86
Sara, Nils P.   232
Sargent, Lori A.   180
Sarker, Niladri   321
Sarkissian, Henry A.   48
Sarnoski, Kim   122
Sartin, Coetta   98
Sass, Frank   40
Saunders, Lorin C.   284
Saunders, Margarette Combs   124
Savage, Donna S.   260
Sawyer-Shepard, Sarah G.   124
Saxton, Ellwood F.   133
Schachter, Jason   231
Schaefer, Michael D.   236
Schaeffer, Fenella   275
Schalit, Robert   8
Schamp-Mack, Heather   325
Scharschmidt, Rosie   203
Scheerer, Deborah L.   177
Schelosky, Virginia   70
Schenk, Kay   221
Schiess, Meryl M.   26
Schilling, Mimi   173
Schillinger, Beverly I.   161
Schlaefer, Eileen   100
Schmerz, Lyle L.   261
Schmidt, Bonnie A.   267

Schmidt, Bud J.   113
Schmidt, Erika   288
Schneider, Charita   162
Schronce, Michael   3
Schultz, Kris   138
Schultz, Ruth Ellen   90
Schulz, Pat   132
Schulz, Stephen Paul   299
Sciaretta, Danielle   31
Scott, Phyllis M.   118
Scoughton, Karie   146
Sedelmarer, Norman Wayne   221
Seed, Neysa E.   227
Seerattan, Frank   137
Segal, Greg   178
Seibold, Michael   97
Seifert, Gary F.   58
Sellers, Dean   175
Sellers, Karmen   31
Serna, Ernest   6
Serrao, Lorrie   247
Serviss, June   65
Sewell, Sabrina   269
Seymour, Benjamin   316
Sforzo, Kristin   26
Shadix, Jay   244
Shafer, Joyce E.   28
Shaffer, Barbara   216
Shaffer, Verina   256
Shalom, Ethan   341
Shanahan, Donald G. Jr.   181
Shareghi, Amanda   121
Sharp, Elizabeth   63
Shaw, Jacklyn L.   152
Sheets, Sunni L.   95
Shepherd, Richard J.   149
Sheppard, Ruby   119
Sherkat, M. K.   33
Sherman, Amy   34
Sherman, Faith   196
Sherrod, Philip   20
Shields, Larry   75
Shimkus, Liz   47
Shoemaker, Anna K.   51
Shonk, Joan A.   39
Shortt, Carrianne   278
Shoshani, Shmuel   82
Showers, Angeline   216
Shuck, Hazel L.   94
Shuda, Jeffrey J.   252
Shufutinsky, Anton   316
Sidorenko, Michael   195
Siegel, Ben   201
Sile, Jennifer   257
Silek, Laura Spencer   41
Simes, Lisa Kamillia   84
Simmons, Susie   16
Simon, David Clarence   68
Simon, Diane R.   73
Simon, Mary Ann   285, 321
Simpson, D. Sean   120
Simpson, Deidre   344
Sinclair, Debbie   313
Sinclair, Walter E.   321
Sir Louis, Diana L.   205
Sisson, Marilyn   62

Skeeters, F. D.   225
Skiles, Benjamin   265
Skirpan, Clement A.   200
Slasten, Guennadi N.   33
Slee, E. McIntire   9
Slichter, Jamie   246
Sloan, John J.   18
Smallwood, Jullian   80
Smedley, Donna Wood   58
Smit, Linda   117
Smith, Ann Elizabeth   225
Smith, Celestine H.   23
Smith, Charles R.   37
Smith, Dee Dee   142
Smith, Dianne Marie   102
Smith, Flavia V.   135
Smith, Gary W.   279
Smith, Janice   24
Smith, Jean Marie   308
Smith, Jennifer   223
Smith, Jo Dell   144
Smith, Joseph N.   312
Smith, Kristy   25
Smith, Rodric   70
Smith, Thomasine Fant   220
Snead, William L.   269
Snodgrass, Marilyn M.   118
Snow, George Edward   319
Sofer, Michael F.   191
Sommerville, Lisa   168
Sorensen, Lisa   29
Sowers, Anita G.   27
Spadafora, Melita   53
Spangler, Elois L.   125
Spaulding, Larry   218
Spears, Deana   245
Spellman, D. R.   176
Spencer, Joyce Stiles   211
Spencer, Sharon E.   305
Spencer-Braden, Helen   88
Springer, Dondi   144
Springfield, Cherie   136
Spurling, Brettioes   27
St. Cyr, Catherine   330
Staley, Elizabeth   143
Stambaugh, Deborah   298
Stangland, Katy   151
Steel, Larry   83
Steele, Carol   34
Steele, Lois M.   186
Stein, Corinne   89
Steinkraus, Chris   210
Steinmann, Holli   167
Stephens, J. Patrick   18
Stephens, Jan   241
Sterling, Jerome   327
Sternberg, Denny   74
Stessin, Alexander   135
Stevens, Candice L.   171
Stewart, Glyn   286
Stewart, Mattie M.   59
Stockmal, Sarabeth   274
Stoddard, Helen Myrtle   176
Stoffel, James   207
Stolar, Halina   5

Stone, Darling 187
Stone, Melinda 222
Stone, Sheila 233
Stouwie, Diane R. 226
Stover, Summer 220
Stovin, Chantele 273
Stratman, Carol J. 255
Strauman, Lynn E. G. 268
Strawderman, Judy K. 232
Stucky, Vernon 166
Suarez, Ilka 140
Sullivan, Brendan 180
Sullivan, Gwendolyn M. 167
Sullivan, Heather 198
Sullivan, John F. 147
Sullivan, Karen 163
Sullivan, Lois-Margaret 124
Sullivan, Michael L. 237
Sultana, Nilofer 7
Sunday, John Jr. 254
Surratt, Anthony L. 340
Surratt, Doris A. Ray 233
Susmuth, John 280
Swan, Zylpha 291
Szabo, Julie 188

T

T., Sue 334
Ta, Tri Duc 239
Tancordo, Joseph 280
Tapp, Wade Jr 347
Taylor, Francis 145
Taylor, Joann 276
Teachout, Kim C. 208
Tedder, Carolyn 299
Tenzing, Chering 256
Terlap, Kimberly A. 11
Tettmar, Nick 87
Teubert, Judy 204
Theoharis, Evelyn 194
Thomas, Austin 276
Thomas, J. David Jr. 268
Thomas-House, Jeanette 198
Thompson, Audrey K. 193
Thompson, Jil 277
Thorburn, Peter 261
Thorn, Ana Lee 4
Thornton, Jennifer 221
Thorpe, Luanne L. 345
Thrush, Becky 322
Tice, Bradley S. 235
Tinker, Thomas L. 224
Tohlen, Sara D. 179
Tonder, Mickey-Shaun Van 100
Toovey, Rita J. 162
Torres, Rosa 156
Tourangeau, Vera 328
Townsend, Velda R. 217
Trafny, Jason T. 325
Treacy, Jerry 314
Trimm, Jake 206
Trout, Amie 183
Trout, Theresa 3
True, Marcia M. 264
Tsosie, Shirley 211
Tucker, Susan R. 209
Turner, Adrienne Denise 106
Turner, David G. 297
Turner, Huldah M. 10
Turner, Judy 265
Turner, Temple 261
Twister 267
Tyler, Norma 120
Tzelnic, Tania 177

U

Ufford, D. Anne 347
Unsworth, Jane 200
Urdialez, John 228

V

Van Antwerp, Lindie Beth 270
Van Der Zee, Cora M. 226
Van Hoose, Jason 320
Van Houten, John Carl 279
Van-Earl Danso, Robert 264
VanDyke, Bryan 7
Vars, Troy R. 142
Veer, R. Douglas 270
Vena, Jason Anthony John 191
Vermette, Jacqueline 116
Vermuele, Elsie J. 141
Vigil, Beverly 199
Villanueva, Claudia R. 328
Villingham, Russell 230
Vincent, Lorie M. 279
Vine, George 213
Vis, Heather 204
von Uthemann Dorsey,
    Cynthia Monique M. 329

W

Wachtershauser, Ellen 271
Wadsworth, Kyle 266
Waeyenbergh, Sarah 136
Wagner, Jennifer L. 227
Wagner, Mary Ann Blakely, Ph.D. 269
Wakamatsu, Jack K. 271
Wakeland, Sherrie 161
Waldo, L. S. 19
Walker, Matthew A. 181
Wall, Julie 186
Wallace, Rodney C. 174
Walls, Amy E. 222
Ward, Christine 107
Warnick, Teresa M. 262
Washington, Nathan L. 123
Watchek, Marjorie M. 211
Waterman, Muriel 246
Waters, D. 289
Watson, Cletus M. S. 242
Watson, JoDee 162
Watson, Roy 267
Wattel, Jeanne-Helene 81
Weaver, Zelma 210
Webb, Marcia 124
Weger, Amy 239
Wehrle, Gary R. 158
Welch, Becky 177
Weltz, Mike B. 4
Werner, Luetta G. 273
West, Farr North 248
Whipple, Haley 140
White, Barbara Jean 229
White, Deloris 215
White, Joan B. 337
Whitmore, Y. Regina 153
Whitworth, Warren N. 281
Wickund, Barry 219
Wierenga, Dianne 171
Wilcox, Alan 273
Wilder Sr., Marshall C. 215
Wilkins, Bill 155
Williams, Alma Ann 222
Williams, Barb 243
Williams, Cheryl Warren 254
Williams, Edward R. 165
Williams, H. Lee 306
Williams, Mamie Lou G. 25
Williams, Regina Cook 254
Williamson, Michael Quinn 151
Willis, John G. 145
Wills, Christopher R. 210
Wilson, Clyde 62
Wilson, Emerson 174
Wilson, James Edward III 67
Wilson, Rachel 223
Winchel, Judith 259
Winter, Ruth 91
Winters, Melanie 263
Wire, Mary Lou 24
Wireman, Tamara 137
Wise, Christopher 128
Wiseman, Mykel 197
Witt, Pamela 325
Woddell, Michelle K. 300
Wolf, Angela 55
Wood, Kay 142
Woodward, Donald M. 216
Woollybear, Mr. 7
Wright, Gary A. 225
Wright, Jack T. 217
Wright, Jeanette A. 242
Wright, Terrence C. 281
Wyatt, Teresa 139
Wylie, Olive 187
Wynn, Candi Mathews 253

Y

Yancey, Pamela Faye 221
Yeager, Gertrude 348
Yopp, Heather E. 140
Young, C. Loraine Judge 199
Yung, Sandra E. Schlessman 254

Z

Zahrebelny, Tony 115
Zapanta, Jaclyn 313
Zavaletta, Lisa 320
Zdanczyk, Cynthia 163
Zegarelli, Steven J. 67
Zeller, Christopher 178
Zimmerman Prentis, Edna 158
Zimmermann, Daniel 269
Zinke, Bill 323
Zofrea, Sonja Ann 220